The Middle East

A History

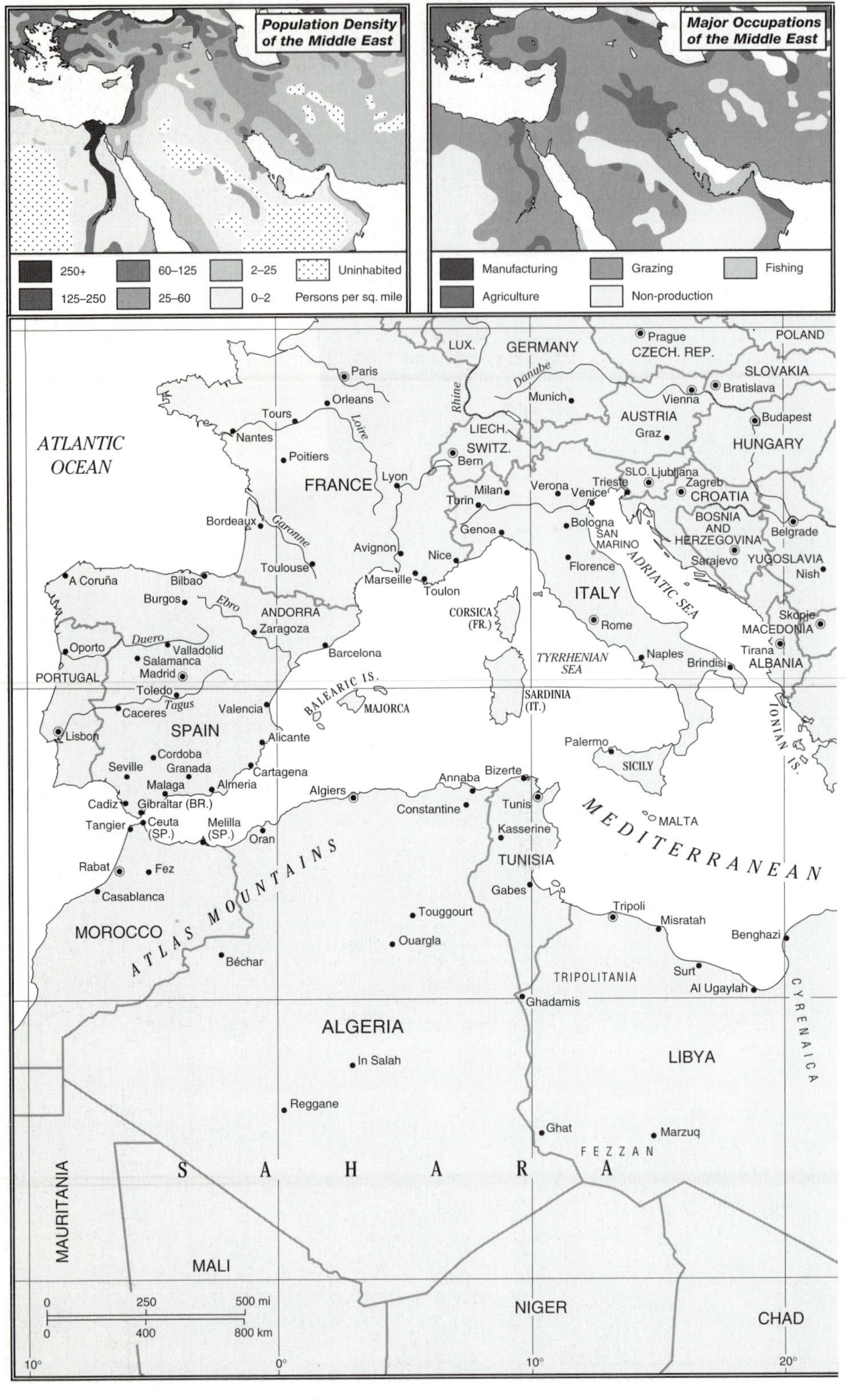
Population Density of the Middle East
250+
125–250
60–125
25–60
2–25
0–2
Uninhabited
Persons per sq. mile
Major Occupations of the Middle East
Manufacturing
Agriculture
Grazing
Non-production
Fishing
ATLANTIC OCEAN
FRANCE
SPAIN
PORTUGAL
ANDORRA
ITALY
GERMANY
LUX.
SWITZ.
LIECH.
AUSTRIA
CZECH. REP.
POLAND
SLOVAKIA
HUNGARY
SLO.
CROATIA
BOSNIA AND HERZEGOVINA
YUGOSLAVIA
MACEDONIA
ALBANIA
SAN MARINO
MOROCCO
ALGERIA
TUNISIA
LIBYA
MAURITANIA
MALI
NIGER
CHAD
TRIPOLITANIA
CYRENAICA
FEZZAN
S A H A R A
ATLAS MOUNTAINS
MEDITERRANEAN
ADRIATIC SEA
TYRRHENIAN SEA
IONIAN IS.
BALEARIC IS.
MAJORCA
CORSICA (FR.)
SARDINIA (IT.)
SICILY
MALTA
Rhine
Danube
Loire
Garonne
Ebro
Duero
Tagus
Paris
Orleans
Tours
Nantes
Poitiers
Bordeaux
Toulouse
Lyon
Avignon
Marseille
Toulon
Nice
Prague
Munich
Vienna
Bratislava
Budapest
Graz
Bern
Milan
Turin
Verona
Venice
Trieste
Ljubljana
Zagreb
Genoa
Bologna
Florence
Rome
Naples
Brindisi
Palermo
Belgrade
Sarajevo
Nish
Skopje
Tirana
A Coruña
Bilbao
Burgos
Zaragoza
Barcelona
Oporto
Valladolid
Salamanca
Madrid
Toledo
Caceres
Valencia
Lisbon
Alicante
Cordoba
Seville
Granada
Cartagena
Malaga
Almeria
Cadiz
Gibraltar (BR.)
Tangier
Ceuta (SP.)
Melilla (SP.)
Oran
Algiers
Annaba
Bizerte
Constantine
Tunis
Kasserine
Gabes
Rabat
Fez
Casablanca
Béchar
Touggourt
Ouargla
Tripoli
Misratah
Benghazi
Surt
Al Ugaylah
Ghadamis
In Salah
Reggane
Ghat
Marzuq
0
250
500 mi
0
400
800 km
10°
0°
10°
20°

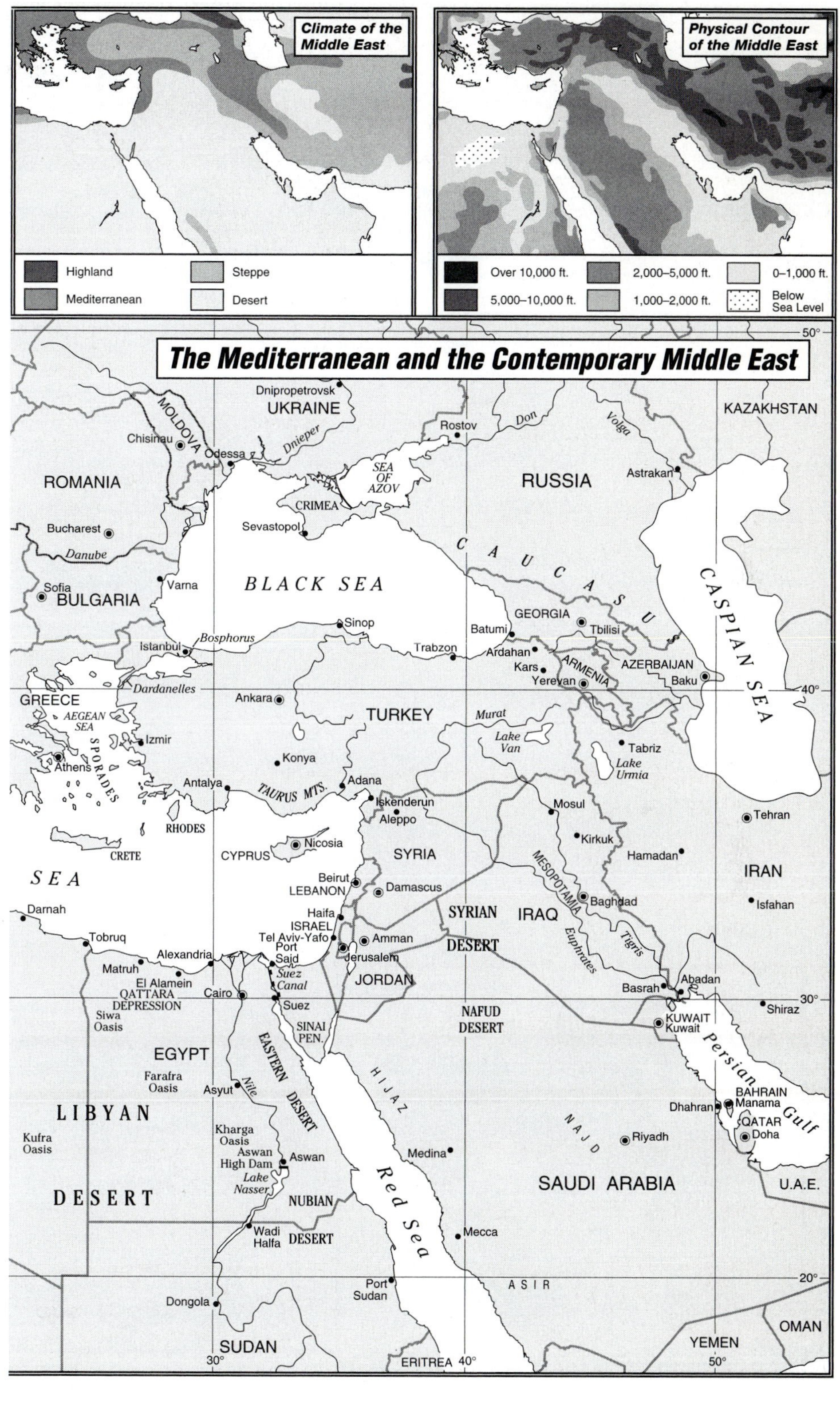

Climate of the Middle East
Highland
Mediterranean
Steppe
Desert
Physical Contour of the Middle East
Over 10,000 ft.
5,000–10,000 ft.
2,000–5,000 ft.
1,000–2,000 ft.
0–1,000 ft.
Below Sea Level
The Mediterranean and the Contemporary Middle East
Dnipropetrovsk
UKRAINE
KAZAKHSTAN
Rostov
Don
Volga
MOLDOVA
Chisinau
Odessa
Dnieper
SEA OF AZOV
ROMANIA
RUSSIA
Astrakan
CRIMEA
Sevastopol
Bucharest
Danube
CAUCASUS
CASPIAN SEA
Varna
BLACK SEA
Sofia
BULGARIA
GEORGIA
Sinop
Batumi
Tbilisi
Bosphorus
Istanbul
Trabzon
Ardahan
ARMENIA
AZERBAIJAN
Kars
Yerevan
Baku
Dardanelles
GREECE
Ankara
TURKEY
Murat
AEGEAN SEA
Lake Van
Tabriz
Izmir
SPORADES
Konya
Lake Urmia
Athens
Antalya
Adana
TAURUS MTS.
Iskenderun
Mosul
Aleppo
Tehran
RHODES
Kirkuk
Nicosia
CRETE
CYPRUS
SYRIA
Hamadan
MESOPOTAMIA
SEA
Beirut
LEBANON
Damascus
IRAN
Baghdad
Darnah
Haifa
SYRIAN
IRAQ
Isfahan
ISRAEL
Tobruq
Tel Aviv-Yafo
Amman
Tigris
Euphrates
Alexandria
Port Said
DESERT
Matruh
Jerusalem
El Alamein
Suez Canal
JORDAN
Basrah
Abadan
QATTARA DEPRESSION
Cairo
Suez
Shiraz
Siwa Oasis
NAFUD DESERT
KUWAIT
Kuwait
SINAI PEN.
EGYPT
Persian Gulf
Farafra Oasis
EASTERN DESERT
HIJAZ
Asyut
Nile
BAHRAIN
Manama
LIBYAN
Dhahran
QATAR
Doha
NAJD
Riyadh
Kufra Oasis
Kharga Oasis
Aswan High Dam
Aswan
Medina
Red Sea
Lake Nasser
SAUDI ARABIA
U.A.E.
DESERT
NUBIAN
DESERT
Wadi Halfa
Mecca
ASIR
Port Sudan
Dongola
OMAN
SUDAN
YEMEN
ERITREA
50°
40°
30°
20°

POLAND
GERMANY
Prague
CZECH. REP.
SLOVAKIA
UKRAINE
Danube
Dniester
Donets
Dnipropetrovsk
Munich
Vienna
Bratislava
AUSTRIA
Graz
Budapest
HUNGARY
MOLDOVA
Pruth
Chisinau
Odessa
Dnieper
Rostov
LIECH.
SWITZ.
SLO.
Ljubljana
Trieste
Zagreb
CROATIA
ROMANIA
SEA OF AZOV
Verona
Venice
Milan
Po
Genoa
Bologna
SAN MARINO
BOSNIA AND HERZEGOVINA
Belgrade
Sarajevo
YUGOSLAVIA
Nish
Bucharest
Danube
Sevastopol
BLACK SEA
Florence
ADRIATIC SEA
ITALY
Sofia
BULGARIA
Varna
CORSICA (FR.)
Rome
Skopje
MAC.
Tirana
ALBANIA
Sinop
Batumi
Bosphorus
Istanbul
Trabzon
TYRRHENIAN SEA
Naples
Brindisi
Dardanelles
SARDINIA (IT.)
GREECE
IONIAN IS.
AEGEAN SEA
Ankara
Erzurum
Murat
TURKEY
Afyon
Lake Tuz
Izmir
SPORADES
Palermo
SICILY
Athens
Konya
Bizerte
Tunis
Antalya
Adana
Urfa
Iskenderun
Aleppo
MEDITERRANEAN SEA
MALTA
RHODES
Kasserine
TUNISIA
CRETE
CYPRUS
Nicosia
Hims
SYRIA
Tadmur
Beirut
LEBANON
Damascus
Gabes
Tripoli
Misratah
Darnah
Haifa
ISRAEL
Tel Aviv-Yafo
Gaza
Amman
Benghazi
Tobruq
Nile Delta
Alexandria
Port Said
Jerusalem
DEAD SEA
JORDAN
Matruh
El Alamein
Surt
El 'Arish
Suez Canal
Ma'an
Al Ugaylah
Cairo
Suez
Eilat
Al'Aqabah
Ghadamis
Gulf of Suez
Gulf of Aqaba
LIBYA
El Minya
EGYPT
Asyut
Nile
El Kharga
Ghat
Marzuq
Red Sea
Medina
Aswan High Dam
Aswan
Lake Nasser
Wadi Halfa
Jidda
Mecca
NIGER
CHAD
Port Sudan
Dongola
Atbara
Haiya
SUDAN
ERITREA
Massawa
Agordat
Asmara
Omdurman
Kassala
Khartoum
Sennar Dam
Adwa
El Obeid
Gonder
Lake Tana
Blue Nile
White Nile
Addis Ababa
ETHIOPIA
30°
Lake Turkana
40°
Population Density
Number of persons per square mile
under 50
50–100
100–150
150–300
over 300

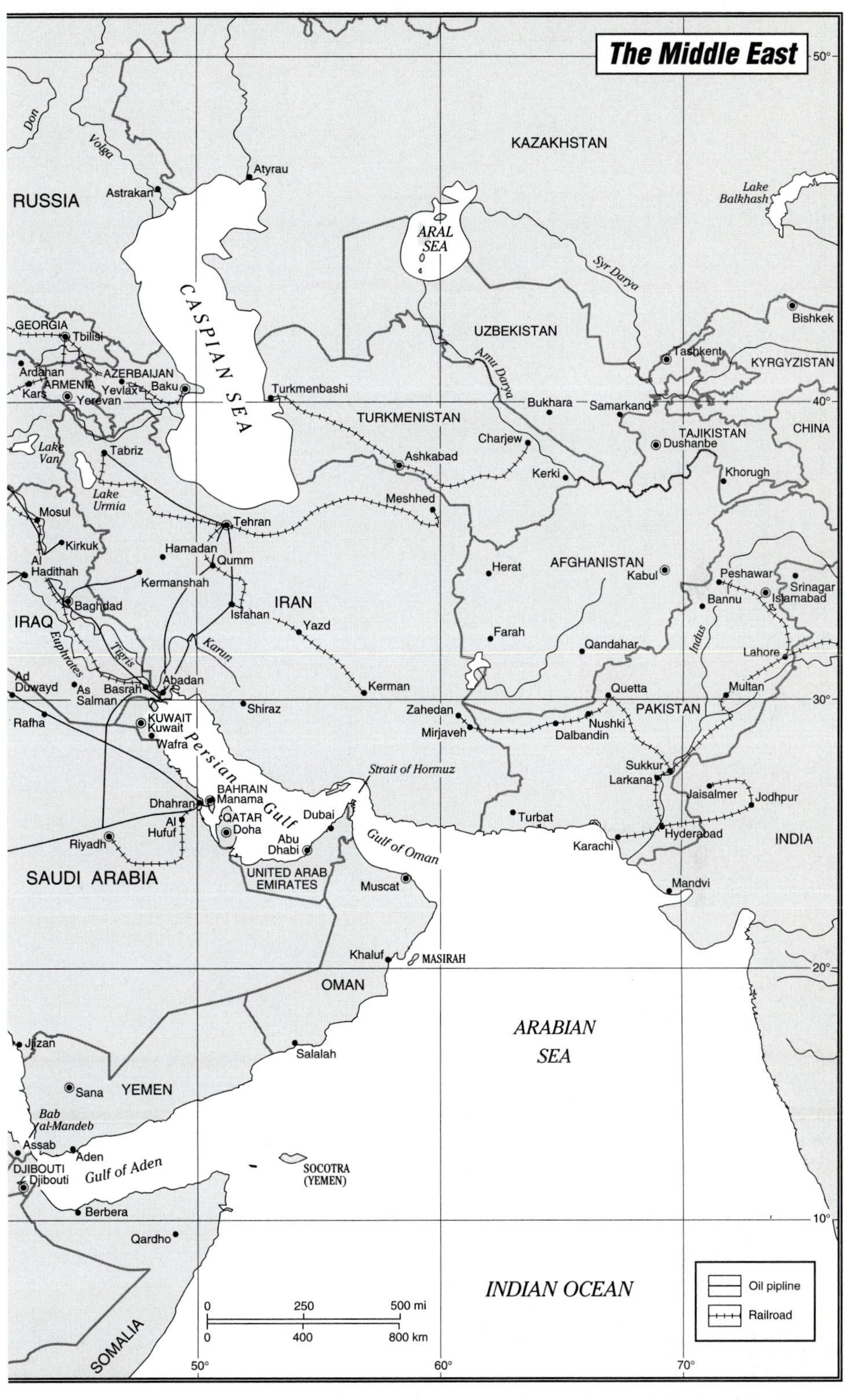

The Middle East
RUSSIA
KAZAKHSTAN
UZBEKISTAN
TURKMENISTAN
TAJIKISTAN
KYRGYZSTAN
CHINA
GEORGIA
ARMENIA
AZERBAIJAN
AFGHANISTAN
PAKISTAN
INDIA
IRAN
IRAQ
KUWAIT
BAHRAIN
QATAR
UNITED ARAB EMIRATES
SAUDI ARABIA
OMAN
YEMEN
DJIBOUTI
SOMALIA
SOCOTRA (YEMEN)
MASIRAH
CASPIAN SEA
ARAL SEA
Lake Balkhash
Lake Van
Lake Urmia
Persian Gulf
Strait of Hormuz
Gulf of Oman
ARABIAN SEA
INDIAN OCEAN
Gulf of Aden
Bab al-Mandeb
Don
Volga
Syr Darya
Amu Darya
Tigris
Euphrates
Karun
Indus
Atyrau
Astrakan
Tbilisi
Ardahan
Kars
Yerevan
Yevlax
Baku
Turkmenbashi
Ashkabad
Bukhara
Samarkand
Tashkent
Bishkek
Dushanbe
Charjew
Kerki
Khorugh
Tabriz
Mosul
Kirkuk
Al Hadithah
Tehran
Hamadan
Qumm
Kermanshah
Baghdad
Isfahan
Yazd
Meshhed
Herat
Kabul
Peshawar
Srinagar
Islamabad
Bannu
Farah
Qandahar
Lahore
Kerman
Shiraz
Abadan
Basrah
As Salman
Ad Duwayd
Rafha
Kuwait
Wafra
Zahedan
Mirjaveh
Quetta
Nushki
Dalbandin
Multan
Sukkur
Larkana
Jaisalmer
Jodhpur
Hyderabad
Karachi
Turbat
Dhahran
Manama
Al Hufuf
Doha
Dubai
Abu Dhabi
Riyadh
Muscat
Mandvi
Khaluf
Salalah
Jizan
Sana
Assab
Aden
Djibouti
Berbera
Qardho
50°
40°
30°
20°
10°
50°
60°
70°
0 250 500 mi
0 400 800 km
Oil pipline
Railroad

The Middle East
A History

SIXTH EDITION

William Ochsenwald
Professor of History
Virginia Polytechnic Institute and State University

Sydney Nettleton Fisher
Late Professor of History
The Ohio State University

Boston Burr Ridge, IL Dubuque, IA Madison, WI New York
San Francisco St. Louis Bangkok Bogotá Caracas Kuala Lumpur
Lisbon London Madrid Mexico City Milan Montreal New Delhi
Santiago Seoul Singapore Sydney Taipei Toronto

The *McGraw·Hill* Companies

THE MIDDLE EAST: A HISTORY
Published by McGraw-Hill, a business unit of The McGraw-Hill Companies, Inc., 1221 Avenue of the Americas, New York, NY, 10020.

This book is printed on acid-free paper.

6 7 8 9 0 FGR/FGR 0 9 8 7

ISBN 978-0-07-244233-5
MHID 0-07-244233-6

Vice-President/Editor-in-Chief: Thalia Dorwick
Publisher: Lyn Uhl
Marketing manager: Katherine Bates
Production editor: David Sutton
Production supervisor: Tandra Jorgensen
Design coordinator: Mary Kazak
Cover design: Asylum Studios
Cover image: ©Nabeel Turner/Getty Images
Compositor: Electronic Publishing Services, Inc.
Typeface: 10/12 Times Roman
Printer: Quebecor World, Fairfield

Library of Congress Cataloging-In-Publication Data
Ochsenwald, William
The Middle East: a history / William Ochsenwald, Sydney Nettleton Fisher.— 6th ed.
p. cm.
Includes bibliographical references and index.
ISBN 0-07-244233-6 (softcover)
1. Middle East—History. 2. Middle East—History—20th century. I. Ochsenwald, William. II. Title.
DS62.F5 2003
956—dc21 2003041213

www.mhhe.com

About the Authors

WILLIAM OCHSENWALD attended the Ohio State University (B.A., M.A.) and the University of Chicago (Ph.D., 1971). He has been a member of the faculty of Virginia Polytechnic Institute and State University since 1971, with occasional leaves for research in Lebanon, Syria, Jordan, Israel, Egypt, Turkey, Britain, and France. He has received grants from the Fulbright-Hays program; the American Research Institute in Turkey; the former United States Department of Health, Education, and Welfare; and the Social Science Research Council and American Council of Learned Societies. In 1979–1980 and 1991 he was an Associate Fellow of the Middle East Centre, University of Cambridge. He is the author of three books, *The Hijaz Railroad* (1980), *Religion, Society, and the State in Arabia* (1984), and *Religion, Economy, and State in Ottoman-Arab History* (1998), and the co-editor of *Nationalism in a Non-National State: The Dissolution of the Ottoman Empire* (1977) and has published many articles, among them essays appearing in *The Middle East Journal, International Journal of Middle East Studies, Die Welt des Islams, The Muslim World, Arabian Studies,* and the *Encyclopaedia Britannica.*

SYDNEY NETTLETON FISHER was born in Warsaw, New York, in 1906 and attended Oberlin College (A.B., M.A.) and the University of Illinois (Ph.D., 1935). He was a member of the faculty of the Ohio State University from 1937 to 1972. Professor Fisher was a member of Phi Beta Kappa, a Fellow of the Royal Historical Society, and a member of the Accadèmia del Mediterràneo. He served as Director of Publications of the Middle East Institute and as editor of *The Middle East Journal* and contributed articles to numerous journals and encyclopedias. He was the author or editor of several books, among them *Foreign Relations of Turkey, 1481–1512* (1948), *Social Forces in the Middle East* (1955), and *The Military in the Middle East* (1963). He died on December 10, 1987.

Contents

Part Two
THE OTTOMAN AND SAFAVID EMPIRES

Part Four
THE MIDDLE EAST AFTER WORLD WAR I

List of Maps

List of Charts and Genealogies

Preface to the Sixth Edition

The issues troubling many parts of the Middle East have sharply increased in severity in recent years, while the impact of the region on the rest of the world has dramatically grown during the period of time since the appearance of the last edition of this book in 1997. The terrible events of September 11, 2001, in the United States have particularly emphasized the importance of increasing the understanding of the Middle East in other parts of the world. A sound knowledge of the history of the Middle East is a prerequisite to viewing its present-day circumstances with understanding and clarity.

This book first appeared in print forty-four years ago. Sydney Nettleton Fisher, who wrote the first three editions (of 1959, 1969, and 1979), provided an immensely useful and widely read guide to comprehending the complex and controversial history of the Middle East. In my revisions for the fourth and fifth editions, appearing in 1990 and 1997, I retained much of his earlier work while also making numerous changes.

For this sixth edition I have again made many changes, affecting almost every chapter. Probably the most important change was the combination of the two volumes of the fifth edition back into one, so as to make the book easier to use. It will now be possible for readers of the early chapters to follow a theme through to the present, while those chiefly interested in modern times can also easily review events from earlier times.

Other important changes include coverage of the dramatic and controversial events that have taken place since the appearance of the fifth edition. Some examples are the September 11, 2001 terrorist attacks in the United States, the subsequent war in Afghanistan, changes in Iranian politics following the election of President Khatami, the collapse of the Israel-Palestinian peace process, and the development of the second Palestinian intifada. In addition, much new research dealing with earlier times has been incorporated into appropriate chapters. Since general studies, monographs, and journal articles of high quality dealing with the history of the Middle East continue to appear in great abundance, I have made changes in the bibliographic references found at the end of each chapter. Unfortunately, due to space considerations I have had to omit mention of many valuable and useful works, an especially frustrating necessity in the flourishing field of Arab-Ottoman provincial history. However, I have been able to include some sites available by computer on the World Wide Web, trying to pick those most likely to contain valuable historical information or analysis rather than polemics or partisanship. The reader should be aware that since web sites frequently change their addresses and even occasionally disappear, the sites mentioned in the text may need to be found using search engines or may no longer be available.

In response to suggestions from readers, I have moved the two chapters on the history of post-1945 Israel, Jordan, and Palestine to an earlier location, thereby providing a better context for the chapters that follow. Many readers also asked me to include a chronological guide to key events, and so I have added a chronology at the end of the volume to provide a general framework for historical changes in the various regions of the Middle East. Throughout the book I have sought more directly to guide the reader's attention to crucial themes and to eliminate superfluous details. I have substantially expanded treatment of the history of women and social and economic history. Finally, I have made considerable revisions to Chapter 19 on the Safavids.

In this edition, I have attempted to provide a somewhat more systematic transliteration system than was employed in earlier versions, but I have not attempted, nor achieved, complete consistency. As Sydney Fisher pointed out in the preface to the first edition, words from Middle Eastern languages have been written in English in different ways, thereby causing much confusion. Most specialists have strongly held but divergent views on proper transliteration. I have usually opted for the simplest and most widely employed methods and spellings. Thus, I have shown ‘ains in Arabic words in only one case (the Ba‘th political party), and only in a few cases have I employed the symbols needed to represent modern Turkish spelling. In some cases, however, I have opted for a spelling that is closer to the original, as in Quran and ulama, rather than Koran and ulema.

I have the pleasant duty of thanking a number of people for their assistance. For all three editions for which I have been responsible, the most important suggestions for revisions came from students taking my classes, who offered frank and useful recommendations that led to many changes. I also owe a debt of gratitude to the following persons for their advice and proposals for change in earlier editions: Karl Barbir, Jean Braden, Linda Darling, Ronald Davis, Justin McCarthy, Donald Reid, Ezel Kural Shaw, and John Voll. For the sixth edition I thank Professor Corinne Blake of Rowan University, who kindly sent me an advance copy of an article providing many insights into web sites and the use of information technology for the study of the Middle East and Islamic civilization. For their very useful suggestions, I also wish to thank reviewers

Nathan Citino, Wittenburg University
Robert Olson, University of Kentucky
Clarence Zylstra, Whatcom Community College
Ismail Abdalla, College of William and Mary
Jon Mandaville, Portland State University
Patricia Risso, University of New Mexico
Elizabeth Frierson, University of Cincinnati
Caroline Marshall, James Madison University
Christopher Vanneson, Pierce College

Once again, professional colleagues who have written other general studies of the history of the Middle East provided important new ideas, data, and interpretations which challenged me to rethink my own earlier work. I found especially useful and stimulating works by Albert Hourani, William L. Cleveland, Arthur Goldschmidt, Jr., and Ira M. Lapidus. For the sixth edition, recent publications by C. E. Bosworth, Bernard Lewis, Glenn E. Parry, and especially Palmira Brummett have been important to me. Of course, I alone am responsible for those faults still remaining in this new edition.

My general approach to the history of the Middle East rests upon foundations established with the help of dedicated teachers and scholars with whom I have studied. They are Sydney Fisher, William McNeill, Marshall Hodgson, William Polk, Richard Chambers, Reuben Smith, Leonard Binder, and Marvin Zonis. I have also gained many insights about general surveys of the history of the Middle East from discussions with Jere Bacharach, Herbert Bodman, Lynne Rienner, and Marilyn Waldman.

My past and present colleagues at Virginia Tech have been of considerable assistance through their stimulating and provocative discussions. I wish to thank Burton Kaufman, Charles Kennedy, Robert Landen, Dean O'Donnell, Djavad Salehi Isfahani, and Peter Schmitthenner. I am especially grateful to Glenn Bugh, whose tactful help on ancient and Balkan history was invaluable. I highly appreciate the assistance of Andrea Kavanaugh, who provided exciting insights into communications technology in the Middle East and North Africa. I acknowledge with gratitude the support of the department of history at Virginia Tech under the leadership of Burton Kaufman, Albert Moyer, and Glenn Bugh. The three departmental secretaries—Linda Fountaine, Jan Francis, and Rhonda Pennington—assisted me patiently and efficiently. The staff of the Interlibrary Loan office of Newman Library worked diligently in providing access to many books and articles.

I am very grateful to friends and family who have provided encouragement and support during the long time needed to complete this new edition. My thanks go in particular to Stewart A. Dean, Elizabeth Fisher, Barbara Kaiser, Donald Miller, Ronald and Joyce Ochsenwald, Jon Miller, and David Starkey.

I can only hope that this sixth edition will be as useful to students and the general public as preceding versions have been. In this way the memory of Sydney Fisher, an inspiring teacher, writer, and friend, will be commemorated.

William Ochsenwald

Preface to the First Edition

For the last two thousand years and more the west has been drawn to, involved in, and fascinated by the culture, religion, resources, and politics of the Middle East. First the Greeks, then the Romans, later the western Europeans, and now the Americans are discovering the Middle East and its peoples. Historically, the area has been labeled the Orient, the East, and Levant, or the Near East; at present the most widely used term is the Middle East.

The United States, because of her great power and world position since the end of World War II, finds herself concerned with the contemporary problems of the Middle East. In general, Americans of today, many of whom have just become cognizant of the existence of the Middle East, find numerous aspects of its life and affairs quite unintelligible. This is particularly true when these complexities are expressed in the various and often conflicting pronouncements of propagandists for the Arabs, the Israelis and Zionism, the imperialists, the oil companies, the internationalists, the isolationists, the various nationalisms of the Middle East, and all sundry interests.

The attempt of this volume has been to present a brief account of the contemporary Middle Eastern scene so that the beginning college student or general reader can place the area in its proper setting and perspective. Many of the present situations and problems cannot be appreciated or evaluated properly without a knowledge and comprehension of the past, since the contemporary civilization of the Middle East probably has deeper and more significant roots in its past culture and experience than many other civilizations.

With this in mind, it was deemed advisable to begin the story, after a short introduction, with the life of the prophet Muhammad and the revolutionary changes that he made upon the society of his time. From this point the narrative has been carried forward, changing the central locus of the scene from Medina to Damascus to Baghdad to Asia Minor to Istanbul and back to the Arab lands as the fortunes of the area have developed, and at the same time examining each era more in detail as the present is approached.

Certain technicalities have been simplified for the beginner. The titles of many positions, past and present, have been translated into English equivalents in order not to confuse the reader with strange words or tire his eyes with unfamiliar combinations of letters and words. The transliteration of Middle Eastern proper names has always presented difficulties. In western literature pertaining to the Middle East, one can find the name of the Prophet rendered as Muhammad, Mohammed, Mohammad, Mohamed, Mahomet, Mehmed, Mehmet, Mehemet, and several other ways. In this book, Muhammad has been used for Arabs, Mehmed for Turks, and Mohammed for some others when individuals spelled the name in that fashion. For most words a spelling has been employed that would render them and their pronunciation most easily adopted by American readers. Where names of places or people have acquired a widely accepted western spelling, those forms have been used.

Since almost every volume concerning detailed or specialized aspects of Middle Eastern life and affairs contains considerable bibliographical material, and because of the excellent and wide coverage provided in Richard Ettinghausen's *A Selected and Annotated Bibliography of Books and Periodicals in Western Languages Dealing with the Near and Middle East with Special Emphasis on Mediaeval and Modern Times* (The Middle East Institute, Washington, D.C., 1952 and 1954), the inclusion of an extensive bibliography has not been felt necessary. The bibliographical entries at the end of the chapters have been supplied to indicate to the beginning student where easily accessible additional material on particular subjects may be obtained. These titles are suggested to serve as second steps for inquiring students who wish to dig more deeply into the many topics discussed only summarily in this text.

In gathering material for this volume it has been necessary to refer to a wide range of books, produced after years of diligent research and study by several generations of scholars in various lands. All will recognize my debt to these; students familiar with the literature of the diverse aspects of Middle Eastern history will appreciate my indebtedness to scholars of other years. This text could not have been written without their labors.

Through the years it has been my good fortune to obtain a closer knowledge of many aspects of Middle Eastern affairs and society through personal conversations and correspondence with many individuals concerned with that area of the world. Without mentioning names, I wish to thank them for the contributions they have made, sometimes unknowingly, to this text. Specifically I desire to pay tribute to inspiring teachers and mentors who have given me a better understanding of general and detailed problems and periods of Middle Eastern history. They are Frederick B. Artz of Oberlin College; Dr. Edgar J. Fisher of Amherst, Virginia; the late Albert Howe Lybyer of the University of Illinois; Philip K. Hitti and the late Walter Livingston Wright, Jr., of Princeton University; and Paul Wittek of the University of London.

In addition to these I am under deep obligation to my colleagues Professors William F. McDonald and John R. Randall for their criticism and aid in regard to certain chapters. Also, Dr. Halford L. Hoskins of the Library of Congress and Professor George G. Arnakis of the University of Texas read the entire volume, offered valuable suggestions, and caught numerous errors and slips. Dr. J. Merle Rife, State University, Indiana, Pennsylvania, was most helpful in assisting in the compilation of the bibliographical references.

However, any faults in fact or judgment which remain are my sole responsibility. Further recognition is due The Ohio State University Graduate School for assistance in the preparation of the manuscript.

This text could not have been prepared without the tolerance and cooperation of my entire family, which has lived with the manuscript for several years.

Sydney Nettleton Fisher

CHAPTER 1

Geographic Prologue

GEOGRAPHY

Since the end of World War II the term Middle East has referred to that area of the world comprising the present political states of Egypt, Sudan, Lebanon, Syria, Israel and the Occupied Territories, Jordan, Iraq, Saudi Arabia, Kuwait, Bahrain, Qatar, the United Arab Emirates, Oman, Yemen, Turkey, and Iran. In addition to this central core region of the Middle East, other nearby localities are now or have been in the past associated culturally and politically with it, including Afghanistan, Pakistan, central Asia, the Caucasus, the Balkan Peninsula, Cyprus, Libya, Tunisia, Algeria, Morocco, and Spain. Many people in the modern Middle East use this term to designate their region even though it originated in Britain and the United States and therefore reflects a geographic definition of world regions as seen from London and Washington. Other terms, such as Southwest Asia and North Africa or the Near East, are also used. In earlier times, the peoples of the Middle East viewed their region as the center of the world, while the lands to the east and west, including Europe and later the Americas, were seen as the peripheries.

Two geographic features of the Middle East have been significant in all periods of history. Its location has given it an important, sometimes strategic, central position between Africa and Eurasia, and between the Mediterranean world and the Asia of India and China. Nations, tribes, traders, armies, and pilgrims—peoples on the move—have traversed the Middle East, finding the land bridge convenient and along the way discovering the wealth of the area and the civilizations of its peoples.

The second important geographic feature is the relative magnitude of the Middle East. Arabia, the central land mass of the Middle East, embraces an area about the same size as that of the United States east of the Mississippi River plus Texas and California. The southern shore facing the Indian Ocean from Aden to Muscat spans the same distance as that between Boston and New Orleans; on the west, the Red Sea is as wide as Lake Erie is long, and the distance from Aden to Port Said is nearly the same as that from New York to Denver. Northward from Arabia proper to the Turkish frontier is roughly 400 miles, or 650 kilometers. When Egypt, Iran, and Turkey are added, the area becomes equivalent to that of the continental United States, or about thirty times the size of Britain.

Stretching out 2000 miles (3200 km.) westward from the mouth of the Nile River to the Atlantic Ocean lies North Africa, culturally a part of the Middle East since the end of the seventh century. Moreover, the delimitation of the Middle East could include the central Asian republics, Afghanistan, and Pakistan, with such historic cities as Bukhara, Samarkand, Kabul, and Lahore. Thus, the physical size of the Middle East becomes impressive to Europeans and Americans who are accustomed to seeing these areas in the framework of maps of Asia and Africa.

PHYSIOGRAPHY

The geologic characteristics of the Middle East show a wide variety of land features, ranging from great bodies of water to low-lying land and swampy regions to rough mountain areas. Over the past 7000 years or so there seems to have been no important physiographic change except that the deltas of most of the rivers have grown and extended the land seaward. In western Turkey, for example, animals now graze on the floodplain of the Meander River in the exact spot where the Persian fleet vanquished the Greeks in antiquity.

Arabia, in general, is a tilted plateau, slanting upward from the northeast to the southwest with a sharp drop in Yemen from 12,000 feet (3700 m.) down to the Red Sea. Central Turkey and central Iran are elevated plateaus, in places reaching an altitude of 8000 feet (2400 m.). Rugged mountains dominate Middle Eastern geography. From a high center in northwestern Iran in the neighborhood of Mount Ararat, mountain ranges up to 18,000 feet (5500 m.) in altitude branch out in several chains: the Elburz group, running eastward south of the Caspian Sea; the Zagros system, a wide series of ranges protruding in a southeasterly direction to Afghanistan and India; and the famed Taurus Mountains, pushing southwestward to the Mediterranean and separating the Anatolian plateau from Syria. The numerous mountains have tended to divide and separate the residents of the Middle East, while allowing relatively small groups of mountaineers to defend themselves easily against armies coming from the plains. Earthquakes in the mountainous zones have often caused great damage, as in 1999, when at least 15,000 people were killed in Turkey.

Rivers have played an important role in fostering political unity and settled agriculture, and they have deeply influenced the development of civilization in the Middle East. Two river systems are basic to the history of the area: the Nile and the Tigris-Euphrates. Flowing from central Africa and Ethiopia, the Nile passes through a relatively flat region in Sudan, where an enormous swamp impedes transportation in the south; the Nile, the world's longest river, then reaches the cataract zone north of Khartoum, where a gorge has been cut. Below Aswan, the Nile flows through a well-developed valley about 6 miles (10 km.) wide to Cairo, where the delta begins. Before the construction of the Aswan High Dam in 1970, the river started to rise in Egypt in August, reaching its peak in September, 18 feet above the low of April and May. Each year tons of sediment, rich in mineral substances, are carried into Egypt, and more than half of this silt formerly reached the delta.

The other great river system, the Tigris-Euphrates, rises in the highlands of eastern Turkey. Winter snowfall feeds both streams, which turn and twist through narrow defiles, emptying out upon the plains of Syria and Kurdistan. Rushing southward, the rivers converge upon Baghdad but meet only about 230 miles (370 km.) farther on where they form the Shatt al-Arab, which flows gently for about 100 miles (160 km.) to the Persian (or Arabian) Gulf. The rivers are at their lowest in September and October but then begin to rise, reaching a flood stage in April for the Tigris and, until recently, in May for the Euphrates. The Tabqa Dam in Syria and the Turkish Keban Dam on the Euphrates control much of the flooding, generate electric power, and extend the arable lands in both countries. Within historic times silt from the Tigris and the Euphrates and two Iranian tributaries of the former filled in the Persian Gulf from near the site of Baghdad to the present shoreline.

Three straits play a major role in Middle Eastern commerce and strategy: the Bab al-Mandeb and the Strait of Hormuz at the entrances from the Indian Ocean to the Red Sea and the Persian Gulf, and the famous straits that form the waterway from the Black Sea to the Aegean Sea. The last of these has historically been the most important. From the Black Sea extends the narrow Bosphorus, a 17-mile (28-km.) waterway. Everywhere the channel is deep. On a point of land in Europe where the Bosphorus empties into the Sea of Marmara stands one of the great cities of the Middle East—variously known as Byzantium, Constantinople, or Istanbul. The Sea of Marmara extends some 125 miles southwestward to the Dardanelles. This historic passage, often called the Hellespont, is 36 miles (57 km.) long and empties into the Aegean. The Bosphorus, Marmara, and Dardanelles separate Europe from Asia yet serve as a strong connecting link between east and west. Economically, politically, and strategically, the straits have been important in controlling passage between the Mediterranean and the Black seas.

CLIMATE

During the fourth glacial period, some 25,000 years ago, when much of Europe and northern Asia was covered with an ice sheet, the southern Middle East and the Sahara regions were moist and dotted with lakes and seas, a well-watered wooded land abounding with animals. As the ice receded, the desert area between the tropical and the temperate zones appeared and gradually grew. Compared with these major events change has occurred in the climate of the Middle East in the past 5000 years only at a slow pace.

Rainfall along the shores of the Mediterranean, Black, and Caspian seas and the southern part of the Red Sea is relatively abundant. Many areas receive an average annual fall of 30 inches (760 mm.) or more. (As one progresses inland, however, the average drops appreciably; most of Egypt and the plateaus of Arabia, Iran, and eastern Turkey have a desert climate.) Moreover, the rains are not only seasonal but almost capricious. Damascus has an average annual rainfall of about 10 inches (250 mm.), but four inches have been known to fall in one morning. The mountainous areas of eastern Turkey and Iran receive more moisture, but here, too, winter is the wet season, with much of the precipitation occurring in the form of snow. The one exception to the winter rain

Danube
CARPATHIAN MTS.
Dniester
Pruth
Donets
DONETS BASIN
Dnieper
ALPS
Po
SEA OF AZOV
CRIMEA
Iron Gate
Danube
APENNINES
ADRIATIC SEA
BALKAN
BALKAN MTS.
BLACK SEA
CAU
CORSICA
PENINSULA
Bosphorus
PONTIC MTS.
TYRRHENIAN SEA
SARDINIA
Dardanelles
ANATOLIA
IONIAN IS.
AEGEAN SEA
Murat
SPORADES
Lake Tuz
SICILY
TAURUS MTS.
MEDITERRANEAN SEA
RHODES
CRETE
CYPRUS
SYRIAN DESERT
Nile Delta
DEAD SEA
TRIPOLITANIA
Suez Canal
CYRENAICA
QATTARA DEPRESSION
NAFUD DESERT
Siwa Oasis
Gulf of Suez
SINAI PEN.
Gulf of Aqaba
EASTERN DESERT
HIJAZ
Nile
Farafra Oasis
LIBYAN
Kharga Oasis
Kufra Oasis
Red Sea
FEZZAN
SAHARA
Aswan High Dam
Lake Nasser
DESERT
NUBIAN DESERT
MANGUENI PLATEAU
TIBESTI MTS.
THAMAH
ENNEDI
Lake Chad
Sennar Dam
MARRA MTS.
Lake Tana
GUERA MASSIF
Blue Nile
BAUCHI PLATEAU
White Nile
ADAMAWA
ETHIOPIAN HIGHLANDS
Lake Turkana
10°
20°
30°
40°

The Geography of the Middle East
THE STEPPES
Don
Volga
CASPIAN DEPRESSION
TURAN LOWLAND
Lake Balkhash
ARAL SEA
Syr Darya
CAUCASUS MTS.
CASPIAN SEA
Amu Darya
TIAN SHAN
Mount Ararat
KARA KUM
Lake Van
KOPET MTS.
PAMIRS
Lake Urmia
KURDISTAN
ELBURZ MTS.
HINDU KUSH
Mount Damavand
ZAGROS MOUNTAINS
KAVIR DESERT
KHURASAN
Khyber Pass
KASHMIR
MESOPOTAMIA
IRANIAN PLATEAU
LUT DESERT
Indus
Euphrates
Tigris
Karun
KHASH DESERT
Persian Gulf
FARS
GREAT INDIAN DESERT
Strait of Hormuz
AL DAHNA DESERT
Gulf of Oman
TUWAIQ MTS.
Rann of Kutch
ARABIAN PENINSULA
RUB' AL KHALI
MASIRAH
ASIR
ARABIAN SEA
HADHRAMAUT
Bab al-Mandeb
Gulf of Aden
SOCOTRA
SOMALI PENINSULA
INDIAN OCEAN
50°
40°
30°
20°
10°
60°
70°
0
250
500 mi
400
800 km

pattern is the monsoon region of southern and southwestern Arabia, which gets most of its rainfall in the months of July, August, and September.

Temperatures depend upon latitude and altitude, and winter in the mountains of Arabia, Iran, and eastern Anatolia can be quite bitter. Summer temperatures in Egypt, Arabia, and Iraq are hot, sometimes over 100°F (38°C) during the day, but nights are cool everywhere except in some of the lower valleys and along some coasts where the humidity is high.

FLORA AND FAUNA

Wood has been a prized building material and, along with animal dung, the principal fuel in the Middle East from the beginning of history until the advent of coal and oil. Over the past 5000 years a process of deforestation has denuded most of the land. Some stands of trees remain on the slopes of the Zagros and Elburz mountains, in coastal Anatolia, and on the Lebanon Mountains, while the systematic planting of trees has restored some of the earlier landscape in Turkey and Israel. Elsewhere the land would be bare but for cypresses in cemeteries and gardens and poplars along streams and irrigation ditches.

Unconcern about land conservation over the past 5000 years has resulted in the destruction of much of the forest and topsoil resources of the Middle East, and pollution of water sources is also now a major problem. But absence of concern cannot be said to have existed with respect to the cultivation of edible flora of the area. Wheat, barley, rye, broad beans, lentils, onions, garlic, figs, grapes, apricots, olives, and dates are the principal foods developed from the vegetation of the area. Industrial crops include cotton, tobacco, and sugar beets.

Domestication of native animals of the Middle East probably began about 8000 B.C.E. It is difficult to tell in what order, but at some very early time the dog (probably first), sheep, goat, pig, ox, and donkey were tamed and used for work or to provide food and clothing. Domesticated horses and camels were introduced into the area from farther east in Asia in the second millennium B.C.E. As the forests became scarcer, the pig was replaced by more economical all-purpose animals such as the ox, goat, and sheep; the arrival of the camel was crucial for habitation in the desert and facilitated Middle Eastern nomadism in Arabia proper.

Middle Eastern waters teem with fish. The Caspian Sea has long been noted for its sturgeon and caviar. The Black Sea and the Arabian Sea have numerous varieties of fish. And the eastern Mediterranean, fed by the vegetable matter of the Nile, has been for centuries a productive spot for fish of all kinds, though the Aswan High Dam and environmental pollution have presented new challenges to fishers.

RESOURCES

The significant natural resources of the Middle East have been, and still are, the availability and interrelationship of water, soil, sun, plants, and animals, allowing for a productive agriculture. Other natural resources are the excellent clays with which the bricks, pots, and finer ceramics of many cultures have been fashioned. Mountains and rock formations laid bare by river erosion have provided extensive quarries for basalt, granite, marble, sandstone, and limestone.

Gold, silver, copper, and iron are extracted in easily workable ores. The presence of other metals such as tin, nickel, and copper led the way to the development of bronze and brass. Deposits of these metals have been worked almost continuously up to the present, and the output has been of considerable value in the economy and life of the area. In the twentieth century other metals have come to the fore. Chromium and manganese are found in sizable deposits, and phosphate rock can be used in making chemical fertilizers. Coal, lignite, and iron ore exist in considerable amounts in Turkey and Iran, and to a lesser extent in Egypt.

The greatest of the natural resources of the Middle East of the present, beyond land and water, are oil and natural gas. Small oil fields have been located in Turkey, Syria, Yemen, and Israel, but the large ones are those of Iran; Iraq; along the Persian Gulf in Saudi Arabia, Kuwait, Bahrain, Qatar, the United Arab Emirates, and Oman; and in Egypt, Libya, and Algeria. No one yet knows the full extent of the oil and natural gas of the Middle East, but the area's known reserves far outstrip those of any other oil-producing region, and the presence of this natural resource has changed the world importance of the Middle East.

PEOPLE

While the Middle East is drier than many other regions of the world, the stereotypical view that it is mostly desert is incorrect. The Middle East, despite its large deserts, was blessed with a warm climate, a fertile soil, animals and plants suitable for food, some waters available for irrigation, and varied mineral resources; it thus was a favorable area for the development of settled life, for the increase in standards of living, and for the growth of organized and complex societies. Most people have tended to live in the well-watered areas, and settlement patterns have been complicated, with many different groups who live close to each other or even together in the same communities.

The earliest known human inhabitants in the Middle East lived at least a million years ago. Although scientists have yet to unravel the wanderings of prehistoric Homo sapiens in the Middle East, it seems certain that around 13,000 B.C.E., as the fourth glacial period terminated, the well-watered regions of Arabia and the Sahara were inhabited by widely dispersed groups of people, most of whom gathered food rather than raised crops. Then, through millennia, as the ice cap was retreating to Scandinavia, Arabia and the Sahara became drier and hotter, and their inhabitants moved northward and seaward.

Much domestication of plants and animals took place in the highlands, with the plow and the wheel being developed in the fourth millennium. With the advent of settled agriculture into the chief river valleys where water was readily available, Middle Eastern civilization had its beginnings. Because rivers flooded annually, renewing the soil with the silt they deposited, agriculturalists could continue to cultivate the same fields year after year, generation after generation. Eventually this development permitted the growth of settled, complex communities, leading to a crucial and long-lasting triple division of social and economic activity that came to influence the way most people lived.

The three economic groups were nomads, who gained their livelihood by herding animals; farmers or peasants, who constituted the bulk of the population in most parts of the Middle East and who raised crops as they resided in villages; and townspeople, who provided services and goods of diverse types. All three groups interacted with each other and were often mutually interdependent. In this context, records accumulated and history in the Middle East began.

REFERENCES

Bacharach, Jere L.: *A Middle East Studies Handbook.* Seattle: University of Washington Press, 1984. Invaluable not only for its maps but also for its chronology, dynastic tables, and lists of heads of state. Excellent for the beginning student and also highly useful for specialists.

Beaumont, Peter, et al.: *The Middle East: A Geographical Study.* 2d ed. New York: Halsted Press, 1988. Covers physical and social geography for the whole region and country by country.

Blake, Gerald, et al.: *The Cambridge Atlas of the Middle East and North Africa.* Cambridge: Cambridge University Press, 1987. Many clear maps show physical, cultural, economic, and political aspects of modern geography.

Coon, Carleton S.: *Caravan: The Story of the Middle East.* New York: Holt, 1951. An excellent anthropological introduction to the Middle East, written in a style easily understood by the beginning student.

Drysdale, Alasdair, and Gerald H. Blake: *The Middle East and North Africa: A Political Geography.* New York: Oxford University Press, 1985. Shows the relationship between political and diplomatic issues and geographic factors.

Fisher, W. B.: *The Middle East: A Physical, Social and Regional Geography.* 7th ed. London: Methuen, 1978. Authoritative; a classic.

Held, Colbert C.: *Middle East Patterns: Places, Peoples, and Politics.* 3rd ed. Boulder, Colo.: Westview, 2000. In addition to country-by-country coverage there is thorough treatment of historical and general factors. The best introductory work available.

Kennedy, Hugh: *An Historical Atlas of Islam.* Revised ed. Leiden: Brill, 2002. Valuable for its extensive coverage, this new edition of William Brice's 1981 atlas includes a searchable CD-Rom.

Robinson, Francis: *Atlas of the Islamic World since 1500.* New York: Facts on File, 1982. Filled with beautiful illustrations, maps, and a historical narrative that is comparative and informative.

Wagstaff, J. M.: *The Evolution of Middle Eastern Landscapes: An Outline to A.D. 1840.* London: Croom Helm, 1985. A thoughtful and elegant study of the impact of society on the environment, with an emphasis on the period up to the rise of Islam.

CHAPTER 2

Pre-Islamic Politics and Society in the Middle East

THE RISE OF CIVILIZATION

The history of the Middle East may be usefully divided into several units: the period of antiquity, stretching from the rise of civilization to the coming of Islam; the classical Islamic period, which extended from the life of Muhammad to the middle of the tenth century; the two parts of medieval Middle Eastern history—from about C.E. 950 to about 1250, and a second part to about 1500; and then the two phases of the history of the modern Middle East—a time dominated by great empires (1500 to 1800) and then recent centuries that saw the integration of the Middle East into world systems.

The first of these historical units began when the civilization of the Middle East started in the Nile valley and in Mesopotamia along the Tigris and Euphrates rivers (located in modern-day Iraq). Archaeologists are also now discovering that significant cultures were independently developed in northern Syria and in Palestine, especially at Jericho after 9000 B.C.E.; in northern Mesopotamia around 8900 B.C.E.; and in the south-central plateau of Anatolia some time before 7000 B.C.E. Botanists and geneticists have shown that in the foothills of western Asia between the Mediterranean and the Himalayas, edible grasses, like wheat and barley, and herd animals, such as sheep, goats, and cattle, had their natural habitats. Small, sheltered groups of people learned to cultivate and domesticate these natural resources and established settled societies. Eventually, large walled towns were built and defended, although the residents of the towns depended ultimately on peasants, nomads, and merchants for food and goods. Civilizations with writing, art forms, religious practices, foreign trade, and social and political norms appeared.

Only when agricultural skills and social techniques had been developed adequately could the complex problems of living on the plains of rivers be solved. Just how and where the transitions occurred has not yet been determined, but they undoubtedly took place slowly over several millennia. In any case, in two centers of highly evolved urban civilizations, along the Tigris-Euphrates and the Nile, it can be shown that each culture arrived in the area already in a transitional stage, that each brought with it domesticated plants and animals (many of which were of common origin), but that each in its new habitat independently developed an urban civilization.

Periodization in the History of the Islamic Middle East

Antiquity: from the rise of civilization to the coming of Islam

Classical Islamic period: from the life of the prophet Muhammad to the middle of the tenth century C.E.

The early medieval era in the Middle East: from about 950 to about 1250

The late medieval era in the Middle East: from about 1250 to about 1500

The early modern Middle East: from about 1500 to about 1800

The modern Middle East: from about 1800 to the present

Somewhat after the year 3500 B.C.E. the Sumerian people arrived in the Tigris-Euphrates valley, where Sumerian city-states evolved around 3100 B.C.E. with society divided into technological-social classes—bureaucrats, priests, traders, farmers, and artisans—divisions that have remained significant in Middle Eastern civilizations. Writing was invented. The peoples of Mesopotamia began to use irrigation techniques to provide water for crops. Other peoples from Arabia were drawn to the prosperous Sumerian cities and to the densely settled countryside. They spoke a language belonging to the Semitic family, which predominated in central Arabia. Thus, very early in history, a mixture of people with different languages and origins influenced events.

Farther north along the middle Euphrates, about 3000 B.C.E., Semitic-language speakers, probably seminomads from the steppes or desert, began to become sedentary in the cities of the region. For a thousand years the ruling families of Sumerian and northern states were ardent rivals, although conflict among the cities in each group was the norm. A larger unit was created about the year 1750 B.C.E. by the union of all of Mesopotamia under Hammurabi of Babylon.

With the rise of warring states, patriarchal values probably became predominant, while the authority of women and female deities decreased. Kingship was usually hereditary within the males belonging to a family, and the dynastic principle dominated political structures. Women could become scribes, and at least some upper-class women were literate; however, most aspects of public life were usually controlled by men.

At approximately the same time that the Sumerians appeared in Mesopotamia, a civilization with its own distinctive language slowly began to develop along the Nile. The nature of the land, the annual flooding of the Nile, the local presence of copper, and the relative isolation of the Nile valley by the surrounding deserts were conducive to the establishment of an absolute monarchy and a flourishing culture. Shortly before 3000 B.C.E. a series of dynasties headed by pharaohs who were considered divine ruled a united Egypt, developed hieroglyphic writing, and constructed enormous pyramids that served as royal tombs. The pharaohs supervised a highly efficient and centralized state. Irrigation projects, preparation for a life after death, and the worship of the gods preoccupied the rulers. Egypt often dominated nearby areas, while its art, commerce, and religions had a wide influence.

Other areas beyond the two great river valleys developed aspects of civilization somewhat later. Yemen experienced settled agriculture about 2000 B.C.E., while Oman saw long-distance trade, cultivation of animals, and sophisticated use of metals by about 2500 B.C.E. Ebla in northern Syria employed cuneiform writing by 2400 B.C.E., and its widespread commerce and diverse gods reflected the open horizons of its population. The changes that affected southern Mesopotamia so greatly also influenced nearby southwestern Persia.

Early in the second millennium B.C.E. peoples from eastern Europe and western Asia began a southward movement, exerting population pressures upon the whole of the Middle East. In a succession of thrusts, these intruders, first equipped with bronze weapons and then with iron weapons, and accompanied by horses and camels, pushed ahead into the Middle East. Invaders included Hittites, Armenians, Greeks, Philistines, Medes, and Persians. Between these invasions and conquests of the northmen, pharaonic Egypt was independent and flourishing, and Semitic-language tribes such as Assyrians, Aramaeans, Phoenicians, Nabataeans, and Hebrews established states in Mesopotamia, Syria, or Palestine.

Around 1000 B.C.E. King David made Jerusalem the capital of the expanding Jewish state; prophets, who built on the experiences of earlier leaders such as Moses, established the foundations of monotheistic faith and a religious-moral code for living. Eventually, the Torah, the books of the prophets, and later scriptures became the basis of what Christians call the Old Testament. Ruled sometimes by judges, then by kings, and often in later centuries controlled by foreign dynasties, the Jewish Israelites strove to preserve their covenant with God by rejecting polytheism.

Each group of invaders, at the time of its arrival upon the Middle Eastern scene and in its first contact with Middle Eastern civilization, was leading a nomadic or pastoral life. The change to an organized life with greater economic specialization and division of labor produced turmoil and strains, but the transition was usually made successfully. Each group added something in religion, the art of writing, metallurgical skills, political organization, transportation, irrigation, or astronomy, and within a brief period the knowledge was disseminated over the entire area.

ANCIENT EMPIRES

By the beginning of the first millennium B.C.E. the Middle East was rapidly becoming one cultural region, the use of iron started to spread, and a number of efforts were made to unite the area politically. Throughout the second millennium B.C.E. the Egyptian pharaohs had sought and from time to time held control of Syria, Palestine, and parts of Sudan. Anatolian kings such as the Hittites, however, vied with the pharaohs for these provinces; and from that age until the present the Syrian coast has been able to maintain its independence only when both Egypt and Anatolia/Mesopotamia have been weak or evenly matched.

Iron weapons, a disciplined army, a well-organized bureaucracy, and battering rams on wheels gave the Assyrians such an advantage in the seventh century B.C.E. that Nineveh held sway from Sinai nearly to the Caspian Sea and from southern Mesopotamia

The Middle East in Antiquity

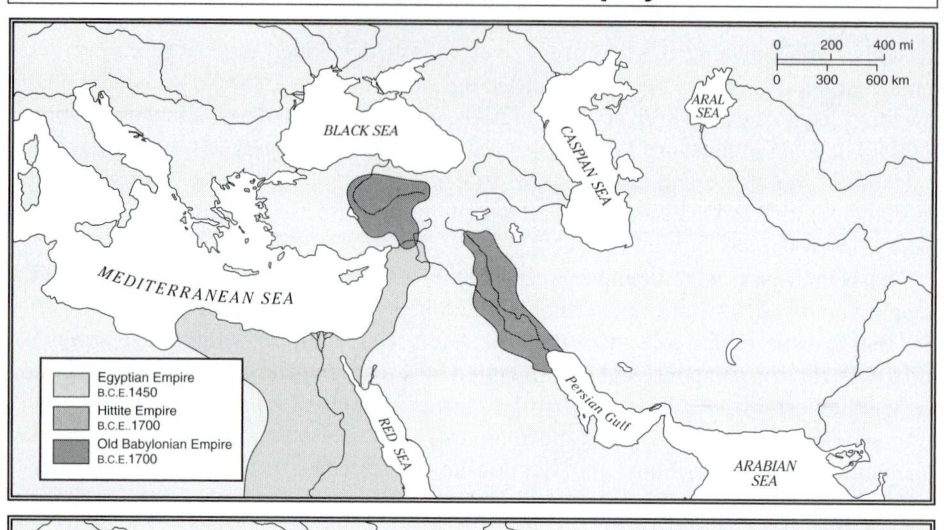

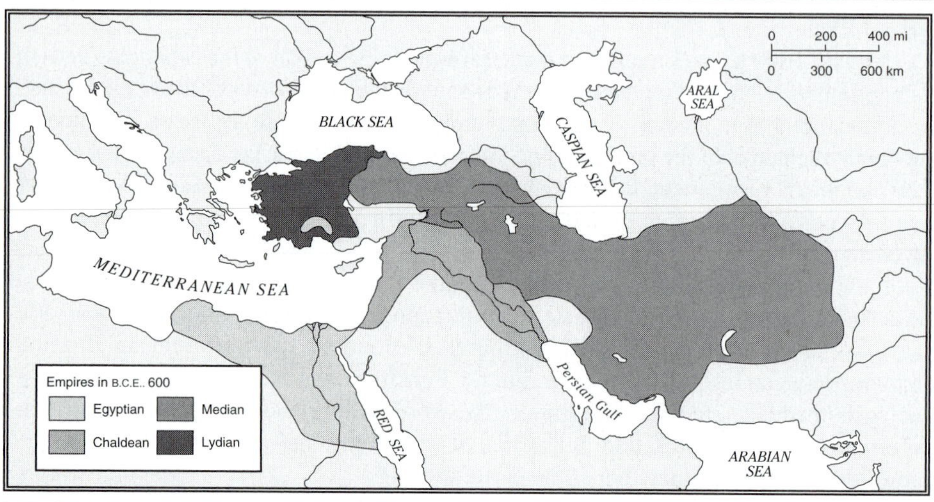

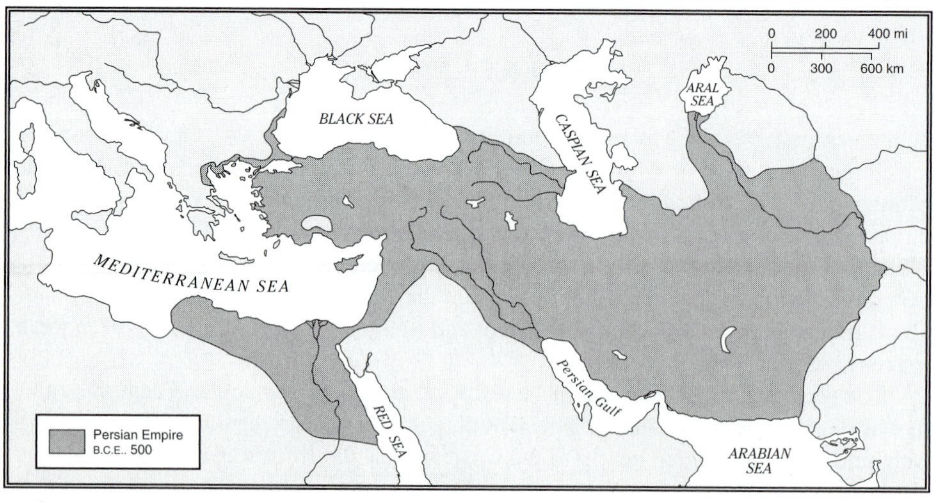

The Middle East in Antiquity

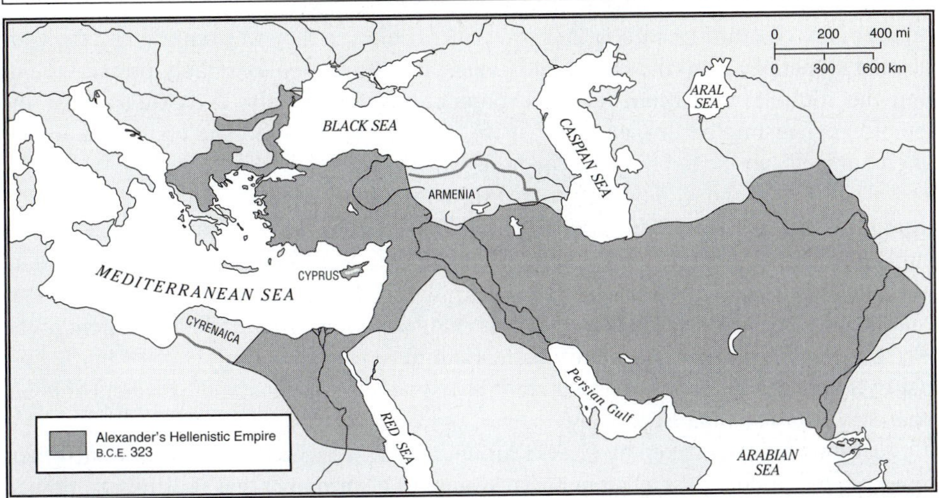

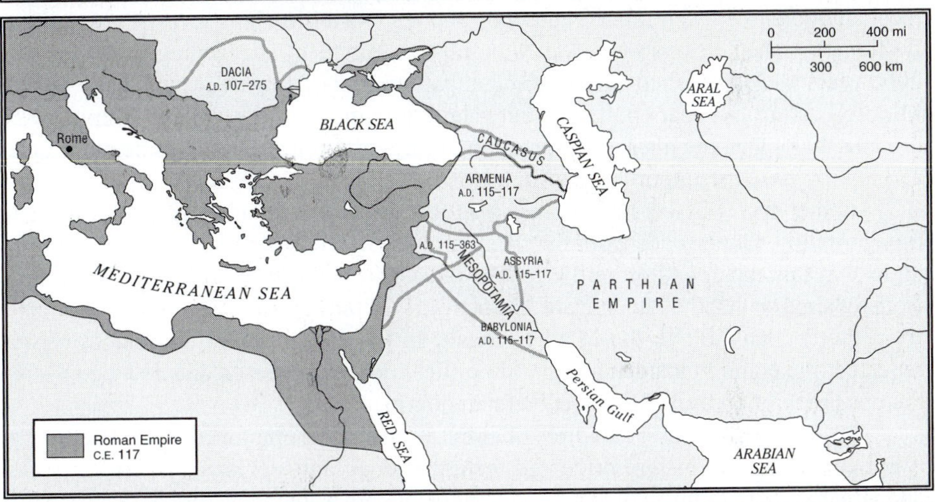

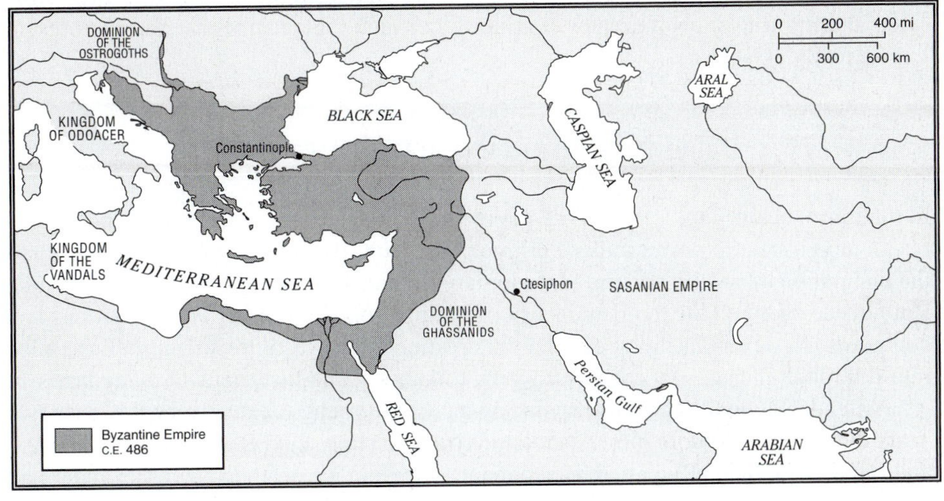

to the plains of central Anatolia. Assyrian rulers believed they were entitled by the gods to rule all peoples, and the tactics the kings used were often extremely brutal, including the forcible relocation of whole populations. Ultimately, overextension of the empire, exhausting battles, and civil strife, coupled with hatred and resistance among their subjects, weakened the army and the government.

The unity of the Middle East was restored by the Persians, a group of Zoroastrian Iranians from the Zagros range, who reunited the areas of the previous Assyrian Empire and added Greek Anatolia, Thrace, the Nile valley to Sudan, Afghanistan, Baluchistan, the Punjab, coastal Oman, and parts of central Asia. The heart of their empire was Persia (later known as Iran) and Mesopotamia (modern Iraq). With the establishment of the Persian Empire in the sixth century B.C.E. Semitic speakers lost rule in the Middle East for over a thousand years. It was not until the rise of the Arabs under the banners of Islam that they regained their hegemony.

Despite being checked by Greeks around 490 B.C.E., the Persians maintained their power in the Middle East by an imperial system of government that skillfully combined local autonomy with centralized authority and responsibility. This form of government fashioned by the Persians was adopted in most essentials by succeeding rulers for over 2000 years and established a governmental pattern that often was accepted as a part of Middle Eastern civilization. The twenty-three provinces of the Persian Empire were organized along ethnic lines, and toleration of local differences was considerable. Taxes and loyalty were the important requirements.

Another secret of Persian success was the advancement of communications and transportation. Good roads from the frontier to the heart of the empire were kept open under constant repair and surveillance. The old canals between the Nile and the Red Sea were repaired so that the Phoenicians, the stalwarts of the Persian fleet, could sail directly from the Persian Gulf to the Mediterranean. In the end, however, the old story was repeated: the empire changed as central political power decreased and new peoples on the periphery of control challenged Persian dominance.

The history of the great empires of antiquity would be employed much later, in the twentieth century, to inspire pride and foster national unity, as Persians, Turks, Arabs, and Israelis used examples of earlier accomplishments from the historical record, while often altering it to show a greater continuity between the ancient past and the present than actually existed.

ALEXANDER AND THE GREEKS

In the fourth century B.C.E. a new people in the Balkans who were related to the Greeks began their ascent to power under Philip of Macedon. By the use of heavier armor and the integration of cavalry and the Macedonian phalanx, Greece was subjected to his rule. But Greece captured the mind and spirit of Philip's son, Alexander. The campaigns and conquests of Alexander the Great and the creation of his vast Greek empire have been retold through the ages by countless poets, romantics, and historians of many lands.

After defeating the Persian army in 334 B.C.E., the young Alexander, only twenty-two years old, swept all before him. Anatolia, Syria, Palestine, Egypt, Mesopotamia, Persia, and India to the Indus River had been conquered before his death in 323. Alexander had hoped to unify the entire Middle East into one lasting empire and he therefore married a Persian princess. But his untimely death left only his chief generals to battle for the empire, which they eventually divided: Ptolemy in Egypt, Antigonus initially in Anatolia and then his successors in Macedonia and Greece, and Seleucus in Syria and Iran.

Following the breakup of Alexander's empire, the Middle East fell heir to a century of international political anarchy and intermittent wars; yet it enjoyed a period of vast trade and wealth as well as many decades of important intellectual and artistic activity. It was the apogee of the brilliant Hellenistic age, which persisted for two centuries more until, with Cleopatra's suicide, the last vestige of Ptolemaic rule in Egypt ended and the Nile valley became a Roman province.

THE ROMAN AND PARTHIAN EMPIRES AND THEIR SUCCESSORS

Rome became the arbiter of Middle Eastern affairs, as the Mediterranean was turned into a vast Roman lake. Except for the Tigris-Euphrates, the plateaus of Persia, and most of Arabia, the Middle East was transformed into Roman provinces and was ruled from Rome until the emperor Constantine transferred his capital eastward to Constantinople, on the shores of the Bosphorus. (The Greek city of Byzantium was traditionally said to have been founded in 667 B.C.E.; renamed Constantinople, it kept that designation until the Ottoman Muslim conquest in 1453, after which it also became known as Istanbul.) From the establishment of Constantinople in C.E. 330 to the defeat of the emperor Heraclius by the Arab Muslim armies in 638, the provinces of the Middle East were important parts of the Byzantine or Eastern Roman Empire, whose history will be more fully discussed in Chapter 13.

In Mesopotamia and Persia in the second century B.C.E. the great Parthian Empire flourished under Mithridates I. All territory east of the Euphrates was seized by the Parthian king of kings, who built his royal palace at Ctesiphon on the Tigris. The Parthian power rested on its nomadic cavalry, Zoroastrianism, and on a cultural reaction against Hellenism, even though the kings knew Greek and had Greek tragedies performed at their court. The Parthians defeated the Romans, who recognized Parthian dominion over all of Mesopotamia.

Early in the third century C.E. internal weakness brought the downfall of the Parthian kings at the hands of a new Persian family, the Sasanians, who used extensive irrigation and international commerce to create a wealthy empire. The founder of the dynasty was a Zoroastrian, and that dualistic faith was vigorously advanced as the official religion of the empire. Wars with the Romans and Byzantines found the religious differences to be as important as the political ones.

From their main residence at Ctesiphon the Sasanians time and again harried the Byzantine provinces of Syria and Anatolia. After the fifth century, when Christianity was tolerated and the Nestorian church had become widespread in the Sasanian Empire, particularly in Mesopotamia, the conflicts with Constantinople were more imperial in nature. The Byzantine emperor Justinian checked the Sasanians temporarily, but exhausting campaigns were resumed under Justinian's successors. Bubonic plague and the decline of urban life further weakened the Byzantine lands.

A powerful Sasanian army erupted into Syria in 613, destroying the Church of the Holy Sepulcher in Jerusalem and pillaging Damascus. A Sasanian army captured the cities across from Constantinople. Evil days appeared for the Byzantines, but the tide turned. Between 622 and 628 Heraclius, the new Byzantine emperor, succeeded in driving the Sasanians from Egypt and Syria, and looted Ctesiphon. But the wars, ensuing destruction, and internal changes left both empires weakened. Syria, Egypt, and Mesopotamia were ripe for picking by the new armies of the Muslim Arabs in the next decade.

PRE-ISLAMIC CIVILIZATION IN THE MIDDLE EAST

For nearly a thousand years much of the Middle East was subjected to the influence of Greek, Hellenistic, Roman, and Byzantine states. Although it would be possible to point out distinguishing characteristics of each of these and to show how each evolved from its predecessor, they form one continuous experience for the history of the later Middle East.

First and foremost among the changes was the adoption of Greek by the educated and by the leaders of society as the language of government, philosophy, literature, and sophisticated communication. Greek colonists—merchants, soldiers, and government officials—settled in most of the Middle Eastern cities and founded many new Greek cities, such as Alexandria in Egypt. Intellectually and artistically, much of the Middle East appeared as one world. Greek philosophies and science became universal throughout the area, although many leaders were not originally Greek speakers.

Roman and Sasanian rule ended the internecine warfare of the Alexandrian successor states and brought a more bountiful material life to the cities of the Middle East. The remains of the almost countless theaters, temples, baths, gymnasiums, and public buildings that dot the Middle East today are silent witnesses of the populous, thriving, and wealthy cities of that age and of the public life that was dominated by men. Urban upper-class women were often veiled in areas influenced by the Greeks and Persians; while rulers frequently had harems, most men were monogamous.

Roman and Sasanian military might and administrative skill could not always control the Middle East. Many people did not adopt Sasanian and Roman ways in speech, dress, food, religion, and manners. As the years passed, the Hellenistic states became less and less Greek, conforming more faithfully to earlier patterns of life in the Middle East. The Ptolemies appeared as pharaohs, and the Seleucids lived as Assyrian and Persian monarchs. Jesus of Nazareth spoke Aramaic, not Greek. Greek and Roman civilization pervaded many of the cities of Syria and Egypt, but not the villages or nomadic areas of the Middle East.

CHRISTIANITY AND ZOROASTRIANISM

The new contribution that came to the cultural stream of the Middle East with Byzantine dominion was Christianity, which received recognition as the official religion of the empire. In Hellenistic and Roman periods people were groping for a philosophy of life and a religion that would answer some of the problems of those rapidly changing and turbulent days. Faith in the power or protection of the Greek gods had largely disappeared by the time of Alexander. The educated neglected the gods and pursued philosophical systems that served as intellectual shelters where distressed souls might take refuge from a materialistic and heartless society.

To the masses these philosophies were meaningless. The formation of large empires deprived the individual of the sense of identity he or she might have enjoyed in a city-state, with its protecting god. As helpless individuals, people needed a personal savior. They therefore turned to the mystery cults of Asia. Here the individual, by witnessing and participating in an esoteric ritual, was initiated into the mysteries of life and death, god and immortality. As the savior-god had lived and died and risen again, so the lonely and helpless individual, living in a tumultuous world, might win eternal salvation by personal union with the god.

In the second century C.E. the greatest change in the Middle East, under Roman rule, came with the rise and spread of Christianity. Taking many of the tenets of monotheistic Judaism, of the Greek philosophies, and of the Asian cults, Christianity added two vital factors that were largely absent in Hellenism and Romanism: Christ offered immortality to all, and his creed was based on love of humanity.

Early Christianity appealed especially to urban Hellenistic society, the language of the church being Greek. After Christianity obtained official status, the Byzantine state rapidly developed into a synthesis of Hellenism and Christianity with earlier influences, and a blending of the political power of the state and the religious authority of the church.

The union of autocracy and theocracy in the Byzantine state ensured the alienation of some of the masses in the Middle Eastern provinces. As new Christian doctrines from the Middle East were branded heresies by the state-dominated church councils, separate native Christian churches evolved. Byzantine Constantinople could not force its type of Christianity upon all the Middle Eastern peoples.

The Nestorian church presented a dualism of good and evil not far distant from Zoroastrian doctrines, a fact that may explain its acceptance in Mesopotamia. Monophysite Christianity certainly embodied some of the Egyptian ideas of human divinity. Heresies opposed to official doctrine flourished in non-Greek areas of the Byzantine Empire and served as basic factors in the almost complete lack of resistance of the Middle Eastern provinces at the time of the conquests by the Muslim Arabs.

When the Arab Muslim armies invaded Iran they also found a reinvigorated version of the long-established Zoroastrian faith, which flourished in the Persian Empire and was later strongly encouraged by the Sasanian dynasty. The prophet Zoroaster is traditionally believed to have lived during the seventh century B.C.E. Zoroastrian beliefs evolved and changed over the centuries but were centered around the idea of a supreme god (Ahura Mazda). He was the source of goodness, the lord of life and wisdom, supported by other eternal spirits and angels, but even though he was opposed by demons and the spirit of evil (Ahriman), it was believed he would ultimately triumph over them. The dualistic struggle between goodness and evil dominated all aspects of human life. Zoroastrians also believed in a life after death in heaven or hell, an individual's freedom to choose ethical behavior in accordance with a divine law of righteousness, and sacred fire as a symbol of truth. Priests conducted rituals such as sacrifices and burial ceremonies. When Alexander the Great conquered Iran, the Zoroastrian holy books were disrupted, but they were partially compiled again by the Sasanian monarchs as the Avesta, consisting of hymns, narratives, prayers, rituals, liturgies, and laws. Zoroastrianism was associated especially with speakers of Persian; a majority of the population of Persia during the Sasanian era consisted of Zoroastrians, while Christians and Jews were minorities there.

THE ARABS

In the first half of the seventh century, the Arabs, under the banners of Islam, descended upon Syria, Egypt, Mesopotamia, and Persia. Coming from an area on the edges of the great empires, the Muslim Arabs seemed to be a new and different force to the peoples of that age.

The Arabs mostly lived along the shores of Arabia, in the southern highlands where there was some rainfall, and in scattered oases; they spoke an Arabic language whose form emerged between 500 B.C.E. and C.E. 500 in central and western Arabia. These desert inhabitants—farmers and nomadic shepherds—were few and insignificant until the advent of a new saddle for riding camels. The peculiar characteristics of this animal made nomadic life in the desert profitable; indeed, the one-humped dromedary was as revolutionary to life in Arabia at that time as oil and the motor vehicle have been in the twentieth century. The camel people became lords of the desert. Above all, the camel welded town and desert life in Arabia into one integrated society, each dependent upon the other.

The use of the camel, moreover, eased many difficulties of the transit trade between India and the Mediterranean. Camel caravans began to carry spices and incense from Yemen to Mecca (Makkah), the Hijaz, Damascus, and the Mediterranean. Other trade routes connected western Arabia with towns on the Euphrates and the Persian Gulf. Cities prospered and small kingdoms were established as the commerce of the Hellenistic, Roman, and Sasanian worlds expanded. Many Arabs moved northward, where they settled in Byzantine-controlled provinces and became Christians; at the same time other Arabs also settled in the Sasanian-dominated northeastern parts of the peninsula. Arabia in the sixth century, the time of the birth of Muhammad the Prophet, was being affected increasingly by events in surrounding states.

WESTERN ARABIAN SOCIETY

In order to understand Muhammad and the people's response to his preaching, it is useful to examine briefly the economic, political, social, and religious forces current in his day in the Hijaz and in Mecca. Mecca, Muhammad's birthplace, was near the caravan routes from Yemen to Syria. Possessing a permanent spring and an ancient sacred shrine, Mecca dominated the Hijaz. It was a pilgrimage site, commercial town, and growing financial center. By the end of the sixth century Meccan merchants were buying and selling wares (especially leather) in markets from Yemen to southern Syria. Mercantile wealth was turning to financial speculation and investment. There is little evidence of local agriculture in Mecca, although there were orchards and cereal production at al-Taif, and dates grew at the oasis of Medina. Mecca itself had a spring, but the unwalled town was set in the midst of a barren, narrow valley.

Nomads—Bedouins, or desert Arabs—dwelled with their herds in the neighborhood of Mecca. Moving about in search of pasturage, they enjoyed a free, open, precarious existence; yet they were exceedingly jealous of their rights in the desert where they roamed. Brigandage to them was perfectly legitimate, whether upon oases or caravans. The Bedouins were good fighters, and when the advent of the north Arabian saddle greatly enhanced their raiding abilities, merchants, towns, and peasants often bought protection by paying tribute. Between the nomads and Mecca an interdependence developed, and the situation of the Bedouins in the Hijaz improved with the growing prosperity of Mecca.

In Muhammad's time the Quraish tribe of Arabs had dominated life in Mecca for more than a century, although families from the older inhabitants still lived in the city. The tribe had split into a dozen or more clans, which were grouped into two federations. Muhammad's clan was the Hashim, so named for his great-grandfather. Membership in a clan was based on kinship through the male line. Security of person and property was a clan responsibility; violation of either was a cause for reprisal by the clan. An irresponsible member was usually disowned by the clan and consequently became a kind of social, political, and economic outcast.

The clans prized the virtues related to desert nomadism—"bravery in battle, patience in misfortune, persistence in revenge, protection of the weak, defiance of the strong." Other values that were expressed in oral poetry were generosity, hospitality, loyalty, and fidelity. A man with honor and moral excellence exhibited the possession of these characteristics and demonstrated his capacity to govern his life by wise judgment. Women in Mecca were not veiled and they could interact with men.

Government in Mecca was simple, direct, unorganized, and exceedingly democratic. An assembly of chiefs and leading men of the clans met as a council, but each clan was independent and could go its own way. Individuals within a clan might differ with the majority and act accordingly, but they were sure to find such action difficult and the results uncomfortable. Unanimity of clan action had to be achieved by personal negotiation among the leaders, who commanded respect because of wealth, wisdom, and strength of character. A few religious offices possessed privileges, sometimes with opportunities for profit, such as control over the water of the sacred well or supplying food to pilgrims.

Political affairs in the foreign field taxed the skill and ingenuity of the Meccan leaders, for the Arabs were buffeted by the contest between the Byzantine and Sasanian empires. Eastern Arabs were satellites of Persia, and such Arabs as the Ghassanids east of the Jordan were on the Byzantine side. Upon the development of a Persian-sponsored rule in Yemen and with frequent battles between Persia and the Byzantines, Meccan regional commerce northward to Byzantine Syria became a touchy enterprise. But Meccan neutrality, religious prestige, and diplomatic and economic shrewdness kept caravan trade going.

Previously, the Hashim clan had operated caravans north to Syria, but in Muhammad's time it began to lose that monopoly. Hashim, Muhammad's great-grandfather, had obtained from the Byzantines protection for Meccan merchants and their goods in Syria and Palestine. To complement this arrangement, Hashim organized what some have labeled the "Commonwealth of Mecca." He and his successors secured a novel partnership with hitherto hostile Bedouin tribes in the northern area of Arabia whereby Meccan commerce prospered through a sharing of the profits between Meccan merchants and leaders of the tribes, as well as the hiring of the tribes to escort the caravans. Other factors in strengthening the Meccan trade position were the innovations of joining investments from poor members of Meccan families to those of their rich brethren and of including some Bedouin goods in merchandise marketed in Mecca and in Syria. Furthermore, many Meccan leaders married daughters of prominent Bedouin leaders. Thus, beginning with Hashim many groups developed a common interest in the Meccan trade enterprise.

Society in Mecca was reeling from the strains of a swift transition. Not only had the emphasis among the Quraish shifted from tribe to clan membership, with intense rivalry developing among clans, but individualism within a clan was growing at a quickening tempo. Business partnerships were being formed across clan lines. And the leaders and powerful men of Mecca were successful businessmen and merchants who did not always live by the long-accepted Arab standards. Common material interests seemed to be replacing common blood in the determination of kinship in the new Mecca. Social maladjustment resulted from the failure of the new economic life to accommodate itself to the old moral values of Arab life. At the same time, the economic disruptions caused in southern Syria by the Byzantine-Sasanian wars of the early seventh century limited trading opportunities.

Pagan Mecca had numerous gods and goddesses, most of whom possessed abstract characteristics. Stones, trees, and other objects were venerated as places in which these deities were thought to reside. Magic and superstition were inextricably interwoven in this paganism, but belief in the gods had begun to fade in Muhammad's time, though brutal social customs like female infanticide were still practiced.

A more forceful religion was one that was bound up with the belief in the immortality of the tribe and clan. Honor, bravery, generosity, and other virtues were characteristics that ensured the survival of the tribe. Fate was believed to govern life in only a few ways, determining, for instance, the length of life, gender, and happiness. Otherwise individuals controlled their own destiny. It was not quite the same for the desert Arab, however, for life in the desert was so precarious that it seemed to be governed by some unfathomable law or whim of a force beyond one's control or responsibility. There was no belief in personal immortality; immortality rested with the tribe.

Finally, in Mecca a conception of monotheism was evolving. The Arab word Allah was derived from the word al-ilah, meaning "the god." Allah, then, was the supreme God, and Muhammad, in using this word, did not have to give his audiences any explanation. The idea, evidently, was in the air at Mecca, though undoubtedly the understanding of monotheism was vague and ill defined in Meccan minds.

The source of the concept of monotheism in Mecca is a hotly debated issue. Judaism and Christianity have had their champions, and certainly the Meccans had had ample opportunities to become acquainted with each of these religions. Later, Muslims argued that their faith was a continuation of a religious tradition that included Judaism and Christianity, whose original revelations had become obscured and needed to be reformed and purified. From that point of view there was no "borrowing" from Judaism or Christianity; rather, Islam was a renewal and a completion of divine inspirations that were the original bases of various monotheistic beliefs.

It is important to note that Muhammad and Meccan society were familiar with monotheistic concepts. As is obvious from the events that followed, they were ready to have these thoughts organized into a systematic religion—a religion that was originally distinctly Arab in character. That was the great work and accomplishment of Muhammad.

REFERENCES

Bulliet, Richard W.: *The Camel and the Wheel.* Cambridge: Harvard University Press, 1975. Discusses the domestication of the camel and how the camel displaced the wheel in transportation in the Middle East.

Crone, Patricia: *Meccan Trade and the Rise of Islam.* Princeton, N.J.: Princeton University Press, 1987. A controversial revision of earlier works on Mecca before Islam; asserts that trade was local and regional and that there was little social upheaval in Mecca at this time.

Freeman, Charles: *Egypt, Greece and Rome: Civilizations of the Ancient Mediterranean.* Oxford: Oxford University Press, 1996. Political, military, cultural, and religious history to the emergence of the Byzantine empire.

Hallo, William W., and William Kelly Simpson: *The Ancient Near East: A History.* 2d ed. Fort Worth, Tex.: Harcourt Brace, 1998. Concentrates on Mesopotamia and Egypt and is the best introductory account of their political histories in antiquity.

Hourani, Albert: *A History of the Arab Peoples.* Cambridge: Harvard University Press, 1991. This beautifully written and truly outstanding work is a magisterial summary of existing knowledge combined with extraordinary insights by the author.

Kuhrt, Amélie: *The Ancient Near East, c. 3000–330 B.C.* 2 volumes. London: Routledge, 1995. Careful evaluations of religion, politics, and economics, including excerpts from original sources.

Lewis, Naphtali: *Life in Egypt under Roman Rule.* Oxford: Oxford University Press, 1983. A witty look at social history and the life of those outside the ruling circles.

Millar, Fergus: *The Roman Near East, 31 B.C.–A.D. 337.* Cambridge: Harvard University Press, 1993. Carefully based on available evidence, this important book examines linguistic, religious, and ethnic factors.

Nigosian, S. A.: *The Zoroastrian Faith: Tradition and Modern Research.* Montreal: McGill–Queen's University Press, 1993. Incisive analysis of Zoroastrian history, scriptures, teachings, and observances.

Roux, Georges: *Ancient Iraq.* 2d ed. New York: Penguin Books, 1980. Introduction to Iraq, or Mesopotamia, from earliest times to the Parthians; includes intellectual, economic, and religious trends.

Saggs, H. W. F.: *Civilization before Greece and Rome.* New Haven, Conn.: Yale University Press, 1989. Useful discussions of writing, cities, the sciences, law, religion, and politics.

Sells, Michael: *Desert Tracings: Six Classical Arabian Odes.* Middletown, Conn.: Wesleyan University Press, 1989. A valuable short introduction to early Arab poetry beautifully translated into English.

Shahid, Irfan: "Pre-Islamic Arabia." In P. M. Holt et al., eds.: *The Cambridge History of Islam.* Vol. 1A: *The Central Islamic Lands from Pre-Islamic Times to the First World War.* New York: Cambridge University Press, 1970. An important survey of the subject by an expert on early Arabian history.

Wiesehöfer, Josef: *Ancient Persia: From 550 B.C. to 650 A.D.* Translated by Azizeh Azodi. London: Tauris, 1996. Sensitive discussion of the Persian, Parthian, and Sasanian empires and the sources needed to understand them.

Yarshater, Ehsan, ed.: *The Cambridge History of Iran.* Vol. 3: *The Seleucid, Parthian and Sasanian Periods.* New York: Cambridge University Press, 1983. Scholarly essays on political, social, religious, and cultural aspects of Iranian history before the rise of Islam.

PART ONE

The Rise and Spread of Islam

CHAPTER 3

Muhammad: His Life and Leadership

"There is no god but God; Muhammad is the messenger of God." The acceptance of this statement as the fundamental truth of life identifies all who follow the teachings of Muhammad. Allah is the God worshiped by Jews and Christians. But who was this man Muhammad?

It has been said that Muhammad was the only great prophet born in the full light of history. However, the first biography of Muhammad was not written until he had been dead for 100 years; others were compiled during the second century after his passing. We have no original sources about the life of Muhammad from non-Muslims. It is from the Quran (Koran), biographies, the oral stories of the early conquests, and the non-Quranic sayings of or about Muhammad (the hadiths) that the traditional accounts of Muhammad's life have come. Most modern scholars, both Muslims and non-Muslims, have been able to establish many points of mutual agreement. By analyzing various early accounts of Muhammad's life and the lives of his contemporaries, and by studying social, economic, political, and religious aspects of the society in which he moved, they have been able to reconstruct the history of this time.

Muhammad was a mortal human being; he never professed otherwise and always emphasized this point to his followers, indicating that he would die like any other man. Nevertheless, as the founder of a great religion, he was revered as a most holy man even within his own lifetime. It is not strange, then, to find his biographies, written five or six generations later, full of unlikely incidents designed to exalt him. Perhaps this traditional figure has been more important than the real one in fashioning the culture and civilization of the Middle East and the Islamic world from his day to our own.

MUHAMMAD'S EARLY LIFE

In the year C.E. 570 (or perhaps somewhat later in the 570s), a male child was born in Mecca to the Hashim clan of the Quraish tribe. He was given the name Muhammad, meaning "highly praised." His immediate family was not one of the wealthier or more

Periodization in the History of the Islamic Middle East
Antiquity: from the rise of civilization to the coming of Islam
Classical Islamic period: from the life of the prophet Muhammad to the middle of the tenth century C.E.
The early medieval era in the Middle East: from about 950 to about 1250
The late medieval era in the Middle East: from about 1250 to about 1500
The early modern Middle East: from about 1500 to about 1800
The modern Middle East: from about 1800 to the present

powerful of the city, nor was it one of the poorest groups. His father, Abd Allah, died before the child was born, and his mother died when Muhammad was about six years old. First as a fatherless boy, and then as an orphan, his lot was not easy. His paternal grandfather, Abd al-Muttalib, cared for and protected him, and upon his grandfather's death Muhammad became the ward of his uncle Abu Talib.

From many of Muhammad's statements it is apparent that his uncle was not a prosperous man and that they lived in modest circumstances. Evidently there was no opportunity for Muhammad in any of the businesses of his uncles; a job had to be found for him outside the family circle. Such a post was located with a rich widow, Khadijah, who had been married twice and had children from each marriage.

Khadijah was older than Muhammad, some say as much as fifteen years, and certainly her social position in Mecca was far superior to his. She was an astute businesswoman and continued her husbands' commercial activities. It is uncertain at what age Muhammad began working for her, exactly what he did, and how old he was when she asked him to marry her. The story of her proposal is probably factual. In Mecca it was not the usual custom for a woman to propose; in this instance, however, because of Khadijah's wealth, her better social class, and her position as employer, it would not have been unlikely. This step altered Muhammad's life greatly, and at this point he becomes a clearer historical personage.

Muhammad had already gained recognition as a successful trader and skilled administrator, and this marriage reinforced his reputation. He and Khadijah had four daughters who grew to maturity and several sons, all of whom died in infancy. Khadijah died about 619, and as long as she lived Muhammad had no other wife. Since he continued to act as Khadijah's commercial agent after their marriage, giving him security, Muhammad now had means and a definite position in the society of Mecca.

HIS CALL

In the Middle East, it has been the custom for people who have some means and who are troubled intellectually and emotionally by the cares and ills of society to retreat to a lonely spot to think and to seek answers for problems of the day. A number of people

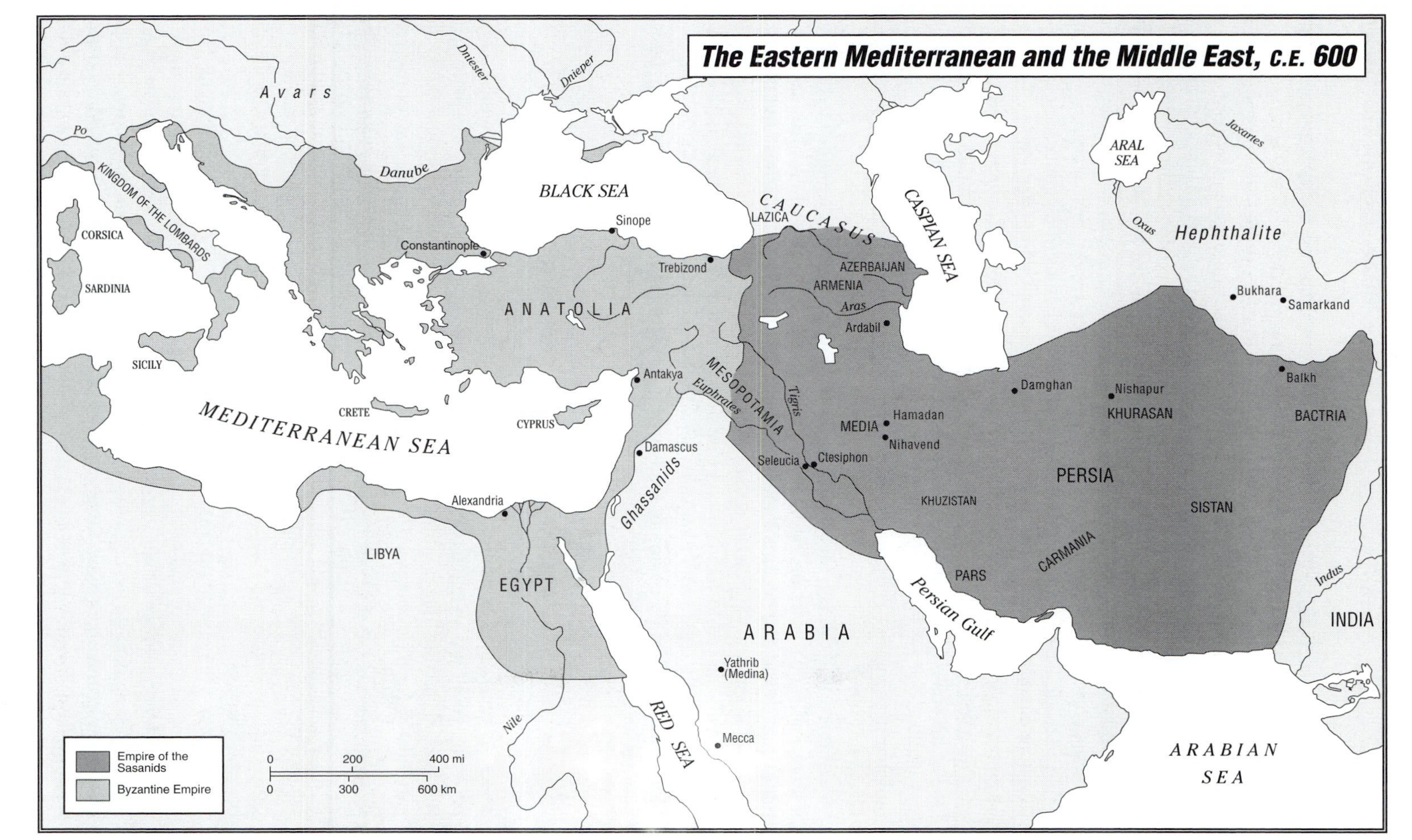
The Eastern Mediterranean and the Middle East, C.E. 600
Avars
Dniester
Dnieper
Po
Danube
KINGDOM OF THE LOMBARDS
CORSICA
SARDINIA
SICILY
BLACK SEA
Sinope
Constantinople
Trebizond
ANATOLIA
CRETE
CYPRUS
MEDITERRANEAN SEA
Antakya
Damascus
Ghassanids
Alexandria
LIBYA
EGYPT
Nile
RED SEA
LAZICA
CAUCASUS
CASPIAN SEA
AZERBAIJAN
ARMENIA
Aras
Ardabil
MESOPOTAMIA
Euphrates
Tigris
MEDIA
Hamadan
Nihavend
Seleucia
Ctesiphon
KHUZISTAN
PERSIA
PARS
CARMANIA
Persian Gulf
ARABIA
Yathrib (Medina)
Mecca
Damghan
Nishapur
KHURASAN
SISTAN
ARAL SEA
Jaxartes
Oxus
Hephthalite
Bukhara
Samarkand
Balkh
BACTRIA
Indus
INDIA
ARABIAN SEA
Empire of the Sasanids
Byzantine Empire
0
200
400 mi
0
300
600 km

in Arabia in the sixth and early seventh centuries were searching for such greater insight. Muhammad, after his marriage, began to follow this practice.

Perhaps it was in the year 610 that Muhammad had a sudden and unusual experience in the form of thoughts flooding upon him. In the language and understanding of his time it was a revelation, and he ultimately accepted it as such. (This occasion is celebrated each year by Muslims as the "night of power.") Probably occurring in a cave on one of the hillsides outside Mecca, the message commanded Muhammad to preach the truth to his fellow Meccans. This was his call.

Muhammad on frequent occasions heard other revelations. Certainly he fully believed them; he was his own first convert. The revelations often concerned ideas that were being widely discussed in Arabia and that he had contemplated earlier. There can be no real doubt of his sincerity and conviction that the messages were from God.

With respect to religion, Muhammad had grown up in the pagan society of Mecca. One of his sons, Abd Manaf, bore a pagan name. Mecca was a pilgrimage destination and a holy place, famed for the Kaba, the earthly abode of many gods and the only stone building in the town. The Quraish had a special relationship and certain responsibilities to this temple.

At this time, however, Mecca and the Hijaz were experiencing a gradual trend toward a more intellectual religion. Moreover, the ideas and teachings of Judaism and Christianity had spread and become known in Mecca through slaves, pilgrims, and traders as the small town grew somewhat more prosperous and its life more settled. Repeatedly, Muhammad referred to Judaism and Christianity, and to help demonstrate the truth of the revelations he showed a congruity between Islam and those older faiths. Although Muhammad apparently could not read anything other than the simplest writing, he was familiar with many of the ideas of the Monophysite sect of Christians in Syria.

PREACHING AND CONVERTS

The first revelations presented quite a simple religion. God was represented as all-powerful, good, and loving. Created existence was transitory; the creator was permanent. But God, in creating humans, implanted in them moral responsibility for themselves and, particularly, for their fellows. There would be a final judgment on the day of resurrection. Pure individuals were those who were grateful to God, worshiped him, appealed to him for the forgiveness of sin, offered frequent prayers, helped other people, avoided all forms of cheating, led chaste lives, and had cleansed themselves from love of wealth. Such persons, then, would recognize the goodness and power of God and their dependence upon God. This was Islam—the surrender to God—and the pious who thus purified themselves became Muslims.

At first, Muhammad was reluctant to tell many people about the revelations. However, the heavenly truths had been revealed to him and duty compelled him to remind the Arabs of Mecca of these truths in order to save them from divine wrath on the approaching day of judgment. In the beginning his preaching brought no firm opposition. His first converts were members of his family: his wife Khadijah, his young cousin Ali, and Zaid, a former slave. The most important of the others were Abu Bakr, Umar, Uthman, and Zubair.

Some of the early converts were younger sons of influential men of the leading families and clans of Mecca. The father of one was the most prominent financier in Mecca; another's father had been a religious leader prior to Muhammad's time; two others were nephews of the head of the Makhzum clan, the wealthiest and dominant family among the Quraish. The majority, however, were men of no great social standing. Some had neither family nor clan ties, and the families of others had ceased for one reason or another to afford them protection.

Early Islam was a movement of people mostly well under forty years old and from the middle socioeconomic groups of Mecca. They were individuals who felt their positions to be inferior when they compared their wealth and influence with the fortunes and power of those at the top. Such a generalization certainly implies that economic, social, and political conditions in Mecca had a hand in fostering the development and growth of Islam. In the century before Muhammad's call, life in Mecca had been changing. The rapid growth of commerce had widened the gap between rich and poor and between the influential and their dependents. Wealth and the life of a merchant promoted individualism as contrasted to family and clan solidarity. Kinship based on money was supplanting that of blood, a substitution that did not satisfy the less successful. Nomadic virtues were hardly those valued in a mercantile society. Old ideals of generosity, honor, the moral responsibilities of family and clan, and the group's accountability for crimes against its members were seriously challenged in the evolving individualistic society. Seemingly, anything could be obtained through money and power. Also, in the last few decades before Muhammad's call, military conflict between Byzantines and Sasanians had decreased commercial opportunities while increasing the risks involved in long-distance trading.

Muhammad and his early converts, however, were not consciously frustrated men seeking solace in religion. In these first days, they were conservatives preaching against the abandonment of the old virtues. Nevertheless, Islam did recognize individualism as a permanent aspect of society. The last judgment concerned individuals; for it was said that on the day of the last judgment "one shall have no influence on behalf of another." Salvation came from the mercy of God, but one should take care of poor relatives, make sure of the well-being of orphans, and be generous to the poor. For the rich the new faith meant sacrificing and cooperating with the poor.

PERSECUTION

Muhammad and Islam entered a new period of development in 615. Monotheism was plainly recognized, and opposition and persecution began. Muslims were subjected to all manner of verbal insults. Garbage was dumped at their doors. Unprotected individuals were beaten, as were Quraish Muslims by their fellow clansmen. Some Muslims went to Ethiopia, seeking refuge from the persecution. Economic pressure was exerted by refusal to pay debts and by a severe boycott that harmed many, including Muhammad's closest friend, Abu Bakr. Muhammad warned his opponents that God had sent earlier messengers and warners, that they, too, had been persecuted, and that God had then punished the people who had ignored the divine revelations.

Abu Jahl, the head of the Makhzum clan, declared economic war upon the Muslims and asserted that every one of them would be ruined financially. He coaxed and threatened Abu Talib, Muhammad's uncle and the leader of the Hashim clan, to try to get him to abandon Muhammad. Failure in this approach led to the formation of an alliance of all the Quraish clans to pursue an economic boycott of the Hashim clan and its closest ally, the al-Muttalib clan. There were to be no business dealings and no intermarriage with any member of either clan. Apparently, during this boycott, the Hashim maintained their own caravans to Syria and withstood the pressure. After two years the grand alliance was dissolved and the economic sanctions lapsed, since they had proved unsuccessful in destroying Muhammad.

More significant was the verbal assault, which indicated the opinions held by those in opposition. They scoffed at the idea of the day of last judgment and ridiculed Muhammad's preaching of the resurrection of the body after it had moldered in the grave. They kept asking scornfully, "When is the Hour?" Muhammad's conviction that God was one and only one and that all idolatry was evil disturbed Meccan society because, to a considerable degree, this meant forsaking the religion of the forefathers. Muhammad tried to counter this with the contention that he was following in the steps of the religion of Abraham and the prophets of old, and thus, that Muslims were only regaining the old Arab religion.

The opposition jeered at Muhammad's claim to prophethood, calling him a magician, a poet possessed by spirits, and even a madman. If God had desired to reveal the truth, they asserted sarcastically, he would have selected someone more important than Muhammad for this role. And why was not the full revelation made all at one time? How else could Muhammad explain the driblets of revelation except that he and some assistants were busy making up the verses!

Traditionally, the opposition to Muhammad by the leaders of Mecca centered around his preaching of the unity of God and his rejection of the use of idols. Some rich Meccans objected to his message that the rich should help the poor among them. They also feared that the adoption and practice of these beliefs would ruin Mecca as a modest commercial center, if they caused it to lose its shrine and thereby its role in drawing Bedouins to the town. Abu Jahl, the most ambitious financier of Mecca, recognized the threat of Islam to his way of life and realized that widespread acceptance would give the leadership of the city to Muhammad. Other leaders opposed Muhammad as an innovator who was disrupting the social order of Mecca.

It was at about this time that Muhammad, according to Muslim belief, underwent a mystical experience—he was transported during a night journey to Jerusalem, and from there he visited heaven, before returning once again to Mecca. Jerusalem thus would eventually become one of the holiest places in the world for Muslims.

Possibly this experience and the ending of the economic boycott in 619 were interpreted as indications that success was at hand. But one incident after another quickly dashed such optimism and brought Muhammad close to the breaking point. Khadijah died, and then his uncle and protector, Abu Talib, followed her. Abu Lahab, another uncle, who now became the leader of the Hashim, refused to continue protection. Several years had elapsed since any important person had accepted Islam. There was no Muslim in Mecca with sufficient stature to offer Muhammad protection. How easily Islam could have perished! Muhammad's only alternative was to leave the city.

HIJRAH TO MEDINA

Muhammad first visited the neighboring town of al-Taif to explore the possibilities of establishing residence and the headquarters of Islam there. He was met with a quick rebuff and upon leaving was stoned.

Some 200 miles (about 320 km.) to the north and east lay the town of Yathrib—later called Medina (the city, i.e., the city of the Prophet) by the Muslims. Yathrib comprised an area of date oases, fertile lands, and scattered settlements. Numerous tribes occupied quarters of the town and had been engaged in bloody and exhausting civil war, in part over the limited cultivated lands of Yathrib. The most important clans were Aws, Khazraj, Nadir, Quraizah, and Qainuqa, of which the last three adhered to Judaism.

During the pilgrimage of 620 and following his rebuff at al-Taif, Muhammad discussed Islam with several pilgrims of the Khazraj tribe of Yathrib and raised the question of asylum. The following year, additional people from Yathrib participated in the pilgrimage and more discussions occurred. One of Muhammad's trusted supporters returned with them, and converts were obtained from every important family except one. In 622, a number of Medinans made the famous Pledge of al-Aqabah to protect Muhammad. Furthermore, there was some agreement concerning the migration of the Muslims, including Muhammad, from Mecca to Yathrib and the establishment of an alliance between Muslims and the people of Yathrib. Later additions to the pledge in the so-called constitution of Medina granted Muhammad sufficient authority to form the commonwealth of Medina. Pagan Arabs from Yathrib saw Muhammad as a holy man and arbitrator who might end the continual feuding of the clans.

As soon as agreement had been reached, Muhammad urged all Muslims to go to Yathrib. Over a period of weeks they left secretly in small groups until only Muhammad, Abu Bakr, Ali, and a handful of Muslims remained in Mecca. After all who planned to migrate had gone, Muhammad and Abu Bakr slipped away at night, hid in a nearby cave for a couple of days until the search for them had relaxed, and then proceeded to Yathrib (Medina). On September 24, 622, they were joyously greeted at the outskirts of the city.

This migration, or hijrah (hegira), was a dangerous move on the part of the Muslims, for they were abandoning the protection of their families and their town for the untested protection of strangers. Almost overnight their position was so changed that the hijrah came to mark the new era. The lunar Muslim religious calendar A.H. 1 begins on July 16, 622, the first day of the year in which the hijrah occurred and the year in which the new Muslim community of believers was founded. In Mecca, Muhammad and the preaching of Islam had failed to win a majority of the population, but in Medina, Muhammad immediately became the acknowledged political and social leader of the whole town, as well as the religious head of the small community of Muslims.

Residence in Medina placed new demands on Muhammad's diplomatic and executive talents. He could count definitely on the full support of the Muhajirun—the "emigrants" from Mecca—and the converts of Medina, called Ansar, or "helpers." For protection and sustenance, as well as for religious reasons, Muhammad created a new kind of community, which emphasized the mutual obligations of Muslims to each other. The problems and the affairs of the Muslim community were to be brought before God and

Muhammad, whose judgments had to be obeyed. Herein lay the basis for the establishment of Muslim theocracy. God was Muhammad's guide and protector, and the disobedient would suffer the agonies of hell. The revelations received in Medina turned more to social and political matters; forms of worship and religious ideas that had been revealed in the Meccan prophecies were now stressed to a much lesser degree.

To help the Muhajirun and to establish rules for economic development, Muhammad encouraged regulations for sharecropping, hiring farm labor, new ways of allocating water, land reclamation, and the creation of a central market to replace several small markets.

Feuds among the disparate groups in Medina were rekindled quickly. The Jews soon began to quiz and mock Muhammad because of their knowledge of the Torah. He had expected that they would testify to the validity of his message, but they could not accept an Arab as the Messiah, even though Islam accepted Abraham and Moses as prophets. Islam had a distinctly Arab cultural flavor. This aspect came to be emphasized with the beginning of Muhammad's Medina residence.

In the first days following the hijrah the Muslims had adopted several of the Jewish rites. They prayed facing Jerusalem; they observed midday prayers and Jewish fast days; and Friday, market day as well as the Jewish day of preparation for the Sabbath, became the most important Muslim day of public prayer. Later, when relations with the Medina Jews became tense, Muslims, in accordance with new revelations, turned away from some of the Jewish forms. In worship the faithful now faced the Kaba sanctuary in Mecca; an annual pilgrimage to Mecca (the hajj) was prescribed for Muslims and a period of fasting (the month of Ramadan) was ordered.

CONFLICT WITH MECCA

During the winter of their first year in Medina, Muhammad and his followers were busy establishing their new homes. When spring and summer came and the Meccan caravans began to pass northward toward Syria, armed Muslim bands from Medina menaced the merchants. No booty was taken, and the caravans were so well protected that these incidents served only as reconnaissance missions. However, the need to provide a livelihood for the expatriates of Mecca forced Muhammad to direct attacks upon the passing caravans. It was a normal expediency in Arabia.

Late in 623 a handful of Muslims under orders from Muhammad surprised a small Meccan caravan on the road between Mecca and al-Taif. One Meccan was killed and much booty was captured. Nevertheless, sentiment in Medina was divided. The Medinans had promised the emigrants from Mecca protection from attack but had not agreed to let their city serve as a base of operations against Mecca. The success of the venture, however, invited other and larger expeditions.

Muhammad decided to ambush the main caravan of the Quraish upon its return from Syria. Muhammad himself led a group of about 300 to waylay the caravan under Abu Sufyan, the head of the powerful Umayyad family. At Badr, 20 miles (about 32 km.) southwest of Medina, Muhammad was challenged by a force of some 800 or 900 armed Meccans. The fighting was fierce and bloody, but the smaller force of Muslims was victorious. Although the battle of Badr was hardly more than a minor fracas (Muhammad lost fourteen men; the Meccans lost fifty), some have called it one of the decisive battles of history. To the Muslims it was a miracle, positive proof that God was supreme.

Henceforth Muhammad was a marked man, for the news of this victory traveled quickly to many parts of Arabia. Moreover, the battle set the stage and the pattern of the future: a fifth of all booty was assigned to Muhammad to be allotted to the needy or used by the state. The commonwealth of Medina now became a real possibility. From the moment of victory there could be no peace until the supremacy between pagans and Muslims was decided. Within two decades Muslims came to appreciate the importance of this battle; those who had participated in it were the "nobility of Islam"; and a cloak that had been worn at the battle of Badr was a most distinguished robe of honor.

This victory by no means guaranteed to Muhammad an easy path to his now clearly recognizable goal: control over Mecca and the incorporation of all its inhabitants into his Muslim community. Indeed, although the battle showed the Muslims that such a goal was attainable, it also goaded the leaders of Mecca into a real effort to annihilate the Muslim community.

Muhammad, taking advantage of his success, moved to consolidate his position. Alliances were made with a number of neighboring Bedouin tribes. The Qainuqa tribe, the weakest of those adhering to the Jewish faith, was driven from Medina. In 625, however, Abu Sufyan, the new leader of Mecca since the death of Abu Jahl on the battlefield of Badr, set forth with an army of 3000 for revenge. Electing to meet the enemy outside the town at the foot of the hill of Uhud, the Muslims appeared at first to be winning but were subsequently overrun by the Meccan cavalry. In the melee Muhammad was wounded but managed to escape. Torn by dissension as usual, the Meccan army neither pursued the Muslims nor pressed on to Medina. Two years later, Abu Sufyan returned again with an even larger Bedouin and Meccan army. Forewarned, Muhammad ordered a wide ditch dug in front of the less protected sides of Medina. After a two-week siege, the withdrawal of the Meccans was prompted by bad weather, persistent quarrels, and the disaffection of some of the nomad allies. In addition, the Meccans claimed that the Muslim trench was a dishonorable trick to which no Arab would resort. The "battle of the ditch," along with Badr and Uhud, were the three battles where lines were drawn between the pagans and Muslims. The battles were in some measure part of a civil war. Participants on each side were well known to each other. Old slights and grudges were remembered, and emotions and the spirit of vengeance ran high.

Following each of these failures by pagan Mecca, Muhammad moved quickly to solidify the Medina community. When the Medina Jews had failed to hide their delight over the Uhud misadventure, the Muslims attacked the Jewish Nadir clan and drove them from Medina to Khaibar. After the third battle the men in the Jewish tribe of the Quraizah were killed, and the women and children were sold as slaves, because the Muslims felt the Quraizah had betrayed them. Citizens of Medina who, until now, had neither accepted Islam nor recognized Muhammad as their leader joined the Muslim band. This meant that by the end of 627 Muhammad had established Medina as a united community with one religion as its cohesive force.

The next spring Muhammad was advised that some of the men of Mecca wished to arrange peace with the Muslims. With this information Muhammad called for an advance upon Mecca during the month of a minor pilgrimage. His Bedouin allies would not join him, and Mecca sent forth an armed force to contest his entry. A compromise was reached stipulating that the Muslims might participate freely in the lesser pilgrimage the following year, and marking Muhammad's first success in his peaceful conquest of Mecca. Later that year, the Muslims captured the fertile oasis of Khaibar, largely inhabited by Jews. This acquisition made the Muslims wealthy, since the lands were most productive. The inhabitants were not exiled but remained on their lands, paying yearly taxes to the conquerors and establishing a precedent for the years and centuries to come—when other monotheists paid tribute and accepted Muslim supremacy, they could live in peace and practice their faiths.

VICTORY

In March 629 Muhammad led more than a thousand of his men into Mecca to perform the rites of the lesser pilgrimage, as agreed upon the previous year. A number of Meccans joined him, recognizing Muhammad as the coming leader. Two of the most redoubtable military figures of Islam were among those who joined at this time: Amr ibn al-As and Khalid ibn al-Walid. Even Abu Sufyan, in secret negotiations, tried to adjust to the inevitable.

As more Bedouin tribes joined the Muslims, Muhammad began to insist that they accept Islam and become an integral part of the community rather than serve merely as military allies. However, the sense of completeness and fulfillment of the Muslim community was lacking so long as Mecca did not recognize Muhammad as the leader and refused to accept Islam. Mecca was the site of the Kaba, the religious sanctuary and holy shrine. It had also been the home of the leaders of the Muslim community.

An insignificant incident brought Muhammad and the Muslims to Mecca to do battle in 630. Hardly anyone in Mecca was disposed to fight, however. Abu Sufyan came out from the city to pay homage to Muhammad, and Muhammad granted amnesty to him and most of the Meccans. Upon entering the city Muhammad demanded the destruction of all idols; he then prayed at the Kaba. He had merged his commonwealth with that of Mecca.

Muhammad's astuteness in politics and diplomacy was revealed by his decision not to settle again in Mecca but to return to his adopted city of Medina. The Quraish were a proud people, and it had not been easy for them to acknowledge Muhammad as the leader. He did not tarry to remind them too plainly of their new position. Moreover, the rapid spread of Islam and the increasing numbers of Muslims were presenting a multitude of problems. A rather unsuccessful campaign occurred in Transjordan, and missions went as far as Yemen, Bahrain, and Oman. There were small Muslim groups to be found in most parts of Arabia, but many still denied that Muhammad was God's messenger. (In areas where Muslim political authority had penetrated, Christians, Jews, and Zoroastrians were tolerated on the condition that they concede political rule to the Muslims.)

Muhammad could now see that Arabia was rapidly becoming one great united religious community (in Arabic, ummah). In this community it was religion rather than tribal identity, blood, language, customs, or economics that held the people together; there were no distinctions among the believers except their degree of piety. It is probable, however, that some professed Islam not because they submitted to the will of God but because they feared not being a Muslim or because they wanted the political, social, and economic advantages of being one.

Although Mecca acknowledged Muhammad as its leader, many in the host of visitors to the Kaba in the month of great pilgrimage were still pagan Arabs. Muhammad declined to go on the great pilgrimage in 631 and sent Abu Bakr at the head of the Muslims. Ali, Muhammad's cousin and son-in-law, was deputized to announce that after four months no pagan would be permitted to participate in a pilgrimage to Mecca and that all political alliances between Muslims and Arab tribes would be revoked if Islam were not accepted.

Thus, the stage was set for Muhammad to lead the reformed pilgrimage in March 632. Only Muslims would be present, and the veneration for the one God would be complete. Since Muhammad died soon after this pilgrimage, it has been called the farewell pilgrimage, and the events of the occasion are steeped in tradition. Muhammad eliminated many of the pagan aspects from the ceremonial rites that had been performed at the Meccan sanctuary in earlier days. His every move and act have been described and followed by devout pilgrims. He knew the significance of this first solidly Muslim pilgrimage; in his address, as leader, he must have said something like "Today I have perfected your religion and completed my favors for you and chosen Islam as a religion for you."

Three days later, he departed for Medina and in less than three months (on June 8, 632) he died from fever. He had no sons still living, and, according to most Muslims, no provision had been made for a successor as leader of the Muslim community-state. Genuine bewilderment reigned in Medina. For a whole day Muhammad's body lay disregarded. He was finally buried under the floor of the hut of his wife Aishah.

The personality and private life of Muhammad remain to be considered. In general his tastes were quite simple. There is no evidence that his standard of living changed greatly upon the successes and the growth of the Muslim community. Perhaps the only significant change was his practice regarding marriage. After Khadijah died, Muhammad married several times. At one time he had nine wives. Without question, his favorite was the daughter of Abu Bakr, Aishah, whom he married soon after the hijrah (while she was still a child). His disposition was usually kindly and gentle, and he made no distinction in his treatment of people. The frailties of human nature were well appreciated, and Muhammad never expected too much from his converts. When he found wrongdoing, he upbraided the culprits for their actions but was lenient and cautious in his condemnations.

Most outstanding, however, were Muhammad's personality and character. The loyalty and compliance rendered naturally and generously to Muhammad by his companions in Mecca and Medina stemmed from the charisma of his being. His great intelligence, his display of a sense of justice, and his revelation of religious truth centered the attention of the citizens of Medina upon him. His converts, from first to last, testified to something special and irresistible in his nature. Lacking this quality, Muhammad's stand as a prophet of God would surely have been ignored by the worldly townspeople of Mecca.

REFERENCES

Akkad, Moustapha, director: *The Message: The Story of Islam.* This 220-minute-long, 1976 film sensitively presents the story of the life of Muhammad in Mecca and Medina.

Bamyeh, Mohammed A.: *The Social Origins of Islam: Mind, Economy, Discourse.* Minneapolis: University of Minnesota Press, 1999. A sociological interpretation of Meccan society provides a theoretical framework for understanding the life of the Prophet.

Buhl, F., and A. T. Welch: "Muhammad." *Encyclopaedia of Islam.* New ed. Vol. 7, pp. 360–376. Leiden: Brill, 1993. In this first part of the article on Muhammad the authors deal with his life; later sections by other writers discuss Muslim popular piety and European critics. Indispensable.

Cook, Michael: *Muhammad.* Oxford: Oxford University Press, 1983. A short and simply written account of the life of Muhammad; it includes views that are critical of the sources often used.

Haykal, Muhammad Husayn: *The Life of Muhammad.* Translated by Ismail al Faruqi. Philadelphia: North American Trust Publications, 1976. The first Arabic edition of the book appeared in 1935; it is perhaps the most influential of the modern biographies of the Prophet written by a Muslim.

Hodgson, Marshall G. S.: *The Venture of Islam: Conscience and History in a World Civilization.* Vol. 1: *The Classical Age of Islam.* Chicago: University of Chicago Press, 1974. Written in a difficult style, this, the first of three volumes, brilliantly covers pre-Islamic and early Islamic history, with an emphasis on religious thought, philosophy, and literary developments.

ibn Ishaq, Muhammad: *The Life of Muhammad.* Edited by Abd al-Malik ibn Hisham. Translated by Alfred Guillaume. New York: Oxford University Press, 1955. Ibn Ishaq was born about 705 and died in 768 in Baghdad. His work is the earliest known biography of the Prophet. The original is lost but remains in the edited version by Ibn Hisham, who died in 833. This is the source of most traditional accounts of Muhammad's life.

Peters, F. E.: *Muhammad and the Origins of Islam.* Albany: State University of New York Press, 1994. Contains extensive excerpts from early materials dealing with Mecca, the life of Muhammad, and the religion of Islam.

Rodinson, Maxime: *Mohammed.* Translated by Anne Carter. New York: Pantheon, 1971. The author uses a psychological approach in analyzing stories and events to explain and interpret the Prophet's life.

Schimmel, Annemarie: *And Muhammad Is His Messenger: The Veneration of the Prophet in Islamic Piety.* Chapel Hill: University of North Carolina Press, 1985. The views of later generations of Muslims in regard to Muhammad are shown through developments in philosophy, poetry, and theology.

Shaban, M. A.: *Islamic History, A.D. 600–750 (A.H. 132): A New Interpretation.* Cambridge: Cambridge University Press, 1971. This is a most significant volume, giving many ideas about developments during this formative period in the Middle East.

Watt, W. Montgomery: *Muhammad: Prophet and Statesman.* London: Oxford University Press, 1961. A thorough and scholarly study of the life of the Prophet and his social setting.

CHAPTER 4

The Establishment of the Muslim State

The leadership or caliphate of the Muslim community in the nearly thirty years after the death of Muhammad went in turn to Abu Bakr, Umar, Uthman, and Ali. Even though all four of these figures faced considerable administrative difficulties, the Muslim state expanded enormously and enjoyed a tremendous period of success. A number of crucial decisions were made about basic matters of faith and government even as differences of opinion among certain Muslim groups threatened the unity of the community.

THE CALIPHATE

Muhammad's position as a prophet of God precluded the nomination of a successor, even though his other roles as head of state, chief judge, and commander of the army did warrant some provisions for his replacement. Muhammad had sought counsel and taken advice from his companions as situations demanded. After his death in 632, his most frequent and trusted counselors agreed that Abu Bakr should be the leader of the Muslims. Muhammad's closest friend, Abu Bakr had led the prayers in the mosque and presided over the gatherings of Muslims in the last days when the Prophet had been too ill to perform these functions of leadership. When news of Muhammad's death spread through the city, the native Medinans nominated one of their own as head of their community, but the Meccan Quraish prevailed upon all to accept Abu Bakr as their commander. The following day in the mosque, even before Muhammad was laid to rest, the assembled Muslims swore allegiance to Abu Bakr as the successor of Muhammad.

This outcome was neither unusual nor startling. Chiefs in Mecca and Medina, as well as in Arab tribes, were chosen on the basis of consensus by the heads of families. Leadership often passed to another within the same family but without any idea of inheritance or of legal claim; the power and prestige of a family influenced the decision in its favor. In this instance Abu Bakr commanded the support of many of the Muslims who had emigrated to Medina, and that fact won his election. Other aspirants would have been from the Makhzum or Umayyad families of Mecca, from a prominent family of Medina, or from Muhammad's immediate family, but the election of one of these would not have been based on religious considerations. Authority passing into the hands of Abu Bakr, one of Muhammad's close companions, meant the survival of the Muslim community. The consensus of the community became a key ingredient in the political and religious realm.

Khalifah Rasul Allah ("Successor of the Messenger of God") was the name frequently used to describe Abu Bakr and his position. Abu Bakr probably used it himself as a title. From this appellation came the title and institution of the khalifah (caliph), present for centuries in the Muslim world. It implied the assumption of all the duties and prerogatives exercised by Muhammad except those connected with his role as prophet. The caliph was head of the state, supreme judge, leader in public worship, and commander of the army. Muslims also called the caliph commander of the faithful. If he did not actually occupy the pulpit in the mosque, the sermon was delivered in his name and he issued authoritative rulings on law. His name appeared on coins. And it was he whom Muslims revered.

ABU BAKR

Abu Bakr, about three years younger than Muhammad, had probably been the first convert outside Muhammad's immediate family. A prosperous merchant from one of the lesser Quraish families and totally devoted to Muhammad and Islam, Abu Bakr maintained his position of great respect because of a gentle personality coupled with a clear head in matters of judgment and advice. It was a wise selection in that Abu Bakr pursued Muhammad's ways and thoughts. No innovator, he succeeded in holding together the remarkable and talented people who had risen to prominence in this new community.

The first significant task facing the new leadership was to maintain the degree of centralization in Arabia already established by Muhammad. Except in Medina, Mecca, and a few other nearby places, most Arabs questioned the political and taxation authority of Medina. Some even denounced Islam, seizing the end of personal allegiance to Muhammad as an opportunity to cast off the yoke of submission.

Abu Bakr viewed these actions as apostasy, and he met their challenge with the vigor and fire of the Prophet. Khalid ibn al-Walid, a general and a fortunate choice, subdued the tribes of central Arabia, many of which had not given their allegiance to Muhammad. Encouraged, other Muslim generals suppressed revolts and more thoroughly established Islam throughout Arabia, including Bahrain, Oman, and Yemen. Usually treating the vanquished and renegade with mercy, Abu Bakr subjugated most of Arabia in less than a year. The riddah (apostasy) wars were quickly and decisively won.

Indirectly, the Islamization of the Hijaz and the domination of the Arabian peninsula by the Muslims led, in the years 633–634, to military expeditions into Syria and Mesopotamia (Iraq). Although fighting among Muslims was contrary to the principles of the new society, raiding was an economic necessity as well as a frequent activity of most Arab tribes; thus, ventures into adjacent lands were to be expected. Muslims also wished to expand the faith through jihad (holy war; also, internal and spiritual struggling for Islam). With little direct encouragement from Medina, Khalid finished the conquest of northeastern Arabia and then, joining some Arab Muslim tribes, spilled over into the Sasanian lands.

For the ex-merchants of Mecca and Medina who directed the Arab Muslim armies, Syria was more important than Mesopotamia. Their caravans went there; it was more accessible; and to them it was a land flowing with milk and honey. Forces led by Amr ibn al-As defeated the Byzantine governor of Palestine near the Dead Sea and destroyed his fleeing troops near Gaza early in 634. To oppose the fresh Byzantine levies Abu Bakr ordered Khalid to cross the desert from Mesopotamia to Syria. Appearing almost miraculously, Khalid defeated the Byzantine army in 634, in the historic battle at Ajnadain, near Jerusalem, thus opening all of Palestine to the Muslims.

The news of this victory reached Medina after the death of Abu Bakr. His passing, however, hardly caused a ripple across Arabia, for Umar immediately assumed the power of leadership that he had already been exercising behind the scenes. Recognition and fealty were given to Umar publicly by all. But the two-year caliphate of Abu Bakr must not be considered as a brief empty interlude between two glorious periods, nor should Abu Bakr be seen as a shallow, colorless figure. He made the important distinction between state property and the privy purse of the ruler, even though this action irreconcilably alienated Muhammad's daughter Fatimah. Perhaps most important, when war booty was first coming to Medina from outside of Arabia, Abu Bakr held fast to Muhammad's rule on the spoils of war—all true believers, whether at the front or at home in Arabia, had equal rights.

UMAR

Umar's accession to the caliphate by consensus in 634 marked the opening of the ten-year administration of an energetic and brilliant man, then only forty-three years old, whom Muslims consider the second founder of Islam. An early convert, Umar, like Abu Bakr, belonged to one of the less important families of Mecca. Leadership in the hands of Umar signified that Muslim aspects of the community continued.

The affairs most pressing upon Umar at his accession were the military campaigns in Syria and Mesopotamia. Umar's accession to the caliphate did not change Muslim activities in Palestine or Syria. Several Arab forces converged on Damascus in 635, which surrendered on terms to Khalid. The emperor Heraclius (r. 610–641), ruler of the over-extended Byzantine state, gathered a large army, but it, too, succumbed to Khalid in 636 at the decisive battle of Yarmuk. Upon receiving the news of this disaster Heraclius left Syria and Palestine to the Muslims; north Syria fell from 637 to 647, and Jerusalem also surrendered in 637. Muslim Arab tribes entered the Jazirah between the Euphrates and the Tigris in the north and ruled that vast and fertile area.

The Muslims had conclusively occupied these provinces of the Byzantine Empire. Mountains to the north discouraged further advance into Byzantine lands or the vigorous pursuit of the emperor's armies. Arab generals and many tribes, however, looked for new opportunities. Amr ibn al-As decided upon an expedition toward Egypt. Although Alexandria, the second city of the Byzantines and an important naval base, was strongly tied to Constantinople by sea routes, the loss of Syria and Palestine cut Egypt off from the rest of the empire. Egypt, the chief granary of Constantinople and one of the richest and most populous areas of the Middle East, was very inviting to an ambitious general

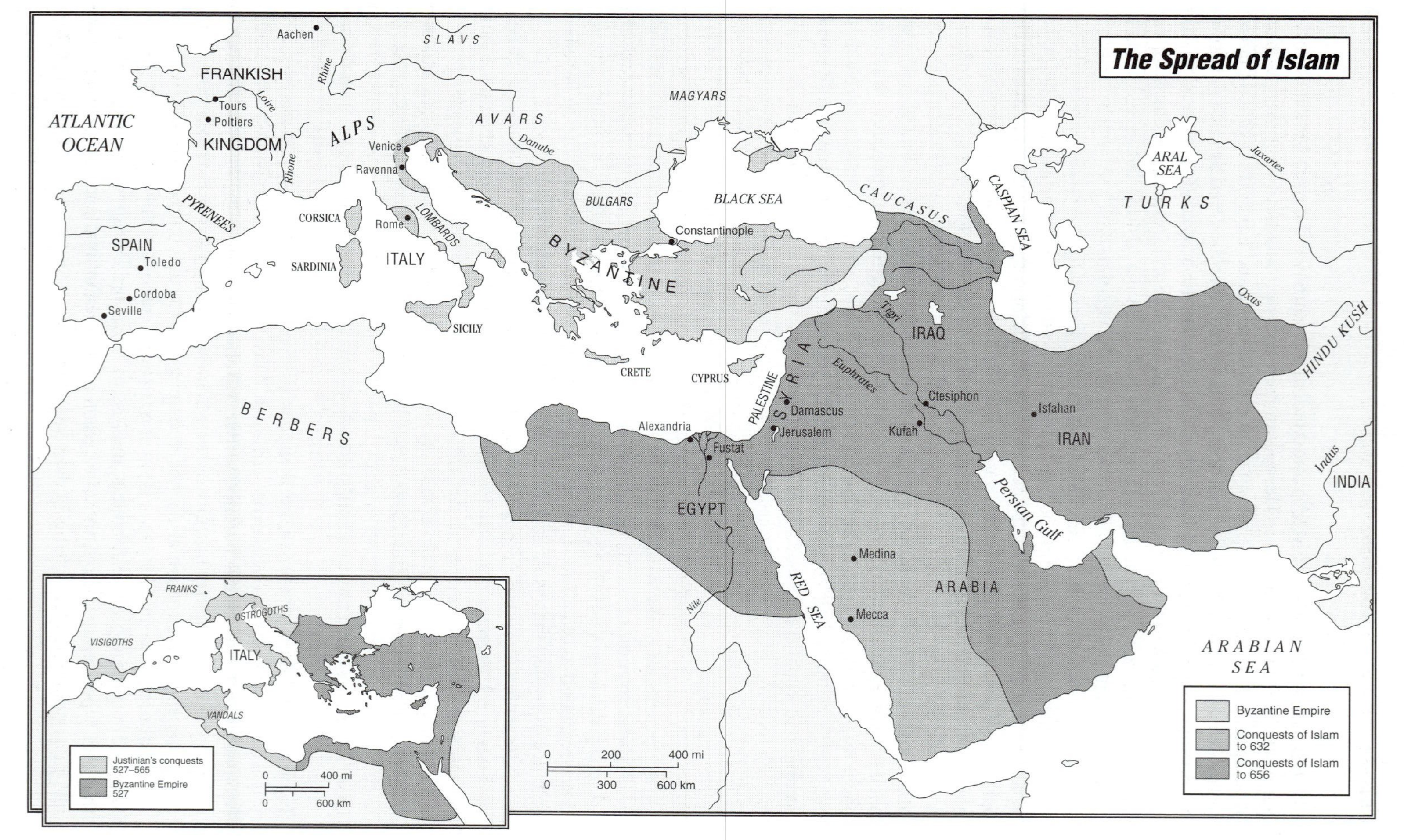
The Spread of Islam
ATLANTIC OCEAN
FRANKISH KINGDOM
Aachen
Tours
Poitiers
Loire
Rhine
Rhone
SLAVS
ALPS
AVARS
Danube
MAGYARS
BULGARS
BLACK SEA
Constantinople
BYZANTINE
CAUCASUS
CASPIAN SEA
ARAL SEA
Jaxartes
TURKS
Oxus
HINDU KUSH
Indus
INDIA
PYRENEES
SPAIN
Toledo
Cordoba
Seville
CORSICA
SARDINIA
Venice
Ravenna
Rome
LOMBARDS
ITALY
SICILY
CRETE
CYPRUS
PALESTINE
SYRIA
Damascus
Jerusalem
Alexandria
Fustat
EGYPT
Nile
BERBERS
Tigri
Euphrates
IRAQ
Ctesiphon
Kufah
Isfahan
IRAN
Persian Gulf
Medina
Mecca
ARABIA
RED SEA
ARABIAN SEA
Byzantine Empire
Conquests of Islam to 632
Conquests of Islam to 656
0 200 400 mi
0 300 600 km
FRANKS
VISIGOTHS
OSTROGOTHS
ITALY
VANDALS
Justinian's conquests 527–565
Byzantine Empire 527
0 400 mi
0 600 km

like Amr. Umar gave his assent to the campaign, but reluctantly. Amazed at the extent of the territory already occupied by his armies, he was fearful lest they be spread too thinly.

Leaving Palestine by the historic route along the coast, Amr entered Egypt late in 639 and then moved toward the apex of the Nile delta. Joined by a larger Arab contingent under one of the Companions of the Prophet ("those who knew Muhammad"), Amr moved on Alexandria and forced its surrender in 642. It was a great and rich metropolis whose public buildings, harbor facilities, and defense walls and towers were a cause of wonder to the desert and town Arabs. To protect his position Amr pushed on westward into Libya and received tribute from tribes around Tripoli. Egypt, from Alexandria south up the Nile to a point well beyond modern Cairo, was now a Muslim possession.

Umar also conducted extensive military campaigns in the east. At the moment of Umar's accession to the caliphate, the brilliant Bedouin general al-Muthanna, commander of the Muslim armies in Mesopotamia, was in Medina pleading for reinforcements. He begged that troops be raised among the Arab tribes guilty of opposing the Muslim state upon Muhammad's death, rightly judging that, however weak and chaotic Sasanian society and government might be, surrender to the Arabs would not occur without a struggle.

Although the lifting of the ban against former apostates brought streams of warriors into Mesopotamia, superb Persian generalship, the use of elephants, the size of the armies, and the wealth available to the Sasanian kings more than matched the fervor of al-Muthanna's tribesmen. Ravaging far and wide, even to the gates of Ctesiphon, the Sasanian capital, the Arab forces acquired vast herds and immense stores of grain. Yet they had to retire from Mesopotamia into the western desert when finally faced by an organized Persian army under royal leadership.

Umar soon recognized that to hold Mesopotamia and secure its borders it would be necessary to destroy the main Persian army and reduce the capital at Ctesiphon. A major force gathered and, in a decisive four-day battle at Qadisiyyah in 637, routed the Persian army. Ctesiphon capitulated, and other battles—especially at Nihavend in 642—destroyed the Sasanian forces. There ensued the consolidation of Muslim control over the lands bordering on the Tigris and Euphrates rivers as far north as Mosul. These years saw the permanent conquest and occupation of Mesopotamia (now to be called Iraq).

With the booty that fell to them, the Arabs suddenly enjoyed great wealth and unknown luxuries. After the battle of Qadisiyyah each soldier received 6000 pieces of silver; at the fall of Ctesiphon each received 12,000 pieces. Gold became as common as silver, and fabulous objects, such as a life-size silver camel with a rider of gold or a golden horse with trappings of gold, emeralds for teeth, and its neck set with rubies, became the prizes of the day. One Bedouin who sold a female slave for 1000 pieces of silver was chided by another for having sold her for so little. The excuse offered was that he had not known any sum larger than ten hundred. From the palace of Ctesiphon the army sent to Umar the royal banquet carpet, measuring 105 by 90 feet (32 by 27 m.) and portraying a landscape. The ground was represented by gold and the paths were silver; meadows were made of emeralds; streams were cascades of pearls; trees, flowers, and fruits were depicted by diamonds, rubies, and other precious stones. Some suggested that the carpet be kept as a trophy, but when many pointed out that earthly goods were but passing things, the carpet was cut into pieces.

Over the next several years Muslim parties raided Khuzistan and advanced toward Isfahan. Persian forces rallied at Hamadan, but with the removal of Umar's ban on advances into Persia (now to be called Iran), Muslims overran most of that land. In the ten years of Umar's caliphate Muslim armies had in an almost unbelievable sweep conquered Iraq and western Iran. They repeatedly crushed armies that only a few years previously had been able to conquer much of the Byzantine Empire. This success was even more remarkable when one considers that other Arab armies at the same time were engaged in conquering Syria and Egypt. During Umar's caliphate Iran, Iraq, Syria, Palestine, and Egypt became parts of the Muslim world. They, together with Arabia (and later Anatolia), constituted the heartland of the Islamic Middle East.

ADMINISTRATIVE ACCOMPLISHMENTS

These conquests alone would have assured Umar the position of second founder of Islam. But Umar's orders regarding the occupation and administration of the new territories were equally important in setting a pattern that persisted. Except in some parts of Syria and a few other places, the people of the conquered provinces continued to work and live as they had for centuries, generally with the initial advantage of paying less in tribute than they formerly paid in taxes. Armies were destroyed and administrators either departed or were employed in similar capacities by the Muslims, but most inhabitants were hardly touched. The strife, destruction, and plagues of the time when the Byzantines and the Sasanians fought each other incessantly were ended, and reconstruction and stability began to take effect.

Indeed, in some instances, Arab domination was not only tolerable but welcome. In Syria and Palestine urbanites had acquired a Hellenistic orientation and many of them, especially in Syria, left with the defeated Byzantine armies; but the local peoples had retained contact with desert and town Arabs, thus easing the transition to Arab rule. In Iraq, native tribes rejoiced in the Sasanian defeats. In Iran, however, the Arabs were never as fully accepted, and the rapidity of the Muslim conquest can be attributed in part to the collapse of the Sasanian dynasty and royal government.

In Syria, Palestine, and Egypt, heavy Byzantine taxes and the arrogant, high-handed attitude of officials from Constantinople embittered the provinces. More aggravating and more emotional were the persecutions inflicted upon local Christians and Jews. The orthodox Council of Chalcedon in the year 451 condemned the Monophysite doctrine, according to which divinity and humanity make one compound nature in Christ. This Monophysite approach to Christianity was persecuted savagely by many emperors. Thus, when it became apparent that Muslim rule meant religious freedom as well as lower taxes, the Arabs had little difficulty in obtaining cooperation from some of the local peoples. Since at this time Muslims paid no taxes, this toleration of taxpaying Christians and Jews is the origin of the often repeated but little understood Muslim formula of the three-way choice—Islam, taxes, or death—offered to conquered peoples.

Except in Iran, the armies of occupation were held aloof from the established urban centers as much as possible. Umar ordered that camps be placed in the open near the desert. Later, camp cities were established in the newly won provinces—Basrah in lower Iraq, Kufah in central Iraq, Jabiyah in Syria, Ramlah in Palestine, and Fustat in Egypt.

In Syria, Muslim soldiers and local Arabs took over partially deserted towns and some lands whose owners, being Byzantine supporters, had departed. Some 20,000 of the Muslims moved into Hims and Damascus, but the Christians were more numerous. Jealousy and strife arose over available houses and lands, so much so that Umar visited Syria and made an evenhanded redistribution among everyone.

In all the conquered territories the caliph appointed governors to collect taxes and maintain order. Only a handful of administrators accompanied the governors, and, in general, bureaus of government were staffed by previous officials. Non-Muslims could not bear arms and were subject to their own laws, a practice that established Islamic society as one of the most tolerant of all ages and developed into the famous millet (or semi-autonomous religious community) system of the Ottoman Empire. Arabs from Arabia were eventually not permitted to own agricultural lands in conquered territory. Later, this injunction evolved into a complex system of landownership and rights of tenancy. Considering all aspects of life, the conquered peoples of the Middle East were disturbed very little by Muslim occupation.

Many other developments occurred during Umar's caliphate. The character of Mecca and Medina began to change as wealth from victories poured in. There was great building activity, particularly in Medina, where apartments were needed for retired soldiers, administrators, and others who flocked to the capital city as well as for the old inhabitants whose wealth had now greatly increased. Umar decreed that grazing grounds in Arabia would be restricted to horses and camels that would be used in the holy wars.

Umar again enunciated Muhammad's policy that although prisoners and movable property belonged to the soldiers who won them, land and taxes from conquest belonged to the whole Muslim community, and one-fifth of all income from conquered territory was to be forwarded to Medina. To facilitate distribution among the Muslims, Umar had a census taken in Arabia and a register (diwan) made of the sum each was to receive annually from the public treasury. The list included male and female Muslims of all ranks, from Aishah and other members of the Prophet's family down to the least prestigious ranks of women and children of non-Arab warriors. Aishah received 12,000 dirhams (a silver coin); Companions of the Prophet, 5000; and a child of non-Arabs, 200.

Perhaps Umar's regulation of the calendar best showed the belief that a new state and community had been born. Numbering the new era with the Prophet's immigration to Medina, Umar decreed that Muslim dating should be counted as so many lunar years after the hijrah and that he had therefore become caliph in the year A.H. 13.

As the years went by and wealth and opportunity grew, Umar had more and more difficulty with his provincial governors and their administrations. Since he had little power to enforce his will, the governors were nearly independent. Consequently, the required income from conquered lands was not always forthcoming; Syria, in fact, never sent any. Among the leaders of Islam, Umar was only first among equals. This was especially true in the camp cities of Kufah and Basrah, inhabited by many nomad warriors who were proud, hardy, political Muslims, resentful of Quraish rule. Al-Mughirah, Umar's governor of Basrah, was a brilliant, tough, scheming native of al-Taif, just the sort of rough-and-ready genius that a new city would require. But when he was caught in adultery, the protests from Basrah were so vociferous that he was recalled to Medina for trial. Although al-Mughirah escaped punishment by slipping through a legal loophole, Umar relieved him of his post. Later al-Mughirah was able to wangle the appointment to Kufah, which he retained for many years, augmenting its power and scope until he became one of the most powerful men in the Muslim world.

In 644, at the very height of Umar's power and prestige, he was assassinated at worship in the mosque of Medina by an Iranian Christian slave who had a personal grudge to settle. On his deathbed Umar selected six leading notables of Medina, all ex-Meccans, to choose his successor. Shortly after he had been buried beside Muhammad and Abu Bakr, the notables, probably on the basis of seniority and a pledge to follow the policies and practices of Umar, selected Uthman ibn Affan, who ruled as caliph from 644 to 656. The other leading candidate, popular with the older Medina families, was Muhammad's cousin Ali, who was passed by because he would not promise to follow in Umar's footsteps.

UTHMAN

Uthman was a member of the prominent and powerful Umayyad family of the Quraish. Noted for his mild manner and piety, his only distinction as a Muslim leader was having been a respected Companion of the Prophet. His three predecessors as leaders of the community had belonged to lesser Quraish families, as had most of the immigrants to Medina. Perhaps it was because of this that they had ignored the traditional Arab policy of nepotism and regarded all Muslims as members of one community and one brotherhood. This new social philosophy was one of the revolutionary aspects of Islam.

Although Uthman was seventy and not particularly energetic when he became caliph, he nevertheless sought greater control over the provinces. He was fortunate to have at his command within his own clan a number of vigorous governors and generals to carry forward the banners of Islam. His foster brother Abd Allah was appointed governor of Egypt with financial and civil control, while the conquering Amr was left as commander of the Muslim army. Outraged, Amr immediately went to Medina and refused to serve, with the acid remark "To be over the army and not over the revenue was like holding the cow's horns while another milked her." Abd Allah's great contribution was the development of a Muslim fleet, including at least some Coptic Christian sailors. In 652 the Muslim navy repulsed a Byzantine armada before it could attack Alexandria.

In Syria, Uthman had as governor his shrewd and aggressive cousin Muawiyah ibn Abu Sufyan, one of the greatest administrators in Muslim history. Umar had appointed him governor of Damascus, and as other governorships in Syria fell vacant they were added to Muawiyah's territory until under Uthman he became the powerful ruler of all of Syria. He rebuffed a large Byzantine army and sent raiding parties into Anatolia. He, too, built a fleet; he gained influence over Cyprus in 649, attacked the island of Rhodes, and in 655, in conjunction with Abd Allah's ships, destroyed a large part of the Byzantine navy.

Other cousins of Uthman were appointed as governors of Kufah and Basrah; during these years they led Arab armies in Iran, continuing to fan out eastward. Fars was fully subdued by 650; parts of Khurasan were taken in 651; inroads were made into eastern Armenia in the 640s; and before the end of Uthman's caliphate, expeditions reached central Asia and Afghanistan.

Even though the caliph might not be personally aggressive, the ability of the Muslim army and navy were no longer questioned in the Middle East. The growing problem was the impact of the new empire upon the Muslim community, which had so recently emerged from Arab society. Most of the original emigrants who still lived were now notables and exceedingly wealthy. One reputedly had 1000 slaves and a palace in each of the great cities; another left a fortune of 400,000 dinars; many had villas in Mecca and Medina or in the hills nearby.

A second generation was coming to full adulthood. The amusements and luxuries of Alexandria, Damascus, Ctesiphon, and the camp cities of Basrah, Kufah, and Fustat were tempting. Wine, women, and gambling were the undoing of many young men. Gone were the days when, as Aishah easily recalled, Muhammad considered wheat bread a rare treat and usually made a meal of dates or milk but never had the luxury of both at the same time. Sumptuous living, however, was not the only change. Personal politics and the desire for power and prestige began to eat at the vitals of Muslim society, and certainly Uthman was not strong enough to stem the process that was disrupting the consensus of the community.

MUSLIM POLITICAL FACTIONS

Three political factions were developing in the area ruled by Muslims. The first considered itself the party of Muhammad. Led by members of the less important families of Mecca, it was composed of those who had established the Muslim community. Abu Bakr and Umar had been members of this group, and in most circles Ali, as the husband of Muhammad's daughter Fatimah, was looked upon as the leader. The strength of the party, sometimes called legitimists, lay in Egypt and Iraq.

Leaders of the second faction were members of the Umayyad family and their associates among the Quraish. It had been one of the two wealthiest and most influential Meccan families in the pre-Islamic period—a family that had bitterly attacked Muhammad and had led the campaigns against the Muslims in Medina. Uthman was an Umayyad, as were Muawiyah in Damascus, Abd Allah in Egypt, and Marwan, who served as Uthman's executive secretary in Medina. Though latecomers to Islam, they possessed great managerial talent and were rapidly surging to the fore in administering the empire. Umar had used them and controlled them, but the legitimists contended that the Umayyads controlled Uthman through their great power and wealth in Syria.

The third faction was composed of Arab soldiers who had joined the Muslims just before or after Muhammad's death. They outnumbered the other two groups, but they were unorganized and their leaders did not have the prestige of the Quraish. Yet it was their swords that had been responsible for the rapid expansion of the domain of Islam, and since Islam acknowledged no distinctions among peoples or individuals, this faction resented the inferior political position forced upon them. The third party had followers everywhere, but their forces were concentrated in Arabia and the two great military cities in Iraq.

Having lost the election that followed Umar's death, the legitimists carped at Uthman for his policies and his inaction. He was censured for enlarging the square around the Kaba in Mecca and for rebuilding and embellishing the mosque in Medina. Even his standardization of the Quran (still the canonical text today) was attacked, with many feeling that he had no superior religious insight for such an undertaking. But the most severe criticism was leveled at him for appointing so many members of the Umayyad family to high office and for distributing unjustly the spoils of war. His political opponents claimed that he was reverting to the old order of Arab society where blood ties had ruled. Muhammad had preached earnestly to create a unitary Muslim community wherein all members would be like a family and where social, economic, and political equality would prevail, yet a mere dozen years after his death the traditional preference for the family reasserted its consuming role.

Malcontents across the empire fed on stories regarding the sale of positions and the power and wealth of favorites. Kufah first raised the banners of revolt. When opponents arrived in Medina from Egypt and Iraq and surrounded Uthman's residence, the caliph would not permit an army to be raised in his defense and commanded Muawiyah not to come to his rescue. After a siege of several months in 656 the rebels, including Abu Bakr's son, stormed the palace and murdered Uthman. Anarchy reigned in Medina until a group of notables, under pressure from the rebels, elected Ali to the caliphate and restored order.

ALI

Ali, Muhammad's cousin, adopted son, and son-in-law, was a pious and esteemed Muslim who as an individual soldier in his younger days had shone as one of the great heroes of Muslim battles. He had already been disappointed three times in not being selected caliph, and he may have known of the move to kill Uthman. Generally throughout the Muslim world he was recognized as the caliph, although with reluctance. The new governor appointed by him for Syria was rejected by Muawiyah, who refused to resign. There were many individuals who did not acknowledge Ali as caliph, largely because of jealousy or shock over the murder of Uthman.

Some of the legitimists, aided by Aishah, who bitterly opposed Ali, hatched a rebellion in Mecca on the grounds that Ali had implicated himself by not punishing the regicides. In 656, Ali led his army from Medina, which from that day onward ceased to be the residence of any caliph, and defeated the insurgents near Basrah in the renowned "battle of the camel," when the fighting swirled around Aishah on her camel. (Women had earlier, during the days of the Prophet, participated in battlefield activities and others would later take part in the struggle between Ali and Muawiyah.) In this first battle of Muslim against Muslim neither booty nor reprisal against the vanquished was taken. Many illustrious Companions of the Prophet were killed. Aishah was captured but was permitted to retain an honored status in Medina, where she served as a source of religious information as she lived on for twenty-two years in her apartment—the place where, beneath the floor, Muhammad, Abu Bakr, and Umar had been buried.

Denouncing Ali as an associate of the murderers of his uncle, the caliph Uthman, Muawiyah met Ali's forces at Siffin on the banks of the Euphrates in northern Syria in 657. In the midst of battle, fighting between Muslims was dramatically halted upon agreement that the contest would be decided by referring to the Quran. Arbitration was unsuccessful; Muawiyah refused to accept Ali as caliph until Ali punished the murderers of

Uthman, and Ali could not kill his supporters, nor would he abdicate. Each force, however, retired from the field, and a stalemate ensued.

Following the "battle of the camel," Ali had made his capital at Kufah. His episode with Muawiyah was, in part, a revival of the persistent rivalry between Syria and Iraq for dominance in the Middle East. It was also a struggle between the Umayyad Quraish, now located in Syria, and the settled Arab tribesmen of Iraq and the Hijaz.

At the "battle of the camel" so many of the legitimist party perished that it disappeared from the annals of Islam, leaving Ali, in Kufah, at the mercy of the dominant local and religious groups. In fact, some members took the name Kharijis ("Seceders") and revolted against Ali in protest against his willingness to arbitrate. Ali destroyed their force in 658 but was assassinated in 661 by a Khariji in Kufah on the way to prayer. Hasan, Ali's eldest son, was declared caliph in Kufah, but Muawiyah was recognized as caliph in Damascus. A few months later Hasan reached an agreement with Muawiyah and retired on a royal pension to his palace in Medina. Muawiyah, thenceforth, was accepted throughout the Muslim Empire as the sole caliph, and the center of the state shifted to Damascus.

Thus ended the short consensual era of the caliphate in which the rulers were selected for reasons other than birth or military might. Throughout the bulk of this period Medina still served as the capital of the Muslim world, and the leaders of the community had known the prophet Muhammad personally. It was an Arab state; the conquered provinces were ruled by a relatively small minority of Arabic-speaking Muslims. Most Muslims of later times looked back upon this era as a golden age, when Islam was extraordinarily successful and a mostly united community of believers was governed with great piety and wisdom. With the transfer of the seat of authority to Damascus and the caliphate to Muawiyah of the Umayyad family, a new era was born.

REFERENCES

References cited at the end of Chapter 3 are pertinent to this chapter as well.

Arnold, Thomas W.: *The Caliphate.* Oxford: Clarendon Press, 1924. A classic discussion of the formation and history of the rule of the Muslim state.

Donner, Fred McGraw: *The Early Islamic Conquests.* Princeton, N.J.: Princeton University Press, 1981. The standard account of the Muslim conquests of Syria and Iraq, this work also contains a valuable analysis of the relations between nomadic tribesmen and the Medina government.

Firestone, Reuven: *Jihad: The Origin of Holy War in Islam.* New York: Oxford University Press, 1999. The author carefully shows the evolution of the concept of jihad during the seventh century.

Ibrahim, Mahmood: *Merchant Capital and Islam.* Austin: University of Texas Press, 1990. An intriguing essay on the early history of Islam up to the Umayyad dynasty, emphasizing the role played by merchants.

Kaegi, Walter E.: *Byzantium and the Early Islamic Conquests.* Cambridge: Cambridge University Press, 1992. Carefully traces both military and other causes of Islamic expansion based on Byzantine and Arabic sources. An excellent study.

Keddie, Nikki R., and Beth Baron, eds.: *Women in Middle Eastern History: Shifting Boundaries in Sex and Gender.* New Haven, Conn.: Yale University Press, 1991. A wide variety of essays dealing with the theoretical and practical aspects of the history of women in the Islamic Middle East, including a discussion of Aishah.

Kennedy, Hugh: *The Prophet and the Age of the Caliphates: The Islamic Near East from the Sixth to the Eleventh Century.* London: Longman, 1986. This detailed political history incorporates scholarly research as well as original sources; the author considers, but ultimately rejects, revisionist historians who have attacked the reliability of the primary sources.

Lewis, Bernard: *The Arabs in History.* Oxford: Oxford University Press, 1993. A concise account of the rise of the Arabs, emphasizing the broad economic movements through the ages and correlating these developments with historical processes among the Arabs.

Madelung, Wilferd: *The Succession to Muhammad: A Study of the Early Caliphate.* New York: Cambridge University Press, 1997. A detailed history sympathetic to Ali and critical of the Umayyads.

Shoufani, Elias: *Al-Riddah and the Muslim Conquest of Arabia.* Toronto: University of Toronto Press, 1973. A study of the wars in Arabia upon the death of Muhammad, showing that Arabia was far from united at the time of the Prophet's death.

Spellberg, D. A.: *Politics, Gender, and the Islamic Past: The Legacy of 'A'isha bint Abi Bakr.* New York: Columbia University Press, 1994. Discusses later views of Aishah's life and importance.

Vaglieri, L. Vecchia: "Ali ibn Abi Talib." *Encyclopaedia of Islam.* New ed. Vol. 1, pp. 381–386. Leiden: Brill, 1960. This article, like the following one by W. Montgomery Watt, shows the high standards and thorough scholarship of the authors in the *Encyclopaedia of Islam,* a basic reference tool for all who are concerned with the Islamic Middle East.

Watt, W. Montgomery: "Abu Bakr." *Encyclopaedia of Islam.* New ed. Vol. 1, pp. 109–111. Leiden: Brill, 1960.

CHAPTER 5

The Spread and Organization of the Muslim Empire under the Umayyads

The death of Ali left no serious rival to Muawiyah and his leadership as caliph over all Muslims. He established the rule of the Umayyad dynasty over the Muslim community and state, replacing the consensual system of the first four caliphs. The Umayyad Empire lasted only ninety years, but Muawiyah and his heirs accomplished much in the political, military, and administrative areas while at the same time providing the prerequisites for both cultural accomplishments and religious and factional variations and disputes.

Proclaimed caliph at Jerusalem in 661 while in his fifties, Muawiyah established Damascus as his chief residence and seat of government. Until his death nineteen years later, he managed the provinces through energetic, capable, and forceful governors, who tried to maintain a strong discipline over the proud and turbulent Arab soldiers. In Iraq, however, the crowded garrison cities and determined leaders declared their autonomy so vigorously that Muawiyah had a limited degree of control. Muslim soldiers held the province and the Sasanian governmental lands as theirs by right of conquest and rarely sent any part of the income to Damascus.

At home Muawiyah ruled confidently and with good judgment as the first among equals. He discussed policies of state with the notables about him, frequently explaining the course of government publicly from the pulpit of the mosque. In truth, his power rested upon the personal loyalty of the Syrian army, which was the strongest and best organized of any in the state. More and more he built an administration in the Sasanian and Byzantine tradition; less and less was he the tribal Arab shaikh governing purely on a personal basis. He was the first Muslim ruler to execute a fellow Muslim for political reasons.

Five years before his death, Muawiyah induced the leaders of the empire to recognize his son Yazid as his successor. This procedure was definitely a dynastic custom. Essentially, this method of succession made the position of caliph a hereditary one, or at least a family prerogative, and overtly established the Umayyad Empire, which lasted until 750. Succession was among the males of the Umayyad family, but not necessarily from father to eldest son; instead, the incumbent ruler could designate his heir, or power might be seized by the ablest male in the family. Female members of the Umayyad royal family did not play a prominent part in public life (as Aishah had done earlier), but they helped link together the generations. Atika, daughter of Yazid I and wife of Abd al-Malik, was closely related to twelve different Umayyad caliphs.

In general and by comparison with other ruling families, the Umayyads produced a dynasty of talented, competent caliphs. They were much maligned by later Muslim historians, especially the pious religious scholars who wrote under the patronage of the succeeding dynasty and depicted the Umayyads as wine-bibbing, luxury-loving, worldly minded usurpers of the caliphate. But the Umayyads organized the Muslim state into a centralized force that once again carried forward the banners of Islam into distant places. They were realists who could not always follow the principles of government and law being formulated by theologians and jurists in the holy city of Medina. However, the military successes of the Umayyad dynasty were balanced by the development of new concepts and dogmas within Islam that gave birth to numerous Muslim sects. Under the Umayyads the unity of theology, as well as politics, was lost in the Muslim world.

CAMPAIGNS AGAINST BYZANTIUM

The nearest and greatest rival power of the Umayyad state was the Christian Byzantine Empire with its capital at Constantinople; the nearest and richest land for the Muslims to raid was Anatolia, the heart of the Byzantine lands. Muawiyah, as governor of Syria, had already driven Byzantine armies from north Syria and defeated Byzantine fleets. He repeatedly raided Armenia, which was forced by 662 to pay tribute to Damascus. Muawiyah's army exploited the weakness of the rule from Constantinople by annual summer excursions through the passes into Anatolia. After he became caliph, Muawiyah's forces roamed far and wide over Anatolia, and he attacked Constantinople, but the land and sea walls of the city proved too great a barrier for the Muslim Arabs.

Another assault upon Constantinople was launched by the Umayyad caliph Sulaiman. His forces occupied both shores of the Bosphorus and held a tight siege of Constantinople for months. In 717, however, he was foiled by Greek fire and the brilliant defenses of the new emperor, Leo the Isaurian, and by the ravages of disease, hunger, and an unusually severe winter. The new caliph, Umar II, strongly opposed to all expansionist policies, ordered the siege lifted and the Muslim forces withdrawn. Several generations elapsed before the Muslims appeared again before the walls of Constantinople, which proved too thick and too strong for the Arabs to penetrate without the aid of gunpowder. (Byzantine history will be discussed more thoroughly in Chapter 13.)

NORTH AFRICA AND SPAIN

The records do not disclose any planned pincers movement on Europe by the Umayyads, although simultaneously with their attacks upon Constantinople the greatest westward movement of Islam was being executed. Amr ibn al-As, governor of Egypt, sent a Muslim force into North Africa and resumed raids into Libya in the 660s. A camp city whose construction was begun in 670 at Qairawan in Tunisia served as headquarters to subdue

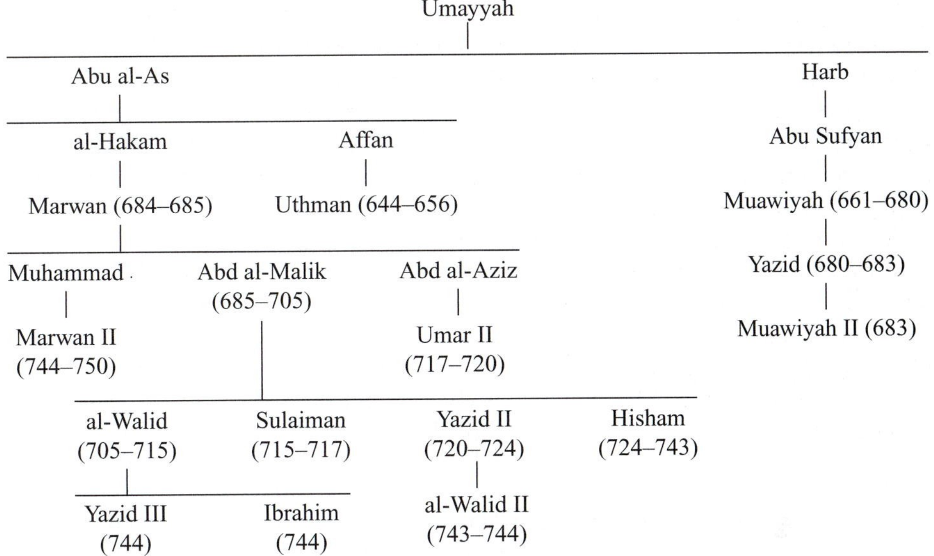

The Umayyad Caliphs

Berber tribes and the coastal cities dependent upon Constantinople. Toward the end of the century Byzantine rule over the coast was ended by a joint army-fleet maneuver, as the new city of Tunis was founded. Appointed governor of northwest Africa sometime between 698 and 705, Musa ibn Nusair consolidated the region and added greatly to his military force by recruiting from among the Berber-speaking tribesmen. Most of Morocco, however, subsequently remained beyond the effective control of the Umayyad governors for decades.

The Berber freedman Tariq crossed the Strait of Gibraltar on his celebrated raid in the early summer of 711 with several thousand men, mostly Berbers, and established a base on the strong height that still is called Tariq's mountain—Jabal Tariq, or Gibraltar. Crushing the Visigothic Christian forces of Spain, Tariq fanned out northward at will. Tariq soon found himself master of half of Spain, with an almost unlimited amount of booty at his disposal.

Scolding Tariq for acting independently, Musa joined his henchman in 712. Within two years nearly all of Spain had been overrun by Muslim forces. From Galicia, Musa looked down upon the waters of the Atlantic. At this time, a messenger ordered Musa to appear before the caliph in Damascus. Accompanied by Tariq, Musa made the long trek overland and presented to the court his trophies and many male and female Visigothic captives. Shortly thereafter a new caliph stripped Musa of his wealth and degraded him, perhaps because of fear or jealousy of Musa's great popularity. Musa died in poverty a few years later, a strange fate for one who had opened Europe to the Muslims.

Within six or seven years the conquest of Spain was completed. The Arabs called the province al-Andalusia ("Land of the Vandals"), and it, or some part of it, remained a Muslim land for almost eight centuries. The Arab-Berber-Muslim (Moorish) culture left its indelible mark on Spain, which in turn had a profound influence on Islamic society. The speed and ease with which Spain was conquered indicated that it had been in a state of near anarchy following a struggle over succession to the Visigothic throne.

In 720 Arab-Berber invaders seized Narbonne on the Mediterranean and established an arsenal and base for operations north of the Pyrenees. Raiding columns rode out of Narbonne every year, terrorizing the countryside and carrying off rich booty, especially from churches and convents. The greatest of these expeditions was the renowned foray led by the governor of Spain, Abd al-Rahman. The raiders turned back from their northward course only after the loss of their leader in the determined, bloody resistance put up by Charles Martel in 732. Never again did an organized expedition of Muslims approach so near to Paris.

Although Narbonne was not abandoned until 759, the Arabs and Berbers of Spain never fashioned a real hold upon southern France because of their lack of manpower, the distance from Damascus, and a running feud between Berber and Arab that led to violent insurrection in North Africa and Spain. Conversions to Islam among the Berbers were so extensive as to compromise the relationship between conquerors and vanquished in North Africa. Many Muslim Arabs looked down on the Berbers, who upon becoming Muslims anticipated equality with the proud Arabs. When the expected treatment was not forthcoming, rebellion burst out everywhere. From 739 to 742 North Africa was in flames from one end to the other. Berbers claimed that they were given semiarid plateau lands in Spain while the Arabs acquired all of the fertile areas.

In addition, factional strife among the Arabs existed at every turn. Political, religious, and family quarrels were at this moment rocking the Islamic world from the Pyrenees to the Indus, making incursions beyond well-established frontiers wholly ineffective. Furthermore, rivalry developed between Arabs from Arabia and the more recently arrived Syrian army sent to subdue Berber uprisings; their bickerings with the Arab governors and lords were interminable. From 732 to the landing of the Umayyad prince in Spain in 755, the term of the governorship of Spain averaged twelve months. With such turmoil, uncertainty, and anarchy, permanent conquests in France were impossible.

EXPANSION IN ASIA

While the Umayyads were extending Islam westward into North Africa and Spain, a similar expansion carried Muslim rule to the Indus River and the frontiers of China in central Asia. Often territory was peacefully surrendered by treaty rather than conquered. Becoming viceroy of the eastern lands of the caliphate in 695, al-Hajjaj, a schoolmaster of al-Taif, gave his governor of Khurasan Arab troops to establish a strong base at Merv (Mary). These were added to the thousands of Arabs from Kufah and Basrah that Muawiyah had sent to settle in the oases around Merv; moreover, local Persian landowners, volunteers, and clients swelled the ranks of the Muslim forces. The army crossed the Amu Darya River (known then as the Oxus) and in a series of brilliant campaigns brought large parts of central Asia under Muslim domination. Bukhara and Samarkand in Uzbekistan and adjacent areas were subdued between 705 and 712 and soon became Islamic strongholds; Buddhist temples and monasteries were destroyed. The Umayyads also conquered Herat and Kabul in Afghanistan. Native Turkish and Persian rulers were left in charge of civil affairs, although Muslim military inspectors represented the imperial authority. A generation later another caliph sent an Arab general beyond the Amu Darya River as far as Kashgar, on the borders of China, to reconquer the area and bring the Turkish rulers, some of whom had accepted Islam, again under caliphal authority.

Farther south, al-Hajjaj's son-in-law was authorized to lead a column toward India. The Arab Muslims controlled the territory of modern Pakistan after 711 (and continued to rule there until 1026). Steady conversion to Islam, especially among Buddhists, eventually made this northwestern corner of India an important part of the Muslim world. Expansion beyond Sind to the east, or beyond central Asia to the east and north, did not take place for many of the same reasons as mentioned in connection with the situation of the Arab Muslims in southern France. In addition, the Muslims faced strong opposition from the military and political forces of Hindu Indian states as well as the power of China.

FISCAL DEVELOPMENTS

This wave of Muslim expansion under the Umayyads brought to a head certain economic and fiscal problems that had been developing at an accelerated pace. From the time of the hijrah in 622, Muslims had been subject to a small tax to support their poor and unfortunate brethren, but there was no general taxation. Toward the end of the seventh century, with Arab Muslims scattered over the face of the earth and conversions among conquered non-Arab peoples growing by leaps and bounds, questions of state annuities to worthy Muslims, landownership, and taxation arose to vex one caliph after another and ignited serious disturbances in Muslim society.

Besides the state's share of booty, which in the Umayyad era was very sizable, the principal source of revenue came in taxes from subject peoples and land. Each free non-Muslim was required to pay for protection a poll tax (jizyah) of four, two, or one gold dinar or the equivalent in goods, according to wealth and position.

Land taxes were far more complex. In the days of the earliest conquests Muslim Arabs were forbidden to possess land outside of Arabia proper. Domain lands of ousted Byzantine and Sasanian governments and vacant lands fell to the caliph as agent for the Muslim community, and the income went into provincial coffers, with all surplus supposedly being forwarded to Damascus. As the Umayyad rulers established irrigation and agricultural development projects, the ensuing revenues from the provinces proved a valuable supplement to taxation. Ownership of other land was mostly not changed, so peasants or local landlords who had owned the land under the Byzantines and the Sasanians usually continued in possession. In most cases the taxes (kharaj) remained the same and were collected by the same agents. As Arab Muslims acquired properties in Syria, Iraq, and other areas outside Arabia, freedom from land taxes usually prevailed. The state leased domain land to Muslim Arabs, who bought and sold the rights so that the land had the appearance of private property. Consequently, Arab laws governing landownership and tenure adhered generally to Byzantine and Sasanian customs, thereby assuring to tillers of the soil throughout the Middle East a continuity that changed only slowly.

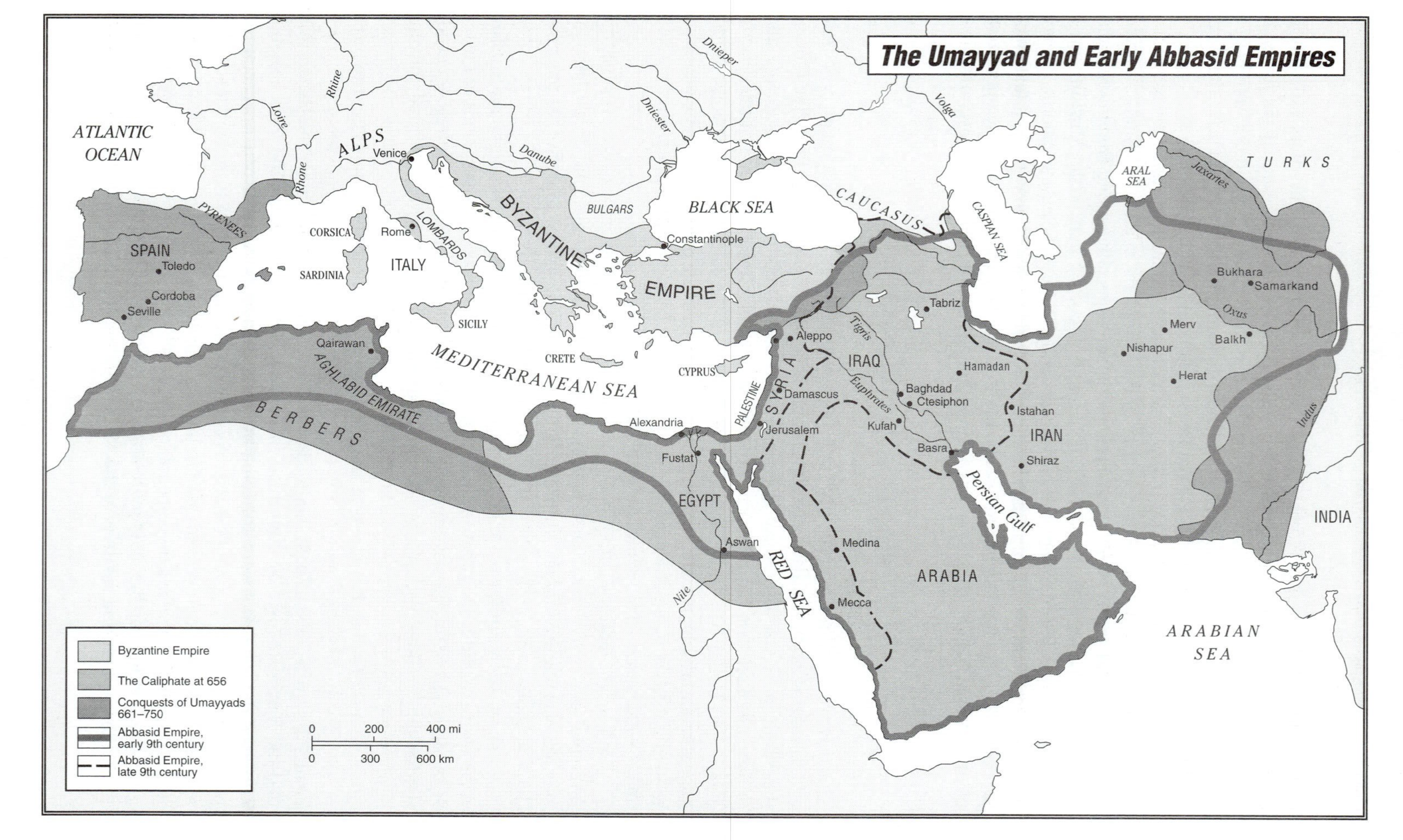
The Umayyad and Early Abbasid Empires
ATLANTIC OCEAN
ALPS
Venice
Danube
Rhine
Loire
Rhone
Dnieper
Dniester
Volga
BULGARS
BLACK SEA
CAUCASUS
CASPIAN SEA
ARAL SEA
Jaxartes
TURKS
PYRENEES
SPAIN
Toledo
Cordoba
Seville
CORSICA
SARDINIA
Rome
ITALY
LOMBARDS
SICILY
BYZANTINE EMPIRE
Constantinople
CRETE
CYPRUS
MEDITERRANEAN SEA
Qairawan
AGHLABID EMIRATE
BERBERS
Alexandria
Fustat
EGYPT
Aswan
Nile
RED SEA
PALESTINE
SYRIA
Aleppo
Damascus
Jerusalem
Tigris
Euphrates
IRAQ
Baghdad
Ctesiphon
Kufah
Basra
Tabriz
Hamadan
Istahan
IRAN
Shiraz
Persian Gulf
Medina
Mecca
ARABIA
Bukhara
Samarkand
Oxus
Merv
Nishapur
Balkh
Herat
Indus
INDIA
ARABIAN SEA
Byzantine Empire
The Caliphate at 656
Conquests of Umayyads 661–750
Abbasid Empire, early 9th century
Abbasid Empire, late 9th century
0 200 400 mi
0 300 600 km

As the number of non-Arab Muslims increased through conversion, most deserted the land for the city in the expectation of receiving state annuities as Arabs did. They paid no taxes on the land left behind in the village and ceased to pay the poll tax. This disastrously affected the treasuries, especially in North Africa, Iraq, and Khurasan—a large and rich province in northeastern Iran and central Asia.

Furthermore, in order to eliminate the increasing resentment of non-Arab Muslims and to prevent incipient revolutions in several of the provinces, the Umayyad caliph Umar II decided to free Muslims, irrespective of origin or state, from paying poll and land taxes. The result was a lowering of revenues that upset the fiscal system of the government. Caliph Hisham withdrew the order and instituted the policy, generally permanent in Muslim lands ever since, that although poll taxes "fell off" upon conversion to Islam, land taxes did not. Hisham also used land surveys and population censuses as part of the taxation system. At that time in the provinces the old tax measures were considered by non-Arab Muslims, the principal landowners, to be very inequitable. Great disaffection led to civil war in North Africa and proved to be a major factor in the overthrow of the Umayyad regime by the troops from Khurasan.

SOCIAL ORGANIZATION

As the Arabs and the native inhabitants of the conquered territories began to coalesce, there arose four social classes: Muslim Arabs; clients, mostly Muslim non-Arabs; non-Muslim free persons (Christians, Jews, Zoroastrians); and slaves. The most numerous were the non-Muslim free persons—even at the end of the Umayyad Empire about 90 percent of the population was still non-Muslim.

The Muslim Arabs were the leaders of the Islamic order, and the Quraish of Mecca claimed to be the noblest of the Arabs. Wherever Islam spread, Muslim Arabs regarded themselves as the rightful leaders of society, and at first only they could live in the new garrison cities such as Qairawan and Kufah. Most Muslim Arabs outside Arabia lived in cities. Although Islam taught the equality of all believers and disavowed family connections in favor of religious ties, Muslim Arabs everywhere retained pride in their lineage: clan and tribe feelings ran high, and marriage between a Muslim Arab woman and a non-Arab man was considered a serious mistake. The children of an Arab Muslim man and a non-Arab woman were often considered to be inferior in status. In the Umayyad period most Muslim Arabs were enrolled in the imperial registry, each receiving regular payments from the state treasury on the theory that the receipts of the Muslim community should be divided among all its members. In practice the Muslim Arabs acted as if it were decreed that the Arab minority would rule the non-Arab majority, Muslims as well as non-Muslims.

By the beginning of the eighth century, clients (mawali, singular mawla) outnumbered the Arab Muslims in most parts of the Umayyad Empire except Arabia. Most of the clients were non-Arab Muslims who became affiliated with an Arab Muslim tribe; in addition, even some poor Arab Muslims were not considered to be in the ruling Arab elite. Many clients were freed slaves. The masses in lower Iraq, Syria, and the cities of

Khurasan were converted so rapidly that revenues in those provinces had dropped conspicuously. Rarely were these converts accepted as equals by the Muslim Arabs, and usually they attached themselves to a member of an Arab tribe or family (thus the term "clients"). Yet the converts were in many instances trained and educated individuals with skills not possessed by many Arabs. As several generations passed, because of the adoption of the Arabic language and considerable intermarriage, the Arabs from Arabia who had migrated to conquered territory had become intermingled among a variety of peoples, who jointly participated in a new common culture in sections of the Middle East. In areas such as Syria and Iraq, where many Arab Muslims settled, non-Arab Muslims were absorbed relatively quickly, and Arabic became the dominant language of the masses. In more distant lands such as central Asia, India, and Spain, the few ruling Muslim Arabs dominated society and Islam spread, but indigenous languages prevailed in the long run. Non-Arab Muslims had a large role in cultural formation in the core areas of the Middle East; in the outer periphery of the Muslim lands they played an even more significant part.

Non-Muslims—Christians, Zoroastrians, Jews, pagan Berbers, and a few scattered others—were called dhimmis and were protected and recognized legally as second-class subjects on condition that they acknowledged the political supremacy of the Muslims. They were judged almost entirely in their own courts in accordance with their own laws and were permitted to worship in their own way and to live their personal lives as they wished. They were, nevertheless, greatly circumscribed in matters of civil rights and community affairs. Non-Muslims could not bear weapons; instead, they paid taxes. They were subject to many distinctive regulations concerning clothing, types of saddles, and manner of riding. While dhimmis could not hold the highest public offices, many served in bureaucratic positions or as advisers to high Muslim Arab officials. In the Middle East many non-Muslims learned to speak Arabic in addition to the language they had earlier used, but the change to Arabic was slow and gradual and by no means universal. For a time Christians and Jews continued to produce theological thinkers of high quality, although as more and more of the population converted to Islam minority groups tended to become less innovative. Often the brightest and most ambitious members of the minorities were among the first to convert to Islam, and the lower social status of the dhimmis discouraged new thinking.

At the bottom of the social ladder were the slaves. Slavery in the middle east and throughout the rest of the world had existed for many centuries before the birth of Islam in Mecca. Although Muhammad openly condemned it, saying that freeing slaves was pleasing in the sight of God, he declared slavery legal. In Islamic society, no Muslim could be enslaved legally; acceptance of Islam, however, did not give a slave freedom. Children of a slave woman remained slaves unless the male owner of the slave acknowledged them as his children. Marriage between master and slave was not permissible, although concubinage was. A concubine who gave birth to her master's children could not be sold, was accorded special recognition as the mother of his children, and gained her freedom upon his death.

Slave trading was an active and profitable business in the Middle East under the Umayyads. Most slaves were acquired as booty in victorious campaigns and successful raiding expeditions, but many were purchased through regular slave channels. Greeks, Armenians, Turks, Kurds, Spaniards, Iranians, black Africans, and Berbers predominated, but there were slaves of every race and description. Prices rose and fell with the supply. Wealthy Arab Muslims frequently counted their slaves in the thousands.

POLITICAL ADMINISTRATION

When Muawiyah became caliph, his first task was to effect a systematic administration for the empire. Obviously following the practices of the Byzantine Empire formerly current in Syria, Muawiyah organized his government along three main functional lines: political and military affairs; tax collection; and religious administration, including courts and endowments. He also established rapid government messengers, the office of chamberlain, and a corps of guards.

The caliphs divided the empire into several provinces, each with a governor appointed by the caliph; the provinces were often subdivided, merged, and reorganized. The religious officials, tribal army leaders, military police, and civil administrators in each province acted upon the authority of the governor. Administration was located in buildings that were usually next to the chief mosque; government employees engaged in holding prisoners, supervising the treasury, and collecting taxes were housed together. Local expenses were defrayed by taxes collected in the provinces, with only the tax balances being forwarded to Damascus. Toward the end of the Umayyad regime, when the administration began to weaken, provincial governors built up great personal fortunes by neglecting to forward the full balance to the caliph. Viceroys even remained in Damascus, hiring agents to go to the provinces to perform their functions. Frequently, special officers were sent directly by the caliph to collect taxes and to be responsible solely to him rather than to the viceroy, who resented the implied lack of confidence.

As the empire expanded, problems of trained and loyal personnel, of communications, and of money came to the fore. The number of qualified Arabs was too small to fill the positions required to keep the government functioning. In Syria, Iraq, and Egypt, Muawiyah retained the services of most of the government employees he found there upon the conquest. These employees used Greek, Persian, and Coptic to keep their records. Not until the time of Abd al-Malik was the conversion to Arabic as the language of government systematically begun. By the end of the Umayyad era, however, government affairs were recorded in Arabic, and clerks were Arabic-speaking and usually Muslim in faith. Mawali filled many prominent administrative posts, and there were even contingents of these Muslim clients in the army.

At the time of their conquest, the Byzantine and Sasanian empires largely relied on a money economy, with gold, silver, and copper coins in wide circulation. The Muslims took these over as mediums of exchange, sometimes with a phrase from the Quran stamped on the coins. True Muslim-Arabic coins, first minted at Damascus in the reign of Abd al-Malik, were similar in value to coins already in circulation. The gold ones were called dinars after the Roman denarius; the silver, dirhams, from the Greek drachma.

Muslim judges (qadis) for the various cities of the empire were usually chosen by the provincial governors and were responsible to them. Since these qadis were concerned only with the Muslims, there was little occasion for judges in towns at this time. Caliphs and provincial governors also held court and handed out justice personally.

OPPOSITION AND OVERTHROW

As long as Muawiyah lived, his firm hand checked the development of opposition to the Umayyad dynastic rule of the Muslim community. After the death of his son Yazid I in 683 a civil war broke out; it was only resolved by the efforts of Marwan I and the reestablishment of Umayyad rule during the long reign of his son, Abd al-Malik, from 685 to 705.

Arab Muslim society tended to separate into two great groups, which were allegedly related to tribal groupings present in the Arabian Peninsula before Islam. Under the Umayyads with the rule of Abd al-Malik and his ruthless viceroy, al-Hajjaj, party strife reached a high point and influenced many aspects of political life in the empire. Reminiscent of the famous popular factions of the Byzantine Empire, the rivalry of the Arab parties became keen and often bitter. Although each group went by a variety of names, the two main divisions were often called the South Arabians and the North Arabians. Between the two parties most differences had long since disappeared; only tribal rivalry remained to perpetuate the factions. Nevertheless, the feuding between the two groups was very real, as is attested by the oft-told incident of the two-year war in Damascus that was touched off because a member of one party stole a watermelon from a garden belonging to a member of the other party.

Beginning with Abd al-Malik until the downfall of the Umayyads, differences between the two parties became fixed upon two central issues, one political and one social. The first was the question of military campaigns of expansion. The South Arabians were generally opposed to these campaigns. Umar II, a staunch supporter of this nonexpansionist view, stopped every campaign in 717 when he became caliph. His successors, however, were mostly expansionist North Arabians, and al-Hajjaj lieutenants were reappointed to high positions. They believed that the social and economic ills of the empire, such as pressures for equality in taxation, fiscal policies of stipends for all Arabs, and civil disturbances caused by some Arabs' refusing to go on campaigns, could be met by expansion on the frontiers, which would occupy the soldiers and avert civil wars, at the same time bringing in booty for soldier and imperial treasury alike.

The social difference was over assimilation—the granting of full status to non-Arab Muslims. The South Arabians believed that Islam recognized equality between Arab, Iranian, Berber, Egyptian, and all Muslims. The North Arabian view, on the other hand, held that Arabs formed a special elite. In general, South Arabians, as exemplified by Umar II, felt that successful rule could be effected only by the consent and cooperation of those ruled. The North Arabian faction tended to rely more on authority, force, and favoritism to maintain order and peace. (In spite of their views concerning equal rights, the South Arabians excluded non-Arabs from their leadership, as did, of course, the North Arabians. For example, the caliph Abd al-Malik raised thirteen sons, but only the six born of Arab mothers could be considered as possible successors; even the capable Maslamah was ineligible because his mother was a non-Arab. This prejudice against Umayyad princes whose mothers were not Arabs lasted almost to the end of the dynasty in Damascus.)

Another source of opposition to the Umayyads emerged from two grandsons of the Prophet, the children of Ali and Fatimah—Hasan and Husain. Upon the death of Hasan, who had relinquished his caliphate in Kufah to make way for Muawiyah, his brother

Husain became the head of the house of Ali. He remained at peace with the Umayyads until Muawiyah's death; then, refusing to recognize Yazid as successor and caliph, he rebelled openly. Husain set out for Kufah with a meager force and at Karbala in Iraq was surrounded and cut down by Umayyad supporters on the tenth of Muharram, A.H. 61 (October 10, 680). Although at the time it caused hardly a ripple across the Muslim body politic, his death was later observed by the Shii sect of Muslims, who came to regard Husain and his brother Hasan as martyrs for the faith and as the rightful heirs to the leadership of the Muslims. Karbala has become a most holy spot, and frequently a kind of passion play is enacted by Shiis on the tenth of Muharram.

Husain's martyrdom left the opposition to the Umayyads in a very weakened position. When Medina, the center of remaining opposition, surrendered to Yazid's army, the rebels sought the protection of the supposed inviolability of Mecca but were pursued by the Syrian forces. In the midst of siege operations, which shattered the Kaba, news of Yazid's death led the Syrian army to withdraw. The North Arabian party in Mecca thereupon openly supported Abd Allah ibn al-Zubair, who was recognized as caliph throughout Arabia, Iraq, Egypt, Iran, and even in parts of Syria. Had he been willing to transfer his residence to Damascus, it is possible that all Muslims would have accepted his rule. Instead, Ibn al-Zubair's followers were defeated by the South Arabians in Syria, and the elderly Marwan, Muawiyah's cousin and formerly executive secretary to the earlier Umayyad caliph Uthman, took power. Nine months later Marwan was dead, and the task of reuniting the state fell to his son Abd al-Malik. In 692, eight years later, a Syrian army led by al-Hajjaj defeated Ibn al-Zubair after another destructive siege of Mecca; thus ended the second Muslim civil war.

This violent struggle of the Umayyads with Husain and Ibn al-Zubair was more than personal or dynastic; it was even more than a bitter outbreak of political party rivalry. In the first instance, the lesser families and clans of the Quraish of Mecca still resented the power that the Umayyad clan had possessed in the decades just prior to the hijrah. Added to this jealousy was indignation over the fact that most of the Umayyads had opposed Muhammad almost to the very end; in fact, Muawiyah's father had driven Muhammad and the Muslims from Mecca and Muawiyah's mother was famous for her hatred of the Muslims. That this family should inherit Muhammad's mantle was more than many could stomach.

More serious in the long run was the moving of the center of the state to Syria. It was inevitable that the wealth and worldliness of that province would affect the ruling elite living there. Visitors from Arabia and religious scholars from Kufah were shocked at the elegance and pomp of the Damascus court and scandalized by the flow of wine, the singing girls, and the devotion to hunting they saw. The Umayyads built luxurious hunting palaces in the desert, and many princes became patrons of poets, singers, musicians, and horse trainers. All these practices seemed far removed from the teachings of Muhammad. As the wealth and power of the ruling society increased, idleness, pleasure seeking, and disregard for Muslim virtues multiplied. Al-Walid II was the most shocking of the rulers among the pious; famous for his bathing in a tub of wine, he was extravagant, eccentric, sensual, and irreverent.

Such antics and increasing centralization alienated the provinces. The regime in Damascus, starting with the reign of Abd al-Malik, introduced greater centralization in government, an army reorganization, and more Arabization in the operations of the bureaucracy. Iraqis, in particular, disliked Syrian rule. In a sense it revived the old enmity seen in the wars of the Sasanian and Byzantine empires.

Shiis and Kharijis rejected the Umayyad family's claims to the hereditary rule of the Muslim community, each claiming that they had a better right to rule and to define the nature of being a Muslim. Pious Muslims in general were offended by the personal immorality of some of the Umayyads, but Shiis and Kharijis actively opposed the regime, especially in Iraq, Iran, and Khurasan. Shiis, who held the view that the mantle of the Prophet rightfully belonged to the family of Muhammad and Ali and objected to the idea that might makes right, formed the nucleus of the opposition. At this time they were joined by the Kharijis, centered in southern Iraq, Iran, and the Arabian peninsula. The Kharijis were religious democrats with a radical social vision who proposed that piety be the basis for selecting the leader of the Muslim community. They objected to prior designation or inheritance, as claimed by the Umayyads and the Shiis. Instead, the consensus of the faithful should determine the leader. Both groups were poorly organized and included people with a wide range of opinions on religious and political matters.

The third subversive party was that of the Abbasids, led first by Muhammad, a great-grandson of al-Abbas, who in turn was an uncle of the Prophet. This Muhammad circulated the story that one of Ali's grandsons on his deathbed had transferred the rights of the Alids (followers of Ali) to the Abbasid family. Beginning about the year 740, Abbasids claimed the leadership of the house of Hashim—Alid as well as Abbasid—and from their headquarters south of the Dead Sea gathered under their standard all anti-Umayyads of Islam. The Umayyads should have seen the handwriting on the wall when many Arabs in Syria, finding life too comfortable, refused to answer the call to arms.

The most valuable support to Alids and Abbasids came from Arab and non-Arab Muslims of Iran and Khurasan, who objected to an inferior position, demanded the equality preached in Islam, and rebelled against Umayyad policies of expansion and authoritarian rule. The organizational structure of the Umayyad Empire was decaying rapidly, as the Syrian troops that were the bedrock of military support for the Umayyads were spread thinly throughout the extensive lands of the empire. An atmosphere of petty, vicious, and sometimes murderous rivalry surrounded the court; and in every corner of the empire there was strife between the two Arab parties. Such violent partisanship, coupled with what was viewed as the immoral life of many Umayyads, invited rebellion everywhere and played into the hands of non-Arab Muslims. The Abbasids utilized these factors to the full in their propaganda in the east and gathered Iranians, Khurasanians, Shiis, and others around their banner, for which they chose the color black. (The Umayyads' and Alids' banners were white; that of the Kharijis was red.)

In 747 the Abbasids raised the standard of revolt. Despite the execution of the initial leader, Abu al-Abbas, a great-great-grandson of al-Abbas, and his Iranian agent succeeded in directing a band of Iranians, Khurasanians, and South Arabians who took the city of Merv. Iraq fell in 749, and Abu al-Abbas was recognized in Kufah as caliph. Marwan II met the rival force early in 750 on the bank of the Zab, a tributary of the Tigris. The great Abbasid victory there opened all Syria, which had few soldiers in it, and Damascus surrendered in April. Abu al-Abbas moved the capital of Islam from Damascus to Kufah, establishing Iraq as the center of the Abbasid empire and placing a new family on the throne as leaders of the Islamic community.

At an infamous banquet near Jaffa some eighty Umayyads were murdered; others were hunted from one end of the empire to the other in an Abbasid attempt to wipe out the entire Umayyad family. Among the few who escaped was Prince Abd al-Rahman, who made his way to Spain and established an Umayyad state there. The political unity of the Islamic community was shattered from that time onward.

REFERENCES

References cited at the end of Chapters 3 and 4 are pertinent to this chapter as well.

Bashear, Suliman: *Arabs and Others in Early Islam.* Princeton, N.J.: Darwin Press, 1997. A complex analysis of the connections between Arab identity and Islam based on the Quran and the sayings of the Prophet Muhammad, concentrating on the eighth century.

Blankenship, Khalid Yahya: *The End of the Jihad State: The Reign of Hisham ibn Abd al-Malik and the Collapse of the Umayyads.* Albany: State University of New York Press, 1994. Emphasizes military defeats as the chief cause of the overthrow of the Umayyads.

Crone, Patricia: "Mawla." *Encyclopaedia of Islam.* New ed. Vol. 6, pp. 874–882. Leiden: Brill, 1991. Treats the history of the clients in law, and for the Umayyad and Abbasid periods.

Crone, Patricia, and Martin Hinds: *God's Caliph: Religious Authority in the First Centuries of Islam.* Cambridge: Cambridge University Press, 1986. A detailed examination of the use of the title "caliph," and a revisionist interpretation of the role of the Umayyads as religious leaders.

Glubb, John B.: *The Great Arab Conquests.* Englewood Cliffs, N.J.: Prentice-Hall, 1964. A military history by an English general with long experience in the Middle East.

Hamilton, Robert: *Walid and His Friends: An Umayyad Tragedy.* Oxford: Oxford University Press, 1988. A vivid account of the life of Walid II, with an emphasis on poetry.

Hawting, G. R.: *The First Dynasty of Islam: The Umayyad Caliphate, A.D. 661–750.* 2nd ed. London: Routledge, 2000. This is a careful and balanced political and military history with especially important information on tribal relations with the Umayyads.

Lewis, Bernard: *Race and Slavery in the Middle East: An Historical Enquiry.* New York: Oxford University Press, 1990.

Morony, Michael G.: *Iraq after the Muslim Conquest.* Princeton, N.J.: Princeton University Press, 1984. The continuity of Sasanid with Islamic Iraq is examined in the areas of administration, taxes, and ethnic and religious groups.

Roded, Ruth, ed.: *Women in Islam and the Middle East: A Reader.* London: Tauris, 1999. A wide variety of texts dealing with Muslim women from the seventh century to the present is introduced, analyzed, and presented by the editor.

Shaban, M. A.: *The Abbasid Revolution.* Cambridge: Cambridge University Press, 1970. A detailed history of the Arab conquest of Iran and Khurasan; highlights the importance of assimilation between Arabs and Iranians up to the Abbasid victory.

Sharon, Moshe: *Black Banners from the East: The Establishment of the Abbasid State—Incubation of a Revolt.* Jerusalem: Magnes Press, 1983. The tangled early history of the Abbasids and their use of propaganda to gain victory over the Umayyads are thoroughly traced.

al-Tabari, Muhammad ibn Jarir: *The History of al-Tabari.* Vol. 18: *Between Civil Wars: The Caliphate of Muawiyah.* Translated by Michael G. Morony. Albany: State University of New York Press, 1987. This monumental and vitally important chronicle has been published in many volumes, translated and annotated by various authors. They are essential original sources on which most subsequent historians have based their own work.

Taha, Abdulwahid Dhanun: *The Muslim Conquest and Settlement of North Africa and Spain.* London: Routledge, 1988. Detailed military and political history.

CHAPTER 6

The Flowering of the Muslim World under the Early Abbasids

The destruction of the Umayyads marked the opening of a new age in the history of the Muslim community in the Middle East—the rule of the Abbasid dynasty in its early phase, which lasted until the middle of the tenth century. The Abbasids were Arabs whose relationship to the prophet Muhammad provided their chief claim to legitimacy. During the early Abbasid empire the state witnessed a variety of trends: the continuing importance of pre-Islamic imperial traditions and their adaptation to Islamic values; a cultural, economic, and religious flowering; the moderately successful organization of government institutions; and a growing decentralization of power, ultimately resulting in the ruling dynasty's loss of control.

The political center of Islam shifted eastward to the Tigris-Euphrates valley, since Arabia proper had become less significant in power and wealth and Damascus, in spite of its interior lines of communication and transport, no longer held an advantage as the capital of such an empire. Iraq was more productive than Syria and profited from extensive trade with India, China, and central Asia, whereas commerce languished in the Mediterranean and Europe. The markets of India and China were fabulous and their production was varied; the economy of the west, except for Spain and Constantinople, was yielding rapidly to the demands of a self-subsistent agricultural life.

As has been pointed out, the Abbasids had shrewdly capitalized on the many grievances that various factions held against the Umayyads and, in an adroit propaganda campaign among the Muslim ummah, posed as the champions of each disgruntled group. However, hardly was Abu al-Abbas, the first of the line, seated on the throne than he openly showed the insincerity of Abbasid promises. Though he surrounded himself with theologians and pretended to take their advice, positions of authority and power were filled by Abbasids or by trusted family agents. The chief executioner, who was a new governmental official, always stood near the caliph's throne. The Alids, who were the leaders of the Shiis, were sometimes honored but powerless; Kharijis, who had generally opposed the Umayyads, received little consideration; viceroys, generals, and ministers who became too wealthy or too popular were executed. Indeed, many of the very leaders who had engineered the Abbasid revolution were liquidated in the first years of the new regime by Abu al-Abbas, who was known as al-Saffah ("the bloodletter"). Abbasid rulers governed more imperiously than their predecessors.

It was at the end of Abu al-Abbas's reign that the true installation of the new empire occurred, with the ascension to the caliphate in 754 of Abu al-Abbas's brother, Abu Jafar. This ancestor of the next thirty-five caliphs took the name al-Mansur (meaning "rendered victorious").

Like many of the Abbasids who followed, al-Mansur faced a struggle over the question of succession to the throne inside the royal family. Often the heir apparent was sent to Khurasan or Syria as governor, to learn how to be an able administrator. Succession did not necessarily go from father to eldest son; instead, rule might be transferred to any among the able male relatives. This was an issue that increasingly served as a vehicle by which social and governmental groups could strive for power. To obtain recognition for his son al-Mahdi, al-Mansur gave prodigious bribes to his cousin, who had been named to the line of succession by al-Saffah. Nonetheless, al-Mahdi's elder son and designated heir, Musa al-Hadi, was almost passed over by the generals and court ministers in favor of his more popular younger brother, Harun al-Rashid. The court intrigues involving the accession of later caliphs grew even more heated as time passed. By the close of the ninth century, the question of succession overshadowed every act of the caliph. By the tenth century, caliphs were removed, blinded, and turned out into the streets to beg.

Succession to the caliphate was not, of course, the only internal issue for the Abbasid government. Simultaneously, issues concerning theology and jurisprudence added fuel to the political fires. The religious scholars preached that the life of state and society should be based on the Quran and the practice of the prophet Muhammad, whereas the other main contestants for the caliph's ear, the civil secretaries and governing officials, looked for a political structure tending toward absolutism so that their decisions would be enforced. The latter group desired the guidance of an absolute ruler; the pious sought security in the collective wisdom of the community.

Al-Mansur discovered that his personal safety was in question since his residence was so close to hostile Kufah. The danger led him to build, in 762–766, a new capital on the Tigris, only 30 kilometers north of Ctesiphon, where a personal bodyguard of several thousand was on hand at all times. This new circular fortress-palace of al-Mansur grew within a few decades into the fabled luxury-filled city of Baghdad, which has thrilled the imagination of people from that time onward.

THE GLORY OF BAGHDAD

During the first century of the Abbasid caliphs Baghdad was the hub of the Middle East, with a population numbering about 1 million. Baghdad was a circular garrison fortress, situated on the west bank of the Tigris near a canal connecting with the Euphrates. The central area had a mosque and a green-domed palace with an audience hall 130 feet (40 m.) in height; it was surrounded by a wall, a deep moat, and two thick outer brick walls. Numerous other luxurious palaces for princes and ministers of state were erected, and beyond these rose the busy center of the Muslim world.

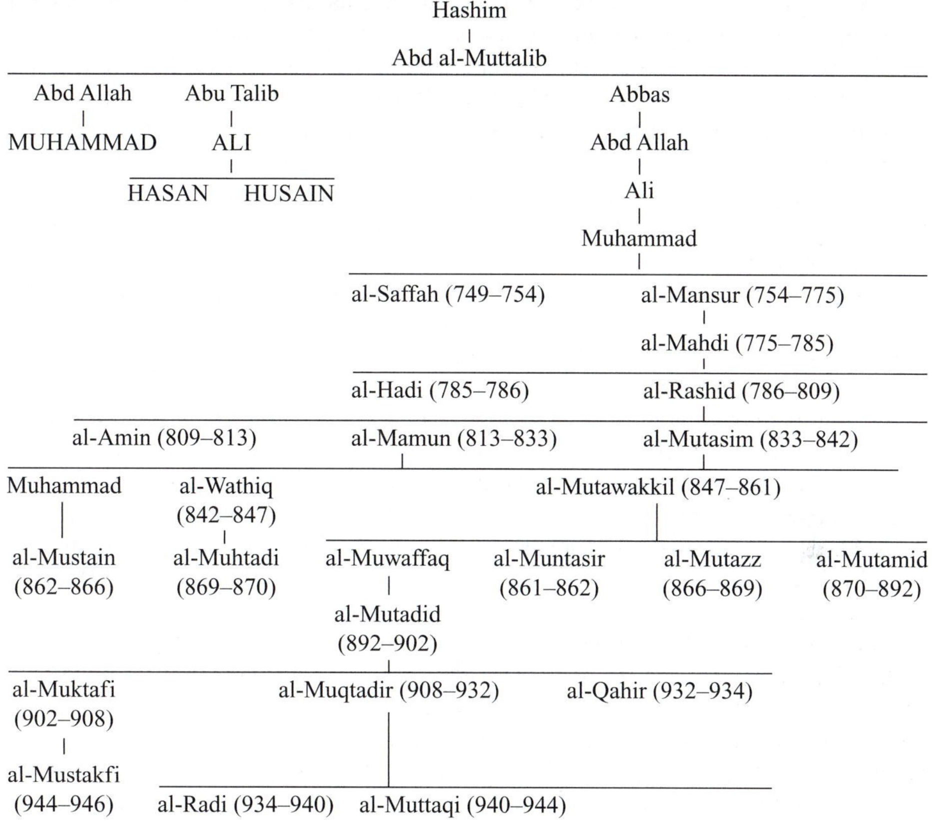

The Early Abbasid Caliphs

The setting of the Abbasids in the lavish fortress capital of Baghdad ensured that their rule would follow the pattern of the monarchies of earlier days. In comparison to the unabashed prodigality of royal life in Baghdad and to the difficulty an ordinary Arab had in approaching the caliph, the rule of the Umayyads seemed the essence of frugality and simplicity.

The wealth and magnificence of the court of al-Rashid (786–809) were renowned in his own day, and through the tales of the *Arabian Nights* the splendors of his court and life in Baghdad have captured popular fancy in later ages, although, in fact, he often resided elsewhere. The center of display was the palace of the caliph, where Zubaidah, al-Rashid's favorite wife, held sway. She insisted that all dishes be made of gold and that tapestries be studded with precious gems. She outfitted several hundred of her most attractive maidservants as pageboys (a fashion that was soon all the rage in Baghdad), largely to amuse her son and to divert his affections from a favorite eunuch. At a festival celebrating the marriage of a prince, a thousand matched pearls were showered upon the couple as they sat upon a jewel-encrusted mat of gold.

In Baghdad, the wheel of fortune turned easily. This aspect of Abbasid rule had been exemplified in the life of Khaizuran, a slave from Yemen and the mother of al-Rashid. Given to al-Mahdi, she became his favorite and ultimately his wife, and her sons were recognized at an early age as the heirs to the throne. The intelligent and able Khaizuran exerted considerable influence in the capital: she had her family brought to court; her brother became governor of Yemen; and her sister married a prince whose daughter was the famous Zubaidah. Before Khaizuran died she held vast properties bringing in an annual income of more than 160 million dirhams. The preference of the generals and courtiers for al-Rashid over al-Hadi was stimulated considerably by Khaizuran's acknowledged favor for the former. (Although Khaizuran's fortunes seemed to have steadily improved, wealth, position, and favor in Baghdad were always precarious, as the sudden fall of many favorites and advisers attested.) While Khaizuran's life demonstrated the influence women could exercise, the system of segregating upper-class urban women from men in public places was already being developed, as shown by al-Mansur's construction of a separate bridge across the Euphrates designated for women only.

At the court any word or act of flattery, a song or poem that pleased, or a deed well done was rewarded handsomely: 60,000 dinars tossed to the singer of a pleasant tune with complimentary lines; 100,000 dirhams to a poet who beguiled at the right moment; a landed estate to an entertainer or a dancer! For a sonnet extolling Harun al-Rashid on a trivial occasion a poet was given 5000 gold pieces, a robe of honor, ten Greek slave girls, and a horse from the imperial stables.

From the four corners of the known world came royal embassies bearing gifts and seeking the caliph's favor. Most publicized of these, at least in the west, was the mission sent by Charlemagne in 797 to secure greater safety for Frankish pilgrims to Palestine. The trophies brought back from the journey, the most fantastic being an elephant, so magnified the incident for the west that Baghdad became a romantic, incredible, and fabulous place.

Intellectual interests of the Abbasids, hand in hand with imperial patronage, produced a great cultural flowering. The learning of the Greco-Romans, the Iranians, and the Hindus was translated into Arabic and assimilated into Muslim culture. Arabic became the common language not only for theology and jurisprudence but for philosophy, science, and the humanities. History, political treatises, literature, poetry, and etiquette came largely from Iran; astronomy and mathematics, from India; philosophy, medicine, and science, from Greece. Royal patronage set the stage for translations and the expansion and dissemination of knowledge. Many princes, governors, and high officials followed the same course and became, on a lesser scale, patrons of scholars.

ADMINISTRATIVE ORGANIZATION

The Khurasanian soldiery was the power that had raised the Abbasids to the caliphate, and for several generations a Khurasan bodyguard maintained imperial authority in Baghdad and elsewhere. Even in this time, however, some army units still consisted of Arabs from Syria and Iraq. In the first decade of Abbasid rule the army conquered the area south of the Caspian Sea. Harun al-Rashid later launched his army against the Byzantine capital of Constantinople, but two sieges failed to take the walled city on its fortified peninsula. By the 830s, mawali clients formed some units in the Abbasid army, along with free and slave groups recruited originally from non-Muslim peoples, as the army became diverse in its origins.

Iranian influences grew apace at the court. After the building of Baghdad, Iranian dress, manners, and techniques spread quickly throughout the empire, especially in fashionable society, although Arabic remained the language of administration and court culture, while the earliest bureaucrats to work for the Abbasid dynasty were often drawn from the same Arab families that had served the Umayyads. Converts to Islam no longer needed to become the clients of Arab Muslims, though freed slaves often continued to affiliate themselves in this way.

The Umayyads had advisers and ministers heading various departments of the government. Under the Abbasids, however, there arose the office of chief minister, the vizir, who became the alter ego of the caliph. The vizir's power was almost unlimited, and the office was frequently handed down from father to son. The first family of vizirs was the famous Barmakids of the second half of the eighth century. Khalid ibn Barmak, son of a Buddhist chief priest, held the confidence of al-Saffah and al-Mansur. Khalid served as minister of finance and then as governor, became a general, and acted as guardian of al-Rashid. Khalid amassed a great fortune; on one occasion he was forced to pay 3 million dirhams of taxes which as governor he had not forwarded to Baghdad. His son, Yahya, served al-Mahdi as vizir but fell into disfavor and was imprisoned by al-Hadi.

The apogee of Barmakid fortunes was reached under al-Rashid. Yahya, freed from prison, became the first true grand vizir, issuing orders and managing the empire with great skill and profit. He favored a policy of strict centralization, in both provincial government and taxation. He became alienated from the military, who generally preferred decentralization, which advanced their interests in the provincial garrisons. Yahya's sons al-Fadl and Jafar also exercised great power. Al-Fadl followed in his father's footsteps as governor and vizir, while Jafar became al-Rashid's boon companion and confidant. The Barmakids lived in a sumptuous manner, and their generosity to their own favorites and clients became proverbial throughout the Islamic world. Yahya, however, was distressed by Jafar's personal and intimate relationship with al-Rashid, fearing that it would bring disaster. The family could not hope for social, political, or religious equality with the Abbasids. In 803, without warning, Jafar was beheaded because of policy differences in regard to Khurasan and because he had used al-Rashid's friendship to impinge too far upon royal prerogatives; Yahya, al-Fadl, and two others were imprisoned; and the Barmakid fortune—palaces, lands, and some 30 million dinars in cash—was confiscated.

Other families of vizirs rose and fell, and with them rival generals and armies. Under the Abbasids, generals were a significant force in obtaining the throne. Following al-Rashid's reign, intense rivalry rose between two of his offspring, the sensual al-Amin, son of the famed Zubaidah, and the more serious and steady al-Mamun, son of an Iranian slave girl. Al-Mamun had the better generals, and with the full support of the Khurasanian army he attacked Baghdad and beheaded his caliph brother. Al-Mamun's twenty-year rule was marred by insurrections that were overcome only very slowly. Egypt was brought to obedience by 827; the Aghlabids in Tunis paid tribute, but most of North Africa was lost to the empire. On the other hand, mountainous Azerbaijan and the Caspian shores were conquered.

By 861, the succession to the throne was to be decided for a time by the leaders of the army. The rulers al-Mamun and al-Mutasim had brought Turks and Persians, mostly slave mamluk soldiers, to Baghdad and Samarra (a city in northern Iraq and the capital from 836 to 892) in such numbers that they dominated the imperial bodyguard, which in turn controlled the caliph.

After the beginning of the tenth century, the Abbasid caliphs receded into the background as puppet rulers. Diverse groups from the geographic margins of the empire began to influence its center. The old elites, including the Arab tribal leaders, the descendants of the Khurasanians long settled in Iraq, and the Abbasid family, declined in importance. Arab ancestry was still a source of pride, but more and more often non-Arab Muslims became leaders of society. Powerful captains in the eastern and western provinces, some Arabs and some non-Arabs, seized authority and established autonomous Muslim states. The political unity of Islam, which had already been cracked in the 750s by the establishment of the Umayyad state in Spain, was gradually shattered, starting with the advent of the military groups who controlled the Abbasid caliphate.

ECONOMIC AND SOCIAL LIFE

The bases of Abbasid wealth were agriculture and a century of relatively capable, honest, and stable administration of the provinces. Caliph al-Mansur established such a vigilant and judicious system of government throughout the empire and enforced such thrift that it took more than a century of spending to dislocate the state budget. In central Iraq the ancient canal system initially was operated so efficiently and extended to such a degree that productivity rose. In that same century imperial revenues from Egypt, Syria, and Iran showered great wealth upon the ruling circles.

As a natural corollary to this organized agriculture and governmental stability, there arose flourishing commerce and, for that age, advanced technical production. Most commerce was in the nature of domestic trade. Caravans plied the trade routes from the Indus to the Pyrenees, distributing the goods of each province throughout the empire and exchanging manufactures of Iran for those of Egypt, carpets of Tabaristan for paper of Baghdad. Handsome profits were realized, but great fortunes were as easily lost.

The bulk of foreign trade was with East Asia. From Baghdad and Basrah, Muslim merchants carried their goods by sea via the Persian/Arabian Gulf to China and India, while the main overland route to China went through Samarkand and central Asia. A flourishing trade across the Sahara developed between North African Khariji Muslims and the populations of the Senegal River region. Although trade with western and eastern Europe was undoubtedly profitable, it seemed so trivial that Muslim traders left it for the most part to Christian and Jewish itinerants. Goods from the Middle East were expensive, and Europe beyond the lands of the Byzantines had little other than furs to offer in exchange.

A type of banking with letters of credit and double-entry bookkeeping arose to facilitate the extensive commerce that stretched across much of the eastern hemisphere.

Concurrent with the rich agriculture and brisk commerce of the Abbasid empire, there developed an active artisanal production in every province. Artisanal traditions of the ancient Middle East revived and expanded. Textiles of linen, cotton, silk, and wool were the most important. Although each area produced high-quality fabrics of many types, every city or province excelled in some particular pattern or technique; carpets from Bukhara, linens from Egypt, damask from Damascus, and brocades from Shiraz gained fame. Special skills were often localized, and families guarded trade secrets, which were passed on as prized possessions through the centuries.

The science of papermaking was acquired from China, and by the tenth century paper mills existed in Iran, Iraq, Arabia, and Egypt. Paper made from flax facilitated the production of books on an enormous scale. Private and public libraries spread widely; paper was even made that was light enough to be transported by carrier pigeon. Fine glass was produced in Egypt, and the glass industry flourished in Syria. The ceramic industry in the Middle East reached back into the most distant past, and the Abbasid era created some of the finest potteries and glazed tile; tin glazing and luster painting were used to create painted ornamentation. Samarkand, Baghdad, and Damascus won fame for their decorated porcelains and their fine shades of blue, green, and turquoise. Middle Eastern artisans were equally skilled in metalwork using iron, steel, copper, brass, silver, and gold; the ewers made at this time were especially famous. Other crafts included making dyes, perfume, jewelry, leather, inlaid and decorated wood, and enamelwork on wood and metal. Soap manufacture in Syria produced hand soaps and colored, perfumed toilet soaps.

The Middle East in the eighth and ninth centuries utilized many of the arts and techniques of China, India, Iran, and the Byzantine Empire, and those of the early civilizations of Greece, Egypt, and Mesopotamia. The synthesis of these influences gave great life to Muslim civilization and production, which was regarded in Europe as the marvel of the ages. The slow movement of Middle Eastern know-how across the Mediterranean and over the Pyrenees gave rise to the development of similar handicrafts in Europe.

The Abbasid championing of non-Arab people within the Muslim Empire ironically took place at the same time as a rapid Arabization of the empire. Iranians, Berbers, Syrian Christians, Egyptian Copts, Jews, and others began to speak Arabic in their daily lives. Science, philosophy, literature, and books of knowledge from other cultures and tongues were rendered into Arabic. And an Islamic civilization evolved in which poets, scholars, musicians, merchants, soldiers, vizirs, and concubines were considered cultural Arabs; little heed was given to parentage or birthplace for Muslims, and non-Muslims also contributed substantially to society and culture.

Local rulers followed the common patterns of Abbasid government and administration, and Muslim civilization continued to prevail. Political loyalties might differ as, more often than not, religious doctrines did; but artists, men of letters, scientists, merchants, and travelers were as much at home in Cordoba as in Cairo, Baghdad, or Samarkand. Provincial governors imitated as sumptuously as they could the Baghdad court. From India to Spain palaces and mosques were built where petty princes lived in the grand manner among poets, scholars, soldiers, dancing slaves, and fawning courtiers.

DECENTRALIZATION UNTIL 945

Although Islamic civilization prevailed in the Abbasid era from the borders of China to the Pyrenees, there was never more than a fleeting political unity. The Shii followers of Ali and his descendants were never completely mollified, and more and more religious sects arose to battle against authority. As more of the subject population became Muslim, the cohesion of the Muslim ruling elite and its mutual loyalty declined; instead, local attachments and loyalties grew, while allegiance to the central government and the caliphate relatively decreased. Social and economic ills periodically disturbed the empire. The caliphs starting with al-Mutawakkil frequently allocated the right to collect taxes from a given region to army generals. Ambitious soldiers sought to carve out their own principalities, whose armed forces increasingly were based on professional cavalry, often recruited from Turks or Berbers. Centered upon a land area, communications and transportation over most of the Abbasid empire were costly, slow, and tedious. Distant provinces were difficult to control, and, as caliphs grew less and less concerned with the grueling task of governing, even nearer provinces defied the wishes of the Abbasid rulers. Revenues declined by about one-half from 788 to 915. The increasing salinity of the soil in central Iraq sharply reduced agriculture and the taxes derived from it—resources located at the center of the empire and formerly very important. The canals in Iraq were not properly maintained; taxes were raised and collected in a harsh manner, often through a system of tax farming; and the insurgencies of the late ninth century created widespread havoc. When Abbasid caliphs became mere puppets in the hands of bureaucrats in Baghdad and then were dominated by generals, governors and soldiers in the provinces opted for local autonomy.

Shii claimants to the leadership of the community emerged in several places. With the death of the eleventh imam or leader of the chief Shii lineage in 874 and the apparent disappearance of his son shortly thereafter, one source of opposition to Abbasid claims was temporarily removed, but other groups, both Sunnis and Shiis, posed many challenges to the Abbasid caliphs.

In the west—Spain and North Africa—Abd al-Rahman, grandson of the Umayyad caliph Hisham, escaped from Abbasid vengeance, and, making his way in disguise through Syria, Egypt, and North Africa, reestablished the Umayyad dynasty in Spain in 756. First as amirs and then in the tenth century as caliphs, the rulers maintained at Cordoba a court that rivaled the Abbasids in Baghdad. Many distinguished scholars, scientists, and literary figures in the Muslim world flourished under their patronage. At its zenith in the tenth century, Cordoba had more than 100,000 inhabitants, 700 mosques, 300 public baths, and a royal palace comprising 400 rooms that ranked second in size and splendor only to those at Baghdad. The Umayyad state in Spain resembled the contemporary Abbasid caliphate in witnessing many conversions to Islam, economic growth but fiscal difficulties, the professionalization of the army, uncertainty about succession to the throne, and regional separatism. Abd al-Rahman III (r. 912–961) brought about a political, military, and cultural revival, but Umayyad power began to deteriorate thereafter. Muslim Spain disintegrated into many small states after 1031.

In 788 in Morocco, Idris, a descendant of Ali, established an independent Sunni regime. From their capital at Fez the Idrisids ruled most of Morocco for two centuries, firmly implanting Islam in that corner of Africa and establishing a flourishing trade with sub-Saharan Africa. Arabic became the dominant language in the towns, while Berber was used widely in the countryside. The Idrisids ultimately succumbed to the Umayyads of Cordoba.

Harun al-Rashid appointed Ibrahim ibn al-Aghlab governor of Algeria and Tunisia in 800. For a century the Aghlabids ruled as free amirs from Qairawan in Tunisia. Their fleets ravaged the coasts of Italy and France, seizing Malta, Sicily, and Sardinia; by 835 the Aghlabids had learned how to use the 'Greek fire' liquid incendiary, which had first been employed by the Byzantines in 674, in naval warfare. The great mosque of Qairawan was built by the Aghlabids and soon became for western Muslims a venerated shrine, next in importance and holiness to Mecca, Medina, and Jerusalem. But in 909 the Aghlabids were engulfed by a Shii uprising that placed on the throne the Fatimid dynasty.

Meanwhile, beginning with the middle of the ninth century, a succession of governors and two short-lived Turkish dynasties ruled Egypt in the name of the Abbasids, who received some revenues from that province but exercised no real power there. Conversion to Islam had been slow, and the Muslims remained largely an urban-based minority group. Foreign slave and mercenary armies were recruited by the new dynasties. In the second half of the tenth century Egypt was conquered by the Shii Fatimids of North Africa, whose claim of descent from Ali and Fatimah persuaded many to accept them as the valid leaders of the Muslim community.

South and east of Baghdad the Abbasid empire was likewise succumbing to the laxity of the caliphs' rule and falling into the hands of aggressive soldiers and leaders who founded local dynasties, even though some of these groups acknowledged the nominal overlordship of the Abbasids. The greatest dangers were south of Baghdad and closest to hand: the rebellions of the Zanj and the Qarmatians.

Since early Islamic times the marshlands of southern Iraq, a perfect area for guerrilla warfare, had been the scene of a kind of slavery, based on large-scale agricultural estates, which was not seen elsewhere in the empire; the slaves, who were harshly treated, were mostly of east African origins. Under the leadership of Ali ibn Muhammad, an Arab from Iran, and with the help of Arab tribal allies, they rose against their owners in 869, took Basrah, and were a major threat to the Abbasid political and social order as they espoused Kharijism. In 883, the Abbasid caliph finally conquered the Zanj in southern Iraq, but the prosperity of that region was ruined.

The Qarmatians were Ismaili Shiis (like the Fatimids in Egypt) who, starting in the ninth century, steadily attempted to overthrow Abbasid power, basing their forces in Kufah, among the nomadic tribes of Syria, and in Bahrain and eastern Arabia generally. In 923, they conquered Basrah, and in 930 the Qarmatians raided Mecca and carried off the sacred Black Stone from the Kaba. Internal disputes stopped their expansion, the Black Stone was returned to Mecca, and the Qarmatians became a local force enjoying peace and prosperity until the late tenth century. Although their enemies accused them of practices contrary to Islamic morality, they were most noteworthy for the existence of an advisory council whose opinions the ruler was obliged to consider, as well as approaches to gender relations based on equal treatment for men and women.

To the east, the Abbasids succeeded in crushing a peasant revolt based in Azerbaijan, but they lost effective power in their easternmost provinces of Sind and Makran, on the borders of India and Pakistan, after the middle of the ninth century.

In central Asia Turkish-speaking, horse-raising, nomadic tribes who worshiped many gods and spirits had established a loosely organized empire as early as the middle of the sixth century. Independent of both China and the Muslim state in the ninth century, the central Asian Turks served as trade intermediaries with both, dealing especially in silk and slaves, including the military guards sought by the Abbasids. In later times, Turks in central Asia who became Muslims would have a tremendous impact on the core regions of the Middle East when they moved into those areas.

Three local dynasties dominated the eastern part of the empire in the ninth century. The Tahirids, starting in 820, extended their sway from Merv to the frontiers of India. They were a family of local governors who sent extensive taxes to the Abbasid caliphs, and they played a major role in the internal political life of Baghdad. From 867 the Saffarid dynasty spread outward from Sistan, destroyed the Tahirids, invaded and conquered most of eastern and southern Afghanistan for Islam, and ruled with the investiture of the caliphs until 900, when they were reduced to only a local influence in southeastern Iran. Also in the late ninth century the truly independent Persian Sunni Samanid dynasty was acknowledged by the caliphs as local governors; by the tenth century, they seized all of Khurasan but settled in central Asia, establishing Bukhara as their capital and Samarkand as the leading city of the state. Culture and the economy continued to flourish under Samanid rule, and the new forces were quickly assimilated, as illustrated by the Samanid ruler who invited the young Ibn Sina (Avicenna) to Bukhara and gave him free run of the state library. Under the Samanids, Firdawsi wrote his first poetry, marking the rebirth of Persian literature. From the Muslim conquest to the Samanid period, Arabic had been the language used everywhere by scholars; this new era signaled the advent of brilliant works of Muslim Iran, written in Persian as well as Arabic.

In Baghdad itself, the authority of the Abbasid caliph vanished almost completely. Only the title and some of the prestige remained. Turkish captains of the bodyguard deposed caliphs almost at will; at one time three blind ex-caliphs were beggars on the streets of Baghdad. Taking the title *amir al-umara* (literally, "commander of commanders," but better, "prince of princes"), the de facto ruler imprinted his name on coins and insisted that his name be coupled with that of the caliph in the Friday prayers.

In 945 a Shii Iranian, Ahmad ibn Buya, entered Baghdad with a strong army and was recognized by the caliph as the commander of commanders. Making and unmaking caliphs openly, the Buyid control of the Abbasid caliphate publicly and clearly changed the nature of political power and ushered in another new era in the political history of the Islamic Middle East. Before these new political changes took place, the development of Islamic theology, law, and philosophy, along with the creation of a complex and flourishing Islamic civilization, had already provided elements of continuity and creativity for the peoples of the Middle East, whose lives had been considerably changed as a result.

REFERENCES

References cited at the end of Chapters 4 and 5 contain material pertinent to this chapter as well.

Abbott, Nabia: *Two Queens of Baghdad: Mother and Wife of Harun al-Rashid.* Chicago: University of Chicago Press, 1946. Not only does this volume discuss the lives of Khaizuran and Zubaidah, but it is full of the life of Baghdad in the eighth and ninth centuries.

Abun-Nasr, Jamil M.: *A History of the Maghrib in the Islamic Period.* Cambridge: Cambridge University Press, 1987. An excellent survey.

Amabe, Fukuzo: *The Emergence of the Abbasid Autocracy: The Abbasid Army, Khurasan and Adharbayjan.* Kyoto: Kyoto University Press, 1995. Detailed essays on Abbasid military history and politics.

Asimov, M. S., and C. E. Bosworth, eds.: *History of Civilizations of Central Asia.* Vol. IV: *The Age of Achievement: A.D. 750 to the End of the Fifteenth Century.* Part One: *The Historical, Social and Economic Setting.* Paris: UNESCO Publishing, 1998.

Bligh-Abramski, Irit: "Evolution Versus Revolution: Umayyad Elements in the Abbasid Regime 133/750–320/932." *Der Islam* 65 (1988): 226–243. As the author makes clear, there were some links between Umayyad practices and the new Abbasid state.

Choksy, Jamsheed K.: *Conflict and Cooperation: Zoroastrian Subalterns and Muslim Elites in Medieval Iranian Society.* New York: Columbia University Press, 1997. A sensitive analysis of majority-minority relations, changes, and adaptations including political, religious, and material culture issues.

Daniel, Elton L.: *The Political and Social History of Khurasan under Abbasid Rule, 747–820.* Minneapolis: Bibliotheca Islamica, 1979. This book follows the victory of small landowners in a key province and their subsequent fate, with attention to tax policy and regional particularism, as well as rural unrest.

Frye, R. N., ed.: *The Cambridge History of Iran.* Vol. 4: *The Period from the Arab Invasion to the Saljuqs.* London: Cambridge University Press, 1975. Seven chapters on Iran's political history, followed by other chapters on social, cultural, religious, and intellectual history.

Gordon, Matthew S.: *The Breaking of a Thousand Swords: A History of the Turkish Military of Samarra (A.H. 200–275/815–889 C.E.).* Albany: State University of New York Press, 2001. A detailed history of the Turkish military role in the Abbasid state.

Hourani, George F.: *Arab Seafaring in the Indian Ocean in Ancient and Early Medieval Times.* Revised and expanded by John Carswell. Princeton, N.J.: Princeton University Press, 1995.

Kennedy, Hugh: *Muslim Spain and Portugal: A Political History of al-Andalus.* London: Longman, 1996. An excellent account of political and military events.

Lassner, Jacob: *The Shaping of Abbasid Rule.* Princeton, N.J.: Princeton University Press, 1980. Essays cover the topics of crises over the succession to the throne, the clients of the Abbasids, the army, the city of Baghdad, and the royal palace.

Shaban, M. A.: *Islamic History: A New Interpretation.* Vol. 2: *A.D. 750–1055 (A.H. 132–448).* Cambridge: Cambridge University Press, 1976. This occasionally polemical book centers on the themes of trade, taxes, and regions.

Waines, David: "The Third Century Internal Crisis of the Abbasids." *Journal of the Economic and Social History of the Orient* 20 (1977): 282–306. In the ninth century an internal economic and political crisis gripped the Abbasids; the crisis is ably analyzed and shown to be as important as the external threats to the empire's central authority.

Zaman, Muhammad Qasim: *Religion and Politics under the Early Abbasids: The Emergence of the Proto-Sunni Elite.* Leiden: Brill, 1997. Studies relationships of caliphs and religious authorities from 750 to 809.

CHAPTER 7

Islam

THE RISE AND SPREAD OF ISLAM

Throughout the centuries that followed the life of the prophet Muhammad the central beliefs of Islam remained consistent, easy to understand, and inspiring to the growing numbers of Muslims in the ummah as it spread in the Middle East. Despite increasing theological sophistication, splits in the community, and ensuing differences of interpretation, there nevertheless remained a considerable common core. The central belief of all the approaches to Islam remained the simple monotheistic religion preached by Muhammad. Even though the rapidity of expansion and conversions admitted to Muslim society many whose knowledge of Islam was limited, the core of the faith remained, as the interpretation of the basic elements of Islam became richer and more varied.

During the rule of the four early caliphs in Medina and in the era of the Umayyad Empire, Muslims gained access to the Hellenistic philosophy and theology of Egypt and Syria, which rapidly affected Islamic theology. Ultimately the new concepts and dogmas within Islam gave birth to different Muslim sects; under the later Umayyads and early Abbasids the complete unity of theology, as well as politics, was lost in the Muslim world.

Acceptance of monotheism was the most important facet of religion to Muhammad. To be a Muslim was to profess the unity of God, to surrender to the will of God, and to accept Muhammad as God's messenger. God had ninety-nine names, each with a related attribute. The mere recitation of some of these would remind humanity of God: omniscient, omnipotent, the judge, the mighty, the creator, merciful, compassionate, forgiving, magnificent, everlasting, most generous, and most high.

Of the infinite qualities of God, Muslims constantly stressed everlastingness. God was the creator of creation and existed through all eternity. All people were God's creatures, and God "misleads whom He will and guides whom He will." Fear of God and the day of judgment was particularly emphasized in the early revelations in Mecca to impress the materialistic society there; but God was also visualized as a loving, bountiful, and forgiving protector, "closer to a man than his own jugular vein." The Quran repeatedly refers to God as merciful and compassionate. A third important attribute of God was mystical in nature: God was termed the light of the heavens and of the earth. In later centuries theologians developed this quality into various organized mysticisms that served as powerful forces in the spread and influence of Islam.

THE QURAN

The basis for Muslims' views of God and religion and for the central beliefs of Muslims of every sect rested upon the Quran ("lecture" or "recitation"), the collection of revelations sent to the prophet Muhammad. Consisting of 114 chapters, called *surahs,* made up of 6236 verses (77,934 words), the earliest versions were assembled soon after Muhammad's death. Most of the revelations had been written down in his later years by his secretaries; these and other revelations were memorized and recounted word for word by his companions. Tradition has it that after a battle in which many reciters of the Quran perished, the caliph Abu Bakr ordered the full Quran to be committed to parchment so that it would not be lost. Later, Uthman established the copy held in Medina as the true Quran. In the tenth century the methods of reciting the text were regularized from different readings that had arisen because of the lack of vowels and diacritical marks in the early Arabic script.

Except for the first, which is a short prayer, the chapters were arranged according to length, so that the later but longer Medinan chapters are located at the beginning. The Quran is about two-thirds the length of an Arabic version of the Christian New Testament.

Muslims regard the Quran as the word of God, transmitted to Muhammad by the angel Gabriel. It furnished the basis for law in the Islamic world. It also prescribed a pattern of daily individual and community living that distinguished Islamic civilization from all others. Since translations were frowned upon, Quranic Arabic served as a common religious language and a bond for all Muslims from one end of the world to the other. The Quran was also a schoolbook, and committing it to memory was standard practice for children. The very sound of the Arabic words stirs the emotions of Muslims; read silently, the Quran loses much of its power.

The major part of the Quran is concerned with God, whose attributes are cited and powers proclaimed; the individual's relations to God are defined. Associated with a vivid explanation of the day of judgment are portrayals of the resurrection, paradise and hell, and angels and devils. Religious and ethical paths to follow in life are sometimes presented directly, but for the most part they are contained in parables and stories, many of which are similar to those in Jewish and Christian holy books and their associated literature. Adam, Noah, Abraham, Joseph, Moses, David, Solomon, Elijah, Job, Zachariah, John the Baptist, Mary, and Jesus are all set forth so as to show that God rewards the righteous and punishes the wicked.

A perusal of the Torah, the Christian Bible, and the Quran discloses a number of very similar passages. Surah 21, verse 105, is identical to Psalm 37, verse 9: "For evil doers shall be cut off; but those that wait upon the Lord, they shall inherit the earth." The Christians of Europe branded Islam as a Christian heresy—a castigation that led to the abhorrence of Muslims and an exaggeration of the differences between Christianity and Islam. In reality, Judaism, Christianity, and Islam have a great deal in common. The dissimilarities are more in language, style, and form than in substance. Through each of these three religions runs a strong message of personal salvation for righteous individuals. This message of hope gives to the individual a sense of significance and equality that is not ordinarily available in cultures where other religions prevail.

HADITHS

Following the Prophet's death it became obvious that God's revelations did not provide an answer to every problem that arose in daily life. Muhammad always distinguished carefully between his own individual thoughts and divine revelation. God's word was law; Muhammad's words were only guides to a wise and holy life.

As the years slipped by, leaving fewer and fewer Muslims who knew from their own memories what Muhammad had said and done, collections of his comments and deeds were considered vital for following his precedents. Hadiths by the hundreds of thousands appeared; these reported the sunnah, the custom, usual procedure, or behavior of the Prophet. The sunnah of the Prophet in turn became a most important guide to life and belief for Muslims. Each of the different sects and parties that developed in Islam accepted certain hadith reports and rejected others as forgeries to prove the correctness of the party's views, no matter whether the contention affected militarism or pacifism, predestination or free will, mysticism or realism, asceticism or worldliness.

By the second or third century after the hijrah, hadiths had become very intricate in response to the philosophical and theological demands of the scholars of the time. In the early days of Islam, the hadiths had consisted of the simple, unvarnished ideas and stories that Muhammad had voiced or that his friends had repeated word for word. They are on varied topics, for Muhammad had definite opinions on all types of subjects. On one occasion he said, "God curse the woman who wears false hair and the woman who ties it on." When his wife Aishah acquired a pictured cushion, Muhammad exploded: "Verily, the makers of these pictures will be severely punished on the Day of Resurrection." On slavery he remonstrated, "A slave must not be given a task which he is unable to perform." Muhammad sometimes perceived the difference between legality and righteousness, as when he observed, "Of the things which are lawful the most hateful to God is divorce." In a similar vein he declared, "There is no man who receives a bodily injury and forgives the offender but God will exalt his rank and diminish his sin." Having been an orphan, Muhammad was always concerned with such unfortunates and proclaimed, "The best house amidst the Muslim community is that which contains an orphan who is well treated, and the worst is that wherein an orphan is wronged." Perhaps best known is the attitude Muhammad held toward moneylenders. In commenting on persons paying or charging very high rates of interest, he proclaimed, "They are equally culpable." Among Muslims one of his often quoted commands indicated Muhammad's views that sexual activity and piety could coexist: "No monkery in Islam!"

BELIEFS

Muhammad was not a systematic theologian, but after his death Muslim theologians and philosophers classified the faith into three fundamentals: religious beliefs (iman), religious duties (ibadat), and good works (ihsan). The first fundamental is religious beliefs, and first and foremost among them is the belief that God is one and has all of the attributes ascribed to God. It has never been clear, however, how the attribute of omnipotence ought to be interpreted, and this problem has engendered controversy among Muslims from the day of the first caliphs to the present. In the early unaffected period, God's omnipotence simply meant that the individual is completely subordinate to God and can do nothing unless God permits it. Yet all persons are responsible for what they do and will be rewarded or punished accordingly. Muhammad preached incessantly on this point and declared that people would fall into evil ways if they did not believe in God. Submission to the will of God is the key to Islam.

Muhammad and the first Muslims referred so frequently to the day of judgment and the resurrection that belief in these two has become one of the significant aspects of Islam. When the cataclysmic day comes, the faith and deeds of each man and woman will be weighed, one's body will rise, and one will either enter paradise or be cast into hell. Martyrs for the faith do not wait for the day of judgment but immediately enter paradise. The latter is clearly described as a beautiful garden by a flowing river where the blessed rest on silken couches, partake of heavenly food and drink, enjoy spiritual joys, associate with their families, and are entertained by dark-eyed maidens and wives of perfect purity. The terrors of hell are almost beyond description. Waters boil; sinners' bellies are filled with molten brass. Into this fiery hell go the unbelieving, the covetous, and those who worship other gods.

Another basic point in the religious belief of Muslims is the role played by angels and jinn. Heaven and earth are populated by these invisible spirits who serve as God's messengers and record one's deeds. Gabriel is recognized as the leading angel and the spirit who brought the Quran to Muhammad. Rebellious jinn are devils and, like humans, will be cast into hell on the day of judgment. The leading devil did not bow down to Adam and continues to seduce people into evil ways until the resurrection.

Muslims believe that God has sent many human messengers to teach the world and that the last and greatest was Muhammad. The Quran specifically mentions twenty-eight prophets besides Muhammad, including four Arabs and one Greek (Alexander the Great); three (Zachariah, John the Baptist, and Jesus) are also in the Christian New Testament; the remainder are mentioned in the Torah or the Christian Old Testament. The most important of all the prophets are Adam, Noah, Abraham, Moses, and Jesus. Of all these, the last is Muhammad, whom God sent as the "Seal" of all. Prophets did not perform miracles except on special occasions when God gave them these powers. Divine revelation was granted to Moses in the Jewish Torah, to David in the Psalms, to Jesus in the Gospels, and to Muhammad in the Quran, which was his only miracle. All of them preached salvation through the recognition that God is one.

Muslims are to accept and believe all of these scriptures, for they are the word of God and they corroborate each other. The final word of God, the Quran, attests the revelations in the other scriptures, clarifies all previous uncertainties, and brings perfect truth. After some controversy, Muslims came to feel that the Quran is eternal and uncreated; its earthly reproduction is identical in language and spelling to the heavenly original, every word and letter of which is sacred and divine.

DUTIES

The second fundamental in Islam as taught by Muhammad, after religious beliefs, is religious duties. These actions are less obligatory than those of faith, but their performance constituted the individual's recognition of the omnipotence of God. These duties have usually been termed the "five pillars" or acts of worship of Islam. They are the easiest to observe once one has achieved ritual and spiritual purity. While the five pillars are very important, many uninformed non-Muslims and even some Muslims have mistakenly ignored the key significance of faith, belief, and intention that should give them spiritual meaning.

The first and foremost pillar is the open profession of faith. Often reduced to the Quranic formula "There is no god but God, Muhammad is the messenger of God," this declaration is used throughout a Muslim's life and suffices to ensure one's acceptance as at least a nominal Muslim.

Muhammad emphasized worship as the second obligation for Muslims. The Quran mentions directly no set ritual for worship but bids the faithful to worship frequently. Before Muhammad's death it had become customary for Muslims to pray formally five times daily: just before daybreak, at noon, in the midafternoon, at sunset, and in the evening. A Muslim should pray wherever he or she may be, but it is preferable to pray in unison with others and in a mosque if possible, with one acting as leader (imam) and the others standing in rows behind, all facing Mecca. Each prayer is composed of a certain number of bows: two at daybreak, three at sunset, and four at the other times. Each bow consists of seven distinct acts: (1) placing the open hands at each side of the head and repeating, "God is most great"; (2) standing upright and repeating the opening prayer of the Quran and at least one other Quranic passage; (3) bending from the hips and touching the knees with the hands; (4) straightening up, saying, "God listens to the one who praises Him"; (5) falling to the knees and prostrating oneself with the forehead touching the ground; (6) sitting on the haunches; and (7) a second prostration. Most Muslims include individual prayers to God, and devout Muslims pray frequently at other times during the day and night. Certain events such as burials, eclipses, serious decisions, and religious celebrations demand special prayers. The Friday noon prayer is the great congregational prayer at which a sermon (khutbah) is usually delivered. At first the sermon was delivered by Muhammad, then by the caliph or his representative, and now by a learned Muslim, who also offers a prayer on behalf of the ruling head of the state.

At the time of prayer one must be in a state of spiritual and physical purity, which is determined in various ways. Usually before prayers, simple purity, as defined in the Quran, is achieved by washing the hands and arms to the elbows, the face, and the feet up to the ankles. In the absence of water, sand may be used.

Prayer in public has been a democratizing force for men. Side-by-side at prayer are common soldier and general, prince and pauper, merchant and holy man. The proudest men bow in humble prostration to the omnipotent God. While women attended prayers in mosques at the time of the prophet Muhammad, by the time of the Abbasids most legal thinkers argued that women should pray at home, rather than in public.

The third pillar of Islam is almsgiving. Muhammad at first regarded giving to the poor and needy as a personal atonement and a means of salvation. Sometime in the Medinan period of his prophecy almsgiving was regularized to become a 2.5 percent voluntary tax on all produce and revenue of each Muslim above a certain minimum of goods. Termed *zakat,* the proceeds were used to support the poor, to erect religious buildings, and to help defray government expenses. Alms are also to be given generously for various religious and human charities such as mosques, hospitals, poorhouses, and schools. Likewise, beggars and the destitute are not to be turned away empty-handed. An ethical and egalitarian society is envisioned where excess wealth will be used for the benefit of the whole community.

Fasting, the fourth pillar of Islam, was enjoined upon all Muslims during Ramadan (the ninth lunar month), a month of fasting. From the very first flush of dawn to nightfall, food, drink, and smoke are not to pass the lips; sexual intercourse is also forbidden. When Ramadan fell during the summer months, compliance with fasting was particularly difficult in the Middle East. Voluntary sacrifice reinforced the spiritual commitment of the faithful. Fasting is also considered the best means of expiating one's sins of the year.

The fifth pillar of Islam, that of the yearly pilgrimage to Mecca (hajj), stands as the symbol of Muslim unity. It was assumed that each Muslim, man and woman, should participate in the pilgrimage each year if possible. Later, as the Muslim world grew, it became too arduous for many to go from Iraq, Syria, and Egypt; when Islam had spread to India and Spain, the pilgrimage became obligatory only once in a lifetime and only for those who could afford it.

Muslim women went on pilgrimage to Mecca more often than they traveled to other distant locations. Prominent female pilgrims included Khaizuran and Zubaidah of the Abbasid caliphal family. Elite women demonstrated their personal piety through acts of charity in Mecca and for the pilgrims who were going there.

Occurring in the twelfth lunar month, the pilgrimage ritual is celebrated on certain days by elaborate rites at the Kaba in Mecca and at other sacred spots nearby. Since Muhammad's farewell pilgrimage in 632, non-Muslims have not been permitted to be present in Mecca during the pilgrimage; in general they are forbidden entry into both Mecca and Medina.

Throughout Muslim history the pilgrimage has been a valuable unifying factor within Islamic civilization. Pilgrims have come to Mecca from the four corners of the Muslim world. The acquisition of knowledge, the exchange of products, and the interplay of political forces in Mecca have been factors in maintaining a common Muslim link among the diverse peoples embracing Islam.

To some Muslims a sixth pillar of Islam has been added: that of jihad, which can be striving on an individual basis for one's own correct behavior or striving for the faith in holy war. Many consider that every Muslim bears the duty to expand the frontiers of Islam, by force if necessary, until the entire world has been won.

GOOD WORKS AND SINS

It might well be thought that after professing the religious beliefs of Islam and performing the various duties of a Muslim, the circle of religion had been completed. In addition, however, the Quran imposes upon all a course of righteous living and doing good works. There is a religious character for both private and public acts; only in a just society can one easily be a good Muslim, while it is the duty of a Muslim to strive for justice in society.

From the virtues extolled, Islam can be seen as moralistic and sometimes puritanical. In the area of marriage, the Quran limits the number of a man's wives to four and then adds "But if you fear that you will act unjustly among them, then marry only one." Many other commandments raised the status of women in Arabian society. Support is required for a woman if she is divorced; a widow can marry whomever she wishes; and the burying alive of daughters is prohibited. Personal modesty in clothing is urged upon men and especially upon women; the caliph Umar decreed that men and women should pray separately from each other, so as to preserve modesty during the ritual. Some women mentioned in the Quran are meant to serve as examples of virtue or sin for the believers.

Spiritual and earthly penalties are promised for murder, adultery, homicide, theft, armed robbery, fraud, perjury, libel, and in general corruption. Injunctions are delivered against gambling, usury, and monopolistic practices. The use of wine and the eating of pork are forbidden. Idolatry is most sinful, and the making of images is only one step removed from worshiping other gods. Most of these declarations of right living are injunctions against practices that were common in the pagan society of Mecca at the time of Muhammad. Instead of this behavior the Quran and the hadiths encouraged alternatives, leading to just behavior according to the shariah, the holy law of Islam.

In view of the comprehensive scope of the faith with respect to religious beliefs, religious duties, and virtues, the early Islam of Muhammad must be regarded as very successful. Since Islam required individual belief and morality, the tribal morality of pre-Islamic Arabia was replaced by the personal responsibility of the individual Muslim as a member of the universal Muslim community. By the end of the early Abbasid period in 945 the core of Islamic belief was clear. The approach to understanding God, the belief about God's will for this earth, and the way of salvation were soundly established. Ultimately they changed the life and philosophy of hundreds of millions of people in the Middle East and the wider Muslim world.

REFERENCES

References cited at the end of Chapters 3 and 4 contain material pertinent to this chapter as well.

Ali, Abdullah Yusuf: *The Holy Qur'an: Text, Translation and Commentary.* Washington, D.C.: Islamic Center, 1978. One of the best translations, with comments and analysis, and the English and Arabic texts facing each other.

Arberry, Arthur J.: *The Koran Interpreted.* New York: Macmillan, 1955. The translation catches much of the majesty and beauty of the original; it should be used in conjunction with Watt's *Companion to the Qur'an,* cited below.

Ayoub, Mahmoud: *The Qur'an and Its Interpreters.* Vol. 1. Albany: State University of New York Press, 1984. This presentation and analysis of the first two chapters of the Quran shows the ways Muslims have analyzed the text.

Blake, Corinne: "Teaching Islamic Civilization with Information Technology." *Journal for MultiMedia History* 1 (1998) at www.albany.edu/jmmh/vol1no1/teach-islamic. Direct links to, and critical discussion of, on-line sites for the Quran, hadith, Shiism, Sufism, Islamic literature, and art.

Denny, Frederick Mathewson: *An Introduction to Islam.* 2d ed. New York: Macmillan, 1994. This general survey of Islam, still the best available for the beginning student of the religion, deals with all aspects of the subject, with an emphasis on mysticism and personal faith as well as historical developments to the present.

Esposito, John L., ed.: *The Oxford History of Islam.* New York: Oxford University Press, 1999. A lavishly illustrated series of essays by leading authorities on the faith of Islam and its history, culture, institutions, expansion, renewal, and contemporary situation.

Peters, F. E.: *A Reader on Classical Islam.* Princeton, N.J.: Princeton University Press, 1994. This work provides basic sources on early Islamic thought.

Rahman, Fazlur: *Major Themes of the Qur'an.* 2d ed. Minneapolis: Bibliotheca Islamica, 1989. Spiritual insights into Quranic discussions of God, humanity, society, nature, revelation, the day of judgment, evil, and the ummah written by a profound Muslim thinker.

Robinson, Neal: *Islam: A Concise Introduction.* Washington, D.C.: Georgetown University Press, 1999. This simply written but sophisticated introduction includes very useful chapters on the Quran, prayers, zakat, fasting, the pilgrimage, law, and Islamic groups.

Ruthven, Malise: *Islam in the World.* 2d ed. New York: Oxford University Press, 2000. A clear and sympathetic account of early and contemporary Islam.

Schimmel, Annemarie: *Islam: An Introduction.* Albany: State University of New York Press, 1992. A general survey of Islam, with an emphasis on India and Sufism.

Stowasser, Barbara Freyer: *Women in the Qur'an, Traditions, and Interpretation.* New York: Oxford University Press, 1994. This sophisticated book includes views of early, medieval, and modern Muslims about women mentioned in the Quran.

Waines, David: *An Introduction to Islam.* New York: Cambridge University Press, 1995. Valuable for understanding the early Islamic period.

Watt, W. Montgomery: *Companion to the Qur'an: Based on the Arberry Translation.* London: Allen and Unwin, 1967. Certain sections of the Quran are explained or put in context.

Welch, A. T.: "Al-Kur'an." *Encyclopaedia of Islam.* New ed. Vol. 5, pp. 400–429. Leiden: Brill, 1981. A complete account of the various controversies, the arrangement of the text, the meaning of different sections, the final compilation, and the importance of the Quran for Muslims.

Williams, John Alden, ed.: *The Word of Islam.* Austin: University of Texas Press, 1994. A very useful reader; includes excerpts from the Quran, hadith, shariah, mysticism, theology, and various sects.

CHAPTER 8

Muslim Theology and Law

The uncomplicated, direct, and ethical religion and law preached and practiced by Muhammad appealed to the townspeople of Mecca and Medina and to the nomads of the desert. In general, they were easily adjusted to the needs of the theocratic state under Muhammad and the first four caliphs who immediately followed him.

When Islam, Muslim rule, and the need for law based on the faith spread beyond Arabia, Muslims faced unforeseen conditions. Succeeding generations of Muslims were exposed to the philosophies and law codes current in the acquired provinces and developed a finely drawn Islamic theology and varied views on how to interpret law. A mystical approach to Islam and the separation between Sunni and Shii Muslims also became prominent during the Umayyad and early Abbasid periods.

THEOLOGY

Though the political capital of Islam was transferred to Damascus and then to Baghdad, Medina maintained its ascendancy as a center of Muslim theology for several centuries. Opinions not subscribed to by the thinkers of Medina were declared to be in error. Divergent views led to the formation of a number of groups with a wide variety of interpretations of Islamic theology and philosophy, which in many cases were branded as heretical by the Medinan theologians. Three schools of thought—the Kharijis, Murjiis, and Mutazilis—were especially influential in the classical Islamic period.

At the time of the dispute between Ali and Muawiyah, the Kharijis broke away, rejecting the concept of compromise that Ali proposed. They believed that might does not make right and that only God can judge among people. A Muslim who committed great sins was no longer a Muslim. They professed their way of life to be the right way; however, when they quoted the Quran ("be patient until God judges between us") they meant that the fight should be continued until God granted them victory. The Kharijis were against both Ali and Muawiyah and opposed the growing organized structure of society in which they were being enveloped. Coming from a nomadic background, they found settled life in large groups alien to their spirits. The Kharijis eventually evolved into a sect that held that good works are the measure of faith and the only path to salvation. They also insisted on openly and literally pursuing egalitarianism and the commandment to preach to all persons a righteous life and to restrain them, by the sword if necessary, from doing evil. Their emphasis upon the centrality of the Quran influenced all other Muslim groups.

The laxity of life in Damascus induced others to uphold belief in the adequacy of inherent faith in attaining personal salvation. In essence, these Murjiis, as they were termed, were the opposite of Kharijis, for they readily accepted rulers whose conduct was sinful. They held that as long as persons profess God's unity, they should not be judged because of their sins but should be accepted as believers. In the first two centuries of Islam, the Murjiis' concern was to preserve the unity of the Muslim community. Rebuked by Medina, they eased their ethics to political accommodation under the Umayyads. When the Abbasid revolution approached, Murjiis supported the Umayyad claim to the caliphate, but once the Abbasids had won, they found no reason to oppose them.

In the formative period of Muslim theology Mutazilis held a view between these two extremes. By the time of the Abbasid caliph Harun al-Rashid, Mutazilis, accepting the doctrine of free will, were entangled in Aristotelian and Hellenistic Christian philosophies and engaged in adjusting Islam to Greek logic. Adhering to rationalism, free will, and philosophical theology in the ninth century, they lost much of their following by the tenth century.

A myriad of theological questions appeared for these three groups as for others, several arising over and over again. Foremost was the question of God's omnipotence in relation to human responsibility or, as it devolved to the religious plane, the problem of predestination and free will. The second great problem related to the nature of the Quran: Was it uncreated and eternal or was it created? The third troublesome subject centered upon the nature of God and his attributes. If God could hear, see, and speak, was not his unity in doubt?

Mutazilis held that if God rendered punishment for deeds that had been predetermined, he would be an unjust God, and that therefore the human being does have free will. They professed that the Quran had been created in time by God and that between God and his creation, the human being, there is no resemblance. On other points Mutazilis believed that God does not forgive the grave sinner except after repentance and that, being just, he punishes all persons equally. They stood between Kharijis and Murjiis with regard to the Umayyads and their sins, saying that judgment should not be rendered. On the question of one's duty to judge others, they asserted that one should command one's fellows to follow the right path. Wrongful actions should be forbidden—which meant that armed revolt against an unjust ruler was justified when there was a chance of success.

According to the theologian al-Ashari (d. 935), the apparent contradiction embodied in the concepts of predestination and free will was explained by the doctrine that human beings are responsible for their actions but only because God has so willed it. For al-Ashari and others, the Quran was preexistent and eternal; the words or expressions were created and revealed by the angels to the prophet Muhammad only as guides to the eternal word. The apparent contradiction between the unity of God and his other, more human, attributes referred to in the Quran was explained by the belief that God is one and eternal but that his existence is not the same as existence in the world; therefore, one should not seek to specify how the Quran's descriptions of God in human terms can be reconciled with God's infinite character.

Many other theological points were established by al-Ashari, including the dogma that right and wrong are what they are because God declared them to be so, and that God could inflict pain in this world or in the next without being unjust. Even al-Ashari, however, was criticized by the religious men of Medina because they considered his theology too rationalistic and too far removed from the Islam of Muhammad. Followers of al-Ashari remained unpopular in Baghdad until the advent of al-Ghazali, whose writing and teaching united the modified Greek logic and philosophy of al-Ashari with Muhammad's religion to create a faith that has remained the basis of the mainstream of Islam to the present day.

SUNNIS AND HADITHS

When the word of the Quran did not appear to give the answer to some specific problem, the men of religion (ulama; singular, alim) of Medina and the pious throughout Islam looked for guidance in the words and actions of Muhammad or in those he had allowed. Arab tribes were devoted to traditions and normal practice, and custom (sunnah) was a powerful force in their lives. In the new community established by Muhammad and severed from many tribal customs, the life of Muhammad served as the touchstone for proper Muslim thought and conduct.

Early in Muslim history believers put together collections of the statements and deeds of Muhammad. Aishah was the source of hundreds, which Sunnis accepted and Shiis often rejected. The city of Medina, where a great many Companions resided, became a center of the compilations. Each saying was called a *hadith,* or a report, and the whole body of these traditions was known as the *hadiths.* Each hadith eventually had an introduction giving its full pedigree of transmission. Scholars developed a science to establish which of these hadiths were authentic and which were spurious. Many reports were fabricated, particularly in Iraq, starting in the eighth century, and the task of selecting which ones were sound and which were forged became a difficult one. Each sect of Islam and each theologian chose the most suitable hadith on which to base some contentions or to press a point.

The first written collections were begun for judicial ends. By the ninth century the literature on the subject had grown so voluminous that it brought about the science of hadiths. The scholar al-Bukhari (d. 870) published a collection of over 7000 hadiths that was generally pronounced the most authoritative source of tradition. One of the largest collections was that of Ahmad ibn Hanbal, who assembled nearly 30,000 hadiths to form a corpus that served as the basis of his legal and theological ideas. Each major Muslim city or province eventually adopted as standard practice the collected hadiths of one of the noted theologians.

Acceptance of a body of hadiths in time led to the establishment of the sunnah—the custom and behavior of the prophet Muhammad—and to the holy law of Islam. Attachment to the hadiths and a willingness to abide by the consensus of the community and its religious ulama identified Muslims as following the Islamic sunnah and thus gave them the name of Sunnis. This meaning of the term became clearly articulated only by the tenth century, as Sunni acceptance of Abbasid claims to the caliphate grew clearer and Sunni rejection of Kharijis and Shiis increased.

MUSLIM LAW

Early Muslims, pious and devout, perceived hardly any difference between law and religion. Only God knew the law, right behavior, and justice. Islam pointed the "right path" (shariah) to an individual's salvation; divine law recognized good and evil. Law and justice were the chief duties of the state. If the state failed to enforce the law, the state's validity ceased. The caliph as head of the state was charged principally with the enforcement of law. Shariah was theoretically unchanging, although understanding of the law was fluid and changed in the early Islamic period. Law upheld the common good of the community and served individual interests only when these conformed to those of the Muslim community as a whole.

Muslim systems of law, both Sunni and Shii, grew largely from two roots: the Quran and the hadiths. However, caliphs and their judges, even in Medina, discovered early on that the Quran and the hadiths did not address many situations with which they had to deal. In the absence of a definite statement, judges resorted to the use of analogy to some instance in the Quran or the hadiths in deciding cases brought before them. Although the strictest judges did not practice analogy, on the grounds that it left too much to human judgment, it was nevertheless adopted widely in the eighth century as a legal aid and became an integral part of the shariah. In the same century Malik ibn Anas, a jurist-theologian of Medina, compiled a book of hadiths that incorporated many of the local juridical customs and practices. This procedure introduced the institution of consensus (ijma), which at first was reserved to Medina.

In the next generation the jurist al-Shafii drew together these several elements and expanded consensus to include the Muslim community at large. In thus helping to establish Sunni Islam, al-Shafii was instrumental in advancing the idea of following the practice as recognized by the ulama. Questions of law were to be resolved, ultimately through four fundamental means: the Quran, the hadiths, analogy, and consensus. Al-Shafii's general doctrine became widely accepted, with the modification of restricting consensus to that of ulama rather than to the whole ummah. The inclusion of consensus in the principles of the shariah established the classical Sunni theory of the roots of jurisprudence and enabled Islam through the centuries to adapt its institutions to a changing world.

An additional source of Muslim law has been private opinion (ray), which was never quite accepted as a fifth principle of the shariah but was widely practiced. Early caliphs employed it extensively until bitter complaints that human legislation corrupted divine law forced its near abandonment. Nevertheless, most caliphs and later rulers were compelled by administrative necessity to issue laws and decrees that were sanctioned almost wholly by opinion; such laws and regulations were later termed kanuns. In addition to the theoretical and theological bases of the law and the decrees of the rulers, Islamic law in the Middle East was also influenced in practice by the preexisting Roman and Sasanid laws of the provinces conquered by the Muslim armies.

FOUR SUNNI SCHOOLS OF LAW

The Sunni jurists all accepted the shariah but differed as to which hadiths were genuine and the weight that ought to be allowed to analogy, consensus, and opinion in establishing a viable Muslim code of law. The Umayyad and early Abbasid caliphs did not codify the diverse laws in the empire; instead, local particularisms initially won the day and numerous systems prevailed among the Muslims. Four schools of legal practice, named after their founders and systematized by later generations of scholars, eventually emerged as dominant among Sunnis.

The most important of the early schools of law was the Hanafi, which was supported by the Abbasids. Named after Abu Hanifah (d. 767), a legal scholar of Kufah and Baghdad, the Hanafis held a tolerant view on the use of analogy and consensus and particularly emphasized the value of private opinion and judgment by those administering the law. By the eleventh century, however, a strong conservative movement somewhat closed the door on further individual reexamination of the bases of law (ijtihad). After this time, many judges felt they could allow only previously rendered opinions and were required to adhere closely to Hanafi precedent. The Hanafi rite was the established procedure followed in the Ottoman Empire, parts of India, and central Asia.

Next to the Hanafi school in general acceptance has been that of the Shafii. The jurist al-Shafii studied under Malik ibn Anas in Medina and taught in Fustat (Cairo), where he died in 820. The Shafii rites permitted wider use of consensus than did those of the Malikis, and al-Shafii asserted that consensus was the safest and highest legislative authority in Islam. The Shafii school of law dominates legal practice in Lower Egypt, eastern Africa, western and southern Arabia, parts of India, and Indonesia.

The Maliki approach to law was named after Malik ibn Anas of Medina, who died in 795. He and his successors codified the bases of law and acknowledged the consensus of the community of Muslims in Medina. Maliki jurists, however, stood against general consensus, private opinion, and the broad use of analogy. The Maliki school was accepted in Muslim Spain and still prevails in North Africa and Upper Egypt.

The Hanbali school was the fourth and smallest among the orthodox schools. It was named after Ahmad ibn Hanbal, a student of al-Shafii who rebelled against the teachings of his master. The Hanbalis accepted neither private opinion nor analogy and scorned the use of consensus. They maintained that the only valid basis of Muslim law, besides the Quran, was the hadith. For his refusal to disavow his views Ibn Hanbal was beaten and persecuted by al-Mamun and al-Mutasim. Despite Ibn Hanbal's apparent personal appeal, as suggested by the hundreds of thousands of mourners who attended his funeral in Baghdad in 855, Hanbalism outside Baghdad was too rigid to be popular or practical over the centuries and had only scattered followers. After the Ottoman conquest the doctrine was revived in the eighteenth century by the Wahhabis in central Arabia.

In addition to the four principal codes of law, another body of law evolved from a court practice of submitting the summary of involved and important cases to a learned jurist (a mufti), as a consultant, for an opinion known as a fatwa. Fatwas, which presented the legal issues and indicated the proper decision, were later collected and used as guides to the courts in rendering judgments. Until the advent of the Ottoman Empire, muftis more or less remained free from control or restraint by the government.

RATIONALISM

In essence, all of these ulama were attempting to fashion a system of law by a synthesis of Islamic truths and the highly refined and developed rationalism of the Greek philosophers. In the Umayyad period, those favoring the introduction of Hellenistic logic into Muslim theology were Mutazilis. The arguments regarding the nature of God and the Quran rocked the empire. The debates lasted for several centuries, and the particular views of the reigning caliph determined which opinion flourished at any given time. Caliph al-Mamun persecuted all but Mutazilis and ruthlessly suppressed those who did not support free thought. Al-Mamun insisted that the ulama accept the Mutazilis' views and the doctrine of the createdness of the Quran. He initiated an inquisition to force his views on theologians such as Ahmad ibn Hanbal. Caliph al-Mutawakkil, then, in turn ousted the Mutazilis. Eventually, theologians under al-Ashari and the learned founders of the schools of religious law brought the controversy to rest and established theology, tradition, and law as separate from, and occasionally antagonistic toward, the caliphate and the state apparatus it controlled.

The great philosophical efforts, however, had the effect of taking Islam away from the people and ran the danger of destroying it as a practical religion. People desired a living experience of God, not a metaphysical or conceptual discussion of religion. To the simple Muslim, God was a personage always near at hand. One could talk to God, as a Bedouin's prayer in a time of drought attested: "O God of the devotees, what is the matter with us and You? You used to give us water—What has possessed You? Do send rain down on us. Exert Yourself!"

ASCETICISM AND MYSTICISM

In the first years after Muhammad, piety in Islam sometimes took the form of asceticism. Pious Muslims seeking knowledge of God and salvation for themselves adopted and preached asceticism. Study of the traditions of the Prophet, prayer, fasting, solitary meditations, and prolonged vigils would lead the soul to God. Poverty, humility, patience, repentance, and silence in this world would save believers seeking godliness from eternal chastisement and permit them to come into the presence of God by means of the annihilation of the self, to taste the joys of paradise, and to abide there to eternity.

In spite of a waning of ascetic tendencies in the Abbasid period, asceticism linked to mysticism remained strong among both male and female Muslims across the centuries. Sultans, generals, rich merchants, judges, and scholars might not adopt ascetic practices themselves, but they usually paid deference to those who did.

Toward the end of the eighth century, mysticism entered into Islam with a great force. Theology and philosophy had not greatly affected the masses, and after the first half of the ninth century the majority of the literate community found little of interest in the hairsplitting of the ulama. For religious experience the masses turned to mysticism. Knowledge of God was to be achieved by the inner light of the individual soul, not by the intellectual methods of the philosopher.

Muhammad the Prophet came to be seen as the perfect or ideal human being, without sin, and popular piety viewed him as a model for what human life should be. The major roots of Islamic mysticism were the Quran and the hadiths of Muhammad; to them were added the quietism and occult practices and beliefs of Buddhist stories, Hindu monism, Zoroastrian dualism, Gnostic ideas from Iraq, and miracles from the Gospels. The second coming of Christ became the doctrine of the coming of the Mahdi, the rightly guided one, who would bring complete victory to Islam.

The essence of mysticism was love, an ecstatic communication with the divine, and final absorption into the godhead. Nothing existed but God. To know and love God and to be united with him, without any thought of reward or salvation, was an emotional means of purifying the soul. God was eternal beauty, and the path leading to him was love. The mystic sought to lose the self in life with God, and he or she felt a sense of union with the godhead that offended nonmystical Muslims. The process of commingling self with God could best be achieved by love and thought of God.

Until the twelfth century, popular preachers who based much of their message on mysticism and won their wide appeal through mysticism and miracles were despised by philosophers and theologians and were frequently judged guilty of heresy. Then, as al-Ashari had made rationalism and Islamic theology compatible, so al-Ghazali led the learned and pious doctors and jurists to accept mysticism.

Born in Iran in 1058 and appointed professor at the Nizamiyah at Baghdad in 1091, the legal scholar Abu Hamid al-Ghazali had the court and the scholars at his feet, and for four or five years his fame spread far and wide. Apparently secure for life, he then experienced some sort of personal admonition and abandoned everything to become a mystic. After about a decade of wandering, contemplation, and writing, he returned to society and taught at the Nizamiyah at Nishapur, and eventually died in his hometown of Tus in 1111. His great contribution, largely through his writings, was initially viewed by early medieval Muslims as his works on law, but in the longer run he energized Sufism and Islam by making personal experience and emotion a part of religion. Islam began to live again for the ordinary man, through both law and mysticism.

FRATERNAL ORDERS

At the time of the appearance of mysticism a holy man was called a sufi, meaning "one garbed in wool." Sufis preached to the masses, and they lived a life of example for their admirers. Without question the conversion to Islam of many on the frontiers of the Muslim state was the accomplishment of the Sufis.

For several centuries Sufism was an unorganized movement throughout Islam. Certain Sufis obtained a devoted following on a personal basis. Before the end of the twelfth century, however, groups of Sufis formed compact brotherhoods. The master Sufi, or shaikh, was the teacher and initiated disciples into the order. The members, by study, ritual, and piety, proceeded up the ladder of the order until they were ready to leave to establish a branch center.

By the fourteenth century, thousands of lodges dotted the Muslim landscape from Morocco to India. Each order had its own peculiar ritual and liturgy (dhikr). Some were elaborate and others simple, but all were mystical efforts to reach God. Most fraternities had hundreds, sometimes thousands, of lay members who went about their normal occupations in city or town. At stated times they met at the lodge to observe their ceremonies. Some Sufi lodges consisted solely of women. A few of the orders increased the mystical stimulus by an accompaniment of music or by dancing or whirling.

It was not possible to know how many different orders existed at any one time; new splinter fraternities sprang into being and others disappeared at regular intervals. One of the best known was the Qadiriyah, founded by the Hanbali Abd al-Qadir al-Jilani in the twelfth century, which had its center in Baghdad and spread throughout Islam. More conservative than most, its members have been noted for their philanthropy and humility. Another order, the Rifaiyah, was famed for glass eating, fire walking, and self-mortification. In Anatolia, the two best-known orders were the Bektashi, to which many Ottoman soldiers belonged, and the Mevlevis, whose members were popularly called "whirling dervishes" because of certain aspects of their ritual. In the central and eastern parts of the Middle East, there was the Naqshbandiyah order.

As a great social and religious development, the significance of the fraternal orders lay in the members' extensive participation in the spread and popularization of Islam, resulting in the majority of the people in North Africa, Sudan, Anatolia, central Asia, certain parts of India, and Indonesia becoming converted to Islam. In this process, much to the horror and disapproval of Muslim theologians, local beliefs and religious customs were grafted upon the original doctrines to form a popular Islam. In most instances, therefore, popular Islam in different parts of the world became exceedingly diverse in form and practice. Sufis could also be either Sunnis or Shiis, although most mystics apparently were Sunnis.

SHIISM

Differences of opinion and belief have usually been accepted in Islam. Variations in practice and doctrine among the four main Sunni legal systems, the many conflicting interpretations of hadiths in vogue throughout the Muslim world, and the confusing welter of exotic ideas rampant in popular Islam have made a definitive imputation of heresy difficult to verify on purely theological grounds.

Until comparatively recently, rulers throughout the world usually persecuted subjects whose religion was at marked variance with theirs. Nonetheless, Islam was relatively tolerant, as the treatment of Christians and Jews testifies, and the caliphs permitted many types of religious deviation. In general, deviation became a serious matter only when religious doctrines denied to the caliph the right of his position and his power. Therein lay the true seeds of accusations of heresy.

Following the death of Ali and the ascension of the Umayyad caliphs, Alids contended that the rulers were usurpers and that the imamate, as they called the leadership position for the Muslim community, should be lodged in the house of the prophet Muhammad, through Ali and Fatimah. Within that family, succession to the imamate could be decided according to one or more criteria: strictly hereditary succession from Ali's son Husain; designation by the previous imam, which would be given to a member of the family but

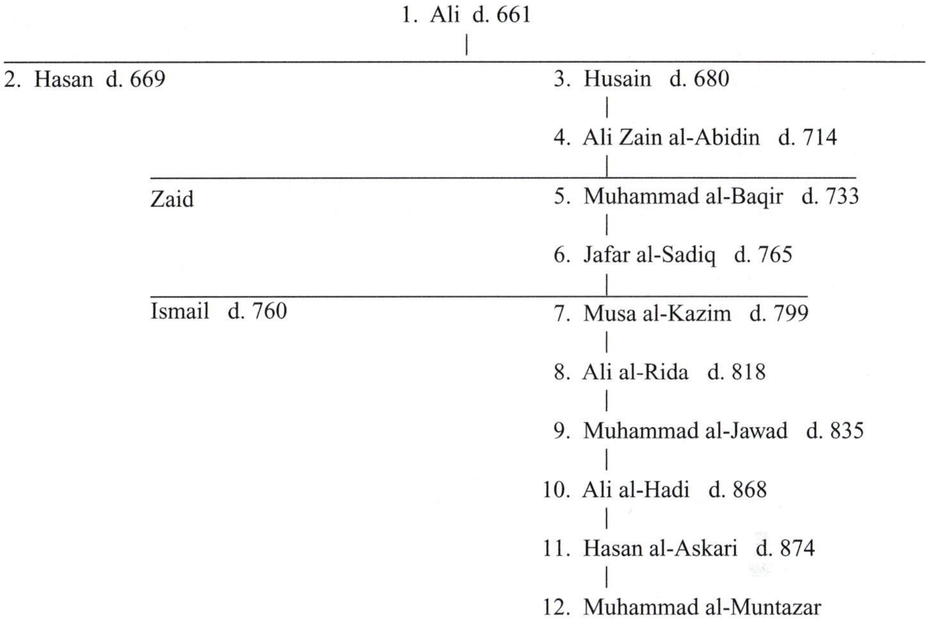

The Twelve Imams

not necessarily the eldest son; self-designation through action against the enemies of the family, as Alid pretenders rose against the Umayyad and Abbasid caliphs. For more than two centuries, intermittent political and military attempts were made by the Shiis (the partisans, or sect, of Ali) to unseat the caliph. Constant opposition to established authority, along with the growing consensus inside the Shii community, made the Shiis into an umbrella movement that attracted numerous social and economic groups antagonistic to caliphal policies and the existing order. Although successful in reaching political power in some places at certain times, the Shiis usually were ruled by Sunnis. The Shiis gradually developed an intricate theology, heavily influenced as of the eleventh century by Mutazili thought, which engendered some beliefs opposed by Sunnis.

The Shiis held that Ali had been the legitimate imam ("leader") and that the imamate was rightfully transmitted to his descendants. Ali had been given an esoteric power to interpret the Quran, a knowledge that was handed on, in turn, to his sons and grandsons. (Later, some extremists even professed that God's revelations had been intended for Ali but that the angel Gabriel had mistakenly given them to Muhammad.) Ali's descendants, therefore, ruled by a divine right that was handed down to them from Adam; they were infallible, impeccable, and certainly beyond human censure, and therefore not subject to the consensus of the Muslim community.

To substantiate their theological and political claims, the Shiis offered their own interpretation of the early history of Islam. Shiis elevated the importance of Fatimah and downplayed the role of Aishah in events. Shiis rejected the legitimacy of the first three caliphs and claimed that Muhammad had announced in 632 that Ali was his rightful successor. Muawiyah and the Umayyads in general were particularly criticized by the Shiis because they had overthrown Ali, and they were responsible for the murder of Ali's son, Husain, in 680, as he led an unsuccessful rebellion against the caliph Yazid. The tragic martyrdom of Husain became the most fervently celebrated event in the Shii religious calendar, and martyrdom was a major impetus for the spread of the faith.

The Shiis have been divided into numerous sects since the eighth century. The majority, the Twelvers, adhered to the belief that there was a succession by prior designation of twelve imams to Muhammad al-Muntazar ("The Expected"), who in the 870s disappeared in a cave and who will return as the savior (Mahdi) of humanity. In his absence the law and the creed were interpreted originally by four agents who acted for him, but upon the death of the last of these in 940 the "great occultation" or concealment began, and no definitive interpretation of the will of the imam was possible. This meant that historical precedent and the faith could not be interpreted in an absolutely binding way after 940, and intellectual speculation and judicial ingenuity (ijtihad) could be exercised by Shii scholars and jurists. Thus, in law, the Twelver Shiis accepted only the Quran, the sunnah of the prophet Muhammad, those hadiths of Muhammad narrated by a recognized imam and the imams' own views on law and theology as compiled in the tenth and eleventh centuries, and a scholar's or judge's personal opinion when it could be upheld by hadith or precedent established by an imam. Justice was strongly emphasized, and oppression and tyranny were considered to be great evils. The ulama restricted analogy and consensus, and their use was not widely accepted until a much later time.

Aside from a few minor differences between Sunni and Shii rituals, the chief practices accepted by Shiis but rejected by Sunnis were the allowance of temporary marriage and the practice of dissimulation. The latter permitted Shiis to deny their faith to avoid persecution when Sunnis attacked them for opposing the authority of the caliphs.

Twelver Shiis held power only occasionally before the sixteenth century, as in the Buyid dynasty that controlled the Sunni Abbasid caliphate in Baghdad at the close of the classical Islamic period, and several Syrian and Iraqi tribal dynasties. However, other types of Shiis established themselves in various parts of the Middle East in the ninth and tenth centuries, while in the early twenty-first century the majority of Muslims in Iran and Iraq are Twelver Shiis.

The most conservative of the Shiis are found in Yemen. In parts of northern Yemen the Zaidi sect, which arrived there in the ninth century, at about the same time the sect was also flourishing in northern Iran, recognized a series of imams who were descended from Zaid, a son of the fourth imam. The Zaidis allow for little supernaturalism in their theology; succession to the imamate was by ability, among the descendants of Ali and Fatimah, and not by designation by the incumbent imam.

More extreme Shii groups included a score or more of divergent sects. Of these the Ismailis, or Seveners, have had the greatest following. Ismail was the rightful seventh imam. Jafar al-Sadiq, the sixth imam, had first named Ismail, his eldest son, as successor, but then Jafar designated another son, Musa, as successor. The Seveners rejected this substitution, arguing that the imam was incapable of erring and his original choice must have been correct. Seven became a sacred and mystical number. The essence of the universe came in seven steps: God, universal mind, universal soul, matter, space, time, and earth and the human being. Since Muslims needed guidance, there must be an imam present to lead the community at any given time.

The Ismailis were masters of organization and tactics. Sent out from Syria, missionaries traveled through the Muslim world, preaching that the language of the Quran was an occult veil covering an inner and true meaning that could be revealed only to the adept. Initiation of the novice proceeded in seven graded degrees, wherein was divulged secret knowledge such as transmigration of souls, the divinity of Ismail, and the coming of the Mahdi. One part of the Ismaili sect established its rule in North Africa early in the tenth century. The Fatimids, who claimed universal domination as their goal, ruled much of the western portion of the Muslim world, while the Qarmatians, who were also Ismailis, ruled much of eastern Arabia, although the majority of the Muslims of the Middle East remained Sunnis.

Another Ismaili sect was the notorious Assassins, founded in Iran by Hasan ibn al-Sabbah, who studied Ismaili rites and doctrine in Fatimid Egypt and then returned to his home as a missionary. In 1090, near Qazvin in the Elburz Mountains, he seized the fort of Alamut, which became the residence of the grand master of the order. Below him were priors and propagandists; at the lowest rank stood the fidais, who risked death for the faith. Their familiar name, Assassins, was derived from the Arabic word for hashish, which they were said to use in their fearless raids from mountain fortresses. Exact knowledge about these Ismaili groups is lacking, however, because many of their records and books were destroyed in 1256 when the Mongols razed Alamut. Spreading westward earlier, the Assassins in the twelfth century held numerous castles in north Syria. The assassination of the famous vizir Nizam al-Mulk in 1092 was the first in a series of assassinations of prominent individuals. The western branch of the order was eliminated by the Mamluks in 1272.

Other Ismaili sects were the Nusairis or Alawis of northern Syria and the Druzes of Lebanon, Syria, and Jordan. The Nusairis were devotees of the eleventh imam but nevertheless adhered to the main tenets of the Seveners. They looked upon Ali as the incarnation of God and possessed a liturgy with many Christian borrowings. The Druze sect was an eleventh-century splinter group from Fatimid Egypt. Its members settled in Syria and the Lebanon mountain region, where they developed an elaborate ritual and a pattern of life distinctive even in minor detail. Both the Druzes and the Nusairis maintained strict secrecy with respect to their faith and practices.

Probably the best-known Ismaili in the twentieth century was the incomparable Agha Khan III of Bombay, London, Paris, and the Riviera, who traced his descent through the last grand master of the Assassins at Alamut to the seventh imam. Regarded as infallible and impeccable by his followers in Syria, India, Pakistan, and Zanzibar, he received a tenth of their revenues.

In addition to the sects and divisions of these branches of Islam already described, there have been many more. Thus, the Quran and the sayings of the prophet Muhammad passed through the fires of Greek logic, Hellenistic Christianity, and Persian dualism to evolve a finely drawn legal system and intellectual theology, a highly charged supernatural religion, and a flourishing mystical tradition. The apocryphal words of Muhammad have apparently been fulfilled: when told that there were seventy-two varieties of Christianity, the Prophet was supposed to have said that Islam would have seventy-three!

REFERENCES

References cited at the end of Chapters 3 through 7 contain material pertinent to this chapter as well.

Arberry, A. J.: *Sufism: An Account of the Mystics of Islam.* New York: Harper and Row, 1970. This succinct book by an expert in the field looks at the Quran, Muhammad, and Sufis.

Burton, John: *An Introduction to the Hadith.* Edinburgh: Edinburgh University Press, 1994. The author discusses the politics, study, theology, verification, collection, and evaluation of hadiths.

Daftary, Farhad: *A Short History of the Ismailis: Traditions of a Muslim Community.* Princeton, N.J.: Markus Wiener, 1998.

Fakhry, Majid: *A Short Introduction to Islamic Philosophy, Theology and Mysticism.* Oxford, England: Oneworld, 1998. A general review of the links among these topics.

Hallaq, Wael B.: *A History of Islamic Legal Theories: An Introduction to Sunni Usul al-Fiqh.* Cambridge: Cambridge University Press, 1997. Subjects include the evolving principles of jurisprudence, the foundations of law to the eleventh century, and the relationship of theory to practice, with a last chapter on modern legal interpretation.

Jafri, Husain M.: *Origins and Early Development of Shi'a Islam.* London: Longman, 1979. The author follows events from the days of Muhammad to Jafar al-Sadiq from the point of view of Shii Islam.

Juynboll, G. H. A.: *Muslim Tradition: Studies in Chronology, Provenance and Authorship of Early Hadith.* Cambridge: Cambridge University Press, 1983.

Khalidi, Tarif: *Classical Arab Islam: The Culture and Heritage of the Golden Age.* Princeton, N.J.: Darwin Press, 1985. Thoughtful essays on a broad range of subjects, including Sufism, reason, nature, and the prophet Muhammad.

Knysh, Alexander: *Islamic Mysticism: A Short History.* Leiden: Brill, 2000. The lives and spiritual biographies of leading Sufis.

Massignon, Louis: *The Passion of al-Hallaj: Mystical Martyr of Islam.* Vol. 1: *Life.* Translated by H. Mason. Princeton, N.J.: Princeton University Press, 1982. A moving account of the life of one of the most extreme and famous of the mystics.

Melchert, Christopher: *The Formation of the Sunni Schools of Law, 9th–10th Centuries* C.E. Leiden: Brill, 1997. Based on biographical dictionaries, this revisionist work argues that the Sunni schools of law were developed by the successors of the persons for whom they were named.

Momen, Moojan: *An Introduction to Shi'i Islam: The History and Doctrines of Twelver Shi'ism.* New Haven, Conn.: Yale University Press, 1985. Shiism as a political, religious, and intellectual movement is thoroughly examined.

Renard, John, ed.: *Windows on the House of Islam: Muslim Sources on Spirituality and Religious Life.* Berkeley: University of California Press, 1998. Original texts and illustrations dealing with Quran, the beliefs of Islam, devotions, literature, institutions, patronage, teaching, and accounts of religious experiences.

Rippin, Andrew: *Muslims: Their Religious Beliefs and Practices.* Vol. 1: *The Formative Period.* London: Routledge, 1990. A revisionist introduction that casts doubt on many accepted interpretations.

Schacht, Joseph: *An Introduction to Islamic Law.* New York: Oxford University Press, 1964. A classic in the field and more than an introduction, as the author sheds light on the importance of al-Shafii.

Schimmel, Annemarie: *Mystical Dimensions of Islam.* Chapel Hill: University of North Carolina Press, 1975. This is a synthesis of Sufi theory and practice, its history, psychological and social significance, and literary output.

Watt, W. Montgomery: *Muslim Intellectual: A Study of al-Ghazali.* Edinburgh: Edinburgh University Press, 1963. A full study of this great theological philosopher.

———: *The Formative Period of Islamic Thought.* Edinburgh: Edinburgh University Press, 1973. A detailed study of Islamic ideas from 632 to 945. This important work closely relates the effect of the development of ideas and beliefs upon political events.

———: *Islamic Philosophy and Theology: An Extended Survey.* 2d ed. Edinburgh: Edinburgh University Press, 1985. An excellent short introduction and summary.

World Wide Web: The following on-line sites constitute useful and searchable resources for the study of Islam.

Ahlul Bayt Digital Islamic Library Project: www.al-islam.org/organizations/dilp, for many Shii works, guides, and references

Muslim Students Association of the University of Southern California: www.usc.edu/dept/MSA/fundamentals, for hadiths and sunnah

Qadiri-Rifai Tariqa: www.qadiri-rifai.org, for the history, leaders, and beliefs of a Sufi brotherhood

CHAPTER 9

Muslim Civilization in the Middle East

The Muslims burst from the cities of the Hijaz and the deserts of Arabia into the existing complex civilizations of the Middle East. Everywhere they demonstrated a remarkable genius for appropriating and assimilating various attributes of existing cultures and blending them with their own to form a new and varied Muslim civilization. For the classical Islamic period during the first few centuries following the death of Muhammad in 632, Arabic remained the universal language; non-Arab Muslims and non-Muslims alike, if they learned the Arabic language, could and did participate in most aspects of Muslim culture. Jews, Christians, and others made substantial contributions to the development of the new civilization that often transcended religious as well as political and geographic differences.

The unity arising from participation in the new, cosmopolitan Muslim civilization helped to preserve and further develop a sense of unity in the Muslim community despite increasing political, military, and sectarian fragmentation. Islamic civilization linked together Muslims who were as far apart geographically as those in Spain and central Asia. A jointly held Muslim civilization helped differentiate the Muslims in the Middle East from their neighbors in China, India, Europe, and Africa, even while Islamic philosophy, medicine, science, and art helped foster interconnections with the other civilizations of the Eastern Hemisphere.

Despite the changes that altered the nature of Muslim governments in the early medieval period from 950 to about 1250, the development and refinement of Muslim civilization in the Middle East accelerated. There was little specialization in knowledge; most thinkers were accomplished in several fields of research. The cultural and intellectual accomplishments of the Muslims in the Middle East included major advancements in human knowledge in diverse fields, spanning various arts and sciences.

PHILOSOPHY

Greek logic was studied during the Umayyad era. Not until the reign of the Abbasid al-Mamun, however, was the bulk of Hellenistic thought and science translated into Arabic.

Beginning with a majority of the works of Aristotle and Plato, translators soon rendered most earlier philosophers into Arabic. It was upon this base that Muslim philosophy was erected.

The earliest of the prominent Arab philosophers was the Iraqi al-Kindi (d. ca. 865), a tutor to the son of the caliph al-Mutasim. He excelled in the study of optics, chemistry, medicine, and music, but above all he was a philosopher. Al-Kindi studied the ideas of Aristotle and Plato. He intermingled philosophy and theology, holding that the world of intelligence is supreme. Immortality results from having the correct knowledge of God and the universe. A century later, al-Farabi (d. 950), a Turk from central Asia who lived much of his life in Aleppo, blended Aristotelian, Platonic, and Sufi mystical thought. He presented his philosophy in a political treatise by describing a model city where the ruler was a moral and intellectual being and the happiness of all was the governing force. Al-Farabi's classification of the sciences influenced Muslim scholars for centuries to come. However, he shocked Muslims by claiming that the world was not created and had no beginning.

Muslim philosophers better known to the Western world were Ibn Sina (d. 1037; known as Avicenna) and Ibn Rushd (d. 1198; known as Averroës). The former, called by the Muslims "the shaikh and the prince of the learned," was born in 980 in a village near Bukhara. An Iranian, Ibn Sina lived as a young man in Bukhara, where he acquired an encyclopedic knowledge of medicine, mathematics, astronomy, and philosophy. Since he was able to write concisely, yet in a popular style, Ibn Sina's numerous works on diverse subjects had a wide vogue among Muslims and greatly influenced the advancement of philosophical thought in medieval Europe. Pursuing Aristotelian philosophy, Ibn Sina developed and passed on to the west the notion that there are two intelligibles—the concept of an object such as a chair, and the pursuant or logical concept of a chair in relation to its abstract universal concept. He taught that the idea of a chair existed before the chair was created, and that in each chair existed the idea of chair and that from many chairs came the idea of chair.

Ibn Rushd, the Maliki Muslim judge and philosopher, lived in Cordoba, Seville, and Marrakesh. He wrote in the fields of philosophy, medicine, mathematics, law, and theology. As the last of the classical Muslim philosophers of Spain, he built on the systems of al-Farabi, Ibn Sina, and his fellow countrymen. He declared that active human reason and possible reason or knowledge are one and present in everyone. Ibn Rushd's commentaries on Aristotle were more popular and influential in Christian Europe than they were in the Muslim world.

Muslim scholars, writing in Arabic, had a profound influence on Christian philosophers of medieval Europe. More significant to the Middle East, however, was their permanent impact upon Muslim intellectuals. Summaries and commentaries on these philosophers and scores of others less well known were read and discussed. Scientific method itself became a field of controversy where philosophers, theologians, and the practitioners of the individual sciences fiercely debated theories of knowledge and investigation.

MEDICINE

Muhammad supposedly declared that there exist two sciences: theology and medicine. Consequently, throughout classical and medieval Islamic history most Muslim philosophers and scientists were students of medicine; frequently they were also practicing physicians. Muslims first became aware of medical knowledge at the Damascus court of the Umayyads, through their Greek, Syrian, and Iranian physicians, whose skills were based almost exclusively on works of Greek scientists. A few Greek or Syriac treatises were translated into Arabic, and the Alexandria medical school was transferred from Egypt, first to Antioch and later to Iraq.

Great strides in medicine were made under Abbasid rule in Baghdad. The medical works of Galen and Hippocrates were especially important when translated into Arabic. Galen was highly influential in forming medical theory. Several schools of medicine developed, and a physician took state examinations to obtain a license to practice his profession. In the year 931, there were 869 physicians registered in Baghdad; they swore to work for the benefit of humanity and for the relief and cure of the sick and not to give deadly medicines. Some traveling clinics for the poor were supported by the state, and hospitals were introduced into the Muslim world by the Abbasid caliph Harun al-Rashid. Most physicians were general practitioners, but there was specialization in ophthalmology and surgery. On most of his campaigns the Seljuk Turkish sultan Malikshah had with him a mobile hospital, carried on forty camels. Pharmacists were also examined and licensed, and schools of pharmacy and drugstores were established.

In 765 the Nestorian Christian Jurjis ibn Bukhtishu, dean of the academy of medicine of Jundishapur in southwestern Iran, came to the court of al-Mansur to cure the Abbasid caliph's stomach ailment. Fortunes were made by court physicians, who passed on their professional skills and practices as valued possessions from father to son for generations. Ibn Bukhtishu's grandson understood psychiatry; through a form of hypnosis, he cured one of al-Rashid's slave girls of hysterical paralysis by pretending to disrobe her publicly. Descendants of Ibn Bukhtishu served the Abbasid court for nearly three centuries.

The arrival of physicians from Jundishapur opened the way for medical investigations beyond the works of the ancient Greeks, and the ninth century in Baghdad was a period of many advances in medical knowledge. The compendium by Thabit ibn Qurra of Harran (d. 901) discussed general hygiene. It stated causes, symptoms, and treatment for diseases of the skin and every part of the body from head to foot. Infectious diseases were classified; fractures and dislocations were described; and the importance of climate, food, diet, and sex was explained.

The most ingenious Muslim physician was the Persian al-Razi (d. 925), chief of the Baghdad hospital from about 902 to 907, then a practicing physician and philosopher in Rayy. Considered the best original mind and clinician of the medieval period, he treated bladder and kidney stones, and presented the first clinical report on measles and smallpox. He had some fifty-six monographs on medicine and surgery to his credit. His comprehensive medical encyclopedia was based on clinical observations and experimentation.

The most famous Muslim medical work was al-Qanun, written in the eleventh century by Ibn Sina, whose philosophical accomplishments have been mentioned earlier. Encyclopedic in character, it showed the advances of Muslim knowledge and the originality of Ibn Sina in this field. Among other things, it explained the contagious nature of tuberculosis, showed that disease could be spread through water, recognized pleurisy, and described 760 different drugs. Al-Qanun, along with the works of Galen and Hippocrates, was among the chief medical books of the Middle East and western Europe from the twelfth to the seventeenth century.

With the decline of Abbasid power and patronage, Baghdad's importance in medicine decreased and regional centers of medical excellence became more important. Muslim Spain possessed superior physicians and surgeons. The ablest surgeon was Abu al-Qasim of Cordoba, who practiced the art of crushing bladder stones, cauterized wounds, and advocated dissection of bodies, even though Muslims generally did not engage in dissection. His surgical writings were translated and became the surgical manual at the medical schools of European centers. At the time of the Black Death in the middle of the fourteenth century, a Muslim physician of Granada, Ibn al-Khatib, recognized the disease's contagious character. He noted that a patient's symptoms were identical to those of the person from whom he had been infected. Although religious law denied contagion, Ibn al-Khatib held that "experience, investigation, the evidence of the senses and trustworthy reports" established without a doubt the reality of infection from the afflicted.

Building on earlier sources, Muslim physicians expanded the frontiers of medicine. Their practice, monographs, and compendiums demonstrated originality and ingenuity up to the thirteenth century. The diversity and number of their works, translated into Latin and eventually printed, further established the place of Muslim physicians in the history of world medical science.

MATHEMATICS AND ASTRONOMY

Muslim scholars also found mathematics an attractive and useful science, especially in company with astronomy and astrology. By far the greatest achievement of the Arab mathematicians was the adoption and wide use of "Arabic numerals," which were brought from India. These numerals, including the use of zero and the placing of the digit in a series to denote units, tens, hundreds, and so on, made "everyday arithmetic" possible and simplified calculations, enabling Muslims to take the square and cube roots of numbers with ease. The word *cipher,* meaning zero, was taken directly from the Arabic *sifr,* meaning "empty."

Building on Indian and Greek works, Middle Eastern scholars advanced mathematical knowledge considerably. Muhammad al-Khwarazmi of Khurasan (d. 850) did a study on Indian numerals that later circulated in the west. Through his name came the word "algorism." He wrote on the solution of quadratic equations, and from part of the title of one of his books was derived the word *algebra* (al-jabr: "integration"). In the same century, the mathematician, astronomer, and physician Thabit ibn Qurra developed new propositions and studied irrationals. The Syrian al-Battani (d. 929) was the first to present ideas on trigonometric ratios.

One of the most distinguished mathematicians was the Iranian poet Umar Khayyam (d. 1130). He advanced far beyond al-Khwarazmi, establishing procedures for the solution of cubic and quadrinomial equations and developing analytic geometry in numerous ways. The last great medieval mathematician of the Middle East was the Iranian Nasir al-Din al-Tusi (d. 1274), who assembled his astronomical laboratory in northwestern Iran under the patronage of the Mongols. Here he wrote his famous *Treatise on the Quadrilateral* and conducted his brilliant studies in the field of spherical trigonometry.

Mathematics and astronomy were closely related, especially since in the construction of any mosque it was necessary to fix the direction of Mecca, and accurate timekeeping was important to determine the occasions for prayers. Furthermore, since astrology was popular and the latitude and longitude of one's birthplace entered into one's horoscope, the movement of the stars was significant. Folk astronomy was used for fixing the lunar months and calculating times of prayers, while mathematical astronomy was more specialized. Muslim astronomy started from Iranian, Greek, and Indian contributions.

When the Abbasid caliph al-Mansur decided to build his new palace in Baghdad, the Iranian astronomer Naubakht was employed to draw the plans. Many palaces in Baghdad had private astronomical observatories. The main professional observatories were at Jundishapur and Baghdad. Scientists at the time of al-Mamun measured a degree on the meridian precisely, with only a 2 percent error. Although the Muslim religious calendar was based on lunar months, rather exact astronomical tables and solar calendars were also prepared.

Thabit ibn Qurra determined the altitude of the sun and computed the length of the solar year and an analysis of motion. Muhammad al-Battani recorded his observations on the appearance of the new moon, the inclination of the ecliptic, and eclipses of the sun. The astronomer and geographer al-Biruni (d. 1048), while at Ghaznah in Afghanistan, proposed the idea that the earth rotates on its axis and reckoned quite accurately latitudes and longitudes for every important city in the Middle East, as well as writing excellent cultural geographies.

Near Cordoba lived the great astronomer al-Bitruji, who computed the length of the Mediterranean and found it to be 42° of longitude, a nearly correct measurement. He advanced the idea of diurnal movements of the earth and explained the movement of the stars by the turning of the earth on its axis as well as by its circling about the sun.

The Arabic names of many stars and constellations and the Arabic origin of such words as *azimuth, nadir,* and *zenith* vouch for the brilliance of the Middle Eastern astronomers and the acceptance of their contributions by the west. Besides assimilating and transmitting to posterity the mathematics and astronomy of the ancients, Middle Eastern scholars up to the fifteenth century made many original contributions in the practical and theoretical branches of the subjects. The widespread use of numerals gave arithmetic an everyday value. Algebra became an exact science, and solid foundations were laid in the fields of analytic geometry and plane and spherical trigonometry. Through Spain and Sicily most of these ideas passed at an early date to the western world, where they influenced the science of Europe, while the same knowledge was also passing to the great civilizations of India and China.

SCIENCES

In addition to medicine, mathematics, and astronomy, Middle Easterners investigated and frequently brought about fundamental redefinitions in the basic and natural sciences. A scientific culture and a community of scientists helped foster the unique contributions of great individual scholars. It is not possible here to detail the various advances made in each science. Some examples would include works on botany, chiefly in connection with drugs for the pharmacist and physician. Zoological studies were made, some for use by veterinarians. Al-Masudi, who died about 957 in Cairo, discussed earthquakes, described windmills, and advanced a theory of evolution. In his book on geology, Ibn Sina suggested several ideas about earthquakes, winds, climate, and geologic sedimentation.

However, the greatest strides in the sciences were taken in chemistry and physics. The word *chemistry* is derived from Arabic. Chemistry was studied in connection with alchemy, although some famous scientists, such as Ibn Sina and al-Kindi, did not believe in the transmutation of metals. Alchemy was founded on the belief that all metals contain the same essences and that it is possible to transmute one to another. Further, it was believed that gold is the purest form of metal and that some substance exists that can transform baser metals into gold. Throughout the Muslim world and elsewhere, countless individuals engaged in the search for this substance and the technique of its use. Celebrated philosophers and physicians gave their time and genius to the quest. One of these men, al-Razi, distinguished volatile and nonvolatile bodies and classified all matter as vegetable, animal, or mineral. Others in their research determined the specific weights of stones and metals.

The greatest chemist, or alchemist, was Jabir ibn Hayyan, who lived in Kufah toward the end of the eighth century and died in 815. Jabir advocated experimentation and recognized the importance of confirming by careful observation theories that are based only on previous writings and hypotheses. He was able to prepare arsenious oxide, lead acetate, sulfide of mercury, and sal ammoniac. Jabir presented new and improved methods of evaporation, filtration, sublimation, melting, crystallization, and distillation. His works, translated into Latin in the twelfth century, proved to be the foundation of western alchemy and chemistry. The Arabic origin of such words as *alkali* and *alcohol* attests to western dependence upon Middle Eastern discoveries in this branch of science.

In physics the widest interest lay in theoretical and applied mechanics as related to problems of irrigation, the construction of mills, and the flow of water. Waterwheels and water clocks were built in many cities of the Middle East, some of the clocks being exceedingly ingenious in design. (Clock design was one of the very few areas of science and technology where European innovations were brought into the Islamic world; generally, the flow of knowledge went the other way.) In the twelfth century, al-Khazini observed the greater density of water when it was nearer the center of the earth, and he displayed a strong preference for experimentation rather than theorizing.

The most significant developments in physics, however, were in the field of optics. Many prominent scientists of the age investigated the subject. The most outstanding was Abu Ali ibn al-Haitham (d. 1039), who flourished in Cairo at the time of the Fatimids and who also extensively studied momentum and gravity. He refused to accept Euclid's and Ptolemy's theory that the eye emits visual rays; instead he advanced the theory that vision is due to the impact of light rays. Experimenting with reflection and optical illusions, he studied refraction through spherical segments filled with water. He also proposed that light is fire reflected at the spherical limit of the atmosphere; from observing phenomena at twilight he reckoned the atmosphere to be about 10 miles (16 km.) high. Ibn al-Haitham's studies greatly influenced, through translation, the works of such Europeans as Leonardo da Vinci.

GEOGRAPHY

The religious obligation of a pilgrimage to Mecca once in a lifetime undoubtedly reinforced a desire among many in Islamic lands to travel and see the world. Because geographic data were needed by these travelers as well as by traders and administrators, travelers wrote detailed books on where they had been and what they had seen. Geography became one of the most popular pursuits of the medieval period of Islamic civilization in the Middle East.

Muslim geographers had difficulty in freeing themselves from earlier Greek, Persian, and Indian concepts of the world. The scientist al-Khwarazmi, at the caliph al-Mamun's command, prepared a great map of the earth and a companion text that was used by geographers until the fourteenth century. Largely following the ancient Ptolemy, al-Khwarazmi pictured the world encircled by a continuous ocean from which the Mediterranean and the Indian Ocean branched to separate the land of the earth, which was divided into seven climate zones. The western prime meridian ran through the Canary Islands, and the easternmost area discussed was China. Iraq was considered to be in the center and the most fortunate of places.

Fortunately, the conservative and classical geographers were ignored by travelers and sailors who recognized irregular coasts strewn with gulfs and peninsulas and stated that the Indian Ocean, in certain directions, has no limit. The tales of these voyagers came down through the ages as the stories of Sindbad the Sailor. They described China in the ninth century and Russia in the tenth. Their road books were a mine of historical topography and economic and political geography. The tenth-century scholar was frequently on the move. The greatest globe-trotter was al-Masudi (d. 956), who visited most of the countries of Asia, Zanzibar, and much of North Africa. His thirty-volume work became one of the two recognized geographic and historical encyclopedias of the medieval period. One of the last discerning voyagers was Ibn Battutah of Morocco. Living in the fourteenth century, he was on the move for nearly three decades. He made four pilgrimages to Mecca and visited India, Byzantine Constantinople, and parts of Africa.

The most noted geographer of the Muslim world was al-Idrisi, born in Ceuta in 1100 and for many years the chief geographer for the Christian King Roger II of Sicily. In his writings and discourses in Arabic, he summed up the ideas and contributions of Ptolemy, al-Khwarazmi, and al-Masudi. Using silver, al-Idrisi constructed for his patron a celestial sphere and a disklike map of the earth; the latter distinctly showed the source of the Nile to be a lake in central Africa.

The last eminent medieval Muslim geographer was Yakut ibn Abd Allah al-Hamawi, a Greek slave from Anatolia who was educated and given his freedom. Before his death in 1229 Yakut compiled a famous and vast encyclopedia of geographic information. Arranged alphabetically, it summed up the whole fund of knowledge available to him in this field and thus became an invaluable source book for all scholars.

POETRY AND LITERATURE

Poetry was the single most important expression of literature in the Islamic world, although other genres also flourished. In pre-Islamic Arabia poetry was a favorite vehicle of expression. A talented poet was highly esteemed, and the cultured person was one who appreciated fine poetry and could recite an endless quantity of verse. Muhammad found much of this poetry distasteful, since the way of life extolled was not the way of Islam.

The advent of the Umayyad regime set the stage for the return of poetry to its pre-Islamic popularity. The poet Umar (d. 712) wrote with charming grace of free and erotic love in Mecca, and his directness and simplicity influenced generations of Arab poets. Singers and entertainers found his style well suited to their ballads. Lyric poetry reached its height in the Majnun-Laila romance. The author-hero became mad (majnun) because of his burning passion for a woman whose father compelled her to marry another. The deranged lover roamed the world seeking his beloved. Ever after, Majnun was the typical hero of unrequited-love poems throughout the Middle East. In addition, there reappeared in the Umayyad period many writers of eulogistic and epic poetry of the pre-Islamic style. Noted for their erotic language and political invective, these poets pleased their patrons and their poetry revealed the life and morals of the age. Many Umayyad caliphs were themselves poets.

With the coming of the Abbasids, the court moved to Baghdad and the poets followed. Persian influence and rich caliphal patronage introduced an elegance and an openness in sexual matters. One of the first poets in this period was the blind Bashshar ibn Burd (d. 783), whose paeans of love were so popular and so apt for singing that the caliph al-Mahdi had him executed for endangering public morals. The boon companion of Harun al-Rashid was the sparkling and lusty Abu Nuwas (d. 811). Not all poetry, however, dealt with wine, women, and song; much political poetry was also written.

At the court and in wealthy society poetry was on the lips of all, and every elegant household had its poet. The immediate material rewards were great, as was, consequently, the quantity of verse, much of it praising a patron or meant only for the moment. Since the golden days of Baghdad the poetry of that classical age has retained its favored position among educated Arabic-speaking Middle Eastern peoples.

The ballad and folk song developed in Muslim Spain were popularized and spread by wandering minstrels. The epoch of the troubadour in northern Spain, Italy, and France was largely dependent upon this Spanish development; the idealization of the lady and love found in the troubadour songs was a Christian characterization of themes prevalent in Arabic lyrics of the Muslim world.

At the other end of the Muslim world, in the province of Fars and especially in Shiraz, there arose the school of Persian-language poets. Firdawsi, who died in 1020, presented his epic Shahnamah, or book of kings, written in Persian, to the ruler Mahmud of Ghaznah. No poetry has ever stirred the soul of the Iranian people as has Firdawsi's Shahnamah; even today illiterate people recite legends and history from Firdawsi's poetry with great emotion.

The famous Iranian scholar and poet Umar Khayyam wrote a set of quatrains; this Rubaiyat as translated into English, even though often far from the original texts, has come in the west to be popularly regarded as the very best of Middle Eastern poetry. Khayyam's poems beautifully expressed the hope for love accompanied by disillusionment of twelfth-century Nishapur but were merely a side thought of Khayyam, an illustrious mathematician.

Besides Firdawsi, the other poets regarded as truly gifted by Iranians were Nizami (d. 1209), whose romantic stories were exceptionally popular and whose rendition of the Majnun-Laila theme was depicted in countless miniature paintings; Jalal al-Din

Rumi, the mystic poet who founded the Mawlawi (Mevlevi) Sufi order and died at Konya in Anatolia in 1273; Sadi of Shiraz, another mystic whose writings were among the favorite poems of Iran; and the fourteenth-century Hafiz, the master of Persian-language lyricists, a materialist yet a mystic, whose love for the shady gardens, wine and women, and the laughter-loving people of Shiraz was shown in his collection of odes.

The Umayyad period featured letters addressed to the caliphs and others, often written by the newly Arabized bureaucrats and secretaries in Damascus. The Arabic language was thoroughly studied, and its grammar and style were analyzed as many dictionaries were compiled. Under the Abbasids government officials and others composed administrative manuals, collections of biographies, and "mirrors for princes" that were written to inform the young about how to govern. Another literary form was represented by the ninth-century essayist, humorist, and litterateur al-Jahiz of Basrah (d. 869)—a notable and witty example of the cultivated writer of polite and amusing stories who set high standards for subsequent authors.

For the most part, the literature of the medieval Middle East consisted of the writings of men who were famous philosophers, theologians, bureaucrats, geographers, historians, and travelers. They wrote under the patronage of rulers and officials. Prose fiction and advice-to-kings literature were not so highly regarded among the Muslim Arabs; not until the tenth century did Persian contacts influence the general taste to produce Arabic literature of this type. Rhymed prose emphasized elegant form over substance; it was often embellished with unusual words. In Muslim Spain a type of anecdote, frequently introducing a moral lesson through the adventure of some dashing hero, became the prototype of the Spanish picaresque novel. In his rhetorical tales al-Hariri of Basrah (d. 1122), whose works became enormously popular and were often illustrated by miniature painters, subtly criticized the existing social order.

A number of delightful anthologies, treasuries of poetry, literature, and history, serve as invaluable sources for the study of Muslim civilization. An example is the twenty-volume *Book of Songs* gathered by Abu al-Faraj al-Isfahani (d. 967).

Of all the literature of the Middle East the most colorful, fanciful, and noteworthy through many centuries has been the *Arabian Nights.* Taking the core of the stories and names of leading characters from old Indian and Persian tales, al-Jahshiyari in the first half of the tenth century in Iraq blended local color and current episodes and romances of the courts of al-Rashid, al-Mamun, and other caliphs to produce the great *Alf Lailah wa Lailah (One Thousand and One Nights,* known as the *Arabian Nights).* Its present form was achieved in the fourteenth century in Mamluk Egypt. Subsequently translated into other languages than Arabic, it has delighted many children and adults throughout the world, while it also can provide much information on social history.

HISTORY

The Muslims of the Middle East produced a number of notable historians. Political controversies in the early days of the Muslim ummah led to an emphasis on history writing. Shiis were especially active in writing history, as reference to the early history of Islam was crucial to their political and theological positions.

Umayyad historians were largely suppressed by the succeeding Abbasid dynasty. By the middle of the eighth century, historical works, especially biography and genealogy, attracted the attention of Muslim scholars. The most important early biography of the prophet Muhammad was composed by Ibn Ishaq, who died in 767. In the ninth century, accounts of the early battles of Islam, tales of the astonishing Arab Muslim expansion, and biographical dictionaries of historical figures appeared. The two best were those of Ibn Abd al-Hakam (an Egyptian), the story of the conquest of Egypt, North Africa, and Spain, and of al-Baladhuri (an Iranian), a carefully compiled and balanced narrative of Muslim expansion.

The histories produced in the Abbasid era were numerous and varied. Every century and court had professional chroniclers. One of the more noted was al-Tabari (838–923), who traveled widely and studied at many important Muslim centers. A most prolific writer for more than forty years, al-Tabari left a commentary on the Quran but is most noted for his monumental historical chronicle, often used by subsequent generations of historians. His contemporary from Baghdad, the Twelver Shii al-Masudi, dealt with the same material but treated the unfolding of civilizations topically instead of chronologically as al-Tabari had done. Written after years of travel, al-Masudi's work ran to thirty volumes.

Probably the best known of Muslim historians is the Tunisian Ibn Khaldun (1332–1406). A citizen of the Muslim world, he studied and held important political positions in Fez, Granada, Algeria, and Cairo. His history of the Muslim states and peoples, especially the sections about North Africa, was a significant contribution to knowledge. But Ibn Khaldun's fame rested on his history's first volume, entitled *Muqaddimah (Prolegomena),* in which he presented his philosophy of the cyclic development of civilization, social solidarity, and the relationship of nomadic and settled groups, and explained how the historian should record and study the interrelated forces of society. Since he considered climate, geography, economics, and culture as the basic causes of major events, so as to provide lessons and rules about the patterns of history, Ibn Khaldun can be called the first modern historian.

ISLAMIC ART

In the whole field of the decorative arts Muslims in the classical Islamic and early medieval periods advanced the skills and techniques of antiquity in a notable fashion. The Umayyads helped develop an eclectic, experimental, and propagandistic approach to the arts along with basic concepts in designing mosques, palaces, and the applied arts. Abbasid prosperity led to an explosion of artistic creativity. The Abbasid era saw great advances in polychrome painted stucco, the building of enormous mosques, creation of outstanding textiles, innovations in pottery, and the writing of beautiful Qurans in Kufic script.

Far ahead of western Europe in each of the minor arts, at least until the European Renaissance of the fifteenth century, the Middle East produced outstanding rugs, silk and cotton textiles, leatherwork, fine glass, highly glazed ceramics of many types, and exquisite metal pieces in gold, silver, copper, brass, and bronze, many of the pieces heavily inlaid with other metals. The painting of miniature pictures developed into a fine and precise art. Skilled penmanship produced a calligraphy so graceful and so pleasing that it became the predominant decorative art form, with many different decorative and cursive regional styles. Images of living beings were not present in religious buildings, but in secular life they were sometimes depicted. Elaborate arabesque designs based on intricate geometric and vegetal patterns were used in many different media.

Between the seventh and thirteenth centuries, proof of the real unity of the Muslim world was the ease and extent of exchange of knowledge and movement of individuals. Such a circulation dictated a considerable universality of Muslim civilization, and Islamic art is an excellent example. From Spain and North Africa in the west to central Asia in the east, each of the great cities boasted reputable craftsmen and artists in all of the arts who were supported by male and female patrons.

From the foregoing survey of the many aspects of Muslim civilization and its development in the classical Islamic and early medieval periods, it can be seen that Muslim civilization was formed in its most important aspects during the times of the Umayyad and Abbasid empires. In the early medieval period Islamic civilization reached new heights. The Muslims appropriated and adapted from other civilizations and societies valuable ideas, experiences, and skills to create Muslim civilization, while innovative and original contributions were also made by Muslim and non-Muslim artists, writers, and scientists.

Few civilizations have been able to endure for long or to pursue any dynamic course when isolated either geographically or intellectually. Cultural growth is accelerated by the exchange of knowledge among peoples; the greater the exchange, the faster the acceleration. During the Umayyad and Abbasid empires many diverse groups were brought into close contact. Although by the end of the classical Islamic period the power of the central government had greatly lessened, the history of culture and intellectual activity in the early medieval Muslim Middle East reveals a continuing refinement and growth. In the later medieval period of the thirteenth to fifteenth centuries scientific and cultural productivity continued but slowed substantially; cultural development would reach another peak of creativity in the great empires of the early modern period.

REFERENCES

Among the volumes already cited, those of particular value for this chapter are in Chapters 7 and 8.

Ahmad, S. Maqbul: "Djughrafiya." *Encyclopaedia of Islam.* New ed. Vol. 2, pp. 575–587. Leiden: Brill, 1965. A useful survey of geography.

Allen, Roger: *An Introduction to Arabic Literature.* Cambridge: Cambridge University Press, 2000. This abridged version of the author's *Arabic Literary Heritage* (1998) succinctly examines literary tradition, the Quran, poetry, prose, drama, and criticism.

Ashtiany, Julia, et al., eds.: *The Cambridge History of Arabic Literature: 'Abbasid Belles-Lettres.* Cambridge: Cambridge University Press, 1990. Twenty-four chapters on all aspects of literary history.

Beeston, A. F. L., et al.: *The Cambridge History of Arabic Literature: Arabic Literature to the End of the Umayyad Period.* Cambridge: Cambridge University Press, 1983. A thorough study of the subject written by several authors.

Brend, Barbara: *Islamic Art.* Cambridge: Harvard University Press, 1991. Sophisticated analysis of art in each period and region, with many illustrations.

Cooperson, Michael: *Classical Arabic Biography: The Heirs of the Prophets in the Age of al-Ma'mun.* Cambridge: Cambridge University Press, 2000. Critical evaluation and biographies of an Abbasid caliph, a Shii imam, a legal scholar, and a Sufi.

Duri, Abd al-Aziz: *The Rise of Historical Writing among the Arabs.* Edited and translated by Lawrence I. Conrad. Princeton, N.J.: Princeton University Press, 1983. Especially valuable for developments in Medina and Iraq during the seventh, eighth, and ninth centuries.

El-Hibri, Tayeb: *Reinterpreting Islamic Historiography: Harun al-Rashid and the Narrative of the Abbasid Caliphate.* Cambridge: Cambridge University Press, 2000. Discusses the sources for, and the reigns and personalities of, al-Rashid, al-Amin, al-Mamun, and al-Mutawakkil.

Grabar, Oleg: *The Formation of Islamic Art.* Rev. ed. New Haven, Conn.: Yale University Press, 1987. A very sensitive, thought-provoking, and outstanding treatment of the subject.

al-Hassan, Ahmad Y. , and Donald R. Hill: *Islamic Technology: An Illustrated History.* Cambridge: Cambridge University Press, 1986. One of the very few works on this topic—although written by specialists it is accessible to beginners in the field.

Hillenbrand, Robert: *Islamic Art and Architecture.* New York: Thames and Hudson, 1999. This profusely illustrated book is a good place to begin when reading about Islamic art and architecture.

Humphreys, R. Stephen: *Islamic History: A Framework for Inquiry.* Rev. ed. Princeton, N.J.: Princeton University Press, 1991. An outstanding introduction to the sources and problems of Middle Eastern history from 600 to 1500, and an excellent guide to further reading.

Irwin, Robert: *The Arabian Nights: A Companion.* London: Allen Lane, 1994. The best introduction to the stories and their context.

Islamic Arts and Architecture Organization: www.islamicart.com. This site features discussions of Islamic coins, rugs, wood and metal objects, and the decorative arts.

Khalidi, Tarif: *Arabic Historical Thought in the Classical Period.* Cambridge: Cambridge University Press, 1994. Perceptive essays on historiography from the eighth to the fourteenth century.

Kraemer, Joel L.: *Humanism in the Renaissance of Islam: The Cultural Revival during the Buyid Age.* Leiden: Brill, 1986. Buyid political history is related to religious and cultural life.

Kritzeck, James: *Anthology of Islamic Literature from the Rise of Islam to Modern Times.* New York: Holt, Rinehart and Winston, 1964. Discusses all forms of literature from the Quran and early commentaries to political theory, history, stories, and Ottoman puppet plays.

Leaman, Oliver: *An Introduction to Medieval Islamic Philosophy.* Cambridge: Cambridge University Press, 1985. Al-Farabi, Ibn Sina, al-Ghazali, Ibn Rushd, and Maimonides on the creation of the world, immortality, God's knowledge of particulars, ethics, and happiness.

McNeill, William H., and Marilyn Waldman, eds.: *The Islamic World.* New York: Oxford University Press, 1973. Original sources in translation, dealing with poetry, history, literature, and so on.

Morrison, George, Julian Baldick, and Shafii Kadkani: *History of Persian Literature from the Beginning of the Islamic Period to the Present Day.* Leiden: Brill, 1981.

Nasr, Seyyed Hossein: *Science and Civilization in Islam.* Cambridge: Harvard University Press, 1968. A discussion of the development of science, technology, and scientific methodology in medieval Islam.

Rahman, Fazlur: *Health and Medicine in the Islamic Tradition: Change and Identity.* New York: Crossroad, 1987. Very readable general account of religion and medicine; emphasizes earlier time periods.

Turner, Howard R.: *Science in Medieval Islam: An Illustrated Introduction.* Austin: University of Texas Press, 1997. A readable and useful survey of Islamic philosophy, mathematics, astronomy, geography, and medicine.

Ullmann, Manfred: *Islamic Medicine.* Edinburgh: Edinburgh University Press, 1978. Brief review of translations of medical works, and of physiology, anatomy, pathology, disease transmission, dietetics, and the occult.

Young, M. J. L., et al., eds.: *The Cambridge History of Arabic Literature: Religion, Learning and Science in the 'Abbasid Period.* Cambridge: Cambridge University Press, 1990. Superb essays on a wide variety of cultural fields.

CHAPTER 10

Social Patterns

By the end of the early Abbasid period in the middle of the tenth century, Islamic civilization in the Middle East gradually had evolved certain social patterns that became associated with political, religious, economic, and cultural institutions to form a long-lasting synthesis. These patterns involved a number of groups and issues, such as the role of women in society and gender relationships. The places and buildings in which people lived and the ways they earned their livelihood also profoundly influenced the social history of the era. Keys to understanding social patterns were the education and recreation available for the population.

While some information is available about these subjects, relatively little is known about the life of the bulk of the population, who lived in the countryside in villages, or about the smaller number of people who earned their living by herding animals as nomads. Most historical accounts dealt with city people and chiefly the prominent male individuals among them. Social patterns also differed from region to region as well as from era to era. Tracing significant changes and then relating the patterns of social history to political, religious, economic, and cultural events is extremely difficult to do.

THE ROLES OF WOMEN AND MEN

Unfortunately, very little is known about the history of most women in the classical Islamic period, but it does seem clear that by the tenth century the role of wealthy and middle-class urban women in the family and in society had undergone a marked change from earlier times. Veiling, seclusion of upper-class urban women in a harem, and the general segregation of women from men were practiced by Muslims and by many non-Muslims in the Middle East. The origins of these practices and the reasons for their introduction are not certain, but indications point to Byzantine civilization as the main influence. Initially only the wives of the prophet Muhammad were secluded, but gradually this pattern of living became more widespread. Most people placed a high value on privacy and society became highly patriarchal.

Some urban women still shopped for goods, and Muslim women who were escorted by male relatives continued to make the pilgrimage. With the general and wide acceptance of concubinage, the rank of the actual wife was greatly elevated, though elevated rank did not translate to greater freedom. On the contrary: slave girls might sing, dance, and entertain quite openly and freely for the guests of their masters, but not wives. Thus, the veil and seclusion grew as a protection and a mark of distinction, although these institutions were also, paradoxically, an indication of the subordinate status of women.

Both men and women were obliged by religious values to dress modestly. Clothing often reflected social, class, ethnic, and regional variations as well as gender differences, but a fairly standard Islamic clothing system emerged by Abbasid times. Clothes for women and men consisted primarily of one or more undergarments, such as a body shirt or a dress, and one or more overgarments, such as a coat or mantle, plus sandals and a head covering. Abbasid males adopted the caftan, a robe that included sleeves and buttons down the front, from earlier Persian styles. In the early medieval period new garments, especially headgear, reflected increasing social stratification, while in later medieval times rulers in Egypt tended to enforce, more strictly, requirements for religious minorities to wear distinctive clothing or symbols. Governing elites used embroidered robes of honor as gifts for prominent men.

The freedom and the public role of women such as enjoyed by Aishah, the wife of Muhammad, and in early Abbasid times by Khaizuran and Zubaidah, lessened. The social segregation of the sexes encouraged the widespread expression of male homosexuality, which was often celebrated in verse, even though condemned by theologians. Al-Wathiq, an Abbasid caliph, devoted much of his poetry to a male lover. Muslims also condemned prostitution, adultery, and suicide; people engaged in prostitution and adultery were subject to rigorous punishments, sometimes including death.

Despite gender segregation, women appeared in courts, where their testimony was accepted, though it carried less weight than that of men. The legal status of Muslim women varied in part according to which one of the Sunni schools of law they and their families followed; Hanafis were particularly open to interpretations that favored the status of women. In accordance with religious law, a woman's share in an estate was usually only about one-half that of a man. It seems likely that in some cases male-dominated families denied women their due rights so as to reduce the splintering effect of the division of estates or simply because of greed.

Women's roles in society were affected by the practice of birth control, through both contraception and abortion. Scientific, legal, and popular literature was written on the subject, and the authors assumed a free wife could choose to avoid contraception so as to have children, if she wished, while the rights of a slave wife were somewhat limited, and those of a concubine in this area were nil. The ulama, or men of religion, differed on the issue of abortion, with some holding that abortion during the first four months of pregnancy was permitted, while the majority held that it should not take place at all unless the life of the mother was threatened. Women and men regarded childbearing, and particularly having sons, as a way of improving the social status of individual women and benefiting the family's future economic situation.

Most men and women entered into marriages during their teenage years; chastity before marriage was socially expected. Families would usually consult with matchmakers to arrange marriages. If one marriage partner died, remarriage usually took place in a short time, since widows and especially widowed mothers of young children would often be poor. Marriage was a legal contract and was governed by religious laws. Society expected that women would obey their husbands, but actual practice in this and many areas of gender relations must have varied widely depending on economic status and personal tastes, abilities, and preferences. While Muslim men could theoretically marry as many as four wives at one time if they treated each wife equally, in practice very few men were polygamous. Only rich men could afford the expenses involved in marrying and maintaining several wives.

Although men were legally dominant in marriage, women retained the marriage settlement as their own property in the event of a divorce, which could be instituted by the husband or, very rarely, by the wife. Divorce was viewed as abhorrent and a last resort for couples. Marriages were arranged and contracted between individuals or families of roughly equal status; the marriage of a Muslim woman to a non-Muslim man was uniformly opposed by the legal scholars. Prestige in marriage seemingly came chiefly from the man's family, but the status of the woman's family also influenced the esteem enjoyed by the couple. Families were the central unit of society, and for most people loyalty to the family was far more important than the loyalty owed to any other social group.

Women could and did own property; however, the management of real estate and commercial investments was sometimes difficult because of social restrictions on women. Many occupations were limited entirely to men, including such important posts as judges, clerks, and soldiers. Usually women worked inside the home; peasant women probably also worked in some capacities in the fields, and nomadic women helped with the herds. Urban women were employed as servants, entertainers, midwives, and perhaps as assistants to males engaged in craft production. Men often passed on their skills to related females, so, for instance, in a family of calligraphers one would occasionally find women who became expert writers. Urban women worked with other women, serving as brokers of goods to households, religious teachers for women, secretaries, and professional mourners at funerals. Many women worked in spinning and weaving textiles and in food preparation, for instance as bakers.

Some wealthy women established endowed family charitable foundations (awqaf; singular, waqf). Women members of the Ayyubid dynasty in twelfth-century Damascus and Aleppo commissioned numerous religious buildings, including schools and Sufi gathering places. Perhaps about one-third of all awqaf were established by women.

Some women, including female religious scholars and teachers, became prominent despite the difficulties placed in their way. Examples include the eighth-century celibate mystic Rabiah al-Adawiyyah of Basrah (d. 801), who was one of the most influential of the early mystics and ascetics. In later times other famous Sufis were women. Several female poets gained some renown, especially the eleventh-century Spanish Umayyad princess Walladah. Some women were included in biographical lists: at least 400 of 1000 women mentioned in an Egyptian biographical treatise had studied Islam by memorizing the Quran, working with a scholar, learning hadith, and receiving a certificate of completing a course of study. Shii Muslims placed great emphasis on the devotional role of Fatimah, daughter of the prophet Muhammad and wife of the caliph Ali. Asma al-Dajai (d. 1498), a female alim in Yemen, was a Quran reciter, a recounter of the hadith of the prophet Muhammad, and an expounder of the meaning of religion. She mostly taught other women, but even a local male ruler consulted her. More frequent, though still rare compared with the total number of women in society, were the female students who sought instruction from male and female teachers of religion, although outside the higher institutions of learning, whose formal students were exclusively males.

A few women who influenced the politics of various Muslim Middle Eastern states will be discussed in later chapters. Exceptionally, two queens who were members of the Shii Sulayhid dynasty in Yemen ruled in the eleventh and twelfth centuries. Women played a relatively large role in pre-Islamic Turkish groups and this pattern of behavior may have carried over to Muslim Turkish dynasties in the Middle East and northern India, where several women actually ruled. More often, though, women played an influential role behind the scenes, sometimes acting as regents for their male children.

CITIES AND MOSQUES

The peasants who lived in villages constituted the majority of the population in most parts of the Middle East. It was the villagers, along with the animal-raising nomads, who jointly provided the agricultural surplus of production above consumption that fed the cities. Villagers and nomads themselves needed some goods and services from the cities and the skilled craftsmen who lived in them, so there were mutual interchanges among all three locales. And some people worked and lived in intermediate ways, including those who resided in settled villages and then in other parts of the year moved with herds of animals from one grazing place to another, city-based traders who visited both villagers and the nomads who came to marketplaces, and nomads who might occasionally live for periods of time in the outskirts of cities. Trading and marketing provided an economic base supplemented by artisanal handicraft production in the cities. Urban-based government, religion, and culture also provided services, including education and law, while extracting resources from the countryside.

In the larger cities of the Islamic Middle East general patterns for organizing work and living existed across the area, although to refer to these frequently found characteristics as constituting "the Islamic city" implies more uniformity than actually existed. Almost all cities were walled, for instance, and most cities were organized into quarters or districts, often named after the chief market in the vicinity or after a local mosque or Sufi saint's tomb. The incidence of epidemic diseases in cities was very high, with the plague sometimes carrying off one-quarter of the population, as in Basrah in 749. Gender segregation and Islamic laws affecting ownership of property also helped shape common urban characteristics. Middle Eastern cities were administered directly by the central government with few local corporate institutions, so city-states or urban republics did not exist. Yet despite these and many other similarities, differences also existed, as, for instance, between relatively new cities such as Cairo (founded in 969) and much older cities such as Damascus.

Residential areas with a few hundred or a few thousand people were the norm, and they had a strong sense of local identity that was reinforced by a mutual responsibility for maintaining law and order. While the poor lived in huts, middle-income people lived either in apartment buildings of three or more stories or in separate homes usually built around courtyards. Homes were designed so as to provide maximum privacy; they generally contained little furniture. Religious and ethnic minorities and new immigrants to the city tended to live in separate areas, but a wide variation in housing patterns could exist, where people of varying backgrounds would live side by side. Craftsmen and shopkeepers who dealt in similar goods usually worked in the same neighborhood. Differences in status were reflected in style of housing but also in clothing, by which a person's religion, gender, and standing in life often could be judged visually.

Skills were passed from one generation to the next and the units of production were small, with only a few larger factories employing animal power or sometimes water power. New occupations emerged as the division of labor increased and economic prosperity created a thriving economy, but technological and administrative changes originating in one place diffused at only a slow rate throughout the Middle East. Crafts differed in prestige, with some occupations such as tanning leather regarded as obnoxious because of the smells associated with the work, while others such as working in precious metals carried greater social approval. Since streets were winding and narrow, so as to provide shade from the sun and to keep the size of the city within its walls small, porters (as well as donkeys) carried goods from one place to another. Many poor people had no permanent employment, while the rich and powerful enjoyed extraordinary luxuries.

Government, soldiers, and rulers usually resided outside the city center in fortified and somewhat isolated palaces and compounds. A web of interests linked the governing elite to the city people; each needed the other. Some examples of this interdependence included the ruler's need for urban tax revenues and the merchants' need for market inspectors to regulate business. Intermediary officials between the rulers and people facilitated communication and the maintenance of order. Leaders of city quarters, the heads of guilds, representatives of the Christian or Jewish minorities, spokesmen for the merchants, and prominent ulama all put forward the respective needs and desires of the rulers to the people, and the requests and complaints of the people to the rulers.

Muslims of all backgrounds and occupations often went to worship in mosques. The first mosque was none other than the house of Muhammad in Medina, which resembled the typical house of the town Arab in Muhammad's time—a simple enclosure, usually square, with a few huts along the edge. Before he died it assumed a public character, for here the followers congregated to pray with Muhammad. Along one side palm trunks were set up and covered with palm leaves as a protection from the sun. Muhammad stood on a piece of a palm trunk so as to be heard. A pointer indicated the direction of Mecca so that prayers could be made facing the Holy City. Bilal, an early follower of Muhammad, stood upon a rooftop to call the Muslims to prayer. Thus were established the essentials of a mosque.

As the Arab Muslims expanded into other lands, they employed local craftsmen in the building of mosques. Consequently, techniques and materials differed from place to place. But the fundamentals of a congregational mosque remained unchanged. A large part of the mosque area was an open courtyard, usually with a fountain where ablutions could be performed and sometimes with a narrow covered arcade on three sides. On the fourth side was the mosque proper. In most mosques in Iraq, Syria, Egypt, North Africa, and Spain, the mosque proper consisted of a system of arches supported by piers or columns arranged in series of parallel aisles and upholding domes, vaults, and a roof. Where the dome covered a square chamber or area, a transition from the arch was necessary. Stilted and horseshoe arches appeared early in the development of Islamic architecture, largely because the available cut columns taken from older structures were not long enough to hold the roof at the desired height. At Cordoba this problem was met by using a series of columns and arches superimposed upon another series.

At one or more of the corners of the enclosure there stood a minaret, a square tower-like structure from which the call to prayer was given. Round or pencil-shaped minarets did not develop until late in the medieval period, although circular ziggurat-type minarets are known to have existed in ninth-century Iraq and Iran.

In the wall of the mosque on the side toward Mecca a mihrab, or niche, was constructed to indicate the exact direction of the Holy City. This was particularly helpful in converted churches, since they were often not correctly oriented. A pulpit (minbar) was a necessary piece of furniture of a congregational mosque, enabling the person who delivered the Friday sermon to be seen and heard by all. The façade encasing the main entrance of the mosque enclosure, as well as the inner façade around the doorway to the mosque itself, in time was elaborately decorated, taking on the appearance of an external mihrab. Semidomes, vaults, marble paneling, and molding surrounded these entrances and made peerless approaches for the mosques. In Iran and the east some mosques had unusually lofty and imposing portals. The prevalence of the distinctive stalactite or honeycomb vault occurred in the late eleventh century.

The exterior and interior decoration of the mosques was based upon matched and quartered panels of marble and other types of stone, different-colored stones being used in alternate courses in the walls. Spaces were often covered with finely carved geometric and floral patterns; in many instances the walls were given color, warmth, and depth by the use of plain or figured tiles. One of the most frequent and pleasing patterns employed in stone, wood, or ceramics was that composed of highly stylized Arabic letters, almost invariably a verse from the Quran. Human and animal figures almost never appeared in a mosque, although human figures were depicted in palaces and in book manuscripts.

Some of the imposing mosques of the Middle East that date from the classical Islamic period are the Umayyad mosque of Damascus, begun in 706; the Mosque of Ibn Tulun in Cairo, finished in 879; the Great Mosque of Qairawan, built about 836; the Great Mosque of Cordoba, begun in 785 (now the cathedral); and the Friday Mosque of Isfahan, built about 760 but much changed at later times. Although it is not a mosque, probably the most widely known sacred building in the Muslim Middle East is the revered Dome of the Rock in Jerusalem. A ringlike structure, it was begun about 685 by the Umayyad caliph Abd al-Malik to cover and enshrine the spot from where Muhammad made his nocturnal journey to heaven; it is also close to the spot where the Jewish temple had stood in antiquity. The Dome of the Rock comprises an octagon surmounted by a dome that rests upon an interior circle of piers and columns. The space between the inner circle and the octagonal wall was too wide to be spanned by beams, necessitating an intermediate octagon of arches borne by piers and columns. Thus were formed two rings that were used for ceremonial circumambulation. Originally the upper part of the exterior was covered with mosaics, but these were replaced with decorated tiles. The style of the building was a composite of Syrian, Roman, and Byzantine traditions and contained a number of novel adaptations. The style, however, was followed in later Muslim architecture only in technical and decorative details and not as a general model for other structures.

In the east the Ghaznavid and the Seljuk dynasties in the early medieval period used mud brick or baked brick to rapidly build monumental structures, usually decorated with stucco or stone, including mosques with a courtyard surrounded by four vaulted niches framing a portal. The dramatic height of the portals and niches contrasted with the smaller proportions of the courtyard at ground level. Mausoleums were usually square chambers covered by domes; they also came in the form of tomb towers, towers with conical roofs.

Although mosques and great mausoleums have been the most permanent of Middle Eastern buildings of the classical and early medieval period, various books contain descriptions of numerous libraries, hospitals, bazaars, palaces, forts, shrines, and public baths in Baghdad and other cities. One of the most famous, enduring, and beautiful of the palaces was the Alhambra of Granada, Spain. Begun in the thirteenth century, the fortified residential palace became world-renowned for its luxurious gardens, spectacular views, and sumptuous decorations. Some of these structures were open for all to visit, but many were intended solely for the wealthy patrons who constructed and maintained them. In any case, few peasants or nomads visited such urban sites.

EDUCATION

Formal education was similarly linked primarily to the cities, although much training and exchange of information took place informally in the family, while working on the job as apprentices, and in social institutions and organizations. In the early days of the Muslim ummah, the ruling Arabs held that a man was educated if he learned the basics of religion, to read and write, to use the bow and arrow, and to swim. A man should be taught courage, endurance, justice, hospitality, honesty, and generosity, while women were expected to attain skills relating to the household as well as the basics of the faith. By the opening of the eighth century most leading Muslims employed tutors or owned slaves to teach their children. The only education available for the masses was that obtained from Quran readers in the mosques.

In the Abbasid period, the number of elementary private schools increased, so that many children, especially in the cities, were taught to read and write. The curriculum centered on the Quran, allied religious texts, and Arabic grammar, and memory achievement was the goal. Children of wealthy and prominent families continued to get rigorous and comprehensive individual instruction. It was still not easy to acquire an advanced education, although to make one's way about the Muslim world in quest of great teachers was less arduous than in earlier days. Various study groups, academies, and mosques where one could study existed, some with waqf charitable endowments, but they were unorganized and did not furnish any systematic education. Children began systematic study inside the family or as apprentices at an early age, perhaps around eight years old; when urban children ultimately mastered a given craft, skill, or book of knowledge the supervising instructor or master craftsman issued the student or apprentice a certificate.

One of the most famous of the Islamic institutions for advanced study was al-Azhar in Cairo, founded by the Fatimids in the latter part of the tenth century. Through the centuries al-Azhar maintained a reputation for scholarship and a high quality of education, especially in the fields of theology and law, which it still has to this day. College-mosques often provided residential facilities for students and teachers. Sufi groups had separate educational locations, where mystics studied traditions, their own approach to law, and the mystical path to knowledge. A bureau for translation, a library, and an observatory in the Abbasid caliph al-Mamun's House of Wisdom in Baghdad served as a kind of collegiate institution, while libraries were widespread throughout the cities of Islam.

The honor of creating one of the first centers of learning in the east fell to Nizam al-Mulk, the ingenious eleventh-century vizir for the Seljuk dynasty. His Nizamiyah in Baghdad, intended as a private institution to teach Shafiis religion, was part of a trend that led throughout the Muslim world to construction of many madrasahs—schools for higher education chiefly in religion and law. In the leading cities of the Middle East, near each of the larger mosques, eventually there were privately organized and funded madrasahs, where religious and legal subjects predominated. Waqf pious foundations provided the money to support teachers and students. Professorial chairs were endowed, and fellowships were granted to advanced students. Philosophy, mathematics, medicine, and the natural sciences were taught in the homes of scholars, bookstores, hospitals, and sometimes in the madrasahs as auxiliary to religious subjects. Despite the popularity of the madrasahs, education continued to be available in many other settings, including homes, mosques, study groups, and religious festivals.

Rote learning and an emphasis upon the transmission of knowledge without much questioning until one mastered approved approaches to issues predominated—as in most educational establishments elsewhere throughout the ages. But the need to acquire dialectical skills and to defend viewpoints while deriving legal opinions encouraged analysis and synthesis for some thinkers. The obligation to show the relation between the ideas they imparted and the ethical and social requirements of society was recognized by noted Muslim teachers.

RECREATION

The great mass of people in the medieval Middle East, as in all other regions and in other periods except for the present, had little time or energy for higher education or for recreation and entertainment. However, people of moderate means, including villagers, nomads, and city people alike, could enjoy certain kinds of recreation, while other types were in practice reserved for the urban wealthy and the elite. Among the more widely accessible were poetry and some kinds of music.

Although many religiously oriented people criticized music, which was often associated with moral laxity, song and music from various instruments were exceedingly popular. Chanting the Quran was a valued skill. Religious poetry was often sung, and sometimes it was accompanied by musical instruments, especially among the Sufi mystics. In secular arenas, and in particular at the courts of rulers, accomplished musicians were praised, highly rewarded, and accepted as companions in high society. Slaves with musical talent and training commanded high prices. The elite themselves sometimes performed, and the Abbasid caliph al-Rashid's brother Ibrahim was regarded as a truly accomplished musician. Musical theorists included many prominent thinkers such as al-Farabi, al-Jahiz, al-Masudi, and al-Ghazali, who have already been discussed in Chapter 9 in other connections. The principles of performance and composition were based on improvising; dividing into clear internal units; repetitively reformulating earlier motifs, phrases, and sections; following a single melodic line; using few long notes; and constructing short but seemingly infinite patterns of musical expression. Performers used a wide variety of instruments such as the short-necked lute, flute, drums, and fiddles.

Upper-class urban men and women, separately, relaxed at home or at a public bath that served as their club, open for the sexes on alternating days. Baghdad in its heyday boasted several thousand such establishments. After soaking and steaming and a vigorous massage the patron might sip cool sherbet, listen to music, and engage in a game of dice, backgammon, or chess. Inside the home chess and playing cards were used for recreation. Chess was an ancient Indian game that came to Christian Europe by way of Iran and the Muslims. Playing cards also came from India to the Middle East, probably around 1300.

Outdoor sports were many; favorites were archery, javelin throwing, fencing, polo, and a ball game that may have been the ancestor of tennis. Hunting, with its allied sports of hawking and falconry, was much in vogue in the Umayyad and Abbasid eras, and later as well. The art of falconry was greatly refined, and there were numerous books on the subject. Caliphs and generals organized great hunts in which thousands participated in driving the game into confined quarters where the hunters could shoot the quarry without much effort. However, certain wild game at close range frequently provided a dangerous sport, as depicted in painting and ceramic decoration.

The most royal of all sports in the Middle East was horse racing. In ancient times, racing was the sport of kings and the favorite of the masses. The Arabs loved and prized horses, and the Muslim rulers quickly took to racing their horses in Syria, Iraq, and Egypt. Caliphs had their own stables, and al-Rashid apparently took great pleasure in seeing his horses win their races. Betting accompanied horse racing, as it did other sports, and made the races and games more exciting. Pedigrees and an interest in the breeding of horses advanced to the point where Arabian horses were recognized and valued throughout the Muslim world.

While only the rich could engage directly in such activities, everyone had to eat, and dining provided a form of recreation when family members and friends visited each other. Picnics were a particularly frequent pastime. Rural and provincial town cuisines were imported into the governing centers, and new delicacies soon became known throughout the whole region. The earliest still extant Islamic-era cookbook dates from about 800. Professional chefs working for the rich prepared lamb, chicken, game, and fish, especially by stewing; many vegetables and fruits were served; and a variety of spices were employed. The key foods for the poor were wheat bread, olive oil, and vegetables.

AGRICULTURE

Most of the first Muslims in the Hijaz were not farmers; however, intensive and irrigated agriculture was widespread in parts of Yemen and Oman, areas that contributed many soldiers to the Muslim armies and settlers in the newly conquered empire. In the rich agricultural lands of Iraq, Syria, and Egypt, the Muslims quickly came to appreciate the methods needed to efficiently cultivate the soil. As the native populations of these provinces and other fertile areas (such as Spain and Khurasan) were converted to Islam, Muslims were engaged directly in agriculture. Accordingly, the governing classes, the landowners, and the actual farmers or peasants all were concerned with agricultural progress. Most peasants had little margin for experimentation, however, because of their poverty; sharecroppers were especially poor because much of the profit of their operation went to landowners, who often provided seeds as well as the right to farm the land.

In the Middle East in Islamic times, the prime factor in agriculture has been water; the need for irrigation increased as new crops were introduced that required water in the summer when little rain fell. Problems of irrigation and canal building were public issues, and everywhere rulers paid attention to digging, reopening, and repairing water channels. Under Muslim governments gardens flourished, with many different plants, vegetables, and fruit trees being propagated. Rulers often sought to acquire new plants, and Arab manuals on farming and botany were written. The Arabs had known numerous varieties of dates, and families treasured their own species with favored qualities of flavor, sweetness, and moisture. The same interest and care were given to other produce of the land as Islam spread into new areas and new crops were grown, mainly fruit trees, grains, and vegetables.

Agricultural productivity rose with higher-yielding crops and more specialized land use, including greater development in rotation of crops, labor-intensive methods, and a summer growing season. The agricultural surplus became so great it could support much larger rural and urban populations.

Cultivators were interested in improving the quality, cash value, and variety of their crops, and they took specimens wherever they went. Many crops were introduced from India through sailors and merchants from Oman and Yemen who carried knowledge of irrigation technology as well as seeds and cuttings from South Asia to the Middle East. On pilgrimages to Mecca, and on other travels, people exchanged information on agriculture. Thus, the best varieties of plants were distributed far and wide. The cultivation of cotton, sugarcane, apricots, peaches, and rice was introduced even as far as Spain on the distant edge of the Islamic world. Spanish authors produced many treatises on agriculture; one of the best-known and most beautiful gardens of the world was near the Alhambra. The technique of controlled pollenization was known and frequently practiced with special and prized varieties of the date palm and fruit trees. European Crusaders learned to value Middle Eastern agriculture and acquired a taste for many of its products. Yet it was largely through Sicily, Spain, and Cyprus that agricultural knowledge and skills slowly passed to Christian Europe.

The patterns of social activity that had appeared by the end of the classical Islamic period around 950 were further elaborated and developed during the early medieval era, when new political and military structures reshaped the public life of the Muslim community.

REFERENCES

References cited in Chapters 4 through 9 contain material pertinent to this chapter as well.

Abu-Lughod, Janet: "The Islamic City—Historic Myth, Islamic Essence, and Contemporary Relevance." *International Journal of Middle East Studies* 19 (1987): 155–176. After a considered evaluation of methodological debates, the basic nature of cities is discussed.

Ahmed, Leila: *Women and Gender in Islam: Historical Roots of a Modern Debate.* New Haven, Conn.: Yale University Press, 1992. An excellent, balanced view of the topic, valuable especially for its discussion of Egypt.

Ahsan, Muhammad Manazir: *Social Life under the Abbasids, 170–289 A.H.* 786–902 *A.D.* London: Longman, 1979. The author examines costume, food, housing, hunting, games, and festivals, and gives many specific examples.

Creswell, K. A. C., and James W. Allan: *A Short Account of Early Muslim Architecture.* Rev. ed. Aldershot, England: Scolar, 1989. A detailed survey of Creswell's earlier works, covering Umayyad and Abbasid days.

Ettinghausen, Richard, and Oleg Grabar: *The Art and Architecture of Islam: 650–1250.* New York: Penguin, 1987. Specialized analysis with many valuable illustrations.

al Faruqi, Ismail, and Lois Lamya al Faruqi: *The Cultural Atlas of Islam.* New York: Macmillan, 1986. Broad coverage of nearly all aspects of culture and history makes this work a useful introduction to many topics.

Goitein, S. D.: *A Mediterranean Society: An Abridgement in One Volume.* Revised and edited by Jacob Lassner. Berkeley: University of California Press, 1999. This summary of the six-volume original monumental work of scholarship studies the life of Jews in the Arab world for the eleventh through the thirteenth centuries, but also illustrates general social, gender, and economic history.

Hambly, Gavin R. G., ed.: *Women in the Medieval Islamic World: Power, Patronage, and Piety.* New York: St. Martin's Press, 1998. Includes specialized studies of medieval women as well as those living in later times in Iran, the Ottoman Empire, and India.

Makdisi, George: *The Rise of Colleges: Institutions of Learning in Islam and the West.* Edinburgh: Edinburgh University Press, 1981. Includes the role of religion, curricula, students, the position of professors, and a variety of aspects of the topic.

Musallam, B. F.: *Sex and Society in Islam: Birth Control before the Nineteenth Century.* Cambridge: Cambridge University Press, 1983. A valuable and unusual study of an often neglected subject.

Nashat, Guity, and Judith E. Tucker: *Women in the Middle East and North Africa: Restoring Women to History.* Bloomington: Indiana University Press, 1999. An outstanding survey from antiquity to the present and the best beginning point for reading about the topic.

Roded, Ruth: *Women in Islamic Biographical Collections.* Boulder, Colo.: Lynne Rienner, 1994. An essential discussion of Muslim women from early Islam to about 1500.

Shatzmiller, Maya: *Labour in the Medieval Islamic World.* Leiden: Brill, 1994. This study of occupations illustrates the economic history of the Arab lands from the early Islamic empires up to the fifteenth century.

Stanton, Charles Michael: *Higher Learning in Islam: The Classical Period, A.D. 700–1300.* Savage, Md.: Rowan and Littlefield, 1990. A clear introduction to contents and methods of education.

Stillman, Yedida Kalfon: *Arab Dress, A Short History: From the Dawn of Islam to Modern Times.* Edited by Norman A. Stillman. Leiden: Brill, 2000. An important work for the social history of women and men, including illustrations.

Waines, David: *In a Caliph's Kitchen.* London: Riad El-Rayyes, 1989. Entertaining analysis enlivens a short book of medieval recipes.

Walther, Wiebke: *Women in Islam.* Updated edition. Princeton, N.J.: Markus Wiener, 1993. Emphasizes art, poetry, and social history.

Watson, Andrew M.: *Agricultural Innovation in the Early Islamic World: The Diffusion of Crops and Farming Techniques, 700–1100.* Cambridge: Cambridge University Press, 1983. A significant breakthrough in research on Islamic agriculture, this work is crucial reading.

Wright, J. W., Jr., and Everett K. Rowson, eds.: *Homoeroticism in Classical Arabic Literature.* New York: Columbia University Press, 1997. Eight essays on aspects of male homosexual literature.

CHAPTER 11

The Early Medieval Middle East

The early medieval Middle East from 950 to 1250 was marked by political fragmentation. Even before 950, local dynasties of Muslim rulers had emerged in many parts of the Abbasid Empire. After 950 the Abbasid caliphs still ruled in Baghdad but only in name; real power there was in the hands of the Buyid dynasty. However, the unity of newly emerging Islamic civilization and social patterns preserved a sense of common identity for the ummah despite political fragmentation and military divisions. The Abbasids lost their power while keeping a kind of prestige basically because the territories they controlled were too large and diverse to be ruled centrally, given the technology of the age, and because they could not find a means of keeping the support of the Muslim community. An enormous gap developed between the Islamic ideals of political life and the reality of government, a gap that neither Sunni nor Shii rulers could easily close.

A bewildering series of successor states to the Abbasids was sometimes more successful in providing a government suitable to local conditions than had been the all-encompassing empires of the Umayyads and the Abbasids. Power fell into the hands of regional dynasties that were often drawn from or based upon foreign military groups, converts to Islam, and aliens to the vast majority of the people whose lives they controlled. Regional rulers exercised nearly absolute power in return for upholding Islam, the shariah, and the prerogatives of the ulama. Political legitimacy based on Islam became stronger in this era as conversion accelerated in the countryside, where Muslims now became the majority of the population. While most people withdrew from public life, the new Islamic civilization flourished despite political diversity bordering on chaos. Not until the appearance of the Ottoman Turks and the Safavids in the sixteenth century did the Middle East again experience large and centralized Muslim empires that reunited political, military, and cultural accomplishments on the scale of the Umayyads and Abbasids.

Muslim successor states in the early medieval period should be seen not only in comparison to the enormous empires that preceded and followed them but also in their own terms. The accomplishments of many regional dynasties particularly set off the early medieval period from the somewhat lesser achievements of the late medieval era after about 1250. Comparisons of the early medieval period in the Middle East with the

Periodization in the History of the Islamic Middle East

Antiquity: from the rise of civilization to the coming of Islam

Classical Islamic period: from the life of the prophet Muhammad to the middle of the tenth century C.E.

The early medieval era in the Middle East: from about 950 to about 1250

The late medieval era in the Middle East: from about 1250 to about 1500

The early modern Middle East: from about 1500 to about 1800

The modern Middle East: from about 1800 to the present

medieval period in western and central Europe are also useful, but it is important to note that the characteristics that define early and late medieval times for the Islamic Middle East differed somewhat from the structures of medieval European history.

SPAIN AND NORTH AFRICA

In the eleventh century, resurgent Christian Spain began a long and difficult series of campaigns that finally ended in 1492 with the capitulation of the ruler of Granada, the last Muslim prince in Spain. Sardinia, Sicily, and Malta also fell to Christian rule in the eleventh century.

Two Muslim dynasties in Spain and North Africa resisted the Christian advance. Also in the middle of the eleventh century a reformist and fundamentalist religious-military-tribal group, the Murabit dynasty (Almoravids), conquered western Algeria, Morocco, and southern Spain and established Marrakesh and Seville as their capitals. The Murabits governed with the support of the Maliki ulama and the military backing of the Berber tribes. When Christians began to take districts in Spain from the Murabits, their legitimacy declined while their dogmatism offended many Muslims. Murabits in the twelfth century were replaced by the Muwahhids, a band of Muslim Berber reformers originating in Morocco. The founder of the Muwahhids claimed to be the Mahdi (the expected deliverer), and he reinforced this religious claim with tribal military alliances. His successor, Abd al-Mumin (r. 1130–1163), destroyed the Murabits and conquered part of Spain. Responding to the Norman expansion from Sicily into North Africa, he gained control of Algeria and Tunisia, and took Tripoli in Libya. He then established the principle of succession to power through dynastic inheritance within his family, and thereby transformed the nature of the state. The Muwahhids became patrons of philosophers. They united most of northwestern Africa economically, providing prosperity and the basis for considerable accomplishment in architecture and the

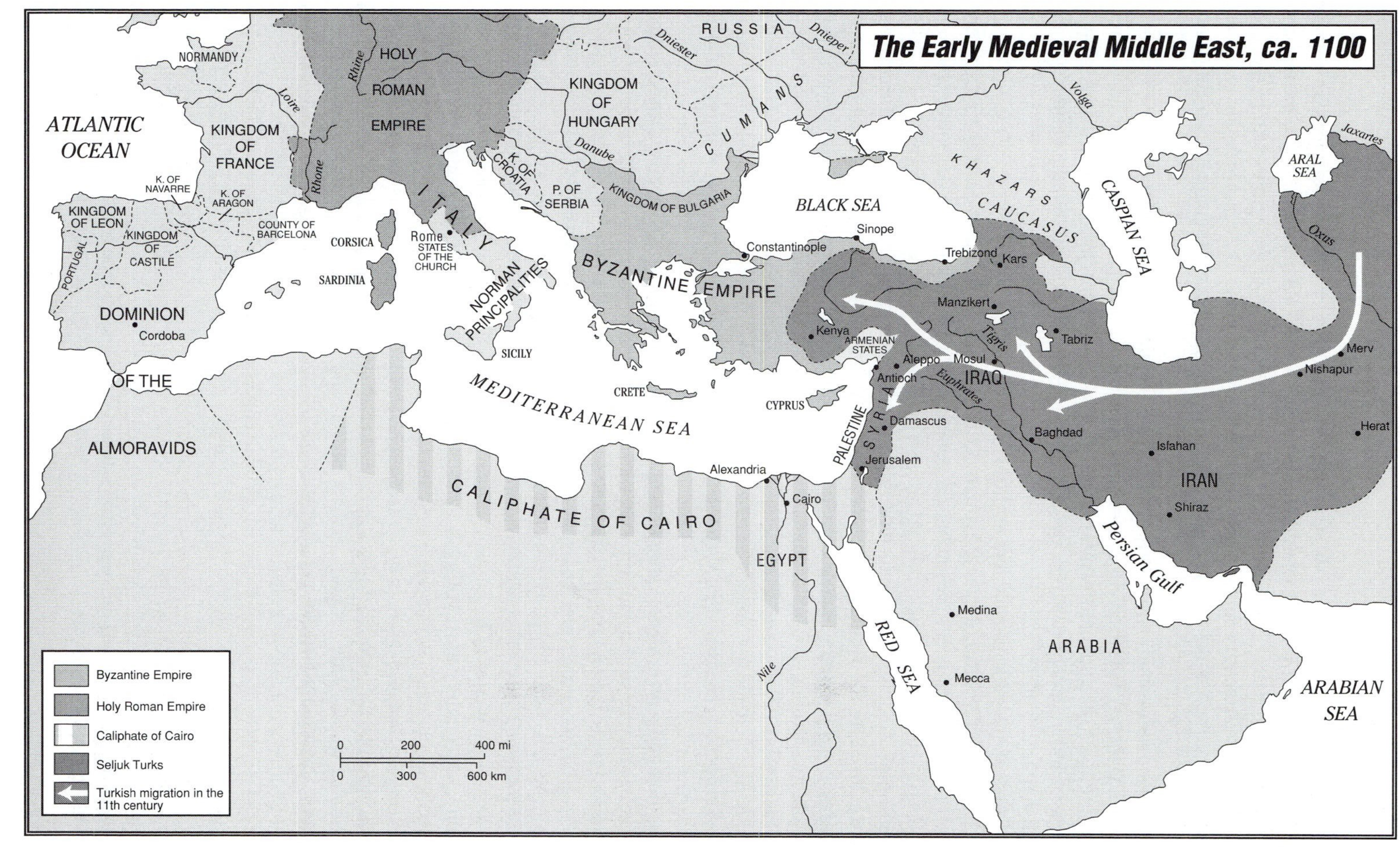
The Early Medieval Middle East, ca. 1100
ATLANTIC OCEAN
NORMANDY
KINGDOM OF FRANCE
Loire
K. OF NAVARRE
K. OF ARAGON
COUNTY OF BARCELONA
KINGDOM OF LEON
KINGDOM OF CASTILE
PORTUGAL
DOMINION
Cordoba
OF THE
ALMORAVIDS
HOLY ROMAN EMPIRE
Rhine
Rhone
ITALY
Rome
STATES OF THE CHURCH
CORSICA
SARDINIA
NORMAN PRINCIPALITIES
SICILY
KINGDOM OF HUNGARY
Danube
K. OF CROATIA
P. OF SERBIA
KINGDOM OF BULGARIA
RUSSIA
Dniester
Dnieper
CUMANS
KHAZARS
CAUCASUS
Volga
BLACK SEA
Sinope
Constantinople
Trebizond
Kars
BYZANTINE EMPIRE
CASPIAN SEA
ARAL SEA
Jaxartes
Oxus
Merv
Nishapur
Herat
Manzikert
Tabriz
Tigris
Kenya
ARMENIAN STATES
Aleppo
Mosul
Antioch
IRAQ
Euphrates
SYRIA
PALESTINE
Damascus
Jerusalem
Baghdad
Isfahan
IRAN
Shiraz
Persian Gulf
CRETE
CYPRUS
MEDITERRANEAN SEA
Alexandria
Cairo
CALIPHATE OF CAIRO
EGYPT
Nile
RED SEA
Medina
Mecca
ARABIA
ARABIAN SEA
0 200 400 mi
0 300 600 km
Byzantine Empire
Holy Roman Empire
Caliphate of Cairo
Seljuk Turks
Turkish migration in the 11th century

decorative arts. Rebellions in Tunisia, the inevitable gap between religious ideals and political reality, tribal disaffections, deportation from Spain, and the rise of new and vigorous alternative leaderships led to the disintegration of the Muwahhids in the middle of the thirteenth century. Only a small province in the southeast of Spain remained in the hands of Muslim rulers, who nevertheless constructed there the beautiful palace of the Alhambra.

The Shii Ismaili Fatimid dynasty had also begun its rule in North Africa in the early tenth century. With the help of North African Berber troops, the Fatimid dynasty overcame the Aghlabids and various Sunni and Khariji forces, built a navy, and recruited slaves for an expanded army. Upon their conquest of Egypt in 969, the Fatimid imams also took the title of caliph and transferred their capital from Tunisia to the new city of Cairo, which they planned and built.

Under the Fatimids, the Egyptian court and its society experienced prosperity and a great burst of accomplishment in commerce, art, culture, and learning. One outstanding example of their cultural policy could be seen in the Azhar mosque-university complex in Cairo. Elaborate processions, public rituals, inscriptions, and patronage organized by the Fatimids also provided legitimacy to the regime. Fatimid prosperity came from the peace and security given to the peasants of Egypt, and from imports of gold from Nubia, a sound coinage, textile manufacturing, and a flourishing international trade, especially by sea. The majority of the population became Muslims at this time, but they were mostly Sunnis, unlike their rulers. The Fatimids helped create institutions of urban governance based on a codification of Shii law, a hierarchy of judges, market inspectors, a police force, prisons, and a separate appeals process for complaints against the government. Fatimid Egypt participated greatly in the artistic and intellectual endeavors of the Muslim world; many outstanding works of early medieval Muslim art and architecture still extant in Egypt date from the Fatimid period.

The Fatimids gained control of territory beyond Egypt: Syria, Palestine, the Hijaz, and Yemen. With difficulty, they ultimately defeated the Qarmatians in Syria and various nomadic and Turkish groups. Thus, at their height, about the year 1000, the Fatimids ruled most of the western Muslim world except Spain, while northern Syria was under Byzantine control; the Fatimid caliph's name was mentioned in the Friday prayers from Tunisia to the Euphrates. Their influence acting through Shii agents even reached as far as India. However, because of eccentric rulers, quarrels among the various ethnic units in the armies, and the inability to convince the masses of the central Middle East that Fatimid Shiism was the true version of Islam, the Fatimid rulers lost power in the eleventh century. Vizirs dominated the caliphs by the 1070s, and these ministers became heads of both the military and civil branches of government. The assassination of the caliph al-Amir in 1130 opened a period of internal strife over power when no single military faction could gain a lasting degree of success. Salah al-Din al-Ayyubi (Saladin) eventually ended the Fatimid rule in Egypt in 1171. To a considerable degree it was the disintegration of the Fatimids that permitted first the continuation of Byzantine power in northern Syria and, second, the late eleventh-century incursion of the western knights called Crusaders, who captured and held the Christian Holy Land of Palestine and the Syrian coast in the twelfth and thirteenth centuries.

TURKISH DOMINANCE IN THE EASTERN AND CENTRAL REGIONS

In the first years of the early medieval period the Buyid, Ghaznavid, and Seljuk ruling dynasties controlled the eastern and central lands of the Muslim Middle East. This era witnessed the eventual triumph of Sunni Islam over various Shii challengers and the incursions of Turkish-speaking nomadic groups who decisively influenced the subsequent history of the central and eastern regions.

An exception to the Sunni and Turkish dominance was the Shii Persian Buyid federation of rulers, who controlled the caliphs in Baghdad. After 945 the Buyids were usually led by the member of the dynasty residing in Shiraz, who took various titles such as "king" or "king of kings," thereby alluding to the pre-Islamic Sasanian dynasty. The Buyids beautified Shiraz and brought to it many learned men, while the dynasty portrayed itself as an heir of the pre-Islamic Persian kings. For a century Shiraz rivaled Baghdad, Ghaznah, Bukhara, Cairo, and Cordoba in culture and splendor, while massive irrigation projects improved agriculture in the countryside. In Iraq, however, Buyid administration was less successful as nomadic groups gained control of most of the countryside. The Buyids assigned the revocable right to collect government revenues (iqta; pl. iqtas) as grants to specific employees of the state, so as to pay for services. This system—sometimes mistakenly called feudalism—was subsequently adopted with modifications by other dynasties such as the Seljuks and became a crucial factor in decentralized administration throughout the Middle East. In the middle of the eleventh century Buyid fought against Buyid for the position of king; this, along with the internal disagreements of their troops and the diversion of international trade to the north and south of the Buyid lands, made them easy prey for the Turks riding in from the east.

The Turks were a pastoral people located in central Asia, Mongolia, and western China and were organized into tribes that lived off their flocks of animals. Even before the early medieval period the Turks had interacted with Muslims in the Middle East, when some Turkish-speaking troops, both slave and free, had been part of the Abbasid armies. In the late tenth century Turkish nomads from the Kazakh steppes in central Asia wandered into the Khurasan region and became partially settled there. Unlike earlier Turks who had served individually as professional soldiers, the new arrivals came as tribal groups, preserving their identity and seeking permanent control of grazing lands for their animals. Their military prowess gave impetus to a general trend throughout the Middle East, whereby cavalry replaced infantry as the more crucial element in armies, except for sieges. Women played a large role in Turkish tribal life and even occasionally took part in combat. Turkish dynasties such as the Ghaznavids and Seljuks dominated the central and eastern Middle East.

The Ghaznavid dynasty began with a Sunni Turkish leader among the slave soldiers of the Samanid dynasty named Alptigin, who rose through the ranks to struggle for power. Forced to flee from the Samanid domain, he captured Ghaznah and in 961 began to establish the famed Ghaznavid empire of Afghanistan and the Punjab in India. The most eminent of the Ghaznavid family was Mahmud (998–1030), who led nearly a score of expeditions into India and laid the foundations of the permanent Islamization of north and northwest India. The Ghaznavid role in expanding Islam and Islamic civilization beyond the core area of the Middle East continued the role of the Umayyads in western Europe and foreshadowed future steady expansion by other Muslim groups into sub-Saharan Africa, southeastern Europe, and southeastern Asia.

Loot from Hindu temples gave Mahmud of Ghaznah the material strength to help destroy the Samanids and extend his state to include most of the eastern provinces of the Muslim world. The army was so important an element in providing the basis for government that in effect it became the state. Although a vestige of the Ghaznavid empire remained at Lahore until 1186, decline followed rapidly on the death of Mahmud in 1030. Muslim independent states in India broke away, the Persian-speaking peoples of central Asia became independent, and the Seljuk Turks appeared in western areas of what had been the Samanid and Ghaznavid states.

One of the chieftains, or khans, under the Samanids was named Seljuk. For three centuries his Sunni and strongly pro-Hanafi dynasty played an outstanding role in the Muslim world from Syria eastward and led Turkish elements to victory. The true founder of the dynasty, Seljuk's grandson Tughril (r. 1038–1063), ascended to power rapidly in Khurasan. Defeating the Ghaznavids and ejecting the Buyids from Iran, Tughril entered Baghdad with an army in 1055. The Abbasid caliph of the day recognized him as king of the east and the west and sultan (the holder of power), and Tughril married the caliph's daughter. Henceforth, these Seljuk Sunni Turkish-speaking rulers adopted *sultan* as their chief official title. They dominated but did not totally control the Abbasid caliphs in Baghdad, who preserved an occasional local autonomy.

Tughril's nephew Alparslan followed as sultan and succeeded in gathering within his domain the vast lands of the Muslim world from the frontiers of China to the Mediterranean. Having expanded into Armenia and taken the Byzantine emperor prisoner in the decisive battle of Manzikert in 1071, Alparslan opened Syria and Anatolia to his Turkish and Kurdish nomads. His horsemen were astride the commercial and pilgrim routes of Anatolia. His son, Malikshah, pushed southward, taking Damascus, Jerusalem, and parts of Arabia, and threatening Fatimid Egypt, while making Isfahan his capital.

As the Seljuks became strong, they encountered numerous rivals, including Kurds, Ismaili Shiis, and nomadic Chinese non-Muslim rulers in central Asia (the Qara-Khitai). The Kurdish tribal states were established in the Zagros Mountains, the mountains of northern Syria and southeastern Anatolia, and in Azerbaijan, subsequent to the decline of the Abbasids between 950 and 1050. The Kurds, who had their own language and culture, established their rule based on nomadic groups and brought a good deal of economic prosperity to the diverse regions they controlled. They were in deadly competition with the nomadic Turkish tribes for pasturage—a competition won by the Seljuks, in part because of their superior political organization. As nomads expanded their grazing areas, peasants suffered and the amount of land under cultivation shrank. The Ismaili Shiis called Assassins also opposed Seljuk rule and killed several prominent Seljuk officials. In the case of some opponents the Seljuks would use marriage as a means of forming an alliance or deflecting potential enmity.

The political genius through the reigns of Alparslan and Malikshah was Nizam al-Mulk, their principal vizier. A cultured and versatile Iranian, Nizam al-Mulk founded the renowned Nizamiyah, an academy in Baghdad, and wrote the Siyasatnamah, a scholarly work on the science of government. Nizam also revised the calendar and is perhaps best known as a patron of the Persian astronomer-poet Umar Khayyam and the famous

al-Muti (946–974)
|
al-Tai (974–991)

al-Qadir (991–1031)
|
al-Qaim (1031–1075)
|
Muhammad
|
al-Muqtadi (1075–1094)
|
al-Mustazhir (1095–1118)
|

al-Mustarshid (1118–1135)
|
al-Rashid (1135–1136)

al-Muqtafi (1136–1160)
|
al-Mustanjid (1160–1170)
|
al-Mustadi (1170–1180)
|
al-Nasir (1180–1225)
|
al-Zahir (1225–1226)
|
al-Mustansir (1226–1242)
|
al-Mustasim (1242–1258)

The Later Abbasid Caliphs

thinker al-Ghazali. While Nizam al-Mulk was the most famous of the bureaucrats who served the Seljuks, the rulers cleverly utilized the administrative skills of other civil servants, while also allying themselves with the urban notables, the Sunni ulama, and an army divided between Turkish nomads, freedmen, and Turkish slave soldiers.

The Seljuks were famous patrons of the arts and architecture. Book illustration, metalwork, and textiles reached new heights under their influence. Chinese porcelain exports reaching the Middle East by sea increased substantially, and Seljuk-era potters tried unsuccessfully to produce their own porcelain in competition with that made in China.

Unity among the Seljuks vanished in 1092 on the death of Malikshah and the assassination of Nizam al-Mulk. In prior years, there had been numerous civil wars among members of the family; upon the demise of these two leaders what little central control that had existed over the various petty western Seljuk states was gradually lost. The chief reason for the collapse of the central Seljuk state was the difficulty the dynasty had in balancing so many contradictory groups and forces (nomads, soldiers, bureaucrats, and ulama) while also maintaining a delicate balance of power among the members of the royal family. One son succeeded to the sultanate in Baghdad. A brother held Damascus and Aleppo, although these cities were soon seized by different sons. A cousin ruled Anatolia from Konya; others possessed Jerusalem, Mosul, Diyarbakir, Amasya, and Edessa (Urfa). Soon afterward, the appearance of the Crusaders from the West disrupted Seljuk rule in Syria even further, though the main branch of the dynasty maintained its hold upon Baghdad until about 1152, and Sanjar (1118–1157) kept the eastern provinces relatively united and prosperous for a time. Ultimately the Qara-Khitai dynasty gained control of much of central Asia and even defeated the Seljuks in 1141; northern Iran also gained independence under another dynasty.

Economic productivity in Iraq under the Seljuks fell as agricultural conditions for the peasants worsened. The iqta revenue grants system the Seljuks borrowed from the Buyids evolved into a form whereby the soldiers or administrators who received grants sometimes became powerful local magnates who governed autonomously.

The death of Malikshah and the collapse of the central Seljuk state heralded for early medieval times the end of a Muslim political entity strong enough and sufficiently organized to dominate the eastern and central Middle East. Under the rule of Malikshah, a merchant could travel alone unmolested with his goods from Samarkand to Aleppo. But within a few years of his death intraregional political anarchy, religious rivalries, and disastrous military chaos helped lure the Crusaders eastward and, much later, the Mongols westward.

CRUSADERS AND AYYUBIDS

In preaching the Crusade, or holy war, in 1095, Pope Urban II was unquestionably governed by religious spirit. Christian pilgrims returning from Jerusalem brought tales of the woe that recent Seljuk Turkish warfare had inflicted upon them in Syria. They also reported that disunity and internecine warfare among the petty Muslim states of Syria would make possible a victory. Furthermore, Emperor Alexius Comnenus sent a desperate appeal for help and promised the cooperation of the Byzantine army and fleet.

The western European feudal Catholic states had developed economically, socially, and politically to a degree that they could outfit and send expeditionary forces overseas. Gathering at Constantinople as an advance base, the Crusaders, almost always called Franks by Middle Easterners, departed for Palestine in 1097. Taking by force Iznik (Nicaea) and Eskishehir, the Crusaders were next welcomed with enthusiasm by the Armenian Christians in Edessa. The main Frankish army conquered Antakya (Antioch). Then the Crusaders successfully stormed the walls of Jerusalem on July 15, 1099. After the conquest, Muslims and Jews were barred from living in the city. In the ensuing decade one after another of the coastal cities of Palestine and Lebanon fell to the merchant fleets of Pisa, Venice, and Genoa, the allies of the Crusaders.

Shortly after the conquest of the Holy City, Godfrey of Bouillon became the "defender of the Holy Sepulchre," where Jesus had been buried, and the titular head of the kingdom of Jerusalem. Other prominent Crusaders scattered along the coast to become the count of Edessa, prince of Antioch, and count of Tripoli in Lebanon, these newly created principalities being held as fiefs of Jerusalem. Most of the Crusaders returned home as soon as the first victories were won, and those who stayed on were continuously hard-pressed to retain their possessions. In fact, they were a minority of the total population (where there was a Muslim majority), and the Crusaders would have been lost at an early date had not a stream of knights appeared from the west and had not the merchant cities of the western Mediterranean helped them.

Eventually the kingdom of Jerusalem was extended eastward across the Dead Sea and southward in a narrow tongue of land to touch the Gulf of Aqaba. In the north the county of Edessa reached eastward to the headwaters of the Tigris. Elsewhere, the Franks clung close to the coast, in some places holding a strip barely ten to fifteen miles wide. They never gained possession of such interior cities as Aleppo or Damascus.

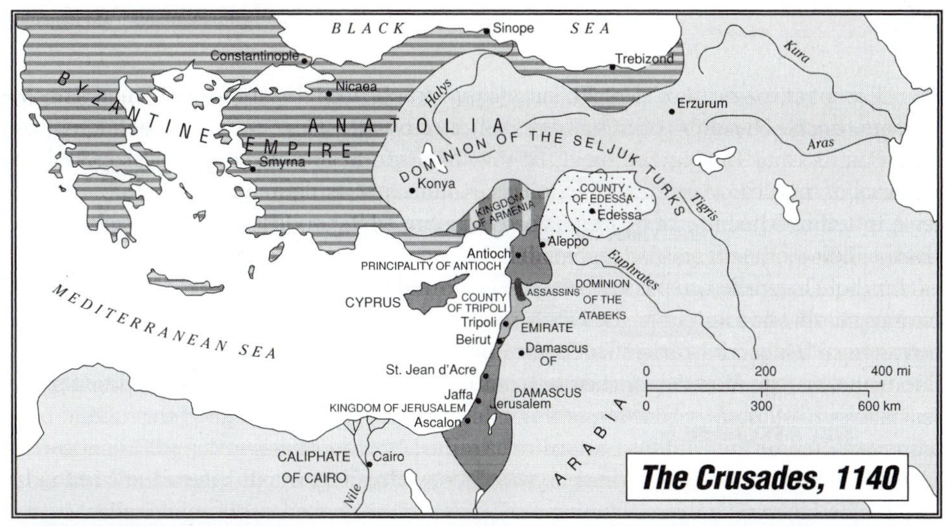
BLACK SEA
Sinope
Constantinople
Trebizond
Kura
BYZANTINE EMPIRE
Nicaea
Halys
Erzurum
ANATOLIA
DOMINION OF THE SELJUK TURKS
Aras
Smyrna
Konya
COUNTY OF EDESSA
Edessa
KINGDOM OF ARMENIA
Tigris
Aleppo
Antioch
PRINCIPALITY OF ANTIOCH
Euphrates
MEDITERRANEAN SEA
CYPRUS
COUNTY OF TRIPOLI
ASSASSINS
DOMINION OF THE ATABEKS
Tripoli
Beirut
EMIRATE OF DAMASCUS
Damascus
St. Jean d'Acre
Jaffa
KINGDOM OF JERUSALEM
Jerusalem
Ascalon
ARABIA
CALIPHATE OF CAIRO
Cairo
Nile
0 200 400 mi
0 300 600 km
The Crusades, 1140

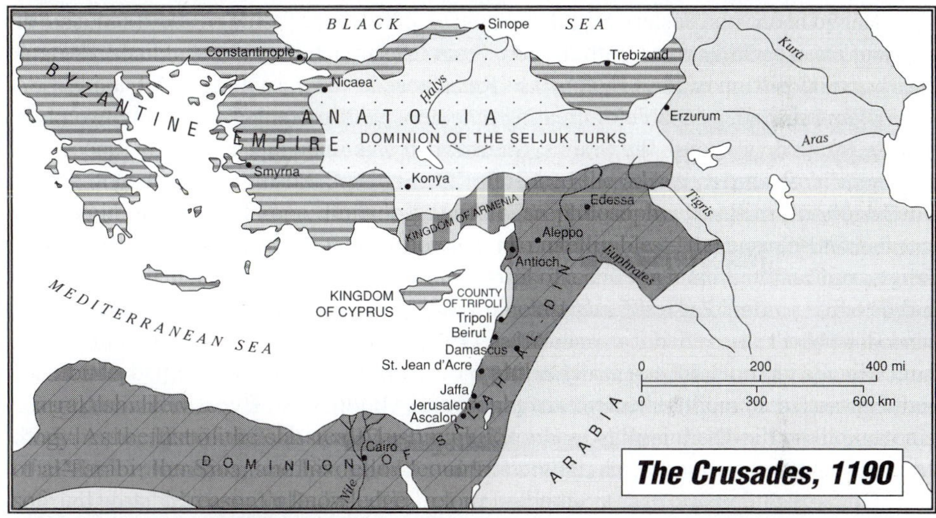
BLACK SEA
Sinope
Constantinople
Trebizond
Kura
BYZANTINE EMPIRE
Nicaea
Halys
Erzurum
ANATOLIA
DOMINION OF THE SELJUK TURKS
Aras
Smyrna
Konya
Edessa
KINGDOM OF ARMENIA
Tigris
Aleppo
Antioch
Euphrates
MEDITERRANEAN SEA
KINGDOM OF CYPRUS
COUNTY OF TRIPOLI
Tripoli
Beirut
Damascus
St. Jean d'Acre
Jaffa
Jerusalem
Ascalon
DOMINION OF SALAH AL DIN
ARABIA
Cairo
Nile
0 200 400 mi
0 300 600 km
The Crusades, 1190

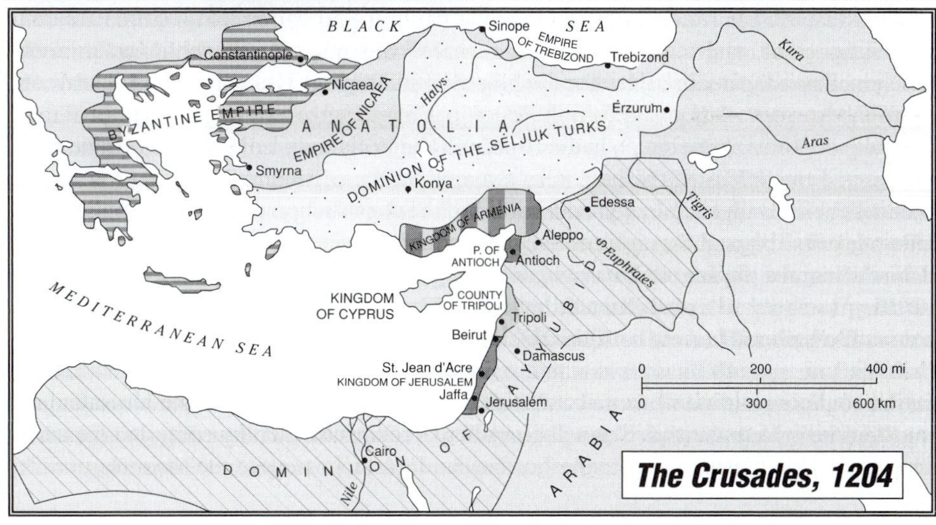
BLACK SEA
Sinope
EMPIRE OF TREBIZOND
Trebizond
Constantinople
Kura
Nicaea
Halys
Erzurum
BYZANTINE EMPIRE
ANATOLIA
EMPIRE OF NICAEA
DOMINION OF THE SELJUK TURKS
Aras
Smyrna
Konya
Edessa
KINGDOM OF ARMENIA
Tigris
Aleppo
P. OF ANTIOCH
Antioch
AYYUBIDS
Euphrates
MEDITERRANEAN SEA
KINGDOM OF CYPRUS
COUNTY OF TRIPOLI
Tripoli
Beirut
Damascus
St. Jean d'Acre
KINGDOM OF JERUSALEM
Jaffa
Jerusalem
DOMINION OF
ARABIA
Cairo
Nile
0 200 400 mi
0 300 600 km
The Crusades, 1204

The great majority of western successes sprang from the complete disunity of the Muslim rulers. The amirs of Syria were delighted by the Crusaders' defeat of the Seljuks in Anatolia, and during the siege of Antioch emissaries from Egypt proposed an alliance of the Crusaders and the Fatimids. Alliances by Muslim princes with Crusaders against fellow Muslims, or by Franks with Muslim amirs against fellow Crusaders, were commonplace.

Before a decade had passed only newly arrived Crusaders carried the religious spirit and fervor that had launched the First Crusade. In the Middle East the European knights reverted to the search for fiefs and the constant fighting they had known in the west. Nevertheless, the more advanced civilization of the Middle East began to influence the barbarous westerners. Crusader nobles emulated the ways and adopted the higher standard of living of the Middle Eastern ruling classes, thus opening the way for some of the knowledge of the east to find its way to western Europe and hasten the coming of the Renaissance.

Baghdad and the eastern Seljuk sultans were hardly bothered by the inroads of the Crusaders, especially since within a few years the latter followed the general preexisting political pattern of the Middle East. Resistance to the west awaited the appearance of a vigorous leader capable of creating an extensive Muslim state that might serve as a base for an attack upon the Franks. Such a man was Imad al-Din Zangi, Turkish lord of Mosul. Consolidating the northern arc of the Fertile Crescent from Mosul to Aleppo into one Muslim state, Zangi stormed and took Edessa in 1144, an act that touched off the Second Crusade, whose chief effect was to bring fresh recruits to ward off other blows and hold the line. The Zangid principality subsequently augmented its power as both Seljuk rule in Baghdad and Fatimid power in Cairo waned. Zangi's son, Nur al-Din (r. 1146-1174), added Damascus to his state, conquered all of the county of Edessa, and wrested territory from Antioch and Tripoli. Popular sentiment for jihad or holy war now increased among the Muslims of the central Middle East. Bypassing the Franks in Jerusalem, Nur al-Din's armies forced the Fatimid caliph of Egypt to surrender control of that still Muslim region to a Zangid lieutenant, Salah al-Din al-Ayyubi (Saladin).

Of Kurdish family origins, Salah al-Din sought to unify Islam and destroy the Crusaders. In 1171, he refused to recognize the Fatimid Shii caliph and restored Egypt to the Sunni creed, and the Abbasid caliph's name was once again mentioned in public prayers. Upon the death of the Zangid Nur al-Din, Salah al-Din married his widow and used the Kurdish, Turkish, and Arab Bedouin army to seize Syria. Eventually Salah al-Din was accepted as the sultan in the Hijaz and Yemen as well. Long-distance trade flourished, and the spices of the east were a major source of wealth. Salah al-Din and the Zangids before him encouraged education and the construction of schools, hippodromes, and other buildings in the cities of Syria. Salah al-Din's newly constructed citadel above Cairo remained the seat of government in Egypt from his day until 1874. The historian Ibn al-Athir (d. 1234) documented the record of the Zangids and Salah al-Din, while drawing on a wide variety of sources.

Turning upon the Franks, Salah al-Din wiped out the cream of the knights' armies at the battle of Hattin on July 4, 1187. This victory enabled him to retake Jerusalem and most of the principal cities. Salah al-Din's new fleet unsuccessfully contested control of the eastern Mediterranean with the Europeans. Jerusalem's fall to the Muslims initiated the Third Crusade, which gave rise to more romantic episodes in the history and literature of Islam and western Christendom alike than any of the other Crusades. Philip Augustus, Frederick Barbarossa, and Richard the Lionhearted could not recapture Jerusalem, but after a siege of two years Acre (Akka), which became the new Crusader capital city, fell to Richard in 1191. When the demanded ransom was not forthcoming, Richard decreed the execution of the garrison of 2700 soldiers. This was in sharp contrast to Salah al-Din's clemency following the fall of Jerusalem, when all who were not ransomed were set free. An armistice was concluded, leaving a narrow coastal area and the island of Cyprus in possession of the Crusaders.

Upon the death of Salah al-Din in 1193 the usual political dismemberment developed, and his Ayyubid dynasty lasted only about fifty more years. One son held Damascus; others governed at Cairo and Aleppo. A brother ruled Jordan and conquered Syria and Egypt. Upon his death, division and anarchy again ruled the Ayyubids' principalities until their own slaves destroyed them in 1250.

The recurring Muslim turmoil seemed to play into the westerners' hands, leading to the Fourth Crusade, whose most significant triumph was the conquest of Orthodox Christian Constantinople in 1203, and eventually the Fifth Crusade's vain attempt to conquer Egypt. Salah al-Din's nephew, al-Malik al-Kamil, forced the Crusaders to abandon Damietta, where they had landed hoping to seize Egypt and the Red Sea, and their commerce with India and the east. Nevertheless, he made friendly treaties with the Italian city-states, entertained and discussed theology with Saint Francis of Assisi, and gave Jerusalem to Frederick II, the Holy Roman Emperor, as part of the Sixth Crusade in 1229. In Palestine, disputes over succession to the throne of Jerusalem and quarrels of Venetians against Genoese and of baron against baron prevented lasting Crusader achievements.

Louis IX's Seventh Crusade to Egypt fell victim to the plague in 1249; at that same time the Ayyubid family of Salah al-Din in Egypt was supplanted by Turkish generals from its slave army. A new era in Muslim history was emerging—the Mamluk (slave) period. Baibars, the fourth Mamluk sultan, captured much of Palestine and Antioch. In 1291 another Mamluk took Acre. This was the signal for the few remaining Crusader towns to surrender. An episode in the history of the Middle East had ended.

The significance of the Crusades for western Europe was mixed. Most of the Crusaders remained in the Middle East a short time and profited little from the experience. Trade between east and west in the Mediterranean did, however, increase markedly, especially via a network of Jewish merchants in Cairo. Exports of sugar extracted from sugarcane were especially valuable eastern goods in western markets. Furthermore, returning crusaders created an expanded western market for eastern goods, since even those who remained in the Middle East only a brief time often acquired a taste for Oriental foods and a preference for its superior manufactured goods such as textiles, cutlery, metalwares, and leather goods. However, the main channels of Muslim influence upon western Europe were through Sicily and Spain. The concept of crusading continued even after the Europeans were expelled from Palestine; subsequent Crusades were launched in Spain, the Balkans, and elsewhere.

The effects upon the Muslims of the Middle East were much less significant. They became convinced that the westerner was a ruthless soldier, semibarbarous in nature, ignorant, and uncivilized. For centuries, Crusaders' castles dotted the landscape, but these did not alter in any measurable degree local military architecture. The incessant fighting, particularly in Palestine, had severely weakened the local economy. Indigenous Christians were the object of suspicion by their Muslim rulers, and their position in society declined after the departure of the Crusaders. The Middle East was politically disunited when the Crusaders arrived; it was still in fragments when they departed. In the interim, to be sure, the Ayyubids and then the Mamluks united the Muslims from the Nile to the Tigris, but this had little relationship to the Crusades; it was only an example of the recurring pattern of centralizing and decentralizing political forces continually at work in the area. In general, it can be said that the memory of the Crusades heightened antagonism between the Muslim Middle East and western Europe, and that the Middle East was poorer because of the Crusading experience.

The power of Muslim rule in the Middle East was threatened by Christian Europeans in Spain and the eastern Mediterranean area, but this challenge was successfully met by the Ayyubids and their successors. Many other issues and challenges were also at least tentatively resolved during the early medieval period. Sunni Muslims repressed the attempt of various Shii groups to gain control, although Shiism by no means disappeared from the Middle East. Militarily, the early medieval period usually saw the victory of nomadic groups—the Seljuks and Berbers, to name two—over settled societies. The economic prosperity of the central Middle East continued, especially in the twelfth century, although the turmoil that accompanied the incessant fighting among the Seljuks challenged the well-being of merchants, peasants, and townspeople alike.

Throughout the early medieval Middle East the political and military fragmentation that followed the loss of effective power by the Abbasid caliphs was accompanied by cultural, economic, and religious accomplishments. Even with the introduction of the Turkish peoples and the revival of the Persian language, Arabic remained a common tool for high culture, religion, and government. Certain common institutions, such as pious endowments, iqtas, and concepts of justice, also served to link the Islamic Middle East. In the later medieval Middle East the Mongols from central Asia, disease, and the rule of slave soldiers posed new challenges to the established order.

REFERENCES

Many volumes already cited bear upon this chapter, including several in Chapters 4, 6, 8, 9, and 10.

Ashtor, E.: *A Social and Economic History of the Near East in the Middle Ages.* Berkeley: University of California Press, 1976. An extremely important synthesis of earlier work, with discussions of agriculture, city life, Iraq and the Mediterranean areas, and the Mamluks.

Bierman, Irene A.: *Writing Signs: The Fatimid Public Text.* Berkeley: University of California Press, 1998. Analyzes the means by which the Fatimids, and later Ayyubids and Mamluks, used inscriptions to justify their legitimacy.

Boyle, J. A., ed.: *The Cambridge History of Iran.* Vol. 5: *The Saljuq and Mongol Periods.* Cambridge: Cambridge University Press, 1968. Beginning with the political and dynastic history of Iran from 1000 to 1217, the volume describes the internal structure of the Seljuk empire and its religion. It continues with a discussion of the Il-Khans, the Ismaili state, and the Mongols. Chapters on poetry and prose, the arts, and sciences are most useful.

Ehrenkreutz, Andrew S.: *Saladin.* Albany: State University of New York Press, 1972. Still an extremely interesting study of Salah al-Din, this work examines his liquidation of the Fatimid dynasty in Egypt, the establishment of his house as a princely family, and the unification of Egypt and Syria.

Finlay, Robert: "The Pilgrim Art: the Culture of Porcelain in World History." *Journal of World History* 9 (1998): 141–187. Stresses the interconnections between China and the Middle East.

Halsall, Paul: *Internet Islamic History Sourcebook–Islamic History Section of Internet Medieval Sourcebook* at www.fordham.edu/halsall/islam/islamsbook.html. A very useful web site that includes maps, primary sources, and secondary articles on Islamic history.

Hillenbrand, Carole: *The Crusades: Islamic Perspectives.* Chicago: Fitzroy Dearborn, 1999. A lengthy and profusely illustrated treatment of the impact of the Crusades on the Middle East; especially important for the question of jihad.

Hodgson, Marshall G. S.: *The Venture of Islam: Conscience and History in a World Civilization.* Vol. 2: *The Expansion of Islam in the Middle Periods.* Chicago: University of Chicago Press, 1974. The author discusses the establishment of the international Islamic civilization.

Holt, Peter M.: *The Age of the Crusaders: The Near East from the Eleventh Century to 1517.* London: Longman, 1986. This broad and detailed work examines all aspects of the subject.

Humphreys, R. Stephen: *From Saladin to the Mongols: The Ayyubids of Damascus, 1193–1260.* Albany: State University of New York Press, 1977. This author explains the Ayyubid confederation of principalities.

Lambton, Ann K. S.: *State and Government in Medieval Islam.* Oxford: Oxford University Press, 1981. An authoritative look at religion, politics, law, community, the individual, and the state.

———: *Continuity and Change in Medieval Persia: Aspects of Administrative, Economic and Social History, 11th–14th Century.* New York: Bibliotheca Persica, 1988. Very useful for the Seljuks and Mongols.

Lev, Yaacov: *State and Society in Fatimid Egypt.* Leiden: Brill, 1991. Detailed discussion of Fatimid government, military, and society.

Lewis, Archibald R.: *Nomads and Crusaders, A.D. 1000–1368.* Bloomington: Indiana University Press, 1988. This book adroitly presents a broad picture of the eastern hemisphere; useful for putting the Middle East into the general historical scene.

Morgan, David: *Medieval Persia: 1040–1797.* London: Longman, 1988. In this short book the author gives a useful overview and a starting point for subsequent reading.

Mottahedeh, Roy: *Loyalty and Leadership in an Early Islamic Society.* New ed. London: Tauris, 2001. This fascinating exploration of the values prevalent in Buyid society examines patron-client relationships, social categories, and the role of the king as arbiter in society.

Petry, Carl F., ed.: *The Cambridge History of Egypt.* Vol. 1: *Islamic Egypt, 640–1517.* Cambridge: Cambridge University Press, 1998. The crucial source for political, military, religious, monetary, and cultural history of Egypt up to the Ottoman conquest.

Pipes, Daniel: *Slave Soldiers and Islam: The Genesis of a Military System.* New Haven, Conn.: Yale University Press, 1981. In a broad essay, the author examines the evolution of Muslim military history.

Riley-Smith, Jonathan: *The Crusades: A Short History.* New Haven, Conn.: Yale University Press, 1987. The best short introduction now available.

Sourdel, Dominique: *Medieval Islam.* Translated by J. Montgomery Watt. London: Routledge and Kegan Paul, 1983. The author provides a sophisticated discussion of a number of disputed interpretations.

Tsugitaka, Sato: *State and Rural Society in Medieval Islam: Sultans, Muqta's and Fallahun.* Leiden: Brill, 1997. Analysis of the iqta system and the relationship between the state and peasants for Iraq, Syria, and Egypt from the Buyid era to about 1325.

Wink, André: *Al-Hind: The Making of the Indo-Islamic World.* Vol. 1: *Early Medieval India and the Expansion of Islam, 7th–11th Centuries.* 3d ed. Leiden: Brill, 1996. A wide-ranging discussion of the eastern Islamic world.

CHAPTER 12

The Late Medieval Middle East

From about 1250 to 1500 the late medieval Middle East witnessed a considerable variety of political and military regimes. In the thirteenth century Mongols from central Asia conquered most of the eastern regions and destroyed the Abbasid caliphate in Baghdad. At about the same time Mamluk slave soldiers established in Egypt and adjacent lands an unusual but long-lasting regime that for a time provided security and prosperity. While the Mongol devastation was in many ways repeated under the conqueror Timur, his descendants ruled only a relatively small area. And in Anatolia the growing power of the Ottoman state projected a regional force that subsequently dominated most of the central Middle East in the early modern period.

Disease, destruction, internal strife, and other factors weakened the chief political units, especially after the middle of the fourteenth century. By the fifteenth century much of the Middle East was poorer than it had been since the rise of Islam, although cultural contributions were still being made in some centers of art and religion such as Cairo and Herat. Few areas other than Granada in Spain were permanently lost to non-Muslim control; the contrary was true—Islam was expanding dramatically on the margins of the Middle East and in areas beyond it.

THE MONGOL INVASIONS

In the early thirteenth century, as the Crusades were waning, devastation rode in upon the Muslim Middle East, China, and Russia from central Asia. Born about 1167 near Lake Baikal, Genghiz Khan came to rule over shamanistic Mongol nomad horsemen. He consolidated military power in his hands by adding to his army the tribal cavalry he had defeated. Genghiz and his army of bowmen moved westward to Iran in 1219, conquering all lands in their path. Merv, Nishapur, Herat, and many other centers of civilization were stormed and sacked. Inhabitants were slain by the hundreds of thousands, perhaps millions.

Iraq, Syria, and areas to the west were spared by Genghiz's death in 1227 and by the subsequent division of the empire among his sons. But heirs maintained the great

Periodization in the History of the Islamic Middle East

Antiquity: from the rise of civilization to the coming of Islam

Classical Islamic period: from the life of the prophet Muhammad to the middle of the tenth century C.E.

The early medieval era in the Middle East: from about 950 to about 1250

The late medieval era in the Middle East: from about 1250 to about 1500

The early modern Middle East: from about 1500 to about 1800

The modern Middle East: from about 1800 to the present

empire and pressure continued upon the Middle East. The Seljuk Turks in Anatolia were defeated in a ruinous battle in 1243, and the Mongols levied tribute upon them. Under Mongke, the third successor to the position of Mongol supreme khan, a great expedition moved westward under the direction of Mongke's younger brother Hulegu. Starting in 1252 to rid the world of the Shii Assassins and to destroy the Abbasid caliphate, Hulegu Khan razed Alamut, the Assassin headquarters.

The Abbasid caliph al-Nasir, who reigned from 1180 to 1225, had managed to restore some real political power to the caliphate in Iraq. But now in 1258 Baghdad and the Abbasids were to come into the hands of the non-Muslim Mongols. Following a siege of several months, the city fell and was given over completely to the troops. Destruction continued for a month, and the Abbasid caliph was killed, thus ending the Abbasid line's long rule in Baghdad. Some of the Mongol armies, including local auxiliaries from the Middle East, then proceeded westward as far as Damascus. They were halted by Baibars, a Mamluk leader of Egypt, in a battle in 1260 at Ain Jalut, near Nazareth, as the Crusaders stayed neutral. Egypt was spared Mongol violence; Baibars, who became sultan, pressed his victory, freeing Syria from Mongol control.

In their conquests the Mongols pillaged widely, often destroying what they had to leave behind. They could not garrison the cities adequately, and the first generations neither understood nor appreciated the cultures and civilizations of the peoples they conquered. Ulama who fled the Mongols subsequently made major contributions to Islam in places as far apart as India, Anatolia, and Egypt. The effects of the devastations wrought by the Mongols lasted in some areas for centuries. Millions of people perished; cities vanished; canals silted and irrigation decreased; lands became barren and deserted; governments disintegrated; civilization foundered; and life returned to the bare essentials. Taxes were sharply increased and collected in an unusually brutal fashion. Since the initial Muslim conquests, conquering armies and peoples had come and gone as customs, religions, knowledge, and culture had been modified, developed, and altered. But through all this time the Middle East had never suffered such a cataclysmic shock as it received from the Mongol invasions.

MAMLUK RULE BEGINS IN EGYPT

Untouched by the Mongol devastation, Egypt suddenly became the great stronghold of Muslim civilization, even though it had just entered into a new and different era of its own domestic history. Upon the death of the Ayyubid sultan in 1250, his widow Shajar al-Durr gained power. After she had a second husband—a Turkish slave general—murdered seven years later, she was beaten to death by his slave soldiers. The rule of Egypt then passed briefly to his son and then to other slave generals, one after another until 1517, when Egypt was conquered by the Ottomans. This long period of two and a half centuries of Egyptian history was termed the Mamluk ("slave") era. Until 1382 the Mamluks were mostly Turkish and Mongol in origin, and they were called Bahri ("river") Mamluks. Between 1382 and 1517, they were generally Circassians and were known as the Burji ("citadel") Mamluks. The Mamluks were not a dynasty.

Begun by the later Ayyubids as a slave bodyguard of foreign origin, the Mamluks evolved into a Turkish-speaking, self-perpetuating urban slave military oligarchy. The recruit was purchased, usually in a Black Sea slave market, by the agent of a general or officer and transported to Egypt by Christian Italian merchants. In Egypt, he became a Muslim and was rigorously trained in the arts of war, especially cavalry, within a household where he would form a sense of common identity with his fellow Mamluks. As he developed and progressed toward the top, he would be freed, though in turn he would make new purchases of slaves, who would become the next generation of Mamluks. (The sons of the Mamluks might become part of the army, but they usually lacked the prestige and special position of their fathers; they were not Mamluks themselves.) Some Mamluks served in the civil administration, though most were in the military. A score of generals or amirs at the summit intrigued and battled for supremacy, held the chief posts of government, and chose the successor to the late Mamluk sultan. Sometimes during Bahri times the sultan would name one of his relatives as his successor, an example being the descendants of Qalawun (r. 1279-1290), many of whom subsequently became sultans. Under the Burjis a ruler picked on this basis would not rule long before he was ousted by an ambitious general. Many of the wives of the Mamluks were brought to Egypt from the Black Sea region, although in the Burji era intermarriage with Egyptians was more widespread. Some Mamluks never bothered to learn Arabic and were Sunni Hanafi Muslims in name only. Aloof from the native Egyptians, whom they despised, the Mamluks usually showed toleration for religious minorities although conversion to Islam was widespread. The Mamluks supervised the pilgrimage to Mecca, many went to the Holy City themselves, and they dispensed charity to the poor of Cairo.

Although frequently illiterate, the Mamluk sultans were usually good at barracks politics, and some were capable organizers and outstanding generals. Nevertheless, their lives were fearfully uncertain, the average reign of the forty-seven Mamluk sultans being less than six years. The most resourceful, and one of the most enduring, Sultan Baibars (r. 1260-1277), the real founder of the Mamluk system, not only turned back the Mongols in Palestine but also cracked the strength of the Crusaders in Syria. He established friendly relations with Sicily and Seville, sent envoys to the Byzantine emperor, and made an alliance with the Kipchak Turks of the Volga River basin (his own birthplace) against the Mongols of Iran and Iraq. He reestablished the Abbasid postal and spy system for quickly taking news to Cairo. Bringing from Damascus a refugee Abbasid prince, Baibars originated the practice of having an Abbasid in Cairo as caliph but without actual power. Abbasid caliphs resided there up to the time of the Ottoman conquest, and their presence gave Mamluk rulers a degree of legitimacy.

Under the Mamluks (as earlier the Buyid and other dynasties), a system of iqta revocable government grants to individuals in return for services spread in Egypt and elsewhere in their domains. In the tenth and eleventh centuries, as the power of the Abbasid government had declined, military officers and various civilians were assigned provinces and estates from which they collected taxes for their own support. For these privileges and benefits they were expected to serve the caliph or sultan, often in a military capacity. Land grants of this type were frequently changed from one individual to another under the Mamluks, especially after a cadastral survey to fix agricultural land ownership. The fate of peasants in Mamluk Egypt was perhaps particularly harsh, as the state constantly increased exactions from them. Gradually most of the revenue from the lands of Egypt was granted to Mamluk officers who had to support, equip, and ensure the service of a number of soldiers, the number depending upon their rank and the size of the grant. However, after 1315, about one-half of the revenues from these grants was assigned to the sultan himself, for the same purposes.

THE IL-KHANS AND TIMUR

The major portion of the central Middle East under the Mongol Empire was split into a variety of provinces; all of these regions were part of the Mongol domain in the Middle East, but other branches of the royal family also ruled in China, Mongolia, and southern Russia. Genghiz Khan's family felt that destiny had chosen them to be the rulers of the world. Contests with other Mongols as well as the Mamluks of Egypt dominated foreign policy, while government and wealth tended to move eastward. From time to time in the century following the conquests of Hulegu, peace among Genghiz Khan's descendants allowed for passage of traders and travelers such as Marco Polo (d. ca. 1324) and Ibn Battutah (d. ca. 1378). But the persistent military violence, direct or threatened, harmed middle-class merchants and tradesmen. In Herat a local Persian dynasty ruled and flourished from 1245 to 1383 while accepting Il-Khan sovereignty, while at the other side of the Mongol Middle East, the Armenian state in southeastern Anatolia also acknowledge Mongol supremacy.

Domestic policy was based initially on the fact that the Il-Khans, or Mongol rulers of Iran and Iraq, with their chief capital at Tabriz, remained non-Muslims and were tolerant protectors of the Christian and other minorities of the region. The Mongols themselves were subject to their own separate law, but Muslims and other groups continued to be tried according to their preexisting religious systems. After a period of strife over the succession after 1282 was ended, with the accession to the throne of Ghazan in 1295, the dynasty became Muslim and sympathetic to Sufism. The shariah once again was the law backed by the state, although Mongol customs undoubtedly continued. Revenue-yielding iqta land grants to soldiers probably became more widespread, as Ghazan reformed and regularized taxation, administration, and succession to the throne. Turkish began to replace Mongol as the language of the elite. Persian speakers dominated the civil administration, whose

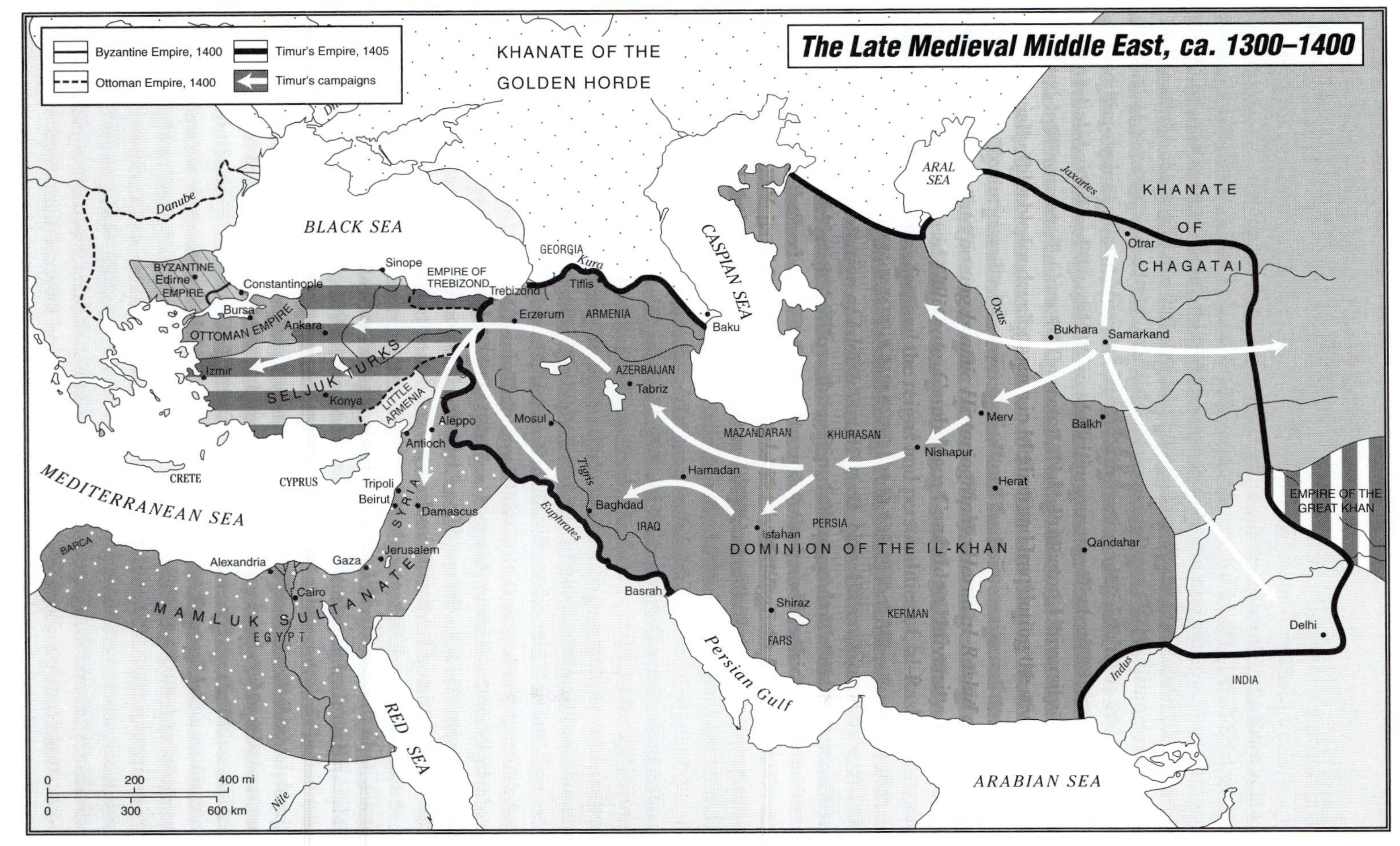
The Late Medieval Middle East, ca. 1300–1400
Byzantine Empire, 1400
Ottoman Empire, 1400
Timur's Empire, 1405
Timur's campaigns
KHANATE OF THE
GOLDEN HORDE
KHANATE
OF
CHAGATAI
BLACK SEA
CASPIAN SEA
ARAL SEA
MEDITERRANEAN SEA
RED SEA
Persian Gulf
ARABIAN SEA
Danube
Kura
Jaxartes
Oxus
Tigris
Euphrates
Indus
Nile
BYZANTINE EMPIRE
Edirne
Constantinople
Bursa
OTTOMAN EMPIRE
Ankara
Izmir
SELJUK TURKS
Konya
LITTLE ARMENIA
Sinope
EMPIRE OF TREBIZOND
Trebizond
GEORGIA
Tiflis
Erzerum
ARMENIA
Baku
AZERBAIJAN
Tabriz
Mosul
Aleppo
Antioch
CRETE
CYPRUS
Tripoli
Beirut
SYRIA
Damascus
Jerusalem
Gaza
Alexandria
Cairo
BARCA
MAMLUK SULTANATE
EGYPT
Baghdad
IRAQ
Basrah
Hamadan
MAZANDARAN
KHURASAN
Isfahan
PERSIA
DOMINION OF THE IL-KHAN
Shiraz
FARS
KERMAN
Nishapur
Merv
Herat
Balkh
Bukhara
Samarkand
Otrar
Qandahar
EMPIRE OF THE GREAT KHAN
Delhi
INDIA
0
200
400 mi
0
300
600 km

chief function was to extract taxes for the benefit of the Mongols. New Turkish nomadic groups also entered the Middle East during the Mongol period, and nomads gained ground from peasant agriculturalists, while much land was simply abandoned.

Abu Said (r. 1318–1335) was the last of the Mongols to rule over a united Iran and Iraq. He even succeeded in making peace with the Mamluks, but he left no heir to the throne, so civil war and puppet rulers followed each other after his death, and small and ephemeral dynasties came to rule a disease-racked area where the Mongols had once dominated. Moreover, in 1368, the founder of the Ming dynasty in China conquered the Mongols there and closed the overland Silk Road trade routes from central Asia into China, diverting commerce with the Mediterranean to the sea route through the Indian Ocean, the Red Sea, and Egypt.

Some cultural accomplishments took place under Il-Khanid Mongol rule: the Persian historian and statesman Rashid al-Din (1247–1318) wrote a famous world history; the study of astronomy was widespread; and great writers such as Sadi (d. 1291) and Hafiz (d. 1390) produced beautiful literature. Chinese medical texts were translated and used in Iran, while in the visual and plastic arts blue-and-white pottery and exquisite tiles became famous. Architecture was marked by the use of glazed bricks, more colorful decorations, and carved plaster. Female members of the royal family were patrons of the arts, sciences, and religion.

The final blows to the highly developed Muslim culture and civilization of the late medieval period in Iraq, central and eastern Anatolia, and parts of Iran were administered by the Mongolian Turks. From 1370 to 1405 the east was in turmoil because of the eruption of the Mongolian Turks led by the Sunni Muslim Timur Leng ("Timur the Lame," or Tamerlane). Son of a Turkish-speaking chieftain of Mongolian extraction, Timur first won control of much of central Asia, which served as a base for expansion both eastward and westward. He called himself by the title *amir,* while retaining the fiction of Mongol overlordship by descendants of Genghiz Khan. Timur and his successors also married female descendants of Genghiz Khan. In 1380, his steppe cavalry archers began the conquest of Afghanistan, Iran, and Kurdistan. In rapid succession he captured Baghdad, Isfahan, Aleppo, Damascus (where he interviewed the historian Ibn Khaldun), and Ankara—but not Egypt. Beyond the Middle East, Timur conquered Delhi in northern India in 1398 and was planning an invasion of China when he died in 1405 at the age of about seventy. Timur's death and the subsequent disputes among his heirs brought relief to the Middle East, but the desolation wrought at his hands was difficult to repair. His most notorious custom was the construction of pyramids of human heads after the sacking of cities; at Isfahan 40,000 heads were built into such markers. Schools, libraries, and mosques were destroyed, and only the walls of the famed Umayyad mosque in Damascus were left. Skilled artisans and their families were deported to Samarkand, Timur's capital, where they erected magnificent buildings.

DECLINE IN IRAN AND EGYPT

Simultaneously with the development of the iqta Middle Eastern revenue grants system came the spread of a more self-subsistent economy. As the uncertainties of government mounted and the difficulties of transportation and communication increased, industry and commerce were depressed and the money economy was greatly weakened. Political anarchy and civil wars destroyed the controls over the nomads within the Middle East, and the perpetual battle between the "desert and the sown" was resumed as agricultural production in most parts of the Middle East decreased. A number of factors contributed to this: the overuse of resources; an inability or unwillingness to overcome technical barriers so as to deal with past farming problems, such as increased salinity of the ground; a social conservatism that opposed most forms of innovation; and reduced social mobility as many judicial and educational posts were held for long periods by the same family. Widespread disease, as in the case of the Black Death in the middle of the fourteenth century, and subsequent plagues killed millions of people, disrupted urban life, and at least temporarily decreased long-distance commerce. The Middle Eastern lands entered into this new era piecemeal over a long period of time.

After the death of Timur, three major regions still dominated in the Middle East: a fragmented Iran; a broken and reduced Ottoman state; and the wealthy if tumultuous Mamluk state of Egypt. Fifteenth-century affairs in the Middle East revolved around the economic, political, and international problems and relationships of these three powers.

In about 1409 eastern Iran came under the rule of Timur's son Shah Rukh (d. 1447), who made his capital in Herat and established a peaceful and prosperous regime. Until 1506 the succeeding Timurids were able to rule most of eastern Iran, central Asia, and Afghanistan, where they were great patrons of the sciences and arts. Miniature painting reached a brilliant stage of accomplishment in Herat, and a new calligraphic script and mosaic tilework flourished. Trigonometry, astronomy, and history were extensively studied. Sufi themes in poetry were frequent, as in the works of the biographer and poet Jami (d. 1492). The later Timurids, however, battled among themselves to such an extent that they were unable to control the Turkish nomadic tribes of the area. Despite some attempts by Timurid rulers to undo the damage done by the Mongols and by Timur himself, the general economic situation was bleak. New groups and families arose to divide Iran and to render it impotent in the struggle for power in the Middle East. Raids by Uzbeg tribes led the center of population and importance to shift westward, although one of the Timurid princes went south, where ultimately he and his descendants founded a new empire—the Mughal dynasty of India.

In the westward regions of the Caucasus and the highlands of eastern Anatolia, Turkish tribes under the leadership of the Qara Quyunlu (Black Sheep Turkomans) seized control of Armenia and Azerbaijan. For a time in the fifteenth century after the death of Timur, the Qara Quyunlu ruled Baghdad and western Iran, establishing Tabriz as their capital and building the famous "Blue Mosque" there. Other Turkish tribes in a Sunni Aq Quyunlu (White Sheep Turkomans) federation were established in Armenia and northern Iraq with Diyarbakir as their capital. The pinnacle of Aq Quyunlu power came under Uzun Hasan, who ruled Iraq, much of eastern Anatolia, and nearly all of Iran from about 1467 until his death in 1478. Married to a daughter of the Greek emperor of Trebizond (Trabzon), Uzun Hasan through his in-laws was approached by Venice to fight battles against the Ottomans. However, he found the Ottoman sultan Mehmed II a formidable foe, especially since Venice made no move to engage the Ottomans in another quarter. After the death of Uzun Hasan the Aq Quyunlu state disintegrated, preparing the ground for the rise of the Safavid dynasty under Shah Ismail.

The fortunes of the Ottoman state are considered in more detail elsewhere in this volume. Here it is sufficient to point out that the Ottoman state was reunited by Sultan Mehmed I within fifteen years after the debacle of his father at the battle of Ankara in 1402, when Timur captured the Ottoman sultan. The process of building an empire by adding provinces in the Balkans and Anatolia was resumed, with Constantinople finally falling to Sultan Mehmed II in 1453. Following that renowned event, the Ottomans in their expansion southward and eastward came into conflict with both Iranians and Mamluks. Mehmed II in 1473 turned back Uzun Hasan of Iran, and Selim I soundly trounced Shah Ismail, clearing Anatolia of most of the Iranian sympathizers and fellow Shiis. Under Mehmed II border disputes flared in southeastern Anatolia between the satellites of the Mamluks and the Ottomans. In the 1490s Bayezid II was engaged in several indecisive campaigns against the Mamluks. Twenty years later (1517) the Ottoman Sultan Selim I and his army marched victoriously into Cairo.

Before the Ottoman conquest the Mamluk Empire remained as a vibrant society, although it had declined in some ways from the earlier days of its foundation and strength in the late thirteenth and fourteenth centuries. Egypt controlled most of the east-west commerce, especially in spices, after the collapse of the central Mongol Empire. The trade of south and southeast Asia passed to Europe through the Red Sea and to the Mediterranean either by way of Egypt or by the historic caravan routes in the Hijaz to Jordan and Syria. As this trade grew steadily in the fourteenth century, it, together with the natural productivity of the Nile valley and the skilled artisanal manufactures of Egypt, gave to the Mamluk-Arab society a brilliance unrivaled in any other Arab land.

What cultural life and quest for knowledge remained in the Arab world found refuge and patronage in Cairo, probably the largest city in the Middle East and one that drew scholars and students from many parts of the Muslim world. Mamluk Egypt and Syria in the fourteenth century excelled in the production of beautiful enameled and gilded glass, especially mosque lamps; and Quranic calligraphy, heraldry, and bookbinding flourished. Inlaid metalwork, as in brass candlesticks, was also noteworthy, while decorated textiles and carpets later became valued exports to Europe. Although originality had largely passed, religion, science, and literature were cultivated by students and supported by the court and the wealthy. In Damascus the theologian Ibn Taimiyya (1263–1328) contributed substantially to Hanbali interpretations of Islam, criticized Sufism, and emphasized the basic elements in the faith. The general urban public enjoyed processions, festivals, Sufi activities, carnivals, tournaments, archery displays, polo games, and shadow puppets, as well as such earlier genres as the recitation of poetry and tales. Judging from condemnations of such behavior by the ulama, urban women sometimes defied the goal of seclusion in the household by mixing with males in bazaars, selling their own handmade goods, and listening to sermons in mosques. Village women often took part in agriculture, especially tasks involving silkworms, as well as engaging in handicraft production such as weaving.

The greatest activity was in the construction and endowment of madrasahs, Sufi residences, and mausoleum-mosques in the great cities of the Mamluks, in particular Cairo and Jerusalem. Of these the most outstanding in Cairo was that of Sultan Qaitbay, who ruled from 1468 to 1496. Noted for its alternate red and white stone courses, the mosque-tomb-school has a stately high dome over the tomb chamber. The exterior of the dome is covered by an elaborate geometric pattern interspaced with intricate floral designs. The minaret, several stories high, is one of the most handsome in Cairo.

Yet, despite all the trade and wealth and the escape from invasion and devastation, society and civilization in Egypt were changing in ways that adversely affected most people. Government was uncertain. Mamluk sultans usually succeeded each other with frequency and violence. In the fifteenth century, there were twenty-two changes of sultan; on one occasion there were three sultans in a single year. The system of training Mamluk officers and soldiers broke down, and the quality of new slaves deteriorated as it became more difficult to purchase slaves in the Volga and the Black Sea areas. Law became the whim of the ruler, and the ruling class was beyond the law. Graft, corruption, and inefficiency within the Mamluk order mushroomed. As land revenues declined, civilian government officials grew more corrupt.

Sultan al-Nasir's death in 1340 signaled the end of a period of clear economic growth and of the tight control of government by the sultan, and began a time of internal strife. The Black Death of 1347–1350 killed tens of thousands of people in Cairo alone, and many more died in the rest of the Mamluk domains. (However, even the much reduced population of Cairo was still some three or four times larger than that of contemporary Paris or London.) After 1382 the Circassian Mamluks' regime brought even more factionalism. Bedouin unrest, increased taxation, state monopolies that reduced business flexibility, outbreaks of disease and subsequent depopulation (especially among the Mamluks themselves), the devastation of Syria in the period of warfare initiated by Timur, inflated prices, neglect of irrigation by the government, and famine all contributed to a decline of the Mamluk state.

The Mamluk Empire included the Hijaz and Syria as well as Egypt, and in the 1370s the Armenian state in southeastern Anatolia was added. The outlying provinces were held through semiautonomous amirs. Syria was loosely tied to Cairo when the sultan was weak, and frequently at such moments the amirs played the dangerous game of flirting with the reviving Ottoman state or with whatever prince ruled in Iran. Border disputes were inevitable, and when a war broke out between rivals for the throne of Dhu al-Qadr (Dulgadir) in southeastern Anatolia in 1485, the Ottoman sultan Bayezid II backed one contender while the Mamluk sultan Qaitbay supported the other. During the subsequent wars at one time the Ottomans occupied Aleppo; at other times Mamluk generals penetrated Anatolia. The Mamluks won the battles but could not achieve victory, and in 1491 peace was arranged.

Within a decade after this successful defense of the distant frontiers of the state, Mamluk good fortune was irretrievably lost. The Mamluk households' loyalty to their leaders declined and was replaced by insubordination and mutiny. Training for the Mamluk cavalry was of poor quality, and the Mamluks were reluctant to use cannons and handguns on the battlefield. Repeated attacks of disease also devastated Egypt and Syria. Then the Portuguese rounded Africa and strongly established themselves in the Indian trade, where they could afford to pay higher prices for goods than the Mamluks. Portuguese ships threatened the port of Jidda on the Red Sea, and in 1506 the Portuguese occupied and fortified the island of Socotra near the entrance to the Gulf of Aden. The small Mamluk fleet was damaged in 1509 by the Portuguese, but with Ottoman help the Red Sea was defended against further incursions.

When the Ottoman sultan Selim I arrived in Syria, conditions in the Mamluk Empire were in disarray. Selim quickly crossed the Taurus Mountains, and routed the Mamluks at Marj Dabiq in August 1516. Previously, the Mamluk army had been well paid and well equipped, but the force before the Ottomans here was a sullen and dispirited mob using obsolete armament, whereas the Ottoman armies had powerful and mobile cannons. Selim proceeded southward, taking all of Syria with ease. Cairo was taken by assault in January 1517, and the last Mamluk sultan was seized and hanged. Egypt became an Ottoman province, and the Abbasid puppet caliph, al-Mutawakkil, was taken to Istanbul.

With Selim I's destruction of the Mamluks and his temporary defeat of the Safavids of Iran, the political, economic, and cultural center of the Middle East shifted to Istanbul and the Ottoman Empire. An age had wearily come to an end. Turkish or Mongol sultans, generals, and slaves had ruled in Arab countries and Iran for several centuries, and the newly dominant power in the Middle East was still another Turkish empire, that of the Ottomans. The Ottomans and other successful dynasties employed gunpowder weapons and destroyed states that did not adopt them.

Other general characteristics of the late medieval period included the relative decline in importance of Arab Iraq and the growth of celebrated literatures in Turkish and Persian. Cultural creativity continued in Arabic, which remained the chief language for the study of religion, but Arabic's near monopoly of high culture was expanded to include other languages. Sufi mystical brotherhoods, some now structured and organized, others engaging in radical forms of behavior, became even more prominent than earlier. The Sufis spread Islam widely. While a majority of the population had converted in the early medieval period, now a much larger majority of the people were Muslims. Christians and Jews persisted as small minorities.

Economic decline affected many areas but was not universal. Peasants were particularly hard hit by the violence and exactions of oppressive governments, yet pastoral tribes often benefited from the same events that injured the villagers. City people probably suffered even more than peasants or nomads from the frequent bouts of epidemic disease that devastated so many parts of the Middle East during the late medieval age.

REFERENCES

References already cited bear upon this chapter, including several in Chapters 6, 8, 9, 10, and 11.

Abu-Lughod, Janet L.: *Before European Hegemony: The World System A.D. 1250–1350.* New York: Oxford University Press, 1989. A brilliant essay on the interconnections of eastern hemisphere societies and merchants, including the Middle East.

Atil, Esin: *Renaissance of Islam: Art of the Mamluks.* Washington, D.C.: Smithsonian Institution Press, 1981. Beautifully illustrated, with chapters on manuscripts, metalwork, glass, ceramics, and textiles.

Berkey, Jonathan: *The Transmission of Knowledge in Medieval Cairo: A Social History of Islamic Education.* Princeton, N.J.: Princeton University Press, 1992. Instruction, the role of women, relations with Mamluks and the general public are all touched upon in a careful analysis.

Blair, Sheila S., and Jonathan M. Bloom: *The Art and Architecture of Islam, 1250–1800.* New Haven, Conn.: Yale University Press, 1994. An excellent general survey.

Daniel, Norman: *Islam and the West: The Making of an Image.* Oxford: Oneworld, 1993. This revised version of a 1960 classic work recounts Christian Europe's views of Islam and Muslims, chiefly during the medieval period.

Dols, Michael W.: *The Black Death in the Middle East.* Princeton, N.J.: Princeton University Press, 1977.

Dunn, Ross E.: *The Adventures of Ibn Battuta: A Muslim Traveler of the 14th Century.* Berkeley: University of California Press, 1986. Ibn Battutah (1304–1368) journeyed through most of the Muslim world; his lively and entertaining observations form the basis of this work.

Irwin, Robert: *The Middle East in the Middle Ages: The Early Mamluk Sultanate, 1250–1382.* Carbondale: Southern Illinois University Press, 1986.

Jackson, Peter, and Laurence Lockhart, eds.: *The Cambridge History of Iran.* Vol. 6: *The Timurid and Safavid Periods.* Cambridge: Cambridge University Press, 1986. A detailed examination of the political history of the age is followed by discussions of administration, European contacts, trade, social affairs, sciences, religion, art and architecture, and literature. Invaluable for all serious readers.

Karamustafa, Ahmet T.: *God's Unruly Friends: Dervish Groups in the Islamic Later Middle Period, 1200–1550.* Salt Lake City: University of Utah Press, 1994. Discusses the radical Sufi groups; particularly useful for the early Ottoman Empire.

Lapidus, Ira Marvin: *Muslim Cities in the Later Middle Ages.* Cambridge: Harvard University Press, 1967. Centered on Cairo and Damascus, this book is extremely important for Mamluk social history.

Manz, Beatrice Forbes: *The Rise and Rule of Tamerlane.* Cambridge: Cambridge University Press, 1989. A biography with an emphasis on tribal and military factors.

Morgan, David: *The Mongols.* Oxford: Basil Blackwell, 1987. A well-written and balanced introduction to the subject with useful illustrations.

Petry, Carl F.: *The Civilian Elite of Cairo in the Later Middle Ages.* Princeton, N.J.: Princeton University Press, 1981. The quantitative methodology employed here for fifteenth-century Cairo represents one of the relatively few attempts to use these analytic tools in the study of the medieval Middle East.

———: *Protectors or Praetorians? The Last Mamluk Sultans and Egypt's Waning as a Great Power.* Albany: State University of New York Press, 1994. A thorough account of the last years of the Mamluk system.

Soucek, Svat: *A History of Inner Asia.* Cambridge: Cambridge University Press, 2000. The best introduction to the subject from the early beginnings of Turkish states to the post-Soviet era.

Spuler, Bertold: *The Mongol Period: History of the Muslim World.* Princeton, N.J.: Markus Wiener, 1994. This reprint of the 1969 edition discusses the Mongols and their influence on the Mamluks, Timur, India, and Russia.

Thorau, Peter: *The Lion of Egypt: Sultan Baybars I and the Near East in the Thirteenth Century.* Translated by P. M. Holt. London: Longman, 1992. Examines critically all aspects of his life.

Woods, John E. *The Aqquyunlu: Clan, Confederation, Empire.* Revised and expanded ed. Salt Lake City: University of Utah Press, 1999.

PART TWO

The Ottoman and Safavid Empires

CHAPTER 13

The Byzantine Empire

Throughout the centuries in which the faith of Islam spread in the Middle East, the Christian Byzantine Empire persevered as rival, enemy, and sometime trading partner. For over 1100 years the Byzantines ruled in parts of the eastern Mediterranean, Anatolia, the Balkans, and the Black Sea region. As discussed in earlier chapters, from the seventh century on the Byzantines profoundly influenced the Middle East: during the early days of the Islamic ummah, the Umayyad and Abbasid dynasties, and the early and late medieval periods. In architecture, institutions, culture, imperial customs, economic structures, and many other aspects of life the Byzantine historical experience affected not only the empire's earlier contemporaries but also its chief successor—the Muslim Ottoman Empire, which at last destroyed the Byzantine state in the fifteenth century.

ESTABLISHMENT OF THE STATE

In a sense the Byzantine Empire was the continuation and heir of the Roman Empire after the last western emperor in 476, but with three significant differences from the old Roman Republic and Empire: the Byzantine state was Christian, not pagan; its dominant language was Greek, not Latin; and its center was in the eastern Mediterranean, not in Italy. Byzantine history begins with the era of the emperor Constantine and his dedication of the new city of Constantinople on the site of ancient Byzantium in 330.

Except for a period in the thirteenth century when western European knights of the Fourth Crusade occupied it, Constantinople was the hub of the Byzantine or Eastern Roman Empire until its fall to the Ottomans in 1453 (after which the city was known as either Istanbul or Constantinople). In choosing a site for a new imperial capital, Constantine placed his chief residence close to the populous part of the empire and in a situation for the defense of the Balkan (southeastern European) provinces.

The eleven centuries of Byzantine rule witnessed, especially in Constantinople, the preservation and propagation of the Christian faith and its theology; the knowledge of the Roman and Hellenistic ages; the art and architecture of the ancient world; and many techniques of government discovered through centuries of Roman rule. In Constantinople, the emperor was the absolute monarch. Except in a very few provinces, civil and military powers were separated, and a regular civil service system for the various bureaus of government was expanded on the basis of merit and seniority. Starting with Constantine, the emperors and the Christian churches of the east closely cooperated. They participated in Christian affairs by calling general councils of the church, and they used their imperial power to try to achieve uniformity in Christian doctrine.

From its first days, therefore, the Byzantine state embodied Roman imperial tradition, Christian orthodoxy, and Hellenistic culture—forces that gave direction to government, religion, and society in Constantinople for a thousand years.

POLITICAL HISTORY

Following Constantine, more than seventy emperors or empresses belonging to several dynasties held the imperial throne of Constantinople before its fall in 1204 to Fourth Crusaders. A relatively large number of these rulers were capable leaders; many were outstanding. Theodosius I (r. 379–395) made Christianity the official and sole religion of the empire. Theodosius II (r. 408–450) published the code of Roman law bearing his name and constructed the land walls of Constantinople, which stretched from the Sea of Marmara five miles to the Golden Horn. Without a doubt this formidable barrier on countless occasions saved the imperial city, and therefore the empire, from northern barbarians and the Muslims.

Justinian I (r. 527–565) was particularly noteworthy. Many of his structures still stand in Istanbul (the former Constantinople), such as the incomparable Church of Hagia Sophia. Equally celebrated were the Justinian codes of laws. These codes remained the foundation of law through the years in the Byzantine Empire; they appeared in Italy in the twelfth century and served as the basis for the reintroduction of Roman law in western Europe. Probably the main reason for publication of the laws was Justinian's need for rigorous control of the empire and efficient collection of taxes to provide funds for his military campaigns in North Africa, Italy, and Spain.

The next gifted emperor, Heraclius (r. 610–641), an Armenian soldier, was the reviver of the empire. It was under him that Greek became the official language of the empire. Upon his accession he found disturbed conditions, with Slavs and Sasanians threatening the empire's existence. By reuniting church and state, by revitalizing the army and navy, and by reinstituting strict economy, Heraclius defeated the Sasanians in a series of brilliant campaigns and freed Syria and Egypt from their control. However, the financial strain of these wars and the cost in manpower left him vulnerable and the recovered provinces were lost to Islam in Heraclius's last days.

During the remainder of the seventh century the frontiers contracted under the rule of the Heraclian dynasty; North Africa was lost, to be followed by the Byzantine portions of Italy in the next century. Local rulers maintained control of many parts of the Balkans from the seventh to the eleventh centuries. The economy of the state materially weakened as population decreased. Muslim armies ravaged Anatolia, camped near Constantinople, and took to the sea in the eastern Mediterranean. But Leo III (r. 717–740) preserved the empire despite these problems. He favored legal and religious reforms and advanced the military system of themes, by which free soldiers were granted land to support and arm themselves for the battles against the Muslim Arabs.

A contemporary of the Abbasid caliph Harun al-Rashid, the empress Irene (r. 797–802) was the Greek wife of Leo's grandson and the power behind the throne for twenty years. Irene blinded her son and ruled alone as emperor until overthrown by a revolution. She paid tribute to the Abbasid caliph Harun al-Rashid, an indication of the decline of Byzantine power. Domestically, she gave her support to factions in the capital that favored icons, disclosing the deep-seated religious division that persisted in the empire. Many with Monophysite Christian tendencies, especially those from eastern reaches of the empire, were iconoclastic; that is, they objected to icons, images, and pictures in church services. Leo III, over the protests of many clergy, forbade the use of icons, an act pleasing to the soldiery of his eastern themes. Irene made a political alliance with orthodox churchmen, and for their favor in her struggle for power she pursued orthodox doctrines of anti-iconoclasm. The debate over iconoclasm racked the empire not only in Irene's reign but for a period of about 125 years, from 717 to 843.

The empire suffered a loss of power until the ascent of Basil the Macedonian (r. 867–886). Maintaining its supremacy until 1056, his Macedonian dynasty led the empire during one of the more brilliant periods of its long life. Basil, of peasant origin, rose from the imperial stables, where his feats of prowess attracted the attention of the emperor. Soon co-ruler, Basil I took the next step and had his patron murdered. Nevertheless, he and his successors, particularly Basil II (r. 976–1025), were capable emperors, publishing codes of laws, restoring harmony in the church, sponsoring a classical cultural revival, and pursuing a vigorous expansion of the state against Arab Muslims, Armenians, and Bulgarians. Byzantines controlled northern Syria for over a century after 969, and they added Crete, Cyprus, eastern Anatolia, and much of the Balkans to the empire as well. The strength of the Byzantine army was due to the development of a new corps of guards, recruitment of a mobile field army, and strengthening the theme system by uniting military and civilian provincial administration. Byzantine culture, religion, and commerce also spread to Russia, Bulgaria, and Serbia.

From the death of Basil II until the fall of Constantinople to the Fourth Crusaders in 1204, a series of calamities befell the Byzantine state, reducing its effective power to an alarming degree. Beginning in the tenth century, transformation of the rural society and economy proceeded relentlessly. The free peasant and the free landholding soldier, especially in Anatolia, were disappearing as a result of the expansion of great estates held by the landed military aristocracy and the church. Even though there was a clear increase in economic activity between 1000 and 1200, and the population grew, especially in the European provinces, heavy taxes, famine, and insecurity caused the peasants to lose their lands to powerful lords. The stronger the magnates became, the more certain they were to obtain privileges, reduced taxes, and many other concessions from the central authorities. In turn, these events weakened the Byzantine fiscal position, lowered the available supply of loyal soldiers, harmed the theme military system, and created a powerful class in the provinces that was able to threaten an unwary or uncooperative emperor. By the middle of the tenth century, emperors began to issue decrees to halt this process, but to no avail.

When the strong hand of Basil II was removed in 1025, intense rivalry between the landed military aristocrats of the provinces and the powerful bureaucrats of the capital flared openly in the competition for the throne. From 1025 until 1057, the civilian government thwarted some thirty rebellions and exiled, executed, or blinded a long list of generals who had mounted these insurrections. But the bureaucracy, looking for compliant emperors, found for the most part incompetents.

Since the main strength of the great Anatolian families lay in their control of the armies stationed in their midst, the bureaucrats set out to dismantle these local troops by withholding financial support from them, dismissing competent generals, and commuting military duty into cash payments. The army became increasingly staffed by foreign mercenaries, who lacked loyalty to the Byzantine state. This was done at a time when Seljuk Turks were pressing on the frontiers in the east, the Normans of southern Italy were expanding, and others were invading the Balkans. In addition to the ease with which they changed sides, the mercenaries frequently ravaged the Anatolian countryside and reduced the flow of taxes to the imperial treasury. The economy of the empire sagged and the power of the state ebbed as the rival parties for political power, in spite of all consequences and at all costs, vied for supremacy.

With the accession of Alexius I Comnenus to the throne in 1081, the generals began a reign that lasted until the fall of Constantinople in 1204. During most of that time the Comneni dynasty ruled the empire, spanning the years of the early Crusades. Despite the successes of Alexius, under his heirs civil wars continued unabated, with generals and leading families feuding among themselves and seeking to establish semi-independent principalities. Not least among these rivals were former mercenary leaders, many of them Normans and Turks. Alexius's daughter, Anna Comnena, left a most interesting account of the arrival of the First Crusade at Constantinople; the contrast in culture and civilization of the two Christian societies of her day was sharply drawn. In 1054, the western Christian church, led by the bishop of Rome, had officially declared the eastern church, headed by the patriarch of Constantinople, to be schismatic. The division between the two parts of Europe—the Catholic west and the Orthodox east—was even more emphatic in light of the flourishing of Byzantine culture, especially in the areas of rhetoric, history writing, theology, and the making of icons and other forms of art.

During most of the twelfth century the Comneni contained the dangers from the west, using a strong fleet against the Normans, tactful diplomacy against the papacy and Crusaders, and a balance-of-power strategy with Venice. In the east, the Byzantines allied with Orthodox Georgia and traded peacefully with the Seljuks of Anatolia, but they faced strong opposition from Armenians and the Crusader states. In the 1180s internal quarrels and foreign reverses began a downward spiral. A large influx of western Catholics into Constantinople coincided with many influential government positions being given to them, much to the displeasure of the local bureaucracy. A strong popular antiwest reaction ensued. In 1204 Constantinople fell to Venetians and Fourth Crusaders, an act that ended the true Byzantine Empire. What later passed for that empire proved to be only a shell of its former power, grandeur, and significance.

THE ORTHODOX CHURCH

Before discussing this later phase of the empire, it may be well to study a few institutions of society as they were at the height of Byzantine glory, for their forms persevered into the weak last days and even beyond, into the Ottoman period. The strongest and most vital arm of the emperor was the Christian church. After the demise of paganism in the fourth century, Constantinople, the Balkans, and Anatolia were devoted in their support and loyalty to the church. The church's organization, with the patriarch at its apex, gave powerful support or presented determined opposition to the emperor and government. Consequently, the emperor tried to control the selection of the patriarch, while the patriarch had a strong influence with the emperor; there was a close and intricate relationship between the two posts.

Church monasteries and convents were socially, economically, and religiously important, and the monks were often popular heroes. Frequently, the government found it necessary to follow doctrines espoused by the populace, even though other dogmas would have been preferable for reasons of imperial policy. Whenever an emperor compromised with what was deemed heresy, to mollify a distant province or the army in some Asian theme, or entered into an understanding with the Roman papacy regarding the universal Christian church, orthodox voices in Constantinople were heard in opposition. And the Orthodox church strongly opposed Islam, condemning it on theological as well as political grounds.

In a way, the church resembled an administrative department of the government, and the patriarch acted as a minister of state in charge of religion. A dynamic emperor chose, appointed, and dismissed patriarchs; an energetic patriarch bent weak emperors to his will—yet at most times, the emperor was supreme and the church was subordinate to the state.

GENDER, AGRICULTURE, AND THE ECONOMY

Historical records for the Byzantine Empire are relatively scanty, particularly those dealing with aspects of social and economic history beyond the realms of the Orthodox Church. Men produced most of the information passed down to subsequent generations and the society was patriarchal in its values and institutions. Male writers often portrayed women negatively.

Most women had far more limited opportunities than did men, as in education and law. Law courts favored men in issues relating to divorce and as witnesses. Nevertheless, Byzantine women did have equal rights to inherit property. Many wealthy women became patrons of the arts, the church, and charity. Parents arranged marriages for their children; society regarded childbearing and child rearing as the chief purpose of women's lives. Weaving clothes and preparing food were major occupations for most women in their households.

Middle- and upper-class urban women were generally secluded, often veiled, and had little interaction with men outside their immediate families. Poorer urban women and the vast majority of the female population who lived in the villages were not as secluded and they interacted much more often with men. Many women were sellers of goods and some owned businesses. Women shared with men a strong interest in worship, pilgrimages, and religious controversies such as iconoclasm. Poor women whose spouses died would often seek refuge and support in a convent.

The sometimes prominent role of women in the imperial family should not obscure the fact that most women had no major part in public life. However, Byzantine empresses occasionally acted as regents, they could transmit dynastic legitimacy through their marriages, and they often influenced policy, though only three women ruled directly on their own.

The provision of food for urban men and women became more difficult after the loss of Egypt to the Muslims. Now Constantinople, the largest city of the empire by far, had to draw its wheat, olives, grapes, and domesticated animals from Anatolia and nearby Thrace.

The life of the peasants living in villages was difficult, and few envied them. Given the problems of disease, heavy taxation, moneylenders, and many other ills, peasants appealed to the saints for help. The growth of great estates at the expense of the small freeholding peasants in the twelfth century especially increased their oppression. Yet they seldom lacked the bare essentials of life, and private churches, monasteries, and rich families provided charity to the poor.

Land was fundamental to the economy. Livestock such as oxen increased productivity, while monasteries had enough economic stability to provide many with a living. Urban dwellers often bought and held land as an investment.

Although agriculture was the mainstay of the empire, artisanal production and commerce gave it wealth and luxury. In the cities of the empire compact populations were engaged to a considerable degree in making articles of everyday use. Many, too, produced luxury goods of great value, which were used in the rituals and services of thousands of churches and monasteries and were vital to the pageantry of the imperial court. Sumptuous living was much enjoyed, and the wealth of silk fabrics, gold brocades, jewelry, enameled wares, fine glassware, and all the precious and refined luxury of the age dazzled visitors. The crafts and skills of Hellenistic artisans prevailed for a thousand years in the Byzantine world.

The most active commercial city of the Byzantine Empire, Constantinople, was filled with warehouses, depots, banks, money changers, and other aids to foreign and domestic commerce. Trade from the Black Sea area and most of Russia centered upon Constantinople. Goods from the Far East and western Asia passed down the Bosphorus to quays on the Golden Horn. Domestic imperial production also gravitated to the capital for exchange and transshipment. Ships plied regularly between Constantinople and Trebizond, Salonica, Venice, and Genoa. A standard tax of 10 percent, levied on all imports and exports, brought to the imperial government a large part of its revenue. Italian cities, however, found it possible to obtain tariff concessions from the emperors, which allowed them to dominate long-distance trade.

Commerce and artisanal production were strictly regulated by the government. Controls were exercised over prices, quality, and quantity of goods produced or imported, profits, locations of business, labor conditions, and movement of workers. Implementation of these controls was effected by individual guilds, which were highly organized and fully developed before C.E. 900. Governments granted most guilds special privileges and monopolies. To some extent guilds were restrictive and conservative in character. Yet they prevented speculation and collusion, protected rights of individuals in local and distant markets, and performed many social and legal functions for members. The state appointed the heads of the guilds, and by regulating their activities, it controlled much of the urban economy.

THE CRUSADES

In 1071, when Emperor Romanus IV Diogenes was defeated by the Seljuk sultan Alparslan at the battle of Manzikert near Lake Van, the rout was so complete that soon eastern and central Anatolia were overrun with Turkish bands. Food supplies and raw materials, revenues, commerce, trade routes, and manpower supplies were lost; this further contraction of the empire ultimately spelled its doom.

When Romanus IV Diogenes marched out to meet Alparslan, not only was his military equipment woefully inferior but half of his soldiers were merely untrained city youths and the other half were unreliable mercenaries. On his way to battle he had to subdue his own unruly Germans; his predecessors also had alienated many Armenians. In the heat of the battle the leader of the contingent of bureaucrats in the emperor's army spread the word that Romanus was being defeated and withdrew his men. Turkish forces, witnessing the anarchy, attacked the Byzantine army in flight and captured the emperor. It had been more than 250 years since an emperor had been taken prisoner in battle!

The humiliation of the battle of Manzikert accelerated the fragmentation of society. When the Turks set Romanus IV free, civil war over the throne erupted, further destroying military power in Anatolia and creating a power vacuum. Petty independent states sprang up everywhere: Normans in Bithynia; Seljuk Turks at Nicaea; Armenians in the southeast; and Turkish (Turkoman) tribes everywhere. As a result, Byzantine cultural borrowing and military dependence increased. Before the able general Alexius I Comnenus seized the imperial throne in 1081, several contenders had even relied on Turkish armies in their battles against each other. These actions and the encouragement of Alparslan to Turkoman tribes to invade Anatolia brought Turkish sieges of many walled towns and the general ravaging of the countryside in every corner of Anatolia.

At last Alexius I Comnenus sent out a desperate call to western Christendom for aid. The Crusades were the response, but in the long run they did more harm than good for the Byzantine Empire. The west expended little sentiment over the Byzantine Empire, as the Fourth Crusade demonstrated. The fall of Constantinople to Venetian merchants and soldiers in 1204 abruptly terminated the Byzantine Empire, and its society and civilization collapsed. The Orthodox church was Latinized; monasteries disappeared; the wealth of the churches was carried off; learning and literature vanished; and works of art were destroyed.

The flight of the Byzantine court and ruling classes from Constantinople in 1204 had the immediate effect of producing several independent Greek principalities in the Byzantine provinces. Meanwhile, the new Latin empire of Constantinople hardly had a chance. Fraught with internal feuding and largely deserted by the west, the Crusaders were hemmed in by the expanding second Bulgarian kingdom (founded around 1186) and by Byzantine states. Finally, in 1261, Michael Palaeologus, a general, overthrew the Latins and reestablished the Byzantine state in Constantinople under Palaeologi rule. Greece and the Aegean, however, continued as several Latin-ruled states.

THE END OF BYZANTINE RULE

From 1261 to 1453 Byzantine rule held in Constantinople, but it cannot justly be regarded as a restoration of the Byzantine Empire. It was never more than a small Greek kingdom, and for the final half century nothing more than the capital city itself. The old empire was broken beyond repair. Furthermore, the Mongol invasions weakened the Seljuks of Anatolia, who controlled much of Anatolia. The resulting power vacuum opened the way to the new Ottoman state, which was built upon the Seljuk and Byzantine legacies.

The Palaeologi tried to maintain a style of imperial government unjustified by the extent of their actual domain. Only a small part of northwestern Anatolia remained in their hands, and most of the Balkans were held by Bulgarian and Serbian rulers. The Byzantines now had no imperial navy. Land revenue was extremely low, as fiscal, judicial, and administrative affairs increasingly fell into the hands of the church and local landlords. Revocable government grants of revenue became hereditary, and the services owed by the grant holders were frequently ignored. The peasants in the fourteenth century were becoming poorer as the central government lost power and authority. Indeed, with so much trade passing to western Europe through Mamluk Egypt the imperial crown jewels had to be pawned in Venice. Most of the Byzantine population realized the empire they considered to be protected by God was in decline; a mood of grim persistence dominated the public.

One mediocre ruler succeeded another; palace poverty and intrigue spawned civil wars and revolutions. Toward the middle of the fourteenth century the poor rose in Constantinople and massacred the aristocracy, while in 1347 bubonic plague devastated Byzantine cities. Interminable strife also marked the history of the church. The Palaeologi, in their desperation for aid, repeatedly made bids to subordinate the Orthodox church to the pope of Rome. Monks, churchmen, and the people objected, and religious unity with the west was continually being postponed or abandoned.

Foreigners gained more power in the empire. From their docks and counting houses of Galata, a suburb across the Golden Horn from Constantinople, the Venetians and Genoese yearly grew more powerful and more insolent in their dealings with the Palaeologi. The most spectacular group of foreigners that came to the Byzantine state was the mercenary Catalan Grand Company of soldiers, who were hired in 1302 to combat the mounting aggression of the Turks. The emperor, however, was soon more terrified of the Catalans than he was of the Turks. No longer could the state afford a regular standing army; the mercenaries, smallholders, and heavy cavalry grant holders could be paid and supported only when a crisis arose or a threat appeared.

In the century and a half preceding the fall of Constantinople, international politics in the Byzantine area consisted almost entirely of constantly shifting alliances and realignments among the Byzantine successor states, of which the Greek state was only one. However, when Venetians and Serbs banded together to seize Constantinople, Orhan, the Ottoman ruler, was given the hand of Theodora, the daughter of the emperor John VI Cantacuzenus, as partial inducement to bring his forces across the Dardanelles into Europe to defend Thrace from that combination. A rival emperor in alliance with the Genoese drove the Ottomans back to Asia and sent his predecessor to a monastery, where he spent the rest of his days writing his brilliant memoirs. Deposed by his own son and the Genoese, the new emperor called for Ottoman support, which returned him victoriously to Constantinople in 1379.

From that time on Ottoman sultans were deeply involved in Byzantine affairs. Emperors frequently recognized sultans as their overlords and sent their sons as hostages to the Ottoman court. Sultans plotted palace revolutions in Constantinople, and emperors sponsored rivals to the sultan's throne and intrigued with other Turkish principalities against the Ottomans. Manuel II (r. 1391–1425) and Mehmed I personally discussed affairs from their respective galleys on the European shores of the Bosphorus and then crossed to the Asiatic side for a picnic. When an emperor died childless in 1448, Murad II approved the selection of Constantine XI, whose niece married Mehmed II. The various groups in the area had much in common, despite religious differences; their leaders and societies were coming to resemble each other in many ways. Still, the Ottoman Muslim dynasty was a rival to the Byzantines.

At first the Ottomans were invited and hired by Byzantine emperors to fight in battles against Serbs, Bulgars, and Italians or for one faction of Palaeologi against another. Later they settled in Europe, and before the close of the fourteenth century they had become masters of Thrace, Macedonia, Bulgaria, and parts of Serbia. Constantinople was isolated but obtained a fifty-year reprieve from Timur's crushing defeat of the Ottomans at the battle of Ankara in 1402. Constantinople was all that remained of the Byzantine Empire. That it did not fall to the Ottomans after their state was re-created under Mehmed I can be credited almost wholly to its superb defensive position. Protected by water on three sides and the marvelous Theodosian wall between the Golden Horn and the Sea of Marmara on the fourth side, the inhabitants of Constantinople felt secure.

By building castles on the European shore of the Bosphorus in 1452, the Ottoman ruler Mehmed II was able to blockade Constantinople by sea. Control of the Balkans gave him complete freedom to mass an army equipped with heavy artillery before the land walls in the spring of 1453. When the walls were breached and his navy transported from the Bosphorus over the hills of Pera to the Golden Horn, the fate of Constantinople was sealed. Constantine XI died on the walls, Muslim prayers were recited in Hagia Sophia, and bells tolled in Europe. The once great and vigorous Byzantine Empire finally succumbed after a long and painful illness. The young Ottoman Empire ushered in a new day for the great imperial site on the Bosphorus.

Through the ages and up to the present, writers have maligned the Byzantine Empire, its civilization, and particularly its rulers. Intrigue, court politics and palace revolutions, the sharp business acumen of the merchants, and the mercenary character of some aspects of its life all led historians to use the word *byzantine* in a derogatory manner. Nevertheless, a close study of Byzantine records reveals a complex society that possessed an efficient government and excellent public services, managed and directed by an educated and sophisticated bureaucracy, and protected by an army of high tactical ability. At a time when western Europe was semibarbaric, some inhabitants of the Byzantine Empire were enjoying literature, philosophy, urban social culture, and a much higher standard of living. Certainly the Byzantine Empire had a great impact on the peoples and governments of the Middle East and especially on the Ottoman Empire.

REFERENCES

References cited at the end of Chapters 4, 5, and 11 are also pertinent to this chapter.

Angold, Michael: *Church and Society in Byzantium under the Comneni, 1081–1261.* Cambridge: Cambridge University Press, 1995.

Bartusis, Mark C.: *The Late Byzantine Army: Arms and Society, 1204–1453.* Philadelphia: University of Pennsylvania Press, 1992. Excellent detailed examinations of military matters and their political and social impacts.

Browning, Robert: *The Byzantine Empire.* Rev. ed. Washington, D.C.: Catholic University of America Press, 1992. A profusely illustrated general introduction.

Cavallo, Guglielmo, ed.: *The Byzantines.* Chicago: University of Chicago Press, 1997. Among the various essays, those by Alice-Mary Talbot on women and Alexander Kazhdan on peasants are especially worthwhile.

Halsall, Paul: *Internet Medieval Sourcebook* at www.fordham.edu/halsall/sbook.html. Contains many documents, particularly relating to religious issues, as well as links to other sites.

Harvey, Alan: *Economic Expansion in the Byzantine Empire, 900–1200.* Cambridge: Cambridge University Press, 1989. This complex revisionist analysis finds general economic and demographic growth, in opposition to the prior view of decline and contraction.

Hussey, J. M. *The Orthodox Church in the Byzantine Empire.* Oxford: Clarendon Press, 1986. The story of patriarchs and emperors, theology, and the spiritual life of the church.

Mainstone, Rowland J.: *Hagia Sophia: Architecture, Structure and Liturgy of Justinian's Great Church.* New York: Thames and Hudson, 1988. A beautifully illustrated historical introduction.

Mango, Cyril: *Byzantium: The Empire of New Rome.* London: Weidenfeld and Nicolson, 1980. Social history is related with care, as the author discusses cities, heresies, the economy, monasticism, education, and intellectual life and self-image.

Nicol, Donald M.: *The Last Centuries of Byzantium, 1261–1453.* 2d ed. Cambridge: Cambridge University Press, 1993. A perceptive account of late Byzantine political history.

Ostrogorsky, George: *History of the Byzantine State.* New Brunswick: Rutgers University Press, 1969. The standard political history of the Byzantine Empire.

Treadgold, Warren: *A Concise History of Byzantium.* New York: Palgrave, 2001. An updated and shorter version of the following book.

———: *A History of the Byzantine State and Society.* Stanford, Calif.: Stanford University Press, 1997. Though primarily an excellent chronologically arranged treatment of military and political events, the author also analyzes religion, society, the economy, and administration of the empire.

Vasiliev, A. A.: *History of the Byzantine Empire, 324–1453.* Madison: University of Wisconsin Press, 1952. A valuable general introduction.

Whittow, Mark: *The Making of Byzantium, 600–1025.* Berkeley: University of California Press, 1996. The author critically examines many doubtful points in Byzantine history and puts the empire into a larger geographic context.

CHAPTER 14

Ottoman Origins and Early History

The Ottoman Empire destroyed the Byzantine state, but the major role the Ottomans played in the history of the Muslim Middle East should be viewed in the context of a broad range of accomplishments. This empire lasted for more than 600 years, it ultimately ruled over large parts of three continents, and its ruling family became the best-known and most important example of a Muslim dynasty in the Middle East during the early modern and modern periods.

Throughout its long history the Ottoman Empire was marked by three characteristics: allegiance to the imperial dynasty founded by Osman, adherence to Sunni Islam, and dominance by a Turkish-speaking elite. Although the capital of the empire changed, the center of the state and the economy was constant, located where Asia and Europe met, and where the Black Sea and the Mediterranean-Aegean seas joined.

The origins of the Ottomans have been the subject of much scrutiny, not only because of the historical importance of the Ottoman Empire but also because so few sources are available about its early history that many different hypotheses could be entertained. The chief elements that enabled the Ottomans to establish themselves as a leading dynasty were the legacy of the Seljuk Anatolian experience, Byzantine weaknesses, the process of Turkification, competition with other Turkish dynasties, and the contribution of frontier warrior and tribal values. Once established, the Ottoman principality flourished not only because of these factors but also because of the personal abilities and policies of its rulers.

THE TURKISH SELJUKS IN ANATOLIA

The battle of Manzikert in 1071, in which the Seljuk Alparslan routed the Byzantine army, ranks as a decisive historical event: it opened Anatolia to Turkish settlement and created the first element in what was to become the Ottoman Empire—the Seljuk experience as a model. A second factor in explaining the rise of the Ottomans existed at about the same time as the Seljuk Anatolian state flourished—a power vacuum around Constantinople resulting from the weakness of the Byzantine Empire.

Within ten years Turkish forces fanned out over Anatolia. The ease with which Turks conquered much of Anatolia resulted not only from their war skills but also from popular resentment against Byzantine policy. March warriors and Armenian areas were disaffected, and gave the Byzantines little aid. Turkish Muslim frontier warriors (ghazis), independent Turkoman nomads, and other Turkish princely dynasties overran Anatolia.

The First Crusade helped Byzantine forces to stem the Turkish tide. Nicaea was retaken, and western sections of Anatolia were restored to Byzantine control, while central and eastern Anatolia remained Turkish. It was only during the reign of the Seljuk Kilij Arslan II (1156–1192) that a truly local Seljuk administration in Anatolia was created, with its capital at Konya, as the administration of the central Seljuk empire to the east collapsed. Kilij Arslan II subdued other ghazis and obtained from Emperor Manuel Comnenus recognition as the commanding lord of Anatolia. However, the central power of the Anatolian Seljuks declined once Kilij Arslan II assigned governorships to his twelve sons, who declared their independence in their father's declining years.

Because of the great prestige of the Seljuk name, Konya attracted ulama to teach in its schools; mystics, Sufis, and poets frequented its court. The Seljuks established Muslim financial administration throughout their state and built mosques, mausoleums, schools, palaces, and caravanserais. Christian churches and monasteries remained in many urban centers, even though they owed their allegiance to the Orthodox patriarch in Constantinople. A mixed culture prevailed in rural areas, in former ghazi districts, and definitely at the frontiers toward the Byzantine Empire.

As the Seljuks expanded their rule, some Greeks fled westward; others were killed or enslaved; many became Muslims and gradually learned to speak Turkish. A decisive victory by the Seljuk sultan over the Byzantines in 1176 meant the Byzantine emperors gave up any idea of reconquering Anatolia, and the Seljuk sultans felt secure from any serious attack from Constantinople. Now the Seljuks, other Turkish rulers, ghazi bands, and Turkomans controlled Anatolia except for a small district around Trebizond on the Black Sea coast and the area near Constantinople.

Thus, through most of the century from 1150 to 1250, the Seljuk sultanate of Konya shone brightly. Muslim and Christian traders frequented its markets, and a considerable share of Far Eastern trade passed through the area to enrich various treasuries. Schools were crowded and the arts flourished. Armenian stonecutters, Persian poets, and Arab calligraphers practiced their crafts. Ghazis settled down, Turks became villagers, communities were established, stone caravanserais were built, and life in central and eastern Anatolia prospered.

Early in the thirteenth century, refugees fleeing the Mongols settled in Seljuk Anatolia, which was soon invaded. At the fateful battle of Kosedagh in 1243 the Seljuk armies were crushed and the Seljuk rulers, thenceforth, were only puppets or vassals of the Mongols to whom they had to pay a high yearly tribute. All respect for Seljuk rulers by other Turks of Anatolia vanished, and the dynasty itself disappeared in the early fourteenth century. Since the Mongol Il-Khan state collapsed after 1335, their invasion politically fragmented the peninsula but did not lead to any permanent new order. Mongol traditions and governmental practices did, however, ultimately influence the small Turkish states that succeeded the Seljuks, including the Ottomans. Almost simultaneously with the Mongol conquests the Byzantine emperors regained Constantinople from the

Crusaders and became involved immediately in Balkan affairs, so that their Asian provinces were neglected. Turkish ghazis and Turkoman tribes discovered not only that the restraining hand of the Seljuk sultan could be ignored but also that Byzantine frontiers could be easily penetrated.

TURKIFICATION OF ANATOLIA

The third element in creating the prerequisites for the emergence of the Ottoman state was the transformation of Anatolia from a Greek and Armenian Christian society to a Turkish Muslim land. Throughout the twelfth and thirteenth centuries and on into the fourteenth, pressure was exerted on every aspect of Christian life and society. Decisive victories for Muslim armies, continual marches across the land by soldiers, sacking of cities, and scorched-earth policies generated massacres, flight, enslavement, plague, and famine. Those Christians who remained were filled with insecurity and a sense of helplessness.

As various areas fell into Turkish Muslim hands, certain factors made it fairly easy to assume the customs and manners of the victors. In the first place, non-Muslims were tolerated but nevertheless discriminated against in many ways with regard to dress and life; unquestionably they were second-class subjects. Converts, on the other hand, escaped discrimination—as well as many taxes. Furthermore, Christian communities became leaderless at a time of great psychological and economic crisis. Consequently, whole villages turned Muslim overnight, at first in the interior and later along the coasts of Anatolia. By about 1300 a majority of the population of Anatolia was Muslim.

The Seljuk state also actively supported Islamic institutions. Within a few decades Anatolia was blanketed with mosques, madrasahs (advanced schools), hospitals, and caravanserais. Most of these were endowed as waqfs by leading Turks or by the state from confiscated Christian property and the income from Christian villages. Moreover, Anatolia was saturated by Sufis who preached a mystical popular Islam that reached the people. They presented a kind of religious syncretism that equated Islamic practices and holy men with those of the Christians. The twelve apostles became the twelve imams and the Trinity came to consist of God, Muhammad, and Ali. This phenomenon of cultural change continued in Anatolia until the mid-fifteenth century when the Ottoman Turks captured Constantinople, recognizing the patriarch as subject to the sultan and in essence institutionalizing and protecting the Orthodox church as a part of the state. As a consequence, Christian communities could look to the patriarch and bishops without fear of reprisal, and the church hierarchy felt responsible for its flock throughout the Ottoman domain.

OTHER TURKISH STATES

A fourth element in the rise of the Ottomans was the long competition between that family and other small Turkish Muslim dynastic states whose political and social patterns dominated Anatolia for several centuries. Originally the amirate founded by Osman near Eskishehir was quite insignificant, even though eventually it conquered or annexed all the others. Probably the most important of these was the Karaman principality, a successor to the Seljuks, with its capital at Konya. The founder of the dynasty, Karaman, was the son of a Sufi mystic. Other Turkish principalities along the Aegean coast established navies that raided commerce.

Ibn Battutah, the fourteenth-century Moroccan globe-trotter, visited Anatolia and left a record of his impressions of these amirates. Entertained at the courts of many, he reserved no special tribute for Orhan, Osman's son. It was the competitive struggle among the principalities that helped the Ottomans evolve patterns of behavior and institutions that subsequently held them together through times of adversity.

GHAZI SOCIETY

A fifth factor in bringing about the later success of the Ottomans was their leadership of ghazi warriors. The Ottoman dynasty, in addition to its desire for expansion and glory, also sought to foster Islam by armed force. (The ghazi traditions and attributes were not limited to the Ottomans; indeed, most Muslim dynasties on frontiers with non-Muslim peoples had something resembling the Anatolian ghazi experience.)

Ghazi war bands brought back rich plunder, including slaves. Ghazis were equal socially and politically; aristocracy was derived from actions and leadership rather than from blood. It was a typical rough frontier society. Another feature of ghazi life was acceptance of the futuwwa, a set of rules by which the virtuous should live. Mutual fidelity among the membership was particularly emphasized. Likewise, almost every ghazi brotherhood recognized a spiritual leader; in most cases this leader was a Sufi.

Ghazi society lacked administrative, institutional, and governmental apparatus and stability that could maintain control once conquest ceased. This problem confronted the Ottomans constantly in their meteoric path across Anatolia and the Balkans. The success with which they solved this continuing problem determined, in considerable measure, the permanent character of Ottoman conquests.

OTTOMAN ORIGINS: OSMAN AND ORHAN

In addition to the external factors that helped open the way to the rise of the Ottoman dynasty, the personal abilities of the rulers and their individual accomplishments played a very important role in the establishment and growth of the state. Osman, founder of the Ottoman state, was the son of a Turkish frontier warrior on the western edge of the Seljuk domains, probably one of the countless seminomadic Turkomans looking for a place to settle in Anatolia.

Raids into Byzantine territory began in the 1290s. This was presumably after Osman had married the daughter of a Sufi leader. Osman established ties with ghazi groups and their futuwwa moral and ethical ideas. (The word *Ottoman* was an Italian corruption of *Uthman,* the originally Arabic name Turks pronounced as Osman; in Turkish the dynasty was often called the sons of Osman.)

Osman, as a leader of tribesmen, began to acquire by capture or alliance a number of small towns. Between 1300 and 1320 Osman seized the countryside west of the Sakarya

Osman (?–1324)
|
Orhan (1324–1360)
|
Murad I (1360–1389)
|
Bayezid I (1389–1402)
|
Mehmed I (1403–1421)
|
Murad II (1421–1444; 1446–1451)
|
Mehmed II (1444–1446; 1451–1481)
|
Bayezid II (1481–1512)
|
Selim I (1512–1520)
|
Suleiman I (1520–1566)

Ottoman Rulers to 1566

River, and west and north to the Sea of Marmara. Yet he was not strong enough or sufficiently well equipped to take the walled towns. Not until after Osman died in 1323 or 1324 did his followers, under the leadership of his son Orhan, take Bursa (Brusa), which surrendered without a struggle after several years of siege. Bursa became the Ottoman capital and center of government. The fall of Bursa to the Ottomans was the signal for Byzantine collapse in that corner of Anatolia. Orhan occupied Nicaea (Iznik) in 1330. Later, he dispossessed the quarreling sons of a neighboring Turkish amir and placed Ottoman rulers over still another amirate. Thus, by 1345, the Ottoman state included the entire northwestern corner of Anatolia from the Aegean to the Black Sea.

Several factors prepared the way for this accelerating growth of the Ottoman state. The personality and spirit of Osman counted heavily since his followers were loyal and devoted to him. Byzantine force weakened rapidly, and such towns as Bursa and Iznik were summarily abandoned to their fate. Unlike other nearby Muslim dynasties, the Ottomans kept their lands intact under one ruler, rather than dividing them among various family heirs.

A most important element in the growth of Ottoman forces was the policy of welcoming any and all fighting men as part of the fluid, open religious and social atmosphere of the Anatolia of that time. Mikhal, a Greek who became a Muslim, was one of Osman's favorite comrades. His descendants (the Mikhaloglu) held prominent positions through centuries of Ottoman history. Osman and Orhan used slave soldiers who were part of their household entourage. In 1305, some of the Catalan Grand Company joined the Ottoman camp; defeated Mongol raiders, given clemency, joined Orhan. Fighting men from various tribal, ghazi, and Byzantine Christian backgrounds flocked to the Ottoman infantry and cavalry as their successes multiplied. Some Christians worked as bureaucrats for the Ottomans in the early fourteenth century. Orhan also accepted the Muslim practice of allowing Christians and Jews to live in a Muslim land by paying taxes and special tribute.

In the first half century under Osman and Orhan, Ottoman expansion was gradual enough to permit the organization of some governmental administration. Moreover, the Muslim world was in such disorder that Muslim artisans, merchants, bureaucrats, theologians, teachers, and scribes were attracted by opportunities in this new frontier Muslim state. Schools of theology were built in Bursa and Iznik soon after their capture, and Bursa remained the center of learning and philosophical discussion for the Ottomans.

Furthermore, the immigrant artisans and merchants who were known as akhis formed corporations somewhat like European guilds. These akhi guilds were closely knit bodies subscribing to specific futuwwa codes of conduct very similar to the ghazi code of honor. A close alliance and understanding between ghazi and akhi gave to Ottoman society an economic strength that was lacking in other ghazi states. Silver coins were minted, and a lively trade developed in the prosperous towns, while charitable foundations (waqfs) were endowed. The early arrival of Muslim judges, theologians, and ulama expanded the social structure beyond the ruling ghazi and Turkoman family circles. Thus, at an early date social and economic disturbances in towns passing into Ottoman hands were largely minimized. Life went on in much the same way, with considerable intermingling of people. Orhan himself married Nilufer, a daughter of the Greek lord of a captured town. By the middle of the fourteenth century Orhan had become amir, or prince, of a sizable state facing the historic Straits and Europe beyond.

OTTOMAN EXPANSION: ORHAN AND MURAD I

Turkish ghazis were long accustomed to raiding parties in Thrace and Macedonia. An example of this raiding took place when Orhan and his men became allies of the Byzantine emperor John VI Cantacuzenus in 1345 to fight against a rival emperor. Part of Orhan's bargain was the privilege of plundering; another part was the hand in marriage of Theodora, Cantacuzenus's daughter. Six thousand Ottomans ravaged the hinterland of Constantinople and were instrumental in taking Adrianople (Edirne). In most years thereafter Ottoman soldiers amassed fortunes in booty through raids in Thrace and the southern Balkans. Byzantine resistance to Ottoman expansion was also weakened by the Black Death, which reached Constantinople first in 1347, and by a severe earthquake in 1354, which demolished the walls of Gallipoli on the European shore of the Dardanelles. Ottoman forces in Europe rushed into Gallipoli, asserting that God had given it to them, and Ottomans colonized the city, much of whose population had been carried off by the Black Death.

From this bridgehead in Europe, Ottomans stormed over eastern Thrace, seizing all areas between the Aegean and the Black seas except, of course, the imperial city of Constantinople. The Serbian empire collapsed in 1355 and Bulgaria became weak in the 1360s, also opening the way to Ottoman expansion. Adrianople surrendered in about 1361 to Murad, third in the Ottoman line of rulers, and for nearly a century that city (which the Turks called Edirne) stood as the chief Ottoman city in Europe.

Murad I, the younger son of Orhan and Nilufer, followed in his father's footsteps, vigorously pushing one campaign after another northward and westward into the Balkans. Rival emperors of Constantinople, Serbian and Bulgarian tsars, independent princes of Greece, the city-states of Venice and Genoa, popes, and Crusaders kept the Balkans in such constant turmoil and confusion that Murad in his expeditions did not have to worry about facing a consolidated offensive and usually had several Christian allies in his camp. Under Murad's leadership (r. 1360–1389), Ottoman armies and raiders succeeded in conquering most of Bulgaria, Macedonia, and parts of Serbia.

Likewise, Murad made extensive advances in Asia. He took Ankara and, through a combination of prestige, power, money, and diplomacy, nearly doubled his Anatolian possessions. Marriage of his son Bayezid to the daughter of an amir brought the town of Kutahya as a dowry. Murad forced another Turkish amir to "sell" most of his domain and will the balance to the Ottomans. Campaigns were launched against the Karaman princes but with little success, perhaps because ghazis fought with less enthusiasm against fellow Muslims. In these Anatolian campaigns, Murad's most loyal supporters were contingents of his Slavic allies and mercenaries. Western Crusaders also were involved in conquests in Anatolia: from 1344 to 1402 Izmir, an important port, was held by them, not the Ottomans.

During the battle of Kosovo in 1389 against the Serbs, Murad lost his life. When Bayezid I succeeded as ruler or sultan of the Ottomans, he inherited a state that in the brief span of a century had grown from a petty principality to a dominant power stretching from the Danube River in Europe to the Taurus Mountains in Asia.

BAYEZID I

Bayezid I seized the reins of government on the field of Kosovo in 1389. His only brother, Yakub, was assassinated by the supporters of Bayezid, leaving him the only male alive in the Ottoman royal family. Having the example of bitter and destructive rivalries in the Byzantine and Seljuk dynasties before him, Bayezid judged that executing his brother was for the best. This procedure later became a means of helping to guarantee the permanence of succession to the throne.

With the rise of modern nationalism, Kosovo was viewed by Serbs as a catastrophic defeat despite an equality in losses, but in 1389 no great ill feeling seemed to be generated. A Serbian royal princess was married to the victorious Bayezid, who became devoted to her; and Serb contingents remained loyal to Bayezid throughout his reign. In succeeding years Ottoman forces raided Bosnia and Hungary, and Bayezid brought greater numbers of Turks into Europe, especially into Thrace.

Indeed, beginning in 1391, all of Thrace was occupied up to the very walls of Constantinople: the city was virtually blockaded from the land side. Bayezid attempted to close the Bosphorus and the Dardanelles to ships destined for the imperial city. But attacks, first in Europe and later in Asia, saved Constantinople for half a century.

Sigismund, then king of Hungary, but later Holy Roman Emperor, was concerned over Ottoman aggressions. The building of an Ottoman navy, which began depredations in the Adriatic Sea, helped lead Europe to heed Sigismund's cries for a crusade. The crusade of Nicopolis of 1396 was the result. Nobles from England, France, and the German states, and armies from Hungary and Wallachia, all laden with wine and women, joined as if on a picnic. They foolishly charged the center of the Ottoman forces, commanded personally by Bayezid, who had left the siege of Constantinople to meet the knights of Europe. Utterly outmaneuvered, the western nobility fell on the battlefield

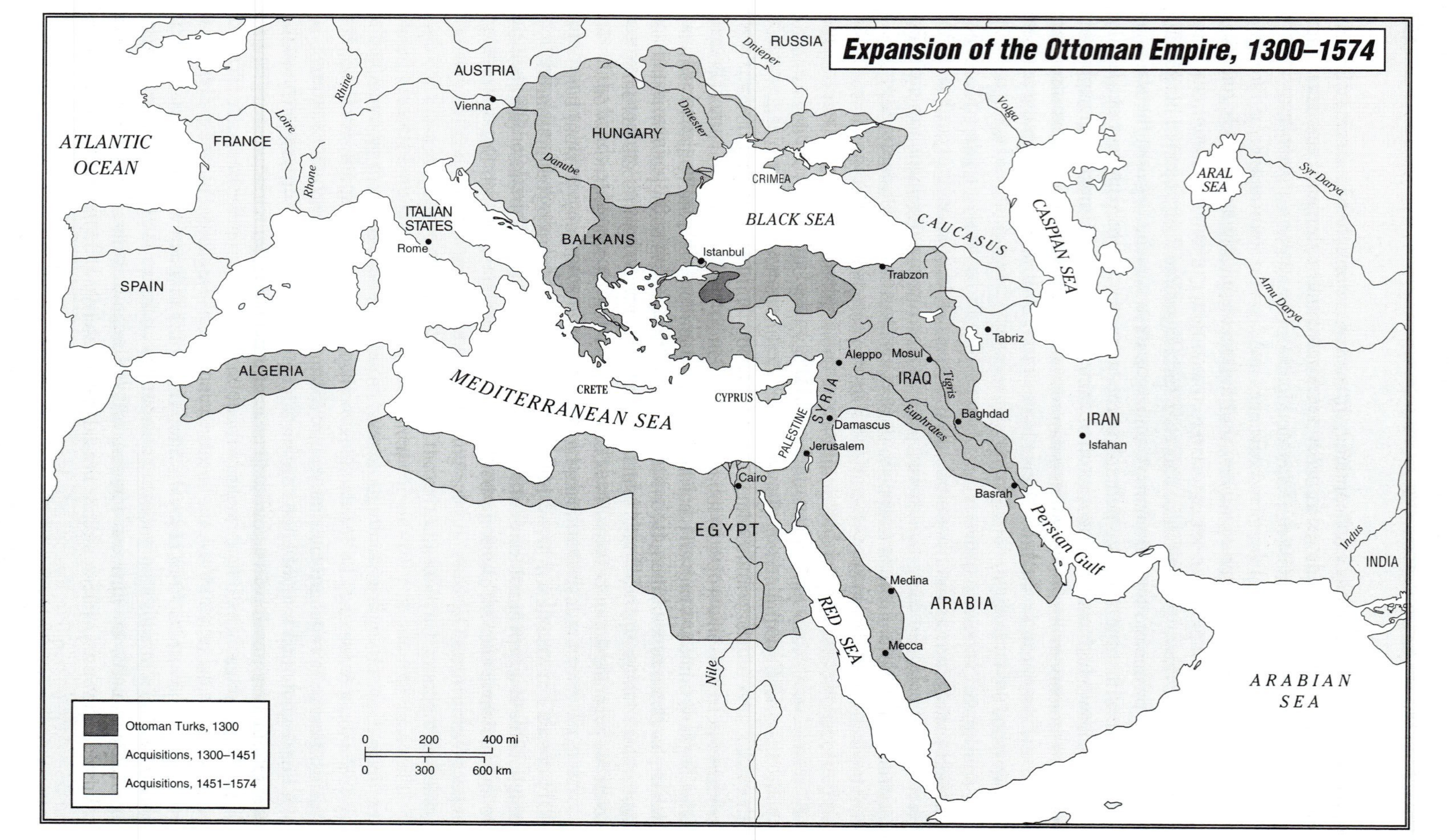
Expansion of the Ottoman Empire, 1300–1574
RUSSIA
Dnieper
AUSTRIA
Vienna
Rhine
Loire
ATLANTIC OCEAN
FRANCE
Rhone
HUNGARY
Danube
Dniester
Volga
CRIMEA
BLACK SEA
CAUCASUS
CASPIAN SEA
ARAL SEA
Syr Darya
Amu Darya
ITALIAN STATES
Rome
BALKANS
Istanbul
Trabzon
SPAIN
Tabriz
ALGERIA
Aleppo
Mosul
IRAQ
Tigris
CRETE
CYPRUS
SYRIA
MEDITERRANEAN SEA
PALESTINE
Damascus
Euphrates
Baghdad
IRAN
Isfahan
Jerusalem
Cairo
Basrah
EGYPT
Persian Gulf
Indus
INDIA
Medina
ARABIA
RED SEA
Mecca
Nile
ARABIAN SEA
Ottoman Turks, 1300
Acquisitions, 1300–1451
Acquisitions, 1451–1574
0 200 400 mi
0 300 600 km

of Nicopolis, and thousands were captured. Those under twenty years of age were taken for the janissary corps or the sultan's court. Many were held for ransom, and others were impressed to row in the galleys as ordinary slaves.

Bayezid turned his attention to Greece, where Ottoman armies overran Thessaly, entered the Peloponnesus, and captured towns and smaller cities. Ottomans were settled in the northeastern corner of the Peloponnesus, then called Morea, and land grants were handed out in northern Greece. But fortified cities that could be supplied from the sea were, like Constantinople, still beyond Ottoman reach.

Bayezid's involvements in Europe and the attempts at choking Constantinople did not deter him from campaigns in Anatolia. His burning ambition was to unite under his rule all Muslim lands of Anatolia and perhaps of the entire Middle East. Although this sort of goal was common in the expansion and unification attendant upon the rise and growth of a new state, Bayezid's haughty manner and ruthless tactics plus the rise of a brilliant enemy spelled his eventual ruin.

In rapid succession between 1390 and 1397 Ottoman forces, frequently led by Bayezid in person, captured and annexed Turkoman amirates such as Karaman. The dispossessed princes, instead of being given responsibilities to weld them into the Ottoman system, fled with revenge in their hearts to the court of Timur Leng (Tamerlane). With Bayezid engaged in subduing Bulgaria and besieging Constantinople, the Karaman leaders judged that a revolt might be successful. However, Bayezid transferred his troops to Asia with amazing speed and destroyed the Karamans in front of Bursa. He did this so completely and so quickly that his soldiers dubbed him Yildirim (meaning "thunderbolt" or "lightning").

Except for a few walled towns like Constantinople and Athens, Bayezid was now master of the land from the Adriatic and the plains of Hungary to the Euphrates. In barely a decade he had doubled his Asian possessions and gained recognition as lord of the Balkans. In 1395 Serbian princes and Byzantine emperors rendered homage. The uncomplicated Ottoman state of Osman and Orhan had vanished.

ECONOMIC, SOCIAL, AND POLITICAL CHANGES

Two great trade routes met in Anatolia, and as the Ottomans conquered the peninsula they gained control of this rewarding commerce. The extension of the Mongol Empire into Anatolia in the thirteenth century had established profitable east-west trade routes, especially for Chinese and Persian silks. At the same time, merchants following north-south routes brought spices and fabrics to Konya and then to the principal markets of Anatolia and to Constantinople. In the fourteenth century, with the disintegration of the Mongol state and the rise of the Ottomans, more and more of this trade found its way to Bursa, which by the year 1400 had become the most important trading city in Anatolia. As Bayezid extended his rule, merchants could travel safely from Tabriz and Aleppo to Bursa, where merchants from the Italian cities bought grain, slaves, and alum and sold cloth. The Ottoman realm was now part of the Mediterranean trading economy.

The Ottomans were interested in commerce and industry, and the akhi groups were influential members of their society. Ibn Battutah noted in 1333 that Orhan, because he held Bursa, was the richest Turkish ruler in Anatolia. And as early as 1340 Orhan had built a bazaar and an enclosed market in Bursa where valuable goods could be safely stored and sold. Such interests had greatly aided the Ottoman successes.

In the time of Murad I the government began to grow; under Bayezid I expansion was rapid. The first cadastral registers, designed to record land revenue assignments, were compiled. Government organization by religious leaders and graduates of the schools of Bursa and Iznik introduced more efficiency yet also more rigidity in administration. At the same time evolution of the post of grand vizir or chief minister in the hands of Kara Khalil Chandarli aroused considerable opposition among most Ottoman soldiers, accustomed for generations to great freedom.

Dismay also stemmed from Bayezid's dreams of empire. In 1394 he sent an embassy to the Mamluk-controlled Abbasid caliph in Egypt, requesting to be invested with the title sultan of Rum (Anatolia). Even Bayezid's grandfather had used that title, and eventually it was commonly applied to Bayezid. Yet he wished recognition from the older Muslim world, perhaps because numerous Turkoman amirates that he engulfed looked upon him as a tyrant. Some ghazis may have objected to his Asian campaigns; Bayezid learned that in operations against fellow Muslims he could be sure only of his janissaries and contingents sent by his European Christian vassals. Many Muslims in Asia could hardly escape questioning Bayezid's own faith when he led Christian soldiers against Muslims.

There were other ways in which Bayezid's actions alienated his subjects. The cultural background of Ottoman leaders left them open for many innovations. Discussions among religious leaders of various sects within the Ottoman state even led to proposals for a common religion from a composite of Islam, Judaism, and Christianity. Undoubtedly this trend can be seen in the names of Bayezid's younger sons—Musa (Moses), Isa (Jesus), and Mehmed (Muhammad). Other sons were called Ertogrul (Turkish name), Mustafa (Muslim mysticism), Kasimir (Balkan Christian), and Suleiman (Solomon).

Even more objectionable to many Ottoman subjects were Bayezid's personal habits. Increasingly, he took on the ways of Balkan and Byzantine rulers and nobles. Manners and dress changed; court ceremony became more elaborate. Many still remembered the ease with which they could approach Orhan and contrasted the simplicity of Orhan's establishment to the complexity of Bayezid's. Bayezid, though brilliant and energetic, fell under the spell of sumptuous living. He drank wine and engaged in homosexual behavior, both of which scandalized many Muslims. His harem was large, and he began to follow in the footsteps of the caliphs of old. Earlier Ottoman rulers had married both Christian and Muslim women, including princesses; by the days of Bayezid, males in the royal family more frequently had concubines than wives, and it was these non-Turkish concubines who were the mothers of the next generation of rulers.

DEFEAT AT ANKARA

Timur invaded Anatolia in part because of the unrest among Bayezid's subjects and the request to do so by exiled Anatolian amirs who were in his entourage. In addition, Bayezid had invaded territory beyond the Euphrates to the Tigris and given indications of ambitions in Syria, thereby threatening Timur's vassals.

Surprisingly overconfident, Bayezid moved leisurely to meet the threat. In the face of so great a danger he organized a huge hunting party, wasting valuable time and tiring his men. The contest came in 1402 at Ankara, where only the janissaries and the Christian vassals of the Balkans stood fast. Bayezid was taken prisoner and brought before Timur, who honored him until his haughtiness became insufferable. Within a few weeks he died, and his body was returned to Bursa, the chief Ottoman burial site.

Following his great victory, Timur marched across Anatolia to Izmir on the Aegean. He showed little desire to hold Anatolia directly, however. Ottoman conquests in Europe and the early holdings of Osman and Orhan in Asia were divided among Bayezid's remaining sons: Suleiman, Musa, Isa, and Mehmed. Anatolian amirates taken by Murad and Bayezid were restored to their previous hereditary families. Bayezid had a dream of empire, but it was shattered at Ankara. The Ottoman family was left only in possession of those holdings that were considered legitimately theirs. Bayezid's sons and all other amirs of Anatolia swore allegiance to Timur but when Timur died three years later, the amirs of western Anatolia and the four heirs of Bayezid renounced all dependence upon the Timurids.

The duration of the united Ottoman state, from about 1300 to 1402, had been equivalent to that of many other Muslim dynasties in the late medieval Middle East. Thus the destruction of the Ottoman army and the ensuing disunity were typical of what had happened often in the past to other groups, and the disappearance of the Ottoman state could be expected. What was surprising was that the empire was soon reunited and in fact became far more successful in the fifteenth century than it had been earlier. Causes for this revival can be found in many of the circumstances that had enabled the Ottomans to expand their principality between 1300 and the battle of Ankara, and in particular their dynastic, military, diplomatic, institutional, religious, and cultural accomplishments.

REFERENCES

References cited at the end of Chapters 12 and 13 are pertinent to this chapter as well.

Alderson, A. D.: *The Structure of the Ottoman Dynasty.* Oxford: Clarendon Press, 1956. An important volume on the Ottoman family and the lives of the individual sultans.

Cahen, Claude: *Pre-Ottoman Turkey: A General Survey of the Material and Spiritual Culture and History, c. 1071–1330.* Translated from the French by J. Jones-Williams. London: Sidgwick and Jackson, 1968. The most important work on the subject.

Cook, M. A., ed.: *A History of the Ottoman Empire to 1730.* Cambridge: Cambridge University Press, 1976. Seven chapters by different authors; the essays are drawn from the *Cambridge History of Islam* and the *New Cambridge Modern History.*

Faroqhi, Suraiya: *Approaching Ottoman History: An Introduction to the Sources.* Cambridge: Cambridge University Press, 1999. An important introduction to historiography and advanced research in Ottoman history.

Fleet, Kate: *European and Islamic Trade in the Early Ottoman State: The Merchants of Genoa and Turkey.* Cambridge: Cambridge University Press, 1999. Examines money, commodities, slaves, grain, wine, alum, cloth, and metals and concludes that the early Ottomans actively supported traders.

Imber, Colin: "Othman I." *Encyclopaedia of Islam.* New ed. Vol. 8, pp. 180–182. Leiden: Brill, 1995.

———: *The Ottoman Empire 1300–1481.* Istanbul: Isis Press, 1990. Detailed political and military history is based on scrupulous analysis of primary sources; this is now the best beginning point for the time period and subjects covered.

Inalcik, Halil: *The Ottoman Empire: The Classical Age, 1300–1600.* 2d ed. New Rochelle, N.Y.: Caratzas, 1989. Thorough history by an outstanding scholar. In addition to political matters, the author discusses law, economic and social life, and culture.

Itzkowitz, Norman: *Ottoman Empire and Islamic Tradition.* New York: Knopf, 1973. This excellent introduction to the Ottoman Empire deals with the early history leading to the formation of the empire.

Kafadar, Cemal: *Between Two Worlds: The Construction of the Ottoman State.* Berkeley: University of California Press, 1995. This book, which emphasizes the importance of ghazis in early Ottoman affairs, should be read in connection with the work by Rudi Lindner cited here.

Kramers, J. H.: "Murad I." *Encyclopaedia of Islam.* New ed. Vol. 7, pp. 592–594. Leiden: Brill, 1993. A brief but useful account.

Lindner, Rudi Paul: *Nomads and Ottomans in Medieval Anatolia.* Bloomington, Ind.: Research Institute for Inner Asian Studies, 1983. The author discounts the ghazi and emphasizes the tribal identity of the early Ottomans. There is also an account of the treatment of Anatolian nomads by the Ottomans in the middle period of the empire's long history.

Olnon, Merlijn: *Memalik-i Mahruse—The Ottomanist's Domain* at http://members.lycos.nl/molnon. Based at Leiden University, this site includes recent book and article citations, sections on transliteration and paleology, and information on Ottoman court music.

Pitcher, Donald Edgar: *An Historical Geography of the Ottoman Empire: From the Earliest Times to the End of the Sixteenth Century, with Detailed Maps to Illustrate the Expansion of the Sultanate.* Leiden: Brill, 1972. Emphasis is on political geography.

Shaw, Stanford: *History of the Ottoman Empire and Modern Turkey.* Vol. 1: *Empire of the Gazis: The Rise and Decline of the Ottoman Empire, 1280–1808.* Cambridge: Cambridge University Press, 1976. This contribution by a leading scholar in the field analyzes the many forces that produced the Ottoman Empire.

Sugar, Peter F.: *Southeastern Europe under Ottoman Rule, 1354–1804.* Seattle: University of Washington Press, 1977.

Vryonis, Speros, Jr.: *The Decline of Medieval Hellenism in Asia Minor and the Process of Islamization from the Eleventh through the Fifteenth Century.* Berkeley: University of California Press, 1986. A landmark in scholarship for its concepts of developments in later Byzantine times.

CHAPTER 15

The Winning of the Ottoman Empire

Even though the Ottoman Empire was dissolved by Timur in 1402, by 1413 Mehmed I reunited it, in the process overcoming both internal and external enemies. As the strengthened state then expanded, the Ottomans encountered challenges on all fronts. One of the chief means by which they overcame these difficulties was their army, while diplomacy and the personal abilities of the ruling sultans also played a large role in their successes. The renewed Ottoman state evolved from an egalitarian, frontier, ghazi orientation toward an urban and bureaucratic empire. Finally, the Ottomans aimed at capturing Constantinople, the great imperial city whose conquest had been the goal of several earlier Muslim dynasties.

MEHMED I REUNITES THE STATE

Timur's capture of Sultan Bayezid I at the battle of Ankara in 1402 destroyed the unity of the Ottoman Empire, causing the remaining Ottoman provinces to be apportioned among his sons. Timur recognized Mehmed as governor of Amasya. Isa was designated as lord of Bursa, the former capital of the Ottomans. Suleiman, the eldest son, went to Edirne and ruled the Ottoman possessions in Europe. Musa, taken prisoner by Timur, was placed on parole at Kutahya. Shortly afterward, he was authorized to take his father's body to Bursa for burial and was then sent to the court of his brother Mehmed.

The transitory character of Timur's conquest permitted the four sons to quarrel among themselves over their patrimony. At first Mehmed and Musa teamed up against Suleiman and Isa, striking their first blows in Asia. Fleeing to Constantinople, Isa was encouraged by Suleiman, himself under pressure from Musa, to make a bid to regain his city. Isa was, however, beaten by Mehmed and vanished.

Suleiman, meanwhile, having escaped from the Ankara disaster with Ali Pasha Chandarli and the leader of the janissaries, arrived at Edirne, European headquarters for the Ottoman family. With the richest part of the state in his hands and supported by his father's chief ministers, Suleiman in 1403 claimed to be ruler of the Ottomans, and he extended his reign to include most of Ottoman Anatolia. But Mehmed and Musa refused to acknowledge his supremacy.

Rivalry among the three brothers endured for a decade. Its genesis was the example set by Bayezid I in killing his own brother. But competition among Suleiman, Musa, and Mehmed also arose from opposition to their father's attempts to consolidate and centralize the state.

The imperial clique found its candidate in Suleiman. Supported by the Chandarli and Evrenos families, by the governmental machinery in Edirne, and by the janissaries who survived the rout at Ankara, Suleiman reigned until 1411. Treaties with Venice and the Byzantine emperor recognized him as Ottoman ruler and facilitated trade and commerce in Europe, affairs in which the Chandarli family was personally interested.

With the aid of discontented Serbs and Wallachians, Musa carried the struggle against Suleiman to Europe in 1410. Unsuccessful in the first attempt, Musa caught Suleiman the next year in a surprise raid upon Edirne and had him strangled. Ibrahim Chandarli, the Evrenos family, and the court immediately transferred their loyalty to Musa, who was now recognized as lord of Europe. Mehmed remained supreme in Anatolia.

Besides Balkan vassals and Ottoman European officialdom, Musa was supported by freethinking religious groups popular at that time. As chief judge in Ottoman European territories, he appointed one of the leaders of these Sufi groups, Shaikh Badr al-Din Simavni, who held views leading toward an egalitarian society. Some years later Shaikh Badr al-Din led an unsuccessful rebellion against the state, and in the mid-sixteenth century his views were still being preached by one of his descendants.

Musa was an energetic individual who sent out raiding parties into Europe and resumed the siege of Constantinople, but Mehmed aided the Byzantine emperor against his brother. Musa's support of Christian vassals and royal slaves drove many of his supporters, such as Ibrahim Chandarli, over to Mehmed, who carried on an active campaign for allies among high-placed Ottoman lords in Europe. Most of these went over to Mehmed; and in 1413, after Mehmed gained fresh troops from the Serbs and Dhu al-Qadr, Mehmed caught up with Musa. Musa perished, and his body was returned with honor to Bursa to be buried beside Sultan Murad I.

In looking for factors in the success of Mehmed, his having first governed in Amasya, heartland of the old ghazi district, helped make him the champion of the ghazis. With the favor of this powerful faction, essentially the military foundation of the state, propaganda for him among frontier raiders and Ottoman colonists in Europe took root easily, while the slave troops, Christian vassals, and officials were lowered in position and rank. Mehmed represented the "good old days" of Osman and Orhan.

Another factor in the personal success of Mehmed was the role of his tutor and his early education. As was customary, Mehmed was sent as a boy to govern a province and learn the art of ruling. A high official accompanied the prince to advise in all matters. In this instance, the tutor was Bayezid Pasha, an Albanian by birth and a war captive raised at court. Bayezid Pasha proved to be an outstanding general and a devoted slave to Mehmed, winning battles, organizing campaigns, and above all leading Mehmed to the task of reuniting the Ottoman state. Bayezid Pasha was one of the very first of a new type of high Ottoman official who in his attachment to his masters, the Ottoman family, showed his desire for a centralized state.

In strongly identifying himself with Anatolia and the old ghazi way of life, Mehmed avoided the mistakes of his father and his brother Suleiman in their European manners. He chose for his wife a daughter of the amir of Dhu al-Qadr, a Turkoman amirate of the Syrian frontier. Mehmed grew to be revered by the Ottomans for his gentleness, integrity, and modesty.

THE OTTOMAN ARMY

The institution of the Ottoman army also proved to be an important factor in helping to preserve the Ottoman dynasty and to overcome the factionalism and divisions following 1402. Military traditions, processes, and history provided pressures for unity. The army had become more sophisticated and differentiated since the early days when under Osman criers simply went through the villages announcing that anyone who wished to participate in a raid should meet at a given place at a specific time.

The army was organized on a basis of units of 10, 100, and 1000 men, with a responsible officer over each group. This was as true of irregular infantry and tribal horsemen and cavalry scouts as it was of regular cavalry (sipahi) and the janissaries (yeni cheri). Officers of the immediate family and entourage of the Ottoman ruler were placed in overall charge of the armies. The word *pasha* was a title used at this time by Ottoman officers.

The institution of the janissaries held a special place in Ottoman annals. The origin of this corps has been much debated since they were so important in Ottoman victories through several centuries. Janissaries as an Ottoman institution probably began in connection with the custom of Muslim states, beginning in the time of the prophet Muhammad, that the ruler usually received one-fifth of the booty of war. Since human beings had long been valuable prizes of successful campaigns and since their lot was often one of slavery, the Ottomans under Orhan and Murad found more slaves on their hands than they knew how to employ. The answer was to turn them into soldiers to fight for their captors.

In the past caliphs and sultans had slave bodyguards, and in late medieval Egypt the ruling Mamluks had been slaves. Seljuk rulers used slaves by the thousands who were trained as soldiers, led their armies, and rose to become high officials. Most of them were Greek youths of Anatolia taken as prisoners or levied as a tribute from the Greek subjects. Youths captured in battle were kept as slaves by the Ottoman sultans as well. Normally converted to Islam, they were banded together and trained as special corps in the army about the sultan. Their name, yeni cheri ("new soldier"), was corrupted to "janissary" by Europeans, who learned to fear their discipline, their esprit de corps, and their prowess with arms. Many younger captives were "farmed out" as apprentices to Ottoman officers for a number of years. During these years they learned some Turkish and how to fight.

In the days of Murad I the janissaries probably numbered around 1000; by the time of Bayezid I they had increased to about 5000. They were paid a small daily wage and did not marry while serving as active soldiers. Living together in barracks, drilling, training, and dressing alike gave the janissaries the status of a standing army. Some were cavalry; most were infantrymen; others were members of a specially honored left-handed guard. Many rose through the ranks and became high officers and trusted civil officials; a few were beheaded for dishonesty or disobedience. Before a century passed, only those who became regular infantry were known as janissaries. Other ranks and other corps had their own special designations.

The most important group were the sipahis, who answered the need for regular cavalry, for colonization of newly won lands, and for local provincial administration. Adapting Seljuk iqtas, Ottoman rulers rewarded fighting men with the revocable grants of the right to collect tax revenues from land farmed by peasants; the sipahis derived their living from these revenues. By the sixteenth century these grants tended to become hereditary. Each year when a campaign was announced, sipahis left their estates and appeared equipped to fight under a local officer whom they elected. Sons went along on campaigns with their fathers and learned the profession of arms. They were eligible to become cavalrymen, and often they were awarded at least a part of the family holdings. By settling and rearing families on the land, the sipahi cavalry served as the first Ottoman colonizers and administrators of new territories.

In certain areas where the frontier had long been a battleground, as in Bosnia and Albania, a society emerged similar to those of earlier frontier areas in Anatolia. A thorough mixture of Ottoman warriors with local populations occurred, giving rise in the Balkans to some Greek-, Serb-, and Albanian-speaking Muslims.

All these groups—janissaries, sipahis, frontier raiders, urban volunteers, and others—felt that the religious ideal of frontier warfare for Islam, their own particular and organizational interests, and the success of Ottoman Muslim society were intertwined with the glory and unity of the Ottoman Empire, which needed strong leadership. With the victory of Mehmed I the Ottoman state was reunited in 1413.

EXPANSION IN ASIA

There were in Anatolia many Turks, however, who were not considered Ottomans and who did not accept the idea of one united state. The Karaman prince, the prime Ottoman rival in Anatolia, besieged Bursa when Mehmed was destroying Musa in Rumeli. (The European part of the Ottoman state was referred to as Rumeli—the land of the Romans, i.e., Byzantines.) The Karamans were defeated in 1415, but their state was not conquered.

Most of the other Anatolian states now recognized the dominant position of the Ottomans in central and western Anatolia. However, the disruption of society resulting from Timur's invasion and continued by the civil wars of Bayezid's sons generated many mystical sects in Anatolia. A number of Sufi orders founded by holy men from Iran date their origin from this period. Social unrest, too, was common. In 1416, Bayezid Pasha had to raise levies from most of Anatolia to quell a socioreligious egalitarian movement in Anatolia and in Europe—a movement led by the mystic Badr al-Din Simavni, one-time European army judge under Musa.

Mehmed could not ignore Europe, especially since Rumeli produced far greater revenue for the Ottoman government than did Anatolia. Mehmed intervened in Wallachia, built fortresses north of the Danube, and conquered parts of southern Albania reaching the Adriatic Sea, although the sultan refused to resume the attack upon Constantinople.

Mehmed reestablished Ottoman unity approximately to the extent that it had existed in his father's time. But a truly complete Ottoman Empire was not yet created, and it could not be created without Constantinople, geographic and economic center of the area. Mehmed's death from a stroke in 1421 may have saved the city from attack.

MURAD II

The idea of the continuity of the state and the sultan's relationship to governmental power had so grown that Mehmed's closest advisers, of whom Bayezid Pasha was one, concealed his death for forty days until his son and successor Murad II arrived in Bursa to take charge. Nearly eighteen years old, Murad had resided with his advisers and tutors at Amasya. At the time of his father's death, Murad had three surviving brothers—two were blinded and therefore made ineligible for the succession; the third, Mustafa, afraid that Murad would kill him as Bayezid had strangled Yakub, fled from his Anatolian governorship with his tutors to the protection of the Karaman family in Konya.

Murad surrounded himself with representatives of old Ottoman families such as the Chandarli and Evrenos families, and with leaders of the new courtiers like Bayezid Pasha, although this latter group was less numerous. At the very outset of Murad's reign the Byzantine emperor freed the old pretender Mustafa, supposed son of Bayezid I, who defeated and killed Bayezid Pasha, gained backers among the nomads, seized Gallipoli with the emperor's aid, and invaded Anatolia. Murad rallied and drove them back to Europe. In 1422 Genoese cooperation in transporting his troops across the Straits permitted him to catch and kill the pretender Mustafa and the rebels in Edirne.

Murad raged at the emperor for his duplicity and ordered resumption of the siege of Constantinople. With prodigious effort, much enthusiasm, and the use of breaching cannon for the first time in Ottoman history, Murad and his soldiers stormed the walls. After two months of failure Murad lifted the siege to meet a new threat in Anatolia: Byzantine diplomacy with the Karamans had brought Murad's brother Mustafa from his refuge in Konya to an unsuccessful attack upon Bursa.

Though Mustafa was caught and hanged, and the threat of a new lengthy civil war averted, Murad never resumed the attack upon Constantinople. The emperor agreed to pay the Ottomans a yearly tribute and surrender most Byzantine territory outside the walls. In Anatolia, Murad judiciously alternated between diplomacy and force. Murad married the daughter of one amir, and by 1430 he had brought all of western Anatolia fully under Ottoman control. Although the Karaman amir sued for peace, there was an uneasy relationship with Karaman.

Murad's greatest efforts were expended in Europe, and there lay his greater gains. The sultan encouraged privateers whose ships in the Aegean Sea raided commerce, while he also organized an Ottoman fleet into which the privateers were ultimately incorporated. Using this naval strength based at Gallipoli as well as the army, in 1430 Salonica was retaken from Venice after a long struggle. Upon the accession to the throne of Hungary of Ladislaus, king of Lithuania and Poland, he invaded Ottoman territory, in 1443 winning numerous strongholds and bringing Murad to the edge of ruin. Nevertheless, Murad and King Ladislaus concluded a peace in 1444. Murad had also temporarily defeated the Karamans and John Hunyadi, Ottoman vassal governor of Transylvania.

Evidently Murad felt that since he had made peace with his enemies the time was right for retirement from an active rule. He was forty years old and had been sultan for twenty-three years. Murad abdicated in favor of his young son, Mehmed, who went to Edirne with Khalil Pasha Chandarli as grand vizir. Murad himself withdrew to his residence in Manisa, where he intended to live in ease and peace with poets, mystics, theologians, and men of letters. He wished to pursue the futuwwa, the ideal life, studying and writing in quiet contemplation.

It was the time of an incipient Turkish renaissance. The Turkish language, as spoken at the Ottoman court and in western Anatolia, became a medium of cultured expression. Konya and Bursa in Anatolia and Edirne in Europe were its centers; its patrons were the Karaman and Ottoman families and their courts. Persian and Arabic were the languages of poetry, records, and education. But Turkish was growing more popular. Many Persian and Arabic works were translated into Ottoman Turkish, and poets were held in high esteem. Sufis were numerous and venerated.

Ottoman history was first cultivated under Murad, when a "romantic" movement arose. Until this time, Ottoman chronicles were legendary sagas of ghazis and their great deeds. Under Murad, there developed a new and more formal Ottoman history, which included stories of illustrious ancestors going back to the most noble of Turkish tribes. Beautiful tales were written of Osman's ancestors riding with 400 horsemen into Anatolia. In this manner the Ottomans are supposed to have received their start! It must be remembered that at the time of Murad's retirement about 150 years had passed since Osman's first conquests, and that in a new and rapidly evolving society not many people could correctly relate the exploits of their great-great-great-grandfathers.

Murad's intellectual and cultural concerns were reflected in the education of his children. He employed distinguished scholars, many of whom also held important army or administrative positions, as teachers for the princes. Included with the princes in the palace school were other boys, some of whom were captives of war or sons of distinguished vassals of the sultan. Murad desired not only to educate his own sons but also to train other youths who might serve state and sultan intelligently and faithfully. Proof of the value and thoroughness of this school was first demonstrated in the education and ability of Murad's son, Mehmed.

MILITARY DEVELOPMENTS

After Murad's retirement, the Hungarians broke the peace in 1444. Murad was recalled from his retirement and crushed the crusader invaders near Varna on the Black Sea. King Ladislaus lost his life, and his army was defeated and dispersed.

The Ottomans now easily overran Serbia and Bosnia. Since Ottomans were tolerant of Christianity whereas Hungarians in their brief sway had begun to impose Catholic rites upon Serbian and Bosnian Orthodox churches, many fortresses freely opened their gates to Murad.

With this affair apparently settled, Murad abdicated a second time in 1445 and returned to Manisa. It was not long, however, before rebellion against Mehmed II by janissaries seeking back pay brought Murad back to active rule in Edirne. The ringleaders were executed and the sultan's authority was restored.

This episode was a sign of future grave difficulties that Ottoman sultans would experience with janissary and other imperial troops, who were hardened professional soldiers. Simply educated, reared and trained for warfare, and not too well paid because of the expectation that they would be richly rewarded from plunder won on campaigns, the janissaries felt their power and importance and were easily induced to demand favors of many kinds. Between them and other groups of Ottoman supporters—the sipahi cavalry and old families who provided administrators like those closest to Murad—rivalry was often bitter.

For this reason, in about 1430 Murad had reinstituted a draft (devshirmeh) procedure for the janissary corps. Every few years army officers toured the rural districts, conscripting Christian boys between the ages of ten and fifteen. These youths were brought to Edirne and were parceled out among court officers, the sipahis, and the sultan himself. After a few years of growth, toughening, Islamization, and Turkification in language and customs they were returned to Edirne, where they received military training and were assigned to a janissary barracks. The more favored were attached to the palace; the very best attended the princes' school, whereupon any position in the state was open to them. At first employed to augment the ranks of the janissaries when wars and raids failed to yield sufficient captives, the draft was justified as another form of taxation for the subject communities, analogous to poll taxes, except that these taxes were paid in boys! More significant was the fact that the most vigorous and capable youths were being removed from their villages and raised as Ottomans. Some observers remarked that this policy helped to keep the Christian population in subjection by drawing away future leaders. Some families turned to Islam rather than lose their sons.

It was also the custom for vassal Christian princes who were permitted to retain their lands to send sons as hostages to the sultan's court. One such hostage was George Kastriota, who was sent to Murad II. He was educated in the princes' school, served in various responsible posts under Murad, but deserted in 1443. Skanderbeg, as he was now called, returned to his native Albania, where for twenty-five years he led resistance movements and guerrilla warfare against Murad and Mehmed II.

After the janissary revolt of 1445 was put down, Murad did not again retire but engaged in campaigns in Europe. Twice he entered Albania in pursuit of Skanderbeg. Bulgaria was fully absorbed into the Ottoman system of direct rule, and much of it was settled by Turkish-speaking nomads. In 1448, Murad drove John Hunyadi (now in control of Hungary) out of Serbia, defeating him on the plains of Kosovo. Early in 1451, the aged warrior (about fifty years old) died in Edirne. The young Mehmed, now grown to manhood, when apprised in Manisa of his father's death, supposedly leaped on his horse and raced to the capital, Edirne, to take charge.

MEHMED II

In some ways Mehmed II's character was an extension of his father's. Since he had the benefits of the princes' school, his mind was well trained. He knew literary Turkish, Arabic, Persian, and Greek, and was able to converse in Serbian and Italian. He enjoyed philosophy and poetry, and was familiar with the classical poetry of Iran, Greece, and Rome. Mehmed was an accomplished poet himself and gathered about him poets from the Muslim world. He loved history, particularly biographies of Alexander the Great and the Caesars. The study of war and of everything associated with war aroused his interest greatly. Ottoman males in the royal family had a trade—perhaps because of the akhi heritage—and Mehmed was an accomplished gardener. Later, between campaigns and for relaxation, he worked in the gardens of the royal palace.

With regard to administration, however, Mehmed was quite unlike his father. Thoroughness and efficiency combined with great energy and promptness became the order of the day. Mehmed was known for his furious temper. He showed remarkable tolerance in religious matters.

In many respects Murad had not been very businesslike in his administration, and Mehmed spent the first year of his reign reorganizing the government, particularly the treasury. Tax rates were raised, monopolies established, and pious foundations (Arabic, waqf/awqaf; Turkish, vakif/evkaf) were confiscated to the benefit of the imperial treasury. The entire administration of the royal palace was surveyed, registers of the troops scrutinized, and soldiers' pay increased. One unhappy episode was Mehmed's order that his only brother, an infant, be drowned in his bath, thus perpetuating the custom begun by Bayezid I of eliminating rival heirs.

CAPTURE OF CONSTANTINOPLE

With the coming of 1452 Mehmed began his plans for taking Constantinople. Peace with Serbia, Hungary, and the Karamans had been arranged, so as to deter their aiding the Byzantines. Munitions were gathered: armor, bows, arrows, mortars, cannons, gunpowder, timbers, and war articles of every sort. Although Ottoman siege cannons were rather clumsy, they were quite effective and technologically equivalent to those first used by French forces in the 1430s. At Gallipoli a fleet was assembled and new ships built. To control the Bosphorus Mehmed ordered the construction of a fortress on its European shore opposite the fortifications built on the Asian side half a century earlier by his great-grandfather.

While the siege began in 1452, the true attack upon Constantinople started in April 1453. More than 50,000 of the best soldiers that Mehmed could muster were assembled for the assault. The Ottoman fleet numbered about 200 ships. For fifty-four days cannonballs pounded the land walls of the city. The sea walls were bombarded by the fleet, but the walls along the Golden Horn could not be reached. Mortars from the shores of the Bosphorus did sink some Greek ships on the Golden Horn, but a heavy chain from Galata to Constantinople effectively closed the Horn to Mehmed's ships. Not to be thwarted, Mehmed constructed a greased wooden runway from the shore of the Bosphorus up the hill of Beyoglu (Pera) and down the slope to the Golden Horn. About seventy ships of the Ottoman fleet were hauled up over the incline and slid down to the Golden Horn, from where they threw their stone cannonballs on the city walls.

Cut off completely and bombarded from every side, the few defenders of Constantinople still resisted the attacks. The Genoese and other Italians in Galata and Pera gave little assistance, and most of the 50,000 inhabitants of the once great city seemed indifferent to their fate, perhaps because Emperor Constantine in desperation had called for aid from the west and announced submission to the pope in exchange for promises of soldiers. A few came, but help was entirely inadequate.

A stupendous assault was launched on May 29, 1453; cannon fire breached the walls, and the city was taken. Following the custom of that age, the conquering troops had complete license to pillage the city and enslave its inhabitants, except that no public buildings could be touched. Mehmed entered the city, and the plundering ceased. He went to Hagia Sophia, where Muslim prayers were said. A governor was appointed; inhabitants were encouraged to remain by exempting them from taxes and by giving them back their houses; the sultan ransomed many on the condition that they would stay; the army was disbanded; and Mehmed temporarily returned to Edirne.

The economic, military, and cultural effects of the capture of Constantinople have usually been exaggerated. Later centuries developed a myth that the fall of Constantinople blocked the trade routes to the Far East, thereby forcing the age of discovery and the voyages of Columbus. According to another legend, the fall of Constantinople resulted in the migration of Greek monks and manuscripts to Italy, thus initiating the Renaissance. Another story has related that the fall of Constantinople removed the Balkan bastion, at once enabling the Ottoman Turks to conquer the whole peninsula of southeast Europe. All three of these myths have been exploded.

Nevertheless, the emotional impact of the fall of Constantinople on the people of the fifteenth century should not be minimized. To Christian Europe, both Orthodox and Catholic, the great imperial city had fallen. In a sense the Roman Empire had finally come to an end. Now Ottoman expansion seemed a more threatening and immediate danger. To Muslims, the fall of Constantinople was a great and glorious achievement that Islamic rulers and armies had attempted many times in the past. To them, Constantinople was the majestic city of imperial tradition whose conquest had been a goal of the great caliphs. Now a Muslim state had accomplished the impossible, and consequently Mehmed II received acclaim and respect. To the Ottomans, it was the conquest of the natural capital and center of their state.

Since the time of Bayezid I the incorporation of Constantinople in the Ottoman state had been a logical and necessary step, but it had been long in coming. Its acquisition served as the keystone in the Ottoman Empire, which would now enter into a long period of dynamic expansion and development.

REFERENCES

References cited at the end of Chapters 13 and 14 are pertinent to this chapter as well.

Babinger, Franz: *Mehmed the Conqueror and His Time.* Edited by William C. Hickman. Translated by Ralph Manheim. Princeton, N.J.: Princeton University Press, 1978. This classic biography emphasizes diplomacy and military and political history.

Inalcik, Halil: *The Ottoman Empire: Conquest, Organization and Economy.* London: Variorum, 1978. A collection of sixteen articles dealing with Ottoman conquests and organization, the economy, and decline and reform.

Kritovoulos: *History of Mehmed the Conqueror.* Translated by Charles T. Riggs. Princeton, N.J.: Princeton University Press, 1954. A contemporary account by a Greek in the service of the Ottomans.

McCarthy, Justin: *The Ottoman Turks: An Introductory History to 1923.* London: Longman, 1997. An excellent general survey with emphasis on the Turkish population's political, military, and social history.

Runciman, Steven: *The Fall of Constantinople, 1453.* Cambridge: Cambridge University Press, 1969. The author has scoured the sources and presented in great detail and with much understanding a very readable account of the taking of the city.

Tursun Beg: *The History of Mehmed the Conqueror.* Translated by Halil Inalcik and Rhoads Murphy. Minneapolis: Bibliotheca Islamica, 1978. In addition to a facsimile text of a manuscript of the work by Tursun Beg in the original Turkish, the translators have provided a summary translation and a discussion of the author.

CHAPTER 16

Expansion of the Ottoman Empire

The reestablishment of the Ottoman Empire after Timur's destruction and then the conquest of Constantinople opened the way for rapid expansion of the imperial borders. Three rulers—Mehmed II, Bayezid II, and Selim I—directed the wars and diplomacy that resulted in a doubling of the size of the state. Despite struggles over succession to the sultanate, advances were made in rebuilding Constantinople (now called Istanbul) as the imperial capital and making institutional arrangements for the governance of the many non-Muslim subjects added to the realm.

MEHMED II'S CONQUESTS

Beyond taking Istanbul in 1453, the young Mehmed II, called Fatih ("the Conqueror") by his subjects, extended the periphery of his empire substantially. Campaigns were scheduled almost every year. Operations were conducted in the Balkans and Anatolia, and from Venice and southern Italy to Iran and the Crimea. Affairs of any one area involved those of others, and Mehmed was unable to isolate his many international and domestic problems to deal with one at a time. Moreover, Venetian envoys were plotting at every court to bring his downfall.

Ottoman campaigns, colonization, and government had been proceeding in the Balkans for a century. Nonetheless, Ottoman rule was still not effective in several regions, and many provinces that were tied to the Ottomans by a kind of vassalage or alliance were not integrated units of the state. Byzantine practices persisted in local administration, especially on church and monastery lands. Conversion to Islam was very slow; the languages of the conquered peoples persisted even when Ottoman judicial, fiscal, and landholding structures were introduced. The Ottomans ruled about 4 million non-Muslims in the Balkans, whose territory provided much of the revenue of the state. The sultan enacted a number of reforms; probably the most important was a land reform in the entire empire, whereby the state regained direct control of the taxes of thousands of villages that had fallen into private hands (this reform was reversed under Mehmed's successor). In addition, semiautonomous local lords were ousted in parts of the Balkans in favor of more direct rule, and Christians were retained as holders of some revocable land grants, although most of these grants were given to Muslims. The sultan chose slave recruits from the Balkans for high offices while decreasing the role of men from the old Turkish families, many of whom were forced to move to the Balkan region.

Pressure on the Balkans, however, was maintained continuously. Greece, except for a few Venetian ports, was conquered, with Athens falling to the Ottomans in 1456. In the 1460s Serbia and Bosnia were subjected to Ottoman rule and organized as regular imperial provinces. Wallachia and Moldavia were forced to become allies. Skanderbeg was checked in Albania, and after his death in 1468 much of Albania and Herzegovina became provinces of the empire.

Mehmed also pursued a vigorous policy in Anatolia and the east. The most resistant foe to the Ottomans had been the Karaman dynasty of the Bursa region; in 1468 Karaman opposition was broken. Later Cilicia in southeastern Anatolia was acquired, and as his reign closed Mehmed became involved in family quarrels of the Dhu al-Qadr of Diyarbakir. The entire Mediterranean coast of Anatolia was now in Ottoman hands. Since Istanbul and the Straits were now Ottoman, Mehmed moved northward and eastward, hoping to control the Black Sea shores. In 1461, with the cooperation of the navy from Gallipoli, Mehmed forced the surrender of the Greek emperor of Trebizond, thus obliterating the last remnant of the Byzantine Empire.

These activities led the Ottomans into conflict with the Aq Quyunlu, who dominated parts of Iran, Armenia, and eastern Anatolia. Venetian ambassadors traveled to the court of the Aq Quyunlu leader Uzun Hasan at Tabriz and encouraged war against Mehmed, so as to lessen Ottoman pressure upon Venice and its European territory. The danger to the Ottoman state was great, since the alliance of Venice, Hungary, Uzun Hasan, and the Karaman ruler threatened the empire on all fronts in the 1460s and early 1470s. However, Mehmed II collected a mighty army of more than 200,000 soldiers, including his two sons, Mustafa and Bayezid, his grand vizir, and Gedik Ahmed Pasha, a burly general who had risen from the ranks of the ordinary janissaries. Using cannons and handguns to which the Aq Quyunlu were unaccustomed, the sultan defeated Uzun Hasan in 1473 in eastern Anatolia; after this defeat the Karaman pretenders finally disappeared. Next the Crimea, which was ruled by Turkish Tatar khans, accepted Ottoman sovereignty in 1475. Except for the coast between the Crimea and the Danube River, the Black Sea was now an Ottoman lake.

To the south of Istanbul in the Aegean Sea, conflict between Venice and the Ottoman Empire grew. To ensure control of the Aegean coast of Anatolia and permit Ottoman conquests in southern Greece, it was necessary to incorporate the Aegean Islands into the empire. This was particularly important because Venetians and pirates used these islands as bases to harry the Ottoman coast. Mehmed's fleet, therefore, captured these islands, and for fifteen years (1463–1478) he was at war sporadically with Venice. The Ottomans were unable to defeat Venetian fleets at sea, but they captured strategic bases that would later enable them to extend their naval power substantially.

Pressure on Venetian outposts along the Dalmatian coast in the Adriatic Sea area was also constant. In 1477 Ottoman raiders descended to the Italian plain north of Venice. At night Venetian senators from the roof of St. Mark's could see Ottoman campfires and burning villages. When autumn came the Ottomans returned home laden with booty. Venice concluded peace with Mehmed and recognized his island acquisitions.

In 1480 an Ottoman army under Gedik Ahmed Pasha crossed the Adriatic and took Otranto in the heel of the Italian peninsula, thus establishing a bridgehead for the conquest of Italy. Gedik Ahmed wintered there, but upon Mehmed's sudden death in May 1481 the expedition to Otranto was withdrawn, never to be launched again. The conqueror was dead. Secrecy was maintained in the Ottoman Empire until a successor could ascend the throne. Bells pealed in Europe when the news arrived.

ISTANBUL AND THE ORTHODOX PATRIARCHATE

Constantinople/Istanbul in 1453 was only a half-populated city, which had been dying slowly for more than two centuries. Mehmed II viewed the task of repopulating the city as even a mightier one than the actual conquest. He freed many prisoners, encouraged others to remain, exempted many from taxation, and conducted a census in 1455. In later conquests inhabitants of other towns were ordered to move to Istanbul, so that by the end of the century Istanbul became the most populous city in the Middle East. Mehmed also supported the bazaar merchants by building many shops. Many pious endowments (awqaf) were established to promote the welfare of Muslims. The Christian population, as in most Ottoman cities, was not subjected to the devshirmeh.

When Mehmed "Fatih" entered Istanbul, he learned that the Orthodox Christian patriarch was dead. Appreciating the need for the election of a new patriarch, Mehmed indicated confidence in the teacher and philosopher George Scholarius. Duly elected, Scholarius took the name Gennadios. Mehmed recognized him as leader of the Christians in Istanbul. Gennadios was charged with responsibility for the obedience, conduct, and life of the Greek Orthodox people and their relationship to the Ottoman government. Thus, in many ways Orthodox Christians were encouraged to reside in Istanbul and allowed to live according to their own laws as long as they did not come into conflict with the administration of the government and the lives of Muslim subjects. In like manner, Mehmed II recognized a head of the Armenian Christian community in Istanbul, as well as other Armenian religious leaders for other regions. The chief Jewish rabbi of Istanbul was treated as preeminent among the rabbis of the empire, while the heads of local Jewish communities in other cities were acknowledged as locally autonomous leaders.

Islam and Muslims nevertheless received priority in government policy. Public buildings were reserved for the state, and many churches were converted into mosques; nearly 200 new mosques were built by the imperial authorities. The outstanding example was Justinian's great church Hagia Sophia, which became the Muslim Aya Sofya. Mehmed II and his successors gave much church-owned land to Sufi establishments. During the siege the Ottomans discovered what they claimed to be the burial site of the hero Abu Ayyub al-Ansari (Eyup), the standardbearer of the prophet Muhammad, who had died in 668 during an earlier siege near the walls of Constantinople in the days of the caliph Muawiyah. Ayyub's remains were entombed in a mosque-mausoleum-Sufi residence near the Golden Horn, where subsequent Ottoman sultans were ceremoniously girded with the sword of their authority.

As his first residence Fatih built a large palace in the most populous part of the city; he occupied it for about twelve years whenever he was in Istanbul. Here, about the year 1465, a new palace was completed, which remained the chief domicile of sultans until the nineteenth century. The new palace was erected on the site of the acropolis of ancient Byzantium on the point of land between the Golden Horn and the Sea of Marmara. Facing the entrance to the Bosphorus, it was the most beautiful and spectacular spot in the city for an imperial residence. It was soon popularly called Topkapi Saray ("Cannon Gate Palace") because of the heavily fortified gate at the tip of the point of land. Yet Fatih passed many seasons at the palace in Edirne or in Bursa. Edirne remained the favorite summer headquarters of sultans until the eighteenth century.

BAYEZID II AND JEM

When Mehmed II died in 1481, he left two sons. Bayezid II, aged thirty-three, was governor of Amasya, the old ghazi center. Jem, aged twenty-one, was governor of Konya, the former Seljuk capital. Since Amasya was eight days' ride from Istanbul whereas Konya was only four, the younger son had an advantage in obtaining control of the central administration. The janissaries, the pages of the palace, and the government officials who were slaves of the sultan and recipients of the palace school training preferred Bayezid. Mehmed's last grand vizir, however, belonged by birth to the old Muslim families of Anatolia and was partial to Jem. He tried to conceal Mehmed's death and secretly dispatched couriers to Jem. However, Mehmed's death became known, whereupon the slave officials and the janissaries seized control, murdered the grand vizir, impaled his messengers to Jem, and awaited Bayezid's appearance. They chose the latter because they considered his residence of twenty-five years or more at Amasya as wedding him to the ghazi tradition, of which they were fast becoming the heirs. Moreover, Bayezid had cleverly attached through marriages and political friendship several figures of the government hierarchy to his candidacy. Jem's chief difficulty was his comparative youth; Bayezid for years had been gathering his party for the eventual day. To break through a cordon of officers blocking the gate to the imperial palace of Topkapi, Bayezid pledged a handsome gift of money to every janissary, declared an amnesty for all crimes committed in the interregnum, and most significantly, agreed to appoint to the vizirship only men who were soldiers or palace slaves.

Jem, with forces from Karaman and Konya, occupied Bursa and challenged Bayezid for the throne. Gedik Ahmed was recalled from Otranto and with the army that Mehmed II had gathered defeated Jem, who fled to Mamluk Egypt whence he made the holy pilgrimage to Mecca. Bayezid offered him a princely income if he would live peacefully in Jerusalem, but Jem returned in 1482 and made a second vain attempt at the throne. Escaping to the protection of the Knights of St. John on the island of Rhodes, he was held in custody by them and used to obtain a favorable treaty of peace with the Ottomans. The knights subsequently moved him to their castles in France, where he fell into the hands of Charles VIII. Later, Jem was presented to the pope, then was borrowed by Charles in 1494, from Pope Alexander VI, ostensibly to participate in a crusade against the Ottomans. Jem, however, died of a fever in Naples the next year.

WARS OF BAYEZID II

Between 1482 and 1495, Bayezid's fear of his brother's return somewhat restricted his foreign activities. Yet the organization of the Ottoman state was conditioned to aggressive expansion. When campaigns were not in progress, sipahis, janissaries, and the court became uneasy. During these years, therefore, a number of expeditions along the Dalmatian coast and into Hungary were undertaken and a large navy was built. Although these raids were usually indecisive, they were rewarding in plunder. Akkerman, on the Black Sea at the mouth of the Dniester River, was taken, and Wallachia and Moldavia were subdued.

In this early period of Bayezid's reign, war broke out with the Mamluk sultans of Egypt. Persistent dynastic difficulties among the Dhu al-Qadr involved the Mamluks and Ottomans in disputes. In 1484, after aid and asylum had been given to Jem, open war broke out. The peace concluded in 1491 left Egypt in possession of the disputed border areas, but no difficulties appeared for two decades.

Following Jem's death, Bayezid pursued a more aggressive policy in the west. The tempo of Ottoman raids along the Dalmatian coast increased; ports rang with the noise of carpenters constructing war galleys. When war broke out with Venice in 1499, the Ottoman navy of about 250 vessels defeated the Venetian fleet in a great sea engagement at Navarino. Peace was not concluded until 1503. The war further eclipsed Venetian power in Greece and the eastern Mediterranean, and Ottoman sea power became strongly established. Thereafter in Bayezid's reign, contingents of the Ottoman navy raided throughout the Mediterranean, and Ottoman merchants prospered throughout the great inland sea.

Back in the east, about the time the war with Venice ended, a new figure emerged on the Ottoman frontier—the Shii Shah Ismail of Iran, who kindled a religious and military enthusiasm in the peoples of Iran and eastern and southern Anatolia. Shah Ismail's doctrines proved popular, and open revolt among the Turkoman tribes developed in 1511. Ismail's followers were called qizilbash ("red head") because of the red hats they wore. Pro-Safavid rebels besieged and took Konya, seized Kutahya (Ottoman Anatolian army headquarters), and impaled the Ottoman commander in chief. Despite the eclectic nature of Ottoman Sunni Islam and the fact that Bayezid II was enough of a mystic that one of his nicknames was Sufi, the Ottomans could not permit the religious ideas of a foreign monarch free rein within their state. The Safavid rebels were defeated in a battle against an army that included 4000 janissaries under the grand vizir and three Ottoman princes.

SELIM'S SUCCESSION

After the end of the Venetian war Bayezid suffered poor health and was often carried on a stretcher so that the troops might see him and know he still lived. With each illness his sons became exceedingly nervous about the future. Of his eight sons, only three remained in 1511: Korkud at Manisa; Ahmed at Amasya; and Selim, the youngest, at Trabzon. Each was jockeying for advantages and seeking favors and strategic appointments for friends and sons as the protracted struggle for power weakened the central government. The janissaries and the soldiers preferred Selim, since he was the most devoted to warfare. High officials advanced Ahmed as a solid administrator. The poets, philosophers, and theologians supported Korkud, for he was one of them.

Selim moved his forces to Edirne, and when Bayezid and his close advisers began granting authority to Ahmed, Selim seized that city, but was ousted by his father. The empire was on the verge of civil war as the external challenge by Safavid-backed forces in Anatolia increased. The staunchly Sunni Bayezid called Selim to Istanbul in 1512 and abdicated in his favor. Bayezid died while en route to retirement.

For thirty-one years Bayezid II, a peace-loving, scholarly, and contemplative person, had governed the Ottoman Empire. He spent years in organizing the administration of the government and took great interest in the palace school, often quizzing the students himself. Trade flourished, with merchants from Venice and Genoa thronging to Istanbul, and merchants from the east and the Arab lands coming to Bursa. The Ottomans exported copper and timber and imported silk, wheat, and spices. Bayezid and many janissaries and court officers belonged to Sufi orders, yet he was strict with Muslims because his father's unorthodox ways had disturbed him. One of Bayezid's first acts as sultan was to clear from the palace the pictures of his father painted by Gentile Bellini. Despite this religious rigor, during his reign about 200,000 or more Jews came to Istanbul, Izmir, Edirne, Salonica, and Palestine when they were driven from Spain, even before but especially during 1492.

Selim I (nicknamed Yavuz, meaning "stern" or "inflexible") gave a bonus to each soldier upon his accession, as had become the custom in securing the throne. But he entered the palace by a side gate in order not to bow openly to their demands. The facts were that he held only Rumeli with Istanbul, Ahmed controlling most of Anatolia from Amasya. Selim crossed to Asia and carried the attack against Ahmed, who fled to Safavid Iran, returned, and was defeated and executed. Meanwhile, five of Selim's nephews and his brother Korkud were similarly disposed of. Because Ahmed had obtained considerable support from the qizilbash of Anatolia, Selim decided to curb the growth of the sect, particularly since it was popular in the difficult mountainous and frontier areas of Karaman and Diyarbakir. Later in 1513, Selim stationed troops in all parts of the empire, and at a given notice about 40,000 qizilbash were cut down. By transporting others to Europe, Selim hoped that he had eradicated religious dissent in Anatolia.

WAR AGAINST SAFAVID IRAN

In this ferocious way Selim acted against Shah Ismail in Anatolia, where he was supported by qizilbash and regarded by many as a holy saint. Ismail had interfered in the affairs of Dhu al-Qadr and the Ottoman succession, but he posed a more general and serious challenge to the basic legitimacy of the Ottoman dynasty and to Sunni Islam. Selim sent the fleet with his commissariat to Trabzon. With several thousand janissaries, the grand vizir, and troops of Rumeli and Anatolia, supported by batteries of light artillery, he marched eastward. Shah Ismail scorched the earth as he retreated; Selim's soldiers complained as they were driven on, but Selim would not turn back. In August 1514 at Chaldiran, northeast of Lake Van, Selim's cannon and his army's superior numbers turned the tide against the Iranian cavalry. Ismail fled, leaving even his harem to be captured.

Although the victory at Chaldiran momentarily settled Selim's problems on his eastern frontier, in no way did it destroy the new state arising in Iran or eliminate the Safavid dynasty and its spreading of Shii Islam. (Safavid Iran will be discussed at greater length in Chapter 19.)

THE CONQUEST OF EGYPT

With Shah Ismail's defeat, Sultan Selim began to use the title shah and sometimes shahinshah ("king of kings"), or padishah ("father of kings"). More important, the balance of power among the three largest Middle Eastern Muslim states—Safavid Iran, Mamluk Egypt, and the Ottoman Empire—was fully upset in favor of the last. Ismail had written to the Mamluk sultan for aid against Selim, and in 1516 the Mamluks at last marched into Syria in full force. Selim as usual took the offensive, crushing the Mamluk army at Marj Dabiq, north of Aleppo. Again it was a victory of artillery and muskets in the hands of a well-disciplined, well-paid, and well-supplied army over an undisciplined and disloyal motley force. Aleppo, Damascus, and Jerusalem opened their gates to the Ottomans. New governors were appointed everywhere, but little else was changed. Taxes continued to be farmed; the amirs of the Lebanon Mountains became only nominal vassals; and Jews and Christians were treated well.

By January 1517, Selim I and his army were on the outskirts of Cairo, which they stormed and took after several days of fighting. A quarter of a century earlier, the Mamluk power had defeated the Ottomans in several campaigns over successive years. Now Selim captured the Mamluk Empire in one campaign. The Mamluk government had become impoverished and could no longer meet its commitments or protect the state.

Selim was sultan from the Danube to the cataracts of the Nile. By extension, he became sovereign of Mecca and Medina, along with Jerusalem the principal holy cities of Islam. With the conquest of Egypt Selim's influence now extended into the Red Sea and the Indian Ocean, directly engaging the expansionist Portuguese, who sought to dominate the spice trade. Shah Ismail hastened to congratulate him on his new territories, and in most parts of the Middle East the Ottoman Empire was now the dominant power after the conquest of the central Arabic-speaking lands.

By midsummer 1518, back in Istanbul after an absence of two years, Selim faced the question of the meaning of the extensive conquests. At Aleppo the puppet Abbasid caliph al-Mutawakkil, whom the Mamluks brought along on the expedition, fell into Selim's possession. Selim took the caliph to Istanbul, where he was confined to the state prison. Much later, in 1543, he was permitted to return to Cairo, where he died, thereby finally ending the last shadow of the Abbasid dynasty. The Ottoman rulers had unofficially used the title of "caliph" since Murad I, a title that was now nearly meaningless. With the new dominions, they added to their titles "servant of the two holy sanctuaries" of Mecca and Medina, and saw themselves as protectors of Islam and the pilgrimage to the Hijaz, and as the most powerful of the Muslim rulers, in accordance with the will of God.

In Selim's long absence his only son, Suleiman, wielded power in Edirne; Piri Pasha, the great admiral, managed Istanbul; Bursa was governed by Hersekoglu Ahmed Pasha, several times grand vizir and cavalry officer under Mehmed II and Bayezid II. Even under such able guidance the affairs of state suffered and the treasury was depleted. Selim remained in Edirne and Istanbul, straightening out accounts, collecting back taxes, and preparing a navy adequate for an attack upon Rhodes. However, cancer struck him in the spring of 1520 and he died that autumn.

SELIM I

Yavuz Selim was a controversial figure. Yavuz means "good," "just," "stern," "inflexible," "ferocious"; he was all of those. He massacred many thousands of qizilbashs in his land. Vizirs and generals lost their heads at seemingly the slightest failure. A standard curse came to be, "May you become Selim's vizir!" He was an excellent general, a brilliant poet, and a skillful administrator. His court supported philosophers, historians, theologians, and literary figures of many kinds. His tastes were simple; he read widely, slept little, and was uninterested in his harem. Some attributed his moods to an addiction to opium, but there is no evidence that he used the drug before cancer troubled him.

In Selim's brief reign of eight years Ottoman territory increased greatly—almost exclusively in Asia at the expense of other Muslim states. Dominating the Middle East, the Ottoman Empire became the outstanding Muslim empire of the area, heir of the Umayyad and Abbasid empires, and ruler of the Muslim holy lands. Selim's sole male heir, Suleiman, would reign over the Ottomans for forty-six years. The fabric of society and the sources of power and wealth, however, were well fixed by the time of Selim's death. The eminence of Suleiman's period rested on the firm building of his ancestors. A new stage in the history of the Middle East would begin as the Ottoman Empire and its great Muslim rival, the Safavid Empire of Iran, entered into the early modern era.

REFERENCES

References cited at the end of Chapters 12, 13, 14, and 15 are pertinent to this chapter as well.

Brummett, Palmira: *Ottoman Seapower and Levantine Diplomacy in the Age of Discovery.* Albany: State University of New York Press, 1994. An excellent account of commerce, diplomacy, and warfare during the reigns of Bayezid and Selim.

Fisher, Sydney Nettleton: *The Foreign Relations of Turkey, 1481–1512.* Urbana: University of Illinois Press, 1948. Deals with the period of the reign of Bayezid II.

Hathaway, Jane: "Problems of Periodization in Ottoman History: The Fifteenth through the Eighteenth Centuries." *Turkish Studies Association Bulletin* 20:2 (1996): 25–31. A useful essay on how to approach the study of Ottoman history.

Hodgson, Marshall G. S.: *The Venture of Islam: Conscience and History in a World Civilization.* Vol. 3: *The Gunpowder Empires and Modern Times.* Chicago: University of Chicago Press, 1974. This concluding volume in a magisterial survey of the Muslim world's history emphasizes the period from about 1500 to 1900.

Inalcik, Halil: "Istanbul: An Islamic City." *Journal of Islamic Studies* 1 (1990): 1–23. Istanbul is described during its first years as an Ottoman city, including discussions of Mehmed II's policies and urban institutions.

———: "Selim I." *Encyclopaedia of Islam.* New ed. Vol. 9, pp. 127–131. Leiden: Brill, 1995.

Inalcik, Halil, and Donald Quataert, eds.: *An Economic and Social History of the Ottoman Empire, 1300–1914.* Cambridge: Cambridge University Press, 1994. With outstanding contributions by the editors, Suraiya Faroqhi, Bruce McGowan, and Shevket Pamuk, this lengthy work is a crucial source of information for the history of the Ottoman Empire and its peoples.

Lewis, Bernard: *Istanbul and the Civilization of the Ottoman Empire.* Norman: University of Oklahoma Press, 1963. A brilliant survey of the city at its heyday.

Mihailović, Konstantin: *Memoirs of a Janissary.* Translated by Benjamin Stolz, with historical commentary and notes by Svat Soucek. Ann Arbor: University of Michigan Press, 1975. This volume contains the Czech original along with the translation. Very interesting and illuminating.

Runciman, Steven: *The Great Church in Captivity: A Study of the Patriarchate of Constantinople from the Eve of the Turkish Conquest to the Greek War of Independence.* Cambridge: Cambridge University Press, 1968. The author contends that under the sultans the patriarch became a lay ruler of a state within a state and that the church endured as a great spiritual force.

CHAPTER 17

Institutions of the Ottoman Empire

At the same time the Ottomans dramatically increased the size and power of their empire through military and diplomatic successes, they also maintained and developed institutions that preserved and strengthened the state. The sultan was at the apex of society through his military leadership, assertion of legitimacy, and supervision of the administration of justice. By using the elaborate imperial palace services, including training facilities in the palace school, the sultan gave direction to a differentiated and flexible system of government. Military, administrative, scribal, financial, and religious officials functioned efficiently, while non-Muslim subjects and foreign residents were regulated.

Ottoman institutions changed and evolved over the six centuries the dynasty ruled, but the sultans in the fifteenth and sixteenth centuries kept certain basic patterns of government intact. Other large empires, such as the Safavids of Iran and the Mughals of India, had somewhat similar institutions. Thanks in large part to its government structure, the Ottoman Empire was a formidable power in the eastern hemisphere.

THE SULTAN

At the head of the Ottoman Empire and at the pinnacle of the various social strata stood the sultan. In the west his government was called the Sublime Porte, presumably because edicts emanated from the principal gate of the palace, called the Gate of Felicity or the Exalted Gate. The sultan's authority derived from the military power that he controlled, from the allegiance and obedience his subjects gave him, and from his religious legitimacy for Sunni Muslims. In earlier years the sultan had to share power with Turkish notable families, but for about a century after the conquest of Constantinople the sultanate had so much prestige and the rulers were so competent they controlled the institutions of the state without major challenges.

All military power was under his command. Whether slaves, sipahi cavalry, irregular infantry, vassal troops, or sailors of the fleet, all were supposed to obey his orders. Not that they always did, of course. Groups frequently went on unauthorized raids into

Christian lands, often to the embarrassment of the sultan. On numerous occasions the army insisted on abandoning arduous campaigns that took them from the pleasures of Edirne and Istanbul during winter months or from their homes in the provinces. And the janissaries came to demand bonuses from the sultan upon his accession to the throne.

Nevertheless, the armed services were generally loyal, and certainly they were more obedient than similar forces in western Europe were to their kings and emperors. Upholding the sultan was the long Turkish-Mongol tradition of leadership by family; no other family possessed the prestige of the Ottoman dynasty. Moreover, the slave status of most of the commanding officers and the nature of their rearing gave the sultan such a hold over their lives that deviation from his wishes was risky.

The sultan was head of the Islamic state, defender of the faith, protector of the pilgrimage to Arabia, executor of sacred law, and preserver of the holy relics associated with the prophet Muhammad captured in Cairo by Selim I. Sultans constructed notable buildings and used court ceremonies, special clothing, banners, thrones, and other symbols that emphasized their glory, power, and wealth, and thereby helped create a sense of awe and allegiance. Sunni Muslims in the empire rendered obedience to the sultan as the most important leader of the faith. Indirectly, Christians and Jews did likewise, since the sultan appointed some of the leaders of their communities.

The great institutions of the state were accepted as emanating from God or from the sultan's supreme will; in no sense were they considered to flow from the will of the people. The procedures of government were not identical from one century to the next. Ceremonial forms may have often remained the same, but the power, realities, relationships, and types of personnel varied from period to period. All the personnel and their families can be said to have belonged to the ruling class.

At the time of the accession of Suleiman I in 1520 there were four principal divisions of government: the palace services; the military-governing administration; the scribal-financial bureaucracy; and the religious-judicial establishment. In theory and in practice the sultan supervised all of these, and the officials in each were directly or indirectly answerable to him. In common speech all the officials belonged to the military category or askeri, and in fact many went on campaigns with the sultan, even if they were not trained to fight. This terminology was used to differentiate them from the reaya category—the "flock" or those Muslims and non-Muslims who did not belong to the Ottoman service and system. The leaders and upper echelons in these four branches of government were the elite of state and society, even though many members of these branches, except those of the religious establishment, were technically the slaves of the sultan.

THE PALACE SERVICES

Since the sultan was the supreme head of the government with absolute power, the center of the government was wherever he happened to be. Thus his household gained a special significance and power through the influence that could be exercised upon him. Technically, individuals of the ruling category, with the exception of the land-grant holders, enjoyed membership in the sultan's court and were expected to be a part of his retinue on ceremonial occasions and sometimes in camp. More specifically, the court consisted of the harem of the women, the Inside Service, and the Outside Service.

Until about 1540 there were relatively few in the harem, which was quartered in the Old Palace in Istanbul or in the palaces in Edirne and Demotika. It formed a palace within a palace and included consorts of the sultan (whether wives or concubines), other female relatives, female servants of the court, eunuchs, and girls in training, who ultimately were married to court officers unless they had moved up the well-defined hierarchy in the harem. The greatest woman of the harem was the sultan's mother (valide sultan); after her came the mother of the sultan's firstborn son, and then mothers of other sons.

Until the middle of the fifteenth century Ottoman sultans had sometimes married foreign princesses, but only concubines gave birth to the sultans' sons. By policy, concubines in the harem who gave birth to a son no longer had sexual relations with the sultan. The mother of a possible heir was to devote herself to her son's rearing. At the age of sixteen the son (along with his mother) would be sent to govern a provincial town and gain experience in administration. The mother of a sultan's son played a large role in his education, training, and advancement.

Male functionaries who took care of the sultan's personal affairs constituted the Inside Service, which was also a kind of harem, in the sense that it preserved the same sense of privacy as the harem of the women. Chief of the entire Inside Service was the general of the gate, a white eunuch. He was invariably a high state dignitary, who served also as grand master of ceremonies for the palace, director in chief of the palace school, and confidential agent of the sultan.

Aside from the white eunuchs, members of the halls were called pages and were young men usually chosen from the elite of the captives and tribute children. Those who did not obtain advancement joined the sultan's cavalry at various levels or received other appointments. The pages remained as court officials or were appointed as provincial governors, high officers in the janissary corps or cavalry, or as officials in the Outside Service or another principal branch of government.

Whereas the Inside Service controlled the relations of the sultan's life within the palace, the Outside Service coordinated his relations with the world outside. In the Outside Service the most important officials for the military-governing administration were the grand vizir and the remaining vizirs. Other high functionaries included the commanders of the janissaries and the sultan's cavalry divisions; officers responsible for palace security, discipline, and protocol; the kitchen service; gardeners; tent pitchers; masters of the hunt and equerries; the treasurer and record keepers; the personal bodyguard; and learned associates of the sultan. These learned associates were members of the religious-judicial establishment, constituted by the sultan's religious teacher and adviser, preachers, muezzins, readers, astrologers, physicians, and surgeons. The bodyguard was drawn from sons of high officials, graduates from the Inside Service, and veteran janissaries—in all about 400 men. Many palace guards were responsible officials, including ambassadors and executioners. The treasurer and record keepers were members of the scribal-financial bureaucracy, which was just beginning to form at this time. Others tended the palace gardens or rowed the sultan's boats on Bosphorus excursions.

At the time of Suleiman I the sultan's court with its three services numbered in the neighborhood of 10,000 persons. Earlier Ottoman sultans lived more simply; several accounts of public ceremonies in mosques and other places report that it was difficult to distinguish the sultan from his attendants. In the court of Mehmed II, magnificence in ceremony appeared. After the conquest of Istanbul, Mehmed II introduced into his bodyguard a company of 100 halberdiers, copied in arms, costumes, and manners from the Byzantine emperor's bodyguard. Rituals of each section of the services became elaborate and rigid.

Until the reign of Suleiman I the court and its personnel seldom directly affected government and administration. The court served the personal needs of sultan and palace. However, insofar as court officers had direct access to the sultan, they could be influential persons whose favor was eagerly sought. To have a friend highly placed at court was a precious asset.

THE PALACE SCHOOL

In the years of Mehmed II's reign the expanding state, with its growing diversity of population, needed more trained personnel to operate the government. Murad II had faced a similar problem and had resolved it by placing the most promising of his young slaves in a school beside his own sons. Mehmed met the crisis by creating the palace school of Istanbul, which maintained continuous operation until the twentieth century. Students, called pages, were selected after a very careful screening from the boys between ten and fourteen years old among war captives and those drafted from Christian provinces. At the palace school, they received a thorough education in languages, literature, music, law and theology, military science, mathematics, administration, finance, physical training, personal conduct, and sports. It was thought fitting that each should learn a trade in case he should some day have to earn a living as a craftsman. Only the very best lasted through the ten to twelve rigorous years of the course.

Graduates were appointed to administrative posts in various sections of the government. The instructors were drawn from the finest teachers in mosque schools of Bursa, Edirne, and Istanbul and from high administrative offices of the government. All in all, a tremendous spirit was induced in the students; graduates of the palace school formed a firmly knit group that stood apart in conduct and loyalty to the sultanship. Trained by one sultan, they often served his son or held the government together until a successor was determined. At the time of the great success, efficiency, and strength of the Ottoman central government, the entire system was based on merit, personal connections, and political skills. Training and merit would bring appointment to government office and subsequent promotions.

THE MILITARY-GOVERNING ADMINISTRATION

The administrators in the sixteenth century who ran the government and the army were usually products of the Inside Service of the palace. From the end of Mehmed II's reign through most of the following century, the great majority were recruited chiefly, though not entirely, from the tribute and captive children. At the top was the vizir, or chief minister;

later, when four ministers had the title of vizir, one was designated first vizir or, under Suleiman I, grand vizir. The sultan delegated his political and executive authority only to his vizirs. When they were in the provinces or on campaign, they could even impose the death penalty. The grand vizir by the law of Mehmed II had power and ceremonial precedence greater than all others and was the sultan's absolute deputy. He was also entrusted with the sultan's personal seal (the taking away of which signaled dismissal from office). The grand vizir was responsible for a wide array of duties, including personally inspecting the bread supply of Istanbul, so as to make sure that the people of the capital city would have enough to eat.

Murad I had appointed the first grand vizir from one of the prominent Ottoman families. Murad II chose vizirs from the religious-judicial establishment and from the army. Mehmed II picked them from the graduates of the palace school and from Ottoman families of Anatolia, but from the accession of Bayezid II until late in the sixteenth century all were from some part of the palace service.

The vizirs, under the chairmanship of the grand vizir, made up a council, or divan, with whom the sultan conferred on matters of state. Other members of the divan, also often called vizirs, were the head of the janissaries; two chief judges—one for Anatolia and one for Rumeli; two defterdars, or treasurers, again one each for Anatolia and Rumeli; the chief secretary of state; and the chief admiral of the navy. The divan met with the sultan for several hours every Saturday, Sunday, Monday, and Tuesday to decide all matters of government. Analogous to a modern cabinet meeting but also bearing some resemblance to a supreme court, the divan meeting served as a kind of union and capstone to the several branches of the Ottoman government. However, by the time of Mehmed II the sultan, rather than attending divan meetings himself, after each session would receive the divan members to consider their decisions.

It was a rule that no one, not even the other vizirs, could be privy to the grand vizir's dealings with the sultan and to their secret decisions. Yet there were many checks on the authority of the grand vizir, for he was obliged before making any important decision to consult with the other members of the divan. Failure to abide by this procedure was an important factor in the dismissal and execution of the grand vizir Ibrahim in 1536. In addition, the heads of the janissaries, the treasury, and the judiciary also dealt directly with the sultan. (As stated by Mehmed II, not a single penny would enter or leave the treasury unless the head of the treasury ordered it.) The various vizirs and other officials maintained households similar to that of the sultan, with the number of slaves, pages, and aides usually dictated by the position. Rustem Pasha, one of Suleiman's grand vizirs, had 1700 slaves at the time of his death.

Among the various functional divisions of government supervised by the vizirs, the military was the most important. (The earlier conditions of the army were discussed previously in Chapter 15.) By the middle of the sixteenth century the armed forces numbered more than 100,000. The heart of the Ottoman army was the janissary corps of over 10,000, many of whom used handguns in battle. The janissaries were commanded by an aga (general) who was directly responsible to the sultan. Usually this aga was an officer trained in the palace, although sometimes he rose from the ranks like other janissary officers. In addition to the ordinary janissaries there were a number of specialized units.

The regular cavalry, generally called sipahi of the Porte to distinguish it from the sipahi land-grant holders, was drawn principally from the ordinary janissaries and the pages of the palace. One special battalion consisted of non-Ottoman Turks, Kurds, Arabs, Christian renegades, and horsemen from sources outside the sultan's court.

The Ottomans gave special attention to the technical services, and European observers at that time marveled at the equipment, food, transport, and routes provided for Ottoman armies. Most important were the artillery corps and ordnance services, which cast cannon and manufactured gunpowder. These branches more than any other brought victory after victory to Ottoman armies.

Beginning with Murad II, the navy became an effective division of the armed services. Development of sea power advanced reign by reign until under Selim I and Suleiman I the navy applied its force widely. Ships were built at many different ports from the Black Sea to the Adriatic, even in the Red Sea. Master shipbuilders working with Greek and Turkish builders, frequently by flares at night, kept the navy in fighting trim. The navy was manned by experienced seafaring men from North African coasts and the eastern Mediterranean area who maintained fleets of 300 to 400 ships. Some Ottoman corsairs raided civilian shipping in much the same fashion as cavalry on land raided Carinthia and Styria, but most of the navy was used for protecting commercial ships and for regular warfare against the enemies of the empire. Like the sipahi land-grant holders in the army, high naval officers also held such grants or timars on land to pay their salaries and expenses.

One of the most important parts of the Ottoman army came from the provincial sipahis. Whenever a campaign was announced, the governors of most provinces assembled the cavalry who held land grants from the sultan, although some areas of the empire such as Egypt were not part of the sipahi system. Each sipahi came with a predetermined number of warriors in his entourage. They elected their own immediate leaders, although their provincial commander was an appointee of the sultan (after the time of Murad II, frequently a graduate of the palace school). Prior to the period of Suleiman I, supreme command of these cavalry rested on the shoulders of two generals—the beylerbey of Anatolia and the beylerbey of Rumeli. (At a later time additional beylerbeys were designated for areas such as Syria, Hungary, and Baghdad.) These two generals acted as vizirs, attended meetings of the divan when convenient, and commanded the wings of the army in battle.

Other branches of the armed forces included irregular, unpaid, volunteer cavalrymen or foot soldiers who answered the call to arms in hopes of booty or the gift of a land grant for valor. In any battle these soldiers usually were used as frontline troops to absorb the first shocks of contact with the enemy.

THE SCRIBAL-FINANCIAL BUREAUCRACY

The scribal-financial bureaucracy consisted of private secretaries, a corps of scribes, and personnel attached to high posts. On a broader base, however, three main branches of the bureaucracy evolved into the executive office of the divan, the chancery, and the treasury. In the early days, individuals holding these offices had usually come from the palace, but by the middle of the sixteenth century most were recruited from the families of Ottoman officials and their clients and from relatives of members of the bureaucracy. Clerks entered the bureaus as apprentices and learned on the job, often simultaneously taking courses to enhance their knowledge of laws and religious sciences. Promotions in the bureaus came at regular intervals, and diligent and intelligent clerks could work their way to the top. Changing from one bureau to another was possible but unlikely except when one had reached a fairly high position.

The divan had a secretarial staff, and as time passed a regular bureau was formalized to draw up orders. The head of this bureau, in turn, became the first secretary of the grand vizir, and in later centuries became a minister of state and foreign minister. The chancellor, who was a member of the divan, checked on all appointments to office (including the assignment of grants of land revenue); had responsibility for the land surveys and censuses; kept records of salaries; and recorded all ordinances and commands of the sultan, the divan, the vizirs, and other officials, affixing the seal of authority and the sultan's signature to official documents. The treasurer collected state income and was charged with accounting for all receipts and expenditures of the central government. Until the time of Mehmed II, collection of taxes was generally administered directly by the treasury, chiefly through the land-grant holders, but there was also tax farming. The Ottoman Empire was greatly decentralized financially; provincial governments collected and spent their own funds; and the religious establishment was supported by revenues from waqf properties granted as endowments and not always funneled through the treasury. Total revenue for the central government in the 1520s has been estimated at about 9.7 million ducats, a greater sum than that spent by contemporary governments in France, Spain, and Iran. The treasurer, like the chancellor, was a member of the divan and responsible only to the sultan.

In addition to these main departments of government, there were a number of others, including the mint, the customs bureaus, commissionerships, governors in the provinces, courts, and endowments that developed bureaucracies of their own. Consequently, there were thousands of secretaries and scribes in the Ottoman Empire in the sixteenth century—as evidenced by the tons of records still in the archives in Istanbul.

THE RELIGIOUS-JUDICIAL ESTABLISHMENT

Parallel with the three main branches of government already described stood the religious-judicial establishment. In many ways it was quite separate from the others but not fully independent of them. Since Islam was the religion of the government (with the sultan responsible for the enforcement of Islamic law) and all officials by this time were Muslims, every aspect of government was touched by the religious-judicial establishment. Government personnel at the top levels often moved to other branches of government, particularly from the religious-judicial group into the others. Functionally, this establishment had three main divisions: religion, education, and law.

In general, Ottomans followed the law of Sunni Islam as developed by earlier Muslims. Four distinct bodies or sources of law existed. Foremost and supreme over the other three stood sacred law (shariah), in accordance with the interpretation of the Hanafi school. Sultan and judges were bound by sacred law, and to ignore it invited disaster. Second stood kanuns, or decrees of sultans, which either were administrative in character or were said to be supplementary to the shariah. Kanuns, for example, dealt with intricate ceremonial law of the Ottoman government and with military, financial, taxation, and police law. Last in the strata of law were adet and urf. Adet was customary law as observed by Turks from time immemorial, by Ottomans, and by peoples conquered by them. Thus, adet in Bosnia might be different from adet in Greece, and both might be different from adet in Ankara. Urf, the sovereignty or will of the ruling sultan, might contravene adet. Kanuns could change adet and urf and could annul or amend other kanuns. Shariah, however, was thought of as inviolable.

The learned ulama included such religious functionaries as preachers, mosque caretakers, muezzins, professional leaders of prayers in mosques, heads of Sufi brotherhoods, and sharifs and sayyids. Waqf mosque endowments provided for regular attendants and leaders in mosque activities on a full-time basis. Sufis preached holy wars, spread the faith, and inspired emotional public demonstrations. Sharifs and sayyids traced their descent from Hasan and Husain, grandsons of the prophet Muhammad, wore green turbans, and had numerous personal prerogatives. One was the sultan's standard-bearer and ranked above all officers of the army.

Every mosque, large and small, had a primary, or reading, school, where pupils studied reading, writing, Arabic, and the Quran. Schools of higher learning, called madrasahs (medreses in Turkish), taught grammar, logic, metaphysics, geometry; advanced madrasahs gave courses in law and theology. Students were partially supported by waqf religious endowments; those in law were completely subsidized. Madrasahs were numerous throughout the empire, and in Istanbul every sizable mosque had one or more attached to it. Each stage of education was rigidly graded; those who completed the courses belonged to the learned class. A graduate received a degree and became qualified to teach in a primary school. Further study raised the holder to higher ratings, which permitted him to be a professor, jurist, or judge.

A learned individual who completed a law course, especially those given in Istanbul, usually received an appointment as a teacher, then as a judge (qadi in Arabic, kadi in Turkish) or as a legal consultant (mufti), or as an assistant in the office of one of these. In cities and large towns the sultan appointed a judge who exercised juridical control over the surrounding territory. Judges also carried out and registered imperial decrees, supervised tax collection, and made records of wills and marriage contracts. Slaves of the sultan, sharifs, and sayyids had their own judges and courts. Except in cases that involved Muslims, foreigners and non-Muslims were subject to their own laws. Sometimes non-Muslims used Muslim courts when they felt their cases might be judged more favorably there. Local officials, beylerbeys, and vizirs also administered justice in their courts except in cases involving the shariah.

The hierarchy of judges was based on carefully classified grades, and advancement usually proceeded from one grade to another. At the top of the system of judges were two judges—one for Europe and one for Asia—who nominated all the other judges of the empire. Appeals progressed from court to court, and sentences were executed by the civil authorities.

Associated with the judge of many cities was a mufti, who was assigned to interpret sacred law for the judge and government officials. Appointed for life, the muftis had no initiative of action. When a judge, or even a private citizen, was faced with a legal problem, he or she submitted the question to the mufti for legal opinion. The mufti examined the law and gave his answer. In Istanbul the mufti of the Hanafi Sunnis, who was usually selected from the ranks of the judges and teachers rather than other muftis, ranked above the judge; and since the sultan and vizirs might pose important questions vital to the life of the whole empire, he became a significant official. Mehmed II added to the mufti's dignity by conferring upon him the title shaikh al-Islam (Şeyhülislam in Turkish), "Leader of Islam," and in ceremonies he took precedence over the grand vizir.

The Muslim religious-judicial establishment within the Ottoman Empire, from the shaikh al-Islam to the lowliest teacher in a mosque primary school, welded the empire together under one type of education and one body of law. Any male Muslim child, if he studied hard and passed the various examinations, might rise in the ranks, just as fighting men and the sultan's slaves advanced on merit in their branches of government. Poverty was no barrier to advancement, but important friends or relatives did help.

Perhaps one-third of the land of the empire was set aside as waqf endowment for various religious activities. In Anatolia and Europe cash endowments were also established, despite the opposition of some men of religion. The money that constituted the basis of the foundation was lent to peasants and townspeople, leading to their increasing indebtedness. Both sorts of endowments, in land and in cash, could be given by sultans and private individuals, and were, at least theoretically, intended for the support of some specific mosque, library, school, almshouse, hospital, bridge, inn, or fountain. The imperial treasury actually handled the funds established by the sultan, and an official was designated as trustee. Private donors often stipulated in the deed of transfer that their own descendants should be administrators of the endowment; thus, much of the revenue from the endowment could be diverted for private and personal gain. Slaves of the sultan found this method a convenience in providing perpetual and inalienable income for their descendants. However, in many cases the property and wealth of men of the state were confiscated by the sultan upon their deaths.

GUILDS AND PEASANTS

Government institutions directly affected urban members of guilds and the vast majority of the population that consisted of peasant farm families. Ottoman guilds were like European associations of artisans, who made one sort of item or engaged in a certain craft in a town. In addition to links with the Sufi orders, the guilds interacted closely with local government officials, who often assisted the guild masters in trying to maintain levels of quality, set prices for raw materials and finished products, and control competition. Nevertheless, the guilds managed most of their own affairs internally, as in electing their own leaders.

While the Ottoman government did not have a systematic approach to economic issues, the authorities did tend to prefer a conservative maintenance of existing institutions, acting through such means as government-appointed market inspectors who helped sustain the guild structure. The central government tried to forbid the export of gold and silver, goods deemed to be vital for the economy. Although relatively little was spent on developing certain kinds of infrastructure, expenditure for security purposes tended to help merchants, and the building of caravanserais also assisted them.

Throughout most of the Ottoman central lands peasants in villages managed and farmed small-sized land holdings that were carefully analyzed in cadastral surveys undertaken by the government. Ownership of land was usually vested in the state and peasants were tenants who inherited the right to farm the land. Timar holders had some supervisory responsibilities over the peasants, who were required in theory at least to request permission before moving elsewhere. To assist in collecting taxes, a detailed record was made of the village households and their property, especially oxen used in ploughing. The settlement of nomads, increased security of life and property, limits on over-exploitation by tax farmers or timar holders, and honest regulation of the coinage were all policies employed by governments that helped the peasantry. The sultan was particularly concerned that peasants could grow enough food to feed the imperial capital of Istanbul.

NON-MUSLIM SUBJECTS AND FOREIGNERS

Ottomans were tolerant of non-Muslims in the fashion of the older Muslim world. Christian and Jewish groups were given their religious and cultural freedom; many Balkan communities preferred such autonomy under the Ottomans to the religious and cultural restrictions and persecutions suffered under Hungarian and Hapsburg Catholic rule. In the first centuries of the empire's existence, some non-Muslims served as holders of iqta or timar revocable land grants and warriors; by the late sixteenth century this practice seems to have stopped. By the 1530s probably less than one-tenth of the population of Anatolia was Christian or Jewish, but in the European provinces the proportion was reversed and only one-fifth of the population was Muslim, while the vast majority of the subjects in the countryside were Christians.

The various religious groups were termed *communities* (and, much later, *millets*), which meant a group of people with a particular religion within the Ottoman Empire. Each community—while considered inferior to the Sunni Muslims—still had the right to use its own language, develop its own institutions, collect taxes and render them to the imperial treasury, and maintain courts for trying members in all cases except those involving public security and crime. Each millet had a leader or leaders (such as the Orthodox Patriarchs) who were responsible to the sultan for the payments of taxes and for the good behavior of members of the community. Christian and Jewish subjects of the state, resident non-Ottoman Muslims, and non-Muslims who were subjects of other Muslim states were all subjected to a special extra poll tax. Shii Iranians began to be treated as a separate category in at least some of the Ottoman provinces in a later time.

Paralleling these religious communities were groups of foreigners, chiefly merchants residing in Istanbul, such as the Genoese residents in Galata across the Golden Horn. Each group lived under provisions of a formal treaty drawn up between the sultan and the foreign authority; the agreements were periodically renewed. The trading privileges or capitulations that the French had enjoyed under the Mamluk sultans in Egypt since 1251 were reconfirmed by Suleiman in 1528; and a regular treaty with France was concluded, though not formally ratified, in 1536—a treaty similar to those made with Venice, Florence, and Hungary by Mehmed II and Bayezid II.

The general tenor of these treaties was exemplified in the Treaty of 1503 between Bayezid II and Venice. Among other things, the sultan agreed that a Venetian consul might come to Istanbul with his family and reside there. Venetians could live in certain designated cities of the empire for a limited time. The consul should settle all cases and disputes among Venetians; and Venetian testimony was recognized as valid in courts of Christian and Jewish Ottoman subjects. In criminal cases Venetians were guaranteed justice in regular Ottoman courts.

These treaties recognizing certain rights and obligations for European residents in the Ottoman Empire were based on the assumption that since foreign Christians could not fare well under the shariah, they would have to live by their own laws. However, in later years, when the balance of power between western Europe and the Ottoman Empire shifted, such arrangements evolved into the famous capitulatory treaties, which gave nationals of other governments a privileged position in the Ottoman Empire. Those years were still far away, however, in the fifteenth and sixteenth centuries, when Ottoman governmental institutions provided the empire with great resilience, legitimacy, efficiency, and power.

REFERENCES

In addition to general studies on Muslim institutions, references in Chapters 14, 15, and 16 are of particular importance.

Andrić, Ivo: *The Bridge on the Drina.* Translated by Lovett F. Edwards. Chicago: University of Chicago Press, 1977. A gripping historical novel that is set in sixteenth- and nineteenth-century Ottoman and Austrian Bosnia and includes a description of the devshirmeh.

Bilkent University (Ankara, Turkey), Department of History: "The Topkapi Palace Museum" at www.ee.bilkent.edu.tr/~history. Omer Nezih Gerek, Russel Johnson, and Mehmet Kalpakli have compiled an attractive site for the Ottoman imperial center, featuring historical background, a virtual tour, discussion of the collections, and bibliography.

Birge, John Kingsley: *The Bektashi Order of Dervishes.* Hartford, Conn: Hartford Seminary Press, 1937. A significant work on this Sufi order and its relationship to Ottoman society.

Braude, Benjamin, and Bernard Lewis, eds.: *Christians and Jews in the Ottoman Empire: The Functioning of a Plural Society.* 2 vols. New York: Holmes and Meier, 1982. This excellent collection of twenty-nine articles emphasizes the late Ottoman period and deals extensively with the Arab lands as well as the central government.

De Busbecq, Ogier G.: *Turkish Letters.* Translated by Edward S. Forster. Oxford: Clarendon Press, 1927. De Busbecq was an ambassador to the Ottoman Empire for many years; his observations were singularly objective and discerning.

Gibb, H. A. R., and Harold Bowen: *Islamic Society and the West: A Study of the Impact of Western Civilization on Moslem Culture in the Near East.* Vol. 1 (in two parts): *Islamic Society in the Eighteenth Century.* London: Oxford University Press, 1950,

1957. While subject to much valid criticism, this work remains a penetrating study of Ottoman institutions.

Goodwin, Godfrey: *The Janissaries.* London: Saqi, 1994. A popularly written account of janissary life and how the janissaries affected Ottoman events.

Knolles, Richard: *The Generall Historie of the Turkes. . . .* London, 1603. This is still the most extensive and longest Ottoman history in the English language, written by an Englishman, long a resident in Turkey. There are many later editions.

Lewis, Bernard: *The Jews of Islam.* Princeton, N.J.: Princeton University Press, 1984. A thorough and well-written treatment of the subject.

Mandaville, Jon E.: "Usurious Piety: The Cash Waqf Controversy in the Ottoman Empire." *International Journal of Middle East Studies* 10 (1979): 289–308. An interesting examination of the flexibility of Ottoman legal thinking.

Masters, Bruce: "Trading Diasporas and 'Nations': The Genesis of National Identities in Ottoman Aleppo." *International History Review* 9 (1987): 345–367.

Mitler, Louis: "The Genoese in Galata: 1453–1682." *International Journal of Middle East Studies* 10 (1979): 71–91.

Necipoglu, Gulru: *Architecture, Ceremonial, and Power: The Topkapi Palace in the Fifteenth and Sixteenth Centuries.* Cambridge: MIT Press, 1991. This beautifully illustrated volume provides a detailed examination of every part of the imperial palace and of the rituals and symbols that inspired awe and allegiance.

Repp, Richard C.: *The Müfti of Istanbul: A Study in the Development of the Ottoman Learned Hierarchy.* London: Ithaca Press, 1986. Traces in an extremely careful and detailed way career patterns and lives of individuals who held the post of mufti.

Robinson, Francis: "Ottoman-Safavids-Mughals: Shared Knowledge and Connective Systems." *Journal of Islamic Studies* 8 (1997): 151–184. This comparative study of Iran, India, and the Ottoman Empire focuses on education, Sufism, and the role of the ulama.

Simsar, Muhammed Ahmed: *The Waqfiyah of Ahmed Paşa.* Philadelphia: University of Pennsylvania Press, 1940. A fine translation with notes on a perpetual trust established in 1511 by Ahmed Hersekoglu Pasha, who was the son of the last duke of Herzegovina and who became an Ottoman vizir.

CHAPTER 18

The Ottoman Empire as a World Power

During the early modern period of Middle Eastern history, from about 1500 to about 1800, the Ottoman empire dominated the region and much of the eastern hemisphere in terms of institutional, political, military, religious, and cultural accomplishments. Other states existed in Morocco and elsewhere in the Middle East, but only the Safavids in Iran and the Hapsburg dynasty in western and central Europe provided a real challenge to Ottoman supremacy.

The sixteenth-century reigns of Suleiman I and Selim II were particularly noteworthy for their success in using gunpowder weapons for military expansion to both the east and the west, by both land and sea. Changes in the organization of the court and in administration also marked the era from 1520 to 1574, while imperial sponsorship of architecture, art, and literature helped create remarkably beautiful symbols of Ottoman glory.

SULEIMAN I

The institutions and personnel of the Ottoman Empire were so well organized, capable, and effective under Mehmed II, Bayezid II, and Selim I that the government could function well even without much direction from a sultan. When combined with an extraordinary leader, the Ottoman state could accomplish even more, as took place during the long reign of Suleiman I. Since Selim I left only one son, for the first time since the accession of Mehmed Fatih the transfer of authority in 1520 generated no civil war or execution of royal relatives. Suleiman, moreover, was born in the year A.H. 900, the opening year of the tenth century of Islam, and was the tenth of his dynasty. Because of these portentous beginnings his subjects believed he was destined to rule over a great part of the world.

The youthful Suleiman, only twenty-five years old when he became sultan, was called "the Magnificent" by Europeans and Kanuni ("the Lawgiver") by his own people. He appeared as a magnificent sovereign, certainly the match of his contemporaries Ismail I of Safavid Iran, the Mughal Babur of India, Charles V of the Hapsburg family

Periodization in the History of the Islamic Middle East
Antiquity: from the rise of civilization to the coming of Islam
Classical Islamic period: from the life of the prophet Muhammad to the middle of the tenth century C.E.
The early medieval era in the Middle East: from about 950 to about 1250
The late medieval era in the Middle East: from about 1250 to about 1500
The early modern Middle East: from about 1500 to about 1800
The modern Middle East: from about 1800 to the present

of Holy Roman Emperors, Francis I of France, and Henry VIII of England. Suleiman reigned for forty-six years. During those years the Ottoman Empire reached its height as a conquest state in terms of power, wealth, and brilliance.

During the latter years of Bayezid II's reign Suleiman was assigned as governor of Kaffa in the Crimea, where his mother, daughter of a khan, had been reared. After his father seized the throne, Suleiman was called to govern Istanbul, while Selim fought against brothers and nephews. Suleiman then governed Edirne during his father's long wars in Iran and Egypt. Only upon Selim's return to Istanbul in 1517 was Suleiman sent to rule the province around Manisa in western Anatolia. Thus Suleiman attended the pages' school in Istanbul and resided for more than five years at the palaces of Istanbul and Edirne. In addition, he had nearly six years of experience as provincial governor. No prince of his time had better training for the responsibility of ruling a great empire.

SULEIMAN'S COURT

After initial military campaigns against Belgrade and Rhodes, for the following three summers Suleiman remained in Edirne and Istanbul enjoying peace. He loved the gardens of the palace, and one of his greatest pleasures was boating on the Bosphorus and the Sea of Marmara.

It was also during these years that a slave girl named Hurrem caught his fancy. She soon completely captivated Suleiman, became his legal wife, and dominated him until her death in 1558. Suleiman's mother ruled his harem until her death in 1534; after that date Hurrem became Suleiman's confidant and counselor. Her chief rival, the concubine Mahidevran, mother of Suleiman's oldest living son, Mustafa (b. 1515), left for Manisa in 1533 in the company of her son when he was established there as governor. As a concubine Hurrem departed from Ottoman tradition not only by marrying the sultan but also by bearing him more than one child. She ultimately gave birth to several children, including Mehmed; Selim (b. 1524); Bayezid; Jihangir, a hunchback; and a daughter, Mihrimah. Hurrem did not leave Istanbul, as had Mahidevran. Competition in the harem for Suleiman's affections and intense rivalry among the mothers for the advancement and protection of their sons brought affliction upon Suleiman in later days, but the royal family also provided a source of strength as the sultan's female relatives were married to prominent vizirs.

In 1523 Suleiman advanced to the grand vizirate his favorite and boon companion, Ibrahim. The son of a Greek sailor, Ibrahim had been captured by pirates and sold to a lady of Manisa, who gave her slave an excellent education. As a prince in Manisa, Suleiman recognized Ibrahim's talents, enjoyed his violin playing, and brought him to Istanbul as chief falconer and head of the pages of the inner chamber. For the following thirteen years Ibrahim governed the empire, year by year relieving his brother-in-law Suleiman of more of the tiresome duties of ruling. He even took the title of seriasker-sultan ("commander in chief of the armies," with the power of sultan). He dined with Suleiman, was with him at all hours, and even slept in the sultan's apartments.

Unfortunately, Ibrahim's rapid advancement to grand vizir ran counter to the system of promotions based on merit and service. There could be no question that Ibrahim was a brilliant and successful administrator and adviser. Still, others who had proved their abilities through service were passed over by the sultan's personal favorite.

The first demonstration of Ibrahim's genius came in Egypt. The second vizir in 1523 had asked for and received as a consolation the governorship of Egypt. Within months after his arrival in Cairo he was deeply involved in treason and was murdered in his bath by loyal Ottomans. Other revolts by Arab tribes and Mamluks led Suleiman to commission Ibrahim to go to Egypt to inaugurate a stabler regime. Finances, administration, law, and trade procedures were thoroughly overhauled, and future Ottoman governors were given more responsibility. Ibrahim went on to show his abilities in many subsequent activities.

Eventually, however, Suleiman came to feel that Ibrahim was amassing too much power. One evening in 1536 Ibrahim dined as usual with Suleiman and retired for the night to his customary place in Suleiman's apartments. The next morning his strangled body was found. No explanation was ever given. His immense wealth reverted to the sultan, since he was Suleiman's slave. In later years Suleiman tried to avoid promoting officers too rapidly or elevating them too obviously over the heads of their seniors.

BELGRADE, RHODES, AND VIENNA

Suleiman expanded the size of the empire significantly, both in the Balkans and against eastern foes. His numerous European campaigns began with the goal of taking Belgrade in 1521. At Sofia, he gathered his army and supplies, including 3000 camels carrying ammunition and 30,000 laden with grain. At least 10,000 wagonloads of grain were requisitioned locally, and 300 cannon were brought up the Danube from Istanbul.

As expected, there was little opposition from Europe. The Hapsburg Charles V was busily engaged preparing for war against Francis I of France and also deeply involved with Martin Luther and imperial problems. Belgrade held out for three weeks until Ottoman cannon ended all resistance; many Serbs were transplanted to the outskirts of Istanbul. The capture of Belgrade opened the Hungarian plains and the upper Danube basin to the Ottomans.

The following year, Suleiman assembled his forces in Asia for the heralded attack on the island of Rhodes. Rhodes lay only 6 miles off the coast of Anatolia, astride the sea route from Istanbul to Alexandria, where the Knights of St. John had continually harassed Ottoman trade. Rhodes was a highly fortified port, and large contingents of knights arrived to defend the citadel. (Venice sent its fleet, but to protect Cyprus!) Massing 200 ships and 200,000 men, Suleiman personally led the attack, which lasted from July until December. Thousands of stone cannonballs bombarded the walls, and a few rudimentary explosive shells were hurled into the town. Effective attacks were launched in conjunction with sapping and mining operations against the walls. The knights surrendered on Christmas Day 1522. They were allowed to depart with all who desired to leave.

The janissaries and palace troops then grew restless with several years of inactivity and little booty. In April 1526, Suleiman, Ibrahim, and other vizirs set out from Istanbul with 100,000 men and several hundred cannon. Early in August the Ottomans crossed the Drava River and moved toward Mohacs, where a crushing victory opened all of Hungary. Early in September, Buda surrendered to Suleiman. But the expedition into Hungary ended as only a magnified raid. Suleiman did not possess adequate manpower to garrison such distant cities as Budapest and Mohacs. Hungary remained a political vacuum.

Subsequently, John Zapolya, duke of Transylvania, occupied Budapest and was crowned king of Hungary. Then Ferdinand of Hapsburg, archduke of Austria, defeated Zapolya in 1527 and claimed to be the Hungarian king. In desperation, Zapolya turned to the Ottomans. Suleiman moved in 1529 to oust the Austrians from Hungary. Not until the middle of May did the army leave Istanbul, and continuous drenching rains impeded its march. The larger cannon had to be abandoned along the way. Mohacs was reached only in mid-August; Budapest was reached a month later. Soon afterward Ottoman raiders penetrated into Austria like swarms of locusts, and the attack upon Vienna opened on September 29.

Ottoman mining operations and assaults raged day after day. On October 12, 1529, mines seriously damaged the walls, and infantry attacks almost succeeded. Both sides grew weary, however, and on October 15 the Ottomans retired. To the defenders of Vienna it seemed miraculous, for they were on the point of surrender. In truth, the retreat was forced by the janissaries, who wanted to reach Edirne and Istanbul before winter. Ferdinand recognized Suleiman's hold upon Hungary in a peace treaty in 1533.

Vienna had not been taken by Suleiman because his communications were so extended that his forces could not be effective. Incessant rains in the Balkans and in Austria made the long marches arduous and the hauling of the heavy cannon that took Belgrade almost impossible. Having left Istanbul only after the mud dried late in April, the army insisted upon returning before the winter began in November. Neither the janissaries nor the sipahis wanted to campaign in the winter. Vienna was thus beyond Ottoman reach, although Christian Europe failed to appreciate the full facts of the sultan's limitations.

NAVAL ACTIVITIES

While Suleiman was engaged in Hungary combating the Hapsburgs, the French looked to him as a useful ally in their struggle against the Hapsburg Holy Roman Emperor, Charles V. Relations with the French led the Ottomans to extend their interests to the entire Mediterranean. Since the conquest of Istanbul Ottoman navies had grown in competence. In 1480 Mehmed II was able to support an expedition across the Adriatic to the heel of Italy. Under Bayezid II, Ottoman sea power came of age, controlled the eastern Mediterranean, and repeatedly plundered the shores of Spain. Under Suleiman the navy occupied and added much of North Africa to the empire.

The key figures in this conquest were the Barbarossa brothers. While Selim I was conquering Egypt, Aruj Barbarossa and his more famous brother, Khair al-Din, appeared in Tunis to lead fleets against Christian Europe. Their father was an Ottoman grant holder from Rumeli and they followed the sea-ghazi tradition. After retaking Algiers, Aruj lost his life in an assault upon Tlemcen. Khair al-Din, who inherited his brother's name of Barbarossa, sent word that he would consent to Selim's overlordship. Appointed beylerbey of Algiers and North Africa with absolute authority to rule those provinces and to raise and organize a janissary army, Barbarossa went to Istanbul in 1533; he would exercise Ottoman power in the Mediterranean until his death in 1546. His ships raked the coasts of Spain and maintained unceasing pressure upon Charles V. Barbarossa's men were of all backgrounds, and thus truly Ottoman, but his personal bodyguard was composed exclusively of Spanish renegades.

Barbarossa's conquest of Tunis in 1534 was soon challenged by Charles V, who employed a large fleet and a powerful army to dislodge the Ottomans from Tunis. But Barbarossa escaped with a score of his ships to Algiers. Then he proceeded with his loot to Istanbul—where Suleiman appointed him admiral and made him responsible for all naval activities. After the treaty with France in 1536, French ships frequently cooperated with Ottoman fleets in the western Mediterranean. In the winter of 1543, the harbor of Toulon was given over entirely to Barbarossa's ships and men as the inhabitants moved out.

After Khair al-Din died in 1546, his role was filled by Turgut (Dragut), Piyale Pasha, and Khair al-Din's son Hasan. Tripoli of Libya was stormed and became the headquarters of Turgut, who was named its beylerbey. The strategic island of Jerba off the coast of Tunisia fell to Piyale Pasha. The Ottomans now ruled nearly all of North Africa, except for Morocco, which under the Saadian dynasty used gunpowder weapons to successfully defy both Ottoman and Iberian invaders. Morocco never did become part of the Ottoman Empire.

In 1565, Suleiman sent Piyale with 200 ships and a landing force of nearly 30,000 men to take the strategic island of Malta from the Knights of St. John, whom he had driven from Rhodes more than forty years earlier. After several months of costly assaults upon the island fortresses, the Ottomans had to withdraw. Despite this failure, Ottoman supremacy upon the Mediterranean continued for many years after Suleiman's death.

EASTERN CAMPAIGNS

On several occasions in the early years of Suleiman's reign, there were difficulties with the Safavid shah of Iran. The Ottoman court, being Sunni, looked with contempt upon the Shiis of the east. They also feared any successes of the Shii Safavid followers who lived in various parts of the Ottoman Empire. Although Selim I had defeated Shah Ismail and killed thousands of his followers, border chieftains in eastern Anatolia vacillated in their loyalty from the Safavid capital of Tabriz to Istanbul and then back to Tabriz again as advantages shifted from one to the other. Such changing allegiances helped cause large conflicts between the two great empires and also perpetuated minor engagements, all of which tended to cause the depopulation of the border districts of the Caucasus.

The first eastern campaign conducted personally by Suleiman was in 1533–1535. The Ottomans took Tabriz, but since they were not able to come to grips with Shah Tahmasp, they moved southward and captured Baghdad. There Suleiman passed the winter, arranging the administration of this new addition to his empire. In 1547 Shah Tahmasp's brother appeared in Istanbul, seeking help in a bid for the Iranian throne. Suleiman left Istanbul in 1548, recaptured Tabriz, wintered in Aleppo, and spent all of 1549 pillaging cities and pursuing the elusive Tahmasp, who never dared risk a battle.

Again in 1553, perhaps believing that the Ottomans were fully engaged in Europe, Tahmasp adopted an aggressive policy and seized Erzurum from the Ottomans. Rustem Pasha, the grand vizir for most of the years from 1544 to 1561, headed a large army against the Safavids. Despite numerous victories the Ottomans recognized the futility of trying to hold all their eastern conquests, so they arranged a peace that allowed them to retain Iraq, including Baghdad, and a port on the Persian Gulf, as well as most of Kurdistan and western Armenia.

Suleiman also took an interest in developments in the Red Sea area and along the shores of the Arabian Sea. In 1538, an Ottoman admiral sailed from Suez, installed governors in Aden and Yemen, and then passed on to the Malabar coast of India, where he landed and unsuccessfully besieged Diu. Suleiman also found that the Portuguese blocked the exit from the Persian Gulf, in part nullifying his capture of Baghdad and Basrah. When the famous geographer–sea captain Piri Pasha failed to oust the Portuguese from the Strait of Hormuz, he was beheaded for cowardice. (The Portuguese kept Hormuz from 1515 to 1622.) Nonetheless, the Ottomans retained a loose control over the Persian Gulf, Aden, Yemen, and the Red Sea, including the coastal areas of the Sudan and portions of Ethiopia, while the spice trade to Egypt through the Red Sea then revived.

HUNGARY AGAIN

Suleiman had too many irons in the fire to press his eastern campaigns vigorously. In the latter half of his reign he became involved again in Hungary, occupying Budapest in 1541 and for the first time merging central Hungary directly into his empire. Some twenty-five provinces were formed, each with a governor under the beylerbey of Budapest. Peace treaties were signed in 1547; each party retained the lands in its possession, and Austria paid a tribute to the Ottomans. The Hapsburgs, however, violated the peace, and in 1552 Suleiman's forces incorporated the Banat of Temesvar (Timishoara), northeast of Belgrade, into the empire.

Maximilian II succeeded his father, Ferdinand, in 1564. He, too, refused to pay the tribute and attacked Ottoman territory. When governors clamored for support in 1566, Suleiman set forth on his seventh campaign into Hungary. Over seventy years of age and no longer able to ride a horse, he traveled in a carriage. On the night of the fall of the fortress at Sziget—the eve of the consolidation of Hungary, the fulfillment of the conquest that had begun with the fall of Belgrade in his first year of campaigning—Suleiman died. Mehmed Sokollu, the grand vizir, kept Suleiman's death a secret for over three weeks while he sent a messenger to Kutahya to summon his father-in-law, Selim, to the succession.

THE SUCCESSION OF SELIM II

Suleiman had had eight sons, but only one outlived him. The four most important included Mehmed, Suleiman's favorite, who died in 1543 at the age of twenty-one. In 1553 elements of the army apparently began to suggest that the sultan's eldest son, Prince Mustafa, should take the throne, so as to respond to attacks launched by the Safavids. Egged on by Hurrem, who was plotting for the succession for one of her sons, Suleiman took the field, then summoned Mustafa to Eregli, where he was strangled. Thus, for the first time since Murad I, a sultan executed an adult son.

The remaining two rivals, Selim and Bayezid, were Hurrem's sons. Selim, the elder of the two, formerly governor of Konya and Manisa, drank to excess. The soldiers preferred Bayezid, who resembled Suleiman. Each brother had a following at court, and rivalry between the two had been intense. Selim and his friends employed every means to advance his power. Especially after Hurrem's death in 1558, Selim's fortunes were watched over by the grand vizir Rustem Pasha. The latter was the husband of Hurrem's and Suleiman's daughter Mihrimah, who had as much power over her father as her mother did. Civil war between the brothers broke out in 1559. Suleiman ordered the provincial governors in Anatolia to give active support to Selim, who was then victorious. Bayezid fled to the court of the Safavid Shah Tahmasp. Eventually, on the payment of 400,000 ducats, he and his sons were turned over to Suleiman's agent, who executed all of them. Thus, when Suleiman died, there remained of his sons only Selim, known as "the Drunkard."

IMPERIAL ADMINISTRATION

The succession of Selim II was symptomatic of the rapidly changing dynamics of imperial government. Expansion into eastern Anatolia, Syria, and Egypt by Selim I was followed without much breathing space by Suleiman's conquests in Serbia, Hungary, North Africa, and Iraq. The result was that in two decades the empire experienced an astonishing increase not only of power and wealth but also of responsibilities.

More provinces were created, with more governors, judges, tax collectors, and clerks. The janissary corps doubled in size. The imperial household became larger and more complex, and power became centralized within it. As wealth poured into Istanbul, high officers of the court adopted a life of pomp and splendor. (To celebrate the circumcision of Mustafa, Mehmed, and Selim in the summer of 1530, high dignitaries gathered in Istanbul for festivities that lasted three weeks.) Each vizir had a magnificent court of his own, modeled after that of his master. Mehmed Sokollu, the grand vizir at the time of Suleiman's death, had become Suleiman's slave when the chief treasurer was executed and his property confiscated in 1534. Ayas Pasha, Ibrahim's successor as grand vizir and a slave of Albanian origin, lived in the grand manner. At his death from the plague, it was noted that he left 120 children!

As governmental administration became more complex, institutions, standards, and values began to change. The situation was abetted by the haphazard growth of Ottoman law and legal procedures. Suleiman, therefore, reissued and modified numerous kanuns, or decrees, dating from his predecessors' reigns, and codified old kanuns, particularly those affecting the provinces, in an attempt to regularize his administration. (It is on the basis of this legal activity that he has been known in Ottoman history as Suleiman Kanuni—"the Lawgiver.") Many laws related to matters of inheritance, salary, rank, and ceremony for officers of the court. Clothing and guild regulations were modified, and one of the greatest collections of laws was that fashioned for the land-grant holders in 1530. It was designed to make sure that all grants were made directly by the central administration and not by the beylerbeys.

A social problem also emerged in connection with the relatively new drink, coffee, which had come into general use in the fifteenth century. Opposition to coffee first emerged among some governmental and religious circles in Mecca and Cairo, despite the economic advantages created by the trade in coffee during the sixteenth century. Popular coffeehouses were viewed with suspicion by the central Ottoman government officials as likely to lead to sloth and sedition, but despite condemnations the coffeehouses spread ever more widely and increased the male public's opportunities for social interaction.

Suleiman's revenues were greater than those of any contemporary monarchs in Europe. Income was derived from many sources. Since the Ottomans usually followed the customs that were practiced in a province before its conquest, the sources varied from one province to another. Tithes on land, poll taxes, special taxes on lands of non-Muslims, trade, animals, produce, markets, mines, confiscations, and booty annually brought Suleiman about 12 million ducats. Even so, Suleiman was often hard-pressed for funds, and in his later years he forced gifts from his officers upon their appointment to a higher position.

SELIM II

Throughout his reign of eight years Selim II retained his father's last grand vizir, Mehmed Sokollu, who administered the government and might well be called the actual ruler. Selim generally deferred to him and to other high officials of proven abilities. Selim was highly emotional, sensitive, and a truly gifted poet, but he was also self-centered.

Since Sokollu continued as grand vizir throughout Selim's reign and on into that of his successor, there was no break in governmental procedure or policy, although there was some difficulty at the onset. Selim did not understand the power of the janissaries, and at first he declined to give the customary accession donations to the soldiers. Complaints and a show of force followed until Selim promised the money.

Otherwise, the course of events proceeded as it had under Suleiman as military expansion took place. Piyale Pasha took the island of Chios from the Genoese, peace was made with Austria and Poland, and more of Yemen was subjugated. An ambitious project was undertaken in 1569: forces were sent to conquer Astrakhan at the mouth of the Volga River at the Caspian Sea. Meanwhile, engineers started digging a canal to connect the Don River and the Volga at a point where they are only about 30 miles apart. The purpose was to enable ships and military supplies to be sent from the Black Sea to the Caspian Sea so as to support attacks upon Iran. The garrison at Astrakhan withstood the storm, however, and an army drove away the overextended Ottomans. The enterprise was abandoned, and peace between Muscovy and the Ottomans was reestablished.

Sokollu had a similar dream of cutting a waterway across Suez to link the Mediterranean and Red seas, but affairs in Yemen and Arabia and then Selim's insistence upon war against Venice for the conquest of Cyprus stopped the work. The whole island of Cyprus was subdued at heavy cost by 1571. Cyprus became a part of the unified empire.

The attack on Cyprus and the extraordinary naval preparations of the Ottomans not only alarmed Venice but instigated the formation of a powerful naval league that included Spain, Venice, Savoy, the pope, and the Knights of Malta. The Christian fleet met the Ottomans at the Gulf of Lepanto in 1571. A furious battle ensued, with the Ottomans losing over 150 ships and many men. The allied fleets suffered less, and victory was theirs. To the Ottomans the battle of Lepanto was a severe loss in a long series of naval engagements. However, a new fleet was built that winter in the naval yards of Gallipoli and Istanbul; by the spring of 1572 the Ottoman naval position was largely repaired. To the Christians, it had seemed a notable victory; it gave them courage and proved that the Ottomans were not invincible upon the sea. Nevertheless, in 1574 Tunis joined Algiers and Tripoli as Ottoman strongholds on the north shore of Africa and remained an Ottoman possession until the nineteenth century; in the eastern Mediterranean only the island of Crete remained outside Ottoman control. Ottoman maritime commerce prospered and flourished.

Late in 1574, while inspecting a new bath at the palace, Selim fell on the floor and suffered a brain concussion. His death, followed a year later by the assassination of Mehmed Sokollu, terminated an era in Ottoman history. The expansionistic Ottoman Empire soon turned into a stabler and more satisfied but still powerful state, with new policies and procedures in the seventeenth century.

OTTOMAN ARCHITECTURE AND ART

In the period of Ottoman history during the reigns of Suleiman and Selim (and including some of their successors), the most viable and lasting example of the empire's greatness and magnificence was the Topkapi imperial palace, whose human-scale buildings provided a splendid setting for lavish ceremonies, while giving its inhabitants the opportunity to view one of the most beautiful land- and seascapes imaginable. More open to the Muslim public were the equally majestic mosques that still silhouette much of the skyline of Istanbul. Sultans, grand vizirs, princes and princesses, and women of the harem—all built impressive pavilions, tombs, mosques, and mosque complexes (the latter centered around the mosque but including madrasahs, hospitals, etc.) to memorialize themselves. Most of the prominent mosques of the empire, and of Istanbul in particular, date from the sixteenth century, beginning with the mosque of Sultan Bayezid II (completed about 1500) and ending with the Blue Mosque of Sultan Ahmed I (1617). They surpassed the already high standard of imperial architecture established at Bursa and Edirne.

The simplest style and form, exemplified by the mosque of Sultan Selim I in Istanbul, consisted of a plain square building carrying one large dome. The transition between square and circle was accomplished by pendentives. The second type of imperial mosque evolved in the mosques of Bayezid II and Suleiman I. These mosques showed that Ottoman architects studied Hagia Sophia and appreciated its solution to the problem of building a domed open square or rectangular structure suitable for congregational worship. In these two mosques, the great rectangle was roofed by a large dome on pendentives that effected the transition from the dome to the four broad pointed arches resting upon four piers. The dome was abutted by semidomes fitted to their rectangles by pendentives or small semidomes, which in the Suleimaniye mosque were anchored to their corners by stalactite pendentives. The pendentives confused the eye and thereby hid the awkwardness, thus serving much the same function as the colored mosaics of the Byzantines. The strong buttresses in the lateral walls were admirably concealed by external porches.

Sinan (d. 1588), a janissary and a military architect, became the master designer of all sorts of buildings. Sinan contended that his early Shehzade mosque in memory of Suleiman's son Mehmed was the work of an apprentice; his later mosque for Suleiman was the work of a journeyman; and Sultan Selim II's mosque in Edirne, completed in 1574, was the work of a master. In Shehzade, Sinan presented a new style aimed at opening the entire edifice into one spacious congregational hall so that every worshiper could see the mihrab. The post-Sinan great mosque of Sultan Ahmed I (built 1609–1616) followed the same principle and achieved its goal by replacing the small domes of the lateral aisle with one large semidome. The central dome at Ahmed was supported by large circular piers. Upon entering Ahmed, one noticed immediately that the whole area was unified and that the central space was vaster than in Hagia Sophia.

At the mosque of Sultan Selim II in Edirne, Sinan developed another type of imperial mosque. The dome, 31 meters across, was supported by an octagon of arches, penditives of stalactite corbels, and eight sturdy paneled piers, which Sinan called "elephant feet." In all these mosques the flood of light that entered the central halls played a large role in the fascination and admiration felt by so many worshipers and other visitors.

The internal centers of the domes were usually decorated with flowered and calligraphic frescoes, and the walls were embellished by panels of colored and veined marble or colored ceramic tiles. The Ottomans were more conscious of aesthetic external lines and composition than were Byzantine builders, and this accounts for the architectural evolution that gave to the Istanbul horizon its splendor of domes and slender minarets. A distinctive Ottoman architecture spread from Istanbul throughout the empire, serving as a source of visual unity.

Mosques and palaces were furnished with the richly colored and geometrically patterned carpets and rugs for which the Ottoman Empire became so famous, and also with pottery, whose style was initially influenced by Chinese porcelain models. By the middle of the sixteenth century, Ottoman pottery and tiles, especially those produced at Iznik and Damascus, developed a variety of beautiful colors and motifs that dazzled as they pleased.

Calligraphy was an art form that was favored by the sultans and had close connections to the Sufi mystics. The imperial court also sponsored bookbinding and miniature painting. Styles of painting were influenced by Safavid artists in the early and middle sixteenth century; later Ottoman artists developed a more independent style. The "minor" arts also flourished; Sultan Suleiman was himself a goldsmith and a calligrapher, as well as a patron of art on an enormous scale. Ottoman silk weavings were much sought after in Europe. All the various forms of art were largely produced in workshops organized by the imperial government, which consumed most of their production. Officials of the state, leaders in the provinces, and the wealthier members of the religious minorities also patronized similar artisans.

OTTOMAN LITERATURE

The sixteenth century led in architectural achievement, but it was also a period of brilliant literary activity. Suleiman had a strong historical feeling; he emphasized the parallelism of Ottomans and Byzantines, so that Mehmed II and the emperor Constantine were viewed as similar, and Suleiman equated himself with Justinian. Like the Byzantine emperor Justinian, Suleiman was lawgiver and law codifier, builder of remarkable religious edifices and aqueducts, leader of armies, and generous patron of scholars and men of letters.

A quarter of all the eminent Ottoman poets and writers belonged to the period of Suleiman and Selim II. Poetry and history were the outstanding forms of literary effort. Lyric poetry often had a Sufi content and was expressed in forms heavily influenced by Sufi mysticism. Many themes were persistent for centuries—the garden; the lover/beloved; an urban orientation, especially toward Istanbul; and images of roses, nightingales, and wine. From an earlier time the female writer Mihri Hatun (d. 1506) produced exquisite love poetry, while Jem, son of Mehmed II, wrote poetry reflective of his life and its melancholy circumstances. The Turkish-Iraqi poet Mehmet Fuzuli (d. 1556) produced a panegyric on Suleiman's conquest of Baghdad and became famous for his romantic poems. Sufi poets and wandering minstrels recited poetry for the masses in the countryside, poetry that strikingly differed from that of the palace and the capital city. Both Suleiman and Selim were accomplished poets themselves, Suleiman writing in Persian and Turkish under the pen name Muhibbi (one who loves). The shining lyric poet of that age and perhaps of the Turkish language of all ages was Abd al-Baki, whose elegy for Sultan Suleiman was his greatest public work.

Historians flourished. Their works were sometimes general in scope and sometimes specific, describing only one phase or incident of the period, and were often sumptuously illustrated with miniature paintings. Early histories had been straightforward and written in a popular style, but Sultan Bayezid II commissioned a more ornate comprehensive history of the Ottomans. The ornate style first involved works written in Persian and Arabic, and later an infusion of words and grammatical units from those languages into Turkish. Cultural intermingling, amalgamation, and synthesis were reflected in language, but the gains in literary elegance were counterbalanced by the increasing gap between the style of the imperial court and the learned elite on the one hand, and the great mass of Turkish speakers on the other. The latter often could not understand the new high-flown rhetoric of the imperial style.

Among the historians, Ramazan wrote of the capture of Rhodes; Kemalpashazade, whose career included service as a sipahi and, much later, as shaikh al-Islam, narrated the victorious campaign of Mohacs, and wrote a general history of the dynasty. One of the most revered of Ottoman historians appeared late in the sixteenth century in the person of Saad al-Din. Tutor of Suleiman's grandson Murad III, he wrote and compiled *The Crown of Histories,* which, in numerous volumes and an analytic manner, covered the gamut of Ottoman history. The prolific bureaucrat, poet, and historian Mustafa Ali of Gallipoli (d. 1600) wrote an important book of counsel for sultans and a history of the world and the Ottoman Empire, begun in the year 1100 after the hijrah (C.E. 1591–1592). For such writers, historical chronicles were literary accomplishments, reflecting the increasingly complex and rich nature of Ottoman Turkish, as well as following the format of chronologically arranged annals.

The conquests chronicled by the historians were due in large part to Ottoman success in using gunpowder weapons and to the flexibility the empire demonstrated in adapting its military to new needs. Ottoman history in the sixteenth century and the nature of its rulers were typical of the range of experience found in other Middle Eastern and European countries of the time. Selim I had been harsh, brilliant, demanding, and energetic; he set the government in motion toward momentous conquest. Suleiman I was a dignified, orderly, just, conscientious, and artistic soldier and gentleman who gave the Ottoman Empire a sense of distinction and cultural urbanity. Selim II was a talented, irresponsible, emotional, dissolute drunkard who helped hasten the transformation of the state in new directions. Through all three reigns the Ottomans accomplished much in cultural areas as well as in the military and administration. During the sixteenth and seventeenth centuries they successfully met the threat posed by the Shii Savafids of Iran.

REFERENCES

Most titles already cited for the chapters discussing the Ottoman Empire are relevant to this chapter. Especially noteworthy are those in Chapters 14 and 16.

Andrews, Walter G., et al.: *Ottoman Lyric Poetry: An Anthology.* Austin: University of Texas Press, 1997. These beautifully translated Ottoman poems are arranged by themes and chronologically.

Atil, Esin: *Süleymanname: The Illustrated History of Süleyman the Magnificent.* New York: Harry N. Abrams, 1986. Lavish display of miniatures with a history of the sultan.

———: *The Age of Sultan Süleyman the Magnificent.* New York: Harry N. Abrams, 1987. The text and pictures illustrate all aspects of the art of the age.

Cook, Weston F., Jr.: *The Hundred Years War for Morocco: Gunpowder and the Military Revolution in the Early Modern Muslim World.* Boulder, Colo.: Westview, 1994. A thoughtful analysis of Moroccan events in the sixteenth century that also provides comparative insights into Ottoman and Safavid history.

Fleischer, Cornell H.: *Bureaucrat and Intellectual in the Ottoman Empire: The Historian Mustafa Ali (1541–1600).* Princeton, N.J.: Princeton University Press, 1986.

A sophisticated analysis not only of the life of this particular historian but of historiography for the entire period.

Goodwin, Godfrey: *A History of Ottoman Architecture.* Baltimore, Md.: Johns Hopkins University Press, 1971. Reissued, London: Thames and Hudson, 1992. An outstanding work, covering Bursa, Edirne, Istanbul; includes Sinan's works and an excellent chapter on the Ottoman house.

———: *Sinan: Ottoman Architecture and Its Values Today.* London: Saqi, 1993. A short but valuable introduction to the superb Ottoman architect and his work.

Guilmartin, John Francis, Jr.: *Gunpowder and Galleys: Changing Technology and Mediterranean Warfare at Sea in the Sixteenth Century.* London: Cambridge University Press, 1974. A masterful study on ships, sea battles, and their influence on politics and economy.

Hattox, Ralph S.: *Coffee and Coffeehouses: The Origins of a Social Beverage in the Medieval Near East.* Seattle: University of Washington Press, 1985. This charming book is an excellent example of research on Ottoman social history.

Kortepeter, Carl Max: *Ottoman Imperialism during the Reformation: Europe and the Caucasus.* New York: New York University Press, 1972. A study of relationships of political units in the great span between Europe and the Caucasus.

Kuran, Aptullah: *The Mosque in Early Ottoman Architecture.* Chicago: University of Chicago Press, 1968. Develops the idea that the basic unit in early Ottoman architecture was the domed square. Scholarly and authoritative.

Murphey, Rhoads: *Ottoman Warfare, 1500–1700.* New Brunswick, N.J.: Rutgers University Press, 1999. This is a general history of the Ottoman army, with especially valuable analysis of activities in the European region.

Norton, Claire, and Marios Hadjianastasis: *The Ottoman Studies Resource Index* at www.ottoman-links.co.uk. Contains many useful links to sites for a wide variety of subjects, including Ottoman chronology, flags, literature, and the study of the Middle East.

Peirce, Leslie P.: *The Imperial Harem: Women and Sovereignty in the Ottoman Empire.* New York: Oxford University Press, 1993. This outstanding analytic work concentrates on the period from 1520 to the middle of the seventeenth century; an indispensable work of historical revisionism.

Pryor, John H.: *Geography, Technology and War: Studies in the Maritime History of the Mediterranean, 649–1571.* Cambridge: Cambridge University Press, 1988. While covering a wide array of groups, this book is especially interesting on the fifteenth- and sixteenth-century Ottomans.

Rogers, J. M.: *Islamic Art and Design, 1500–1700.* London: British Museum, 1983. Treats Ottomans, Safavids, and Mughals of India comparatively.

Veinstein, G.: "Süleyman." *Encyclopaedia of Islam.* New ed. Vol. 9, pp. 832–842. Leiden: Brill, 1995. A full discussion of the life and accomplishments of the sultan, with a useful bibliography.

Woodhead, Christine: "Selim II." *Encyclopaedia of Islam.* New ed. Vol. 9, pp. 131–132. Leiden: Brill, 1995. A concise summary of the reign of this Ottoman sultan.

CHAPTER 19

The Flowering and Collapse of Safavid Iran

In the early modern period of Middle Eastern history the Shii Safavid dynasty dominated Iran, establishing a large empire beginning in 1501 that lasted for about 220 years. During this time Iran gained a religious and political identity separate from that of its Sunni neighbors—the Ottomans, the Mughals of India, and the Uzbegs of central Asia. Military competition with the larger Ottoman Empire strongly affected the Safavids, whose vigorous rulers such as Ismail and Abbas the Great often fought the sultans of Istanbul, even while interacting with them culturally. In the two centuries up to its abrupt demise in 1722, the Safavid state usually witnessed a capable administration, religious conversion on a large scale, economic prosperity, and cultural flowering.

ESTABLISHMENT OF THE SAFAVIDS IN IRAN

As the Mongol Il-Khan state declined in the late thirteenth and fourteenth centuries, many Turkoman tribes became autonomous. At about the same time numerous independent Sufi orders appeared. Some of the Turkoman tribes and the Sufi orders converted to Shiism, as Sufi leadership became hereditary and combined religious and military roles along with a frontier heterodoxy.

After the Mongols destroyed the city of Ardabil in northwestern Iran in 1220, it subsequently revived but only as a small provincial town. A Sufi order in Ardabil was called Safavid after its first leader, Safi al-Din, a Sunni, who died in 1334. The tomb of the Safavid leader became a shrine, and the complex of buildings around it served as a place of pilgrimage. Political chaos, which disturbed northwestern Iran, enabled the Safavid family to maintain their local freedom and gain great wealth. They became Shii at some time after 1392 and by the 1450s were seeking political power as allies of the Aq Quyunlu Turkomans. Raids against Christian Georgia earned the Safavids the title of ghazi. Following the death in battle of the Safavid Haidar in 1488, his son took the title padishah (king or emperor), and in the late fifteenth century the charismatic Safavid rulers claimed to be the Hidden Imam of the Twelver Shiis, who came to that position

Ismail (1501–1524)
|
Tahmasp (1524–1576)
|

Ismail II (1576–1578)

Muhammad Khudabanda (1578–1588)
|
Abbas (1588–1629)
|
Safi Mirza
|
Safi (1629–1642)
|
Abbas II (1642–1666)
|
Suleiman (Safi II) (1666–1694)
|
Husain (1694–1722)
|
Tahmasp II (1722–1732)

The Safavids

as a result of inheritance and not by designation of a predecessor. In time, powerful Turkoman clans and Sufi groups in western Iran and eastern Anatolia accepted and supported the Safavid order. (As mentioned earlier, the Sufis were called qizilbash, or "red head," a term derived from their distinctive hat—a scarlet cone-shaped affair with twelve scallops, or gores, one for each of the twelve Shii imams.)

Ismail, a younger son of Haidar, became the leader of the Safavid dynasty. With the aid of Turkish-speaking qizilbash tribes and a small group of advisers, Ismail defeated his maternal relatives, the Aq Quyunlu, took Armenia and Azerbaijan in 1501, and, at the age of fourteen, was proclaimed shah in Tabriz.

As leader of the Safavid religious order, Ismail regarded himself in his poetry—and was accepted—as a divine reincarnation. He was worshiped during his lifetime as a saint who possessed supernatural attributes and who, consequently, was invincible; his subjects prostrated themselves before him as before God. His state was based on the principles of Twelver Shiism, and his task in Iran was to spread that sect. Wherever his edict reached, the choice was fixed: conversion to Shiism or death. Though most Iranians had been Sunni Muslims, Ismail's cruelty, coupled with his policy of confiscating properties of Sunnis, expropriating endowments of Sunni Sufi orders, executing or exiling Sunni religious leaders, bringing into Iran Shii scholars from the Arab world (especially from southern Lebanon), and the already existing Shii sentiment in Qumm and Khurasan and among guilds, all changed Iran into a Shii state by the time of Ismail's death in 1524. His power was based on the support of the Turkish clan leaders, held by a mystical allegiance and tied to urban populations who were devotees of the Safavids. The tribal and Sufi leaders together could be called a kind of religious fraternity. In return for soldiers and revenue, each qizilbash chief was given a province, with the power of life and death over its people and the obligation to convert all to Shiism.

Claiming descent from the prophet Muhammad, Ali, and the seventh Shii imam and also from Aq Quyunlu Turks and Byzantine emperors, Ismail united Iranians, Turks, and

Shiis in devotion to his mystical being. Ismail established a theocratic state in western Iran with his principal strength in the north. Ismail gained control of central and southern Iran in 1503, and of Baghdad and southwest Iran in 1508. To the west, he seized most of the Tigris-Euphrates basin including Diyarbakir in 1507, and later he reached Dhu al-Qadr and the frontiers of the Ottomans. Expanding eastward, he successfully waged war against the Sunni Uzbegs of central Asia, killing Muhammad Shaibani, their chieftain, in 1510. Herat now became the second most important city in the state and the residence of the heir to the throne, despite the temporary resurgence of the Uzbegs in 1512.

Ismail sent religious-political agents to Anatolia, where they took advantage of the economic distress of the Turkoman tribes to urge revolt against the Ottomans. To overawe the Ottoman sultan Bayezid II, Ismail had the Uzbeg chieftain's skin stuffed with straw and sent to him as a warning. (In an even more typically macabre gesture Ismail had that same victim's skull rimmed with gold and set with jewels, using it for a while as his drinking cup.)

A governing apparatus of three main divisions was formed: military, religious, and bureaucratic. At first, no sharp distinction in the ruling establishment existed between military and civilian officers: all were members of the monarch's household. (The only real distinction was that most of the military spoke Turkish and most of the civilians spoke Persian). As political centralization gained momentum, the reins of government were gathered into the hands of Ismail's associates and officials.

At the top of the somewhat fluid hierarchy stood the viceroy, who exercised both temporal and spiritual authority. He took a leading role in political affairs, acted as a military commander, and influenced the selection of officials. The viceroys spoke Persian, a fact deeply resented by the qizilbash Turkish leaders. In the midst of a battle against the Uzbegs in 1512, the qizilbash forces deserted, guaranteeing the defeat and death of the viceroy. After another viceroy was killed in the battle of Chaldiran in 1514, the position was limited to supervision of the bureaucracy and the civil administration. Next in line stood the commander in chief, a post that was originally held by the viceroy and that, in addition to controlling the military, had considerable influence in administrative and political matters. In 1509, Ismail chose an obscure officer for this post in an obvious move to weaken the power of the Turkoman leaders. Persian-speaking individuals also held the posts of supervisor of the ulama and vizir. Naturally there developed among these officials a great deal of rivalry for power and for Ismail's favor.

When Selim I seized the Ottoman throne in Istanbul in 1512, he became involved in the raging quarrel in Anatolia over the qizilbash tribes. Selim set out to destroy Ismail. At the battle of Chaldiran in 1514 the Ottomans outnumbered the Safavids; in addition, the Ottoman forces enjoyed the superiority of janissary muskets and Ottoman artillery over the Safavid swords, spears, and bows. (The Safavids had used cannons in sieges, but they were reluctant to use cannons and handguns, and had not as yet successfully integrated handguns and artillery into their military; the Ottomans, on the other hand, adapted their warfare to the new technology.) Most Turkoman qizilbash leaders and many high Iranian officials were killed. The Ottomans temporarily occupied the Safavid capital of Tabriz, but the long lines of transportation back to Anatolia, the opposition of the soldiers to such a distant campaign, and the bitter cold induced Selim to retreat. The Ottomans did, however, gain and keep Diyarbakir and most of eastern Anatolia.

Ismail's spirit was crushed. It is said that he never smiled again, and he began to drink excessively. Henceforth the Turkoman leaders tended to doubt Ismail's claim of supernatural powers. But with Selim seizing Kurdistan and Diyarbakir, and wiping out qizilbash rebellion in Anatolia, the Turkoman qizilbash seemed to have had no choice but loyalty to Ismail. The shah never again led troops into battle. He tried to put civilians into positions of trust and power in order to break the might of the qizilbash leaders, although he could not control all the provinces, especially Khurasan. With his death in 1524 at the age of thirty-six, the full extent of the decline of the ruling institution became apparent.

SHAH TAHMASP I

Because when Ismail died his eldest son, Tahmasp, was only ten years old, Turkoman leaders were able to regain their power. Civil war among the Turkoman tribes kept the state in turmoil until Tahmasp subdued the rebellions and ended the strife by seizing power for himself and appointing an Iranian viceroy in 1533. Tahmasp then established his personal authority, civilian rule as set by Ismail became dominant, and the Safavid state survived. The Sufi organization was unsuccessful in penetrating or subverting the administrative system of the Safavid government. The Safavid family tended to marry prominent women and men from the Turkoman qizilbash tribes. During this period in Iran the main lines of monarchy were worked out, the capital was fixed first at Qazvin and later in Isfahan, and Shiism became the established official religion.

Despite this political turmoil, textiles, ceramics, calligraphy, and miniature painting flourished during Tahmasp's reign. The shah himself was a noted poet, calligrapher, and painter. Illustrations for Firdawsi's *Shahnamah* commissioned by Ismail and Tahmasp were especially splendid and they celebrated royal grandeur. Chroniclers, theologians, geographers, and astrologers flourished. Safavid-era madrasahs emphasized sciences such as medicine, logic, and scholastic theology, while royal patronage encouraged the study of religious law, hadith, and mathematics. In religious matters, Tahmasp did not regard himself as being semidivine; instead, he designated a leading cleric as the deputy of the Hidden Imam (a concept later called the mujtahid of the age).

External enemies threatened the Safavid lands. The Uzbegs took Khurasan but were defeated by Tahmasp in 1528, in large part thanks to cannons provided by the Portuguese. To the west, when the Ottoman sultan Suleiman I threatened Iran over its support of various Turkoman chiefs, Tahmasp in vain sent envoys to Charles V for aid. In 1534 the Ottomans invaded, sacking Tabriz and Gilan, and capturing Baghdad. (Central Iraq remained in Ottoman hands for ninety years.) Another campaign occurred in 1548 when Tahmasp's brother induced the Ottomans to send an invading army that seized Azerbaijan. Peace was arranged in 1555, but the shah lost Iraq to the Ottomans. Although a shortage of artillery and muskets was a disadvantage to Tahmasp, his scorched-earth strategy, distances from Istanbul, and difficult terrain stopped the Ottoman forces from permanent conquest. Thus, Tahmasp was able to enforce his rule from the Tigris to central Asia and from the Persian Gulf to both sides of the Caspian Sea. Border provinces lost their autonomy and were directly incorporated into the state.

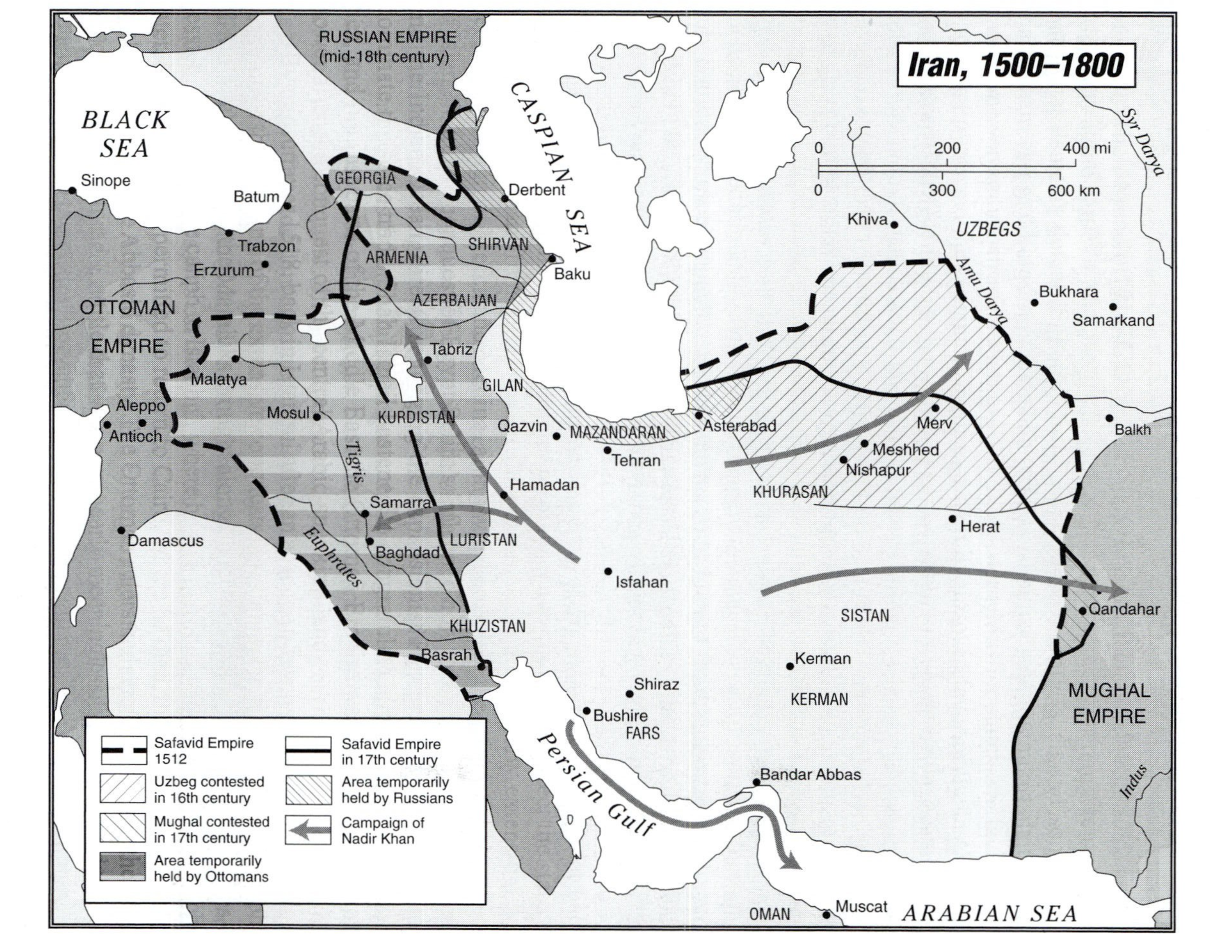
Iran, 1500–1800
0 200 400 mi
0 300 600 km
RUSSIAN EMPIRE
(mid-18th century)
BLACK SEA
CASPIAN SEA
Sinope
Batum
Trabzon
Erzurum
OTTOMAN EMPIRE
GEORGIA
ARMENIA
SHIRVAN
AZERBAIJAN
Derbent
Baku
Tabriz
GILAN
Malatya
Aleppo
Antioch
Mosul
KURDISTAN
Qazvin
MAZANDARAN
Tehran
Asterabad
Tigris
Hamadan
Samarra
Baghdad
LURISTAN
Damascus
Euphrates
Isfahan
KHUZISTAN
Basrah
Shiraz
Bushire
FARS
Persian Gulf
Bandar Abbas
OMAN
Muscat
ARABIAN SEA
Khiva
UZBEGS
Amu Darya
Syr Darya
Bukhara
Samarkand
Merv
Meshhed
Nishapur
KHURASAN
Balkh
Herat
SISTAN
Qandahar
Kerman
KERMAN
MUGHAL EMPIRE
Indus
Safavid Empire 1512
Safavid Empire in 17th century
Uzbeg contested in 16th century
Area temporarily held by Russians
Mughal contested in 17th century
Campaign of Nadir Khan
Area temporarily held by Ottomans

Within the Safavid lands there was competition between the qizilbash Turkomans and Persian-speaking groups. Shah Tahmasp attempted, as his father had before him, to find an alternative to the power of unreliable Sufis and qizilbash. Nearly every province was held by one of their leaders, and their incomes and retainers gave them an independence difficult to offset. Between 1540 and 1544 Tahmasp sent four expeditions to Georgia, bringing back 30,000 prisoners, most of whom were boys who would be trained as ghulams—slaves to serve in his army or in administration. The girls served as concubines whose sons also entered the shah's service. This policy of creating a Georgian, Circassian, and Armenian counterweight to the qizilbash in the end proved disastrous, as civil war broke out between them in 1572 when Tahmasp grew old and feeble.

Tahmasp's mother competed for influence over the shah with her daughter, Mahin Banu (d. 1562), who played a substantial role in state matters. Mahin Banu, an excellent calligrapher, was actively engaged in writing about foreign relations with both the Ottomans and the Mughals. She was also a patron of Shii shrines and she established numerous charitable waqfs, including some that helped orphaned girls. Several other later female members of the Safavid royal family also were prominent in government affairs, in part because of their being educated by tutors inside the imperial harem. Other elite urban women similarly contributed to Safavid and Shii shrines and were engaged in the economy through owning interests in homes, baths, caravanserais, shops, water wells, and land. Gender relations for most urban women seem to have been based on patterns of living derived from patriarchal values in society, gender segregation, shariah mandates, veiling, and arranged marriages.

The women of the royal family and their many sons began to intrigue for the succession to the throne toward the end of Tahmasp's life. Two leading candidates were Prince Ismail, whose mother was a Circassian, and Prince Haidar, whose mother was a Georgian. In the end the qizilbash declared they would support sons of Turkish or Circassian mothers only.

In 1576, Tahmasp was poisoned and the qizilbash had the power to put Ismail II on the throne. Having been incarcerated for twenty years by his father, he was brutal toward his royal relatives. He killed all the royal princes except Prince Muhammad Khudabanda, who was nearly blind and not considered a threat. The shah attempted to return Iran to Sunnism and executed many qizilbash and Sufi leaders who had supported his brothers. Ismail finally gave orders to have his sole remaining brother executed. Before the deed could be committed, however, the shah died mysteriously; it is possible he was poisoned.

Shah Muhammad Khudabanda ruled as a puppet in Turkoman hands for ten years until 1588. During this time of Safavid weakness the Ottomans began a war that lasted from 1578 to 1590 and resulted in their reconquest of Tabriz. Shah Muhammad was overthrown and killed by Turkoman leaders who seized Qazvin, the capital, and who put his sixteen-year-old son, Abbas, on the throne. Ruling for forty-one years, Abbas ushered in a new age in Iranian history. By 1587, religious zeal for Safavid rule had lessened, and over the century the shah's position as the head of a secular state dominated. There had been a gradual change and evolution under Tahmasp, with acceptance of the idea of a central government. He strengthened the state by moving the capital from Tabriz to Qazvin, which was safer from Ottoman assault. Moreover, Shii doctrinal unity had been achieved to a great extent, making religion much less of an emotional issue. One could now recognize the consolidation of Safavid Iran into a state of considerable permanence.

SHAH ABBAS THE GREAT OF ISFAHAN

Only about one-half of the Safavid Empire was still intact when Abbas came to the throne. After the qizilbash chieftains left Herat for Qazvin to install Abbas on the Safavid throne in 1588, the Sunni Uzbeg tribes had invaded and captured Herat. Shah Abbas met them at Meshhed, but crucial rebellions of local princes in his western provinces demanded his immediate return. With combined forces of local qizilbash tribes and an army improvised from Georgian prisoners and held together by his personal leadership, Abbas was able to put down a serious uprising in Shiraz and soon had central Iran pacified. The Ottoman attack in the west could not be thwarted, however, and by the peace of 1590 with Murad III, Tabriz, some Caspian ports, and surrounding areas were ceded. In the same year Abbas moved the capital to Isfahan.

During the following seven years Abbas consolidated his position and power, his initial step being the weakening of qizilbash forces. Their leaders were killed and their provinces and lands confiscated. With the income from these holdings plus the funds of the royal household, Abbas formed a standing army of 10,000 horsemen from the qizilbash and Persian-speaking tribes and 12,000 foot soldiers from prisoners and slaves from Armenia and Georgia. In addition to this strengthening of manpower, Abbas significantly improved his firepower.

In 1598, Robert Sherley, along with other Englishmen, arrived in Isfahan, the new capital, to discuss trade and an alliance against the Ottomans and the Dutch. The Englishmen helped Abbas train musketeers and taught his men how to cast cannon. Abbas also bought weapons from Russia and Venice. Within a few years, Abbas had a force of 12,000 artillery men equipped with 500 brass and bronze cannons, with which he effectively challenged the Ottoman armies as well as internal dissidents. A new corps of 12,000 mounted musketeers was raised from the peasantry, and another 10,000 Georgian prisoners were added to the army. Throughout his reign Abbas continued the policy of turning prisoners of war into soldiers and administrators: on one occasion 20,000 Armenians were taken from the region of Erzurum and pressed into service; on another, an expedition into Georgia, tens of thousands of prisoners were taken and moved into his state in various areas and capacities.

By 1602, Abbas cleared the eastern frontiers of challengers. He drove the Uzbegs from Meshhed, Herat, and Khurasan and moved eastward to Balkh. Abbas attempted to stamp out Sunnism in eastern Iran. To defend Khurasan he transported thousands of Kurdish horsemen and their families to the frontier, establishing them so securely that many of their descendants still reside in that area. War against the Ottomans erupted in 1603, and Tabriz was recaptured. With the decline of Ottoman military force in eastern Anatolia, Abbas took Kurdistan and Shirvan from Ahmed I and in 1623 recaptured Baghdad, Mosul, and Diyarbakir, restoring to Iran the territories held at the time of Shah Ismail. On other fronts, Abbas defeated the Mughals of India, taking Qandahar (Kandahar) in Afghanistan; seized the Bahrain Islands in the Persian Gulf; and drove the Portuguese from Hormuz in 1622, founding the important Persian Gulf trading post of Bandar Abbas. When Shah Abbas died in 1629, his lands enjoyed peace and prosperity. In contrast, the Ottoman Empire had been defeated, Russia was recovering from its Time of Troubles, and the Mughals in India were beginning to lose hold of south Asia.

ADMINISTRATION AND TRADE UNDER ABBAS

By the year 1606, Shah Abbas had established his direct rule over most of the provinces of Iran. Warfare was relegated to the frontiers and was fought by professional soldiers as well as qizilbash. The administration of most of the provinces was overseen by governors subservient to the royal will. Like Allahverdi Khan, governor of Fars and one of Abbas's first appointees, many of these officials were slaves. Eventually more than a fifth of the central government came from the ghulam slave ranks. Still, a majority of the civil administration was drawn from Persian-speaking free people.

Over one-half of the population consisted of peasant farmers living in villages; the next largest economic group was made up of nomads and seminomads, organized usually into tribes; and the smallest category consisted of town and city dwellers. Most imperial revenues came from the tax on land. A village's harvest was divided into shares which were paid to its several owners, whether landlords, iqta holders, or managers of waqfs. Peasants were obliged to stay in the villages, whose land they farmed communally. Sometimes they fled when the burden of taxation or payments to landlords became too great. In theory the shah owned most of the land on behalf of the Hidden Imam. Iqtas or revocable grants of revenue constituted the chief form of payment for government officials and soldiers, along with exemptions from taxes. The central government set tax rates and procedures, but the actual collection of taxes was decentralized. Strong villages, guilds, landlords, and tribes made special arrangements, thereby pushing more of the tax burden onto weaker groups. Abbas and earlier shahs coopted leaders into their service by giving them the right to collect taxes from the peasants. These leaders also were in charge of law and order locally and had to muster troops in the event of war. Often local elites held these privileges on a hereditary basis, thereby giving them a base of political power. From the beginning of the Safavid dynasty, a system of tax farming was also used, especially for collecting indirect taxes; special religious taxes were collected directly by the ulama. Guilds collected taxes from consumers. The numerous craft guilds met with city officials to debate taxes and matters of general concern; on occasion they protested government restrictions and officials' repression.

The shah created numerous religious endowments as symbols of his commitment to Twelver Shiism. Abbas enhanced the post of sadr, an administrative official and head of the religious and judicial hierarchy, who gained in power by becoming charged with the administration of many waqfs. Madrasahs, courts, and mosques were flourishing, but they were not as efficiently organized and as subservient to imperial authority as in the Ottoman Empire. The shah ordered the compilation of a legal treatise that became the basis of law for the century. Shii ulama were brought to Iran from the Arab theological centers of southern Lebanon and Bahrain, and the shah persecuted most Sufi orders. The great philosopher and metaphysician Mullah Sadra Shirazi (d. 1640), writing in Arabic, espoused Gnostic views. As a result, he was strongly attacked by the Shii ulama.

Abbas had a special concern for commerce, both domestic and foreign. To connect all major cities, Abbas provided a network of roads that every 20 miles (30 km.) or so had a secure caravanserai where several caravans could spend the night safe from marauders. The shah and other prominent government officials traded on their own account. Often elite figures would force merchants to buy or sell goods on highly beneficial terms, with government having the right of first purchase of a commercial shipment. Commerce was difficult in Iran because of the numerous mountains and deserts, as well as the relatively small and dispersed population, but Abbas and his successors helped organize a variety of merchant groups and trading routes to encourage trade. The shah showed initiative with regard to the important and highly profitable silk trade. Since Armenian communities were basic in the silk trade, with one of their centers at Julfa on the Aras River in Azerbaijan, Abbas imported 3000 Armenian families and created New Julfa for them on the outskirts of Isfahan. A monopoly over the silk export trade was established, with the Armenians running it for the shah. They prospered so greatly that some Armenian merchants lived in the style of the Safavid imperial court. Armenian religious manuscript illumination reached new heights, and the printing of Armenian secular works began in 1608.

To exploit European enthusiasm for fine porcelain from China, Abbas brought 300 Chinese potters to Isfahan to create pottery in the Chinese style. Not only was an additional export developed but an important tradition was established, for the most skillful and resourceful potters since the seventeenth century have been in Isfahan.

It was not long before Iranian artisanal goods were highly esteemed and their quality and artistry became legendary. Among the more important were silk and wool carpets and textiles of all types, porcelains, miniature paintings and albums, enamelwork, glassware, lacquered woods, bookbindings, leather goods, gold and silver plates, vases, and fine steel swords. Since many of these items were the product of court workshops, they were of a design and workmanship that were nearly always superb. As commercial relations with Europe and India increased in the seventeenth century, export goods declined somewhat in quality and were more influenced by foreign motifs.

Undoubtedly the best-known articles have been the Persian carpets. The finest of these carpets were made in court workshops for the court and the wealthiest patrons, few if any being exported. Only materials of the highest quality were employed in their manufacture. Sheep were specially bred for their delicate wool and were tended like children so that the wool would never be soiled or roughened. Even the water for washing the wool was important. Court painters designed the carpets, often using medallion patterns and also employing refined stylized motifs that incorporated gardens, animals, and pools. Rugs manufactured for export, though of a lesser quality, were nevertheless rich in color, design, and fabrication, most coming from workshops closely allied to the court. Outside the imperial capital the carpet weaving of nomads and villagers followed the old traditions and was often of high quality, particularly in the making of plain-weave, lightweight kilims used for travel.

Skills in other arts were also highly developed. Velvets, brocades, and embroideries were produced with the greatest care. Painting and the decorative arts were of a highly intricate style that displayed a keen sense of blending floral and geometric patterns to create a pleasing whole. Potters learned how to decorate their wares in many colors, often firing seven or more colors at once on large tiles. Shah Abbas was so fond of fine calligraphy that he is said to have personally held a candlestick so that his favorite artist could see better as he wrote.

THE SPLENDOR OF ISFAHAN

The internal stability established by Shah Abbas the Great encouraged a vast increase in trade, raised levels of production, opened wider avenues of opportunity for many, and ensured prosperity for much of the population. At the court in Isfahan the resulting wealth transformed the style of life to a degree of lavishness seldom seen. European visitors gave descriptions of the dazzling opulence: Abbas on his throne surrounded by several hundred courtiers clothed in gold and silver with an array of gray, scarlet, yellow, green, plum, blue, and maroon silks embroidered with the rarest of jewels.

In the center of the new, planned district of Isfahan, Abbas surrounded a great open square, 560 yards by 174 yards (512 m. by 159 m.), with magnificent buildings. The square was used for polo—the popular sport of the courtiers at that time—horse races, religious processions, fireworks displays, and executions. On one side of the square was the Ali Kapu, an entrance to the imperial palace, featuring a lovely pavilion in which Abbas liked to lounge with his courtiers and watch the festivities of the square. On another side was the imperial mosque, Masjid-i Shah, masterpiece of Safavid architecture. An impressive pointed archway more than 80 feet (24 m.) high led to an inner courtyard surrounded by a graceful two-storied arcade. Opposite the entrance was another portal leading to the mosque proper, whose walls carried a large dome, the exterior of which was covered by exquisite polychrome tiles with arabesque patterns in dark blue and green on a sky-blue background. On another side of the area was a great covered bazaar with a monumental arched entrance. The dome of the imperial mosque served as a landmark of the center of the heavily walled city, which eventually had 600,000 inhabitants and boasted 1802 caravanserais, 162 mosques, 273 public baths, 48 colleges and academies, and numerous coffeehouses. Isfahan, with its pools, bridges, and watercourses, was a flower lover's paradise, its gardens displaying roses, jasmine, lilies, irises, poppies, and many other flowers. Abbas himself laid out the gardens, planned the buildings, and even gave detailed instructions to the workmen.

UZBEG CENTRAL ASIA

At the time when the Safavids were accomplishing much in the cultural and military arenas, in the arid steppelands of central Asia the heirs of Timur were driven into India, where they subsequently created the Mughal Empire. In their place, the Shaibanid and Tuqay Timurid descendants of the Mongol conqueror Genghiz Khan established Sunni states based on Uzbeg Turkish-Mongol tribes. Succession in the royal families to the position of khan or leader usually went to the senior male in the family, and military and fiscal power often was decentralized among various royal princes. The Turkish Uzbeg and Persian Tajik nomadic, village, and urban populations also provided military and Sufi leaders. Administration was less formal and thorough than in the Safavid Empire; for instance, the rulers did not have a formal standing army. Holders of revocable grants played a large role in tax collection and provincial administration. The Hanafi rite of Islam dominated the shariah courts as supported by the political leadership.

Muhammad Shaibani Khan, the grandson of an earlier Uzbeg leader, rose from a cavalry soldier to governor of Tashkent by 1494. He based his claim to power on descent from the Mongol conqueror Genghiz Khan. After Muhammad Shaibani's capture of Samarkand in 1501 he expanded the new Uzbeg state to Herat in 1507, but following his defeat and execution by Shah Ismail the khanate was more limited geographically, including chiefly Bukhara, Samarkand, Tashkent, and Balkh. Although the Shaibanids defended themselves against Mughal and Safavid attacks, internal divisions limited their military power. Civil wars between 1550 and 1582 ultimately resulted in the victory of one Shaibanid clan, which united all of the region. Abd Allah Khan (1583–1598) overcame the Safavids and seized Herat and most of Khurasan, but upon his death and the assassination of his heir, anarchy ensued. The Safavid Abbas the Great regained eastern Iran, while in central Asia the Shaibanid dynasty disappeared.

Rule over Uzbeg central Asia fell into the hands of another group of descendants of Genghiz Khan, the Tuqay Timurid clan. They consolidated their power during the decade of the 1600s, gaining their capital Bukhara, as well as Samarkand and Balkh, but ultimately ceding Tashkent to the expanding power of the Kazakhs. The long and relatively peaceful reign of Imam Quli Khan (1612–1642) was followed by civil war and Mughal invasion, and finally the reestablishment of the Tuqay Timurids, who ruled from both Bukhara and Balkh. In the last half of the seventeenth century the Tuqay Timurids maintained their state against numerous foes, supported the ulama and Sufis, and fostered the pilgrimage to Mecca.

Both branches of the Genghiz Khan family, the Shaibanids and the Tuqay Timurids, built mosques, madrasahs, Sufi centers, and royal palaces in central Asia. The Tuqay Timurid khans endowed shrines with waqf properties to provide money for expenses. Literature written in eastern Turkish dialects and Persian poetry provided a basis for a common culture heavily influenced by Safavid Iran, and miniature painting modeled on the style of Herat flourished in Bukhara, which was the intellectual capital of Muslim central Asia.

In the first half of the eighteenth century central Asia experienced a general crisis, including political disintegration, economic decay, urban collapse, the enhancement of tribal power, and the decline of settled agriculture. Government revenues lessened as commerce decreased, while local groups successfully challenged the power of the various royal families. Samarkand was completely abandoned and devastated. The Tuqay Timurid khans in Bukhara lost all real power, although they remained symbols of legitimate rule. Kazakh tribes expanded their influence, while Turkmen groups moved into Khurasan and parts of central Asia. As a result, an ethnic and linguistic patchwork of settlements emerged, where widely varying groups of people lived side by side.

SHAHS SAFI AND ABBAS II

South of Uzbeg central Asia in Iran, the last century of Safavid rule began with the relatively uneventful reigns of Shahs Safi and Abbas II, who preserved the basic institutions and boundaries of the empire between 1629 and 1666. Personally the shahs were capricious and cruel, and, as was perhaps to be expected, they could not maintain the level of rule of Abbas the Great. During this time a transition took place from an expansionist military and foreign policy to a more internally oriented leadership; for most Safavid subjects the change was probably at first beneficial.

The empire was preserved intact by a multitude of factors: the widespread acceptance of Shiism as a common bond among the people, the strength of the administration, the quality of many officials, the vitality of commerce, the general peace, the internal tranquility, and the weakness of opponents beyond the frontiers. Without these, the dynasty and the state might well have become weak earlier than was actually the case.

A decline in the experience and ability of the rulers was caused by Abbas I. Because he feared the popularity of his own sons, he had his eldest executed and two others blinded, making them ineligible to rule. In addition, he instituted the practice of keeping the royal princes as prisoners within the palace, in the company of women and servants who satisfied their every sensual whim. The royal princes no longer governed provinces as training for possibly ascending to the throne. Instead, they were catapulted to power after years of polite imprisonment in Isfahan. Court officials, women of the harem, and slave retainers influenced them strongly. Queen mothers played an especially great role at court. Effective control of administration frequently fell into the hands of the grand vizir. The royal family now tended to arrange marriages of Safavid princesses with members of the ulama, bureaucrats, and descendants of the prophet Muhammad.

In 1629 Abbas was succeeded by his young grandson, Shah Safi, who murdered his mother, a sister, his favorite wife, army generals, provincial governors, and many of the court officials. Nevertheless, the government under Safi did have the strength and will to repel Uzbeg incursions into Khurasan and suppress rebellions in Gilan, although the Mughals repossessed Qandahar and the Ottomans retook Baghdad in 1638. There ensued a peace treaty that ended the incessant Safavid-Ottoman wars—at the cost of Iraq becoming Ottoman. The shah was a noted patron of miniature painting, thus continuing Isfahan's reputation as the center for great successes in this art form.

Safi died from drinking too much and was followed in 1642 by his ten-year-old son, Abbas II, who started with real promise and at the age of sixteen showed vigor and flashes of his great-grandfather's character by leading an army in the recapture of Qandahar. Despite this success, Abbas II usually chose peace with his neighbors. During his reign an intellectual form of Sufism reached a high level. He appointed slave ghulams who were converts to Islam to high posts in the provincial governments, while the shah personally took a direct interest in the administration of justice. Still more lands were taken from the governance of notables and directly administered by the central authorities. The shah fostered the economic growth of Isfahan. Abbas II's rule was marred, however, when he turned to drink and personal indulgences, murdering many around him and forcing the conversion of Isfahan Jews to Islam.

Some cultural and artistic successes were achieved. In ceramics, textiles, miniature paintings, and drawings, works of considerable beauty were still being created. However, European styles began to influence painting by the late seventeenth century, and literature and poetry were in decay, despite new opportunities for poets and folktale reciters in coffeehouses. The ruling dynasties of India and the Ottoman Empire offered many inducements to Persian writers, prominent thinkers, and artists to leave Iran. The sciences in Iran were stagnant, except for limited advances in medicine and in the production of astrolabes.

THE DECLINE AND END OF SAFAVID RULE

In addition to a steady decline in the quality of the shahs, the power of the central government over distant regions weakened. The economy contracted as the value of exports fell, foreign competition increased, the plague killed thousands, silver flowed out to India, and insecurity on the trade routes worsened. Silk production decreased, although wool exports increased. Transportation of bulky goods continued to be so expensive that while grain surpluses existed in some areas, famines took place elsewhere. The government debased the coinage and reallocated spending away from the military so that close to one-half of expenditures went to the harem and the royal family. Customs collections were farmed out to tax collectors, a practice that in the long run contributed to budgetary woes. Most important of all, the number and effectiveness of tribal cavalry soldiers fell even as spending on the ghulam standing army was also cut.

Moreover, at the same time as this economic and military decline, Shiism became ever more widespread among the peoples of Iran. The shariah-minded Shii ulama gained more influence at court and among the faithful. At the instigation of the ulama many of the Sufi orders were repressed by the state and Sunnis were harassed. As the shahs lost legitimacy and backing, the Shii ulama gained support.

Upon the death of Abbas II in 1666, his seventeen-year-old son first took the title Safi II but because of disasters chose to take a new regnal name and was recrowned the following year as Shah Suleiman. He reigned for twenty-eight long years, dying in 1694. Shah Suleiman was a drunkard who loved peace and thought little about the state: once, when told that an attack was expected, he replied that it made no difference to him, as long as he could keep Isfahan. Perhaps inadvertently this policy of peace worked well, and Iran enjoyed years of respite from foreign wars.

In 1669 Shah Suleiman built the famous palace called "Eight Paradises," known for its pavilions and tile work. The shah had many government officials executed, leaving more of the administration to his ghulam palace cronies, although he employed an able grand vizir. When he died, he had already executed his eldest son and left the choice between his other sons to the eunuchs and courtiers of the palace. They chose Husain. Having been shut up in the harem of the palace for twenty-six years, Husain was ignorant, superstitious, and easily influenced—just the kind of shah the courtiers desired.

Husain inaugurated his reign by prohibiting the use of wine: he had all the wine jars in the palace broken and would not permit the Armenians who controlled the wine trade to sell in Isfahan. As a youth he had become a partisan of religious teachers and leaders, or mullahs, so much so that many jokingly called him Mullah Husain. Religious minorities—Christians, Jews, and Sunnis—were persecuted. An edict issued by the shah forbade music, dancing, coffeehouses, gambling, and chess. Women's activities were strictly limited. As the ulama gained more influence in Isfahan, the shariah was rigidly implemented and patriarchal values curbed a more open society. In 1706, the shah organized a pilgrimage to the holy shrine at Qumm, the site of the family tombs, accompanied by over 60,000 people. This venture proved so enjoyable that he went with an equal number of retainers on the 600-mile (around 950 km.) pilgrimage to Meshhed, remaining there a whole year. The extravagance of this expedition not only emptied the treasury but ruined all the provinces through which it passed.

Thanks to an aunt who prevailed upon him to permit her to drink in the palace, Husain did not remain abstemious for long. Soon wine flowed freely everywhere. Husain became licentious, and his agents were constantly on the lookout for attractive faces to kidnap for his harem. Unable to curb his lavish habits and faced with the mounting cost of maintaining a standing army with cannon and muskets, the shah's ministers had to find additional income. Government officials created artificial bread shortages in the capital of Isfahan and then made fortunes selling grain at inflated prices. Another lucrative device was to squeeze more revenue from the provinces. Even before this, provincial administration had already suffered under Safi I and Abbas II, when many provinces had been transferred to the royal household and their governorships sold to court favorites, who reimbursed themselves by gouging the inhabitants. The right to collect revenue was sold more and more often, thereby also increasing the tax burden on the peasants. A general economic crisis affected Iran.

Upon the raiding of Qandahar by Baluchis, Shah Husain sent a Georgian general as the new governor in 1704, who adopted such severe measures against the Sunni Ghilzai Afghan inhabitants that they rose in revolt under Mir Vays in 1709. Shah Husain sent an army from Isfahan in 1711 to destroy Mir Vays, but being poorly paid and divided by jealousies among three different components, it was routed in front of the walls of Qandahar. Mir Vays thus became an independent ruler, calling himself regent of Qandahar.

In 1715 Mir Vays was succeeded by his sixteen-year-old son, Mahmud, an ambitious youth who began to attack the shah's kingdom, advancing to a point close to Isfahan. The battle for the Safavid capital was joined in 1722, with Mahmud occupying the Armenian suburb of New Julfa and investing the city. After a six-month siege that saw 60,000 inhabitants killed by starvation or epidemics and 20,000 killed in fighting, Husain surrendered. In a humiliating ceremony Husain went out to Mahmud's headquarters and there, with his own hands, took from his turban the imperial plume of heron's feathers set with jewels—the sign of sovereignty—placed it on Mahmud's head, and bade him rule. Safavid power had collapsed.

During the siege Tahmasp, one of Husain's older sons, escaped from Isfahan and made his way to Qazvin, where he was recognized as Shah Tahmasp II. Affairs were not, however, favorable to his candidacy for rule. The Ottomans seized Tiflis, Tabriz, and Hamadan. Peter the Great of Russia, outfitting a fleet on the Caspian Sea, took Shirvan and Gilan, and compelled Tahmasp II to sign a treaty in 1722, ceding to Russia Darband, Baku, Gilan, Astarabad, and Mazandaran in exchange for Peter's commitment to drive the Afghans from Isfahan. When Mahmud learned of the proposed Russian incursion to place Tahmasp II back on the throne in Isfahan, he had all the members of the Safavid family assembled in the palace courtyard; he and two of his friends then hacked them to death, except for Husain and two small children whom Husain shielded with his own body. Mahmud, who had rapidly grown insane, died in 1725, being succeeded by his cousin Ashraf. The Ottoman armies pressed forward into Iran, asserting that they planned to restore the Safavids to their rightful possessions. Ashraf thereupon had Husain executed and sent his head to the Ottoman commander to forestall his attack on Isfahan.

Meanwhile, Tahmasp II gathered an army in Mazandaran in 1727, being supported by two qizilbash tribal leaders: Fath Ali Khan, the chief of the Qajars, and Nadir Khan of the Afshars, each bringing several thousand experienced soldiers. They marched into Khurasan and recaptured Meshhed and Herat from the Afghans in 1729; along the way Nadir Khan murdered his rival, Fath Ali, and thus became the sole commander of the royal army. Nadir routed the Afghans under Ashraf, expelling them from Isfahan and Shiraz. Tahmasp II returned as shah to Isfahan but gave most power to Nadir. In 1732 Nadir dethroned him and sent him as a prisoner to Khurasan, where he was later killed. Nadir put Tahmasp's infant son on the throne as Abbas III, but the child died in 1736 and Nadir assumed the title shah, the powers of which he had been holding for several years. Safavid rule had ended.

The Safavids left a profound legacy for Iran, as they determined its Shii religious identity, established many of its borders, encouraged a cultural flowering, and provided stable government. Notable Safavid shahs—Ismail, Tahmasp I, and Abbas the Great—arranged a balance of power among their backers so that qizilbash, ghulams, ulama, and bureaucrats functioned effectively. Isfahan during the reign of Abbas I was especially splendid. The collapse of the Safavids, however, ushered in a long era of chaos and catastrophes for the people of Iran. During the seventeenth century the Ottoman Empire faced many of the same challenges and opportunities encountered by the Safavids and the Uzbegs of central Asia, but the Ottomans were more successful in responding to changes. While the Safavid and Uzbeg dynasties collapsed, the Ottomans endured for several more centuries.

REFERENCES

References cited at the end of Chapters 10, 11, 12, and 18 are pertinent to this chapter as well.

Blake, Stephen P.: *Half the World: The Social Architecture of Safavid Isfahan, 1590–1722.* Costa Mesa, Calif.: Mazda, 1999. Describes the cityscape in general and in particular the palaces, mansions, gardens, bazaars, and madrasahs.

Floor, Willem: *A Fiscal History of Iran in the Safavid and Qajar Periods, 1500–1925.* New York: Bibliotheca Persica, 1998. A lengthy and detailed but valuable discussion of taxes, administration, and fiscal issues based on a political-economic approach.

———: *Safavid Government Institutions.* Costa Mesa, Calif.: Mazda, 2001. A thorough review of the posts, functions, and practice of Safavid administration, especially useful for the army's history.

Foran, John: "The Long Fall of the Safavid Dynasty: Moving beyond the Standard Views." *International Journal of Middle East Studies* 24 (1992): 281–304. Adds new dimensions to the analysis presented in the book by Laurence Lockhart cited below.

———: *Fragile Resistance: Social Transformation in Iran from 1500 to the Revolution.* Boulder, Colo.: Westview, 1993. This important sociological and historical study puts Iran's experiences into a comparative framework.

Keyvani, Mehdi: *Artisans and Guild Life in the Later Safavid Period: Contributions to the Social-Economic History of Persia.* Berlin: Klaus Schwarz, 1982.

Lockhard, Laurence: *The Fall of the Safavi Dynasty and the Afghan Occupation of Persia.* New York: Cambridge University Press, 1958. Deals largely with the eighteenth century; excellent for political history.

Matthee, Rudi: "Administrative Stability and Change in Late-17th-Century Iran: The Case of Shaykh 'Ali Khan Zanganah (1669–89)." *International Journal of Middle East Studies* 26 (1994): 77–98. An interesting account of the life and policies of a Safavid grand vizir.

Matthee, Rudolph P.: *The Politics of Trade in Safavid Iran: Silk for Silver, 1600–1730.* Cambridge: Cambridge University Press, 1999. A sophisticated and thorough examination of international and regional commerce, concentrating on the relationship between merchants and the Safavid political elite.

McChesney, Robert D.: *Waqf in Central Asia: Four Hundred Years in the History of a Muslim Shrine, 1480–1889.* Princeton, N.J.: Princeton University Press, 1991. The economic, social, and political history of Balkh is splendidly illuminated by this thorough study.

———: "Central Asia vi. In the 10th–12th/16th–18th Centuries." *Encyclopaedia Iranica.* Vol. 5, pp. 176–193. Costa Mesa, Calif.: Mazda, 1992. Valuable detailed discussion of political and military history.

Monshi, Eskandar Beg: *History of Shah 'Abbas the Great.* 2 vols. Translated by Roger M. Savory. Boulder, Colo.: Westview, 1978. A monumental "insider's" look at Safavid court history.

Quinn, Sholeh A.: *Historical Writing during the Reign of Shah 'Abbas: Ideology, Imitation, and Legitimacy in Safavid Chronicles.* Salt Lake City: University of Utah Press, 2000. Useful for understanding the styles, point of view, and message of basic sources for Safavid history.

Rochefort, Thomas C.: Isfahan Web Server at http://isfahan.anglia.ac.uk/. Photos and descriptions of buildings in Isfahan are artfully combined with historical descriptions, links to other sites, and a bibliography.

Savory, Roger: *Iran under the Safavids.* Cambridge: Cambridge University Press, 1980. In addition to political events, there is full discussion of foreign policy, the arts, the city of Isfahan, social and economic history, and intellectual life. A brilliant and impressive work, crucial for the era.

Titley, Norah M.: *Persian Miniature Painting and Its Influence on the Art of Turkey and India.* Austin: University of Texas Press, 1984. Includes Mongol, Timurid, Safavid, and Qajar art, with an emphasis on individual painters and their styles.

Turner, Colin: *Islam without Allah? The Rise of Religious Externalism in Safavid Iran.* Richmond, England: Curzon, 2000. Contrasts and analyzes Twelver Shii beliefs and Safavid political practice in regard to religion.

Welch, Stuart Cary: *A King's Book of Kings: The Shah-Nameh of Shah Tahmasp.* New York: Metropolitan Museum of Art, 1976. Sumptuous and beautiful.

Zarinebaf-Shahr, Fariba: "Economic Activities of Safavid Women in the Shrine-City of Ardabil." *Iranian Studies* 31 (1998): 247–261.

CHAPTER 20

The Transformation of the Ottoman Empire

Unlike the Safavids, the Ottomans were able to adapt to changing situations while retaining both internal legitimacy and military prowess. Historians used to view the Ottoman Empire during the time between 1574 and 1699 as in a state of decline verging on collapse. More recent research and analysis instead seems to show an empire going through a gradual transformation. Many in the ruling Ottoman elite viewed the changes in leadership, the military, the economy, and society as a decline from earlier times, but it is possible to see them as a readjustment with some positive as well as negative characteristics. In the fifteenth and sixteenth centuries the Ottoman state had been expansionist, with sultans who were activist warriors. Now the empire expanded only slightly even though it fought many long wars, and its sultans were for the most part less competent and usually sedentary in Istanbul. Power was shared in a different way in the capital, while in the provinces the transformation favorably affected the interests of some groups while harming others.

THE TRANSFORMATION OF THE SULTANATE

The Ottoman political system, with an absolute sultan as the keystone of the arch of power, changed as the military, administrative, and religious establishments rearranged power. A dozen sultans ruled during the period discussed, and many of them were personally incompetent and in some cases even disastrous rulers. The causes of this obvious change in the quality of the sultans were in part the need for a regency for the four who were under sixteen years of age when they succeeded to the throne, and also the fact that most of the rest of these sultans were undisciplined young men with little training to be rulers. Transformation of the sultanate was an evolving process discernible for a number of years rather than an abrupt change associated with the personalities or characteristics of a single ruler.

As the sultanate changed, the women of the royal family, especially the mothers of the sultan and the sultans' favorite concubines, gained great influence and even on occasion formulated policy. One example was Sultan Murad III (1574–1595), who was controlled

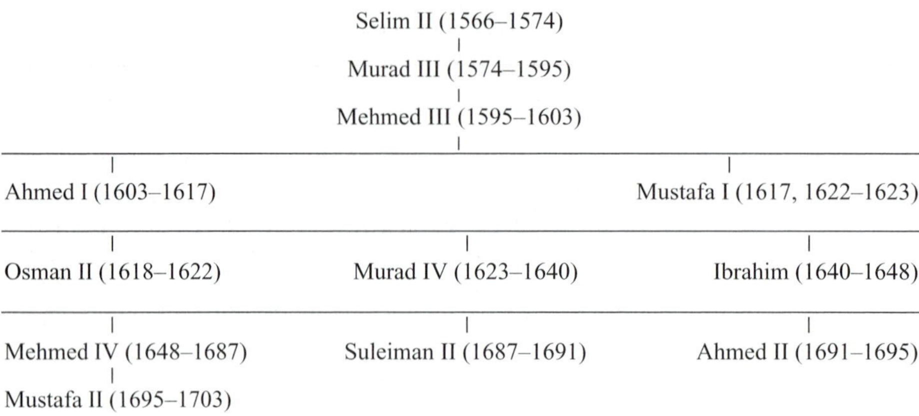

Ottoman Rulers, 1566–1703

by his mother and by his harem favorite, Sultana Safiye. It was Safiye who actually ruled the empire later while her son Mehmed III (1595–1603) occupied the throne. For a time Murad was so faithful to Safiye that his mother and sister, the wife of Sokollu, fretted over her undue power and made presents of pretty slaves to distract Murad's attention. In at least one respect they were obviously successful: Murad fathered over 100 children, of whom 20 sons and 27 daughters survived him.

The women of the harem also used the marriage of princesses to state officials as a means of cultivating loyalty and influence. Women in the royal family became prominent philanthropists, sponsors of elaborate buildings, and creators of waqf foundations. A sultan's mother served many roles: regent during the minority of a young sultan, protector of her son against intrigues, adviser to him, and a channel whereby outsiders could pass on information.

Another transformation took place in the succession to the throne. In most earlier cases, Ottoman royal princes battled for their father's sultanate, with the victors executing the losers. Selim II and Murad III sent only their eldest sons to be provincial governors. Mehmed III was the last Ottoman ruler to have had this useful training. Ahmed I (1603–1617), upon his accession to rule, decided upon a new procedure where succession was based on seniority. Unlike his father, who had had his own nineteen brothers strangled, Ahmed allowed his nearly insane brother, Mustafa (1617, 1622–1623), to be his heir and to live closeted in the palace. Royal princes were kept in the palace, so the sultans came to the throne without experience of outside life, but the new system did stop the violent struggles for succession among the princes. The sultans were now sedentary in Istanbul and not often leaders in battle, which allowed them to stay in the center of power rather than risk their lives in battles on the distant frontiers of the empire. Only a reigning sultan was allowed to father children; royal princes no longer had children. While in the prior fourteen generations of Ottoman sultans succession went from a father to a son, for the next three centuries the eldest male of the dynasty, usually a brother or nephew of the incumbent, succeeded upon the death, deposition, or abdication of the sultan.

The sultans were surrounded by fawning officials and courtiers. In such an atmosphere intrigue flourished. Personal spies, intercepted letters, and gossip became acknowledged techniques of government. Sultans usually found it impossible to differentiate the important from the petty and frequently were mentally ill.

The saddest chapter in seventeenth-century Ottoman history was the period embracing the reign of Ibrahim (1640–1648) and the minority of Mehmed IV (1648–1687). Ibrahim, the only male of the royal family alive in 1640, initiated a reign of eight years that was one long series of wild caprices. Among many other things, Ibrahim disrupted divan meetings. Ibrahim had a great passion for furs and commanded that the floors and walls of his apartments be carpeted and covered with sable. The sultan commissioned a trusted woman of the harem to make the rounds of Istanbul baths to seek out special beauties who were then installed in his harem. No person and no property were secure against Ibrahim; he even seduced the daughter of the shaikh al-Islam. In 1648 the janissaries and ulama, led by the shaikh al-Islam, deposed Ibrahim as unfit to rule and placed his seven-year-old son on the throne. Ten days later, when the sipahis rioted in favor of Ibrahim, the executioners were sent to his cell. For eight years the Ottoman central government had been the scene of intrigue, military insubordination, judicial venality, local oppression, and provincial revolt. Turbulence continued until Sultana Turhan, Mehmed IV's mother, saved the day for her son by appointing in 1656 an old, experienced, and honest official (Mehmed Köprülü) as grand vizir with absolute power and authority.

Even before the advent of Köprülü there were flashes of the earlier style of sultanic leadership, as, for instance, in the reign of Murad IV (1623–1640). At Murad's accession the treasury was empty, the coinage debased, and the soldiery of Istanbul unruly and lawless. His mother had talent and preserved the sultan's authority for several years until he came of age. In 1632 the sipahis rose in revolt and called for the heads of high officials, including the shaikh al-Islam and the grand vizir. For two months terror reigned at the palace. Murad IV perceived that his own turn might easily come unless he acted swiftly. Obtaining the support of the janissaries and the judges, he executed the leaders of the rebellious sipahis and through vigorous measures restored order.

Twice Murad personally led expeditions eastward. In 1638, he reconquered Baghdad from the Safavids, personally performing prodigious feats with his sword, but in the same year Yemen was lost to the Zaidi Shii imams. As time passed, however, he grew hardened to the presence of the executioner. Frequently through mere caprice he removed someone's head, perhaps just for crossing the road in front of him. Furthermore, he took to drinking bouts that carried him to the grave at the age of twenty-eight.

FISCAL, ADMINISTRATIVE, AND MILITARY TRANSFORMATION

Among the most important causes of the transformation of the central government were economic and financial issues. From its earliest days, the Ottoman state supported itself in considerable part from raids and conquest, but as frontiers in Europe and Asia were extended, campaign costs became staggering. The booty obtained hardly met expenses, and little was left for palace extravagances, which nevertheless continued. Fireworks, public festivities, processions, and sumptuous luxury were on display to the public in Istanbul and Edirne, especially for the circumcision ceremonies of the royal princes. The widow of Sultan Ibrahim ordered the construction of a large mosque complex beside the Golden Horn, and Murad IV added impressive new buildings to the Topkapi Palace. Such expensive buildings and ceremonies were designed to show the legitimacy, power, and glory of the ruler.

A gradual shift in world trade from the Mediterranean to the Atlantic stopped the increase in Ottoman revenues from international trade. Simultaneously, Europe and the Mediterranean world were experiencing a continuing monetary inflation. Government income never quite met expenditures most years.

To make up for the loss of revenue, officials were obliged to give liberal sums to the sultan upon promotions. During the reign of Murad III the sultan obtained bribes for appointments, and by the time of Sultan Ibrahim there was open sale of offices. An example was the Orthodox Christian patriarchate, which saw sixty-one changes in office in the seventeenth century, with bribes and appointment fees accompanying each new patriarch. Such a personnel system quickly filtered down to the lowest officials, so ability became less important than access to cash.

With the doubling of the size of the empire in the early sixteenth century, administrative problems became more and more difficult. As the work of governing increased to overwhelming proportions, the sultan left more affairs of state to the grand vizir, whose role in decision making naturally increased. In 1654 Mehmed IV finally gave the grand vizirs a residence and set of offices outside the imperial palace.

Later sultans frequently were unwilling to perform any onerous duties as head of the state and gave themselves up to a life of voluptuousness and frivolity. Since the sultans nevertheless could dismiss and even execute any official, there resulted an unfortunate separation between power and responsibility. Meanwhile, leading officers drew unprecedented power into their hands. Beginning with Murad III, the sultans gave high office to their favorites, who were usually ill fitted for the jobs to be done.

As the slave recruiting system fell out of use, personal loyalty to the sultans also declined somewhat and greed played a larger role in motivation. The corruption and venality should not, however, be overly emphasized, for despite a transformation in values and the other changes appearing in the Ottoman central government, there persisted a remarkable devotion to the dynasty and the state among a substantial body of capable, trained, and loyal officials. Such leaders helped in a new collection and revision of the imperial decrees, or kanuns, in 1673 so as to take into account the transformation of the state. And the administration of justice according to the shariah in the major towns remained swift, flexible, equitable, and fair even to the poorer groups in society.

For about three centuries the Ottomans had expanded continuously. But now campaigns in Austria, Russia, Iran, and North Africa were proving too costly to be pressed fully. Further expansion would not pay. When the conquests ended, ambitious members of the military and civil elites had to readjust their expectations as opportunities decreased.

Compounding this problem was the increased military sophistication of European enemies, which created a growing need for improved Ottoman manpower and weaponry. Between Suleiman's accession to the throne in 1520 and the end of the century, the janissaries increased from 8,000 to 37,000 and the sipahis of the palace from 5,000 to 21,000.

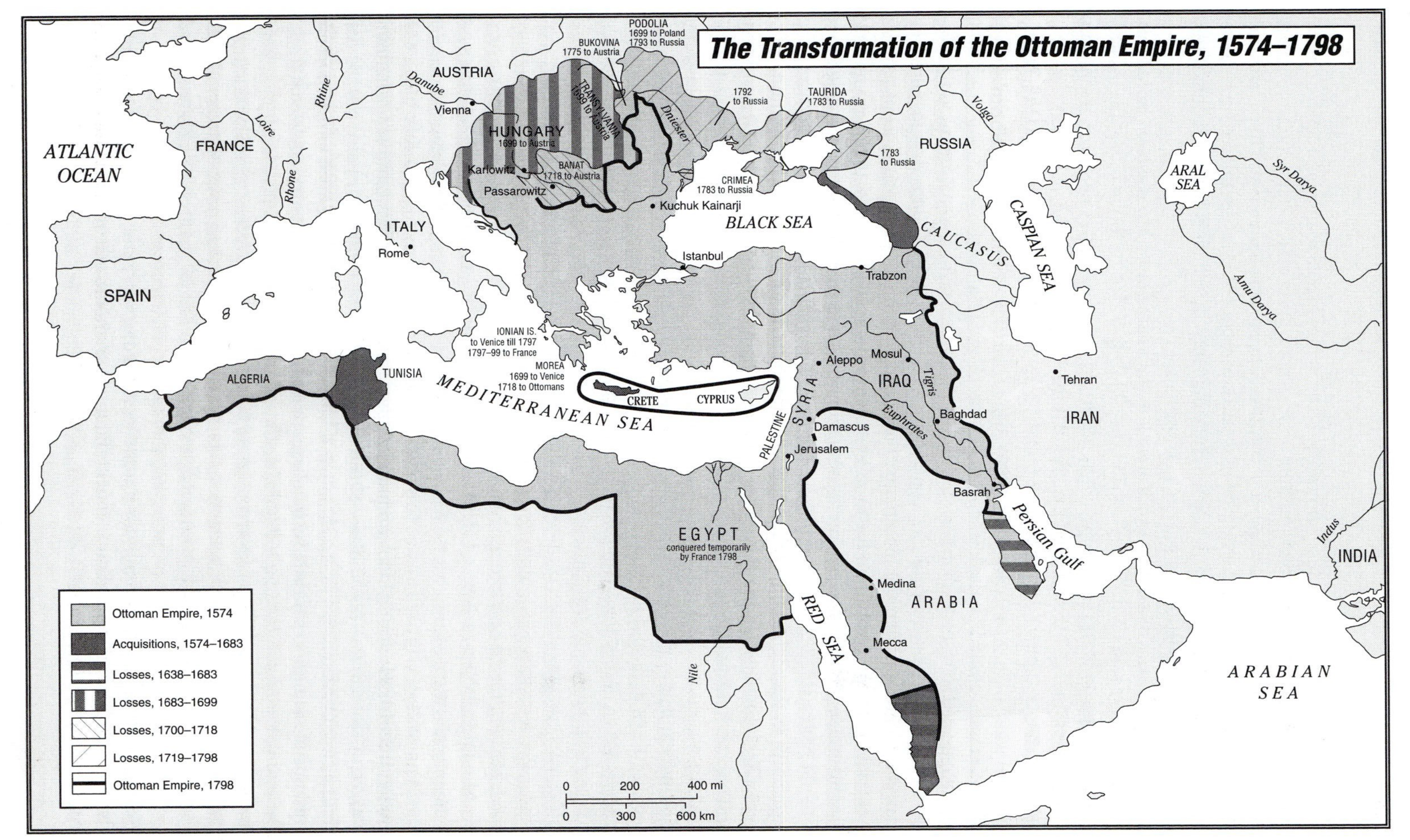
The Transformation of the Ottoman Empire, 1574–1798
ATLANTIC OCEAN
FRANCE
SPAIN
ITALY
Rome
AUSTRIA
Vienna
Danube
Rhine
Loire
Rhone
HUNGARY
1699 to Austria
TRANSYLVANIA
1699 to Austria
BANAT
1718 to Austria
Karlowitz
Passarowitz
BUKOVINA
1775 to Austria
PODOLIA
1699 to Poland
1793 to Russia
Dniester
1792
to Russia
TAURIDA
1783 to Russia
CRIMEA
1783 to Russia
1783
to Russia
RUSSIA
Volga
Kuchuk Kainarji
BLACK SEA
Istanbul
Trabzon
CAUCASUS
CASPIAN SEA
ARAL SEA
Syr Darya
Amu Darya
IONIAN IS.
to Venice till 1797
1797–99 to France
MOREA
1699 to Venice
1718 to Ottomans
ALGERIA
TUNISIA
MEDITERRANEAN SEA
CRETE
CYPRUS
PALESTINE
SYRIA
Aleppo
Mosul
IRAQ
Tigris
Euphrates
Baghdad
Damascus
Jerusalem
Tehran
IRAN
Basrah
Persian Gulf
EGYPT
conquered temporarily
by France 1798
Nile
RED SEA
Medina
Mecca
ARABIA
Indus
INDIA
ARABIAN SEA
Ottoman Empire, 1574
Acquisitions, 1574–1683
Losses, 1638–1683
Losses, 1683–1699
Losses, 1700–1718
Losses, 1719–1798
Ottoman Empire, 1798
0
200
400 mi
0
300
600 km

By 1600, the total of the sultan's household troops had grown to around 85,000. Unlike the provincial sipahis who held land revenue grants, the sultan's standing army had to be paid in cash. The provincial sipahis continued to provide about 100,000 cavalry, but the heavy casualty rates they endured as a result of frequent wars decimated their ranks. During the seventeenth century they more often stayed in their local grant area rather than be transferred from one province to another.

The central and provincial governments formed new troops in Anatolia called sekbans, who were trained in the use of firearms. Money had to be found to pay the salaries of larger armies, at the same time when government income was declining. As payless days arrived the sekbans ravaged the countryside. Joined by landless villagers and penniless students, they, under the name of jelalis, menaced Anatolia for many years, beginning in 1595. Their rampages left many dead and large areas deserted. Government troops finally gained control, integrated many of the jelali leaders into the governing elite, and tried to resettle abandoned villages; the government also inaugurated the policy of stationing salaried janissary contingents in the provinces. Almost immediately the janissary leaders joined the merchants, the guild masters, and the ulama as provincial notables. They amassed great fortunes by tax farming, acquiring vast tracts of land and forcing villagers to become sharecroppers. Sons of janissaries became janissaries. From this janissary infusion came many of the local dynastic families that dominated the provinces in the eighteenth century, weakening the central government still more.

These changes among the sultans, the high officers of the state, and the military invited insubordination and rebellion from the rank and file of the armed forces. By the time of Mehmed II the janissaries and sipahis of the palace were already headstrong groups that had to be placated by gifts at festivals and, especially, at accessions of new sultans. Even in the days of Bayezid II and Suleiman I the janissaries had frequently dictated policies. Beginning with the reign of Murad III, soldiers often stormed the palace to demand the head of a particular official, usually one who was corrupt and whose rapacity or incompetence inflicted hardship and injury upon them. Once this type of action proved successful, ambitious officials through clever appeals instigated movements among the troops to remove rivals.

Equally debilitating were civil wars between different branches of the services and open revolts of garrisons or local forces in the provinces. Bad blood developed between the janissaries and the sipahis of the court. In the reign of Murad III warfare broke out in the streets of Istanbul. Under Mehmed III the janissaries, at the bidding of his mother, Safiye, broke the insubordination of the sipahis. Wishing to weaken the power of the janissaries, Osman II (1618–1622) entered into war against Poland with the purpose of thinning the janissaries' ranks; he then intended to gather an army from Anatolia to fight the janissaries, a project that led to his dethronement and murder.

THE FUNDAMENTAL CAUSES OF TRANSFORMATION

Social, cultural, and economic developments helped bring about the transformation of the sultanate and the central government. Population growth was one of the most important of these factors.

Until about the 1580s, life and society in the Ottoman Empire, especially in Istanbul and the central provinces, seemed to be stable and secure. Incomes were ensured, prices were relatively constant, and food and goods were abundant. With this well-being, the population had increased in some parts of the empire over the sixteenth century—by 40 percent in villages, 80 percent or more in some towns. Population pressure on the available land began to be felt, and deforestation ensued in much of Anatolia and the eastern Mediterranean area. The influx of people into cities was altering their character.

Likewise, a smugness and an opposition to innovation arose among so many of the ulama that they developed a dislike for inquiring creatively into theology and intellectual sciences. Those supporting innovation in thought or belief were condemned by popular preachers from Istanbul pulpits. Society was much affected by the use of tobacco, a new product brought to the Middle East by the English; it soon spread, and smoking was associated with the flourishing coffeehouses, despite the objections by the men of religion, many of whom despised it. Coffee from Yemen, song, tobacco, and intellectual sciences were attacked by some of the anti-Sufi ulama in the same breath with luxury, lax morals, and injustice, all as factors supposedly undermining religious faith. (An uprising led by these preachers was quelled by Mehmed Köprülü, who exiled them.) Despite this intellectual conservatism, the Ottomans maintained sophisticated technical skills in such fields as mining. Information and knowledge were transmitted by networks of travelers, theologians, Sufis, geographers, merchants, and diplomats.

One example of cultural stagnation could be seen in the reaction against Murad III's building an astronomical observatory in 1579. Shortly thereafter an outbreak of the plague was attributed to God's vengeance against those who had penetrated divine secrets. The shaikh al-Islam petitioned the sultan to have the observatory dismantled, and the janissaries leveled it to the ground. Fanaticism and stagnation triumphed along with anti-intellectualism.

The cultural and artistic life of the imperial court continued at the high standards of the mid-sixteenth century for some decades. It was only in the late seventeenth century that decline became noticeable in a number of areas. Originality of design and fineness of execution in Iznik pottery and tiles deteriorated, although miniature painting took the new form of studies of single figures, which were often beautifully drawn. Court music changed in the mid-seventeenth century away from styles shared with Iran toward musical genres more distinctively Ottoman in nature. Several sultans were noted both for their own calligraphy and for their patronage of calligraphers. Creative genius still remained, as could be seen in the work of the great calligrapher Hafiz Osman (d. 1698), who created a style that served as a basis of imitation for later generations; he influenced the imperial court directly as a teacher of Mustafa II (1695–1703) and Ahmed III (1703–1730). In some of the provinces governors and notables imitated the sultans as patrons of the arts.

The following, if not the root causes of all these changes of fortune, as some economic historians contend, were at least major complicating factors: the massive influx of gold and silver into Europe and the Middle East from the Americas; the ensuing monetary and price inflation; debasement of the imperial coinage; and the failure of the Ottomans to adopt a mercantile economy. The biggest impact of these changes came in the 1580s, producing tremors felt throughout the next century. Silver began to flood the market. In 1580, one gold coin equaled 60 silver ones; by 1590, it took 120 silver coins to buy a gold coin; by 1640, it took 250. During the sixteenth century the price of wheat increased nearly twenty times. Urban wage earners and people on fixed incomes—central government officials, judges, janissaries, sipahis, waqf endowment holders—were ruined unless they turned to bribery and corruption. For the central government it was fully as disastrous. In 1534 the treasury had an income of 5 million gold ducats, but by 1591 it was only half that, for taxes were levied in silver.

To counteract the fall in revenue, new taxes were added, more tax farming was tried, and local communities were asked to make lump sum tax payments. Increased revenues from higher taxes, however, went mostly to intermediary authorities rather than to the central government. During the seventeenth century tax farmers usually held the right to collect taxes for only three years, but in 1695 the central government in some provinces also authorized the sale of the right to collect taxes from the peasants for the lifetime of the tax farmer. Many of these measures had the effect of increasing the decentralization of the empire, and thereby exacerbating the fiscal crisis.

Domestically, the government sometimes tried to hold down prices in the face of tremendous increases. The resulting price differentials stimulated the smuggling of significant quantities of wheat, copper, wool, and other raw materials from the empire, producing local shortages and even greater inflation. Because of the enormous profits to be had, peasants and landowners conveniently located for this trade began to be oriented to a commercial agrarian regime. This export orientation in some regions did not change the basic organization of agriculture: small peasant farmers, not large landlords, continued to predominate in most regions during the seventeenth century, while much land was turned into waqf property. Local craft production continued, with credit available at interest rates of 10 to 20 percent; a higher rate of annual interest was labeled by the courts as usury and was condemned. International commerce was centered around Istanbul, Izmir, Aleppo, and Cairo. The balance of trade was probably negative; precious metals flowed to India and Iran in return for spices, textiles, and rice. As people lost faith in the value of the money, Ottoman mints nearly stopped producing new coins in the middle of the seventeenth century; instead, foreign coinage was widespread.

Against new western mercantilist policies the Ottomans clung to old ideas, concerned primarily with providing the home market with necessities such as food. The empire encouraged imports and discouraged exports, prohibiting the export of certain commodities for fear of domestic shortages. It saw no danger in extending capitulations to foreigners, since in the seventeenth century foreigners and their local aides were still under the control of the empire. Ottoman subjects dominated most aspects of trade by land, and guilds were widespread. Artisanal production was not yet substantially disrupted by European competition.

Social patterns and gender relationships apparently remained intact, without major change. In seventeenth-century Istanbul, Egypt, Syria, Anatolia, and Cyprus, as presumably throughout the empire, urban women took part in court cases, frequently were owners and administrators of real property (mostly in the cities but occasionally including village farmland), inherited estates, and lent money. Women engaged in cottage industry but seldom belonged to guilds, and males maintained their legal and political superiority. While gender relations were often based on local patriarchal customs, muftis' decisions on implementing the shariah also played a large role in creating a flexible space for women to exercise some rights. While men were privileged in many matters, such as divorce, women had such rights as to be supported economically by their husbands and a right to choose their spouse. Many urban women obtained provisions in their marriage contracts that limited their husbands' rights following the wedding ceremony. The goal of government was to regulate sexuality so as to create a socially stable and peaceful environment ensuring legitimacy and inheritance for children based on paternity.

The Ottomans saw little reason to change their society. In cultural, religious, social, and economic matters they were still convinced of their superiority.

CHANGES IN THE PROVINCES

The political situation in the provinces varied tremendously from one region to another. As the central Ottoman government in Istanbul lost much of its power, local elites in many of the provinces gained more autonomy. They welcomed the transformation of the sultanate and the administration because it often resulted in an effective transfer of authority to themselves, as leaders of the great cities or tribes, and as provincial tax farmers or officeholders.

If the imperial court retained the ability to name governors on its own, rather than bowing to the wishes of local elites, the governorships were often given to court favorites and estates were left vacant so that their income would devolve upon the governor. Governorships were for shorter terms than formerly; they were sold to new courtiers every year or two, and a succession of governors seeking the money payments needed by Istanbul often led to overtaxation. The elaborate households of the provincial governors were an added expense. Many peasants fled the high taxes; some peasants became nomads.

Local leaders usually remained within the Ottoman system: they acknowledged the overlordship of the sultans, used their names in the Friday noon prayers, remitted some revenues to Istanbul, provided troops for the imperial armies when asked, and made no attempt to establish an independent foreign policy or to mint coins in their own names. (The same Ottoman gold coins circulated throughout the empire, but different regions had differing silver coins.) The provinces closest to Istanbul, which were crucial to the provisioning of the capital and to providing money to the treasury, were especially closely supervised. At least some of these areas, such as Bursa, were as prosperous in the seventeenth century as they had been in the sixteenth. They were more fully integrated into the Ottoman political and military structures than were the more distant lands.

Some local leaders did not follow this pattern. A prominent example was Ali Janbulad (Jumblat), who led a rebellion in northern Syria aiming at real independence, suppressed only with the greatest difficulty in 1607. The Manid amir of southern Lebanon, Fakhr al-Din, similarly sought so much freedom of action in running his local administration as to provoke an Ottoman invasion and his ouster in 1633. Southern Iraq was autonomous for the first half of the seventeenth century, as tribes and local notables directed affairs, but it was brought more closely under Ottoman control after 1668.

Egypt was reorganized in the 1520s after revolts, and the Ottomans controlled the country during the rest of the sixteenth century. The viceroy of Egypt was appointed by the sultan, while the revenues of local districts, especially those along the upper Nile, were farmed out to tax collectors. The sipahi and revocable land-tax system was not established in Egypt. During the seventeenth century, competition for power among households and factions turned the Ottoman governors into figureheads; real authority resided with military leaders drawn from diverse backgrounds, some slaves and some free men. Occasionally, when the local forces grew too anarchic or were perceived in Istanbul to be too strong, the central government would directly intervene. Following an insurrection in 1711, Ottoman power decreased. However, justice was enforced in Ottoman Egypt in the seventeenth century with remarkable fairness; both holy law and secular decrees provided the bases for social legitimacy. The population of the larger Arab-Ottoman cities such as Cairo increased from the sixteenth through the eighteenth centuries, despite political uncertainties and rivalries. Other signs of the relative social peace and prosperity of Egypt included the integration of the tribes of upper Egypt into the local governing system, the flourishing of Sufism, the development of guilds, and more students at al-Azhar university. Merchants prospered in Cairo as they conducted trade with other parts of the Ottoman Empire, Europe, and the Indian Ocean region. Wealthy Egypt provided much-needed revenue to the sultan in Istanbul.

Great distances, mountains, deserts, the slowness of transportation, and the dispersed settlement patterns inherent in Middle Eastern geography all combined to encourage decentralization and to limit the power of the Istanbul authorities. A nearly autonomous province was the Crimea, whose khan would send a large contingent of between 40,000 and 100,000 troops to assist in Ottoman campaigns. Other vassal states in the northern Balkans, Moldavia and Wallachia, represented another pattern of provincial control—they were tributary to the Ottoman Empire. They acknowledged Ottoman overlordship, and in return the Ottomans granted them the right to select their own rulers as long as they paid tribute, supplied food to Istanbul, and permitted some Ottoman garrisons on their territories. The local princes and nobles otherwise controlled their own affairs.

EXTERNAL AFFAIRS: EUROPE, THE MEDITERRANEAN, AND THE EAST

Despite the numerous difficulties posed to the Ottomans by their military transformations, the empire remained intact and, on balance, even expanded slightly. The Ottomans fought numerous long, exhausting wars and suffered heavy casualties, but until the end of the seventeenth century they won most of the time or the wars ended in a draw.

A revolution in military technology in western Europe involved new equipment, regularized firepower, infantry organized in regiments, new styles in fortifications, and a much larger standing army. These changes led to longer and more expensive wars.

The war with Austria from 1593 to 1606 was marked by a great victory of Ottoman arms in 1596 at Mezö Keresztes, which kept the Hapsburgs at bay. Since each side was worn out, peace was signed in 1606 on the basis of the status quo. This was the first time an Ottoman peace treaty had been negotiated outside the empire, as well as the first time the Hapsburg ruler was recognized as a fellow emperor who did not have to pay tribute. Fortunately for the Ottomans, whose depleted treasury would have made further military engagements precarious, the Thirty Years' War engulfed the Hapsburgs and other European powers between 1618 and 1648.

The question of the security of the eastern Mediterranean was perennial. Wheat, barley, and other vital supplies came from Egypt, as did an annual surplus revenue, sometimes amounting to half a million ducats. In 1645 the Ottomans began a war aimed at capturing Crete from Venice; the ensuing conflict lasted until 1670. In 1656, one in a series of inept admirals, whose only qualification was his position as son-in-law of the sultan's mother, led the fleet out of the Dardanelles to total destruction. Venice blockaded the Straits, and Istanbul was in a panic as prices of foodstuffs soared. Later, the grand vizir, Ahmed Köprülü, turned his attention to the island of Crete, where Candia, the modern Herakleion, had resisted sporadic Ottoman assaults for twenty years; to the Ottomans it had become like a running sore. Köprülü conducted a three-year siege of Candia until it fell in 1669; Crete, in Venetian hands since the Fourth Crusade, finally was incorporated into the Ottoman Empire.

On the outer peripheries the empire was under attack from all quarters. Ottoman naval power could no longer be projected into the Indian Ocean. The empire was able to maintain some control in the Red Sea, although English and Dutch pirates began to operate there in 1613 and Ottoman forces in the Persian Gulf became ineffective. Cossacks raided at will north of the Black Sea. Meanwhile, the sultans increasingly lost their hold on North Africa, which came to grant only a nominal acknowledgment of Ottoman legitimacy.

From 1578 to 1639 the Ottomans often had successful military adventures in the east. Aid from the Crimean khan kept them at Darband on the Caspian Sea, and Kars was converted into a fortress in 1579. Baghdad, Mosul, and all of Iraq were formally annexed in 1586, and a favorable treaty in 1590 with Iran left Tabriz in Ottoman hands. But then Shah Abbas I began the war of 1603–1618, in which the shah captured Tabriz, much of the Caucasus, and Kars. In 1623 another Ottoman army was crushed, and Abbas took Baghdad and the rest of Iraq. By the middle of the next decade, however, Murad IV seized Erivan and recaptured Baghdad in 1638. The peace that was arranged in 1639 settled eastern affairs for many years, leaving Iraq and Kars to the sultan and Azerbaijan to the shah.

MILITARY RESURGENCE UNDER THE KÖPRÜLÜS

When Mehmed Köprülü assumed office as grand vizir in 1656, he inaugurated a period of traditional reforms, centralization, and military expansion. He was filled with a ruthless determination to purge the government. In 1658, he repressed the rebel Anatolian governors who had defied the power of Istanbul since the 1620s. In five years of his grand vizirate some 30,000 officers, officials, judges, and theologians were executed for acts contrary to the interests of the sultan. His son Ahmed Köprülü succeeded to the post and remained grand vizir until his death in 1676. Restoration of central control under these two vizirs revealed that the coercive strength of the state had not been sapped beyond repair.

Although Mehmed IV gave himself up completely to hunting and to the harem, he remained steadfast in his support of the Köprülüs. In 1663 Mehmed placed the battle standard in the hands of Ahmed Köprülü, who then led the largest force assembled since the campaigns of Suleiman I to Belgrade and beyond. However, Ahmed Köprülü was repulsed at the renowned battle of St. Gotthard in Austria. Ahmed succeeded, however, in capturing Crete and thereby successfully ending the long war with Venice.

Next, the scene shifted to Galicia and the Ukraine. Cossacks of the Dnieper River region threw off Polish rule and sought Crimean and Ottoman protection. When the cossack leader came to Istanbul in 1672, he received a two-horsetail standard and was named leader of the Ukraine. Poland protested, and the grand vizir led an army that forced Poland to surrender its Ukrainian territories and to pay an annual tribute. Several more campaigns followed, and a treaty in 1676 incorporated the western Ukraine into the empire.

Three days after the signing of this treaty Ahmed Köprülü died. Unfortunately, Mehmed IV filled his place as grand vizir with his court favorite, Kara Mustafa, who was also related by marriage to the Köprülü family. In 1683 he organized the last attack upon Vienna. Early in the spring the ambitious Kara Mustafa gathered about 150,000 men and reached Vienna in the middle of July. For two months the army mined and bombarded the walls of Vienna, which were defended by a force of only 15,000 men. As September approached, the weakness of Vienna and the depletion of its garrison were obvious. The janissaries felt confident that Vienna would fall, but Kara Mustafa held back, hoping that the city would surrender: if it did, its wealth would be his, whereas if the soldiers took the city by storm, it would be theirs to loot. Meanwhile he ignored the approach of King John Sobieski of Poland with an army of 76,000 to relieve the city. When Sobieski encamped on the heights outside Vienna, Kara Mustafa virtually dismissed his presence. The Ottomans were thoroughly defeated on September 12, 1683, with only about one-half of the army escaping. Kara Mustafa was subsequently executed by the sultan for incompetence.

MILITARY DEFEATS

In the next four years one military calamity after another descended upon the empire. Venetians captured southern Greece and Athens. In the siege of Athens the Ottoman defenders made their last stand on the acropolis, which the Venetians shelled, exploding the beautiful Parthenon, which was serving as a powder magazine. The Austrian forces followed up their victory at Vienna by a lengthy war in which they took Budapest and seized Hungary. In 1687 the loss of Mohacs so infuriated the Ottoman soldiers that they forced Mehmed's deposition and placed his younger brother on the throne as Suleiman II (1687–1691). The new sultan, who had been incarcerated in the palace for forty-five years, did not know how to cope with the situation. Janissaries and sipahis rioted in Istanbul and partially sacked the city; a sort of civil war broke out between sekbans and janissaries. Belgrade fell in 1688, as did Vidin and Nish in 1689.

Previously when Ottomans had suffered reverses, they recouped their losses quickly and returned to fight in strength. This was notably true before Vienna in 1529 and at Lepanto in 1571. But the transformations of the seventeenth century had weakened the military. By the late seventeenth century, when the call for a campaign was sounded, the sipahis hid on their estates or bribed a commanding officer to excuse them. At one time a census was ordered, compelling all sipahis in Europe to register in order to expose unfit and fraudulent grant holders, but the inspectors were incompetent and no one was caught. However, the sipahis were no longer as important as they had been, since few were equipped with up-to-date firearms and they lacked the new skills needed in warfare. Instead, many land grants were sold or rented by the imperial government so as to gain the money to pay the sekban musketeers. By the eighteenth century there were fewer than 25,000 sipahis, and they were relegated to digging trenches and hauling cannons.

The changes among the janissaries, the sipahis of the court, and palace soldiers were no less substantial. Captive boys and renegades diminished in numbers as the seventeenth century progressed since there were so few new territories added to the empire. The drafting of Christian boys ceased entirely during the reign of Murad IV. In his attempt to restore the vigor of the state, Ahmed Köprülü reinstituted the program and collected 3000 boys in 1675, but the policy was suspended after his death. Free local Muslims, the sons of janissaries, and even unsuited persons joined the ranks. Worst of all was the practice of ignoring merit in questions of promotion, for it meant that officers were not skilled in military affairs. Many janissaries had other occupations and were members of the corps only on payday, although it should be noted that janissary engagement in commerce and leasing shops was traceable as far back as the early sixteenth century. European commanders in the late seventeenth century observed the mediocre leadership of Ottoman armies and outmaneuvered them time and time again. By the beginning of the eighteenth century the janissaries had become an ill-disciplined, turbulent gang, frequently more dangerous to their own government than to foreign aggressors.

After the loss of Nish in 1689 Suleiman II recognized the desperate plight of his empire and appointed as grand vizir Mustafa Köprülü, brother of the late Ahmed Köprülü. The genius of the Köprülü family ran strong in the new grand vizir. He instituted financial measures that made it possible to assemble an army and regain Nish and Belgrade. Köprülü attempted again the following summer to drive the Austrians farther back but lost his life in battle.

The energy of Mustafa II, an opponent of the Köprülü faction, brought a series of minor Balkan victories; but when faced by Prince Eugene of Savoy in 1697 at Zenta, the Ottoman units were crushed, and Hungary and the lands north of Belgrade were lost forever.

TREATY OF KARLOWITZ, 1699

In the face of these reverses Mustafa called to the grand vizirate Husain Köprülü. Negotiators met at Karlowitz, north of Belgrade, where the hostile participants agreed on the general principle that each power should retain what it possessed and concluded in 1699 the Treaty of Karlowitz. In addition, the sultan pledged to give his Christian subjects consideration and protection, as he customarily had. Venice gave up Athens but retained part of southern Greece and Dalmatia. Austria obtained most of Transylvania and Hungary. Poland received back parts of the Ukraine the Ottomans had earlier taken. Russia opted for a truce but in 1700 accepted the Karlowitz arrangement as a basis for peace. Karlowitz underlined the military weakness of the state and thereby encouraged rebels in 1703 to depose Mustafa II.

Karlowitz marks a definite change in the relations of the Ottoman Empire and Europe. Since it was largely arranged by England, the treaty seemed to acknowledge that many European states were rightfully concerned with Ottoman issues. It recognized the special interest and importance of the Russian state with respect to the Ottoman Empire. The treaty showed how the sultan's Christian subjects would become a major concern of European foreign offices.

At the peace conference of Karlowitz, European emissaries worked largely through the Ottoman-Greek interpreter, Alexander Mavrocordatos, and carried away the erroneous impression that he was chief of the Ottoman delegation. But his important role signified a transformation in the Ottoman civil service. For a century the great majority of Ottoman officials had been Turkish-speaking Muslims, many of whom did not know much about Christian Europe. Many were not educated in the palace, and their schooling was less secular than in previous generations, so they became dependent upon Christian subjects, chiefly Greeks residing in Istanbul, for interpreters and counselors.

As for Europe, Karlowitz ended the fear of an Ottoman invasion of central Europe and opened an avenue for European expansion toward Istanbul. When Europe was engaged in its own internal struggles, Ottoman forces were still able to win victories, but from the beginning of the eighteenth century, Ottoman armies and navies would be no match for first-rate European soldiers. No longer was the Ottoman Empire a grave military question. As one writer aptly put it, its importance became diplomatic.

Despite the military and diplomatic weakness the treaty of Karlowitz signaled, the transformations the Ottoman Empire had undergone between 1574 and 1699 also had some favorable consequences. Most subjects were still loyal to the sultanate, Ottoman institutions functioned reasonably well, religion provided a strong basis of identity, local groups using gunpowder weapons were integrated into provincial elites, and some areas even flourished. The Ottoman Empire responded flexibly to new circumstances. However, the incompetence of many sultans, the recurring fiscal crises, the insubordination in the military, the social and intellectual resistance to technological change, and the rapid growth of European power presented grave threats for the future.

REFERENCES

References cited at the end of Chapters 14, 16, 17, and 18 are pertinent to this chapter as well.

Abou-El-Haj, Rifa'at 'Ali: *Formation of the Modern State: The Ottoman Empire, Sixteenth to Eighteenth Centuries.* Albany: State University of New York Press, 1991. This extended essay raises many theoretical questions about Ottoman history.

Barkey, Karen: *Bandits and Bureaucrats: The Ottoman Route to State Centralization.* Ithaca, N.Y.: Cornell University Press, 1994. The author shows how jelalis were incorporated into the Ottoman structure.

Chelebi, Evliya: *The Intimate Life of an Ottoman Statesman, Melek Ahmed Pasha (1588–1662) as Portrayed in Evliya Chelebi's Book of Travels (Seyahat-Name).* Translated and with a commentary by Robert Dankoff. Albany: State University of

New York Press, 1991. A grand vizir's biography that also vividly illustrates life in Istanbul and the provinces.

Cook, M. A.: *Population Pressure in Rural Anatolia, 1450–1600.* London: Oxford University Press, 1972. Examination of population trends of the period and their effects.

Daly, M. W., ed.: *Modern Egypt, from 1517 to the End of the Twentieth Century.* Vol. 2 of *The Cambridge History of Egypt.* Cambridge: Cambridge University Press, 1998. An indispensable introduction to the subject.

Darling, Linda T.: *Revenue-Raising and Legitimacy: Tax Collection and Finance Administration in the Ottoman Empire 1560–1660.* Leiden: Brill, 1996. This specialized study based on extensive use of Ottoman records argues against the decline paradigm and instead demonstrates the flexibility of the central government.

Faroqhi, Suraiya: *Subjects of the Sultan: Culture and Daily Life in the Ottoman Empire.* New York: Tauris, 2000. Examines the social role of everyday culture, with discussion of many topics, mostly for the period from 1570 to 1730, but with some analysis up to 1908.

Gerber, Haim: *The Social Origins of the Modern Middle East.* Boulder, Colo.: Lynne Rienner, 1987. Traces the impact of landholding patterns in the Ottoman Empire from early days up through the twentieth-century Middle East.

———: *State, Society, and Law in Islam: Ottoman Law in Comparative Perspective.* Albany: State University of New York Press, 1994. Examines the way courts operated in Bursa and Istanbul during the seventeenth and eighteenth centuries.

Goffman, Daniel: *Izmir and the Levantine World, 1550–1650.* Seattle: University of Washington Press, 1990. Interesting account of changes brought about by European traders in western Anatolia.

Griswold, William J.: *The Great Anatolian Rebellion 1000–1020/1591–1611.* Berlin: Klaus Schwarz, 1983. A wide-ranging study of this question, including discussions of Syria and Ottoman policy toward the Safavids.

Hanna, Nelly: *Making Big Money in 1600: The Life and Times of Isma'il Abu Taqiyya, Egyptian Merchant.* Syracuse, N.Y.: Syracuse University Press, 1998. A well-written account not only of one person, but of his social, economic, and political environment.

Hathaway, Jane: *The Politics of Households in Ottoman Egypt: The Rise of the Qazdaglis.* New York: Cambridge University Press, 1997. Emphasizes the similarities of military households in Egypt with those in the central Ottoman lands rather than seeing them as a revival of the earlier Mamluk system.

Holt, Peter: *Egypt and the Fertile Crescent, 1516–1922.* Ithaca, N.Y.: Cornell University Press, 1966. Authoritative on Ottoman-Arab relations.

Kafadar, Cemal: "The Question of Ottoman Decline." *Harvard Middle Eastern and Islamic Review* 4 (1997–1998): 30–75. A careful analysis of arguments against and in favor of this concept based on Ottoman perceptions and realities.

Kunt, I. Metin: *The Sultan's Servants: The Transformation of Ottoman Provincial Government, 1550–1650.* New York: Columbia University Press, 1983. An outstanding study of Ottoman administration.

Masters, Bruce: *The Origins of Western Economic Dominance in the Middle East: Mercantilism and the Islamic Economy in Aleppo, 1600–1750.* New York: New York

University Press, 1988. A superb example of the trend toward detailed social and economic histories of seventeenth-century Ottoman provinces, as also seen in excellent studies by Daniel Crecilius, Haim Gerber, Halil Inalcik, and Ronald C. Jennings.

Pamuk, Şevket: *A Monetary History of the Ottoman Empire.* Cambridge: Cambridge University Press, 2000. An excellent discussion of coinage, fiscal policies, and the political and economic repercussions of monetary issues.

Raymond, André: *Cairo.* Translated by Willard Wood. Cambridge: Harvard University Press, 2000. A description and discussion of the city itself and in its Egyptian setting.

———: *The Great Arab Cities in the 16th–18th Centuries: An Introduction.* New York: New York University Press, 1984. A refreshingly written and informative survey.

Tietze, Andreas, trans. and ed.: *Mustafa 'Ali's Counsel for Sultans of 1581.* Pt. 1. Vienna: Austrian Academy of Sciences, 1979. Ottoman self-view of the causes of decline and corruption.

Tucker, Judith E.: *In the House of the Law: Gender and Islamic Law in Ottoman Syria and Palestine.* Berkeley: University of California Press, 1998. Examines marriage, divorce, mothering and fathering, sexuality, and other issues based on a careful reading of muftis' decisions.

Winter, Michael: *Egyptian Society under Ottoman Rule, 1517–1798.* London: Routledge, 1992. Excellent account of social and political matters, including discussions of Sufism, guilds, tribes, ulama, minorities, and life in Cairo.

Zilfi, Madeline C.: *The Politics of Piety: The Ottoman Ulema in the Postclassical Age (1600–1800).* Minneapolis: Bibliotheca Islamica, 1988. Discusses Sufism and puritanical movements as well as the careers of the ulama.

CHAPTER 21

The Retreat of the Ottoman Empire Begins

The changes that transformed the government of the Ottoman Empire in the seventeenth century continued into the next century, but the challenges the empire faced increased as the power of its European adversaries grew, leading to the beginning of a retreat of the Ottoman state. By the end of the period 1703 to 1789 the Ottoman Empire was weak in comparison with its two chief military challengers, Russia and Austria. Internally, local elites in the provinces gained more and more autonomy, thereby decreasing the effectiveness of the central government. Despite these factors, the Ottomans still attained some success in military, cultural, and economic fields.

THE SULTANATE

Power in the central government was allocated in the same way as in the seventeenth century: the palace dominated administration, and the sultans were greatly influenced by those closest to them.

The five sultans who ruled in the eighteenth century lacked the education and training to enable them to be leaders. They were unable to cope with the growing corruption, inefficiency, and incompetence that marked the period. Each of the sultans came to the throne after decades of confinement; none had an opportunity to learn the art of statecraft. Usually, his mother or the harem favorite dominated the sultan. Females in the royal family often married important officials so as to increase their loyalty to the dynasty. The rulers could not bring about substantial changes so that the central government could adapt itself to new times. The sultans were still the ceremonial leaders of the army, but they did not participate in battles.

Increasingly, the grand vizir and sultan called special councils, composed of prominent officials, to debate the severe problems facing the empire. By this means, responsibility for difficult decisions could be spread among a wider number of people. Sultans also changed their grand vizirs so frequently (their terms averaged around seventeen months) that few were able to carry out any long-range projects. Ability within the Muslim religious establishment declined, and posts of high authority went to unqualified favorites of the ruler. Training of about one-half of government officials took place in the households of major officeholders rather than inside the palace. Household factions dominated key posts.

Many of the rulers were artists. Ahmed III (1703–1730) was interested in his tulip gardens, and also was a calligrapher and a patron of poets. Like Louis XIV of France, Ahmed spent fortunes on festivals and illuminations for the women of the court. Ahmed also had a more serious side—by playing his enemies against each other he regained a good deal of power for himself. He then embarked upon a naval reorganization, and he expanded the rural sipahis and the standing armed forces.

Sultan Mahmud I (1730–1754) loved literature and surrounded himself with poets and men of letters. The rest of his energy was devoted to building mosques, palaces, and kiosks. Osman III (1754–1757), Mustafa III (1757–1774), and Abdulhamid I (1774–1789) were all well along in years when they ascended the throne; they proved to be mild, ineffectual rulers. Abdulhamid may at least be commended for the freer life he permitted his nephew Selim, the heir apparent, for with Selim's accession in 1789 began the more vigorous attempts at reform that marked the nineteenth century.

WARS WITH RUSSIA AND AUSTRIA

Austria and Russia contested the power of the Ottomans throughout the eighteenth century. During the period 1711–1739 the Ottomans lost little territory, even though they were often defeated.

Tsar Peter of Russia (r. 1682–1725) was not content with the 1699 Treaty of Karlowitz: the Black Sea, the Straits, and, most important, Istanbul all beckoned the Russians on against the Ottomans. However, when Peter led his army across the Pruth River in 1711, he fell into an Ottoman trap. To escape, he restored to the sultan the territories and privileges gained at Karlowitz. Ahmed III dismissed the grand vizir for agreeing to such easy terms when the Ottoman army might have destroyed Peter and crushed the Russians.

Peace with Russia and Austria freed the Ottomans to regain their possessions lost to Venice at Karlowitz. The grand vizir swept Venice from southern Greece in 1715. These victories enticed Austria to break with the Ottomans, and Prince Eugene won several smashing engagements, capturing Belgrade. Then Britain arranged the Treaty of Passarowitz of 1718, which ceded to Austria all the conquered territory in Serbia but permitted the Ottomans to retain the lands taken from Venice.

In response to Russian provocation, the Ottomans declared war in 1736. Russia overran the Crimea, and Austria entered the fray. As an Ottoman resurgence in 1739 pushed the fighting back to the walls of Belgrade, the French ambassador skillfully engineered the amazing Treaty of Belgrade, which returned that city to the Ottoman Empire. Even though Russia won great victories, it gained little.

During the thirty-five years from 1739 to 1774, there was peace in Europe for the sultans, although they fought wars against Iran during that time. As a result, the growing weakness of the Ottomans compared with European states remained unrevealed. In fact, by "depriving" the Ottomans of military experience for a full generation, the Treaty

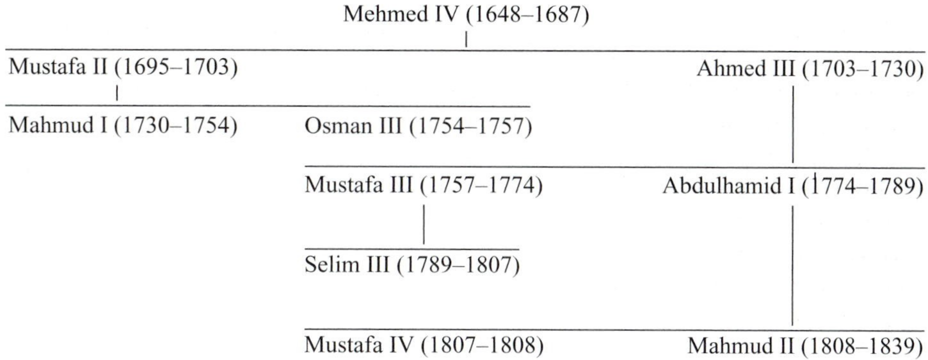

Ottoman Rulers, 1703–1839

of Belgrade accelerated Ottoman weakness. Even though the Ottoman forces adopted some European-style technical reforms, the military gap between the skills and abilities of western and central Europeans and the Ottomans increased throughout the century. Another factor causing Ottoman military decline was internal: Ottoman soldiers rejected the use of new weapons, such as the bayonet, because they would hurt the vested interests of the officers.

COMMERCE AND THE CAPITULATIONS

While internal commerce inside the empire was most important, trade with Europe increased substantially in the eighteenth century. European merchants were governed by a series of agreements known as capitulations. France and England, and to a lesser extent the Netherlands, had valuable commercial interests in the Middle East. Ottoman wars with Austria and Russia disturbed their trade, a factor that animated English, French, and Dutch mediation in Ottoman wars.

Ottoman commerce with India was probably equal to European trade. The Ottomans exported precious metals to India and various commodities, such as cotton, olive oil, and tobacco, to Europe. In the Red Sea and Black Sea most merchants were Ottoman subjects, but in the Mediterranean Europeans gained control of trade. Much commerce remained in the hands of Ottoman Armenians, Jews, and Greeks. Traders on land were mostly Ottomans, not Europeans, while textile production remained steady despite European competition.

Earlier capitulations granted by the sultans to various Europeans and especially to the French were reaffirmed. As of 1740, capitulations changed from temporary trading arrangements granted by the sultan in expectation of reciprocal rights for Ottoman merchants to relatively permanent arrangements given European countries in return for their diplomatic support of the empire. The significant points of a treaty of 1740 with France, to which almost all similar treaties of later dates refer, granted the French the right to travel and trade in any part of the empire. French diplomats had jurisdiction over French subjects. The French were allowed to possess churches of their own and to worship freely, special considerations being made for French Christians in Palestine.

Most important was the article that gave France the privilege of enrolling under its protection foreigners who had no ambassador or consul at Istanbul. All Roman Catholics were treated as French, giving them a special consideration among Christians in the Ottoman Empire. Furthermore, France and other nations that had such an article in their treaties (England, Austria, the Netherlands, and later Russia) could bestow trading privileges to Ottoman subjects, usually Christians and Jews. As a result of these circumstances, a large portion of the exterior trade of the Ottoman Empire was beyond imperial control.

TREATY OF KUCHUK KAINARJI

Upon the termination of the Seven Years' War in 1763 the powers of Europe were free to turn their attentions to Poland and the Ottoman Empire, with unfortunate consequences for both. Upon the advice of the French ambassador, Mustafa III unwisely rushed into war against Russia in 1768 when his demands with respect to Poland were not met. Since the Ottoman armies were unprepared, the Russian armies occupied Bucharest and within two years held all of Moldavia and Wallachia. Meanwhile, a Russian fleet sailed from the Baltic Sea around western Europe to the Aegean Sea, where it proceeded to destroy the Ottoman fleet. Nonetheless, the Ottomans, with French advice, had repaired the fortifications along the Straits leading to Istanbul sufficiently to thwart the Russians.

Russian successes in the Danubian Principalities caused the Austrians to sign a secret treaty with Istanbul in 1771, pledging military support if the Russians crossed the Danube. Informed of this maneuver, Prussia prevented war between Austria and Russia by speeding the partition of Poland among its three neighbors and simultaneously inducing Catherine II of Russia (1762–1796) to relinquish her conquests from the Ottomans. Partition of the Ottoman Empire was saved by the sacrifice of Poland! Desultory fighting came to a halt in 1774 upon the signing of the Treaty of Kuchuk Kainarji. This famous treaty was a landmark in Russo-Ottoman relations for more than a century. The sultan regained possession of Moldavia, Wallachia, and the Aegean islands, but Russia's political (though not religious) control of the Muslim-populated Crimea was confirmed. Navigation on the Danube was freed, and the Black Sea was opened to Russian shipping. A permanent Russian ambassador was accepted at Istanbul.

Of particular significance for the future were articles that stated in vague terms that the sultan promised to protect the Christian religion in his empire. More important, Russia as a "neighboring and sincerely friendly Power" could offer the sultan representations on behalf of his Christian subjects in Moldavia and Wallachia. These two articles served Russia in the nineteenth century as useful devices to advance its ambitions in the Balkans.

Since Austria had diplomatically supported the Ottomans against Russia, the Austrians demanded from the sultan the province of Bukovina as a reward. When Vienna ordered the occupation, the sultan recognized his helplessness and ceded Bukovina to the Hapsburgs.

The Ottomans reacted to the new military situation with a naval construction campaign, the raising of new regiments of cavalry and infantry, the building of a more modern artillery corps, changes in military education, and a purge of the janissaries so as to eliminate those who were soldiers in name only. French advisers provided new approaches to warfare, and traditional reforms were also undertaken.

For a decade and a half the sultan was left in peace, while Russia and Austria discussed the possibility of further Ottoman disintegration. The "Greek project" of Catherine II and Emperor Joseph of Austria in 1782 marked the first specific design for partitioning the Ottoman Empire. The fate of the Crimea was established when Russia annexed it in 1783, thereby discarding the limited rights of the Ottoman sultan.

Still another war broke out in 1787. Austria and Russia won initial victories, but international complications in Europe and serious internal disorders in the Hapsburg realm enabled the Ottomans to obtain peace with Austria (1791) and with Russia (1792). Russia advanced its frontier to the Dniester River. The outbreak of the French Revolution in 1789, the partitions of Poland, and the death of Catherine II of Russia (1796) gave the new Ottoman ruler, Selim III (1789–1807), a short relief from European expansion.

DOMESTIC CHANGES

Internally, the Ottoman court supported cultural accomplishments, while bringing about changes in taxation and the status of non-Muslims. A new system of governing Moldavia and Wallachia had particularly important consequences.

Peace between Russia, Austria, and the Ottomans in 1718 allowed the fun-loving Ahmed III to begin a period known for its luxury, its love of flowers (especially tulips), its imitation of European styles, and its translations of works from Persian, Arabic, and European languages into Turkish. Cultural innovations of all types flourished. An Istanbul printing press began to issue a small number of nonreligious books in Ottoman Turkish in 1729, although few were printed after 1745; Jewish and Christian groups had printed books in other languages even before the eighteenth century. Rococo and, later, baroque decoration modeled on that of Europe abounded in the capital, just as Ottoman styles influenced western European art. The new imperial mosques, fountains, and kiosks that were built reflected the elegance, grace, and lightheartedness of the rococo style as modified by Ottoman traditions. Public festivities, parks, and mosque illumination at night helped create greater freedom and space for women in Istanbul. Wall paintings and some miniature paintings showed western conceptions of perspective. Later, the famous poetess Fitnat (d. 1780), a member of a distinguished ulama family, wrote sonnets that celebrated classic themes such as the beauty of tulips, though she found it necessary to adopt the same poetic discourse as male poets.

Some cadastral surveys for fiscal demarcation were reinstituted after a lapse of a century. This and other measures raised money needed for the imperial court, but they also caused mounting opposition to the sultan's policies. Ahmed III was overthrown in 1730 after suffering a defeat by Iran, and his changes were temporarily suspended.

The eighteenth century up to the 1770s was marked by a degree of economic growth in the Ottoman Empire. Agriculture, artisanal production, and regional commerce grew. From the 1720s to the 1760s imperial budgets were usually balanced, with even occasional surpluses. Silver production increased and new Ottoman coins became the standard means of payment. However, wealthy persons increasingly sought to avoid confiscation or heavy taxation of their assets by the state through establishing waqfs.

In the seventeenth and eighteenth centuries some provincial administrators, sipahis, and managers of pious endowments hired tax farmers to manage the collection of revenues. As the power of the central government's bureaucracy decreased after 1695, some tax farms auctioned in Istanbul were converted to positions whose incumbents held them for life; these tax farms became quasi-hereditary. It was hoped that the increased security of tenure would encourage the tax farmers to foster economic growth, but the life-term tax farm tended to weaken the Istanbul administration.

Other changes took place among religious groups. Christian and Jewish religious minorities came increasingly into contact with their coreligionists outside the empire. Most Ottoman Christians remained members of Orthodox churches, but the Roman Catholic Church established small Uniate churches that, while linked with Rome, also preserved their own liturgies. Ottoman authorities tended to support Orthodox leaders against Catholics, while the Orthodox patriarchs tried to extend their influence throughout the empire. Jews suffered from lawless attacks by janissaries and also from prejudiced treatment by Christian Ottomans and foreign European Christians. The Ottoman central government in the eighteenth century reissued rules about clothing non-Muslims could wear, but these regulations were usually circumvented by bribes to officials. Among Muslim ulama, especially those in Mecca and Medina, there was a broadening of interest in reform of the faith. This found expression in a renewed study of hadiths and a strengthening of Sufi brotherhoods.

One of the more significant developments in Istanbul was the rise of the so-called Phanariotes. In the seventeenth century the Orthodox patriarch lived in a district bordering the Golden Horn, taking its name Phanar from the Greek word meaning "lighthouse." Earlier, most Greeks who served the sultan had become Muslims, but by the end of the seventeenth century it was no longer necessary for Greeks to adopt Islam to hold office. Out of this circumstance grew the term *Phanariot,* used to designate a Greek or Hellenized Christian in Ottoman service. (Most Orthodox Ottoman Christians were thoroughly under the control of the Greeks, even though such peoples as Bulgarians, Arabs, and Romanians were not Greek-speaking.)

The ascendancy of the Phanariotes took place gradually in the last half of the seventeenth century. From the Phanariotes and their associates came Orthodox patriarchs, merchants, bankers, government translators, ambassadors, and the governors of Moldavia and Wallachia from 1714 to 1821. Of these posts, the most lucrative and therefore the most expensive to purchase were the governorships. Consequently, Phanariot governors found it necessary to rule over their subjects in an extortionate fashion. The prosperity of Moldavia and Wallachia in the seventeenth century were ended as local armies were abolished, requisitions of food increased, and landlords controlled a majority of the peasants. By the end of Phanariot rule the peasants and nomads had fallen to an estate lower than any in the Balkans.

Yet the Danubian Principalities (and Bulgaria) remained the larder of Istanbul. The empire as a whole was self-sufficient in food, but the capital city needed to import grain and store it in case of emergency. Wheat, butter, cheese, honey, and cows were transported by the central authorities, and more than 500,000 head of sheep were moved every year. As the production of Anatolia became less available, the Danubian Principalities assumed greater importance as an imperial granary. Nevertheless, the frequent wars of the eighteenth century fought on Danubian soil and four Russian occupations increased the misery of the peasants.

The Danubian Principalities were freer from the political and financial control of the Ottoman central government than many provinces of the empire. However, by the middle of the eighteenth century the process of disintegration had reached a point where an energetic and ambitious governor in many of the provinces could build up his own independent military, political, and economic power and even try to defy the sultan. Throughout the empire, the local wealthy, urban, elite families gained power as the central government was progressively weakened, and the nomads moved into cultivated areas, thereby decreasing the number of villages and the taxes paid by them.

REBELLIOUS PROVINCES

To describe each one of the petty provincial lords and to relate the incidents of his local government would be superfluous. In Europe the best known were Ali Pasha of Janina, who ruled Epirus from 1788 to 1822, and Osman Pasvanoglu of Vidin, who terrorized the lower Danube from Belgrade to the sea. Both recognized the sultan's theoretical sovereignty and occasionally sent Istanbul tribute; yet, unlike seventeenth-century local leaders, each also regularly defied the central government and entered into diplomatic relations with European powers. They established order in their own areas, and their rule, though harsh, was at least less destructive than the circumstances created by the near anarchy that prevailed where robber bands and ex-janissaries held sway.

The most famous of the quasi-independent lords in other parts of the empire were the rulers of the city-states of North Africa. Even in the sixteenth century, at the heyday of the sultan's power, the authority of the Ottoman central government in Algiers, Tunis, and Tripoli was never very substantial. In the eighteenth century, North African local dynasties and corsairs recognized the sultan's overlordship but retained local control in their own hands, as could be seen in Tripoli under the Qaramanli dynasty from 1711 to 1835.

More significant in the process of the weakening of Ottoman central government and in its loss of revenue were developments of the eighteenth century that occurred in Egypt, Iraq, Syria, and Anatolia. Once the reins from Istanbul were loosened, a neo-Mamluk household military system flourished in Egypt from 1711 to 1798. Initially the households included both free-born Muslims and Mamluk slaves, but after about 1750 the Mamluks predominated. Cairo was prosperous for most of this time but disease, famine, and political disputes weakened the economy after 1780. Ali Bey, the Mamluk leader of Egypt from 1760 to 1772, secured military and fiscal power, centralized the civil administration, expanded contacts with Europe, and directed Egypt on an independent course, even minting coins using his name rather than the sultan's. In 1786 the Ottoman central government conquered Egypt again but was unable to directly govern such a distant province, so it reverted to Mamluk control and ensuing economic decline.

From 1704 to 1831 Baghdad was in the hands of a Mamluk dynasty, and Mosul was held for more than a century by the Jalili family. The al-Azm family ruled strongly on behalf of the central government in Damascus and adjacent areas of Syria, where they created private homes of great splendor as well as some degree of public order. Other families held Jerusalem, and the province of Aleppo was so torn with strife and civil wars that between 1765 and 1785 hundreds of villages disappeared.

The most adventurous career was that of Ahmed Jezzar (Ahmed the "Butcher"). Of Bosnian origin, he obtained his nickname from his ruthless tactics while employed by Ali Bey of Egypt. Gaining the favor of Istanbul, he became pasha of Sidon and Acre along the Mediterranean coast (1785–1805), later augmenting his territory to include Damascus. Ahmed Jezzar Pasha maintained a private army, built a fleet, suppressed the nomads, drastically increased taxes on the peasants, established monopolies, made commercial agreements with western merchants, and created an efficient governmental organization. All this was done in the name of the sultan, and his policies gained Ahmed the approval of Istanbul.

Even in Anatolia, closer to Istanbul, a similar situation existed in the eighteenth century. Derebeys (valley lords), who were leaders of local families, seized power. The central government was compelled to appease them to obtain any compliance with respect to law, taxes, and military support.

SEARCH FOR REFORM

Beset by foreign powers and enfeebled by internal political decentralization, the empire nevertheless retained the support of many groups as its leaders considered reforms. In Istanbul and other cities the many trade and craft guilds served as a powerful bonding agent, giving individuals a sense of security and a definite place in society. (There were even guilds for prostitutes and pickpockets!) Guild members found their lives regulated by their guild, experienced their social life in the guild, and had their contacts with government chiefly through guild leaders. In the countryside, landowners avoided political association as much as possible, and peasants were concerned only with their landlords. Simple village life was the chief aim of the peasants.

Many Ottomans in the scribal bureaucracy believed the state was stagnating and falling behind European states. They predicted that the empire was surely doomed unless reforms were undertaken. In sciences such as astronomy Ottomans kept informed about European discoveries in a timely fashion, but military defeats spurred ex-officials of the government to write treatises deploring corruption and inefficiency. Notable essays on these points appeared in 1616, 1630, 1657, 1725, 1772, and 1780; each condemned the selling of offices and recounted specific abuses by officials from the sultan down to the lowliest scribe. In a book written in 1725, a former imperial treasurer prescribed as a remedy a return to the higher values that had allegedly prevailed two centuries earlier in the reign of Suleiman I.

No reforms could be initiated with success unless they were supported by the sultan. Many sultans of the eighteenth century desired reforms but did not know how to inaugurate them. A reorientation of the government also demanded the labor of dedicated persons who understood Ottoman conditions in relation to developments in Europe, such as the Ottoman ambassadors sent to European capitals. Unfortunately, money needed for military reforms was in short supply as the revenues available to Istanbul declined and at the same time the needs of the state grew.

In the early part of the eighteenth century the Ottomans enjoyed some diplomatic successes and witnessed cultural growth. By the end of the century, however, internal disagreements and rebellious provincial leaders bedeviled the Ottomans, and their chief challenge came from Russian and Hapsburg Austrian expansionism. As of 1789 the need for administrative change and military reform was great, although many groups still opposed it or were unsure how to bring it about.

REFERENCES

References cited at the end of Chapters 14, 16, 17, and 20 are pertinent to this chapter as well.

Abou-El-Haj, Rifaat Ali: *The 1703 Rebellion and the Structure of Ottoman Politics.* Istanbul: Netherlands Historical-Archaeological Institute, 1984. In addition to an account of the rebellion, this valuable work contains an analysis of the Ottoman Empire in the seventeenth century.

Aksan, Virginia H.: "Ottoman Political Writing, 1768–1808." *International Journal of Middle East Studies* 25 (1993): 53–69. Useful analysis of reformers' ideas on military change and westernization.

———: *An Ottoman Statesman in War and Peace: Ahmed Resmi Efendi, 1700–1783.* Leiden: Brill, 1995. An excellent account of the life of this Ottoman statesman, ambassador, and signer of the Treaty of Kuchuk Kainarji.

Anderson, M. S.: *The Eastern Question, 1774–1923: A Study in International Relations.* London: Macmillan, 1966. A classic study of European diplomacy as it related to the Ottoman Empire.

Atil, Esin: *Levni and the Surname: The Story of an Eighteenth-Century Ottoman Festival.* Istanbul: APA Tasarun, 1999. Lavish illustrations by the miniature painter Levni of the festival celebrating the circumcision of four sons of Ahmed III in 1720.

Barbir, Karl: *Ottoman Rule in Damascus, 1708–1758.* Princeton, N.J.: Princeton University Press, 1980. An excellent book showing the subtlety of Ottoman-provincial relations.

Cohen, Amnon: *Palestine in the 18th Century: Patterns of Government and Administration.* Jerusalem: Magnes Press, 1973. Authoritative.

Crecilius, Daniel: *The Roots of Modern Egypt: A Study of the Regimes of Ali Bey al-Kabir and Muhammad Bey Abu al-Dhahab, 1760–1775.* Minneapolis: Bibliotheca Islamica, 1981.

Feldman, Walter: *Music of the Ottoman Court: Makam, Composition and the Early Ottoman Instrumental Repertoire.* Berlin: Verlag für Wissenschaft und Bildung, 1996.

Fisher, Alan W.: *The Russian Annexation of the Crimea, 1772–1783.* Cambridge: Cambridge University Press, 1970. Based on Russian and Ottoman archival materials, this work shows that the idea of Russian liberation of the Crimea was a myth.

Fleet, Kate, ed.: *The Ottoman Empire in the Eighteenth Century.* Rome: Istituto per l'Oriente, 1999. A special edition of the journal *Oriente Moderno* with 18 chapters on Ottoman economy, administration, religious groups, literature, and historiography by experts in the field.

Grant, Jonathan: "Rethinking the Ottoman 'Decline': Military Technology Diffusion in the Ottoman Empire, Fifteenth to Eighteenth Centuries." *Journal of World History* 10 (1999): 179–201. A useful introduction to a subject also treated in other works by Virginia Aksan and Rhoades Murphey.

Hitchins, Keith: *The Romanians, 1774–1866.* Oxford: Clarendon Press, 1996. Discusses economic, social, intellectual, and political issues.

Inalcik, Halil: "Imtiyazat ii.—The Ottoman Empire." *Encyclopaedia of Islam.* New ed. Vol. 3, pp. 1179–1189. Leiden: Brill, 1971. An important discussion of the capitulations by a leading scholar.

Itzkowitz, Norman: "Eighteenth Century Ottoman Realities." *Studia Islamica* 41 (1962): 73–94. Still essential reading for an understanding of Ottoman government.

Jelavich, Barbara: *History of the Balkans.* Vol. 1: *Eighteenth and Nineteenth Centuries.* Cambridge: Cambridge University Press, 1983.

Khoury, Dina Rizk: *State and Provincial Society in the Ottoman Empire: Mosul, 1540–1834.* Cambridge: Cambridge University Press, 1997. The author argues that in the eighteenth century many of the local leaders in northern Iraq were linked to Istanbul as a kind of provincial service elite.

Marcus, Abraham: *The Middle East on the Eve of Modernity: Aleppo in the Eighteenth Century.* New York: Columbia University Press, 1989. An exceptionally valuable and richly rewarding picture of social life in all its manifestations.

Murphey, Rhoades: "Provisioning Istanbul: The State and Subsistence in the Early Modern Middle East." *Food and Foodways* 2 (1988): 217–263.

Naff, Thomas, and Roger Owen, eds.: *Studies in Eighteenth Century Islamic History.* Carbondale: Southern Illinois University Press, 1977. Sixteen chapters by various experts on government, economy, and culture, mostly in the Ottoman Empire.

Panzac, Daniel: "International and Domestic Maritime Trade in the Ottoman Empire during the 18th Century." *International Journal of Middle East Studies* 24 (1992): 189–206. Especially valuable for discussion of Mediterranean trade.

Salzmann, Ariel: "An Ancien Régime Revisited: 'Privatization' and Political Economy in the Eighteenth-Century Ottoman Empire." *Politics and Society* 21 (1993): 393–423. A sophisticated and thorough examination of the life-term tax farming institution and its political ramifications.

Shaw, Stanford J.: *The Jews of the Ottoman Empire and the Turkish Republic.* New York: New York University Press, 1991. A well-written and thoroughly researched account.

Thomas, Lewis V.: *A Study of Naima.* Edited by Norman Itzkowitz. New York: New York University Press, 1972. A perceptive study of the life, ideas, and contributions of the great Ottoman historian and chronicler of the late seventeenth and early eighteenth centuries.

Zilfi, Madeline C.: "Elite Circulation in the Ottoman Empire: Great Mollas of the Eighteenth Century." *Journal of the Economic and Social History of the Orient* 26 (1983): 318–364. In this and later articles the author carefully examines Ottoman administration, legitimacy, and religion.

Zilfi, Madeline C., ed.: *Women in the Ottoman Empire: Middle Eastern Women in the Early Modern Era.* Leiden: Brill, 1997. Chapters including case studies as well as general analyses for the period 1650–1830, often based on legal registers.

PART THREE

The Nineteenth-Century Middle East

CHAPTER 22

The Era of the French Revolution and Napoleon

Three crucial events marked the end of the early modern era and the beginning of the modern period in Middle Eastern history: the accession of the reform-minded Selim III as sultan of the Ottoman Empire in 1789, the 1798 invasion of Egypt by Napoleon Bonaparte, and the establishment of the new Qajar dynasty in Iran around 1794. The reforms undertaken by Selim III, based in part on trends already seen in the eighteenth century, brought about many changes in the military. A rapid French conquest of Egypt opened the way for multifaceted struggles and changes along the Nile during the next decades and showed the Ottomans how weak they were compared with western Europe. Qajar rule in Iran ended the chaos and fragmentation that had devastated much of that land since the destruction of Safavid rule in 1722.

The Ottoman Empire, Egypt, and Iran had to respond to the political, military, and economic challenges of Europe. A common factor linking the central Ottoman lands, Egypt, and Iran was a perceived need for military reforms along western European lines. The far-reaching wars and diplomacy of the era of the French Revolution and Napoleon from 1789 to 1815 emphasized the military imbalance between Europe and the Middle East. Despite this, some groups, such as the Saudi dynasty in central Arabia and the Ottoman janissary corps, reacted against European encroachments by opposing any type of reform, even limited military modernization.

THE REFORMS OF SELIM III

In the 1790s the Ottoman population grew to around 30 million, the economy underwent major strains, the empire fought costly wars, and government spending increased so that deficits became regular events. Selim III became Ottoman sultan in 1789, just before the outbreak of the French Revolution. The new ruler desired to restore the power of the sultanate over other institutions and groups in Istanbul and to establish governmental authority in the provinces. That he thought of himself as a reformer in a modern sense is doubtful. But he did understand that techniques pursued in Russia and the

Periodization in the History of the Islamic Middle East

Antiquity: from the rise of civilization to the coming of Islam

Classical Islamic period: from the life of the prophet Muhammad to the middle of the tenth century C.E.

The early medieval era in the Middle East: from about 950 to about 1250

The late medieval era in the Middle East: from about 1250 to about 1500

The early modern Middle East: from about 1500 to about 1800

The modern Middle East: from about 1800 to the present

west had placed great power in the hands of the ruler and his government. Selim, a talented musician and poet, was in 1789 twenty-seven years old and had studied more widely than most of his immediate predecessors. At first, wars with Austria and Russia tied his hands. The French Revolution, however, distracted the European powers, gave the Ottoman Empire a few years of respite from western imperialism, and offered Selim an unexpected opportunity to show his true character.

In the central government Selim sought to curb the powers of the grand vizirs by reorganizing the imperial divan and by commanding that it be consulted on all important measures. Specialized commissions and advisory councils were formed. One of the greatest difficulties in administering any reform was the lack of officials who thought of their position as anything but an opportunity for personal profit at the expense of the state.

In the provinces Selim found that his word received little heed and foresaw that reforms would be ineffective unless a thorough transformation could be carried out in the army. The janissaries and standing sipahi cavalry had for some time been of little value; the training and weapons of all were obsolete. Following the Peace of Jassy in 1792, Selim recruited a corps of 600 men, who were outfitted in European military garb and trained in European tactics. When Selim suggested to the divan that the janissaries adopt similar uniforms and be drilled in the same manner, he was able to appease mutineers only by withdrawing the request.

Selim instituted similar reforms in the old army units by reorganizing the financing of the army and giving the administrative duties of the commanders to other officers, thus allowing the janissary agas to concentrate on military effectiveness. Fortunately, French revolutionary governments sent several of the latest pieces of artillery, artillerymen, and army engineers to advise in the use and manufacture of the new weapons and to organize and train a new Ottoman army.

A new force, called the Nizam-i Jedid (Army of the New Order), came into being about 1792 and grew slowly. By 1801 there were over 9000 men in the new army; in 1807 there were 22,000. But because of the rapidity of this expansion, training and discipline were superficial. The janissaries refused to adopt any "Christian" devices and objected to serving alongside the Nizam-i Jedid. Thus these troops played only a token role in the 1806 and 1807 campaigns against the Serbs and Russians, leaving the main fighting to the relatively ineffective janissaries and sipahis.

Selim encouraged the founding of schools, especially engineering academies, which he felt were necessary adjuncts to any military reform. The Imperial Naval Engineering School included courses in naval architecture, and the arsenal was improved. By 1806, forty-five naval vessels had been launched. In all, there were twenty ships of the line and twenty-five frigates with 40,000 sailors. The navy could compete with European fleets whereas the army could not, though it was perhaps equal in quality to Russia's much larger army. A cannon foundry was built and a new gunpowder plant set up. Other scattered technical improvements included the founding of the naval school of medicine and the reintroduction of printing establishments that made possible the printing of mathematical and technical books.

Military reform was a limited goal, with no evidence that Selim felt a need for innovative political, social, and economic reforms to support the military and technical changes. To improve foreign policy, permanent Ottoman embassies were sent to London, Paris, Vienna, and Berlin. The published reports of many of the Ottoman ambassadors contributed to the limited, but growing, Ottoman knowledge about conditions in Christian Europe. Ottoman artists also came to follow European conventions and methods in some fields, as seen in book illustrations, landscape painting, and architectural decoration but not in such cultural areas as music and literature.

Selim sought greater governmental efficiency and therefore issued orders to reduce the number of officials, doing away with the positions of many who did no work. He increased taxes, debased the coinage, seized private property, and melted down gold and silver utensils, sending the bullion to the mint. But these measures merely led to inflation and economic disaster. In Istanbul earlier decrees to regulate costumes of persons according to creed, profession, trade, and position were openly flouted. To reduce violence and disorder on the streets, Selim demanded that laws be enforced, including those regarding rules for clothing according to personal status, and even went out in disguise to catch offenders himself. Another attempt to bring law and order to the capital and to reduce its burgeoning population was an edict to cut down on the number of taverns and coffeehouses and to send idlers back to their villages. When grain became scarce, Selim controlled the supply and the trade: bakers had to buy their grain and sell their bread at fixed prices. Many of the reforms failed because of the sultan's personal weakness and lack of determination; the reforms lapsed entirely when General Napoleon Bonaparte invaded Egypt.

NAPOLEON INVADES EGYPT

The sultan's authority in Egypt had been only nominal for nearly a century. As the power of Istanbul waned, Mamluks grew wealthy and independent. Ostensibly, Bonaparte invaded Egypt to destroy the Mamluks, who were proving so troublesome to his supposed ally Sultan Selim III. However, Bonaparte's real objective was probably to attack the route to British-controlled India, while the possession of Egypt would widen the French commercial sphere in the Mediterranean. In view of Napoleon's known regard for the importance of Istanbul, perhaps he also intended to take Egypt as a base for moving upon the Ottoman capital.

In any case, Bonaparte, accompanied by engineers, historians, archaeologists, architects, mathematicians, chemists, and Egyptologists, set sail in May 1798 to take Malta and Egypt. He took Alexandria on July 2, and defeated the outnumbered Mamluks at the famous battle of the Pyramids outside Cairo on July 21. The rapidity of the French defeat of the Mamluks can be explained by the technical superiority of the revolutionary armies of the Republic, the military genius of their general, and the dreadful economic circumstances of Egypt in the 1790s. Napoleon's victory was partially overcome, however, when his fleet was destroyed by the British; his line of supply was thus cut and his freedom of action impeded. Nevertheless, the French were able to suppress revolts in Cairo by the Egyptians.

Since Egypt was a province of the Ottoman Empire, the attack brought a declaration of war from the sultan, who joined with England and Russia in a coalition against France. This alliance scandalized the ulama, who considered the treaty as too subservient to the infidels and contrary to the shariah. Selim gave Ahmed Jezzar, governor of Sidon and Acre, command of the army in Syria, and a fleet and army were collected at Rhodes for the relief of Egypt. Napoleon marched on Syria in 1799. He took Gaza and Jaffa, where in cold blood he murdered 3000 Ottoman prisoners. But Jezzar, with reinforcements landed by an English squadron, held off Napoleon's attack at Acre. Repulsed there, Napoleon hurried to Egypt to meet a landing of Ottoman infantry and cavalry. These he drove into the sea, regaining his heavy-handed mastery of Egypt. He then deserted his troops and sailed for France, where he executed his famous coup d'état and seized power in the government.

The French forces remained in Egypt until 1801. Several Ottoman expeditions, in collaboration with an English army and naval squadron, forced the surrender of the French and gave them a guarantee of safe-conduct home. British forces then held Egypt as a way of securing the route to India, and the British kept the several local competing factions from open warfare, until a short peace in 1802 required their departure. At that point Mehmet Ali (Muhammad Ali), leader of one of the Ottoman factions, took advantage of the prevailing political and military anarchy and set the course of his meteoric ascent. His rise was of great significance for the Middle East, but it separated to a degree the affairs of the Nile from those of Istanbul.

At the time of the 1802 peace, agreement was reached between Selim III and Napoleon. Selim was also at peace with England, Russia, and Austria. The Russians and British, however, used every device to offset French influence and to gain the Ottomans as allies for their European policies. Trade revived in Ottoman ports, and shipping was brisk on the Black Sea and the Mediterranean.

UPRISINGS IN SERBIA AND ARABIA

Upon the general establishment of peace in Europe, Selim expected to proceed with his reforms, but calamity befell him in Serbia and the holy cities of Arabia. The combined effect of these rebellions contributed mightily to his eventual overthrow and execution.

The Dissolution of the Ottoman Empire, 1798–1914

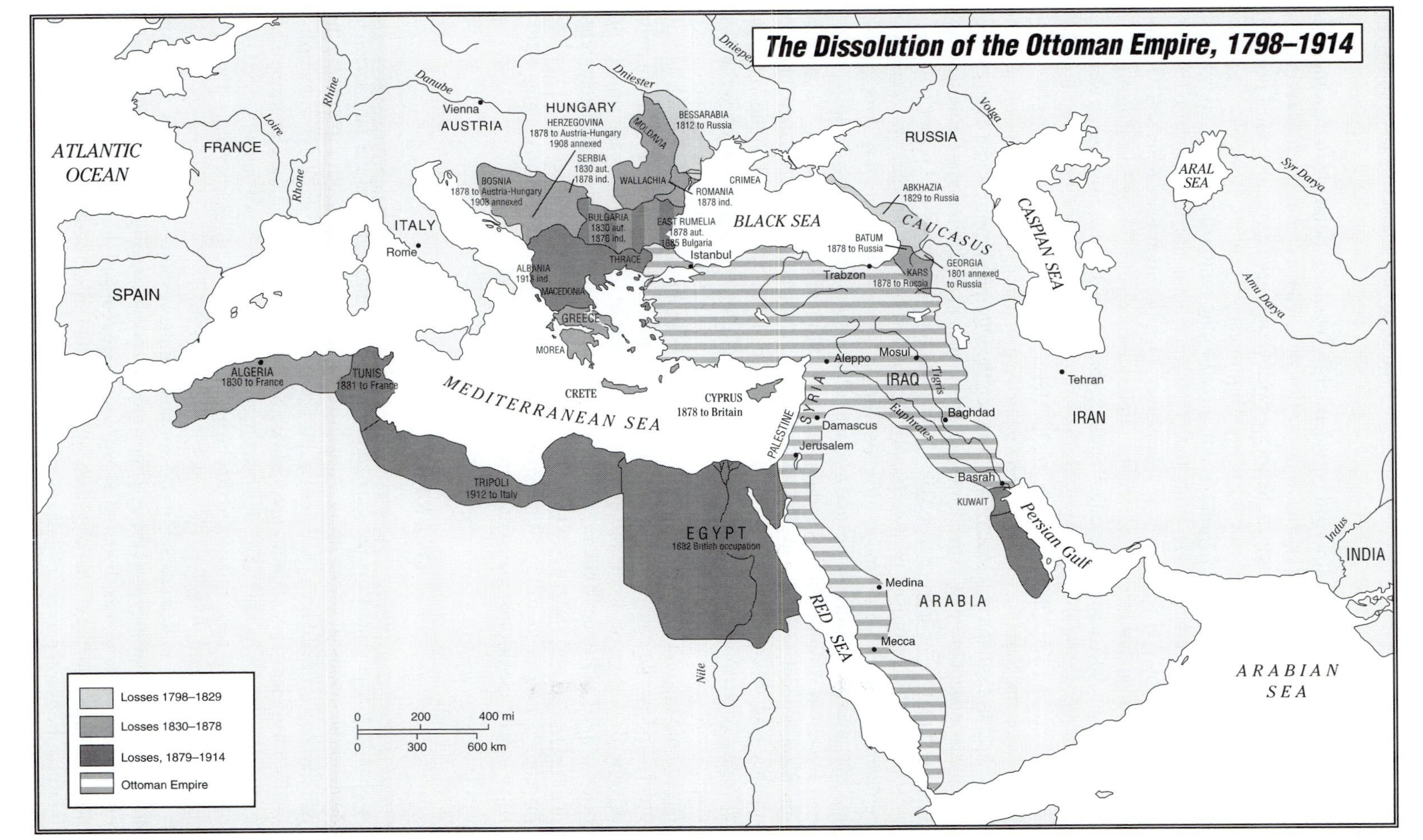

The 1791 peace of Sistova had provided for the return of Belgrade to the sultan, but it also stipulated that the janissaries, who previously ruled the area in a ferocious manner, would not be permitted to return. Selim's new governor gave Serbia the most peaceful, prosperous, and enlightened rule it had known for nearly a century. However, to appease Osman Pasvanoglu Pasha of Vidin, Selim agreed to the return of the janissaries to Belgrade in 1799. Murdering the enlightened governor, janissary leaders defied Selim's authority and divided Serbia among themselves. Outrage upon Christians and Muslims followed outrage, until there occurred the famous uprising of 1804 against janissary rule.

Aided by Austrian arms and led by the Serbian Kara George, insurgents were successful in destroying the janissaries. Selim sought to reestablish Ottoman rule in Belgrade. When the Serbs then turned to Russia, the Ottomans sent troops against the rebels. Victorious, the Serbs organized a provisional autonomous regime and defeated the Ottomans. In 1806 the outbreak of war between the Ottoman Empire and Russia enabled Serbia to clear Ottoman arms from the entire province. Thereupon Serbian affairs became a part of the European tangle of international diplomacy and power politics.

When Selim removed the two pro-Russian governors of Wallachia and Moldavia, replacing them with pro-French officials, Russia invaded the Danubian Principalities in 1806, and the Ottomans declared war and closed the Straits to Russian ships.

In central Arabia, well beyond the reach of Ottoman soldiers, Prince Muhammad ibn Saud, a local prince in the small oasis town of Diriyyah, in 1745 concluded an alliance with Muhammad ibn Abd al-Wahhab (d. 1792), a Hanbali Sunni religious reformer. Muhammad ibn Abd al-Wahhab and his followers (usually called Wahhabis) emphasized the unity of God, sought to return Muslims to the practices of the earliest days of the ummah in Medina, opposed so-called innovations in the faith such as Sufi orders, and energetically sought to expand their control. From the Saudi-Wahhabi point of view, the Ottomans were among the chief enemies of true Islam. By the time of the death in 1765 of Prince Muhammad ibn Saud, the Saudi-Wahhabi group had conquered much of central and eastern Arabia. Saud I (r. 1803–1814) captured Mecca and Medina, thereby taking control of the pilgrimage from the Ottoman Empire and causing Selim III to order expeditions to be sent from Egypt against Saud.

OVERTHROW OF SELIM

A change of equipment for the garrisons on the Bosphorus incited the janissaries to demand the dismissal of the divan. And since payments due them were in arrears, the janissaries overturned their soup kettles, the traditional sign of revolt. The ensuing uprising by unruly janissary trainees precipitated Selim's deposition and the elevation of his cousin Mustafa IV in May 1807. Formal charges against Selim were that he incited revolution by military innovations and that he had fathered no children after more than seventeen years of rule.

As had been indicated, Selim did not possess the resolute ruthlessness necessary to cope with the turbulence of the age. Surrounded by self-seeking, dishonest, and insubordinate officials, he was thwarted at every turn. He realized that his only hope was to play one faction against another. Each suggested innovation jeopardized some vested interest, the most perceptibly threatened group being the janissaries whose distress brought his downfall. The masses were agitated over prices and by fears of uprisings in many of the provinces. French and Russian threats kept everyone on edge.

Mustafa IV was an ineffectual person, the puppet of those who had overthrown Selim. Although the French officers and technicians were dismissed, the new sultan and Napoleon concluded a truce which ironically was disastrous for Mustafa and the rebellious janissaries, since it freed the Ottoman armies on the Danube. An Ottoman army of Bosnians and Albanians, commanded by Bairaktar, governor of Ruschuk, marched on Istanbul and camped near the capital. Bairaktar called many leaders to his camp and in July 1808 moved upon the city and the palace. Before Bairaktar's men could force the gates, Mustafa executed Selim and gave orders for the strangling of his own brother Mahmud. The insurgents, however, quickly imprisoned Mustafa and placed on the throne Mahmud II, who had been hidden in an empty furnace of the palace.

MAHMUD II AND THE NAPOLEONIC WARS

Mahmud II gave the office of grand vizir to Bairaktar, and the movement for reform proceeded along the lines drawn by Selim. After the organization of a new Europeanized army, Bairaktar permitted his Bosnians and Albanians to return home. Thereupon the janissaries rose up and destroyed Bairaktar. Civil war raged in the streets of Istanbul for a week, with fires, explosions, and chaos, during which Mustafa was executed. Mahmud, now the sole surviving male of the Ottoman dynasty, was fairly safe, but friends of the janissaries controlled the government, and military reforms were out of the question.

The French and Russians were furious as Mahmud seemed to favor Britain; the tsar sent his troops to the Danube and into the Caucasus, taking several towns. Fortunately for Russia, the 1812 Peace of Bucharest with the Ottoman Empire was signed a month before the French attack on Russia was launched. As a result of the treaty, the Ottomans gained back most of the territory they had lost, except Bessarabia (Moldova), which came under the control of Russia. Mahmud II dismissed the grand vizir and executed the negotiators for giving Bessarabia to the tsar, but the Peace of Bucharest did permit the Ottomans to stay neutral in the enormous struggle between Russia and the French Empire.

The treaty also abandoned the Serbs to the sultan, who pledged that Serbs could manage their own internal affairs. The Russian regiment left Belgrade, and the Ottomans attempted to rule the province. Although Kara George departed, a new leader, Milosh Obrenovich, continued the Serbian revolt. The Congress of Vienna in 1815 allowed the Serbs to retain their arms and gave them a voice in the management of their own government through an elected parliament. As a result, the sultan's sovereignty over Serbia was hardly more than a legal fiction, and most of the taxes that the Serbs collected remained in Serbia. The empire had lost effective control over several peripheral provinces, but its core remained intact, although in need of military strengthening.

NADIR SHAH AND CHAOS IN IRAN AND CENTRAL ASIA

While the Ottoman Empire witnessed a relative decline in its power compared with most of Europe, the fate of Iran in the eighteenth century was far worse. After the fall of Isfahan to the Sunni Afghans in 1722, Safavid Shii Iran disintegrated. Even though the military adventurer Nadir Shah temporarily established a large empire, neither he nor the capable Karim Khan Zand was able to stop the impoverishment and anarchy that affected most of Iran and central Asia.

In 1731 the weak Safavid shah Tahmasp II had to cede Iranian holdings in the Caucasus to the Ottomans. The real power in the land, Nadir Khan Afshar, removed Tahmasp from the throne, and then Nadir managed to revitalize his forces and effect the recovery of Azerbaijan and the southern Caucasus. The Russians evacuated Gilan, Baku, and Darband. Nadir, crowned shah in 1736, placed his capital at Meshhed, not far from where he had been a shepherd boy of the qizilbash Afshar tribe.

Nadir owed his position to the strength of his army and his ability to lead it, rather than to internal prosperity and popular support. Under his rule for several decades the state's economy worsened. Taxes on the peasants doubled, waqfs were confiscated, and internal trade was impaired by constant warfare. A standing army with artillery and muskets was so expensive that the only way Nadir could keep his regime in funds was through conquest and loot. First he successfully pressed the Bakhtiyari chieftains in the southwest to accept his rule, many of them enrolling their tribal followings under his banner. In 1738 he took Qandahar after having laid siege to it for over a year.

Nadir proceeded to Kabul, and through the Khyber Pass to India. Here he found rich stores of money with which to support his army. In 1739 he defeated the Muslim Mughal emperor at the battle of Karnal. Victory allowed him to proceed triumphantly into Delhi, where the emperor handed over his immense wealth. (The most famous trophy in this loot was the peacock throne, built of gold and covered with priceless pearls and jewels, which became the throne for the ruler of Iran.)

In 1745 Nadir defeated an Ottoman army and captured its artillery and military stores, but then concluded peace with Mahmud I. The shah began to build a navy in the Persian Gulf, but this attempt was ultimately without result since the state Nadir had fashioned was crumbling. A military adventurer, Nadir never appreciated the relationship between military means and political ends. He administered the state poorly and the bureaucracy was neglected. His experiment in the reconciliation of Shii with Sunni Islam was a failure, and the independence of the Shii ulama actually increased. By the time of his assassination in 1747, he had become a tyrant who marked his triumphs by having his victims' skulls stacked into high pyramids.

Immediately upon Nadir's murder, his army broke up into segments under tribal leaders. One chief, Ahmad Shah Durrani, subsequently became ruler of Afghanistan (1747–1773). For most of the following half century, Iran suffered under a frightful anarchy among contenders for the throne. The land was rife with massacres and wholesale blindings. When Kerman fell to Aga Muhammad, for instance, he ordered that 20,000 pairs of eyes be presented to him!

In central Asia, the disintegration of the Tuqay Timurid state in the first half of the eighteenth century matched the chaotic and dangerous conditions of Iran, but no local figure equal to the conqueror Nadir Shah emerged as descendants of Genghiz Khan lost some of their legitimacy after 500 years of rule. On Nadir's return from India he occupied Herat, and in 1740 he invaded the lands of the Uzbegs, taking Bukhara and Khiva, which he controlled loosely thereafter. Upon the death of Nadir two tribally based Uzbeg dynasties gained power, and, as trade with Russia increased, a certain degree of prosperity returned to parts of central Asia in the late eighteenth century.

There was a hiatus to the savagery following the death of Nadir for some parts of Iran with the rule of Karim Khan Zand, who maintained his capital at Shiraz. Karim upheld justice, was a patron of music, and gave much of Iran two decades of internal peace, low taxes, and general prosperity. He temporarily extended Iran's control over Basrah in southern Iraq and unsuccessfully tried to assert Iranian power in Oman, all the while continuing his modest fiction of simply being the deputy of a puppet Safavid prince. But upon Karim's death in 1779 confusion again engulfed Iran, with cities falling to one attacking force after another, in many cases suffering devastation that was felt up to the twentieth century. In 1794, Aga Muhammad, the leader of the Qajar qizilbash tribe, won over all rivals, and his chief residence of Tehran thus became the capital of Iran. This shah, who had been castrated at the age of six by Nadir's nephew, nevertheless established a Qajar rule that held sway in Iran until 1925.

THE QAJAR DYNASTY

The Shii Qajar tribe of northern Iran was a major player in the chaotic struggle for power in eighteenth-century Iran. Aga Muhammad Shah of the Qajars, who won out in 1794 over other rivals for the throne of Iran, had gained ascendancy in the leading Qajar clan as a young man and then passed many years as a political hostage at the court of Karim Khan. After Karim's death, Aga Muhammad made his way to the north, where he organized a force, drove the Russians from the southern Caspian coast in 1781, established his capital in Tehran by 1786, and had so strengthened his position that with the fall of Kerman in 1794 major resistance to Qajar rule was eliminated in the central Iranian lands. In 1796 Aga Muhammad crowned himself shah and girded himself with the sword of the Safavid Shah Ismail.

Aga Muhammad, attacking the Georgians and their Russian allies, took Tiflis and Erivan, before conquering Meshhed. When the Russians in 1796 occupied Baku and Darband, his position would have been hopeless had not the death of Catherine the Great that year brought about a Russian withdrawal. He managed to pacify Kurdistan and subdued parts of Khurasan and fortified it against Uzbeg forays.

Aga Muhammad was generally recognized to have had four passions: power, avarice, revenge, and hunting, the greatest being power. He was often ruthless and cruel, but was very effective in establishing justice in the countryside. He was murdered by his personal servants in 1797.

The shah had chosen as his successor his nephew Fath Ali. Governor at Shiraz at the time of his uncle's assassination, Fath Ali hastened to Tehran. Scions of the Afshar and Zand tribes made bids for the throne, but Fath Ali's army gave him sufficient edge to overwhelm them. When the early Qajar shahs died, several contenders might battle for the imperial turban and plunge the state into disorder. Two centuries earlier the central government's acquisition of artillery and muskets gave the opposition little chance, but at the outset of the nineteenth century many groups in Iran possessed these weapons and could question the succession of even a designated heir. Eventually, however, the throne passed more peacefully to later rulers, even though the government's army, consisting largely of cavalry, was weak. British and Russian contingents more or less guaranteed a regular succession, since they wanted to avoid a civil war.

Fath Ali Shah maintained a close association with many of the ulama and welcomed, at times, their participation in governmental matters. He knew that an appearance of piety was useful and so he built mosques and commissioned theological works. To the great pleasure of the ulama, he also suppressed the Sufi orders.

The monarchy was the dominant feature of Iranian politics, and the shah's word was final within the central government. If he made prudent decisions, the state prospered; if he made unfortunate ones, all suffered. The shah appointed some of his numerous sons to be provincial governors, where they gained experience in administration, and the central bureaucracy was increased in size. But Iran was not truly unified: there was little social cohesion, so the absolutism of the shah was limited. Within the royal family and among the elite there was a mixture of self-interest and self-indulgence often combined with considerable efficiency and effectiveness in administration.

DIPLOMACY IN IRAN

For Fath Ali and his ministers, Russian power and aggression engendered apprehension throughout his entire reign. During the French Revolution and the Napoleonic Wars in Europe, French, British, and Russian envoys and military missions journeyed to Tehran, vying for Iranian alliances. The French were looking for aid against the British in India, and the British were cajoling Iran to stand firm against France. The Russians sometimes were allies of the French and usually opposed the influence of the British. Britain also had an interest in Iranian policies since to a certain degree British India's northwest frontier was more peaceful when Iran blocked Russia and held the Afghans in check.

In addition to these issues of grand strategy, for Iran the fate of the Caucasus helped determine its alliances. Russia annexed Georgia in 1801, added portions of the western Caucasus in 1803–1806, and gained some of the eastern Caucasian khanates and Baku between 1804 and 1813. Since Iran considered the southern Caucasus to be an integral part of its own domain, this caused considerable friction with Russia.

French approaches in 1805 proposed that Fath Ali sever his undertakings with the British and invade India with French support. At the same time an alliance against Russia was suggested with the idea of French aid in regaining Georgia from Russia. Napoleon and Iran signed the Treaty of Finkenstein in 1807. By its terms, Iran pledged to declare war on Great Britain, to incite the Afghans to attack India, and to grant French troops right of passage across Iran; the French meanwhile recognized Iran's right to Georgia and committed a military mission to Tehran. General Claude Gardane and seventy officers and technicians soon arrived to train the Iranian army in European warfare. This was a monumental task, compounded by the poor pay of the soldiers, the absence of any heavy artillery, and the tribal composition of the fighting units.

Sorely disappointed by the Franco-Russian Treaty of Tilsit because it contained no mention of Iran, Fath Ali did not declare war against Great Britain. In 1809 the British envoy signed a treaty that promised an annual subsidy to Iran as long as Great Britain was at war with Russia and pledged a mission of British officers to train the Iranian army. General Gardane was replaced by British officers. One in particular, Captain Henry Lindsay Bethune, an artillery officer who was 6 feet 8 inches tall, so captivated the Iranians that he remained there for many years and became commander in chief of the Iranian army. The shah sent one of the princes to London to learn how the substantial subsidy was to be paid, and from these negotiations the Treaty of Tehran of 1814 was signed. According to this treaty all alliances between Iran and European powers hostile to Great Britain were null and void; Iran agreed to induce the rulers of Bukhara to prohibit armies from marching against India; frontiers between Iran and Russia were to be determined by Iran, Russia, and Great Britain; and a large subsidy was to be given each year to Iran by the British. Frequently called the Definitive Treaty, this arrangement was the basis of relations between the two countries for many years.

The costly Russo-Persian War of 1804–1813, which was declared a jihad by the ulama, finally ended with the humiliating Treaty of Gulistan, by which Iran ceded Georgia, Baku, Shirvan, and other areas in the Caucasus to Russia, with the stipulation that Iran would have no navy on the Caspian Sea. The Treaty of Gulistan also committed Russia to support Prince Abbas, son of Fath Ali Shah, for succession to the throne.

REFORM IN IRAN

Even before the Gardane mission arrived in Iran, Prince Abbas as governor of Azerbaijan had been reorganizing the Iranian army along European lines. Russian officers were employed to train the soldiers of this new army, the Nizam-i Jedid, who were recruited on a permanent basis with fixed pay, disciplined and dressed as European troops, and equipped with modern weapons. They were similar to the Nizam-i Jedid, the new army of Selim III in Istanbul, and the ulama in Iran, who were gaining in power and self-confidence, objected to them just as those in the Ottoman Empire had. (Prince Abbas drilled with the new soldiers but had to do so in private so that his religious faith would not be questioned.) French officers replaced the Russians in 1808, only to be replaced in turn by the British, who continued in the role of military advisers for several decades. Prince Abbas began many other reforms in Tabriz and was energetic in improving the systems of taxation and justice. He also encouraged the production of local cloth.

The Qajar dynasty began a new era of recovery from the devastation of most of the eighteenth century. Modern Iranian history commenced with the establishment of the Qajars, their diplomatic activities during the wars of the French Revolution and Napoleon, and their halting steps toward military reforms.

The Ottoman Empire by 1815 had also, on balance, successfully weathered the cataclysms of the 1789–1815 period. It was true that Bessarabia was lost, a semiautonomous regime was legalized in Serbia, Egypt was recovering from foreign occupation, and the Hijaz in Arabia was dominated by the Saudis; also two sultans had been slain by military revolts. Little change resulted in the internal organization of the empire, and Selim's military changes seemed dead along with him. Nonetheless, the seeds of reform were sown by wide movements of people and ideas. The Ottoman Empire, Iran, and Egypt were on the threshold of a new age.

REFERENCES

References cited at the end of Chapters 19, 20, and 21 are pertinent to this chapter as well.

Aksan, Virginia: "Selim III." *Encyclopaedia of Islam.* New ed. Vol. 9, pp. 132–134. Leiden: Brill, 1995. An excellent supplement to the work by Stanford Shaw cited below.

Amini, Iradj: "Napoleon and Persia." *Iran: Journal of the British Institute of Persian Studies* 37 (1999): 109–122. A detailed diplomatic account.

Anderson, Robert, and Ibrahim Fawzy, eds.: *Egypt Revealed: Scenes from Napoleon's Description de l'Egypte.* Cairo: American University in Cairo Press, 1987. A good introduction to the massive publication on Egypt compiled by the French scholars accompanying Napoleon in 1798.

Atkin, Muriel: *Russia and Iran, 1780–1828.* Minneapolis: University of Minnesota Press, 1980.

Avery, Peter, et al., eds.: *The Cambridge History of Iran.* Vol. 7: *From Nadir Shah to the Islamic Republic.* Cambridge: Cambridge University Press, 1991. Twenty-four chapters cover all aspects of the period; indispensable.

Dallal, Ahmad: "The Origins and Objectives of Islamic Revivalist Thought, 1750–1850." *Journal of the American Oriental Society* 113 (1993): 341–359. Compares Wahhabis with other Muslim religious reformers.

Fasa'i, Hasan-e: *History of Persia under Qajar Rule.* Translated by Heribert Busse of Farsnama-ye Naseri. New York: Columbia University Press, 1972. This detailed account of the Qajar dynasty and rule to 1882 is factual, anecdotal, and illuminating.

Hurewitz, J. C.: *The Middle East and North Africa in World Politics: A Documentary Record.* Vol. 1: *European Expansion, 1535–1914.* New Haven, Conn.: Yale University Press, 1975. The first of three volumes; indispensable for diplomatic events.

al-Jabarti, Abd al-Rahman: *Napoleon in Egypt: Al-Jabarti's Chronicle of the French Occupation, 1798.* Translated by Shmuel Moreh. Princeton, N.J.: Markus Wiener, 1993. This account vividly conveys how an Egyptian scholar regarded the invasion and, along with other items printed in the book, is extremely informative.

Kelly, J. B.: *Britain and the Persian Gulf, 1795–1880.* Oxford: Clarendon Press, 1968. A monumental work dealing with British activities on all sides of the Persian Gulf.

Lewis, Bernard: *The Muslim Discovery of Europe.* New York: Norton, 1982. A fascinating discussion of Muslim views of Europe as seen in language, media, scholarship, religion, and culture, and on a personal level.

Perry, John R.: *Karim Khan Zand: A History of Iran, 1747–1779.* Chicago: University of Chicago Press, 1979. Outstanding discussion of political, military, provincial, economic, and external events as they affected Iran in the second half of the eighteenth century.

Shaw, Stanford J.: *Between the Old and New: The Ottoman Empire under Sultan Selim III, 1789–1807.* Cambridge: Harvard University Press, 1971. A comprehensive description by a leading authority.

Yapp, M. E.: *The Making of the Modern Near East 1792–1923.* London: Longman, 1987. This history concentrates on political and economic events; it is especially useful for comparing one region with another.

CHAPTER 23

Mahmud II: Greek Nationalism and Ottoman Reform

The Ottoman Empire, Egypt, and Qajar Iran sought military reforms along European lines, but they faced many obstacles. These three large units formed the most important elements for analysis in the history of the Middle East in the nineteenth century. Issues of political identity and how to respond to the growing military power of Europe profoundly affected the governments and peoples of the Ottoman Empire, Egypt, and Qajar Iran.

In particular, ethnic nationalism, another western European innovation, caused difficulties for the multiethnic, religiously based, dynastic Ottoman state. Nationalists challenged the basic identity of the state and its reason for being. The first of many anti-Ottoman nationalist movements arose in Greece. Revolution there brought about the intervention of Europe directly in Ottoman internal affairs, greatly complicated the military reform efforts of Sultan Mahmud II, and increased the tension between semi-autonomous Egypt and the central Ottoman authorities.

THE GREEK REVOLUTION

The French Revolution of 1789 and the ensuing reorganization of much of Europe along nationalist lines contributed to the rise of Greek nationalism. Eighteenth-century liberal Europeans wished to emulate ancient Greek culture; they particularly admired Greek political ideas. Therefore, as Greeks increased their contacts with Europeans in the eighteenth century, they were impressed with their own heritage and fostered an intellectual renaissance in Greek communities from Odessa to Marseilles. Before 1820, over 2500 books had been published in modern Greek.

Greek intellectual patriots roused their countrymen to arms and formed a society to cast off Ottoman rule. They glorified the heroic deeds of ancient Greeks and advanced the reconstruction of modern Greek by condemning colloquialisms that had crept into the ancient tongue. The labors of such patriots were aided by the Greek Orthodox Church, which had preserved the religious identity of the Greek community, and by Greek schools, which trained churchmen and taught many people to read and write Greek.

As the military power of the central Ottoman government in its provinces decreased in the eighteenth century, many outlaw bands emerged in the mountains of Greece. They created a nucleus of Greeks familiar with the handling of weapons. Also, as in antiquity, many Greeks were drawn to the sea and foreign commerce.

In 1814, a group of Greeks founded a secret band named the Philike Hetaeria (Friendly Society) to organize a rising against the Ottomans. Similar to contemporary European secret societies, the Philike Hetaeria grew rapidly with the commercial depression after 1815. In 1821 Alexander Ypsilanti, a distinguished Phanariot Greek and a general in the Russian army, unfurled the banner of revolt. He crossed the Pruth River from Russian Bessarabia into Moldavia, but this was not the most propitious spot from which to launch a Greek revolution. When an Ottoman army drove him from Bucharest, he fled to Hungary.

Within a few weeks of the crossing of the Pruth, the revolution was in full swing in the Peloponnesus of Greece, where Greek speakers constituted a majority of the population. Ottoman Turks were massacred and the population of surrendered towns put to the sword. When the Ottoman provincial capital fell, over 8000 Ottoman Turks were butchered. Athens, except for the acropolis, was conquered by the insurgents. Immediately the Ottomans fought back; on Crete and some of the Aegean Islands reprisals and counterreprisals were common among Ottoman Muslims and Greek Christians.

The rebellions in the Danubian Principalities and the Peloponnesus led Sultan Mahmud II (r. 1808–1839) to take action against suspected Greek nationalists in Istanbul. A number of leading Phanariotes were executed, and on Easter Sunday the Greek patriarch was hanged from the gate of his residence by janissaries despite his denunciation of the rebels.

Of all the Aegean Islands, Chios was the wealthiest, and its inhabitants showed no interest in the uprisings on the mainland. Early in 1822, however, Greek adventurers took over the island against the wishes of the Chiotes. Thereupon, an Ottoman admiral landed and the Ottomans leveled villages, put Chios to the torch, and massacred nearly 25,000 Greeks. Shortly thereafter, Ottoman soldiers surrendered the acropolis in Athens on the pledge that their lives would be spared. The promise was not kept.

One of the factors that had led to these uprisings was Sultan Mahmud's decision to settle some scores with Ali, the rebellious Albanian pasha of Janina in northern Greece. Indeed, because Ottoman forces were dispersed, Mahmud's withdrawal of the best of his soldiers to subdue Ali virtually ensured Greek success. A mixture of eighteenth-century European Enlightenment, pro-Sufi sentiments, and devotion to ancient Greek literature, Ali had ruled as a benevolent tyrant for thirty years, corresponding with Napoleon and the British. In 1820, Mahmud sent an army to Epirus to bring in Ali's head. During this campaign the Ottoman garrisons in Athens and other Greek towns were reduced to the minimum, leaving the towns defenseless against a popular uprising. When, however, Ali Pasha's head and those of his sons and grandsons were exhibited on a silver platter outside the sultan's palace in Istanbul in 1822, Mahmud's forces began the long but ultimately successful campaign to restore Ottoman authority in Albania. They also could intimidate the Greeks since, although the sultan's forces were exhausted, the Greeks were torn already with dissension.

INTERVENTION BY EGYPT AND THE GREAT POWERS

The European Great Powers (Great Britain, France, Prussia, Austria, and Russia) looked upon the Greek activities with considerable misgivings, but pro-Greek committees in England and France compelled their governments to take an interest. Considerable romantic publicity accompanied the enlistment of European volunteers; the most famous of these was the English Lord Byron, whose death in 1824 in Greece created more sentiment for the Greek nationalists than any other single event in the long struggle.

In 1824, Mahmud commissioned his powerful vassal of Egypt, Mehmet Ali (Muhammad Ali), to aid in suppressing the insurrection. His son Ibrahim, appointed governor of the Peloponnesus, proceeded to establish his authority by fire and sword. Meanwhile, an Ottoman army subdued western Greece and recaptured Athens. Greek independence seemed very doubtful.

The victories of Mahmud's lieutenants hastened the intervention of the Great Powers. The Treaty of London, signed in 1827 by Britain, Russia, and France, demanded an armistice from the Ottomans and the Greeks and the mediation of any differences. Since Mahmud refused to declare an armistice, the British navy intercepted supplies and reinforcements destined for Ibrahim. The battle of Navarino on October 20, 1827, completely shattered Egyptian and Ottoman naval forces, and a French army then compelled Ibrahim to withdraw from Greece.

Russian interests in Greece were tied to the affairs of Serbia and the Danubian Principalities. Even before Russia agreed to the London treaty, an ultimatum had been delivered to Istanbul demanding cession of Kars and other eastern provinces; evacuation of Moldavia and Wallachia, whose governors would be elected by the Romanian aristocracy and could be removed only upon Russian consent; and immediate autonomy for Serbia. On the last possible day Mahmud accepted the terms, which were incorporated in the Convention of Akkerman of 1826.

After the destruction of the Ottoman navy at Navarino, Russia could not resist taking advantage of Ottoman weakness. A peculiar kind of war was declared in 1828; Russia became a belligerent in the Balkans and the Black Sea but remained a neutral in the Mediterranean. One Russian army advanced in the Caucasus with considerable success, taking Ardahan and Erzurum; another took Varna on the Black Sea, crossed the Balkans, and entered Edirne.

TREATY OF ADRIANOPLE

Upon the advice of Prussian and British envoys Mahmud sought peace. The Treaty of Adrianople (Edirne) of 1829 reestablished the frontiers much as they had been before the war, yet it also compelled the Ottomans to pay a heavy indemnity to Russia. The Straits were open again to Russian trade. The two Danubian Principalities no longer had to supply grain and sheep to the sultan's government; only the annual tribute to Istanbul was continued. Governors held their posts for life and ruled in consultation with native assemblies. The ties with the Ottomans were reduced to a minimum, and Russia moved into the vacuum.

Other provisions of the treaty stipulated that the articles of the Convention of Akkerman should be put into immediate effect. Another article declared that the Ottomans adhered to a second Treaty of London, which England, France, and Russia had concluded earlier in 1829 and which established an independent Greek kingdom. In consequence of its inclusiveness the Treaty of Adrianople was an important landmark in Balkan development as well as in the relationship of the Ottoman Empire to the great European states. Greece became an independent state in 1832, but it was small, with most Greek speakers still living outside its borders.

DESTRUCTION OF THE JANISSARIES

An event of vaster proportions and ramifications, however, preceded the Treaty of Adrianople and was in part responsible for it. In 1826, Mahmud destroyed the janissaries. For many years Ottoman sultans had found the janissary corps unruly, and since the beginning of the seventeenth century these soldiers frequently vetoed policies of state, and grand vizirs were beheaded at their behest. Through the eighteenth century several of the sultans contrived to modernize the army and equip the janissaries with more efficient weapons, but each attempt was rebuffed. Since the sultan's authority in the provinces was weak, a reliable standing army had to be created before he could reassert his power. Although Ali Pasha of Janina and Mehmet Ali of Egypt possessed competent standing armies, the sultan depended upon janissaries, irregular levies, and the remnants of the sipahis. The modernization of the army became even more urgent as Ottoman units met with Austrian and Russian regiments, to which they compared adversely.

Selim III had earlier lost his life in the attempt to modernize the army, so Mahmud II plotted more warily. The sultan had to maneuver into key positions officials who would support him and his policies. Ottoman artillery was carefully improved, and more than 14,000 artillerymen were gathered in Istanbul. When the blow was readied, Mahmud had the loyalty of the artillerymen, the grand vizir, the shaikh al-Islam, the chief of the janissaries, and a sizable force of Anatolian levies stationed across the Bosphorus.

In 1826, Mahmud ordered some janissaries to drill in European fashion. An uprising broke out, as was expected. The artillery mowed down the janissaries as they charged the palace and then shelled their barracks into a mass of ruins, burying 4000 beneath the rubble. Victory was followed up in the provinces, where many janissaries were either killed or completely scattered. New troops were assembled, and Mahmud planned to organize and train an army of 40,000. Although the Russian attacks in 1828 and 1829 were launched before the new troops were trained, Mahmud rid his state of an anachronism that had retarded the process of military modernization in the empire. It was a first step in destroying the power of the governors in outlying provinces and in rebuilding centralized control. Military spending represented about 70 percent of the government's expenditures, but now other reforms could also occur.

MEHMET ALI AND MAHMUD II

But there was hardly any time for sound reform. Peace was no more than established when Mahmud faced rebellion and serious attack by Mehmet Ali, his governor of Egypt. The actions of this dynamic newcomer affected the Ottoman Empire profoundly, particularly in its relationship to the Great Powers.

For lending aid to the sultan, Mehmet Ali had been given Crete and the governorship of the Peloponnesus for his son Ibrahim. The latter promise could not take effect, however, because the Great Powers established the kingdom of Greece; so Mehmet Ali diverted his attention to Syria, which he requested for Ibrahim in place of the Peloponnesus. When Mahmud refused, Mehmet Ali invaded Syria.

Ibrahim, meanwhile, waged a combined land and sea attack upon Acre, which finally fell in 1832 after a prolonged siege. Ibrahim easily routed an Ottoman army collected in central Syria; and in rapid succession Damascus and Aleppo in Syria, and Adana and Konya in Anatolia were occupied by the Egyptian army. Up to this point the Great Powers were unconcerned; France even looked with favor upon the expansion of Mehmet Ali's territory. Ibrahim defeated the main Ottoman army and pushed on to Kutahya in western Anatolia, on the route toward Istanbul. At this point Mahmud grew frantic and begged the Great Powers to rescue him. Only Russia responded. Early in 1833 a Russian fleet anchored in the Bosphorus, and Russian marines landed to protect Mahmud from Mehmet Ali.

Meanwhile, Russian and Ottoman envoys in Cairo were discussing peace terms with Mehmet Ali, while French diplomats were pressing Mahmud to accept some of the Egyptian demands. Compromises were effected. Syria was assigned to Mehmet Ali; he was also to retain Adana, which would give him easy access to the Taurus passes and Anatolia. Ibrahim's troops were recalled from Anatolia. The Russian fleet, however, postponed its departure from the Bosphorus. Two days before the Russians reembarked from the Bosphorus village of Hunkiar Iskelesi, a treaty was signed that achieved for Russia a long-sought goal. The Treaty of Hunkiar Iskelesi of 1833 was a straightforward alliance between Russia and the Ottoman Empire. The provocation lay in a secret article stating that upon Russian request the sultan would close the Straits to the extent of not allowing any foreign vessel of war to enter.

MAHMUD'S REFORMS

Mahmud II used the peace he had so dearly purchased to carry forward the reform of the government. Reform was pushed beyond purely military and technical changes to include government administration and a broad array of policies. Destruction of the janissaries and the formation of new troops, known as Muslim Soldiers, were only the most publicized aspects of his military innovations.

The 1831 attempted abolition of the sipahi system ruined the cavalry and levies upon which sultans had depended and which had proved valuable for Mahmud. Income from land grants to support sipahis now went directly to the treasury, and officers of the sultan enlisted recruits from these areas. The best sipahis were enrolled in four new squadrons of cavalry and the rest were pensioned, while in 1834 a national militia was organized to give rudimentary military training in the provinces. A group of Prussians participated in training Ottoman officers.

Military and medical colleges were opened in 1830. Connected with these colleges and previously established engineering schools were primary and secondary schools where a mostly secular education was given to prepare students for advanced training. In 1824 Mahmud declared a primary education compulsory for all, but means for carrying out this decree never materialized. The best primary-secondary school was the one attached to the medical college at Galatasaray. With instruction given in Turkish and French, it became a leading source of elite education in the latter part of the nineteenth century. Medicine, mathematics, and physics now began to be understood as in western Europe; old concepts in these fields gradually faded away.

Since the ulama had opposed previous attempts at reform, Mahmud attempted to weaken them and the Sufis, and symbolically to change traditional culture. In 1826 he gave an office building to the shaikh al-Islam and appointed him as head of a regular department of government; courts for Muslim subjects came under its authority. However, the appointment of teachers and the control of schools passed to the new Ministry of Education and the selection of judges and the administration of law went to the Ministry of Justice. Even more damaging to the ulama, and to the chief officers of the state who also had their own pious endowments, was the creation of a Ministry of Pious Foundations to which was given the income of most religious and charitable endowments. This ministry paid out what was needed to the various foundations, placing the remainder in the treasury. The financial independence of Sufi orders was attacked. Bektashi Sufi leaders were exiled and the order's buildings confiscated, supposedly because of the order's heretical views but actually as part of the suppression of the janissaries, with whom many Bektashis had been associated. However, Bektashis secretly continued to operate in parts of the empire, even in Istanbul, until the twentieth century.

The fez was adopted as the new headgear for government officials, regardless of rank or religion. The frock coat was also adopted, and within a few years the fez, the frock coat, trousers, and black leather boots became the standard clothing for men in urban centers. When the shaikh al-Islam objected, Mahmud removed him, giving public notice of his earnestness in these matters. On the other hand, Mahmud was not completely opposed to earlier culture: he was himself a master calligrapher.

As spending for reforms increased, so did government deficits. Total spending by the central government more than doubled between the 1790s and 1840. Debasement of the silver content of coins as a source of revenue became a necessity for some years after the destruction of the janissaries.

Changes in the military were used to centralize power in Istanbul. Independent local lords in Anatolia, the Balkans, and the Arab provinces were checked. Iraq was subdued in 1831, and other governors began to feel and respect the sultan's authority. In 1835 the Ottoman army occupied Tripoli in Libya, thereby ending the local autonomous rule of a prominent family; however, it would take the Ottomans twenty more years of campaigning to bring the whole of Libya under direct imperial control. To a certain extent the war with Egypt resulted from Mahmud's desire to project his power into every corner of the realm. As a further curb on local rulers, governors were forbidden to execute anyone without referring the case to Istanbul.

In addition to ministers already cited, two bureaus within the office of the grand vizir were formed into ministries: foreign affairs and civil affairs. This development took away the power of the grand vizir as an all-powerful deputy of the sultan and made him a prime minister, for a number of years holding this title instead of that of grand vizir. One of the more important innovations came after the Greek revolution when Greek Phanariotes were no longer trusted to serve as translators and interpreters. Within a few years a translation bureau was attached to the Ministry of Foreign Affairs, and officials in this bureau became significant members of the government, many later in the century rising to be grand vizirs. Departments of government were staffed by better-trained civil servants, whose higher salaries tended to lessen bribery, and more attention was given to promotion on merit.

To a significant degree the changes that were instituted came as a result of closer contact with western Europe. The first steamship arrived in Istanbul in 1828, and within a few years regular schedules were established between Istanbul and western Mediterranean ports. The length of a trip from France was cut from a month to twelve days. Thus, the 1830s saw an influx of western visitors, merchants, and missionaries joining Istanbul and other Ottoman coastal cities such as Izmir to the west as nothing previously had done. As a result, European techniques were studied and employed in many ways.

The end of the wars with Russia and Egypt left the empire almost bankrupt. Foreign observers commented on the wealth and produce of the country, but inefficiency in the collection of taxes reduced the sultan to penury. Under new procedures the central government tried to assume direct responsibility and sent out its own agents, thereby reducing the number of hands through which the taxes passed. Lifetime tax farms were eliminated, but farming or auctioning the right to collect certain taxes for shorter periods of time continued. Non-Muslims had to pay higher poll taxes. New roads improved trade, and Muslims were encouraged to enter business. Creditors felt less personal danger in pressing the government and its high officials for the payment of debts. In general, these measures were effective by the end of Mahmud's reign in 1839, despite numerous outbreaks of epidemic diseases and some recurrent famines.

Mahmud also recognized the stimulus to reform that a general circulation of books and newspapers would generate. Presses were established in Istanbul and Izmir, publishing with those of Mehmet Ali in Egypt several thousand books in Turkish and Arabic between 1830 and 1840. The military and medical colleges introduced many young Ottomans to French and German literature. Newspapers in French were founded in Izmir in the 1820s; and in 1832 the first Turkish-language newspaper appeared in Istanbul with official support from Mahmud.

Mahmud II's reforms broke the conservative grip of the janissaries and ulama upon government. The increase in the power of the central government was a mixed blessing since some groups were adversely affected—nomads lost much of their freedom, villagers' taxes were increased, provincial notables were no longer as influential—while other segments of society, especially merchants and townspeople, benefited from the increase in law and order.

Military and administrative reform did not accomplish its chief goal of acquiring equality with the European powers or Egypt, as shown in the Treaty of Adrianople and an 1839 defeat of Mahmud's forces by Mehmet Ali. Also, the success of Greek nationalism was only a beginning: nationalist movements in other parts of the empire later grew and flourished, posing increased dangers to the state. Nevertheless, after Mahmud's changes a return to the old order was impossible, and a commitment to reform would prevail.

REFERENCES

References cited at the end of Chapters 21 and 22 contain material pertinent to this chapter.

Barnes, John Robert: *An Introduction to Religious Foundations in the Ottoman Empire.* Leiden: Brill, 1986. An excellent discussion of the origins of pious foundations, the Ottoman land system, and the actual administration of the foundations.

Clogg, Richard: *A Short History of Modern Greece.* 2d ed. Cambridge: Cambridge University Press, 1986.

Findley, Carter V.: *Bureaucratic Reform in the Ottoman Empire: The Sublime Porte, 1789–1922.* Princeton, N.J.: Princeton University Press, 1980. An able analysis of the transformation of the scribal service into a civil bureaucracy; also discusses with great insight the general political transformation of the Ottoman Empire.

Fleming, K. E.: *The Muslim Bonaparte: Diplomacy and Orientalism in Ali Pasha's Greece.* Princeton, N.J.: Princeton University Press, 1999. Concentrates on diplomacy, culture, and a critique of Orientalism affecting how Ali Pasha was viewed.

Landen, Robert G.: *The Emergence of the Modern Middle East: Selected Readings.* New York: Van Nostrand Reinhold, 1970. Even though out of print, this book is still useful for its collection of original documents in translation.

Lewis, Bernard: *The Emergence of Modern Turkey.* 3rd ed. New York: Oxford University Press, 2002. An important account of the development of the Ottoman Empire in the nineteenth century.

Quataert, Donald: *The Ottoman Empire, 1700–1922.* Cambridge: Cambridge University Press, 2000. A clear introduction emphasizing social and economic issues; argues against Ottoman "exceptionalism" and in favor of similarities between Ottoman experiences and those in other parts of the world.

Ralston, David R.: *Importing the European Army: The Introduction of European Military Techniques and Institutions into the Extra-European World, 1600–1914.* Chicago: University of Chicago Press, 1990. Comparative studies of military modernization in Europe, Russia, the Ottoman Empire, Egypt, China, and Japan.

Shaw, Stanford J., and Ezel Kural Shaw: *History of the Ottoman Empire and Modern Turkey.* Vol. 2. *Reform, Revolution, and Republic: The Rise of Modern Turkey, 1808–1975.* Cambridge: Cambridge University Press, 1977. This substantial volume touches upon every aspect of change in the Ottoman Empire and Turkey.

Zürcher, Erik J., ed.: *Arming the State: Military Conscription in the Middle East and Central Asia, 1775–1925.* London: Tauris, 1999. Discusses chiefly the Ottoman military along with some chapters on Egypt, Iran, and Central Asia.

CHAPTER 24

Mehmet Ali, Ismail, and the Development of Egypt

Nineteenth-century Egypt was largely the creation of Mehmet Ali. Mamluk leaders of Ottoman Egypt in the 1770s and 1780s had increased contacts with Europe, and some social and economic changes commenced before 1805, but it was Mehmet Ali and his descendants, acting as Ottoman governors of Egypt, who created the basic administrative, military, and economic structures that marked a new period in Egyptian history. The complex and contested relationship between the Ottoman central government and Mehmet Ali involved the challenges and opportunities posed to each of them by growing European military and economic strength as well as their mutual interactions in regard to reforms, in which Egypt usually led the way for the larger and more decentralized Ottoman state. Mehmet Ali and his descendants sought autonomy within the framework of the Ottoman Empire. Egyptian military reform and expansion threatened the central Ottoman government and were ultimately curbed by the European Great Powers, but domestic reorganization and development continued until bankruptcy opened the way for a British occupation in 1882.

RISE OF MEHMET ALI

Mehmet Ali arrived in Egypt in 1801 as second in command of part of an Ottoman army sent by Sultan Selim III against Napoleon. Mehmet Ali was a Sunni Muslim Ottoman, probably of Albanian descent and then about thirty-two years old. (His name as spelled here follows the Turkish form, by which he referred to himself; in Egypt and the Arab world he is called Muhammad Ali.)

His political talent was manifested in Egypt, where he was soon responsible for several thousand Albanian and Bosnian troops. At that time three major powers existed in Egypt: the Ottoman governor, who ruled in the name of the sultan; the Mamluks, who held landed estates and were split in factions; and the Albanians. The people of Cairo constituted a weak fourth.

Mehmet Ali played his cards extremely well. When the British left Egypt in 1803, he sided with the Mamluks and drove the Ottoman governor from Cairo. Mehmet Ali

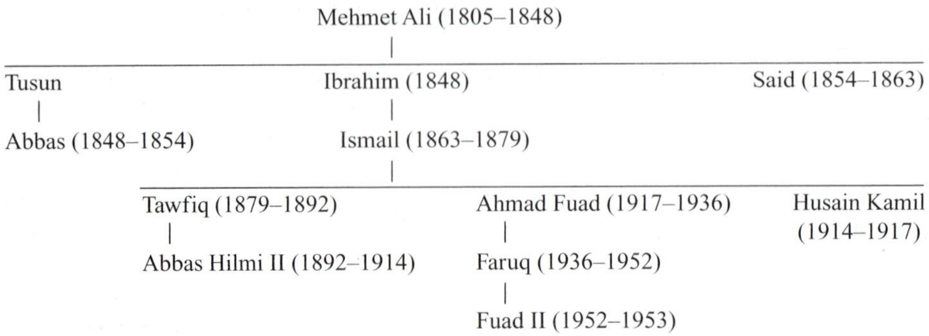

Dynasty of Mehmet Ali

then turned one Mamluk faction against another. Finally, with the aid of the Cairo populace, he chased the Mamluks into the desert and was recognized as governor by the citizens of Cairo. In 1805 Mehmet Ali asserted his submission to Sultan Selim, who reluctantly appointed him governor of Egypt.

Affairs in Europe in 1807 pushed the Ottomans and Mehmet Ali along with them into the French camp. In league with Mamluk remnants, the British occupied Alexandria but were defeated and withdrew. Mehmet Ali was now the actual as well as the titular holder of power in Egypt.

Finances cramped him severely. On several occasions even Mehmet Ali's own Albanians, their pay considerably in arrears, shot at him as he passed in the streets of Cairo. The economic catastrophes of the 1790s and repeated wars had disrupted agriculture and trade, thereby lessening taxes collected. Under the Mamluks taxes had supported an Egyptian army, but Mehmet Ali found revenues to be quite insufficient. Consequently, he ordered a detailed cadastral survey of all landholdings and confiscated properties with irregular titles. Later he seized many land grants, modified the system of land tenure, collected taxes more harshly, and expropriated tax farms. Taxes on land usually produced over half of his revenues. Even awqaf belonging to religious institutions were appropriated. Despite all these measures, real revenues increased only gradually during the next twenty-five years, after accounting for inflation.

As land taxes increased, Mehmet Ali turned his attention to commerce and established a government monopoly on the export of grain. In several of these years the Nile valley possessed the only exportable surplus available to the British. Demand was brisk, and profits in the grain trade often reached 500 percent.

Mehmet Ali's power and the loyalty of his troops rose in direct proportion to his improved finances. One long-standing score remained to be settled, not only for himself but for the authority of his sovereign, the Ottoman sultan. The Mamluks, particularly those in Upper Egypt, had never been fully subjected. Mehmet Ali's entreaties induced many to settle near Cairo, and in 1811 they were tricked into entering the citadel of Cairo, where the Albanian soldiers slaughtered them. A year later another thousand were executed in Upper Egypt. The destruction of most of the Mamluks confirmed Mehmet Ali as the chief authority of the land.

ARABIA, THE SUDAN, AND GREECE

Organization of the finances of Egypt and destruction of the Mamluk power enabled Mehmet Ali to consider widening his rule to nearby areas. Since the Ottoman central government was challenged by the Saudi-Wahhabi uprising in Arabia (discussed in Chapter 22), Mehmet Ali willingly responded to an order from Istanbul to send his new armies there. The sultan was eager to suppress the Saudis so as to restore Ottoman control of the Meccan pilgrimages and to reestablish Ottoman prestige as protector of the holy cities of Mecca and Medina, while Egypt sought to restore its Red Sea trade.

In 1811 Mehmet Ali's son Tusun headed an expedition to subdue the Hijaz. Not until 1818, however, under the able leadership of Mehmet Ali's son Ibrahim, did the troops from Egypt turn the scales against the Saudi-Wahhabi forces. The Saudi capital was taken and razed, and the Saudi ruler was conveyed to Istanbul, where he was executed. Ibrahim became governor of the Hijaz and Ethiopia, the latter consisting then of a few Red Sea ports that served as outlets for the Sudan.

Mehmet Ali looked upon the Sudan as a boundless area full of gold and slaves. He also believed that he could develop an army of black slaves from the Sudan, thereby securing independence from his unruly Albanians. An expedition went southward in 1820. The Sudan was politically divided and had become the refuge for some Mamluks who had fled Egypt. The sedentary tribes along the Nile capitulated after little resistance, and the Funj sultanate was conquered, but gold proved to be relatively scarce. Khartoum became the capital of Egyptian administration.

The experiment with an army of Sudanese slaves proved a failure. Disease and fatalities among the Sudanese constrained Mehmet Ali to build an army around Egyptian soldiers and Turkish, Circassian, and European officers. Over 30,000 Egyptian peasants were in a short time drilled into effective soldiers, and eventually a military of over 150,000 was conscripted (at great cost to the lives of the soldiers' families). The new army was modeled along Selim III's Nizam-i Jedid. Meanwhile, Mehmet Ali assembled a fleet.

While these developments were in progress, the Greek rebellion upset the eastern Mediterranean area (as discussed in Chapter 23). Sultan Mahmud II offered the governorship of Crete and part of Greece to Mehmet Ali and his son Ibrahim, whose army of 17,000 men and a navy of sixty-three ships left Alexandria in 1824. Various islands were attacked and plundered, Mehmet Ali replacing his losses with new ships from France and Italy; he even bought some from Greek shipbuilders! Ibrahim landed in Greece in 1825, but that adventure was extremely costly for Mehmet Ali: his fleet was ruined, and his trained and disciplined army returned to Egypt crippled.

CONQUEST OF SYRIA

But Mehmet Ali was not a ruler to be discouraged easily. From his ready income provided by the changed tax base he rapidly reconstituted an army. And by 1829 the new naval arsenal at Alexandria had begun to turn out frigates, corvettes, and other men-of-war.

Syria was economically inviting, especially since its districts were pledged to Mehmet Ali as payment for his undertaking in Greece. Mehmet Ali sent Ibrahim against Acre, which fell in 1832. He then turned upon the Ottoman forces, reaching northward

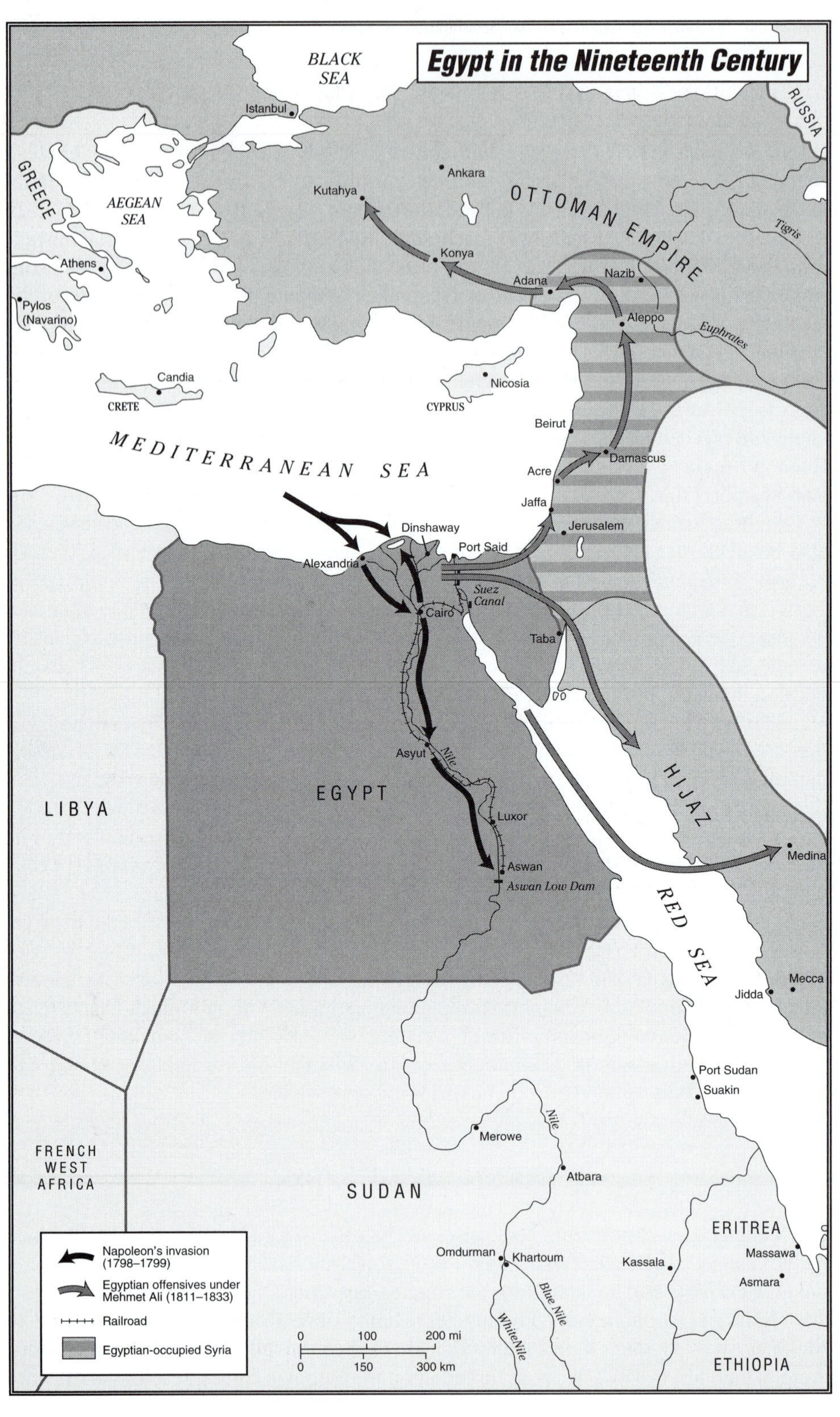
Egypt in the Nineteenth Century
BLACK SEA
RUSSIA
Istanbul
Ankara
GREECE
AEGEAN SEA
Kutahya
OTTOMAN EMPIRE
Tigris
Athens
Konya
Nazib
Adana
Pylos (Navarino)
Aleppo
Euphrates
Candia
CRETE
Nicosia
CYPRUS
Beirut
MEDITERRANEAN SEA
Damascus
Acre
Jaffa
Jerusalem
Dinshaway
Port Said
Alexandria
Suez Canal
Cairo
Taba
Asyut
Nile
HIJAZ
EGYPT
LIBYA
Luxor
Aswan
Aswan Low Dam
Medina
RED SEA
Mecca
Jidda
Port Sudan
Suakin
Nile
Merowe
Atbara
FRENCH WEST AFRICA
SUDAN
ERITREA
Massawa
Omdurman
Khartoum
Kassala
Asmara
Blue Nile
White Nile
ETHIOPIA
Napoleon's invasion (1798–1799)
Egyptian offensives under Mehmet Ali (1811–1833)
Railroad
Egyptian-occupied Syria
0 100 200 mi
0 150 300 km

to the outskirts of Konya in Anatolia. Ibrahim's devastating victory at Konya carried him on to Kutahya, where peace between Mahmud and his rebellious viceroy was concluded in 1833. Egypt, Syria, Adana, Tarsus, and Crete were assigned to Mehmet Ali, for which he agreed to pay a tribute to Istanbul.

Ibrahim governed Syria for eight years. Taxes were regularized, justice was more secure for the religious minorities, commerce was encouraged, education was stimulated, and law and order were more prevalent. The harsh rule that Mehmet Ali created in Egypt was also attempted in Syria. Conscription was resisted, the new taxes were hated, and rebellion faced Ibrahim on several occasions. Mahmud was rebuilding a modern army to threaten Mehmet Ali. Since the governorships of Egypt, Syria, and Crete were granted for only one year at a time, Mehmet Ali considered maintenance of an ever-ready army a prime requisite for his own safety.

Ottoman forces invaded Syria but were destroyed at Nazib by Ibrahim in June 1839. Five days later Mahmud II died, and before July was out the Ottoman fleet deserted to join the Egyptians at Alexandria. Mehmet Ali was now master of the situation, and the Ottomans prepared to surrender to his demands of hereditary control for all territories then in his possession.

DEFEAT OF MEHMET ALI

A joint note from the European Great Powers—Austria, Great Britain, France, Prussia, and Russia—recommended to the Ottomans that no action be taken on Mehmet Ali's claims without their approval. The British feared that Russia would call into operation provisions of the Treaty of Hunkiar Iskelesi or that France through Mehmet Ali would dominate Syria and Egypt and control all routes from the Mediterranean to India. The British, therefore, preferred a united action and they prevailed upon Russia, Prussia, and Austria to sign the Treaty of London in 1840. This treaty was a diplomatic defeat for France, which nevertheless eventually agreed to its terms. The 1840 treaty allowed Mehmet Ali the hereditary governorship of Egypt if he agreed to the settlement.

Since Mehmet Ali refused to budge, the only recourse was force. British agents in Lebanon and Syria helped raise a rebellion against Ibrahim, while a combined British-Austrian fleet landed troops at Beirut and captured Acre. Mehmet Ali was forced to recall Ibrahim from Syria and accept British terms. He also withdrew from central and western Arabia, allowing the Wahhabis and Saudis to return to power in the central regions, and the Ottomans to regain Mecca. Egypt was left as a hereditary province to Mehmet Ali and his heirs, but the size of his army was limited to no more than 18,000 men.

ORGANIZATION OF EGYPT

The defeats of 1840 and the diplomatic negotiations of 1841 gave Mehmet Ali full political power in Egypt. He lapsed into senility in 1847 and died one year later. For forty years Mehmet Ali had ruled Egypt, and every phase of life and society had interested him at one time or another. He had created a new government and developed a cabinet.

Real power, however, had never slipped from the hands of the Pasha, as Mehmet Ali was known. Most of the top officials were related to him or were personally associated with his household. In the 1830s, when councils of notables were appointed to discuss governmental affairs, western travelers were greatly impressed. But the Pasha never intended that his rule be other than that of a benevolent despot.

In economic matters Mehmet Ali attempted to make many changes. Exports were partially oriented away from the rest of the Ottoman Empire and toward Europe. The trade monopoly for grain was extended to include cotton and tobacco, although the British terminated the monopoly system after the 1838 commercial treaty for the Ottoman Empire was eventually forced upon Egypt. He also extended the corvée, or forced labor of the peasants, which by 1840, along with various acquisitions of land, brought the state—that is, Mehmet Ali, his extended family, and newly established notables—control of about half of the cultivable land in Egypt. Peasants received less than the free-market value of their crops, with the government pocketing the difference. Some peasant rebellions took place; the government attempted to rigorously and directly monitor peasant life. The ruling family controlled the domestic market through state enterprises, and for more than a decade there was a monopoly over imports as well as exports. By the treaties of 1840 and 1841, however, Mehmet Ali was forced to abide by the sultan's laws, especially the capitulations and commercial privileges held by the Great Powers. Since taxes were paid in kind, the Pasha's government continued to be the principal participant in the export trade.

To promote agriculture, corn and rice were introduced. In many areas steam pumps and better canals allowed summer irrigation, compelling the peasants in the villages to double the yield by growing two crops a year. Great attention was given to the science of irrigation. Swamplands were drained, old canals opened, and new ones built. About one-third more land was brought into cultivation, but the amount of work required from peasants dramatically increased. North of Cairo a great barrage on the Nile was constructed to raise canal levels, especially in years of scanty floods. However, since the engineering work was not sound, it proved ineffective until rebuilt in the 1880s.

The age of Mehmet Ali in Egypt coincided with rapid industrial growth in western Europe, and the Pasha became convinced of the value of industrialization. He built textile plants and sugar refineries. But technical knowledge, capital, suitable labor, power-drive machines, and supplies of coal and iron were lacking, while European pressure also restricted Egyptian opportunities. Even before Mehmet Ali died, the failure to industrialize Egypt was apparent.

Mehmet Ali's centralization adversely affected the status of urban and some rural women, but it did improve public health. The Pasha tried to centralize weaving in government factories, thereby damaging the interests of women who were weavers. Many middle- and upper-income women were hurt by changes in waqfs and tax farming, while poorer women were burdened by additional work loads or increased poverty because of conscription of men for the army and corvée. New government bureaucracies and functions, such as education, tended relatively to decrease opportunities for women as they increased opportunities for men. Great plagues raged every year, and annual deaths from smallpox, cholera, and bubonic plague sometimes rose to 10 percent or more of the population. Midwives were trained, a more effective quarantine was organized, and the foreign consuls in Alexandria were appointed to a board of sanitation. After 1840 health conditions in general improved somewhat, except for cholera outbreaks. A notable increase in the population was largely attributed to advances in public security, agriculture, and health.

The first new government schools were for the military—infantry, cavalry, engineers, navy, and artillery. Most of the instructors in these schools were French, and boys were sent to study in France. In 1833, however, the Polytechnic School was founded with a staff composed almost entirely of Egyptian teachers. Soon preparatory schools for the Polytechnic were organized in Cairo and Alexandria, although the vast majority of school-age children either attended traditional elementary religious schools or had no formal education at all. In connection with the government schools an official press was set up near Cairo; most of its publications were translations of European technical works. Newspapers printed in both Arabic and French not only gave urban society access to western ideas but also made Egypt a leader in the new intellectual life of the Arab world.

A neoclassical cultural revival along indigenous intellectual lines also took place in the early years of Mehmet Ali's reign. The notable historian and religious scholar Abd al-Rahman al-Jabarti, who was antagonistic toward the ruler, compiled a massive and sophisticated history of the era. Turkish remained the language of the ruling elite and most government records throughout the Mehmet Ali era.

Mehmet Ali was impatient and tried to change society rapidly without a sufficient number of sympathetic officials. Many of his innovations were too hurried and too shallow to endure, and by the middle 1840s even he ended or slowed down many of them. Still, construction of canals brought Nile trade and traffic from Cairo to Alexandria and helped turn the latter into a cosmopolitan boomtown whose population increased from 5000 in 1806 to 100,000 by 1850. During his reign, Mehmet Ali had ruthlessly established local autonomy for Egypt and even sown the seeds for the establishment of a separate state. Incredibly, this was done without incurring any substantial foreign debts.

ABBAS AND SAID PASHAS

Much of Mehmet Ali's work was undone by his successor, his grandson Abbas Pasha (r. 1848–1854). A conservative pro-Ottoman, Abbas Pasha disliked Europeans and resented their presence in Egypt, but he also realized that his interests paralleled those of the British. He shunned Frenchmen and permitted many of his grandfather's innovations to lapse. Uneconomic factories were abandoned, and schools were closed. Western influences and culture were weakened under Abbas. Aggressive policies were curtailed, and Albanian mercenaries were brought into the army. Although a British firm constructed the first railway between Alexandria and Cairo, Abbas opposed French proposals to build a Suez Canal to join the Mediterranean and Red seas. Egypt's economy was linked more closely to Europe, despite the policies of Abbas.

Upon Abbas Pasha's murder in 1854, authority passed to his uncle Said (1854–1863), Mehmet Ali's favorite son, who had headed the Egyptian navy for many years and who was pro-French. Said initially cut the size of the army from about 80,000 or more under

Abbas to about 70,000, and even further by 1860 to about 25,000. Abbas and Said sent an army of 20,000 to help the central Ottoman government during the Crimean War, and Said borrowed large sums of money from European bankers, beginning thereby an ultimately disastrous process. Some reforms were initiated, including the opening stages of the Suez Canal, but the reigns of both Abbas and Said saw relatively few changes compared with the age of Mehmet Ali before them or Ismail after them. For most common Egyptians the period from 1849 to 1863 was uneventful and a welcome relief from the wars, exactions, and rapid Europeanization under Mehmet Ali.

In Said's youth he had formed a friendship with Ferdinand de Lesseps, son of the French political agent in Egypt, and shortly after his accession Said granted his friend a concession to construct a canal at Suez. The 1855 news touched off a long diplomatic struggle. The British government opposed the scheme, believing it would deliver control over the easiest means of trade and communications with their empire in India into the hands of the French and Egyptians.

In 1856 an international commission of engineers surveyed the land and reported on the proposal, setting an estimate of £6 million as a maximum cost. Some stock in the Suez Canal Company went to Said for granting the concession and for furnishing the labor required to dig the canal. Other shares were held by the organizers or were given without cost to influential persons.

Until 1858 Napoleon III, emperor of the French, seemed unconcerned with the Suez Canal project, but de Lesseps gave a substantial number of shares to members of Napoleon's court, if not to the emperor and empress themselves. Although Said warned that construction of the canal should not begin until approved in Istanbul, digging started in 1859. The British protested over the use of forced labor and were able to keep the sultan from ratifying the concession. Little work had been accomplished when Said died in 1863 and Ismail, Ibrahim's oldest living son, became Ottoman governor of Egypt.

THE SUEZ CANAL AND ISMAIL

At his accession Ismail accepted the commitments concerning the canal, and by 1866 the British no longer opposed it. Under pressure from Napoleon III the Ottomans gave their authorization. Ismail paid an indemnity for not supplying forced labor, and the construction proceeded rapidly. When the canal was finished in 1869, Ismail spent £1 million on the lavish opening ceremonies. Empress Eugénie was the guest of honor among 6000 guests. Verdi's famous opera *Aïda,* composed for this event, was later performed in Cairo at the opera house built for the occasion; the opera emphasized the glory of the ancient Egypt of the pharaohs.

For the first several years the Suez Canal operated at a loss, and the company was perilously close to bankruptcy. However, traffic increased, the canal showing profits continuously after 1875. The cost of the canal to Said and Ismail was estimated at £11.5 million, for which Egypt received little return. Egypt also spent large sums of money on other infrastructure projects. Ismail ordered the digging of thousands of miles of irrigation canals, the doubling of the railroad network, and the building of an extensive telegraph system. A government-run postal service used steamboats on the Nile.

ISMAIL'S RULE

Ismail was thirty-three years old when he gained power in 1863. He had been educated in Paris. From the moment of Ismail's accession until his deposition in 1879, life at the court in Egypt was sumptuous: money flowed like the waters of the Nile. Ismail showered lavish gifts upon all, and his trips to Europe and Istanbul were extravagant in every detail. Presents to the sultan on the order of £1 million and a diamond-encrusted solid-gold dinner service were not unusual. Ismail possessed a charismatic personality that dispelled opposition.

Shortly after Ismail's accession, Sultan Abdulaziz visited him in Egypt, being the first Ottoman sultan to come to Cairo since its capture in 1517. (It should be pointed out that these two rulers, who resembled each other in many ways, were cousins, their mothers being sisters.) In 1866–1867 Ismail visited Istanbul, where through gifts he won the title khedive (prince) and recognition of the succession to control of Egypt by the law of primogeniture, rather than the previous system whereby the eldest male descendant of Mehmet Ali had succeeded to the governorship. At the same time, for the doubling of his tribute he was allowed to strengthen his army, coin money, and bestow decorations and titles on his own. In 1869 he was received, entertained, and decorated by the crowned heads of Europe. However, Ismail was rapidly falling into the clutches of unscrupulous moneylenders and European bankers.

Before detailing Ismail's bankruptcy his reign should be examined to provide a balance by acknowledging his imagination and leadership. Egypt in 1879, the end of Ismail's rule, was a far cry indeed from the Egypt of 1863. Perhaps the most apparent change during Ismail's reign was the Europeanization in sections of some Egyptian cities. He forcibly changed parts of the cities by constructing some European-style residential quarters, squares, and parks along with water service, gas supplies, and street lighting. The social and cultural gap between the cities and the countryside widened greatly, as by 1880 as many as 100,000 Europeans were living in Egypt, mostly in Cairo and Alexandria. By 1882 the total population of Alexandria grew to more than 230,000. The bulk of the population, however, continued to live in villages and engage in agriculture.

Meanwhile, the leading citizens of Egypt sent most of their sons to Europe to be educated. Ismail's fondness for saying that Egypt was a part of Europe was not without foundation. In fact, it was the Europeanized elite, participating in government, education, and general culture, who maintained his programs and sustained most of his works.

In military and government matters, Ismail drastically increased the size of the military, which reached 35,000 in 1865 and ultimately more than 120,000. Egypt sent a contingent to participate in the Russian-Ottoman War of 1877–1878. New officers were recruited: the upper ranks were reserved for Turks and Circassians, but some Egyptians also became officers. While many in the ruling elite still spoke Turkish, most government records were now written in the Arabic language. In 1866 the khedive inaugurated the Assembly of Delegates, a quasi-parliamentary body, most of whose members came from the category of wealthy and influential village headmen. The assembly served Ismail as a kind of constitutional shield to offset the Turkish elite that was evolving from the privileged army officer and government official classes. Until 1875 the assembly meetings were under Ismail's thumb, but then the financial crisis emboldened the members to criticize foreign powers and to demand responsibility over government ministers. In a session in 1876 it suggested that the assembly supervise government expenditures, and in 1879 Ismail dissolved the assembly.

The economy under Ismail was dominated by cotton, a labor-intensive crop. Long-staple cotton had been introduced in 1821 from the Ethiopian-Sudanese border, and Mehmet Ali had eagerly spread its cultivation. By 1850, a total of 35 million pounds (about 16 million kg.) was being grown annually, as Egypt became integrated into the world market dominated by Europe. During the American Civil War production soared to 250 million pounds (113 million kg.) per year, and the price increased by 400 percent to a total of over £25 million because Britain could no longer obtain cotton from the American south.

The rich especially profited from this bonanza, but with the end of the war prices tumbled and peasants were thrown into a miserable condition of mortgage foreclosures and indebtedness. By the 1870s about one-third of the peasants were landless laborers. Village headmen, foreigners, and prominent officials improved their own position by lending to their bankrupt neighbors. The dominance of the headmen in the assembly, formed at a time of peasant hardship and depression, was not a coincidence. Since cotton was a cash crop, it tended to destroy the old communal economy of the village; and in steps under Said and Ismail, family proprietorship with an individualistic economy began to prevail. The state monopoly over agricultural products was terminated, and in 1871 Ismail gave full right of ownership to villagers. Still, with heavy taxes a peasant flight from the land persisted. Big estates flourished and were subject to taxation only after 1854, though at a low rate. Village headmen remained important in the political, economic, and social life of the country, and their sons, subject to conscription under Said, began to improve the quality of the rank and file in the army and even to change its character as some higher ranks were opened to them. Large estates, swollen by abandoned lands, were owned by the khedivial family and the Turkish-speaking elite. Yet there was also a certain fluidity in ownership caused by personal mismanagement and indebtedness and the fractioning of landholdings under Muslim laws of inheritance. Ismail's economic policies and actions, including the building of roads, railroads, and canals, and the bringing of over a million acres (400,000 hectares) of new land under cultivation, were efforts to increase his own income; nevertheless, they did benefit the whole nation, as the population growth during his sixteen years of rule testified.

In the sphere of international affairs, Ismail had certain autonomous rights granted by the sultan but also many burdensome obligations. In addition to the ability to contract loans, Ismail could negotiate with foreign governments but only through consuls, never ambassadors. As a part of the Ottoman Empire, Egypt was subject to capitulatory treaties with fourteen countries, whose abuse ensured that law cases were settled by diplomatic pressure rather than on the basis of merit. The variety and number of foreign nationals residing in Egypt made cases of one foreigner against another difficult to adjudicate. Ismail's foreign minister, the Armenian Nubar Pasha, proposed a mixed court staffed by Egyptians and foreign judges, which would administer codes based on French law. It would deal with civil and criminal cases. Eventually a conference in Istanbul in 1873 authorized the Mixed Courts. The courts began in 1875 with a majority of foreign judges, and the French language used in all proceedings. Judges, Egyptian and foreign, were appointed by the khedive, although foreigners were nominated by participating governments. Establishment of the Mixed Courts, however, weakened the government and frequently frustrated its operation. They did not end the capitulations but modified them in an important way. Personal law for Muslim Egyptians remained the Islamic shariah.

Ismail's boldest foreign venture was the extension of Egyptian rule into the Sudan. Mehmet Ali had conquered parts of the region, and in 1842 the sultan had recognized him as governor-general of the Sudan. During the middle of the century under Abbas and Said, interest lapsed. Ismail was Europeanized to the extent of considering Egypt as a participant in the exploration and partitioning of Africa, and he devised ambitious schemes of expanding Egypt to the equator and including all of the basin of the White Nile. In 1869, he declared that steps were being taken to end the slave trade in the Sudan and set up a government in the equatorial region. Expeditions to the equatorial lakes district resulted in the attachment of Bahr al-Ghazal to the Sudan. Ismail sent the Briton General Charles George Gordon toward Ethiopia in 1875 and 1876. Gordon was so successful in curtailing the slave trade as to disturb the local economy and dislocate the principal occupation of local leaders. Gordon departed in 1877, and by 1879 the Sudan was left in a state of near anarchy. Taxes throughout the period of Egyptian rule were high, and the depopulation of many areas and the disruption of much of the economy ensued. Without financial resources from Cairo, Egyptian governors were no match for the uprising led by Muhammad Ahmad of Dongola, who declared himself Mahdi, the expected savior, in 1881.

Ismail admired the social and cultural life he saw in his European travels, and he tried to create a similar society in Egypt. Hardly any facet escaped his attention. Societies were organized for archaeology, music, and poetry, for the construction of libraries (the Khedivial Library in 1870) and museums (the Egyptian Museum in 1863) for the advancement of Egyptology, and in 1875 the Khedivial Geographical Society for African exploration. Newspapers were encouraged, and the famous daily *Al-Ahram* (meaning "the pyramids") was born in 1876, while postage stamps had been used for the first time in 1866.

As neighborhoods, guilds, and religious groups began to be affected by change, the role of men in society remained predominant. However, many midwives were professionally trained, and some women participated in the new education or worked in factories. Women were active in the court system, and they took part in the general economy—buying, selling, inheriting, lending and borrowing, and pursuing debtors. As conscription and forced labor for the state increased in the country, family life was often disrupted. A frequent, though unintended, consequence of the reforms was to decrease the freedom of social action of many women.

Above all else, Ismail believed firmly that education would westernize his state. A Ministry of Education was established and headed at times by Ali Pasha Mubarak, a scholar and administrator. In 1873 the first school for girls was established. Specialized schools were started for military officers, lawyers, engineers, and administrators; Teachers College was founded in 1872; and the renowned School of Languages was reopened under the direction of Rifaa al-Tahtawi, a scholar and author who was to inspire many of the leaders of Egyptian public life for the following half century. During Ismail's reign literacy had climbed to perhaps 5 percent, and many more children were now taking part in formal education, whether in religious, government, or foreign schools.

BANKRUPTCY AND EUROPEAN INTERVENTION

At Ismail's accession Egypt had a combined foreign and domestic debt of £7 million. Thirteen years later it had a foreign debt of £68 million and a domestic debt of £30 million, which made Egypt on a per person basis one of the most indebted countries in the world at that time. Of the debt, nearly 35 percent was incurred in the form of discounts and commissions, none of which could be used for investment in Egypt. Interest charges amounted to £5 million per year, more than half the total annual revenue of the government. Ismail flogged the peasants to increase taxes and sought new sources of income. In 1874 he sold his shares of stock in the Suez Canal to the British government for nearly £4 million. But this only delayed the day of reckoning, which came in 1876 when Ismail ceased payment on his debts and Egypt became officially bankrupt.

There is no question that Ismail was exceedingly extravagant, although most of the proceeds from the loans were spent on useful and productive projects. The capitulations practically condemned Egypt to the role of an agriculturally based economy, which in the period following the Crimean War and the American Civil War reduced it to a level of relative inferiority compared with industrialized nations. Hard times following the European financial panic of 1873 hurt Ismail; further loans were impossible to obtain, and state revenues were inadequate to cover interest payments.

To extricate himself, Ismail conducted a losing battle against European bondholders and their governments. In 1876 the debt was unified, and Ismail agreed to set up a public debt authority with foreign directors (the British member was Evelyn Baring of the Baring banking family, who later became Lord Cromer).

But Ismail had also been forced in 1876 to appoint dual controllers who became the real rulers of Egypt. A law was enacted squeezing the debt down to £85 million and reserving £4.5 million of the annual government income for the budget. All excess income, then estimated at £4 million, was to be employed to retire the debt. Unfortunately for the future development of Egypt, expanding revenues resulting from increased productivity and hard work would not benefit Egyptians or improve services of the government.

An international commission demanded that Ismail accept a civil list for himself and the idea of ministerial responsibility. Times were hard; government expenditures were greatly curtailed; and the Nile flood of 1877–1878 was exceedingly low, drastically reducing crop yields. The crisis encouraged activity by many social groups, including the Assembly of Delegates, military officers, ulama, the press, artisan guilds, peasants, and nationalist clubs; all these played a role in the opposition to European control of Egypt.

Ismail appointed in 1879 an all-Egyptian cabinet. A draft constitution was submitted to the assembly, giving it, among other things, full control of finances. There was great jubilation when the assembly accepted the constitution. The British and the French, however, were determined that Ismail be deposed. The European powers persuaded the sultan in Istanbul to send a telegram on June 26, 1879, addressed to the "former" khedive Ismail informing him that rule had passed to his son Tawfiq (r. 1879–1892). Ismail left for Italy, where he died in 1895.

Soon after Ismail's deposition authority passed to the revived dual controllers, who cut expenditures to the bone. The size of the army was reduced to 36,000; many officers were retired; civil budgets and personnel were pared. Yet a sizable number of foreign administrators came in at inordinate salaries. Opposition quickly formed in Egypt. The evolution of society under Ismail had brought four parties to the fore: a weak reactionary group; a vigorous Islamic modernist faction developed by Muhammad Abduh; a constitutional party of wealthy Europeanized Egyptian landowners organized by Sharif Pasha from membership in the assembly and from other groups; and an army group composed of Egyptians in the lower officer echelons and inspired by Colonel Ahmad Urabi. Only the first party acquiesced in the foreign dual control, preferring it to any of the Egyptian groups. The army was the most violent in its opposition because high-ranking officers were Turks or Circassians and the dual control did not remove these officers to the extent that it curbed the rise of native Egyptians.

When in January 1882 England and France presented a joint note to the khedive Tawfiq protesting the formation of a constitutional government, the army partly gained control of the cabinet. The army's leaders sought reforms within the context of Egypt's continued local autonomy inside the Ottoman Empire. England and France had to occupy the country or give up the dual control, and riots in Alexandria served as the pretext. A change in the French government, however, altered French policy; and England alone intervened. The British occupied Egypt in July 1882 to overthrow Colonel Urabi and reestablish European control through their influence on Tawfiq. Alexandria was shelled; the British navy occupied the Canal cities; and in September, British troops defeated the Egyptian army and took Cairo. At this point resistance to European control in Egypt collapsed.

European power and influence were increasing throughout the Middle East in the nineteenth century, even while Egypt, the central Ottoman Empire, and Qajar Iran engaged in military and economic modernization. As Egypt became incorporated into the European-dominated world economy, the Suez Canal made this Ottoman province led by the family of Mehmet Ali more and more important, both strategically and commercially. Britain would remain in control of Egypt for more than seventy years after 1882.

REFERENCES

References cited at the end of Chapters 20, 21, 22, and 23 are pertinent to this chapter as well.

Abu-Lughod, Ibrahim: *Arab Rediscovery of Europe: A Study in Cultural Encounters.* Princeton, N.J.: Princeton University Press, 1963. A study of Arab travelers and students in Europe in the century after Napoleon.

Cannon, Byron: *Politics of Law and the Courts in Nineteenth-Century Egypt.* Salt Lake City: University of Utah Press, 1988. Especially useful for new views on the Mixed Courts.

Chicago, University of, Joseph Regenstein Library: Photo Archive at www.lib.uchicago.edu/e/su/mideast/PhotoArchive.html. Early photographs, especially of Cairo, Jerusalem, Damascus, and Istanbul.

Cole, Juan R. I.: *Colonialism and Revolution in the Middle East: Social and Cultural Origins of Egypt's 'Urabi Movement.* Princeton: Princeton University Press, 1993. A sophisticated and convincing discussion of Egyptian social, economic, and political history in the middle decades of the nineteenth century.

Crabbs, Jack A., Jr.: *The Writing of History in Nineteenth-Century Egypt.* Detroit: Wayne State University Press, 1984. A very useful contribution to the historiography of the Middle East.

Cuno, Kenneth M.: *The Pasha's Peasants: Land, Society and Economy in Lower Egypt, 1740–1858.* Cambridge: Cambridge University Press, 1992.

Fahmy, Khaled: *All the Pasha's Men: Mehmed Ali, his Army and the Making of Modern Egypt.* Cambridge: Cambridge University Press, 1997. A revisionist study that emphasizes the Ottoman character of Mehmet Ali through a careful examination of his control and management of soldiers. For an opposing view see the works of Afaf Lutfi al-Sayyid Marsot cited below.

Farnie, D. A.: *East and West of Suez: The Suez Canal in History, 1854–1956.* Oxford: Clarendon Press, 1969. A monumental work, derived from a vast range of western-language sources.

Goldschmidt, Arthur, Jr.: *Modern Egypt: The Formation of a Nation-State.* Boulder, Colo.: Westview Press, 1988. The bibliography is especially valuable in this clear, concise, and thoughtful analysis of Egypt from Mehmet Ali to Mubarak.

Gran, Peter: *Islamic Roots of Capitalism: Egypt, 1760–1840.* Austin: University of Texas Press, 1979. Stimulating discussion of Egyptian economic conditions and intellectual life.

Hunter, F. Robert: *Egypt under the Khedives, 1805–1879: From Household Government to Modern Bureaucracy.* Cairo: American University in Cairo Press, 1999. This reprint of the 1984 first edition is a detailed study of the growth and changes in government and administration.

al-Jabarti, Abd al-Rahman: *Abd al-Rahman al-Jabarti's History of Egypt.* Edited by Thomas Philipp and Moshe Perlmann. Stuttgart: Franz Steiner, 1994. This three-volume translation of al-Jabarti's chronicle is especially valuable as a primary source on the events of Mehmet Ali's career.

Jankowski, James: *Egypt: A Short History.* Oxford: OneWorld, 2000. A rapid survey from the pharaonic age to the present.

Kuhnke, LaVerne: *Lives at Risk: Public Health in Nineteenth-Century Egypt.* Berkeley: University of California Press, 1990. An excellent study of medical theory and practice.

Landes, David S.: *Bankers and Pashas: International Finance and Economic Imperialism in Egypt.* Cambridge: Harvard University Press, 1958. A significant case study of private banking in Egypt in the 1860s.

Lane, E. W.: *Manners and Customs of the Modern Egyptians.* New York: Dutton, 1923. Still the most valuable source for the social history of nineteenth-century urban Egypt, this book, originally printed in 1835, is full of interesting observations on life in Cairo.

McCarthy, Justin: "Nineteenth-Century Egyptian Population." *Middle Eastern Studies* 12 (1976): 1–40. A sophisticated analysis of a complicated issue, showing that substantial population growth was caused largely by civil order and political stability.

Marsot, Afaf Lutfi al-Sayyid: *Egypt in the Reign of Muhammad Ali.* Cambridge: Cambridge University Press, 1984. A valuable political biography that analyzes most aspects of Egyptian history of the period.

———: *A Short History of Modern Egypt.* Cambridge: Cambridge University Press, 1985. An excellent introduction to the subject.

———: *Women and Men in Late Eighteenth-Century Egypt.* Austin: University of Texas Press, 1995. This perceptive work includes a chapter on the nineteenth century.

Morsy, Magali: *North Africa 1800–1900: A Survey from the Nile Valley to the Atlantic.* London: Longman, 1984. Especially useful for discussions of the Sudan and the role of the Sahara in the history of North Africa.

Owen, E. R. J.: *Cotton and the Egyptian Economy, 1820–1914: A Study in Trade and Development.* Oxford: Clarendon Press, 1969. A stimulating and scholarly analysis of the Egyptian economy.

Reimer, Michael J.: *Colonial Bridgehead: Government and Society in Alexandria, 1807–1882.* Boulder, Colo.: Westview Press, 1997. An excellent account of this flourishing port.

Rivlin, Helen Anne B.: *The Agricultural Policy of Muhammad Ali in Egypt.* Cambridge: Harvard University Press, 1961. An outstanding work that considers the entire economy of Egypt.

Schölch, Alexander: *Egypt for the Egyptians! The Socio-Political Crisis in Egypt, 1878–1882.* London: Ithaca Press, 1981. The best study of the political factors in the fall of Ismail and the rise of Urabi.

Toledano, Ehud R.: *State and Society in Mid-Nineteenth-Century Egypt.* Cambridge: Cambridge University Press, 1990. A more favorable evaluation of Abbas Pasha and the social history of his time, emphasizing elite ties to Ottoman culture and fascinating insights into everyday urban life.

Tucker, Judith E.: *Women in Nineteenth-Century Egypt.* Cambridge: Cambridge University Press, 1985. A pathbreaking work of great value for the urban history of Egypt and the role of women in Egyptian society.

Vatikiotis, P. J.: *The History of Modern Egypt: From Muhammad Ali to Mubarak.* 4th ed. Baltimore, Md.: Johns Hopkins University Press, 1991. A detailed book on nineteenth- and twentieth-century Egypt. Strong on social and intellectual movements in the rise of Egyptian nationalism.

CHAPTER 25

Ottoman Tanzimat and European Ambitions

Between 1839 and 1876 the Ottoman Empire undertook a series of reforms while struggling against the growing power of European imperialism. During the nearly forty years of this reform period, which was known as the Tanzimat, the military and civil sections of the central government witnessed many substantial changes. The reforms, nevertheless, did not uniformly affect all regions; some were far removed from the effective reach of the reformers. Throughout the whole period the empire also faced a series of external challenges. Those in the Ottoman elite who favored internal reforms believed that the changes were inherently worthwhile since they would promote the modernization or Europeanization needed to save the state from being swallowed up by its enemies. At the same time reforms might gain favor with some European countries, particularly Great Britain, and thereby advance the diplomatic interests of the empire. The pattern of alternating and intersecting internal reforms and foreign crises sometimes made it difficult to focus successfully on one or the other.

HATT-I SHARIF

The reforms of the Ottoman sultan Mahmud II had strengthened the authority of the central government. After the destruction of the janissaries a more effective army was developed and many autonomous provincial governors were subdued. Mahmud's struggle with Mehmet Ali of Egypt, however, resulted in a disastrous defeat in 1839. With Mahmud's death in 1839, his sixteen-year-old son, Abdulmejid (r. 1839–1861), faced military catastrophe, only to be saved by the European Great Powers. The new sultan had only a scanty education. Since his view of the world hardly extended beyond the palace walls, his understanding of the problems of his empire was rudimentary. His personal whims led to constant shifts of grand vizirs, frequently at the instigation of powerful ambassadors. He and the other sultans of the Tanzimat period—Abdulaziz (r. 1861–1876) and Murad V (r. 1876)—remained the source of political legitimacy and sovereignty, yet they played only a small role in governing, as power tended to gravitate toward the chief bureaucrats and grand vizirs.

Shortly after his accession Abdulmejid declared the Hatt-i Sharif (Illustrious Rescript), theoretically changing many aspects of Ottoman political life. It abolished capital punishment without a trial; guaranteed justice to all with respect to life, honor, and property; and continued the Supreme Council of Judicial Ordinances, whose purpose was to frame laws. Mixed tribunals, composed of Muslims and non-Muslims, were formed to handle commercial cases involving foreigners. Most significant, testimony by a non-Muslim against a Muslim was made admissible in the courts. The second reform measure of the Hatt-i Sharif was designed to end the system of tax farming and expand the direct collection of taxes by government officials. (In reality, some tax farms continued until World War I.) The decree's provisions pertained to all subjects, regardless of religion.

The Hatt-i Sharif was a demonstration to Europe that the Ottoman Empire was capable of self-preservation and reorganization to withstand pressures from Christian ethnic groups for independence. Its issuance made enactment of the London treaties of 1840 and 1841 concerning the integrity of the Ottoman Empire appear more reasonable and just. The Ottoman foreign minister, Mustafa Reshid, had served as ambassador in London and Paris, and recognized the appeal that the Hatt-i Sharif would generate in European capitals. Whether the Hatt-i Sharif was intended primarily for foreign consumption or as part of an internal reform process has been much debated. Reshid became an advocate of both internal reform and a pro-British foreign policy.

The new spirit of reform was soon curbed. As soon as the Great Powers decided to drive Mehmet Ali back to Egypt, reaction set in. Reshid had introduced a new penal code, based somewhat on French models, but after he fell from office in 1841 over discussions of the new commercial code, which eventually was decreed in 1850, the course of reform took a different direction, emphasizing chiefly military matters. Under Riza Pasha, a conservative court favorite and commander in chief of the army, a more rigorous conscription among Muslims was effected and some foreign officers were hired. (Christians were excluded from conscription.) The regular army and the reserves were increased, although in practice Ottoman forces were often tied down in police operations. The currency was threatened by the issuance of excessive amounts of paper currency in the 1850s and 1870s, but generally monetary policy came to be based upon a stable gold, silver, and copper coinage.

EUROPEAN INTERESTS IN THE OTTOMAN EMPIRE

Throughout the nineteenth century, Britain, France, Austria, and Russia maintained a continuing interest in the Ottoman Empire. Toward the end of the century Germany became the fifth major European imperialist power involved in the Middle East.

Britain and France thought of the Ottoman Empire in terms of commerce, imperial geopolitical strategy, and military and naval alliances. France was interested in imperial expansion in North Africa and the Mediterranean; the French conquered Algiers in 1830. Since England rivaled France in the east and in southeast Asia, whichever power gained secure access to Middle Eastern routes could threaten and block the communications of the other. In 1839 Britain annexed the important trading center of Aden in Yemen. Britain tended to support the maintenance of the Ottoman Empire as a means of blocking Russian entrance into the Mediterranean. This policy impelled England to oppose partition of the Ottoman Empire and to seek to strengthen the sultan's government.

Dynastic expansion at the expense of the Ottomans motivated Austrian and Russian conquests. Austria and Russia were also apprehensive that each might gain Ottoman territory at the expense of the other.

Russia, the most consistent enemy of the Ottoman Empire, dreamed of gaining Istanbul and reestablishing a Christian empire in the city of Constantine. Russia also was expanding in central Asia and the Caucasus areas; felt a religious interest in Jerusalem; was concerned over the welfare of Ottoman Orthodox Christians; and sought the creation of friendly Slavic Christian satellite states in the Balkans. In 1840–1841 the European powers agreed that any Russian occupation within the Istanbul region to protect the sultan from Mehmet Ali had to be only temporary. With the expiration of the Treaty of Hunkiar Iskelesi no European state had any special privilege that others did not possess, even though Russia, on the basis of various agreements with the Ottomans, enjoyed specified rights in the Balkans and among certain Christian groups throughout the empire.

The study of the Middle East or Orientalism grew in all the European states. Scholarship concentrated on the study of languages, ancient history, and religion, while many university professors also advised their governments about current foreign policy.

COMMERCE AND THE CAPITULATIONS

While most of the commerce of the Ottoman Empire consisted of local trade among Ottoman subjects, international commerce was steadily increasing throughout the nineteenth century, and this area of the economy was coming under the control of foreigners and Ottoman minority groups protected by foreigners. In 1838, the signing of the British-Ottoman commercial convention gave English merchants favorable terms for trading; other European merchants soon gained the same privileges. Furthermore, government monopolies were abolished on goods exported from the empire, a provision that specifically included Egypt. The effects of the convention for Ottoman traders were unfortunate, but the consequences were lessened when the agreement was ignored or circumvented in some provinces.

International commerce increased dramatically throughout the whole world during the nineteenth century. The 1838 commercial convention marked a definite upsurge in commerce between the Ottoman Empire and western Europe. As a result, port cities such as Beirut and Izmir grew rapidly in population and wealth. After 1846, the grain trade of the Ottoman Empire and especially of the Danubian provinces rose to unprecedented heights. Within a few years Britain was obtaining as much grain from the Ottomans as from Russia. In 1827 British exports to the Ottoman Empire were worth about £500,000; in 1849 they were more than £2,400,000. Britain became the chief trading partner of the Ottoman Empire.

Growing industry in western Europe found in the Middle East a source of foodstuffs and raw materials that could be obtained in exchange for the products of the new machines of the west. This trade affected cloth production in the Ottoman Empire, in some areas substituting machine-made textiles from western Europe for local homespun cloth and thereby helping to cause a decline in guild membership by the end of the century. Ottoman industry also suffered from a lack of capital, although in various fields of production Ottoman artisans and manufacturers proved to be adaptable to new circumstances, thereby retaining and even expanding their sales of goods.

Great Britain forced the Ottoman Empire, Egypt, and Iran to stop almost entirely their commerce in slaves. In the 1840s and 1850s the British secured measures to stop the importation of African slaves by sea and the public sale of slaves. By the 1880s the slave trade was officially banned and only small numbers of slaves were being smuggled into the Ottoman Empire. (Abolition of slavery, however, had to wait until the next century.)

Use of machines and new types of power made it possible for the west to forge far ahead of the Middle East in matters of material welfare and wealth. Industrial capitalism, the earlier agricultural revolution, vast strides in science and technology, new military techniques, and the political strength deriving from nationalism all contributed to the increasing power of western Europe. The imbalance of power and prestige of western countries over the mostly agricultural Middle East became more preponderant with each decade. The central government of the Ottoman Empire and the coastal regions of that state (and their immediate hinterlands) became closely linked to western Europe. The privileges known as capitulations hastened this process.

With great increases in trade and shifting power relationships in the nineteenth century, the capitulations allowed foreigners special privileges. Some Ottomans gained the status of foreign citizens, and outright sale of citizenship and passports was practiced by unscrupulous consuls. Since foreigners had the right to be tried in their own consular courts and Ottoman officials frequently relied upon the advice of powerful European ambassadors, consuls could usually have criminal cases against their nationals dropped. Foreigners were exempt from local taxes and were thus able to conduct business with less interference from the government and at a lower cost than Ottoman subjects. In the first half of the nineteenth century sultans granted special privileges to selected Ottoman merchants to help them compete with European traders.

Export tariffs were also established by the capitulations and could not be changed except by consent of each party in a specific treaty. Since each treaty also contained a "most favored nation" clause, it was necessary to change all treaties at once to make any successful change at all: to get all to agree was virtually impossible. Such a situation enhanced the commercial exploitation of the weak Ottoman Empire by the powerful European nations.

RELIGIOUS ISSUES

Into this picture of the capitulations was injected an additional feature: religion. France claimed to represent the interests of all Roman Catholics inside the Ottoman Empire, and Russia asserted a similar claim to protect all Orthodox Christians. European powers increasingly intervened in Ottoman domestic affairs on behalf of religious and ethnic minorities. This helped lead to an identification of religious creed with ethnic nationality, which seemed to make nationalism synonymous with sectarian religion.

Prior to the recognition of Greek independence, there were still only three millets (semiautonomous religious communal groups) in the Ottoman Empire. But by 1914 there were seventeen, and almost all enjoyed the sponsorship of a foreign government. Not entirely responsible for this movement but certainly encouraging it were foreign missionaries. Christian missionaries from Europe, especially Roman Catholics, had labored in the Middle East for centuries, but their number increased greatly in the nineteenth century. Different denominations established schools, churches, hospitals, printing presses, and a variety of service groups to carry the Christian message and western concepts of society to Middle Eastern peoples. Almost completely unsuccessful in converting Muslims, they concentrated their efforts upon indigenous Christian groups but sought to influence Muslims by westernizing them. Many Orthodox Christians in Anatolia became more prosperous and took part in a cultural flowering separate from the efforts of the missionaries and still within the framework of the Ottoman political system.

In 1860, with the founding of the Alliance Israélite Universelle, Jews in Europe began to better the welfare of Jews in the Middle East, especially through education. Most Jews in the Middle East did not have the diplomatic protection granted Christians by European governments; as a result, they suffered less from the rising antagonism directed by some elements of the Muslim population against minorities who depended on foreigners for advancement and security.

The Christian European governments often subsidized Christian Ottoman groups for ulterior, political aims. Russia and England, for instance, competed for the Armenians, and neither wished to see American missionaries enter the field. The greatest rivalry occurred in Palestine between the Russians and the French. Since medieval times Catholic clergy had attended the holy places in Bethlehem, Jerusalem, and Nazareth. Orthodox churchmen dated to the seventeenth century their right to protect the Holy Sepulchre, where Jesus had been buried. They protested against French claims. In 1842, when the cupola of the Church of the Holy Sepulchre needed repair, a great commotion arose over which sect should enjoy the privilege, and actual fighting broke out in 1847 in Bethlehem, where Catholic and Orthodox monks attacked each other with candlesticks and crosses at the Church of the Nativity. The Ottoman governor of Jerusalem posted soldiers inside the Church of the Holy Sepulchre to prevent bloodshed.

TANZIMAT

In the midst of these crises, Mustafa Reshid returned to office as foreign minister in 1845 and became grand vizir the following year. He reinvigorated the Hatt-i Sharif by favoring the Tanzimat (meaning "reforms"), a movement for reorganization, and he found an eager ally in the British ambassador.

Earlier military reforms continued and cost large sums of money. The regular Ottoman army grew from 24,000 in 1837 to 120,000 in 1850; during the Crimean War of 1853–1856 reserves were also mobilized, bringing the total force to about 250,000. A major difficulty arose from the insufficient number of trained officers and the inadequacy of support services.

The Tanzimat spirit was also manifested in the growing number of Ottomans who were educated in the west or in a western manner and who became more secular in their outlook. The best evidence of this growth was the newspapers and books that appeared in the 1840s. Politics, history, biography, and philosophy were popular subjects, and new ideas appealed to some in the younger generation. Everywhere in Europe revolts against conservatism were stirring, and Istanbul, on the edge of Europe, felt this movement. Nationalist sentiment among Greeks, Armenians, Bulgarians, and others could not fail to arouse Ottoman patriotism, too. A secular attitude was injecting new ideas of law and education into the Muslim as well as the non-Muslim communities: the individual was coming to be regarded as having rights outside of the group. Although many Muslims still opposed the idea, Ottomanism promised equality for all subjects, and Ottoman Christians and Jews were appointed to the reform councils.

Some of Reshid's reforms were extended beyond the capital and appeared in measures regarding equal justice, withdrawal of capital punishment from the hands of local governors, an increase in the size of the bureaucracy, and creation of elected local assemblies. These assemblies were usually composed of wealthy, influential notables and conservatives; ironically, they often prevented changes from being adopted. In addition to provincial assemblies, the grand vizir checked on actions of the governor by sending out commissioners to inspect a province and receive petitions from local groups.

No longer was the state to be viewed solely as an instrument for the sovereign to collect revenue, raise armies, and administer justice. Matters of education, public works, and economic development were of some concern to the rulers. This Tanzimat "reordering" spirit was also manifested in the modernization of law and diplomacy. Government administration was more efficient (except in finance), the number of bureaucrats increased substantially, and civil servants were recruited more broadly than in the past. No law or ordinance could become effective until it had been discussed by the Tanzimat Council and approved by the Council of Ministers. The Judicial Council, including Christian as well as Muslim members, served as a court of appeals for cases arising from new, westernized civil laws, but not those arising from religious laws, as these were handled by millet courts. Many innovations were introduced, including the standardization of weights and measures under the metric system, postage stamps, a new nationality law, a lending bank for small businesses, and a reorganization of public instruction.

THE CRIMEAN WAR

Ottoman leaders could not concentrate exclusively on domestic reforms—they also had to deal with urgent foreign policy disputes. The Ottomans tried to satisfy both Russia and France in their argument over the Christian holy places in Palestine, but the Russians came to feel that they had been duped by the sultan. In 1853 they demanded full Orthodox privileges in Palestine, including the Russian right to repair the cupola of the Church of the Holy Sepulchre as well as a special treaty guaranteeing privileges for Ottoman Orthodox Christians and conclusion of a secret defensive alliance with Russia. Compromise was reached on some matters, while the sultan refused demands regarding Russian protection of Orthodox Christians, for to do so was tantamount to giving Russia the right to govern between 10 and 12 million inhabitants of the Ottoman Empire.

When the Russian tsar ordered the occupation of the Danubian Principalities, the British and French supported the Ottomans. Bolstered by the recent arrival of a large Egyptian fleet at the Golden Horn, the Ottomans rejected new European proposals, declared war in 1853, and attacked the Russians on the Danube. Inconsequential Ottoman successes were obtained there and in the Caucasus, but real victory was won by the Russians when the Ottoman navy was destroyed in the Black Sea. Then the British and French governments sent their combined fleets into the Black Sea.

In 1854 Austria and Prussia joined against Russia by requesting assurances of the integrity of the Ottoman Empire. The Russian army retired from the Ottoman Danubian Principalities since the tsar was not prepared to face all Europe. British and French troops occupied Athens to force the Greeks to abandon an attack upon the Ottoman Empire. But sentiment in England and France, on the streets and in the governments, was for further war.

Acting with a treaty of alliance between Britain, France, and the Ottoman Empire, the three powers waged war against Russia. There is no need to dwell on the Crimean War here, since it was primarily a European rather than a Middle Eastern war. Ottoman monetary debts to English and French bankers mounted as costs mushroomed. Cholera weakened the armies more than did battles, but the will to fight persisted. War continued until the fall of Sevastopol in the Crimea to the allies and the fall of Kars in Anatolia to the Russians in late 1855. Peace was speedily concluded at Paris in 1856.

The Treaty of Paris and additional agreements declared that the Ottoman Empire was a European power. In a separate treaty England, France, and Austria agreed to respect, defend, and guarantee the empire's independence and integrity. The Black Sea was demilitarized. Equally important was European acceptance of a new edict already promulgated by Sultan Abdulmejid, the Hatt-i Humayun, guaranteeing many reforms for Ottoman Christians. Domestic change was accelerated greatly by the Crimean War.

Special vassalage status was conferred upon the Ottoman provinces of Wallachia and Moldavia, with the hope that a more independent rule for the Danubian Principalities would enable them to serve as a better buffer between the Ottoman Empire and Russia. In 1866 a member of the Prussian royal house, Carol (Charles) of Hohenzollern, became prince of a united Romania.

HATT-I HUMAYUN

Before the Treaty of Paris could be completed, a new reform document was issued. This was the Hatt-i Humayun (Imperial Rescript) of 1856, which reendorsed the Hatt-i Sharif and the Tanzimat. But it was far more specific in its details and more extensive in scope than previous reform measures. The imperial decree was in the main concerned with the Christian and Jewish population; it granted non-Muslims the rights and privileges that the Muslim subjects possessed. Patriarchs and heads of communities (millets) were to be appointed for life, and through self-chosen assemblies each community was to control its own administration. Freedom of worship was declared, and no one could be compelled to change religion. Religion or ethnicity could not be a hindrance to holding public office, employment by the state, entry into a school, or service in the army.

In matters of justice and court procedures, commercial and criminal cases between Muslims and non-Muslims and among non-Muslims of different sects were referred to mixed tribunals whose proceedings were open to the public. Equality of taxes among the various religious groups was pronounced, and foreigners were permitted to own real property in the sultan's realm.

On paper the Hatt-i Humayun contained the essentials necessary for a strong revival. The Ottomans sought to show this strength by extending their power over areas, such as Yemen, that had long been independent of Istanbul. In 1849 they had landed there, and in 1872 they took Sana in the interior. But in Yemen and many of the other more distant provinces, such as the Hijaz in Arabia, the Tanzimat reforms were unpopular and were for the most part not applied.

To make the reforms work, both in the central government and in the provinces, required the commitment of more people than were available. Moreover, the Hatt-i Humayun ignored the rising tide of nationalism among non-Muslim nationalists who accepted the concept that people could only enjoy the greatest happiness when governing themselves. The capitulations in the Ottoman Empire, including Egypt, gave political, social, and economic privileges to foreign nationals. Thus the Hatt-i Humayun, in spite of the efforts of such men as Fuad and Ali Pashas, was doomed to failure almost from the beginning. Too many were opposed to it. On the other hand, the wars in Europe from 1859 to 1871 that accompanied the unification of Italy and Germany and the reforms that occupied Russia usually allowed the Ottoman Empire to follow its own political course.

LEBANON AND SYRIA

A series of bloody events in Lebanon and Syria furnished one pretext for European intervention in internal Ottoman problems. Since the time of Napoleon, Amir Bashir Shihab, the leader of a local dynasty that had been paramount in the area of Mount Lebanon after 1697, had ruled with ruthless calculation. His loyalty to Mehmet Ali allowed the Ottomans to replace him in 1840 with an incompetent nephew. Maronite Christians and Druzes soon fell to fighting. European pressure elicited a new arrangement from the sultan in 1843: the northern regions of Lebanon were governed by a Maronite, supported by the French; the southern portion was left to the Druzes, who were favored by the British.

An uneasy peace and prosperity reigned. However, a new and weak governor in the Maronite district, installed in 1854, permitted local notable families to abuse villagers, and population pressures were felt keenly. In 1858 a kind of social upheaval broke out, while in 1860 in the Druze-governed district, where many of the peasants were Maronites, and in the city of Damascus, massacres of Christians took place. The Great Powers permitted Napoleon III of France to send a force of 6000 to restore order there. The Ottomans, however, firmly stopped the violence before the French arrived, and the Ottomans reestablished direct control over Syria as a European commission drew up a statute for autonomous rule in Mount Lebanon. Signed by Sultan Abdulmejid in 1861, it provided for an Ottoman Christian governor appointed with consent of the Great Powers. He was to have full executive power and was to be assisted by a central administrative council composed of members of all important sectarian communal groups. The first governor proved exceptionally able as a diplomat and administrator; and rule under the statute, redrawn in 1864, remained in effect with a great degree of success until the Ottomans assumed direct control during World War I.

SOCIAL CHANGES AND POLITICAL REFORMERS

Western European influence was indirect as well as direct; it could be seen in books and secular ideas, which affected political affairs more and more noticeably after the Crimean War. By the early 1870s about 160 books were published each year, chiefly in Istanbul. Many elite Ottomans, including especially members of the religious minorities, imitated French poetry, art, philosophy, and social forms; nationalism was discussed; European-style plays were performed; and Persian elegance of phrasing became outmoded. French manners, urbanity, and sophistication were now the fashion. The effect, however, of this innovative group upon Ottoman society as a whole was still limited to the urban areas, and some earlier cultural expressions, such as calligraphy and puppet shadow plays, continued to be quite popular.

More immediately, European style was influential in the design of new imperial palaces. Ponderous, opulent, and westernized in their interior decoration, these palaces marked a transformation of Ottoman imperial artistic traditions. The sultans of the Tanzimat era moved from the beautiful Topkapi Palace in old Istanbul to the new Dolmabahche Palace along the Bosphorus in 1853. Many parts of Istanbul were changed as streets were widened and straightened, transportation was improved, and urban services were increased.

A conservative influence came from the millions of Muslim immigrants who arrived in the Ottoman Empire from the provinces that had been lost to Russian and Balkan state expansionism. Resettlement of the refugees from the Caucasus, the Crimea, and the various Balkan regions was a costly process, but one that the Ottoman government welcomed. The refugees were viewed as a source of additional agricultural labor to work on productive land that had been vacant. One consequence of the refugee settlements was that the proportion of the Ottoman Empire's population that was Muslim substantially increased. The total population probably remained roughly constant despite this immigration, since endemic diseases, occasional starvation, war casualties, and outward migration tended to counterbalance the number of immigrants.

The Ottoman Land Law of 1858 enabled the new immigrants and others already settled on the land to obtain deeds and more security of tenure. Land ownership in most parts of the Ottoman Empire probably remained in the hands of small holders, although some large estates were created by nomadic leaders who registered as their own property enormous amounts of land that had been collectively utilized by their tribes. The central government also sold land in public auctions, and large sections could be accumulated by absentee investors, especially in regions newly brought under the effective control of the state. The land law and protection from raids by nomads enabled peasants to extend their planting of crops into outlying regions, as in Syria, Jordan, and Iraq.

Some of the Tanzimat changes affected the role of peasant and urban women. Some wealthy urban women were especially affected; for instance, their clothing became similar to that worn in western Europe. The central government began to train midwives, and thousands of girls attended new public and private schools by the end of the century. A women's teachers training school was established, and female education was supported by some male political leaders and reformers, although primary education remained in the hands of the relatively conservative ulama. Most families continued to be nuclear in structure, with a wife and husband and their children living together. New factories often hired women, especially in silk-reeling mills, and paid them very low wages, while many village and urban women worked in their homes producing such products as yarn, cloth, and carpets. Many western Europeans favored a change in the status of women, with the result that in the minds of conservative Ottomans feminism became associated with foreign claims of cultural superiority.

The Ottoman reformers were led by Reshid Pasha, who died in 1858. He had been for twenty years the most commanding figure in the Ottoman government, having held all the high offices at one time or another. As was the custom, he found young, talented men in the government service and advanced them to higher positions if their views agreed with his. Two, Mehmed Emin Ali Pasha and Kechejizade Mehmed Fuad Pasha, came to be regarded as Reshid's chief disciples. Both Ali and Fuad were liberals, reformers, and Freemasons; together they dominated the Ottoman government for fifteen years following the Hatt-i Humayun. Both were born in 1815, and for the decade from 1861 to 1871 one was always foreign minister while the other was usually grand vizir.

Ali Pasha, the son of an Istanbul shopkeeper, entered government service at the age of fifteen, moved into the famed translation bureau in 1833, became ambassador to London in 1841, foreign minister in 1846, and grand vizir in 1852 at the age of thirty-seven. During the Crimean War he served as foreign minister, and then in 1855 as grand vizir again. In 1856 he attended the Paris Peace Conference as the Ottoman envoy. When Reshid Pasha died in 1858, Ali was named grand vizir yet again.

A small, frail person who spoke hardly above a whisper, Ali Pasha knew when to be silent and possessed complete self-control. Ali, as an Ottoman leader, endeavored to uphold order in the state, to ensure prosperity for all, and to initiate gradual changes in government and society. He believed in mixed schools where Muslims and Christians could study together, and hoped for the development of a full equality among Ottomans. He was, however, opposed to the introduction of an elected constitutional government, arguing that the people were not sufficiently educated for that.

The only rival permitted in Ali Pasha's circle was his fellow moderate liberal, Fuad Pasha, who teamed so well with Ali yet differed from him in so many ways. Fuad, who belonged to a well-known Istanbul family, graduated from the Galatasaray medical school, where instruction was in French, and then served in the army medical corps. His fluency in French was such that his witticisms in that language became famous throughout Europe. Entering the translation bureau in 1837, he soon became its highest officer. Fuad lived in London and conducted special negotiations in Spain, Russia, and Egypt.

Fuad was tall, handsome, talkative, and much more westernized in his habits than was Ali. Nevertheless, Fuad was also devoted to the service of the Ottoman state. He strongly believed that to survive, the Ottoman Empire would have to change its political and civil institutions to keep pace with progress in Europe. Feeling that Islam was out of date in some respects, he argued that it should accept new truths. He moved to dampen the growing nationalisms in the Balkans by calling for an Ottoman identity and equality, with liberties for all non-Muslims. Fuad accompanied Sultan Abdulaziz and his nephews Murad and Abdulhamid in 1867 when they visited Paris and London, a trip that helped persuade the sultan to support Tanzimat reforms.

Fuad and Ali were the guiding hands of the late Tanzimat period, but ultimate legitimacy and power remained in the hands of the sultans of the Ottoman dynasty. Though others might carp at the Tanzimat leaders for pushing too slowly for changes, Fuad and Ali recognized that politics is the art of the possible and that change must be gradual.

YOUNG OTTOMANS

The Tanzimat was opposed by conservative Muslims in society and in the palace. On the other hand, there were those who chafed at the slow progress: by the mid–1860s quite a number of young Ottomans, both Muslims and non-Muslims, who had studied in Europe felt this way. Young army officers, medical students, junior government officials, and others criticized the shortcomings of the government in the newspapers. Following the terminology of such groups in Italy, France, and elsewhere, Europeans labeled them the Young Ottomans. Foremost among them was Namik Kemal, whose father was court astronomer (astrologer). Namik Kemal, a poet and an Ottomanist patriot, was a clerk for a time in the translation bureau but left this job for journalism. In 1873, his play *Vatan* (*Fatherland*) created such a stir that it was shut down by the government and Kemal was exiled.

Uprisings in Crete and appeasement of the Cretans by Istanbul infuriated the Young Ottomans. Abdulhamid Ziya joined Namik Kemal, turning his pen and influence against Ali, with whom he had a personal quarrel. An admirer of western science and Persian poetry, Ziya was an Ottoman patriot who in 1867 was exiled to Cyprus.

Many of the Young Ottomans went into exile in Europe, where they agitated for reforms in their homeland. Their lack of internal cohesiveness made it easy for the central government in the late 1860s and early 1870s to secure their services and separate them one from another.

MIDHAT PASHA AND THE CONSTITUTION

Those government officials who most strongly favored westernization and reform were led by Ahmed Midhat Pasha (1822–1884), an able provincial administrator. After he put many reform ideas into practice as governor of Nish, Midhat was recalled in 1864 to Istanbul, where he helped draw up new regulations for the provinces. The empire was divided into twenty-eight large provinces (vilayets), with mixed tribunals for cases involving

Christians and Muslims and assemblies of notables to counsel the governor. Yet, since the power of appointing the governor rested in the hands of the sultan or his advisers, the quality of administration enjoyed by a province depended almost wholly upon the governor's personality and the sultan's backing.

The energetic Midhat returned to Bulgaria, where for a few years he served as governor of the new Province of the Danube. He established roads, bridges, orphanages, schools, hospitals, agricultural credit cooperatives, and an official newspaper. Even more important was his securing of law and order and his just treatment of the Christian population. On the other hand, Midhat Pasha ruthlessly suppressed outbursts of nationalism aimed at self-government and independence. In rapid succession following the Bulgarian assignment, Midhat chaired the imperial council of state and was governor of Baghdad, where he also enacted many modernizing reforms. He became grand vizir for three months in 1872, held the governorship of Salonica, and then retired to private life in Istanbul.

The government of the Ottoman Empire had lacked strong leaders since the death, in 1869, of Fuad Pasha and, in 1871, of Ali Pasha. Bankruptcy and uprisings in the Balkans, with their corollary of European intervention, heartened Midhat Pasha to engineer the deposition of the incompetent Abdulaziz and install as sultan his nephew, Murad V, on May 30, 1876. In August Murad had a nervous breakdown and was replaced by his brother Abdulhamid II (r. 1876–1909), meaning that the Ottoman Empire had three sultans in one year. Midhat mistakenly assumed that Abdulhamid would support liberal political changes.

Under the direction of Midhat Pasha as grand vizir, on December 23, 1876, Abdulhamid proclaimed a written constitution that Midhat and others had been formulating since the deposition of Abdulaziz. Accepted with great rejoicing among the liberals of Istanbul, the constitution provided for a cabinet and an elected parliament. It reaffirmed that all subjects of the sultan were equal, regardless of race or creed. Freedom of religion, education, and the press were guaranteed.

The outbreak of war with Russia enabled Abdulhamid in 1878 to suspend parliament, exile Midhat, and quietly ignore the constitution. By the end of the war and the settlement at the Congress of Berlin, Abdulhamid and his entourage had control over the central government. In 1884 the sultan ordered Midhat to be strangled. Modernization through liberal political reform was killed along with Midhat.

OTTOMAN FINANCES

No matter which sultan reigned, the expenses of the state increased throughout the century. The central government in Istanbul needed increasingly large sums of money to pay for wars, military modernization, and other changes. Beginning with the Crimean War, the Ottoman government contracted loans to meet the extraordinary expenses of the army and navy.

Between 1854 and 1875 the Ottoman Empire borrowed about $1 billion from western Europe; at the end of that period almost nothing remained to show for such a vast sum—except debts. The tax system was still antiquated, increasing income could not keep up with the costs of government, and there was a yearly excess of imports over exports. The great bulk of imports were consumer goods, and loans did not bring in the capital goods that in the end might have expanded Ottoman productivity and facilitated repayment of the loans.

Once the habit was fixed, loans were contracted almost every year. Interest rates were high, and as long as confidence could be maintained, European bankers had little difficulty in floating bonds, with enormous profits to be made. The theory of the right of European governments to intervene in Ottoman affairs grew with the series of loans.

By 1875 Ottoman foreign debts had risen to £200 million, bearing annual charges of £12 million, while the total revenue was only £22 million. This meant that the empire had one of the highest debts per person of any country in the world at that time. Severe famines in central Anatolia and a financial crisis in Europe contributed to the Ottoman dilemma; the government had to partially suspend payments of interest. The empire was bankrupt.

The growing financial crisis affected every part of the empire. The burden of the debt left the treasury a diminishing sum with which to meet expenses of government. Officials who went unpaid resorted to corrupt practices, while the government adopted harsher methods of taxation. Peasants everywhere were squeezed; the most serious rebellion burst in Bosnia.

BALKAN PROBLEMS

About one-half of all Ottoman subjects lived in the Balkans, where many local Muslim leaders had resisted the Tanzimat innovations. Bosnian Muslims rebelled in 1849, only to be subdued in 1850. Financial difficulties called for rigid collection of taxes in Bosnia in 1875, even though there had been a scanty harvest the previous year. Serbian Christians in Herzegovina and other Balkan areas erupted over the stringent measures. Christian insurgents tasted considerable success—and Pan-Slavs in Russia and Serbia were jubilant.

The Balkan revolt spread to Bulgarian districts, where economic prosperity and a cultural revival had opened the way to ethnic nationalism. Long centuries of Ottoman rule had permitted Muslim notables and Greek Orthodox clergy to have local authority. By the 1830s Bulgarian schools, history, language, folklore, and national consciousness began to develop rapidly as the Bulgarian region became linked economically to western Europe. With the creation of a Bulgarian Orthodox Exarchate in 1870 nationalism grew ever faster and Macedonia became a battleground between Greek and Bulgarian. Further unrest arose when Muslim refugees from the Crimea and the Caucasus settled in Bulgarian regions; the refugees terrorized peasants and kept villages in a state of perpetual siege. Christian peasants also wished to gain control of agricultural land owned by Muslim notables. Irregular Ottoman militias perpetrated massacres, most notably upon the villagers of Batak, who were preparing to join in an uprising. Perhaps 5000 individuals out of 7000 in Batak were killed. Reports from correspondents, describing many shocking incidents, appeared in London newspapers.

Montenegro and Serbia declared war against the Ottoman Empire in July 1876, but Ottoman armies defeated the Serbs, whereupon Russia gave the sultan an ultimatum, leading to a December 1876 conference of the Great Powers in Istanbul to discuss peace between Serbia and the Ottomans.

At the beginning of the conference, the sultan proclaimed a written constitution for his empire. Counting on the friendship of Britain, the Ottomans refused to go along with the Great Powers, and the conference broke up in January 1877. Peace was signed directly between Serbia and the sultan in February upon the basis of the status quo.

RUSSIAN-OTTOMAN WAR

Hoping to gain territory and influence, Russia declared war in April 1877. The Ottoman navy dominated the Black Sea, but Romania declared full independence from the Ottoman Empire and aided the Russians, who passed the Danube and appeared to be on their way to Edirne and Istanbul. Then the Ottoman general Osman Pasha dug in near Plevna in Bulgaria, resisting the Russian siege from July until December. The Ottomans mobilized armies totaling about 250,000 men on the European and Caucasian fronts. Meanwhile, Ottoman forces were defeated at Kars by a Russian general, in Herzegovina by the Montenegrins, and at Nish by the Serbs. The Ottomans threw themselves upon the mercy of the European powers as Russia, Romania, Serbia, and Montenegro continued the war, occupying Edirne in January 1878. Muslims fled before the advancing armies, since Russian and Balkan armies were as brutal in their atrocities as Ottoman irregulars had been at Batak.

As the Russians approached Istanbul, they placed their headquarters at the village of Yeşilköy (San Stefano), only a few miles from the Ottoman capital. Under this threat, the Ottomans signed the disastrous Treaty of San Stefano in March 1878, recognizing the independence of Montenegro, Serbia, and Romania, each of which received considerable territory at Ottoman expense. Bosnia and Herzegovina obtained autonomous rule. Russia solidified its control of the whole Caucasus region, acquiring Batum and Kars, and eastern Anatolia up to Trabzon and Erzurum. Bulgaria was created within the Ottoman Empire as a large, self-governing Christian principality from the Aegean Sea to the Black Sea and westward to Albania, including Macedonia. As a final blow the Ottomans were to pay a large indemnity to Russia.

THE CONGRESS OF BERLIN

Almost before the ink dried, objections to San Stefano arose. The creation of "Big Bulgaria" produced a storm—Greece, Serbia, Romania, and Montenegro protested, and representatives of Albanian groups petitioned to be heard. Britain and Austria demanded a new settlement. First, the Anglo-Ottoman convention of June 1878, ceding the administration of Ottoman Cyprus to Britain, was announced; then at Berlin, on July 13, 1878, a galaxy of statesmen concluded new arrangements for the Balkans.

The Treaty of Berlin reduced the "Big Bulgaria" of the Treaty of San Stefano to a smaller autonomous principality, where the prince would be chosen by an assembly of Bulgarian notables and confirmed by the sultan. The province of Eastern Rumelia was constructed, where the governor-general was appointed by the sultan with consent of the Great Powers. Macedonia remained Ottoman rather than becoming part of Bulgaria.

Romania, Montenegro, and Serbia became independent; and Austria-Hungary occupied and administered Bosnia and Herzegovina. Kars and Batum were given to Russia. Finally, the Ottomans pledged religious liberty and civil equality for the sultan's subjects in Europe and Asia alike.

The loss of so much territory in Europe, bankruptcy, three sultans in one year, declaration of a constitution, and the cumulative effect of nearly forty years of reforms and foreign policy crises left the Ottoman state reeling by the time of the Congress of Berlin. European imperialism seemed stronger than ever. While Ottoman military reforms and expenditures had increased the power of the army, they had not been sufficient to defend the empire against Russia. Only foreign diplomatic intervention had stopped the humiliating San Stefano agreement from being put into effect; the Congress of Berlin arrangements, while an improvement, were still a major defeat for the Ottoman Empire.

Using the Hatt-i Sharif and the Hatt-i Humayun, the leaders of the Tanzimat had succeeded in reforming many bureaucratic practices, while Ottoman commerce increased dramatically and the Ottomans became part of the world economy. By the 1870s the reforms began to reach beyond the cities and towns to affect some of the peasants, although most of the villagers and the nomads were still unaffected. But European influence inside the empire was also growing, often by means of minority religious groups who identified their interests with those of external governments. The success of the Tanzimat was also limited by the size and complexity of the empire. Decreeing reforms in Istanbul was one thing, but executing the changes throughout the enormous empire was another. Since by the late 1870s the Ottoman Tanzimat seemed insufficient to save the empire from destruction, another approach to government, reform, and foreign policy seemed to be essential.

REFERENCES

Many volumes mentioned in earlier chapters concerned with the Ottoman Middle East relate to subjects discussed in this chapter. Works cited in Chapters 16, 17, and 20 through 23 are especially pertinent.

Augustinos, Gerasimos: *The Greeks of Asia Minor: Confession, Community, and Ethnicity in the Nineteenth Century.* Kent, Ohio: Kent State University Press, 1992. A sensitive treatment of the subject for the period 1840–1880.

Black, Cyril E., and L. Carl Brown, eds.: *Modernization in the Middle East: The Ottoman Empire and Its Afro-Asian Successors.* Princeton, N.J.: Darwin, 1992. Highly useful summaries of current knowledge; the first part deals chiefly with the late Ottoman period, while the second part covers the twentieth century.

Çelik, Zeynep: *The Remaking of Istanbul: Portrait of an Ottoman City in the Nineteenth Century.* Seattle: University of Washington Press, 1986. An excellent study of urban change.

Clay, Christopher: *Gold for the Sultan: Western Bankers and Ottoman Finance 1856–1881: A Contribution to Ottoman and to International Financial History.* London: Tauris, 2000. A lengthy and detailed account of the Imperial Ottoman Bank and Ottoman finances.

Davis, Fanny: *The Ottoman Lady: A Social History from 1718 to 1918.* New York: Greenwood, 1986. Along with charming anecdotes of upper-class Ottoman women, there are numerous bits of information on economic, cultural, and political activities of women in Ottoman cities, especially Istanbul.

Davison, Roderic H.: *Reform in the Ottoman Empire, 1856–1876.* Princeton, N.J.: Princeton University Press, 1963. Still the best available study of this time period.

———: "Midhat Pasha." *Encyclopaedia of Islam.* New ed. Vol. 6, pp. 1031–1035. Leiden: Brill, 1991. An introduction to this leading figure of the Tanzimat.

Devereux, Robert: *The First Ottoman Constitutional Period: A Study of the Midhat Constitution and Parliament.* Baltimore, Md.: Johns Hopkins University Press, 1963. This work, with those by Davison and Mardin, makes a fine trilogy.

Fawaz, Leila Tarazi: *Merchants and Migrants in Nineteenth-Century Beirut.* Cambridge: Harvard University Press, 1983. Traces the growth of the city and the changes in its social and economic composition.

Findley, Carter Vaughn: *Ottoman Civil Officialdom: A Social History.* Princeton, N.J.: Princeton University Press, 1989. An impressive study of how the central bureaucracy changed from 1789 to World War I.

Finnie, David H.: *Pioneers East: The Early American Experience in the Middle East.* Cambridge: Harvard University Press, 1967. Concerned with all American interests, from diplomats to navy men, shipbuilders, scholars, and missionaries.

Issawi, Charles: *The Economic History of Turkey, 1800–1914.* Chicago: University of Chicago Press, 1980. A wide variety of readings drawn from foreign and Ottoman sources that illustrate economic history.

———: *An Economic History of the Middle East and North Africa.* New York: Columbia University Press, 1982. An outstanding volume that concentrates on the nineteenth century.

Jelavich, Charles, and Barbara Jelavich: *The Establishment of the Balkan National States, 1804–1920.* Seattle: University of Washington Press, 1977. An excellent survey of the various Balkan countries.

Karpat, Kemal H.: *Ottoman Population, 1830–1914: Demographic and Social Characteristics.* Madison: University of Wisconsin Press, 1985. Very useful statistical information and fine analysis.

Lewis, Norman N.: *Nomads and Settlers in Syria and Jordan, 1800–1980.* Cambridge: Cambridge University Press, 1987. A stimulating study of nomadic tribes and their interactions with Ottomans and the national states of the twentieth century.

Makdisi, Ussama: *The Culture of Sectarianism: Community, History, and Violence in Nineteenth-Century Ottoman Lebanon.* Berkeley: University of California Press, 2000. Deals with sectarianism as a practice and a discourse, as well as the impact of Ottoman modernization and European colonialism from 1840 to 1860.

Ma'oz, Moshe: *Ottoman Reform in Syria and Palestine, 1840–1861.* London: Oxford University Press, 1968. A well-balanced description of political, social, and religious conditions.

Mardin, Şerif: *The Genesis of Young Ottoman Thought: A Study in the Modernization of Turkish Political Ideas.* Syracuse, N.Y.: Syracuse University Press, 2000. This reprint of the 1962 edition is still the best study of early Turkish nationalism.

Masters, Bruce: *Christians and Jews in the Ottoman Arab World.* Cambridge: Cambridge University Press, 2001. A fine study of social status, sectarian relations, and political identities with an emphasis on Syria.

Ochsenwald, William: *Religion, Society and the State in Arabia: The Hijaz under Ottoman Control, 1840–1908.* Columbus: Ohio State University Press, 1984. Points out that many Tanzimat changes were not put into effect in distant provinces.

Owen, Roger: *The Middle East in the World Economy, 1800–1914.* Rev. ed. London: Tauris, 1993. An excellent study.

Palairet, Michael: *The Balkan Economies c. 1800–1914: Evolution without Development.* Cambridge: Cambridge University Press, 1997. The author argues that in some cases the Balkan states that became independent were better off economically under Ottoman rule.

Pamuk, Şevket: *The Ottoman Empire and European Capitalism, 1820–1913: Trade, Investment and Production.* Cambridge: Cambridge University Press, 1987. A sophisticated analysis, based on the "dependency school" approach, which sees the Ottoman Empire as part of Europe's periphery.

Polk, William R., and Richard L. Chambers, eds.: *Beginnings of Modernization in the Middle East: The Nineteenth Century.* Chicago: University of Chicago Press, 1968. Twenty papers by distinguished scholars on the many facets of change in the nineteenth-century Middle East.

Quataert, Donald: *Ottoman Manufacturing in the Age of the Industrial Revolution.* Cambridge: Cambridge University Press, 1993. A convincing essay showing that Ottoman household and workshop textile production adapted to new circumstances despite European competition.

Rosenthal, Steven T.: *The Politics of Dependency: Urban Reform in Istanbul.* Westport: Greenwood Press, 1980. Traces the European-supported reform in municipal government in parts of Istanbul during the Tanzimat.

Ruggles, D. Fairchild, ed.: *Women, Patronage and Self-Representation in Islamic Societies.* Albany: State University of New York Press, 2000. Interesting chapters on Ottoman and Safavid women's history.

Said, Edward: *Orientalism.* New York: Pantheon, 1978 and subsequently reprinted. A highly influential and controversial work which examines western scholars who studied the Middle East.

Shields, Sarah D.: "Take-off into Self-Sustained Peripheralization: Foreign Trade, Regional Trade and Middle East Historians." *Turkish Studies Association Bulletin* 17 (1993): 1–23. Argues that Ottoman internal trade was more important than commerce with Europe.

Toledano, Ehud R.: *Slavery and Abolition in the Ottoman Middle East.* Seattle: University of Washington Press, 1998. Examines slavery as a phenomenon and how it has been interpreted by contemporary as well as more recent thinkers.

CHAPTER 26

Abdulhamid II and Autocratic Reform

Sultan Abdulhamid II, who ruled the Ottoman Empire from 1876 to 1909, was the last of the Ottoman sovereigns to exercise real power. He was viewed by Ottoman and European liberals as a tyrant, and he did in fact suppress the constitution of 1876, oppose nationalism, and construct an elaborate system of spies. On the other hand, he also continued many elements of the Tanzimat, with an emphasis on technical, educational, and military modernization. Earlier reforms had begun slowly; now they finally began to take effect. The sultan sought to increase central control over the provinces despite growing nationalist opposition to Ottoman rule. In exercising political power Abdulhamid resembled his grandfather, Mahmud II, more than his Tanzimat-era father, Abdulmejid. Among Sultan Abdulhamid's chief policy concerns were European imperialism, the state's finances, and building railways.

ACCESSION OF ABDULHAMID II

The remarkable year 1876 witnessed three sultans ruling the Ottoman Empire. Abdulhamid II became ruler in a period of intense crisis. Internally, the tragic situation in Bulgaria and Bosnia had provoked rebellion and severe repression. A year earlier, in 1875, the empire had to suspend payment of interest on its bonds. International events set in motion by these events, which have been discussed earlier, included the Russian-Ottoman War, the Treaty of San Stefano, and the Congress of Berlin. By 1878 about one-third of the territory of the empire had been lost.

Faced with these problems, two political groups favoring different solutions had emerged. One was distinctly liberal and pro-western European in its desire for constitutional government, fiscal reforms, and industrial and commercial expansion. The other was conservative and favored strong rule by the monarch. The liberals were led by Midhat Pasha and Husain Avni Pasha.

On May 31, 1876, Midhat and Husain Avni deposed the extravagant Abdulaziz and brought Murad V to the sultanate. Two popular liberal journalists, Abdulhamid Ziya and

Namik Kemal, became the sultan's private secretaries. Midhat proceeded to draft a constitution that limited the power of the sultan, created a parliament, and appealed to liberals in Europe. Unfortunately for the Ottoman liberals, the former sultan Abdulaziz committed suicide, a crazed officer broke into a cabinet meeting and assassinated four officials, and the strain of rule proved too much for Murad, who became incapable of governing. Affairs of state stood still until in August Midhat deposed Murad in favor of Abdulhamid II.

The new sultan promised to support the liberal party, but he had much more sympathy for the conservatives. Abdulhamid did make Midhat grand vizir and promulgated the constitution. However, Midhat was soon placed aboard the sultan's yacht and carried away to exile. Parliament met in March 1877, but Abdulhamid obtained its adjournment after a few weeks and, with the Russian army almost in Istanbul in February 1878, adjourned it and suspended the constitution. Until 1908 the constitution was printed each year in the official register but remained ignored. The war with Russia served as the excuse for its suppression and became the pretext for Abdulhamid to rule in the fashion of his pre-Tanzimat predecessors.

OTTOMAN PUBLIC DEBT ADMINISTRATION

Bankruptcy in 1875, followed so closely by defeat in the war with Russia, compelled Abdulhamid to accept measures limiting Ottoman sovereignty. In 1881, the Ottoman central government arranged with European bondholders' groups to reduce and consolidate the £210 million of the external debt of the empire to £106 million. The Council of Administration of the Ottoman Public Debt was authorized to collect and disburse revenues and taxes on behalf of the bondholders. The Public Debt Administration regularized Ottoman finances and eventually reestablished the sultan's credit, although large sums of money had to be transferred abroad. By the late 1880s about one-fifth of all revenues were paid as interest on the debt.

Within a few years after its inception, the Ottoman Public Debt Administration became more than merely a collecting and banking agency. Slowly, debts began to be liquidated and, even more important, Ottoman credit was rehabilitated so that money could be found to build railways and other western innovations. In almost every case in which Ottoman credit was involved, an agreement provided that the Ottoman Public Debt Administration should act for the government.

Sometimes the Ottoman Public Debt Administration served as an instrument of economic imperialism. By and large, however, it recognized that the interests of the bondholders would be best served by an improved economy. Sill later, after World War I, the Turkish Republic accepted the validity of the Ottoman debts but refused to accept the kind of foreign intervention implied in the Public Debt Administration; the latter died quietly in 1923, when the Treaty of Lausanne omitted all reference to it.

CONTINUING REFORMS

Abdulhamid II eliminated the internal political opposition and stopped political liberalism. Some opponents were bought, while Midhat Pasha was secretly strangled in Arabia and other illustrious Ottomans died in exile. Abdulhamid, who eventually came to live in terror of his own overthrow, had an elaborate system of spies. He took refuge at Yildiz Palace in Istanbul, which he enhanced and rebuilt.

Faced with so many problems, Sultan Abdulhamid embarked on a new policy that aimed at securing internal and external support for him as the caliph of the Muslims and the leader of the Pan-Islamic cause. Unlike most of his ancestors, who had viewed the title of caliph as only a minor one among many honorifics, Abdulhamid emphasized a claim to be the successor of the prophet Muhammad and leader of the ummah everywhere. Within the Ottoman lands this was an effective means of gaining legitimacy with many Sunni Muslims, especially the growing middle class, as well as new refugees from areas seized by Christian states. The empire's population now consisted of a majority of Muslims, because of the loss of many Christian-inhabited regions in the Balkans.

Pan-Islam, as opposed to the secularizing tendencies of the Tanzimat, stressed the role of the sultan-caliph in upholding the shariah and Hanafi Islam. Abdulhamid carefully used Islam and its symbols as a way of legitimizing his rule while also building international acceptance of the Ottoman Empire by participating in international congresses and expositions. The sultan argued that all Muslims should rally to defend the Ottoman Empire—the largest remaining independent Muslim state. Abdulhamid encouraged the growth of Pan-Islam by enlisting Sufi orders, using Ottoman diplomats abroad, subsidizing newspapers, and sending emissaries to all parts of the Muslim world. Some support for Pan-Islam emerged in areas such as India, Africa, and southeast Asia, thereby threatening the European imperial powers who controlled those regions and making them more willing to try to conciliate the Ottoman state.

Despite his firm determination to centralize all power in his own hands, in many ways Abdulhamid continued elements of the reforms that had characterized the Ottoman Empire since the days of Selim III. The sultan strongly favored military modernization and new weapons procurement. He employed Germans to train the army, while England was engaged to organize a police force. Fine new ships for the navy were ordered in England, France, and the United States.

Changes in government administration and society proceeded in those areas where Abdulhamid was not categorically opposed to reform. Government bureaucracy and revenues increased dramatically, even though the sultan was often not able to pay civil servants on time. As a result, employees often became corrupt and inefficient. In 1879, Abdulhamid appointed the minister of justice, Mehmed Said Pasha, as grand vizir, with the hope that Said would meet the pressing problems of the empire in a traditional fashion. Said had earlier reorganized the Ministry of Justice.

While minister of justice, Said Pasha had written a memorandum to Abdulhamid proposing financial reforms to strengthen the state and improve the army, administrative reforms to end the drift toward local autonomy, and educational reforms to achieve greater allegiance to Abdulhamid from his Muslim subjects. By this initiative Said Pasha became grand vizir, a post he held eight different times.

Said Pasha also understood the need to adjust the Ottoman system to the realities of Europe, which were pressing upon the empire. After 1885, however, Said Pasha had difficulty in overcoming Abdulhamid's suspicion of innovation; Said's power waned, and his later terms as grand vizir were of short duration.

WOMEN, THE PRESS, AND EDUCATION

Many changes were also underway in areas beyond administrative reforms. A particularly controversial issue for the Ottomans was the status of women. Political liberals favored female education, while conservatives were opposed. About one-third of school-age girls attended primary schools by 1900, and some women became school teachers. Upper-class urban Muslim women still wore veils in public, but in the 1890s the veils became lighter and more transparent. Elite urban married couples began to visit the homes of other couples on social occasions. Some exceptional women wrote poetry or essays and learned foreign languages. Women in the 1890s began to publish illustrated magazines and newspapers specializing in women's issues and promoting Ottoman services and manufactured goods. It was fashionable in Istanbul and other large cities to have professional photographers take family pictures. Women also preserved a varied oral culture centered around ceremonies such as weddings.

Poorer women sometimes worked in new circumstances, such as in newly established small factories, where women tended to receive lower wages than men. However, most village, nomadic, and urban women apparently continued to work in traditional occupations, especially in the home, assisting in the fields or with the herds, and in handicraft production, as in the rapidly expanding area of carpet manufacture.

The press had a difficult time during the reign of Abdulhamid, even though circulations increased. In the 1860s several Turkish-language newspapers had been launched, most of which were liberal in their attitudes toward government. Ziya and Namik Kemal were the most noteworthy and capable editors and writers. But Abdulhamid enforced censorship, and newspaper work meant "patriotic martyrdom," since editors and authors were almost invariably exiled. Ziya died a broken man in 1880 in Adana and Namik Kemal followed in 1887. Many writers lived and published their works abroad and sent them into the Ottoman Empire through the protection of the various foreign post offices established under the capitulations. Abdulhamid controlled the press and suspended opposition papers as they appeared. But he did not have enough spies to police the entire empire.

Yet the effects of writers reached beyond the strictly political, educating the literate population to developments and thoughts in the outside world. Over 300 books were published in 1890, many of them exciting French novels translated into Turkish that introduced Ottomans to a very different world. And phonographs and films reached the urban centers of the empire shortly after their invention, providing new media for cultural diffusion and entertainment.

Two authors, Tevfik Fikret and Ahmed Midhat, left their marks during these decades of Abdulhamid's rule. Fikret, whose writings flowered later, was editor from 1895 to 1901 of the *Servet-i Fünun* (Treasury of Science), which at first was an illustrated scientific and literary supplement to an Istanbul evening newspaper and then was an independent periodical. This pictorial newsmagazine was directed to the educated elite and contained articles on biography, art, science, and literature. Because of censorship and the strict prohibition of even indirect political comment, Fikret and other authors attacked social ills through fictional writing and introduced readers to European cultural and intellectual life.

The most prolific author of the period was Ahmed Midhat, the son of a humble cloth merchant of Istanbul. Educated by his elder brother in a simple elementary school, Ahmed

Midhat entered government in the civil service, which he left in 1871 at the age of twenty-seven to be a printer and a writer. He fell in with liberals and found himself deported to Rhodes for four years, returning with most of the exiles upon the deposition of Abdulaziz. In 1877 he published a book vindicating Abdulhamid's accession and title to the throne, an act that won for him the directorship of the state printing press. For the next thirty-one years this mediocrity made a great contribution to the development of Ottoman society.

Ahmed Midhat edited a daily newspaper, *Interpreter of Truth,* that had a weekly supplement distributed to the students of the nation's elementary schools. Most of the stories were written or translated by Ahmed Midhat, who at the same time was writing books, more than 150 in all, on history, ethics, religion, philosophy, and science, as well as producing many works of fiction. He also wrote separate histories of European countries and a three-volume world history. These were the first serious efforts to give the ordinary reader of Turkish a view of history beyond the Islamic world. Because Ahmed Midhat did not possess outstanding style or distinction and had little originality, men of literary talent were contemptuous of his work. Yet his prodigious outpouring of books, periodicals, and newspapers—particularly those for schoolchildren—probably did more to change the outlook of the Ottomans, educating them for a more secular and European world, than the work of any other author.

Public education for boys and girls was promoted in 1880 when, in a lengthy memorandum, the grand vizir Said stressed the importance of an improved and greatly extended educational system. Throughout the provinces the number of elementary and secondary schools was greatly increased and teacher training schools were established. The new schools often had ulama teachers, emphasized Islam in the curriculum, and sought to strengthen loyalty to the sultan-caliph. There were a million students in the public schools by 1895, plus tens of thousands in foreign educational institutions, while the literacy rate increased steadily throughout the nineteenth century—reaching perhaps 5 percent by 1876 and 15 percent by 1914. Said opened a school for training civil servants for the government. Eighteen new professional schools or faculties were founded in Istanbul, teaching law, finance, fine arts, commerce, civil engineering, and veterinary medicine. Finally, the Imperial University in Istanbul opened in 1901.

The spread of western thought and the mixing together of pupils from many locales in Ottoman schools swelled the ranks of the discontented, some of whom fled as exiles to western Europe. Despite this, Abdulhamid continued to found many schools and even supplied the students with pocket money in hopes they would remain loyal to their patron. Perhaps because the teachers in the government medical and military schools had had the most European experience, their students were the most unsettled of all. In pursuing their studies many were exposed to French or German, which immediately opened to them the ideas of nineteenth-century Europe. As a result, army officers and medical men came to hold positions of political leadership all out of proportion to their numbers in society.

THE ARMENIAN QUESTION

Many Europeans disliked Abdulhamid most because of his treatment of the Armenian minority. As national aspirations had earlier stirred Serbs, Greeks, Romanians, and Bulgars, so some Armenians were moved in the latter half of the nineteenth century to seek a separate identity. Most of the Ottoman Empire's Armenians lived in its eastern Anatolian provinces; many Armenians were also subjects of the Russian Empire, living in the regions of the Caucasus close to the Ottoman border.

Muslim Turks and Kurds, Greeks, and Armenians in Anatolia were relatively prosperous between 1878 and 1911, as the peninsula's population increased by about one-half. Of the 17 million or so people living in Anatolia in 1911–1912, about 1.5 million were Armenians and about the same number were Greeks, while a large majority, about 14.5 million, were Muslims. Of the latter, most were Turkish speakers, but in the eastern provinces there were many Kurdish speakers and users of other languages as well.

Encouraged by the Russian government and stimulated by European and American missionaries, the three Armenian Christian religious communities—Gregorian, Catholic, and Protestant—and their respective educational institutions worked to develop national consciousness. Political societies flourished, and visions of an independent Armenia were encouraged by revolutionary committees in Russia.

Abdulhamid became frightened of the Armenian situation. He feared that six or more eastern provinces forming the Armenian highlands, where most of the Armenians were concentrated, and Little Armenia, or Cilicia, might become separated from the empire. To subdue the Armenian nationalists and forestall the possibility of an Armenian state, from 1894 to 1897 violent attacks upon the villages and massacres were perpetrated especially by Kurdish irregular Ottoman forces. Killings of Armenians occurred in many places, even in Istanbul. In all, perhaps 100,000 or more Armenians lost their lives.

These government atrocities had a very deep effect. The few revolutionary societies were wiped out; Armenians were cowed; and many thoughtful Ottomans were genuinely depressed by their government's action. Charitable foreign aid societies provided some relief, but emigration appeared to be the only solution. Economic life in many areas was disrupted. The British, French, Italian, and American governments protested in vain against Ottoman treatment of Armenians. Newspapers, magazines, churches, and lecture halls echoed to stories of the "Terrible Turks." As a result, for several decades western governmental and diplomatic actions in the Ottoman Empire were guided to a considerable degree by unfriendly public opinion in the west.

CRETE

Anti-Ottoman feeling was already widespread on the island of Crete even before Abdulhamid became sultan. The quality of government on Crete varied greatly, since the distance of the island from Istanbul left governors considerable autonomy. In the 1860s the better-educated subscribed to Greek nationalism, the first outburst for union with Greece taking place in 1866. Desultory fighting and Ottoman countermeasures persisted until 1870.

In 1885, a concentration of European naval units at Crete placed a damper on Greek preparations for war against the Ottomans and discouraged Cretan enthusiasts for union with Greece. Nonetheless, disorders of various origins continued to maintain tension. In 1896 and 1897, after bloody battles on the streets of Canea between Greeks and Turks brought matters to a head, Prince George of Greece cut off Ottoman reinforcements and the Great Powers occupied Canea. Boiling national sentiment in Athens compelled the king to initiate a war against the Ottoman Empire. The Greco-Ottoman War of 1897 was a series of Greek disasters. Only the intervention of the Great Powers saved Athens from an Ottoman occupation. The Peace of Istanbul, which restored the boundaries, placed a heavy indemnity upon Greece. Even though the Ottomans won the war, the European powers in Crete recognized Prince George as high commissioner under the suzerainty of the sultan. The Muslim minority gradually emigrated from Crete; by 1908, when union with Greece was finally achieved, less than 10 percent of the population was Muslim.

MACEDONIA

Problems with Armenians and in Crete were enough to keep the Ottoman state embroiled with the European powers and to stampede the sultan into some unwise and bloody decisions. It was the complex affairs of Macedonia, however, that sealed his fate and substantiated the charge that the Balkans were the powder keg of Europe. Populated by Bulgarians, Turks, Greeks, Albanians, and other groups, Macedonia became the focus of the competitive nationalisms of the Balkans. When the Bulgarian Orthodox church permitted churches in Macedonia to choose between Greek and Bulgarian affiliation an explosion ensued, as nationalism and religion interacted. Nationalistic schools, newspapers, and books, as well as raids, village burning, kidnapping, and assassination, were employed to achieve nationalist ends.

A committee to advance a movement of "Macedonia for the Macedonians" was formed in Sofia, Bulgaria. It suggested the organization of an autonomous Macedonia with its own government at Salonica. The obvious intention was a repetition of the Eastern Rumelia episode and a union of Macedonia with Bulgaria. The proposition was rejected by all except the Bulgarians, and Macedonia sank into chaos. Ottoman police forces and the imposition of martial law were unable to cope with the situation. In 1903 the Mürzsteg Program, suggested by the Great Powers, went into effect. Accordingly, the British, French, Italians, Austrians, and Russians each policed an area of Macedonia. Although some regions were excluded from the agreement, European control was sufficiently successful to induce the Great Powers in 1908 to extend the Mürzsteg Program for another six years.

RAILWAYS AND ECONOMIC GROWTH

Despite international and internal turmoil, direct foreign investment in the Ottoman Empire tripled between 1890 and 1914, and France and Germany were the leaders in the development of the Ottoman infrastructure that ensued. It should be noted that Germany did not participate in the pacification of Macedonia. Until this era German imperial interests in the Ottoman Empire were small, since German leaders viewed the area as worthless to Germany, instead wanting only to keep Russia and Austria from fighting each other over the Balkans. But with the accession of Emperor Wilhelm II in 1888, Germany's role changed. In that year the Oriental Railway was completed from Vienna through to Istanbul, while a newly formed German syndicate, the Anatolian Railway Company, was granted a concession to construct a railroad from the Bosphorus to Ankara in central Anatolia; it was in operation by 1893.

German interest in the Ottoman Empire increased with the official visits of Emperor Wilhelm to Istanbul in 1889 and again in 1898; on the latter trip he also went to Jerusalem and Damascus, where he uttered a famous speech promising Muslims that the German Emperor would be their friend. But above all else, German interests focused upon railway concessions, which blossomed into the much-publicized Berlin-to-Baghdad venture.

Sultan Abdulhamid believed that railways would unify the empire and bring the central government more effective power over outlying regions. More of the resources of Anatolia and the Arab provinces would be developed, guaranteeing economic prosperity. The military capacity of the state would be improved and independence protected. Although railways and other such facilities, like telegraph networks, ports, and roads, were costly enterprises, it was thought that the results would amply repay the effort and money expended.

In the case of the Hijaz Railway, which linked Syria to Ottoman western Arabia, the Ottoman government itself financed and built a railroad between 1900 and 1908, reaching Medina by 1908. This project had a special religious character since it helped facilitate the Muslim pilgrimage to the holy cities. Other railways were foreign-built and foreign-owned. A favorite project of the sultan was building a railway from Istanbul's Asiatic suburbs to the Persian Gulf. British and French companies already had built and were operating several lines connecting Izmir with the Anatolian hinterland when the Anatolian Railway Company took over the British railroad from the Bosphorus to Izmit and extended it to Ankara. In 1896, other existing Asiatic railways included Jaffa-Jerusalem, and Beirut-Damascus-Aleppo lines. The government naturally desired to link all these together to form an integrated system, and also to push on to Iraq and the Persian Gulf.

The railway concessions usually called for a government subsidy to the construction firm, a guarantee of a minimum annual revenue, or both. For the line to Ankara, money was to come from the taxes of several provinces, the collection of these taxes being assigned to the Public Debt Administration.

Abdulhamid insisted that the railway should not approach the Mediterranean, where gunfire from enemy fleets could interrupt traffic. The Germans, therefore, proposed to proceed from Konya to Adana, then eastward to the valley of the Tigris near Mosul, and down the river past Baghdad, ending with a terminal on the Persian Gulf. British and French capitalists accepted the idea that the concession would be awarded to the Germans, and their governments were fully satisfied. In 1899 Britain safeguarded its military preponderance in the Gulf by an agreement to conduct all foreign relations for the shaikh of Kuwait; this permitted England to block the railroad's best terminus on the Persian Gulf and to gain an unofficial protectorate over Kuwait.

The Ottoman Empire paid tremendous sums not only for building the railway but also for guaranteeing annual operating receipts. In October 1904, the first section was opened. Building cost less than was expected, and profits were high. In 1909 a construction company was organized to undertake the second leg across difficult mountainous terrain. Certain bridges and tunnels in the Taurus Mountains were still not finished at the outbreak of war in 1914. Thus, a through route to northern Iraq or Syria from Anatolia was not opened completely to traffic until the post–World War I period.

The railways brought an agricultural revolution to Anatolia and Syria. New settlements were formed, greater amounts of produce were marketed, tax revenue from crops was increased, and more land was cultivated; grain and other heavy commodities were now much cheaper to ship. By 1910 guarantees for annual receipts were no longer necessary and railways were even paying profits into the Ottoman treasury.

By opening up vast areas to inexpensive transportation, the railways changed local economic conditions and helped integrate many districts into the world economy. The railways also helped Ottoman growth in general, although an international economic depression between 1873 and 1896 lowered the world prices for Ottoman exports, especially grains. Ottomans enjoyed a long period of economic upturn from 1889 to 1911, except for temporary setbacks in 1894–1897 and 1907–1909. A sign of the times was the opening of modern bank offices in many distant provincial towns, although most credit to local enterprises was still offered by traditional lenders at high rates of interest. Immigrants continued to come into the domains of the sultan, including Muslims fleeing European Christian control and persecution in such areas as the Balkans, Algeria, Crimea, and the Caucasus. Emigration was also substantial, especially from Lebanon and Syria; hundreds of thousands of Christians (and some Muslims) from those regions went to the Americas, including the United States, seeking greater opportunities. Some emigrants subsequently returned to Lebanon, where they formed the beginning of a rurally based, westernized middle class.

Despite the prosperity that was linked in large part to infrastructure development, the Ottoman government was constantly short of money to pay its troops, and the peasants who had to pay the agricultural tithe to tax farmers bore much of the burden of the empire's expenditures. By the 1900s, the Ottoman Empire had to pay about one-quarter of all spending for the interest and part of the principal of its debt, while expenditures on the military consumed 40 percent or more of the budget. Government civilian employment expanded to about 500,000 people.

The railways helped bring not only economic growth but also German influence, which many Ottomans found to be a relief from British and French colonialism. Usually Germans were more tactful and considerate of Ottoman feelings. But German inroads into the Middle East frightened the British, who after 1904 and 1907 convinced the French and Russian governments to cooperate with them in trying to block German aspirations.

Sultan Abdulhamid II was able to block most of the European states who sought to gain direct control of the central Ottoman Empire. After the disastrous losses at the beginning of his reign, little additional territory was taken from the Ottomans. Indeed, the only war the empire subsequently fought during his reign was marked by the victory over Greece. However, indirect European influence grew in the Ottoman Public Debt Administration, and in Macedonia and Crete, while most of the new railways were built by foreign capital. The sultan's Pan-Islamic policy became known to many foreign Muslims, but its chief effect was to reinforce the sense of loyalty of Ottoman Muslims.

Internally, the power of the central government was extended to many regions that had been part of the Ottoman Empire in name only; in Palestine, Iraq, and southern Syria, and in certain sections of Libya, the Hijaz, and Yemen Ottoman authority was established on a firmer basis. Even in autonomous Mount Lebanon the Ottomans managed to secure a long period of peace. But growing nationalism and political opposition threatened to overthrow the sultan. Autocratic reforms in such areas as railway construction were insufficient in the eyes of the young army officers who in 1908 sought a new path toward Ottoman reinvigoration.

REFERENCES

Many readings touch upon this chapter. Those cited in Chapters 16, 21, 22, 23, and 25 are particularly pertinent.

Akarli, Engin D.: "Economic Policy and Budgets in Ottoman Turkey, 1876–1909." *Middle Eastern Studies* 28 (1992): 443–476.

———: *The Long Peace: Ottoman Lebanon, 1861–1920.* Berkeley: University of California Press, 1993. An excellent study of political history.

Berkes, Niyazi: *The Development of Secularism in Turkey.* London: Hurst, 1998. This reprint of the 1964 edition remains a stimulating book on the subject.

Deringil, Selim: *The Well-Protected Domains: Ideology and the Legitimation of Power in the Ottoman Empire, 1876–1909.* London: Tauris, 1998. An examination of the means used by Sultan Abdulhamid to help legitimize his rule.

Edib, Halidé: *Memoirs.* New York: Century, 1926. The life of a western-educated Ottoman Turkish woman.

Frierson, Elizabeth B.: "Unimagined Communities: Women and Education in the Late-Ottoman Empire, 1876–1909." *Cultural Matrix* 9 (1995): 55–90.

Graham-Brown, Sarah: *Images of Women: The Portrayal of Women in Photography of the Middle East, 1860–1950.* New York: Columbia University Press, 1988. Numerous photographs demonstrate aspects of life and gender relations in the Ottoman Empire, Egypt, and Iran.

Haddad, William, and William Ochsenwald, eds.: *Nationalism in a Non-National State: The Dissolution of the Ottoman Empire.* Columbus: Ohio State University Press, 1977. Essays on the development of nationalism in the Ottoman Empire.

Karpat, Kemal H.: *The Politicization of Islam: Reconstructing Identity, State, Faith, and Community in the Late Ottoman State.* New York: Oxford University Press, 2001. Expands upon and modifies many of the points made by Jacob Landau in the work cited below.

Khater, Akram Fouad: *Inventing Home: Emigration, Gender, and the Middle Class in Lebanon, 1870–1920.* Berkeley: University of California Press, 2001.

Landau, Jacob M.: *The Politics of Pan-Islam: Ideology and Organization.* Oxford: Clarendon Press, 1994. This authoritative study begins with Ottoman Pan-Islam but also discusses later developments.

Ochsenwald, William: *The Hijaz Railroad.* Charlottesville: University Press of Virginia, 1980. Examines one aspect of Abdulhamid's Pan-Islamic policy and political centralization.

Quataert, Donald: *Social Disintegration and Popular Resistance in the Ottoman Empire, 1881–1908: Reactions to European Economic Penetration.* New York: New York

University Press, 1983. Excellent essays on various aspects of European economic investments in the Ottoman Empire. Especially valuable on the Anatolian railways.

Quataert, Donald, ed.: *Consumption Studies and the History of the Ottoman Empire, 1550–1922: An Introduction.* Albany: State University of New York Press, 2000. This interesting work concentrates on Istanbul with discussions of the history of such topics as food, fashion, photography, and newspapers.

Rogan, Eugene L.: *Frontiers of the State in the Late Ottoman Empire: Transjordan 1850–1921.* Cambridge: Cambridge University Press, 1999. An excellent analysis of the expansion of Ottoman power into Jordan and the consequences for its inhabitants.

Salt, Jeremy: *Imperialism, Evangelism and the Ottoman Armenians, 1878–1896.* London: Frank Cass, 1993. Using chiefly British and U.S. sources, this highly controversial work emphasizes the role of foreign promises and Armenian revolutionaries in provoking violent incidents.

CHAPTER 27

The Young Turks and Nationalism

In the years before 1908 a broad movement arose against the absolute power of Ottoman Sultan Abdulhamid II. This Young Turk opposition included a wide array of Ottomans, but its core consisted of Turkish-speaking Muslim army officers organized in the Committee of Union and Progress, who first limited the sultan's authority and then, in 1909, deposed him. During the short time from 1908 until the outbreak of World War I in 1914, the new government faced many foreign policy problems, including war with Italy and several wars in the Balkans. Domestically, there was a struggle for control of the central authority and a continuing process of defining the basic ideology of the state, with Ottoman, Islamic, and Turkish identities overlapping and in dispute.

The ethnic nationalist separatism that had started with the independence of Greece and the autonomy of Serbia continued in the last years of the Ottoman Empire as Arabs and other Ottoman subjects of different linguistic, ethnic, and religious backgrounds agitated for new cultural and political roles. When the Committee of Union and Progress leaders learned of Arab nationalism, they sought to suppress the Arab secret societies, arguing that the desperate situation of the empire by 1914 necessitated unity.

SECRET SOCIETIES

The Young Turk revolution of 1908 was a reaction to the political absolutism and repression during the long reign of Sultan Abdulhamid II. Added to this was the growing westernization of certain Ottomans and the effect of European liberal ideas upon Ottoman youth. After the suspension of the constitution of 1876, dissident Ottomans living in exile in Europe dreamed of governmental reform at home.

In 1889, at the Istanbul Military Medical College, a group of students organized a secret society, the Ottoman Unity Society, which subscribed to reformist ideas. Membership spread to other government schools. Society members who escaped to Europe joined with other Ottoman malcontents. The best known of these was Ahmed Riza (1859–1930), whose newspaper became the society's official publication. The society's programs of action were as varied as its membership, but most of the members denounced any thought of overthrowing the reigning family; it preached reform and the value of science, promoted westernization, favored secularism, and advocated Ottomanism and a strong government. Abdulhamid II should be removed, the constitution restored, and all would be well.

A series of arrests nipped in the bud the society's coup planned for 1896. The sultan shattered the now renamed Committee of Union and Progress.

Nevertheless, every class at the Military Academy was infected with the virus of revolution. At the General Staff Academy in 1905 a young leader named Mustafa Kemal (1881–1938; subsequently president of the Turkish Republic) was arrested as a revolutionary agitator on the very day he was commissioned. Later, when released and stationed in Damascus, he helped organize a secret revolutionary society among officers in Syria. Because Macedonia and its cosmopolitan center of Salonica were susceptible to revolutionary propaganda, Kemal sought a transfer there in 1907. In Salonica an influential secret society included in its earliest membership Mehmed Talat Bey and Colonel Jemal Bey. This group spread rapidly throughout the European provinces. Pledged to overthrow Abdulhamid and establish a just government, the society drew to its ranks liberal and freethinking Turks.

In 1907 fugitives from Salonica won over Ahmed Riza in Paris to the possibility of armed revolution. Abdulhamid's enemies joined them in a congress of Ottoman liberals, at which even an Armenian revolutionary society was represented. After this meeting the Paris and Salonica groups merged under the earlier-used name Committee of Union and Progress.

THE REVOLUTION

The real revolution began in the Middle East, not in Paris. Army mutinies became frequent in 1906, largely because of miserable conditions and arrears in pay. When rebellions were seen to bring immediate improvements, many more occurred in 1907, with civilians joining to protest against corrupt officials. In 1907 and 1908, there were crop failures in wide areas of the empire; the prices of grain and meat rose very sharply. Real income fell, and inflation increased. Beginning in June 1908, mutinies broke out in Macedonia, as Russia and England planned additional reforms that might end Ottoman rule there. Majors Enver and Niyazi and other officers took to the hills. Messages from scores of cities and towns poured into Istanbul, and meetings of soldiers and civilians proclaimed the constitution. After a fateful telegram on July 23 announced that the units in Macedonia would march on Istanbul on behalf of the constitution, Abdulhamid reluctantly restored it and ordered elections for members of the Chamber of Deputies.

The summer of 1908 was spent in preparing for the elections and readjusting government ministries in accordance with the wishes of the Committee of Union and Progress. Even though the committee wanted to depose the sultan, crowds in Istanbul cried out, "Long live the constitution!" and "Long live the sultan!" And Abdulhamid pretended that he was happy over the turn of events! The committee was not fooled but recognized that it did not have the force to depose him. Abdulhamid, following the committee's wishes, appointed Kamil Pasha grand vizir, and thus the committee indirectly controlled state affairs; the palace was isolated.

On December 17, 1908, in the chambers where Midhat's parliament had met thirty-one years earlier, Abdulhamid opened parliament. Major religious and national groups of the empire were represented. The best-organized group was the Macedonia branch of the Committee of Union and Progress, but it was far from having complete control of the situation. Ahmed Riza, who was chosen president of the Chamber of Deputies, served as a valuable figurehead for the anonymous members of the committee.

Members of parliament coalesced into three political groups. In addition to Union and Progress, there were the Liberal Unionists, who believed the solution to the ills of the empire could be found in creating a loosely federated state of locally autonomous provinces. The third group was the Muslim Association, which supported Pan-Islam and religious law. Union and Progress, however, showed its power in February 1909 by causing the downfall of the grand vizir on a motion of no confidence.

FAILURE OF THE COUNTERREVOLUTION

The Young Turks, led by the Committee of Union and Progress, held many different views on policy, and they were inexperienced in government. They retained a conspiratorial approach to exercising power. The committee members tended to favor an authoritarian interpretation of the constitution, economic nationalism, anti-imperialism, and general reform. Some of them came to view themselves as the saviors of the state, whose extreme peril in the next few years would, they argued, justify extreme measures to save the empire from destruction.

Initially the Committee of Union and Progress did not clearly dominate affairs. Freedom of the press increased, and satirical newspapers ventured to criticize both the former absolutism and the new regime. Social unrest was seen as Anatolian Railway Company workers and tens of thousands of other laborers went on strike, with both Muslims and non-Muslims often successfully acting together for economic goals. However, most of the people of the Ottoman Empire who lived in Anatolia and the Arab provinces were not prepared to abandon the system of the millets and the political superiority of Muslims as compared with non-Muslims. "Under the same blue sky we are all equal; we glory in being Ottomans,"—these often-quoted words of Enver, one of the committee members who later rose to fame, stirred emotions but were not accepted as fact.

A counterrevolution struck on April 12, 1909, and leading members of Union and Progress went into hiding. Developing among lower-level ulama and soldiers in Istanbul, the counterrevolution was inspired by the cries of "Down with the constitution," "Down with the committee," and "Long live the shariah." Abdulhamid gave his blessing to the counterrevolution.

The Committee of Union and Progress, however, acted decisively. Mahmud Shevket Pasha, commander of the army in Macedonia, was invited to Istanbul to defend the constitution. On April 24, Istanbul was occupied, and a few days later parliament deposed Abdulhamid, having obtained approval from the shaikh al-Islam. The new sultan, Mehmed V, a mild gentleman born in 1844, declared he had not read a newspaper in the last twenty years. He had been completely surrounded by his brother's spies and had lost all initiative. He was the perfect constitutional monarch for the committee. And the constitution of 1876 was amended to give greater authority to the parliament, which was dominated by the committee.

WAR WITH ITALY OVER LIBYA

The tasks before the new government would have staggered the most experienced administrators. Internal problems commanded the highest priority as many bureaucrats and army officers sympathetic to the old order were purged, but foreign affairs and war rose to occupy the minds of the committee and consumed the meager funds available. In October 1908, Bulgaria cut all ties with the sultan, Austria-Hungary announced annexation of Bosnia, and Crete declared union with Greece.

A far greater shock was delivered by the Italian ultimatum of September 1911, demanding that the Ottoman Empire cede Libya to Italy. The Italian government had been seeking overseas territories in Eritrea and Ethiopia. After Italy declared war, Ottoman forces were driven from the coastal areas of Libya, although guerrilla warfare continued in the interior. Because of its naval superiority Italy was able to occupy Rhodes and the Dodecanese Islands and shelled the Dardanelles. Sentiment ran high in the empire. Enver Bey, along with other officers of later distinction like Mustafa Kemal, made their way with difficulty to Libya, where they organized and for a time led a resistance movement in cooperation with the Sanusi Sufi organization.

As Ottoman victory was hopeless, and when it appeared that the Balkan states were plotting a common war against the Ottoman Empire, the Ottomans hastily signed a treaty with Italy on October 18, 1912. Under the terms of the treaty the Ottoman Empire withdrew from Libya, while Italy withdrew from the Aegean Islands. Italy, however, refused to evacuate its island conquests, while the Ottomans continued to incite guerrilla warfare in Libya. By 1914 Italy had control of most of Libya.

THE COMMITTEE OF UNION AND PROGRESS

Shortly after the deposition of Abdulhamid in 1909, the Committee of Union and Progress held a party congress and established a central executive committee that remained active until the party was dissolved at the end of World War I. The executive committee ruled the party and, when the party was in power, the government and the ministers. Provincial branches of the committee consisted of local notables, professionals, merchants, guild leaders, landowners, and soldiers, mostly Muslims and Turkish-speakers.

The many activities of the Union and Progress party began to tell on its popularity. Even before the defeat by the Italians, to stop a defeat in the Chamber of Deputies the committee had Mehmed V dissolve the chamber and call for a new election. The new chamber was also closed in August 1912, when radical young leaders of Union and Progress attacked a cabinet composed of men of more experience and prestige. A Liberal Unionist party government tried to curb the power of the Union and Progress group.

The government, however, succumbed to a coup d'état by the Union and Progress party in January 1913, when extremists rebelled at surrendering Edirne to the Balkan states. From that moment until the end of World War I leaders of Union and Progress maintained firm control over the government.

The desires of Union and Progress flowed out in every direction. Their intention was to examine all the institutions of their society, changing any that had become outdated. The Finance Ministry was reorganized, tax farming was abolished, and strikes were outlawed. General Liman von Sanders headed a German mission to transform the army under the direction of Enver. Secular law was gaining as the ulama were brought under the control of the state.

The Committee of Union and Progress changed the legal rights of women, and magazines and newspapers increasingly published essays dealing with the status of women. Women gained the right to work in the postal offices and telephone exchanges. During World War I reformers achieved basic changes in marriage laws, which now came under the Ministry of Justice. The writer and educator Halidé Edib (Adivar) and other women founded several women's organizations, while in 1916 the University in Istanbul admitted women students.

These Union and Progress leaders sought to improve the well-being of the great mass of Ottoman subjects. They deplored their poor quality of life and wished to give pride and dignity to the people. They recognized that the empire remained an exporter of foodstuffs and raw materials, and an importer of manufactured goods, with few heavy industries. They wanted to create a national consciousness; however, the society lacked ethnic, religious, linguistic, and national homogeneity. Village, nomadic, and urban cultures and manners were so foreign to each other that little overlap seemed to exist.

OTTOMANISM, ISLAMISM, AND TURKISH NATIONALISM

Reformers debated the bases of the state, identity, and nationalism and at various times emphasized one factor over another. Because of the complex and variable nature of group identity at the time, three overlapping yet distinct cultural and political expressions developed: Ottomanism, Pan-Islamism, and Pan-Turkism.

Ottomanism possessed the greatest attraction in the earlier days of the revolution. It was based on loyalty to the dynasty, a territorial basis of identity, a commitment to the fatherland, and the unity of all Ottoman peoples, despite their mixed ethnic character. Since Turkish was viewed as a common language among the political elite, linguistic diversity was not, according to supporters of Ottomanism, a barrier to their success. They pointed to a common history and culture that upper-class Ottomans shared, whether Turks, Greeks, Arabs, Kurds, or Armenians.

But ethnicity soon triumphed. Often non-Turks in the Chamber of Deputies voted as a bloc in opposition to the Turks. So-called programs for Ottomanization were branded as attempts to Turkify all others. By 1910 such moves provoked a revolt in Albania, where the tribes and nationalists resisted fiercely. Equality in the army, holding government posts, and paying taxes went against the customs and views of too many groups in the empire to be accepted voluntarily for very long. As centralization increased, differences were highlighted and proved insurmountable.

The next move was toward religion and Pan-Islamism. Abdulhamid II had sought greater rapport among Muslim states and peoples and hoped to strengthen the position of the empire by building wider support for the Ottoman sultans as caliphs. Pan-Islamic missions were sent to Kabul, and Abdulhamid subsidized Jamal al-Din al-Afghani (1839–1897) in his work of preaching for reform in Islam. Many Turks found some satisfaction in Pan-Islamic dreams, even though most of the Committee of Union and Progress leaders were not very pious. Unfortunately, Islam as the basis of the state was seen as implicitly discriminatory against non-Muslim minorities inside the empire. Full responsibility for the atrocious massacres of Armenians in Cilicia in 1909 was never ascertained, but some blame should probably be shouldered by Ottomans who were Pan-Islamic.

The third form of identity appeared in Pan-Turkism, which espoused the cultural connections and political union of all Turkish peoples, including those in central Asia. The main efforts of the Pan-Turkists were devoted to the policy of Turkification of all non-Turks and to the task of instilling a national, historical, and linguistic common feeling among all Turks within the Ottoman Empire. In literature, music, and cultural matters generally, Turkish nationalists espoused reforms that would emphasize what they saw as the Turkish core of Ottoman identity. To accomplish this the Committee of Union and Progress sponsored a program of adult education aimed at developing a national consciousness.

ARABISM

In the many Ottoman provinces where Arabic speakers formed a majority of the population at the opening of the twentieth century, the question of an Arab political nationalism distinct from Ottoman or Egyptian patriotism was in the minds of only a very few. However, a cultural revival using Arabic had been under way for some decades. The cultural and the later political aspects of Arab nationalism at first affected mostly urban upper-class Ottoman subjects, especially those most in contact with Europeans and European thought. Initially, peasants, artisans, and nomads were largely untouched by both cultural and political nationalism.

In Syria and Lebanon, from its founding in 1866, the Syrian Protestant College (known later as the American University of Beirut) played an important role in training Muslim and Christian Arabs. Catholic missionaries, largely from France, settled in Syria in great numbers; in 1875 the University of St. Joseph in Beirut opened. Later, Ottoman and Egyptian state schools played an even more important role than the missionary institutions in spreading secular and patriotic concepts.

Numerous writers, thinkers, and teachers influenced the growth of Arab nationalism. Two of them were Christian Arabs from Lebanon. Nasif al-Yaziji taught Arabic near Beirut until his death in 1871. His masterly writings in Arabic pioneered a style, manner, and vocabulary suitable for expressing the life and ideas of the modern world and paved the way for an Arabic renaissance. Butrus al-Bustani (1819–1883) assisted American Protestant missionaries in translating the Bible into Arabic. His dictionary, encyclopedia, and periodicals helped to create a modern Arabic prose that could present the concepts of contemporary thought in language simple enough for use in newspapers; he is the father of so-called newspaper Arabic. He was at the same time both a Syrian Arab patriot and an Ottoman loyalist, and he seemingly saw no contradiction between these two positions.

In Egypt, still nominally part of the Ottoman Empire even after its occupation by Britain in 1882, an educational and literary renaissance was also under way. Cairo drew many intellectuals from every part of the Arab world. Books and newspapers published there spurred nationalism. British control ironically freed nationalists from the Ottoman sultan's surveillance. Egypt, along with France and Switzerland, became a haven for exiled Arab nationalists. One of these exiles was Abd al-Rahman Kawakibi of Aleppo (1854–1902), whose works analyzed the world of Arab society and called for a return to early Islam. Kawakibi attacked the ignorance of the masses and the obscurantism of the ulama who dominated the educational field. He was also one of the first to separate Arab national revival from Pan-Islamism.

In the last half of the nineteenth century, Arabic presses in several Ottoman cities were publishing original works and many translations of European books. From outside the empire ideas of patriotism, nationalism, Islamic reform, and European science were being developed, while the threat of expanding western Christian imperialism made new ideologies an urgent matter.

THE BIRTH OF ARAB NATIONALISM

For centuries Muslims in the Middle East had felt superior to westerners. After the Napoleonic Wars economic, cultural, military, and political contacts between the Middle East and western Europe expanded greatly, and the wealth and power of Europe became evident. Nineteenth-century thinkers such as Nasif al-Yaziji and Butrus al-Bustani put their faith in an educational revival as a means of catching up. Differences between Arabs and Turks were barely considered. Islam and Islamic civilization were regarded as the valid bases of the society that had produced the wondrous ages of the past. Accepting the fact that Arabic was the language of religion and Turkish the language of government and politics, the early thinkers supported the Ottoman Empire and argued that it would be necessary only to borrow certain things from the west, such as the natural and physical sciences (as in the case of the Darwinian theory of evolution), and the gap would close.

As the years passed and the obvious gap between the strength of the Middle East and the west widened, more penetrating questions began to be raised about Middle Eastern culture. Al-Afghani, his Egyptian pupil Muhammad Abduh (1849–1905), and the modernist Muhammad Rashid Rida (1865–1935), asserted that Islam was in a deplorable condition because over the centuries society had corrupted true original Islam. They believed in Pan-Islam and that Muslims should exercise reason and examine the bases of faith so as to be truly modern. None of these reformers was prepared at this time to overturn the Ottoman caliph-sultan.

Arab nationalists countered the Pan-Islamists by proclaiming that Islam was only one of the glories of the Arab nation. They favored religious tolerance among Arabs and called for ejecting alien influences from the Arab scene. After the revolution of 1908 many Arab thinkers became suspicious of Ottomanism and Pan-Islamism, though most Arab leaders remained loyal to the Ottoman Empire until the end of World War I.

THE YOUNG TURKS AND ARAB NATIONALISM

An early test of the judgment of the Committee of Union and Progress in regard to policy in the Arab lands arose when it insisted that Abdulhamid designate Sharif Husain of the prophet Muhammad's Hashimite family as prince of Mecca. Although Husain had resided quietly for fifteen years in Istanbul, the sultan astutely judged the man to have ambitions to rule an autonomous Arab state and warned the Committee of Union and Progress of the folly of its recommendation. In September 1908, however, Abdulhamid appointed Husain to the post.

After the counterrevolution of 1909, centralization of government, Ottomanism, and secularism became objectives of the committee. As political societies were suppressed, the Arabs, among others, went underground. Here, then, was the birth of passionate Arabism among the new professionals who were teachers, students, journalists, civil servants, military officers, lawyers, and local notables. Many such Arabs feared the loss of Arab Libya to Italy in 1911–1912 indicated that the Ottoman Empire could no longer protect other Arab provinces from European imperialism

In Palestine, another source of Arab nationalism appeared in addition to ethnic, cultural, intellectual, and political factors. Jewish nationalism, or Zionism, created a strong backlash as Arab Muslims and Christians who composed a majority of the total population in Ottoman Palestine felt increasingly threatened by Jewish settlers and their foreign supporters. Zionism had originated in Europe during the nineteenth century in response to new, more liberal circumstances for western European Jews, and also as a reaction against the harsh repressions directed against eastern European Jews. Some Russian, Polish, and other Jews argued that it was imperative to end their diaspora and reestablish themselves in their ancient homeland and religious center of Palestine, where they could fully develop themselves culturally, politically, and spiritually. The possibility of massive numbers of Jewish settlers arriving in the area was disturbing to Ottoman officials and Arab residents alike, who feared that in the long run the Zionists might aim at gaining independence from the empire. As Zionists actually settled in parts of Ottoman Palestine, their aspirations became more real and substantial. Ottoman Jews were divided in their views of Zionism, with many favoring it and others opposed.

Palestinian and other Arab representatives in the Ottoman parliament after 1908 joined the Arabic press in harsh criticism of what they felt might be a Zionist goal for unilateral control of the land. Since the Ottoman authorities usually shared the views of the Arab nationalists on this question, many barriers were placed in the way of Zionism in Palestine before World War I—barriers that were often evaded with the help of European powers.

ARAB SECRET SOCIETIES

As usual in the development of ethnic nationalism, a welter of small societies sprang into being among Arabs in Istanbul, Damascus, Beirut, Cairo, Baghdad, Aleppo, and other Arab cities. An important open group was the Ottoman Decentralization party, established in Cairo in 1912 by Syrian Arab Muslim and Christian public figures. Its objectives were to mobilize Arab and Turkish public opinion for the organization of an

Ottoman Empire based on a federal system. The Decentralization party enjoyed partial success during the last half of 1912 when the Union and Progress party was out of power. Lebanese patriots who wanted to enhance the special status of Mount Lebanon within the empire worked together to agitate for new policies by the central authorities.

One interesting secret society was called al-Qahtaniya. (Qahtan was a legendary ancestor of the Arabs.) It advocated the creation of a dual Turko-Arab empire, much like the Austro-Hungarian Empire.

Suppression by the Committee of Union and Progress drove many Arabs abroad. Like the Turks a decade earlier, they flocked to Paris. In 1909 Arab refugees and students formed the society known as al-Fatat (Youth). A secret society, al-Fatat eventually rejected the idea of any integration within the empire and worked for full Arab freedom and independence. It became the most widespread and effective force among Arabs.

In view of these activities and the Arab enthusiasm they evoked, the Union and Progress leaders adopted stringent measures to combat them. A committee of reform in Beirut in 1913 publicly announced a program for Arab home rule and won such wide acclaim that the government suppressed it. Under the leadership of al-Fatat a congress of Arabs held in Paris adopted the platforms of the Decentralization party.

Major Aziz Ali al-Misri (1879–1965) of the Ottoman general staff initiated a new society called al-Ahd (the Covenant). Aziz Ali had been a member of Union and Progress before 1908. Al-Ahd was composed exclusively of army officers and became for the military what al-Fatat was for civilians. In 1914, the Young Turks arrested Aziz Ali and condemned him to death. Public opinion became so indignant, especially in Egypt, that the British protested to Istanbul. Aziz Ali was pardoned and sailed for Egypt as a public hero.

THE ARAB PRINCES

Not only did the Ottoman Turks have difficulty with Arab nationalists and their many patriotic societies, but they also discovered that Arab semiautonomous rulers employed every means to resist centralization. Unsuccessful expeditions were sent to bring the inner sections of Yemen, then under the rule of Imam Yahya, and Asir, ruled by Muhammad al-Idrisi, to heel. Tiring of the continual drain on resources, the central government reached an accord with the two, granting them many local powers. In central Arabia the Istanbul authorities found their support of the Rashid family unavailing against the young Saudi ruler Abd al-Aziz, who drove the Ottomans from the rich province of al-Hasa in eastern Arabia in 1913.

Had it not been for the Hijaz Railway, which connected Syria with Medina, Ottoman authority over Sharif Husain in Mecca would have been even weaker. However, the Hijaz was too dependent upon religion and the pilgrimage to welcome secular Arab nationalism. Husain did find substantial local help in his opposition to the centralization of power, the attempted introduction of conscription, the extension of the Hijaz Railway to Mecca, and the Europeanization espoused by the Committee of Union and Progress. Early in 1914, Prince Abd Allah, Husain's second son, an Arab member of the Ottoman parliament, hinted vaguely to the British as he passed through Cairo that his father would be open to rebellion against the Ottomans. These discreet overtures indicated that Husain was considering a treaty similar to that which the British had with Arab princes in the Persian Gulf area. Such treaties provided for British recognition of the Arab ruler's independence and protection, in exchange for British conduct of all foreign relations.

Suspicion that Husain was harboring these intentions drifted back to Istanbul, where the authorities planned to build the Hijaz Railway south of Medina toward Mecca and assigned a new governor to the Hijaz with instructions to destroy Husain. In the spring of 1914, the Ottomans came to understand that Husain had consolidated his position with the townspeople and tribes of the Hijaz; the new governor was ordered to make peace, and the railway extension was stopped.

Probably no substantial connection existed between the various Arab princes in the Arabian peninsula on the one hand and the revolutionary societies of the Ottoman Arab world on the other. Some foreign governments were friendly to the secret societies; British and French officials in Beirut and Egypt gave encouragement to them.

When World War I began in 1914 the Union and Progress government realized that defection in Arab provinces was likely, but divisions of interest among the Arabs and a strong commitment to Islam would save the day. Most Arabs remained loyal to the Ottoman Empire, either because they felt loyalty to it or because they feared its destruction would lead to the dissolution of the only remaining barrier against European imperialism. Equally apprehensive were the various princes, each of the other. But it was only a question of time before Arab nationalism would flare into the open.

THE BALKAN WARS

Other non-Turkish communities also bitterly resisted centralization. In several districts in Anatolia trouble arose with Greeks and Armenians, whose boycotts and attacks caused serious dislocations of commerce. A violent storm broke in Albania, when the government took steps to enforce a decree forbidding the possession of arms. Albanians also objected to a census, taxes, and the drafting of young men to serve in Yemen (which was called the graveyard of Ottoman armies). The Albanian rebellion was quelled early in 1911 after a grant of considerable local autonomy.

Concessions to the Albanians, however, aroused hopes among other nationalities; the Macedonian Bulgarians particularly hoped for the establishment of a regime similar to the one in Eastern Rumelia. These concessions also excited the ambitions of officials in Greece, Bulgaria, Serbia, and Montenegro, who declared war on the Ottoman Empire in October 1912, after agreeing on the division of Macedonia. Within a month after the start of the war these allies, who possessed a decided numerical advantage over the Ottoman armies, overran most of Ottoman Europe. Bulgaria took Edirne after a lengthy siege. Military casualties on all sides in this war were substantial, while hundreds of thousands of civilian Ottoman Muslims and Jews fled the territories that came under the control of the European Christian states, with many dying from disease and deprivation.

In December an armistice was signed, and the five belligerents met to negotiate peace. The European powers demanded the cession of Edirne to Bulgaria, but when it became apparent that Kamil Pasha, the grand vizir, and the Liberal Unionists were willing to pay that price for peace, Enver Bey and about 200 members of Union and Progress staged a successful coup d'état. They assassinated the minister of war and returned to power. In February 1913 war was resumed. Edirne fell, and the Greek navy defeated the Ottoman forces outside the Dardanelles and occupied a number of the Aegean Islands.

In April a second armistice was arranged, and a peace treaty ceded to the victors almost all Ottoman European possessions. Then the establishment of Albania upon the insistence of the Great Powers goaded Greece and Serbia to demand a revision of their previous understandings with Bulgaria. Failure to reach agreement brought war between Bulgaria and Serbia on June 30, 1913. Greece, Montenegro, and then Romania entered the war against Bulgaria. In July 1913, the Ottomans invaded Thrace, and Enver Bey reoccupied Edirne. The Treaty of Bucharest ended the Second Balkan War in August.

When the Libyan and Balkan wars ended, the Ottomans had lost almost all their possessions in Europe and North Africa. The empire had ceded about a quarter of its population and 10 percent of its territory, including lands it had ruled for hundreds of years!

THE TRIUMVIRATE

The radical wing of the Committee of Union and Progress had seized power in January 1913, and Mahmud Shevket Pasha became grand vizir. But his assassination in June and the succeeding grand vizirate of Said Halim Pasha, a mild and weak Egyptian prince, permitted the reins of government to fall into the hands of a collective leadership headed by a triumvirate of the committee: Talat, Enver, and Jemal.

Talat Bey (1874–1921), now minister of the interior, was born of a poor family near Edirne and began work as a telegraph operator in the government office at Salonica. Possessing a brilliant mind, he was one of the organizers of the revolutionary movement in Macedonia and served as minister of the interior in several cabinets. He was a dedicated man who stayed poor and remained modest throughout his career. Ruthless in his tactics, he made a distinction between personal and national morality, believing that many acts that would be entirely immoral and cruel if perpetrated by an individual were perfectly moral if performed in the interests of the state.

Enver Bey (1881–1922), minister of war, came from a lower-middle-class family and received a military education. Catapulted to public attention by his flight to the Macedonian hills in the first stage of the revolution in 1908, Enver loved the heroics of Turkish nationalism. He was a man of action and hasty decisions. As an attaché in Berlin, Enver fell under the spell of Prussian militarism and believed in the superiority of the German military machine. He, more than any other, brought the Ottomans into World War I as German allies. As he rose to power, he became vain—a development many of his former friends deplored. As one remarked: "Enver Pasha has destroyed Enver Bey." An advocate of Pan-Turkism, Enver died pursuing this policy in central Asia after the end of World War I.

Jemal Pasha (1872–1922), governor of Istanbul and later minister of the navy, was an early member of Union and Progress. He came from an old Ottoman family and had been a Pan-Islamist, but in the days of the triumvirate he became an ardent Turkish nationalist. The weakest of the three, Jemal served as a kind of policeman for the Young Turks, maintaining discipline and holding the faltering in line.

To the day of the entry of the Ottoman Empire into World War I, the young and rash leadership ruled with a strong hand. Disobedient party members were punished, opponents were eliminated, and terror returned to government circles. Thus, even before the carnage of World War I, the internal violence and external wars of the period from 1908 to 1914 created an atmosphere seemingly so threatening to the existence of the state as to justify extreme repression and radical reform.

The rejoicing that had greeted the Young Turks in 1908 faded away by 1914. Although the Committee of Union and Progress did succeed in dominating the central government, its military leaders lost several wars and a great deal of territory during this short time. Continuing uncertainty about the allegiances linking the people to the state also weakened the regime. However, Arab nationalists and other ethnic groups seeking independence or autonomy had as yet little popular support among most of the subjects of the sultan. *Din ve devlet*—religion and the state, or Islam and the sultanate of the House of Osman—still commanded the loyalty of most of the population, except for some of the religious minorities who became increasingly alienated by the Young Turks. In Egypt, however, the fiction of Ottoman overlordship had been undermined since 1882 by the reality of British supervision. The already somewhat separate path of historical development Egypt had pursued since Mehmet Ali's days diverged even more from the central Ottoman experience in the three decades before the outbreak of World War I.

REFERENCES

Many references mentioned in preceding chapters are important for this chapter; those of particular note are in Chapters 23, 25, and 26.

Ahmad, Feroz: *The Young Turks: The Committee of Union and Progress in Turkish Politics, 1908–1914.* Oxford, England: Clarendon Press, 1969. This important study points out that the committee did not hold absolute power during this period and was able to adapt to altering circumstances.

Ahmida, Ali Abdullatif: *The Making of Modern Libya: State Formation, Colonization, and Resistance, 1830–1932.* Albany: State University of New York Press, 1994.

Antonius, George: *The Arab Awakening: The Story of the Arab National Movement.* New York: Hamilton, 1938. Still a key work on this topic; its controversial conclusions have been revised by many scholars, as in the works of Dawn, Kayali, and Khalidi, cited on page 334.

Arai, Masami: *Turkish Nationalism in the Young Turk Era.* Leiden, The Netherlands: Brill, 1992. Illustrates nationalist thinking through a study of periodicals.

Brummett, Palmira: *Image and Imperialism in the Ottoman Revolutionary Press, 1908–1911.* Albany: State University of New York Press, 2000. An intriguing analysis of Istanbul newspapers' cartoons.

Cleveland, William L.: *The Making of an Arab Nationalist: Ottomanism and Arabism in the Life and Thought of Sati' al-Husri.* Princeton, N.J.: Princeton University Press, 1971. The life of an Ottoman Arab who chose to be an Arab nationalist after World War I.

Dawn, C. Ernest: *From Ottomanism to Arabism: Essays on the Origins of Arab Nationalism.* Urbana: University of Illinois Press, 1973. Shows the subtle aspects of the Arab revolt and its relationship to Arab nationalism, bringing out many of the misconceptions about it.

Gawrych, George: "Tolerant Dimensions of Cultural Pluralism in the Ottoman Empire: The Albanian Community, 1800–1912." *International Journal of Middle East Studies* 15 (1983): 519–536.

Hall, Richard C.: *The Balkan Wars, 1912–1913: Prelude to the First World War.* London: Routledge, 2000. Emphasizes the tactics, battles, and diplomacy of the Balkan wars.

Hanioğlu, M. Şükrü: *Preparation for a Revolution: The Young Turks, 1902–1908.* New York: Oxford University Press, 2001. Along with his earlier work, *The Young Turks in Opposition,* the author presents an exhaustive and definitive history of this group.

Hourani, Albert H.: *Arabic Thought in the Liberal Age, 1798–1939.* New York: Oxford University Press, 1962. Brilliant, authoritative treatment of Arabic thought and Arab nationalism.

Howard, Douglas A.: *The History of Turkey.* Westport, Conn.: Greenwood, 2001. This excellent brief survey covers both the Ottoman Empire and the Turkish Republic.

Kayali, Hasan: *Arabs and Young Turks: Ottomanism, Arabism, and Islamism in the Ottoman Empire, 1908–1918.* Berkeley: University of California Press, 1997. The author examines in a sophisticated way Arab politics in relationship to the central government, with many useful examples.

Khalidi, Rashid: *Palestinian Identity: The Construction of Modern National Consciousness.* New York: Columbia University Press, 1997. Excellent discussion of the dynamic changes in the multiple loyalties of Palestinian Arabs, their interactions with Zionism, and their newspapers.

———: "Arab Nationalism: Historical Problems in the Literature." *American Historical Review* 96 (1991): 1363–1373. This excellent bibliographic essay is a good beginning point for reading about the topic.

Khalidi, Rashid, et al., eds.: *The Origins of Arab Nationalism.* New York: Columbia University Press, 1991. Essays on all aspects of the topic, concentrating on Syria, Iraq, and the Hijaz.

Khoury, Philip S.: *Urban Notables and Arab Nationalism: The Politics of Damascus, 1860–1920.* Cambridge, England: Cambridge University Press, 1983. An analysis of the governing elite, who among them came to be Arab nationalists, and why.

Kushner, David: *The Rise of Turkish Nationalism, 1876–1908.* London: Frank Cass, 1977. This is a brief study of the intellectual origins of Turkish nationalism in the last decades of the nineteenth century.

McCarthy, Justin: *The Ottoman Peoples and the End of Empire.* London: Arnold and Oxford University Press, 2001. Discusses the period of the late empire through the initial establishment of the successor states.

Macfie, A. L.: *The End of the Ottoman Empire, 1908–1923.* London: Longman, 1998.

Shimoni, Gideon: *The Zionist Ideology.* Hanover, N.H.: University Press of New England, 1995. A thorough history of the social origins of Zionism and different approaches to it, up to 1948.

Tauber, Eliezer: *The Emergence of the Arab Movements.* London: Frank Cass, 1993. Surveys of each group and analysis of their views and effectiveness.

Turfan, M. Naim: *Rise of the Young Turks: Politics, the Military and Ottoman Collapse.* London: Tauris, 2000. In this lengthy study the author emphasizes the military elements in the Committee of Union and Progress.

Zeine, Zeine N.: *The Emergence of Arab Nationalism.* 2d ed. Delmar, N.Y.: Caravan Books, 1973.

Zürcher, Erik Jan: *The Unionist Factor: The Role of the Committee of Union and Progress in the Turkish National Movement, 1905–1926.* Leiden: Brill, 1984. A stimulating, revisionist interpretation that stresses the continuity between the Union and Progress period and that of the Turkish Republic.

CHAPTER 28

British Occupation of Egypt and the Sudan

From 1882 to 1914 Britain occupied Egypt, chiefly to control the Suez Canal and to stop Egypt from falling into the hands of any other country. Despite maintaining the fiction of Ottoman sovereignty and the governorship of Mehmet Ali's descendants, Britain gradually consolidated its military occupation, domination of civilian government, and influence on the economy. Opposition to the British presence increased, and Egyptian nationalism came to have a considerable impact on political and cultural affairs.

STABILIZATION OF BRITISH CONTROL

The British army occupied Cairo and took control of Egypt in September 1882. The British administration presumed that its occupation would be of short duration, hoping to put Khedive Tawfiq (r. 1879–1892) in a powerful position and then to withdraw. But the British cabinet argued that certain aspects of Egyptian government needed to be stabilized before evacuation was possible. For this purpose Lord Dufferin, British ambassador to Istanbul, was sent to Egypt to advise the khedive in establishing authority. Colonel Ahmad Urabi, the national hero, who had surrendered to the British, had been turned over to the frightened and vindictive khedive for trial. Urabi was found guilty of treason and sentenced to be executed, but the British intervened and insisted instead that he be exiled to Sri Lanka.

Lord Dufferin spent months forcing changes in the Egyptian government. First the army and the police were reorganized. A new Egyptian army, provisionally set at 6000, was created under an English general. The British army of occupation was cut from 12,000 to 9500. In the cities a police force was formed, commanded by Europeans.

The British believed that financial reforms were the second step to ensure stability and tranquility. A British financial adviser became fiscal master of Egypt. Also Dufferin placed in key ministries British advisers whose recommendations had the force of commands. In the provinces civil and criminal codes, based on Napoleonic codes, were adopted, and between 1883 and 1889 a system of lower courts and courts of appeal was decreed. However, then and for a long time thereafter, the secular courts were poorly understood by most Egyptians, who continued to regard them as unjust and foreign.

One of Lord Dufferin's more lasting reforms was the bringing in of engineers as irrigation advisers to the Ministry of Public Works. They set to work to rehabilitate the old Nile Barrage built by Mehmet Ali at the apex of the delta. In 1884, after the barrage was restored, the cotton yield was 30,000 tons greater than in the previous year. This increased Egypt's cotton income by over £1 million; the cost of the renovation had been only £26,000.

In the long run revenues from these and similar changes greatly increased; as a result, public and private profits made the British occupation of Egypt acceptable to the Great Powers and their bondholders and tolerable to Egyptian landlords.

LORD CROMER AND EGYPTIAN GOVERNMENT

In September 1883, Sir Evelyn Baring (1841–1917) became British agent and consul general in Egypt. Elevated to the peerage as Lord Cromer in 1892, he controlled Egypt autocratically from 1883 until his retirement in 1907. His negative views of Egyptian national character served as a means of justifying English control of Egypt, while many Egyptians resented his condescending attitude toward them. He faced an interlocking and complex series of problems, including the indefinite status of Egypt and its desperate financial situation.

Egypt's status was not clearly defined: the dynasty founded by Mehmet Ali governed nominally as Ottoman appointees, and Egypt was supposedly part of the Ottoman Empire; locally, the khedive was formally in control of the autonomous area of Egypt; and several European countries claimed special privileges inside the country. In reality, though, England controlled Egypt, despite the fact that no formal machinery for control was established. The capitulations remained, as did the Mixed Courts, and the public debt. Khedive Tawfiq continued as head of the administration, the cabinet and the ministries functioned, local officials governed the cities and provinces, and the courts and judiciary performed their duties. The ultimate power of decision, however, resided in the British agent. This indirect rule was facilitated by an unspoken alliance fashioned early between Lord Cromer and Tawfiq, in which Egyptian ministers either followed the advice of the British agent or lost their posts. Several prime ministers served under Cromer. Mustafa Fahmi served the longest continuous period and was so subservient to the British that he antagonized many Egyptians.

Lord Cromer and his British advisers and officials determined and administered trade policies, agriculture, communications, irrigation, health, and foreign affairs in addition to Egypt's army and finances. Education failed to fit into any program. The illiteracy of the masses was hardly touched, and the number receiving a secondary education was very limited. Sufi brotherhoods were brought more closely under the control of the Egyptian state; religion was one of the few areas that remained largely outside the sphere of the British.

In the short run the British occupiers faced a desperate financial situation. The French, embittered by Britain's unilateral occupation and the abolition of the dual control, used every device possible to embarrass the British. Revenues continued to be collected, but funds for the administration of government and payment of tribute to the Ottoman sultan were insufficient. By the end of 1883 government workers' salaries were in arrears, and the floating debt had doubled. British proposals to reduce interest payments on the debt and transfer some funds to pay for administration were vetoed by the French.

Finally, at a London conference in 1885, agreement was reached to float an internationally guaranteed loan to pay off the current debt, to reduce interest payments, and to provide for Egyptian irrigation needs. Any surplus funds were to be divided equally between the administration and debt funding. By 1891 the Egyptian treasury began to show surpluses.

With Egypt's finances seemingly adjusted, the British turned to the thorny problem of withdrawal from the country. England tried to conclude in 1885 a withdrawal agreement in concert with Sultan Abdulhamid II and with the other European powers. The French and Russians protested so strenuously against British proposals that Abdulhamid failed to ratify the agreement. As a result, the British remained in Egypt, although with an anomalous status, until 1914. British imperial military and diplomatic strategy shifted its focus to Cairo and Suez from Istanbul, where German influence was mounting. British withdrawal from Egypt was now pushed to some nebulous future.

KHEDIVE ABBAS HILMI II VS. LORD CROMER

Mustafa Fahmi became prime minister in 1891. An elegant Turk, honest, hardworking, an ally of Ismail, a friend of Urabi, and devoted to Tawfiq, Fahmi continued as prime minister, with some interruptions, until Cromer's retirement in 1907. Affairs moved so smoothly during Fahmi's stewardship that Cromer allowed that he was almost bored. With imports and exports on the rise, treasury surpluses building up, and the cabinet and khedive docile, the British occupation appeared to be succeeding. Then, in January 1892, Tawfiq fell ill and died. His son and successor, Abbas Hilmi II, not quite eighteen years old, was studying in Vienna. Cromer realized that the "alliance" had been broken; he would have to start afresh to educate the new khedive to reality.

Abbas had some acquaintance with French liberal ideas, and he tended to be suspicious of England. The new khedive wanted to show his independence of Cromer and evidently hoped that France would aid him in getting rid of the British.

Soon, Abbas decided to replace the seriously ill Fahmi with a prime minister of his own choosing. With London's backing, Cromer forced Abbas to dismiss the prime minister designate and declare that he would willingly adopt British advice.

Suddenly Abbas became a hero to many of the budding Egyptian nationalists, who saw in him a young and vigorous voice for "Egypt for the Egyptians." Abbas now had the sympathies of many of the Egyptian people and especially of the Egyptian army. In 1894, though, he discovered that the rather small army might hail him at one moment but abandon him in a contest of will with the British. Abbas and Horatio Kitchener (1850–1916), commander of the Egyptian army, were making a tour of inspection when Abbas remarked disparagingly to Kitchener on the performance of some troops. Kitchener took offense and demanded a public apology. Sensing this as a suitable opportunity to put Abbas in his place, Cromer supported Kitchener's stand. Abbas was forced to retract his remarks.

EGYPTIAN NATIONALISM

For support in his opposition to British occupation, Abbas then turned to the Egyptian nationalists, who had been increasing in number and influence. Cromer, never worried very much about Egypt's educated minority, had permitted a free press to exist. Now a number of teachers, lawyers, and writers, most of whom had studied or lived in Europe, were involved in the creation of a sense of Egyptian territorial patriotism or Pan-Islam, but not yet Arab nationalism. Few Egyptians identified themselves with the Arabic-speaking people to the east of Egypt, even though several Arab nationalists from the Syrian region were active in Cairo.

Egyptian nationalists began to appear early in the nineteenth century. One of the first advocates was Rifaa Rafi al-Tahtawi (1801–1873), who had studied at Cairo's al-Azhar University and then in 1826 was sent by Mehmet Ali to Paris as the religious guardian of a group of Egyptian students. He remained there for five years, learning French and reading widely. After his return to Cairo, al-Tahtawi taught two generations of Egyptian students and wrote and translated many significant books. These works championed the love of Egypt but pointed out that Egypt's destiny could not be attained until the ulama were modernized and the schools offered a more secular education.

Many other writers contributed to the intellectual and ideological ferment in Egypt in the time of Said and Ismail. One was Jamal al-Din al-Afghani, who lived, taught, and conspired in Cairo from 1871 to 1879. A Shii from Iran, he posed as a Sunni from Afghanistan (in Afghanistan he claimed to be a Turk). He had studied in Iraq and lived in Istanbul before coming to Cairo. Jamal al-Din's life can be summed up in a phrase used as the title of a book about him, *An Islamic Response to Imperialism.* In Egypt he found adherents who were swept up by his compelling personality, his lucid and persuasive presentation of ideas, and the innovation and dedication of his beliefs. He argued that when the Muslim ummah returned to the truth of Islam, society would cease to be weak; only then would there be a regeneration. Jamal al-Din believed that the essence of Islam was identical to that of modern rationalism. He believed that one should use one's mind freely to know and test all. Furthermore, every mind was capable of providing the individual with self-respect and a sense of equality. Lastly, Jamal al-Din was convinced that Islam was an active way of life; it was not a passive resignation to whatever might come but a responsible activity in doing the will of God.

These preachings, which were debated privately, were heady stuff. They were aimed against Christian imperialistic attacks upon Islam and against westernizing influences and materialism. Jamal al-Din al-Afghani was a Pan-Islamist who wanted to reform Islam by means of education and to adapt Islam to the conditions of modern life. He did not see how this could be done without revolution, the political unity of the Muslim world, and freedom from foreign domination. Wherever he went, whether in Cairo, Istanbul, or Tehran, he vigorously stirred the minds and imaginations of Muslims to react in defense of an embattled Islamic society and against its debasement by Christian Europe. He became so influential in Egypt that the government asked him to leave. The remainder of his life was spent in Iran, France, England, and Istanbul, where he died in 1897.

Jamal al-Din's most illustrious pupil was Muhammad Abduh, born into a peasant family, who had a distinguished career as a mystic, journalist, judge, and teacher. Differing from his mentor, Muhammad Abduh deplored the use of violence and believed that true reforms came only as a gradual process. He advocated a reform of Islam that would return it to its earliest, purest dogma, permitting a more flexible interpretation than was allowed in al-Azhar University. Abduh also worked for the development of Arabic into a more unified language, attempting to draw newspaper Arabic and the spoken vernacular together and bring both nearer to classical Quranic Arabic.

Abduh supported the Urabi movement and was exiled along with Urabi. He found his way to Paris to join al-Afghani; together they edited a short-lived but influential Pan-Islamic journal. At Cromer's urging, Abduh was allowed by Tawfiq to return to Egypt in 1888. He was appointed a judge in a local court and in 1899 became grand mufti of Egypt, from which post he helped reform the religious courts and codify the shariah until his death in 1905. In France, Abduh had concluded that Egypt's poverty-stricken traditional society could neither mount a successful revolution nor drive out the British. Henceforth he taught that reason and the pragmatic accommodation of Islam to the modern world must supersede customary practice and belief; one should adopt what is reasonable and just for society.

Abduh and Cromer respected each other and met frequently. Abduh felt Egypt needed a benevolent despot. Cromer backed Abduh against the vindictiveness of Tawfiq and Abbas, which made them dislike and distrust Abduh. Abbas circulated such rumors about Abduh that only after Abduh's death was he fully accorded his rightful honors as a patriot, scholar, teacher, judge, and reformer.

No nationalist was more fiery than Mustafa Kamil (1874–1908). Coming from the new educated class, he entered the School of Law in 1891 and went on to France, where he graduated in law in 1894. Returning to Egypt in 1896, he spent the remaining years of his life working for Egyptian national independence. A spellbinding orator who fired audiences with his ideals and ideas, Mustafa Kamil pleaded with all Egyptians of whatever origin or religion to unite into one nationalistic force to eliminate ignorance and to support the khedive as a rallying point against the occupation. His slogans, such as, "Had I not been born an Egyptian, I would have wished to become one," instilled in his followers a love of Egypt and a pride in its past glories. Kamil worked to erase the defeatism and the sense of inferiority generated by the capitulations and the occupation. In 1900 he founded the radical newspaper *al-Liwa* (The Standard) and created the Nationalist party shortly before his death. Something of a Pan-Islamist, whose goal was to achieve liberation of Egypt from British rule and autonomy within the Ottoman Empire under the sultan-caliph, he accused the British of impairing the authority of the khedive, destroying Arabic as the language of the educated, depriving Egypt of the Sudan, exploiting Egyptian agriculture, and excluding Egyptians from top government positions. Cromer called him a fanatic.

CHANGES IN GENDER RELATIONS, THE ECONOMY, AND CULTURE

Debates over the status of women and cultural issues, along with changes in the economy, agriculture, and population, played a role in the public life of Egypt. The actual status of most Egyptian women perhaps deteriorated in the late nineteenth century, especially as

Hanafi Islamic law replaced earlier, more flexible approaches to the regulation of family life. At the same time, however, many modern middle-class Egyptian nationalists and some British liberals agreed on the desirability of education for women. They favored more schooling for women, abolishing the veil (although rather few Egyptian women wore it in any case), and making polygamy more difficult. Qasim Amin's controversial book of 1899, *The Liberation of Women,* was especially influential, as it presented the argument that European political and scientific superiority was, in part, based on the relatively better-educated condition of women in Europe. Women's ignorance also created a harmful intellectual gap between wives and husbands and lessened the national strength of Egypt. Despite these and other arguments, very few women were enrolled in public elementary schools by World War I. A government primary school for girls in Alexandria, the second-largest city in Egypt, was opened only in 1917. On the other hand, traditional Muslim religious schools for girls had about 17,000 students by 1908; Christian and Jewish girls also were enrolled in religious community schools. Muslim benevolent societies provided increased educational opportunities in the 1890s, but mostly for males. Women's associations played a considerable role in literary and charitable enterprises, especially after 1908, as women's magazines promoted education and discussed gender relations. Still, men continued to dominate public life, including culture.

Some aspects of popular culture remained as in earlier times; for instance, Quranic schools were the chief source of education for most students, while the majority of the population still lived, as in earlier periods, in villages near the Nile. However, European civilization did heavily influence new cultural genres and life in the major cities. Starting in the 1840s, plays were produced; often they were translations of European works, but by the end of the century original plays flourished. Newspapers by the 1870s gained a considerable audience among the minority of the population that could read. Foreign-run schools played a prominent role in education, while the nearly 1000-year-old al-Azhar theological institution nevertheless continued to be influential throughout the Sunni Muslim world. The sons of elite families often went to Europe for higher education. A Museum of Arab (later Islamic) Art, which opened in 1884, supplemented the Egyptian Museum's specialization in the pharaonic period. European architects in Cairo designed buildings along European lines while incorporating some elements of Islamic design in surface decorations. European scholars of ancient Egypt often supported imperialism while ignoring Egyptians who wanted to study the history of Egypt.

The British encouraged the government to invest large sums of money in irrigation projects, making perennial irrigation and two or three crops a year standard practice in many parts of Egypt. The British also paid the workers on these projects and sought to abolish forced labor under the lash. A dam at Aswan opened in 1902 made perennial cropping possible in large parts of Egypt, guaranteed water for summer irrigation, and ensured a high and increasing cotton yield. Overall agricultural production substantially increased, even when calculated on a per capita basis. However, in the long run, perennial cropping posed an unintended but serious health and ecological hazard to the farmworkers and to the soil itself. The water-borne disease bilharziasis came to affect as many as half of the peasants of northern Egypt.

Ownership of much of the agricultural land was concentrated in the hands of an elite: some 12,000 people owned about 40 percent of the cultivated area. On the other hand, a peasant-based middle group of small to medium landowners had about one-third of the cultivated area; they often rented land and also had to find work on land belonging to other people. And about one-third of the peasants owned very little or no land at all in 1896. The British occupiers organized a cadastral survey of the land, and agricultural taxes were equalized and reduced.

Egypt became a net importer of food as cotton was by far the greatest crop grown in the country. Food needs increased because of rapid population growth, especially in the cities, in which about one-tenth of the population resided by 1897. Despite several cholera outbreaks, the population of Egypt increased from about 8 million people in 1882 to more than 12 million in 1917.

The more than 100,000 foreigners resident in Egypt strongly welcomed British control, since the British in effect supported foreign domination of Egyptian finance, banking, and the export trade (including cotton). Technical and commercial modernization was part of, and a contributor to, the further integration of the Egyptian economy into the world economy. Some examples included the establishment of the first telephones in Egypt in 1884, construction of more railways, and the founding of the first European-style insurance company in 1890.

THE ANGLO-EGYPTIAN SUDAN

Throughout the nineteenth century the governing forces in Egypt maintained a lively interest in the Sudan, just south of Egypt along the Nile River. Mehmet Ali sent an expedition into that area in 1820, and in 1842 the Ottoman sultan recognized him as governor-general of the Sudan. During the middle of the century the chief activities with regard to the Sudan consisted of conflicts with Ethiopia over Red Sea ports. A regular commerce in ivory and slaves developed, despite vigorous measures taken later by the khedive Ismail against the slave trade. Ismail extended Egyptian control up the Nile, to the east and west of the great river, and toward Ethiopia. Many of his appointees in the Sudan were European Christians who did not know Arabic and who were greeted with great hostility by the Sudanese. At the time of Ismail's ouster from office and the crisis over Urabi and the finances of Egypt, affairs in the Sudan were beginning to be difficult to manage.

In 1881 Muhammad Ahmad (ca. 1841–1885) of Dongola, an ascetic Sufi leader, proclaimed himself to be the Mahdi, the religious leader sent to complete the work of the prophet Muhammad and to signal the last days of the world. He gained support among the northern tribes and the western nomads, and he preached a message filled with appeals to revolutionary justice and Sunni fundamentalism. He claimed to be recreating the circumstances of the early Islamic community in Mecca and Medina. He said Egypt and the "corrupt" Islam practiced there were the enemy. The harsh rule of the Sudan by Mehmet Ali and his successors provided a powerful sense of resentment that fueled the Mahdist movement among the Sudanese. When revolt broke out south of Khartoum, affairs in Egypt were so chaotic and finances so desperate that the Sudan was left alone. However, in 1883 Khedive Tawfiq sent an Egyptian army to the Sudan. It was cut to pieces by the forces of the Mahdi, and the English insisted upon complete Egyptian withdrawal from the Sudan, largely for financial reasons. Charles George Gordon was then sent in 1884 to arrange for the evacuation of Khartoum, but he delayed the operation and a relief expedition from Cairo arrived too late. In 1885 Khartoum fell to the Mahdi, and Gordon and his men were slain.

For the following decade the Sudan was an independent theocratic state under the Mahdi and his successors. The Mahdi established a judicial system based on his own unique position as the recipient of communications from the prophet Muhammad. Sufi fraternities were outlawed, and the pilgrimage to Mecca was forbidden because Mecca was under the control of the Ottoman Empire. The Mahdi minted coins, collected the Quranic taxes, and permitted slavery and the slave trade once again to flourish. Following the Mahdi's death in 1885, the caliph Abd Allah of the western tribes overcame a series of revolts, bad harvests, and the outbreak of disease. He sought to conquer Ethiopia and Egypt but was disastrously defeated by the Anglo-Egyptians in 1889. Taxes were increased, and the major government positions were assigned to members of Abd Allah's tribe as the state authority came to resemble personal rule exercised through a bureaucracy rather than the charismatic appeal of the Mahdi.

In the 1890s, the Italian war in Eritrea and French pressure upon Ethiopia led the British to consider the reconquest of the Sudan. Kitchener took Dongola in 1896. Two years later, with the support of Indian and English troops, the Egyptian army moved up the Nile under the leadership of Kitchener, taking Omdurman and Khartoum and completely routing Caliph Abd Allah's forces.

In 1899, the Sudan Convention established what soon came to be known as the Anglo-Egyptian Sudan. Theoretically, it was a condominium, or joint rule, but the Egyptian voice in ruling the Sudan remained only nominal. Military and civil power was vested in a governor-general chosen by the British. Egyptian law was not valid in the Sudan, nor were the mixed judicial tribunals extended there. Import duties were not levied on goods coming from Egypt, and the slave trade was prohibited.

By World War I, the borders of the Sudan with its neighbors were determined. But within the country, British control was limited by vast spaces, the heterogeneous population, and inadequate funding. Egypt paid for the armed forces and provided a subsidy until the Sudanese budget was finally balanced in 1913. British officers in the Egyptian army and Egyptian civilians were the main sources of government employees. Personal law came from the Islamic holy law; tribal law dominated the nomadic tribal countryside; and secular law began to prevail in criminal matters. The southern Sudan was treated differently than the rest of the country: the English language was encouraged, missionaries were supported, and Islam, the Arabic language, and Arab customs were opposed. The condominium built railroads linking Khartoum to Egypt and to a new port on the Red Sea, and by the beginning of World War I the British were planning for massive irrigation projects that would enable a dramatic increase in the growing of cotton. Although the British and Egyptian flags were flown side by side over all public buildings, no one ever doubted which power ruled the Sudan.

TABA AND DINSHAWAY

Though the diversion of some resources to the conquest of the Sudan and nationalist attacks in the press made life more difficult for Cromer, he expected that improved economic conditions would blunt the campaigns of the educated few who mounted the opposition and would allay the antagonisms of the Egyptian masses. Events seemed to be working in his favor and dashing the hopes of Abbas, Kamil, Abduh, and others. Kitchener had secured the Anglo-Egyptian condominium over the Sudan. Meanwhile, there had been an inconclusive showdown between Kitchener and French officers at Fashoda, as part of the European scramble for control of Africa. The Anglo-French Agreement of 1904, part of a general understanding called the Entente Cordiale, stated that the French accepted the indefinite postponement of British evacuation. Two years later, however, three inflammatory incidents rekindled the nationalist fires, setting the stage for Cromer's retirement.

In January 1906, Ottoman forces landed at Taba, a desert spot near the head of the Gulf of Aqaba, and established a post there. The British protested that Taba was in the territory of Egypt, but the Ottomans disagreed, arguing that Taba was in the Sinai peninsula and that it was part of Syria. Mustafa Kamil and other Egyptian editors came out strongly in support of the sultan and bitterly attacked Cromer and the British for trying to humiliate the caliph and Islam. Cromer considered the pro-Ottoman clamor only another anti-British outcry. Istanbul succumbed to a British ultimatum to delimit the frontier in Egypt's favor.

Almost before the Taba affair was concluded the students at the School of Law, ardent followers of Kamil, went out on strike, the first demonstration of its kind in Egypt. In the end Cromer had to arbitrate the matter. By 1908 student and labor union strikes would become ordinary occurrences.

Then, in May 1906, the Dinshaway affair altered irrevocably the course of political life in Egypt. A group of British officers went to Dinshaway, a village near Tanta, to shoot pigeons, a favorite sport of theirs. Without securing permission from the village headman, they greatly antagonized the villagers, who regarded the pigeons as their domesticated birds. A fire broke out, a gun went off, a village woman was shot, British officers were mauled and one died from heat exhaustion, and a peasant was beaten to death before order was restored. The British judged that stern measures were needed and at Cromer's insistence set up a special tribunal to try the Dinshaway villagers on charges of murder. Composed of Butros Pasha Ghali, the minister of justice, the British judicial adviser, the British vice president of the courts, the Egyptian president of the native courts, and a British army judge, the special tribunal imposed on various villagers sentences of death, public lashings, life imprisonment, or long jail terms. Punishments were carried out immediately, in public view, in the village. The severity of the judgment stunned Egypt and shocked Europe.

For many Egyptians the naked display of power at Dinshaway led to the birth of nationalist feeling and the formation of political parties. Mustafa Kamil set up the Nationalist party, and followers of Muhammad Abduh organized the Party of the Nation, Hizb al-Ummah. All these urged the institution of representative government in Egypt, replacement of European officials by Egyptians, and transfer of criminal jurisdiction over foreigners from consular courts to the Mixed Courts. Though Cromer secured the appointment of Saad Zaghlul, a leading member of al-Ummah, as minister of education, Cromer's style of governing Egypt now was unsuccessful, and he resigned in 1907. Kamil, on the occasion, wrote in his paper that Cromer had negated the khedive's authority, seized the Sudan with Egyptian men and money and then stripped Egypt of any influence there, denied Egyptians any power at home, insulted Islam, forced Egyptians to be governed by Englishmen, and converted Egypt into a British colony. Kamil's condemnation was widely accepted in Egypt, and Cromer ultimately came to be seen as epitomizing British imperialism, which was viewed by most Egyptians as a negative phenomenon despite a few positive accomplishments.

THE LEGISLATIVE ASSEMBLY AND SAAD ZAGHLUL

Despite the crises of 1906 and financial difficulties in 1907, no popular uprising surfaced. The alliance of nationalists and the khedive against the British was ineffective. Many educated Egyptians, especially among the Coptic Christian minority, supported the Party of the Nation (al-Ummah), a moderate group under the leadership of the scholar and lawyer Ahmad Lutfi al-Sayyid. The leaders of al-Ummah, although wanting a British departure, recognized that Cromer had established financial equilibrium, doubled government revenues, organized an orderly and tolerably efficient government, and instituted considerable justice in the administration and the courts. For this they were thankful. Life was not bad enough to warrant a revolt.

To replace Cromer, London sent Sir Eldon Gorst, who had been in Egyptian government service from 1886 to 1904. Gorst had instructions to win over Abbas, break the alliance between the palace and the nationalists, and prepare Egypt for self-rule. Gorst began by opening up more administrative positions for Egyptians. He extended the power of the provincial councils but would not consider the nationalists' call for true legislative institutions and a constitution, even though the Ottoman constitution was restored in 1908.

In 1908, Mustafa Fahmi bowed to pressure on all sides and finally resigned as prime minister. In his place Gorst installed Butros Pasha Ghali, a leader of the reformist group inside the Coptic Christian community. (His grandson, Boutros Boutros-Ghali, a prominent Egyptian diplomat, became secretary-general of the United Nations in 1992.) For the nationalists a worse choice could not have been found, since as a cabinet minister Butros Pasha Ghali had signed the Anglo-Egyptian condominium over the Sudan and as a judge he had sat at the Dinshaway trial. Also, in 1909, the Suez Canal Company, whose concession ran until 1969, offered to pay the Egyptian government £1 million a year to extend the concession an additional forty years, but with more profits going to Egypt. Many thought this to be an attractive proposition and, urged on by al-Ummah leaders and by Gorst, Butros requested the Legislative Council's approval. The debate over the extension was vehement; Butros was accused of selling Egyptian property and of perpetrating a dishonorable arrangement; in 1910, before the request was rejected, he was assassinated.

These events broke Gorst's spirit; overcome by ill health, he returned to England, where he died in 1911. He was replaced by Lord Kitchener, who had served in Egypt in various capacities from 1883 to 1899. Kitchener's appointment indicated the end of Gorst's policies. International tensions mounted rapidly with the Italian invasion of Libya, just to the west of Egypt. The resulting Ottoman-Italian war reinforced Egyptian feeling against European imperialism. In 1913 a new Legislative Assembly joined together the old Legislative Council and General Assembly. Most of the new legislature's members were elected; by occupation the members were predominantly rich landowners and lawyers; no seats were reserved for religious minorities; and the Party of the Nation, al-Ummah, held a majority.

Saad Zaghlul (d. 1927) now became the most prominent Egyptian nationalist spokesman in the legislature. The son of a village headman, he was educated at both al-Azhar and the khedivial law school; Zaghlul was a lawyer, judge, and government official with connections to such important figures as Prime Minister Mustafa Fahmi, his father-in-law. Zaghlul won a seat in the Legislative Assembly with a program for attaining justice in the courts, spreading public education, and increasing freedom of the press. Despite opposition from Kitchener, Zaghlul was popularly designated as the natural leader of the opposition, and he became vice president of the assembly. However, the khedive asked Husain Rushdi and not Zaghlul to form a cabinet, which remained in office until the end of World War I in 1918. The assembly seemed on the verge of gaining real power over the cabinet and government administration when it adjourned in June 1914, but the outbreak of war in Europe stopped this process.

During the summer of 1914, Kitchener became minister of war in London; Abbas Hilmi, who was in Istanbul, was not permitted to return to Cairo; and martial law was invoked in Egypt. In December Great Britain declared a protectorate over Egypt and the Sudan. Kitchener's mission as British agent had failed. By 1914 the efficiency of British officials in Egypt could be legitimately questioned, for their effectiveness was weakened because they were not Egyptians.

Between 1882 and 1914 Britain had succeeded in stabilizing its control over Egypt and extending its military power into the Sudan as well. This period witnessed substantial economic growth and the development of infrastructure, especially in the production of cotton and the increase of irrigation, while the Suez Canal had become even more important commercially and strategically. As the decades passed and Britain gave no sign of leaving, opposition to British personnel, policies, and power steadily expanded, among both the political elite and the Egyptian masses. Incidents like that at Dinshaway starkly showed the negative side of British imperialism; as a result, Egyptian nationalists such as Saad Zaghlul appealed to a wide range of people.

The opportunities and problems the Egyptians were to experience in the post–World War I period were coming quickly to the fore even before 1914. The population was growing very rapidly, and social changes, such as the emergence of the new professionals, the disappearance of the guilds, and debates over gender relations, placed even more pressure on the existing political structure. Only the outbreak of war and subsequent strong military occupation prevented Egyptian nationalists from openly attacking the British position. Such action was reserved for the time following the war.

The British occupation of Egypt and the Sudan was part of a trend throughout the Middle East and North Africa by which European powers gained total control or great influence; this could be seen in France's actions in Tunisia and Morocco, Britain's movement into Cyprus, and the Italian conquest of Libya. Even in the Ottoman central lands and in independent Iran European powers became more and more influential in the decades leading up to World War I.

REFERENCES

References cited at the end of Chapters 10, 24, 26, and 27 are also pertinent to this chapter.

Amin, Qasim: *The Liberation of Women: A Document in the History of Egyptian Feminism.* Cairo: American University in Cairo Press, 1992. An important work by a male Egyptian writer, originally published in 1899.

Baer, Gabriel: *Studies in the Social History of Modern Egypt.* Chicago: University of Chicago Press, 1969. A study of the social background that helps mold political events.

Baron, Beth: *The Women's Awakening in Egypt: Culture, Society, and the Press.* New Haven, Conn.: Yale University Press, 1994. Concentrates on the years 1892–1919 as the author examines public and family issues.

Berque, Jacques: *Egypt: Imperialism and Revolution.* Translated by Jean Stewart. New York: Praeger, 1972. A description of the rise and decline of British power in Egypt, or the interrelated processes of colonization and decolonization, 1882–1952.

Brown, Nathan J.: *Peasant Politics in Modern Egypt: The Struggle against the State.* New Haven, Conn.: Yale University Press, 1990. Examines social structure, images, and actions taken by peasants from 1882 to 1952.

Cromer, Evelyn Baring: *Modern Egypt.* 2 vols. London: Macmillan, 1908. Cromer's account of his rule in Egypt; invaluable.

Holt, P. M.: *The Mahdist State in the Sudan, 1881–1898: A Study of Its Origins, Development and Overthrow.* 2d ed. Oxford, England: Clarendon Press, 1970.

Holt, P. M., and M. W. Daly: *A History of the Sudan from the Coming of Islam to the Present Day.* 5th ed. Harlow, England: Longman, 2000. A classic discussion of the subject by two authorities on the Sudan.

Keddie, Nikki R.: *Sayyid Jamal ad-Din "Al-Afghani": A Political Biography.* Berkeley: University of California Press, 1972. A definitive biography of the political activist and publicist.

Lloyd, George Ambrose L.: *Egypt Since Cromer,* 2 vols. London: Macmillan, 1933–1934. Lord Lloyd was an official in Egypt.

Marlowe, John: *Cromer in Egypt.* New York: Praeger, 1970. Covers Egyptian finances and British negotiations with other European powers as well as the details of Cromer's administration.

Mitchell, Timothy: *Colonising Egypt.* Cambridge, England: Cambridge University Press, 1988. A subtle examination of European and Egyptian attitudes and language in such fields as education, the effects of which were to foster British control.

Reid, Donald Malcolm: *Whose Pharaohs? Archaeology, Muslims, and Egyptian National Identity from Napoleon to World War I.* Berkeley: University of California Press, 2002. A thorough study of cultural and institutional history.

Richards, Alan: *Egypt's Agricultural Development, 1800–1980: Technical and Social Change.* Boulder, Colo.: Westview Press, 1981. Excellent treatment of the social impact of agricultural and technical changes; emphasizes importance of drainage and shows the damage caused by its neglect.

Al-Sayyid, Afaf Lutfi: *Egypt and Cromer: A Study in Anglo-Egyptian Relations.* New York: Praeger, 1968. The nationalist movement and the British reaction to it. The author had access to many private papers of nationalist leaders.

Seikaly, Samir: "Coptic Communal Reform, 1860–1914." *Middle Eastern Studies* 6 (1970): 247–275. A fine study of a neglected subject, this article shows that the Christian Copts of Egypt went through many of the same changes as the religious millets in the other parts of the Ottoman Empire in the late nineteenth century.

Sonbol, Amira, tr. and ed.: *The Last Khedive of Egypt: Memoirs of Abbas Hilmi II.* London: Ithaca Press, 1998. The khedive's own story.

Sonbol, Amira El-Azhary: *The New Mamluks: Egyptian Society and Modern Feudalism.* Syracuse, N.Y.: Syracuse University Press, 2000. Discusses the divisions between the elite and most Egyptians from the days of Mehmet Ali to Anwar Sadat.

Tignor, Robert L.: *Modernization and British Colonial Rule in Egypt, 1882–1914.* Princeton, N.J.: Princeton University Press, 1966. A balanced and fair evaluation written in a clear and orderly fashion; the best general study of this period.

Voll, John: "The Sudanese Mahdi: Frontier Fundamentalist." *International Journal of Middle East Studies* 10 (1979): 145–166. Valuable for putting the Mahdi into a broad analytical framework.

CHAPTER 29

Qajar Iran and Reform

Beginning in the 1790s, the Shii Qajar dynasty under its first two rulers, Aga Muhammad and Fath Ali, reestablished the political unity of Iran while preserving its independence. As discussed in Chapter 22, the Qajars sought to centralize political and military power in their new capital of Tehran, but they had to deal with the increasingly powerful influences of Russia and Britain as well as internal factors that limited their effectiveness.

Qajar legitimacy and administration were based on Shii Islam, a patrimonial role for the all-powerful shahs, and employment of the royal princes as provincial governors. During the nineteenth century Iran under the Qajar shahs attempted to modernize its army, civil administration, and economy, but with only limited success. Iran had to watch as Russia and Britain intervened in neighboring territories in central Asia and Afghanistan. Shii ulama and nationalists came to question the shahs' Europeanizing reforms. The long reign of Nasir al-Din Shah (r. 1848–1896) particularly witnessed many initiatives designed to improve the strength of the country and to defend the homeland.

MUHAMMAD SHAH AND THE ULAMA

Abbas, the reform-minded crown prince of Iran, died in 1833, and the next year Fath Ali Shah Qajar also died, leaving his grandson Muhammad (r. 1834–1848) as the heir, but some of the numerous Qajar royal family refused to recognize him as shah. The British and Russian ministers in Iran cooperated to fund Muhammad's armed supporters, who assured him the throne. The new shah appointed his tutor, Hajji Mirza Aqasi, as chief minister, a post he held throughout Muhammad's rule. Hajji Mirza had studied under the famous Sufis of the time and had himself been a wandering Sufi. One English observer called him lewd, ignorant, fanatic, and avaricious, whereas the shah believed he could perform miracles and had direct contact with God.

The legitimacy of the Qajars, including that of the new Muhammad Shah, rested on Shii Islam, the military strength manifested in the dynasty's founding years, and in Iranian cultural-national unity. The Persian language, a shared history, and cultural

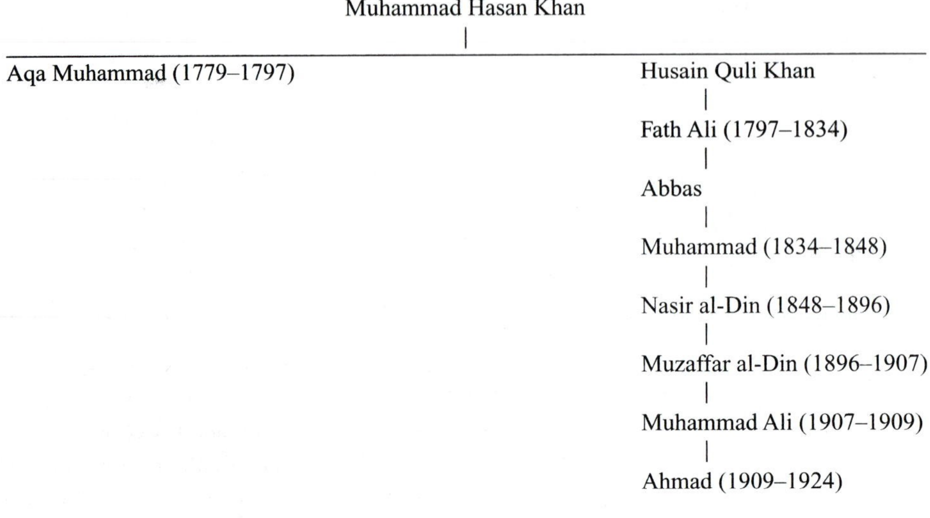

The Qajars

accomplishments helped unite the country under the Qajar dynasty, even though various linguistic, ethnic, and religious minority groups persisted inside the Iranian realm. Forces working toward the weakness of the state included tribal groups and the ulama.

Many Shii Iranians increasingly looked to their religious leaders for inspiration and guidance. Ulama held considerable power for several reasons. Shii theology allowed leeway for them to interpret the Quran and the traditions of the prophet Muhammad and the twelve imams, and gave their rulings on legal and political matters a considerable impact. The ulama frequently mediated confrontations arising between cities and provinces. The ulama also possessed great wealth derived from the taxes that all Shiis were obligated to pay directly to them, as well as from rich endowments (awqaf) scattered across the land. Another factor in the power wielded by the ulama was that the recognized center of Shii thought lay in shrines in Ottoman Iraq outside of Iran, and beyond the reach of Qajar power.

Throughout his reign Muhammad Shah and his minister favored Sufis and Sufism against the established, conservative Shii ulama. The shah's subjects found themselves caught between the realities of monarchical power and the religious authority of the ulama, a conflict that was not resolved. By enhancing Sufism, Muhammad Shah strengthened the state and the central government. He proceeded to remove many types of cases from religious courts, subjected provincial governors to closer scrutiny from Tehran, continued modest military reforms, issued decrees banning torture as a means of punishment, and abolished the slave trade by sea. An abstainer, he prohibited the sale of alcohol as well.

THE CAUCASUS, CENTRAL ASIA, AND AFGHANISTAN

Another problem facing the new shah was Russian and British expansionism in central Asia and Afghanistan. During the 1826–1828 war initiated by Iran, Russians had captured the Iranian-influenced sections of the Caucasus, and even Tabriz in Iran proper. The Treaty

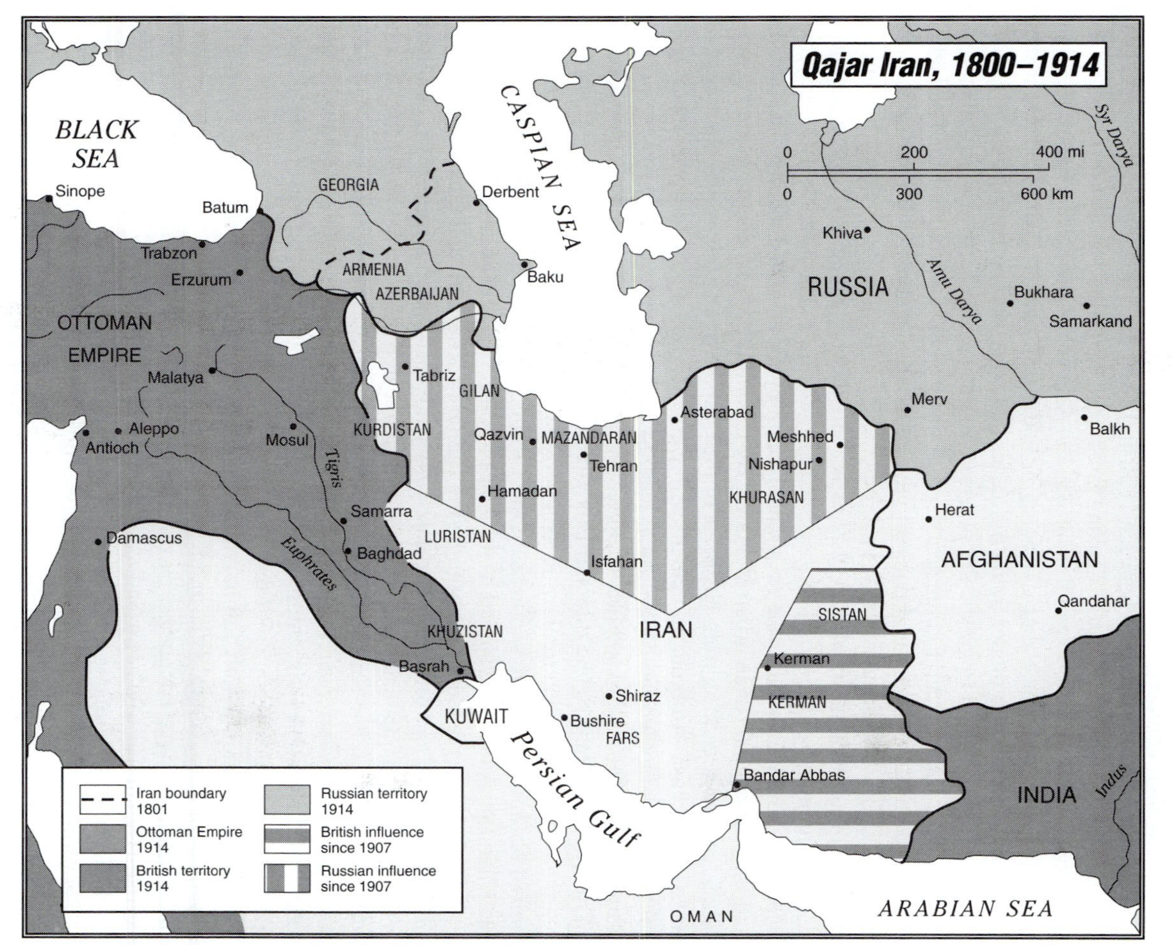
Qajar Iran, 1800–1914
0
200
400 mi
0
300
600 km
BLACK SEA
CASPIAN SEA
Persian Gulf
ARABIAN SEA
Syr Darya
Amu Darya
Tigris
Euphrates
Indus
RUSSIA
OTTOMAN EMPIRE
IRAN
AFGHANISTAN
INDIA
KUWAIT
OMAN
GEORGIA
ARMENIA
AZERBAIJAN
KURDISTAN
GILAN
MAZANDARAN
KHURASAN
LURISTAN
KHUZISTAN
SISTAN
KERMAN
FARS
Sinope
Batum
Trabzon
Erzurum
Malatya
Aleppo
Antioch
Mosul
Samarra
Baghdad
Damascus
Basrah
Derbent
Baku
Tabriz
Qazvin
Tehran
Hamadan
Isfahan
Asterabad
Meshhed
Nishapur
Khiva
Bukhara
Samarkand
Merv
Balkh
Herat
Qandahar
Kerman
Shiraz
Bushire
Bandar Abbas
Iran boundary 1801
Ottoman Empire 1914
British territory 1914
Russian territory 1914
British influence since 1907
Russian influence since 1907

of Turkmanchay of 1828 signaled the loss of the Caucasus to Russia, provided indemnities to the tsar, and, most significant, gave Russians capitulatory commercial and legal rights in Iran, rights that soon were extended to other Europeans.

Russia then embarked on a systematic expansion into the Caucasus, provoking a fierce resistance led by Shamil between 1836 and 1859. By 1864 the Russians had brutally suppressed most opposition, causing hundreds of thousands of Muslims to flee the Caucasus. Russia also was expanding into central Asia, where in the first half of the nineteenth century three new Uzbeg dynasties in Bukhara, Khiva, and Khokand established central power based on modernizing militaries and increased bureaucracies, while ruling over ethnically and linguistically diverse populations. Eastern Turkish dialects and Persian were the two chief languages used in government and urban life. The Uzbeg rulers undertook conquests and raids into the steppes and against China and Qajar Iran, but the Uzbeg states quarreled with each other and could not fully integrate the various nomadic groups into their political systems, leaving the region open to Russian conquest.

Muhammad Shah's successors saw Russia seeking political control, commercial expansion, and increased leverage against Britain by moving first against the Kazakhs and then the central Asian urban khanates. By the middle 1850s Russia gained control of a large area stretching from northeast of the Caspian Sea to the Aral Sea and beyond to Lake Balkhash. A border agreement with China in 1864 opened the way to successful Russian campaigns in central Asia, leading to the annexation of Tashkent (1865), Samarkand (1868), Khokand (1876), and Merv (1884), and their organization as units of the Russian Empire. The rulers of Bukhara and Khiva became vassals of Russia but maintained some local autonomy. Russia built railways and encouraged cotton production in central Asia, while suppressing the Turkoman tribes that had often raided Iranian Khurasan. And Russia spread its influence toward Afghanistan and northeastern Iran.

The Qajars considered Herat to be the capital of Khurasan and thus a rightful part of their realm, as had often been the case for past dynasties, but this area was contested by independent Afghanistan and by Britain, which feared negative developments near its territories in India. The Sadozai dynasty based on Durrani Pashtun tribal groups had ruled Afghanistan and adjacent areas from its capital at Kabul throughout most of the late eighteenth and early nineteenth centuries, but Amir Dost Muhammad (r. 1826–1863) founded a new Muhammadzai branch of the Durrani dynasty that would rule Afghanistan until 1973. While predominantly Sunni Afghanistan was sorting out its rulership, peripheral provinces in India, central Asia, and Khurasan (still under the Sadozai Durranis) became independent or were conquered by other groups. British India intervened in the first British-Afghan war to place a Sadozai Durrani ruler on the throne in Kabul from 1839 to 1843, but Dost Muhammad returned triumphant and then set out to establish his central government's authority over all the former provinces of Afghanistan, including Herat.

In 1836–1837 Muhammad Shah Qajar of Iran had attacked Herat. The British tried to dissuade him from the campaign because they felt it would open Afghanistan and the approaches to British India to Russian interference through a pro-Russian Iran. An English artillery officer successfully contrived Herat's defense, and the British went to war with Iran, occupying portions of its territory along the Persian Gulf. After a peace was arranged in 1838 the British established a kind of protectorate over Herat.

Iran under Nasir al-Din Shah (r. 1848–1896) attacked and occupied Herat in 1856. The British in India declared war and sent a naval force, cavalry, and artillery into the Persian Gulf, taking Bushire and the island of Kharg. In 1857, at the conclusion of the Crimean War, Nasir al-Din's envoy in Paris negotiated a settlement with the British to end the second Anglo-Iranian war. By the terms of the treaty Iran withdrew from Herat and recognized it as a part of Afghanistan, and the British evacuated the Iranian territories they had occupied in the Persian Gulf. The treaty also assigned special commercial privileges to the British and gave standard capitulatory rights to British nationals in Iran.

Sher Ali (r. 1868–1879) held Herat for Afghanistan while also beginning to modernize the administration of the country. His reforms in tax collection, provincial administration, and education were interrupted by the second British-Afghan war of 1878–1881, which resulted in British control of Afghanistan's foreign policy and the positioning of the country as a buffer state between Russian Central Asia, British India, and Qajar Iran. Sher Ali's nephew Abd al-Rahman (r. 1880–1901) used British subventions to support a policy of harsh centralization inside secure borders. Despite numerous tribal rebellions against him, he succeeded in systemizing tax collections, rebuilding the paid army, and establishing some state-run industries. Abd al-Rahman united the mountainous regions occupied by Afghanistan to a greater degree than had been the case before, although local groups still retained a great deal of autonomy.

BABISM AND BAHA'ISM

Although Muhammad Shah devoted much attention to foreign policy, particularly in central Asia and Afghanistan, the rise of a new religion in Iran also preoccupied him. Babism began in Shiraz with the preaching and teaching of Sayyid Ali Muhammad (b. 1819), a merchant who had spent his youth in religious study. In 1844, one thousand lunar years after the disappearance of the Twelfth Imam of the Shiis, his followers hailed him as the Bab, or "Gate," between the world of the flesh and that of the spirit. Only through him, the Bab, was the Twelfth Imam in touch with the world. He assumed the role of point of manifestation of the divine essence and called for universal peace, improvement of the life of women, destruction of many status distinctions, and a society that followed the spirit rather than the letter of religion.

Iran was witnessing considerable social and intellectual unrest at the time. Outbreaks of cholera, military losses to Russia and Britain, economic difficulties, and the brutality and inefficiency of Qajar rule all contributed to an environment where a new religion could flourish. Also, as Shii theology became more restricted and narrowly defined, theologians with new interpretations and views found it difficult to gain acceptance among the mainstream ulama.

At the time of Muhammad Shah's death the Bab was imprisoned in Tabriz and had been interrogated by the crown prince. The Bab now claimed to be the Mahdi-Imam, and he and his followers seceded from Islam. In 1850 the new shah, Nasir al-Din, experiencing serious insurrections by devotees of the Bab, with the approval of three ulama ordered that he be put to death.

Two years after the Bab had been executed, a member of the sect attempted to assassinate the shah. As a consequence, many Babists were massacred throughout Iran. Some leaders of the new religion escaped from Iran to establish two branches of the faith: one became headquartered in the European part of the Ottoman Empire but ultimately died out; the other was centered in Acre and Haifa in Ottoman Palestine. It later spread widely in Europe and the United States under the name of the Baha'i faith and thrives to this day. It renounced the use of force, even when persecuted, as in Iran during the nineteenth century and some parts of the twentieth century.

FIRST YEARS OF NASIR AL-DIN SHAH

When Muhammad Shah died in 1848, Qajar family rivalries were held in check by British and Russian officers. The British legation induced a group of notables to form a regency council for the sixteen-year-old Crown Prince Nasir al-Din while he made his way to Tehran from administering Tabriz. Nasir al-Din Shah appointed his tutor Mirza Taqi Khan Amir-i Kabir as first minister. Taqi was the son of the cook of a high government official, who had given him a fine education. Prior to his elevation to his high post, Taqi had been in Erzurum, where he had learned about the Ottoman reforms of the Tanzimat. He had also participated in a mission to St. Petersburg, the Russian capital. Taqi became known as a man of stern integrity who possessed great zeal for reform. Naturally, the palace courtiers and the queen mother, who dominated the harem, disliked him. With an empty treasury and a serious revolt in Khurasan, Taqi faced a difficult situation.

Though Taqi's predecessor was superstitious, he was aware of the economic and agricultural changes creeping across the 20 percent of the land that could be farmed. Hajji Mirza recognized that cotton, opium, silk, dried fruits, and nuts had become cash crops for export to foreign markets, tempting the landlords to press their peasants severely in order to garner profits. Land now produced more wealth in addition to the high social status it had previously conferred. Taqi extended this policy and became the merchants' friend. He built the great bazaar in Tehran and encouraged the growth of a mercantile class.

In these years three politically active strata arose beneath the royal court. There was the old elite, landed aristocratic nobles who relied for their power on inherited privileges, extortion, and intrigue. The second stratum consisted of the ulama, who controlled the courts, justice, morals, education, religion, and intellectual life in Iran. The third stratum consisted of the new merchants, many of whom had traveled abroad to the Ottoman lands, Russia, Egypt, India, and even China, and brought home not only wealth but ideas of a wider world.

In suppressing the rebellion in Khurasan, Taqi formed an army of about 20,000 soldiers who were paid on time. Believing that the ulama should not participate in politics, he sent the army to Tabriz in 1850 and carried off the chief religious figure. But Taqi had gone too far, and in 1851 Nasir al-Din was induced by the ulama, the court, and his mother to dismiss the chief minister and to agree to his murder shortly thereafter. Taqi was replaced by Mirza Aqa Khan Nuri, a mediocrity who managed diplomacy and public affairs for his own advantage. Nasir al-Din was never happy with him. Because of Aqa Khan Nuri's failed policies in Afghanistan and the war with Britain, he was dismissed in 1858.

THE AGE OF ATTEMPTED REFORMS

Nasir al-Din ruled for a long time with few rebellions against his authority, and he undertook many reforms while borrowing very little money from abroad, but at the same time most of the reforms turned out to be far less effective than those begun earlier by the Ottomans and Mehmet Ali of Egypt. One factor that ironically promoted both the longevity of his rule and his lack of success in reforms was the competition between the British and the Russians, with each of the two powers fearing that the other might gain an advantage in Iran. Also working against Nasir al-Din's success were his own inconsistency, the falling value of silver used as Iran's currency, a decline in real revenues coming into the government, his inability to find competent administrators, the primitive state of transportation and infrastructure, the great famine of 1869–1872, which killed hundreds of thousands of people, the nearly autonomous condition of several parts of the country, and the high status of the ulama.

With Iran at peace Nasir al-Din made a trip in 1870 to the Shii holy places in Ottoman Iraq. He was escorted by Prince Husain Khan, the Iranian ambassador in Istanbul, and met Midhat Pasha, then governor of Baghdad, with whom he discussed Ottoman reforms. Husain accompanied the shah back to Tehran, where he became first minister, attempted some reforms, and dominated much of the government for the next ten years. The journey to Iraq was so pleasant that Nasir al-Din subsequently made three visits to Europe, nearly bankrupting the Iranian treasury. The shah was impressed with the display of vast wealth in Europe. He returned home convinced that foreign money invested in Iran would develop the country into a prosperous state similar to those he saw in Europe.

Modern infrastructure was largely missing: between the urban centers of the central provinces there were vast stretches of mostly barren countryside controlled by nomadic and seminomadic tribes. The central government in Tehran found it impossible to completely control the tribes, even when the sons of tribal leaders were kept as hostages at the shah's court, until the advent of the airplane after World War I finally gave the central authorities more military strength. Outside of Tehran the government could do little beyond collect revenue, and not much of that! However, the building of telegraph lines across Iran, in the main to connect London to India, played an important role in opening Iran to the world. The first line was merely a toy to impress the shah, but within a few years Tehran was connected with several other parts of Iran. The rights to the international lines were sold to English companies beginning in 1862, and a local line, alongside the international ones, carried Iranian messages. No longer was Iran isolated.

The shah and the ministers, always short of funds, soon learned that Europeans would pay handsome sums in ready cash and give enormous bribes for a privilege or concession. In 1872, the shah granted to Baron Julius de Reuter a seventy-year economic concession for the development of Iran's economy and industry. So much clamor against this monopolistic concession was raised in all sectors of society in Iran, and in Russia as well, that obstacles were placed in de Reuter's way to prevent his compliance with the contracts. The money guarantees accrued to the shah, the bribes were kept, and Russia and the populace were satisfied by the concession's termination and appeased by the dismissal of Prince Husain Khan as first minister. But concession hunting continued.

In 1888, Sir Henry Drummond-Wolff arrived in Tehran as the new British minister. He intended to open the Karun River to international steamer traffic to meet possible Russian railway building in the north. Sir Henry gave the shah a written guarantee that England would prevent infringement of the integrity of Iran by any other power. With this guarantee against Russian actions, the shah issued decrees permitting foreigners to operate commercial steamers on the Karun River and to establish the Imperial Bank of Persia, which for sixty years would have the right to issue money in Iran and to engage in financial and commercial transactions.

Russian influence, however, was not completely lost. On the shah's second trip to Europe he was frequently escorted by impressive Russian cossacks. He obtained from the tsar some Russian military instructors, who were to reform and improve the army. By 1879 the shah could see an Iranian Cossack Brigade, with Russian and Iranian officers. For a number of years its leadership was rather poor, but in 1894 it again became a disciplined and effective instrument of Russian pressure in Iran, lasting until 1921. It was the only effective modern unit in the Iranian army, the balance of which consisted for the most part of irregular tribal cavalry and provincial forces coming from the villages and under the command of local governors. In the early 1900s the infantry numbered only about 13,000 (including the small Cossack Brigade); the regular soldiers were conscripted for life and were poorly armed and paid. Tribal irregular warriors also numbered about 13,000 and were perhaps better armed than the regular army. (Iran had no navy at all until 1885, and thereafter only a very small one.)

Russia also had a letter from Nasir al-Din in 1887 engaging Iran not to give any concession for building a railway without consulting Russia. In 1890 Iran agreed to Russia's demand that no railway would be built for the next ten years; in 1900 the convention was renewed. Thus, by 1914 practically no railways existed in Iran.

Nasir al-Din Shah did accomplish some centralizing and modernizing reforms. Government operations were reorganized several times, and various ministries and advisory councils were created. The shah consolidated in the capital the minting of coins and set up a European-style police force in Tehran, while postage stamps were introduced in 1870. Some factories were built by the government in the 1850s and 1860s, but they were failures economically. The shah, largely in response to pressure from the British, took measures against the importation of slaves and the slave trade. A modern government hospital, managed by Germans, was opened in Tehran in 1869. Nasir al-Din Shah also sent students to Europe to study at government expense, although from 1811 to 1911 only about 100 Iranians graduated from European universities. Government officials opened public elementary schools for boys starting in 1873, military high schools in 1882, and a public school for girls in 1918, but most education was still conducted in private primary institutions by the ulama, who opposed government intervention in education.

Culturally, Nasir al-Din Shah's long reign saw the decay of Iranian art in such fields as ceramics, but new art forms, especially photography, and revivals of traditional music and painting lacquer items were supported by the royal court. Old architectural traditions were perpetuated in building palaces, although they were somewhat modified by European influences. The shah and various notables built religious theaters decorated with paintings and murals and dedicated to enacting ceremonies related to the martyrdom of the Imam Husain. Persian writers, including the shah himself, adopted a more comprehensible literary style; the flowery and elaborate forms of earlier days were gradually simplified and clarified. A modern Persian journalistic style of writing came into use. An official newspaper was published; an establishment of higher education, the Dar al-Funun, was founded; a translation bureau was created; French became the chief foreign language studied; and about 160 books were printed in the country during the century.

Many announced reforms were only partially implemented or, after the fall of their sponsors from government office, abandoned. Nasir al-Din was unable to push through major innovations in government and the military, and the number of reform-minded government leaders was too small to allow them to assume control of the process. Powerful vested interests, including foreign powers, saw the reforms as a threat to their positions, while most Iranians perceived the reforms and the reformers to be too Europeanized. The population of Iran grew somewhat, even though economic, agricultural, and health factors limited natural increase. And many provinces remained in the hands of semihereditary rulers or officials who purchased the right to hold positions; provincial revenues were kept largely in the provinces and not sent on to Tehran. Provincial officials resisted the shah's centralizing, as in the case of attempted judicial reforms, so urban legal procedures remained as before, with criminal cases handled by the police and religious judges dealing with personal law.

THE ECONOMY AND THE TOBACCO CONCESSION

Half of the population of around 10 million lived in villages; perhaps one-quarter of all the people were nomads, and about one-quarter inhabited cities. The economy depended chiefly on crops, so that when prices for agricultural products and raw materials fell dramatically throughout the world after the mid-1870s, this produced financial crises in many countries, including Iran. The amount of wheat exported in 1894 was eight times what it had been a quarter of a century before, but the price had decreased so much that total receipts for wheat exports remained the same.

It was different for some exported commodities, such as opium, cotton, and rice, whose production and value rose sharply in the 1870s. Agriculture became more diversified and more oriented toward exporting cash crops, as Iran became partially integrated into the world economic system. In response to demand from Europe, knotted pile carpet production became a major industry employing mostly young girls, although European imports nearly destroyed the cotton- and wool-weaving textile industries in southern and central Iran. With the opening up of the country to world trade, imports and exports doubled and then tripled. Prices rose rapidly as the value of the silver coinage decreased. Despite some limited increases in agriculture, year by year the government, the shah, public officials, wealthy merchants, and the lower ranks of the ulama found it more difficult to make ends meet.

Aside from the element of greed, fundamentally the idea behind the granting of most of the concessions to Europeans was to try to consolidate and centralize the economy and to entice foreign capital and expertise to develop the resources of the state. The hope of attracting foreign capital was one motive for the shah's trips to Europe. Unfortunately, the entire process was riddled with corrupt practices and managed by unscrupulous adventurers. Iran was being sold bit by bit to foreigners.

In England in 1889, Drummond-Wolff introduced the shah to a Major Gerald Talbot, who asked for the monopoly to buy, sell, and manufacture tobacco in Iran for fifty years. Generous bribes were handed to the shah and others, and the concession was given in 1890. The company to be formed would pay the Iranian treasury £15,000 and 25 percent of its net profits annually; in return the company would control the entire traffic in tobacco—even members of the tobacco sellers' guilds would have to obtain permits from the company to engage in local trade. For many farmers this would mean selling their tobacco to the company and then buying it back.

The Imperial Tobacco Corporation of Persia bought the concession from Talbot and set out to implement the monopoly. By 1891 a nationalist, popular, mass campaign was organized against the government and concentrated on the tobacco issue, for of all the concessions granted to foreign capital this one touched the most people directly. Jamal al-Din al-Afghani, who had returned to Iran in 1889 upon the shah's invitation, was one of the leaders. Jamal al-Din so aroused the shah's ire by preaching openly against the government that he had to take sanctuary in the shrine of Shah Abd al-Azim outside Tehran. From there he continued his attack, scattering leaflets throughout the capital, until Nasir al-Din ordered him removed from the shrine, thus violating sanctuary. He was deposited across the Ottoman frontier.

But the eviction did not end the crisis. Merchants rebelled; warnings of violence against those who used tobacco spread across the land; and some merchants burned their entire stock rather than sell it to the company. Ulama petitioned the shah against the monopoly, stating that the Quran prohibited infidels to have control over Muslims. Soldiers dispelled the crowds of protesters in several cities, and some people were killed. Women participated significantly in the protests. A religious decree, promulgated apparently by the leading Shii theologian at the holy places in Iraq, calling upon all Muslims to abstain from smoking, was observed everywhere in Iran. Even the shah's wives refused to smoke! The shah canceled the concession. This popular victory over the government and the shah by the religious and city leaders made further movements of this nature possible. Moreover, a loan to the government to pay indemnities arising from the cancellation of the tobacco concession opened the door to more such loans in the following decade, leading Iran closer to the brink of bankruptcy.

In the midst of the anti-British tobacco crisis Russian nationals obtained concessions for insurance companies, lumbering, and other endeavors. One of the more important privileges granted Russia was permission to open the Discount and Loan Bank of Persia, which, in fact, was a branch of the Russian ministry of finance. The bank made loans on easy terms to princes, officials, ulama, and merchants; by 1900 it was said that Russia had bought off nearly all the ruling elite. In the middle 1890s there was a standoff between England and Russia in their diplomatic and economic maneuvers in Iran; Russian activity centered in the north, while the British dominated the south.

Pessimism was the paramount mood even in high circles in Iran, as the shah's energy and interest waned. The shah's brother suggested that Iran was like "a lump of sugar in a glass of water" gradually melting away, while the shah's third son, as commander in chief, neglected and robbed the troops. In desperation the first minister, Ali Asghar Khan, even suggested to the British minister that England bribe the shah to reform! Then on May 1, 1896, Nasir al-Din was assassinated by Jamal al-Din al-Afghani's servant and follower at the Shah Abd al-Azim shrine, where his master's sanctuary had been violated.

Iranian reformers, in evaluating the reign of Nasir al-Din Shah and their country's lack of success in Europeanizing reforms as compared with Egypt or the Ottoman Empire, often pointed to the difficult mountainous geography of Iran, its distance from Europe, the lack of infrastructure, an opposition by many religious Iranians to the reform movement, and the frustrating interventions of Russia and Britain. However, unlike central Asia and Egypt, which were conquered by Russia and Britain, Iran was able to keep its independence. Iran began to develop a sense of territorial identity inside defined borders. And during the reigns of Muhammad Shah and Nasir al-Din Iran did experience some centralization of government and the introduction of new cultural trends, while preserving Shii Islam against the inroads of a new world religion. Mass opposition to the tobacco concession opened the way in the next decade to a new stage of popular involvement in governmental affairs.

REFERENCES

References cited at the end of Chapters 12, 19, and 22 are especially important for this chapter.

Algar, Hamid: *Religion and State in Iran, 1785–1906.* Berkeley: University of California Press, 1970. An important volume for understanding the political and religious system of Iran.

Amanat, Abbas: *Resurrection and Renewal: The Making of the Babi Movement in Iran, 1844–1850.* Ithaca, N.Y.: Cornell University Press, 1989. A thorough and balanced study of religious and social conditions.

———: *Pivot of the Universe: Nasir al-Din Shah Qajar and the Iranian Monarchy, 1831–1896.* Berkeley: University of California Press, 1997. This excellent biography covers chiefly the shah's reign from 1848 to 1871.

Arjomand, Said Amir: *The Shadow of God and the Hidden Imam: Religion, Political Order, and Societal Change in Shi'ite Iran from the Beginning to 1890.* Chicago: University of Chicago Press, 1984. A review of religion and politics from a social scientist's viewpoint.

Avery, Peter: *Modern Iran.* New York: Praeger, 1970. A very substantial, detailed work that begins with the mid-nineteenth century.

Bakhash, Shaul: *Iran: Monarchy, Bureaucracy and Reform under the Qajars: 1858–1896.* London: Ithaca, 1978. A comprehensive treatment of all aspects of the subject.

Balland, D.: "Afghanistan: Part X. Political History." *Encyclopaedia Iranica.* Vol. 1, pp. 547–558. London: Routledge, 1982. An excellent review from the eighteenth century to 1979.

Bayat, Mangol: *Mysticism and Dissent: Socioreligious Thought in Qajar Iran.* Syracuse, N.Y.: Syracuse University Press, 1982.

Bosworth, Edmund, and Carole Hillenbrand, eds.: *Qajar Iran: Political, Social and Cultural Change, 1800–1925.* Edinburgh: Edinburgh University Press, 1983. Twenty-one essays dealing with a wide variety of subjects.

Bregel, Yuri: "Central Asia: Part VII. In the 12th–13th/18th–19th Centuries." *Encyclopaedia Iranica.* Vol. 5, pp. 193–205. Costa Mesa, Calif.: Mazda, 1992. The best short treatment of the subject.

Daniel, Elton L.: *The History of Iran.* Westport, Conn.: Greenwood, 2001. A useful survey from antiquity to contemporary times.

Diba, Layla S., with Maryam Ekhtiar, eds.: *Royal Persian Paintings: The Qajar Epoch, 1785–1925.* London: Tauris, 1998.

Gilbar, Gad: "Demographic Developments in Late Qajar Persia, 1870–1906." *Asian and African Studies* 11 (1976): 125–156. One of a series of thoughtful and judicious analyses of Iran's economic and social history by the author.

Issawi, Charles, ed.: *The Economic History of Iran, 1800–1914.* Chicago: University of Chicago Press, 1971. Contains valuable documentary material needed for writing a coherent history of the Iranian economy.

Kashani-Sabet, Firoozeh: *Frontier Fictions: Shaping the Iranian Nation, 1804–1946.* Princeton, N.J.: Princeton University Press, 1999. A discussion of the influence of geography on shaping national identity.

Kazemzadeh, Firuz: *Russia and Britain in Persia, 1864–1914: A Study in Imperialism.* New Haven, Conn.: Yale University Press, 1968. A detailed chronicle and interpretation of diplomatic history, using primary sources.

Keddie, Nikki R.: *Religion and Rebellion in Iran: The Iranian Tobacco Protest of 1891–1892.* New York: Humanities Press, 1966. An important work on mass movements against foreign concessions.

Litvak, Meir: *Shi'i Scholars of Nineteenth-Century Iraq: The Ulama of Najaf and Karbala.* Cambridge, England: Cambridge University Press, 1998. Includes information on Iranian linkages, Shii theology, and the impact of the ulama locally.

Mahdavi, Shireen: *For God, Mammon, and Country: A Nineteenth-Century Persian Merchant, Haj Muhammad Hassan Amin al-Zarb (1834–1898).* Boulder, Colo.: Westview, 1999.

Nashat, Guity: *The Origins of Modern Reform in Iran, 1870–80.* Urbana: University of Illinois Press, 1982. A thorough discussion of the reforms of Prince Husain Khan and his experiences.

Noelle, Christine: *State and Tribe in Nineteenth-Century Afghanistan: The Reign of Amir Dost Muhammad Khan (1826–1863).* Richmond, England: Curzon Press, 1997. The state's establishment, expansion, and interaction with tribes.

Sheikholeslami, A. Reza: *The Structure of Central Authority in Qajar Iran, 1871–1896.* Atlanta: Scholars Press, 1997. Emphasizes the patrimonial nature of administration.

CHAPTER 30

Iran's Constitutional Revolution

*B*y the time of the assassination of Nasir al-Din Shah in 1896, the Qajar dynasty and the peoples of Iran had undergone only a very limited degree of modernizing Europeanization. Still, efforts to create a new intellectual climate, the more substantial involvement of Iran in world economy, reforms in the military and civil government, and the imperialist encroachments of Russia and Britain were all leading to a new phase in Iranian history. The popular, religious, and nationalistic opposition to economic concessions to Europeans continued into the reigns of Muzaffar al-Din Shah and his successor, Muhammad Ali Shah, culminating in widespread support for a constitutional revolution. The constitution was preserved despite strong opposition, but civil war and foreign intervention threw the country into great turmoil in the years leading up to World War I.

MUZAFFAR AL-DIN SHAH AND THE CONSTITUTIONAL REVOLUTION

The Russians and the British recognized Muzaffar al-Din as the new shah in 1896. He ordered Ali Asghar Khan to remain as prime minister. The transfer of power was peaceful and indicative of the long stability in the reigns of the Qajar shahs to this point: in the century from 1797 to 1896 only three shahs had ruled—Fath Ali, Muhammad, and Nasir al-Din.

Muzaffar al-Din (r. 1896–1907) was a sickly, uneducated, good-natured forty-three-year-old prince who was bored and baffled by governmental affairs and preferred the company of his wives, astrologers, and favorites. His first thought after his enthronement was a trip to Europe.

Ali Asghar Khan Amin al-Sultan, prime minister for more than a decade of hard times, had collected so many enemies that they were able to prevail upon the weak shah to dismiss him, but he had to be recalled before long because only he could secure the money needed for the shah to travel in Europe. Payments to the troops and the salaries of most officials were at least six months overdue. It was said the minister of taxation "took no bribes, which was thought foolish, and he gave none, which was thought wicked." Ali Asghar Khan's first act was to reorganize the customs offices with Belgian officials in charge and to take a loan from Russia. After paying Iran's debts, Muzaffar al-Din and his retinue set out for Europe, visiting several health spas for his kidney ailment. By the time he arrived back in Tehran the treasury was again empty. The natural recourse was another loan.

A new commercial agreement with Russia lowered the tariff on many imports from Russia and gave it a powerful grip on Iran's finances and trade. All tariffs on cotton cloth were removed, thereby ruining most Iranian cloth manufacturers. Some of the 1.5 million Iranians who worked at various times in Russia, especially in the Caucasian oil fields around Baku after the petroleum boom began in the 1870s, transferred revolutionary social ideas gained from Russian democrats and leftists back to Iran.

Internally, after the shah ordered a pension of £3000 a year for the court astrologer because he had saved the shah's life when the shah dreamed he was drowning, Ali Asghar Khan lost his temper and said he had "raised large sums to pay for the Shah's tours and toys, but must protest paying for his dreams." A new prime minister was named: Prince Abd al-Majid, Muzaffar al-Din's son-in-law and a grandson of Fath Ali Shah. But a change in prime ministers was not a cure for the ills of Iran. Agitation by the ulama against the ministers and the arrogant efficiency of the Belgian customs officials was easily blunted by Abd al-Majid, for the central government was stronger in 1903 than it had been in 1890 at the time of the tobacco affair.

A bad harvest, cholera, the Russo-Japanese War, the high cost of food, and unemployment in the cities helped bring about the important Constitutional Revolution of 1905–1906. A growing number of Iranians opposed the tyranny of the shahs, favored freedom, desired national unity, and sought reforms as a way of regaining the former glories of ancient and Safavid Iran. An eclectic assortment of groups—intellectuals, government employees, journalists, merchants, religious minorities, and some leaders of the Shii ulama—sought political changes. Secret societies spread the ideas of constitutional government, while many reformers pointed to the poverty and humiliation endured by so many Iranians. In 1905 poor peasants in Quchan, located in Khurasan, were so affected by heavy taxation they had to sell their daughters into slavery, while Sunni Turkoman tribes from across the Russian frontier raided the district, capturing women who also became slaves. The weak autocracy of the Qajars could not protect the nation. Several demonstrations took place protesting against the government, but the direct cause of the Constitutional Revolution occurred in December 1905, when several bazaar merchants in Tehran were ordered to be flogged for allegedly raising the price of sugar. Immediately, the merchants closed the bazaar and went on strike. The government ordered them to open the shops or have all their goods confiscated. Thereupon, about 2000 merchants, joined by ulama, fled to the shrine of Shah Abd al-Azim. Supported by Ali Asghar Khan and the crown prince, they insisted upon the removal of Abd al-Majid and other ministers, the ousting of the governor of Tehran, the dismissal of the Belgians from the customs offices, and the convening of a "House of Justice," to be composed of merchants, landowners, and ulama. In January 1906 the shah acceded to their demands, and they returned to Tehran.

In the spring, amid further turmoil, the shah had a stroke. Authority was weakened and responsibility diffused. Recognizing that religious sanctuary was no longer being respected, merchants, guild members, and ulama took sanctuary at the British legation on July 19, 1906. Soon some 14,000 protesters were camping in the legation garden. Giant cauldrons were brought in to prepare food. Russia did not protest, and the British tolerated the invasion. Abd al-Majid was dismissed, and the shah, after being nudged by the British, called for a representative assembly. On September 17, 1906, the shah signed the imperial decree calling for parliamentary elections. It appeared that Iran had taken a step toward limiting the power of the shahs and democracy, pushed not by an armed intervention or a revolution but by passive resistance.

Elections were held early in October, with the eligible voters being male property owners over 30 years old. The members of parliament had to be able to speak and read Persian. Not waiting for the representatives from the provinces, the successful candidates from Tehran, including many merchants, met to write a constitution and enact basic laws for a legislative body. Tehran was dramatically overrepresented in the parliament, as compared with the more distant provinces. By this time, the shah had recovered sufficiently to return to the capital to open the assembly (majlis). A new prime minister found the treasury empty, tax returns at a low ebb, salaries unpaid for six months, and sentiment in the majlis utterly opposed to any foreign loan. In the end the majlis voted unanimously to float a loan internally.

On December 30, 1906, the constitution was signed by Muzaffar al-Din Shah and Crown Prince Muhammad Ali, who had come to the capital since all knew that the shah was dying. The constitution provided for an elected majlis of 60 representatives from Tehran and 100 to 140 representatives from the provinces, and a senate of 60 members, half to be elected and half appointed by the shah. The majlis was the dominant body and would control finances and foreign affairs.

A supplementary fundamental law was added to the constitution in October 1907. The constitution called for an independent judiciary, mandatory education, and freedom of the press. Equality before the law was guaranteed for all subjects, irrespective of religion, but enactments of the majlis were supposed to be in accordance with the shariah, and Shii Islam was the official religion.

The British applauded the formation of the constitution; the Russians found it distasteful. The crown prince, who was openly pro-Russian and even spoke Russian, frankly loathed the constitution. Muzaffar al-Din Shah had died January 8, 1907, and Muhammad Ali was soon crowned as shah. With an enemy on the throne the constitution's future was in jeopardy.

MUHAMMAD ALI SHAH AND THE COUNTERREVOLUTION

Had the majlis been well organized by skillful and experienced leaders, a patriotic representative government under a constitution might have succeeded in managing Iranian affairs and found a way to avoid bankruptcy. As the members elected in the provinces joined the majlis, however, it became less and less coherent. The members were of varying backgrounds: guildsmen, merchants, ulama, bureaucrats, landowners, and professionals. Most opposed aspects of the old system of government, yet rival leaders also quarreled over old antagonisms. A member of a prominent Tehran family was elected president of the majlis, while his personal enemy led the opposition. The members from Tabriz were radical in their views, as they had been affected by revolutionaries fleeing from Russia. Political societies (anjumans) formed in every locality to influence events; some felt that the majlis was the largest anjuman of all. Within a few months even local anjumans split—in Tabriz between senior and junior clergy and in Meshhed between merchants and shrine officials. The majlis sitting in Tehran could not enforce authority in the provinces, but it prevented local governors from doing so. Local anjumans defied the majlis, the central government, and the local administration. Land taxes went unpaid, and no one collected road tolls. Smuggling prevailed. One force remaining in the provincial cities was the ulama, who claimed they represented justice since they dispensed the holy law while the government with its laws symbolized injustice, an idea that played a decisive role in the thinking of the anjumans; some of the ulama opposed the constitution, while many favored it, at least initially. Some urban women formed anjumans, demonstrated on behalf of the constitution, founded schools to promote female education, donated funds to the proposed national bank, and encouraged the production of locally made cloth. All groups who favored the constitution had to deal with the uncertainty surrounding its implementation. No one knew how the constitution would be applied in practice, so the balance between legislature and executive powers was unclear and contested.

Bankruptcy was never admitted, and the total foreign debt remained far below that accumulated by the Ottoman Empire or Egypt. When the finance minister made his report to the majlis, itemizing necessary expenditures, the majlis authorized him to borrow the required funds from the National Bank, which, however, did not exist! It was generally recognized that no government could function without cooperating with the majlis, but it became apparent that the majlis had difficulty functioning at all.

In March 1907, when bankruptcy was near, all agreed that Ali Asghar Khan, the ingenious, detested negotiator of the two Russian loans, should be invited back from exile. He nearly had arranged a loan with Russian, French, German, and British backing when on August 31, 1907, he was assassinated by a radical anjuman member from Tabriz. This blow eventually led to the demise of the majlis.

The constitutionalists suffered a second fatal injury the very same day with the signing of the Anglo-Russian Convention in St. Petersburg. In part, the document set aside the northern portion of Iran, including Tabriz, Tehran, and Meshhed, as a sphere of influence for Russia, and a small, southeastern portion from the Afghanistan border to the Persian Gulf near Bandar Abbas as a British zone; neither power would be paramount in the land between the two zones. London was more concerned with the security of India than with any interests in Iran. Russia obtained a free hand, which the constitutionalists in Tehran feared. Prince Abd al-Qasim Khan, who soon succeeded Ali Asghar Khan, could not comprehend how his British friends could abandon the constitutionalists.

Muhammad Ali Shah, though he swore three times to uphold the constitution, did not tolerate it for long. The shah suggested that Russian forces be called in to prevent riots, leading to a split within the royal family itself. The shah left the capital, gathered his forces, and moved on Tehran on June 23, 1908, where the Cossack Brigade bombarded the majlis building, arrested many leaders, and executed three of them. Muhammad Ali Shah, hand in hand with the Russians, was now the absolute ruler of Iran.

MUHAMMAD ALI SHAH ABDICATES

The shah's victory gave him control of the government in Tehran, but it also handed him full responsibility for the country's dire problems. His close friends took over the various ministries and filled their pockets as rapidly as possible to pay personal debts incurred when they had not been in control. Pressed to find a loan, the government received the same message from the Russians and British as before—reform the finances first.

Throughout Iran it was anarchy that reigned, rather than Muhammad Ali. The shah did not have much control or influence outside of Tehran. Religious leaders dominated the local anjumans and city councils. In Tabriz the anjumans and constitutionalists revolted and gradually came to rule the entire city. The shah besieged Tabriz for nine months without much success until Russian troops surrounded and invaded the city in April 1909. Rebellious forces by this time held Meshhed and Isfahan, and the entire south had slipped away. In Isfahan, power had been seized by Najaf Quli Khan, chief of the Bakhtiyari tribes, whom the shah had tried to remove. In league with the anjumans, Najaf Quli Khan revived the constitutional drive and set out with a small cavalry force for Tehran.

The shah's party in Tehran, along with British and Russian diplomats, failed to grasp the extent of the opposition. Bakhtiyaris from the south joined forces from the north to encircle Tehran, which fell in July 1909. The new government executed the highest ranking alim in Tehran, who had succeeded in adding to the Constitution a provision giving the ulama veto power over secular legislation. (Much later, in the 1980s, the ulama leaders of the Islamic Republic of Iran would see in the conservative but pro-Constitution ulama of the 1900s their heroic precursors.) The constitution was restored; Muhammad Ali Shah abdicated and took sanctuary in the Russian legation. Granted a pension, he left Tehran for Russia.

CONSTITUTIONAL GOVERNMENT, 1909–1911

A few days after Muhammad Ali abdicated, his twelve-year-old son took the throne as Ahmad Shah (1909–1924). Weeping when taken from his parents, Ahmad promised that he would be a good shah. A Qajar prince was named regent. In Tehran leaders designated a group to serve until constitutional government could be reestablished, and elections to the second majlis were held in August.

Constitutionalism was supported by Iranian nationalists of all hues and at first even by most of the ulama. As weeks passed the majlis divided into Social Moderates and Democrats. The Democrats believed in the separation of civil and religious power, compulsory conscription, universal education, and land reform; the Social Moderates, the majority, were more conservative in their ideas and supported the ulama, the nobility, and the landowners. Considerable political maneuvering divided the Democrats and Social Moderates, as when Abd al-Qasim Khan was elected the new regent for the young shah.

Russian troops never withdrew from the northern provinces; in 1910 there were still several thousand stationed from Tabriz to Khurasan. Russian demands were greater than any Iranian minister could meet, while Britain accepted the situation. Russia and Britain blocked a new loan; they both evidently intended to limit Tehran until Iran's leaders recognized the overriding position of Russia in every aspect of their affairs. When a somewhat radical cabinet took office in 1910, and even more radical nationalists began to assassinate moderate leaders, the Russians backed attacks on Tehran anjumans, which were driven from the city. The central government was able to create a gendarmerie or national police force, with Swedish and upper-class Iranian officers.

A neutral party, W. Morgan Shuster, an American, was hired in 1911 to be financial adviser to the government. Neither Russia nor England was ever pleased with Shuster's presence in Tehran, and they acted to make his position untenable. Shuster took the view that the Iranian government as dominated by radical members of the majlis was virtuous, and that all Iranians and foreigners who opposed reform were bad. Favoring the Democrats and disappointing the Bakhtiyaris, Shuster pressed the majlis to give him the authority to collect and disburse all revenues. Russia opposed reforms that might strengthen the independence of Iran, and the British and Russians openly warned bankers against making loans to Iran. Shuster then began to collect taxes from notables in Tehran who had not paid their taxes in years. Many of these now sided with the foreign legations against the American.

During the summer of 1911 Iran was torn asunder. In the middle of July ex-shah Muhammad Ali, with Russian aid and British agreement, crossed the Caspian Sea and with Turkoman supporters seized control of the province of Mazandaran. Many provinces revolted against Tehran and declared for Muhammad Ali, while in Tehran Najaf Quli Khan and the Bakhtiyaris took control. Government troops loyal to the majlis and financed by Shuster defeated the ex-shah, who returned to Russia in 1912. The Russians invaded Iran after an ultimatum in November 1911, in which they demanded the dismissal of Shuster and stipulated that the Tehran government could not hire foreigners without Russian approval. Najaf Quli Khan was ready to comply, but the majlis voted to reject the ultimatum. Twelve thousand Russian troops captured Tabriz and prepared to take Tehran. The cabinet expelled the majlis from its building on December 24, 1911, not to meet again until World War I, and Shuster was fired the next day.

THE STRANGLING OF IRAN

When Shuster returned to America in 1912, he wrote a book about his experiences in Iran, entitled *The Strangling of Persia,* a phrase used to describe the period extending from Shuster's dismissal to the outbreak of World War I. Shuster's departure was a blow to the Democrats from which they never recovered. Bakhtiyari leaders controlled the government, and their chieftains ruled from behind the scenes. Over the next three years a series of prime ministers proceeded through that office. Many Bakhtiyari khans received lucrative provincial governorships and ministries. The state disintegrated rapidly; local authority soon superseded central rule. Roads were unsafe, and the company that had the concession on the Karun River and overland traffic to Shiraz had to pay local brigands for protection. Trade came to a standstill in many provinces.

In March 1912 the Russian government gave up on Muhammad Ali and attempted to disperse his sympathizers gathered at Meshhed. The city was bombarded and the sacred

Shii shrine there looted and shattered, sending a traumatic wave across Iran and destroying any possibility of an understanding or genuine cooperation with Russian officials.

In May 1912 Abd al-Qasim, the regent, left for Switzerland and found excuses for not returning. According to the constitution, his appointment as regent could only be terminated by the majlis and only he could convene it. The Russians and British brought many pressures on the ministers in 1913 and 1914 to grant major concessions for building railways across Iran, but no concession was valid unless approved by the majlis. Abd al-Qasim refused to come home to call it; the two powers were quietly stalled.

The British discovery of oil in southwestern Iran increased British willingness to grant the Russians a free hand in the north. Among the concessions granted at the turn of the century, one signed in 1901 gave to a British subject the exclusive rights to search for and develop natural gas and petroleum in all of Iran except the five northern provinces. Oil was struck in May 1908, and the Anglo-Persian Oil Company was organized the next year. The British bought land on Abadan Island in the Shatt al-Arab to build a refinery, and they obtained rights-of-way for pipelines. All these negotiations with local groups were carried on without authorization from Tehran. In this area the British were as independent as the Russians in the north and had fewer obstacles and greater success. Britain was deeply concerned about oil and access to it; the British admiralty purchased a majority interest in the company in 1914 as the navy was turning from coal to oil.

During the strife of the Constitutional Revolution, the counterrevolution led by Muhammad Ali Shah, and the "strangling" of Iran by Russia and Britain, little could be done to carry out modernizing reforms in the country. Instead, civil war was followed by foreign invasions, the effects of both being catastrophic for Qajar Iran. Any real constitutional regime and the restoration of peace and economic renewal would have to await the end of the world war that had started in Europe in 1914.

REFERENCES

References cited at the end of Chapters 19, 22, and 29 are especially important for this chapter.

Afary, Janet: *The Iranian Constitutional Revolution, 1906–1911: Grassroots Democracy, Social Democracy, and the Origins of Feminism.* New York: Columbia University Press, 1996. Seeks to show the social, cultural, ethnic, class, and gender aspects of the Revolution, especially in regard to the anjumans.

Bakhash, Shaul: "Iran." *American Historical Review* 96 (1991): 1479–1496. An excellent historiographical review, centering on Shiism, economic growth, and revolutions in the nineteenth and twentieth centuries.

Bayat, Mangol: *Iran's First Revolution: Shi'ism and the Constitutional Revolution of 1905–1909.* New York: Oxford University Press, 1991. Emphasizes the roles of dissident ulama, liberals, and social democrats in causing the revolution.

Browne, Edward G.: *The Persian Revolution of 1905–1909.* New ed.; Abbas Amanat, ed. Washington, D.C.: Mage, 1995. A new impression of the 1910 edition with a useful introduction. This full and sympathetic account of the Revolution is a classic source.

Garthwaite, Gene R.: *Khans and Shahs: A Documentary Analysis of the Bakhtiyari in Iran.* Cambridge, England: Cambridge University Press, 1983. This anthropological and historical treatment is especially valuable for the late nineteenth century.

Jamalzadeh, Sayyed Mohammad Ali: *Isfahan Is Half the World: Memories of a Persian Boyhood.* Translated by W. L. Heston. Princeton, N.J.: Princeton University Press, 1983. Lively and beautiful accounts of life and Sufis in Iran before World War I.

Kashani-Sabet, Firoozeh: "Hallmarks of Humanism: Hygiene and Love of Homeland in Qajar Iran." *American Historical Review* 105 (2000): 1171–1203. Discusses health issues and the way by which tyranny came to be seen as a disease by 1907.

Keddie, Nikki R.: *Roots of Revolution: An Interpretive History of Modern Iran.* New Haven, Conn.: Yale University Press, 1981. A brilliant summary and analysis of Iranian history.

McDaniel, Robert A.: *The Shuster Mission and the Persian Constitutional Revolution.* Minneapolis, Minn.: Bibliotheca Islamica, 1974. A thorough study of the revolution in Iran in 1906 and the failure of the Shuster mission in 1911.

Martin, Vanessa: *Islam and Modernism: The Iranian Revolution of 1906.* Syracuse, N.Y.: Syracuse University Press, 1989. An examination of the major ulama in Tehran during the Constitutional Revolution.

Najmabadi, Afsaneh: *The Story of the Daughters of Quchan: Gender and National Memory in Iranian History.* Syracuse, N.Y.: Syracuse University Press, 1998. A fascinating and lively reconstruction of gender issues and the Constitutional Revolution.

Said, Kurban: *Ali and Nino.* Translated by Jenia Graman. New York: Pocket Books, 1972. An exciting novel set in Baku and Tehran ca. 1900–1920 that gives a personal view of the impacts of modernization.

Shuster, W. Morgan: *The Strangling of Persia.* Washington, D.C.: Mage, 1987. A reprint of the 1912 book on Iran before World War I.

Taj al-Saltana: *Crowning Anguish: Memoirs of a Persian Princess from the Harem to Modernity, 1884–1914.* Edited by Abbas Amanat. Translated by Anna Vanzan and Amin Neshati. Washington, D.C.: Mage, 1993. This frank autobiography of a daughter of Nasir al-Din Shah says much about court life of the time.

Wright, Denis: *The English amongst the Persians during the Qajar Period, 1787–1921.* London: Heinemann, 1977. Colorful and full of anecdotes that illustrate the personal side of the relations of the two peoples.

CHAPTER 31

Impact of World War I upon the Middle East

The history of the modern Middle East is divided into two parts: an early modern period dominated by the Ottoman and Safavid empires (C.E. 1500–1800) and the modern era beginning around 1800, which has been marked by the integration of the Middle East into evolving world systems. Within the last two centuries, World War I marks a definite division between the long nineteenth century and the contemporary age.

Between 1914 and 1918 World War I profoundly affected political, diplomatic, military, economic, and social matters in Iran, Egypt, and the central lands of the Ottoman Empire. For the Ottomans the war had especially important effects, since much of the fighting took place on Ottoman soil. Military casualties were enormous, and millions of civilians were also killed in massacres or by starvation and disease. When the combat stopped in 1918, the ordeal of the Middle East continued, as the victors sought to allocate among themselves the people and lands of occupied countries and regions.

The shot at Sarajevo fired by a Serbian nationalist killed the Archduke Franz Ferdinand of Austria on June 28, 1914, and it ricocheted around the world. It proved fatal as well to the Ottoman Empire, while greatly influencing Iran and Egypt. Austria-Hungary and Germany formed the Central Powers, and opposed to them were Serbia, Russia, France, and Great Britain—the Entente group. Many other countries were at least initially neutral, including Italy, Bulgaria, the United States, the Ottoman Empire, and Iran.

IRAN AND EGYPT DURING THE WAR

Ahmad Shah was crowned on July 21, 1914, and ten days later Europe was engulfed in war. In November the shah declared strict neutrality for Iran. When the Ottomans joined the war in November, they said they wished to respect Iranian neutrality but could not as long as Russian troops remained in neighboring Azerbaijan. When Iran requested a Russian withdrawal, Russia demanded promises from the Ottomans that they would not attack. Such guarantees were not forthcoming. Ottoman Kurds invaded Iran, and more Russian troops poured into northern Iran. The third majlis opened on January 4, 1915, but Iran was no longer in control of its own affairs.

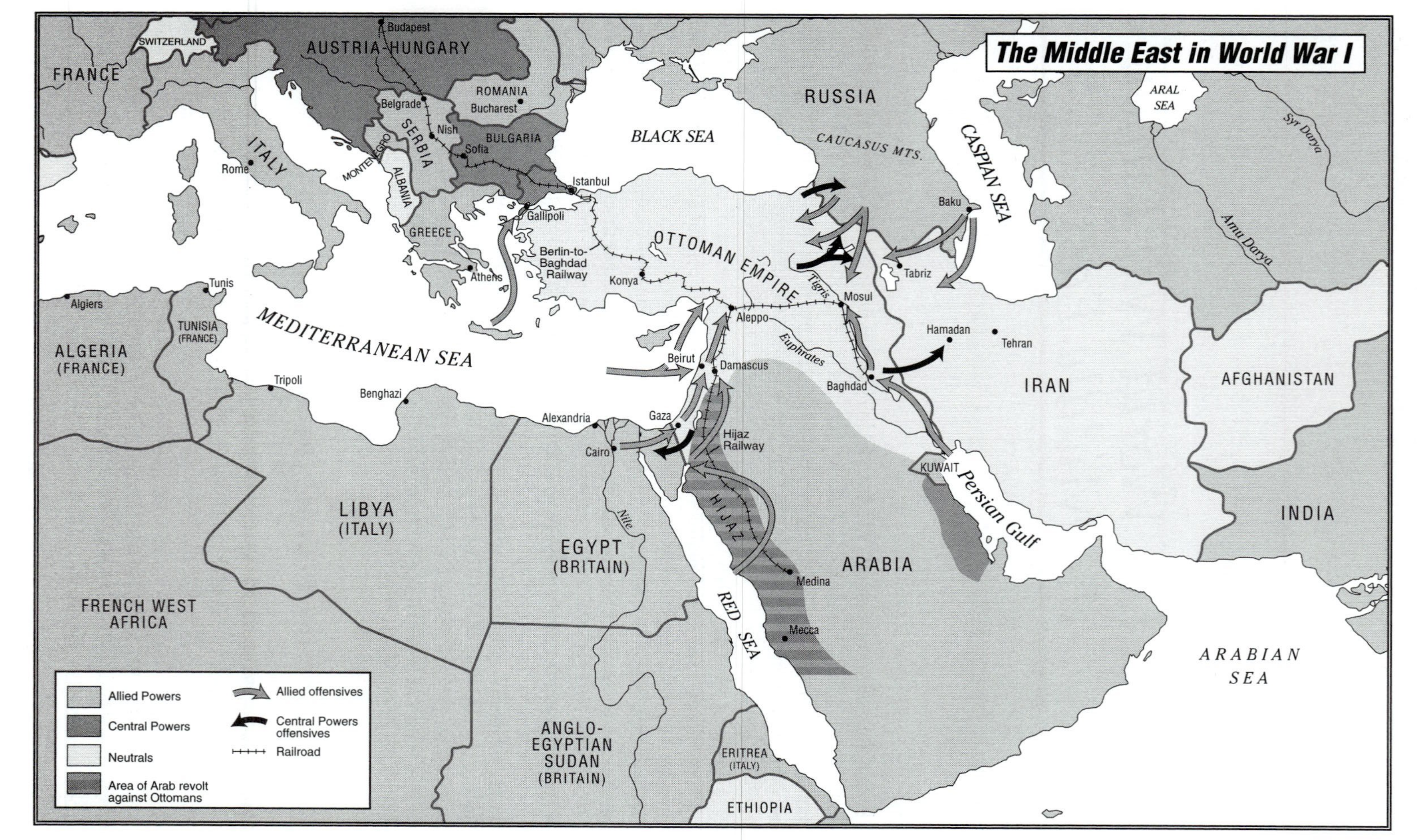
The Middle East in World War I
FRANCE
SWITZERLAND
AUSTRIA-HUNGARY
Budapest
ROMANIA
Bucharest
Belgrade
SERBIA
Nish
BULGARIA
Sofia
MONTENEGRO
ALBANIA
GREECE
Athens
ITALY
Rome
Istanbul
Gallipoli
Berlin-to-Baghdad Railway
Konya
BLACK SEA
RUSSIA
CAUCASUS MTS.
CASPIAN SEA
Baku
Tabriz
ARAL SEA
Syr Darya
Amu Darya
OTTOMAN EMPIRE
Tigris
Euphrates
Mosul
Aleppo
Beirut
Damascus
Baghdad
Hamadan
Tehran
IRAN
AFGHANISTAN
INDIA
KUWAIT
Persian Gulf
ARABIA
ARABIAN SEA
Gaza
Hijaz Railway
HIJAZ
Medina
Mecca
RED SEA
Alexandria
Cairo
Nile
EGYPT (BRITAIN)
ANGLO-EGYPTIAN SUDAN (BRITAIN)
ERITREA (ITALY)
ETHIOPIA
MEDITERRANEAN SEA
Tunis
TUNISIA (FRANCE)
Algiers
ALGERIA (FRANCE)
Tripoli
Benghazi
LIBYA (ITALY)
FRENCH WEST AFRICA
Allied Powers
Central Powers
Neutrals
Area of Arab revolt against Ottomans
Allied offensives
Central Powers offensives
Railroad

When World War I burst upon the Middle East, Iran was already experiencing chaotic problems involving internal political and constitutional developments, financial and economic turmoil, and intense imperial rivalry between Russia and Great Britain. After 1911, Iranian nationalists believed that Germany offered the only hope of avoiding an impending partition of Iran by British and Russian imperialists. During the first months of the war Germany concluded a secret treaty with the Iranian government promising arms, ammunition, and money in return for cooperation.

Britain and Russia acted swiftly to hold Iran in their power. Russian troops moved to the outskirts of Tehran. Supporters of the Central Powers then fled to Kermanshah, where an anti-Entente Iranian government lasted into 1916. Ahmad Shah remained in his capital with his cabinet, and technically Iran maintained its neutrality, as the shah received subventions from Britain. A German consul stirred the Qashqai and Bakhtiyari tribes in southern Iran and threatened British oil operations. To counter this danger and protect the oil wells, whose production increased during the war, the British eventually sent Sir Percy Sykes to organize a military force. In 1917, in cooperation with Russian cossacks from the north, they occupied Kerman, Isfahan, and Shiraz. Russia's collapse, however, left the northern provinces open; for a time German and Ottoman troops held Azerbaijan, but they were recalled at the end of the war and the British remained dominant in Iran. A famine further devastated northern Iran, and the country experienced great difficulties.

On December 18, 1914, Great Britain unilaterally declared the establishment of a protectorate over Egypt, thus ending Egypt's flimsy association with the Ottoman empire. Although the announcement carried a pledge of ultimate self-government, a protectorate was humiliating to Egyptians. Khedive Abbas Hilmi II, pro-Ottoman and anti-British, had not returned from Istanbul when hostilities broke out. He was deposed; his uncle, Husain Kamil, was proclaimed sultan of Egypt.

For nearly four years Egypt served as a military base for hundreds of thousands of British and other Entente forces. Troops requisitioned supplies, taking camels and donkeys from peasants. Starting in 1917 Egyptians were drafted into an army that fought alongside the British, and ultimately many men served in the armed forces. Inflation was rampant, and fortunes were made by illegal practices. The price of cotton more than tripled, and wheat became scarce and costly. As the British military ignored Egyptian sensibilities, the public blamed the British for every ill that befell Egypt. World War I spurred Egyptian nationalism forward in the years between 1914 and 1918.

THE OTTOMAN EMPIRE ENTERS THE WAR

Sentiments in the Ottoman Empire were mixed regarding the war. Influential people desired an alliance with one of the two groups lining up for the war, since the Ottomans had been isolated during the damaging Italian and Balkan wars. In conversations with the Entente for a possible alliance the Ottomans asked about terminating the capitulations. Russia coveted Istanbul and the Straits leading to the Mediterranean Sea, and the Entente powers held the military strength of the Ottomans in low esteem and were not willing to offer the Ottomans the assurances they demanded.

A hard core of army officers, dominant in the Committee of Union and Progress, had come under the spell of German military genius. Guided by Minister of War Enver Pasha, who was confident that Germany would quickly win, key members of the Ottoman cabinet signed with Germany on August 2, 1914, a secret alliance directed against Russia, and the Ottomans then began to mobilize their armies. Pro-German Ottomans feared Russia's desire for Istanbul and hoped to regain effective control of the Aegean Islands and Egypt, while Pan-Turkish leaders wanted to annex Turks living under Russian control. The Ottoman-German alliance was reinforced by the surprise entry into the Straits of two German cruisers, which were taken into the Ottoman navy even though they were still staffed by Germans, in place of two powerful Ottoman ships built in England but kept there on the outbreak of war in Europe. The leaders of the Committee of Union and Progress and the government—Enver, Talat, and Jemal—told Germany that if it would shoulder a major share of the burden of war materials, transport, and financing the Ottomans would join the war. By October 16, shipments of the promised German gold reached Istanbul.

On October 29 the Ottoman fleet, including the formerly German ships, shelled Russian Black Sea ports. Russia formally declared war on November 2; England and France soon followed. The sultan pronounced a jihad, or holy war, hoping this might induce Muslims under the French in North Africa, under the British in Egypt, the Sudan, and India, and under Russia in central Asia to rebel, but there were no revolts of any significance. One reason for the failure of the call to jihad was that the Ottoman sultan-caliph was allied with the Christian powers of Germany and Austria-Hungary.

With the formal entry of the Ottoman Empire into the war Germany became very influential. Though transportation, food supplies, finance, and many other highly important wartime problems were in Ottoman hands, German officials regularly acted as they pleased.

The immediate reaction of Arab subjects to Ottoman entry into the war was threefold. One group looked upon the outbreak of war as an opportunity to obtain a united and independent Arab national state. A second group, consisting largely of some princely Arab families and their clients, regarded the war as a time to rebel against the Ottoman sultan and establish independent Arab kingdoms. Most Arab Ottomans viewed the Ottoman state as the only protection against European imperialism and the preserver of Islamic independence, and thus continued to support the empire until its defeat.

GALLIPOLI CAMPAIGN

The Entente powers assumed the offensive against the Ottomans in 1915. Britain, at the suggestion of Minister of War Lord Kitchener (formerly British representative in Egypt), agreed to send a force to break through the Straits, take Istanbul, drive the Ottomans out of the war, and open a supply route to Russia. After unsuccessful attacks in February and March by British and French naval forces, an Australian and British army began operations on the Gallipoli peninsula in April 1915. The attackers met withering fire and stubborn defense by Ottoman forces led by Mustafa Kemal (Atatürk) and some German officers under the overall command of General Liman von Sanders. Both sides suffered huge losses. The half-million British imperial and French forces, joined by the Italians in August, clung on and nearly succeeded in a breakthrough. Lack of cooperation by the Russians at the Bosphorus end of the Straits, skillful tactics on the part of the Germans and Ottomans, and faulty intelligence work by the offensive forces led first to a stalemate and then to Entente withdrawal from the Straits and defeat in January 1916.

OTTOMAN WAR OPERATIONS

The overly ambitious overall Ottoman war plan called for an attack upon the Russians in the east and an expedition to drive the British from Egypt, while countering the Entente attacks on the Dardanelles and Iraq meant the Ottomans were fighting on four fronts. In addition, after Bulgaria joined the Central Powers in 1915, Ottoman troops were sent to fight in eastern Europe. The offensives were carried out by soldiers who were usually poorly paid, often dressed in rags, suffering from widespread illness, and not fed sufficiently. Most soldiers were illiterate and therefore did not have easy access to news from home. Military transportation was poor, and death rates were high for the troops even before they reached the battlefields.

During the last months of 1914, Ottoman forces moved east against Russia under the command of the rash Enver. The Ottomans had to fall back—nearly 90 percent of the Third Army had been lost to frostbite, disease, and enemy action. Enver relinquished his command and returned to Istanbul. All news of the disaster was censored.

In the campaigns of 1915–1916, with the aid of Armenian revolutionaries and irregular forces, the Russians captured Erzurum, Van, and Trabzon in the east. In 1916 Mustafa Kemal came to that mountainous Caucasus front, but little was accomplished. Transportation was next to impossible; ammunition and supplies of every kind were scarce; and disease was rampant. In February 1917, forty-two Ottoman army surgeons died of spotted typhus alone, and thousands of soldiers died of starvation. The dreadful casualties of Enver's first campaign and the considerable depopulation of the eastern areas as a result of the Armenian massacres and deportations in 1915 created such a weakness on the front facing Russia that it would have been fatal had not Russia been so hard-pressed in the European war theaters from 1915 to 1917.

The revolutions in Russia in 1917, especially the Bolshevik Communist Revolution in the autumn, markedly affected the Caucasus front. All the Russian troops except for the Armenian and Georgian divisions melted away. The Ottomans advanced rapidly to occupy eastern Anatolia, which the March 1918 Treaty of Brest Litovsk gave to the Ottomans. And by September 1918 the Ottomans captured Baku on the Caspian Sea, killing many Armenians in the process, and occupied Azerbaijan. Germany felt the Ottoman inroads into the Caucasus were going too far and opposed them.

The second ambition of Enver was the conquest of Egypt. Jemal Pasha, Ottoman minister of marine and one of the triumvirate, took command of the Fourth Army and assumed responsibility for Syria, including Palestine. In February 1915, his forces made a surprise attack upon the Suez Canal, but, possessing inadequate strength to hold the eastern bank, they retired. Raids on the Suez Canal compelled the British to maintain a large force; however, the morale of the Ottoman armies was low because they inevitably had to retreat.

When Italy joined the war on the Entente side in May 1915, the Ottomans and Germans sought to attack Italian-controlled Libya; with the assistance of the Sanusi Sufis, an operation was even launched from Libya against Egypt. The British counterattacked, however, and the Ottoman-Libyan forces ultimately could only engage in limited raids on Entente forces.

A massive Ottoman assault against the Suez Canal from Palestine was ordered for February 1916, but poor transport delayed the attack until the hot weather of midsummer. The assault proved a failure, and from that moment until the end of the war the Ottoman armies were on the defensive in this theater of operations. In March and April 1917 at the famous battles of Gaza, Ottoman and German forces withstood heavy British fire and drove the enemy back to a line in Sinai, while the city of Gaza was largely destroyed. Later that year a German-directed operation, including some German combat units as well as Ottoman troops, attempted to gain a favorable decision in Palestine, but again failure of transport, sabotage of supplies, continuing harassment by Arab desert bands, and a buildup of British forces under General Allenby brought disaster.

Another area of major hostilities in the Middle East was Iraq. British contingents from India seized Basrah so as to protect nearby Iranian oil operations. A sizable force captured Kut al-Amarah in 1915, but it was defeated just south of Baghdad and fell back to Kut al-Amarah, where the Ottomans forced a humiliating British surrender in 1916. However, the British and Indians reestablished their hold on southern Iraq. A railroad was built, and superior concentrations of men, artillery, and supplies enabled the British to retake Kut al-Amarah and capture Baghdad in 1917. At the time of the armistice in 1918 the British had not yet reached Mosul in the north.

THE ARMENIANS

While World War I was unfolding in the Middle East and shattering the Ottoman Empire, some members of two national groups within the state, the Armenians and the Arabs, suffered greatly as a result of the war and openly aided the enemy. Christian Armenians were located in both the Russian and Ottoman empires, caught between the mighty armies that swept back and forth through the Caucasus and eastern Anatolia during the world war.

The fate of the Ottoman Armenians in 1915–1916 has been the subject of much dispute, both at the time and subsequently. Historical records still do not permit a totally clear account of all the circumstances surrounding responsibility for the undoubtedly brutal massacres of hundreds of thousands of civilian Armenian-Ottoman men, women, and children.

By the late nineteenth century a growing minority among the Armenians were nationalists, basing their identity no longer on religious and historical ties within the multi-ethnic Ottoman, Russian, and Iranian Empires, but instead turning to linguistic, secular, cultural, and territorial factors. These nationalists claimed that the Russian tsar was the protector of all Armenians. On the other hand, some Ottoman Armenians insisted that their people should support the Ottoman government in the war. In Istanbul and the western cities Armenians complied with war orders, but in eastern Anatolia some of the Ottoman-Armenian population, often following Armenian radical nationalists and remembering persecutions in the recent past, aided Russia by collecting intelligence and rebelling. In April 1915, an Armenian government was proclaimed in Van. In some districts, part of the Muslim population was killed by the Armenians.

The Ottoman central government in early 1915 felt that imminent military defeat was possible in the light of Russian advances and the Entente attack at Gallipoli. The deep suspicions felt by the Committee of Union and Progress leaders about possible Armenian disloyalty combined with a desire to secure the military situation in eastern Anatolia. As a result, the central authorities ordered in June 1915 the deportation of the Armenian population, which led to the massacres of 1915 and 1916.

An estimated 1.5 million Armenians had lived in Ottoman Anatolia at the outbreak of the war. The great preponderance was in the eastern regions. The transfer of all non-Muslims away from points of military concentration was authorized, and non-Muslims in the military forces were relegated to rear service units without weapons. Many of the latter were murdered. Thousands of civilian Armenians also had already died.

During the deportation, disease and inadequate provisions in the Syrian deserts, the general destination, led to the death of tens of thousands from exposure, illness, exhaustion, and starvation. Many were marched off into the desert to die. Ottoman government officials ordered the killing of many Armenian civilians. Local gendarmes, Ministry of the Interior forces, and marauding bands of Kurds and Turks perpetrated numerous atrocities against Armenians. Representatives of neutral governments protested to Istanbul, and German officials privately lamented the action. Talat, Enver, and the Ottoman government, however, were deaf to all pleas, since influential individuals in the government were actually bent on exterminating the Armenian population in eastern Anatolia. Perhaps 600,000 or more Armenians (about 40 percent of the Ottoman-Armenian population) perished, while hundreds of thousands fled elsewhere. Almost no Armenians were left in their ancient homeland in eastern Anatolia. Although some Turks did shield and protect Armenian individuals from the Ottoman authorities, the Armenian deportations and massacres were dreadful blots on the record of the Ottoman Empire.

ARAB NATIONALISM

The other pressing ethnic nationalist problem confronting the leaders of the Ottoman government was the loyalty of the Arabs. No open break occurred until June 1916, when Sharif Husain of Mecca proclaimed his revolt in the Hijaz. Even before that, Jemal Pasha found in Syria documents implicating numerous Muslim and Christian Arab leaders in treasonable activities. When Enver called upon Jemal for troops for the Gallipoli campaign, Arab divisions, including many leaders of the al-Ahd secret society of Arab nationalists, were sent in order that more reliable Turkish troops might control Beirut and Damascus. In April 1916, about 200 Arabs were arrested for treason and 22 were hanged; tens of thousands of suspects were deported to Anatolia.

Before further examining the moves for independence made by the Arabs in Syria and the Hijaz, it is important to place British relations with Arabs elsewhere in their proper setting. Arab states existed along the western shore of the Persian Gulf and the southern coasts of Arabia. Almost every one of these protectorates had a treaty of friendship with Great Britain, which exercised power over foreign relations, while a British resident agent advised on all governmental matters.

When war became imminent, the British persuaded Abd al-Aziz ibn Abd al-Rahman (known as Ibn Saud) of eastern Arabia to enter into a standard British-Arab agreement: Abd al-Aziz placed his foreign affairs in British hands and accepted a generous subsidy. In return Abd al-Aziz would be at least neutral, and might well engage in actions against the Ottomans in central Arabia.

A rival of Abd al-Aziz was Husain, the Ottoman co-governor of Mecca in western Arabia and a sharif, or lineal descendant, of the prophet Muhammad. Since Husain feared Ottoman centralization, the British raised with him and his son Abd Allah the question of an alliance. Thus began the celebrated correspondence between Sharif Husain and the British in Egypt. Husain found himself in a delicate situation with the Ottomans close at hand and not sure about the ultimate intentions of the British or the attitude of the Arab secret societies in Damascus and Beirut. Exchanges of letters between Husain and Sir Henry McMahon, high commissioner for Egypt and the Sudan, brought to a head the issue of Arab independence. Britain promised, upon the successful conclusion of the war, to agree to the creation of an Arab state. The area of the state was to be bounded on the north by a line drawn eastward from Alexandretta to the Iranian frontier and then southward to the Persian Gulf and was to include much of the western Arabian peninsula. Excepted from this were certain areas west of the districts of Damascus, Hims, Hama, and Aleppo; although the meaning of this was often disputed, the exceptions seemed to be the regions where France had interests, thereby implying that perhaps part of Palestine would be included in the area promised to the Arab state.

Husain's son Faisal had conferred clandestinely in Damascus with leaders of the Arab movement, and in 1915 he presented the secret Damascus Protocol to his father. This document defined the Arab state's frontiers as Husain later insisted upon them with McMahon. Although Husain of Mecca was not an Arab nationalist, but rather more like Abd al-Aziz and other Arab princes who feared Ottoman centralization, in a sense he did represent the Arab nationalists of Syria as he dealt with the British. Husain declared a revolt against the Ottomans in the Holy City of Mecca in June 1916 and began a campaign in the Hijaz with the help of the British.

THE SECRET TREATIES

While these negotiations with Husain were in process, the Entente powers were engaged in formulating secret treaties, dividing among themselves the Ottoman Empire. Russia was to obtain Istanbul as well as the Straits, and in return Britain would add to its sphere of influence the neutral zone in Iran. Later the Pact of London was signed to bring Italy into the war. This pact promised Italy sovereignty over the Dodecanese Islands, the elimination of all rights of the Ottoman caliph yet remaining in Libya, and Antalya in Anatolia.

The most far-reaching of the secret treaties—the Sykes-Picot Agreement of May 16, 1916—allotted to Russia the already promised Straits area and most of eastern Anatolia. France was granted the northern coastal strip of Syria and southeastern Anatolia. Britain obtained an enclave about Haifa and Acre on the Mediterranean, and part of Iraq from

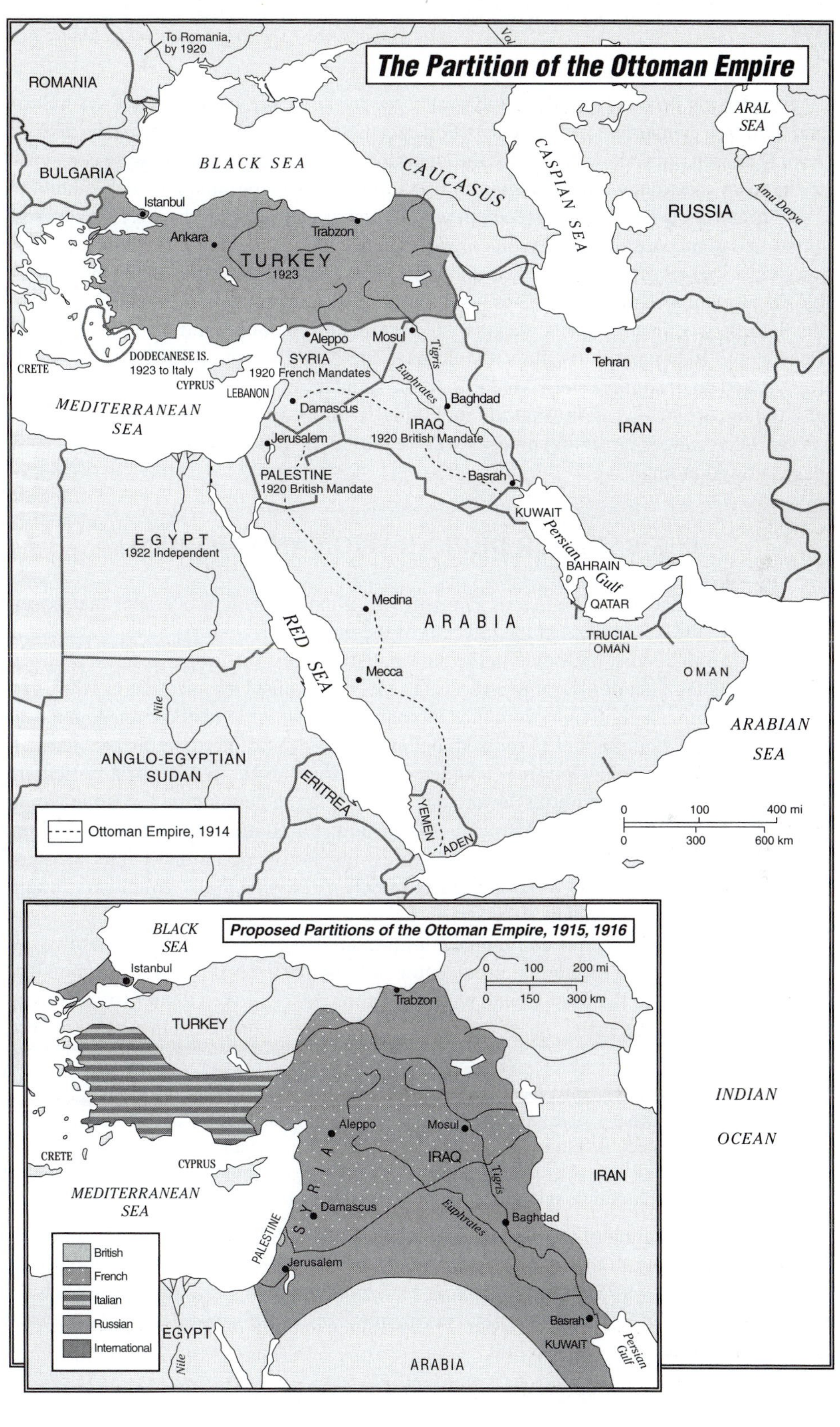

The Partition of the Ottoman Empire
To Romania, by 1920
ROMANIA
BULGARIA
BLACK SEA
CAUCASUS
CASPIAN SEA
ARAL SEA
Amu Darya
RUSSIA
Istanbul
Ankara
Trabzon
TURKEY
1923
DODECANESE IS.
1923 to Italy
CRETE
CYPRUS
LEBANON
Aleppo
Mosul
Tigris
SYRIA
1920 French Mandates
Euphrates
Baghdad
Tehran
MEDITERRANEAN SEA
Damascus
IRAQ
1920 British Mandate
IRAN
Jerusalem
PALESTINE
1920 British Mandate
Basrah
KUWAIT
Persian Gulf
EGYPT
1922 Independent
BAHRAIN
QATAR
Medina
ARABIA
RED SEA
TRUCIAL OMAN
Mecca
OMAN
Nile
ARABIAN SEA
ANGLO-EGYPTIAN SUDAN
ERITREA
YEMEN
ADEN
Ottoman Empire, 1914
0 100 400 mi
0 300 600 km
Proposed Partitions of the Ottoman Empire, 1915, 1916
BLACK SEA
Istanbul
Trabzon
0 100 200 mi
0 150 300 km
TURKEY
INDIAN OCEAN
Aleppo
Mosul
IRAQ
CRETE
CYPRUS
IRAN
MEDITERRANEAN SEA
SYRIA
Damascus
Tigris
Euphrates
Baghdad
PALESTINE
Jerusalem
British
French
Italian
Russian
International
Basrah
EGYPT
KUWAIT
Persian Gulf
Nile
ARABIA

Baghdad to the Persian Gulf. Palestine west of the Jordan River was cut from French Syria and promised an international administration because of the holy places. The Arabs of Syria from Damascus and Aleppo eastward through Mosul to the Iranian frontier were consigned to French protection, while the region from Kirkuk to Aqaba became a British sphere.

The secret Sykes-Picot Agreement was signed only a few months after agreements embodied in the Husain-McMahon correspondence were concluded. Husain learned of the Sykes-Picot Agreement and was unhappy with it, but he had little choice but to trust his far more powerful British allies until after the war ended. When Italians learned of the Sykes-Picot arrangements, they insisted upon gaining more land. In 1917 England, France, and Italy agreed that Italy should have the districts around Izmir, Antalya, and Konya, and all of southwestern Anatolia. At the same time, Greece was promised Cyprus and the territory of western Anatolia including Izmir as an inducement to join the war on the Allied side. Conflicting pledges with regard to the future of the Middle East were beginning to mount!

THE BALFOUR DECLARATION AND ZIONISM

Zionist claims had yet to be heard. Zionism was a nationalistic movement that developed among European Jews in the last half of the nineteenth century. Savage attacks in Russia and anti-Jewish prejudice in the nationalistic states of Europe fostered political Zionism and led Theodor Herzl to establish the World Zionist Organization in 1897. The Zionists had repeatedly sought from the Ottomans a Jewish settlement company in Palestine, but Sultan Abdulhamid II refused, believing this would increase his problems of nationalism. The Zionist Congress had declined a British offer in 1903 of a settlement in Uganda, for Zionism without the ancient land of Zion in geographic Palestine would be a paradox. At the outbreak of war in 1914, Zionist activities were centered in Germany. Upon the division of Europe into two camps, however, another center arose in London, led by Dr. Chaim Weizmann (1874–1952). Jewish Zionist volunteers fought as units of the British army in Palestine.

The Zionists lobbied for an Entente commitment to create a Jewish commonwealth in Palestine. Slowly an influential group came to favor the Zionist position, arguing that Palestine, so close to the Suez Canal, would be more closely linked to the British sphere of influence. Success came on November 2, 1917, when Lord Balfour wrote to Lord Rothschild:

> His Majesty's Government view with favour the establishment in Palestine of a national home for the Jewish people and will use their best endeavours to facilitate the achievement of this object, it being clearly understood that nothing shall be done which may prejudice the civil and religious rights of existing non-Jewish communities in Palestine or the rights and political status enjoyed by Jews in any other country.

The exact meaning of the declaration has been much debated, but it was in all probability contrary both to the Sykes-Picot Agreement and to the Husain-McMahon correspondence. Reasons for its issuance included a British desire to gain support from Jewish circles in the United States and Russia. Husain of Mecca was dismayed when the news of the Balfour Declaration reached him.

THE FOURTEEN POINTS

Another Allied promise made during the war took place when Baghdad and Jerusalem fell to British forces in 1917: the victorious generals announced that any future settlement would be made with the consent of local populations. These statements foreshadowed the broad concepts of United States President Woodrow Wilson's Fourteen Points of January 1918. Although the United States was fighting Germany and had not declared war against the Ottoman Empire, Wilson's twelfth point stated that the Turkish parts of the Ottoman Empire should have a "secure sovereignty" and that other nationalities should be given security of life and an opportunity for development. Greeks, Armenians, and Arabs built their hopes upon this point. Some Arabs naively believed that Wilson's declaration recognized their aspirations as proposed by Husain and that the Fourteen Points nullified the Balfour Declaration and all secret treaties made under the duress of total war.

ENTENTE VICTORY

Failure of an Ottoman campaign in the summer of 1917 opened the way for the British in Egypt to move into Palestine. Jerusalem fell to General Allenby in December 1917. Entente forces proceeded northward along the coast in late 1918, taking Beirut. The Arab revolt of June 1916 had shattered the Ottoman regime in the Hijaz, and Arabs under Faisal east of the Jordan River paralleled the actions of Allenby. Under the encouragement of such British liaison officers as Colonel T. E. Lawrence (known as Lawrence of Arabia), and receiving British equipment and gold, the Arabs captured Aqaba and then entered Damascus in October 1918, at about the same time as British imperial forces. (Lawrence became a war hero in Britain; this and his literary skills enabled him to play a role in forming 1920s British policy in the Middle East along lines favorable to Faisal.) The Ottomans under Mustafa Kemal nevertheless held the Entente forces north of Aleppo.

German failures on the western front in Europe during the fall of 1918 and the imminent collapse of Germany, Austria-Hungary, and Bulgaria spelled the end of warfare in the Middle East. Without German assistance the Ottoman Empire could not maintain effective resistance. Ottoman defeat became clear when Entente forces broke out of Salonica and moved toward Istanbul, which was almost undefended. Although the army still had almost one million men under arms, the new Ottoman government contacted the British off Mudros on the island of Lemnos in the Aegean Sea and on October 30, 1918, signed an armistice ending the war. It was nearly an unconditional surrender, since Ottoman forces were to be demobilized, and the Entente was to control the Straits and could occupy any areas it wished. The three leaders of the Committee of Union and Progress government fled the country.

The war, four years long almost to the day, brought many changes to Ottoman society, which disintegrated so fully under the terrible wartime conditions that the British leader Asquith declared, "The Sick Man had really died this time." The larger cities were disturbed more than the villages, and Istanbul most of all. The Committee of Union and Progress controlled railway transportation and therefore the sale of wheat; the government also encouraged the development of Muslim Turkish merchants and artisans, while prominent individuals made fortunes through war profiteering.

Shortages of every kind developed; foreign goods could not be imported; domestic produce and animals used in agriculture were largely requisitioned by the government; the amount of land under cultivation steadily declined; physical suffering among the masses became widespread; disease and famine were everywhere; and the generally low standard of living deteriorated rapidly, as inflation lifted the prices of everything without much change in wages. About 2.5 million Ottoman Muslims died in Anatolia from 1914 to 1922; hundreds of thousands of the minority communities also died. About one-fifth of the total population of Anatolia died. And starvation, disease, and destruction were widespread in the other parts of the empire as well.

Ottoman military casualties during World War I were difficult to calculate but were certainly enormous. In 1915 alone the number of killed, seriously wounded, and missing was around 500,000. Of the 2,900,000 men mobilized by late 1918, about 750,000 died from disease or in battle, while 300,000 more were seriously wounded.

The Ottoman government did enact some desired changes despite these terrible conditions: the capitulations were abolished in 1914; the taxation system was reformed; more women were brought into higher education and the workforce; the Ottoman Public Debt Administration was terminated; the powers of the religious communities were limited; and the war-burdened government assumed control over many unaccustomed activities. Despite these and other reforms, the end of the Ottoman state seemed obvious by late 1918.

The war encouraged anti-Ottoman nationalists. As the power of the Ottoman government waned, Arabs, Greeks, Armenians, and other nationalities gave more open expression to their nationalism. For Ottoman Armenians, it led to destruction. To the Greeks, it brought a temporary fulfillment of cherished dreams. And among the Arabs, it created revolt and new Arab states. For the Turks, uncompromising nationalists, such as Mustafa Kemal, now had an opportunity to be heard.

Of the other effects of the war, the presence of many British, French, Italian, and German soldiers meant that thousands of Middle Easterners saw westerners and their manner of living for the first time. The impact of the west upon the Middle East in every facet of its living, from transportation to religion, was more profound and penetrating in these four war years than in earlier contacts through religious, commercial, and intellectual missions from the west. A new age for the Middle East was born as European-style territorial states replaced the multi-ethnic Ottoman Empire, a state that had been based on loyalty to the dynasty and to Islam.

THE PARIS PEACE CONFERENCE

Less than two weeks after the Mudros armistice halted World War I in the Middle East, Germany signed the armistice with the Entente and war officially ceased. The fate of the Middle East devolved then upon "the smoke-filled rooms" of Paris, where diplomats, statesmen, generals, journalists, and representatives of every special interest gathered to make peace. The Middle East, however, was only a small part of the total settlement. Problems with respect to Germany took precedence over all others, and disagreements on European issues delayed the verdict on the Middle East.

The prime conflict concerning the Middle East appeared in the disparities among the London Pact of 1915, the Sykes-Picot Agreement, the Balfour Declaration, the Husain-McMahon correspondence, the Fourteen Points, the liberation statements at Baghdad and Jerusalem, and the "make the world safe for democracy" slogan. Britain and France, the dominant military powers, sought to advance their own national and imperial interests rather than the desires of the smaller countries and nationalistic groups that also flocked to Paris. British Prime Minister David Lloyd George and his advisers viewed practically the entire Middle East as a prize. The French leader Georges Clemenceau, on the other hand, stood for a French hold upon Syria and southern Anatolia, hoped to dominate the Straits, and dreamed of having a French adviser at the elbow of the Ottoman sultan. President Wilson discussed plans for peace in the Middle East that would fulfill the pledge made in his Fourteen Points.

The Big Three—Lloyd George, Clemenceau, and Wilson—held major decisions in their hands; many others, however, had greater personal or national interests in the Middle East. Prince Faisal came to Paris to represent his father, Husain of Mecca, and his Kingdom of the Hijaz. Two groups of Armenians presented conflicting claims for their nation. Eleutherios Venizelos (1864–1936), the prime minister of Greece, sought to obtain Entente promises with respect to the Greek "Great Idea," that is, restoration of the Greek empire to include western Anatolia, Constantinople (Istanbul), and the Straits. Prime Minister Orlando of Italy intended to receive the Dodecanese Islands, southwestern Anatolia, and an area in and about Izmir.

Bankers, oil men, merchants, bondholders, missionaries, and humanitarians of sundry types also converged at Paris to lobby for their respective interests. Everyone was there except the Ottomans, although the grand vizir was permitted on one occasion to deliver a statement.

Zionists were able to incorporate a version of the Balfour Declaration in the peace treaties and gain approval of it from the new League of Nations. The Wilsonian policy of the right of national self-determination, however, seemed to block Zionist aims, since Jews constituted not more than 15 percent of the population of Palestine, and a policy of counting heads would have favored the Arab majority, possibly leading to Palestine's inclusion in a larger Arab state. As a result, Wilson proposed to the supreme council that a commission of inquiry go to Syria, Palestine, Iraq, and Armenia to obtain information about national self-determination. At first the French, British, and Italians agreed, but later they refused to cooperate. Therefore, President Henry C. King of Oberlin College and businessman Charles R. Crane, the American appointees, proceeded alone in the spring of 1919 with a staff of experts; their King-Crane report of late 1919 was suppressed because it ran counter to arrangements already dictated between England and France.

SAN REMO AGREEMENTS

No permanent decisions regarding the Middle East could be reached in Paris in 1919. The signing of a peace treaty for the area seemed more uncertain than ever because of several factors, including the opposition of America to accepting a mandate for any territory. Russia was going through a civil war, while Italy was suffering from internal dissension and disillusionment. Questions of the Middle East, therefore, lay squarely between England and France. Meanwhile, armies of occupation governed the Middle East, whose peoples grew restless waiting for their fate to be decided. British forces under Allenby controlled Egypt, Palestine, and Lebanon; Husain and Faisal held sway over the Hijaz and inner Syria, including Damascus; and Britain controlled Iraq.

In the last months of 1919 British contingents in Lebanon were replaced by French units in accord with the Sykes-Picot Agreement. Arab nationalist opposition to this action, anti-Jewish riots in Jerusalem and Jaffa, the election of Faisal as king of Syria and of Abd Allah as king of Iraq by the Arab National Congress in Damascus, growing tension in Baghdad, and insurrection in Egypt—all drove Britain to realize that a treaty for the Middle East was now imperative.

One of the sensitive questions in the settlement between England and France revolved around the division of Mosul oil. The Sykes-Picot Agreement assigned the district of Mosul to France, but Britain pressed the French to allow Mosul to be attached to British-controlled Iraq. In February 1920, an agreement provided that France could buy 25 percent of the crude oil from Iraq. With this in hand the Allied negotiators journeyed to San Remo, Italy, where on April 24, 1920, they reached an agreement on oil, pipelines, mandates, and united action with respect to the Turks and Arabs.

Britain secured mandates for Iraq and Palestine, and France obtained mandates in Syria (and Lebanon); both Britain and France would be supervised by the new League of Nations in the administration of their mandates. Palestine included the lands on each side of the Jordan and extended to the Gulf of Aqaba; the Balfour Declaration was written into the mandate authorization. In addition to the oil understandings, France was given a free hand to deal with Faisal and the Arab Syrian kingdom with force—to crush them if necessary. At San Remo Britain and France also accepted the independence of the Hijaz under Husain of Mecca, although Husain rapidly rejected both the San Remo agreements and the Treaty of Sèvres as well.

THE TREATY OF SÈVRES

The San Remo agreements prepared the way for a peace settlement with the Ottoman Empire, and the Treaty of Sèvres was signed on August 10, 1920. This treaty gave Greece western and eastern Thrace, including Edirne and territory close to Istanbul, and Izmir for at least five years. Armenia was established as an independent state. Kurdistan, east of the Euphrates River, obtained local autonomy. Although Istanbul remained under Ottoman sovereignty, the Straits area was to be controlled by an international commission. The Ottoman Empire would maintain an army of only 50,000. Minority rights were to be respected. New, humiliating articles were added to the reestablished capitulations. And the Ottoman Public Debt Administration was given almost absolute control over economic, financial, and budgetary matters. Equally galling to the Turks was the announcement of the Tripartite Agreement among England, France, and Italy, dividing what remained of Turkey into three spheres of influence almost exactly along the lines marked by wartime secret treaties. The Treaty of Sèvres left Turkey prostrate.

As for the rest of what had been the Ottoman Empire, by this treaty the Ottoman sultan recognized the separation of Syria, Iraq, Arabia, and Egypt. A British protectorate over Egypt was allowed, and the independence of the Arab rulers and their states, subject to treaties of friendship with Britain, was accepted. Provisional independence for Syria and Iraq under a mandatory power was acknowledged.

The Treaty of Sèvres was obsolete before it was drawn, and because of its sections dealing with Turkish portions of the Ottoman Empire it was never fully ratified. Theoretically, then, final arrangements in the Middle East awaited the Treaty of Lausanne in 1923; yet divisions, boundaries, and the disposal of non-Turkish parts of the Ottoman Empire in that final treaty varied only slightly from the transfer of legal authority that was proposed at San Remo and Sèvres. The mandates bargained for at San Remo dictated Arab political and economic life for the next twenty years, and Britain and France immediately took action in their respective spheres.

There was one additional settlement in this era of treaties and engagements. In March 1921, Winston Churchill, who was then colonial secretary, held a lengthy conference in Cairo with most of the British Middle Eastern experts and especially T. E. Lawrence. They put Faisal, ousted by the French from Damascus, on the throne of Iraq and carved from the part of Palestine east of the Jordan the state of Transjordan for his brother Abd Allah, who originally had been promised Iraq. This created a British-controlled route from Mosul to the Mediterranean.

ENTENTE OCCUPATION OF TURKEY

The Entente powers took control of Istanbul on November 13, 1918, when a combined fleet dropped anchor in the Golden Horn; soon an Entente army entered the city. British, French, Italian, and American high commissioners assumed responsibility for the four zones established in the city. In this fashion the capital of the 600-year-old Ottoman state, under Muslim control since 1453, fell into the hands of foreign Christians.

Istanbul witnessed drastic inflation, but Greeks and Armenians there welcomed the Entente allies as liberators, who rolled back time to 1914: the capitulations were restored; the Ottoman Public Debt Administration functioned again; and concession hunting once more became the sport of the day. Tens of thousands of refugees found refuge in Istanbul.

At first Turks were relieved that the fighting had ended, as they were genuinely weary of war. As the occupation proceeded, however, thoughtful Turks grew dismayed at the occupiers' lack of justice, understanding, and political wisdom. Although some government ministers, women's associations, guilds, and members of parliament in Istanbul were independent enough of foreign control that they were able to help the nationalists in Anatolia, it soon became apparent that Sultan Mehmed VI (r. 1918–1922) was only a puppet. It also became clear that Anatolia would be carved up, if the Allies could agree on partition.

Britain moved northward from Mosul; France claimed southeastern Anatolia as an extension of Syria; and Italian forces landed at Antalya to assure that promises would be fulfilled. Greek troops landed at Izmir to take possession of what the Greeks had been awarded. Supported by Britain and France, Venizelos began the Greek occupation on May 15, 1919. Organized Turkish resistance occurred almost immediately; Muslim Turkish acceptance of Christian Greek rule in Anatolia was impossible.

TURKISH NATIONALISTS

Following the Greek landing at Izmir, Mustafa Kemal, appointed as inspector general of the Third Army by the sultan, sailed for the Black Sea coast with orders to demobilize troops. Kemal resigned his commission and convened national congresses at Erzurum and Sivas, calling all patriotic Turks to join the Association for the Defense of Rights in Europe and Anatolia. Many former leaders of the Committee of Union and Progress and other nationalists had already formed local Turkish resistance organizations.

The Greek landing at Izmir produced extensive demonstrations and strikes in Istanbul. As the strength of the nationalists grew in the capital, the British in March 1920 occupied the city. Nationalist leaders were sent to Malta. Then, in April 1920, a Grand National Assembly met at Ankara and elected Mustafa Kemal as its president—the Turkish resistance was now fully committed to fight for independence.

Mustafa Kemal and the nationalists in Ankara seemed to be in a hopeless situation. They faced the British in Istanbul and the Straits, the Greeks at Izmir, the Italians at Antalya, the French at Adana, the British in Kurdistan, the Armenians in the northeast, and a hostile Ottoman puppet sultanate in Istanbul. Fortunately for the Turkish nationalists, the enemy never presented a concerted attack, and they were able to meet them one by one.

At Ankara in 1920, Mustafa Kemal defied the victors of World War I. He commanded only the scanty resources of central Anatolia and the veterans of several scattered armies. However, the undefeated Ninth Army, which had operated in the Caucasus and marched to the Caspian Sea, served as his nucleus, and Kemal organized a force about them. Then the Turks under Kazim Karabekir captured Kars, Ardahan, and Mount Ararat from the Armenian republic; the Russian Bolsheviks gained control over the Armenian state, which was incorporated ultimately into the Union of Soviet Socialist Republics. In December 1920 Turkey ceded Batum to Russia in exchange for Russian acknowledgment of Turkish control over the provinces of Kars and Ardahan. A few months later the Treaty of Moscow confirmed this new frontier and pledged Russian aid. In the spring of 1920 the Turks drove the French back to Aleppo and signed an armistice removing them from the combat. In March 1921 Kemal reached an agreement whereby the Italians, in return for economic concessions, evacuated Antalya. Consequently, by the opening of the summer of 1921 Kemal faced only the Greek army and some weak British contingents on the Straits.

TURKISH-GREEK WAR

Since June 1920 the Entente allies, through British insistence, had assigned to the Greeks the task of enforcing the peace terms. Greek armies advanced in Thrace and Anatolia, taking, in about a year, Edirne in Europe and sections of western Anatolia. The only victories Kemal could show were two battles at Inönü, where Colonel Ismet (1884–1973) won lasting fame in 1921.

Time, however, was on Kemal's side. Britain was undergoing economic and political turbulence and wanted to reduce the size of its armed forces serving in the Middle East and drastically cut overseas spending. Britain also quarreled with France over problems in Europe. A secret treaty of peace and friendship between France and the Turkish nationalist government was concluded in October 1921, with France hoping to gain economic advantages. Kemal was also aided by political developments in Greece when King Alexander died from the bite of his pet monkey in October 1920 and was succeeded by his father, Constantine, who was recalled from exile. The British distrusted King Constantine, while Turkish nationalists were obtaining war supplies from France, Italy, and Russia.

The Greek advance was checked by the three-week battle of Sakarya, which ended in September 1921. Stubborn Turkish resistance and extended Greek lines of communication decided the issue, although the Turks needed a whole year to regroup their forces for the victorious rush upon Izmir. After a Turkish victory in August 1922, the rout became general: Mustafa Kemal soon entered Izmir, and by September 19 all Greek forces were cleared from Anatolia. Mustafa Kemal won the title of ghazi, warrior for the faith and for the Muslim community, as the Turkish armies became victorious.

The war with Greece had been won, but intense bitterness remained. The Greek army in retreat pursued a scorched-earth policy and committed atrocities against defenseless Turkish villagers in its path. Shortly after the occupation of Izmir, fire broke out and destroyed nearly half of the city.

From Izmir the Turkish nationalists turned to the Straits. Britain signed an armistice with the government of the Turkish Grand National Assembly in October. Eastern Thrace with Edirne was ceded to the Turks, and the idea of a new peace treaty was accepted. Kemal had won; the British postwar policy for Turkey collapsed, taking David Lloyd George with it.

LAUSANNE CONFERENCE

Invitations to meet at Lausanne were issued both to Kemal and to the sultan's government in Istanbul, compelling the Grand National Assembly to pass a law deposing Mehmed VI. In November, the nationalists took over control of Istanbul, the sultan fled aboard a British cruiser, and the Grand National Assembly chose Mehmed's cousin, Abdulmejid II (r. 1922–1924) as caliph, but without the title of sultan. The Ottoman sultanate had come to its end.

Convening on November 20, 1922, the Lausanne Conference had a stormy course before its final acts were signed on July 24, 1923. England, France, Italy, Russia, Japan, Bulgaria, Romania, Yugoslavia, Greece, and Turkey participated in the deliberations and signed one or more of the several documents that were drawn up. Lord Curzon, the British foreign minister, dominated the conference; his tall figure was a sharp contrast to that of the Turkish delegate, Ismet, an Ottoman army officer and hero of battles against the Greeks, who was only 5 feet 4 inches tall. Ismet proved to be a stubborn yet skillful negotiator who knew that the Turks were willing to fight again if necessary to obtain independence, whereas the British had just sacked their prime minister rather than run the risk of further war. Frequently, when Lord Curzon would arrogantly deliver some advice, he would become infuriated almost to the breaking point when Ismet, who was a trifle deaf, would cup his bad ear and ask him in French to repeat what he said: "Répétez-vous, s'il vous plaît?"

At the Lausanne Conference eastern Thrace with Edirne went with full sovereignty to Turkey. Of the Aegean Islands, Tenedos and Imbros went to Turkey, the Dodecanese to Italy, and the remainder to Greece. The settlement with regard to the Straits gave Turkey sovereignty over the area; however, each shore would be demilitarized for 15 kilometers. The Mosul frontier was left to be negotiated at a later date. In regard to the Armenian and Greek minorities Turkey accepted articles similar to minority clauses inserted in treaties with Austria, Hungary, and Bulgaria, and the Greeks agreed to a compulsory exchange of populations, excluding the Greeks of Istanbul and the Turks of western Thrace. The capitulations were abolished entirely. Financial questions were settled by ending the Ottoman Public Debt Administration and by a proportionate assumption of Ottoman government debts by all successor states. Turkey agreed not to alter its tariff for five years. Ismet went home to Ankara with the knowledge that Turkey was recognized as an independent free nation, except for the demilitarization of the Straits and the undefined border with Iraq.

The exchange of populations between Turkey and Greece, begun in the summer of 1923 under the League of Nations, proceeded over many months. About 1 million Greeks and half as many Turks were moved, at considerable hardship to the individuals involved. The impact upon Greece was most serious. Turkey lost many merchants and businesspeople, but Ismet argued at Lausanne that such a loss would be more than offset by the advantages of a united Turkish nation.

The Treaty of Lausanne was ratified during the summer of 1923. On October 29, 1923, just nine years after the Ottoman Empire entered World War I, the Grand National Assembly in Ankara declared Turkey a republic and elected Mustafa Kemal its president.

IRAN'S POSTWAR PROBLEMS

While the British and their Greek allies were attempting to dominate western Anatolia, London also had dreams of a British zone that would extend from the Mediterranean to India. With Iraq and Palestine already conquered by 1918, Iran was the missing link. An Iranian delegation went to the Paris peace talks, but being anti-British, it was not permitted to attend or to state Iran's case, though Iran did join the League of Nations. A less hostile delegation negotiated and signed, on August 9, 1919, an Anglo-Iranian treaty, which virtually transformed Iran into a dependency of the British Empire. Iranian government departments, finances, and the army would be in British hands. Iran already received a monthly subsidy from Britain and would now gain a loan of £2 million; in return, its tariffs would be controlled by the British as collateral against the loan. The Iranian assembly (majlis) refused to ratify the treaty, and Britain withdrew its forces from Iran.

Communist Russia had denounced the capitulations and tsarist treaties with Iran. Soviet forces conquered formerly Russian Azerbaijan in 1920; while pursuing a tsarist general they also occupied Iranian territory north of the Elburz Mountains and refused to depart until all British military were evacuated. A Soviet Republic of Gilan was established, but Moscow alleged it had no authority over it.

Iran's protests to the League of Nations about Soviet intervention were fruitless, so Iran concluded an agreement with Russia in February 1921. The frontiers and independence of each country were to be respected; Iranian debts to Russia were canceled; all concessions were relinquished, except the Caspian Sea fisheries (since even Communists had to have caviar); and if a third power occupied any part of Iran, Russia might send troops. Russia then withdrew its troops from the Soviet Republic of Gilan, which promptly fell because of internal disputes and an Iranian military expedition.

The independence of Iran was confirmed by the rejection of the Anglo-Iranian treaty of 1919, the withdrawal of British troops, and the Soviet-Iranian treaty of 1921. However, Iran was still torn with strife and economic disorder. Disease, poverty, chaos, and corruption prevailed everywhere. The installations of the Anglo-Persian Oil Company were flourishing, but they were under the thumb of the British government. World War I left Iran in a seemingly hopeless situation.

This devastating war changed not only Iran but the whole of the Middle East in many ways. The rash Ottoman entry into the war sealed its fate, already challenged as it was by competing nationalisms. The Entente distribution of Ottoman lands, the British domination of Egypt and Iran, the continuing French-British-Italian control of North Africa, and renewed Russian Soviet annexation of the Caucasus and central Asia marked what seemed to be the total success of Europe, as the Middle East was incorporated into European-dominated world economic and political systems on terms dictated by the victors in World War I.

From 1919 to 1923, however, some Middle Eastern groups rejected the Entente's terms and brought about revisions in the postwar settlements. Popular uprisings among Arabs, political opposition expressed by the Iranian majlis, and, most remarkably, the vigorous military and diplomatic efforts of Turks succeeded in putting limitations on the dominance of Europe in the Middle East during the two decades following 1918.

REFERENCES

References cited at the end of Chapters 21, 23, 26, 27, 28, and 30 are pertinent to this chapter as well.

Busch, Briton Cooper: *Mudros to Lausanne: Britain's Frontier in West Asia, 1918–1923.* Albany: State University of New York Press, 1976. A study of British policy in the area between the Straits and central Asia after the breakup of the Ottoman and Russian empires and the emergence of a new balance of power.

Criss, Nur Bilge: *Istanbul under Allied Occupation.* Leiden, The Netherlands: Brill, 1999. Discusses political and social history, Entente administration, and nationalist resistance.

Dadrian, Vahakn N.: "The Documentation of the World War I Armenian Massacres in the Proceedings of the Turkish Military Tribunal." *International Journal of Middle East Studies* 23 (1991): 549–576. In this and other works the author carefully examines records establishing the involvement of the Committee of Union and Progress in the Armenian massacres.

DeNovo, John A.: *American Interests and Policies in the Middle East, 1900–1939.* Minneapolis: University of Minnesota Press, 1963. A thorough work that includes all aspects of American interests.

Djemal Pasha, Ahmed: *Memories of a Turkish Statesman, 1913–1919.* New York: Doran, 1922. The autobiography of one of the Ottoman triumvirate during the war.

Edib (Adivar), Halidé: *The Turkish Ordeal.* New York: Century, 1928. Written by a woman who participated in the Turkish struggle for independence.

Erickson, Edward J.: *Ordered to Die: A History of the Ottoman Army in the First World War.* Westport, Conn.: Greenwood Press, 2001. This indispensable work is solidly based on the Turkish Army's archives.

Fromkin, David: *A Peace to End All Peace: The Fall of the Ottoman Empire and the Creation of the Modern Middle East.* New York: Avon, 1989. A popular account of wartime diplomacy, centering around British activities.

Helmreich, Paul C.: *From Paris to Sèvres: The Partition of the Ottoman Empire at the Peace Conference of 1919–1920.* Columbus: Ohio State University Press, 1974. Objective and very well organized topically and chronologically.

Hovannisian, Richard G.: "The Historical Dimensions of the Armenian Question, 1878–1923." In Richard G. Hovannisian, ed., *The Armenian Genocide in Perspective,* pp. 19–41. New Brunswick, N.J.: Transaction Books, 1986. An able summary of evidence supporting Armenian claims of Ottoman guilt in the massacres as well as a general discussion of Ottoman-Armenian relations.

Hurewitz, J. C., compiler, trans., ed.: *The Middle East and North Africa in World Politics: A Documentary Record.* Vol. 2: *British-French Supremacy, 1914–1945.* 2d ed. New Haven, Conn.: Yale University Press, 1979. This volume contains significant documents for this crucial period.

Kedourie, Elie: *In the Anglo-Arab Labyrinth: The McMahon-Husayn Correspondence and Its Interpretations, 1914–1939.* 2d ed. London: Frank Cass, 2000. A thorough examination of the correspondence and the conversations, followed by a full analysis of the various interpretations and historical reports of them.

Kent, Marian, ed.: *The Great Powers and the End of the Ottoman Empire.* 2d ed. London: Frank Cass, 1996. Seven authors evaluate the diplomatic history of the Ottoman Empire, Austria, Italy, Russia, Germany, France, and Great Britain from around 1900 to 1923.

Klieman, Aaron S.: *Foundations of British Policy in the Arab World: The Cairo Conference of 1921.* Baltimore: Johns Hopkins University Press, 1970. A first-rate account of this prestigious meeting, drawn from official sources.

Lawrence, T. E.: *Seven Pillars of Wisdom.* London: Jonathan Cape, 1935. The full story of Lawrence of Arabia's activities among the Arabs during the war; a literary masterpiece whose historical accuracy has been much debated.

McCarthy, Justin: *Death and Exile: The Ethnic Cleansing of Ottoman Muslims, 1821–1922.* Princeton, N.J.: Darwin, 1995. Discusses the forced migrations of Muslims and mortality among the refugees.

McKale, Donald M.: *War by Revolution: Germany and Great Britain in the Middle East in the Era of World War I.* Kent, Ohio: Kent State University Press, 1998. Useful especially for the author's analysis of perceptions about jihad held by the British and Germans.

Monroe, Elizabeth: *Britain's Moment in the Middle East, 1914–1971.* 2d ed. Baltimore: Johns Hopkins University Press, 1981. A comprehensive and classic survey.

Moorehead, Alan: *Gallipoli.* New York: Harper, 1956. The story of the famous campaign.

Olson, William J.: *Anglo-Iranian Relations during World War I.* London: Frank Cass, 1984. An excellent treatment of British policy and Iranian governments up to 1920.

Sachar, Howard M.: *The Emergence of the Middle East: 1914–1924.* New York: Knopf, 1969. A well-documented account of the area from a European rather than a Middle Eastern view.

Simon, Rachel: *Libya between Ottomanism and Nationalism: The Ottoman Involvement in Libya during the War with Italy (1911–1919).* Berlin: Klaus Schwarz, 1987. A detailed examination based on Ottoman archival sources.

Sonyel, Salahi Ramsdan: *Turkish Diplomacy, 1918–1923: Mustafa Kemal and the Turkish National Movement.* London: Sage, 1975. A clear study of international diplomacy centering around the diplomacy of the nationalists. Based on primary sources in Turkish and western languages.

Storrs, Ronald: *Orientations.* London: Nicholson and Watson, 1937. Storrs was the Oriental secretary to the British high commissioner in Egypt during the war.

Suny, Ronald Grigor: "Empire and Nation: Armenians, Turks, and the End of the Ottoman Empire." *Armenian Forum* 1 (1998): 17–51. A balanced sketch of the history of Armenians, the development of nationalism, and the massacres of World War I.

Swietochowski, Tadeusz: *Russian Azerbaijan, 1905–1920: The Shaping of National Identity in a Muslim Community.* New York: Cambridge University Press, 1985. An excellent account of political, military, and national history that includes the World War I period.

Tauber, Eliezer: *The Arab Movements in World War I.* London: Frank Cass, 1993. A thorough discussion of Arab nationalists and their connections with the Arab Revolt.

Toynbee, Arnold J.: *Survey of International Affairs, 1925.* Vol. 1: *The Islamic World Since the Peace Settlement.* London: Oxford University Press, 1927. By the renowned historian who wrote world historical studies, as well as works dealing with the Middle East.

Trumpener, Ulrich: *Germany and the Ottoman Empire, 1914–1918.* Princeton, N.J.: Princeton University Press, 1968. Largely based on German sources, this outstanding book discusses the alliance of 1914, the conduct of the war, financing, Armenian persecutions, German economic efforts, and political evolution of the alliance.

Vital, David: *Zionism: The Crucial Phase.* Oxford, England: Clarendon Press, 1987. An excellent account of Zionist internal organization and relationships with Britain and France from 1907 to 1919.

von Sanders, Liman: *Five Years in Turkey.* Baltimore: Williams and Wilkins, 1928. The record of a German commanding general stationed in the Ottoman Empire during the war.

Wilson, Jeremy: *Lawrence of Arabia: The Authorized Biography of T. E. Lawrence.* New York: Atheneum, 1990. This lengthy work shows careful consideration of the controversial life of its subject.

Yasamee, F. A. K.: "Ottoman Empire." In Keith Wilson, ed. *Decisions for War, 1914,* pp. 229–268. New York: St. Martin's Press, 1995. Weighs carefully considerations and explanations for the entry of the Ottoman Empire into World War I.

Zürcher, Erik Jan: "Between Death and Desertion: The Experience of the Ottoman Soldier in World War I." *Turcica* 28 (1996): 235–258. What the war was like for most Ottoman soldiers.

PART FOUR

The Middle East after World War I

CHAPTER 32

The Turkish Republic under Atatürk

Many reforms carried out in the Turkish Republic began in the last years of the Ottoman Empire. Especially during World War I, the radical reformers in the Committee of Union and Progress government accomplished much along these lines, such as abolishing the capitulations, reorganizing religious courts, and enacting a new family law. To a degree, then, Mustafa Kemal and the other leaders of the new republic carried on the programs of Europeanization and modernization that had marked the Ottoman Empire since at least the reforms of Sultan Selim III in the 1790s. And the republic also benefited from the trained personnel, substantial infrastructure, and sense of identity created in Ottoman days. But the Kemalists viewed the Ottoman legacy with great suspicion, pointing to the defeats, debts, and deadening of initiative they thought pervaded late Ottoman history. Instead, they wanted to create a new centralized nation-state, with a new capital and a radically new approach to life, based on Turkish identity.

To a certain extent the revolutionary changes developed without a systematic plan, but they ultimately became associated with six basic principles: republicanism, secularism, populism, nationalism, economic statism, and reformism. The Turkish state under the leadership of Mustafa Kemal and the Republican People's party, supported by the armed forces and reinforced by a period of international peace after the earlier devastating wars, created a transformed Turkish society.

MUSTAFA KEMAL

Modern Turkish nationalism, conceived in the latter part of the nineteenth century and nourished in the Young Turk period inside the framework of the Ottoman Empire, was born in 1919 and 1920. It first saw the light of day on the plateaus of central Anatolia, and its birth pangs were a series of wars for independence against several enemies.

The chief leader of the Turkish nationalists was Mustafa Kemal, born in 1881 in Salonica (then part of the Ottoman Empire but later located in Greece). He belonged to the lower middle class and attended military schools, where he distinguished himself in mathematics. As an Ottoman officer, he served in Damascus and the Balkans and took an active part in various revolutionary societies. He also served in Libya in the war against Italy and participated briefly in the Balkan wars. During World War I he became a hero in the Gallipoli campaign, and by 1918 he had commanded armies on several fronts.

Mustafa Kemal combined a brilliant mind with a perfectionist approach. An early teacher had given him the nickname Kemal ("perfection"), a name he eventually came to use almost exclusively. Kemal was contemptuous of pomp and ceremony; he was a devoted nationalist with energy, an indomitable will, and an incorruptibility that was frightening to many.

ESTABLISHMENT OF THE REPUBLIC

Between September 1911 and September 1922, there were five wars and only twenty-two months of peace for the Ottoman Empire and Turkey. About 20 percent of the population of Anatolia died, and there were millions of refugees in the country. Overcoming those problems posed major difficulties for the new Turkish Republic as it sought reforms.

On October 29, 1923, the Grand National Assembly voted approval of a declaration asserting that "the form of government of the Turkish State is a Republic." That same day it elected Ghazi Mustafa Kemal Pasha president of the republic. The idea of a republic was not entirely novel; its declaration revealed an evolution ongoing since 1919 and the resistance against the Entente plans to carve up Anatolia among the victors in World War I. The Grand National Assembly meeting in April 1920 at Ankara recognized the prisoner-like status of the Ottoman sultan in Istanbul and declared that there was "no power superior to the Grand National Assembly." Kemal became its president, and a council of state was elected to serve as the executive arm of the Ankara government, as it was called.

The Grand National Assembly continued to debate whether it was a permanent or provisional government until early 1921, when it passed amendments to the 1876 Ottoman constitution. These articles established the Assembly as a permanent institution and served as the basis of government until 1924, when a new constitution was adopted. Meanwhile, a new Assembly elected in April 1923 gave Kemal and his cohorts a small majority. It was this second Assembly in Ankara that proclaimed the republic and later adopted the constitution. Support for Kemal, the Grand National Assembly, and the Ankara government came chiefly from the military, civilian bureaucrats, large landowners, the ulama, and professionals, but there was popular enthusiasm among many peasants and townspeople as well. Kemal had military officers resign their commissions and become civilians before serving in the Assembly, thereby formally separating the armed forces from politics.

Meanwhile, Kemal's Association for the Defense of Rights in Europe and Anatolia evolved by 1923 into the Republican People's party. Kemal, as party president, used frequent party caucuses for debate and formulation of policy. At these meetings, which often continued through the night, actual government policy decisions were made. After the Mudanya armistice, Kemal used every wile and force at his command to carry through his points. Anatolian party leaders counseled direct military action against the British in Istanbul as the best solution. This step, which would have been highly successful initially, was skillfully countered by Kemal, who understood that Britain had overwhelming force at its command.

Before the constitution was adopted, a fundamental change had been made in the religious and political structure of the state. When Sultan Mehmed VI left Istanbul for Malta in 1922, the Grand National Assembly deposed him and ended the sultanate, while declaring the caliphate vacant and electing to that office an Ottoman prince, Abdulmejid. However, a caliph without the temporal power of a sultan was an anomaly. Kemal eventually proposed that the caliphate also be abolished, and in March 1924, despite strong opposition, the Assembly did so. In addition, the Ottoman imperial family was banished from Turkey, and the shariah (Muslim sacred law) courts were abolished. The functions of the ministries governing waqfs (pious foundations) were transferred to a newly created presidency of religious affairs.

The new constitution of the republic was promulgated on April 20, 1924. Drawn up without too much controversy, it stated that sovereignty resided in the Turkish nation, whose representative was the Grand National Assembly. It declared all Turks equal before the law and forbade special privileges for groups or individuals. A Turk was defined as anyone who was a citizen of the Turkish Republic, without distinction as to ethnicity or religion. Freedom of speech, thought, press, and travel were guaranteed. The religion of the state was declared to be Islam; the language, Turkish; and the seat of government, Ankara.

The government established by the constitution was in form a democracy but in fact—at that time and for more than twenty years to follow—a one-party government controlled by Kemal and his close political associates. The Grand National Assembly was elected for a four-year term by universal male suffrage; women were granted suffrage as of 1934. Although the president of the republic was elected by the Assembly for a similar term, the prime minister was appointed by the president. Until 1945, the machinery of government was almost entirely in the hands of the Republican People's party. Candidates for election as deputies from the various districts to the Grand National Assembly were nominated by that party, and only one slate of names was presented to voters.

Mustafa Kemal was correctly labeled a dictator: he determined high policy, selected key officials of state, and forced his will on the party and nation. But in most matters, he was careful to prepare the people by skillfully organized speeches before action was taken. Kemal was convinced that he knew what was best for the Turkish people and the best way to obtain it. His abiding ambition was for the Turkish people, not for himself. In this way he was a benevolent dictator and extremely popular with most, though not all, citizens.

KURDISH REBELLION

Throughout the numerous wars and upheavals of this time, the Kurdish-speaking population of Anatolia had generally supported first the Ottoman Empire and then the nationalist government in Ankara. Kurds resided in a broad area extending into the Caucasus, northern Syria, Iraq, and Iran; the largest single group resided in Turkey. The Kurds of Turkey included mostly Sunnis and some Alevi Shiis, and many belonged to Sufi orders. They were also divided among speakers of several dialects and along tribal lines, and many spoke Turkish as a second language. Kurds participated in the Ottoman armies even before World War I, and they took part in the armed struggles that convulsed eastern Anatolia during the war, suffering heavy civilian and military casualties. The Kurdish role in the massacres of Armenians was prominent. Most Kurds apparently supported the nationalists during the war against Greece, although a small Kurdish rebellion did break out in 1921. After the Turkish-Greek population exchange, the Kurds constituted by far the largest single non-Turkish group in the country, comprising between one-tenth and one-fifth of the total population of 13 million.

Nationalism developed among the Kurds relatively late compared to other Middle Eastern societies, but by the 1920s, some degree of ethnic-national awareness was arising among them. In 1921 Kurdish military leaders founded the Azadi society, a nationalist organization. The Treaty of Lausanne had given Kurds the possibility of autonomy, but the collapse of that treaty allowed the authorities in Ankara to opt for a policy of tightly centralized authority in the provinces. Actions taken by the government that infuriated Kurdish opinion included forbidding the teaching of Kurdish and its use in public, forcibly resettling Kurdish tribal chiefs, and abolishing the caliphate.

Early in 1925 Shaikh Said, a Naqshbandiyah Sufi leader, led many Sunni Kurdish tribal groups in a rebellion aimed at autonomy or even independence for eastern Anatolian Kurds. His followers blended together religious and nationalist opposition to Kemal and the Ankara government. Kurdish Alevi Shiis, however, tended to support the secularist Ankara regime on the grounds that it would be more tolerant toward Shiis than a religiously based Sunni Kurdish authority. Rapid military action taken by Kemal soon crushed the rebellion, and Shaikh Said was arrested and executed, although other Kurdish groups continued to fight until 1930.

Because of the outbreak of the revolt, Ismet Pasha, prime minister almost continuously from 1923 to 1937, pushed through a law for the maintenance of order under which a Tribunal of Independence was set up. Kurds and other opponents were tried and hundreds were executed, while thousands of Kurds were relocated to western Anatolia. A small Kurdish rebellion that broke out in 1937 was crushed with even more severity. Turkish nationalists decided Kurdish identity had to be denied and suppressed so as to maintain the unity of the country and the state, while many Kurds voluntarily assimilated to the Turkish majority.

SIX PRINCIPLES OF THE REVOLUTION

Reforms touched every aspect of life and society in Turkey in the 1920s and 1930s. In the earlier period, change was rapid and followed no clear pattern of planned or coordinated development. In response to criticism, Kemal consolidated and classified these rather haphazard reforms and adopted a clearer course of modernization in 1931. Terming the entire program *Kemalism,* he defined his reforms along six broad classifications: republicanism, secularism, populism, nationalism, statism, and reformism. These six became the party's campaign platform for the elections of 1935 and were adopted as the basic principles of the new Turkish nation when they were incorporated into the constitution by amendment in 1937.

Republicanism

The first principle, republicanism, was demonstrated in Article 1 of the constitution: The Turkish State is a Republic. Kemal could have made himself king or sultan, but he insisted on a republic because it was more Western and more democratic and because he believed it suited Turkey. Although conservative elements, clients of the Ottoman family, the religious hierarchy, and the devout clung to the old order in many aspects, few people then or later favored a restoration of the Ottoman family as monarchs.

Secularism

The second reform principle was the secularization of the state and society. Islam pervaded most aspects of life in Turkey, and Kemal and many other leaders subscribed to the theory, learned from their contacts with the West, that Islam's hold on society retarded development and created the difference between West and East.

Abolishing the caliphate and closing the shariah courts did not in themselves change the religious basis of law in Turkey. Law reforms in the late nineteenth century had westernized the commercial and criminal laws, but civil law and family matters were still tied to sacred law. In 1925, a new law school opened in Ankara to instruct lawyers and judges in the fundamentals of Western laws. Then in 1926, the Grand National Assembly adopted the new civil code, based on Swiss law; the new penal code, taken from Italian law; and the new commercial code, which was a modification of the German code.

The republic adopted a series of other measures designed to curb the power of organized religion and change the social expression of Islam in public life. Friday, the Muslim holy day, was made a compulsory day of rest throughout the land in 1924, in part to give the day another emphasis. In 1925 Sufi orders were forbidden, and their centers and shrines were closed. Rather than simply disappearing, however, Sufi groups illegally continued as underground organizations. Most startling of all was the law forbidding men to wear the Ottoman fez and ordering male headgear to have a brim or a visor. The armed services were outfitted in Western-style military caps. The fez was considered a Muslim symbol, although when it was adopted at the time of Sultan Mahmud II, it had been regarded as a symbol of modernizing reform. The wearing of veils by women was never outlawed, but it was discouraged in every possible way.

Up to this point the Muslim lunar calendar was employed by the general public. The dating of years ensued from the prophet Muhammad's emigration from Mecca to Medina in the earliest days of Islam. Both the lunar calendar and the dating system were now abandoned and replaced by the Western Gregorian calendar. Everywhere the Muslim year of 1342 became 1926. The Muslim calendar was still employed, however, in calculating Ramadan, the month of fasting, and all other Muslim religious holidays.

A far-reaching effect of Western law was the official end of polygamy and a new status for women. Since not many men had been able to afford to maintain more than one wife, the prohibition against polygamy was not an enormous change. More important for both men and women were equal rights of divorce and equality in inheritance and in courtroom testimony. Nevertheless, the husband was still considered the head of the family in law. Job opportunities for women became wider in the cities, and some women, with the permission of their husbands, entered the new textile factories and also the professions; the first Turkish woman physician began practicing medicine in 1922. Many of the legal and employment changes were ignored or opposed in rural areas; they took effect at first primarily in the cities. Family life also changed first in the cities. Starting as early as the 1880s but accelerating in the days of the republic, Istanbul families had far fewer children, women married later in life, birth control was more widely practiced, and the quality of child care improved more rapidly than among families in the countryside.

Secularization went so far that in 1928 the constitution was amended, removing the statement that Turkey is an Islamic state and providing that government officials, on being inducted into office, would swear on their honor, rather than before God, to fulfill their duties. Later, in 1935, the day of rest was changed to Sunday, and the weekend was established by law as extending from Saturday at 1:00 P.M. to Sunday midnight.

Kemal probably was an atheist, but many of his advisers were sincerely religious. Despite this, by the 1930s all deemphasized the place of religion in national life, even though Islam had been used as a bond to promote solidarity in the war against the Greeks in the 1920s. By the end of this period, fewer individuals observed religious days; in Istanbul and Ankara many persons paid no attention to Ramadan, and many children were not taught prayers. Religious instruction was gradually removed from public and private schools. The faculty of theology at the University of Istanbul enrolled so few that it was consolidated in 1933 with the department of literature. By 1939 Turkey was a secular state, as typical in this respect as France, Germany, or the United States.

Populism

In the Ottoman Empire the capitulations and the millet system gave special privileges to foreigners and to many religious minorities. In the republic, however, the constitution stated that all Turks are equal before the law and that all "privileges of whatever description claimed by groups, classes, families, and individuals are abolished and forbidden." It was this idea that Kemal incorporated in the word *populism.*

The new republic of Turkey was won by the peasants, who constituted about 80 percent of the total population, and to them the new Turkish society was dedicated. Tax burdens on them had been inordinately heavy, so Kemal promised them relief on this score in payment for their efforts in the national struggle. The Grand National Assembly in 1925 abolished the tithe on their lands, and taxes on agriculture were lightened in order to stimulate greater production. In the 1930s world prices for Turkish exports fell as the Great Depression hurt peasants and merchants. Taxes on peasants effectively rose once again as unemployment in the cities increased. Despite these problems, life expectancy was higher, and land was still available for agricultural expansion.

Primary education in government-supervised schools became obligatory as free and universal education was established as another expression of populism. In conformity with the goal of universal education, schools were built by the thousands during this era. Emphasis at first was placed on adult education and teacher training schools, since a lack of teachers handicapped the program's success. Each village was required to have a primary school of five grades. Secondary schools were constructed in the towns to prepare students for various vocations and for entrance to lycées, which were the equivalent of American high schools and junior colleges. Beyond the lycée was the University of Istanbul and, later, Ankara University and specialized schools.

With the illiteracy rate at an estimated 90 percent, the ability to read became a privilege that Kemal desired for all Turks. The Arabic script was never satisfactory for the Turkish language, in which vowels not present in Arabic play an important part in word formation. Writing and spelling were arduous exercises. In 1928, the Grand National Assembly adopted a new, strictly phonetic Turkish alphabet based on Latin characters; it became compulsory January 1, 1929, and after that date everything in writing—all public signs, newspapers, books, and so forth—was in the new script.

The work involved in the changeover was staggering. New textbooks had to be printed for every subject; in the autumn of 1928 schools opened several weeks late because books were unavailable. The literate had to learn to read and write all over again, and the heritage of the past, written using the old alphabet, gradually became unavailable to the young, who knew only the Latin letters. Kemal and members of the Grand National Assembly traveled about the country giving public reading lessons in the Latin characters. Changing headgear was relatively easy in comparison to the alphabet transition, but the campaign was effective. Millions learned to read, particularly in the cities and towns, and the literacy rate tripled by 1945. Newspapers multiplied, typewriters became less complex, and a modern national life embracing a majority of the population was born.

Nationalism

The fourth point in the Kemalist program was the development of nationalism. Kemal was a fiery Turkish patriot, proud of being a Turk. He renamed the country Turkey and renounced the identity of the Ottoman Empire. Kemal set out in his program to make Turks proud of their folk heritage, while limiting the national community to those living within the new borders, thereby excluding Turkish speakers living in central Asia, Iran, or elsewhere. And Kurdish ethnic or national identity inside Turkey was rigorously repressed.

Although all the reforms of the Kemalist regime were tinged with nationalism, none was more pointed than the new histories written in the Latin alphabet for elementary and secondary schools. The books minimized the history of the Ottoman Turks, in order to forget the centuries after Suleiman I, but they set out for the Turks a glorious and significant past. Sumerians and Hittites became Turks; most non-Semites of Middle Eastern antiquity were claimed as Turks; indeed, all peoples who came from central Asia were classified as Turks. Since the Turkish word for man is *adam* and since Adam traditionally was the first man, it was popularly said that Adam was Turkish and therefore that all peoples are Turkish. Individuals who viewed these theories critically were berated, so most skeptics remained silent. Many Turks found genuine satisfaction in these theories, which helped generate a more dynamic Turkish national feeling.

For centuries Turkish literature and, more recently, even newspaper Turkish had been filled with many words taken from Arabic and Persian. Since many of these words were not used in conversational Turkish, they made written Turkish unintelligible to the great majority. After the adoption of the new alphabet, the drive to free Turkish from an Arabic and Persian vocabulary and to resurrect obsolete Turkish words made great headway. New words also came into Turkish from French and other European languages.

For a period of several years in the mid-1930s, the government published a list of new Turkish words and their old equivalents every few weeks. Since all government publications used these often artificial new words and since communications to the government containing old words were often ignored, business concerns and foreign organizations frequently employed someone just to keep up with the rapid language changes. As a result of all these changes, Turkish lost the richness, variety, and history of written Ottoman forms, while the government consciously sought also to turn the new generation away from Arabic, the language of the Quran, toward Turkish. The written language closely resembled the everyday vernacular, becoming almost entirely phonetic in its spelling.

One of the more dramatic and publicized events in Kemal's program of Turkish nationalism was the forced adoption and use of family names. Only a few of the old Turkish families had names. The Grand National Assembly gave to Kemal the name of Atatürk ("Father of the Turks"), to Ismet the name of Inönü in honor of his two victories there, and other appropriate names to party leaders. The head of each family went to precinct police headquarters and selected the family name from a list of approved Turkish words and names. Most names had a meaning, such as Biyiklioğlu ("son of the man with a mustache"), Üstündağ ("mountaintop"), and Kirkağaçlioğlu ("son of the man with forty trees").

At times nationalism seemed to engulf the Turks, and certainly it made them extremely sensitive to criticism. Whether Atatürk believed in all the theories he supported is debatable, but he certainly believed in the necessity of not tolerating public debate about them. In any case they worked, and his slogan, "Turkey for the Turks and the Turks for Turkey," was accepted by most of the nation.

Statism

At Lausanne bitter wrangling took place between Britain and Turkey over the capitulations and European economic imperialism. Economic independence was compromised by the promise not to tamper with the tariff for five years, while the new government had to spend much of its budget every year after 1929 on paying off the debt burden inherited from the Ottoman Empire.

Kemal's advisers desired to develop the economic resources of Turkey and to inaugurate industrialization without foreign influence. The unfortunate experience that the Ottoman Empire had suffered from foreign loans, capital investments, and concessions conditioned Kemal against any repetition for the republic. His idea was that Turkey would develop its own resources and industrialize behind a strong protective tariff that could become effective in 1929. Within a short time, the Turks discovered that imports and exports could be more easily regulated through exchange control than by tariffs and quotas and that a managed economy could be introduced.

With the worldwide depression of the 1930s, Turkey's exports dropped. When Nazi Germany proposed an attractive compensation trade agreement, the Turks readily accepted. Trade with Germany boomed, and in 1936 over 50 percent of Turkey's exports went to Germany.

Kemal understood that agriculture was the principal occupation and resource of his nation, and he strove to increase the output. He established a model farm near Ankara, where the latest techniques and machinery were demonstrated for all to see, and activities of the Bank of Agriculture, founded by the Ottomans in 1889, were greatly expanded. The world depression, however, cut agricultural prices by one-half, so the government began to support them in 1932. Perhaps the greatest spur to increased agricultural production was the security and peace provided in the countryside after years of wars and devastation. Agriculture by 1929 had recovered almost to the level of production in 1912.

Gross national product per capita grew substantially, increasing at the rate of about 8% per year between 1923 and 1929. The Depression slowed this increase to about 3% per year from 1929 to 1939.

Kemal felt that advances in industry, in contrast to the progress in agriculture, moved too slowly. Too few people had any industrial know-how, and those with capital tended to follow the traditional practice of investing in buildings or land. The middle class had been devastated by the destruction, deaths, and exile caused by the Balkan wars, World War I, the Armenian massacres, and the war against Greece. Since many of the most active industrialists, merchants, and technicians had been members of the religious minorities who were no longer present, Turkey had many barriers to economic growth. On the other hand, government monopolies in matches, tobacco, alcohol, and salt and the government operation of railroads and electric utilities were highly successful. Expansion programs were effective, and railroad lines were extended in several areas. From state monopolies and public works Kemal turned to state economic enterprises; thus, in 1934 the government inaugurated a five-year plan for the development of industry and created banks to own and operate such enterprises. A score of factories were built to produce textiles, paper, glass, and steel.

In Turkey this policy of planning and state enterprises, created and managed by the government, was called *statism* and gave rise to some debate. Some branded the course as a step toward communism, whereas others claimed it was a kind of autarchy as preached by Hitler and Mussolini and thus linked Atatürk with the two dictators, pointing to such similarities as a ban on trade unions. Kemal opposed Marxist class analysis, claiming that class conflict should not be allowed to appear in Turkey; he outlawed strikes. Different views on various economic issues were held even in high places in the Republican People's party.

Reformism

The sixth and final arrow of Kemalism stood for reformism. By this Atatürk meant opposition to blind conservatism and to a rigid adherence to the status quo. He did not believe in change for change's sake, but he knew all too well how reformers grow old and conservative, especially when they hold responsible government posts. Kemal wanted his revolution to be a continuing process, evolving and expanding. The program with respect to women fell into this category. He wished more than just a change in their legal status and costume. Upper- and middle-class urban women found new opportunities as Kemal compelled wives of cabinet ministers to learn to dance, encouraged girls to become actresses and airplane pilots, and opened the way for women to become lawyers, doctors, bankers, and public officials. Of 399 members elected to the Grand National Assembly in 1935, 18 were women. About one-third of all students were female.

In cultural matters, the Ottoman past was to be superseded by European styles and usages. Ottoman art music was banned from the government radio service, and in 1936 in Ankara a new conservatory for actors, ballet dancers, opera singers, and musicians was opened. Both Turkish folk music and Western classical and popular music were encouraged, including the tango and the Charleston. Atatürk secured the services of experts from central Europe, many of whom were refugees, for enterprises in such fields as music, medicine, and archaeology. Novels and poetry became extremely diverse in style and substance; many writers discussed political themes and the new reforms of the republic. Atatürk personally encouraged touring theatrical groups whose plays were intended to spread new values and ideas, and he even dictated changes to some of the plays. The old religious opposition to sculpture was suppressed, and idealized and heroic monuments were erected. Painters used impressionist and other European-inspired styles, and portraits and narrative paintings designed to commemorate the revolution and war of independence flourished. Turkish architects initially continued a revival of Ottoman styles, but in the 1930s the government employed foreign, especially German, architects whose buildings were of the new, stark, international style. Young Turkish architects soon adopted this new approach while blending it with Turkish national characteristics.

Another important change was in regard to sports. Early Ottomans were keen sports enthusiasts and held competitions in archery, polo, horse racing, wrestling, and many other sports. Later there was a reversal; many in the elite looked on physical exertion as degrading and sports participation as undignified. Before Atatürk died in 1938, every city had several sports clubs. The Ottomans had already sent entries to the revived modern Olympics starting in 1912. And soccer (called *futbol* in Turkish) became the new national sport, which boys and girls throughout the country played with great enthusiasm.

The old Ottoman government was very corrupt. Bribes and tips were widespread. Kemal was ruthless in his treatment of this custom, and although it did not disappear entirely, anyone in the government found guilty of accepting bribes was speedily dismissed and prosecuted. When it was suggested that one of Kemal's secretaries of long service accepted a silver cigarette case for some service rendered, he was soon thereafter recalled and dismissed.

One of the most fruitful reforms had to do with the idea of the role of destiny in human affairs. If some unpleasant circumstance developed or an unfortunate event occurred, the natural reaction of most people in earlier times was to shrug their shoulders and blame God and fate. Through persistent education and practical demonstrations in sanitation, orderly government, and mental habits, people's attitudes changed so that many accepted responsibility for their own destiny rather than blame supernatural forces.

TURKISH POLITICS

Although there was only one political party under Kemal through most of this period and most politicians supported the six points of Kemalism, it should not be assumed that there was no politics in Turkey. The Progressive Republican party was organized in 1924 by members of the nationalist movement and former generals in opposition to Kemal. Some were conservatives, some were personally ambitious, and others were liberals who disliked Kemal's dictatorial methods and hoped for more democratic procedures, such as direct elections rather than the two-tiered indirect system then in use.

Kemal and Ismet, the prime minister, used the emergency created by the Kurdish revolt of 1925 to disband the Progressive party. Some opponents of the reforms and of Atatürk, many of whom were also former leaders of the Committee of Union and Progress, were tried as enemies of the state and executed. Others were exiled. Newspapers were closed. The liberal writer Halidé Edib and her husband, Adnan Adivar, left Turkey until the exile laws were repealed and political amnesty was declared in 1938 to all, even to Ottoman royalty. In addition to the few liberal opponents, underground Sufi groups and a new religious fellowship founded by Said Nursi, a Kurdish Islamic modernist, quietly persisted in spreading their messages, which were diametrically opposed to the principles of Kemal.

At a congress of the Republican People's party in 1927, Kemal made a historic six-day speech, reviewing in detail the events of 1919 to 1924 and claiming that he and his political party were solely responsible for the independence and nature of the new Turkey. Feeling more secure, Kemalists withdrew the laws for the maintenance of order in 1929; the following spring Kemal invited Fethi Okyar, former ambassador to France, to form an opposition party. The Free Republican party called for more free enterprise and less statism. The party was successful enough to frighten the Republicans, and Kemal judged that the time had not yet arrived when Turkey might have more than one party. Fethi's party was disbanded in 1930. Subsequently all other organizations that might provide an independent basis for criticism of the government were disbanded or, in the case of Istanbul University, reorganized so as to support the regime.

In October 1937 Ismet Inönü resigned again as prime minister, to be replaced by Celal Bayar. Although Kemal and Ismet had worked together for seventeen years, they were basically of very different temperaments. Their shared belief in party discipline, strong public authority, and central control had kept them together. But differences of opinion about foreign affairs relating to Italy in the Mediterranean led to the break.

Atatürk died in Istanbul on November 10, 1938. Excessive drinking and a profligate personal life eventually undermined his iron constitution. His death was a shock to the nation, and the emotional wave it unleashed demonstrated the devotion that he had won from most of the Turkish people. Inönü was elected president the following day, and the Republican People's party carried on with only a slight break. A new Grand National Assembly was elected in 1939, and Inönü became president for a full term. Inönü was soon faced with the events leading up to World War II.

INTERNATIONAL AFFAIRS

The remarkable internal changes in Turkey were paralleled by success in the foreign field. Atatürk's chief international goal was "peace at home and peace abroad," so as to allow the republic to recuperate from its enormous losses.

The Treaty of Lausanne left the undetermined frontier with Iraq to be settled directly with Great Britain as trustee for Iraq. Negotiations dragged on and reached a tense point in 1925. The Mosul province, the area in dispute, had a large Kurdish population whose leaders wanted an independent Kurdistan. On several occasions, war over Mosul was debated in party caucuses in Ankara, but peace prevailed. In 1926, a treaty was signed and ratified by England and Turkey, giving Mosul to Iraq; however, the treaty also gave Turkey 10 percent of all oil royalties paid by the concessionaire to Iraq for the following twenty-five years. Turkey promptly settled for a cash payment from Iraq.

Relations with Greece after the exchange of populations improved rapidly. Prime Minister Venizelos made a state visit to Turkey and was received with much fanfare. In 1934 the Balkan Pact was signed with Greece, Yugoslavia, and Romania, guaranteeing all frontiers and pledging collective security.

In 1932 Turkey was admitted to membership in the League of Nations. Turkey took an active part in League affairs, cooperating with efforts to control illicit traffic in narcotics and maintain collective security.

Almost immediately after Italy's attack on Ethiopia in 1935, Turkey entered into diplomatic action for changing the demilitarized status of the Straits. The Lausanne signatories met at Montreux in 1936, when Turkish policy gained a compromise: Turkey's right to erect fortifications and full sovereignty over the Straits. Turkey, Great Britain, France, Japan, the Soviet Union, Bulgaria, and Romania all signed the agreement governing the Straits. When he received news of the Montreux agreement, Atatürk in full dress attire was seen on the sands in front of his villa near the Sea of Marmara doing handsprings and cartwheels in celebration of his triumph.

Turkey gained a heightened sense of international security through the conclusion of a nonaggression pact with its Asiatic neighbors. In 1937 Turkey entered into the Saadabad Pact with Iran, Iraq, and Afghanistan in much the same fashion as it had in the earlier Balkan Pact with its European neighbors. In effect, the Saadabad Pact organized a neutral buffer zone along the southern Asian border of the Soviet Union.

Turkey's most troublesome frontier was to the south with Syria. In obtaining the mandate for Syria, France promised to give Alexandretta, where more than 90,000 Turks resided, a separate administration. When France was apparently preparing to give Syria some degree of independence in 1936, Turkey was concerned about the future of Turks in Alexandretta. In July 1938, a Turko-French condominium for Alexandretta was established, and later that year the population gave pro-Turks twenty-two seats out of forty in the provincial assembly. Voting themselves autonomy, the deputies proclaimed the Republic of Hatay and immediately sought a union with Turkey. France, despite bitter protests from the Arabs of Syria, acquiesced in this action; Hatay was annexed to Turkey in June 1939. This territorial acquisition was the only exception to a general Turkish policy of preserving the status quo and peace with its neighbors.

In 1939, as maneuvering among the powers in the diplomatic prelude to World War II became more tense, Turkey's international position grew in importance. Britain and France secured a military alliance and nonaggression pact. In May a "declaration of mutual guarantee" was made that was generally recognized as a veiled alliance. Meanwhile, in connection with the annexation of Hatay, Turkey signed a nonaggression pact with France. Thus, in World War II Turkish leaders found themselves in a neutral position between Germany, the Soviet Union, and the West yet most friendly to England and France.

Turkey's emphasis on a peaceful foreign policy was an indication that in foreign policy, as in most other aspects of government and public life, the Turkish Republic and its leaders sought new policies. Although the republic was in a sense the heir of the Ottoman Empire, it deliberately repudiated the Ottoman legacy and embarked on an emphatic Europeanization. Mustafa Kemal Atatürk molded the new government into a vehicle for top-down modernization. Most Turks, especially the townspeople, enthusiastically supported the new order, although some villagers, religious conservatives, and Kurds remained opposed. The government obtained numerous changes in most aspects of life. Turkey's success inspired secular reformers and nationalists in Iran and other parts of the Middle East, although during the 1920s and 1930s few other countries in the area went through as radical a transformation as did Turkey.

REFERENCES

References cited at the end of Chapters 23, 26, 27, and 31 are valuable for this chapter as well.

Abadan-Unat, Nermin, ed.: *Women in Turkish Society.* Leiden, The Netherlands: Brill, 1981.

Ahmad, Feroz: *The Making of Modern Turkey.* London: Routledge, 1993. An outstanding survey of Turkish history from 1908 into the 1990s.

Barlas, Dilek: *Etatism and Diplomacy in Turkey: Economic and Foreign Policy Strategies in an Uncertain World, 1929–1939.* Leiden, The Netherlands: Brill, 1998. A thorough discussion of both topics.

Bozdogan, Sibel: *Modernism and Nation-Building: Turkish Architectural Culture in the Early Republic.* Seattle: University of Washington Press, 2001. Traces the impact of nationalism and modernism on architectural style, 1908–1950, with many illustrations.

Brown, L. Carl, ed.: *Imperial Legacy: The Ottoman Imprint on the Balkans and the Middle East.* New York: Columbia University Press, 1996. A collection of essays on the impact of the Ottoman experience.

Duben, Alan, and Cem Behar: *Istanbul Households: Marriage, Family and Fertility, 1880–1940.* Cambridge, England: Cambridge University Press, 1991. A sociological discussion of Muslim family life during a period of rapid changes.

Edib (Adivar), Halidé: *Conflict of East and West in Turkey.* 2d ed. Lahore, Pakistan: M. Ashraf, 1935. A personal account of the revolution.

Hale, William: *Turkish Foreign Policy, 1774–2000.* London: Frank Cass, 2000. The author analyzes Turkey's behavior as a "middle power" mostly after 1918.

Heper, Metin: *Ismet Inönü: The Making of a Turkish Statesman.* Leiden, The Netherlands: Brill, 1998. Discussion of his life, characteristics, and policies.

Keyder, Çağlar: *The Definition of a Peripheral Economy: Turkey, 1923–1929.* Cambridge, England: Cambridge University Press, 1981. An important example of the new light that can be cast on Turkish history by "dependency school" scholars.

Kinross, Lord (Patrick Balfour): *Atatürk: A Biography of Mustafa Kemal, Father of Modern Turkey.* New York: Morrow, 1965. Full and well documented from Turkish sources; a lengthy and excellent biography.

Lewis, Geoffrey: *The Turkish Language Reform: A Catastrophic Success.* Oxford, England: Oxford University Press, 1999. Shows the excesses and failures as well as the successes of the alphabet and terminology changes.

McCarthy, Justin: "Foundations of the Turkish Republic: Social and Economic Change." *Middle Eastern Studies* 19 (1983): 139–151. A brilliant study that analyzes changes among the people that permitted some acceptance of radical innovations.

McDowall, David: *A Modern History of the Kurds.* 2d ed. London: Tauris, 2000. Extensive and well-informed exposition of the subject.

Mango, Andrew: *Atatürk.* Woodstock, N.Y.: Overlook Press, 2000. An outstanding biography that in many ways replaces the work by Lord Kinross cited on page 405.

Mardin, Şerif: *Religion and Social Change in Modern Turkey: The Case of Bediüzzaman Said Nursi.* Albany: State University of New York Press, 1989. Traces the life, times, and thought of this religious leader from 1876 to 1960.

Olson, Robert: *The Emergence of Kurdish Nationalism and the Sheikh Said Rebellion, 1880–1925.* Austin: University of Texas Press, 1989. A thorough examination of all aspects of early Kurdish nationalism in Turkey.

Renda, Günsel, and C. Max Kortepeter, eds.: *The Transformation of Turkish Culture: The Atatürk Legacy.* Princeton, N.J.: Kingston Press, 1986. Discusses the arts and culture during and after Atatürk's days.

Volkan, Vamik D., and Norman Itzkowitz: *The Immortal Atatürk: A Psychobiography.* Chicago: University of Chicago Press, 1984. An attempt to explain the major events of Kemal's life on the basis of his personal character.

Weiker, Walter F.: *Political Tutelage and Democracy in Turkey: The Free Party and Its Aftermath.* Leiden, The Netherlands: Brill, 1973. The period of "tutelage" was from 1923 to 1946, when there was but a single political party responsible for both modernization and democracy.

Yapp, M. E.: *The Near East Since the First World War.* London: Longman, 1991. A broad survey, especially valuable for discussion of political and economic matters.

Zürcher, Erik J.: *Political Opposition in the Early Turkish Republic: The Progressive Republican Party, 1924–1925.* Leiden, The Netherlands: Brill, 1991. A short but definitive monograph on this group.

———: *Turkey: A Modern History.* Rev. ed. London: Tauris, 1997. An excellent comprehensive study, concentrating on political events.

CHAPTER 33

Iran between the Two World Wars

Iran and its eastern and northern neighbors—Afghanistan and Soviet central Asia and the Caucasus—enacted a series of changes during the 1920s and 1930s that were more substantial and radical in nature than their earlier attempts. Although the wars and revolutions associated with World War I exhausted and impoverished much of this region, Iran, the Soviet Union, and, to a lesser extent, Afghanistan secured many of their goals. All three regimes sought independence from foreign control, centralization of political power, heavier taxation, military modernization, economic development, and substantial social change. Iran and Afghanistan followed roughly the same path; in the Soviet-controlled Caucasus and central Asia, a more revolutionary pattern emerged.

IRAN

Reza Khan Becomes Reza Shah

By the end of 1920 Iran was in a desperate situation. The Constitutional Revolution of 1905–1906, the counterrevolution led by Muhammad Ali Shah, massive intervention on the part of imperial Russia and Great Britain—all these had contributed to the misery of the country even before World War I. Despite its claim to neutrality, a weak and defenseless Iran was invaded during the war, and near anarchy reigned. Great Britain had forced a quasi-protectorate on Iran in 1919, and the Russian civil war spilled over into northern Iran, both provoking an increase in nationalist resistance to foreign domination. It was into this situation that in February 1921 Reza Khan (1878–1944), an officer of the Iranian cossack troops, led his men into the capital of Tehran and with a coup d'état forcibly took over the reins of government. A self-educated soldier with a keen nationalist feeling, Reza rose from the ranks of the Russian-officered Iranian cossacks and became one of their leaders when the Russian officers were ousted in 1920. On his march on Tehran in 1921, he was advised and aided by British officers; consequently, opponents charged, though incorrectly, that Reza was simply a pawn in British imperialistic ambitions.

For two decades Reza Khan and his army controlled the Iranian government. Initially a fiery journalist, Sayyid Ziya al-Din Tabatabai, became prime minister, and the Anglo-Iranian treaty of 1919, which would have made Britain dominant in Iran, was finally put to rest. Several others succeeded to the post of prime minister until Reza himself, who had also taken command of the gendarmerie, assumed office in 1923 and manipulated the various political parties and factions against each other. He invited the nominal ruler of the country, Ahmad Shah of the Qajar dynasty, to take "an extended and prolonged tour" of Europe. Reza encouraged republican sentiment as he looked westward to pattern his state after the new Turkey. But in 1924, when the stage was set in Iran for the declaration of a republic, the Turkish assembly abolished the caliphate and advanced along its secular path. Frightened Iranian Shii ulama raised such a storm that Reza met with a group of religious leaders. Thereafter, public mention of a republic was forbidden. In 1925, Reza Khan, with the support of the parliament and the ulama, became shah, taking the dynastic name of Pahlavi (a name for the early Persian language). One of the few members of parliament to vote against ending the Qajar reign was the young Muhammad Mosaddeq, a liberal lawyer related to the Qajars, who was subsequently barred from politics by the new shah. Reza officially crowned himself as shah in 1926.

The problems facing Reza Shah in Iran were similar to those before Kemal in Turkey, only far more difficult to solve. Iran differed from Turkey in many ways. For example, it lacked the large number of trained bureaucrats, soldiers, and diplomats Turkey inherited from the Ottoman Empire. Its geography had made constructing infrastructure such as railways and paved roads difficult, and it was more distant from Europe than Turkey and therefore had been less integrated into the growing world economy dominated by the Europeans.

Financial Changes and Political Centralization

The two most pressing problems facing Iran were reestablishment of a recognized central governmental authority and reform of national finances. The former was largely a matter for Reza and the army to resolve; the latter remained the work of an American, Arthur C. Millspaugh, formerly economic adviser to the U.S. secretary of state. Employed by the Iranian government in 1922 as administrator-general of finances, he held the power and authority of a cabinet minister. Unlike the pre–World War I experience of W. Morgan Shuster, another American adviser to the government of Iran, Millspaugh was able to act decisively. With vast powers and the staunch support of Reza's military force, Millspaugh balanced the budget by reorganizing the tax structure and enforcing the collection of taxes. State enterprises were inaugurated, and economic conditions improved gradually. However, he was frequently tactless and too rigid in his manners. In 1927 he and his American staff departed after he refused to renew his contract except on the same terms of power and authority as before.

One stipulation between Reza and Millspaugh provided that the budget of the Ministry of War would always be met, for Reza understood that the source of his power was the army. By 1926, Reza had personally led his army to end rebellions in Azerbaijan and Khurasan and had defeated some of the nomadic tribes, even while using tribal levies in the army during the 1920s. Eventually he forcibly settled, conscripted, and disarmed the nomadic tribes; he deprived them of their livelihood and earned their bitter hatred, as expressed in such events as the unsuccessful rebellions of the Qashqai confederation in 1929 and 1932. Reza's greatest success along these lines was achieved in ending the nearly independent rule of Shaikh Khazal of Mohammerah (Khorramshahr), with whom the British had a working agreement with respect to the operations of the Anglo-Persian Oil Company. The government created many small provinces to help break the local identity of the old districts.

An unpopular system of conscription of young males into the army began, and the military consumed close to half of revenues. However, the imposition of Reza's authority over the distant provinces, peoples, and governors of Iran increased state revenues and made Millspaugh's policies more effective and widespread. This in turn ensured a more certain execution of royal government.

According to the constitution of 1906, which remained in force even after the dynasty changed from the Qajars to the Pahlavis, the power of the nation was vested in the shah, the senate, and the majlis or assembly, which by 1926 was filled with Reza's supporters. The senate was appointive, but Reza never called it. In theory, the majlis nominated a prime minister who was appointed by the shah, but in fact Reza determined who would serve as the ministers of state, and the political system was a royal dictatorship.

Reforms

Reza and his associates undertook a wide range of reforms, including dramatic changes in the military, the role of Islam, law, education, gender relations, culture, and infrastructure. Reza Shah was personally involved in administration. He tried to create an enthusiastic attitude toward work among the personnel of the ministries. Sometimes he would appear at a government office early in the morning to see if the officials were on duty and on time.

The shah's first reforms were aimed at the military. The Iranian army increased in size and strength, especially following the enactment of conscription in 1925. In 1921 when Reza seized Tehran, the Cossack Brigade had only about 4000 men, but in the 1930s the number of troops in the imperial army rose to more than 100,000. Initially officer candidates were largely trained abroad, especially in France. Later, training schools were also opened in Tehran. Despite the large sums dedicated to the military, most conscripts in the army were poorly paid, suffered from bad health conditions, and had low morale. Military trucks used the newly built highways, and small numbers of aircraft, tanks, and warships were also acquired. Increased security allowed a freer circulation of people and goods and thus boosted economic growth.

As the army grew, the government turned its attention to the role of religion in public life. Veneration given to religious leaders had proved a potent force in many earlier periods of Iranian history. Reza thus attempted to relegate religion, its institutions, and its leaders to a less influential position in national life, particularly after the Shii ulama raised such an effective furor over republicanism in 1924. Sufi orders were banned, and the Muslim lunar calendar was replaced by a solar-based system. The government prohibited presentations in urban areas of the passion play in memory of the death of the Imam Husain, grandson of the prophet Muhammad, who was martyred by the Umayyads in 680. Other acts also showed the supremacy of Reza over the clergy. In 1928, when a religious leader in the mosque at Qumm criticized female members of the royal court for unveiling their faces, Reza hurried there with two armored cars, entered the mosque without removing his boots, and imprisoned the offending preacher.

More important in the long run was the confiscation of many religious properties and endowments (waqfs), the income from which went to the support of schools, hospitals, and other public enterprises. No longer were religious leaders and teachers (mullahs) completely independent, and some of their schools were closed. However, the Shii theological schools at Qumm, southwest of Tehran, were rebuilt and renovated, and they attracted the leading religious authorities. Much of the ulama's livelihood henceforth came from the state, and their hold over the population was diminished. Reza also found that some of the upper ulama could be persuaded to support the government; others opted out of public life, waiting for a better day or disliking too close an involvement with politics.

Religious influence in law and education was decreased by a policy of secularization. A mixture of the shariah and French judicial principles was enacted in the new law codes of 1925–1928; religious law was limited in scope and in authority. By 1931, religious courts exercised jurisdiction only over domestic relations, personal status, and notary public matters. Theological students were subjected to military conscription, and education became a public responsibility under the supervision and regulation of the central government, which broke the ulama's monopoly in teaching. From 1922 to 1940 the number of students in government schools increased eight times, despite a shortage of qualified teachers. Tehran University, founded in 1935, was also expanding; additionally some 1500 students were sent abroad. Textbooks used in the public schools taught the values of patriotism and loyalty to the new dynasty.

Reza Shah encouraged changes in the status of Iranian women. The first government school for girls had already been opened in 1918, but female education at all levels rapidly increased under the new shah. Whereas no girls had finished the twelfth grade in the public schools in 1921, over 300 graduated in 1936. Tehran University admitted women as students in 1937. Wearing veils was outlawed in 1936 as government-controlled newspapers announced a "women's awakening" designed to encourage a public role for women and their working outside the home. Still, men retained a legal superiority over women, and the government envisioned female participation in society taking place under male guardianship.

Intellectual life had begun to change during World War I, when poets, novelists, and journalists emphasized romantic Iranian nationalism by alluding to the glories of the pre-Islamic empires of Iran, such as that of the Sasanid dynasty. New forms of cultural expression included the cinema, which drew many viewers. The first Iranian-made film was shown in 1930, although most films continued to be imported. The government began radio broadcasts in 1940.

In literary and linguistic issues, some writers began to experiment with new forms, including the use of colloquial idioms, while others dealt with new themes such as the emancipation of women. Often such authors were heavily influenced by European schools of expression. Strict censorship and repression of opposition by the government of Reza Shah led many authors either to go into exile or to limit the circulation of their publications to a small circle of friends; by the 1940s many intellectuals felt a sense of deep isolation. Neoclassicists favored old forms with new content; they often backed mild reform measures and enjoyed the support of political authorities. The shah did everything possible to spread the Persian language, the first language of about half the population, and to lessen the use of other languages, such as Turkish, Kurdish, and Arabic, that were spoken in various regions of Iran. An Iranian-language academy created in 1935 was given the nearly impossible task of eliminating words in Persian that were of Arabic origin and creating new words for scientific discoveries.

Other cultural changes included new styles in clothing for men mandated in 1928. The wearing of Western-style hats and the custom of removing them inside public buildings was enforced in the 1930s, leading to a uniformity in attire, at least in the cities, that replaced earlier regional and religious variations. Resistance to this and other reforms was strong, as witnessed in the government suppression of opposition in Meshhed, leading to the death of perhaps hundreds of people in 1935. Still another cultural change was the requirement, similar to one enacted in Turkey, that all citizens had to use family last names. Western-style music was sponsored by the regime, with the first Iranian conductor leading a concert in 1925.

Reza Shah was an Iranian nationalist, who constantly strove to increase the power of the country. He decreased the influence of foreigners in 1928, when the capitulations, which granted rights to foreigners, were abolished. In 1935 Reza insisted on use of the word *Iran* for the country rather than the European-inspired term *Persia.*

One of Reza Shah's permanent accomplishments stemmed from his need for better transportation to bring the more distant parts of his realm within his power. There may have been 2000 miles (3200 km.) of roads in Iran on the day of his coup d'état; by the outbreak of World War II the road system had been extended to about 17,000 miles (27,000 kms.). As the trucks that used the new roads became bigger and more rugged, the cost of transporting passengers and shipping goods fell by about 80 percent. In view of Iran's role in the supply line to Russia in World War II, perhaps Reza's most far-reaching achievement in the area of infrastructure was the construction of the trans-Iranian railway from Bandarshapur on the Persian Gulf to Bandarshah on the Caspian Sea, a distance of 865 miles (1394 km.). Completed in 1938, it was an engineering marvel, consisting of 224 tunnels and passing from sea level to an altitude of nearly 9000 feet (2700 m.) and then down again to below sea level. This very expensive railway was entirely financed by Iran. Its route pleased neither Russia nor Britain. From their points of view, it began nowhere, passed through Tehran, and again ended nowhere, since it had no links to the frontiers of Russia, Iraq, India, and Turkey. But as the Iranians saw it, the railroad connected the northern fertile provinces with the south and by passing through nomad country facilitated the movement of the shah's military strength while potentially aiding the economy. And it was a positive advantage to Iran that the railway did not connect with those of its neighbors, thereby decreasing the chances of their using it for an invasion!

Economic Development

Like Mustafa Kemal Atatürk in Turkey, Reza felt the need of industrialization and economic development. Iran had an agricultural economy, and most of the labor force was engaged in farming. A majority of the total population of about 12 million people consisted of sharecropping peasants who lived in villages scattered throughout the countryside. To be effective, thoroughgoing reforms would have had to include the peasantry and changes in the system of landownership. Although a census and a cadastral survey were undertaken, new crops were encouraged, and some beneficial results were obtained, progress fell far short of the envisaged goals, largely because two-thirds of the arable land was held by absentee landlords who were satisfied with the old techniques and demanded an immediate high return on their investment. Reza did not change the basic system of landownership. Also, one of the new reforms actually hurt the peasants: registration of landownership claims implicitly favored the rich landowners. Economic development aided the cities at the expense of the countryside.

During the 1930s the population of Iranian cities started to increase dramatically, with Tehran doubling its population, to 540,000, between 1930 and 1941. More jobs and better health care drew peasants and townspeople to cities. New urban neighborhoods featured modern amenities, but older neighborhoods became very crowded as little housing was built for the relatively poor arrivals from the countryside.

In 1928, when Iran was fully able to set its own tariffs, import duties were increased so as to raise more revenue and protect Iranian industry. A new national bank was established, thereby limiting the importance of British banks. New factories were built for refining sugar and for spinning and weaving cotton, silk, and wool. Most of these were state enterprises and varied widely in efficiency and capacity. Prices for the goods produced were high, but a state monopoly over most frontier trade rendered competition with imported goods negligible. Nonetheless, since Iranian industry suffered from a shortage of technicians and plant managers, industrial development under Reza proved unsatisfactory.

The world economic depression of the 1930s made the value of Iran's primary exports sink, while the cost of imports increased. Reza created a state trading mechanism under which much of foreign trade was managed by the government. Various other monopolies instituted for special purposes produced about one-third of all revenues; monopolies on sugar and tea, for instance, helped finance the building of the trans-Iranian railway.

The Oil Industry and Great Britain

By far the most important industrial enterprise in Iran during the period of Reza Shah's rule was the Anglo-Persian Oil Company (subsequently, the Anglo-Iranian Oil Company), which by agreement paid Iran 16 percent of its profits. During World War I the company property, installations, and pipelines had been protected by a light infantry force organized by the British. After the war the question of what profits to include while calculating the Iranian government's 16 percent was bitterly debated.

The difficulty originated from the fact that Iran had no control over the quantity of oil produced and no guaranteed annual income from the concession. With the complexity of oil operations and the multiplicity of subsidiaries internationally, Iran lost confidence in the integrity of the company's bookkeeping practices. Fluctuations in the amounts received by Iran—ranging from a low of about £300,000 to a high of about £1.4 million—left the finances and the budget of the government completely at the mercy of the company. In 1931, the Iranian government received only about half of the amount the British government was obtaining from the company. Furthermore, Great Britain went off the gold standard, and Iran's funds were hard hit at the same time that the depression reduced world demand for oil. Finally, a new concession was negotiated in 1931 by the Iraq Petroleum Company, giving more favorable terms to Iraq. Since the Anglo-Persian Oil Company was one of the principal owners in Iraq, the Iranian government felt it should have equally favorable treatment.

After bitter wrangling, sharp notes, and the dispatch of British warships to the Persian Gulf, England took the case to the League of Nations council. Iran informed the company that Iran might agree to the granting of a new concession.

The new concession was signed in Tehran in 1933. The area covered was immediately reduced by half, located entirely in the far southwest of Iran, close to Iraq and the gulf. Iran would receive 4 shillings per ton on all oil sold in Iran or exported. Iran would be paid 20 percent of all dividends over a certain minimum, and the company guaranteed that total annual payments to Iran would never be under £750,000. The Iranian government oil commissioner had the right to examine the company's books. As production of Iranian oil increased later in the 1930s, the revenues of the central government grew substantially. However, the new concession gave the company rights for a longer period of time, set the Iranian payments at a flat amount per ton even if the price of oil increased, and eliminated Iran's prior share in company profits—all to the detriment of Iran's long-term interests.

Undoubtedly, Reza Shah viewed this agreement as a diplomatic victory. Some observers at the time believed that Iran, by this stroke, obtained real independence from Great Britain. Certainly Iran's oil income was placed on a more sustaining basis, although it seemed clear that the British admiralty was still able to purchase Iranian oil more cheaply than could the Iranian government.

International Affairs

Reza Shah in his foreign policy maintained friendly relations with his small and relatively weak neighbors, while dealings with the British, the Soviet Union, and Germany remained paramount. The crowning achievement of his Middle East policy was the signing of the Saadabad pact in 1937 with Turkey, Iraq, and Afghanistan, providing for mutual cooperation and nonaggression.

Even before the 1933 concession for the Anglo-Persian Oil Company, Iranian-British relations were positively affected by the treaty of 1928. Imperial Airways was allowed to fly planes over Iran, Britain recognized the end of the capitulations and the central government of Iran became the protector of the oil pipelines, and Iran recognized British rule in Iraq. Britain, however, retained the opportunity to deal directly with tribes such as the Bakhtiyaris and the Qashqais. Except for Iran's claim to Bahrain, all outstanding matters were considered, and anti-British feelings in Iran temporarily lessened. Such feelings could easily be brought to the surface, however, for twisting the British lion's tail was a sporting event for all Iranian nationalists. Britain remained Iran's chief trading partner in the 1920s, but the Soviet Union and Germany assumed more importance in the 1930s.

Reza Shah's relations with the Soviet Union were more complicated, especially since the two countries had a long common frontier. In a 1921 treaty, the Soviets had formally renounced all earlier Russian concessions in Iran, although keeping the right to intervene if Iranian territory was used by a hostile third party. In the 1920s and again in the 1930s, the Soviet Union protested vehemently when Iran granted oil concessions in the northern provinces to others. Northern Iran's exports went primarily to the Soviet Union, which could and frequently did exert great pressure on Iran by closing its frontiers to Iranian goods. The shah's government outlawed the Communist party, and Reza placed all foreign trade in Iran under state monopoly and control. This device and Germany's return to the Iranian scene when Hitler assumed power gave Iran some freedom from economic domination by the Soviet colossus to the north.

Caught between the British in the south and the Soviets in the north, Iran turned to Germany as a counterpoise. German technicians were invited in great numbers, advising various ministries. When new agreements were concluded in 1935, the volume of trade between the two countries jumped. In 1939 over 40 percent of Iran's foreign trade was with Germany. Iranian schools hired German professors, and numerous Iranians took advanced degrees in German universities. German influences were felt even in Iranian architecture.

AFGHANISTAN

Iran's neighbor to the east, Afghanistan, experienced a somewhat similar historical development. Reza Shah followed developments in Afghanistan closely, but Iran could do little directly to affect them. Iran's and Turkey's changes during the 1920s and 1930s did, however, indirectly serve as models for Afghanistan.

The Muhammadzai branch of the Durrani Pashtun dynasty continued to rule mountainous, mostly Sunni Afghanistan from Kabul. Central governments in Afghanistan were usually weak in the face of strong tribes, a variety of ethnic groups, and an absence of modern communications and transportation. Rulers before 1914 had varying degrees of success in their drive for modernization and centralization of the disparate country. Afghanistan was prudently neutral during World War I. In 1919 the amir (later shah), Aman Allah (Amanullah), rejected British domination of Afghanistan's foreign policy. After a short war with British India, he was successful in gaining freedom of action in foreign affairs, although Britain stopped financial aid to the amirs of Afghanistan. In 1921 the Soviet Union, Britain, Turkey, and Iran concluded treaties with Afghanistan, thereby accepting the independence of the country. Aman Allah tried to defend Bukhara in central Asia against Soviet expansionism but ultimately failed in his efforts.

Domestically, a series of reforms along the lines of earlier Ottoman and contemporary Turkish and Iranian programs was planned. The Afghan military brought in Turkish officers as advisers and purchased some weapons abroad, but its overall size was not greatly increased at this time and its effectiveness in enforcing centralization was open to question. Afghanistan adopted its first constitution in 1923 and attempted to enforce a considerable array of changes, such as the education of women, the abolition of tax farming, and the use of a solar calendar. The government established new schools throughout the country and sent some students abroad for advanced training, newspapers were encouraged, a telegraph system was developed, and in 1925 limited radio broadcasts began. Aman Allah managed to build some roads, but he could not obtain the capital to construct railways. Since the reforms were enacted chiefly in the cities, the majority of the population, which lived in the countryside, was unaffected by them. Many tribal leaders, ulama, minority ethnic groups, and regional notables strongly opposed the reforms and especially Aman Allah's proposals for a radical program of changes in 1929. Rebels seized Kabul and overthrew Aman Allah, who abdicated the throne and went into exile.

Nadir Shah (r. 1929–1933), who had been commander in chief of the royal army, reestablished the dynasty by appealing to Pashtun tribal groups. He unified Afghanistan, finally gaining control of Herat in 1931. However, he reversed many of Aman Allah's policies; Nadir Shah favored Great Britain, issued a new constitution, and slowed or ended most domestic reforms. Nadir actively sought the support of the ulama, whose conservative views on education, law, and the status of women became the basis of government policy in those areas. The shah did, however, pursue military modernization and some initiatives in education. By the end of his reign, the Afghan army was on a sound basis. Customs duties provided most of the revenue, although the Great Depression of the 1930s curtailed Afghanistan's foreign commerce. The government opened Kabul University in 1932, and Afghanistan was admitted to the League of Nations in 1934.

After the assassination of Nadir, his young son, Muhammad Zahir Shah (r. 1933–1973), accepted the supervision of several older uncles, who favored a slow and gradual modernization that was acceptable to the ulama. About half the national budget went for the military, which by 1941 numbered about 90,000; to a certain extent the tribes remained the basis of its organization. Pashto replaced Persian as the official language of government in 1937, although Persian (and Arabic) were still taught in the small number of urban government schools. Most young people either received no formal education at all or attended traditional primary-level religious schools. Radio broadcasts reached the whole country in 1940, but only one public cinema was opened. The government sought to promote economic development through establishing investment banks, improving the roads, encouraging cotton production, and coordinating exports.

Afghanistan's foreign policy aimed at achieving good relations with both the Soviet Union and Great Britain, yet also establishing friendly ties with Turkey and Iran. Germany became an active partner in developing Afghanistan's economy. Aghanistan regarded Germany as less threatening than either the Communist Soviet Union to the north or the British Indian empire to the south.

SOVIET CENTRAL ASIA AND THE CAUCASUS

Culturally, economically, and politically, central Asia and the Caucasus had been associated with the Middle East for many centuries before Russia conquered those areas in the nineteenth century. During Russian Imperial and Soviet control, their history followed a different path from that of Iran, Turkey, and Afghanistan, only to regain more links to the Middle East much later, following the breakup of the Soviet Union in 1991.

As Imperial Russia collapsed during World War I, its possessions in central Asia and the Caucasus gained local control and even, for a brief time, independence. Subsequently, as a result of the bitter and protracted struggle between the Communists and their conservative Russian and foreign opponents, the new Soviet Russia regained power in central Asia and the Caucasus, conquering Bukhara and Armenia, for instance, in 1920, and Tajikistan by 1924. Soviet policy sought to create or reinforce ethnically based administrative regions using such groups as Tajiks, Uzbegs, Kazakhs, Armenians, Georgians, and Azeris, although various ethnic groups often lived interspersed among each other.

Real political, economic, and military power was concentrated in Moscow, in particular, in the hands of the leaders of the Communist party, who undertook radical change even more far-reaching than that underway in Turkey and Iran. Soviet power was based on an officially atheist ideology, so many religious schools were closed, and the Arabic alphabet used in central Asia was replaced by first the Latin and then eventually the Cyrillic alphabet. Marxist class analysis indicated the necessity of a complete reformulation of society. Reforms included confiscation of waqfs, the expansion of education so as to spread literacy, and equal rights for women.

In central Asia, in particular, there was great opposition by many Muslims against such changes as the brutal collectivization of agriculture that started in 1929. The Soviets emphasized oil production in Baku and cotton growing in central Asia. The settlement of ethnic Russians resumed. Between 1928 and 1936 about 1.7 million non-Muslims moved into Soviet central Asia. In general there was little support for communism among the indigenous peoples of central Asia and the Caucasus.

IRANIAN AND AFGHAN REFORMS EVALUATED

Reza Shah's reforms in Iran were more popular than the Communist revolution in central Asia, though many Iranians had good reason to oppose them. Iranian policy was based on autocratic modernization, supported by an expanded and more powerful army and bureaucracy, and using dramatically increased government resources.

Reza Shah Pahlavi was an uneducated soldier who expected his will to be followed exactly. The subtle nuances of traditional Iranian officialdom frustrated him into direct and ruthless conduct. There was a vast amount of work that needed to be done in Iran and too few people to do it, and Reza became immersed in a welter of programs too numerous for him to carry through alone. Taking so much responsibility on his own shoulders discouraged initiative in those about him. Forced Westernization and modernization from the top down were Reza Shah's basic means to the goal of strengthening the country and maintaining his own power. Many Iranians who favored nationalism, a strong central government, and reforms supported Reza as the best means for achieving these goals, although quite a few of his supporters in the early years of his reign became disillusioned later. He was opposed particularly by the ulama, some of the large landowners, political liberals, and the nomadic and seminomadic tribes.

In the end Reza became interested in acquiring a great personal fortune in money and land. He grew tired, his temper rose, his sensitivity to criticism mounted, and his power became more absolute as he purged the government of even his closest associates in the early 1930s. On the other hand, chaos had been replaced by order, Iran was stronger in 1939 than it had been in 1919, and economic development had begun. Modernization from above was underway when World War II violently changed the political situation in Iran.

Aman Allah's rule in Afghanistan from 1919 to 1929 witnessed many of the same goals, methods, and degrees of success as shown in Reza's Iran, but Aman Allah was overthrown while Reza Shah survived until World War II. In Afghanistan there was even less support among the population for modernization along European lines than in Iran, and the Afghan central authorities and army were considerably weaker than similar organizations in Iran. Aman Allah's successors did not abandon his goals, but they were far more cautious than he had been, particularly in regard to respecting the views of the ulama.

In both Afghanistan and Iran, political, military, economic, and social changes were important, but they took effect chiefly in the cities; people residing in small towns and villages were far less affected. The national governments were most successful in gaining greater independence from foreign domination, a goal widely shared by most of the peoples of the Middle East.

REFERENCES

References cited at the end of Chapters 12, 22, 29, 30, and 31 are pertinent to this chapter as well.

Amin, Camron Michael: "Propaganda and Remembrance: Gender, Education, and 'The Women's Awakening' of 1936." *Iranian Studies* 32 (1999): 351–386. Based on interviews with women who lived through these times.

Banani, Amin: *The Modernization of Iran, 1921–1941.* Stanford, Calif.: Stanford University Press, 1961. This study, based largely on Iranian sources, gives a detailed survey of the impact of Reza Shah.

Beck, Lois: *The Qashqa'i of Iran.* New Haven, Conn.: Yale University Press, 1986. An excellent study that includes the nineteenth and twentieth centuries.

Cottam, Richard W.: *Nationalism in Iran.* 2d ed. Pittsburgh, Penn.: University of Pittsburgh Press, 1979. A comprehensive, systematic, and stimulating study emphasizing the interrelated themes of liberal nationalism and the policy of the United States toward Iran.

Cronin, Stephanie: *The Army and the Creation of the Pahlavi State in Iran, 1910–1926.* London: Tauris, 1997. An excellent account of the gendarmerie, the army, and their leaders.

Ehlers, Eckart, and Willem Floor: "Urban Change in Iran, 1920–1941." *Iranian Studies* 26 (1993): 251–275. In addition to this article, in the same issue of *Iranian Studies* other very useful studies also deal with Iran during the 1920s and 1930s.

Ewans, Martin: *Afghanistan: A New History.* Richmond, England: Curzon Press, 2001. Informative especially on the role of Britain in Afghanistan.

Faghfoory, Mohammad H.: "The Ulama-State Relations in Iran: 1921–1941." *International Journal of Middle East Studies* 19 (1987): 413–432.

Ferrier, R. W.: *The History of the British Petroleum Company.* Vol. 1: *The Developing Years, 1901–1932.* Cambridge, England: Cambridge University Press, 1982. An official history based in part on the company's own archives.

Ghani, Cyrus: *Iran and the Rise of Reza Shah: From Qajar Collapse to Pahlavi Rule.* London: Tauris, 2000. Based chiefly on British sources, this is a very useful study of the subject that is favorable to Reza Shah; compare to the work by Homa Katouzian cited below.

Ghods, M. Reza: *Twentieth Century Iran: A Political History.* Boulder, Colo.: Lynne Rienner, 1989. Especially useful in regard to the history of leftist groups.

Gregorian, Vartan: *The Emergence of Modern Afghanistan: Politics of Reform and Modernization, 1880–1946.* Stanford, Calif.: Stanford University Press, 1969. A valuable source of information.

Issari, M. Ali: *Cinema in Iran, 1900–1979.* Metuchen, N.J.: Scarecrow Press, 1989. A thorough survey of the subject.

Jones, Geoffrey: *Banking and Empire in Iran: The History of the British Bank of the Middle East.* Vol. 1. Cambridge, England: Cambridge University Press, 1986. An excellent account of the bank from its beginning in 1889 until its end in 1952, based on internal records.

Katouzian, Homa: *State and Society in Iran: The Eclipse of the Qajars and the Emergence of the Pahlavis.* London: Tauris, 2000. Places the last Qajars and Reza Shah in the context of an analysis of Iran's history as alternating between chaos and arbitrary rule.

Keddie, Nikki R.: *Qajar Iran and the Rise of Reza Khan, 1796–1925.* Costa Mesa, Calif.: Mazda, 1999. A clear survey of the time period; a useful introduction.

Kia, Mehrdad: "Persian Nationalism and the Campaign for Language Purification." *Middle Eastern Studies* 34 (1998): 9–36.

Lenczowski, George, ed.: *Iran under the Pahlavis.* Stanford, Calif.: Hoover Institution, 1978. A very favorable view of Reza Shah's dynasty and its accomplishments.

Millspaugh, Arthur C.: *The American Task in Persia.* New York: Century, 1925. An account of the author's first tour of duty in Iran.

Rezun, Miron: "Reza Shah's Court Minister: Teymourtash." *International Journal of Middle East Studies* 12 (1980): 119–137. One of the very few studies of a prominent member of Reza Shah's entourage.

Rywkin, Michael: *Moscow's Muslim Challenge: Soviet Central Asia.* Armonk, N.Y.: M. E. Sharpe, 1982. A useful general survey.

Talattof, Kamran: *The Politics of Writing in Iran: A History of Modern Persian Literature.* Syracuse, N.Y.: Syracuse University Press, 2000. Detailed examples of episodes in the interaction of Iranian literature with nationalism, Marxism, Islamism, and feminism.

Volodarsky, Mikhail: *The Soviet Union and Its Southern Neighbours: Iran and Afghanistan, 1917–1933.* London: Frank Cass, 1994. A short but important work based on Soviet archival sources.

Wilber, Donald N.: *Iran: Past and Present.* 9th ed. Princeton, N.J.: Princeton University Press, 1981. A classic summary of Iran's history, largely since 1921.

——: *Riza Shah Pahlavi: The Resurrection and Reconstruction of Iran, 1878–1944.* New York: Exposition Press, 1975. An account of the shah's life almost week by week.

Yarshater, Ehsan, ed.: *Persian Literature.* Albany: State University of New York Press, 1987.

CHAPTER 34

Egypt, the Sudan, and Libya

The three most important countries in the Middle East after the collapse of the Ottoman Empire in World War I were non-Arab Turkey and Iran, and Arab Egypt. During the interwar period, 1919 to 1939, these nations had substantial populations, considerable economic resources, and effective governments. In addition, all three obtained national independence, although Great Britain retained a great deal of military control and political influence in Egypt. Whereas the governments of Turkey and Iran undertook radical steps aimed at Europeanization, modernization, and secularization, Egypt pursued chiefly the struggle against Britain.

Egypt was the most central and influential of the Arab states. Its importance was related to such factors as its relative stability; the earlier development of infrastructure, such as the Suez Canal; and the strength of national sentiment among its people. A long and frustrating struggle with Britain for complete independence would not be successful by 1939, but much was accomplished in the meantime. Domestic politics centered around the triangular contest for power among Egyptian nationalists, the Mehmet Ali dynasty, and the British. The growth in population affected most aspects of society, as seen, for instance, in the difficulty of providing mass public education. Egypt retained its place as the cultural center of the Arab world, and Egyptian artists were nearly as preoccupied with the national struggle for independence as were the elite landowners, middle-class professionals, and politicians who led the governments.

There was a stark contrast between the history of Egypt and that of its neighbors, the Anglo-Egyptian Sudan and Italian Libya. The Sudan and Libya were poorer, had far smaller populations, and were considerably less Europeanized than was Egypt. Britain ruled the Sudan with a relatively light hand compared to the harsh administration of Libya by the Fascist Italians. Egyptian nationalists were particularly concerned about developments in the Sudan since engineering projects there could affect the Nile River, virtually the lifeblood of Egypt.

EGYPT

Egyptian Nationalism, the Wafd, and Independence

In 1918, two days after the end of the war in Europe, Saad Zaghlul Pasha, an ardent nationalist who had been minister of education, presented the British high commissioner with a list of demands for Egyptian independence. Zaghlul asked permission to proceed with his delegation (wafd) to London to discuss his independence program. British officials refused, supposedly because Zaghlul did not officially represent the government of Egypt, but they also declined to allow the Egyptian cabinet to send emissaries. (Authority was in the hand of Egypt's ruler, Sultan Fuad, who succeeded to the throne after the death of his brother Husain in 1917.)

Zaghlul and his delegation organized committees throughout the country and stimulated vigorous nationalistic feeling against the British. In March 1919 Zaghlul and other leading Wafd party members were arrested by the British military (Egypt still being under martial law) and deported to Malta. Egyptian reaction was spontaneous. Insurrection and violence spread to all districts within days and included Muslims and Christians; trade unionists, other workers, and capitalists; urban dwellers and peasants; women and men. The patriotic revolutionaries sought independence for Egypt, an independence they felt was justified by the long history of the country and by the right of national self-determination. British military forces rushed to Egypt and crushed the revolt.

The British suddenly awoke to the fact that something needed to be done. General Edmund Allenby was appointed British high commissioner in Egypt, and Lord Milner was designated head of a commission of inquiry to report on the nature of the protectorate. Zaghlul and his fellow prisoners in Malta were freed to lay their demands before the peace conference in France, but their demands were ignored.

A memorandum containing the principles on which a treaty of alliance between Egypt and England might be drawn was composed in August 1920. It recognized Egypt as a sovereign independent constitutional monarchy with representative institutions. Britain would undertake to defend Egypt, and Egypt would offer all assistance within its borders to England. Egypt would have diplomatic representation abroad but would coordinate its policies with those of Britain. Egypt would appoint British judicial and financial advisers, abolish the capitulations, and permit Britain to maintain a military force in Egypt. The final point pledged Egypt to call a constituent assembly to ratify the treaty and to adopt a constitution. Zaghlul argued that the memorandum would have to be approved by the people of Egypt before he could go ahead, and conversations were broken off completely.

Allenby, appreciating that no treaty that Britain would be prepared to sign would be acceptable to Zaghlul, deported him. Still the British cabinet did not agree to recognize Egyptian independence; it took a personal trip to London by Allenby to impress on England the necessity of accepting the commitments made in the 1920 memorandum.

On February 28, 1922, the day of Allenby's return to Egypt, he gave out the unilateral British declaration ending the protectorate and elevating Egypt to the rank of an independent sovereign state. England, however, reserved for its own control the security of communications, Egypt's defense, the protection of foreign interests and minorities, and the affairs of the Anglo-Egyptian Sudan. Egyptian nationalists were annoyed that their country's independence was declared by another state and limited by reservations.

The Constitution of 1923

Sultan Fuad became king of Egypt, and a succession of men passed through the chambers of the prime minister. Politics became a three-way conflict among nationalists, the king, and the British.

The residency pressed Fuad to appoint a prime minister who would present a constitution for the new sovereign state. Finally, a constitution was drawn up, and elections for a parliament were held. According to the constitution, Islam was the religion of the state, but all Egyptians (including the Christian and Jewish minorities) were to be equal before the law. The constitution gave to the king considerable powers. He could dissolve parliament and veto its acts. He appointed and dismissed ministers and could issue decrees in the absence of parliament. He was commander in chief of the armed forces. In reality, a determined king could be chief executive of the state. Ministers were responsible to parliament, but since they held office at the pleasure of the king, they found it difficult to serve two masters. Two-fifths of the senators were appointed by the king; three-fifths were elected. Fuad even had his portrait appear on Egyptian stamps and coins.

Nowhere in the constitution was Great Britain mentioned. But with British troops and many British advisers in Egypt and with an Englishman as commander in chief of the small Egyptian army, Egyptians were fully justified in doubting that they had attained real independence.

Egyptian Politics

Zaghlul returned to Egypt in time for the elections. The Wafd gained a large majority of the seats in the chamber of deputies, and Zaghlul became prime minister, although his Wafdist program was decidedly anti-British: English troops and advisers must go, the Sudan must be "returned" to Egypt, and any British claim to share in protecting the Suez Canal must be abandoned. The government in effect supported demonstrations against the British. Similar stirrings, to which the British reacted strongly, were encouraged in the Sudan. The situation was anomalous. As prime minister, Zaghlul was responsible for the maintenance of law and order in Egypt; as head of the Wafd, he was in open defiance of law and order as the British understood them.

In the summer of 1924, Zaghlul went to London, where he presented his entire program as unequivocal demands. No treaty was signed. In November Sir Lee Stack, governor-general of the Sudan and commander in chief of the Egyptian army, was assassinated in Cairo. Zaghlul immediately pledged swift action to bring the culprits to trial. Nevertheless, the deed was the logical, if indirect, result of open invitations to violence instigated by Zaghlul and the Wafd. Subsequent judicial proceedings demonstrated that leading Wafdists were implicated.

Escorted by a regiment of British cavalry, an angry Lord Allenby called at the offices of the council of ministers; Allenby took every opportunity to display force and humiliate Zaghlul. Allenby placed blame for Sir Lee Stack's murder on Zaghlul and asserted that the Egyptian government was held in contempt by all civilized peoples. Egypt was given about 30 hours to meet a long list of demands, including an apology for the crime, suppressing public political demonstrations, paying a large fine, recalling all Egyptian army units from the Sudan, and permitting the Sudan to increase irrigation. Zaghlul, the king, and the parliament accepted some of the demands. Allenby notified the Sudan government to take all necessary actions and ordered the British army to occupy the Alexandria customs offices. Zaghlul resigned, and the next prime minister accepted Britain's control.

In new elections the Liberal party, led by intellectuals and elder politicians descended from Ottoman Turkish families long resident in Egypt, and a new Unionist party made up of the king's friends, combined with numerous independents from the provinces to defeat the Wafd. Nevertheless, the chamber of deputies elected Zaghlul its president in 1925. This act led the king to dismiss parliament immediately. He was now determined to crush Zaghlul, who seemed to be growing more prominent than the king. The new British high commissioner made common cause with the Wafd to force the king to call for still more elections, in which the Wafd again obtained a sweeping victory. Despite the victory, the Liberal party headed the new cabinet.

In August 1927, Zaghlul died and was succeeded as Wafd leader by Mustafa al-Nahhas Pasha. Fuad forced Nahhas to resign by exposing a political scandal. The next prime minister, Muhammad Mahmud, dissolved parliament and suspended the constitution for three years, thereafter governing as a mild dictator with bitter opposition from the Wafd. Mahmud reached agreement with the British over the Nile waters, the old Ottoman debt, and other financial matters.

But desire for a treaty with Great Britain remained paramount, and in 1929 Mahmud and the British negotiated an agreement that would have met many of the Egyptian nationalists' demands. However, England would only recognize a treaty ratified by a freely elected Egyptian parliament. Elections returned the Wafdists to power, and Nahhas Pasha again became prime minister. His position was impossible, since he had denounced the draft treaty obtained by Mahmud, and the British declared that they had reached the "high-water mark" of concessions. Treaty negotiations were dropped temporarily. King Fuad, fearing the apparent alliance of the Wafd and the residency, engineered the resignation of Nahhas and appointed Ismail Sidqi Pasha as prime minister.

The Constitution of 1930

Parliament was adjourned, Nahhas incited riots, and the British sent warships. Sidqi, protesting against foreign intervention, restored order. In this coup d'état of June 1930 Sidqi appeared as the strong man. The constitution of 1923 was abrogated, and a new constitution with a new electoral law rigged to keep Wafdists out of office was quickly adopted. Sidqi organized a new political party, the People's party. In coalition with the Unionists and independents, the People's party defeated a Wafdist-Liberal united front, which boycotted the election. Sidqi was able to establish his dictatorship only through the ineptitude of the British government, which maneuvered both Liberals and Wafdists into indefensible positions. Sidqi sent the students back to their studies, politicians muttered rather meekly, and the wealthy landowners gladly supported the new rule, for they were fed up with the quibbling, vindictiveness, and arrogance of the nationalistic Wafd lawyers whom they had largely created. No treaty with England was attempted; prime ministers who tried always fell from office, and both Sidqi and Fuad preferred British troops in Egypt to the Wafd. Furthermore, Sidqi must have understood that the British government would not interfere in Egyptian domestic politics as long as British imperial interests were not directly jeopardized.

Fuad again did not intend to permit a potential rival to remain in office very long. Sidqi fell from power in September 1933, and a procession of ineffectual prime ministers followed. Power rapidly gravitated to the king, who was also amassing a great fortune.

The Anglo-Egyptian Treaty of 1936

An external crisis arose in 1935 when the Fascist Italians, who already ruled in Libya to the west of Egypt, invaded Ethiopia, to the south of the Sudan. Britain increased its military establishment in Egypt. Popular pressure in 1935 caused the king to reissue the constitution of 1923. In 1936 King Fuad died, and his only son, the young Faruq (r. 1936–1952), ascended the throne. In new elections the Wafd party won 166 seats out of 232 in the chamber of deputies and obtained a majority in the senate. With such a solid backing, Nahhas became prime minister with a Wafd cabinet. Since he named the regency, the power of the Wafd was, for once, supreme. Nahhas, chairman of the all-party negotiating delegation, announced the new Anglo-Egyptian Treaty on August 26, 1936. A landmark had been achieved.

Beyond internal Egyptian politics, the chief stumbling blocks to such a treaty had been the Sudan, British armed forces, and the capitulations. Changes in the international situation became so obvious to politicians and the public alike that when the British asked for a wider area in the Suez Canal Zone and more military facilities, Egyptian objection was only nominal. The British occupation of Egypt was changed to a twenty-year military alliance. The Sudan settlement again permitted unlimited Egyptian immigration to the Sudan and the use of Egyptian troops in the Sudan. An end to the capitulations, actually arranged by the Montreux Convention of 1937, proved of the utmost consequence to Egypt. The abolition of mixed tribunals and curtailment of consular courts were not abrupt, but they were to stop in 1949. Foreigners would be subject to Egyptian laws, especially taxation and financial legislation. Increased taxation from this and other sources allowed the army's budget to be doubled in the late 1930s.

The 1936 treaty was immensely popular in Egypt. Parliament ratified it and the unprecedented happened when British troops were cheered on the streets of Cairo. A sign of Egypt's new status was its admission to the League of Nations in 1937. But Nahhas Pasha's popularity waned when King Faruq in 1937 became a political force. Even the treaty was no longer popular, probably because the Italian conquest in East Africa was legitimized and the threat of war in the Mediterranean subsided. Nahhas resigned at the end of 1937. A new election, arranged in 1938, defeated the Wafdists. The wheel turned, so that just before World War II broke out, Faruq and his palace officials gained full power by forming a cabinet from which both Liberals and Wafdists were excluded.

Social and Economic Changes

Domestic politics and getting rid of the British consumed the energies and attention of Egyptian leaders between World War I and World War II, and these were the topics chiefly discussed in Egypt. However, other changes and problems, certainly basic and significant for the Egyptian nation and perhaps even more difficult to solve, did exist. Foremost was the increasing population pressure, especially in Cairo, whose population by 1937 reached 1.3 million. The population of all of Egypt increased from 12.7 million in 1917 to 15.7 million in 1937, although the cultivated area remained constant. Increased agricultural yields, improved irrigation techniques, and intensive cultivation—more crops per year—met the situation in part, but there was probably a general lowering of the standard of living among Egyptian peasants. Sanitation and health conditions were poor and made worse by perennial irrigation, which helped spread the intestinal disease bilharziasis to most of the rural population. The death rate was very high, yet the birthrate was higher. These factors, coupled with a lack of coal and industrial development, gave the waters of the Nile an importance that other nations found difficult to appreciate. This dependence on the Nile explained the critical blow to Egypt intended by Allenby's ultimatum to Zaghlul regarding unlimited irrigation in the Sudan. Although heightening the Aswan Dam and the construction of dams in the Sudan and Uganda augmented water supplies in Egypt, such developments barely kept pace with the growing population.

Tied to this pressure of population were many economic, financial, and commercial problems. Cotton was king, and the government and landowners oriented the entire economy for the benefit of cotton. Agricultural experimentation, types of irrigation, industrialization, trade practices, tenant farm policies, and land reform: all were considered in the light of their relationship to the production of cotton. Taxation in general rested lightly on agriculture and landowners and bore heavily on imports, industry, and commerce. The protective tariff of 1930 helped Egyptian industry compete against foreign goods, but the world economic depression of the 1930s severely cut the international price of cotton. Ownership of land was extremely inequitable. Many peasants were landless or were poor sharecroppers, whereas about 21,000 rich persons owned about half of the land. About 70 percent of the labor force was engaged in agriculture.

Abolition of the capitulations following the Anglo-Egyptian Treaty of 1936 and the Montreux Convention in 1937 began to alter the commercial world of Cairo and Alexandria. A general exemption from taxation had given foreigners advantages that enabled them to dominate Egyptian finance, industry, and commerce. After 1936 the situation was partly reversed: foreigners suddenly found it advantageous to have Egyptians as partners. Some resident foreigners became Egyptian citizens. The Bank Misr group of industries tried to lead the way in Egyptian industrialization in the 1920s and 1930s, but it ultimately came to cooperate with foreign capital.

Education, Gender, and Intellectual Life

Nationalism, population growth, and the presence of a small, rich elite affected education, gender, and intellectual issues. A major development in the period between the two wars was in education. In 1914, with a budget of slightly more than half a million pounds, the Ministry of Education had 15,000 students in all of Egypt. By 1939 the budget more than tripled, and by 1945 the number of students rose to more than 1 million. An educated professional middle class emerged as prominent in the life of the nation. But there was still much to do. Illiteracy was high, and the size of the task ahead was staggering. The stress in education was on literature, languages, and the humanities; the needs of Egypt in vocational training as well as for engineers, scientists, and industrial managers were almost ignored.

Traditional elementary schools to teach the four R's—reading, writing, arithmetic, and religion—were organized in many villages. But after children had finished the village school, they were not prepared to enter a vocational or secondary school. Elementary schools attempted only to stamp out illiteracy. Fees kept many poorer families from sending their children on for higher schooling. The Egyptian (subsequently Fuad I, then Cairo) University, a private school opened in 1908, was put under government control in 1925 and joined to schools of law, medicine, and science. European faculty members played a key role in the 1920s and 1930s until Egyptians who had achieved European advanced degrees and had acquired the methodology of their teachers became dominant. The education system was slowly creating a national consciousness among the various strata of Egyptian society; students demonstrated often on behalf of various political causes.

Gender relations remained relatively stable, although the status of women changed somewhat, as, for instance, when Egyptian women were admitted as students at the Egyptian University in 1928. More than one-quarter of all public school students were females. Organizations of upper-class and middle-class women, who were increasingly not wearing veils, now played a larger role in public life. Women formed a committee to support the Wafd party, and urban women banded together to establish social services. They set up hospitals, dispensaries, clinics, orphanages, and schools for girls, as well as an organization designed to promote feminist issues—Huda al-Sharawi founded the Egyptian Feminist Union in 1923. New laws increased the minimum age for marriage and made it slightly more difficult for men to divorce women, but activist women were unable to reach the majority of poorer rural women and could not yet change the political status of women.

Urban social life included new forms of entertainment. Egyptian state radio began its very popular broadcasts in 1934. For men, relatively new social organizations included sports clubs active in soccer, boxing, and weightlifting. Many urban Egyptians began to attend the cinema—the first authentically Egyptian film was produced in 1925—and phonograph records of Egyptian female and male singers were very popular as well. New means of expression existed alongside older cultural themes and media, such as storytellers, calligraphers, and Sufi ceremonies. Egypt continued to be the Middle Eastern center for cultural production using the Arabic language.

Egyptian intellectuals debated the basic nature of Egypt, and in the 1920s most concluded that its long history and geographic territory had determined the national character. Many Egyptians sought to find the roots of their national existence in the pharaonic period of antiquity, when Egypt was strong and powerful. Interest in ancient Egypt was spurred by the discovery of the tomb of the pharaoh Tutankhamen in 1922. Egyptians who emphasized their connections with ancient Egypt deemphasized an Arab or Islamic identity in favor of putting more weight on territorial nationalism. On the other hand, Egyptian Arab and Islamic identities were also gaining ground in the 1930s, as newly urbanized and educated groups entered into the field of political discourse. Constructing national identity in new ways became more urgent as Egyptians faced the need for political freedom, nation-building, and national unity while confronted with an increasingly corrupt and ineffectual series of governments. The effects of the Great Depression mingled with a disillusionment with the liberal experiment of the constitutional monarchy to create a yearning for morality, social justice, and political activism. Increased contact with neighboring Arab states and especially developments in the British mandate of Palestine helped foster identification with Arab nationalism and Islamic identity. The Young Egypt movement founded in 1933 was a militaristic, anti-liberal, and quasi-Fascist group, popular with urban students. The Muslim Brotherhood founded in 1928 by Hasan al-Banna (1906–1949) was a Muslim fundamentalist or Islamist group, whose goals included the revival of the Islamic community, the purification of Egyptian society, and the return to shariah law. The Brotherhood wanted to expel Britain from Egypt, but it also promoted religious values in education and fostered its own economic enterprises. Al-Banna's movement became increasingly popular and widespread in the 1930s and 1940s. (Ultimately, after World War II, it would serve as a prototype for both peaceful and radical Islamic fundamentalists in the late twentieth century.)

Intellectuals such as Taha Husain tested public limits on freedom of expression by publishing books critical of accepted beliefs. When the ulama reacted with violent criticism, such works were either withdrawn or modified. Liberal and secularly minded humanists advocated controversial ideas such as Darwinian theories of human evolution, socialism, and rationalism. But a change took place in the 1930s as many of these same writers started to produce books about the glories of early Islam and the heroic age of the Muslim conquests.

Literature in the 1920s was still heavily influenced by the neoclassical Ahmad Shawqi (1868–1932), court poet of Abbas II, who was proclaimed by Arabs from throughout the Middle East to be the "prince of poets." However, novelists, journalists, short story writers, essayists, and poets more attuned to new genres, styles, and influences gradually gained ground. Free verse and a romantic and personal approach became popular among the poets of the 1930s. Many novelists participated in a nationalistic and realistic approach to their depictions of life. The novelist and playwright Tawfiq al-Hakim wrote in the 1930s and 1940s works that captured the essence of Egyptian life. Their popularity directed attention to such social problems as the gap between peasants, the middle class, and the Europeanized upper class. Similar results were achieved by Najib Mahfuz, whose historical novels and later works set in Cairo were to be among the greatest modern Arab literature.

National rebirth and a lively interest in the day-to-day life of the average Egyptian were also seen in the sculpture of Mahmud Mukhtar, as in his *Egyptian Awakening* (1928) and two monumental statues of Saad Zaghlul. A neo-Islamic style based chiefly on Mamluk architecture dominated new public buildings constructed in the 1920s and 1930s. Even in music, Egyptian nationalists called for changes that would help raise national consciousness. They rejected the traditional Arab tonal system and urged composers to draw their themes from Egyptian life. Nationalism thus dominated Egyptian culture as well as political activities.

THE ANGLO-EGYPTIAN SUDAN

Whenever Egyptians considered severing British ties, the enormous and poor area of the Sudan loomed impressively in their thinking. In the nineteenth century, the Sudan had been important to Egypt because of the border warfare and slave raids that so frequently characterized their relationship. In the twentieth century, finding solutions to controversies over Nile water, irrigation projects, and immigration became vital for Egypt and its burgeoning population.

During World War I the British relaxed their restrictions on Abd al-Rahman, the son of the Sudanese Mahdi. With his help and that of the Sufi brotherhoods and because of the increasing prosperity of the country, the Sudan remained quiet during the war. Abd al-Rahman al-Mahdi built up a following among the tribes and the young intelligentsia and gained great influence through his religious status, wealth, and intelligence. The British also sought in the years following 1918 to gain additional support by extending more authority to tribal shaikhs, and this policy was somewhat successful in western Sudan but not elsewhere. Nationalist sentiment was steadily although slowly growing among Sudanese military and government officials. So as to reduce contacts with Egyptian nationalism, Egyptian troops and civil servants were forced to withdraw in 1924, after anti-British strikes, demonstrations, and army mutinies were crushed.

The new Sudan Defense Force consisted solely of Sudanese, but this small military group was still financed in part by Egypt. Although some Sudanese entered the government's civil service, taking the places of the departing Egyptians, the top posts were held by Englishmen. Spending on education in the 1920s, already quite low, was cut further as part of a general British policy of reducing expenses. Fewer than 5 percent of children attended elementary schools, and by 1934 there were only about 3000 girls in government schools. Some Sudanese called for a distinctly Sudanese literature so as to foster unity and independence. The first daily newspaper started publication in 1935. The English administrators feared the emergence of Sudanese nationalism among an educated elite.

The British tried to increase the separate cultural identity of the southern districts. English was encouraged and the Arabic language was opposed, and the government tried to close the region to northern, Arabic-speaking, Muslim Sudanese. Education was largely in the hands of foreign Christian missionaries. British administration in the southern Sudan spent very little money and basically neglected the area.

The Arabs of the central Sudan benefited from a change in British policy starting in the mid-1930s: more Sudanese were hired by government. Schools of engineering, agriculture, law, and veterinary medicine were set up and were ultimately merged into a new Gordon Memorial College in 1945 (subsequently the University of Khartoum). Tribalism was now less encouraged by the British administration. Sudanese living on the geographic peripheries of the country saw little social change and economic development; for many of them, government remained simply a tax-collecting agency conducted by and for strangers.

Throughout the interwar years, educated Sudanese debated at length, but with no clear resolution, the nature of the relationship that ought to exist between their country and Egypt. Shortly after the close of World War I, the interrelationship of the Sudan and

Egypt had come to the fore again with the setting up of the Gezira project, the operation of which began in 1925. The scheme envisaged the irrigation of the triangular stretch of land south of Khartoum between the Blue and White Niles. World War I delayed the building of the Sennar Dam on the Blue Nile, and its completion did not come until 1925. Under Allenby's direction the Gezira commission put management in the hands of the Sudan Plantations Syndicate, a British organization. Land tenancies were established at 40 acres (16 hectares) each, and tenants had to comply with the syndicate's directives as to what crops to plant. One-quarter of the land had to be planted in cotton, with the tenant, the syndicate, and the Sudan government receiving 40 percent, 25 percent, and 35 percent, respectively.

The Gezira scheme was initially successful. More exports went by railway through the British-constructed Port Sudan on the Red Sea. But because the cotton crop was exported to Great Britain and Sudan cotton gave the British textile industry a greater independence from Egyptian supply, Egypt grew sensitive to any expansion of irrigated tracts in the Gezira. Also, when the worldwide depression of the 1930s caused the price of cotton to fall, Sudan's economy suffered greatly. The total area planted in cotton increased dramatically, but income was still considerably below the levels seen in the 1920s. Very little economic development took place except that related to cotton and transportation; increased security in the central Sudan did, however, help the economy. Many Sudanese nevertheless were still engaged in subsistence agriculture or nomadic activities, so the fate of the cash crops and the residents in central Sudan did not greatly affect them.

Egyptian leaders maintained their claim that Sudan and Egypt were linked together, chiefly because of the water and the expectation that the undeveloped Sudan would serve as an escape valve for growing population pressures in Egypt. Fears and tensions, however, diminished with the treaty arranged in 1929 to allocate the water of the Nile; the Sudan received an adequate supply, although the vast majority of the water was to go to Egypt. After 1929, Egypt seemed ensured of all the water it could use, and at least for the moment, control of the Sudan ceased to be a major political matter. Many Sudanese objected strenuously to the water agreement and to the 1936 treaty because the Sudan and its interests were not consulted in these arrangements.

ITALIAN LIBYA

Whereas Britain controlled the Sudan and dominated Egypt, Italy imposed a much harsher regime on Libya, the territory lying to the west of Egypt and between it and the French protectorates and territories of Tunisia, Morocco, and Algeria. Italy had conquered coastal Libya from the Ottoman Empire just before World War I, and the Italians overcame Libyan and Ottoman resistance by 1918. Italian officials knew little about Libya, and their attempt to co-opt leaders from among local notables was only partially successful. The fighting between 1911 and 1918 caused many deaths and great destruction in an area already poor; perhaps half of the population died or fled as a result.

The Sanusi Sufi order in eastern Libya had been founded in the mid-nineteenth century as a Sunni Muslim religious brotherhood with many lodges, a centralized administrative structure, and support among both nomads and town dwellers in Libya and the

Sahara region. The Sanusis and a republic based in the western area obtained some autonomy and Italian financial support between 1919 and 1922, when Italian policy was relatively lenient. Italy offered a kind of citizenship to the Libyans and even recognized the Sanusi leader as ruler of the eastern interior region. Internal divisions among the western groups and particularly the differences between the regions of the country weakened the Libyan cause. Idris (1890–1983), the head of the Sanusis, took the title of amir (prince) of all of Libya in 1922, but he then had to flee to Egypt, where he remained in exile for many years. Fascists, who gained political power in Italy in 1922, undertook a series of brutal military campaigns in Libya lasting until 1931 and resulting eventually in the complete conquest of all of Libya. Italian forces enacted drastic measures, such as creating large concentration camps for civilians, so as to stop them aiding the guerrillas, and the army also built a long barbed-wire fence along the border with Egypt to stop infiltration. The Sanusi order was directly attacked, tens of thousands of Libyans died during the guerrilla warfare, and the nomads were especially hard hit as their flocks were decimated.

As the war against the Libyan resistance was winding down, Italian administrators served the interests of European settlers by seizing land from Libyans for Italian immigrants, who by 1940 numbered 110,000. (Despite this, a large majority of the total population still consisted of Muslim Arabs.) The Fascist government spent large sums on building roads, railways, and ports, whose construction necessitated the hiring of Libyans to work in the two chief towns, Tripoli and Benghazi. Revenues were low since the country was so poor in known natural resources; the province cost Italy far more than it gained from taxes or customs duties. Libyans played only a small part in government. All the key posts in authority were occupied by Italians. The contempt felt by Italy for the Muslim population could be seen in its disregard for local education, which was severely limited. Libyans were in despair as their lands were being taken and they were being ruled in a particularly harsh fashion. The people turned back to their tribal identities, until World War II opened both new possibilities for independence and yet also for even more destruction as Libya became a major battleground during that protracted war.

A COMPARISON OF LIBYA, SUDAN, AND EGYPT

A comparison of the history of Libya, Sudan, and Egypt between the two world wars makes it clear that Egypt was by far the most influential of the three. Internally, a liberal experiment in parliamentary rule coincided with a triangular struggle between the kings, the Wafdists, and the British. Britain ran the Sudan, and Italy forcibly conquered Libya. Egypt had more independence than Libya or the Anglo-Egyptian Sudan, but from the point of view of Egyptian nationalists, even the 1936 treaty was far from entailing complete self-rule. Egypt was more prosperous than the Sudan or Libya, though most Egyptians were still poor when compared to most Western Europeans of the time. And Egypt was more Europeanized than Sudan or Libya, whether measured by high culture, economic indicators, or political systems.

In the months and years immediately preceding 1939 many Egyptians (although not many Sudanese or Libyans) could look with pride on the accomplishments of the previous two decades. The Anglo-Egyptian Treaty of 1936 gave Egypt more political freedom and sovereignty; the constitution, if it were applied, ensured political democracy and responsible government; the Montreux Convention of 1937 would remove the bonds of economic servitude and set the stage for industrial, commercial, and financial independence; and the Nile water agreement of 1929 allayed the fears of the Egyptians that a foreign power would be able to force a thirsty Egypt into submission. Poor Egyptians shared in the nationalist successes, but their interests were not being seriously addressed. Elite Egyptians felt Egypt was far better off than the Fertile Crescent region, which was under British and French control. All Egyptians hoped that since they now controlled their own lives and destinies for the first time in over 3000 years, great days lay ahead.

REFERENCES

Numerous works already cited contain material of value to this chapter, especially those in Chapters 10, 20, 24, 27, 28, and 31.

Abdel Rahim, Muddathir: *Imperialism & Nationalism in the Sudan: A Study in Constitutional & Political Development, 1899–1956.* London: Khartoum University Press, 1986. A reprint of the 1969 edition, this constitutional study of the peculiar relationships of the Sudan with Egypt and Britain is comprehensive.

Anderson, Lisa: *The State and Social Transformation in Tunisia and Libya, 1830–1980.* Princeton, N.J.: Princeton University Press, 1986. Useful analyses and comparisons illuminate the history of these two countries.

Badran, Margot: *Feminists, Islam, and Nation: Gender and the Making of Modern Egypt.* Princeton, N.J.: Princeton University Press, 1995. An excellent account of the public roles of women up to 1950.

Botman, Selma: *Egypt from Independence to Revolution, 1919–1952.* Syracuse, N.Y.: Syracuse University Press, 1991. A useful introduction to the subject that includes analysis of politics, economics, religion, and culture.

Brugman, J.: *An Introduction to the History of Modern Arabic Literature in Egypt.* Leiden, The Netherlands: Brill, 1984. A massive and thorough study, including analysis of the growth of literary criticism, with a discussion of nearly every major literary figure up to about 1950.

Carter, B. L.: *The Copts in Egyptian Politics.* London: Croom Helm, 1986. Discusses internal aspects of Coptic church history as well as the relations of the Christian Copts with nationalists and the British; ends with the revolution of 1952.

Daly, M. W.: *Imperial Sudan: The Anglo-Egyptian Condominium, 1934–1956.* Cambridge, England: Cambridge University Press, 1991. This work and the next are invaluable, highly critical studies that include discussions of education, economics, health, politics, and the British.

———: *Empire on the Nile: The Anglo-Egyptian Sudan, 1898–1934.* Cambridge, England: Cambridge University Press, 1986.

Davis, Eric: *Challenging Colonialism: Bank Misr and Egyptian Industrialization, 1920–1941.* Princeton, N.J.: Princeton University Press, 1983.

Gershoni, Israel, and James P. Jankowski: *Egypt, Islam, and the Arabs: The Search for Egyptian Nationhood, 1900–1930.* New York: Oxford University Press, 1986. A thorough examination of Egyptian thought about territorial nationalism.

———: *Redefining the Egyptian Nation, 1930–1945.* Cambridge, England: Cambridge University Press, 1995. Many examples to illuminate the social and intellectual bases of Egyptian nationalism.

Jankowski, James, and Israel Gershoni, eds.: *Rethinking Nationalism in the Arab Middle East.* New York: Columbia University Press, 1997. Fourteen valuable essays on new approaches to the study of Arab nationalism, 1919–1958, covering especially Egypt, Syria, Iraq, and Palestine.

Mahfouz, Naguib: *Palace Walk.* Translated by William Hutchins and Olive Kenny. Garden City, N.Y.: Doubleday, 1990. In this novel, the first of a trilogy, Mahfouz beautifully shows the nature of middle-class life in Cairo.

Mitchell, Richard P.: *The Society of the Muslim Brothers.* New York: Oxford University Press, 1993. A reprint of this outstanding study, which first appeared in 1968.

Niblock, Tim: *Class and Power in Sudan: The Dynamics of Sudanese Politics, 1898–1985.* Albany: State University of New York Press, 1987. Particularly valuable for its treatment of regions, social groups, religion, and the economy, as well as politics.

Ostle, Robin, ed.: *Modern Literature in the Near and Middle East, 1850–1970.* London: Routledge, 1991. A broad overview that analyzes Arabic, Turkish, Persian, and Hebrew writing.

Perkins, Kenneth J.: *Port Sudan: The Evolution of a Colonial City.* Boulder, Colo.: Westview, 1993. A valuable work that illuminates Sudanese history and also contains useful comparisons with other cities.

Reid, Donald Malcolm: *Cairo University and the Making of Modern Egypt.* Cambridge, England: Cambridge University Press, 1990. The author carefully describes the nature of education and professional organizations in this excellent book and in a series of articles dealing with such topics as Egyptology.

Sayyid-Marsot, Afaf Lutfi al-: *Egypt's Liberal Experiment: 1922–1936.* Berkeley: University of California Press, 1977. Outlines the social and economic bases as well as the politics of the period.

Sharkey, Heather J.: "A Century in Print: Arabic Journalism and Nationalism in Sudan, 1899–1999." *International Journal of Middle East Studies* 31 (1999): 531–549. Very useful for the 1914–1945 period.

Smith, Charles D.: *Islam and the Search for Social Order in Modern Egypt: A Biography of Muhammad Husayn Haykal.* Albany: State University of New York Press, 1983. The intellectual and political life of a prominent Egyptian thinker.

Terry, Janice J.: *Cornerstone of Egyptian Political Power: The Wafd, 1919–1952.* London: Third World Centre, 1982.

Tignor, Robert L.: *State, Private Enterprise, and Economic Change in Egypt, 1918–1952.* Princeton, N.J.: Princeton University Press, 1984. A thorough and systematic treatment of the Egyptian middle class and the role of foreign companies operating in Egypt.

Vikor, Knut S.: "Sanusiyah." *Oxford Encyclopedia of the Modern Islamic World* III: 473–474. Oxford, England: Oxford University Press, 1995. A short survey in this excellent reference tool for the study of Islam.

Vitalis, Robert: *When Capitalists Collide: Business Conflicts and the End of Empire in Egypt.* Berkeley: University of California Press, 1995. Discusses the interaction of competing private Egyptian businesses with the Egyptian and British authorities from the 1930s to the 1950s.

Woodward, Peter: *Sudan, 1898–1989: The Unstable State.* Boulder, Colo.: Lynne Rienner, 1990. This introduction to the history of the modern Sudan is a good beginning point for any reader.

Wright, John: *Libya: A Modern History.* Baltimore: Johns Hopkins University Press, 1982. A very good survey of the subject.

Ziadeh, Farhat J.: *Lawyers, the Rule of Law, and Liberalism in Modern Egypt.* Stanford, Calif.: Hoover Institution, 1968. Traces the role of liberal tradition, national independence, and constitutionalism in the work of lawyers in Egypt.

CHAPTER 35

Lebanon, Syria, and Iraq under the Mandate System

The Entente powers defeated the Ottoman Empire during World War I and occupied the devastated Fertile Crescent areas of Lebanon, Syria, Iraq, and Palestine. The men and women living in these regions had endured hunger, trauma, the death of loved ones, and great economic losses during the war. Now they were faced with the need to construct new public identities outside the framework of the Ottoman state that had ruled them for 400 years. The contested definition of new national identities was made more difficult by the complex interactions of elite nationalists and foreign rulers, as well as the emergence of other local groups. Many of the nationalists who had served in the Ottoman army or state bureaucracy carried over to the new countries the attitudes, reforms, and points of view of the late imperial era.

Instead of directly annexing these regions, the Entente used the League of Nations to establish them under its supervision as mandates. Britain and France assumed the duty of training the peoples living in the Fertile Crescent for eventual independence and self-government; in the short term the two mandatory countries administered their mandates more or less as they wished. France was in charge of Lebanon and Syria, and Britain governed Iraq and Palestine. (Palestine and Transjordan are discussed in Chapter 36.)

The historic patterns of the Lebanon, Syria, and Iraq mandates differed sharply for two reasons. First, there were substantial internal economic, social, and political variations among the three countries. Second, France and Britain applied different methods in administering their respective mandates.

FRENCH OCCUPATION OF LEBANON AND SYRIA

When Faisal, the son of Sharif Husain of Mecca, galloped at the head of his cavalry into Damascus in October 1918, a new Arab nation under the leadership of the Hashimite dynasty seemed ensured. Some Arab political and intellectual leaders were deeply stirred by the thought of a modern nation-state, based on the sincere-sounding promises and statements made by British officials. On the horizon, to be sure, were the Balfour Declaration

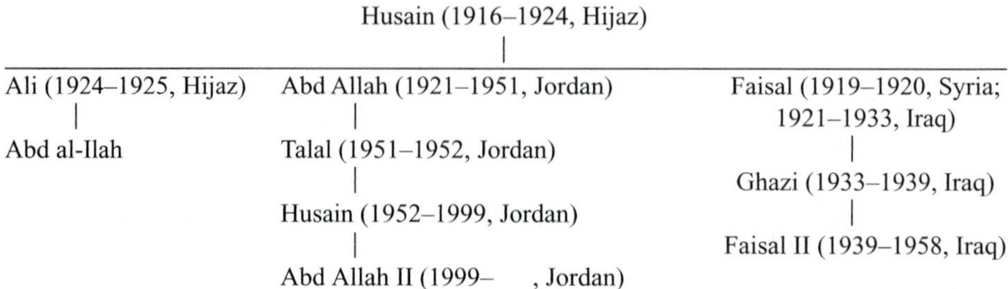

The Hashimites

to the Zionists and the Sykes-Picot Agreement, which seemed to indicate imperialist plans by the British and the French. During 1919 the British controlled the coastal regions of Syria, and Arabs held the interior.

Arab nationalists were disappointed as little headway toward a settlement was made. The Syrian economy was in a state of near collapse, although the British subsidy to Faisal's government in Damascus did keep it afloat financially. The Anglo-French agreement in September of 1919 was a crushing blow because it cut off Palestine and provided for a French military occupation of Syria. By December, General Henri Gouraud and French troops replaced the British in Beirut and along the Syrian coast. The General Syrian Congress, composed of members elected and appointed from all parts of Syria, including Palestine, met in Damascus and passed resolutions that requested independence for Syria with Faisal as king, independence for Iraq with his brother Abd Allah as king, repudiation of the Sykes-Picot Agreement and the Balfour Declaration, and rejection of the mandate idea. In many ways, the actions of the Syrian congress resembled those of the Turkish nationalists.

The General Syrian Congress went even further on March 8, 1920, when it declared the independence of Syria, including Palestine and Lebanon, as a constitutional monarchy under Faisal. The meeting of the Entente supreme council at San Remo answered the Syrian action by acknowledging a French mandate over Syria and Lebanon and separation of Palestine under the British. Many members of the old Syrian political elite now viewed Faisal and the Arab nationalists around him as incompetent newcomers.

Faisal, whose government was nearly bankrupt, was caught between the superior force of the French, the unrealistic national patriotism of the new Arab political elite, and popular small organizations. Gouraud sent Faisal an ultimatum in July 1920, demanding unqualified acceptance of the French mandate. In the face of a French army advancing from Beirut to occupy Damascus, Faisal telegraphed his agreement, but the French added new conditions. A bloody engagement occurred at Maisalun Pass, and accompanied by airplanes, tanks, and the rattle of machine-gun fire General Gouraud captured Damascus. Faisal left within a few days, and the French occupied Syria.

Detailed French administration began at once. General Gouraud, as high commissioner, issued a decree dividing the mandate for Syria and Lebanon into four separate districts: greater Lebanon; Aleppo, including Alexandretta; Latakia; and Damascus. Damascus encompassed the Jabal Druze area in the south and all remaining interior regions. The plan seemed to be to divide and rule.

LEBANON

Mandate for Lebanon

A French decree added the city of Beirut, coastal regions to the north and south including Tripoli, and the Biqa valley to the old Ottoman district of Mount Lebanon to form a new greater Lebanon. Since 1861 Mount Lebanon had had an autonomous political existence under an elected central administrative assembly selected according to religious community. By extending the area of Lebanon in response to pleas from many Lebanese Maronite Christians, the French increased the economic viability of the country but also reduced the preponderance of the Maronite sect by changing population proportions, increasing Sunni Muslims so that the Christians held only a slight overall majority. Maronite Christians represented about one-third of the total population of greater Lebanon, but they dominated the new state. Leading Maronite families exercised political patronage based on their influence on the state, thus continuing the Ottoman-era "politics of notables." Drawing other religious groups into this system, managing conflicts for power among the Maronite leaders, and dealing with the French authorities were the main domestic challenges.

In the new French regime, above the governor of Lebanon stood the high commissioner, who had a government of his own to assist him. Separated into departments such as security, education, and public works, this administration was staffed by the French, who served as the authority to which the Lebanese government looked. In actual practice this system allowed for a fully determined colonialism to operate more or less unmolested behind a semblance of local self-government.

Certain functions of government such as customs, posts, telegraph, railways, public utilities, currency, and local troop levies, were jointly held by the Syrian and Lebanese administrative units. The high commissioner reserved for his own government full supervision of these "common interests." Income from the central operations paid common expenses, and the balance was apportioned among the four state units, always with bickering and dissatisfaction.

French Imperialism

French imperialism manifested itself in Lebanon in many ways. In a number of districts, martial law was established, and throughout the mandate period, the French were quick to decree its use. The press was muzzled effectively, and numerous papers accepted French subsidies. French investors largely owned and operated the railways, public utilities, and banks of Lebanon; the entire fiscal and economic policy was initiated by the French. Concessions granted by the Lebanese government went to French concerns or to Lebanese firms with strong French connections. The new Lebanese currency was tied to the French franc, which had the disadvantage of fluctuating with depreciating French currency. The fall of the franc played an important role in uprisings in Syria and Lebanon in 1925.

French imperialists spoke of their "civilizing mission," a phrase expressing their view of the superiority of French language and culture. The chief work was accomplished through education and the use of French as a second language. All schools taught French, and textbooks had a French coloration on every page. French newspapers were encouraged, and French was an official language in the courts, government offices, and every other walk of life. French archaeologists helped foster through their investigations the idea that modern Lebanon and the Lebanese were not Arab but rather were linked to ancient Phoenicia.

There were, however, many favorable aspects of French rule. Schools improved and increased in number, food and clothing became more plentiful, roads were built, motorcars and transport became available, doctors were trained, disease was controlled, and sanitation and health standards were greatly raised. Striking changes came in the city of Beirut, where numerous new buildings were constructed and the population grew rapidly. Enlarging the port of Beirut helped make the city the gateway for European influence in the area. Beirut became a cultural center, featuring many educational institutions, a national museum, and radio broadcasting facilities. Since most economic development took place in the cities, Christians tended to benefit more than Muslims, and the countryside was neglected. Probably the standard of living and per capita income for Lebanon and Syria together remained stagnant after recovering from the devastating effects of World War I. The Great Depression hit Lebanon's service-oriented economy particularly hard. Emigration abroad declined, as life in Lebanon grew more attractive, despite a decline in silk production.

A desire for independence and true self-government spread. In 1922 a representative council was elected and began meeting. Maurice Sarrail, the new high commissioner in 1925, was noted for his arrogant manners, unwise tactics, anticlericalism, and inopportune appointments. He fomented quarrels with the Maronite church, the Druzes, and many Lebanese leaders. One example was his appointing an unpopular Frenchman as governor of Lebanon after first stating he intended to name a native Lebanese.

When the Syrian general uprisings of 1925, provoked by General Sarrail, refused to burn themselves out, the general was recalled. He was replaced by a more tactful high commissioner, who called on the representative council to draft a constitution. Lebanon still had to acknowledge the mandate and French responsibility for Lebanon's foreign affairs and give the high commissioner veto power and the right to dismiss the executive head of the state and to dissolve the legislature. Beyond those restrictions, the French surrendered to the Lebanese authority over their own affairs. On May 23, 1926, the Lebanese Republic was proclaimed. Charles Dabbas, an Orthodox Christian, was chosen president by the Assembly.

The sheer weight of French military forces kept political agitation under wraps. Moreover, the French encouraged Maronite and other Christian leaders in Lebanon to feel that their security against a Muslim majority required full trust in France and cooperation with French rule.

No major political problem arose until the acute world economic depression; its repercussions on trade, unemployment, and finance in Beirut caused the suspension of the constitution in 1932. A new constitution in 1934 called for the power of the Assembly to be restricted, and the sectarian religious communal basis of election and membership in previous assemblies was ignored. Political life in Lebanon maintained an uneasy calm, until disturbances in 1936 in Syria led France to negotiate a treaty with Syria. Moreover, British concessions to nationalism in Iraq and Egypt encouraged Syrian and Lebanese nationalists.

Syrian-French negotiations for a treaty forced similar actions in Lebanon. France could hardly be less generous to a more friendly Lebanon than it was to a recalcitrant Syria. Inhabitants of the Muslim parts of Lebanon, which the French had added to Lebanon in 1920, were divided in their sentiments in 1936. Many favored union with Syria. Others preferred the more stable political life and higher standard of living in Lebanon. The latter began openly to cooperate with Christian groups. Christian Lebanese in turn emphasized their links to the Muslims—common interests, the Arabic language, and general culture. According to a tacit arrangement, the president of Lebanon was a Christian and the prime minister a Muslim. The Maronites wished to avoid the chances of greater Lebanon's being dissolved, for they assumed that the old Mount Lebanon was too small to survive.

The Franco-Lebanese Treaty of Friendship and Alliance was signed in 1936. It recognized the independence of Lebanon, although Lebanon agreed to respect French interests. French troops were to be permitted in Lebanon without restriction. In 1937, the constitution of 1926 was restored, but difficulties loomed ahead. The French cabinet fell, and the insecure international position frightened French conservatives into refusing the treaties, which the conservatives believed would weaken France. The Lebanese treaty with France was not put into effect.

SYRIA

Mandate for Syria

The other districts created by the French 1920 decree had a life during this period even more varied than Lebanon's. Governments were ordered for Latakia, Damascus, the Jabal Druze, and Aleppo (with Alexandretta attached to Aleppo as a special province). Damascus Syrians never admitted the legality of this fragmentation and continuously called for the unity of all Syria. In 1922, the separation of the Jabal Druze was proclaimed; the remaining states were grouped into a federation. In 1924 the French laid the foundations for a treaty settlement with Syria similar to that which the British gave Iraq. At the same time, they terminated the federation by recognizing a separate government for the Alawis in the Latakia area and amalgamated Aleppo into the state of Damascus, which then became Syria. Alexandretta, though a part of Syria, had its own administration.

French policy was made even worse by the insensitive General Sarrail. In the Jabal Druze, an area beginning to be densely populated, he touched off a bloody uprising by inviting the Druze leaders who opposed the local French administration to Damascus, where they were arrested. Coinciding with economic depression, a revolt flared rapidly across much of the mandate, and severe fighting occurred in the Jabal Druze. In October 1925, Druze columns appeared at Damascus, and the French bombardment of that city caused large damage and considerable loss of life.

This tragedy brought Sarrail's immediate recall, and his successor called for elections. The presidency was offered to Taj al-Din al-Hasani (d. 1943), chief judge of Damascus, but since his program was unacceptable to the French, he refused the post. Every succeeding Syrian request over the following two decades was based on Taj al-Din's platform. He demanded that Latakia and Jabal Druze be joined to Syria, that areas within Lebanon be allowed to choose between Syria and Lebanon, that Syria join the League of Nations, that French troops be evacuated, that a currency reform be enacted, and that Syria be entirely independent in its domestic affairs. Guerrilla warfare continued, and in May 1926 Damascus was again shelled. This time fighting was even more destructive and more savage than in 1925. Both France and the Syrian nationalists began to realize that some compromise was necessary. The latter asked France to forget the past, and the French announced that a constituent assembly would be elected, a Syrian government inaugurated, and a treaty of alliance with France concluded, in that order.

French Imperialism

In 1928, France appointed Taj al-Din president of a Syrian Council of Ministers. He formed a provisional government and held elections for the constituent assembly. Most of the members were Sunni Muslims, and urban-based landowners and merchants were an important part of the membership. (The same groups dominated local Syrian governments throughout the mandate.) A secular nationalist bloc under the leadership of Jamil Mardam began to take shape, and a more radical independence wing was led by Shukri al-Kuwatli. The constituent assembly drafted a constitution, which established a Western-type republic with a president, prime minister, cabinet, legislature, and high court. Syria was pronounced to include Lebanon and Palestine, the official religion was to be Islam, and no mention was made of France as a mandatory power. Since several articles violated French interests and were contrary to League of Nations mandate stipulations, France found the constitution unacceptable.

In 1929 the Assembly was dismissed, but debate over the constitution continued. France later unilaterally set up new governments for Alexandretta, Latakia, and Jabal Druze, simultaneously establishing in Syria a constitution. Nationalists soon took the lead in parliament and pressed for the conclusion of a treaty of independence with France. When a treaty was presented by the French to the parliament, it raised such a howl that the high commissioner suggested its withdrawal. Parliament was dissolved, with the president governing by decree. In 1934 Taj al-Din became prime minister and held on to that post for nearly two years.

In early 1936 Damascus and most of the other towns of Syria became the scene of an organized strike against the French. New groups that had emerged in the 1930s among Syrian women, urban workers, and young people agitated against French control. Negotiations for a treaty were resumed on the basis of Alexandretta's being a part of Syria but Lebanon's being recognized as a separate state. The long discussions ended only after the French agreed that the Jabal Druze and Latakia be incorporated into Syria. Rejoicing, Syria elected the nationalists to power in November 1936. Hashim al-Atasi became president of the republic. The Syrians ratified the treaty but, as with the similar Lebanese treaty, the French government never did ratify it fearing the growing threat of war in Europe and the Mediterranean.

In 1939 the president resigned, and the high commissioner suspended the Chamber of Deputies. The Latakia area and Jabal Druze were once again separated from Syria until their final unity inside Syria was achieved in 1942. Syria was back where it was in 1920 when the mandate began, under the control of the French high commissioner!

French economic policy in Syria assisted the Bedouin shaikhs (nomadic tribal chiefs) in acquiring unsettled lands. The shaikhs and urban-based large landlords dominated agriculture in some areas, but small landowners played a substantial role in other parts of the country. The French conducted a cadastral survey of part of the land and revised the agricultural taxes. About two-thirds of the Syrian population was rural and agricultural during the mandate, and the peasants lived in thousands of villages. Annual variations in rainfall created large fluctuations in grain production. Industry was slow to develop, but textile factories replaced many hand looms. Unemployment and inflation were grave problems.

By 1938 there were about 100,000 children, mostly boys, in schools. The one small university, located in Damascus, admitted women students starting in 1926. Expenditures for education grew substantially in the 1930s. A military academy trained young Syrians, especially those from rural areas and from the religious minorities, such as the Alawis, to become officers in the small army that France permitted to exist. Two-thirds of the total population was Sunni Muslim, and of the remainder half were Christians and half Druzes and Shiis of various types. There were also several thousand Jews.

The bitterest foreign policy event for the Syrians to swallow during the mandate years was the gift of Alexandretta to Turkey. In 1920 the French had declared a special administration for Alexandretta in view of the large Turkish population residing there. When questions over its status were raised by the Turks in 1936, the Syrians objected. As this district of Hatay became independent and then was annexed to Turkey in 1939, Syrian nationalists protested every step of the way. With considerable justification, they declared that the terms of the mandate forbade France from giving any part of Syria to another country.

For two decades France tried to govern Syria but failed ingloriously. Policies dictated by Paris were high-handed, unwise, and based on an almost complete disregard for the situation. The Syrians did not want French rule or even French advisers in the first instance, and the French did little to endear themselves to the Syrians.

IRAQ

The British Create the Kingdom of Iraq

East of Syria and Lebanon, in the valley of the Tigris-Euphrates, the British at the end of World War I occupied Basrah, Baghdad, and Mosul, which had been the seats of three separate Ottoman provinces. There was great uncertainty over the future. When the news from San Remo arrived, a rebellion burst out. For four months in 1920, war raged in Iraq, with resistance forces encouraged by Shii ulama and led by tribal shaikhs in control of the Euphrates region, as well as attacks in some areas north and east of Baghdad. The large cities for the most part did not play a role in the fighting.

Sir Percy Cox was sent to Iraq as high commissioner to provide a permanent resolution to the expensive stalemate in that area. Quickly he organized a provisional Council of State in which Sayyid Abd al-Rahman al-Kailani, Baghdad's naqib al-ashraf (head of the Sunni Arab community), became head. Each minister had a British adviser, and in reality the Council was supervised by these advisers.

The British selected Faisal, ex-king of Syria, as king of Iraq in 1920. Faisal was backed by several hundred Arab officers who had served with the Hashimite Arab revolt in the Hijaz and in Syria. His brother Abd Allah withdrew his own name, and Faisal arrived in Baghdad in June 1921. The Council of State invited him to become king. After a referendum was held, Faisal was enthroned on August 23, 1921. The British provided Faisal, a king without a kingdom, to Iraq, a kingdom without a king!

Faisal served until his death twelve years later. His charm, tact, and broad tolerance made him an admirable choice, as his knowledge and experience made him acceptable to desert shaikhs, landowners, and the townsmen of Iraq. At the same time, Faisal recognized fully the British position of control and appreciated the fact that without British support, he would never have become king.

British Imperialism

In 1922 a treaty was drafted by the British in conjunction with King Faisal and al-Kailani. It defined the special position of Great Britain in Iraq, giving the British military and economic control. British advisers were accepted in all offices. The treaty's many articles justified the objections by the nationalists that it was only a sugar-coated mandate, which, however translated, meant subjection and colonization. King Faisal urged the newly elected constituent assembly to ratify the treaty with Great Britain, pass on the constitution, and enact an electoral law for a parliament—all of which was done in 1924.

Six years later, the highly unpopular and extremely important Anglo-Iraqi Treaty of 1930, which became the prototype of the Anglo-Egyptian Treaty of 1936 and the treaties of France with Syria and Lebanon in the same year, established a twenty-five-year alliance between Iraq and Great Britain. Iraq agreed to consult with Great Britain over foreign affairs and allow the British to station troops in Iraq and establish several air bases. In return, Britain contracted to defend Iraq in case of war. The signing of this treaty cleared the way for Iraq's formal independence and membership in the League of Nations in 1932. The high commissioner became British ambassador, the mandate was terminated, and Iraq stood supposedly as an independent state.

The Government of Iraq

The constitution placed executive administrative power in the hands of a prime minister and cabinet responsible to the Chamber of Deputies, but the king retained extensive powers; he could dissolve the Chamber, and he named the members of the Senate. The Chamber of Deputies was elected indirectly by universal manhood suffrage, with a special provision that four Christians and four Jews were to be elected. The first Chamber was elected in 1925, and elections in 1939 were held for the ninth. Only the Chamber could initiate legislation; in appearance, it was the representative of the people and held the dominant position in the government.

In practice, however, the cabinet was the powerful body, and no cabinet ever fell from a vote of no confidence. The cabinet controlled elections and obtained the dismissal of the Chamber when necessary. Yet there were twenty cabinets from 1925, when the constitution came into force, until the outbreak of World War II in Europe in 1939. A cabinet would promise to obtain full independence from Great Britain, and when it failed, it invited the opposition to try its hand. Ministers moved about from post to post in succeeding cabinets. Nuri al-Said, four times prime minister in that period, appropriately quipped: "With a small pack of cards, you must shuffle them often."

Perhaps the political Ferris wheel would not have been so pronounced had King Faisal lived longer. He died in 1933 and was succeeded immediately by his twenty-one-year-old son Ghazi. Addicted to fast motor cars, Ghazi was killed in an accident in 1939. He was succeeded by his four-year-old son, Faisal II, under the regency of Prince Abd al-Ilah, who was the son of Prince Ali, King Faisal I's oldest brother.

National Unity

Independence and the creation of national identity entailed establishing definite borders as well as building institutions of self-government. Border raids by nomads on the deserts and in the mountains led to difficulties with the states on Iraq's frontiers. Boundary settlements with varying degrees of permanence were made with Kuwait, Saudi Arabia, Transjordan, Syria, Turkey, and Iran. As a further step in regulating the frontiers and relations with Turkey and Iran, the Saadabad Pact was signed by the foreign ministers of Iraq, Iran, Turkey, and Afghanistan at the shah's palace near Tehran in 1937.

Iraq's problems in creating a nation-state were most dependent on the feelings and views of its own population. The mostly Sunni Kurds were about 15–20 percent of the total population. Organized in tribes, they were preponderant in northern Iraq, and with their fellow Kurds in Turkey and Iran they hoped for a peace settlement that would bring forth a Kurdistan. The Kurdish tribes were seminomadic and roamed the mountains and valleys of the northeastern highlands, moving freely from country to country and resisting outside authorities. They had no desire to be taxed or organized. Kurdish deputies in the Iraqi parliament were unsuccessful in obtaining local self-government for the Kurds of northern Iraq. The British and the Iraqi government took punitive measures repeatedly against uprisings in the neighborhood of Mosul in the 1920s and early 1930s. Kurds served in the central government, but real power was in the hands of Sunni Arabic-speaking nationalists.

Another minority group was the Assyrians (Nestorian Christians), who during World War I had joined with the British and fought against the Ottomans. Leaving Turkey at the end of the conflict and finding themselves a homeless minority in Iraq, many had accepted service in the British army. In 1933, incidents between Assyrians (who demanded full local autonomy) and Arabs led to bloody engagements, massacres in Assyrian villages, and looting and suppression of the Assyrians by Kurdish tribesmen as well as by Iraqi army forces commanded by General Bakr Sidqi. Britain helped Iraq obtain a whitewash of the affair before the League of Nations.

The most serious political problem in Iraq arose from the fragmentation of Iraqi society along both ethnic and religious lines. In addition to the ethnic Sunni Kurdish minority and such religious minorities as the Assyrians, there was the lasting schism between Sunni and Shii Arabic speakers. Arabs as a whole constituted something between 70 and 80 percent of the population, but while Shii Arabs were an absolute majority of the total Iraqi population of about 3 million people, the Sunni Arab minority—about one-quarter of the total citizens of the state—dominated government and society. In the 1920s the Shii ulama banned their followers from government employment, but despite this fact more and more of the Shii Iraqis came to regard themselves politically as Arab Iraqis first and adherents of Shii Islam second. By the 1930s the Shii ulama were weakened in several ways: King Faisal and the British tried to curb their effective power, pilgrimages to the Shii holy cities in Iraq and donations to them declined, many Iraqi Shiis turned away from Shii theological schools to government-provided education, and the theological center of Shii Islam moved from Iraq to Iran.

Until Shiis could be brought fully into the national identity, the elite of Iraq necessarily consisted of a small group of Sunni notables who sought power for themselves but held it precariously. The Ministry of Education attempted with some success to create a secular nationalist school system, which aimed at unifying the next generation in its values and Pan-Arab national identity. This was done especially through teaching history that glorified the early period of the Arab empires. The number of students increased rapidly, but from a small base. In 1910 there were only about 10,000 students in the public schools, whereas by 1930 there were about 27,000 boys and 7000 girls, and in 1939 more than 100,000 attended school.

Pending the spread of Iraqi identity among the young, the regime had to depend on the army, which increased from only 3000 in 1922 to 11,000 ten years later and then, using conscription, to 44,000 in 1941. Most officers were Arab Sunnis. Under the leadership of Bakr Sidqi, the military suppressed such occurrences as Shii tribal rebellions in 1935–1936. Breaking the power of the tribes of the middle Euphrates was possible once the army was equipped with the strength and mobility of more mechanized weapons.

Agriculture and Oil

In addition to minorities, there was a grave economic cleavage between the townspeople and the settled and nomadic tribes. The government of Iraq was definitely in the hands of the townspeople, yet the tribes, and particularly their shaikhs, were powerful forces. Every Iraqi parliament had a goodly number of tribal shaikhs as members. They were conservative and usually friendly to the British, in whom they saw a protection from town-dwelling Iraqi politicians.

At least 70 percent of the population won their livelihood from the land, much of which was irrigated. But irrigated soil became salty and channels silted rapidly, compelling peasants to move frequently to new land. In the middle Euphrates area, the tribes also engaged in stock raising, moving their herds from sparse pasturage as the cover was grazed. Thus the tribes had a constant tie with desert Bedouins. The tribal shaikhs were recognized by the British as the responsible heads of the districts, thereby obtaining a quasi-title of ownership of the land, and the land law of 1932 reinforced their power and that of the ex-Ottoman military officers around the king. Many peasants were treated as serfs. A small number of families controlled vast amounts of the land. The cropped area increased nearly fivefold from 1913 to 1943, thanks largely to the introduction of mechanical irrigation pumps, but salinity and drainage problems continued, and the worldwide depression of the 1930s lowered the value of agricultural exports. Crops could be moved to market more quickly by means of new railways, roads, and bridges. The speed and cost-effectiveness of transportation and communications increased dramatically. Processing agricultural goods and serving government needs for textiles and construction provided some impetus for a small industry.

The oil resources of the country promised to supplement agriculture, still the chief source of Iraqi prosperity. Before World War I, the Turkish Petroleum Company was formed in 1912 with German, Dutch, and British ownership to exploit the Mosul fields. The San Remo Conference turned over the German interests to the French, and during the Lausanne Conference the British agreed very reluctantly that the Anglo-Persian Oil Company would also allow American oil firms to join in Iraq.

Oil was behind the dispute between Britain and Turkey in the early 1920s over control of the Mosul region. When in 1925 it appeared likely that Mosul would be awarded to Iraq, that government gave a seventy-five-year concession to the Turkish Petroleum Company. Development, however, moved slowly, with oil operations really beginning in 1927. Whereas the oil production by 1930 in Iran had increased to nearly 46 million barrels, in Iraq it was only 900,000 barrels. By 1940 Iraq's annual production dramatically increased to 20 million barrels, but this was still only about one-third of Iran's. Iraqi leaders charged that Western oil concerns were holding back in Iraq and exploiting their wells in other parts of the world. Although this might be good business for the companies, Iraq was losing revenue it sorely needed.

Iraq gave a new concession in 1931 to the Iraq Petroleum Company (the former Turkish Petroleum Company). The company obtained rights in the Baghdad and Mosul provinces, and it built a pipeline system to Haifa and the Syrian coast and began annual payments of £400,000 against future royalties. By 1939 Iraq was exporting far more oil and thereby gaining greater wealth, but its freedom of action was limited by the power of the Iraq Petroleum Company, which by 1938 held the oil production of all of Iraq in its hands.

Politics

Domestic politics from the very beginning revolved around dynamic individuals, who gathered a clientele, published a newspaper, and organized a political party. Eagerness for personal power, prestige, and position was in some cases linked to the ideology of nationalism and the struggle for independence. Parties were transient, as their members moved from one to another with considerable ease. In the 1920s the most important parties were the National and the People's parties. Each pledged to throw off the treaty-mandate subterfuge and obtain real independence. The People's party was headed by Yasin al-Hashimi, who in the 1930s led his followers into a collective party known as the National Brotherhood. Prime minister twice, he was active in politics and held various ministries until forced into exile. Jafar Abu al-Timman, a Shii merchant who participated in different ministries, organized the National party. Disillusioned by the acts of his political associates, he moved toward the left. In 1933 he joined the Reform party and took an active part in the 1936 coup.

Nuri al-Said, who had concluded the 1930 Anglo-Iraqi Treaty of Alliance, was an Iraqi who had also served in the Ottoman army and then joined the Hashimite Arab revolt during World War I. Returning to Baghdad, he worked for the kingship of Faisal and held office in many cabinets as foreign minister. Prime minister four times before the outbreak of World War II, he was a strong stabilizing force and pro-British.

Nuri's opponents in 1930 joined together under al-Hashimi and Rashid Ali al-Kailani to form the National Brotherhood party, which dominated the government from 1932 until it was overthrown by the 1936 coup. Meanwhile, a Reform party (Ahali) resulted from the meetings and discussions of younger Western-educated men who wanted a more democratic and socialist government. They were disgusted with the corruption of the conservative governments conducted by their elders. For a few years they gained wide influence through their party newspaper, but they soon were eclipsed by experienced politicians.

Realizing that the power of the National Brotherhood government could not be broken and that the cabinet of al-Hashimi and al-Kailani could not be removed without active assistance from the army, Hikmat Sulaiman brought about a cooperation of the Ahali group with disgruntled army officers. The army "hero" proved to be Bakr Sidqi. The plot ripened, and in 1936 Sidqi moved on Baghdad. Al-Kailani, Nuri al-Said, and al-Hashimi escaped into exile; the minister of defense was assassinated; and Hikmat Sulaiman became the new prime minister. This was the first of the occasions when an Arab army seized power in the period of independence; it was the precursor of many other such seizures of power in other Arab states, as well as in Iraq's later history.

Parliament was dissolved, and new elections were rigged so as to seat a great number of deputies who had never served in any previous chamber. Spending on the military increased, and the size and strength of the army grew. (Conscription had been introduced in 1934.) The socialism of the Ahali group led to quarrels with Sidqi and his army officers. Other officers became jealous of Sidqi, and in 1937 he was assassinated. Since the army officer corps was dominated by urban Sunni Arabs, the same religious and ethnic groups continued to control Iraq, as they had done under the preceding civilian regimes. Another army coup d'état soon ended the first, and until 1941 one army coup followed another methodically, while a culture of violence, networks of patronage, and Pan-Arab nationalism dominated politics. Iraq was deeply immersed in this pattern when World War II began in Europe.

THE IMPACT OF THE MANDATE PERIOD

In Iraq, as in Syria and Lebanon, the events of the mandate period had a profound impact on the subsequent nature of the three countries once they became truly independent. Britain and France oversaw the development of institutions, built infrastructure, delimited borders, and helped create other aspects of national identity. Despite this, the two mandatory powers created a deep resentment among most of the population in Iraq and Syria. Because of its heavy-handed policies in Syria, France in particular strengthened an extreme nationalist opposition. Although opinion was more divided in Lebanon, where pro-French feelings prevailed among many of the Christian Lebanese, the French failure to ratify the 1936 agreement seemed to show a bankruptcy in policy ominous for the future.

In all three countries, preoccupation with political process and the struggle for national independence tended to discourage radical economic and social reforms. The growth of commerce and education (and the oil industry in Iraq) nevertheless indicated that the three mandates were definitely part of the world economic system and that Europeanizing modernization was underway. It was in Palestine, however, that nationalism, the struggle for independence, and a desire for economic and social transformation all found their most dramatic expression.

REFERENCES

References cited at the end of Chapters 25, 26, 27, and 31 are pertinent to this chapter as well.

Batatu, Hanna: *The Old Social Classes and the Revolutionary Movements of Iraq.* Princeton, N.J.: Princeton University Press, 1978. A massive and outstanding study of Iraq, centering around the Communist movement but also illuminating many other aspects of the political and economic life of the country.

Cleveland, William L.: *Islam against the West: Shakib Arslan and the Campaign for Islamic Nationalism.* Austin: University of Texas Press, 1985. The ably told story of a Druze writer and leader who became a prominent spokesman for Arab and Muslim independence and Islamic reform.

Dawn, C. Ernest: "The Formation of Pan-Arab Ideology in the Interwar Years." *International Journal of Middle East Studies* 20 (1988): 67–91. An excellent account by a leading scholar.

Devlin, John F.: *Syria: Modern State in an Ancient Land.* Boulder, Colo.: Westview Press, 1983. An outstanding general survey.

Gelvin, James L.: *Divided Loyalties: Nationalism and Mass Politics in Syria at the Close of Empire.* Berkeley: University of California Press, 1998. Examines non-elite, popular bases for constructing nationalism.

Haj, Samira: *The Making of Iraq, 1900–1963: Capital, Power, and Ideology.* Albany: State University of New York Press, 1997. Especially useful on agricultural issues.

Hourani, Albert H.: *Syria and Lebanon, a Political Essay.* London: Oxford University Press, 1946. Examines the rise of Arab nationalism and the French mandate period.

Khadduri, Majid: *Independent Iraq: A Study in Iraqi Politics, 1932–1958.* 2d ed. London: Oxford University Press, 1960. An excellent work on this subject.

Khoury, Philip S.: *Syria and the French Mandate: The Politics of Arab Nationalism, 1920–1945.* Princeton, N.J.: Princeton University Press, 1987. A massive study full of insights on all aspects of the subject.

Longrigg, Stephen Hemsley: *Iraq, 1900–1950.* London: Oxford University Press, 1953.

———: *Syria and Lebanon under the French Mandate.* New York: Oxford University Press, 1958. Covers the period from the end of World War I to the aftermath of World War II. A fair and judicious account with sound conclusions.

Marr, Phebe: *The Modern History of Iraq.* Boulder, Colo.: Westview Press, 1985. A useful general survey.

Nakash, Yitzhak: *The Shi'is of Iraq.* Princeton, N.J.: Princeton University Press, 1994. An excellent account of a seldom-discussed subject; covers the nineteenth century to 1958, with an epilogue on 1991 events.

Russell, Malcolm B.: *The First Modern Arab State: Syria under Faysal, 1918–1920.* Minneapolis, Minn.: Bibliotheca Islamica, 1985. The standard work in English on the topic; full of insights not only for this period but for succeeding periods in Syrian and Iraqi history.

Salibi, Kamal: *The Modern History of Lebanon.* New York: Praeger, 1965. Covers the later centuries in considerable detail.

———: *A House of Many Mansions: The History of Lebanon Reconsidered.* Berkeley: University of California Press, 1988. An able essay on the historical meaning of Lebanon.

Sassoon, Joseph: *Economic Policy in Iraq, 1932–1950.* London: Frank Cass, 1987. Examines finance, agriculture, commerce, oil, and government policies.

Shikara, Ahmad: *Iraqi Politics 1921–41: The Interaction between Domestic Politics and Foreign Policy.* London: LAAM, 1987. Carefully traces the ways domestic factors influenced Iraq's standing with Britain, including analysis of Kuwaiti-Iraqi relations.

Silverfarb, Daniel: *Britain's Informal Empire in the Middle East: A Case Study of Iraq, 1929–1941.* New York: Oxford University Press, 1986. A good book based on British sources.

Simon, Reeva S.: *Iraq between the Two World Wars: The Creation and Implementation of a Nationalist Ideology.* New York: Columbia University Press, 1986. Especially valuable for a discussion of education and the use of history in shaping nationalism.

Sluglett, Peter: *Britain in Iraq, 1914–1932.* London: Ithaca Press, 1976.

Tarbush, Mohammad A.: *The Role of the Military in Politics: A Case Study of Iraq to 1941.* London: Kegan Paul, 1982. A thorough analysis.

Thompson, Elizabeth: *Colonial Citizens: Republican Rights, Paternal Privilege, and Gender in French Syria and Lebanon.* New York: Columbia University Press, 2000. This analytical history concentrates on gender issues and also has much to say on the role of the French, nationalism, culture, and social matters.

Tripp, Charles: *A History of Iraq.* Cambridge, England: Cambridge University Press, 2000. The ably-told history of the Iraqi government and the groups that dominated it after World War I, concentrating on patrimonialism, the political economy of oil, and the political use of violence.

Zamir, Meir: *The Formation of Modern Lebanon.* London: Croom Helm, 1985. Concentrates on the 1920s and the role of the Maronites and the French.

———: *Lebanon's Quest: The Road to Statehood, 1926–1939.* London: Tauris, 1997. A detailed continuation of the book cited above.

CHAPTER 36

Palestine and Transjordan

In the British-governed mandate of Palestine, two national communities—Zionist Jews on the one hand and Palestinian Muslim and Christian Arabs on the other—were in mutual opposition. Britain ruled Palestine for its own purposes, but it was also, according to the League of Nations mandate, under a dual obligation to both communities. The struggle for national independence, the development of self-governing institutions, and the fostering of economic and social change took a very different path in Palestine than in most other parts of the Middle East. Crucial issues were the form and duration of the mandate government, immigration, and land sales. Although Transjordan was connected with Palestine in a variety of ways, its political history between the two world wars was closer to that of Iraq than to the experience of Palestine.

PALESTINE

Zionists, Arabs, and the British

The British and their allies captured Palestine, including the Ottoman district of Jerusalem, in 1917–1918. From then until July 1920, it was occupied and administered by the British army. The future of Palestine remained up in the air until the San Remo Conference in April 1920, when it was awarded to England. Until then, uncertainty nurtured every rumor and fear.

At the close of World War I, the population of this small geographic region was composed of about 620,000 Muslims, 70,000 Christians, and 60,000 Jews. The Muslims and most Christians were Arabic speakers born in the area. Most of the Arab leaders came from prominent landowning families, many of which had provided officials to the Ottoman Empire. Some Jews were cultural Arabs, having lived there for many years. Some had resided there a generation or two, having immigrated to live and work in Jewish agricultural community projects, representing socialist utopian societies. The great majority of Jews, however, were newcomers who belonged to communities living on charity from world Jewry and included elderly Jews of various nationalities who had emigrated to the Jewish Holy Land to pray. The earlier development both of Jewish Zionist national feeling and of Arab nationalism were discussed in Chapter 27.

During the war, immigration ceased, some Jews left Palestine, others were expelled by the Ottomans, and the Jewish population dropped. The Balfour Declaration of 1917 stated that Great Britain "viewed with favour the establishment in Palestine of a national home for the Jewish people," but Zionists hoped for more. In time, they thought, a Jewish national state having all the characteristics of a typical European nation-state would be created.

After 1918, the Arabs of Palestine initially considered their land to be part of Syria and placed their faith in promises made to Sharif Husain of Mecca with regard to an Arab state and in President Wilson's Fourteen Points. Since the Arabs made up a majority of the population, they hoped to become part of the eventual Arab national state. The return of Jews who had fled during the war, accompanied by agitation for Jewish immigration to Palestine, raised a multitude of fears in their hearts.

The British wanted to incorporate Palestine into their empire because of its proximity to the Suez Canal, its suitability as an outlet for Iraqi oil, and its strategic position with respect to Arabia. The British army was occupying Palestine, and there seemed to be no good reason for leaving. A Zionist alliance might serve Britain's imperial interests and prevent the French from holding the entire coast. But procrastination, intrigue, war weariness, and strife plagued the British military administration and intensified public unrest throughout Palestine.

British Mandate

Bloodshed first broke out in April 1920, when many Arab villagers flocked to Jerusalem for a religious celebration. Rumors turned into riots; the British sentenced to prison both Arabs, who inflamed the villagers, and Zionists, who had caches of arms. In July Sir Herbert Samuel, the first high commissioner for Palestine (including the territory to the east of the Jordan River), initiated civilian control.

From 1920 to 1925 four separate yet parallel governments were formed. Most important and most powerful was the British executive government, composed of various departments, over each of which the high commissioner appointed a British director or secretary. Departments were established for public works, education, immigration, customs, excise and trade, antiquities, treasury, revenue, attorney general, police, health, agriculture and forests, posts and telegraphs, lands, and audit. Later, the British also supervised the shariah courts and awqaf (religious endowments). An elective legislative council was projected, but it never came into existence because of disagreement over the ratio of representation between Arabs and Jews.

The Jewish community inaugurated the second government. In 1920 a Jewish National Assembly, including both male and female delegates, was elected. It, in turn, appointed a Jewish National Council, which the high commissioner recognized as representative of the Jewish community in Palestine. The National Council governed the Jews of Palestine in personal, communal, and religious affairs and recommended actions to British authorities. Certain Jews, however, clung to a theocratic concept of

Jewish life and refused to be governed by the National Council. They disclaimed all connections with political and nationalistic Zionism, but they proved too small a minority for the British Palestine administration to recognize. An underground militia, the Haganah, was formed in 1920.

The third government was the international Zionist organization, with headquarters in London. It represented Zionist groups in many parts of the world. A number of its executives who lived and worked in Palestine between 1921 and 1929 were known as the Palestine Zionist executive. Each member was responsible for some department of work: political, immigration, education, industry, health, and public works. Sometimes referred to as a quasi-government, the Zionist executive followed the policies established by the Zionist organization in London. Frequently when the high commissioner's government and the Zionist executive were at odds, the Zionist organization proved more effective in persuading the British cabinet and House of Commons to follow the Zionist course than the foreign or colonial secretary was in obtaining support for the policies of the high commissioner.

These three "governments" represented imperialism, Jewish settlers, and world Jewry, respectively. The fourth government tried to represent the great majority of the people of Palestine—Muslim and Christian Arabs. Arab notables—of which the two most prominent families were the al-Husainis and the Nashashibis—dropped the view that Palestine should be part of Syria, once France gained control of Damascus in 1920. Instead, they opted for a local patriotism added to Pan-Arab nationalism. Following a large Arab congress in December 1920, the Arab executive was born. Musa Kazim al-Husaini, former mayor of Jerusalem, was its chairman until his death in 1934. Although the Arab executive attempted to parallel the activities of the Zionist executive, it never had the latter's extensive resources or personnel. The Arab community was also internally divided and often quarrelsome. Without any effective political muscle or singleness of purpose, this fourth force could not compete effectively with any of the other three. It lost all real authority after 1934, as the al-Husainis and Nashashibis formed their own separate political parties and the radical nationalist Istiqlal (Independence) Party, a pan-Syrian group, emerged. A women's political movement founded in 1929 demonstrated, signed petitions, aided prisoners, and generally helped mobilize support for the Arab nationalists among urban, upper- and middle-class Muslim and Christian women.

In addition to the Arab executive, the British created the Supreme Muslim Council in 1921 to deal with Muslim religious affairs, especially custody of awqaf and administration of Muslim courts. Fines, fees, and patronage gave the Supreme Muslim Council considerable power, and its president, the Mufti Hajj Amin al-Husaini (1895–1974), chosen in 1921, became the leading Muslim political figure in Palestine in the 1930s. A position held for life, the mufti of Jerusalem, like muftis in other cities, gave legal opinions on Islamic shariah.

With four governments in Palestine, each with several parties or groups, and with the eyes of the world on the Holy Land of three religions, Sir Herbert Samuel, who was personally a pro-Zionist English politician, found the task of governing the League of Nations mandate a challenge to human ingenuity. He had to remember Britain's imperial concern for Palestine and the entire Middle East. He had to govern the mandate cheaply and peacefully. He had to fulfill the mission of the mandatory power in instructing the people, most of them Arabs, and in preparing the way for self-government and independence. And he had to follow the instructions of the cabinet in London, which was persistently dogged by political pressure to honor not only the letter of the Balfour Declaration but also its spirit as interpreted by the Zionists, who were already building the foundations for a national state of Israel. The dilemmas posed kept the political scene in Palestine shifting, with first one faction and then another playing the leading role.

Immigration Policies

No other issues weighed more heavily on Palestine than immigration and population. Zionist leaders, who wished to obtain a Jewish majority as quickly as possible, encouraged mass immigration. When a majority was achieved, Great Britain would be asked to relinquish its mandate, and Palestine would become an independent Jewish national state.

From 1920 to May 1921, nearly 10,000 Jewish immigrants entered Palestine. Immigration was suspended then because of serious Arab riots, but a month later immigration was permitted to continue. Winston Churchill, then colonial secretary, announced in a famous memorandum of July 1922 that Britain intended to honor the Balfour Declaration and to allow the Jewish community to increase its numbers through immigration. The pledge, however, would be interpreted so that the volume of immigration should not exceed the economic capacity of Palestine to absorb new arrivals.

In practice, however, it was relatively easy to obtain an entry permit. Immigration increased rapidly, and nearly 35,000 Jews entered in 1925. From 1927 until 1933, however, the number arriving in Palestine did not always offset those leaving. By 1931 there were about 775,000 Muslim Arabs, 90,000 Christian Arabs, and 175,000 Jews. Beginning in 1933 entries rose sharply and in several different years reached 40,000 per year. About half the immigrants were women, a higher proportion than in the past. Many Jewish visitors remained in Palestine illegally, so that the precise number "ingathered" between 1920 and 1939 was unknown, but it was well over 300,000. The total Jewish population rose to about 460,000 in 1939, versus 950,000 Muslims and 120,000 Christians; the Jews were therefore almost 30 percent of the total population, whereas the Muslim and Christian Arabs constituted a large majority of 70 percent. Arab influx and natural growth through a high birthrate did not keep pace with the Jews, who depended primarily on immigrants to keep pace in their desperate population race.

Whenever immigration reached high figures, riots between Arabs and Jews resulted, and the gates would be barred for a few months. Then political pressure in London resulted in the order's being rescinded. Principles of economic absorptive capacity were constantly discussed, but how to apply them and by what standard they could be judged were never determined. To the Zionist organization, any limitation on ingathering appeared fatal to the whole nationalist movement.

Land Policies

A large majority of Jews settling in Palestine came from urban centers in Europe. Yet one of the underlying philosophies of Zionism called for an agricultural society in Palestine, and workers on the land enjoyed an honored position in Zionist society. Zionists pledged that Arab tenant farmers would not be driven from lands purchased by their Jewish National Fund, but this guarantee proved impossible to fulfill. Some of the very best lands in Palestine were purchased at inflated prices from Arab absentee landlords living in Damascus and Beirut. Arab peasants were adversely affected by poor harvests and falling prices for wheat and other products in the 1930s. They also had to deal with uncertain ownership deeds, locusts, indebtedness, droughts, and a rising population that put great pressure on the available land.

Land bought by the National Fund was the inalienable property of the Jewish community, with the provision that only Jews might work the land or be employed upon it. Some Arab tenant farmers who had lived in villages and tilled the land about them were evicted, sometimes summarily. Each tenant farmer feared he would be the next and reacted vigorously against any Jewish immigration.

Land was expensive in Palestine because the population was relatively dense already and in order to expand the cultivable area a considerable outlay of funds was required. In the 1930s farm land cost, on average, about four times what it did in the United States, and the wages of farm labor were so high that general agriculture on a commercial basis was not feasible. Very few private individual farms were set up. The Jewish National Fund purchased most of the farm land and rented it at nominal fees to farmers, who would live in a private village or colony (moshavah), a cooperative village (moshav ovdim), or a collective village (kibbutz). The kibbutz movement reflected an idealistic socialism, which came to serve as an inspiration to many of the Jewish immigrants. Cultivation of citrus fruits was encouraged, and in the years before 1939, annual exports reached 10 million cases, providing Palestine with most of its earned foreign exchange.

The improved agricultural development had a marked effect on the Arab rural community. In the 1930s about 40 percent of citrus exports came from Arab lands. Hill country land that could not be farmed by mechanized equipment was shunned by the Zionist organization and left to Arab peasants. It was marginal farming at best, but the tax structure of the administration bore heavily on the peasants who worked these lands, and their poverty was sharply depicted against the higher Jewish standard of living.

Economic Progress

Up to 1936 the overall economy of Palestine increased substantially, but the rate of growth for Jews was about twice that for Arabs. About three-fourths of the Jews lived in urban communities, whereas only about one-fourth of the Arabs lived in cities or towns. A majority of Jews who worked outside the home were in the service sector; most Arabs were peasant farmers. Per capita income for Jews was roughly two and one-half times that of Arabs. At the end of World War I, Tel Aviv was a small town of 2000 inhabitants on the outskirts of Jaffa; in 1939 it contained over 150,000 inhabitants and was called "the only purely Jewish city in the world." Much of the industry was located there, and it became the center of artistic and cultural life in Jewish Palestine. The Zionist organization had difficulties in persuading immigrants from European cities to settle in rural agricultural villages after they had been sheltered in Tel Aviv.

A relatively large amount of industry developed in Palestine, thanks in part to protectionist tariffs on imports adopted by the government. Up to 1939, industry supplied mostly the local market. Exports from Dead Sea potash and chemical industries were just beginning to show in the trade statistics. Exports of soap made by Arabs were hurt when Egypt applied tariffs to them. In 1935 the pipeline from Iraq began to discharge oil at its terminus in Haifa, but only a small amount was refined locally. Palestinians had visions of supplying the industrial needs of a wide area in the Middle East, but at that time they could not meet even local requirements.

The industrial and labor picture in Palestine was dominated by the General Federation of Jewish Labor (Histadrut), founded in 1920. Owning and operating a number of industries, the Histadrut represented about three-fourths of the Jewish male and female workers, whose wages were higher than those of nonmembers. Most Arab laborers were unorganized, and the obvious wage disparity and discrimination in favor of Jewish workers led to bitter feelings. Yet unemployment figures were low, and many regulations against hiring Arabs were ignored. For example, by 1935 only 28 percent of the labor on Jewish orange plantations was Jewish.

Social and Financial Developments

On social and cultural endeavors, the Zionist organization and many individuals and groups expended much time, effort, and money. From the outset, education was deemed most important. The cornerstone of Hebrew University in Jerusalem was laid in 1918. Schools of every description—primary, secondary, teacher training, vocational, agricultural—came into existence, and before 1939 most Jewish children received at least a primary education. Hospitals, clinics, maternity and infant care, medical research laboratories, and public health campaigns also received much attention. Contributions from abroad, particularly the United States, enabled the Jewish community to maintain a level of public services comparable to those of Western society.

The revival of the Hebrew language as an everyday, spoken language was a major accomplishment of the Jewish settlers in Palestine. Many Jews already knew or learned Arabic, but only a very few Arabs learned Hebrew. Fine arts, theater, newspapers, and writers, such as S. Y. Agnon and Martin Buber, flourished. The Palestine Orchestra and a state radio broadcasting service began in 1936.

Palestinian Arab writers often emphasized Arab nationalism and anti-Zionism, and they used primarily such media as newspaper stories, essays, pamphlets, literary journals, poetry, short stories, and histories. Writers continued to use earlier forms and genres; they did not take an active role in the literary innovations that began to affect poetry and prose in Egypt, Lebanon, and Iraq in the 1930s. Arif al-Arif of Jerusalem epitomized many Arab intellectuals: he founded a newspaper, served in the Palestine civil service, and wrote many histories of towns and cities in that country, including one of Jerusalem.

Public funds from the Palestine government for social services to help the Arab majority of the population were insignificant, though most students who attended government schools were Arabs. Private Arab religious organizations helped meet some unfulfilled needs in the funding of orphanages, health facilities, and education. Life expectancy for men and women increased as infant mortality fell. Many Arabs moved from the villages to the cities, or they continued to live in villages but worked in nearby towns.

The activities of the Zionist organization in purchasing land, supporting new immigrants, building schools and hospitals, and starting industries were made possible by contributions from world Jewry. About $400 million was the cost of the Zionist development in Palestine between 1919 and 1939. Annual exports in the last years before World War II reached only $4 million, most of which were receipts from the citrus industry, while annual imports were more than four times as great. A significant number of settlers brought capital with them in the form of foreign exchange, enabling Palestine to live with this imbalance of imports over exports. Palestine never approached a self-supporting status, and only foreign gifts stabilized Jewish society at a standard of living far above what the country's resources could produce. The worldwide depression initially brought emigration from Palestine. Only the advent of Adolf Hitler to power in Germany and the accompanying Jewish emigration from central Europe saved the Zionist program for Palestine.

TRANSJORDAN

East of the Jordan River, Britain dealt primarily with the Arab inhabitants and Hashimite Pan-Arab aspirations. Although some Zionists believed that territory should also be part of the Jewish national home, most Jewish settlement and interest was centered on the land west of the Jordan. Since the area east of the river was promised during World War I to the Arabs and Sharif Husain, the British found it good policy to grant the administration of that land to Prince (Amir) Abd Allah (1882–1951), who had threatened to attack the French in Damascus. Accordingly, Transjordan was given to Abd Allah in 1921. In 1922 the League of Nations Council exempted it from many provisions of the mandate for Palestine, particularly those referring to the Balfour Declaration and Zionist settlement. The following year in Amman, capital of Transjordan, Sir Herbert Samuel and Abd Allah announced the government of Transjordan, now to be autonomous and separate from the administration of Palestine.

England nevertheless remained in control in many ways. From 1921 onward, the British provided about two-thirds of all Jordanian revenue. Still, Abd Allah could build on a basis for government already established by the prior Ottoman administration. He cleverly managed his relations with the large tribes, securing the cooperation of some shaikhs and mildly punishing others who were contemptuous of government authority. In 1926, Abd Allah convened a group of Arab notables to prepare the way for an elective legislative assembly. In 1927, petitions were submitted to him demanding a national representative council and freedom from British rule. To meet this pressure on Abd Allah, a treaty was concluded in 1928 between Great Britain and the amirate of Transjordan. Legislation and administration in Transjordan were exercised by the prince under authority of the British high commissioner for Palestine through the British resident stationed in Amman. The British were to control the budget, finances, army, economic development, and foreign affairs. Shortly after, Abd Allah issued a constitution providing for a legislative council, which first met in 1929. Some seats in the council were reserved for the Christian minority and the nomadic tribes. Many government officials were not originally from Jordan; they, like Abd Allah, remained Pan-Arab nationalists, who favored the creation of a much larger Arab state under the Hashimite dynasty.

Britain helped Abd Allah establish as his army the Arab Legion, organized in 1923, which defended the frontiers from foreign Bedouin infiltration. Originally it had no desert section and no airplanes, but after 1930 it expanded and blossomed into one of the most significant military forces in the Middle East. Although under the command of the prince of Transjordan, it received five-sixths of its financial requirements directly from the British treasury. The army was the instrument of the British government in the Middle East, but it also provided useful services to Transjordanians. It protected the frontiers of Palestine, Transjordan, and Iraq from raids by Abd al-Aziz (Ibn Saud) of Arabia, and it maintained and policed the corridor between Iraq and Transjordan through which ran the oil pipeline from Iraq to Palestine. The nomadic raids stopped, and Transjordan's borders were accepted by the Saudis.

After the droughts of the 1920s ended, with security better established and new transportation methods available, agriculture expanded as nomads, who had constituted about half of the total population in the 1920s, turned to raising sheep rather than camels. A government cadastral survey gave the peasants and many newly settled nomads more surety of landownership, thereby securing their loyalty.

Transjordan not only was an anchor for the British position in the Middle East but also stood as an important link in its empire. Prince Abd Allah performed well for the British, and they sustained him in a dignified manner, while his policies consolidated the state and aided the people. Abd Allah maintained links with Palestinian political leaders, and the Arab population on both sides of the Jordan River had many interconnections. Although Transjordan was a separate administrative area, with its own government and an increasing sense of identity, its fate was linked closely to that of Palestine.

BRITISH ADMINISTRATION IN PALESTINE

As Transjordan was being severed from the Palestine mandate, during the years from 1920 to 1928 only one serious outbreak of violence, in 1921, occurred between Jews and Arabs. Perhaps a recurrence of the riots was averted by Churchill's White Paper of 1922, which promised the Arab community that nothing would be done to jeopardize Arab rights. Outward peace reigned, and political passions seemed to have cooled.

The League of Nations on July 24, 1922, finally approved the mandate for Palestine; it incorporated the Balfour Declaration in the preamble and recognized the historic association of the Jewish people with Palestine. The League instructed Great Britain to recognize the Zionist organization and to facilitate Jewish immigration and "close settlement by Jews on the land" without prejudicing the "rights and position of other sections of the population." English, Arabic, and Hebrew were designated as official languages. Article 25 of the mandate allowed Britain to exempt all the land of Palestine east of the Jordan River from the execution of some provisions of the mandate.

The terms of the mandate were not easy to fulfill. Every high commissioner from 1920 to 1939 tried to comply with the instructions, but each one discovered how difficult it was to follow the dictates of the colonial office in London, to cooperate with the Zionists, and to maintain Arab rights. British officials in Palestine tended to be anti-Zionist, whereas some central government officials in London were pro-Zionist.

The British attempted to have a constitution adopted and a legislature elected, but they often found Arab leaders, and sometimes Jewish leaders as well, unwilling to cooperate.

Through political boycott and threats to riot, the Arabs hoped to obtain British recognition that their majority entitled them to control any institutions of self-government. Although a currency linked to Britain's pound sterling and an independent Supreme Court were successfully created, most of the time the citizens of Palestine, both Jews and Arabs, lived their lives divided from each other, with few bonds of common identity to bridge their increasingly violent differences. Therefore, no constitution, legislature, or national government came into existence.

THE JEWISH AGENCY

In 1929 the Zionist Congress voted to create the Jewish Agency in Palestine, which would, it was hoped, attract support from cultural as well as political Zionists. Chaim Weizmann (1874–1952), who was the president of the Zionist organization, also served as the president of the Jewish Agency. In actual practice, the Jewish Agency drew in more and more Jews to support its ambitions, finally committing most Jews to the full program.

In addition to the non-Zionist Jews of the Western world who desired full integration into society in Western nation-states, two Jewish groups were opposed to the policies of the Jewish Agency. The more numerous was composed of the rigidly orthodox in Palestine and elsewhere, who felt that the Zionist program, being nationalistic, destroyed the religious basis of Judaism. The other group, led by Vladimir Jabotinsky (1880–1940), rebelled against the Zionist organization's acceptance of the Churchill White Paper of 1922. Calling themselves the revisionists, they demanded immediate fulfillment by the Palestinian government of the national home on both sides of the Jordan River, appealed especially to middle-class Jews, and condemned the inclusion of non-Zionists, whom they regarded as traitors.

THE PASSFIELD WHITE PAPER

Although British armed forces had been reduced as an unnecessary financial burden, the vocal outbursts of these revisionists, along with disturbances in 1928 near the Western Wall, frightened the Arabs and made them more concerned with Muslim rights along the Wall, which was part of the retaining wall around the area containing the Dome of the Rock. (The Wall is all that remains of the structure built near the Second Temple after its destruction by the Romans in antiquity.) Muslim Arabs, agitated by a poor harvest, irritated Jewish worshippers by disturbing religious services. Precedent had been employed for centuries to stake a claim to control areas in Jerusalem, and Arab acts, which to Jews and Westerners seemed intentional aggravations, were efforts to maintain legal rights.

Hostilities broke out in August 1929. A group of young Zionists sang the Zionist anthem and raised their flag at the Western Wall. The next day a Muslim ceremony took place at the same spot, with minor disturbances occurring. In Jerusalem a Jewish boy kicked his football into an Arab tomato patch, and a fight ensued in which the boy was stabbed. Rioting continued for several days; Muslims attacked Jews, and troops were called from Egypt and Transjordan. Jews invaded a mosque in Jerusalem, killing the imam. Later the same day, a Muslim shrine was damaged and the tombs of the prophets desecrated. The British condemned the Arab leadership for the outrages. Over 130 Jews and 116 Arabs were killed, and the mandatory government sentenced twenty-five Arabs and one Jew to death.

Britain and the League of Nations sent out commissions to make recommendations to avert future outbreaks. In 1930 Lord Passfield (Sidney Webb), the British colonial secretary, issued his famous White Paper outlining British policy on Palestine. The Passfield White Paper repeated the same general view presented in 1922 by the Churchill White Paper and emphasized the equal responsibility of the Palestine government to the Jewish and non-Jewish populations. Attention was drawn to the "economic absorptive capacity" of Palestine, and the statement also differentiated between a Jewish national home and a Jewish nationalist state.

Passfield indicated that additional armed forces would be stationed in Palestine for greater security. He condemned the Arabs for noncooperation in establishing a legislative council and promised that steps would be taken to give some self-government to Palestine. The White Paper stressed the poor condition of Arab peasants. It stated that the immediate task of the Palestine administration would be to assist agricultural progress of the Arabs and to close Jewish immigration if it prevented any Arab from obtaining employment.

The storm of protest that arose from the Zionist camp was serious. Pressure on the British government moved the prime minister to write a letter in 1931 to Dr. Weizmann, severely weakening the White Paper. Then the Arabs were up in arms, and the Palestine Arab executive denounced the letter as a breach of faith. British indecision and wavering invited many Arab leaders of the Middle East to reason that the Passfield White Paper resulted from the Arab outbreak of August 1929 and that the prime minister's letter stemmed from Jewish agitation against the White Paper. British prestige suffered; the rewards of violence and threats appeared consequential. Under such conditions, a peaceful future for Palestine looked rather bleak.

PEEL REPORT

Although the political situation remained unsettled, the economic boom into which Palestine entered gave optimists an opportunity to assert that all was well, despite the world depression. Jewish immigration picked up, agricultural and industrial production jumped, government revenue trebled and then quadrupled, citrus cultivation spread, and new capital investments gave greater opportunities for labor, which in turn kept wages at a high level. After 1932, the arrival of German Jewish artisans and capitalists in flight from Hitler provided greater stimulus to the boom.

Legal and illegal immigration swelled. The amazing growth of the Jewish community in the years between 1933 and 1936 affected even remote Arab villages in the hill country of Palestine. Arab peasants shared in some of the economic opportunities of the time, but the amount of land they owned per capita declined in the 1930s and rural poverty was widespread. Arab political leadership coalesced into one united group, which called itself the Arab Higher Committee.

The Arabs in 1935 petitioned the high commissioner to establish democratic government in accordance with the Covenant of the League of Nations and to prohibit Jewish immigration. In response, the British presented details of a legislative council with Arab, Jewish, and British official representation. The Arabs announced they would cooperate; the Jews declared they would not. Outnumbered, they feared they would lose on the immigration issue. It was far better, they thought, to delay self-government for a few years more until a Jewish majority was achieved. The Zionist cause was supported by the English House of Commons. In April 1936 the high commissioner acknowledged that plans for self-government were postponed. At a time when Arab nationalists were moving toward greater independence or increased autonomy in Iraq, Syria, Lebanon, and Egypt, peaceful persuasion in Palestine failed to bring similar concessions.

Violence in Palestine came first from the Arab peasant population, both men and women. Only later was it directed by the Arab Higher Committee. Rioting began and continued in a sporadic way for many months. Strikes ensued, many groups refused to pay taxes, and before the end of April 1936, a general Arab strike spread to all Palestine. The Arab Higher Committee declared the strike would continue until the British agreed to grant self-government, halt Jewish immigration, and prohibit transfer of Arab lands to Jews. Arab rebels, joined by volunteers from Arab states, fought in the hills, and by the end of 1936 there was a full-scale revolt. Bombings and property destruction were frequent, and there were as many attacks directed against the British as against the Zionists.

Palestine had grown important to the British Empire with regard to air routes to Asia and Africa, sea lanes through Suez and the Mediterranean, and oil deliveries from Iraq. The security of these interests was presented to the British public as dependent on the success of Zionism in Palestine. Sentiment in Turkey, Iraq, Egypt, and India sided with the Arabs. Poland and the United States, each with large Jewish groups, pressed England to favor the Zionists.

Great Britain sought to pacify Palestine by sending Earl Peel as head of a commission of inquiry. In October 1936, on pleas from the kings of Iraq and Saudi Arabia—both at that time subservient to British pressure—the Arab Higher Committee called off the strike without obtaining its demands. Zionism and Britain won, but only by giving neighboring Arab governments an active hand in Palestinian Arab affairs.

Without too much difficulty the Peel Report concluded in 1937 that an "irrepressible conflict" had arisen over the question: "Who, ultimately, would rule the country?" The report recommended the division of Palestine and proceeded to suggest frontiers and conditions of partition.

The partition scheme was bitterly assailed by Zionists and by Arabs. Zionists, while not shutting the door on the idea of partition, argued that partition had already been enacted when Transjordan was cut off and that further decrease of the national home was contrary to the mandate. The Arab Higher Committee denounced the principle of partition. With unlimited immigration, the Jewish state would become overpopulated and demand more space from the Arabs. To Arabs, any partition was unreasonable and in violation of the mandate and the Covenant of the League of Nations.

Pursuing the suggestions given in the Peel Report, the Palestine administration curtailed Jewish immigration and used a firmer hand against the Arabs. In 1937, Hajj Amin al-Husaini was removed from the presidency of the Supreme Muslim Council and five of the Higher Committee were deported. (Hajj Amin escaped to Lebanon.) These acts accelerated the Arab rebellion and guerrilla warfare against the British, although numerous attacks on the Jewish community also occurred. To defend themselves, the Jews, with the approval of the authorities, greatly expanded their illegal force, the Haganah, which totaled over 10,000 men, well trained and well armed by the Jewish Agency.

CIVIL WAR

Palestine was in open revolt as bands of Arab rebels attacked police stations. By October 1938 even the Old City of Jerusalem was occupied by the rebels. The Irgun, an illegal and secret national military organization set up by the revisionist Zionists, perpetrated many attacks on the Arabs, and the Haganah increased its membership.

These events coincided with the pressure of Hitler on Czechoslovakia, the Munich Pact, and the decline of British prestige. Nazi Germany and Fascist Italy showered propaganda on the Arabs of Palestine, and England quickly realized how vulnerable its position with the Arab states had become. The new colonial secretary declared that plans for partition were being dropped and invited Arabs and Jews to a conference in London.

Representatives of Egypt, Iraq, Transjordan, Saudi Arabia, Yemen, and Palestine Arabs—Husainis and Nashashibis—came from the Arab side. Representatives of the Jewish Agency and Zionist and non-Zionist Jewish groups from Great Britain, the United States, France, and other countries filled out the roster. The conference opened in early 1939. In essence the British proposed (first to the Arabs and then to the Jews, since the two groups would not sit down with each other) a considerable reduction in Jewish immigration and land purchases and the establishment of a single self-governing Palestine after ten years. The Jews refused to discuss the question further and left, since the terms ruled that Arabs would comprise two-thirds of the population and Jews would forever be a minority in Palestine. Although more favorably disposed, the Arabs declined to accept the proposals because they did not go far enough toward curbing the Zionist presence.

Rebuffed on both sides and with time running out in Europe, Great Britain issued still another White Paper, on May 17, 1939, declaring its unilateral solution of the Palestine dilemma. Partition was rejected, and about 75,000 Jewish immigrants would be allowed to enter Palestine over the next five years; then the doors would be open only with Arab consent. Land sales from Arabs to Jews would be strictly regulated. After ten years, self-rule would be established on lines similar to those already prevailing in Iraq.

The Arab Higher Committee opposed this solution, asking for independence at the beginning rather than the end of the ten-year period. Remembering how the Churchill and Passfield White Papers were disowned by British governments when Jewish pressure was applied, the Arabs could not believe that this White Paper would have a different ending. Jews in Palestine and Zionists throughout the world denounced the White Paper as a treacherous document. David Ben-Gurion (1886–1973), leader of the Histadrut, who had taken over from Weizmann as chairman of the Jewish Agency executive, urged that Jews defy Britain and act in Palestine as though the Jewish Agency were the state.

The history of Palestine in the two decades between the world wars had three component parts: Zionists, Arabs, and the British. Zionists worked hard with great faith, courage, and determination to build the Jewish national home in Palestine. They established institutions as prerequisites for eventual independence and self-government. Zionists also accomplished much abroad by building up support for their goals. Many Zionists ignored, however, the fact that they were viewed by the Palestinian Arabs as intruders in another people's home, and they were insensitive to the distrust and fear they generated in Arab hearts.

Palestinian Arab nationalists believed that an Arab independent state had been promised them. Since Arabs in Egypt, Saudi Arabia, Yemen, and Iraq were independent or were in the process of gaining their independence, was it not strange that they, the Arabs of Palestine, did not have similar freedom? The Arabs, however, suffered from a leadership that mistakenly judged that violence would intimidate the Jews and the British into giving the Arabs independence. Arabs did not establish the institutions of self-government as effectively as did the Zionists.

The third component, the British, saw no profit in investing in Palestine when its permanence within the empire was doubtful and considering how few natural resources it possessed. Instead, the chief British goal was strategic military, political, and economic control. British policy gained enmity on all sides as it failed to meet fully the expectations of either the Zionist or Arab community in Palestine.

Contrary to the general goals of the mandate system of the League of Nations, by 1939 in Palestine the preconditions for national unity, independence, and harmonious self-government did not exist, although the special pro-Zionist provisions of the Palestine mandate had been partially met. In Palestine two rival communities were poised for a continuation of their conflict; in Transjordan the Hashimite ruler, Abd Allah, was consolidating the bases for statehood and possible expansion. The situation in Palestine dramatically changed when World War II broke out in Europe in 1939. Zionists and Arabs alike recognized that the ultimate outcome of the struggle among the great powers would be the determining factor for their future.

REFERENCES

Many works discussing the Middle East in modern times bear some relationship to the events related in this chapter. Of special note are those cited in Chapters 25, 26, 27, 31, and 35.

Abu-Ghazaleh, Adnan Mohammed: *Arab Cultural Nationalism in Palestine during the British Mandate.* Beirut: Institute for Palestine Studies, 1973. One of the very few sources for this topic.

Abu-Lughod, Ibrahim, ed.: *The Transformation of Palestine: Essays on the Origin and Development of the Arab-Israel Conflict.* Evanston, Ill.: Northwestern University Press, 1971. Sixteen scholars discuss the resistance to Zionism among the Arabs during the mandate. Generally sympathetic to the Arabs.

Aruri, Naseer H.: *Jordan: A Study in Political Development (1921–1965).* The Hague: Nijhoff, 1972. Offers insight into the interdependence of domestic and international politics.

Bickerton, Ian J., and Carla L. Klausner: *A Concise History of the Arab-Israeli Conflict.* 4th ed. Upper Saddle River, N.J.: Prentice Hall, 2002. A balanced short survey with excerpts from key documents.

Cohen, Michael J.: *The Origins and Evolution of the Arab-Zionist Conflict.* Berkeley: University of California Press, 1987. A concise and well-written study, especially valuable in regard to British policy up to 1948.

Divine, Donna Robinson: *Politics and Society in Ottoman Palestine: The Arab Struggle for Survival and Power.* Boulder, Colo.: Lynne Rienner, 1994. A useful summary for the period 1800 to 1914.

Farsoun, Samih K., and Christina E. Zacharia: *Palestine and the Palestinians.* Boulder, Colo.: Westview, 1997. A political economy approach to the history of Palestinian Arabs in the twentieth century.

Fischbach, Michael R.: *State, Society and Land in Jordan.* Leiden, The Netherlands: Brill, 2000. This valuable discussion of land ownership, 1851–1967, and especially the consequences of the cadastral survey, is based on exhaustive research.

Fleischmann, Ellen L.: "The Emergence of the Palestinian Women's Movement, 1929–39." *Journal of Palestine Studies* 29 (2000): 16–32.

Graves, Philip P., ed.: *Memoirs of King Abdullah of Transjordan.* New York: Philosophical Library, 1950. Covers the important events of the king's early life.

Kamen, Charles S.: *Little Common Ground: Arab Agriculture and Jewish Settlement in Palestine, 1920–1948.* Pittsburgh, Penn.: University of Pittsburgh Press, 1991. A balanced account of Arab society, Jewish settlers, landholding, and changes in agriculture.

Kayyali, A. W.: *Palestine: A Modern History.* London: Croom Helm, 1978. A political history ending basically in 1939 written from the point of view of the Palestinian Arabs. Shows the emergence of new leaders for that community in the 1930s.

Khalidi, Walid: *Before Their Diaspora: A Photographic History of the Palestinians, 1876–1948.* Washington, D.C.: Institute for Palestine Studies, 1984. Excellent commentary as well as photographs.

Laqueur, Walter: *A History of Zionism.* New ed. New York: Schocken, 1989. A new edition of the 1972 work; a sympathetic but not uncritical account of the prestate period.

Lesch, Ann Mosely: *Arab Politics in Palestine, 1917–1939: The Frustration of a Nationalist Movement.* Ithaca, N.Y.: Cornell University Press, 1979. The best discussion of the subject.

McCarthy, Justin: *The Population of Palestine: Population History and Statistics of the Late Ottoman Period and the Mandate.* New York: Columbia University Press, 1990. A sophisticated analysis by the leading demographic historian of the Middle East.

Mattar, Philip: *The Mufti of Jerusalem: Al-Hajj Amin al-Husayni and the Palestinian National Movement.* Rev. ed. New York: Columbia University Press, 1992. A well-researched account of the life of this very controversial figure.

Metzer, Jacob: *The Divided Economy of Mandatory Palestine.* Cambridge, England: Cambridge University Press, 1998. Convincingly argues that the two communities had separate though occasionally interacting economies.

Miller, Ylana N.: *Government and Society in Rural Palestine, 1920–1948.* Austin: University of Texas Press, 1985. Important coverage of village education.

Morris, Benny: *Righteous Victims: A History of the Zionist-Arab Conflict, 1881–1999.* New York: Alfred A. Knopf, 1999. A massive history concentrating on political, diplomatic, and military events.

Muslih, Muhammad Y.: *The Origins of Palestinian Nationalism.* New York: Columbia University Press, 1988. Traces the early stages of Palestinian Arab identity.

Near, Henry: *The Kibbutz Movement: A History.* Vol. 1: *Origins and Growth, 1909–1939.* New York: Oxford University Press, 1992. A fine history of organizations and the reality of daily life.

Porath, Y.: *The Emergence of the Palestinian-Arab National Movement, 1918–1929.* London: Frank Cass, 1974. A brilliant monograph on the foundations of the Palestinian cause; this work is completed by a book by the same author published in 1978.

Sachar, Howard M.: *A History of Israel from the Rise of Zionism to Our Time.* 2d ed. New York: Alfred A. Knopf, 1996. An excellent general study.

Salibi, Kamal: *The Modern History of Jordan.* 2d ed. New York: Tauris, 1998. Places the political history of Jordan into its broader context; a useful introduction.

Segev, Tom: *One Palestine Complete: Jews and Arabs under the British Mandate.* Translated by Haim Watzman. New York: Henry Holt, 2000. A lengthy work that illuminates the era by focusing on individual experiences.

Shepherd, Naomi: *Ploughing Sand: British Rule in Palestine, 1917–1948.* New Brunswick, N.J.: Rutgers University Press, 2000. Concentrates on British administration, especially education, immigration, health, and security.

Smith, Barbara J.: *The Roots of Separatism in Palestine: British Economic Policy, 1920–1929.* Syracuse, N.Y.: Syracuse University Press, 1993. Shows how British policy favored the creation of a separate Zionist economy in land, immigration, commerce, labor, and industry.

Smith, Charles D.: *Palestine and the Arab-Israeli Conflict.* 4th ed. Boston: Bedford/St. Martin's, 2001. An outstanding survey of the subject with excerpts from original sources.

Stein, Kenneth W.: *The Land Question in Palestine, 1917–1939.* Chapel Hill: University of North Carolina Press, 1984. A meticulous work of scholarship; shows the actual procedures of land sales and their political ramifications.

———: "A Historiographic Review of Literature on the Origins of the Arab-Israeli Conflict." *American Historical Review* 96 (1991): 1450–1465. A useful essay on the vast bibliography dealing with the late Ottoman period to 1948.

Tessler, Mark: *A History of the Israeli-Palestinian Conflict.* Bloomington: Indiana University Press, 1994. This lengthy general study of the issue carefully analyzes the views and actions of each side.

Teveth, Shabtai: *Ben-Gurion: The Burning Ground, 1886–1948.* Boston: Houghton Mifflin, 1987.

Weizmann, Chaim: *Trial and Error: The Autobiography of Chaim Weizmann.* New York: Harper, 1949. The life of the leader of Zionism during the mandate period.

Wilson, Mary C.: *King Abdullah, Britain and the Making of Jordan.* Cambridge, England: Cambridge University Press, 1987. A systematic and thorough evaluation of Abd Allah's role.

CHAPTER 37

World War II and the Middle East

Although World War I had a greater impact on the Middle East than World War II did, some parts of the area were substantially affected by developments between 1939 and 1945. Most of the political units in the region initially were neutral. During the war, almost every Middle Eastern country underwent shortages of goods, inflation, and political strain. A majority of the countries outside the Arabian Peninsula became involved to a limited degree in combat; in North Africa, the fighting was on an immense scale.

The European aspect of World War II started in September 1939 as a war mostly between Nazi Germany versus Britain and France. Following the fall of France to Germany and Fascist Italy in June 1940, two French governments existed: a pro-German neutral French government at Vichy and a Free French movement in London under the leadership of Charles de Gaulle. In 1940–1941 Germany and its allies conquered most of the continent of Europe, including the Balkans, before invading the Soviet Union in June 1941. Britain and the Soviets thus became allies. As a result of the Japanese attack on American and British territories in December 1941, added to the ongoing Japanese war with China, a worldwide war existed. From 1942 to 1945 the chief participants were the Axis powers (chiefly Japan, Germany, and Italy) against the Allies (chiefly the United States, Soviet Union, Britain, China, and Free France). As the Allies defeated the Axis in North Africa, Italy, Eastern Europe, occupied France, and finally Germany and Japan, they planned a new international organization, the United Nations, to replace the old League of Nations.

TURKISH NEUTRALITY

Remembering the catastrophe of World War I for the Ottoman Empire, Turkey again declared neutrality on the outbreak of World War II, but this time with a leadership determined to preserve it. Yet its position was not clear-cut. President Inönü's foreign policy had been veering toward Britain and France. On the other hand, almost 50 percent of Turkish trade was with Nazi Germany. Furthermore, the Nazi-Soviet Pact of August

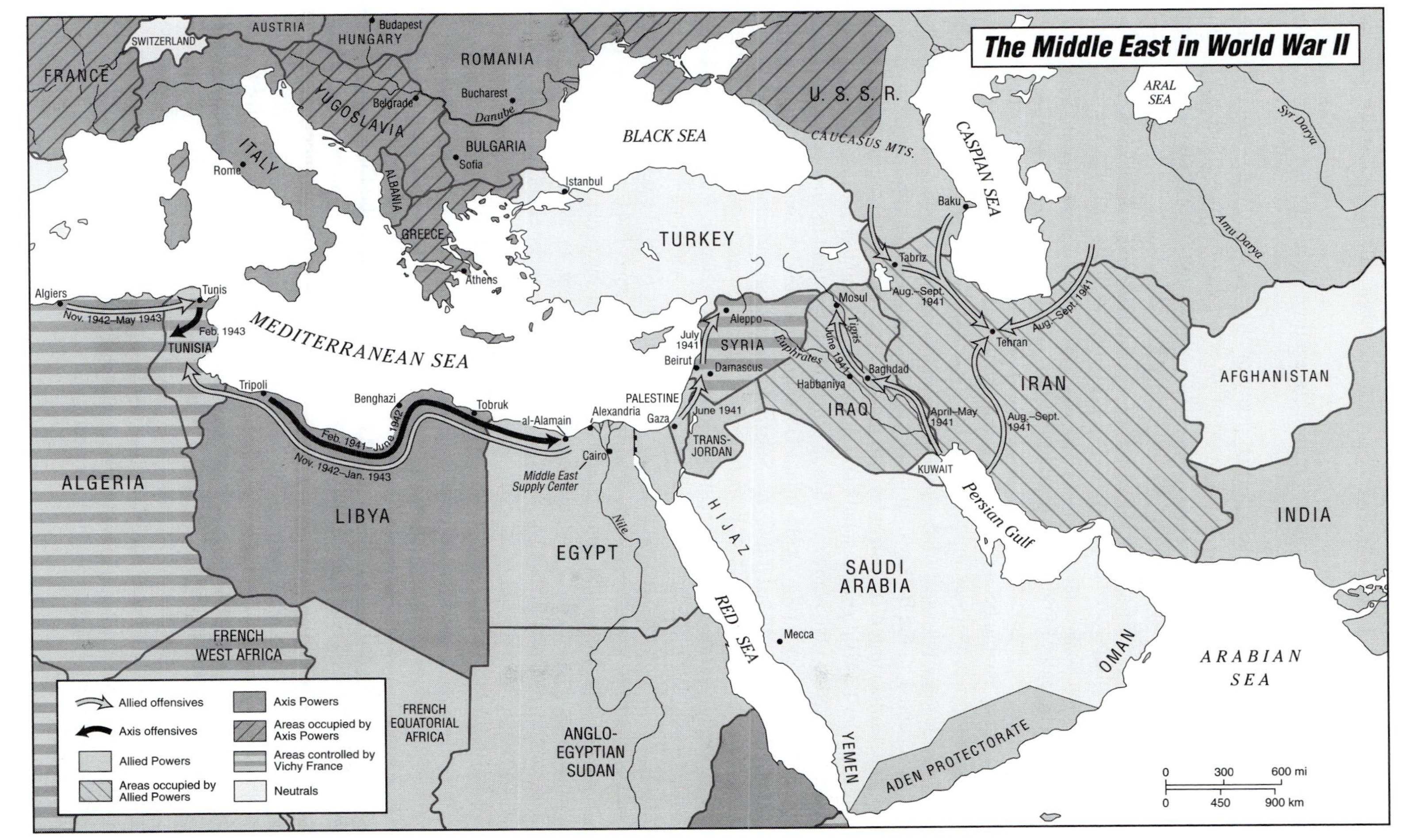
The Middle East in World War II
FRANCE
SWITZERLAND
AUSTRIA
Budapest
HUNGARY
ROMANIA
Bucharest
Danube
YUGOSLAVIA
Belgrade
BULGARIA
Sofia
ALBANIA
GREECE
Athens
ITALY
Rome
BLACK SEA
Istanbul
U. S. S. R.
CAUCASUS MTS.
CASPIAN SEA
Baku
ARAL SEA
Syr Darya
Amu Darya
TURKEY
Tabriz
Aug.–Sept. 1941
Aug.–Sept 1941
Tehran
IRAN
AFGHANISTAN
INDIA
Mosul
Tigris
June 1941
Baghdad
Habbaniya
IRAQ
April–May 1941
Aug.–Sept. 1941
KUWAIT
Persian Gulf
Aleppo
SYRIA
Euphrates
July 1941
Beirut
Damascus
PALESTINE
June 1941
Gaza
TRANS-JORDAN
MEDITERRANEAN SEA
Algiers
Nov. 1942–May 1943
Tunis
Feb. 1943
TUNISIA
Tripoli
Benghazi
Feb. 1941–June 1942
Nov. 1942–Jan. 1943
Tobruk
al-Alamain
Alexandria
Cairo
Middle East Supply Center
Nile
ALGERIA
LIBYA
EGYPT
HIJAZ
SAUDI ARABIA
RED SEA
Mecca
OMAN
ARABIAN SEA
YEMEN
ADEN PROTECTORATE
FRENCH WEST AFRICA
FRENCH EQUATORIAL AFRICA
ANGLO-EGYPTIAN SUDAN
Allied offensives
Axis offensives
Allied Powers
Areas occupied by Allied Powers
Axis Powers
Areas occupied by Axis Powers
Areas controlled by Vichy France
Neutrals
0 300 600 mi
0 450 900 km

1939 gave Turkish leadership every reason for caution, since Russian objectives were difficult to assess.

In October, Turkey signed a formal treaty of alliance with France and the United Kingdom. Its terms held that in the event of an act of aggression on Turkey, its allies would come to Turkey's assistance, that Turkey would enter the war should it come to the Mediterranean, but that under no circumstances would Turkey be drawn into a conflict against the Soviet Union. Britain also had an agreement, which ran until 1943, whereby it could purchase and export the entire output of Turkish chrome ore, essential for making steel.

Upon the fall of France and the entry of Italy into the war, the Turkish government reassessed its international position and decided to remain neutral. It was suspected that Russia, surely having been awarded Istanbul and the Straits by Hitler, might soon move to seize the prize, as it was already doing in Bessarabia. War came to the Mediterranean on Italy's declaration, but Turkey continued its neutrality as Italy and Germany and their allies occupied all the Balkans, up to the Turkish frontier in Europe.

The British urged Turkish entry into the war at the time of the German conquest of Greece. The Turkish leaders steadfastly refused. They pointed out that Britain was no more prepared to give planes and heavy armor to Turkey than to Greece and that recklessness on Turkey's part would invite German retaliation. Also, Turkey as a neutral would serve as a land barrier to Syria, Suez, and the Persian Gulf. Furthermore, the leaders could see no purely Turkish reason for joining in the war.

Hitler's invasion of Russia acutely disturbed Turkey, which feared that a German defeat would leave the Soviet Union the dominant continental power of Europe. The might of Germany from the middle of 1941 to the spring of 1943 awed Turkish leaders. Turkey signed a nonaggression pact with Germany in June 1941, although the Turks insisted on a statement that this pact did not contravene any previous Turkish commitments. Germany and Turkey concluded a trade agreement. In 1943, when the chrome agreement with Great Britain would expire, Germany would be enabled to purchase ore in exchange for war equipment. One reason for President Inönü's reluctance to ally Turkey fully with Britain was his doubts about the future goodwill of Joseph Stalin, the leader of the Soviet Union, with regard to the Straits.

British prime minister Winston Churchill repeatedly pressed the case for Turkish entry and for a concerted attack on Germany through the Balkans as the best way to defeat Germany and save central Europe and the Balkans from the Communists. Russia believed that Turkey should shoulder some of the burdens of the war. But Turkey steadfastly refused to abandon neutrality, recognizing that German bombers from bases in Bulgaria, only twenty minutes from Istanbul, could pulverize that city almost at will, since Turkey's small air force could not successfully defend it. The decisive veto on Churchill's plan was exercised by the United States, which argued that no weapons would be spared from the crucial cross-channel attack on German-occupied France.

In 1944, Turkish chrome shipments to Germany were halted; in August, Turkey severed diplomatic relations with Germany. Finally, in early 1945, in order to become a charter member of the United Nations, Turkey declared war on Germany. But for all practical purposes the war was over.

During the war years, the Turkish economy was subjected to constant pressure from all sides. At times more than 1 million men were under arms, and the Turkish budget called for vast military expenditures. Deficit financing brought inflation, price controls being either absent or ineffective, while the government forced peasants to sell it crops at low prices. Moreover, large sums were thrown about by spies from the belligerent powers. Extensive purchases of Turkish exports by both sides in the war gave Turkey great purchasing power. At this time the importation of consumer articles and capital goods was exceedingly difficult because of a general shipping shortage and the naval warfare in the Mediterranean.

Another cause of inflation was the policy of preemptive buying pursued by England and the United States in Turkey. Several hundred million dollars' worth of goods were bought and stored in Turkey for the sole purpose of keeping them from Germany. The end of the war found Turkey with a sizable fund of foreign exchange acquired from exports and sales that were not balanced by imports. Shipping became more plentiful, Turkish ports were opened, and Turkish products found a ready market in a world apparently short of almost everything.

Inflation and mounting deficits induced Inönü in 1942 to experiment with a capital levy tax in hopes of lowering prices, balancing the budget, and absorbing some of the abundance of money. A law authorized the creation of a special committee in each province to levy a tax on persons according to their capital. Particularly in Istanbul, gross inequalities developed. Greeks, Armenians, Jews, and foreigners were hard-pressed, some being assessed sums nearly equal to their total capital. Those who did not pay were sentenced to hard labor. Representatives of the Allied governments protested to Inönü, but the situation with regard to Turkish neutrality was delicate. Upon official pressure at the highest levels in wartime conferences in 1943, the tax was abolished and those who had not paid were released. The experience left an unpleasant residue of insecurity on the part of non-Muslim Turkish citizens, who regarded the tax as an expression of unbridled nationalism. On the other hand, Turkish diplomats provided considerable assistance to Jewish refugees from Nazi-held Europe.

For Turkey the war period was very difficult. Turkey wished to live in peace with the victorious powers, but during the course of the war, it was not always clear who would win. The standard of living of most Turks declined during the war years. Still, through armed vigilance, able and realistic diplomacy, good fortune, and prudent inaction, Inönü and the leaders of Turkey preserved the state and nation from the disasters that befell most of its neighbors.

OCCUPATION OF IRAN

At the outbreak of World War II, Iran under Reza Shah was deeply involved economically with Germany. Although Iran declared neutrality, official Iranian attitudes were mixed and occasionally pro-German until the Nazi invasion of the Soviet Union in 1941. Reza Shah was decidedly anti-Russian and anti-British, largely because of the imperialism of those powers in Iran's recent history. However, until 1941, Reza feared a Soviet invasion more, and he was willing to view the British as a possible makeweight against Soviet intervention backed by its ally, Germany.

Iran also swarmed with Axis officials, but Hitler's invasion of the Soviet Union in June 1941 changed the diplomatic situation in Iran almost overnight. In July, after the Anglo-Soviet agreement for mutual assistance, the two governments initiated joint pressure on Iran to force the large number of Germans in Iran to depart. Reza was furious at such requests, and no action was taken.

The United States and Britain wished to supply military equipment to the Soviet Union, and one of the few possible ways to do this was by shipping it through Iran, a violation of Iranian neutrality. Great Britain also wished to secure the safety of the Iranian oil fields, as well as those of neighboring Iraq. Also, Iran could not be permitted to become a tool of Germany. After issuing several ultimatums, Britain and the Soviet Union invaded Iran on August 25, 1941. Iran offered resistance for two days, until a new government ordered submission. Since Reza was still defiant, Allied forces occupied Tehran. The shah abdicated on September 17 because of "failing health," and his twenty-one-year-old son, Muhammad Reza, was proclaimed shah. The new ruler thus came to the throne of Iran as a result of British and Soviet occupation and the overthrow of his own father—conditions not promising for his future reign. Reza, the former shah, was eventually taken to South Africa, where he died in 1944. A roundup of Axis agents ensued; the mufti of Jerusalem, Amin al-Husaini, escaped and wound up in Germany, where he hoped to secure support for Arab independence.

For the remainder of the war, Iran had no choice but to cooperate with the Allies. At the 1943 Tehran conference, the Big Three (Stalin, Churchill, and Franklin D. Roosevelt) complimented Iran on the supplying of the Soviet Union. The quantities of goods that passed to the Soviet Union over the trans-Iranian railway and by motor truck through Iran were so vast that the figures of tonnage are nearly incomprehensible. The operations influenced life in the country markedly. In time, more than 30,000 American troops were stationed there, along with many British and Russians. Their expenditures brought quantities of foreign exchange. But the Iranians found little to purchase with these sums, as imports were held to a minimum by the Middle East Supply Center, which controlled Iranian foreign trade. Inflation, already a major problem in the period 1936–1941, now was very serious, with prices for scarce items soaring so high that truck tires sold for $2000 each, famine was widespread, and bread was so expensive there were bread riots. Before the end of the war the general price level had increased nearly 400 percent over 1939, and the dislocation of the Iranian economy became general.

The Allied occupation of Iran meant the removal of Reza Shah's dictatorship over internal governmental affairs. For the next thirteen years Iran was politically volatile, as the various elements in Iranian society that Reza had ruthlessly controlled immediately appeared and played havoc with centralizing processes. Nomads secured rifles and local autonomy, Shii ulama returned to do battle against a secular state and regained control of many pious foundations, wealthy landowners ignored taxation, and liberals and leftists were released from jails. Iranian censorship was relaxed, but the occupying authorities established their own censors. Somewhat free elections for parliament were held, and the new parties represented a wide variety of interest groups, classes, and programs. The Tudeh (Masses) party, representing Marxist views, was founded in 1941. In the provinces and especially in Azerbaijan and Kurdistan, linguistic and ethnic minorities tried to gain power over their own affairs at the expense of the central government.

The American Dr. Millspaugh was invited again to administer Iran's finances. Another American, H. Norman Schwartzkopf, reorganized the police, and an American military mission advised the army, which the new shah managed to keep under his personal control. German undercover activities continued for many months after the forced reversal of Iranian policy. The German military penetration of the Soviet Union and the British retreat in North Africa to al-Alamain encouraged a restlessness among Iranian leaders. General Fazl Allah Zahedi joined a nationalist and pro-German movement and aided in the revolt of the Kurds and the southern tribes. All these activities faded quickly, however, when the Germans began to lose the war against the Soviet Union.

In 1942 in a treaty of alliance with Iran, Great Britain and the Soviet Union acknowledged the independence of Iran and agreed to a withdrawal of their forces not later than six months after the end of the war with the Axis. The supply route to the Soviet Union was the major concern. Nevertheless the Soviet Union used this opportunity to further its imperialistic and communistic interests in Iran. It aided the Tudeh party, intrigued with Armenians and Kurds, and finally in 1944 demanded an oil concession. Iran declared war on Germany in September 1943, thus qualifying at an early date for membership in the United Nations.

In the initial stages of the war, Afghanistan, Iran's neighbor, pursued a similar policy. The Afghan government kept numerous German technical advisers, it proclaimed the country's neutrality, and it feared the possibility of a German approval of a Soviet advance into Afghanistan and Iran. Following the Nazi invasion of the Soviet Union and the joint Soviet-British invasion of Iran, the Afghans agreed to the demand of the Allies to curb the activities of Axis residents. Government spending on the military rose sharply and inflation was prevalent, but Afghanistan maintained its independence, territorial integrity, and freedom from foreign invasion.

EGYPT AND LIBYA IN THE WAR

In other areas of the Middle East, World War II brought even more armies, fighting, and political upheaval. At the very outset, Egypt held a pivotal geographic and strategic position. Egypt severed diplomatic relations with Germany as soon as Britain declared war. In accordance with the 1936 Anglo-Egyptian Treaty, martial law was declared, ports were placed under the authority of the British navy, and censorship was established. Egypt seemingly would give active and willing cooperation to England in defense of Egypt. Some concern arose over the sale of cotton, but demand was brisk, and open market prices climbed higher than those guaranteed by the government. When Mussolini's Italy entered the war in June 1940, Egypt broke off relations with Italy, which then proceeded to attack both Egypt and the Sudan.

In July 1940 Italian forces advanced into the Sudan from Ethiopia, but British, Sudanese, and Indian troops counterattacked, and by May 1941 the Italians were completely defeated and Ethiopian independence restored. In September 1940, Italian forces advanced from Libya into Egypt toward Alexandria and the Suez Canal, resting at Sidi

Barrani until December, when the British drove them west of Benghazi. Then, in April 1941, after contributing heavily to the support of Greece, British forces were forced back toward the Egyptian frontier, although the fortress of Tobruk held. Fighting was in the hands of English and British Empire troops; the small Egyptian army was not directly involved. Damage to civilians in eastern coastal Libya was extensive.

From then until May 1942, Germany's General Erwin Rommel fought a seesaw battle against the British, pushing the front to al-Alamain, only 70 miles (113 km.) west of Alexandria. In October 1942, an important two-week battle at al-Alamain broke the German army, which continued to fall back, as the British 8th Army followed in full pursuit. British, American, and Free French forces, which landed in Morocco and Algeria in November, met the Allied troops coming from Libya and Egypt in Tunisia at the end of March 1943, and the war in North Africa came to its end. Britain and France administered Libya under military controls as enemy-occupied territory.

As war raged in the western desert, life in Egypt changed rapidly. Although a few Britons continued their afternoon cricket matches, most found the tensions of war pressing on them. When the Mediterranean was virtually closed to shipping, a glut of cotton loomed ominously, but Britain solved the problem by agreeing to buy the entire crop at a price Egyptians admitted was generous. The Allies employed about 200,000 civilian Egyptians for army-related work, while tens of thousands of British, Indian, Australian, and other Allied soldiers trained for combat.

Shortages of cereals, inadequate price regulations, inflation, a decline in fertilizer imports, and the lack of import and export controls created hardships for the Egyptian population. A severe outbreak of malaria in already poor upper Egypt killed about 100,000 people. These developments furthered political disintegration and made the anti-British intrigues of King Faruq and some army officers more effective. The British took steps to suppress dissent; Hasan al-Banna, leader of the fundamentalist Muslim Brotherhood, was confined to a residence in a rural area.

British intervention in Egyptian politics was dramatically shown on February 3, 1942, when the British ambassador, in an audience with the king, complained that cooperation with the British had been thwarted at every step, urged that a new government commanding the support of a majority of the country be formed without delay, and suggested that Nahhas Pasha and the Wafd party be called to head the government. The next day an ultimatum by the British demanded that King Faruq make the appointment or accept the consequences. Faruq refused. That evening the British ambassador, accompanied by a tank force, called on the king at Abdin Palace and offered him the alternative of abdicating. The king chose to appoint Nahhas and a Wafdist government rather than be exiled. Egypt was thus humiliated and remained under Britain's political control.

Corruption and inefficiency increased and patronage to "deserving" Wafdists became rife, but the Allies could deal with a cooperative Egyptian government. Nahhas held office until October 1944, although the hatred between Nahhas and Faruq became notorious. Nahhas further weakened his position and his party by favoring his relatives. He quarreled with prominent supporters, many of whom left the Wafd and formed a new party. His dismissal was a foregone conclusion. As soon as the theaters of the war were removed to a distance far from Egypt, British insistence on retaining the Nahhas government could no longer be valid. Pledging cooperation with Britain against Germany and Japan, Ahmad Mahir formed a new anti-Wafd government. On February 24, 1945, he informed the Chamber of Deputies of his intention to declare war on Germany in order that Egypt might become a charter member of the United Nations. As he left, he was assassinated by a young Egyptian fascist, but a formal declaration of a defensive war against Germany and Japan was nevertheless issued. Ironically, Egypt entered the postwar world with both the leading nationalist party—the formerly anti-British Wafd—and the king discredited. The Wafd was seen as too willing to accept power from the British, and Faruq had cravenly accepted the British ultimatum.

UNREST IN IRAQ

World War II found Iraq weak economically and in a highly charged political atmosphere. In 1939 Britain lent Iraq nearly £4 million for armaments and railways, and the Iraq Petroleum Company advanced £3 million to cover ordinary governmental expenses. Nuri al-Said, the prime minister, broke relations with Germany. Although the government declared it would live up to its treaty obligations with Britain, most leaders quietly rejoiced over the embarrassment of England and France. Hajj Amin al-Husaini, the Jerusalem mufti, took up residence in Baghdad in October 1939 and from there continued his campaign to obtain an Arab state in Palestine.

Early in 1940, the lawyer, judge, and cabinet member Rashid Ali al-Kailani became prime minister. Unfortunately, Rashid Ali had little knowledge of the world outside of Iraq. Nuri al-Said led the moderates; Rashid Ali championed the uncompromising nationalists, who thought to use German and Italian arms and money to achieve their anti-British nationalist goals.

In November the British ambassador suggested to the regent that another prime minister be found, which prompted Rashid Ali to look to the Axis for aid. As clandestine relations with the Axis developed, Nuri and other ministers resigned. When a parliamentary vote of no confidence loomed before Rashid Ali, his plea for the dissolution of parliament was denied by the regent, who then left Baghdad to be free from pressures. In the face of such opposition Rashid Ali resigned, despite the support of his middle-class, Pan-Arab nationalist army friends, who were known as the Golden Square.

Rashid Ali grew desperate and worked incessantly to return to power. On the night of April 1, 1941, supported by the army, Rashid Ali returned to power in a kind of coup d'état. The regent was smuggled out of the country, and the British landed an Indian army brigade at Basrah to protect an important air base. The extreme nationalists rejected the wise advice of Saudi King Abd al-Aziz, who suggested that the well-fed lion (Britain) was a safer companion than the hungry vulture (Germany)!

When more British Indian forces were landed at Basrah, the Iraqi army threatened the British units stationed at an air base near Baghdad, who in turn attacked the Iraqis. Bombings and artillery attacks by the Iraqis continued throughout May, until the British and the Arab Legion from Transjordan relieved the air base, destroyed most of the Iraqi air force, and occupied Baghdad. Rashid Ali and his allies fled to Iran and Turkey; German planes, which had just arrived, flew off to Syria; the regent returned with Nuri al-Said and the British; and Nuri eventually became prime minister at the head of a new government.

For the remainder of World War II, relative political peace reigned in Iraq, as the British indirectly controlled the economy, the army, the bureaucracy, and education. Many of the nationalists of the Rashid Ali government were executed, and the army officer corps was purged. Nuri al-Said devoted time and energy to planning an Arab League and promoting Arab unity. Iraq declared war on the Axis in January 1943 and was the first Middle Eastern state to qualify for membership in the United Nations. Iraqi oil and barley were of great assistance to Britain and its allies in winning the war, even though all of the Middle East in 1940 produced only about 5 percent of total world oil production.

Iraq became involved in the process of supplying goods to the Soviet Union, and numbers of British and American troops were stationed there. In 1942, Iraq was made eligible to receive U.S. lend-lease aid. Inflation disrupted Iraq's economy in many ways, as British and American expenditures introduced purchasing power without many imports or local production of consumers' goods. Rationing had to be introduced in 1944. Since Iraq was a member of the sterling bloc, Britain also had an effective instrument for controlling and channeling Iraq's foreign trade to British Empire sources. As World War II came to an end, Iraq was still under a British domination that was increasingly resented by Iraqi nationalists, while the conservative government in Baghdad faced growing opposition from Iraqi Kurds, Shiis, and reformers who sought social justice for the poor.

INDEPENDENCE OF LEBANON AND SYRIA

Iraq was supposedly an independent country, but Lebanon and Syria were still mandates of France at the beginning of the war. The probability of war stiffened the French government's attitude toward them. In July the president of Syria resigned in protest over the gift of Alexandretta to Turkey. The French thereupon dissolved the Chamber of Deputies, suspended the constitution, placed foreign affairs and defense directly in French hands, established a council to govern Syria, and again formed separate regimes for Jabal Druze and Latakia. Although the French appointed a popular general to command their forces in the area, the Lebanese constitution was suspended in September, and France took over the powers of the cabinet.

The fall of France to Nazi Germany in 1940 and the creation of a pro-German French government at Vichy left the situation in Syria and Lebanon (as in French-controlled Morocco, Algeria, and Tunisia) uncertain. Many French officers joined the Free French forces of General Charles de Gaulle. Others collaborated with the new Vichy leadership and with the Axis. German agents flocked into the French mandates and began to prepare them for German control. Economic difficulties, food shortages, and the collapse of the French franc, to which Syrian and Lebanese currencies were tied, led to strikes and political demonstrations. Vichy set up new governments in Lebanon and Syria, but the new arrangements only partially settled the atmosphere, because the leaders of Syria and Lebanon were planning to acquire complete independence at this moment of French weakness and did not relish the thought of falling into the orbit of Germany or Italy.

In the spring of 1941, infiltration by German "tourists" and the use of Syrian airfields for German aid to Iraq posed a serious threat to the British position in the Middle East. British, Australian, Indian, Free French, and Transjordanian forces then invaded the

French mandates in June, just after the takeover of Iraq. Resistance was unexpectedly strong, and the Allied forces had to battle their way into Beirut and Damascus.

Although the Free French appointed a new president of Lebanon and Taj al-Din al-Hasani once again became president of Syria, and France recognized these two states as independent and free republics, in reality the new French authorities wanted to keep control in their own hands. Real power resided in British military forces as Britain incorporated Lebanon and Syria into the sterling bloc. This action and the economic influence of the Middle East Supply Center in Cairo convinced the Free French that Britain opposed French power in Syria and Lebanon, leading to many disputes between the two allies.

These provisions did not satisfy the nationalists, who complained that the people had no hand in them. Widespread demonstrations and strikes by nationalists, labor unions, women, and Communists indicated unhappiness with foreign rule and economic conditions. Under such pressures, the suspended constitutions were reestablished in 1943, and elections were held for legislative bodies. In Syria the leader of the National Bloc, Shukri al-Kuwatli, became president of the republic. In Lebanon Bishara al-Khuri was chosen president. The French, however, found it extremely difficult to relinquish prerogatives such as issuing decrees. Lebanese and Syrians objected to the continuation of colonialism and dropped all references to France from their constitutions. When al-Khuri and the Lebanese cabinet were arrested, a general strike and spontaneous anti-French riots forced the French to give in. The National Bloc in Syria also gained the withdrawal of French controls. In 1944, the Soviet Union and the United States gave full diplomatic recognition of the independence of the two states, which declared war on the Axis, thereby becoming charter members of the United Nations. The actions of the nationalists, Russians, and Americans compelled the weakened French to accept, at least for the moment, Syrian and Lebanese independence.

PALESTINE

Unlike Lebanon, Syria, and Iraq, there was practically no combat by external forces in the British Mandate of Palestine, but World War II nevertheless had a terrible legacy for the struggle between the Arab Palestinians and the Zionist Jews. The 1939 British White Paper was intended to place the future of Palestine on ice for the duration of World War II. Land transfers from Arabs to Jews were halted, and total immigration of Jews for the next five years was fixed at 75,000.

For the moment the Jewish Agency and the Arabs accepted these terms, but few believed that the Palestine problem would not demand a solution immediately at the end of the war. The Jewish Agency and the neighboring Arab states were girding themselves for eventual struggle. Thousands of Palestinian Jews volunteered to fight in British units. Prince Abd Allah of Transjordan allied himself with the British, and on occasion he sent troops to assist them. Arab Palestinian leadership was decimated by the failure of the 1936–1939 revolt and the flight and subsequent discrediting of Amin al-Husaini, who ultimately supported the Axis. Arabs and Jews in Palestine profited economically from the war after 1941, despite the political controversies of the time, since increased demand for food, construction, and military supplies brought them greater income.

The official Zionist position was drawn up in 1942 by a Zionist conference at the Biltmore Hotel in New York City and ratified by the Jewish Agency. This Biltmore program called for the establishment of a Jewish commonwealth in all of Palestine and for unlimited immigration under the control of the Jewish Agency.

The basic argument of Zionism seemed confirmed as the extent of the dreadful Nazi Holocaust in Europe became clearer by late 1942: Jews could be safe only in a Jewish state. Nazi persecution, murder, torture, and robbery of the Jews of occupied Europe horrified the peoples of the Allied countries and had an especially strong effect on the Jews living in Palestine, who frantically sought, where possible, to facilitate the evacuation of European Jews before they would be killed. As a result, Jewish illegal immigration to Palestine multiplied. Crises arose when British authorities would not permit ships carrying Jews to land in Palestine, turned them back, or interned them in Cyprus. One example took place in 1942, when almost all of the 769 visa-less passengers on the S.S. Struma were lost as it sank in the Black Sea. Incidents such as these enraged Palestinian Zionists, who believed it was Britain's moral duty to open the gates of Palestine to the homeless.

As the war in Europe drew to a close, the drive to fulfill the Biltmore program was intensified by pressures from all sides. Jews who were still left alive in Europe fled their homes and found temporary refuge in displaced persons camps. World Jewry in the West, in memory of the 6 million Jews massacred by the Nazis, felt a "divine impatience" over the procrastination in finding homes for these displaced persons. To the leader of the Jewish Agency, David Ben-Gurion, the refugees, if settled in Palestine, would provide the needed majority to ensure a dominant position for the Zionists. The Jewish Agency therefore insisted that the refugees come to Palestine.

An influx of Jews into Palestine found ready opposition from the Arab governments and the Arabs of Palestine. Britain, in the midst of war, was preoccupied with maintaining its military security in the Arab states and Palestine, with an emphasis on access to the oil pipeline and harbor at Haifa. Thus, British policy for Palestine had to avoid provoking an Arab uprising, which the British believed would be certain if Jewish immigration stood at a high level. Since the Zionists feared that time might be against them, they urged the attainment of their program in 1945.

Ben-Gurion had already warned that the British government, should it return to the 1939 White Paper, would be met by violent Zionist opposition in Palestine. But the British faced an Arab as well as a Jewish question. Consequently, the new British Labour party government postponed any changes, with the 1939 White Paper still in effect. World War II left Palestine poised on the edge of civil war.

THE MIDDLE EAST SUPPLY CENTER

World War II brought many innovations to the Middle East. None was more encompassing than the Middle East Supply Center. As military supplies for the British poured in, tonnage for civilian use did not abate. Ports and docks were so choked with goods, many of them luxuries, that at times it seemed certain the war would be lost for want of anchorage and unloading space. Out of this chaos was born, in April 1941, an executive agency that grew and spread its effective control everywhere in the Middle East except Turkey. It allocated shipping, ascertained the types and quantity of goods to be imported, passed on import permits, guaranteed the Middle East at least minimum requirements of scarce commodities, and maintained common stocks of wheat and other items for emergency use.

Initially the Middle East Supply Center was operated entirely by the British. But in 1942, when lend-lease goods went to the Middle East and more and more shipments originated in the United States, American officials participated in the direction of policy at the Cairo headquarters. However, representatives of Middle Eastern governments did not sit on any of the boards or have any voice in determining policy. Officers of the Middle East Supply Center grew to regard their work and the functions being performed not only as an indispensable but also as a benevolent teaching device to be used for techniques of economic planning, area coordination, and development of resources. Middle Easterners questioned the advantages and benefits of the Middle East Supply Center, and as the war drew to a close, its original justification disappeared.

As early as 1944 it became manifest that Britain, through control of imports, use of the sterling area pool, and the denial of dollar exchange, was employing the center as an instrument for maintaining British economic colonialism. Since such acts were contrary to American foreign trade policies, the United States withdrew from the operations in 1945, and the center wound up its affairs. Nothing had been done to bring in Middle Eastern governments or train local personnel to maintain the work. Thus, when the center was abandoned, its possible peacetime usefulness did not materialize, and the Middle East returned to national economic policies. For many states of the Middle East, the demise of the Middle East Supply Center more accurately announced the termination of World War II than did armistices, treaties, or the birth of the United Nations.

CONSEQUENCES OF THE WAR

Within the Middle East, one of the most important aspects of World War II was the success of Turkey and Afghanistan in maintaining their neutrality and independence, especially in comparison to the inability of Iran to do so. Saudi Arabia, Yemen, Oman, and the other states of the Arabian Peninsula were also neutral behind a shield of British protection. Egypt and Libya were deeply involved in the combat, with political ramifications of the 1942 crisis affecting the future of Egyptian politics and the defeat of Italy in the war leading to a new future for Libya. The overthrow of Vichy French control in Syria and Lebanon also introduced greater prospects for real independence, while Britain restored the former regime in Iraq. In Palestine, the Holocaust in Europe had profound implications for the two national communities. All the Arab states eventually took part in the League of Arab States (Arab League), planned in 1944 and formally taking shape in May 1945.

Internally, the war promoted nationalism and radical opposition to imperial control among the peoples of the Middle East. Attempts at liberal constitutionalism in many Middle Eastern countries that were undertaken between the two world wars gave way after 1945 to more authoritarian or revolutionary kinds of governments. The second world war also encouraged urbanization and the growth of small industries, while the area suffered from physical damage resulting from combat and the effects of inflation.

One of the chief consequences of World War II for the entire Middle East was the exhaustion of the political, military, and economic strength of Britain and France. They were eventually forced to withdraw from their imperial control of most parts of the Middle East. The two new superpowers, the United States and the Soviet Union, then extended their political and military influence throughout the Middle East region as the western European countries declined. The preeminent economic and cultural role of the United States in the world gradually became clear to the peoples of the Middle East following 1945. Competition between the Soviet Union and the United States first affected Turkey and Iran. The Cold War became the chief external factor influencing the nationalists of the Middle East in the years after the defeat of Germany, Italy, and Japan.

REFERENCES

References cited in many earlier chapters are useful for this chapter. For instance, readers interested in World War II and Iran should also consult works mentioned at the end of Chapters 29, 30, and 33.

Azimi, Fakhreddin: *Iran: The Crisis of Democracy.* London: Tauris, 1989. Systematic discussions of Iranian cabinets and their policies from 1941 to 1953.

Deringil, Selim: *Turkish Foreign Policy during the Second World War: An 'Active' Neutrality.* Cambridge, England: Cambridge University Press, 1989. Examines all facets of Turkish policy, including military, economic, and historical backgrounds.

Eshraghi, F.: "Anglo-Soviet Occupation of Iran in August 1941." *Middle Eastern Studies* 20 (1984): 27–52. In this and other essays, the author studies chiefly British actions.

Gallagher, Nancy Elizabeth: *Egypt's Other Wars: Epidemics and the Politics of Public Health.* Syracuse, N.Y.: Syracuse University Press, 1990. A careful examination of disease in Egypt during the 1940s that discusses political, economic, and medical aspects of the problem.

Gaunson, A. B.: *The Anglo-French Clash in Lebanon and Syria, 1940–45.* New York: St. Martin's Press, 1987.

Heydemann, Steven, ed.: *War, Institutions, and Social Change in the Middle East.* Berkeley: University of California Press, 2000. Covers the period from World War I onward, with special emphasis on the Arab states.

Hirschfeld, Yair: "British Achievements in Iran, 1 September 1939–25 August 1941." *Asian and African Studies* 14 (1980): 211–240. A revisionist interpretation that shows Reza was at times friendly to Britain and not uniformly pro-German.

Hirszowicz, Lukasz: *The Third Reich and the Arab East.* London: Routledge & Kegan Paul, 1966. A study of the relations of Germany with Arab movements and nations.

Kirk, George: *The Middle East in the War, Survey of International Affairs, 1939–1946.* Vol. 2. London: Oxford University Press, 1953. A still useful work. Thorough, inclusive, and objective.

Kuniholm, Bruce Robellet: *The Origins of the Cold War in the Near East: Great Power Conflict and Diplomacy in Iran, Turkey, and Greece.* Princeton, N.J.: Princeton University Press, 1980. An excellent study.

Lytle, Mark Hamilton: *The Origins of the Iranian-American Alliance, 1941–1953.* New York: Holmes and Meier, 1987.

Mahfouz, Neguib: *Midaq Alley.* Translated by Trevor Le Gassick. London: Heinemann, 1975. A fascinating novel set in Cairo during World War II; shows the impact of the war on poor, urban Egyptians.

Mardam Bey, Salma: *Syria's Quest for Independence.* Reading, England: Ithaca Press, 1994. A detailed political and diplomatic history by the daughter of the Syrian nationalist Jamil Mardam, based on his private papers.

Morsy, Laila Amin: "Indicative Cases of Britain's Wartime Policy in Egypt, 1942–44." *Middle Eastern Studies* 30 (1994): 91–122. In this and other articles, the author shows the nature of British policy.

Ökte, Faik: *The Tragedy of the Turkish Capital Tax.* Translated by Geoffrey Cox. London: Croom Helm, 1987. A frank account of the discriminatory tax by the director of finance of Istanbul during its implementation.

Porat, Dina: *The Blue and the Yellow Stars of David: The Zionist Leadership in Palestine and the Holocaust, 1939–1945.* Cambridge, Mass.: Harvard University Press, 1990. Discusses the controversial issues of how soon Zionists in Palestine became aware of the Holocaust and the effectiveness of their reaction to it.

Roshwald, Aviel: *Estranged Bedfellows: Britain and France in the Middle East during the Second World War.* New York: Oxford University Press, 1990. A detailed account of the two allies' rivalry in Syria and Lebanon.

Rubin, Barry: *The Great Powers in the Middle East, 1941–1947: The Road to the Cold War.* London: Frank Cass, 1980. Concentrates on Anglo-American as well as Soviet relations and includes the Arab countries.

Schulze, Reinhard: *A Modern History of the Islamic World.* New York: New York University, 2000. Covering the period from 1900 to 1998, this general study analyzes the history of Muslim countries, movements, institutions, and thought.

Shaw, Stanford J.: *Turkey and the Holocaust: Turkey's Role in Rescuing Turkish and European Jewry from Nazi Persecution, 1933–1945.* New York: New York University Press, 1993.

Smith, Charles D.: "4 February 1942: Its Causes and Its Influence on Egyptian Politics and on the Future of Anglo-Egyptian Relations, 1937–1945." *International Journal of Middle East Studies* 10 (1979): 453–479.

Wilmington, Martin W.: *The Middle East Supply Center.* Albany: State University of New York Press, 1971. An amazing story of British and American cooperation at a difficult and sensitive time.

CHAPTER 38

Turkey Becomes More Democratic

For almost a half-century after the end of World War II, Turkey and the rest of the Middle East functioned within an international and security framework whose basic outlines were set by the Cold War between the Soviet Union and the United States. Turkey also faced several disputes or diplomatic problems involving Cyprus, Greece, and its Arab neighbors. Given this situation and its imperial and authoritarian past, the Turkish political system's transition toward democracy was remarkable.

Starting in 1950 Turkey entered on a course of multiparty, competitive, democratic politics occasionally interrupted by military intervention. Unlike many other parts of the Middle East, however, the armed forces seized power only for short periods of time. Their chief goal was to reform political circumstances so as to restore civilian control. The pendulum of Turkish politics has swung back and forth several times between liberal parliamentary democracy and authoritarian military rule. National unity has been challenged, however, more by the Kurdish issue than by ideological or military-civilian strife. The political system would also be faced with strains arising from rapid economic growth and social change, involving such phenomena as educational expansion, cultural transformations, and heated debates about the role of religion in public life.

THE DEMOCRAT PARTY

Although the Turkish constitution stated that Turkey was a democracy, in reality only one political party had managed the affairs of the republic since it was first created. This situation seemed to contradict the charter of the United Nations, which Turkey joined in 1945, as well as the goals of the revolution, which had been dedicated in the long run to establishing a West European–style democracy.

President Ismet Inönü gradually opened the way between 1945 and 1950 for competing political parties. Leaders of a new group, the Democrat party, began to organize. The three principal leaders were Celal Bayar, the last prime minister under Atatürk; Adnan Menderes, a Republican People's party deputy; and Fuad Köprülü, of the

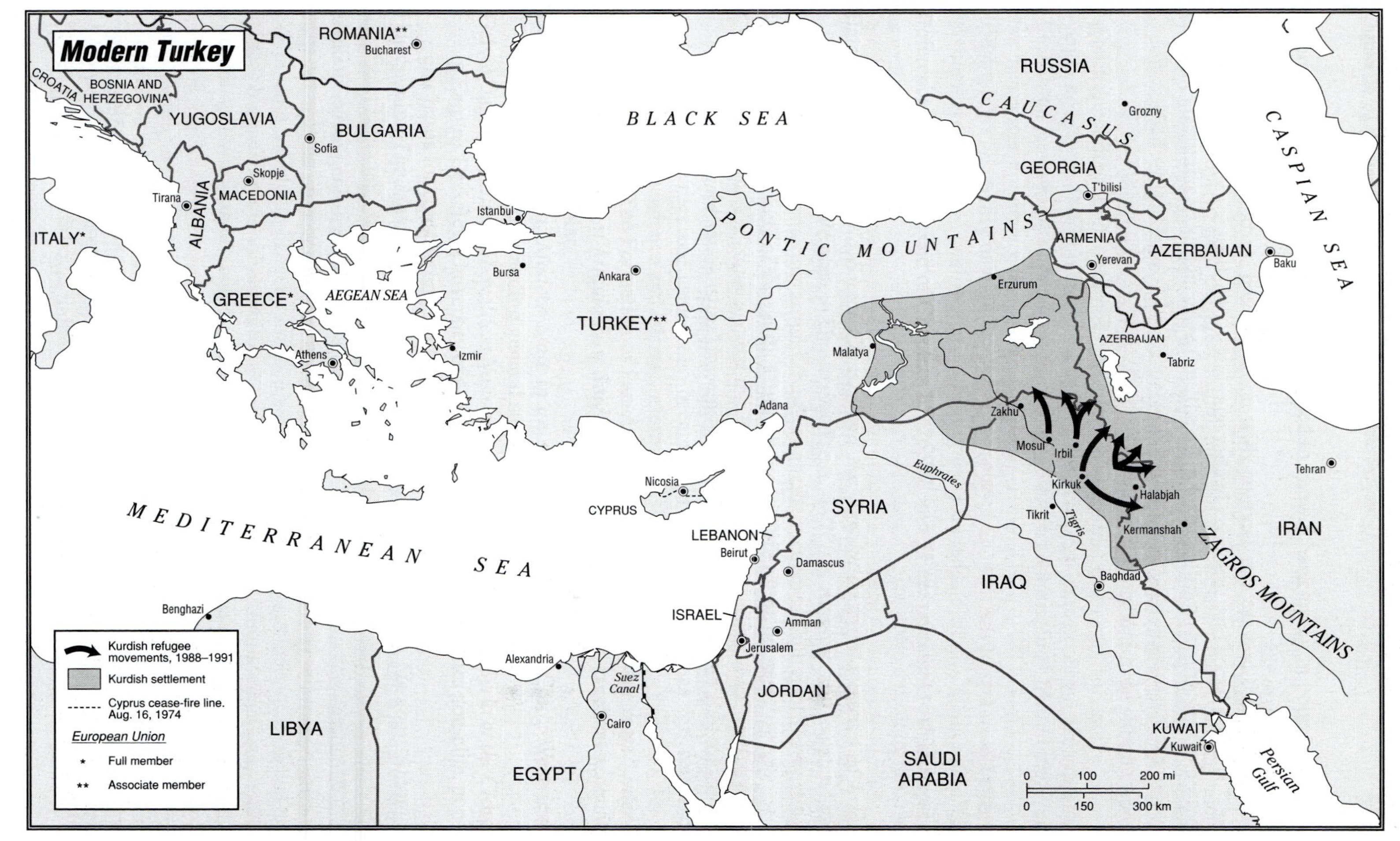
Modern Turkey
ROMANIA**
Bucharest
CROATIA
BOSNIA AND HERZEGOVINA
YUGOSLAVIA
BULGARIA
Sofia
Skopje
MACEDONIA
Tirana
ALBANIA
ITALY*
GREECE*
AEGEAN SEA
Athens
Istanbul
Bursa
Izmir
Ankara
TURKEY**
BLACK SEA
PONTIC MOUNTAINS
RUSSIA
CAUCASUS
Grozny
GEORGIA
T'bilisi
ARMENIA
Yerevan
AZERBAIJAN
Baku
CASPIAN SEA
AZERBAIJAN
Tabriz
Erzurum
Malatya
Adana
Zakhu
Mosul
Irbil
Kirkuk
Halabjah
Tikrit
Kermanshah
Tehran
IRAN
ZAGROS MOUNTAINS
Euphrates
Tigris
SYRIA
IRAQ
Baghdad
Nicosia
CYPRUS
LEBANON
Beirut
Damascus
ISRAEL
Amman
Jerusalem
JORDAN
MEDITERRANEAN SEA
Benghazi
LIBYA
Alexandria
Suez Canal
Cairo
EGYPT
SAUDI ARABIA
KUWAIT
Kuwait
Persian Gulf
0 100 200 mi
0 150 300 km
Kurdish refugee movements, 1988–1991
Kurdish settlement
Cyprus cease-fire line. Aug. 16, 1974
European Union
* Full member
** Associate member

famous family of seventeenth-century Ottoman grand vizirs, deputy, and internationally known historian.

The Democrat party subscribed to the six points of the Republican party, which were, after all, incorporated into the constitution. But the long period of Republican party rule and in particular the recent war years had brought many economic dislocations. Democrats capitalized on these and attracted to their banner all who had any grievance with the government.

Elections for the Grand National Assembly in 1946 gave the Republicans a large majority, but the Democrats were at least now represented. After 1946 several other parties were formed by disgruntled deputies, and concrete election reforms were introduced. In the elections in 1950, the Democrat party won a resounding victory. Celal Bayar was elected president of the republic to succeed Ismet Inönü, who gracefully relinquished the office and power he had held for nearly twelve years. Adnan Menderes assumed the office of prime minister. This marked a peaceful transfer of power as the result of a democratic, contested election.

Thanks in part to American aid programs, the Turkish economy surged forward, and the Democrat party reaped the benefits of that prosperity. In the 1954 elections, the Democrats increased their majority in parliament, with 58 percent of the popular vote. Almost immediately, however, weaknesses in the economy put the Democrats in a poor light. The Democrat leadership reacted vigorously against criticism caused by the economic situation. Because of the ebb in its popularity, the Democrat party did not win a majority of the popular vote in 1957, but it did gain more than 400 seats in the Grand National Assembly, compared to fewer than 200 for the Republicans.

MILITARY COUP OF 1960

Beginning in the mid-1950s, droughts turned wheat surpluses into shortages, upset the balance of payments, and undermined the entire economy. Menderes rashly pursued developments in every sector of the economy. With returns from most of these investments many years away, inflation ensued. By 1959, unemployment, business failures, and shortages were widespread. Vocal opposition to the Democrat regime became commonplace among the urban classes, who were most affected by the economic dislocation.

Menderes was indifferent to the attitudes of the urban elite as long as he retained the support of the villagers, 70 percent of the electorate. In 1959, on an airplane trip, he had quite miraculously walked away unscathed from a crash that killed most of the other passengers. From that moment, Menderes's followers loudly proclaimed that he had been saved by an act of God in order to lead his country, and many Republicans began to despair of ever defeating him.

In 1960, Inönü was stopped on his way to a political meeting by the army, acting on orders from the government. He refused to give way, claiming that the constitution guaranteed freedom of travel to Turkish citizens. The Democrats seemed intent on persecuting their political opponents. University students marched in the streets until they were suppressed by military action. Then on May 27 the army struck. President Bayar,

Prime Minister Menderes, the entire cabinet, and Democrat deputies of the National Assembly were arrested and a bloodless revolution accomplished.

THE NATIONAL UNITY COMMITTEE

General Cemal Gürsel was installed as head of the provisional government. He was a necessary link between the senior officers, the older politicians, and the public on the one hand, and the junior officers who had instigated the coup. Most of these junior officers were young, technologically skilled colonels and majors who held key posts. The military body formed to govern the nation was known as the National Unity Committee (N.U.C.).

The N.U.C. appointed a civilian cabinet, most of whom had not been identified with any political party. To reorient the government was a large order, but to reform the armed services was a task more manageable: thousands of officers were purged by forced retirement.

Within the Committee, a division arose between a moderate majority and a more radical group under the leadership of Colonel Alparslan Türkeş, who advocated pushing through the entire program of the revolution quickly and postponing elections indefinitely. This group was dismissed from the N.U.C. and sent abroad. Instead of military control, a broadly based Constituent Assembly, dominated by members of the Republican People's party, drafted a new constitution, which was approved in 1961 in a national referendum.

From the autumn of 1960 until the summer of 1961, the attention of the nation was focused in large part on the trial of Bayar, Menderes, and many others. Most of those who had voted Democrat in the past were unconvinced by these trials and regarded the evidence as fraudulent. Prime Minister Menderes was hanged; President Bayar's death sentence was commuted to life imprisonment because of his age and poor health.

The new constitution provided for a partially appointed Senate and an elected Assembly, with the two houses meeting together to elect a president for a seven-year term. Ismet Inönü once again led the Republican People's party, and since the Democrat party had been outlawed, a new party was formed with the hope of attracting former Bayar-Menderes followers. The Justice party selected its name to signify the need to ensure justice to the former national political leaders; it openly asked for Democrat votes.

In the election, the Republican People's party won about the same number of votes it had in the elections of the 1950s, and no one could deny that the Justice party had inherited most of Menderes's votes. Because of votes going to small parties, no party held a majority in either house. Cemal Gürsel was elected president.

THE SECOND TURKISH REPUBLIC

Gürsel picked Inönü to head coalition governments, which eventually tried to heal the political wounds resulting from the events of 1960. In this way, the second Turkish Republic, which lasted until 1980, could have a degree of consensus to support its legitimacy by bringing back into the political system the supporters of the former Democrat party.

The armed forces became nearly autonomous; they saw a dual role for themselves: protectors of the nation against enemies abroad and defenders of the republican institutions at home.

Whatever chances Inönü had to maintain the Republican People's party in office were ruined by affairs in Cyprus in 1964. The grievances of the Turkish Cypriot minority incensed the Turkish nation; many Turks felt that their government had the right to intervene openly and blamed Inönü for being too subservient to American diplomatic pressure. Süleyman Demirel (b. 1924), the Justice leader and a former engineer, was appointed to the cabinet. Demirel declared that the Justice party wanted to prove to the military and to the voters that it could govern peacefully and successfully.

During the ensuing election campaign, Inönü, the Republican People's leader, now eighty-one years old, appealed to those in governmental circles, the older established families, dedicated Kemalists, army officers, and many intellectuals to return his party to office. As the campaign progressed, he asserted that his party was somewhat left of center, a position that alienated many Republicans, who did not vote. The Justice party in 1965 won a clear majority over the Republican People's party, and a new leftist Workers party won fifteen seats.

THE JUSTICE PARTY GOVERNS

The dire predictions concerning the advent to power of the Justice party were unfounded. Prime Minister Demirel governed cautiously, although he initiated several new policies. He started the construction of the massive Keban Dam on the Euphrates River. A family planning law passed in 1965 legalized contraceptives, although abortions remained illegal until 1983.

In 1966, President Gürsel, who was ill, was replaced by General Cevdet Sunay. The Republican People's party also elected a new leader: Bülent Ecevit, a vigorous young member of the Assembly who had been minister of labor. Since both Ecevit and Demirel were American-educated, anti-American forces gravitated to other parties.

A euphoria seemed to engulf the nation as tensions lessened, and the economy moved forward with increases in the gross national product, expanding markets in Europe, many Turkish workers sending back income from jobs in Germany, and the widening development of import substitution industry and trade unions at home. In the 1969 Assembly election, the Justice party decisively defeated the Republican People's party.

But the world malaise of the years between 1968 and 1972 affected Turkey. There were miserable shantytowns in Istanbul, Ankara, Izmir, and smaller cities; student disturbances; labor unrest; and many unsatisfied wants in education and land distribution. In 1970 Demirel's governing margin shrank to two votes. With disorders mounting, martial law was established in Istanbul in June.

Opposition became more open. In the first months of 1971, students rioted repeatedly. Terrorist activities by the extreme left and right grew, including bank robberies, bombings, and kidnappings. Demonstrators called for withdrawal from the North Atlantic Treaty Organization (N.A.T.O.) and the Central Treaty Organization. On March

12, 1971, the leaders of the military forces issued a statement that they would take over governmental authority if the situation did not improve immediately.

COUP BY COMMUNIQUÉ

The statement blamed parliament and the government for driving the country into "anarchy, fratricidal strife, and social and economic unrest." It called for an end to politics and for the formation of a strong government to halt the anarchy and to implement reform. Demirel resigned immediately.

President Sunay formed nonparty governments to stabilize the nation. Martial law was imposed in critical provinces, and 2000 persons were arrested and accused of terrorism. For nearly three years, successive caretaker prime ministers and cabinets who tried to govern barely held affairs together. The military leaders again cautioned that they would not tolerate another descent into political chaos. In 1973, President Sunay was replaced after great controversy by still another military figure, Fahri Korutürk, a former admiral.

In the 1973 national elections, the Republican People's party led by Ecevit waged a vigorous campaign, urging state control of the economy and real land reform. Other legal parties included the National Salvation party, which went along with some parts of Ecevit's program but stood for a return to Islamic practices. When the vote was in, the Republican People's party had won more seats than the Justice party, but no party had a majority. In 1974, the Islamic revivalist National Salvation party ultimately joined with Ecevit to form a weak coalition.

Ecevit's leadership became popular after his response to events in Cyprus. He directed the Turkish military landings and occupation of the northern 40 percent of the island, despite the risk of war with Greece and American opposition. In September, at the peak of his triumph, he resigned to get rid of the National Salvation party and force a new general election. But Demirel and the other leaders, recognizing that Ecevit might win a smashing victory, decided to put off elections.

In 1975, a new Justice–right wing coalition was formed amid considerable political controversy, unemployment, poverty, and inflation. There ensued strikes, machine-gun battles between rival student political groups, and kidnappings. A strike by the Revolutionary Trade Unions Confederation was ended by the arrest of its leaders, but the methods of breaking it heightened the tension. Shortages of various commodities were common, largely because a balance of payments deficit had emptied the treasury. Finally, Demirel proposed elections for 1977.

When the final returns were tabulated, the Republican People's party under Ecevit had won in the bigger cities and had gained a plurality but not a majority of the 213 seats, with Justice next, followed by Erbakan's National Salvation party. Demirel and Erbakan put together a short-lived coalition, but Ecevit ultimately formed a weak government that lasted until late 1979, when Demirel once again became prime minister.

Through 1980, inflation continued, and the economy was on the verge of collapse as more money was needed for oil imports. Disorders were not curbed, and pessimism prevailed as martial law was declared in various provinces.

THE MILITARY TAKES POWER AGAIN

By 1980 an average of about twenty people per day were being killed in political assassinations and brawls, inflation was around 100 percent, unemployment was high, and the gross national product, which had been nearly stagnant in 1978 and 1979, now declined. In January 1980 the Demirel government embarked on a severe and far-reaching economic reform program led by Turgut Özal (1927–1993), but it was unable to bring about a cessation of partisan political bickering, which blocked the election of a new president as well as action against violence in the streets.

These immediate crises were made even more tense by a long-range challenge to the political system posed by formerly suppressed groups that now emerged into the political light, such as the Shii Alevis, who constituted almost 20 percent of the population. They had demands and desires that strained the hitherto-existing political consensus. The 6 million or so Kurds, urban workers, displaced villagers who had migrated to the cities, Islamic fundamentalists, and leftist and rightist ideologues expressed ideas or desired the state to adopt policies that were contrary to the consensus Atatürk and Inönü had earlier created. Since the two major political groups—the Republican People's party and the Justice party—were increasingly polarized and would not or could not cooperate with each other, no political remedy for the problems of Turkey seemed to be at hand.

The conflicts of the late 1970s and especially the political crises caused by weak and ineffective governments that could not address the economic and social problems of the country caused renewed military intervention on September 12, 1980, as the leaders of the armed forces seized power again. Parliament was dismissed, a cabinet of technocrats was appointed, and 100,000 people were arrested.

The military clamped down on possible opposition and on groups believed to have caused the chaos that had led to the seizure of power. The old political parties were banned. Violations of human rights of political prisoners, including the (officially unsanctioned) use of torture, were widespread. This and the censorship of the press and intimidation of leftists and rightists gave rise to widespread criticism in Europe of the military government.

Inflation was somewhat reduced in the early 1980s, while exports increased, the trade gap narrowed, and the Turkish currency was devalued. Military spending quadrupled by 1991. The Özal government of the mid-1980s privatized some sectors of the economy and presided over a generally healthy and growing society, but it could not overcome the persistent inflation that hovered around 40 to 50 percent each year.

A new constitution that expressed the military's point of view was adopted by national referendum in November 1982. The constitution upheld the political authority of the state, limited civil liberties in times of emergency, and gave considerably more power to the presidency. Proportional representation in parliamentary elections was retained, but parties that received less than 10 percent of the votes were not to gain seats in the new one-chamber Assembly. The political party that got the largest number of votes also in effect received a bonus number of seats in parliament. General Kenan Evren became president of the republic. Politicians who had been active up to 1980 were banned from running for office. The chief principles of Atatürk were incorporated into the new constitution, thus reaffirming the basic continuity of Turkish politics.

THE THIRD TURKISH REPUBLIC

For the parliamentary elections of November 1983, the generals limited participation to three political parties, including the Motherland party led by Turgut Özal, the engineer and economist who had presided over economic reforms. Despite the clear preference of the military for the other parties, the Motherland party won an absolute majority: 212 of 400 seats, with 45 percent of the popular vote. Its delegation in the Assembly was dominated by businessmen, administrators, engineers, and public servants. The party achieved wide support with social policies that attracted many of the former supporters of the Republican People's party, economic statements that brought it votes from the former backers of the Justice party, and an appeal to Islam as well. Politically, the Motherland party supported the new system and constitution, but since it did not receive the backing of the military, it attracted many voters who wished to oppose the coup.

The other parties that had contested the 1983 elections subsequently dissolved, and new opposition parties appeared in the mid-1980s. These included the moderately leftist Social Democratic party, modeled on similarly named parties in western Europe, and led by Erdal Inönü, son of Ismet Inönü. Another "new" party was the True Path group led by Süleyman Demirel, whose reappearance in politics (along with other banned politicians) was authorized in a national constitutional referendum. Political participation was widespread, but only twelve women were elected to parliament in 1983, a low number that indicated that political participation did not necessarily lead to empowerment.

In the 1987 parliamentary elections, Prime Minister Özal's Motherland party again won an absolute majority of the seats in the Assembly, but it received only 36 percent of the vote. The Social Democrats were second with 25 percent of the vote, and Demirel's True Path party had 19 percent. The other parties, with 20 percent of the total vote between them, had no representation at all since none of them individually had reached the 10 percent minimum vote cutoff. Özal used his renewed authority to put into effect civilian control over the military, appointing his own choice as chief of staff.

Popular support for the Motherland party fell in the late 1980s and 1990s, partially because of its own diversity but also because of growing corruption among its officials, continuing high inflation, and Turkey's difficult role in the Kuwait crisis. Sensing this, Özal opted to be elected president in 1989, while retaining his leading role in the Motherland party and in making domestic policy. He was only the second civilian to become president of the republic.

Elections in 1991 posed a serious challenge to the new president's power when Demirel became prime minister for the seventh time! His True Path party received 27 percent of the popular vote and, in conjunction with Erdal Inönü's Social Democrats, formed a governing coalition in parliament. The vote was fractured, with the Motherland, Welfare, and Democratic Left parties of Özal, Erbakan, and Ecevit also represented.

Despite the ideological closeness of the president and prime minister, both on the rightist side of politics, they disagreed constantly.

Attempts by the military in 1980 to purge the political leaders of earlier times had failed, as became particularly apparent following the death of President Özal and his replacement by Demirel in 1993. On the other hand, Demirel's successor as prime minister marked a remarkable change in Turkish politics: the selection of a woman as head of government. Tansu Çiller, an economist and member of parliament for the True Path party, acted in cooperation with Demirel.

Continuing problems with inflation and the Kurdish fighting plus disputes among the governing coalition parties led to new parliamentary elections on December 24, 1995. The Islamic fundamentalist Welfare party received slightly more votes than did Çiller's True Path party or the conservative Motherland party, with all three groups combined obtaining about 60 percent of the vote. Welfare's leader Erbakan was ultimately able to form a government, since his anti–European Union and pro-Islamic values stands had gained him considerable popularity.

Turkish politics throughout most of the 1990s moved rightward, but the various conservative, pro-business parties split the vote, opening the way for moderate Islamic fundamentalists to seriously challenge the secular basis of the Republic. The Welfare party of Erbakan enjoyed much support in the big cities, appealed to those who sought social justice for the poor, and condemned what it saw as the growing immorality of society and corruption in politics. On the other hand, those groups most committed to secularism, including military officers, strongly opposed the Islamists, as seen in an ultimatum from the National Security Council to Erbakan in February 1997 that at first forced his government to downplay the role of religion in education and hiring for government employment and then helped end his party's leadership in the governing coalition. The Welfare party was outlawed in 1998 and its successor was also banned by the Constitutional Court in 2001, raising concerns among Turks and others about Turkey's commitment to freedom of political expression.

In the face of multiple policy crises dealing with the Kurdish insurgency, economic problems, political scandals, and admission to the European Union, in 1999 the Turkish voters turned out the leading parties and replaced them with two surprising choices: the Democratic Left party led by the veteran Ecevit (22 percent of the vote), and the formerly super-militant Nationalist Action party (18 percent). With the additional support of the Motherland party, Ecevit became prime minister and leader of a solid majority for the coalition into the new millenium. He had to face the consequences of a major earthquake, a debilitating economic crisis, and the need to make numerous adjustments in Turkish public life so as to persuade the European Union that Turkey should be admitted as a full member. Many of these difficulties revolved around the situation of Turkish Kurds and the role of the military.

THE KURDISH PROBLEM

The Turkish population, constitution, national governments, and military emphasized the territorial unity and central administration of the country and outlawed any behavior tending to encourage disunity and separatism. Speakers of Kurdish who were citizens of Turkey were the largest linguistic minority. By the 1980s the Kurds had grown to about 20 percent of the total population. Many Kurds had assimilated into the general population, spoke Turkish fluently, and considered themselves loyal citizens. More than 1 million Kurds lived in Istanbul. Nevertheless, some Kurds yearned for local autonomy in southeastern Anatolia or even independence and union with Kurds in other parts of the Middle East. The Turkish government punished people who spoke Kurdish, even in private, and in general sought to repress Kurdish identity.

The Kurdish Workers party, known as the P.K.K., was established in 1979 and started guerrilla warfare in 1984, using safe havens in Iraq and backing from Syria. Violence steadily escalated as the Turkish army and security forces counterattacked. Thousands of civilians and soldiers died, and abuses of civil liberties were widespread. The disruption of life and destruction of property were great.

Turkey hoped economic growth would lift the standard of living in the poor, rural eastern regions of the country and thereby reduce the appeal of the P.K.K., so the Southeast Anatolia Project for electric production and irrigation was supported. Kurds also enjoyed greater opportunities to participate in politics. In 1991 President Özal, himself half-Kurdish, lifted the ban on speaking the Kurdish language, and for a time both Kurdish and Turkish writers and essayists began to debate long-suppressed issues. But as the guerrilla war intensified in the mid-1990s, feelings hardened; the Constitutional Court ordered the dissolution of the Kurdish-supported Democracy party in 1994.

The P.K.K.'s goals included independence and Pan-Kurdish union. It was a leftist party enjoying much backing among Kurds in Europe, a television service of its own, and some sympathy from Europeans who ignored its brutal tactics and attacks while concentrating on the Turkish government's destruction of villages, employment of gangsters to murder Kurdish leaders, and forced relocations of hundreds of thousands of civilians. The Turkish army succeeded in seriously reducing the effectiveness of the P.K.K. by 1995, but this military achievement was accompanied by heavy-handed repression of Kurdish moderates. Turkey used military threats in 1998 to persuade Syria to expel the P.K.K.'s leader, Abd Allah Ocalan, who was captured by Turkish forces in Kenya in 1999. The Kurdish armed insurgency ended by 2000, but issues associated with Kurdish cultural and linguistic identity and human rights abuses in Turkey continued to be major domestic and foreign-policy concerns as of 2002. Fully integrating Kurds into Turkish public and economic life or adjusting the definition of Turkish identity in a broader way so as to include the use of the Kurdish language remained the preeminent long-range internal issue for Turkish nationalism.

FOREIGN RELATIONS: THE COLD WAR

At the end of World War II in 1945, the Soviet Union demanded the cession of Kars and Ardahan in eastern Anatolia and the granting of Soviet bases on the Straits. The Turks replied with a categorical no. The Soviets maintained strong pressure on Turkey by deploying sizable armies in nearby areas. The solution was found in the Truman Doctrine, proclaimed in 1947, which provided American funds to both Greece and Turkey to bolster them in resisting the Soviet Union and its Balkan satellite states.

American aid was directed at modernizing the Turkish army and improving the systems of communication and transportation so as to give the army greater maneuverability. From 1947 until 1975, between $6 and $7 billion had been expended by the United States on aid. The army was reorganized from top to bottom and new equipment supplied. A new air force was created, and a steady flow of the latest planes kept the Turkish air force an important middle-sized power. American military missions were common, especially along the northern coast, where the most modern eavesdropping and electronic stations were located. By 1970 some 23,000 American military personnel were based in Turkey. Ports were updated, and hard-surface all-weather roads connecting major cities were built. A major airfield was constructed near Adana.

When war broke out in Korea in 1950, Turkey sent a brigade to support the United Nations position. Turkey in 1952 (along with Greece) was admitted to N.A.T.O., although Turkey was far away from the North Atlantic region! The long alliance between Turkey and the United States was, however, strained by the issue of opium smuggling and also the Cyprus dispute; in 1975 the U.S. Congress voted an arms embargo against Turkey because of the action in Cyprus. Later there was an easing of the embargo. Even though Turkey belonged to N.A.T.O., a mutual-defense alliance aimed against Soviet expansion, after the Cyprus problem became prominent Turkey sought to broaden its options by cultivating some ties to the U.S.S.R., which gave the Turks about $3 billion worth of foreign aid in the 1960s and 1970s.

As the tension between the two superpowers lessened in the late 1980s, Turkey's situation changed. Its importance to the United States and Europe remained clear, however, during the Kuwait crisis of 1990 and the resulting 1991 Gulf War. With the disintegration of the Soviet Union, a whole new international environment emerged. By 1999 the United States felt it was no longer necessary to provide military aid to Turkey. Some of the many new possibilities that emerged for Turkey were closer cooperation with all its Black Sea neighbors, epitomized by the 1992 regional Economic Cooperation Zone; support of Turkish-speaking Muslims in the Caucasus and central Asia, particularly in the Azerbaijan-Armenia dispute over Nagorno-Karabagh; and assistance to mostly Muslim Bosnia, part of former Yugoslavia in the Balkans. Most Turks, however, rejected direct expansion at the expense of their neighbors or the renewal of Pan-Turkism. Turkey did extend credits, infrastructure development, educational grants, and private investments to the new central Asian countries.

In the new century, Turkey's foreign policy has been friendly toward the Russian Federation, but chiefly oriented toward issues important in America and western Europe. Turkish governments were concerned with the possible building of new oil and natural gas pipelines from the Caspian Sea region through the Caucasus to Turkey. Relations with Bulgaria and the former Yugoslavia improved dramatically as those countries became more democratic. As a member of N.A.T.O., Turkey had considerable leverage with members of the European Union who wanted to use the alliance as a basis for an emerging European military force. Turkey strongly supported the 2001 United States war in Afghanistan against the Taliban and al-Qaidah and sent peacekeeping troops of its own to Kabul.

GREECE AND CYPRUS

In addition to the Cold War, a serious foreign policy problem for Turkey developed with Greece. On the island of Cyprus, some Greek governments worked in conjunction with Greek Cypriots to effect the union of Cyprus with Greece. Since 20 percent of the population was Turkish and since Cyprus is close to the southern Turkish shore, the Turkish government took a firm stand in opposition to any proposed union.

The British in 1957 broached partition as the only possible peaceful solution to the growing civil war and struggle for independence, but Athens rejected the proposal. Greece and Turkey thus became mutually suspicious, thereby weakening their cooperation as eastern sector partners in N.A.T.O.

In 1959, Greece, Turkey, and Britain signed treaties in London establishing and guaranteeing a Republic of Cyprus. Coming into being in 1960, Cyprus joined the United Nations. Archbishop Makarios, head of the Greek Orthodox church in Cyprus and leader of the Greek Cypriot community, and leaders of the Turkish Cypriot community accepted this settlement. According to the constitution, both partition and union (enosis) with Greece were barred, and the nation was to have two official languages, Greek and Turkish. The Greek Cypriots would elect the president and the Turkish Cypriots the vice president, and both officials would have to sign acts to make them law. Separate Turkish and Greek Cypriot communal chambers were set up to control education, religion, social welfare, and personal affairs, almost like the millets of the Ottoman Empire. In the 1960 elections, Archbishop Makarios became president. Britain retained large bases on the island. No unified Cypriot army was formed because of the ethnic divisions between the two communities. An independent, unified Cyprus was inherently difficult to achieve because of the ethnic, linguistic, religious, cultural, and economic differences that separated Greek and Turkish Cypriots.

In 1963, Archbishop-President Makarios touched off a new crisis by proposing constitutional changes, one of which would terminate the requirement that the vice president approve all legislation. This meant the end of any Turkish veto power. The United Nations Security Council sent a peacekeeping force. At one time when it appeared Turkey would intervene militarily, President Lyndon Johnson sent a stiff note to Inönü warning him of the dire consequences of such an act. Turkish resentment at the note ended automatic cooperation with the United States.

By 1964 the situation in the eastern Mediterranean was grave. Greece intervened to control the Cypriots. In 1968 President Makarios was reelected, progress for peace seemed to be a reality, and signs of economic improvement appeared. However, in 1974 the Greek Cypriot National Guard, with the approval of the junta in Athens, overthrew Makarios, appointing a new president.

On July 20, 1974, Turkey, to prevent enosis, landed 40,000 troops on the northern coast of Cyprus and seized much of the north. The Greek government mobilized but, recognizing the overwhelming superiority of the Turkish forces, agreed to a cease-fire. Then the Athens junta handed over power to a civilian government. A second Turkish army advance ended with nearly 40 percent of the island in Turkish hands. Some 200,000 Greek Cypriots and more than 20,000 Turkish Cypriots became homeless refugees. Both Turkey and Greece denounced the United States for not being impartial, and the United

States imposed a complete arms embargo on deliveries to Turkey. Turkey closed U.S. installations, and the United States later resumed arms deliveries in 1978. Makarios returned to Cyprus, granting amnesty to those who overthrew him but declaring partition unacceptable.

Prime Minister Ecevit presided over the Turkish military action in Cyprus; his immediate popularity did not, however, keep him in office, and Turkish policy fell into the hands of Demirel, who called for a bizonal federal solution in Cyprus. Turkish Cypriots, backed by Ankara, ultimately wanted separate and autonomous Greek and Turkish Cypriot states linked together in a federal union. The Turkish area became quasi-independent, with its own elections and government, secured by Turkish mainland armed forces and substantial financial aid from Turkey. The north declared independence in November 1983 and took the name of the Turkish Republic of Northern Cyprus, but it was recognized diplomatically only by Turkey. Many members of the U.S. Congress attempted to reduce U.S. aid to Turkey because of Turkish support of the new state. Nevertheless, Turkey continued to be a major recipient of U.S. assistance, ranking behind only Israel and Egypt.

In 1977 Spyros Kyprianou, leader of the assembly, became president of Cyprus until 1988, following the death of Makarios, and all attempts at a resolution of Turkish and Greek factions in Cyprus failed. The Greek Cypriots prospered, with tourism and shipping leading the economic growth. In 1988 Cyprus agreed on a customs union with the European Economic Community (E.E.C.) and in 1900 applied to join fully what became the European Union (E.U.). In 1999 the E.U. put Cyprus on a list of countries that might join, but the issue was complex as Greece and Turkey initially took sharply differing positions on this matter. The Turkish Cypriots did not fare as well as their Greek counterparts economically, relying chiefly on farming and some tourist income, while linking their economy and society tightly to Turkey.

In addition to the tension over Cyprus, Turkey and Greece found themselves in a controversy over oil in the Aegean Sea. In 1974, Turkey and Greece disputed the location of the continental shelf in the Aegean, and Greece withdrew from military participation in N.A.T.O. until 1980. With so many Greek-held islands in the Aegean in shallow water close to the Turkish coast, the rights and claims of the two countries overlapped everywhere. Andreas Papandreou, the new prime minister of Greece after 1981, exacerbated tensions with Turkey over a series of issues. In 1988 the Turkish and Greek prime ministers agreed on confidence-building measures, although these were again strained by Aegean disputes in 1996. The United Nations, the United States, and others tried to mediate the Cyprus dispute, but with no success into the 1990s. However, relations between Greece and Turkey became less hostile after Greek assistance at the time of the 1999 earthquake. By 2002 Greece seemed willing to approve the possible admission of Turkey to the European Union, presuming that Cyprus would be admitted to the E.U. as a full member by 2004.

THE MIDDLE EAST

Relations with Turkey's Middle Eastern neighbors usually took second place to the Cold War and issues involving Greece, although trade with the Middle East as a whole surpassed

Turkish trade with Europe by 1981, as relations with Libya, Saudi Arabia, and other oil-producing countries improved. The first serious post–World War II change took place in the mid-1950s when Turkey joined Iraq, Pakistan, Iran, and Britain in a security agreement usually called the Baghdad Pact, in effect linking these countries to the West in the Cold War.

The Iraqi revolution and withdrawal from the Baghdad Pact in 1958 led the members to reorganize it as the Central Treaty Organization. In 1963, however, Turkey announced the abandoning of U.S. missile bases and the return of all the nuclear warheads to the United States, as part of the arrangement whereby the Soviet Union withdrew its missiles from Cuba during the United States–Soviet maneuvering in the dangerous Cuban missile crisis.

Turkey maintained friendly relations with most of the Arab states, except for Syria, where sharp differences existed in regard to the Cold War and border questions. Beginning in 1974, the most vexatious issue was that of the water flow in the Euphrates River. The great Keban Dam produced enormous amounts of hydroelectric power for Turkey, so when the cost of imported oil (mostly from the Arab states) jumped suddenly in 1973, Turkey decided to store water to begin producing more energy. When Turkey reduced the Euphrates' flow below previously agreed levels, Syria complained bitterly because the level was so low. Iraq also had problems, obtaining a mere trickle. Syria subsequently supported Turkish-Kurdish groups to gain leverage in disputes with the Turkish authorities.

Arab support for Turkey over Cyprus was reciprocated by Turkish recognition of the Palestine Liberation Organization (P.L.O.) in 1979, although Turkey maintained low-level diplomatic relations with Israel. Turkey usually sought to remain outside the Arab-Israeli dispute, an ongoing problem that consumed the attention of many other Middle Eastern countries.

Turkish relations with Iraq were cemented by two oil pipelines linking the Iraqi oilfields with Turkish ports, opened in 1977 and 1987. But the outbreak of war in 1980 between Iraq and Iran, both neighbors of Turkey, threatened to drag it into that long and bitter struggle. Turkey went to great lengths to ensure its neutrality, preserving profitable trade with both Iran and Iraq. On many occasions Turkey, acting with the permission of Iraq, attacked Kurdish revolutionary bases in northern Iraq.

Despite internal opposition, Turkey favored the U.S., Saudi Arabia, and United Nations positions after Iraq invaded and annexed Kuwait in 1990. Although Turkey remained officially neutral, it assisted the coalition in many ways. Turkish troops mobilized near the Iraqi border, thus pinning down tens of thousands of Iraqi troops in 1990–1991. Turkey assumed a great financial loss as it closed Iraqi oil pipelines and complied with the United Nations embargo against Iraq. U.S. airplanes used bases in Turkey to launch attacks against Iraq. Iran and Turkey agreed not to intervene directly in Iraq; in effect this guaranteed that neither country would attempt to annex parts of Iraq should it disintegrate.

After the war of 1991 an Iraqi-Kurdish revolt was crushed by Baghdad, and Turkey admitted about 400,000 Iraqi Kurdish refugees, who were helped by Turkish and international authorities before returning to northern Iraq. Turkey assisted in maintaining a "no-fly" zone so as to safeguard Iraqi Kurds from the Baghdad government, but Turkish troops frequently attacked Turkish-Kurdish separatist groups operating in northern Iraq.

Turkey concluded military cooperation and free trade agreements with Israel in 1996–1997, thereby forming a limited alliance with a powerful partner that shared Turkey's opposition to Syrian foreign policy. The Turkish military obliged Erbakan, the Islamist prime minister, to continue the agreements with Israel, despite his reluctance to do so. The tie to Israel helped lead to Syria's expelling Ocalan, the Kurdish leader, as well as increasing Israeli tourism in Turkey and reinforcing links with the United States, a strong supporter of Israel.

THE EUROPEAN UNION

Turkish association with the E.E.C. (subsequently the E.U.) symbolized political, military, and emotional as well as economic ties between the Turkish Republic and the democratic nations of Europe. Most elite Turks saw their country as part of Europe. From the days of the Ottoman reforms in the middle of the nineteenth century to the radical transformations of Atatürk, Turkish elites had been moving the country toward a European identity. This became a more attractive idea when the chief non-communist countries of Europe planned for eventual economic and political union through the Treaty of Rome in 1957.

A Treaty of Association between Turkey and the E.E.C., signed in 1963, provided economic aid and preferential tariffs to Turkey. Some Turks on both the left and right ends of the political spectrum feared these agreements would lead to the increased economic subordination of Turkey to Europe and to the loss of effective national independence, but the major problem in connection with the E.E.C. was the great difference in the basic nature of the Turkish economy as compared to that of the E.E.C. countries.

Greece became a full member of the E.E.C. in 1981 and thus gained a potential veto over any future Turkish application for full membership. The E.E.C. froze relations with Turkey because of the military intervention of 1980 and reopened talks only in 1984, following the restoration of competing political parties. Serious debate within Turkey and among the member states of the E.E.C. about the desirability of Turkish membership persisted, as Turkey formally applied for full membership in 1987. The collapse of communism, the disintegration of the Soviet Union, and the requests of other countries to join the E.U. put a low priority on Turkey's admission. Instead, Turkey obtained in 1996 a customs union as a step toward full membership in the European Union. However, in December 1997 E.U. leaders said they would not accept Turkey as a member, pointing to the Kurdish issue, disputes with Greece, violations of human rights, the role of the Turkish military in politics, and economic problems. Many Turks believed that the most important reason for the E.U.'s decision was religious and cultural—they felt the E.U. was reluctant to admit a large Muslim country to membership in a mostly Christian Europe.

In December 1999 the E.U. reversed its earlier position and officially invited Turkey to become a candidate for admission, though actual membership would be contingent upon a long and difficult process of Turkey making many adjustments in its laws, political processes, military-civilian relations, foreign policy, and economy. The relationship of Turkey to the E. U. will greatly influence the future identity and character of the Turkish state and people.

ECONOMIC PROGRESS

Turkey survived World War II with little damage to its economy, while American aid began to flow in the early days of the Cold War. The purchasing power of the peasants, who constituted the great majority of Turks, was sustained by the government. New industries were sprouting in all regions of the country, roads were built, and agriculture was expanding. However, Turkey lacked capital, trained specialists in the professions, and a tradition of entrepreneurship.

By the mid-1950s the Turkish economy was stagnant. In 1958 grants and loans were obtained from the United States and western Europe to prevent a collapse. However, the shock of the stabilization program was so severe that it was an important factor in bringing on the coup of 1960. Menderes had found an increasing majority clamoring for an ever-larger share of the national product for immediate consumption; after he was gone, the leaders of the Second Republic experienced the same pressures.

The total public debt was over $1 billion, and the nation's foreign debt was about the same, which posed an intolerable burden on foreign exchange earnings. These findings led many businesspeople, even those who had profited from and strongly supported Democrat policies, to appreciate the attempts of Inönü and Demirel to proceed with economic plans and a more orderly development.

Nevertheless, the foreign debt continued to grow, and by 1966 it stood at approximately $2.4 billion, taking about 40 percent of Turkey's foreign earnings to service the debt. The gross national product, however, increased markedly during these years, from $6 billion at the time of the coup to over $9 billion by 1967 and more than four times that figure a decade later. Government budgets jumped yearly, with sums for capital investment often amounting to a quarter of the total. The momentum to develop the economy, set in the Menderes years, was irresistible, and although Inönü, Demirel, Ecevit, and others might deplore its effects on inflation, they did not halt it. Many contended that the extraordinary economic activities and innovations of the controversial 1950s were only now bearing fruit. In spite of inflation and devaluations of Turkish and world currencies, the Turkish economy grew 8 percent a year in real terms from 1963 to 1977, and real wages doubled.

In the 1970s a major economic problem arose with needed oil imports, as energy demands increased. Despite the building of new dams and a constant rise in domestic oil production, 60 percent of local petroleum needs had to be met by imports in 1976. The cost was draining Turkey's economy. This continued into the 1980s. For instance, in 1985 Turkey still spent nearly half of its total export revenues for oil imports.

Exports were needed to earn foreign exchange to pay the oil bills. Turkey successfully encouraged European tourists to visit its beaches, explore its cities and countryside, and view its many antiquities. To attract these tourists, roads, hotels, transportation, and numerous other facilities had to be furnished; along the way the Turkish economy and social fabric began to be transformed. The Justice party governments pushed through welfare legislation, including social security systems.

Similarly, in the 1960s more and more Turkish workers found jobs in western Europe, principally in West Germany. In 1962 there were only 13,000 Turks there; by 1974 there were 800,000; and in 1979, a peak year, over 2.5 million workers and their families lived abroad. Many emigrants returned eventually to Turkey, but others became permanent residents elsewhere. With population in Turkey increasing at a rate of 2.5 percent a year, unemployment and the lack of capital investment to create jobs bred political and social instability and contributed to the weakness of trade unions. In the 1980s, between 1.5 and 2 million Turks were still working in Europe, and hundreds of thousands were also working in various parts of the Middle East, especially in the oil-rich countries. Remittances sent home by these workers continued as a vital part of the Turkish economy.

One major advance was the completion in 1973 of the great suspension bridge across the Bosphorus. Connecting with another heavy-duty bridge over the upper reaches of the Golden Horn, it became the final link in an outer-belt superhighway that bypassed some of the traffic congestion of Istanbul and made practical the trucking of produce from the garden areas of Anatolia to the metropolitan centers of western and northern Europe. Another bridge across the Bosphorus was opened in 1988.

In the 1980s and 1990s, economic change persisted and accelerated. Population grew rapidly, from about 34 million in 1968 to 45 million in 1981, and 66 million in 2001; birthrates were highest in eastern Anatolia. About half of the population was under 20 years of age, which meant that many resources had to be devoted to education and job creation. Industry surpassed agriculture in the gross national product by the early 1980s, and half of the citizenry was living in cities by 1985. Turkey produced a wide variety of industrial goods. Government policy turned away from import substitution toward encouraging exports and allowing more competition in the internal market. National prosperity and a marked increase in the standard of living into the 1990s were tempered by persistently high rates of inflation and unemployment, substantial inequities in the distribution of wealth (by geographic region as well as by economic class), peasants' pressure on the land leading to massive migration to the cities, and the resulting strain on urban services, especially in Ankara and Istanbul. The balance of payments was often negative, and the external debt grew to more than $19 billion in 1984 and $70 billion by 1994.

On the other hand, exports increased remarkably, the currency was realistically devalued, protection of industries by tariffs decreased, construction and tourism activities flourished, life expectancy lengthened, and some uneconomic state enterprises were reformed. The new settlers in the cities often found jobs that provided them with higher incomes than were possible in the villages from which they had come, and their hastily built housing and urban amenities, although lower in quality than those for more long-term residents, were often finer than similar facilities in rural areas.

On the whole, Turkey's economy made impressive strides in the late 1990s, up to the banking-political crisis of November 2000. Between 1987 and 1998 the exports of manufactured goods doubled and private businesses, especially large diversified holding companies, flourished. The standard of living of most Turks increased as the gross national product grew from about $151 billion in 1990 to $210 billion in 1998. Negative factors included high levels of inflation, severe balance-of-payments deficits, the slow pace of privatization of state-owned businesses, the 1999 earthquake, and the felt need to spend enormous sums of money on modernizing the Turkish military's technology. In 2001 banks linked to politicians collapsed, thereby exposing corruption in high places and threatening Turkey's financial system, which had to rely on assistance from the International Monetary Fund.

AGRICULTURE

Production was stimulated in the 1950s after the road-building program opened up many new areas in Anatolia and greatly reduced the costs of transportation, particularly for wheat. A key variable was the weather. In years of abundant rainfall, Turkey could export wheat; when the rains were sparse, it could not.

Part of the early surge in agricultural production may have resulted from land distribution programs, which were approved after bitter debate in 1945 and only slowly implemented. After 1950 the Democrat party reduced but continued the program. The large, wealthy landowners remained powerful allies of Menderes and his commercial and industrial friends. Government provided credit to the farmers, and crops were purchased at high prices—higher than the world market. Peasants and large landowners used the ensuing profits to buy tractors and begin to mechanize agriculture.

As would be expected, the leaders of the 1960 coup treated the agricultural sector of the economy carefully. Agricultural investments continued to hold a high priority, especially under Justice party rule. Nevertheless, in 1961 an income tax was levied on agricultural incomes for the first time.

By the mid-1960s agriculture still accounted for 85 percent of Turkey's exports and about 40 percent of the gross national product. New dams and irrigation systems and the expanded use of fertilizers and farm machinery continued to increase the total output.

With the increase in population, land reform became a more pressing problem. When there were no more vacant lands, the only solution was to take land from large holdings and parcel it out to those who had none, and various reformers over the years sought to do this. A prize-winning Turkish novelist adopted as his theme the life of landless peasants. But the Justice party, supported by large landholders, moved very slowly on land redistribution. Ecevit asserted that it was social injustice to have 4 percent of the farmers tilling 34 percent of the land, leaving 96 percent to work the remaining 66 percent.

Between 1960 and 1980 agricultural output grew by over 3 percent per year as small peasants and large landowners alike increased their productivity. In the late 1970s and 1980s, even as agricultural productivity increased because of the greater use of tractors, seed drills, and combine harvesters, growth in other sectors of the economy meant that the proportion contributed by agriculture shrank. Still, half of the labor force worked in farming, and of the women who worked outside the home, about 90 percent were involved in agriculture. Government measures helped irrigation, the production of new crops, and credit, while government controls over most agricultural prices ended in the 1980s.

The enormous Southeast Anatolia Project, an integrated regional development program, entailed building massive dams to produce hydroelectric power and help irrigate land. It was planned in the 1960s and under construction for decades thereafter. Much of it came into use in the 1990s, with the completion of the Atatürk Dam on the Euphrates, the largest of fifteen dams.

WOMEN, RELIGION, EDUCATION, AND CULTURE

After 1945 remarkable changes in the status of women continued along patterns established in the 1920s and 1930s, as women became more educated, more able to work outside the home, freer to make choices about their lives, somewhat more active in politics, and open to the appeal of a variety of approaches to gender relations, including those espoused by Islamic fundamentalists as well as secularizing Europeanizers. Changes were differentiated by geographic region, by economic class, by rural-urban location, and by degree of social conservatism, with upper-class urban women in western Turkey seeing the greatest amount of change and working-class rural women in eastern Turkey the least. As of the 1990s, most of the female labor force continued to be engaged in unpaid rural agriculture, although more and more urban women also worked at handicrafts in the home. About one-quarter of all professionals, especially in law, education, and state employment, were women.

As the mean age of marriage went up, changes in household responsibilities also took place, although the Turkish legal code still said that men were the head of households. Only in 1992 did married women gain the legal right to work outside the home regardless of the wishes of their husbands. Some women supported Erbakan's Islamic political parties and favored conservative clothing. Wearing a head scarf in government-owned buildings became a highly controversial issue, with most secularly oriented women viewing such attire as a contradiction of the reforms that had revolutionized their status since the 1920s.

Other great changes after 1945 took place in religion and education. The rural population had never really subscribed to Atatürk's program of deemphasizing Islam. As soon as the peasants had a voice in affairs, they insisted that religion be restored to some of its former position in society, although they did not insist that the separation of state and religion be undone. Study of the old Ottoman script became possible, the mausoleums of holy men and the sultans were once again open to the public, new mosques were built, religious days of fasting and feasting were more widely observed, and the call to prayer was again sounded in the traditional Arabic. Radio Ankara presented readings from the Quran, and attendance at mosques increased.

The Democrat party of Bayar and Menderes, including in its program strong attractions for the conservative Islam of the Anatolian villagers, was successful to a degree never possible for the heirs of Atatürk. The Republican People's party was viewed as elitist and antireligious, whereas the Democrats, by contrast, built 15,000 mosques in ten years.

Educated and westernized Turks, especially Republicans, deplored what they called an abuse of religion in order to win votes, and officers cited this as one cause of their revolt in 1960. Although the military and leaders of the Republican People's party rebuked such actions, they too were following a similar practice within a short time: 6000 mosques were built between 1960 and 1964. When Inönü moved his party left of center, Justice campaigners equated this with atheistic Russian communism. Turkish peasants had hated Russians for generations; to this was added the word "Communist," which replaced "infidel" as the common insult to hurl at opponents.

Religion was still a strong political and social force, as the Islamic fundamentalist parties showed. The National Salvation party in the election of 1973 and the Welfare party in the 1980s and 1990s demonstrated substantial appeal. They were the parties of revivalist Islam in regard to education, culture, and religious practices, while also supporting reforms for many socioeconomic problems. They demanded the recognition of Islam as a valid component of Turkish thought and culture. Mainstream politicians also gave Islam greater recognition; for instance, Prime Minister Özal made the pilgrimage to Mecca in 1989 and was linked to the Naqshbandiyah Sufis. Underground Sufi orders gained strength throughout the period after 1960, quietly opening Quran schools and youth hostels. Some new banks followed Islamic rules, paying profits rather than interest on deposits to savers.

In the schools, an awakening in the study of Ottoman history occurred. Atatürk, to strengthen Turkish nationalism, had hurdled all of Ottoman history and found glory for the Turks in earlier epochs. After World War II, writings on Ottoman history began to flourish.

Higher education was advanced by the opening of new universities, including the founding of the Middle East Technical University in Ankara, which soon expanded dramatically. Following the 1960 coup, education at all levels received heavy emphasis. In the election campaign of 1973, both Demirel and Ecevit promised to establish universities throughout the land to enable attendance by every student who wished to enroll. At the elementary level there were nearly 5 million children in 30,000 schools, 200,000 students in 900 vocational schools, and 100,000 in the universities. The government founded even more new universities and increased their size in the 1980s and 1990s. In 2001, for instance, almost 650,000 students were enrolled in higher education. Private sponsors also opened 15 nongovernment universities between 1985 and 2000.

The literacy rate increased, especially for women, so that by 1975 about half were literate, while two-thirds of the men were able to read and write; in the 1990s four-fifths of Turkey's population was literate. By the 1980s 6 million children were enrolled in primary schools. New graduates included large numbers of women. Training in religiously oriented schools also increased considerably after 1980.

A number of educational institutions used a foreign language, often English, as the language of instruction. Turkey has entered into the modern world of universal education. The flood of articles and monographs from the pens of Turkish scholars in almost every field has indicated a flourishing intellectual development. Professional journals publishing articles in these disciplines attest to the arrival of Turkish learning on the world scene.

On the other hand, this major development did not produce a more stable and balanced society. There remained wide gaps between the economic and social levels of Turkish life, and university circles were painfully aware of the chasms. In the late 1950s, demonstrations, riots, and disorders were common. Disruptions of every kind resumed in the late 1970s as student disturbances were widespread. Violent outbreaks between leftist and rightist students helped bring about the military coup of 1980. The new regime purged the universities, suppressed student political groups, and attempted to depoliticize education.

The cultural life of the country and its education were greatly affected by urbanization, a constant feature of modern Turkish history. Between 1950 and 1960 over 2 million people moved to urban areas, followed by millions more later. This led to a direct confrontation of rural, and usually conservative, manners, habits, and values with their urban counterparts. The cultural elite often reflected sharp political divisions between left and right.

Popular culture flourished with the continuation and modification of production in weaving, pottery, woodworking, calligraphy, and other traditional crafts. National and municipal governments sponsored high culture modeled on the accomplishments and heritage of Europe. In most aspects of culture and the arts, the makers of the new forms and artistic products were initially Europeans or Americans, but gradually Turks replaced them. In the 1950s, a state opera and ballet were established in Ankara and Istanbul, and by the 1970s and 1980s they were increasingly performing compositions by Turks and with Turkish themes. Turks had been producing films at a rate of fewer than two each year between 1916 and 1944, but starting in the 1950s, the number and quality of films increased dramatically. In the 1960s more than 200 per year were made; however, their numbers declined later. Despite competition in the 1980s with television, production once again rose.

Regular television broadcasts began in 1968. In the 1970s more than half of broadcasting time was filled with foreign material; in the 1980s more locally produced shows were broadcast although foreign-made programs remained popular; in the 1990s many privately owned stations presented new competition. By 1984 there were more than 6 million television sets in the nation; this number rose to 8 million by 1998.

In the fine arts, a similar pattern has developed. Initially Turkish artists followed the examples of the international artistic environment and then later developed more indigenous and individual modifications. Sculptors and composers of serious music participated in the modernism, abstract, and experimental movements of Europe. Painters became extremely diverse in approach as schools, art galleries, banks, and the public supported different styles. Figure painting was still predominant, but many other methods and techniques were also followed. Poetry flourished after the 1960 revolution, as many young poets were heavily influenced by socialist criticism of society. Novelists, playwrights, and short story writers expressed a realistic criticism of the existing order. This trend was seen especially in the popular novels of Yaşar Kemal (b. 1922), whose stormy career and deep commitment to a political approach to literature epitomized the post-1950 generations.

The international style dominated Turkish architecture and replaced the Turkish National Movement in the 1950s and 1960s. Architects designed buildings for industry and business, as well as for government, and with the growth in the numbers of people engaged in the profession, architecture became more diverse and responsive to popular taste. Since the 1970s, some mosques and smaller buildings that incorporated earlier Ottoman architectural features have been built. Architecture in general, however, remained predominantly influenced by the international style.

Many Turks have viewed their country as a bridge between the West and the Middle East; some have even objected to the inclusion of Turkey in the concept of the Middle East. In the minds of Turkish leaders, N.A.T.O. and the European Union were commitments to a European identity. In more recent times, democratic Turkey has tried to maintain a balanced approach, keeping open its economic and cultural links with the Middle East and other Islamic countries. The end of the Cold War and the collapse of the Soviet Union opened up new foreign policy and economic opportunities for Turkey, even while the Kuwait crisis and tension over water issues created problems nearby.

Turkey was able to maintain a democratic political system after 1950 despite many challenges, including the strained relationship between the military and civilians, bitter quarrels among leading politicians, and the need to integrate the political desires of groups that had been suppressed. Bringing Turkish Kurds and those who favor a bigger role for Islam fully into national politics is the biggest internal issue now facing the Third Republic. On November 3, 2002, the Justice and Development Party, a reformist Islamic political movement, won about one-third of the popular votes but obtained an absolute majority of the seats in parliament. The new government faced many challenges, including difficult relations with the secularist military leadership, continuing economic problems, increasing pressure from the United States to support a war in Iraq, and perplexing questions about the relationship between religion, the state, and society. Economic advances over the decades since 1950 had also transformed Turkish society, with rapid urbanization, population growth, a higher standard of living, and educational expansion marking the half century since the advent of multiparty democracy.

As Turkey and Europe draw nearer to a time when a final decision on Turkish full membership in the European Union will be made, Turkey's rich historical heritage from the Ottoman Empire, Islamic civilization, and Atatürk's republic will play a great role in determining its future identity.

REFERENCES

References cited at the end of Chapters 27, 32, and 37 are pertinent to this chapter as well.

Ahmad, Feroz: *The Turkish Experiment in Democracy, 1950–1975.* London: C. Hurst & Co., 1977. A thorough study of Turkish politics from the end of World War II to 1975.

Arat, Yeşim: *The Patriarchal Paradox: Women Politicians in Turkey.* Rutherford, N.J.: Fairleigh Dickinson University Press, 1989. Also discusses gender roles and values in Turkish society.

Bahcheli, Tozun: *Greek-Turkish Relations Since 1955.* Boulder, Colo.: Westview Press, 1990. A balanced account that deals chiefly with the dispute over Cyprus.

Barkey, Henri J., and Graham E. Fuller: *Turkey's Kurdish Question.* London: Rowman and Littlefield, 1998. Concentrates on the 1980s and 1990s and is policy oriented.

Birand, Mehmet Ali: *Shirts of Steel: An Anatomy of the Turkish Armed Forces.* Translated by Saliha Paker and Ruth Christie. London: Tauris, 1991. Describes all aspects of the life and views of Turkish soldiers and officers.

Davison, Roderic H.: *Turkey: A Short History.* 3d ed. Huntingdon, England: Eothen, 1998. This good introduction, first published in 1968, has been brought up to date with a new concluding chapter by C. H. Dodd.

Dodd, C. H.: *The Crisis of Turkish Democracy.* North Humberside, England: Eothen, 1983. An excellent essay; includes excerpts of the constitution.

Gunter, Michael M.: *The Kurds in Turkey: A Political Dilemma.* Boulder, Colo.: Westview, 1990. The best introduction to the subject.

Hale, William: *The Political and Economic Development of Modern Turkey.* London: Croom Helm, 1981. A useful treatment, concentrating on the period since 1960.

———: *Turkish Politics and the Military.* London: Routledge, 1994. The history of military-political relationships from Ottoman times onward is presented, as well as a comparative theoretical discussion.

Heper, Metin, and Ahmet Evin, eds.: *Politics in the Third Turkish Republic.* Boulder, Colo.: Westview, 1994. Nineteen essays on a wide variety of topics, including education, the economy, and foreign policy.

Kolars, John F., and William A. Mitchell: *The Euphrates River and the Southeast Anatolia Development Project.* Carbondale: Southern Illinois University Press, 1991. This technical study also discusses Syria and Iraq as well as Turkey.

Liel, Alon: *Turkey in the Middle East: Oil, Islam, and Politics.* Translated by Emanuel Lottern. Boulder: Lynne Rienner, 2001.

Makal, Mahmut: *A Village in Anatolia.* London: Valentine, Mitchell, 1954. An important insight into village life in Anatolia.

Mayes, Stanley: *Makarios: A Biography.* New York: St. Martin's Press, 1981. A thorough biography of a crucial figure.

Middle East Institute, Washington, D.C.: www.mideasti.org A site with many links to other resources, compiled by the publishers of the *Middle East Journal.* Especially useful for foreign policy and current affairs.

Moghadam, Valentine M.: *Women, Work, and Economic Reform in the Middle East and North Africa.* Boulder, Colo.: Lynne Rienner, 1998. Important discussion of gender issues, education, and barriers to work outside the home for Turkey, Egypt, Jordan, Syria, and Iran.

Owen, Roger, and Şevket Pamuk: *A History of Middle East Economies in the Twentieth Century.* Cambridge, Mass.: Harvard University Press, 1999. An impressive work of scholarship for Turkey and the whole Middle East.

Özbudun, Ergun: *Contemporary Turkish Politics: Challenges to Democratic Consolidation.* Boulder, Colo.: Lynne Rienner, 2000. A short, clearly written, and excellent overview.

Poulton, Hugh: *Top Hat, Grey Wolf, and Crescent: Turkish Nationalism and the Turkish Republic.* New York: New York University Press, 1997. Carefully discusses concepts of Turkish nationalism in regard to Pan-Turkism, Kurds, Alevis, and Turks living outside Turkey.

Rustow, Dankwart A.: *Turkey: America's Forgotten Ally.* New York: Council on Foreign Relations, 1987. Examines domestic as well as foreign policy.

Salt, Jeremy: "Nationalism and the Rise of Muslim Sentiment in Turkey." *Middle Eastern Studies* 31 (1995): 13–27. A useful and balanced study of many aspects of Islam in Turkey.

Shankland, David: *Islam and Society in Turkey.* Huntingdon, England: Eothen, 1999. A good description based on social anthropology, concentrating on Sufis, Alevis, and Erbakan's political movements.

Tachau, Frank: *Turkey: The Politics of Authority, Democracy, and Development.* New York: Praeger, 1984. An excellent survey with an emphasis on the period of the 1950s and after.

Weiker, Walter F.: *Ottomans, Turks, and the Jewish Polity: A History of the Jews of Turkey.* Lanham, Md.: University Press of America, 1992. A thorough study by a leading scholar of modern Turkey.

Williamson, Bill: *Education and Social Change in Egypt and Turkey.* Basingstoke, England: MacMillan, 1987. Links together educational information with political and economic factors.

CHAPTER 39

Iran: Oil, Nationalism, and Royal Dictatorship

Iran's history differed from that of such neighbors as Turkey in part because of the substantial impact of oil on Iran's politics, diplomacy, military, and economy. On the other hand, both Iranian and Turkish foreign policies were centered around the Cold War between the Soviet Union and the United States. Nationalism was the chief political value in Iran, as in many other parts of the Middle East.

Iranian political history from 1941 to 1977 fell into two parts: from the deposition of Reza Shah in 1941 to the downfall of Prime Minister Mosaddeq in 1953, when parliament dominated Reza's son, Muhammad Reza Shah; and from 1953 to 1977, when the shah controlled the political system. Oil provided wealth to the government during both periods, and the issue of oil control and nationalization was the most important political question. By the 1970s, substantial changes in landowning, industry, culture, the status of women, and education fueled by oil revenues seemed likely to change the basic nature of Iranian society.

THE SOVIET UNION AND AZERBAIJAN

In 1942 Great Britain, the Soviet Union, and Iran provided that Allied forces would be withdrawn from Iran within six months after the end of World War II. At the Tehran conference in 1943, Roosevelt, Stalin, and Churchill signed a statement that their governments desired to maintain "the independence, sovereignty, and territorial integrity of Iran."

After the armistice with Japan on September 2, 1945, Iranian nationalists looked forward to the evacuation of all foreign troops. Their high hopes were soon dashed; in December the Soviets supported a revolution in Tabriz, the chief city of Iranian Azerbaijan, which they had occupied. A new Democrat party, under the leadership of communists, established the autonomous republic of Azerbaijan and declared Azeri Turkish the official language. A small Kurdish autonomous republic was also established. Almost immediately, government troops were sent from Tehran to quell the rebellion, but Soviet troops blocked the roads. Iran appealed to the United Nations. The Soviet Union pursued delaying tactics there, and when the Iranian parliament narrowly chose Ahmad Qavam as the new prime minister, the Western press assumed that Iran was on its way behind the Iron Curtain, since Qavam had earlier befriended the Tudeh (Masses) party, a pro-communist organization outlawed by the shah.

Although U.S. and British troops left, the Soviet military remained and additional Soviets entered Iran in March 1946, when the Cold War began as far as Iran was concerned. And indeed the crisis in Iran became one of the early events in the Cold War, a worldwide struggle between the United States and its supporters versus the Soviet Union and its allies.

Prime Minister Qavam's first task was to cajole the Soviets into removing their troops. He closed down anti-Soviet newspapers and arrested rightist political and army leaders.

In the face of strong British and American statements in support of Iran and the worldwide publicity flowing from the United Nations' first large problem, the Soviet dictator Stalin decided not to use force in Iran. Instead, he announced the planned evacuation of Soviet troops. As part of the bargain, Qavam agreed to form a Soviet-Iranian oil company to exploit oil in northern Iran. Cleverly, Qavam obtained an admission from the Soviet Union that Azerbaijan was an internal Iranian problem with which the Tehran government would deal. Soviet troops actually departed in May 1946.

Qavam played his cards well. Tudeh members were included in a new Qavam coalition cabinet. However, Qavam cautiously led the Soviets into a trap. He pledged his loyalty to the shah and promised to fire the three Tudeh members of the cabinet and liquidate the autonomous Azerbaijan province. He also won a majority for his party in parliamentary elections. Since Qavam declared that elections in all provinces, including Azerbaijan, would be held under the supervision of government forces, the Soviets were presented with a difficult choice. Only if Qavam's Iran Democrats won the election could the new parliament be expected to vote an oil concession to the Soviet-controlled company. Only if an election were held could an oil concession be submitted to an Iranian parliament. But no national elections could be held so long as the Soviet-supported autonomous province of Azerbaijan existed. Tehran's troops entered Azerbaijan and fighting developed; the Soviet Union witnessed the collapse of the autonomous Kurdish and Azerbaijani regimes.

In the elections, Qavam's coalition won handily. In 1947 Qavam informed the Soviet ambassador that the oil agreement was unsatisfactory. Soviet reaction was sharp, and Qavam was accused of treacherously violating his agreement.

During this maneuvering, the Iranian government took heart from the decisive support of the United States. Mohammad Mosaddeq (born in 1882; a politician, lawyer, and landowner, famous for his opposition to Reza Shah) sought real and complete independence of action for Iran. He reminded Qavam of the law of 1944, sponsored by that fiery nationalist, forbidding an Iranian government from granting an oil concession to a foreign state without parliament's consent. With an agreement by the United States to send a military mission, parliament in late 1947 voted to void Qavam's agreement with the Soviet Union.

Iranian leaders breathed more easily; Iranian parliamentary politics returned to normal; and the shah, the army, and the United States gained in status. At the same time Qavam's coalition evaporated on a vote of confidence. He was arrested but allowed to go abroad for "his health."

IRAN LOOKS TO THE UNITED STATES

When the United States supported Iran in the stand against the Soviets, its prestige soared. American help was acceptable to the Iranians because the United States seemed less imperialistic than other powers and was not associated with Iran's past struggles against the Soviet Union and Britain. In the long run, though, United States support of Iran and of the shah offended Iranian nationalists who were suspicious of any foreign power because of the long history of British and Russian imperialism in Iran. American backing would eventually allow the shah to become extremely repressive. However, in the period from 1947 to 1953, power was chiefly in the hands of parliament. Cabinets came and went in Tehran. From 1941 to 1953 prime ministers served on average around eight months.

The general economy was not prospering. The end of World War II and the evacuation of foreign troops had halted a sizable influx of foreign exchange. Receipts from oil payments slumped. Corruption continued unabated, the wealthy and influential ignored their income taxes, and factional politics remained the sport of the great landowners.

NATIONALIZATION OF OIL

Voices had long been raised over the question of oil concessions and, in particular, with respect to royalties. As finances grew desperate, eyes turned toward the prospering Anglo-Iranian Oil Company, which had every appearance of possessing greater wealth and income than the Iranian government. The largest shareholder in the company was the British government.

For the public the oil crisis began in 1948, when the company announced that payments to Iran would remain the same as in 1947, even though the company's net profit after taxation had nearly doubled and the British government profited greatly. Iran asked the company in 1948 for an agreement similar to that which Venezuela had with American companies, which meant 50 percent of the company's profits would go to the government. A supplementary agreement signed in 1949 by the company and the Iranian government increased payments to the government, but when the company's 1948 report showed that Britain received $79 million in taxes and Iran only $38 million in royalties, the uproar was deafening. When the new parliament met in 1950, the question of the agreement fell to a newly created oil committee, headed by Mosaddeq.

When the company finally did agree to reopen negotiations on the basis of a fifty fifty split of the profits, it was too late. Mosaddeq had presented a resolution demanding nationalization of the oil industry. The incumbent prime minister, who reported publicly in March 1951 that nationalization was impractical, was assassinated.

Within a week parliament passed a bill nationalizing the oil industry. Britain objected, but riots, strikes, and demonstrations affected the area of the oil installations. British cruisers appeared in the Persian Gulf, and refineries at Abadan shut down. Mohammad Mosaddeq, hero and chairman of the oil committee, became prime minister in April.

Britain and Iran each believed it possessed the stronger bargaining weapons to back up its position. In addition, each had to be mindful of powerful psychological, political, and economic forces in its own nation. Finally, each side either ignored or was misinformed

Modern Iran
UKRAINE
RUSSIA
BLACK SEA
CAUCASUS
GEORGIA
T'bilisi
ARMENIA
Yerevan
AZERBAIJAN
NAGORNO-KARABAKH
Baku
CASPIAN SEA
Astrakhan
Atyrau
Aqtau
Zhangaözen
Türkmenbashi
KAZAKSTAN
ARAL SEA
UZBEKISTAN
Amu Darya
Samarkand
Bukhara
TURKMENISTAN
Ashkhabad
Merv
Termiz
KYRGYZSTAN
Bishkek
Almaty
Tashkent
TAJIKISTAN
Dushanbe
PAMIR MTS
HINDU KUSH
CHINA
INDIA
New Delhi
Indus
Islamabad
Peshawar
Kabul
AFGHANISTAN
Herat
Qandahar
Quetta
PAKISTAN
Karachi
ARABIAN SEA
TURKEY
Ankara
Adana
Gaziantep
KURDISTAN
IRANIAN AZERBAIJAN
Tabriz
Meshhed
Tehran
Qumm
IRAN
Kermanshah
Isfahan
Kerman
Shiraz
Ahvaz
Abadan
Basrah
KUWAIT
Kuwait
Persian Gulf
BAHRAIN
Manama
QATAR
Doha
Abu Dhabi
UNITED ARAB EMIRATES
OMAN
Muscat
Strait of Hormuz
Gulf of Oman
SAUDI ARABIA
Riyadh
IRAQ
Baghdad
Tigris
Euphrates
SYRIA
Aleppo
Damascus
CYPRUS
Nicosia
LEBANON
Beirut
MEDITERRANEAN SEA
Tel Aviv-Yafo
ISRAEL
Jerusalem
Amman
JORDAN
Port Said
Cairo
EGYPT
Nile
RED SEA
Don
Volga
Dnieper
0 100 200 mi
0 150 300 km
Railroads
Kurdish settlement
Oil fields

about the views, intentions, and strength of its opponent. Also, it was difficult to compromise a struggle based on prestige and power as well as economic matters.

The company asserted that only it could operate the intricate industry. The tottering Iranian economy could not withstand the added shock of a loss of royalties, and political leaders who had benefited from the oil income would quickly force Mosaddeq to come to terms.

On the other hand, the company and the British government failed to comprehend that nationalization of the Anglo-Iranian Oil Company united Iran as nothing else had done since the tobacco concession two generations earlier. Nationalization meant independence, and Mosaddeq had twisted the British lion's tail.

Mosaddeq encouraged Iranians to assume that income from the oil industry would enable them to live in ease, but he did not realize the difficulties he would face in selling Iranian oil without world cooperation. He also expected that the United States would support Iran in its struggle with the company for fear that Iran would drift behind the Iron Curtain. Iran's leaders had studied the legality of the nationalization of industry in Great Britain; they assumed that England would recognize the legality of the same process in Iran. Moreover, they failed to perceive that Britain's acceptance would invite nationalization elsewhere, a thought that gave nightmares to oil officials the world over.

In the ensuing debate between the company and Iran, the position of Prime Minister Mosaddeq was initially strong. Although his National Front party had only 8 out of 136 in parliament when he became leader of the government, his following and influence were widespread. One of his staunchest supporters was a leader of the Shii ulama, Ayatollah Abd al-Qasim Kashani, who hated the British for interning him as a German agent during World War II. In 1949, after an unsuccessful attempt on the life of the shah, Kashani was suspected of inciting such assassinations and was exiled. Elected to parliament in 1950, Kashani worked with the government and used his position to excite popular religious fervor in support of Mosaddeq.

OIL STALEMATE AND GOVERNMENTAL CRISIS

From 1951 to 1953, the drama of the nationalization of oil in Iran had many scenes, a large cast of players, and a constant shift of location. Proposals made by the British, the United States, and international groups to effect a settlement all failed. By the end of the summer of 1951, the oil industry in Iran was shut down; the tanks were full, and no oil was being loaded for export. Production was hurriedly raised in other Persian Gulf oil-producing states.

After these failures the issue was reduced to the amount of compensation, but no agreement could be reached. As the controversy dragged on, Britain and the West adjusted to the loss of Iranian oil. The Anglo-Iranian Oil Company expanded its operations outside Iran. By the spring of 1953, there was a glut of oil on the world market.

In Iran, affairs were descending rapidly to a state of chaos. The loss of royalties was beginning to pinch. Since the great mass of Iranians, however, were not dependent on foreign exchange, life did go on. Nevertheless, Mosaddeq was not nearing any solution. The nationalists were becoming frustrated, the army was being purged by Mosaddeq, the wealthy landowners who governed the country soon discovered that the loss of the royalty revenues hurt them, and the shah was suspicious of Mosaddeq's ambitions.

A crisis developed in July 1952 when parliament opened. Before Mosaddeq would accept the prime ministership, he demanded absolute power for six months. Many members of his own party objected, and so did the shah. Thereupon Mosaddeq resigned, and the shah appointed Qavam to form a cabinet. Qavam publicly branded Mosaddeq a demagogue and Kashani a hypocrite, and he stated that he would settle with the British. Quite understandably, he was forced to resign. But first there were four days of bloody rioting led in Tehran by Mosaddeq, Kashani, and a resurgent Tudeh party.

To avoid civil war the shah sent for Mosaddeq. Kashani was elected speaker of parliament. In August, Mosaddeq became minister of war and was granted unlimited powers; he had reached the pinnacle of his career. Soon the cracks in his structure began to appear. Quarrels within his own party arose over appointments, and in January 1953, when he obtained a continuation of his personal rule for another year, Kashani deserted him. In July, General Fazl Allah Zahedi, his former backer and a retired popular strong man in the army, started plotting Mosaddeq's overthrow.

By this time the government of Mosaddeq had lost the support of many political and social groups in Iran, although he remained enormously popular with the people of the country. His toying with the communists alienated the United States. In 1953 the United States and Britain secretly funded groups that opposed Mosaddeq and split his National Front. Lacking any solid support from the Iranian army, landowners, religious groups, or the shah, Mosaddeq lost out completely.

On August 13, after Mosaddeq decided to dissolve parliament, the shah dismissed him and appointed General Zahedi as prime minister. Mosaddeq refused to be dismissed, however, and remained in office. Muhammad Reza Shah fled by plane to Baghdad and Rome, and Zahedi escaped arrest. But on August 19, crowds in the streets of Tehran began to shout: "Long live the shah!" Zahedi's men, the police, and the military attacked Mosaddeq. This opposition to Mosaddeq was organized and funded by the U.S. Central Intelligence Agency; the United States was convinced Iran was drifting toward the Soviet camp.

The shah soon returned, Mosaddeq was caught and arrested, a new cabinet under Zahedi was approved, and the United States granted aid to Iran. The new government arrested communists and all opponents. Mosaddeq was found guilty of attempted rebellion and sentenced to imprisonment; he subsequently died in 1967. Mosaddeq came to be seen by many as a martyr to the shah's dictatorship and the struggle against American imperialism. The shah told Kermit Roosevelt of the Central Intelligence Agency, "I owe my throne to God, my people, my army—and to you."

THE OIL SETTLEMENT

A consortium of eight major international oil-producing companies was formed: U.S. firms had 40 percent and British Petroleum (the old Anglo-Iranian Oil Company) held the same percentage of the new consortium. Some Iranian nationalists saw American control of almost half of the consortium as a payoff for United States overthrow of Mosaddeq. Key decisions on production and sales were to be made by the consortium, which would extract, refine, and market petroleum for the National Iranian Oil Company. The Iranian company would receive half of the profits and pay compensation for nationalization. Parliament ratified the agreement, and oil began to gush immediately. As the world demand for oil products expanded rapidly, yearly payments to Iran rose sharply to approximately $300 million by 1960.

The island of Kharg in the Persian Gulf was chosen as a convenient base for oil operations, and pipelines were laid between Kharg and the mainland in 1960. Iran acquired its own tankers and began to find markets for its oil. Petroleum operations also were improved by the utilization in the 1960s of the seemingly limitless quantities of natural gas in the oil fields, burned off and wasted for decades.

Oil and gas income to the government soared, and in 1970 it stood at $1 billion. The shah nevertheless complained regularly to the consortium that it was not increasing production fast enough. The consortium agreed to raise the Iranian share of the profits to 55 percent. Iran also gained a greater voice in production and pricing. This action signaled the entry of a new age in the production and pricing of petroleum, not only for Iran but for the entire world.

IRAN AND O.P.E.C.

In 1960, representatives of Iran, Iraq, Kuwait, Saudi Arabia, and Venezuela formed the Organization of Petroleum Exporting Countries (O.P.E.C.) to try to coordinate oil policies regarding levels of production, export prices, and percentages of profits to be paid in taxes and royalties. Over the ensuing decade, meetings of O.P.E.C. were held regularly, but without much world impact. This changed as other oil-producing states, such as Libya, joined, and more and more of the petroleum needs of the world were being met from O.P.E.C. resources.

Iran played a significant role in strengthening O.P.E.C. In Tehran in 1971, during an O.P.E.C. meeting, representatives of the major international oil companies agreed that 55 percent of the profits would accrue to the producing countries. The companies also agreed to a sizable increase in the posted price of crude oil (the base from which profits are calculated) and to change the posted price in accordance with fluctuations in the value of the dollar. By the end of 1972 crude oil was selling for $3 per barrel, almost double the price in early 1970.

World demand for oil appeared insatiable. In 1973 daily world consumption jumped more than 4 million barrels, with most of the increase being supplied by the Persian Gulf area. O.P.E.C. raised the price of oil twice in 1973; by the end of the year the posted price was set at $11.65 per barrel.

Iran did not join the Arab states in their reduction of output during the 1973 Arab-Israeli War, and its average daily production topped 6 million barrels. The shah gained greater control over oil production, exploration, and operations in 1973. As Iran's income from oil grew, so did the sums available for its budget. Oil income provided nearly 90 percent of Iran's annual budget. Revenues for 1973–1974, about $12 billion, dramatically increased to $31 billion in 1974–1975. For 1977–1978 revenues were estimated at $49 billion!

This bonanza could not last forever; oil was a finite resource, and eventually Iran would pump out all of it. The shah therefore was greatly concerned that the oil income be used to generate a balanced economy and self-sustaining industry. His hope was to industrialize Iran and make his empire the equal of any western European country. He spoke of Iran as another Japan.

ECONOMIC DEVELOPMENT

To develop the other natural resources of Iran, the government used petroleum revenue to build dams, hydroelectric power plants, and irrigation systems in arid regions. The vast majority of Iranians were peasants who did not prosper nearly as much as urban dwellers. The government also tried to help industries, provide social services, and finance a wide variety of undertakings, such as road building, but much of this spending was siphoned off to officials in the form of bribes. Industry tended to be concentrated in Tehran.

As oil revenues increased, the government budget grew. The budget for 1968–1969 was $3.6 billion. In each of the following four years, the budget leaped 20 percent or more. Allocations for defense and development were doubled year after year, and the annual gross national product topped $12 billion in 1972.

New projects appeared everywhere, with industrial growth especially prominent during the period 1964–1973. In 1971 the shah invited the world's leaders to ancient Persepolis to celebrate the rebirth of the Persian Empire; he believed he was propelling his people to a time when Iran once again would be one of the world's powers!

THE POLITICAL SYSTEM

In addition to a resolution of the oil issue and attempts at general economic growth, the shah resolved to develop a political system similar to that of his father, in which the monarch would be the chief authority in the state. In 1953, he dismissed parliament and called for new elections, which resulted in the victory of Zahedi's followers and the shah's friends. Elections were held again in 1956. This time the lists of candidates and the manner of the elections ensured a complete victory for conservatives, landowners, and friends of the shah. Former members of the National Front party protested the injustice and mockery of the election.

Beginning in 1961, Muhammad Reza Shah exercised his influence for what came to be termed the "White Revolution," or a revolution from the top down. He appointed an independent, Dr. Ali Amini, as prime minister. Amini was an aristocrat with a keen feeling for social responsibility and the welfare of the masses. Parliament was dismissed, and for the next two and one-half years the shah and the cabinet ruled by decree. With encouragement from the United States, the cabinet issued a land law decree requiring all landowners to sell to the government landholdings in excess of one village and stating that the government would sell such land to villagers. In 1962, when Amini tried to reduce the army's budget, the shah rejected the proposal, and Amini resigned. The shah nevertheless continued these reforms from above, though in a weakened form. From his perspective, land reform would curb the power of the large landowners who had dominated Iran between 1941 and 1953. He presented a program for his White Revolution, based on the breakup of large estates held by religious foundations and individuals and the distribution of these to peasants, the sale of government industries to privately owned companies to obtain funds to compensate the landlords, the compulsory payment of some industrial and business profits to the employees, the forming of a literacy corps from those in military service to go into the villages to teach the illiterate, and the enacting of new electoral laws to eliminate corruption in the elections and to allow women's suffrage.

Both political liberals and Shii religious leaders, including Ruh Allah Khomeini (1902–1989), vehemently protested the regime's corruption and repression, but their censure was suppressed. Khomeini was arrested, causing riots, and eventually he was exiled. He nevertheless spoke against the shah and his reforms and the country's alleged subservience to the United States and to Israel, countries that Khomeini detested. Other opponents of the regime were co-opted; they received comfortable government jobs in return for abandoning their critical attitudes.

During elections in 1963, the old parties were not permitted to present candidates. The New Iran party, organized particularly to support the shah's reform program, handily controlled the parliament, which was now dominated by agrarian reformers and city dwellers, not the great landowners, as in the past. The shah appointed thirty new members to the Senate, including two women, and six women had been elected to the parliament. For the first time in Iranian history, women's votes were officially counted, and in the cities women went to the polls in great numbers.

The shah appointed the former finance minister, Amir Abbas Hoveyda, a New Iran member, as prime minister in 1965. The land reform measures did not progress as rapidly as many had hoped, but eventually about half of village families acquired some land. However, most peasants did not gain much from the land redistribution plans; their expectations were raised, but their real economic positions gradually fell even though production increased. Sharecroppers and landless peasants were hard hit by the new agricultural structure in the countryside. The power of the absentee landlord was now often transferred to the hands of the government.

With Prime Minister Hoveyda working closely with him, the shah supervised all aspects of government and administration and believed he had attained regime stability. Amid a gathering of national leaders and international figures, he celebrated his birthday on October 26, 1967, by placing the crowns of the empire upon his head and that of Queen Farah. Parliamentary elections followed one after the other, and the shah and Hoveyda managed them so as to retain control of the political system in the shah's hands. A large secret police, control of the judiciary, and repression of opposition created a situation where few threats seemed to exist to royal dictatorship. The shah rapidly expanded the size of the government bureaucracy: the number of civil servants doubled between 1963 and 1977.

To enhance the international stature of the shah and the state, the Feast of the Last Twenty-Five Centuries was celebrated in October 1971. At Persepolis, surrounded by all the pomp and circumstance that $100 million can generate, royalty, religious dignitaries, and governmental figures from more than 100 nations gathered to mark the alleged 2,500th anniversary of the Persian Empire. Many criticized the great cost, in view of the poverty suffered by most Iranians.

FOREIGN RELATIONS: THE COLD WAR

In the Cold War, Iran sided strongly with the United States after 1953, while keeping open some communications with the Soviet Union. A U.S. military mission was established to train the Iranian army, and sizable quantities of military equipment were given until 1966, when the United States declared that the Iranian economy had become strong enough to support its army. Iran's secret police and intelligence agencies were also trained and aided by the United States. In the two decades from 1946 to 1966, over $700 million in military aid was given by the United States. By 1966 nonmilitary aid—grants for technical aid, loans from the World Bank, and outright gifts from the United States—totaled over $550 million.

In the mid-1950s the Soviets indicated a desire to settle outstanding boundary and financial controversies. However, Iran joined the pro-Western Baghdad Pact (Central Treaty Organization) in 1955. After the revolution in Iraq in 1958, Iran took on greater strategic value for the United States, and in 1959 Iran and the United States signed a bilateral agreement whereby the United States would render aid in case of any aggression on Iran.

Soviet aid projects therefore moved slowly, but the Soviet Union built a natural gas pipeline from the oil fields of southern Iran to a Soviet port on the Caspian Sea, taking natural gas as payment. The pipeline to Baku was opened in 1970.

After 1970 Iran's expenditures for new armaments skyrocketed. It is estimated that from 1973 to 1976, Iran bought or contracted for $11 billion in ships, tanks, planes, guns, and support equipment from the United States alone. Iran was the United States's single largest buyer of armaments in the world. Thousands of American technicians accompanied such weapons to train Iranians in their use. Iran now had the fifth largest military in the world!

ARAB-IRANIAN FOREIGN RELATIONS

Throughout the first half of the twentieth century, relations between Iran and the Arab states were not particularly warm. The age-old antagonisms between the Arab and Persian cultures and peoples were exacerbated by the running controversies between Sunni and Shii Islam, with non-Arab Iran being primarily Shii and most of the Arab countries' population being Sunni.

After World War II the international oil companies played off the Arab oil producers against Iran. In 1965, increasing friction with Iraq over rights in the Shatt al-Arab waterway border led to the severing of diplomatic relations. During the June 1967 Arab-Israeli War, Iran adopted a mild pro-Arab stance at the United Nations but continued to supply oil to Israel. Iranian and Israeli spies cooperated in exchanging information, and Israel paid for Iranian oil with weapons.

In 1969, when Britain's intention to withdraw its military presence from the Persian (or Arabian) Gulf area became known, the shah proclaimed an increased role for Iran there. When Bahrain sought to become an independent state in 1970, Iran relinquished its claim on Bahrain. However, the shah announced that Iran would prevent Abu Musa and the two Tunb Islands at the entrance to the Persian Gulf from falling into "hostile" hands, claiming that the islands had been seized eighty years ago, when Iran had been weak. These islands occupy a strategic position just inside the Strait of Hormuz, and any unfriendly power holding them could deny passage to tankers laden with Iranian oil. In 1971, the day before the British abandoned them, the shah occupied the islands, leading to strong protests from the amir of Ras al-Khaimah.

Iran's feud with Iraq was aggravated by the fact that both states front on the Shatt al-Arab, a river formed by the union of the Tigris and Euphrates and flowing into the Persian Gulf. Iraq bitterly condemned Iran's occupation of Abu Musa and the Tunbs in 1971 and severed diplomatic relations, deporting 60,000 Iranians from the Shii holy cities of Karbala and Najaf. The shah, in turn, extended military aid to the Kurds, who were in rebellion in northern Iraq, and gave sanctuary to 70,000 fleeing Kurds. Despite these disputes, in 1975 détente between the two was reached, and Iranian support for the Iraqi Kurds suddenly ended, leaving many of them in a precarious position. A treaty signed by Iran and Iraq in 1975 meant that Iran gained control of part of the Shatt al-Arab.

With the support of the United States, which viewed the shah as its local agent and ally in the Middle East, Iran sought to dominate the Persian Gulf and Gulf of Oman. In 1973, at the request of Sultan Qabus of Oman, the shah sent a military force to assist Oman in defeating a rebellion aided by leftist South Yemen. Some 2000 Iranian troops were in Oman by the end of 1974. By 1976 most of the rebellion had been quelled; the troops were withdrawn only in 1979 by a new and very different Iranian government.

WOMEN, EDUCATION, AND CULTURE

Changes in the status of women and in relations between men and women accelerated in the period following World War II, particularly in the cities. Although the basic patriarchal structure of the family did not change, new arrangements in working outside the home, family law, education, and ideas about gender relations did change substantially. Most rural women continued to be unpaid laborers in agricultural production for their families; a growing number were engaged in low-paying village-based jobs such as carpet weaving. As millions of Iranians moved to the cities and experienced public education, women also entered into clerical jobs and the professions, especially as teachers and nurses.

A Family Protection Law passed in 1967 and revised in 1975 changed marriage and family law so as to decrease somewhat men's control over women and to give women more extensive rights, including, for instance, more influence in divorce issues and the opportunity to become judges. Women could be drafted into the army and the police.

The literacy rate of rural women remained quite low, but by 1977 between one-third and one-half of all Iranian women were literate. About one-third of all college students were women. Women's organizations and publications flourished starting in the 1940s and 1950s, as in the creation of the Iranian Women's Medical Association in 1953. The shah's government brought most social organizations under its control or supervision, including those established by women. Royal control of politics meant that when women gained the right to vote in 1963, leading eventually to the presence of nineteen women in parliament by 1978, political advances for women became symbolic of change but without real power, which was concentrated in the person of the shah.

Public education expanded rapidly in the 1960s and 1970s as new universities were founded and old schools were renovated. Elementary schools were built throughout the country, and enrollments grew rapidly to cover about two-thirds of school-age children, though many students dropped out after the first two grades. The literacy rate began to increase. By 1971 roughly half of men were literate, representing a dramatic change since the 1950s. By the mid-1970s, there were about 6 million primary and secondary school pupils in Iran, and about half of them were girls. Ethnic minorities, such as the Kurds, lagged behind the Persian-speaking population in literacy and educational attainment. Only Persian could be used in government affairs, and all education had to be conducted in Persian, so as to help foster centralist nationalism.

The shah set up a parallel educational, financial, and clerical network to rival those features provided by the Shii ulama. Anti-shah clergy and interested laymen began to formulate the intellectual basis for a renovation of Shii Islamic theology and practices so as to counter the government's secularization. The ulama also objected strongly to the "Westoxification," or widespread infatuation with the West, among young people, as well as the growing autocracy of the shah.

Such criticism of the regime was also present in literature. The major themes of most twentieth-century Persian prose were social protest against government tyranny and corruption and attacks on opportunism in all classes of society, including the clergy. Another widespread theme has been the problem of readjustment of foreign-educated Iranians on their return home. Many novels, short stories, and plays concentrated on the lives of ordinary people, and a celebrated Iranian film was set in a village; earlier, village life had often been ignored. During the 1940s and early 1950s a large number of thinkers and artists had been attracted to the Tudeh party. Following its suppression, they turned to village studies, folk art, and the difficulties of the urban poor to find subject matter that would express their commitment to justice, equality, and social and economic reform. Such writers and artists were opposed to the shah's rule. Not only was there new content, but a few poets also wrote using radically new modernist forms. Neotraditional painters found themes in calligraphy, landscapes, and topics drawn from Iranian history, while other painters followed international styles. And theater finally began to provide plays that were popular and successfully depicted Iranian life.

Although engagé thinkers were important in elite circles, popular culture was dominated by political conservatives, and government censors controlled the media. Television broadcasting started in 1958; shows initially featured American programming, although eventually Iranian shows predominated. By the mid-1970s there were about 4 million radios and 1.7 million television sets in Iran, and government control of the media was a significant asset in maintaining control over society. Filmmaking flourished. From 1967 to 1977 about 480 feature films were produced in Iran.

Iran's birthrates were remarkably high; the population grew from 20 million in 1956 to 34 milllion in 1976. The rate of increase in the mid-1970s was over 3 percent per year. Millions of people moved from the villages to the cities, and especially to Tehran, although many of the migrants were transient and periodically returned to the villages. In 1956 about one-third of the total population lived in cities; by 1976 this proportion had risen to nearly one-half. The amenities available to the new migrants, particularly those who were poor, were extremely inadequate. Two-thirds of the population was under the age of 30. Given these circumstances, there was a strong pressure for change.

Whereas Iranian society was changing, Muhammad Reza Shah's political system became increasingly rigid and unresponsive to new circumstances. Still, by 1977, it appeared that Iran was overwhelmingly successful in many fields. In foreign policy, the alliance with the United States had helped preserve the independence of the country, while allowing the purchase of extremely sophisticated weapons. Domestically, the political opposition epitomized by Mosaddeq seemed to have disappeared. Rapidly increasing oil revenues opened many opportunities for industrialization, improvements in education, and raising the standard of living of urban and rural Iranians.

And yet, despite the apparent strength of Muhammad Reza Shah, in less than two years a violent revolution swept him, his military forces, and his political system from power. Iran underwent a radical and unexpected transformation to an Islamic republic.

REFERENCES

References cited at the end of Chapters 22, 29, 30, 33, and 37 are pertinent to this chapter as well.

Abrahamian, Ervand: *Iran between Two Revolutions.* Princeton, N.J.: Princeton University Press, 1982. A detailed political and economic history, with an emphasis on the Tudeh party's development.

Akhavi, Shahrough: *Religion and Politics in Contemporary Iran: Clergy-State Relations in the Pahlavi Period.* Albany: State University of New York Press, 1980. An excellent treatment.

Alam, Asadollah: *The Shah and I: The Confidential Diary of Iran's Royal Court, 1969–1977.* New York: St. Martin's Press, 1992.

Al-e Ahmad, Jalal: *Plagued by the West (Gharbzadegi).* Translated by Paul Sprachman. New York: Caravan Books, 1982. An influential book on Iranian and western cultures.

Bamberg, J. H.: *The History of the British Petroleum Company.* Vol. 2: *The Anglo-Iranian Years, 1928–1954.* Cambridge, England: Cambridge University Press, 1994. The continuation of an earlier work by R. W. Ferrier cited in Chapter 33, based on the archives of the company.

Elm, Mostafa: *Oil, Power, and Principle: Iran's Oil Nationalization and Its Aftermath.* Syracuse, N.Y.: Syracuse University Press, 1992. An account of the diplomatic and political events of the early 1950s; sympathetic to Mosaddeq.

Entessar, Nader: *Kurdish Ethnonationalism.* Boulder, Colo.: Lynne Rienner, 1992. This short survey is a fine introduction to the situation of modern Kurds in Iran, Turkey, and Iraq.

Farman Farmaian, Sattareh, with Dora Munker: *Daughter of Persia: A Woman's Journey from Her Father's Harem through the Islamic Revolution.* New York: Crown Publications, 1992. An autobiography of a leading Iranian woman; covers the late Qajars, Reza Shah, social reforms, and the early days of the Islamic Revolution.

Fawcett, Louise L'Estrange: *Iran and the Cold War: The Azerbaijan Crisis of 1946.* Cambridge, England: Cambridge University Press, 1992. A clear account of internal and foreign ramifications.

Gasiorowski, Mark J.: *U.S. Foreign Policy and the Shah: Building a Client State in Iran.* Ithaca, N.Y.: Cornell University Press, 1991. This sophisticated book goes beyond the scope implied by its title to discuss internal matters and how they were related to foreign policy.

Goode, James F.: *The United States and Iran: In the Shadow of Musaddiq.* New York: St. Martin's Press, 1997. A detailed chronological coverage from World War II to 1978, with an emphasis on the Mosaddeq years.

Hooglund, Eric J.: *Land and Revolution in Iran, 1960–1980.* Austin: University of Texas Press, 1982. An extremely useful study of the issue.

Katouzian, Homa: *The Political Economy of Modern Iran: Despotism and Pseudo-Modernism, 1926–1979.* New York: New York University Press, 1981. Highly critical of Muhammad Reza Shah; economic data are informative.

———: *Musaddiq and the Struggle for Power in Iran.* London: Tauris, 1990. An excellent political biography of Mosaddeq.

MacLachlan, Keith: *The Neglected Garden: The Politics and Ecology of Agriculture in Iran.* London: Tauris, 1988. A fine treatment of water, land reform, and government actions in regard to agriculture.

Middle East Studies Association of North America: www.mesa.arizona.edu This home page of a major academic association for the study of the Middle East has many useful links to a variety of other sources.

Milani, Abbas: *The Persian Sphinx: Amir Abbas Hoveyda and the Riddle of the Iranian Revolution.* Washington, D.C.: Mage, 2000. A sympathetic biography of the long-serving prime minister of Iran.

Moghadam, Fatemeh E.: *From Land Reform to Revolution: The Political Economy of Agricultural Development in Iran, 1962–1979.* London: Tauris, 1996. Based on case studies of villages and large commercial farms, this is a valuable study that puts land reform into its political and economic contexts.

Mottahedeh, Roy: *The Mantle of the Prophet: Religion and Politics in Iran.* New York: Simon and Schuster, 1985.

Najmabadi, Afsaneh: *Land Reform and Social Change in Iran.* Salt Lake City: University of Utah Press, 1987. The author's evaluation of the consequences of land reform is particularly interesting.

Pahlavi, Mohammad Reza: *Answer to History.* New York: Stein and Day, 1980. The shah's own account of his reign and his downfall.

Paidar, Parvin: *Women and the Political Process in Twentieth-Century Iran.* Cambridge, England: Cambridge University Press, 1995. An excellent book that explains the history of Iranian women in the context of political, economic, and social changes.

Poya, Maryam: *Women, Work and Islamism: Ideology and Resistance in Iran.* London: Zed, 1999.

Ramazani, Rouhollah K.: *Iran's Foreign Policy, 1914–1973: A Study of Foreign Policy in Modernizing Nations.* Charlottesville: University Press of Virginia, 1975. Shows the emergence from the desperate 1941–1946 period to the power and position of 1973.

CHAPTER 40

The Islamic Republic of Iran, the Collapse of the Soviet Union, and War in Afghanistan

The reign of the Pahlavi shahs of Iran, which seemed so secure during most of the 1970s, dramatically ended in revolution and the establishment of a form of government new to the Middle East. Once in power, the Islamic Republic of Iran heatedly confronted the United States while being forced into war by Iraq. The Iranian revolutionaries created new policies, institutions, and procedures based on their views of Islam. Even more remarkable and surprising events took place to the north of Iran as the Soviet Union collapsed in the 1990s, thereby liberating the peoples of central Asia, the Caucasus, and Afghanistan from Russian control and communism. In Afghanistan, civil war resulted in the victory of a harsh fundamentalist regime. Taliban-dominated Afghanistan hosted an organization, al-Qaida, which attacked the United States in 2001, leading to a war that overthrew the Taliban.

CAUSES OF THE ISLAMIC REVOLUTION IN IRAN

A multitude of long-term and shorter-range causes led to the dramatic Iranian Revolution of 1978–1979, which in turn resulted in the creation of the Islamic Republic. Like the Constitutional Revolution of 1905–1906, with which it shared many similarities, the revolution of 1978–1979 had political, ideological, religious, economic, and cultural causes. However, the 1978–1979 Iranian Revolution differed from the earlier one in that it came from the radical right, which looked toward an idealized Islamic past, and it was based on the political activism of millions of people and the charisma of one leader, who successfully created a new order.

The structural political causes of the Islamic Revolution included the increasingly centralized nature of decision making in the royal government; the inability of Muhammad Reza Shah to adjust to new political circumstances; the suppression, destruction, or radicalization of moderate opponents of the regime; and the resultant strengthening of the only remaining alternative group, the Shii ulama.

With the abrupt creation of a one-party state in 1975, the shah made very clear his own direct control of the political process. He therefore bore responsibility for any misfortunes that might befall the nation. Iran's seeming economic success, its large role in O.P.E.C., the armaments being purchased so extravagantly, and a close friendship with the United States all reinforced Muhammad Reza Shah's belief in his destiny and ability. He surrounded himself with advisers who told him what he wanted to hear, and he became increasingly unrealistic in his aspirations. The shah tolerated widespread corruption and bribe taking.

New ideas, political programs, and leaders could not easily emerge because of their repression by the shah's secret police. Moderates who simply wanted to implement the constitution were hounded by the regime almost to the same degree as were the "reds and the blacks," that is, the extreme leftists and ulama opponents of change. Yet, despite the all-encompassing nature of the regime, which extended its power in the 1960s and 1970s beyond the cities even to the villagers and the nomad tribesmen, many Iranians remained skeptical about the legitimacy of the shah and the whole system of government.

The shah's right to rule was based ultimately on the army, on being a nationalist, and on his success in administering the government and leading the nation. The armed forces officers were mostly loyal to him, yet many other Iranians doubted the nationalistic claims of the regime. Muhammad Reza had reigned since 1941, when he was installed by his father, the British, and the Soviets. He had ruled since the 1953 overthrow of Mosaddeq, which was engineered in part by the United States and Britain. American influence in oil, the army and police, and the pro-American orientation of Iranian foreign policy all seemed to prove to many Iranian nationalists that the shah was subservient to the United States.

No matter what successes might be achieved in the economy or foreign policy, from the point of view of the ulama, the westernized and secularly oriented shah had to be considered a moral failure. The ulama felt that injustice and secularism were destroying the soul of Iran, while at the same time the shah was selling the country to the United States and Israel. Materialism, Christianity, and Judaism were felt to be corrupting Islam and the people, according to the ulama. Only a revolution, they thought, could overthrow such a regime.

Many Iranians disagreed with such judgments because they had benefited from the shah's programs, yet their support was weak and wavering. Despite the shah's successes, especially in the economy, the political system was so tightly centralized that the upper and middle classes and the wealthier peasants could not find a way of expressing their new status in politics. Iran demonstrated the difficulty of having economic development without political development.

The economy seemed prosperous. An intensified economic transformation overtook Iran in 1973 with the quadrupling of world oil prices. Moreover, all sectors of the economy were rapidly growing. However, the quadrupling of oil prices had itself brought on a world economic recession, which greatly affected affairs in Iran. As the demand for petroleum products slumped badly, a $4 billion trade deficit was entered in 1975. Despite this, per capita gross national product increased five times from 1963 to the late 1970s, even after allowing for inflation. With ever-increasing numbers of factories, the modernization of Iran and its economy seemed to be rapidly underway. Perhaps the predictions of the shah were attainable.

The shah's boasts failed to impress various elements in Iranian society who viewed his travels and self-acclaim and Prime Minister Hoveyda's political structure as idle theatricals.

Iran's cultural patterns of individuality, religious idealism, and contempt for government, along with new ideologies, produced unrest. The secret police, founded in 1957, energetically suppressed and intimidated violent and peaceful opponents of the regime.

Political parties did not possess any allure or dynamism. In 1975 the shah dissolved them, and one political party was formed: the Iranian People's Resurgence party, with Prime Minister Hoveyda as its secretary-general. Political participation under such circumstances appeared futile to many Iranians.

The economic wealth of Iran resulting from oil and development was very unequally distributed, and income inequalities increased with the oil bonanza. Persian speakers in urban areas, the armed forces, some industrial workers, and especially the top government officials were best off. But ethnic-linguistic minorities, rural regions, the unemployed and semiemployed, and most peasants were either worse off or only marginally better off. Since the government fixed prices at a low rate for basic food products, peasants and nomadic shepherds received low returns for their goods. Industrial and energy policy ignored small producers and favored splashy large projects. Those who engaged in commercial distribution through the traditional bazaars resented government favoritism for foreigners and large enterprises. Urban amenities were sadly lacking. Many people in Tehran wondered how Iran could be part of the "Great Civilization" the shah talked about when the most elementary services, such as a workable sewerage system, were lacking!

Cultural westernization, favored by the shah, offended Iranian nationalists, the merchants, and the ulama. Western styles of clothing and music, western views on sex and gender relationships, and western habits in regard to alcohol and gambling offended devout Muslims who saw the cultural westernization of their country as part of political and military imperialism. By 1977 more students from Iran attended American universities than students from any other foreign country. Repression of writers, censorship of the media, and refusal to recognize the cultural and linguistic diversity of the country also offended many intellectuals.

More immediate causes of the revolution centered around economic, personal, and political issues. Inflation was rampant in the mid-1970s. In 1977 a new prime minister replaced the veteran Hoveyda, who had been in office since 1965, and a deflationary program that was launched led to unemployment. Since most people had rising expectations, the new economic situation made them unhappy. The shah knew he was suffering from cancer, so he began to relax his hold on the government slightly. At this time, the new U.S. president, Jimmy Carter, pushed for furtherance of human rights and a strengthening of civil liberty in Iran.

THE REVOLUTION TAKES POWER

A government-inspired newspaper attack in January 1978 against Ruh Allah Khomeini, a charismatic religious scholar famed for his piety, caused a large demonstration of theological students. As the government suppressed the demonstrators, security forces killed at least seventy persons. Massive memorial demonstrations were organized forty days later to commemorate the victims; these occasions again saw new deaths, which led to a new forty-day cycle that was repeated. For Shii Muslims, martyrdom at the hands of oppressors had a strong appeal based on the circumstances surrounding the death of

Husain, the prophet Muhammad's grandson. The implacable Ayatollah Khomeini, in exile, pictured the shah as being like the Umayyads and the people of Iran as like the martyrs at Karbala in the year 680. New martyrs meant still more and larger demonstrations that eventually spread to cities and towns throughout Iran and involved millions of persons.

Banks, shops, and cinemas were attacked by the crowds, which included all sorts of people. The revolutionary movement came to include the ulama, liberals, leftists of various types, trade unionists, bazaaris, the unemployed, many women, the oil workers, and other groups.

The shah attempted to meet the demands of the crowds by appointing reformist prime ministers or, alternately, by using the army to repress the demonstrations. Fortunately for the regime, most peasants remained uninvolved. In the cities, hundreds of people were shot, but the crowds were too large, and the loyalty of the troops too suspect, so the shah decided against a bloodbath of the scale needed against such enormous numbers of demonstrators. Strikes paralyzed the economy and the government in the late summer of 1978, and oil production slumped by 80 percent. Perhaps as many as a million people demonstrated in Tehran on December 11, the anniversary of the death of Husain. Despite this, the United States continued to support the shah's rule.

The pressure finally became too intense, and Muhammad Reza hoped that if he went into exile, the monarchy and army could be preserved under a regency for the crown prince. A nationalistic and moderate prime minister was appointed. But the revolutionary movement was so widespread, and its leadership under the direction of Khomeini was so adamantly antimonarchical, that this policy failed. The shah left Iran on January 16, 1979. Short but intense fighting between the revolutionaries and royalists ended with Khomeini's transition to power on February 11. All of the shah's enormous stockpile of weapons, the attention given to the officer corps, and his nationalistic aspirations for glory and grandeur went for naught. Amid great popular rejoicing, the old system of government was ended, and a new, chaotic experiment began. As in the constitutional revolution of the 1900s, Iranians had determined their own fate, irrespective of the wishes of the great powers.

GOVERNING THE ISLAMIC REPUBLIC

Although the new regime was initially backed by most Iranians and it retained much of its base of support for many years to come, some segments of the revolutionary movement almost immediately became disillusioned with the course of events. Khomeini and his associates had a far more permanent purpose in mind than just ousting the shah; they sought a basic transformation of government and society in all its aspects. The goal of these clerical revolutionaries was the establishment of a populist, godly social order founded on fundamentalist Shii Islam. Others who held a different set of priorities were soon ousted, and the ulama legitimized their own theocratic rule in an uncompromising and heavy-handed fashion. The pace of political-religious change was extremely rapid, but economic and social reformation was slowed by a series of foreign policy crises and especially by the 1980–1988 war with Iraq.

The old regime's leaders were purged. Revolutionary courts quickly executed hundreds. Torture was once again widely employed, and a new version of the shah's secret police was created. The armed forces were purged of those associated with the shah, and the government favored the civilian Revolutionary Guards at the expense of the army. Censorship and suppression of public dissent soon crushed the media. Within a few years, the last vestige of independent and free expression of opinion had disappeared. Minority groups of all sorts were persecuted by the new regime so as to force their acquiescence to its rule. Kurds, Baluchis, Turkomans, Sunnis, Jews, tribal nomads, and others were repressed. Bahāis were forbidden government jobs or attendance in public schools because they were said to be apostates from Islam.

The cabinet of technocrats and reformers charged by Khomeini with the responsibility for governing Iran soon found that real power was located elsewhere. In the chaotic atmosphere of the revolution, neighborhood committees of religious leaders, youths, and radicals soon exercised local control. In late 1979 Khomeini assigned power to the Revolutionary Council, which was composed of ulama and laymen, and a new constitution was approved in a national referendum.

This constitution recognized the guardianship of the chief Shii theologian (at that time, Khomeini) on behalf of the Hidden Imam, who had disappeared in 878. Pending the Hidden Imam's expected return, legitimate political power could be held only by the ulama and among them, by the best as qualified by reason of insight, wisdom, justice, and piety. (This idea was derided by Iranians who believed in popular sovereignty and was also opposed on theological grounds by some Shii ulama.) The constitution set up a formal government of a unicameral legislature, judiciary, and executive. But the president, prime minister, and all other officials were subservient to the theological leader and to the ulama's Council of Guardians, who scrutinized new laws to see if they were in accordance with Islam. Pan-Islam, not Iranian nationalism, became the official ideology of the state.

The presidential election in 1980 resulted in the victory of Abu al-Hasan Bani Sadr, a western-educated social scientist and backer of Khomeini. Bani Sadr was placed in charge of the war effort; his lack of success in repelling Iraq was a signal of his subsequent downfall. In 1980–1981 the Islamic Republican party (I.R.P.) gradually took control of parliament, the courts, and the provinces. This party was dominated by the provincial ulama, many of whom had been students of Khomeini. Its street gangs, known as the party of God (Hizb Allah), intimidated political opponents, and its contacts with guilds and the bazaaris gave it extra strength.

Bani Sadr and other moderates were driven into exile or ousted by the Islamic Republican party and the Revolutionary Guards. The president of the republic fled in 1981 just before he would have been arrested. In subsequent days, I.R.P. members gained power, particularly Ali Khamenei, who was elected president in 1981 and then again in 1985. Disputes in parliament centered over the degree of government control of industry and business and over land reform.

Government ministries, the foreign service, universities, radio and television, and provincial administration were purged, renovated, and revolutionized by the I.R.P. and the ulama. Vigilantes were in charge of justice; the universities were closed; Friday prayer leaders ran the chief provincial cities.

Opposition to this system soon emerged, but it was rapidly decimated. Leftist-religious guerrillas assassinated many of the top leaders of the regime, and they in turn were arrested, tortured, and executed. The Tudeh party leaders were arrested, and the party disbanded in 1983.

Kurds and other ethnic and tribal groups presented a substantial problem. In 1979, Kurdish leaders demanded that the constitution provide local autonomy and recognition of Kurdish as an official language. Khomeini opposed these demands and used the army against the mostly Sunni Kurds. He viewed ethnic regionalism as equivalent to treason and held that loyalty to Islam should be the first political value. Some Kurds aided Iraq during the 1980–1988 war. By 1984 the central government had once again gained control of most of Iranian Kurdistan.

Ayatollah Husain Ali Montazeri, the designated heir to Khomeini, engaged in a struggle for influence against the speaker of the parliament, Hojjat al-Islam Ali Akbar Hashimi Rafsanjani (b. 1934), beginning in 1985. Rafsanjani's role in the I.R.P. seemed at risk, despite his help in securing its resounding victory in the parliamentary elections of 1984. Khomeini intervened in 1987 to abolish the I.R.P. so as to avoid discord among his followers. Despite the official dissolution of the party, its adherents completely dominated the 1988 parliamentary election and retained control of parliament. In 1989 Khomeini dismissed Montazeri as his heir in the leadership of Iran, thereby making Rafsanjani the dominant political figure.

ECONOMIC AND SOCIAL CHANGES

The economy received little attention from Khomeini. Few basic changes in the distribution of wealth were made except for the displacement of the shah and his supporters. Initially, the revolutionaries tried to establish policies for a new Islamic economic order, but the internal struggle for power and the ensuing war with Iraq sidetracked economic policy. The flight of middle- and upper-class opponents of the new regime deprived Iran of a multitude of educated professionals. Revolutionary turmoil, the war with Iraq, and the relatively low price of exported oil in the mid-1980s led to economic austerity, rationing, very high unemployment rates, inflation, government budget deficits, and the spending of foreign reserves to cover deficits. Also, a million Iranian refugees from the war zones had to be clothed, housed, and fed.

Conflicting land reform laws passed between 1980 and 1985 caused confusion in many parts of the country. By the 1990s, land reforms affected only a small number of peasants; the shah's reforms of the 1960s had been far more effective in bringing about the redistribution of arable land. The government provided subsidies so that wheat and other basic commodities would be available at low prices. Despite a general fall in the standard of living, minimum Iranian needs were met, and the rural and poorer urban sectors of society were perhaps slightly better off materially than they had been under the shah.

Oil production gradually rose in the 1980s, reaching about one-half of prerevolutionary pumping. By 1981, Iran earned $8.6 billion from its sale. Iran pushed for higher prices and found itself in this respect, as in most other oil policy matters, opposed to

Saudi Arabia. Because of the Iran-Iraq War, Iranians wished to produce more than their production quota, despite the risks of Iraqi attacks on tankers. Iraq repeatedly attempted to destroy Iran's ability to export oil. Oil revenues in 1983 nevertheless reached a high level. But as the world price of oil fell, so did Iran's income from it; by 1985 it was only $13 billion and by 1987 about $10 billion.

The government nationalized private banks, insurance companies, and large industries as the government's role in the economy became even larger than under the monarchy. Housing was a particular problem because of the war refugees and the million Afghans who fled their own chaotic, war-torn land to settle in Iran.

Social changes included substantial modifications in law and in the role of women. A codification of Shii interpretations of shariah law became necessary. Civil and commercial law codes were adapted from the royal administration, but the criminal law was completely revised in 1982 so as to be based on the shariah. Quranic punishments, including execution for such crimes as adultery and homosexuality, were publicly enforced. And secularly trained judges gradually were dismissed in favor of those educated in religious seminaries.

Many women had participated in the revolution, often while wearing black chadors, a head and body covering, so as to show their opposition to the shah's westernization. In following years, they saw a major emphasis placed on tradition, the extended family, and working in the home. The legal age for women to marry was lowered to thirteen (later, fifteen), and the Family Protection Law of 1967 was annulled, thereby changing once again the legal status of divorce. Government birth control efforts were abandoned until the late 1980s, when a change in policy restored a religiously sanctioned family planning campaign. Abortion under most circumstances was condemned, but birth control was advocated so as to counter a considerable increase in population. Primary school children were segregated by gender. President Rafsanjani called in 1989 for equal pay for equal work by women but said female workers should be separated from men when possible. Women composed about 10 percent of the workforce.

Women were still eligible to run for election to parliament—four were selected in 1980 and nine in 1992—but they could not serve as judges. Modesty, as interpreted by the ulama, was enforced in women's clothing. In legal issues such as child custody and divorce the new regime favored men over women. Swimming areas were segregated by gender, and the government tried to separate men from women at work and in transportation. Nevertheless, in response to the need to replace men at war, by 1986 about 1 million women worked outside the home.

The earlier trend of movement from the villages in the countryside continued. By 1990 more than 60 percent of the population lived in cities. As in other parts of the Middle East, young people, in this case under the age of 17, constituted a majority of the population.

Cultural life changed as many of Iran's leading prerevolutionary writers and artists fled the country. New school textbooks, especially those for literature and history, emphasized Islamic values and the teaching of Arabic rather than English as a second language, and they attacked medieval poets who were viewed as toadying to kings. University faculty who were accused of being secularists or leftists were fired. When universities reopened in 1983, there were far fewer students; women composed a small but increasing proportion of all students. Public school enrollment grew to 13 million by 1989, but the government found it difficult to maintain and expand educational facilities at the rate needed by the rapidly growing population.

The new government sponsored the making of films that promoted its values, especially those dealing with the Iran-Iraq War; such films were often shown on television. In the 1990s filmmaking involved many women, who were depicted in ways supporting the regime's Islamic stance. About half of new books dealt with religious themes. Foreign books, films, music, and television shows were censored or illegal, but gradually they became more available in the 1990s, often through black market sources and videocassettes. In educational and cultural institutions, as in many other fields, the Islamic Republic instituted loyalty tests, used Islamic and ideological criteria to determine employment, and purged those accused of disloyalty or immorality.

THE IRAN-IRAQ WAR

The devastating and lengthy Iran-Iraq War that began in 1980 strongly influenced nearly all aspects of the history of the Islamic Republic. (A fuller account of the war will be found in Chapter 46, in the discussion of modern Iraqi history.) Iraq began the war citing border disputes along the Shatt al-Arab waterway and alleged Iranian interference in Iraqi politics, but behind these issues were Iraq's leader's personal goals, ideological differences between the two countries, power rivalries, and the expectation of a quick and easy victory over the new and inexperienced Iranian regime. The most important events in the war itself were the Iraqi attack that started the war, initial Iraqi military successes, a period of stalemate followed by Iranian advances, and then Iraqi counterattacks as international involvement in the conflict increased.

Despite the military purges of 1979–1980 and the initial Iraqi conquest of parts of southwestern Iran, the revolutionary regime put up a spirited defense. Using Revolutionary Guards as well as the regular armed forces, the Islamic Republic assumed the offensive in 1981. The war had the consequence of uniting many Iranians behind the government, even when Iraqi air attacks damaged cities. Oil revenues went toward the roughly $85 billion the war cost directly; indirect costs for the future would cost billions more. The attention of the regime was diverted from domestic changes to the war. Khomeini rejected mediation attempts, arguing that Iraq must pay reparations to Iran, and that the Iraqi people, a majority of whom were Shiis, should establish an Islamic Republic in Baghdad. Iran also supported Iraqi Kurdish rebels.

The fighting in the mid-1980s reached very large proportions, with hundreds of thousands of troops battling each other in southern Iraq as Iran tried to take the city of Basrah. In February 1986 Iran launched another major offensive and captured the extreme southern part of Iraq. However, Iraq enjoyed superior air power, and the Iraqi armed forces took the offensive with attacks involving hundreds of thousands of troops. Iran's inability to take Basrah and the exhaustion of Iranian troops by 1988 caused it to accept a cease-fire.

The Iranian armed forces surprised Iraq by their determination and willingness to fight despite the chaos caused by the revolution. Recruits and draftees were thoroughly indoctrinated in the regime's Islamic values, and I.R.P. ulama supervised all soldiers. By 1987 the total Iranian armed forces had increased to nearly 800,000, including the regular military, the Revolutionary Guards, and the volunteer martyrs. The Revolutionary Guards also took over internal security.

With international support for Iraq growing and the military position of Iranian armed forces rapidly declining, Khomeini in July 1988 reluctantly accepted a cease-fire proposed by the United Nations. The consequences of the 1980–1988 war were enormous. The economy was nearly in collapse, the population had lost its earlier enthusiasm for fighting, the Iranian armed forces were decimated. About 300,000 Iranians had been killed during the war and more were wounded, often severely. After so many years of death, destruction, and damage, the end of the war was a relief but also a disappointment to many Iranians, since none of Iran's war goals had been achieved and the war ended in a draw.

THE FOREIGN POLICY OF THE ISLAMIC REPUBLIC

Negative equilibrium was the key concept of Iranian foreign policy under Prime Minister Mosaddeq in the early 1950s, and, with some changes, it also became the basis of foreign policy under the Islamic Republic. According to this concept, Iran should keep both superpowers out of Iran's domestic affairs and not ally with either. Khomeini added the view that the United States and the Soviet Union were satanic and that of all the nations of the world, only Iran had a godly political system. He envisioned this system as inevitably spreading elsewhere, to nominally Muslim countries nearby and eventually to the whole world. Nationalism was not the key to Iranian policy; rather, Islam was the determinant. Iran's foreign policy embroiled Iran in repeated clashes with the United States. Two American presidents, Jimmy Carter and Ronald Reagan, were substantially affected by Iranian–United States problems.

Radical revolutionaries organized massive anti-American rallies. When Muhammad Reza Shah entered the United States for medical treatment in 1979, the U.S. embassy was seized, and captured Americans became hostages. President Bani Sadr made arrangements for the release of the Americans, but these deals collapsed because the formal Iranian government did not control the persons holding the hostages. The radicals, with the support of Khomeini, used the hostage crisis as a way of bringing down their domestic opponents and humiliating the United States for its past support of the shah. An American military rescue mission in April 1980 failed. The hostages were at last released, and they arrived in the United States on the inauguration day of President Reagan.

Secret attempts by the United States to reach an accommodation with the Iranian regime in 1986 failed. Those contacts were designed to end attacks on oil tankers, strengthen the moderate factions inside the Iranian government, and win the release of Americans held hostage in Lebanon by pro-Iranian Shii groups. After the sale of American (and Israeli) weapons to Iran and the diversion of the resulting profits to Nicaraguan Contras was discovered, a major internal political debate erupted in the United States. The consequences for Iran included the end of negotiations with the United States. Now Iran turned to China and the Soviet Union for armaments purchases. In 1987–1988 the

United States destroyed a number of Iranian naval vessels and oil platforms in the Gulf, claiming that Iran was responsible for positioning mines there.

These events took place in a regional environment fraught with danger from all sides for Iran. Most Arab countries favored Iraq in the war, except for Saddam Hussein's enemy Syria, which received an oil subsidy from Iran. Iran supported Islamic fundamentalist and revolutionary movements in countries such as Lebanon, Bahrain, and Sudan. The Soviet Union feared that Iranian-exported Islamic fundamentalism might spread into Soviet central Asia, whereas the Iranian ulama strongly opposed Soviet backing of Afghan Communists. Khomeini gained world attention by his condemnation of the novelist Salman Rushdie.

IRAN AFTER KHOMEINI

Iran's foreign policy resulted in diplomatic isolation and the enmity of the United States, but despite numerous crises, the Islamic Republic seemed to be able to overcome its military, economic, and social problems—at least until the challenge to the system posed by the death of Khomeini in June 1989. Although struggle for power seemed likely, a smooth transition took place. President Khamenei took Khomeini's place as spiritual leader, even though he was not regarded as the most authoritative in religious knowledge and judgment of the Shii ulama, and Speaker Rafsanjani was elected president with expanded powers.

Khomeini's institutional and ideological legacy favored both rule by the chief authority among the ulama and a popular voice in electing the political leadership of the Islamic Republic, thereby opening the way for a contest between the two men holding these posts and their backers. The general evolution of politics favored a transition away from charismatic rule toward a more constitutional order based upon widespread acceptance of the new regime by most Iranians. Disputes between Rafsanjani and Khamenei became more noticeable by the mid-1990s, although they usually cooperated. It was the relatively pragmatic Rafsanjani who formed most policies after the death of Khomeini.

Rafsanjani consolidated his power by gaining control of the Council of Guardians as well as another group that selected the spiritual leader. In 1992 his followers dominated parliament, whose election was influenced by the government so as to ensure the victory of its supporters. Whereas the ulama had constituted about half of the members of parliament in 1980 and 1984, by 1992 their presence fell to only one-quarter. Still, they retained ultimate control. Repression of critics and violation of human rights through arbitrary arrest was widespread. Despite this, a loosening of the system did take place. More political criticism was permitted, and a partial relaxation of cultural controls ensued for a time. Antiregime riots and demonstrations in 1992 resulted in a new tightening of controls. Rafsanjani won reelection as president in 1993 as his attention turned to economic difficulties.

After years of revolution and bitter war, Iran desperately needed pragmatic policies on reconstruction, infrastructure development, and economic growth, but its leaders differed on how to accomplish this end. Some favored government activism as in price controls and import limitations; others, usually including Rafsanjani, supported free-market changes and meeting consumer desires. Economic problems abounded. Inflation was persistent; unemployment, especially among young people, was great; birthrates were among the highest in the world (the population reached 60 million in the mid-1990s); and transportation and communications facilities, such as ports and the telephone system, required vast sums of capital investment to improve them. The standard of living of most Iranians was still not back up to what it had been before the revolution. On the other hand, from 1989 to 1994 real gross domestic product increased at about 7 percent per year.

Economic power rested in the hands of the government and the ulama-controlled charities who together controlled about four-fifths of the economy and employed one-fifth of the labor force directly. Patronage networks using these resources made privatization efforts nearly useless. The Islamic Republic also had to deal with the extraordinary long-term costs of the 1980–1988 war, estimated to be as much as $1 trillion. Still, Iran did see some economic successes in the 1990s, including repayment of much of the foreign debt, some investment in the infrastructure, a slower rate of population increase, and cuts in apparent military spending. Oil and natural gas revenues provided most of the government income as the world price of these natural resources varied sharply during the 1990s. Total Iranian production and income from oil and gas adjusted for inflation was still well below that of the late 1970s.

Iranian foreign policy under Rafsanjani was mixed. In some ways he was more moderate than Khomeini. The greatest diplomatic crisis Rafsanjani faced resulted from Iraq's invasion and annexation of Kuwait in 1990. The Islamic Republic condemned Iraq's actions and accepted the United Nations embargo against trading with Iraq, but Iran also vigorously criticized the massive United States intervention. Iraq sought peace with Iran by accepting the old, disputed border between them; diplomatic relations were resumed in 1990. During the 1991 war Iraq sent much of its air force to Iran, which subsequently kept the airplanes. The Islamic Republic unofficially supported the Iraqi Shiis who rose up against Saddam Husain following Iraq's defeat in the war, and Iran accepted many thousands of refugees from Iraq following the suppression of the revolt.

Iran also followed a cautious policy in regard to some of its other neighbors, resuming diplomatic ties with Saudi Arabia in 1991 and intervening carefully in Afghanistan to favor Shii fundamentalist groups. Hundreds of thousands of Afghan refugees fleeing the prolonged civil wars took refuge in Iran. After the collapse of the Soviet Union, Iran was on friendly terms with Russia, from which Iran purchased armaments. Iran along with Turkey, Pakistan, and Afghanistan expanded the Economic Cooperation Organization to include most of the newly independent governments of formerly Soviet central Asia. In 1992 the border with Turkmenistan was officially opened after being closed for seventy years.

What seemed to be a more pragmatic and moderate Iranian foreign policy was deemed by the United States to be only a smokescreen, behind which Iran attacked American interests and allies. Iran's continuing backing of Shii groups in southern Lebanon, its claims to islands in the southern Persian Gulf, and its aid to the new government of the Sudan reinforced American suspicion of the Iranian regime. The United States said that Iran was seeking to develop atomic weapons and long-range missiles to deliver them. As a result, U.S. foreign policy was based on the idea of dual containment, aimed against both Iran and Iraq.

Suspicion of the United States among the ulama was still great, but they were more willing in the 1990s to allow some cultural relaxation from the severity of the early years of the revolution. More books and music were permitted, as long as they remained within the general outlines of Islamic values. Poster art and calligraphy flourished, and cultural-historical figures such as the poet Hafiz now were approved by the government. Iranian nationalism, which had been attacked or ignored earlier, reemerged; nationalist overtones were added to Islam to form a definition for how the political system perceived itself. New dramatic Iranian films caught the attention of audiences and critics worldwide.

The former Minister of Culture and Islamic Guidance, Muhammad Khatami (b. 1943), influenced a cultural thaw in the 1990s that extended to changes in the status of women and to education. Women's magazines were more abundant, and they tested the limits of expression. Female authors played a prominent role in the vigorous discussion of political, religious, and social policies. Although gender segregation and enforcement of conservative clothing became less rigorous, unemployment for women, especially those in the rural areas, was substantial. About one-third of government employees in 1997 were women, but women still needed to obtain the permission of males to work outside the home. Enrollment in the primary grades by the late 1990s was divided equally between boys and girls, and one-third of university students were women. The number of all students grew greatly in the period, so that university enrollment in 1996 was triple that of 1970. However, the quality of instruction declined with the flood of new students into the public school system, and costly private schools increased in number.

KHATAMI AS PRESIDENT

Although the basic structure of the Islamic Republic continued, the moderation of revolutionary zeal also persisted, as noted especially in the May 1997 election of the reformist alim Muhammad Khatami as president, by an overwhelming 70 percent of the 30 million Iranians who voted. He was particularly popular among women, young people, urban dwellers, and all those who wanted to reform the economy and relax the rigors of Islamic fundamentalism while retaining the basic system of ulama rule.

The new president pushed hard for change, urging Iran to support the rule of law, the dignity and freedom of the individual, and a "dialogue among civilizations" that could include the United States. Khatami appointed a woman as one of the vice presidents and decreased newspaper censorship, thereby frightening hard-liners among the ulama clergy, led by Khamenei, who retained control over the army, the Revolutionary Guard, and the judiciary. Opponents of Khatami's reforms closed down liberal newspapers and attacked his supporters, including the mayor of Tehran and university students. Power was shared in an uneasy fashion between Khatami and Khomenei.

Even though President Khatami could not devise successful economic policies to stop inflation, fight unemployment and drought, and revive private businesses, he did receive a bonus as oil prices rose. In 2000 revenues from oil amounted to about $24 billion. Khatami remained popular, as could be seen in the parliamentary elections of February, 2000, in which pro-Khatami candidates won about 200 of the 290 seats. In June 2001 Khatami was re-elected with more than three-fourths of the vote. This popularity was perhaps in part because Iran sought to improve relations with some foreign governments. Iraq and Iran remained enemies, but they did finally exchange all their prisoners of war, and Iran established close ties with Saudi Arabia and a warmer relationship with other O.P.E.C. countries. Iran continued to back revolutionary Shii and Islamic fundamentalist groups in Lebanon and Palestine. However, even though the Taliban government was somewhat similar to that of the Islamic Republic, the two were on bad terms, and Iran did nothing to stop the American invasion of Afghanistan in 2001. The Islamic Republic had clearly entered a more pragmatic and nationalist phase without losing its basic elements of theocratic government, rule by the ulama, and policies based on what it viewed as religious values. In the period after 1979 Iran shared with its neighbors in central Asia, the Caucasus, and Afghanistan a history of radical change.

CENTRAL ASIA AND THE CAUCASUS REJOIN THE MIDDLE EAST

From the seventh century through the eighteenth century, most parts of western central Asia and the Caucasus were politically, militarily, economically, and culturally part of the Middle East. In the nineteenth century, the Russian Empire gradually gained control and annexed these areas, disconnecting them from many of their Middle Eastern connections. After the communists took power in Russia, they created the Union of Soviet Socialist Republics and reconquered central Asia and the Caucasus, enforcing revolutionary new policies as millions of people died in the process. Soviet rule was antireligious in general and anti-Islamic in particular, although often inconsistent in how it actually functioned. Usually the regime acted against the shariah, the ulama, Sufis, and religious education, while still trying to co-opt some Islamic leaders. Under Stalin in the 1930s, persecution of local nationalists and Islam mounted, only to be relaxed somewhat during World War II. Soviet Muslims often operated underground institutions, but their high culture tended to wither away, especially as persecution intensified in the 1960s. A social transformation took place, mostly in the cities, as literacy increased, Russians settled in many areas, the status of women changed dramatically, and government promoted European cultural forms. Population grew very rapidly, especially in the countryside.

The Soviet invasion of Afghanistan and the Islamic Revolution in Iran, both taking place in 1979, affected Soviet Muslims substantially. Khomeini's republic became for a short while an ideal to many, even in mostly Sunni Tajikistan, where Persian linguistic ties to Iran were strong. Muslims had to serve in the Soviet army in Afghanistan as it failed to repress the Afghan guerrillas. Soviet leaders feared the spread of Islamic fundamentalism from Iran and Afghanistan into the U.S.S.R. itself; this fear influenced their determination to stay in Afghanistan despite the heavy cost of doing so.

After Mikhail Gorbachev became the leader of the Soviet Union and its Communist party in 1985, he gradually introduced a series of changes in official ideology and government administration that brought about greater freedom and a restructuring of official society. Communist party leaders in the central Asian and Caucasian republics initially tended to oppose the liberalization in Moscow; eventually many tried to join the bandwagon and thereby retain power. Anti-communist schools, Quran study groups, waqfs, and new political factions began to emerge in the late 1980s, along with secularly minded nationalists and liberals of various types. New mosques and madrasahs opened, and Muslims from the central Middle East helped reacquaint local believers with the faith.

Gorbachev and his successor, Boris Yeltsin, presided over a new foreign policy based on cooperation with the United States and the end of the Cold War. Then economic decline and rapid political change led first to the abolition of communist power and finally to the dissolution of the Soviet Union in 1991. The new Commonwealth of Independent States linked the Slavic states of Russia, Ukraine, and Belarus with the central Asian Muslim republics of Kazakhstan, Kyrgyzstan (Kirgizstan), Tajikistan, Turkmenistan, and Uzbekistan. Of the three Caucasian republics, mostly Christian Armenia joined the Commonwealth immediately; Muslim Azerbaijan and Christian Georgia entered later. Some Muslims still lived in Russia proper, particularly in the northern Caucasus districts, such as Chechnya, which has sought through war to become independent of the Russian Federation.

Enormous ecological problems, such as the depletion of the Aral Sea, faced the new countries, which also found themselves in a rapidly changing international environment. They all had been part of a communist dictatorship running a centrally planned economy that had disintegrated, so economic cooperation and political restructuring seemed to be common problems facing each republic. Other internal issues included dealing with very rapid population growth; economic problems, such as dependence on one commodity (cotton), inflation, and unemployment; and the need to reinvigorate indigenous cultures.

Each of the new states followed its own particular path amid great uncertainty about political, diplomatic, economic, and cultural matters. Some examples of the range of differences included very large Kazakhstan, which possessed a large Russian, non-Muslim population and also inherited a space program and atomic weapons from the former Soviet Union. The much smaller and poorer republic of Kyrgyzstan nevertheless became one of the most democratic of the central Asian states. Turkmenistan retained the old political and economic system longer than the others, featuring a Soviet-style personality cult for the dictator as well as enormous natural gas deposits. Shii Azerbaijan had available the oil of Baku and offshore reserves under the Caspian Sea, but it was locked in a long and costly war with Armenia about ethnic minorities and borders. Georgia and Tajikistan went through civil wars and Russian intervention. Every country had internal minorities, foreign residents, and regional differentiations, which made national unity difficult to achieve.

The foreign policies of the central Asian and Caucasian republics were dominated by their relationships with Russia. Altogether the central Asian states numbered only about 50 million people and the three Caucasian states about 16 million, as compared to the much more numerous Russians. By the mid-1990s the Russians were intent on having close military and economic links with the republics. Russia regarded them as part of the "near abroad," that is, a sphere of influence for itself.

The Turkic republics of central Asia and Azerbaijan sought closer relations with Turkey, having common linguistic, religious, cultural, and economic interests. Many in central Asia and Azerbaijan saw Turkey as the model for their own futures and wanted changes such as the use of the Turkish alphabet; but by the mid-1990s the differences between the Turkish experience and their own circumstances indicated a more cautious approach to borrowing from Turkey's history. Turkey and Iran both provided scholarships for students, some economic credits, technical assistance, and cultural support. The United States, China, Saudi Arabia, Israel, and other countries have also tried to influence the central Asian and Caucasian states diplomatically, commercially, and culturally.

Central Asian Islamic fundamentalists organized into several different groups that became quite popular, especially among the young. These movements constituted part of the opposition that has struggled against the ex-communists who still control many governments. Bitterness at past exploitation, disillusionment with the ruling elites, the decline in the economy and standard of living, and universal uncertainty about public life helped inspire the fundamentalist, Islamist movements. The fundamentalists were strongest in Tajikistan, where a civil war ended with Russian and Uzbeg intervention against them and the restoration of ex-communists to power. Tajik refugees fled to Afghanistan as Russian troops took over the Afghanistan-Tajikistan border. In central Asia and most of the Caucasus, the ex-communists have maintained their control even as more linkages have been established with the Middle East through such practices as the pilgrimage to Mecca, the Saudi provision of millions of Qurans, and students going to study at al-Azhar University in Cairo.

After ten years of independence the ever more authoritarian governments of central Asia and the Caucasus still witnessed rapid population growth, economic decline, and a challenging international environment. Populations grew much faster than social services, providing great problems for education, health, and employment. Privatization of government enterprises usually worked to the benefit of families, clans, and cronies of the incumbent politicians. United States military and economic influence grew, and U.S. military forces were stationed in central Asia close to Afghanistan as part of the 2001 war there. Russia and China approved this role for American troops, based on the assumption that it would be temporary.

Further development of newly discovered oil and natural gas deposits seemed possible if ways could be found to ship these resources out of central Asia and Azerbaijan to markets abroad. Building pipelines was expensive and the price of oil was low through most of the 1990s. New pipelines also involved strategic disputes among various oil companies and countries, with the United States tending to oppose plans favored by Iran or Russia. Little concrete progress was made by 2002 other than Turkmenistan-Iran and Kazakhstan-Russia links. The economic and political development of central Asia was also significantly slowed by happenings in Afghanistan.

AFGHANISTAN: SOVIET INVASION AND WARS

Afghanistan provided a potential threat to Iran's security in the 1980s because of the presence there of more than 100,000 Soviet troops and a communist government. Muslims in Iran and throughout the Middle East regarded this situation as intolerable. Many of the origins of domestic radicalism and Soviet intervention can be found in the earlier history of Afghanistan after World War II.

Landlocked and mountainous Afghanistan was a poor country with few resources. The national government had only a small income, chiefly from taxes on commerce and foreign aid. Numerous regional, ethnic, linguistic, and tribal groupings made it difficult for any central government to control all parts of the country. Technological modernization came to Afghanistan somewhat later than to other parts of the Middle East: radio broadcasts began in 1940 and television in 1977.

King Muhammad Zahir (r. 1933–1973) was dominated earlier in his reign by two uncles and in 1953 by his cousin Muhammad Daud, who became prime minister. Daud followed a relatively conservative domestic policy, but as Afghanistan became friendlier to the Soviet Union, which rapidly increased its economic and military influence, the king became sufficiently alarmed to seize power in 1963. The Soviets and the United States competed in economic development aid to Afghanistan; particularly important was the building of new roads and airports. Conservatives won the elections to parliament, reflecting the population, which was about 85 percent rural in the 1960s.

In 1964 a new constitution was adopted, but the ineffectual king could not resolve disputes over the legalization of political parties, freedom of the press, and the declining economy. Foreign aid from the United States declined, and a drought from 1969 to 1972 severely affected the peasants. Marxist opposition groups drawing members from students in Kabul and from the thousands of army officers educated in the Soviet Union started to plan to seize power. They were preempted by former prime minister Daud, who in 1973 ousted King Muhammad Zahir and declared a republic, with himself as president. The new regime repressed both leftists and conservatives as it initiated steps toward land reform, changes in the status of women, and other reforms.

Continuing economic difficulties and the temporary cooperation of Marxist factions and army officers resulted in a new coup in 1978. Communists killed Daud and seized power. An unrealistic ideology impelled the new government to make revolutionary domestic changes, including land reform. Government education was remodeled along Soviet lines, and the status of women was altered, but internal disputes among the leftists created turmoil, leading to a direct Soviet invasion on behalf of one of the factions in late 1979. The communist reforms were extremely unpopular with most Afghans, who rejected them because they were radically different from earlier practices, and they were seen as being anti-Islamic and imposed by the Soviet Union. Conservatives, tribes, the ulama, Sufis, the Sunni majority, and the Shii minority could all agree in condemning the government in Kabul and its policies. The government in Kabul lost control of much of the country and was heavily dependent upon Soviet troops, advisers, food, and fuel.

The United States, Iran, Pakistan, and many other countries criticized the Soviet invasion and secretly aided anti-communist groups as they fought against the more than 100,000 Soviet troops and the government in Kabul. Since the United States and Saudi Arabia were also supporting the Afghan guerrillas, Iran ironically found itself on the same side as the nations it was vehemently condemning in regard to other aspects of their foreign policy. Millions of Afghans fled the fighting, chiefly to Pakistan and Iran. Militant Islamic guerrilla groups arose in different parts of the country to fight a jihad (holy war), but they had little in common except for their opposition to communism and foreign control of Afghanistan. Combat took place throughout the country; deaths, destruction, and damage were widespread and severe.

One element in the transformation of Soviet policy under its new leadership took place in 1988 when the Soviet Union agreed to withdraw its forces from Afghanistan, where they had been bogged down in a protracted and costly stalemate, which was itself part of the cause for the new policies in Moscow. Soviet troops pulled out in 1989, although the Soviet Union (and the United States) continued to give weapons to their local friends through 1991. The Afghan regime tried unsuccessfully to broaden its political appeal by moderating its policies, and the guerrillas expanded their control of the countryside.

In 1992 the Afghan Communists were finally overthrown. Afghans considered the damages they had suffered during thirteen years of civil war and foreign intervention: about 1.5 million deaths, 6 million refugees, and enormous destruction to the economy. One example of the consequences of the war was the presence of more than 10 million land mines, explosives that routinely claimed the lives of many civilian farmers every year. Volunteers from abroad who had participated in the Afghan guerrilla organizations often continued to fight on behalf of various Islamic fundamentalist groups elsewhere.

But 1992 was not the end to Afghanistan's tragedy. The chief Islamic guerrilla organizations turned to fighting each other for power in Kabul, as small, provincially based governments preserved their own local autonomy. Herat, Jalalabad, and other areas enjoyed some security and economic recovery. Linguistic, ethnic, and religious communities, often supported by different foreign governments, comprised the backing for the rival forces. The quality of life was appalling because of massive destruction of infrastructure, education, and health facilities. The collapse of Soviet Communism and then the dissolution of the Soviet Union did not greatly affect the bleak future Afghanistan faced.

In the context of the political chaos, factional civil war, foreign interventions, economic destruction, and dreadful circumstances prevalent in Afghanistan by 1994, a new group of radical Sunni fundamentalist former religious students known as the Taliban emerged. Enjoying the support of Pakistan and Saudi Arabia, the Taliban were youthful ethnic Pashtuns, many from the Qandahar region, who resented the dominance of other ethnic groups. The Taliban claimed to want a peaceful Afghanistan based on a rigorous interpretation of Islam and the shariah. Qandahar fell to their control in 1994, Herat in 1995, and Kabul in 1996. The Taliban leader Muhammad Umar (Mullah Omar), who adopted the title of Commander of the Faithful in imitation of the early caliphs, initiated a loosely organized government that quickly established order but was also anti-Shii, highly repressive toward women, and quick to brutally suppress any perceived opposition. The Taliban administration was so puritanical that it banned television, music, education for women, and even flying kites. The regime profited greatly from opium exports to Europe.

Russia, the central Asian states, Iran, and India backed various anti-Taliban factions, most notably the Northern Alliance, which held on to a small amount of land as the Taliban extended their rule to most of the country. Foreign antagonism toward the Taliban increased in 1996 when Afghanistan hosted the Saudi radical Usama bin Ladin (b. 1957; Osama bin Laden). Bin Ladin's Islamic fundamentalist terrorist organization, al-Qaida (the Base), had carried out attacks on United States embassies in Africa in 1998, leading to retaliatory U.S. missile attacks against him in Afghanistan. Al-Qaida was a worldwide secret group, now based in Afghanistan, recruiting and training new members in bases there before sending them out on missions. (There is more discussion of both Islamic fundamentalism and terrorism in Chapter 50.) The Taliban government defied resolutions by the United Nations Security Council ordering bin Ladin's extradition, resulting in sanctions in 1999–2000.

On September 11, 2001, al-Qaida members using captured civilian airplanes attacked the Pentagon just outside Washington, D.C., and destroyed the World Trade Center towers in New York City, killing thousands of people. With the support of Pakistan, Russia, N.A.T.O., and the United Nations, the United States first demanded that the Taliban turn over Usama bin Ladin and then, following their refusal to do so, launched air attacks on Afghanistan on October 7. A ground invasion starting on October 19 was closely coordinated with the Northern Alliance Afghan militias and warlords, who took Kabul on November 13. Taliban forces disintegrated, with many surrendering or switching sides, while troops from countries allied with the United States began to arrive. Qandahar fell in December. Both Muhammad Umar and Usama bin Ladin disappeared; their whereabouts were unknown despite vigorous pursuit into the mountains of eastern Afghanistan by American, British, and Afghan forces in 2002.

A new government for Afghanistan slowly emerged following the defeat of the Taliban. Backed by the international community, the chief military factions agreed on the leadership of a Pashtun, Hamid Karzai, who was formally endorsed as interim president by a council of Afghan tribal, religious, and ethnic leaders on June 14, 2002. Afghanistan was entering an uncertain period. Such issues as the allocation of power inside a united Afghanistan, the nature of the new government's policies, the role of foreign countries in assisting the country, and the possible reemergence of the Taliban all remained unresolved.

Unusual and unexpected change has been the dominant characteristic of central Asian, Caucasian, Afghan, and Iranian history since 1979. The new, radical Islamic Republic of Iran founded in 1979 stabilized despite the strains of revolution, war, and the enmity of its neighbors and most of the rest of the world. It seemed likely to endure with its own distinctive political, religious, and cultural identity. Even the death of Khomeini did not disrupt the governing system. In central Asia and the Caucasus, the collapse of communism and the Soviet Union created national independence and opportunities for political, economic, and cultural reformulations as well as increased linkages to the central Middle East. In Afghanistan, the communist seizure of power backed by Soviet invasion similarly brought about a new political and economic system, but one that was overthrown by internal Muslim guerrillas operating with foreign assistance. After the military withdrawal of the Soviets and the ouster of the Afghan Communists, the guerrillas entered a prolonged struggle for power, which greatly hindered economic recovery. The Taliban regime espousing radical Islamic fundamentalism ruled most of the country from 1996 to 2001, before being overthrown by the United States, in response to the terrorist attacks of September 11, 2001. The extraordinary international events and the rapid internal changes of the period after 1979 in Iran, central Asia, the Caucasus, and Afghanistan were in many ways unique, but the complex and controversial history of modern Israel, Palestine, and Jordan was similar in being truly remarkable.

REFERENCES

References cited at the end of Chapters 12, 29, 33, and 39 are also pertinent to this chapter.

Amuzegar, Jahangir: *The Dynamics of the Iranian Revolution: The Pahlavis' Triumph and Tragedy.* Albany: State University of New York Press, 1991. A clearly written book that is a good introduction to the causes of the 1978–1979 revolution.

———: *Iran's Economy under the Islamic Republic.* London: Tauris, 1993. A comprehensive treatment of all aspects of the subject.

Arjomand, Said Amir: *The Turban for the Crown: The Islamic Revolution in Iran.* New York: Oxford University Press, 1988. The author puts the revolution into its historical context while concentrating on the role of religion.

Bakhash, Shaul: *The Reign of the Ayatollahs: Iran and the Islamic Revolution.* New York: Basic Books, 1986. An excellent general survey; clear and relatively concise.

Brumberg, Daniel: *Reinventing Khomeini: The Struggle for Reform in Iran.* Chicago: University of Chicago Press, 2001. Analysis of Khomeini's legacy for the 1990s.

Cordesman, Anthony H.: *Iran's Military Forces in Transition: Conventional Threats and Weapons of Mass Destruction.* Westport, Conn.: Praeger, 1999. By the prolific author of many important studies of modern Middle Eastern military forces.

Goodson, Larry P.: *Afghanistan's Endless War: State Failure, Regional Politics, and the Rise of the Taliban.* Seattle: University of Washington Press, 2001. Explores the devastating effects of war on Afghan society.

Haghayeghi, Mehrdad: *Islam and Politics in Central Asia.* New York: St. Martin's Press, 1995. An excellent account of the subject.

Henry, Clement M., and Robert Springborg: *Globalization and the Politics of Development in the Middle East.* Cambridge, England: Cambridge University Press, 2001. Valuable for economic history since 1945; emphasizes the relatively poor economic performance of Middle Eastern states, including Iran, in the 1990s.

Hiro, Dilip: *Iran under the Ayatollahs.* London: Routledge and Kegan Paul, 1985. A more balanced approach than most other books; well written and organized.

Hunter, Shireen T.: *Iran after Khomeini.* New York: Praeger: 1992. A short but useful survey.

———: *Central Asia Since Independence.* Westport, Conn.: Praeger, 1996. A very useful survey.

Khadduri, Majid: *The Gulf War: The Origins and Implications of the Iraq-Iran Conflict.* New York: Oxford University Press, 1988. Detailed coverage of events from 1979 onward, as well as an introduction to earlier happenings. Presented largely from the Iraqi point of view.

Khomeini, Imam: *Islam and Revolution: Writings and Declarations of Imam Khomeini.* Translated by Hamid Algar. Berkeley, Calif.: Mizan Press, 1981. Includes lectures on Islamic government and on Islam, as well as speeches and interviews.

Kuniholm, Bruce R.: "The Geopolitics of the Caspian Basin." *Middle East Journal* 54 (2000): 546–571. Important for oil and pipeline issues and the role of Russia and the United States in them.

Limbert, John W.: *Iran: At War with History.* Boulder, Colo.: Westview, 1987. A general introduction to the geography and history of Iran.

Menashri, David: *Education and the Making of Modern Iran.* Ithaca, N.Y.: Cornell University Press, 1992. An excellent account of education in Iran from the 1810s to the 1980s.

Milani, Mohsen M.: *The Making of Iran's Islamic Revolution: From Monarchy to Islamic Republic.* 2d ed. Boulder, Colo.: Westview, 1994. Examines causes of the revolution and the nature of the Islamic Republic.

Moghadam, Valentine M.: *Modernizing Women: Gender and Social Change in the Middle East.* Boulder, Colo.: Lynne Rienner, 1993. Features chapters on Iran and Afghanistan as well as other parts of the Middle East.

Moin, Baqer: *Khomeini: Life of the Ayatollah.* New York: St. Martin's Press, 2000. An excellent biography.

Ramazani, Rouhollah K.: *Revolutionary Iran: Challenge and Response in the Middle East.* Baltimore: Johns Hopkins University Press, 1986. Concentrates on Iranian foreign policy and the reaction to it in the Middle East.

Rashid, Ahmed: *The Resurgence of Central Asia: Islam or Nationalism?* London: Zed Books, 1994. An experienced reporter examines political, economic, and religious developments in the 1980s and 1990s.

———: *Taliban: Militant Islam, Oil and Fundamentalism in Central Asia.* New Haven, Conn.: Yale University Press, 2001. An outstanding account.

Ro'i, Yaacov: *Islam in the Soviet Union: From the Second World War to Gorbachev.* New York: Columbia University Press, 2000. A lengthy and meticulous study of government policy based on Soviet archives.

Rubin, Barnett R.: *The Search for Peace in Afghanistan: From Buffer State to Failed State.* New Haven, Conn.: Yale University Press, 1995. Useful for its study of the political and military factions of 1979–1995.

Rumer, Boris, ed.: *Central Asia and the New Global Economy.* Armonk, N.Y.: Sharpe, 2000.

Zonis, Marvin: *Majestic Failure: The Fall of the Shah.* Chicago: University of Chicago Press, 1991. The story of how the psychology of the shah influenced his actions.

CHAPTER 41

The Partition of Palestine: Israel and Hashimite Jordan

Great Britain was so weakened by World War II that it turned over the fate of its Mandate of Palestine to the new United Nations, which then attempted to grapple with the conflicting nationalist claims of Zionist Jews and Palestinian Arabs. The Hashimite dynasty in Transjordan, later known as Jordan, also became closely involved in the partition of Palestine. Ultimately the Arab-Israeli dispute over Palestine became the most contentious international issue in the Middle East and one of the major conflicts in world history after 1945. In the midst of wars and external crises, Israel and Jordan domestically witnessed the gradual evolution of their own political institutions, new economic features, and social transformations, whereas the dispersed Arab Palestinian population did not have their own distinct nation.

FROM WORLD WAR II TO THE END OF THE BRITISH MANDATE

In the 1945 struggle for control over the Mandate of Palestine, the Zionist Jewish paramilitary forces outfought the war-weary British and the Arab nationalists, who had been crushed earlier in the 1936–1939 Arab revolt. David Ben-Gurion (1886–1973), the chief Zionist official, gave his approval to the actions of the three illegal Zionist armed forces in Palestine: the Haganah, the Irgun, and Lehi. The largest of the three, the Haganah (Defense), with a membership of about 60,000, had been organized in 1920 to defend isolated Jewish settlements from Arab attacks. In the 1930s it spread to every Jewish community in Palestine. During World War II it acquired weapons of every description, from small sidearms to tanks. Menachem Begin was the leader of the second largest force, the Irgun Zvai Leumi (National Military Organization); the Irgun and Lehi (Fighters for the Freedom of Israel) were right-wing semimilitary expansionist organizations dedicated to obtaining a Zionist political state that would include all of Palestine, in sharp contrast to the Zionists of the Jewish Agency and the Haganah, who were more likely to be left wing and socialist.

Arab Palestinians had a divided and factionalized leadership consisting chiefly of urban-based notables. Their most important leader was the ex-mufti of Jerusalem, Hajj Amin al-Husaini, who had earlier fled Palestine, cooperated with the Fascists during World War II, and then escaped from Europe to Egypt. The nearby Arab states also intervened in Palestinian affairs, with Egypt and Transjordan playing a particularly active role. Arab Palestinian nationalists rejected the idea of partitioning Palestine; instead, they wanted a unitary, independent state with an Arab majority and character.

The British were caught between Zionist, Arab, and American demands. Zionist military actions against the British included attacks on a British detention camp, thereby freeing illegal immigrants, and other attacks on railway and refinery facilities. Zionists were spurred on by the memory of the Holocaust and by the terrible situation of Jewish refugees still in Europe. The British refusal to admit such refugees into Palestine seemed immoral to them.

Since Britain hesitated to act because of Arab pressures and since the United States was insisting on action without any willingness to shoulder the responsibility of maintaining order in Palestine, an Anglo-American committee of inquiry was appointed to study the question. In 1946, while the committee proceeded, violence in Palestine escalated. The report of the committee recommended granting 100,000 immigration certificates to European Jews and advised that Britain retain the mandate until a trusteeship agreement under the United Nations could be arranged.

Britain was dependent on the United States, and both were concerned about Soviet expansionism in the Middle East. In addition, the cost of maintaining a sizable force of at least 100,000 men in Palestine was a heavy expense for the British. As the British cabinet weighed the dilemma, violence by the Jewish resistance movement grew. Britain arrested Jewish Agency leaders and seized great caches of arms. In retaliation the Irgun blew up the King David Hotel in Jerusalem, British military headquarters.

A new Anglo-American suggestion advocated the creation of separate Arab and Jewish autonomous provinces under a central government that would control Jerusalem, but both sides found this idea unsatisfactory. Still, hope for a solution was in the air until President Truman's announcement in October 1946, just before elections, that the United States strongly supported the immediate entry of 100,000 Jews into Palestine.

PALESTINE BEFORE THE UNITED NATIONS

In 1947 the British decided to refer the question to the United Nations, which selected a Special Committee on Palestine. The committee agreed that the mandate had proved unworkable. Some of its members approved a binational federal state; a majority favored a partition plan with economic union.

Palestine's Arab population in early 1947 was roughly twice the Jewish population: about 600,000 Jews, 1.18 million Muslim Arabs, and 149,000 Christian Arabs. The report recommended partition lines forming three sections of territory for Jews and three for Arabs, with northern and southern points of intersection and communication. Most of the good farmland would be in the Jewish sections. Jerusalem was to be internationalized. As proposed, more than 45 percent of the population in the Jewish state would be Arab,

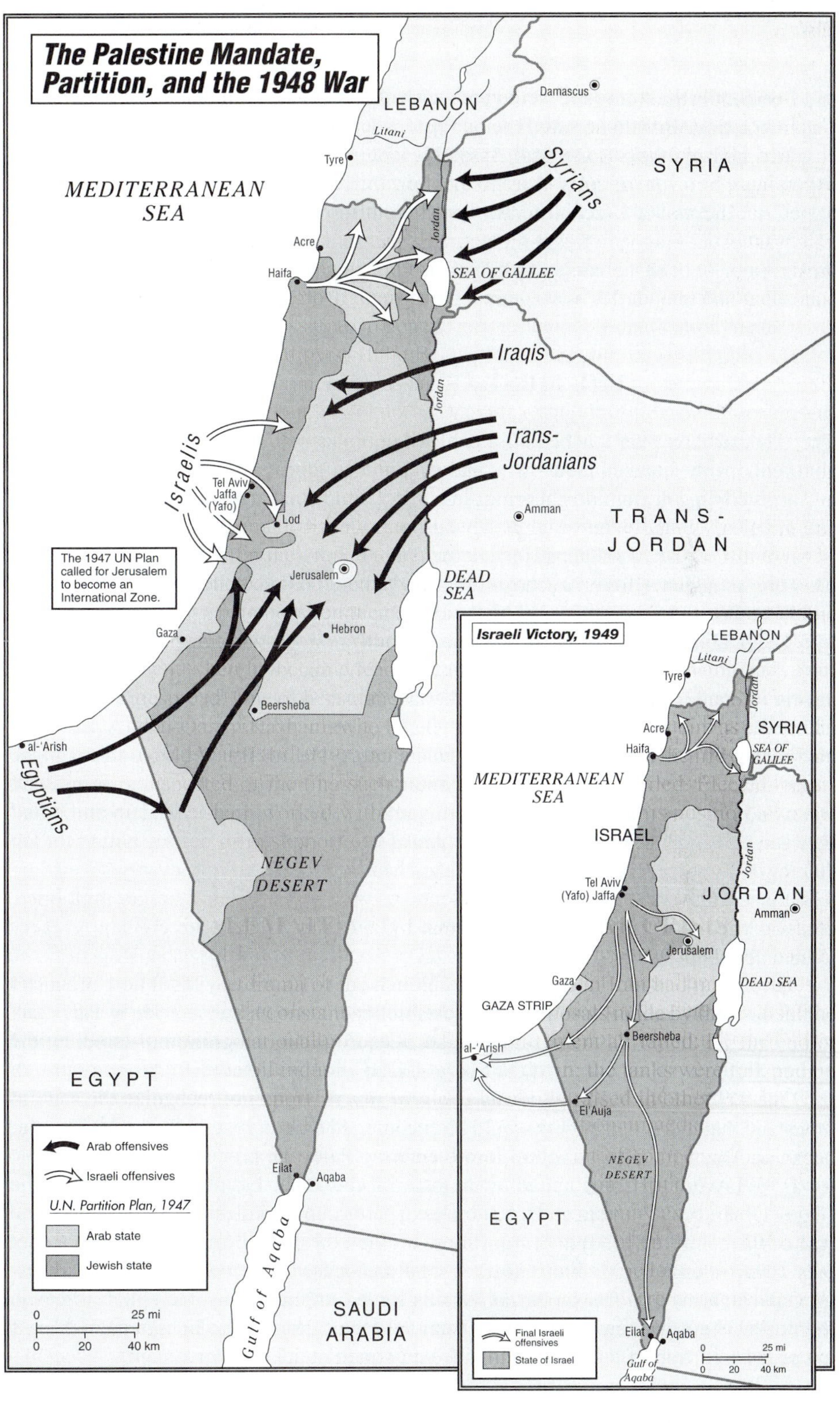
The Palestine Mandate, Partition, and the 1948 War
LEBANON
Damascus
Litani
Tyre
SYRIA
Syrians
MEDITERRANEAN SEA
Acre
Jordan
Haifa
SEA OF GALILEE
Iraqis
Jordan
Trans-Jordanians
Israelis
Tel Aviv
Jaffa (Yafo)
Lod
Amman
TRANS-JORDAN
The 1947 UN Plan called for Jerusalem to become an International Zone.
Jerusalem
DEAD SEA
Gaza
Hebron
Beersheba
al-'Arish
Egyptians
NEGEV DESERT
EGYPT
Eilat
Aqaba
Gulf of Aqaba
SAUDI ARABIA
Arab offensives
Israeli offensives
U.N. Partition Plan, 1947
Arab state
Jewish state
0 25 mi
0 20 40 km
Israeli Victory, 1949
LEBANON
Litani
Tyre
Jordan
Acre
SYRIA
Haifa
SEA OF GALILEE
MEDITERRANEAN SEA
ISRAEL
Jordan
Tel Aviv (Yafo) Jaffa
JORDAN
Amman
Jerusalem
Gaza
DEAD SEA
GAZA STRIP
Beersheba
al-'Arish
El'Auja
NEGEV DESERT
EGYPT
Final Israeli offensives
State of Israel
Eilat
Aqaba
Gulf of Aqaba
0 25 mi
0 20 40 km

and 1 percent in the Arab state would be Jewish. As it became clear that this partition plan was impractical, Britain declared the mandate would be terminated on May 15, 1948.

The United Nations General Assembly voted on partition November 29, 1947, approving it by a vote of thirty-three to thirteen, with eleven abstentions. Both the United States and the Soviet Union voted in favor; Britain abstained. Several days before the vote was taken, it appeared that the partition plan might not obtain the necessary two-thirds majority of those voting, but Zionists and the United States put pressure on five states that had intended to vote against partition.

THE FIRST ARAB-ISRAELI WAR

The U.N. partition plan touched off a civil war in Palestine. Thereafter, Haganah, Irgun, and Lehi openly attacked the British, and Arab forces grew in numbers, with volunteers and arms coming in from neighboring Arab states. Syrian volunteers entered north Palestine in January 1948; by mid-March they numbered fewer than 5000, under the leadership of Fawzi al-Qawukji, a soldier of fortune and Pan-Arab nationalist. Weapons for the Zionists were smuggled in from Czechoslovakia, and no day passed without violence. As more and more British soldiers were killed, the British public clamored to pull out quickly.

The Arab liberation army, augmented by Iraqi and Egyptian contributions, together with detachments of Palestinian Arab units, became engaged in April with the Zionist military organizations. The Jews took Tiberias and Haifa, in the area assigned to a Jewish state by the partition. Heavy mortar attacks by Irgun and Lehi on Jaffa and Acre, which had been reserved for the Arab state, accelerated the flight of Arabs from those cities. Arabs threatened the lines of communication between Haifa, Tel Aviv, and Jerusalem. Irgun and Lehi units attacked the Arab village of Dair Yasin near Jerusalem and killed between 110 and 140 villagers. Then the Arabs attacked a Jewish convoy bound for the Hebrew University and Hadassah Hospital on Mount Scopus, killing seventy-seven doctors, nurses, university teachers, and students. As war spread and its outrages multiplied, civilians tried to escape. Estimates are that by mid-May 1948, Arab civilian refugees totaled about 300,000.

On May 14, 1948, at Tel Aviv, David Ben-Gurion, flanked by his fellow ministers of the national council, proclaimed the establishment of the Jewish state in Palestine, to be called Israel. President Truman announced de facto recognition of Israel by the United States minutes later, and the Soviet Union shortly followed.

The Arab League had previously declared that it would not recognize the state of Israel and that League members would be encouraged to intervene in Palestine. The war began on May 15, 1948. Egyptian forces entering Palestine proceeded along the coast toward Tel Aviv, only to be halted by an Israeli force; other Egyptian units crossed the Negev Desert to Bethlehem and the suburbs of Jerusalem. A Palestinian Arab force held part of the central zone, and an Iraqi force crossed the Jordan and advanced to a spot only 10 miles from the Mediterranean. A small Lebanese token force crossed into Palestine, and an army of a few thousand Syrians served to pin down some Israeli forces in the north. The Arab Legion of Transjordan held the center of the line, occupied areas in the Arab portion of Palestine, and defeated Israeli attacks on Jerusalem.

Although the Arab radio and press claimed victory, the Arab leaders knew this was false. Arab soldiers found their equipment obsolete or defective, their officers were incompetent, and the zeal of the Arab soldier was lacking. Moreover, the Arab Legion of Transjordan was under orders not to move into territory awarded to the Jews by the U.N. partition plan of 1947, since Israel and Transjordan had worked out a secret arrangement to divide up this region.

In the face of widespread Arab attacks, the Israeli military and political leadership won several resounding victories. Remembering the Holocaust in Europe and full of zeal, Israeli troops fought with great enthusiasm. In the early days of the war, bitter controversy developed between Haganah and the smaller military groups, but Ben-Gurion became official commander in chief of the army and crushed internal military opposition.

The 1948 war distressed the major world powers. The U.N. Security Council appointed Count Folke Bernadotte of Sweden as mediator for Palestine, giving him a free hand to bring about an end to hostilities. A truce was arranged that ran from June 11 to July 8, and a second truce began on July 19. In October Israeli forces drove the Egyptians from most of their positions in the Negev, cleared northern Palestine, drove al-Qawukji and his Arab liberation army into Lebanon and Syria, and even occupied some Lebanese villages. In December Israeli mechanized forces pushed the Egyptians into a narrow corridor at Gaza and invaded Egyptian territory in the Sinai Peninsula, compelling the Egyptian government to cease fire.

Without question the Israeli army, under Ben-Gurion's leadership, won the 1948–1949 war. During the hostilities, Israel was a nation in arms fighting for independence and its very existence, and this spirit pervaded the fighting units. Flexibility in tactics, the use of surprise and innovations, speed, and outflanking maneuvers all marked the Israeli forces and contributed to their victory. Pride in the courage of the Jewish soldier in the face of great danger aroused soldiers to extraordinary accomplishments. About 6000 Israelis were killed in the war, roughly 1 percent of the population. A singleness of purpose permeated all levels of society and eliminated most problems of discipline. In contrast, the diversity of aims, personal jealousies, and national self-interest of the Palestinian Arabs, the Arab states, and their leaders deprived the Arab armies of the cooperation and coordination necessary for victory.

In the spring of 1948, the Arab armies as a whole were better supplied and more numerous than the Zionists. But by the autumn of 1948, the situation was reversed: Israel had more troops in the field than did the Arabs. The arms embargo to the area hindered the Israeli effort very little, but the Arabs were not so successful in circumventing it.

ARMISTICES

During the first truce, Count Bernadotte, who was later murdered by Lehi soldiers, made several suggestions for a basis on which peace could rest. Since the second truce was not well observed and the Israelis conquered more Arab territory in the second stage of the war than they had in the first, Israel expanded: it was awarded about 55 percent of the British mandate's territory by the United Nations in 1947, and by 1949 it controlled about 77 percent of what had been the Mandate of Palestine.

In 1949 several armistices between Israel and each Arab state were arranged through the United Nations, but no peace treaty came into being, and the Palestinian Arabs did not participate in the process. The armistice between Israel and Egypt left the small Gaza Strip to Egyptian occupation, but Gaza was not annexed by Egypt. Armistice lines were drawn so that many Arab villages were separated from their farmlands. An armistice between Israel and Lebanon recognized the old international frontier. Syria's armistice kept the frontiers as they were drawn in 1920; the upper Jordan River and the Sea of Galilee were wholly in Israel, but a small part of the nearby marsh area was recognized as a demilitarized zone.

With Transjordan, the settlement was far more complex. Abd Allah of Transjordan took over most of what was left of Arab Palestine: the West Bank area and east Jerusalem. This put him in direct opposition to Amin al-Husaini. Al-Husaini led the short-lived government-of-all-Palestine, proclaimed at Gaza under Egyptian sponsorship, and he bitterly opposed Abd Allah's ambitions. The western part of Jerusalem was taken by Israel, which also pushed south to gain Eilat, a port at the top of the Gulf of Aqaba, next to the Jordanian town of Aqaba, thereby opening the possibility of shipping to the Indian Ocean without having to go through the Suez Canal.

ARAB REFUGEES

After the armistices, the greatest question remaining was that of the Arab refugees. The number of Palestinian Arabs who fled from the area incorporated in Israel and who gathered in surrounding Arab states totaled more than 700,000 by 1949; about 150,000 Arabs remained in Israel, and the balance of the Palestinians lived in their homes, now located in areas held by Jordan and Egypt. The refugee camps with about 500,000 persons were located in the Gaza Strip held by Egypt, and in Jordan, Syria, and Lebanon. Egypt had serious overpopulation problems, east Jordan was quite barren, and west Jordan (the West Bank), the portion of Palestine annexed to Transjordan, lacked the resources to support a large influx of destitute people. In Jordan and Israel, the Palestinians became citizens, but in the Gaza Strip and most other places, they were stateless noncitizens. Israeli Arabs lived until 1966 mostly in areas under military government.

The refugees had left their homes for a variety of reasons. In some places Arabs were expelled when the Israelis took over. And in a number of Arab villages Israeli forces demolished the houses so the Arabs could not return. Probably the most important factor was fear: the massacre at Dair Yasin, the desire to get away from the fighting, and the reprisals of previous years frightened the Arabs and led to panic flight. The collapse of Arab society and the constant tension reinforced a sense of isolation and dread. Hearing over the radio reports that Arab armies would be victorious, some Arabs turned the key in the door, pocketed it, and fled, fully expecting to return shortly. (When this became impossible, most Arab Palestinians supported the Pan-Arab nationalists in the 1950s, and especially Nasser of Egypt. They hoped he could liberate Palestine and allow them to return to their homes.)

The refugee question was also a stumbling block to any peace settlement. Most refugees wished to return, although very few would have felt at home had they been allowed to do so since conditions had changed. But lands, buildings, and bank accounts required compensation if refugees stayed away. Arab leaders lacked the political courage to tell the refugees they could not return, and Israel agreed to discuss compensation and aids to resettlement only in an overall peace arrangement with the Arab states.

In 1948–1949 the United Nations set up a disaster-relief operation to care for refugees, whose numbers were growing rapidly. The United Nations Relief and Works Agency for Palestine Refugees (U.N.R.W.A.) was created for work-relief projects, but the refugee camps acted as breeding grounds for frustration and social revolution. Israel remained adamant about not taking back most of the refugees.

Another issue of contention was the status of Jerusalem. The 1947 partition plan had called for internationalization of the Holy City. The armistice between Israel and Jordan left Jerusalem divided by a barbed wire fence. The eastern part and most of the Old City containing the holy shrines were held by Jordan; the new city to the west came under Israeli control. Israel refused to demilitarize its sector, asserting that it was surrounded by Arab territory on three sides, and Jordan refused to permit Jews access to their holy places in the Old City. In 1950 Israel proclaimed Jerusalem its capital. All government offices moved there except the Ministry of Foreign Affairs, which remained in Tel Aviv to keep in touch with foreign diplomats. Most governments, including the United States, refused to recognize Jerusalem as the capital.

TRANSJORDAN BECOMES JORDAN

East of the Jordan River, Prince Abd Allah ruled his semidesert domain and people under the supervision of Great Britain. The strength of his position was anchored to the financial and diplomatic contributions of Great Britain and was buoyed by the Arab Legion and the Transjordan frontier force, the strongest Arab armies in the Middle East in the 1940s.

Abd Allah's rule was uncomplicated and direct. A new treaty was drafted and signed in 1946, recognizing Abd Allah as king of Transjordan and giving him greater independence from Great Britain. A constitution was promulgated and became effective in 1947, providing for a chamber of deputies and a council of notables appointed by the king.

King Abd Allah was strongly criticized in the Arab League for agreeing to such a subservient position as the treaty established, and Transjordan's application for membership in the United Nations was blocked by the Soviets on the grounds that Transjordan was not independent. Consequently, another treaty was signed in 1948, this one specifying "co-operation and mutual assistance" between Transjordan and Great Britain. Aside from Abd Allah's relations with the British and the annual subvention received from them, his main attention politically centered not on Transjordan but rather on the dream of a greater Syria, including Palestine, over which he would rule.

During the 1948 war, the Arab Legion occupied east Jerusalem against desperate Israeli attacks. Abd Allah's forces held southern and north-central Palestine. King Abd Allah proceeded formally to incorporate the West Bank Arab portion of Palestine into his state, renaming Transjordan the Hashimite Kingdom of Jordan. An election was held in 1950, and a new cabinet was formed composed of ministers from both parts of the kingdom. Most countries refused to recognize the incorporation of East Jerusalem into

Jordan, but the Arab League grudgingly agreed to the annexation of the West Bank and east Jerusalem, although they had threatened to expel from the League any state that took any part of Palestine.

Almost overnight King Abd Allah's role became exceedingly complex. The small state of an estimated 400,000 inhabitants suddenly burgeoned into a kingdom of almost 1.4 million people. More than half of the Arab refugees flocked into Jordan. Those who had means of support, an education, or a skill integrated themselves into Jordanian life or migrated to other Arab lands or to the far corners of the earth. But nearly 500,000 continued to live in refugee camps.

Grave as the refugee situation was, the most significant aspect of this influx and the annexation of Arab Palestine to Transjordan sprang from a transformation in the character of the state. West Jordanians and refugees after 1950 composed more than half the population. On the average they were better educated, more politically minded, more ardent in their Arab nationalism, and more unremitting in their desire to have a second round with Israel and regain mastery in their own state. From this point forward, Jordanian national identity became highly complex. Abd Allah doubled the size of the chamber of deputies in 1950, and half of the members were elected to represent each side of the Jordan. All real power, however, continued to be in the hands of the king.

The Palestinian Arabs, accustomed to blaming their woes on the Zionists and the British, turned their frustration on King Abd Allah. He was a shrewd ruler, as well as moderate and realistic. For these attributes he was despised as too conciliatory toward the Israelis, with whom he had many secret contacts, including even the drafting of a peace treaty. In 1951 he was murdered in Jerusalem by a follower of Hajj Amin al-Husaini.

THE STATE OF ISRAEL

Politics and Population

A provisional government was organized when the state of Israel was proclaimed in 1948 by David Ben-Gurion. In 1949, elections were held for a national parliament and constituent assembly (Knesset), amid conditions of economic austerity and rationing. Mapai (Workers' party), a socialist center group, obtained the largest bloc of seats in the Knesset but not a majority. Although a committee was directed to bring in a written constitution, no such constitution was ever formulated. Instead, in the British manner, a kind of constitution was eventually built up law by law. By doing so, internal debates about the role of religion in the state could be lessened. One of the first laws (the Law of Return) provided for unlimited ingathering of the Jewish people, the immigrants becoming Israeli citizens on their entry. A state of emergency declared in 1948 continued in effect indefinitely.

The Israeli Arab minority could and did vote in parliamentary elections, and some were elected to the Knesset. However, new anti-Zionist Arab parties were not allowed to be formed. Since most of the Arab leadership had fled and those Palestinians who stayed were cut off from the political and cultural trends of the Arab world, Israeli Arabs initially tended to vote for Jewish Israeli parties. Israeli Arabs faced security laws that in effect limited their civil rights in a number of ways until 1966. They were not drafted into the Israeli armed forces, although the Druze Arab minority did voluntarily serve. The greatest problem facing the Israeli Arabs was existential: what did it mean to be a Muslim or Christian Arab in a Jewish state? Jewish Israelis tended to view the Arab-Israeli minority as possible security risks and as alien to the basic Zionist purpose of the Israeli state—the development of the Jewish people in their ancient homeland. Israel's flag and national anthem, for instance, expressed Jewish identity rather than that of an Israeli state in which both Jews and Arabs might be equal citizens.

The Knesset was composed of 120 members elected by proportional representation from national party lists. Elections were usually held every four years, with some exceptions. In every election up to 1977, the Mapai won a commanding plurality and easily formed the government with a coalition of one kind or another. Coalitions were necessary because of basic divisions among the electorate, as reflected in the large number of political parties. Thirteen parties were represented in the Knesset elected in 1951!

If a coalition could not be formed, as in 1961, a new election could be called. David Ben-Gurion provided strong leadership amid the political turmoil until his retirement from the prime ministry in 1963. Ben-Gurion came back to politics when he split from his Mapai party by forming a new party in 1965, as he came to disagree strongly with Levi Eshkol, the prime minister from 1963 to 1969, over policies. Some parties formed coalitions so as to gain more votes in elections. Herut, a right-wing party and heir to the revisionist movement of the 1930s, and the Liberals coalesced for the 1965 election, as did Mapai and a few minor parties. Although seventeen parties presented candidates, Eshkol and his Mapai and associates won forty-five seats.

In addition to the key post in government, the prime ministry, which was determined by the parliament, Israel also had a presidency, an honorific office. Chaim Weizmann was the first person elected to that post, and he served in it until his death in 1952.

Ben-Gurion was prime minister from 1948 until 1954, when he temporarily retired to his home in a kibbutz in the Negev. He was an activist leader, pragmatic, and hawkish in regard to the Arabs. Ben-Gurion believed in Israeli self-reliance, a view he summed up by the phrase, "Our future does not depend on what the Gentiles say but on what the Jews do." Ben-Gurion favored the concept of mamlachitiut or state power, which involved government power over all national institutions, the reduction of factionalism, nonpartisan administration of the civil service and army, secular civil law, and effective political coalitions to build up consensus. Generally he succeeded in putting this concept into effect, thereby greatly strengthening Zionist-Israeli nationalism. However, he was not able to bring most Arabs into the consensus, and he also had to make exceptions in regard to health care, which remained in the control of the trade union federation, and personal status issues in law, which were in the hands of religious authorities.

Ben-Gurion was followed as prime minister for a short time by Foreign Minister Moshe Sharett, another Mapai leader. Sharett was cautious and more willing to seek an understanding with the Arabs than was Ben-Gurion. However, Ben-Gurion returned to the cabinet as minister of defense and then as prime minister in 1955. In 1956 Sharett was relieved of the foreign ministry because he did not favor reprisal attacks on Egypt, Syria, and Jordan. Ben-Gurion remained prime minister until he resigned in 1963. Levi Eshkol, his successor, had been the minister of finance and a prominent member of the powerful Histadrut, the Israeli Federation of Labor.

The Lavon affair that caused so much turmoil in the government started in 1954. Bombs planted in the United States Information Agency library in Cairo exploded, killing several persons. Egyptian investigators traced the act to Israeli agents, who were caught and tried. Egypt claimed that the plot had been an Israeli attempt to anger Americans against Egypt and to effect the cutoff of American support for the Aswan Dam. Pinhas Lavon, Israel's minister of defense at the time, was forced to resign in 1955. In 1960 he was exonerated by the cabinet, which accepted the evidence that Lavon's signature to the documents and orders had been forged.

Although Ben-Gurion had not been prime minister when many of these arrangements were said to have been made but had been closely associated with Moshe Dayan (1915–1981) and other individuals involved, he felt the blame was being shifted to him. Ben-Gurion, with the support of Moshe Dayan, formed his own party, Rafi, and presented a slate of candidates for the 1965 election. The majority of Mapai supported Eshkol, and Rafi placed only ten members in the Knesset. Eshkol formed a new coalition cabinet. When a crisis developed in 1967 over the Straits of Tiran and war was imminent, Eshkol gave the defense ministry to General Moshe Dayan.

Real authority rested in the hands of the prime minister, who usually held simultaneously the post of defense minister. Every cabinet after the first election until 1977 was a coalition centered around the Mapai party, which Ben-Gurion and his successors headed. Various parties joined with Mapai, and these changed through the years except Mapam, a leftist party that was a constant partner.

The National Religious Front, consisting of middle-of-the-road parties with a religious basis, supported Mapai after 1959 until 1977. Several cabinet crises occurred over Jewish dietary beliefs, religious education, and the question of women serving in the armed forces. There were important discussions over the question of who was considered to be a Jew. It was ultimately decided that a Jew is a person born of a Jewish mother who does not belong to another religion, or a convert according to religious law.

Economic difficulties in Israel, resulting from a widening trade gap, greater military expenditures at the expense of development, and a sharp dropping off of capital inflow, brought unemployment, devaluation, and belt-tightening pressures. Furthermore, many eastern immigrants were housed in makeshift camps, and riots occurred over the discriminatory practices of government in housing, jobs, and higher education for the Sephardic Jews. Consequently Israelis began to emigrate in worrisome numbers.

The Israeli Economy

The economy of Israel has been precarious ever since its birth in 1948. Many inhabitants expected and obtained a standard of living comparable to that of central Europe, although Israel was a small and poor country of the Middle East, with few natural resources and major international problems. The relatively high standard of living was made possible by gifts and loans from foreign governments and individual Jews in many countries, plus many sacrifices by Israelis who wanted to build up their country.

Imports for several years ranged from four to five times the value of exports. In most years, Israel has imported more than it has exported. Other economic problems included in agriculture the inefficiencies of the kibbutzim (collective villages), tight state direction of industry, the difficulty of absorbing immigrants, and the necessity of spending large sums on weapons. Because Mapai controlled the Histadrut, the Israeli Federation of Labor, and Mapai dominated the government, there was considerable doubt as to how strong a check any prime minister could maintain on wages, prices, and the standard of living.

The burden of the immigrants on the economy hampered capital development in many ways. New houses were built by the tens of thousands, and the newcomers had to be fed and clothed for many months before they were integrated and absorbed into Israeli society. Construction remained a major element in the Israeli economy for decades. In 1952 some relief came: an agreement with West Germany whereby Israel would gradually receive more than $800 million in reparations for Nazi atrocities.

After the 1956 war, as the number of new immigrants dropped off, the building trades in Israel suffered a slump, with mass layoffs. The conclusion of German reparations in 1965 and the serious decline in charitable gifts from world Jewry made for economic troubles by 1967. During its first ten years, Israel received more than $2.5 billion as imports of capital. Much of this foreign exchange was spent for consumer goods, producing a somewhat artificial standard of living that acted in competition with the need for capital to develop infrastructure projects, such as irrigation canals.

One of the gravest burdens on the Israeli economy was imposed by the economic boycott and closure of the Suez Canal to Israeli shipping by the Arab states. Israel's economy was oriented toward the service sector and also toward industry or mechanized and specialized production, which would have complemented the raw materials and agricultural produce of Arab countries, but the boycott deprived Israel of its natural markets. Iraq shut off the flow of oil in the pipeline to Haifa, forcing Israel to buy higher-priced petroleum from Iran and the Gulf of Mexico. This pressure stimulated a drive to become more independent in matters of transport and commerce, as well as in oil. Eilat on the Gulf of Aqaba was pushed as the gateway to the East. In the 1967 crisis, the closing of the Straits of Tiran by Egypt to Israel-bound shipping carrying strategic goods to Eilat affected Israel and was a cause for war. Interest in Eilat, however, was matched by European and especially Mediterranean commerce. In the 1960s a deep-water port at Ashdod, south of Tel Aviv, was constructed. Ashdod and Haifa became Israel's Mediterranean ports.

The prospect of irrigating the Negev desert and the coastal plain inspired Israeli engineers and planners to build gigantic canals from the north, circumventing Jordan, to the barren southlands. Syria and Jordan protested this unilateral use of Jordan waters, but settlement and irrigation in the Negev continued. The National Water Carrier began to direct water southward through channels and pipes in 1964; Arab attempts in 1965 to divert the headwaters of the Jordan River and thus disrupt the carrier brought about Israeli raids, which were successful in stopping the diversion efforts.

In agriculture and industry there was steady growth in production. In 1950, Israel imported half of its food; by the mid-1960s Israel was self-sufficient in staple foods, and agricultural exports, worth about one-third of total exports, expanded beyond citrus to include cotton, peanuts, and winter vegetables and fruits. Land under cultivation more than doubled between 1949 and 1960. Industrial output increased five times between 1950 and 1969, and it nearly doubled again in the following decade. Tourism grew remarkably. Despite all of Israel's economic problems, the gross national product increased in real terms from 1950 to 1972 at an average annual rate of nearly 10 percent, and output per worker tripled. Unemployment fell steadily, from 10 percent in 1953 to less than 4 percent in 1967, and the standard of living of the average Israeli dramatically improved. Despite this economic progress, imports still exceeded exports, taxes were very high, and inflation was a constant problem.

Social and Cultural Issues

Open immigration into Israel had long been the goal of Zionist leaders. In the first decade after independence, at least 800,000 immigrants swelled Israel's population rapidly; 700,000 came in the first four years alone. In 1958, at the time of the tenth anniversary celebrations, Ben-Gurion announced that the population of Israel had reached 2 million. Since about half of the postindependence immigrants were Sephardic Jews of Middle Eastern origin, their assimilation presented new problems for Israel. Furthermore, because the birthrate in this group was much higher than in others, Sephardic Jews outnumbered the politically dominant Ashkenazi, or European Jews, by about 1965.

The immigrants had to learn Hebrew, one of the two official languages of the state (Arabic was the other). Although Hebrew had been used in religious ceremonies, modern spoken Hebrew had to be learned anew as a living language. As the decades passed, more and more Israelis came to speak Hebrew, and the sabras (native-born Jewish Israelis) tended to forget the languages spoken by their immigrant parents. An Academy of the Hebrew Language was established in 1953 to help regulate the language. Hebrew served to unify the nation and to distinguish it from other nations.

The new immigrants and the new nation witnessed substantial accomplishments, including growth in scientific and technical research, urbanization, and education. Israeli universities and institutes developed strong research agendas in such areas as desalinization of seawater, atomic energy, and aeronautical engineering. Israel spent more on basic and applied research than all of the Arab states combined. Urbanization and the construction industry proceeded rapidly after 1948. At that time, about one-fourth of the Jewish Israeli population was rural and three-fourths urban. As time passed, Israel became ever more urbanized; ultimately 86 percent of the population lived in towns and cities. Most of the growth took place in the coastal areas, and Tel Aviv became the dominant city, with about 25 percent of all Israelis living there. Educational institutions also grew rapidly, for both the Jewish majority and the Arab minority. In 1949 only 1600 students were enrolled in two universities; by 1975, 47,000 students attended seven universities and higher institutes. By 1963, Israel spent 7 percent of its gross national product on education. Between 1948 and 1956, the number of Arab children attending Israeli schools more than doubled. Arabic was their language of instruction, and Hebrew was taught as a second language.

Women participated vigorously in cultural, economic, and political activities. The declaration of independence, Zionist-labor ideology, and the Women's Equal Rights Law of 1951 all emphasized the equality of men and women, although Jewish religious law gave men a superior role, particularly in matters of marriage and divorce. Most women served in the armed forces, and about one-third of Israeli women worked outside the home by the 1970s. Golda Meir was prime minister from 1969 to 1974, but few other women have been prominent in Israeli politics. In most elections, women won about 8 percent of Knesset seats, usually representing leftist parties. Attitudes of Jews from the Middle East were against women working outside the home unless it was absolutely necessary. In this, as in many other aspects of society and culture, Israeli Jews of European background tended to hold sharply differing views.

Partially because of the newness of the country, the diversity of the origins of its people, and the numerous linguistic and intellectual differences among them, a unified Israeli culture was slow to emerge. The Arab minority, for instance, did not share at all in Jewish Israeli culture or its history. Israeli historians generally presented a heroic image of their recent history, based on a widely believed set of interpretations of controversial events and centered on the extraordinary military successes of the State of Israel. (It was only in the 1980s and 1990s that Israeli revisionist historians using newly opened archival sources began to critically re-examine this history by presenting alternative interpretations.)

Many cultural trends and institutions from before 1948 continued for the Jewish majority after independence, as in the theater, but there were also changes in various fields. The Israel Philharmonic Orchestra gained an international reputation, and the Israel Museum in Jerusalem became renowned for its archaeological collections. Archaeology was a national hobby, and many famous Israelis, such as Moshe Dayan, were amateur archaeologists. Archaeology represented a way of reasserting the historical continuity of modern Israelis with the ancient history of the Jews in Palestine. The same connection existed in painting in the 1940s and 1950s, as some artists sought a primitivism in style and content. Other painters moved toward abstract, universal art, especially in the 1950s. Painting in the 1960s was influenced by American trends, whereas public sculpture and murals flourished as memorials were built around the country. Architecture tended to follow Brazilian and French influences in the 1950s and 1960s.

Newspapers flourished, and broadcasting was controlled by the state. Television began in 1965. By 1975 Israel was second in the world in the number of books published per person.

In literature the impact of the Holocaust was strongly felt, and the most famous Israeli writers internationally were those associated with European Jewry. S. Y. Agnon won the Nobel Prize in literature in 1966. The younger generation of writers spoke Hebrew as their first language, were sabras born in Israel, and were more Israel-centered and less interested in the experiences of Jews in the diaspora. In their novels, poetry, and plays, they dwelled on Arab-Israeli relations, wars, materialism, and the antihero.

The Eichmann Trial

In 1960 David Ben-Gurion startled the world by announcing that Adolf Eichmann, head of the German Gestapo Jewish Affairs Bureau during World War II, had been captured and was in Israel, where he would be tried for his war crimes and genocide against the Jewish people. Located in Argentina and abducted by Israeli agents, he had been flown directly to Israel. Eichmann's defense at the subsequent trial was based on the ideas that the kidnapping of the prisoner in Argentina made the trial illegal, that Israel and Israeli law did not exist during World War II, and that no Israeli court could be objective in this case. The Israeli prosecution argued that the manner of bringing the prisoner to trial was irrelevant to the legality of the trial, that no court could be objective in view of the enormity of his crimes, and that there was no international or other national tribunal available for the trial. The trial ended in 1961, after a procession of gruesome photographs, letters, diaries, and witnesses portrayed the dreadful events perpetrated against the Jews, for which Eichmann was held responsible. He was judged guilty by the court and executed in 1962.

Within Israel, the trial spurred greater efforts to build the state. The extensive publicity given to the trial and the horrible details contained in the evidence served to remind the world of the terrible suffering Jews had experienced and to bolster international sympathy and support for Israel.

Foreign Affairs

Israel looked to France, Britain, and the United States for political and financial support. Initially close contacts with the Soviet Union became strained, and Israeli relations with the Arab states, except for Jordan, were consistently hostile.

In 1950 the American, British, and French foreign ministers, meeting in London, signed a tripartite agreement affirming that their states would take action to prevent any violation of frontiers or armistice lines. This guaranteed the safety of Israel as well as the Arab states, while leaving the Palestinian refugees out of the picture. The three powers also declared that they were prepared to stop an arms race between the Arab states and Israel. Britain, France, and the United States in effect accepted the armistice lines and the status quo in the Middle East. Gradually during the next few years, the effectiveness of the tripartite agreement decreased, chiefly because of the growing importance of the Soviet Union in the area.

After the 1956 second Arab-Israeli War and in the face of mounting armaments in Egypt, Syria, and other Arab states, Israel turned to the United States, England, and France for advanced weapons. In 1958 Israel obtained Mystère jets from France; in 1962 the United States supplied Hawk missiles and in 1966 offensive weapons such as Skyhawk bombers. Since Israel could not pay the full cost of such weapons, they were secured at reduced rates. Israelis also relied on the general sympathy among Americans toward the victims of the Holocaust and on American Jews who were friendly to Israel to help secure the diplomatic backing of the United States.

In the early days of the state of Israel, relations with the Soviet bloc were cordial, and sizable shipments of arms from Czechoslovakia were instrumental in Israel's winning the 1948 war. The Soviet Union recognized the legitimacy and existence of the Jewish state. A domestic Israeli Communist party was active, and Mapam subscribed to Marxist philosophy. Israel wished to promote emigration among the 2 million Jews living in the Soviet Union; to do this demanded good relations with the Soviet government. However, Joseph Stalin, the Soviet dictator, became anti-Jewish in his last years. In 1955, when the Soviet bloc began cultivating the Arabs and arms deals were made, Israeli feelings toward the Soviet Union took a sharp turn for the worse.

Relations remained cool, and in the 1960s as Israel looked more to the West for support and sent technicians to aid developing African and Asian countries, the Soviet Union grew more critical of Israel. In 1964 Israel complained of the treatment of Jews in the

Soviet Union. In the 1967 war the Soviet delegate to the U.N. Security Council attacked Israel bitterly as an imperialist and a tool of the imperialists, and the Soviets severed relations with Israel.

KING HUSAIN CONSOLIDATES POWER IN JORDAN

Israel's most important neighbor, Jordan, went through a number of political crises in the 1950s, centering around the issue of royal power. King Abd Allah's eldest son, Talal, was proclaimed king following the assassination of his father, but his emotional stability was questionable, and in 1952 he departed for Europe, leaving the kingdom to his son Husain (also spelled Hussein and Husayn). Husain became king on his eighteenth birthday, in 1953.

Britain continued to support the Arab Legion and heavily subsidized the government. The spread of the Cold War to the Middle East in the 1950s placed Jordan in a critical position. Its Hashimite dynasty belonged to the same royal family as that of Iraq, and Jordan, like Iraq, favored Britain and the United States. But bitter denunciations by Egypt and Syria warned Jordan of the dangers of allying with Britain, America, Turkey, and Iraq. Furthermore, in their campaign to regain possession of the whole of Palestine, Palestinian Arabs were very skeptical of allying with any western state, for it was generally understood that the West would not permit the destruction of Israel.

John Bagot Glubb Pasha, the English head of the Arab Legion, was dismissed summarily in 1956 by the nationalist king and was replaced by Colonel Ali Abu Nuwar. Abu Nuwar became chief of staff, head of the Arab Legion, and a contender for complete power in Jordan. Britain continued financial support, but sympathizers of Egypt's President Nasser rapidly gained in strength and position in Jordan. The ambitious Abu Nuwar viewed himself as the Nasser of Jordan and gathered together a band of young and ardent nationalistic officers.

With the 1956 Suez crisis as a backdrop, the election campaign ensured victory for leftist and Pan-Arab candidates in the relatively free parliamentary elections. The king was too young and inexperienced to control them, as had been the case earlier and as was to occur later. The National Socialists under Sulaiman Nabulsi won eleven seats in the forty-member chamber. Nabulsi's cabinet was installed the day Israel invaded Egypt, and Syrian and Iraqi troops moved in to safeguard Jordan from Israel—and from one another.

Nabulsi frequently suggested that Jordan should ask for arms and aid from the Soviet bloc. Passionately anti-British, he declared that Jordan was ready to terminate its treaty with Great Britain. However, King Husain in 1957 suddenly dismissed Nabulsi, and Abu Nuwar fled to escape arrest. Syrian troops moved to occupy northern Jordan. The fate of King Husain hung in the balance. Showing real courage, Husain rallied his Bedouin troops about him and reestablished his authority. From that point forward, Husain ruled the country and held all political power.

The next crisis arose when Syria and Egypt formed the United Arab Republic. Husain wanted some type of federal union with Iraq. As a result, the Arab Federation was created in February 1958. Then another, and more serious, crisis fell on Husain in July 1958, with the revolution in Iraq and the murder of King Faisal II, of Arab Federation prime minister Nuri al-Said, and of Jordanians in the federation's cabinet. Now technically the head of the federation, Husain proceeded to assert his authority, but Iraq ended the union, abruptly throwing Jordan adrift in a turbulent storm of Arab nationalism. British paratroopers were flown in from Cyprus. The Bedouin troops rallied to Husain's side, and his throne seemed secure.

THE SECOND ARAB-ISRAELI WAR

After the armistice agreements came into effect in 1949, Israeli hopes for peace with the Arab states remained unsatisfied. The growth of Pan-Arab nationalism, particularly in Egypt and Syria, gave Israeli leaders cause to look to the defenses of the state. (For discussion of the wars in regard to Egypt, see Chapters 43 and 44.) The most common expression of Arab leaders in this respect was contained in the idea of a second round, whereby the Israelis would be driven into the sea. On the other hand, some political leaders in Israel, frequently of the Herut party, spoke of the need to expand and incorporate all of Palestine, even Transjordan, into the state of Israel. To many Arabs, the likelihood of expansion by Israel seemed very real.

Thousands of border incidents occurred every year as Palestinians entered Israeli territory, usually because of economic reasons. The nature of many of these incidents changed, starting in 1954, when organized Arab raids from the Gaza Strip into southern Israel were particularly damaging, often characterized by sabotage and murder. Israel reacted to the raids by launching retaliatory attacks designed to intimidate local authorities. Egyptian-supported attacks from the Gaza Strip led to a large Israeli retaliatory raid in 1955.

Until 1956, Israel felt considerable security because of the support of the United States and world Jewry. Israel's military was qualitatively better than those of its neighbors. Jealousies and rivalries among the Arab states, notwithstanding the Arab League, appeared to be Israel's salvation. In 1956, however, there seemed some danger that the balance might be changing in favor of Egypt. The Czechoslovakian Soviet bloc arms deals of 1955, the inability of the West to act in the face of Nasser's nationalization of the Suez Canal, and Nasser's success in aligning Syria, Jordan, and Egypt in a military pact under one command, thus tightening the noose around Israel, led Ben-Gurion to undertake a military buildup in 1956.

It turned out that Israel and France had been harboring grievances against Egypt, and during the summer they plotted an attack. The Egyptian closure of the Straits of Tiran to the Israelis almost strangled Israeli trade with Japan, Asia, and eastern Africa. A direct attack on Egypt seemed the only way out, but Israel needed the collaboration of the French, and it received the grudging cooperation of the British as well. Britain was seriously provoked by the nationalization of the canal, and France was furious over the help Egypt was affording to the rebels in Algeria.

On October 24 near Paris, Ben-Gurion, with Dayan at his side, signed an Anglo-French-Israeli agreement to attack Suez. The plan was for Israel to start the attack on

October 29, 1956. Then England and France would enter the war, bomb Egyptian airfields, seize the canal, and cut off Egyptian forces in the Sinai Peninsula, where they could be utterly destroyed. It all went as planned—except the Anglo-French force did not act quickly enough. No other Arab state came to the aid of Egypt, which fought alone against the combined forces of Israel, Britain, and France.

The Israeli army moved quickly, and by November 7 most of the Sinai Peninsula had been occupied. Sharm al-Shaikh, guarding the Straits of Tiran and the entrance to the Gulf of Aqaba, was taken. British and French troops began heavy bombing of Egypt on October 31 and then attacked the Suez Canal, capturing Port Said and the northern half of the canal, on November 6. The triple allies' war objectives were to weaken the Arab positions and destroy their arms, unseat Nasser by administering a swift military defeat, regain control of the canal for Britain, open the Suez Canal to Israeli use, control the passage of ships into the Gulf of Aqaba, and free the port of Eilat.

As the war progressed the Soviet Union and the United States, usually enemies during the Cold War, agreed on the need to support Egypt. This was particularly noteworthy because the United States was the leading force, along with Britain and France, in the North Atlantic Treaty Organization, which was chiefly directed against the Soviet Union. Internal opinion in Britain was divided; many political leaders criticized the war and sought to end it. President Dwight Eisenhower had telephoned British prime minister Anthony Eden some days before the outbreak to dissuade him from engaging in such measures. The day before the attack, Eisenhower had warned Ben-Gurion against war, and immediately after the attack an emergency meeting of the U.N. Security Council denounced the invasion and demanded a cease-fire.

With the United States, the Soviet Union, and most of the rest of the world ranged against the three invaders, a cease-fire was accepted on November 7. Withdrawal from Suez by the English and French and from Sinai by the Israelis started within a few days. U.N. forces came in to prevent incidents. But Israel refused to surrender the Gaza Strip and Sharm al-Shaikh. Finally, in March 1957 Ben-Gurion agreed to withdraw from both points on the "assumption" that border incidents would halt and that the Gulf of Aqaba would be open to Israeli shipping. The Israeli troops pulled back, Egyptian civil administrators once again took over in the Gaza Strip, and the U.N. Emergency Force was permitted to patrol only the Egyptian side of the frontier, including Sharm al-Shaikh.

Territorially the situation returned to the conditions prevailing before the outbreak of the war. Israel's military victory was reassuring to most Israeli citizens, and the military leaders became heroes. The war of 1956 did show the aggressive side of Israel's foreign policy and its dependence on an alliance with European powers, whereas the Arab states experienced defeat again and, amazed at the might of Israel, felt the urgent need for more military equipment, organization, and cooperation. The Gulf of Aqaba remained open for Israeli shipping, and although Egypt and Saudi Arabia protested its use, they made no move to block the Straits of Tiran.

President Nasser of Egypt emerged as a hero of Pan-Arab nationalism, and many Egyptians were dedicated to seeking revenge eventually for their humiliation. Nasser's reaction was to seek greater influence throughout the Arab world while avoiding direct confrontation with Israel.

ISRAEL, JORDAN, AND OTHER ARAB STATES AFTER THE SECOND WAR

Following the 1956 war, Israel proceeded, with French help, to build secretly and at great expense a nuclear reactor in the Negev to develop atomic bombs. This goal was probably achieved by 1967, thereby guaranteeing Israel military superiority over its Arab neighbors, which did not possess atomic weapons.

With U.N. troops stationed on the Egyptian side of the frontier, clashes after 1957 were rare there. Israel's clashes with Arab neighbors centered on Syria and Jordan. The Syrian border had a neutral demilitarized zone, with both sides asserting the rights of its owners to cultivate it. Each spring Arabs conducted raids on Israelis, who were cultivating land in the demilitarized zone, to which Israel frequently answered with reprisals.

The problem of the infiltration of the Israeli frontier by Palestinian Arab guerrillas such as the al-Fatah group continued. A serious Israeli reprisal occurred in 1966 against the village of al-Samu, Jordan. The U.N. Security Council censured Israel for the deed, and King Husain of Jordan was bitterly criticized by the Arab League and large numbers of his own subjects for not having replied to the Israeli forces. Some feared he might lose his throne as a result of the incident, and even Israel was worried over this possibility, for any new regime in Amman might well be less friendly to Israel than Husain had been.

Husain now seemed to face insurmountable problems: Egypt and Syria were bound together in the United Arab Republic, Iraq had ousted the Hashimite monarchy, Israeli expansionists talked of annexing all of Palestine west of the Jordan River, several thousand British soldiers in Jordan caused Arab nationalists everywhere to call King Husain the tool of the imperialists, and half of his own subjects wished for a different state and a different regime. To make matters worse, nearly 75 percent of Jordan's total revenues in 1958 came from grants and subsidies from Great Britain and the United States. Imports were more than eleven times the amount of exports. Local capital was virtually nonexistent, and natural resources were few. But King Husain was tough and tenacious. He enjoyed the loyalty of his army, which was regarded as the best-trained and best-equipped force among the Arabs. The British troops soon left, and Husain set out to keep his throne. His program consisted of internal economic growth and development; stabilizing the government and expanding the army; and steering an artful course among the jealousies, rivalries, ambitions, and ideologies of his Arab neighbors.

A major economic project was the East Ghor Canal, which was to channel off water from the Yarmuk River and irrigate dry but fertile lands. The first stage was finished in 1961, and it was expanded on later occasions. U.S. economic aid was crucial to Jordanian development. Tourism also became a growing industry as Jordan began to capitalize on a wealth of archaeological remains, as at Petra. Remittances from Jordanians working abroad, especially in the Persian Gulf oil countries, also contributed substantially to the economy. Through this and other development efforts, the economy grew steadily, with the gross national product per person increasing at a rate of about 8 percent a year from 1954 to 1966.

The Jordanian government also devoted considerable attention to social issues, which became important as the population grew rapidly. Amman's population in 1961 was more than 400,000; by 1967 the country's population was about half urban. Education received great attention, with literacy rapidly increasing. The University of Jordan opened in 1962.

Despite social and economic progress, the long-range future of the kingdom seemed uncertain as the Arab states voted in Cairo in 1964 to create an Arab political entity for the Palestinians. Known as the Palestine Liberation Organization (P.L.O.), it was to raise an army that would have a separate identity and operate in each of the Arab host states. Guerrilla attacks by al-Fatah into Israel began to bring Israeli reactive strikes against Jordan, and Jordan became increasingly suspicious of the political motives of Palestinian leaders in regard to the kingdom's unity and leadership.

Vilification of King Husain from some Arab capitals continued. Yet in May 1967, at the height of a new crisis with Israel, Husain flew to Cairo, where Nasser embraced him at the airport. They signed a mutual defense pact, and Jordan pledged its army, should war come with Israel. Husain believed fully that his throne would be lost and he assassinated if his army did not move with vigor on the center front in any new Arab-Israeli confrontation.

THE THIRD ARAB-ISRAELI WAR

The crisis that led Israel to attack Egypt in 1967 and thereby begin the third Arab-Israeli War was caused by several factors. A long cycle of violence, hatred, fear, suspicion, mutual misperceptions, and competition for power and security generally influenced the parties to the Arab-Israeli dispute. More short-term causes were raids by Palestinian guerrillas of al-Fatah, the chief Palestinian Arab group, directed against Israel, and Israeli plans for retaliation. Egypt's Nasser, engaged in a struggle for the leadership of the Pan-Arab nationalist cause, then took a number of warlike steps, bringing about an Israeli attack.

Israeli cabinet members, under great pressure from the public for action, spoke out on the possibilities of an attack into Syria. The Syrians believed they had evidence that an Israeli move was scheduled for May 1967. Alarmed, they called on Egypt to make good on their mutual defense pact as the Soviets also claimed Israel was preparing to attack, although Israel actually was not massing its troops on the Syrian border. Nasser requested that the secretary-general of the United Nations remove its troops from Egypt. This he promptly began to do, and since Israel had refused to accept U.N. troops on its soil in 1957, the frontier was suddenly alive with military forces directly confronting each other. With the U.N. leaving Sharm al-Shaikh at the entrance to the Gulf of Aqaba, Egypt took over there and announced the closing of the Straits of Tiran to Israeli shipping. Egypt claimed that these straits were territorial waters. The loss of free navigation to and from the Gulf of Aqaba was so menacing that Israel declared it would rather fight than go along with this closure.

When it became apparent that neither the United States nor the United Nations was able to effect an immediate opening of the Straits of Tiran, and in order to preclude Egypt and its allies from attacking Israel, the Israelis launched an attack on Egypt. Although Israel warned Jordan and Syria to stay out of the quarrel, they had said they would join with Egypt to form a united front—an extremely threatening situation for Israel. Nasser had begun to mobilize his troops in Sinai even before the U.N. withdrawal. Coupled with his bellicose public speeches, the concentration of Egyptian forces east of the Suez Canal forced Israel to act. General Dayan, the hero of the 1956 Sinai campaign, was brought into the cabinet as minister of defense.

On June 5, Israel, in a surprise attack, destroyed the air capabilities of Egypt and subsequently those of Jordan and Syria. Total Arab strength in artillery, tanks, and other weapons was far greater than that of Israel, but with complete mastery of the skies and superb coordination of all branches of the military, within six days Israeli forces had occupied the Gaza Strip, all of the Sinai Peninsula to the east bank of the Suez Canal, all of Jordan west of the Jordan River (including east Jerusalem and its holy shrines), and the Golan Heights of Syria. Israeli losses amounted to about 1000 killed; the Arab armies lost somewhere between 11,000 and 16,000. When they captured the Old City of Jerusalem, Israelis poured into the streets to rejoice at the seizing of their holy places. They then agreed to a cease-fire called for by the U.N. Security Council.

The possibility of peace was examined throughout the rest of 1967, but the terms envisioned by Israel and the Arab states for an agreement were far apart. Israeli demands, in addition to recognition by the Arabs, were the establishment of definite boundaries, the guaranteed use of the Suez Canal and the Straits of Tiran, and the end of raids and terrorism. Israel also intended to keep permanent control of the eastern part of Jerusalem and cleared structures before the Western Wall so that the many thousands of Jews who came there to pray could be accommodated.

Israel said that Arabs living in east Jerusalem now could choose to be citizens of Israel or Jordan. Most chose to be considered Jordanians. In the Gaza Strip and the West Bank, Israel ruled the Arabs by military force. The Arab Palestinians there did not become citizens of Israel. Unlike Arab citizens of Israel, they had almost no voice in their own governance. Many of them worked in Israel, particularly in construction, and often in low-paying jobs.

At a 1967 Arab summit meeting at Khartoum, the weakened Arab states condemned negotiations with Israel. The Israeli government was faced with the problem of what to do with the occupied territories and the more than 1 million Palestinians; opinion was quite divided. Some favored annexation of all or part of the land by Israel; others favored the return of most of the land to Jordan in exchange for full peace. Each day that no peace settlement was achieved, the status quo of Israeli occupation became more difficult to dislodge.

No resolution of the tensions in the Middle East appeared remotely possible. On November 22, 1967, the U.N. Security Council passed Resolution 242, authorizing a special representative to negotiate peace between Israel and its Arab neighbors. The resolution implicitly recognized Israel's right to exist and called for the establishment of permanent borders, withdrawal of Israeli troops from occupied lands, Israeli use of the Suez Canal and the Straits of Tiran, and a just settlement for refugees, although without specifically mentioning the Palestinian Arabs. Nasser and other Arab leaders would not recognize Israel or enter into direct negotiations until Israel withdrew from the occupied Arab lands. At the same time, Israel repeated that there could be no substitute for direct negotiations. This deadlock meant the continuation of Israeli occupation of the lands taken in 1967.

From the Israeli point of view, the solution to the Arab-Israeli dispute seemed as far away in 1967 as in 1948, since permanent borders, the status of the Palestinians, and Arab acceptance of Israel's legitimacy remained to be settled. Israeli reprisal raids did not seem to be effective against the Palestinians. Most Arab Palestinians, whether living in Jordan or elsewhere, still hoped to create an Arab Palestine with a Jewish minority in the land, but until the mid-1960s, they were not very active in pursuing this vision and did not have a state of their own. Jordan wrestled with the integration of Palestinians with East Bankers, while also facing dependence on external economic and military help. Jordan and Israel alike were engaged in the 1950s and 1960s in building up their societies, economies, and governments, thereby creating the prerequisites for sustained national existence. The second Arab-Israeli War in 1956 demonstrated how regional Middle Eastern issues could involve the great military powers of the world. The Arab-Israeli war in 1967 opened another new phase in the intertwined histories of the Israelis, Palestinian Arabs, and Jordanians.

REFERENCES

The number of books covering this subject is very large and is growing rapidly. Of special significance are references listed in Chapter 36.

Abdallah, King: *My Memoirs Completed.* Translated by Harold Glidden. Washington, D.C.: American Council of Learned Societies, 1954.

Aharoni, Yair: *The Israeli Economy: Dreams and Realities.* London: Routledge, 1991. A comprehensive review of the economy and its relationship to government and society.

Bar-On, Mordechai: *The Gates of Gaza: Israel's Road to Suez and Back, 1955–1957.* New York: St. Martin's Press, 1994. Israeli perspectives on the 1956 war by a firsthand observer.

Begin, Menachem: *The Revolt: Story of the Irgun.* New York: Schuman, 1951. A fascinating story by the Irgun's leader who became prime minister in 1977.

Beilin, Yossi: *Israel: A Concise Political History.* New York: St. Martin's Press, 1993. The author of this informative book is a prominent Israeli political leader.

Ben-Gurion, David: *Israel: Years of Challenge.* New York: Holt, 1963. An account of the founding of the state and the accomplishments of the first decade.

Cohen, Asher, and Bernard Susser: *Israel and the Politics of Jewish Identity: The Secular-Religious Impasse.* Baltimore: Johns Hopkins University Press, 2000. A balanced discussion.

Cohen, Avner: *Israel and the Bomb.* New York: Columbia University Press, 1998. The best study of how Israel developed atomic weapons.

Collins, Larry, and Dominique Lapierre: *O Jerusalem!* New York: Simon & Schuster, 1972. A lengthy and well-written account of the 1948 war.

Dayan, Moshe: *Story of My Life.* London: Sphere Books, 1978. Covers the life of this very important Israeli general and politician up to 1975.

De Atkine, Norvell: "Why Arab Armies Lose Wars." *MERIA: Middle East Review of International Affairs* (electronic journal) 4: 1 (2000).

Dowty, Alan: *The Jewish State: A Century Later.* Updated ed. Berkeley: University of California Press, 2001. Essays by a perceptive political scientist on such issues as democracy, Zionism, institution building, religion, and the Arab minority.

Ghanem, As'ad: *The Palestinian-Arab Minority in Israel, 1948–2000: A Political Study.* Albany: State University of New York Press, 2001. An excellent account, concentrating on political attitudes and activities.

Hazleton, Lesley: *Israeli Women: The Reality behind the Myths.* New York: Simon & Schuster, 1977. A feminist critique of what the author calls the myth of equality in Israel.

Herzog, Chaim: *The Arab-Israeli Wars: War and Peace in the Middle East.* New York: Random House, 1982. A detailed account by a president of Israel who was also a major-general in the Israeli army.

Lowi, Miriam R.: *Water and Power: The Politics of a Scarce Resource in the Jordan River Basin.* Cambridge, England: Cambridge University Press, 1993. Discusses the use of water and political processes pertaining to it.

Luttwak, Edward, and Dan Horowitz: *The Israeli Army.* New York: Harper & Row, 1975. One of the best studies of the Israeli military.

Medding, Peter Y.: *The Founding of Israeli Democracy, 1948–1967.* New York: Oxford University Press, 1990. A good introduction to Israeli politics; features comparisons to other new countries.

Morris, Benny: *The Birth of the Palestinian Refugee Problem, 1947–1949.* Cambridge, England: Cambridge University Press, 1988. An influential interpretation of this controversial issue, showing the multitude of causes while emphasizing the role of panic flight.

———: *Israel's Border Wars 1949–1956: Arab Infiltration, Israeli Retaliation, and the Countdown to the Suez War.* Oxford, England: Clarendon Press, 1993. A careful study of one of the main causes of the second Arab-Israeli War.

Near, Henry: *The Kibbutz Movement: A History.* Vol. 2: *Crisis and Achievement, 1939–1995.* London: Littman Library, 1997. Details the initial successes and later the declining role of the kibbutz and moshav movement in Israeli society.

Ofrat, Gideon: *One Hundred Years of Art in Israel.* Boulder, Colo.: Westview, 1998. A beautifully illustrated review of painting from the 1890s to the 1990s.

Oren, Michael B.: *Origins of the Second Arab-Israel War: Egypt, Israel and the Great Powers, 1952–56.* London: Frank Cass, 1992. A careful examination of Israeli, British, and some Egyptian sources for the subject.

Pappé, Ilan: *The Making of the Arab-Israeli Conflict, 1947–51.* London: Tauris, 1992. Examines the diplomacy and warfare of this period.

Parker, Richard B., ed.: *The Six Day War: A Retrospective.* Gainesville: University Press of Florida, 1996. Interesting comments by participants reflecting upon the 1967 war.

Peretz, Don, and Gideon Doron: *The Government and Politics of Israel,* 3d ed. Boulder, Colo.: Westview Press, 1998. Good on the political parties and the functioning of government.

Reich, Bernard, and Gershon R. Kieval: *Israel: Land of Tradition and Conflict.* 2d ed. Boulder, Colo.: Westview, 1993. An excellent brief introduction.

Rogan, Eugene L., and Avi Shlaim, eds.: *The War for Palestine: Rewriting the History of 1948.* Cambridge, England: Cambridge University Press, 2001. A good example of the revisionist approach to the Arab-Israeli dispute with discussions of the participants in the 1948 war.

Satloff, Robert B.: *From Abdullah to Hussein: Jordan in Transition.* New York: Oxford University Press, 1994. The story of Jordanian politics from 1951 to 1957.

Sayigh, Yezid: *Armed Struggle and the Search for State: The Palestinian National Movement, 1949–1993.* Oxford, England: Clarendon Press, 1997. In this massive study the author presents a thorough picture of the development of Palestinian institutions and nationalism; indispensable.

——— and Avi Shlaim, eds.: *The Cold War and the Middle East.* Oxford, England: Clarendon Press, 1997. Chapters on the major Middle Eastern countries, including Israel, Jordan, and the Palestinians.

Segev, Tom: *1949: The First Israelis.* New York: Free Press, 1986. Captures the flavor of the first year of Israeli independence.

Shlaim, Avi: *The Politics of Partition: King Abdullah, the Zionists and Palestine, 1921–1951.* New York: Columbia University Press, 1990. Demonstrates that Abd Allah and the Zionists had many contacts, including agreements on allocating land in 1948.

———: *The Iron Wall: Israel and the Arab World.* New York: Norton, 2001. Analysis of Israeli foreign policy by a leading revisionist historian.

Troen, S. Ilan, and Noah Lucas, eds.: *Israel: The First Decade of Independence.* Albany: State University of New York Press, 1995. Thirty-three chapters on all aspects of Israel.

Zahlan, Antoine: "The Science and Technology Gap in the Arab-Israeli Conflict." *Journal of Palestine Studies* 1 (1972): 17–36. Shows some of the reasons for Israeli success over the Arabs were in the accomplishments of Israel in science and technology.

CHAPTER 42

Israel, Jordan, and the Palestinians after 1967

Between 1967 and 2002, Israelis, Jordanians, and Palestinians participated to varying degrees in four major wars, substantial changes of political power, considerable economic and social developments, dramatic peacemaking among themselves and with their neighbors, and two intifadas (uprisings). These remarkably eventful circumstances affected all three groups, and their ramifications spread beyond the immediate area to involve much of the rest of the Middle East and the larger world beyond it.

NO PEACE, NO WAR

Between the 1967 and 1973 wars, Israel and the Palestinians living inside it and in the occupied territories experienced major challenges in regard to state finances, social changes, and the nature of the occupation. Israel and Egypt fought a war of attrition along the Suez Canal, and both sides attempted diplomatic maneuvers to secure their goals. Domestic Israeli politics was affected by the situation of no peace, no war.

Financial and budgetary problems included paying the expenses of the war, arms purchases abroad, and the cost of maintaining the occupied territories. All these left Israeli finances in a weak position. The unfavorable trade gap was met from gifts and loans by foreign governments and individuals. Expectation of such annual sums made it possible to live with large budgetary deficits and considerable inflation.

In the six years following the 1967 war, Israel felt compelled to allocate over $6 billion for defense expenditures. Defense spending increased dramatically from 1967 until 1973; enormous defense costs were a crushing burden on Israelis, who accepted them as the price of survival.

By means of several agreements with the European Economic Community (E.E.C.; later, the European Union), Israeli trade with Europe was substantially aided. Foreign trade and aid during the six-year interlude between the wars of 1967 and 1973 helped Israel's economic development and industrialization proceed rapidly, with per capita income rising from about $1000 in 1967 to $2800 in 1973. Production climbed in most sectors of the economy, and capital investment from overseas was impressive. Yet another war in 1973, followed by worldwide inflation, economic recession, and the quadrupling of energy costs, altered conditions negatively.

In the years between the third and fourth Arab-Israeli wars, cynics began to assert that Israel was losing its special character and becoming like other societies. They cited as evidence a growing materialism. The utopian idealism of the kibbutz, the agricultural commune, was waning, and the number of workers in agriculture steadily fell. By 1980 the kibbutzim earned about one-half of their income from industry or services rather than farming. The kibbutz movement steadily lost influence from 1967 to 1973 and subsequently. Nevertheless, Israel's military victories in both wars reassured most of the population and helped produce advances in business enterprise, art, literature, scientific discovery, and archaeology. Life in Israel in 1973 was vibrant, yet many Israelis remained apprehensive about the future.

Events in Jerusalem played a particularly large role in the symbolic and emotional life of the state. After the Arab part of Jerusalem was proclaimed an integral part of Israeli Jerusalem, plans were developed to reconstruct the old Jewish quarter inside the medieval walls, evicting Arabs who had lived there since 1948, when the Jewish inhabitants were evicted. In 1969, after a fire in the very holy al-Aqsa mosque, the Islamic states accused Israel of carelessness. The physical and economic aspects of the city were greatly enhanced, but the Arab inhabitants never felt secure as citizens with rights equal to the others.

In much of the rest of the occupied territories, life went on as before. Trade between Israel and the occupied lands began to provide a substantial market for West Bank produce. In addition, the previous markets in the East Bank remained accessible to the West Bank. On the other hand, Israel placed severe limits on Arab use of water in the West Bank; this was caused by Israel's full utilization of all available water sources by 1970. Arab resentment at living under an occupying force brought incidents of violence and harsh Israeli reprisals.

Soon after the end of the fighting in 1967, Jewish settlers moved into places near Hebron and Jericho from which Jews had been forced to leave in 1948. Many new settlements were established in the occupied lands so as to help make Israeli control permanent.

The cease-fires arranged in June 1967 were never fully observed, and U.N. Security Council Resolution 242, though accepted in principle by all parties, could not be implemented because no agreement could be reached on the meaning and extent of Israeli withdrawal. All semblance of peace disappeared in 1969, when a war of attrition broke out along the Suez Canal. In one fifty-day period, Egypt flew 100 sorties against the Israelis in Sinai, and the Israelis countered with 1000 over Egypt. In 1970, Israel made air raids deep into Egypt; these were curtailed when losses inflicted by newly installed Soviet surface-to-air missiles made the missions too costly. On August 7, 1970, a cease-fire between Israel and Egypt arranged by the United States went into effect.

The tempo of the war of attrition along the canal never rose to the level of the 1967 war, and it gradually ended. Attention shifted to Jordan, where King Husain defeated and expelled armed Palestinian forces in 1970–1971. The Palestine Liberation Organization (P.L.O.) guerrillas settled in Lebanon and began to harass Israel from southern Lebanon. By 1973 peace in the Middle East was as elusive as ever.

Diplomatically and financially, Israel was increasingly dependent on the United States. Diplomatic relations with many other nations, especially in Europe, became more difficult as the Arab cause gained support in various quarters. Israel's occupation policies were criticized particularly by the United Nations.

In domestic politics, Moshe Dayan, a hero of the 1956 and 1967 wars, remained minister of defense. His splinter Rafi party was gradually reintegrated into the dominant labor party, Mapai (Israel Workers' party). Prime Minister Eshkol's death in 1969 led to the selection of Golda Meir as Israel's fourth prime minister. Mapai was united for the election of 1969, joining with Mapam (United Workers party) to form a labor alignment. Although sixteen parties participated in the parliamentary elections, the labor alignment won fifty-six seats, needing only five more seats from coalition partners to gain a majority. Meir enticed the right-wing Gahal party, the National Religious party, and others to join a broad coalition. In 1973 Gahal joined Herut and the Liberals to form a new right-wing bloc, Likud (Unity), in preparation for new elections.

JORDAN AND THE PALESTINIANS AFTER THE THIRD ARAB-ISRAELI WAR

Within a few hours after the beginning of hostilities on June 5, 1967, Israel destroyed the Jordanian air force. Complete mastery of the air gave Israel such an advantage that King Husain's army was ineffective. The entire area west of the Jordan River, including east Jerusalem, was lost, along with its population of 650,000. About 300,000 new refugees fled eastward across the river. Most of the Palestinians of the West Bank and Gaza, however, remained in their homes.

The most productive part of Husain's kingdom was gone, his finances were in shambles, and his armed forces were without equipment. Many Palestinian Jordanians thought Husain and his army had betrayed them by not fighting hard enough. Saudi Arabia, Kuwait, and Libya agreed to aid Jordan financially, and Iraqi troops remained in Jordan to protect it.

Jordan served for the next several years as the staging area for Palestinian attacks on Israel, although King Husain opposed the raids, fearing Israeli counterattacks. The Palestinian nationalists now felt that their earlier dependence on Nasser's Egypt and the other Arab states was futile. If an Arab Palestine would be created, it would have to be done by their own actions, chiefly, they thought, through a guerrilla war of national liberation similar to that undertaken by the Algerians against the French in the 1950s. This idea was especially strong in al-Fatah, led by Yasir Arafat, the largest military organization within the P.L.O. Yasir Arafat, who was born in 1929, was a distant relative of the earlier Palestinian leader, Amin al-Husaini, and was an engineer by training. The P.L.O. overall organization was also headed after 1969 by Arafat, but there was no unity of command.

Since more than half of Husain's subjects were Palestinians, many of them recent arrivals, his policies were condemned by many as traitorous to the Arab people. In any case, throughout 1968, 1969, and 1970 there were countless commando assaults on Israel, followed by reprisals on Jordan and Lebanon. In general, Jordan suffered more than Israel did in these exchanges.

Jordanians were suspicious that the king secretly wanted peace with Israel, in part because of his close ties to the United States. For his part, Husain was suspicious that the Palestinian guerrillas sought power in Jordan. He removed the civilian government, established military rule, and personally took control of his armed forces.

A crisis broke out in September 1970 following the Palestinian hijacking of several airliners and their destruction in Jordan. Husain launched a full-scale campaign against the commando groups. Syrian tanks crossed the border to support the hard-pressed Palestinians, but they withdrew on warnings from Israel and the United States. Husain suppressed the guerrillas, though they remained for a time in Jordan. The Palestinians, angered by their defeat, began to refer to the time as Black September. Jordan in 1971 took control of Palestinian strongholds in the northern hills, thereby eliminating the guerrillas' military forces from the kingdom. Having driven most of the commandos from Jordan to Lebanon, Husain was freer to arrange his own affairs. On several occasions he had secret contacts with Israeli officials and made proposals for peace, but none of them was successful. The United States provided budgetary aid, promised to replenish Jordan's military, and provided help for reconstruction.

THE FOURTH ARAB-ISRAELI WAR

War broke out again on October 6, 1973, as Egypt and Syria, in a surprise, coordinated campaign, attacked Israel on Yom Kippur, Judaism's Day of Atonement. The war also fell during Ramadan, the Muslim month of fasting. Egypt and Syria, with limited help from Jordan, Iraq, and other Arab states, sought to regain the territory they had lost in the 1967 Arab-Israeli War.

Egyptian forces quickly crossed the Suez Canal, and Syrian troops retook much of the Golan Heights. Within a few days, the highly trained Israeli forces were able to beat back the attacks and go on the offensive. Israel by 1973 probably possessed about twenty atomic bombs of its own; knowing this, the Arab states fighting Israel had to be careful not to push too hard. The Israelis contained the Syrian drive and directed air attacks at Syria. Israeli troops reached a point only 22 miles (35 km.) from Damascus, the capital. On the southern front Israeli forces had crossed to the west bank of the Suez Canal, going through the middle of the Egyptian armies, and were driving to surround the Egyptian Third Army, when a cease-fire finally became effective on October 24.

Enormous quantities of weapons were deployed and destroyed on all sides. The Soviets airlifted weapons, tanks, and airplanes to Egypt and Syria in astounding numbers. Israel called on the United States for help and began to receive massive shipments in the midst of fighting. In all it was estimated that Israel lost about 500 tanks and 120 aircraft and suffered 2400 killed and as many wounded. The Arabs lost more than 1100 tanks and 450 airplanes; their numbers killed and wounded exceeded Israel's. The cost to all the combatants was staggering; it has been estimated that Israel alone spent $7 billion.

The magnitude of the war shocked the world, and when the Soviet Union and the United States became indirectly involved as suppliers, the full impact of the war was frightening. The U.N. Security Council could do nothing to stop Israel's fighting, so U.S.

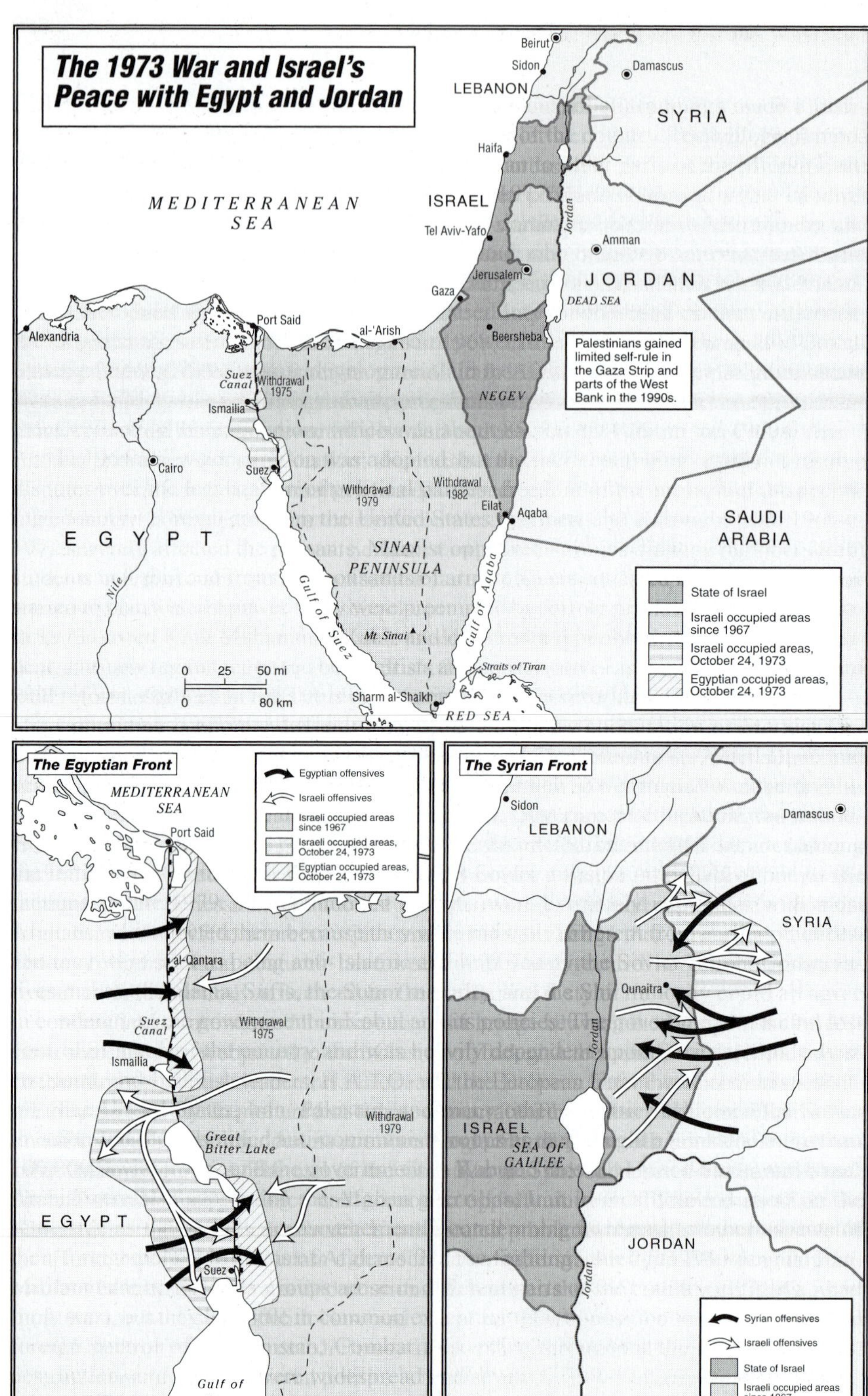

The 1973 War and Israel's Peace with Egypt and Jordan
Beirut
Sidon
Damascus
LEBANON
SYRIA
Haifa
MEDITERRANEAN SEA
ISRAEL
Jordan
Tel Aviv-Yafo
Amman
Jerusalem
JORDAN
Gaza
DEAD SEA
Port Said
al-'Arish
Alexandria
Beersheba
Palestinians gained limited self-rule in the Gaza Strip and parts of the West Bank in the 1990s.
Suez Canal
Withdrawal 1975
Ismailia
NEGEV
Cairo
Suez
Withdrawal 1982
Withdrawal 1979
Eilat
Aqaba
SAUDI ARABIA
EGYPT
SINAI PENINSULA
Nile
Gulf of Suez
Gulf of Aqaba
State of Israel
Israeli occupied areas since 1967
Israeli occupied areas, October 24, 1973
Egyptian occupied areas, October 24, 1973
Mt. Sinai
0 25 50 mi
0 80 km
Straits of Tiran
Sharm al-Shaikh
RED SEA
The Egyptian Front
MEDITERRANEAN SEA
Port Said
Egyptian offensives
Israeli offensives
Israeli occupied areas since 1967
Israeli occupied areas, October 24, 1973
Egyptian occupied areas, October 24, 1973
al-Qantara
Suez Canal
Withdrawal 1975
Ismailia
Withdrawal 1979
Great Bitter Lake
EGYPT
Suez
Gulf of Suez
0 15 mi
0 20 km
The Syrian Front
Sidon
Damascus
LEBANON
SYRIA
Qunaitra
Jordan
ISRAEL
SEA OF GALILEE
JORDAN
Jordan
Syrian offensives
Israeli offensives
State of Israel
Israeli occupied areas since 1967
Israeli occupied areas, October 24, 1973
0 10 mi
0 15 km

secretary of state Henry Kissinger flew to Moscow and reached an understanding that permitted the adoption of U.N. Resolution 338, which called for a cease-fire. When the cease-fire did not hold, the Soviet Union suggested to the United States that the two take action to enforce it. The United States rejected this, and the Soviets then seemed poised to intervene unilaterally. Now President Richard Nixon ordered a partial alert of American forces. The specter of a nuclear world war loomed until the United Nations finally obtained a cease-fire and sent an emergency force, which was placed on the lines between the Egyptian and Israeli armies.

Tensions were also eased when Israeli and Egyptian officers signed an agreement freeing the trapped Egyptian Third Army and providing for the immediate exchange of prisoners, an end to the Arab blockade at the southern end of the Red Sea, and negotiations on a settlement. A conference on an overall peace settlement was convened in Geneva in December by the United States and the Soviet Union, but it was adjourned after one day. Egypt and Israel, prodded by the United States, signed a disengagement agreement in 1974.

A cease-fire on the Syrian front took full effect only in May 1974. After several rounds of shuttle diplomacy between Jerusalem and Damascus, all additional territory on the Golan seized by Israel in the 1973 war, as well as the city of al-Qunaitra taken in 1967, was relinquished to Syria. U.N. observers were placed between the two antagonists on a three-month, renewable basis; they subsequently stayed there indefinitely.

Israel added to its military forces, with the size of the standing armed forces in 1976 tripled as compared to 1966. Men had to serve three years, and women two years, in the active armed forces and many months in the reserves.

Rather than pursue a general peace involving the Soviet Union and all the Arab states, Israel and the United States preferred a step-by-step approach to peace. They reasoned that confidence-building small steps would gradually create an atmosphere of mutual confidence between Israel and Egypt, with the most difficult aspects of the Arab-Israeli dispute, such as the status of Jerusalem, left to the end of the process. Kissinger shuttled between Jerusalem and Cairo until Israel and Egypt signed a Sinai disengagement pact in 1975. Israeli forces withdrew farther eastward in Sinai, with U.N. units stationed between the Israeli and Egyptian zones. Israel agreed to return the oil fields in the Sinai to Egypt, and Egypt promised to permit nonmilitary cargoes bound for Israel to pass through the reopened Suez Canal.

One of the consequences of the 1973 war was an improvement in the electoral appeal of the Likud party in Israel. Parliamentary elections in late 1973 diminished strength for the Labor Alignment, the chief element in the governing coalition, which was blamed for Israel's relatively poor military performance in the early stages of the war. It won just under 40 percent of the popular vote, and its seats in the Knesset, or parliament, were reduced, whereas Likud, the more hawkish group, received more than 25 percent of the votes and increased its seats.

Shortly after the elections, a commission to investigate the conduct of the war issued a report blaming Defense Minister Dayan and Prime Minister Meir for Israel's poor state of preparedness. Golda Meir resigned, and the Labor Alignment chose Yitzhak Rabin to head a new government. Rabin, the first prime minister to be born in the territory that became Israel, had been chief of staff from 1963 to 1967 and ambassador to Washington from 1968 to 1973.

Meir and then Rabin had to deal with the exceptional costs of the war, which dislocated Israel's economy. Then the quadrupling of oil prices brought worldwide inflation and recession. Israel's budget shot up to more than $8 billion in 1974, with over 40 percent for defense, and to $15 billion in 1977, $4 billion of which went for defense. The Israeli pound underwent almost constant devaluation. Taxes then jumped, until it was estimated that Israelis paid about 70 percent of their income to the state.

A great boon to the economy was the development and rapid growth of the armament and electronics industries. Not only did they help to reduce imports of weapons and dependence on foreign sources, but they also provided export revenues. In these industries, Israel showed great skill and ingenuity in redesigning foreign models or in using foreign parts and engines in original Israeli designs, especially those for military aircraft.

After the cease-fires in Sinai and Golan, the major point of conflict shifted to the border with Lebanon, where shellings or incursions from one or another side occurred daily. Many Palestinian camps in southern Lebanon served as staging areas for raids into Israel. In 1974–1975 Palestinian commandos attacked several Israeli towns, killing a great many Israelis. Israel retaliated for these and other raids by shelling the camps and villages where the raiders were based and sending punitive missions into Lebanon. The eruption of the Lebanese civil war in 1975 gave Israel a temporary respite on its northern border. Israel assisted Lebanese rightist Christian groups so as to help break Palestinian control of parts of southern Lebanon.

Who would control the lands in Gaza, the West Bank, and Golan captured in 1967 became an increasingly troublesome problem for Israeli leaders. The pressure of ultranationalist political and religious groups to establish Jewish settlements in the territories, even in defiance of authorities, was relentless. The United Nations, with the United States concurring, condemned such settlements as obstacles to peace.

Within the occupied Arab territories and in Arab-inhabited regions of Israel, the respectable showing made by the Arab armies in the 1973 war stirred the population's latent Arab nationalism. In West Bank elections in 1976 for councils and mayors, pro-P.L.O. candidates won sweeping victories. In 1977 about half of the Israeli Arabs who voted cast their ballots for the communists, the one available vehicle for a protest vote. As a result of increased educational opportunities, new middle-class leaders emerged, to an extent replacing the old notable families.

By 1980, the average family income of Israeli Arabs was about 70 percent of that of Israeli Jews. Arabs were one-sixth of the Israeli population, but they owned no banks and had few newspapers; their infant mortality rate was twice that of the Jewish majority. In most socioeconomic indicators, the Israeli Arabs ranked significantly below Israeli Jews. Israeli Arabs came increasingly to identify themselves as Arabs while at the same time taking part in some aspects of Israeli society.

Another problem facing Israel after the 1973 war was its increased isolation. Many nations severed diplomatic relations with Israel. In 1975 the U.N. General Assembly declared Zionism to be a form of racism, although the U.S government vehemently denounced this stand and secured its repeal much later, in 1991.

BEGIN'S LIKUD COMES TO POWER IN ISRAEL

Prime Minister Rabin was faced with accusations of scandal and leadership challenges from Defense Minister Shimon Peres. New parties began to appear, particularly the Democratic Movement for Change, a party that advocated structural reforms in Israel's government. On May 17, 1977, the Israeli voters gave Likud forty-three seats in the new parliament, an increase of only four from the election in 1973, but the Labor Alignment fell from fifty-one to thirty-two and thus no longer held a plurality. The president invited Menachem Begin, head of the Herut party and leader of Likud, to form a government. With the aid of the Democratic Movement for Change, several religious parties, a few independents, and the defection of Moshe Dayan from Labor to become foreign minister, Prime Minister Begin welded a governing coalition. Begin was the first non-Mapai prime minister in the history of Israel.

In 1976, living conditions in Israel had deteriorated. Inflation was running at nearly 40 percent a year, and the annual trade deficit was nearly $3 billion. Business and industry felt shackled by the red tape of a controlled economy. A combination of wealthy entrepreneurs, poor and disenchanted Eastern Jews, right-wing hawks on Arab issues, young people, and discontented shopkeepers threw out the Labor Alignment to support Likud, which had promised to cure Israel's social, economic, and financial problems. The 1977 election represented an earthquake, a major upheaval in Israeli politics. This election also represented a turning away from an entrenched and privileged Labor Party leadership.

The new government freed the Israeli pound from controls, and its value dropped 40 percent overnight. A conservative free economic system was announced with subsidies ended and many taxes raised sharply. Yet Israel's economic orientation toward a large role for the government in the economy was deeply embedded in its social, political, and geographic resource systems. Inflation continued, few government corporations were sold, taxes remained exceptionally high, and the reform package that Begin espoused was dropped by 1981. Instead, the government, despite its stated desire to curb government, ironically succeeded in extending its role in housing and neighborhood development and in lengthening by three years the tuition-free period of public schooling.

The general economy gained some ground. As the price of oil declined in the mid-1980s, the Israeli economy was helped. Real per capita income rose from 1973 to 1985 at a yearly rate of only about 1 percent, significantly more slowly than in earlier times. Many Israelis saw the acquisition of automobiles as an improvement in their standard of living: private ownership of cars grew from about 400,000 in 1980 to nearly 780,000 in 1990.

The United States in 1981 and in subsequent years changed its economic assistance entirely to grants that did not have to be repaid. U.S. aid sharply increased in the 1980s; in 1980 it was $1.8 billion and in 1983 $2.5 billion. Inflation, however, became an even greater problem in the late 1970s and early 1980s, rising to almost 150 percent in 1983. The foreign debt per capita was the highest in the world and was increasing steadily as the trade imbalance continued.

The limited degree of domestic success enjoyed by the Begin coalition was more than compensated by foreign policy victories, and with the 1981 general election the

Likud bloc again managed to form the government. Likud and Labor received almost exactly the same percentage of the vote and seats in parliament, thus showing a nearly equal split in the electorate. Begin formed a coalition with small rightist parties and particularly with the religious parties. This coalition endured through the 1982 war in Lebanon, raging inflation, and Begin's own resignation in 1983, until the next parliamentary elections were held in 1984.

SOCIAL AND CULTURAL CHANGES IN ISRAEL

From the late 1970s onward, the gap between Eastern and European Jews seemed to widen steadily, and sharp clashes emerged between the two communities, as already seen in the bitter political rivalry of Likud and Labor. Yet this new and increasing difference was largely a question of perception, since the communities had been consistently different in many ways since the founding of the state. Now the Eastern Jews emerged in public with new spokesmen, larger numbers of representatives in parliament, and a driving resentment against European Jewish domination of the social order. In actuality, despite the widespread feelings among Eastern Jews, as the decades passed and intermarriage between members of the two groups increased, and even more as they experienced the same environment in a united Jewish state, their extremely different origins became somewhat muted, though sharp disparities remained in housing and education status.

The Arabs of Israel, on the other hand, seemed increasingly to feel close links to the Arabs of the occupied territories. At the same time, Israeli Arabs became more involved in rapid social change, particularly urbanization. In 1949 only about one-quarter of Israeli Arabs had lived in urban areas; by 1989 almost 90 percent were urban.

Most aspects of culture reflected societal and political concerns. In construction and architecture, for instance, much attention was devoted to new buildings on the eastern outskirts of Jerusalem intended for Jewish settlers. There and in the Old City, aesthetic concepts competed against the pressure to erect tall, massive structures that would alter the skyline. Tel Aviv boomed with new high-rise buildings. Music, poetry, and the theater flourished, and filmmaking eventually moved away from a celebration of heroic nationalism to a wider variety of themes, especially the relationships between Israelis and Arabs, whether at the personal or group level. Painting in the 1980s featured postmodernist and eclectic approaches, embracing performance art, absurdism, and neo-conceptualism. Women became more prominent in all the arts. Painters and sculptors tended to study abroad, and many chose to live outside Israel for a time. Their art generally followed the patterns established in Europe and the United States and used a wide variety of media. Publishing boomed, so that by 1986 about 10 million copies of 5300 book titles were printed in Israel, mostly written in Hebrew. Writers often were sympathetic to Labor or smaller leftist parties; many became highly critical of the Begin regime and its policies. Hebrew as spoken and written in Israel became a more flexible and lively language, with substantial borrowing of words from foreign languages, especially those dealing with the sciences. Israel became a world leader in some scientific and technical fields, two examples being solar power and medical-imaging devices. Israelis published more scientific papers per person than any other nationality in the world.

PEACE WITH EGYPT

Prime Minister Begin's foreign policy started with his firm desire to keep control of Gaza and the West Bank. The latter he called Judea and Samaria (as they were called in biblical times). His intransigent stand seemed in 1977 to be destined for failure, as first the E.E.C. and then the United States and the Soviet Union spoke out for the rights of the Palestinians. In October 1977, a joint American-Soviet declaration called for the reconvening of the 1973 Geneva Conference. Begin asserted that under no conditions would Israel negotiate with the P.L.O., nor would Israel agree to the establishment of a Palestinian state on the West Bank.

Egypt and Israel both opposed the reinvolvement of the Soviet Union in the peace process, as represented by the U.S.-Soviet note. Egypt's president, Anwar Sadat, determined to unfreeze the Arab-Israeli dispute by a bold gesture, flew to Israel on November 19, 1977. In a highly dramatic speech to the Knesset in Jerusalem, he appealed for a peace based on complete Israeli withdrawal from the occupied territories, Israeli recognition of the Palestinians' rights, and full peace between the Arab states and Israel. This extraordinary step provided the psychological and moral impetus for subsequent peace negotiations. In 1978, at Camp David in Maryland, President Carter, Sadat, and Begin established what they hoped would be the basis for peace in the Arab-Israeli dispute. One part of the Camp David agreements comprised principles for a separate Egyptian-Israeli peace, and the other part dealt in rather vague terms with the future of Gaza and the West Bank. This part called for "full autonomy" and a "self-governing authority" for the inhabitants of these areas. Jerusalem was not specifically mentioned, nor were the Golan Heights of Syria.

Prime Minister Begin secured a great victory for Israel by the Camp David Accords of 1978. The effect of a disagreement over interpretation of the accords was to let the present conditions prevail; that is, Israeli control of the occupied territories would persist. Almost immediately, Egypt and the United States disagreed with Israel on implementation, as in Israel's building new Jewish settlements in the territories. Later, Egypt and the United States interpreted such phrases as "full autonomy for the Palestinians" more widely than did Begin, who essentially wanted to annex or keep control permanently of the West Bank and Gaza so as to create a Greater Israel and therefore wished to deny any real autonomy to the Palestinian Arabs.

The P.L.O., Syria, Jordan, most of the other Arab states, and the Soviet Union denounced the Camp David Accords as a separate peace wherein Egypt deserted its Arab allies and the Palestinians so as to regain the Sinai Peninsula. Sadat responded by saying that this was the best compromise he or anyone else could hope to gain.

With extensive new U.S. economic, military, and diplomatic support guaranteed to Israel and Egypt, Begin and Sadat signed the Treaty of Washington on March 26, 1979, and formally established peace between Israel and Egypt. The treaty, simple in its provisions, was based on the exchange of land for peace. Israel returned the Sinai Peninsula to Egyptian control in phases extending to 1982, and in return Egypt established normal diplomatic and commercial ties with Israel. Both countries renounced the future use of force in their mutual relations. Israel had open access for shipping through the Suez Canal and the Gulf of Aqaba. Egyptian control in the Sinai was limited in various ways, and a multinational force, including U.S. troops, was stationed there and in a narrow strip of Israeli territory nearby to supervise the agreement.

The real proof of the effectiveness of the treaty came in 1982 with the Israeli invasion of Lebanon and the fifth Arab-Israeli war, after the turnover of Sinai to Egypt was completed by Israel. Egypt did not mobilize its armed forces. Israel thus gained by the peace treaty of 1979 the neutrality of Egypt in subsequent Arab-Israeli wars, a tremendous military asset. Israel also obtained acceptance and recognition of its legitimacy as a nation from its strongest opponent.

After 1979, Israel undertook a number of military, diplomatic, and political measures that severely tested the peace process. In 1980, the Knesset passed a law declaring Jerusalem to be the united capital of Israel. In 1981, Israeli jets bombed Iraq's nuclear reactor in order to stop Iraq from being able to produce atomic weapons, thereby ensuring that Israel remained the only country in the Middle East to have nuclear weapons of its own. Later that year, Israel extended its "law, jurisdiction, and administration" to the Golan Heights, a move that amounted to Israeli annexation. Israel built more Jewish settlements on the West Bank and in Gaza, east Jerusalem, and the Golan Heights, and it confiscated large amounts of Arab-owned land.

The numbers of Jewish settlers in the West Bank had grown slowly under Labor party governments. Likud governments built suburban settlements for Israeli commuters, and by 1982 Jewish settlers in the West Bank area had increased to 25,000, and 65,000 Jews lived in east Jerusalem. Most Arabs objected vehemently to the Israeli attempt to take over the occupied territories permanently.

In all of the formerly Jordanian territory of the West Bank, the Arab-Jewish ratio was about ten to one. In all of what had been the British Mandate of Palestine (Israel, Gaza, united Jerusalem, and the West Bank), two-thirds of the population was Jewish and one-third Muslim and Christian Arab.

JORDAN AND THE PALESTINIANS AFTER THE FOURTH ARAB-ISRAELI WAR

Jordan did not directly participate in the 1973 war that Syria and Egypt initiated against Israel, although King Husain did send an armored brigade to aid the Syrians against the Israelis. King Husain and Secretary of State Kissinger tried to establish a Jordanian-Israeli withdrawal agreement as part of similar pacts with Egypt and Syria, but Israel would not accept Jordanian and U.S. proposals.

The Arab summit conference in 1974 recognized the P.L.O. as the sole legitimate spokesman for the Palestinians, thereby weakening Jordan's claims to speak for at least some Palestinians. Legislation in 1974 stripped the West Bank of its half of the seats in parliament. This was a somewhat empty gesture, however, since no parliamentary elections were held in Jordan for seventeen years following the 1967 war. Martial law was in effect from 1967 to 1992.

Husain appointed the National Consultative Council in 1978 so as to co-opt leaders and mobilize support for his policies. The Council served many of the functions of a parliament until 1984, when it was dissolved and new partial elections for parliament were held. Those elected from the East Bank then selected delegates from the Israeli-controlled West Bank. Women voted for the first time in 1974.

The 1973 war left few economic traces in Jordan. An immense surge in oil revenues brought wealth to the oil-producing Arab countries, and this sudden affluence of Jordan's neighbors spilled over. In 1975 aid money from the United States and the Arab countries topped $500 million. From 1973 to 1983, Jordan's gross national product grew at about 10 percent per year, the value of exports increased twelve times, and the 350,000 Jordanians (especially Palestinian Jordanians) working abroad sent home large sums—about $1 billion in 1981. More women worked outside the home as a labor shortage developed. As a member of the World Institute of Phosphates, an organization much like O.P.E.C. that was spearheaded by Morocco for phosphate producers, Jordan saw the price of its exports jump. Income from tourism also increased sharply. All of these revenues produced a boom in Jordan. However, inflation, the trade deficit, and the need to import food for the rapidly growing population also rose.

When oil revenues elsewhere fell in the mid-1980s, so did Jordan's economy. Arab aid to Jordan was cut by half, and the country took to foreign borrowing, accumulating a foreign debt of $8 billion by 1989. Many workers returned home, exports fell, and subsidies for maintaining low prices for basic commodities were slashed, an action that produced riots in 1989. Jordan's trade with Iraq became considerably more important during the 1980s as other sources of income started to decrease.

Economic changes particularly affected the Jordanian Bedouins. Most males served in the armed forces, where they were strong backers of King Husain. Another source of income for them was sheepherding, which came in the 1950s and 1960s to include motorized transport of the herds and provisioning of them by water trucks. Very few Bedouins were completely nomadic by the 1970s; nearly all had settled down. Their special legal status was changed so that laws pertained equally to all Jordanians. Deep wells provided water for agriculture, and many tribesmen moved to towns and cities.

Other social changes included increasing urbanization. Half the population lived in Amman, and their need for city services was immense. Intermixing of Palestinian Jordanians and East Bank Jordanians took place more often, leading to a greater sense of common identity. About half of the citizens of Jordan were under the age of fifteen, creating a need for considerable spending on education.

Jordanian education prospered in the 1970s and 1980s as the number of children and youths attending schools steadily grew. Whereas the population increased at a rate of about 2 or 3 percent annually, growth in school attendance was more rapid. In 1966–1968 there were 440,000 students on both sides of the Jordan, including 287,000 on the East Bank. The latter number grew to 460,000 by 1973 and steadily increased thereafter, with nearly equal enrollments of boys and girls. The University of Jordan in Amman was founded in 1962, the Royal Scientific Society in 1968, and Yarmouk University in Irbid in 1976.

King Husain inaugurated television broadcasting in 1968. Government radio and television reached large audiences; by the 1990s about 90 percent of Jordanian households had television sets. Jordanian newspapers published in Amman were subject to the influence of the royal government, and occasionally they were suspended by royal decree. Folklore and archaeology constituted important fields of cultural production. Many aspects of culture were dominated by the political concerns of the day, and especially by the drama and tragedy of the Palestinians. Painting, fiction, and especially poetry have been associated with that history. Palestinian poets in the 1970s and later participated in a revolutionary transformation of poetic style, which was shared by other Arabic-language poets.

THE FIFTH ARAB-ISRAELI WAR

Israel had aided the mostly Christian rightists in the Lebanese civil war of 1975–1976. When Syria intervened in Lebanon in 1976, Israel warned it not to send troops into extreme southern Lebanon, an area Israel wished to keep as a kind of security zone. Palestinian raids into Israel from that area encouraged the government to invade all of southern Lebanon up to the Litani River in 1978. Israel then withdrew, hoping U.N. forces and Israel's Christian Lebanese allies would stop further attacks by the Palestinian commandos. The raids and counterraids resumed, however, until cease-fires were arranged by the United States in 1981.

Prime Minister Begin and Ariel Sharon, the defense minister, decided to invade Lebanon in 1982 to achieve several different objectives. (See Chapter 45.) Their stated goal was to secure peace from raids for northern Israel, but more important aims included destroying the P.L.O. and its headquarters in west Beirut; driving the Syrians out of most of Lebanon; helping to secure the election of Israel's friend, Bashir Jumayyil, as president of Lebanon; and then signing a peace treaty with Jumayyil on the model of the 1979 Egyptian treaty.

Israel invaded Lebanon on June 6, 1982, with about 80,000 troops and pushed rapidly forward north toward Beirut and the Syrian forces in the Biqa Valley, successfully fighting the 15,000 outnumbered but well-armed Palestinians. Bypassing U.N. forces, the Israelis took southern Lebanon easily, in large part because of their complete command of the air and the sea. Syria had 40,000 troops available in Lebanon and an extensive missile and aircraft combat force. On June 7 Israel directly attacked the Syrians in Lebanon. In the following days, Israel destroyed Syrian surface-to-air missile batteries, between eighty-four and 100 aircraft, and 400 tanks. Both Israel and Syria accepted a cease-fire on June 11. Syria did not fight in the 1982 war with all its forces. The Syrian navy, for instance, never left port, and no fighting at all took place on the Golan Heights.

In the Beirut area, Israel continued to fight the Palestinians and Syrians. Israeli forces soon linked up with their Phalangist Lebanese allies, who already held east Beirut. In this manner, Israel completed the encirclement of west Beirut with its civilian population of one-half million people. Israel launched a siege with aerial, naval, and land bombardment designed to force the Lebanese leftists, Palestinians, and Syrians to surrender. This policy was ultimately successful. In short order Israel made Yasir Arafat and his Palestinian guerrillas leave Lebanon by ship; gained the election of Bashir Jumayyil and then, after his assassination, of his brother Amin Jumayyil, as president; brought about the stationing of an international peacekeeping force (including U.S. troops) in west Beirut; and Israeli occupation of that area. Israel had won the war, and at what seemed a relatively moderate cost: 340 killed and some 2200 wounded.

This victory soon turned sour, however. U.S. President Ronald Reagan proposed an American initiative for peace in the Arab-Israeli dispute that was unacceptable to Begin. Another dilemma for Israel arose from the behavior of its rightist Lebanese allies, who massacred hundreds of Palestinian refugees. An Israeli commission, whose creation was demanded by 400,000 Israeli protestors, said indirect responsibility for the massacre fell on Ariel Sharon. Even more worrisome to the Begin government was the growing opposition to the war among Israelis. For the first time a substantial, though minority, opinion among Jewish Israeli men and women opposed the state on a major security-military issue.

Prime Minister Begin and Sharon remained adamant in pursuit of their goals. On May 17, 1983, Israel and President Jumayyil of Lebanon signed a troop withdrawal agreement whose provisions were tantamount to an Israeli-Lebanese peace treaty. Despite U.S. support of Jumayyil, strong internal opposition to him and to the Israelis emerged in Lebanon. Syria also opposed the withdrawal agreement. U.S. troops left Lebanon in 1984, and Israel slowly withdrew its forces as well, leaving just a few troops and some Lebanese proxies in the southern districts by 1985. Jumayyil abrogated the agreement with Israel, Syria gained the upper hand, a pro-Syrian Palestinian group ousted Arafat in 1983 once again from Lebanon, and that unhappy country sank further into chaos and strife. Out of this situation the Likud could point to the P.L.O. evacuation, the dispersion of the Palestinian fighters, and the loss of prestige and control by Arafat, whose new headquarters in Tunis was now far indeed from Israel. Despite this, the 1982 war in Lebanon was, on the whole, not a success for Israel.

ISRAEL IN THE 1980s, 1990s, AND 2000s

Despite the 1982 war, political turmoil, and the first Palestinian intifada, Israel from 1986 up to the second intifada in 2000 generally experienced a period of prosperity. Israeli politics, government finances, and diplomacy in the 1980s reflected an uneasy cooperation between the Likud and Labor parties. In late 1983 Menachem Begin resigned as prime minister and was replaced by Yitzhak Shamir, the foreign minister. Shamir had also been a member of the Irgun, a leader of the Herut party, and a vehement proponent of retaining the occupied territories. The painful withdrawal from Lebanon was underway, and in July 1984 the national parliamentary election took place. Labor won forty-four seats and Likud forty-one, but the voters also elected a number of Knesset members who were more conservative than Likud. More than 70 percent of Eastern Jews voted for Likud, and more than 70 percent of European Jews voted for Labor.

After much maneuvering, Likud and Labor agreed on a joint coalition. The coalition government was deadlocked on most major issues because of the sharp disagreements among its chief parties and their leaders. The two major blocs—Labor and Likud—rotated the most important posts of government for two-year terms, as Shimon Peres of Labor became prime minister and Shamir of Likud was foreign minister. In October 1986 the two reversed their posts.

This coalition inherited an economic crisis: an inflation rate approaching 400 percent, a stock market collapse, and drastic devaluation of the Israeli currency, the shekel. With a national external debt of about $23 billion, increasing unemployment, a trade deficit of at least $4 billion, hundreds of thousands of Israelis living abroad, and expenditures of billions of dollars on the war in Lebanon, Israel was in a dire situation. One source of help was the United States, which increased its aid. Israel now received more U.S. assistance than any other country in the world—almost $4 billion in 1987. The government in 1985 introduced budget cuts, price and wage controls, higher taxes, and a free trade agreement with the United States. Inflation was reduced to a more manageable level of under 20 percent.

The Israeli economy from 1985 to 1995 grew at more than 2 percent per year, slowing down to about 1 percent in the late 1990s. Some real privatization of government-owned enterprises finally took place in the 1990s, so that public spending as a percentage of the gross national product fell from 75 percent in 1985 to about 55 percent in 2000. The economy was boosted by substantial development in computers and related technology. Exports grew sharply, rising from $7 billion in 1987 to $21 billion ten years later. Armament sales abroad were a major component in exports, as could be seen in 1984 when Israel sold weapons worth $1 billion to such countries as Colombia, Zaire, and even to anti-Israeli Iran!

Increasing prosperity helped bring about social changes. Life expectancy was the highest in the Middle East by the 1990s, at about 77 years, and public health was excellent. Changes in the communications media included the rapid growth in the use of cell phones, the commercialization of formerly ideological newspapers, and diversity in the ownership of radio and television. In the 1980s there had been only one government-owned television channel; by the late 1990s cable television made about forty channels available. Many Israelis who were enjoying their new prosperity and opportunities for peace were more receptive to expanding personal liberties. Laws banned discrimination based on sexual orientation and sodomy was decriminalized in 1988. Using the 1992 Basic Law on Human Freedom and Dignity, courts rendered decisions expanding judicial activism, favoring secularist causes, and increasing the human rights of Israelis, including Arab citizens of Israel, but not Arabs living in the occupied territories.

Israeli Arabs became more politically active, economically productive, and successful in articulating their viewpoints in the 1990s and 2000s. By 1988 three-fourths of Israeli Arabs could speak and read Hebrew, allowing them more participation in institutions of higher education, where the language of instruction remained Hebrew. In the 1999 parliamentary elections ten Israeli Arabs were elected, including the first Arab woman to be a member of the Knesset, as well as Arabs who emphasized the central role of Islam in politics.

Technical cooperation with the United States in economic and military matters was crucial to Israel. Both countries worked together on armaments development. The uncovering of Americans who spied for Israel inside the United States did not seriously disturb U.S.-Israeli relations. In 1988, the United States committed itself to pay most of the research costs for a new Israeli missile designed to shoot down Chinese and Soviet missiles possessed by Saudi Arabia, Iraq, and Syria. And Israel was of considerable help to the United States during its secret dealings with Iran, an arms-for-hostages arrangement that became known as the Iran-Contra affair. Israel recognized that both Iran and Iraq were its enemies and sought to keep their conflict in a continuing stalemate.

The collapse of communism in eastern Europe, the ending of the Soviet Union, and the growing prospects of peace in the Arab-Israeli dispute all brought about increased immigration by Jews to Israel. Between 1990 and 1995 more than 600,000 Jews coming from the former Soviet Union to Israel brought short-term problems in absorbing the immigrants, especially in housing and jobs. Israel sought and ultimately obtained U.S. guarantees for loans to build new housing for the immigrants. Russian immigrants gave new life to Israel's hope for the ingathering of the majority of the world's Jews, who still lived abroad, while at the same time putting pressure on Palestinians and Jordanians, who feared that Israel might become more intransigent in its desire for land needed to support the new immigrants.

The power of the Orthodox Jewish groups steadily grew, evidenced by the law banning the sale of pork. Public controversy over the application of religious precepts by government came to the fore and occasionally gave rise to violence between religious zealots and secularists. Religious parties again played an important role as potential partners in building a coalition cabinet following the Knesset election of 1988.

ISRAELI ELECTIONS

Israeli elections revolved chiefly around the issues of security, the future of the occupied territories, and the possibility of making peace with the Palestinians. From 1988 to 2002 the Labor and Likud parties continued to dominate the political scene, but their strength decreased and smaller parties grew with the adoption of a new system for directly electing the prime minister in effect from 1996 to 2002.

In 1988 Likud obtained forty seats and Labor thirty-nine after a bitter campaign that hinged largely on policy issues relating to the uprising of the Palestinian Arabs as well as future peace talks with the Arab countries. Likud was reluctant to take a risk on the exchange of West Bank and Gaza territory for peace, and it proposed many more Jewish settlements in the occupied territories. Labor was more receptive to territorial adjustments for peace. Despite these differences, a new government under the leadership of Likud included the Labor party within its coalition.

In the 1990s the Likud and Labor coalition fell apart. The two parties so profoundly disagreed with each other on policy toward the Palestinian Arabs that in 1990 a vote of no confidence by parliament, the first such vote ever, ousted the coalition and resulted in a right-wing Likud-led coalition government without Labor participation.

National elections in 1992 created a very different result. Voting in new circumstances following the 1991 Kuwait War and in the midst of clear signals from the United States that it would prefer a more accommodating policy on peace, the Israeli electorate restored the Labor party to dominance. Labor with forty-four seats led a narrow coalition with various other leftist and religious parties, and Likud fell to only thirty-two representatives in the Knesset. The reasons for Labor's success were numerous, including such factors as the popularity of the new prime minister, Yitzhak Rabin; the appeal of the idea of land for peace as a way of ending the Palestinian uprising; factionalism inside Likud, which diminished its credibility; and the tendency of new Russian immigrants to support Labor.

Israelis felt increasingly threatened for their own personal security as a result of a wave of suicide bombing attacks by Palestinian Arabs in 1996. Shimon Peres led a Labor party coalition government following the assassination of Rabin, but in May 1996 Peres was narrowly defeated when, for the first time, the voters directly elected the prime minister as well as a new Knesset. Binyamin Netanyahu became prime minister, and his Likud party formed a governing coalition with religious groups and representatives of Russian immigrants. Netanyahu had received support from a majority of Jewish-Israeli voters, almost all the votes of the strongly Orthodox, and many of the 200,000 Jewish settlers in the West Bank and Gaza Strip. He strongly emphasized security issues and pledged a much slower and more suspicious approach to negotiations with the Palestinians, claiming that they had not yet lived up to their earlier commitments. The two major parties together had sixty-six seats and only about one-half of the votes for the Knesset, with gains being scored by the religious parties and Israeli Arabs. Voters apparently felt they could support narrowly based political groups at the Knesset level, now that a separate vote was taken for the office of prime minister.

The various problems of the Netanyahu administration brought on early elections in 1999 as the Likud party nearly disintegrated. Ehud Barak (b. 1942), a former general and chief of staff, and now leader of the Labor party, formed a coalition with smaller groups and won 56 percent of the votes for prime minister, decisively defeating Netanyahu. However, Labor's representation in parliament fell to twenty-six seats, and Likud had only nineteen. Fifteen political parties won seats, a record number, as the religious parties total grew to a combined twenty-seven members in the Knesset. Barak was able to form a broad-based but uneasy coalition favoring peace with Lebanon and Syria and full negotiations with the Palestinian Authority.

THE PALESTINIANS TRY COMPROMISE AND THEN INSURRECTION

The fragmented structure of the Palestinians was a major hindrance in uniting behind a compromise peace with those Israelis willing to deal with them. The Palestinian Arabs were widely dispersed. The experiences of Palestinians in such differing environments as Kuwait, Syria, and the United States influenced their behavior. And the Palestinians living in Israel and, after 1967, those in east Jerusalem, the Gaza Strip, and the West Bank differed again in their experiences. Ideological chasms also existed among the factions: some were radical Marxists; others ignored ideology in favor of a united struggle. The leaders and groups were subsidized by various governments that naturally sought to determine policy as well as lend assistance. Yet despite these variations, nearly all Palestinians had accepted the P.L.O. as their spokesman and had given Yasir Arafat, its leader, their loyalty. The Arab states acknowledged the P.L.O. as the sole legitimate representative of the Palestinians in 1974. Perhaps the major accomplishment of the Palestine Liberation Organization between 1967 and 1992 was the preservation and reinforcement of Palestinian identity. The P.L.O. reaffirmed the political rights of Palestinians and kept the issue of their plight before the world, as it also developed some of the institutions, procedures, and symbols that could be used for eventual national independence and self-government.

In 1977, as the civil war in Lebanon wound down, the Palestinians were weakened by their losses of men and weapons. The Camp David agreements of 1978 between

Israel and Egypt, although inviting Jordanian participation, seemed to King Husain to be a trap. From his point of view, Israel under the Begin government would not agree to terms minimally satisfactory to Jordan or to the Palestinians. Husain denounced the 1979 Egyptian-Israeli peace treaty, but the long Iraq-Iran War of 1980–1988, in which both Jordan and Egypt favored Iraq, helped bring about a restoration of relations with Egypt.

The catastrophe suffered by Arafat and the P.L.O. in the 1982 fifth Arab-Israeli war in Lebanon was reinforced by Syria's determination to manage the Palestinians for its own purposes, leading to a split within al-Fatah, the largest military grouping, and a weakening of Arafat's role. When Syria forced Arafat out of northern Lebanon in late 1983, he turned to Egypt and Jordan, hoping to reach with their help a compromise with Israel leading to the creation of a Palestinian "mini-state" of the West Bank and Gaza in a loose confederation with Jordan. In the 1980s King Husain and Yasir Arafat reached agreement for a joint Jordanian-Palestinian delegation to attend a peace conference with Israel. This failed not because of the king but rather because of Likud or P.L.O. opposition and a lack of sufficient support from the American government.

Instead of peace, raids and counterraids between Israel and the Palestinians continued, as in the Israeli attack on the P.L.O. headquarters in Tunis in 1985 and in various incidents of violence by Palestinians against U.S., Israeli, and other civilians. Israel attacked Palestinian bases in Lebanon as a response to guerrilla raids. Most Palestinians, the Soviet Union, Egypt, and Jordan nevertheless continued to support Arafat as the Palestinian leader.

Within the occupied territories in December 1987, an unplanned Arab uprising against Israeli control, the intifada (literally, "shaking off"), began and rapidly spread. Demonstrations, arrests, deportations, riots, and physical attacks steadily escalated as the twentieth year of Israeli occupation passed with no substantial change in sight. Many Palestinians from Gaza came to support Islamic fundamentalism rather than secular nationalism, but followers of both approaches were united in opposing Israel. Hundreds of Palestinians were killed whereas a much smaller number of Israelis died as a result of the uprising. Thousands of Palestinians were arrested, and general strikes, stone throwing, commercial boycotts, and violent demonstrations persisted into 1993. The uprising gained sympathy among Israeli Arabs and provided clear evidence that Israeli rule was not accepted by the population of the occupied lands.

King Husain saw that Israeli control over the occupied territories was becoming firmer as new Jewish settlements were built with the encouragement of the Likud party, and he also saw a weakening of the already small support of his regime among the West Bank Arabs. Their uprising in late 1987 impelled Husain to sever official Jordanian claims to the West Bank in 1988 on behalf of the P.L.O. In this way the Jordanian option—the Israeli return of some of the West Bank to Jordanian control in exchange for peace—ceased to exist and Israel now faced the need to deal directly with the Palestinians.

Palestinian Arabs had been steadily building organizations, national identity, and cohesion, despite their dispersion among several countries and their numerous internal squabbles about politics. By the late 1980s there were more than 4.5 million Palestinians in the world, and they wanted a country of their own, although most of them realized now that the Zionist state of Israel would also continue to exist. The Palestine National Council in 1988 voted to declare the "establishment of a Palestinian state with

Jerusalem as its capital," but the new state had no control over any territory. Arafat and the Palestine National Council endorsed U.N. Security Council Resolution 242 of 1967, which implicitly recognized the existence of Israel and its right to live within secure and recognized borders. Although renouncing terrorism, the Palestinians also continued to assert their right of armed resistance to Israeli control of the occupied territories, as well as their right of national self-determination. Israel rejected such Palestinian assertions as the United States entered into talks with the P.L.O.

THE PEACE PROCESS BETWEEN ISRAEL, JORDAN, AND THE PALESTINIANS

During the 1990s Israel and Jordan signed a peace treaty, and the Palestinians and the Israelis entered into a series of agreements based on mutual recognition and a promised compromise end to their long and bitter struggle. These unexpected and highly dramatic changes in the Arab-Israeli dispute took place in an international environment dominated by the victory of the United States in the Cold War, the collapse of the Soviet Union, and the diplomatic upheaval associated with the United Nations–sanctioned war against Iraq over the annexation of Kuwait. Palestinians and Israelis were tired by their violent confrontation, deeply affected by the intifada and the controversies related to the occupied territories, and encouraged toward peace by the continued success of the Egyptian-Israeli agreement of 1979.

As the United States and the Soviet Union lessened their differences in the late 1980s, it became clear that the Soviet Union would no longer subsidize its former allies in the Middle East, including the Palestinians, Syrians, and Iraqis. In 1990 Saddam Husain's frantic annexation of Kuwait led to international condemnation, confrontation, and war. As the United States, Syria, Egypt, Saudi Arabia, and some other Arab countries supported the Kuwaiti government in exile and eventually fought Iraq, Jordan tried to mediate the dispute while remaining neutral. The United States and its allies criticized Jordan for being at least implicitly pro-Iraq; Yasir Arafat and the P.L.O., on the other hand, openly favored Saddam Husain on the grounds that only he and the military might of Iraq could balance Israel's stupendous forces.

To preserve the military coalition, the United States successfully urged Israel to remain neutral, even after Iraq attacked it with Scud missiles in early 1991. Saddam promoted the idea of linkage, that is, the concept that the United Nations and the United States had been hypocritical in urging freedom for the Kuwaitis while not doing much to bring about justice for the Palestinians. To counter this claim, the United States pledged that once victory was achieved in Kuwait, it would turn all its efforts toward bringing about a just and lasting resolution to the Arab-Israeli dispute.

The rapid victory of the coalition forces over Iraq had particularly negative consequences for the Palestinians and Jordan. About 400,000 Palestinians were expelled from Kuwait, Saudi Arabia, and other oil states, with most of the refugees going to Jordan. The Gulf Arab governments eliminated financial aid to Jordan and the P.L.O., which were demoralized by the outcome of the Kuwait crisis. Jordan's economy witnessed massive unemployment as sanctions against Iraq curtailed commerce, tourism, and remittances from workers living abroad.

Israel mostly benefited from the new situation. The United States extended extra aid beyond the by-now-usual $3 billion per year, and the defeat of Iraq apparently ended its development of atomic, chemical, and bacteriological weapons. Israeli military superiority had also been enhanced by the launching of its first space satellite on an Israeli solid fuel rocket in 1988, followed in 1995 by a spy satellite, the first to be sent into space by a Middle Eastern country. However, Israeli neutrality in the 1991 Kuwait War demonstrated that it was only one ally among many for the United States in the Middle East. The growing importance attached to oil and developments in the Persian Gulf tended to decrease somewhat Israel's leverage in international affairs.

U.S. President George H. W. Bush fulfilled his earlier pledge to work for peace by arranging for the convening of an Arab-Israeli conference in Madrid, Spain, on October 30, 1991. Israelis, Syrians, Saudis, a joint Jordanian-Palestinian delegation, and many others sat down in public, face to face, to seek peace and justice. Bilateral and multilateral talks ensued, but they achieved little, chiefly because Israel's Likud government would recognize neither the P.L.O. nor the land-for-peace principle. After the Labor party won the 1992 elections, Israel earnestly sought to deal with the Palestinians. Secret talks in Oslo, Norway, led to a dramatic breakthrough: the signing on September 13, 1993, in Washington of an agreement to bring interim self-rule for the Palestinians in the Gaza Strip and a small area of the West Bank around the ancient town of Jericho. Even more important than the terms of the agreement itself was the mutual recognition and acceptance symbolized by Rabin and Arafat exchanging handshakes at the urging of U.S. President Bill Clinton.

Both the Israeli government and the P.L.O. were taking major risks by engaging in peace negotiations with each other. Each faced substantial internal opposition, mutual fear of the other party's sincerity, and the memory of long years of violence. Despite this, many Israelis became somewhat reconciled to the peace process as their diplomatic isolation ended. Russia, China, the Vatican, and several Arab states entered into diplomatic relations with Israel. By the end of 1993 about 135 countries recognized the Jewish state. Prime Minister Rabin, Foreign Minister Peres, and Arafat won the Nobel Peace Prize in 1994. Many Palestinians were also reassured as Israel solidified the 1993 arrangement with lengthy and quite specific understandings on economic relations, withdrawal of Israeli forces, and the creation of a Palestinian police force. In July 1994 Arafat returned to the Gaza Strip and established there a quasi-government, the Palestine National Authority. Israel, however, retained control over external relations, security, and the status of Israeli settlers. The issues of Jerusalem and sovereignty for the Palestinians in the one-fourth of Palestine they still hoped to govern were left open for future negotiations.

In the 1990s opposition to the peace process came from groups on both sides: Israeli religious nationalists and settlers, who wanted to retain the occupied territories permanently, and Palestinian Islamic fundamentalists. The latter were organized chiefly around Hamas (meaning "zeal," and as an abbreviation standing for the Islamic Resistance Movement, an offshoot of the Muslim Brotherhood), and the smaller Islamic Jihad group. Both opposed the secularism, elitism, and corruption of the P.L.O., favored the establishment of shariah as the source of law, and stood against any compromise with Israel. They frequently attacked Israelis, hoping to stop the peace negotiations. Other Palestinians had reservations about Arafat's personal role and suspected that too much had been given away for too little in return. Still another impediment to peace was the slowness of Syrian-Israeli peace negotiations in regard to the Golan Heights, which helped bring about Israeli-Turkish military cooperation implicitly directed against Syria.

Despite these factors, Israel and Jordan signed a peace treaty on October 26, 1994, the second such international pact after the Egyptian-Israeli treaty of 1979. Jordan and Israel ended their state of war, enacted mutual diplomatic recognition, agreed to cooperate in a number of fields such as water, and permitted their citizens to exchange visits. The 1994 treaty was part of the ongoing Arab-Israeli peace process, but it was also part of a series of domestic changes in Jordan associated with political liberalization.

King Husain's severing of Jordanian claims to the West Bank in 1988 opened the way to internal changes designed to gain wider legitimacy for the country. Relatively free elections in 1989 taking place only on the East Bank of the Jordan River resulted in the election of about thirty-four Islamists or Islamic fundamentalists out of the eighty delegates. A national charter adopted in 1991 stated the parliament could override a royal veto under certain circumstances; martial law, which had been in effect since 1967, was ended in 1992. New elections in 1993 and 1997 were again conducted in a mostly democratic manner, and political parties were legalized. Secularists increased their representation at the expense of the fundamentalists, who had campaigned against peace with Israel. For the first time, women were elected to parliament. The results of political liberalization were such as to enable the king to pursue peace with Israel even though most Jordanians were unhappy about it. The United States and its European allies forgave much of the Jordanian foreign debt as a result, and they pledged more direct aid for the future. Slow economic growth in the middle and late 1990s, however, fed into public dissatisfaction with the nature of the Palestinian-Israeli relationship.

The Jordanian-Israeli peace of 1994 was followed in September 1995 by yet another Palestinian-Israeli accord, this time calling for the withdrawal of Israeli forces from most of the West Bank towns and the extension of Palestinian control to them. Momentum for peace was interrupted on November 4, 1995, when a Jewish Israeli religious nationalist assassinated Prime Minister Rabin, thereby calling into question the future direction of Israeli politics and policies concerning the Palestinians.

In January 1996 Palestinians elected a national assembly dominated by pro-Arafat supporters and chose Arafat as president. Nevertheless, Palestinian Islamic fundamentalists succeeded in launching several suicide bomb attacks on Israelis, thereby helping elect Binyamin Netanyahu as prime minister and bringing the Likud Party into power. Likud was determined to slow down the peace process and to limit the freedom of action of the Palestinian Authority led by Arafat. Despite this situation, from 1993 to 2000 the Palestinians in the West Bank and Gaza were able to make some progress toward building up the basis for an independent state. Official radio and telivision services were established; textbooks for the public schools were written; and some Palestinians living abroad returned, bringing capital with them. Government was run in an autocratic manner, even after the election of a proto-parliament in 1996. Arafat established many security services that closely monitored political opponents. He used patronage, ignored a draft constitution until finally signing it in 2002, and centralized all power in his hands as he favored Palestinians who had lived abroad and held high posts in the P.L.O. in exile, rather than Palestinians who had lived in the occupied territories. By 1998 the Palestinian Authority

(P.A.) employed about one-fifth of all those in the labor force; the whole economy, including the government budget, relied heavily on foreign aid. The economic situation of most Palestinians deteriorated in the late 1990s, especially in response to the numerous "closings" of towns by the Israelis, which brought commerce to a halt.

By 1996 the territory of the West Bank and Gaza was divided into three categories. In category A, which existed in a small amount of land but included most of the Palestinian urban population, the Palestinian Authority had complete internal control, including issues related to security. In category B, the Palestinian Authority had some degree of administrative control, but Israel had control over security matters. In category C, which was the largest in area and included the Jewish settlements as well as many Palestinians, Israel had complete control. Categories A and B consisted of many small areas that were like isolated islands surrounded by category C lands.

The new Likud-led Israeli administration of Prime Minister Netanyahu took office in 1996. Although an agreement on the status of Hebron was signed in June 1997, basic disagreements between Israel and the Palestinian Authority caused mutual suspicion and a disinclination to take a further chance on peace. The Hebron arrangement indicated the difficult nature of concessions: whereas the 160,000 Palestinians in Hebron mostly came under P.A. direction, Israeli soldiers retained control of the area occupied by 500 Israeli settlers. Under great pressure from President Clinton of the United States and King Husain of Jordan, an agreement was signed on October 23, 1998, at the Wye River plantation in Maryland. This document called for Israel to turn more territory over to the Palestinians, Arafat to take measures to suppress attacks against Israel, and the United States to provide more aid. Although some parts of the agreement were implemented, major opposition to it emerged among both Israelis and Palestinians. Clinton and Netanyahu suffered from debilitating political troubles, and the religiously based opposition to Arafat was gaining popularity as Israel seemed no longer willing to work for a "peace of the brave."

In many ways Israel by 1998 was much safer than it had been earlier, and it was therefore more receptive to the idea of a compromise peace with the Palestinian Arabs. The peace treaties with Egypt and Jordan, Israeli nuclear strength (at least 50–90 atomic bombs), conventional armament superiority, the growing acceptance of Israel's existence by many Arab states, and negotiations with the Palestinians lessened the possibility of destruction in war. The transformation of the democratic nature of Israel as a result of its occupation and oppression of the Palestinians nevertheless opened the door to negative possibilities, such as the assassination of Rabin.

Israel's identity was bound ever more closely with the national identity of the Palestinian people and the fate of the kingdom of Jordan. The Palestinians were groping toward a realistic understanding with Israel based on mutual recognition, independent national identity, a just resolution of their personal and group claims to land and resources, and the hope of better times ahead. After more than four decades of exile, foreign rule, ruinous warfare, nationalist struggle, self-sacrifice, and institutional development, the Palestinians sought peace, if it could be based on justice. Jordan obtained peace with Israel in 1994 and thereby confirmed the separation of the West Bank and east Jerusalem from Jordan that had existed since the Israeli conquest in 1967. It appeared that the Arab-Israeli dispute might come to a rapid conclusion with a lasting peace between Israel, its neighbors, and the Palestinians.

THE PEACE PROCESS COLLAPSES

Although the peace process between 1996 and 1998 was slow and halting, starting in 1999 the optimism felt by most people and countries began noticeably to falter. Political changes, the bungled diplomatic efforts of the new Israeli government, Syria's reluctance to seize upon peace, attacks by Hamas on Israeli civilians, and other causes led to a catastrophic renewal of outright conflict between an implacable Israel and a desperate Palestinian Authority.

The death of King Husain of Jordan on February 7, 1999, deprived peace of one of its chief proponents. Whereas Husain's son, King Abd Allah II, consolidated his control at home, he cautiously maintained his father's treaty with Israel but could not take major new initiatives. Later, the death of Hafiz al-Asad in June 2000 and the succession of his son, Bashar, to the presidency of Syria created a somewhat similar pattern. The elder Asad had rejected Israel's peace offers; the younger Asad could not yet take a chance for peace, even if he wished to do so.

Israelis elected Ehud Barak as prime minister in May 1999, in part because of his pledge to withdraw Israeli troops from southern Lebanon. On May 24, 2000, Israel completed a unilateral withdrawal from Lebanon, but Lebanon, under the strong influence of Syria, could not move toward peace with Israel until and unless Syria also did so. The Barak administration presented a realistic peace proposal to the Syrians, who ultimately rejected it in early 2000.

In the meantime Barak had decided against a continuation of the step-by-step process of bargaining with the Palestinians, arguing that the last set of issues, including such sensitive topics as the status of Jerusalem and the right of return of Palestinian refugees, had to be dealt with all together. Arafat feared this approach. He maintained that the failure of Netanyahu to return the territory promised to the Palestinians made it imperative first to complete these arrangements and thereby restore trust.

To break the deadlock, in July 2000, President Clinton hosted Barak and Arafat at Camp David, Maryland, the site of the Egyptian-Israeli negotiations in 1978 that had led to the 1979 peace treaty. Although all the details of what transpired during Camp David II are not yet known, it appears that Barak presented the Palestinians with what he considered to be the most generous possible arrangement in regard to the return of land, but they rejected this offer, calling instead for full independence, the right of refugees to return, control of all the West Bank and the Gaza Strip, and a capital in East Jerusalem. The collapse of these talks opened the way to the outbreak of the second intifada.

The chief causes of the outbreak of the second intifada were the long Israeli occupation, the economic decline of the 1990s, the seeming hopelessness of obtaining an independent state, the growing presence of Israeli settlers (now about 200,000), and great dissatisfaction with Arafat's government and tactics. The immediate trigger for the Palestinian uprising was the highly provocative visit by Ariel Sharon on September 28, 2000, to the Temple Mount or Haram al-Sharif in Jerusalem. Palestinians living in the occupied territories embarked upon rioting, demonstrations, and violent attacks on Israelis, especially settlers in the West Bank.

The Israel Defense Forces attempted to suppress the intifada by force as the Israeli government undertook economic sanctions against the Palestinian Authority. Groups associated with Arafat joined Hamas in planting car bombs, killing many Israelis. Prime Minister Barak, in danger of losing his parliamentary backing, resigned, and an election for that post alone took place on February 6, 2001. The leader of Likud, Ariel Sharon, defeated Barak, winning 62 percent of the vote, as most Israeli Arabs boycotted the process. Likud, Labor, and other parties entered into a coalition government led by Sharon, as the security situation steadily deteriorated.

Arafat was unable or unwilling to restrain the suicide bombers, and Sharon was eager to use force to stop the attacks and weaken the Palestinian Authority. Israeli forces entered a Palestinian city in category A territory for the first time in August 2001 and attacked a P.A. police station. During the first year of the second intifada about 600 Palestinians and 180 Israelis were killed in the violence; by September 2002 about 1800 Palestinians and 600 Israelis had been killed and far more were wounded in the violence. Hundreds of checkpoints were erected by Israel at the entrances of Palestinian towns and villages so as to enforce closure and confinement and to try to stop the Hamas and al-Fatah bombers. A particularly gruesome Palestinian suicide bombing of Israeli civilians on March 27, 2002, in Netanya led Sharon to reoccupy the category A areas, surround Arafat in his headquarters, and seemingly end the possibility of negotiations with the Palestinians. On occasion Israel withdrew from some portion of the occupied territories, but it once again moved back its forces following new suicide bombings. Violence between Palestinians and Israelis rapidly escalated, with a corresponding increase in mutual fear, rage, and desire for revenge. The strategy of both sides seemed to be built upon the infliction of pain rather than the desire for a just peace through compromise.

Foreign governments attempted to mediate between the sides, with the United States, Russia, Jordan, Egypt, and Saudi Arabia unsuccessfully proposing various plans for an end to the killings and the resumption of the peace process. The U.S. was particularly involved because its support of Sharon and Israel's policies had an adverse effect on the maintenance of a broad anti-terrorist coalition after the attacks of September 11, 2001, as well as proposed action in Iraq.

The disheartening collapse of the Palestinian-Israeli peace process between 1999 and 2002 strongly influenced international affairs throughout the Middle East. In the long history of the dispute, the United States, the Soviet Union, Britain, France, the United Nations, and many other countries and groups had played a significant role. The dispute was especially important in the modern history of Egypt, an immediate neighbor of Israel and Palestine.

REFERENCES

References cited at the end of Chapters 36 and 41 are pertinent to this chapter as well.

Brand, Laurie A.: "The Effects of the Peace Process on Political Liberalization in Jordan." *Journal of Palestine Studies* 28 (1999): 53–67. A good review of politics in the 1990s.

Cordesman, Anthony H.: *Peace and War: The Arab-Israeli Military Balance Enters the 21st Century.* Westport, Conn.: Praeger, 2002. A very thorough survey of the armed forces of Israel and its neighbors.

Gawrych, George W.: *The Albatross of Decisive Victory: War and Policy between Egypt and Israel in the 1967 and 1973 Arab-Israeli Wars.* Westport: Greenwood, 2000. This excellent military history compares the two wars.

Gowers, Andrew, and Tony Walker: *Behind the Myth: Yasser Arafat and the Palestinian Revolution.* New York: Olive Branch Press, 1992. A biography based largely on interviews.

Gubser, Peter: *Jordan: Crossroads of Middle Eastern Events.* Boulder, Colo.: Westview Press, 1983. A good general survey.

Heikal, Mohamed: *The Road to Ramadan.* London: Collins, 1975. The causes and nature of the 1973 war as told by the Egyptian journalist and political adviser.

Hroub, Khaled: *Hamas: Political Thought and Practice.* Washington, D.C.: Institute of Palestine Studies, 2000. A careful study based on primary sources.

Hunter, F. Robert: *The Palestinian Uprising: A War by Other Means.* Rev. ed. Berkeley: University of California Press, 1993. A clear discussion of the intifada, based largely on interviews with participants.

Jayyusi, Salma Khadra, ed.: *Anthology of Modern Palestinian Literature.* New York: Columbia University Press, 1992. A collection of writings that captures the diverse voices of the Palestinian experience.

Klieman, Aaron S.: *Israel and the World after 40 Years.* Washington, D.C.: Pergamon-Brassey's, 1990. Especially interesting in its treatment of how Israeli foreign policy has been formed.

Landau, Jacob: *The Arab Minority in Israel, 1967–1991: Political Aspects.* Oxford, England: Clarendon Press, 1993. In addition to political matters, this work also features economic, religious, social, cultural, and group identity issues.

Layne, Linda L.: *Home and Homeland: The Dialogics of Tribal and National Identities in Jordan.* Princeton, N.J.: Princeton University Press, 1994. An anthropological discussion of modern Jordanian identity.

Lukacs, Yehuda: *Israel, Jordan, and the Peace Process.* Syracuse, N.Y.: Syracuse University Press, 1997.

Madfai, Madiha Rashid al-: *Jordan, the United States and the Middle East Peace Process, 1974–1991.* Cambridge, England: Cambridge University Press, 1993. Thoroughly presents the Jordanian perspective.

Ma`oz, Moshe: "From Conflict to Peace? Israel's Relations with Syria and the Palestinians." *Middle East Journal* 53 (1999): 393–416. An excellent review of a complex relationship.

Massad, Joseph A.: *Colonial Effects: The Making of National Identity in Jordan.* New York: Columbia University Press, 2001. Emphasizes law and military institutions and how they have helped to define a Jordanian identity.

Meir, Golda: *My Life.* London: Weidenfeld and Nicolson, 1975. A vivid and personal account.

Miller, Aaron David: "The Arab-Israeli Conflict, 1967–1987: A Retrospective." *Middle East Journal* 41 (1987): 349–360. A good summary, full of insight.

Mutawi, Samir A.: *Jordan in the 1967 War.* Cambridge, England: Cambridge University Press, 1987. Based on Jordanian military records and interviews; very useful.

Peretz, Don: *The West Bank: History, Politics, Society, and Economy.* Boulder, Colo.: Westview Press, 1986. Short but full of valuable information.

Quandt, William B.: *Peace Process: American Diplomacy and the Arab-Israeli Conflict Since 1967.* Rev. ed. Berkeley: University of California Press, 2001. An excellent analysis of U.S. actions from a former member of the National Security Council.

Reich, Bernard: *The United States and Israel: Influence in the Special Relationship.* New York: Praeger, 1984. Deals primarily with the period after 1976.

Reiser, Stewart: *The Israeli Arms Industry: Foreign Policy, Arms Transfers, and Military Doctrine of a Small State.* New York: Holmes and Meier, 1989.

Rivlin, Paul: *The Israeli Economy.* Boulder, Colo.: Westview, 1992. A concise discussion of all aspects of Israel's economy.

Robinson, Glenn E.: *Building a Palestinian State: The Incomplete Revolution.* Bloomington: Indiana University Press, 1997. The author demonstrates the political importance of the gap between the experiences and interests of Palestinians living under Israeli occupation and those who had lived abroad.

Sayigh, Yazid: "Israel's Military Performance in Lebanon, June 1982." *Journal of Palestine Studies* 13:1 (1983): 24–65. A fine evaluation of the Israeli military victory by a Palestinian.

Shindler, Colin: *The Land beyond Promise: Israel, Likud and the Zionist Dream.* London: Tauris, 2002. This revised version of the author's 1995 book is an able survey of the period from 1931 to 2001.

Smith, Pamela Ann: *Palestine and the Palestinians, 1876–1983.* London: Croom Helm, 1984.

Sofer, Sasson: *Begin: An Anatomy of Leadership.* Oxford, England: Blackwell, 1988. An exploration of the thoughts and actions of the Israeli prime minister.

Swirski, Barbara, and Marilyn P. Safir, eds.: *Calling the Equality Bluff: Women in Israel.* New York: Pergamon Press, 1991. Forty-three short selections on women and culture, family, war, work, politics, agriculture, and feminism.

Tessler, Mark: "The Political Right in Israel: Its Origins, Growth, and Prospects." *Journal of Palestine Studies* 15:2 (1986): 12–55. A perceptive study of the Likud bloc and religious and other parties.

CHAPTER 43

The Egyptian Republic and Independent Sudan

In 1952–1953 Egyptian military officers under the leadership of Gamal Abd al-Nasser (Jamal Abd al-Nasir; 1918–1970) seized power, established a republic, and erected a long-lasting system of government that became a model for other Arab countries. The Republic's leaders sought real independence from Great Britain, continuing a struggle that had begun with the British occupation in 1882. Nasser subsequently led Egypt through domestic reforms, economic development, wars with Israel, and adherence to the Pan-Arab nationalist cause. Egyptian society witnessed remarkable changes while maintaining its cultural leadership in the Arabic-speaking lands of the Middle East.

The Sudan was considerably affected by both Britain and Egypt, obtaining independence in 1956. An alternating pattern of civilian and military rule soon emerged, but both religiously based politicians and army officers had to deal with difficult economic development issues and the problems of integrating the southern Sudan with the rest of the country.

EGYPT

Egypt, Britain, and the First Arab-Israeli War

Egypt's foreign relations from 1882 to 1956 centered around its relations with Britain and particularly the degree of political and military independence Egypt could exert despite British military control of the country. The status of the Suez Canal, which had been extremely important to Great Britain in both world wars, was the most important ingredient in Anglo-Egyptian relations. Since the new British Labour government, which came to power in 1945, was supposed to be anti-imperialist, Egyptian nationalists thought the moment was at hand for a thorough change of relations with England.

Negotiations with the British bogged down on their evacuation from the country, joint defense in the event of an attack against Egypt, and the status of the Sudan. Egypt held that the British must evacuate all of Egypt; then if war broke out, Egypt could call on England for help. With respect to the Sudan, the unity of Egypt and the Sudan under the Egyptian crown must be recognized. On the other side, Britain was unwilling to withdraw forces from Egypt unless there was an alliance specifying terms for the return of troops. Soviet claims against Iran and Turkey led London to fear for the safety of the Suez Canal. The British refused to budge on the Sudan, stating bluntly that they did not intend to compromise the right of the Sudanese to self-determination. Treaty revision reached a stalemate after much discussion, although British troops did depart from Cairo and Alexandria.

Postwar Egypt also had economic quarrels with Britain. Egypt was relatively prosperous at the end of the war, but Britain held funds belonging to Egypt, until Egypt left the sterling zone by creating its own independently backed currency. In 1951 Egypt established its own central bank.

The future of the Sudan also loomed large in the minds of Egyptians. The water of the Nile passed through the Sudan, and the possibility of dams and water diversion worried Egypt. The Sudan was lightly populated and contained vast areas where the expanding population of Egypt might earn a livelihood. Moreover, cotton culture in the Sudan was considered competition for Egyptian cotton. Egypt wanted to control the Sudan and force the Sudanese economy into a role complementary to its own, thereby bringing about the unity of the Nile valley.

Another foreign policy issue arose with the partition of the British Mandate of Palestine to the northeast of Egypt and the resulting first Arab-Israeli War of 1948, which engulfed Egypt, Israel, the Palestinian Arabs, and various Arab states. King Faruq prompted participation in the war, hoping to maintain Egypt's leadership in the Arab League and gain a clear dominance among the Arab states. Egypt sent two forces totaling about 10,000 troops into Palestine in May 1948. One advanced through Gaza along the coast; the other pushed inland to Bethlehem and the outskirts of Jerusalem. In October the Egyptian forces suffered several reverses from Israeli attacks, which left the Egyptians discredited. Egypt signed the armistice in early 1949, leaving it in possession of the narrow Gaza Strip in what had been Palestine. The armistice was a humiliation for the Egyptians and an experience the soldiers would not soon forgive the politicians in Cairo, who were, the soldiers were sure, responsible for the defeat. Over 200,000 refugees were huddled in the small Gaza Strip, solemn testimony to the defeat of the Arabs. After permitting a short-lived Arab Palestinian government to operate there, Egypt administered the Gaza Strip until 1967, although it did not annex the area.

The Muslim Brotherhood

Nationalists were energized by the 1948 war, which also provided the perfect climate for the growth of the Muslim Brotherhood. Founded in 1928 by Hasan al-Banna, the Muslim Brotherhood grew under the founder's fiery oratory. He exhorted his followers to return to the Islam of the prophet Muhammad, which meant an acceptance of the Quran as the basic law of society. He desired to make Egypt, as well as other Muslim lands, an Islamic theocracy and to stop the trend toward a secular state. But the true strength of the Muslim Brotherhood lay not so much in its ideology as in the energy, devotion, and ruthlessness of its leaders.

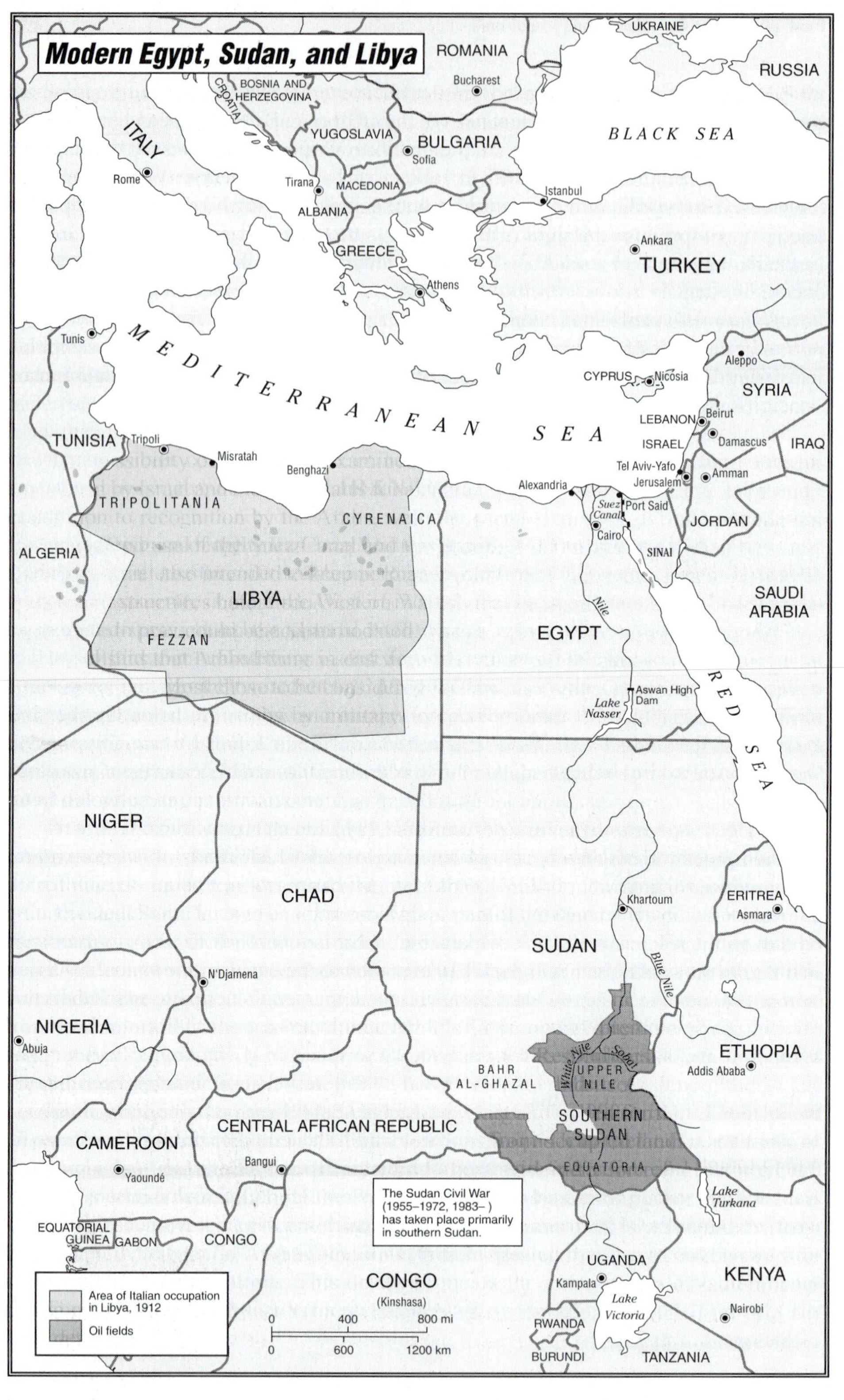
Modern Egypt, Sudan, and Libya
ROMANIA
UKRAINE
RUSSIA
Bucharest
BOSNIA AND HERZEGOVINA
CROATIA
ITALY
YUGOSLAVIA
BULGARIA
Sofia
BLACK SEA
Rome
Tirana
MACEDONIA
ALBANIA
Istanbul
GREECE
Ankara
TURKEY
Athens
Tunis
MEDITERRANEAN SEA
CYPRUS
Nicosia
Aleppo
SYRIA
LEBANON
Beirut
ISRAEL
Damascus
IRAQ
TUNISIA
Tripoli
Misratah
Benghazi
Tel Aviv-Yafo
Amman
Jerusalem
Alexandria
Port Said
Suez Canal
TRIPOLITANIA
CYRENAICA
Cairo
JORDAN
SINAI
ALGERIA
LIBYA
Nile
SAUDI ARABIA
FEZZAN
EGYPT
Aswan High Dam
Lake Nasser
RED SEA
NIGER
CHAD
Khartoum
ERITREA
Asmara
SUDAN
Blue Nile
N'Djamena
NIGERIA
Abuja
White Nile
Sobat
ETHIOPIA
BAHR AL-GHAZAL
UPPER NILE
Addis Ababa
CENTRAL AFRICAN REPUBLIC
SOUTHERN SUDAN
CAMEROON
Bangui
Yaoundé
EQUATORIA
Lake Turkana
The Sudan Civil War (1955–1972, 1983–) has taken place primarily in southern Sudan.
EQUATORIAL GUINEA
GABON
CONGO
UGANDA
KENYA
CONGO (Kinshasa)
Kampala
Lake Victoria
Nairobi
RWANDA
BURUNDI
TANZANIA
Area of Italian occupation in Libya, 1912
Oil fields
0 400 800 mi
0 600 1200 km

In its earlier years the Muslim Brotherhood maintained an active program of social welfare and agricultural cooperatives; in later years it became more militant. Its goal became the remaking of society into a manifestation of Hasan al-Banna's uncompromising concept of early Islamic life. In the 1948 war, the fearlessness of Brotherhood units at the front occasioned many heroic acts, although they in no way changed the outcome of the war. Reprisals, pressure, assassination, and armed gangs gave the Muslim Brotherhood power.

The secular Egyptian government found the Muslim Brotherhood a serious threat and took measures against it, leading to the assassination of the prime minister in 1948. When Hasan al-Banna was murdered, the government took no serious steps to identify his assailants.

Faruq and Politics

Many Egyptians came to the conclusion that economic reforms and social changes were needed. The old exclusive emphasis on the national struggle against Britain was too narrow. Even though national income grew, Egypt was in need of schools, health facilities, and industrialization. Land reform to break up the concentration of land owned by a few was felt to be a necessity. No other country in the Arab Middle East was better prepared to accomplish these changes than Egypt, which had had a progressive society, with a large educated elite. But political power remained in the hands of conservatives who opposed such changes.

The corruptness of King Faruq (who became notorious for his collection of pornography) and his supporters made politics unstable in Egypt. With immense wealth in land at his disposal, his political influence was considerable. Despite the king's usual interventions, relatively free elections held in 1950 showed the strong hold of the Wafd party and its leader Nahhas on Egypt. Nahhas assumed the prime ministership again and remained in office until the riots of January 1952.

Nahhas unilaterally abrogated the Anglo-Egyptian Treaty of 1936 and the Anglo-Egyptian agreements of 1899 that established the condominium over the Sudan. Demonstrations, riots, and limited military engagements broke out at several points in the canal zone.

The 1952 Revolution

In January 1952 Cairo exploded with riots and demonstrations against the British, foreigners, and authority. Martial law was declared, and Faruq ousted Nahhas as prime minister. Despite the king's attempts to retain power, the regime was peacefully overthrown on July 23 by an army coup, seemingly led by General Muhammad Nagib (Najib; born in the Sudan in 1901). Nagib described the goal of the revolution as the ending of corruption and bribery, the causes of Egypt's loss of the first Arab-Israeli War. The economy and political life of the state had to be cleansed thoroughly before Egypt could become a modern state or hope to stand up against Israel. King Faruq was forced to abdicate in favor of his infant son.

A civilian cabinet was formed, political prisoners were released, corrupt officials were arrested, and a land reform program was drawn up. But behind the scenes a very different power situation developed as the Revolutionary Command Council (R.C.C.) played a major role in determining policy. The R.C.C. was made up of young officers from various branches of the armed services. Its most influential leader was Lieutenant Colonel Gamal Abd al-Nasser (Jamal Abd al-Nasir), who had graduated from the military academy in 1938, had fought against Israel in the 1948 war, and was the chief organizer of the military revolutionaries.

Nasser consolidated power under the R.C.C. In September 1952 Nagib became prime minister. The new cabinet decreed that all political parties be purged of corrupt leaders. Hundreds of army officers and bureaucrats were dismissed, and many military officers moved into the various ministries. The head of al-Azhar was replaced by a theologian friendly to the revolution. Nasser tried to break the economic and political power of the large landowners through land reform, which would also, the R.C.C. thought, help end the abject poverty of the masses. Ownership of land had been highly concentrated, with less than 1 percent of the population owning one-third of the farmland while 8 million peasants were landless. The land reform eventually broke the old ruling class and thereby solidified the revolution.

The Struggle for Power

It soon became obvious that Nasser had no special plans outlined when the revolution began, although this revolution became one of crucial importance for Egypt itself and was a model for many others in the Middle East. Army officers in other countries seized power in a similar way and enacted similar reforms. The ensuing struggle for power among the revolutionary army officers in Egypt was also repeated in such countries as Syria and Iraq.

The revolution in Egypt can be seen as three revolutions in one: a "French Revolution," to get rid of a king and form a republic; an "American Revolution," to drive out the British; and a "Kemal Atatürk Revolution," to transform and regenerate society and the economy. For purposes of clarity, each revolution will be examined singly. Yet the interplay of the revolutions and the basic complexity of the situation should never be overlooked in assessing the forces at work in Egypt in the period beginning in 1952.

Once the power of the army was established by the coup, the influence and authority of the king vanished. The deposing and then exile of the unpopular King Faruq were simple matters of informing him that he had to go. A republic was declared in 1953, and the royal house of Mehmet Ali, established in the early nineteenth century, came to an end. Nagib was acclaimed president and prime minister, and Nasser became deputy prime minister and minister of the interior. The R.C.C. announced a transitional period, at the end of which democracy and a parliamentary government would be established.

During this so-called transition toward a purer political system, the military rulers purged their opponents through a new revolutionary tribunal to try enemies of the state and especially Communists, Wafdists, and confederates of the king. Nahhas was put under surveillance, and ultimately several thousand others were sentenced to long prison terms. In 1954 serious fighting broke out between the Muslim Brotherhood and the official party organization sponsored by the army. The Muslim Brotherhood was dissolved. The new regime also outlawed strikes by industrial workers.

Some of the revolutionary leaders, such as Nasser, favored dictatorship, radical reform, and crushing their opponents; others, such as Nagib, wanted to return power to civilians, more gradual reforms, and toleration for opponents. Nasser and his followers believed that the moderates' policies would surely return the old economic and political elite to power and defeat the revolution. Nasser attempted to oust Nagib, but the tank corps forced him temporarily to reinstate Nagib as president. Sentiment for a civilian government was initially very strong, even in the army.

Nasser intrigued against Nagib, bringing military officers into the cabinet and purging the tank corps. Then, using the pretext of an assassination attempt by the Muslim Brotherhood, Nasser relieved Nagib of the presidency and placed him under house arrest. Shortly after, Nasser became acting president. Subsequently, he introduced a constitution, which was submitted to a national plebiscite. Following its approval, the National Assembly met and elected him president according to constitutional provisions. The public then voted its approval of the president, also as outlined in the constitution.

The transition from military rule to constitutional government appeared complete. However, the constitution of 1956 placed extraordinary power in the presidency. Thus, Nasser remained a dictator, ultimately dependent on the backing of the army and what support his actions could ensure. Nasser's popularity in the summer of 1956 belied, at least for some time, doubts regarding the success and permanence of the revolution and the consolidation of all power by one man.

The Sudan, Suez, and Weapons

The second aspect of the Egyptian revolution was getting rid of the British. It had two phases: freeing the Sudan and obtaining full sovereignty over the Suez Canal Zone. In 1952, after conversations with various Sudanese leaders, Egypt signed an agreement approving the establishment of self-government in the Sudan. Great Britain subscribed in principle to this arrangement, and in 1953 an Anglo-Egyptian Agreement was entered into in Cairo, ending the condominium of 1899.

The signing of this Anglo-Egyptian Agreement served as a step in solving Suez difficulties. In 1954 Britain and Egypt agreed on a British withdrawal by June 1956, the ending of the 1936 treaty, the right of British return should Turkey or any of the Arab League states be attacked, and freedom of navigation of the canal.

Nasser throughout his terms as president steadily expanded spending on the military, especially armaments. Modern military machines, however, were so costly that only a nation with a large industrial capacity could afford them, unless purchases could be made at only a fraction of the real cost. Nasser hoped for an arrangement between the United States and Egypt, but Israel and its American friends objected strenuously, and Nasser did not wish to commit Egypt entirely to the U.S. side in the Cold War.

Nasser turned to the Soviet bloc. Nasser's power rested on army officers who demanded first-rate equipment. If he could not satisfy them, they would turn to someone else who would promise to get them arms. Nasser announced in 1955 that an arrangement had been concluded with Czechoslovakia to obtain arms in exchange for cotton. Arab nationalists rejoiced over the news, since they interpreted the turn of events to mean that they were more independent of the western imperialist powers and could at their own convenience attack Israel, which they viewed as the satellite of those same powers.

Nasser Seeks to Dominate the Middle East

Peace between Israel and Egypt remained unattainable. Egypt denied the legitimacy of the Israeli state and supported Arab Palestinian rights. A pattern of infiltrations, border raids, reprisals, bombings, accusations, and denunciations existed between Israel and Egypt, although the two countries also maintained secret diplomatic contacts with each other. Israeli boats and ships of other nations with cargo for Israel were denied passage through the canal; Egypt asserted that any goods that would aid an enemy could legally be denied transit since the canal was Egyptian territory.

The most serious incident occurred in early 1955, when Israelis fell on Egyptian positions near the outskirts of Gaza in retaliation for Egyptian-sponsored raids on Israel. The attack had the effect of forcing Nasser to obtain arms somewhere, regardless of price or strings. This act above all others drove Egypt to the Czechoslovak arms deal.

With regard to the other states of the Middle East, Nasser viewed Egypt as the dominant country in the region. It had the largest population and, with the exception of Lebanon, was by far the most westernized Arab state. Egyptian newspapers, cinema, radio, universities, industry, and commerce outstripped those in other Arab countries. Naturally, Arabs turned to Nasser for leadership. Pro-Nasser groups sprang up in Syria and Jordan, and Nasser gave their leaders encouragement and assistance.

With the Arab League's headquarters located in Cairo, the Cairo newspapers and radio exercised a powerful influence throughout the Arabic-speaking world. Nationalism, sponsored and disseminated by those media, was Pan-Arab in scope. Egyptian and Arab nationalism were equated; if a Syrian or an Iraqi proposed a course of action that might run contrary to the interests of Egypt, he was immediately branded as opposed to Arab national interests.

Nasser and the Arab League looked with sympathy on the actions of Arab nationalists in Morocco, Algeria, and Tunisia who wanted independence from France, and they collected and sent funds to help them achieve their goals. In the Sudan, once the Sudanese attained self-government from Great Britain, the experience of freedom was so sweet they hesitated to exchange it for Egyptian control. Political parties favorable to federation with Egypt cooled their ardor, and political leaders enjoyed the prerogatives of office. In 1955 no agreement was reached over the division or use of Nile water for power and irrigation, and in the program concerning the construction of the high dam at Aswan, no discussions were undertaken over the creation of the lake that would inundate a considerable area in the Sudan.

Nasser especially opposed the pro-British Nuri al-Said of Iraq, his archenemy. Nuri had aligned with Turkey and the west, and Cairo broadcasts vilified him as a British agent. This rivalry was a competition for leadership in the Arab world—a competition extending back through history to early Muslim times and even into antiquity. Egypt and Iraq, and indeed the whole Middle East, had become more power conscious than ever before as England and France, the old colonial powers, withdrew, and the shape of the future balance of power in the region was unclear. Nasser became a leader of the Third World grouping of countries, which sought an independent role between the two superpowers of the United States and the Soviet Union. He articulated the policy of positive neutrality and gained international prestige after playing a significant role at the 1955 Bandung meeting of non-aligned nations.

Domestic Reforms

The third aspect of the revolution was social and economic reform. Many Egyptian leaders contemplated secularism as part of this process, but they proceeded slowly. Religious endowments (waqfs) were ended. Muslim and Christian religious courts in Egypt were abolished in 1956, and cases were heard in secular courts. The decree did not repudiate the shariah, but precepts of sacred law were codified. Sufi organizations came under the tight control of the state, but non-registered brotherhoods also continued to exist and even flourished. Most of the ulama supported the regime, at least tacitly.

The revolution brought benefits in social welfare for the masses. A minimum wage for agricultural workers was set, and relief programs for the destitute were established. Village schools were built, teacher training extended, health services widened, and many projects for agricultural improvement instituted. A steady and pronounced movement of peasants from the villages to the cities, especially Cairo, strained government services. Average real income from 1952 to 1970 probably increased, even taking into account population growth. Economic growth in the 1950s was close to 4 percent per year, while it increased to an even higher level in the period 1960–1965, before falling over the next five years to around 3 percent. Industrial output grew by almost 10 percent per year between 1953 and 1963.

The population in Egypt in 1956 numbered about 22 million and was increasing by 500,000 every year. Life expectancy increased steadily, rising between 1942 and 1975 from 31 to 52 years for men and from 36 to 55 years for women. The standard of living of the majority of the population remained low. Thus, the most pressing problems for Nasser were economic, and especially increasing agricultural production.

Implementation of land reform progressed slowly. But the power of the large landowners, who were the likeliest persons to oppose the new regime, was nevertheless broken. And the small peasantry supported the revolution that helped many of them gain some land. In 1961 Nasser entered a new phase of land reform. As a result of changes then and earlier, more than 8 percent of the arable land was affected. Most of it was distributed to men who were former tenants and local notables; day laborers got practically no land. Overall yields increased as the reforms took full effect. The state strongly encouraged the creation of government-controlled agricultural cooperatives, and it also subsidized the prices of food for city dwellers.

Reforms, social measures, expanded government services and employment, strengthening of the army, and irrigation programs increased the size of annual budgets. Income from taxes fell behind spending. Nasser resorted to loans and artificially low prices paid to peasants for crops rather than drastically increasing taxes.

The economic pressures in Egypt, which the old regime had largely ignored and which helped bring its downfall, were crowding in on Nasser. He described himself as a man in a hurry, comparing his program to that of Atatürk in Turkey. Many things that he wished to do required twenty or forty years to effect, but the peasants and the poor in the cities would not wait that long for a better life.

High Dam at Aswan

It behooved Nasser to give a demonstration of the "promised future." Construction of the high dam at Aswan was pictured as the rational step to revolutionize the Egyptian standard of living. New land would be made available for cultivation and almost limitless electricity generated. Upper Egypt would become industrialized, and population pressure would be relieved. This would give Egypt a balanced and healthy economy.

Egypt was itself too poor to finance the dam. The United States was one possibility. Despite the arms deal with the Soviet bloc, fiery denunciations of the west, and anti-Israeli statements coming out of Egypt, the Americans and Britain announced financial aid for the Aswan Dam project in 1955. But Nasser objected to the secret conditions attached to the aid; this plus his ignorance of the west and his inexperience in foreign affairs made Egyptian diplomacy inflexible. It was announced that the Soviet Union was also offering to finance the building of the high dam at Aswan. To the west it appeared that Nasser was courting the Communist bloc in order to increase the grants from the west.

On June 18, 1956, the last contingent of British soldiers departed from Suez in accordance with the Treaty of 1954. The Egyptian economy worsened as expenditures continued to exceed income, charges for sustaining the expanding military establishment mounted, and gold balances dropped sharply. U.S. Secretary of State John Foster Dulles announced that the offer to finance the dam was withdrawn.

Nasser struck back by nationalizing the Suez Canal Company in July. He had raised great expectations in Egypt about the building of the dam. Without some dramatic move, he was lost. The Suez Canal provided the answer. In his declaration on the canal, Nasser explained that nationalization would provide Egypt with a $100 million annual profit to use in building the Aswan Dam. (In 1955, although gross revenues in tolls were nearly $100 million, the figure cited by Nasser, profits were only $31 million; the Egyptian share was only $2 million.) The boldness, excitement, and drama of the action were heady fare for the Arabs and a much-needed tonic for Nasser's prestige. When England and France threatened to use force against Egypt, all the Arab states, as well as the Soviet Union, rallied to Nasser's support.

Reaction in the west, especially in England and France, to the nationalization was quick. Naval units were moved to the eastern Mediterranean. In London and Paris, government leaders pointed out that Nasser now would be able to subject western Europe to economic blackmail. The bulk of the oil consumed in western Europe was Middle Eastern oil, and 60 percent of it passed through the canal. The British and French also felt that Nasser, backed by the Soviets, had gained so much prestige at their expense as to threaten their positions elsewhere, thereby reducing their influence as great powers, as had happened in Iran just a few years earlier, when Iran had nationalized the Anglo-Iranian Oil Company.

The Second Arab-Israeli War

A possible compromise was upset by the Israeli invasion of Egypt's Sinai Peninsula on October 29, 1956, which began the second Arab-Israeli War. (Many aspects of this event have been discussed in Chapter 41.) England, France, and Israel expected that if they attacked, Nasser's regime would collapse. Britain and France had agreed at a secret meeting to enter the war after the Israeli attack, and the ultimatum that they delivered to Egypt and Israel calling for a halt to the war and insisting that each withdraw to positions away from the canal was a ruse, in part to cloak their collusion and in part to enable them to occupy the canal area without Egyptian resistance. Nasser early in the war ordered his troops to fall back to positions west of the canal, grounded some of his planes, and sent the rest to bases in Saudi Arabia. Israel rapidly conquered the Gaza Strip and the Sinai Peninsula. Nasser refused the British and French ultimatum, and the powers entered the fray.

British and French attacks brought about meetings of the U.N. Security Council, which called for an immediate cease-fire. Britain and France invaded the Suez Canal area, whereupon the Soviet Union warned that it was prepared to use force to obtain the withdrawal of western and Israeli troops from Egypt. In the face of sharp words from the United States and the Soviet Union (these two powers cooperating with each other for once), a cease-fire was ordered on November 7, and U.N. observers entered the canal area. The British and French began their evacuation in December upon the arrival of more U.N. forces, and Israel withdrew from Sinai in January 1957. Only after severe pressure from the United States in March did Israel give up its hold on the Gaza Strip and the Straits of Tiran at the entrance to the Gulf of Aqaba. U.N. salvage crews cleared the canal, which Egypt had blocked in several places during the war, and shipping resumed.

The effects of this episode on Egypt were considerable. A large part of the arms recently acquired from the Soviets was lost in Sinai, and the Egyptian army was again viewed as weak and unprepared, although its defeat was to be expected given the overwhelming power available to its triple attackers. Had not the United States and the Soviet Union rescued Egypt, Nasser might have fallen after the British, French, and Israeli attack. Nasser, however, assumed a bold posture and emerged from the disaster stronger and more popular than ever.

The 1956 war marked a decided loss of prestige for Britain and France, whose roles in the Middle East became far more restricted. United States and Soviet standing rose, as these two countries became the most important external powers in the Middle East. The second Arab-Israeli War also demonstrated their status as the two superpowers, dominant throughout most of the world.

The United Arab Republic

Egypt was now acknowledged as the leading country in the Arab Middle East. Pan-Arab nationalists in Syria urged a merger with Egypt in 1958, despite the hesitations and reluctance of Nasser, who preferred cooperation rather than union.

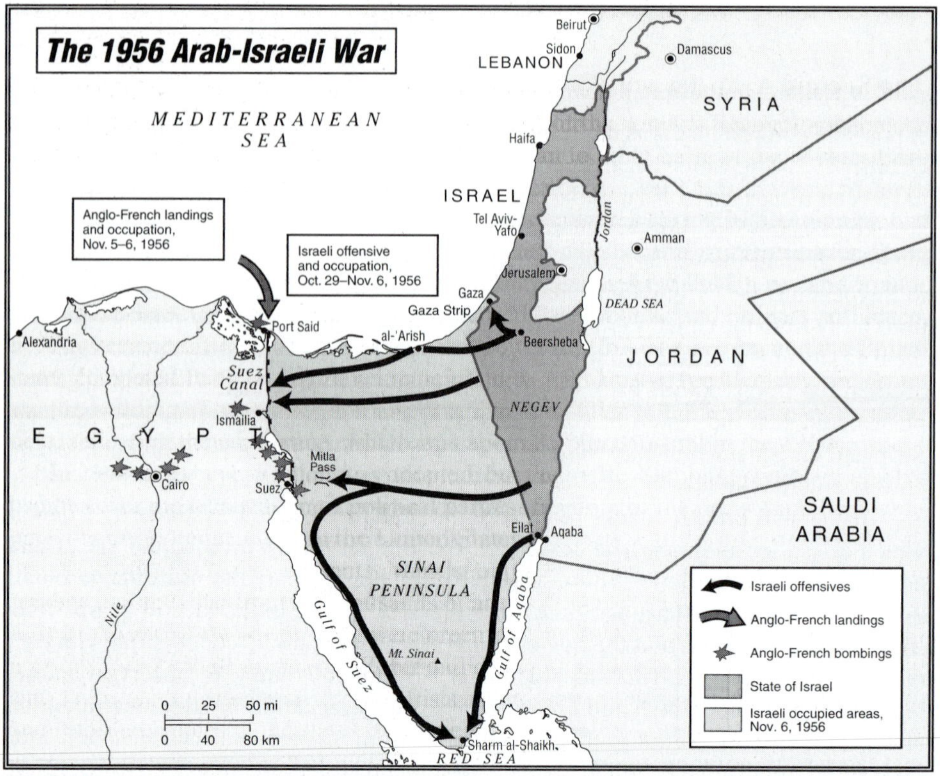

The 1956 Arab-Israeli War

MEDITERRANEAN SEA

Anglo-French landings and occupation, Nov. 5–6, 1956

Israeli offensive and occupation, Oct. 29–Nov. 6, 1956

Beirut
Sidon
LEBANON
Damascus
SYRIA
Haifa
ISRAEL
Tel Aviv-Yafo
Jordan
Amman
Jerusalem
DEAD SEA
Gaza
Gaza Strip
Port Said
al-'Arish
Beersheba
Alexandria
Suez Canal
Ismailia
JORDAN
NEGEV
E G Y P T
Mitla Pass
Cairo
Suez
SAUDI ARABIA
Eilat
Aqaba
SINAI PENINSULA
Nile
Gulf of Suez
Gulf of Aqaba
Mt. Sinai
Sharm al-Shaikh
RED SEA

0 25 50 mi
0 40 80 km

Israeli offensives
Anglo-French landings
Anglo-French bombings
State of Israel
Israeli occupied areas, Nov. 6, 1956

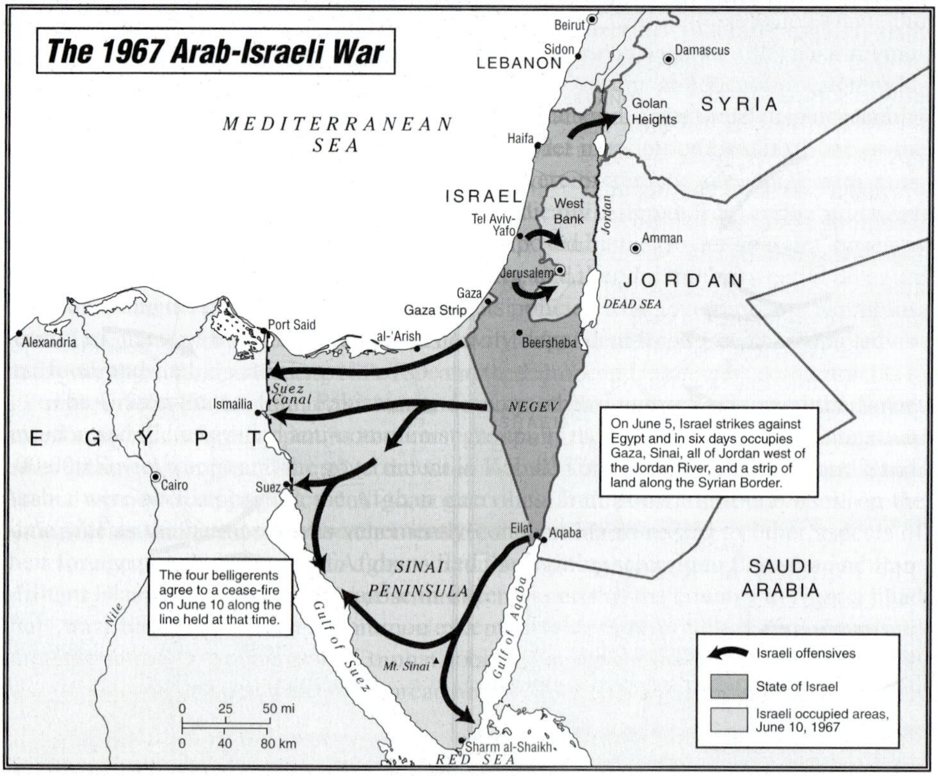

The 1967 Arab-Israeli War

MEDITERRANEAN SEA

Beirut
Sidon
LEBANON
Damascus
Golan Heights
SYRIA
Haifa
ISRAEL
West Bank
Jordan
Tel Aviv-Yafo
Amman
Jerusalem
JORDAN
Gaza
Gaza Strip
DEAD SEA
Port Said
al-'Arish
Alexandria
Beersheba
Suez Canal
Ismailia
NEGEV
E G Y P T
Cairo
Suez
Eilat
Aqaba
SINAI PENINSULA
SAUDI ARABIA
Nile
Gulf of Suez
Gulf of Aqaba
Mt. Sinai
Sharm al-Shaikh
RED SEA

On June 5, Israel strikes against Egypt and in six days occupies Gaza, Sinai, all of Jordan west of the Jordan River, and a strip of land along the Syrian Border.

The four belligerents agree to a cease-fire on June 10 along the line held at that time.

0 25 50 mi
0 40 80 km

Israeli offensives
State of Israel
Israeli occupied areas, June 10, 1967

The United Arab Republic of Egypt and Syria had a new governmental assembly and cabinet. Significantly, Egyptians held the portfolios for defense and foreign affairs.

Conservative, royal Yemen adhered to the U.A.R. nominally, thereby giving lip service to the ideal of Arab unity. Movements similar to Nasserism in Iraq, Lebanon, and Jordan were encouraged, but Hashimite Jordan and Iraq formed a short-lived union of their own. Nasser condemned that federation as the evil doings of "imperialists." Elements in every Arab state looked to him for inspiration and sought to attach themselves to his political coattails. Syrians found the Lebanese borders easy to infiltrate, and Nasser's agents abetted the disturbances that racked Lebanon in 1958. Had not U.S. Marines and British paratroopers landed in Lebanon and Jordan, those states might have fallen to Nasser's partisans and then joined the U.A.R.

In Egypt, and now in Syria, political machinery was devised to eliminate any opposition from political parties and politicians, including the Syrian politicians who had helped propel their country into the merger with Egypt. In 1961, skilled, disgruntled Syrian politicians collaborated with disaffected soldiers, merchants, and landowners to lead Syria out of the union, leaving Egypt as the only member of the U.A.R.

The Syrian secession caused only a slight shock to Egypt, whose political system became clearer in the 1960s. The Arab Socialist Union under Nasser's presidency was launched as the U.A.R.'s sole political party. Elaborate internal security forces were established or strengthened in the 1960s as Nasser became more suspicious of and more isolated from his former colleagues.

Arab Socialism

European Communism, because of its emphasis on dialectical materialism and its atheism, had difficulty in making an appeal in Egypt. This foreign ideology was supported by one of the great powers of the world and therefore suspicious in the eyes of Egyptian nationalists. Nevertheless, governmental control over agriculture and commerce had existed under earlier Egyptian regimes, and in the monolithic structure being devised by Nasser, any different pattern was unthinkable. The state held a responsibility for the economic well-being and advancement of its citizens, and whether it was called state capitalism or state socialism made no difference. The phrase "Arab socialism" had all the right connotations, did not conflict with Islam or the past, and with such a name it was a commodity exportable to neighboring states.

Steadily, the government increased its hold over commerce, industry, and finance by nationalizing many types of businesses. By 1961 all banks and insurance companies had been nationalized, and all newspapers and periodicals were placed under government control. In 1962 estimates showed that 90 percent of all major businesses had been nationalized, including flour mills, transportation firms, and seventy-seven bakeries in Cairo. Foreigners were forbidden to own farm land in Egypt. Over $1 billion in property was taken when the property of Egypt's richest citizens was confiscated. A highly progressive income tax was enacted, and 25 percent of net profits in all businesses had to be distributed to the employees. Egypt gained commercially productive oil wells in the Gulf of Suez and the Red Sea.

Probably the greatest venture was the building of the new dam at Aswan. With Soviet help, construction finally began in 1960. Prime Minister Nikita Khrushchev attended the celebrations in 1964, when the first stage was completed.

Another dramatic development project was the improvement of the Suez Canal. In 1958 a record number of ships used the canal, but oil tankers, nearly half of the ships passing through, were increasing in size to the point where many were unable to use the shallow canal. Once shipbuilders reached the tonnage that was too great for the canal, they would likely start building much larger tankers suitable for rounding Africa. Nasser planned to enable supertankers to navigate the chanal.

Through the years, industrial development in Egypt moved rapidly forward. Agreements were reached with Soviet-bloc countries and China for financial and technical aid to industry. The same was true for western nations. In the 1960s the United States gave large amounts of aid, especially wheat.

The continuing problem of the population explosion was a negative counterbalance to these advances. In 1958, at the time of the formation of the U.A.R., Egypt's population was estimated at 24 million; by 1966 it was 30 million, an increase of 25 percent in only eight years. The annual increase in population was rapidly approaching the 1 million mark, and when the impounded waters of the Aswan High Dam became available to expand the irrigated lands in Egypt, they would hardly feed the numbers added after the project was begun. Any improvement in the standard of living had to come from improved agricultural methods and industrial production.

Nasser and International Relationships

Following the Soviet agreement to aid in building the Aswan High Dam, the U.A.R. became increasingly friendly with the Communist bloc, although it did not become a satellite of the Soviet Union. The Soviet Union supplied large quantities of military goods in exchange for future cotton shipments, even though domestically Nasser actively suppressed Egyptian Communists.

Nasser's relations with the west were fragile because of past European imperialism and the difficulty that Europeans and their governments had in throwing off the concepts on which that imperialism had been based. With Nasser's growing interest in British-controlled south Yemen, relations became strained with London, while Egypt and France were somewhat friendlier.

Nasser was cast as the hero of the modern Arabs, and he had a large and devoted following in every Arab country from the southeastern tip of Arabia to Morocco on the Atlantic. Egypt probably helped plan the revolution of 1962 in northern Yemen, and Egypt sent thousands of soldiers to fight against the Yemeni monarchy in a long intervention. Egypt sustained the republicans to the point that Cairo dictated policies. Estimates were made that Egypt had expended about $1 billion in the effort.

Despite Nasser's charisma and influence, it proved impossible to bring about a new union to replace the Syrian-Egyptian U.A.R. The Arab masses might want Arab unity, but Arab leaders and foreign powers were not prepared to sacrifice their interests and personal positions to Egyptian dominance, even if the union of the Arabs was the only way to defeat Israel. Egypt also lacked the wealth from oil enjoyed by Saudi Arabia and

Iraq, which remained alternatives for the leadership of Pan-Arab or Pan-Islamic groups. Still, Egypt's military might was impressive, and in 1966 Syria joined in a mutual military command, pledged to fight together in the event of war with Israel.

The Third Arab-Israeli War

In May 1967, Syria, fearing an imminent attack by Israel, called on Nasser to make good his pledge for assistance. To support his role as leader of the Arabs, Nasser felt obliged to risk a war with Israel. He secured from the United Nations the removal of its observer forces from the Gaza Strip, the Sinai peninsula, and the Straits of Tiran. Egypt immediately reinstituted the blockade of the Israeli port of Eilat that had been enforced up to 1956. Israel reacted angrily as Egypt mobilized, moving some of its troops into the Sinai area, and Nasser gave impassioned speeches attacking Israel. As the tension mounted, each side prepared for war.

When Israel attacked Egypt in June, Egypt bore the main brunt of the six days of fighting, though Jordan, Syria, Iraq, and other Arab states joined in the fighting. Israel quickly destroyed the Egyptian air force on the ground, sweeping down under Egyptian radar detection. Massive tank battles in the Sinai peninsula were also won by Israel, which rapidly reached the eastern bank of the Suez Canal, thereby conquering the Gaza Strip, all of Sinai, and other territories: the Golan Heights from Syria and the West Bank and East Jerusalem from Jordan. Egypt lost most of its air force and a large part of its tanks and other war matériel. The U.N. Security Council cease-fire of June 10 ended the fighting.

Nasser publicly assumed the blame for the disastrous defeat and resigned, but the general response was so overwhelming that he rescinded his decision. Nasser then blamed the quality of the military leadership and the lack of organization and commitment for the defeat. It was reported that many officers had deserted their posts in the face of the enemy. Several thousand officers were relieved of their commands, and the vice president, a field marshal, was arrested and probably killed, although it was said he committed suicide.

Egyptians' pride and trust in national renovation, military strength, and Pan-Arab leadership collapsed in the face of the abrupt defeat of 1967. But, surprisingly, few real changes took place in the political system of Egypt.

Accusing the United States of participating with Israel in the war against the Arab states, Egypt broke diplomatic ties with the United States, but the chief diplomatic consequences of the war took place at an Arab summit conference in Khartoum, capital of the Sudan. Egypt and the other Arab states joined in pledges to act jointly in any matters concerning Israel, and in particular not to negotiate on a one-on-one basis. Saudi Arabia, Kuwait, and Libya promised Egypt to offset the loss of revenue from the closure of the Suez Canal. In addition, Nasser agreed to end intervention in the Yemeni civil war.

The Soviet Union began to replace much of the military equipment lost or damaged in the 1967 war. For the first time Nasser surrendered to its demands that Soviet military personnel be stationed in Egypt to train officers in the use and maintenance of Soviet equipment and to aid in the organization of a more effective armed force.

Cease-Fires and Stalemate

The cease-fire that ended the 1967 war was shaky from the start. Both Israel and Egypt subscribed publicly to United Nations Security Council resolution 242, which attempted to provide common grounds for ending the Arab-Israeli dispute, but each interpreted it differently. Nasser, insisting that Israel withdraw from the Sinai and all Arab lands, refused to negotiate face to face with the Israelis, as they were demanding, until they had pulled back to the pre-1967 borders; Israel refused to consider doing so until a peace agreement was signed.

Artillery duels and air raids along the Suez Canal, where Egyptian and Israeli forces were very close to each other, became commonplace. A truce in mid-1970 finally ended the large-scale fighting, though each side accused the other repeatedly of violations. Such large amounts of Soviet war matériel had been received by Egypt that it was estimated Nasser's forces were better armed than they had been in 1967, despite considerable economic damage.

Large subsidies from Saudi Arabia, Kuwait, and Libya kept the economy afloat. Oil from the Sinai was not available, the canal was closed, tourists did not come, and the cotton worm infestation was the worst in fifty years. The Aswan Dam was completed without much fanfare in 1970.

Cultural and Social Changes

The revolution of 1952 led to a great number of changes in cultural and social matters, including education, the status of women, and the media. The number of students attending government schools grew rapidly. Between 1952 and 1970 enrollments more than doubled, and in universities they increased threefold. Classes were so crowded that teachers and professors often could not devote much attention to the individual student. Many faculty members left Egypt for employment elsewhere. After 1962 the government guaranteed every university graduate a job, if necessary with the bureaucracy. The famous al-Azhar University in Cairo became a modern university, teaching secular as well as theological subjects under tight government control. Literacy rates improved; by 1976 about 55 percent of men were literate, although only about 29 percent of women could read and write.

The educational system, newspapers, broadcasting, and some of the arts were placed under fairly rigid government control between 1956 and 1964. Television broadcasts began in 1960 and rapidly became highly popular. The regime encouraged the production of films, some with a social realism or patriotic approach; many were commercial successes that were often boisterous melodramas, farces, or musicals.

The status of women improved following the revolution. Middle- and upper-class urban women especially benefited from the expansion of educational and career opportunities. By 1970 about one-quarter of all university students were women. More women worked outside the home in the 1960s than in the 1950s, but this was still a far lower proportion than was the case for males. Although the various constitutions specifically called for equality between men and women, the religiously based personal status laws gave preference to husbands over wives. Women gained the right to vote and to be elected to parliament in 1956, and, by 1967, 1 million women had registered to vote. Women were appointed to the cabinet.

In cultural matters a great chasm continued to exist between the high culture of the elite and the folk culture of the masses. To a certain extent, the cinema, radio, television, and comic strips helped to transcend this difference, particularly since Egypt after World War II was a major producer in all of those media. One example of this cultural expression was filmmaking, which boomed in Cairo, with about fifty films produced each year, many of them exported to other Arabic-speaking countries.

Folk poetry was closely associated with religious festivities, and rural pilgrims returning from Mecca often had the walls of their houses painted with scenes based on their experiences. Painting and sculpture in the western tradition were purchased by the upper classes; some painters used folk-realistic motifs to try to bridge the gap between the poor and the rich. The Egyptian government sponsored conservation of the folk tradition, as in textiles and in Egyptian Arabic music, while the singer Umm Kulthum (d. 1975) became the most famous performer in the Arab world, holding millions of people spellbound during her radio performances.

While some artists followed western styles of expression, much of music, literature, poetry, and drama was preoccupied with political events and social realism, particularly the issues of justice for the poor, nationalism, and the struggle against Israel. Egyptian comic strips, for instance, portrayed Nasser as a hero. Najib Mahfuz (Naguib Mahfouz), the preeminent novelist of the Arab world, who won the 1988 Nobel Prize for literature, initially wrote about the life of middle-class Cairenes; later he turned inward and pursued a more personal vision. The number of books published in Egypt steadily increased, rising from under 1000 in 1948 to more than 2000 by 1960. Political patronage encouraged writers to express support of the state, while censorship restrained dissident opinions unless they were carefully disguised.

Nasser felt the need for measures such as censorship, though he remained immensely popular even after the defeat of 1967. He was the most charismatic and appealing political leader to appear among the Arabs in the twentieth century; his sudden death from a heart attack in 1970 came as a great shock to Egypt and the rest of the world. A tumultuous era of remarkable change had ended.

THE SUDAN

Independence

The history of Egypt and the Sudan was intertwined during the period 1945 to 1970. In addition to direct relationships, they also had somewhat parallel experiences in regard to gaining independence from Britain and uncertainties about the allocation of legitimate political power. However, the large size, diverse society, and relative poverty of the Sudan as compared to Egypt contributed to differences in historical patterns.

At the end of World War II, sentiment in Egypt for unification with the Sudan left the British unmoved, but it attracted the support of Ashiqqa party leaders in the Sudan, largely because they sought to play Egypt off against Great Britain. In 1947 the British announced that a Sudanese-elected legislative assembly with an executive council would be formed. The Ummah party, which gathered its inspiration from the famed nineteenth-century Mahdi, won the election, in large part because Ashiqqa showed friendship for Egypt and boycotted it. Both major political parties were religiously based and under the power of sectarian Sunni Muslim leaders. All the parties in 1950 demanded that Great Britain and Egypt grant the Sudan the right of self-government and self-determination.

Pressure for independence was not a result of economic causes. In fact, the overall economy was growing as cotton exports increased, although this growth started from a low base. The majority of the population engaged in agriculture prospered during this period, although the economy was still sufficiently disparate that some distant provinces experienced famine. In the cities, wages failed to keep pace with food prices, hastening the development of labor unions, particularly among railway workers. The total population was about 10 million, according to the first systematic national census that was conducted in 1956. Literacy was low: perhaps one-quarter of males were able to read and write, and only about 4 percent of women were literate. Radio broadcasting had begun in 1940 and television would start in 1963.

The establishment of independence was made easier in 1952 when Egypt agreed with the Ummah party for the establishment of self-government in the Sudan. The administration, police, and army were to be Sudanized, after which time the right of self-determination would be exercised by the Sudanese. An Anglo-Egyptian agreement ended the condominium of 1899 on the basis of Sudanese self-determination.

The Ummah party declared that it favored the founding of a republic. The head of the party was Abd al-Rahman al-Mahdi, spiritual leader of the Ansar sect of Muslims. The Ummah group favored a slow process of separation from England. Ali al-Mirghani, head of the Khatmiyyah sect, served as titular head of the Ashiqqa party, which now took the name of National Unionist party (N.U.P.). The active leader was Ismail al-Azhari, a teacher of mathematics at Gordon Memorial College in Khartoum, who espoused a close tie with Egypt.

Elections in 1953 resulted in a substantial N.U.P. victory, although voters were split along regional, sectarian, and economic lines. Ismail al-Azhari became prime minister, and Sudanization proceeded rapidly. Sudanese became provincial governors, replacing the customary British civil servants. Very few southern Sudanese were appointed to posts as the British left; instead, northern Sudanese secured the key appointments.

In 1955 the N.U.P. changed its position over the question of the tie to Egypt, coming to favor unfettered sovereignty for the Sudan, but with cultural and economic cooperation with Egypt. Thus the party rejected the union of Sudan and Egypt. The Sudan house of representatives declared Sudan an independent state and requested recognition from Egypt and Great Britain, which they granted on January 1, 1956; Sudan then joined the Arab League and the United Nations.

Nearly 50 percent of Sudan's trade had been with Great Britain, less than 10 percent with Egypt. Cultural ties with Egypt were closer; a great number of Sudanese were educated in Cairo and Alexandria. The problem of the Nile waters was a vital one for Sudan, but doubly so for Egypt. Negotiations between the two states ended in stalemates. With these complex and diverse forces at work on Sudan, a policy of complete independence and neutralism attracted general support.

Military Government

The newly independent Sudan under its civilian government faced many difficulties soon after gaining its new status. In 1956, during the second Arab-Israeli War, the blocking of the Suez Canal hurt Sudan's trade more than that of any other country. Sudanese cotton harvests in 1957 and 1958 were poor, and the world price for cotton fell, thereby creating serious economic problems.

General Ibrahim Abboud, commander of the army, in an easy military coup suspended the constitution in 1958, turned out the cabinet, dissolved parliament and the political parties, abolished trade unions, and declared a state of emergency. A Supreme Council of the Armed Forces proclaimed that it held constitutional authority and that Abboud would exercise all powers. The two religious groups, the Mahdists and the Khatmiyyah, initially supported the army coup.

The conservative Abboud eventually allowed some political participation as economic conditions improved. Relative political stability seemed to indicate support for military rule, although the southern provinces began to see rumblings of nationalist and separatist movements as the military government forcibly imposed measures to integrate the region into the north. One example in 1960 was the changing of the day of rest from Sunday to Friday.

Abboud also tackled the long-standing argument with Egypt over the Nile waters; in 1959 he accepted compensation from Egypt to help resettle those in the Sudan who would lose their lands and homes from flooding caused by the new Aswan Dam. A general agreement was also reached whereby Sudan would be allotted 18.5 billion cubic meters of water annually from the Nile, leaving some 55.5 billion for Egypt. There was genuine satisfaction in Sudan over this division, for it was far greater than Sudan had previously.

Civilian Rule and the Southern Provinces

After six years of military rule, rioting and bloodshed erupted in Khartoum in 1964 as a result of many frustrations, the greatest of which were the continuing unrest and disorders throughout the southern provinces. Sudan's political leaders compelled Abboud to step aside for a civilian caretaker government. The fall of a military-dominated government because of civilian pressure was a most unusual happening in the context of the modern Middle East; Sudan's military lacked the popularity and programs possessed by Nasser in Egypt. Political prisoners were released, censorship ended, political parties legalized, and Khartoum University regained autonomy. Elections for a constituent assembly, in which women for the first time voted, were called in 1965 but held only in the north. A coalition government of Ummah and N.U.P. members was formed.

In 1966 the assembly elected Sadiq al-Mahdi, the new leader of Ummah, as prime minister. Sadiq, thirty years old when he took office, was an Oxford-educated economist and a modernist who had broken with his uncle, the leader of the Ansar sect and descendant of the Mahdi who had thrown out the Egyptians and British in the late nineteenth century. Sadiq, the great-grandson of the Mahdi, advocated neither capitalism nor communism but rather a Sudanese socialism. He also felt that there was a real basis for national cohesion in the Sudan, and the activist southern leaders initially had more confidence in him than in his predecessors. Sadiq went ahead with the first elections in ten years in the south to fill their seats in the assembly. Ummah and the southern Sudan African National Union formed a rather conservative bloc in the assembly.

When the 1967 Arab-Israeli War broke out, Sudan severed relations with Great Britain and the United States. The Arab summit meeting in Khartoum after the war condemned Israel as an aggressor and reaffirmed Arab solidarity. Such emphasis on Arab identity threatened the non-Muslim Sudanese, who objected to any possible union of the Sudan with the Arab states.

Governments tried to extend the infrastructure and build up the military. Some funds were spent on irrigation projects, railway extension, and a national airline, but far more went to pay the burgeoning bureaucracy. Military expenditures increased by almost 400 percent from 1955 to 1967, reaching about 30 percent of the total budget. The state also encouraged the continuing commercialization of agriculture and urbanization, resulting in the growth of greater Khartoum.

Sudan needed domestic political tranquility, and this depended on solving the southern problem. After the declaration of Sudan's independence and the departure of the British, strife erupted between the south and the north. The animistic and Christian blacks inhabiting the southern provinces constituted about one-third of the country's population, while the northern Arab and non-Arab Muslims were a distinct majority. Self-rule, autonomy within a loose federation, secession, and independence: each of these schemes had supporters in the south who mistrusted the government of Khartoum and the Arab politicians and generals. To centuries of distrust and fear was added the new African nationalism. In 1962 large-scale fighting broke out, and it lasted for ten years (and was resumed later, in 1983). Government forces were only partially successful in curbing the uprising in the 1960s, although tens of thousands of rebels fled to other African states. William Deng, leader of the Sudan African National Union, pleaded the southern cause from his exile, but others believed his organization to be too ineffective and favored other groups as the stream of exiles and refugees widened. Bloodshed in the southern provinces pulled down one Sudanese cabinet after another.

Even with southerners in the cabinet, the civil war did not end. Israel provided some assistance to the southern rebels. Fighting in the south also involved Zaire and Uganda, where exiles formed a provisional government. At one time government troops opened roads and secured the towns, but the countryside was fully in the hands of guerrillas.

In Khartoum, the squabbling, factionalism, and incompetence of the chief politicians once again discredited the democratic and parliamentary system. Little was accomplished, and in particular the war in the southern provinces continued. This opened the way to still another military takeover in 1969.

SUDAN AND EGYPT COMPARED

Both Sudan and Egypt had military-led governments by the early 1970s, both had gained real independence from Great Britain in the 1950s, and the size of government in both rapidly increased. The two neighbors also reconciled their interests by the allocation of the Nile River waters. Egypt, however, in accordance with its larger population and more vibrant economy, played a far more significant role in the region and in achieving economic changes, as seen in Nasser's leadership of Pan-Arabism and development of Arab Socialism.

Of the three goals of the Egyptian Revolution of 1952, the establishment of a republic and the ousting of the British were the most successful. The third goal of socioeconomic reform had mixed results, with some successes lessened in their effectiveness by rapid population growth. War and preparation for war also ate up many Egyptian resources as Egypt clearly lost the Arab-Israeli wars of 1948 and 1967, while securing a diplomatic but not a military victory in 1956. The Sudan was spared major international wars, but its internal problems in the south threatened its national integrity while putting great stress on its often deadlocked political system. New leaders in both Sudan and Egypt would try to resolve these dilemmas in the 1970s.

REFERENCES

References cited at the end of Chapters 20, 24, 28, 34, and 37 are pertinent to this chapter as well.

Abd al-Rahim, Muddathir, et al., eds.: *Sudan Since Independence: Studies of the Political Development Since 1956.* Aldershot, England: Gower, 1986. Fifteen essays by political scientists who were associated at various times with the University of Khartoum.

Ali, Wijdan: *Modern Islamic Art: Development and Continuity.* Gainesville: University Press of Florida, 1997. The author reviews the chief artists, schools of painting, and art education; especially useful for Egypt and Iran.

Armbrust, Walter: *Mass Culture and Modernism in Egypt.* Cambridge: Cambridge University Press, 1996. A sophisticated discussion of films, radio, television, and popular culture.

Beattie, Kirk J.: *Egypt during the Nasser Years: Ideology, Politics, and Civil Society.* Boulder, Colo.: Westview, 1994. Concentrates on the way Nasser maintained his power.

Beinen, Joel: *Workers and Peasants in the Modern Middle East.* Cambridge: Cambridge University Press, 2001. The author surveys the subject from the 1820s onward, following the subaltern school of historical writing. His treatment of Egypt is particularly valuable.

Danielson, Virginia: *The Voice of Egypt: Umm Kulthum, Arabic Song, and Egyptian Society in the Twentieth Century.* Chicago: University of Chicago Press, 1997. A wonderful study of the life of the great Egyptian singer.

Douglas, Allen, and Fedwa Malti-Douglas: *Arab Comic Strips: Politics of an Emerging Mass Culture.* Bloomington: Indiana University Press, 1993. A sophisticated discussion of a pervasive cultural form, especially important in Egypt.

Gordon, Joel: *Nasser's Blessed Movement: Egypt's Free Officers and the July Revolution.* New York: Oxford University Press, 1992. A careful account of the early years of the revolution.

Heikal, Mohamed H.: *Nasser: The Cairo Documents.* Garden City, N.Y.: Doubleday, 1973. By an influential journalist and adviser to Nasser.

Hopwood, Derek: *Egypt: Politics and Society, 1945–1990.* 3d ed. London: Routledge, 1993. A useful introductory text that covers politics, economics, ideology, and culture.

Jankowski, James: *Nasser's Egypt, Arab Nationalism, and the United Arab Republic.* Boulder, Colo.: Lynne Rienner, 2002. An insightful analysis of Egyptian nationalism and foreign policy from 1952 to 1961, focused on the merger with Syria.

Khalid, Mansour: *The Government They Deserve: The Role of the Elite in Sudan's Political Evolution.* London: Kegan Paul, 1990. A Sudanese politician and writer discusses political history.

Kyle, Keith: *Suez.* New York: St. Martin's Press, 1991. A detailed, balanced, and well-written study that is particularly useful for understanding British and American actions.

Louis, Wm. Roger, and Roger Owen, eds.: *Suez 1956: The Crisis and Its Consequences.* Oxford: Clarendon Press, 1989. American, Egyptian, Israeli, British, and other authors examine all aspects of the crisis.

Mabro, Robert: *The Egyptian Economy, 1952–1972.* New York: Oxford University Press, 1974. Fine survey of land reform, the Aswan Dam, and industry.

al-Nasser, Gamal Abd: *Egypt's Liberation.* Washington: Public Affairs Press, 1955. A blueprint of the revolution. First issued in Cairo under the title *The Philosophy of the Revolution.*

el-Sadat, Anwar: *Revolt on the Nile.* New York: John Day, 1957. Sadat's description of the events leading to the 1952 revolution.

Sfeir, George N.: *Modernization of the Law in Arab States: An Investigation into Current Civil Criminal and Constitutional Law in the Arab World.* San Franciso: Austin and Winfield, 1998. An excellent comparative study, including the issue of judicial review.

Shibl, Yusuf: *The Aswan High Dam.* Beirut: Arab Institute for Research and Publishing, 1971. A very useful account.

Sullivan, Earl L.: *Women in Egyptian Public Life.* Syracuse, N.Y.: Syracuse University Press, 1986.

Talhami, Ghada Hashem: *The Mobilization of Muslim Women in Egypt.* Gainesville: University Press of Florida, 1996. A general, historical review with emphasis on the 1980s and 1990s.

Vatikiotis, P. J.: *Nasser and His Generation.* London: Croom Helm, 1978. A highly critical and comparative biography.

Voll, John Obert, and Sarah Potts Voll: *The Sudan: Unity and Diversity in a Multicultural State.* Boulder, Colo.: Westview Press, 1985. An excellent short survey that covers economics, geography, history, modern politics, and culture.

Waterbury, John: *Hydropolitics of the Nile Valley.* Syracuse, N.Y.: Syracuse University Press, 1979. Concentrates on water, ecology, and the political and economic impact of the Nile River on Egypt and the Sudan.

———: *The Egypt of Nasser and Sadat: The Political Economy of Two Regimes.* Princeton, N.J.: Princeton University Press, 1983. A thorough study of class, foreign affairs, and political factors.

Woodward, Peter: *Nasser.* London: Longman, 1992. A short introduction to the life of Egypt's leader.

CHAPTER 44

Egypt, Sudan, and Libya after 1970

After Nasser's death in 1970, Egypt seemed to lose its central role in Arab affairs as its leaders turned away from Pan-Arabism, aiming instead chiefly at peace abroad and political stability at home. Egypt's withdrawal from the long confrontation with Israel that had consumed so many resources since 1948 opened the opportunity for a concentrated attack on domestic economic problems. Nevertheless, most of these problems seemed extremely difficult to solve.

Egypt's extraordinarily stable political system was able to extend only some of the benefits of stability to its economy, and social equity was a major dilemma. Economic difficulties helped fuel an Islamic fundamentalist opposition that challenged the entire basis of the state.

Egyptian policies often served as a model to Sudanese central government officials, but they encountered different problems in the southern Sudan, which faced a growing economic crisis and whose role in the country was the source of severe disagreement. The earlier pattern of alternating civilian and military control of government in Sudan was repeated after 1970, with a military-Islamic fundamentalist coalition governing through most of the 1990s.

In 1969 Libya experienced an Egyptian- and Sudanese-style military revolution. Libya's society and government were greatly influenced by the abundant wealth generated by oil, a resource present in smaller quantities in Egypt and exploited only recently in the poverty-stricken Sudan.

EGYPT

Anwar al-Sadat as President of the Arab Republic of Egypt

President Nasser appointed Anwar al-Sadat, one of the original military officers on the Revolutionary Command Council, vice president. When Nasser died in 1970, Sadat became president of Egypt, an office he held for about eleven years, until his assassination in 1981.

Sadat was born in 1918 in a village in the Nile delta. Attending the military academy in 1936, he formed a secret group along with his classmate Nasser to work for the liberation of Egypt from Faruq and the British. Jailed by the British during World War II as a German sympathizer, he participated with Nasser and others in the 1952 coup. He held positions as speaker of the National Assembly and secretary-general of the National Union, the first political party of the revolution.

One of Sadat's earliest actions was to change the name of the country from the United Arab Republic, which remained in effect even after Syria left the union in 1961, to the more locally significant Arab Republic of Egypt, thereby indicating a difference from Nasser's Pan-Arabism. Sadat also had to deal with opponents for power; he arrested several high officials, accusing them of plotting a coup. Sadat, like Nasser, used national referenda to validate this and other changes. Later he dissolved the parliament and brought forth a new constitution that declared Islam the state religion, strengthened civil rights, banned seizure of property, gave women some rights, and maintained the presidential dictatorship. Sadat had taken full power.

In foreign policy, Sadat kept ties to the Soviets, especially for arms purchases. The Soviet-American policy of détente, Sadat decided, meant that he could no longer rely on Moscow to support him in regaining the lands Israel had taken from Egypt in 1967. In 1972 he ordered Soviet military advisers to leave Egypt, a move popular with the Egyptian people. But Sadat began to have second thoughts about alienating the Soviets, and he resumed cooperation.

Although new fields in the desert produced some oil, the Egyptian economy was sustained only by regular gifts from Saudi Arabia, Kuwait, and Libya. Sadat's relations with other Arab states were uneasy. More conservative than Nasser, he disagreed often with the more radical leaders of Syria, leading to the early demise of the nominal Federation of Arab Republics, which had linked the two plus Libya. Sadat and Libya's Muammar al-Qadhdhafi then planned a merger, which also collapsed. To the south, Sadat had so many controversies with the Sudan that he requested Sudanese troops to leave the Suez Canal battle area.

The Fourth Arab-Israeli War

Early in 1973 Sadat decided that stalemate with Israel over the Suez and Sinai could not be ended through Washington or Moscow. Sadat coordinated military operations with Syria, and they jointly attacked Israel and the occupied territories, having the advantage of surprise. Sadat sent Egyptian forces across the Suez Canal on October 6, 1973, in the midst of Ramadan, the Muslim holy month of fasting, and on Yom Kippur, the Jewish Day of Atonement. The main battles terminated on October 25 with a temporary cease-fire on October 22, as called for by the U.N. Security Council.

Egypt was defeated in the war, as Israel now occupied portions of both banks of the Suez Canal and had an Egyptian army surrounded. Israel had also defeated Egypt's ally, Syria, which blamed Sadat for leaving the battle without a joint agreement on actions. On the other hand, Sadat could portray himself on enormous billboards in Cairo as "the hero of the crossing"; since Egyptian troops had crossed the canal and now occupied portions of both banks, Sadat could claim some victory. Egypt had also fought with considerable success in the early days of the war, and for that reason as well Egypt could boast of some success. Egypt had fought far better than in the 1948, 1956, and 1967 wars.

Sadat accepted an American invitation to attend a peace conference in Geneva in December, but it lasted for only a day. After many trips by U.S. secretary of state Henry Kissinger, an interim withdrawal was agreed on in January 1974: Israel pulled back forces east of the canal, Egypt was allowed limited armed units on the east bank of the canal, and U.N. forces patrolled the zone between the two areas. More important, the fourth Arab-Israeli War of 1973 opened the way to the 1979 peace treaty between Egypt and Israel.

A New Egypt

War and steps toward peace did not in themselves change the political and social dynamics of Egypt, but they did open the way for a wide range of initiatives. Although Sadat retained most of the basic framework of the political, social, and economic system, he relaxed many aspects of the Nasser dictatorship, helped change policy in regard to women, and sought to promote economic growth through opening the way for foreign investment.

Sadat's partial success in the war and his need to differentiate himself from Nasser's policies inclined him to open up Egypt's political processes. He released former powerful figures from jail. In the elections for the next People's Assembly, many of the seats were contested; embryonic political parties could be seen, though they were tightly controlled. In the late 1970s, even the old Wafd party was allowed to reappear briefly. A few leftist critics won election to parliament as well, although generally Sadat kept power in his own hands and increasingly curbed any visible opposition.

Changes were also made in the status of women. By 1971 about 40 percent of all university students were female. In 1979 the Sadat government reserved thirty seats in parliament for women and made legal changes favorable to women, but some of these policies were later reversed. Trends in the Egyptian economy in the 1970s and 1980s made it possible for more women to find employment in the service sector, in fields such as banking and tourism, as well as taking positions vacated by Egyptian men who were working abroad. About one-third of those working overseas were themselves women. This trend took place despite high female illiteracy—more than 60 percent, according to a 1990 estimate.

Many women, especially those from the lower socioeconomic groups, participated in the Islamic fundamentalist revival by dressing in a more conservative fashion. Calls for limits on women working outside the home were made in the 1980s and 1990s as unemployment increased with the decline of oil revenues and the return of workers to Egypt. Muslim fundamentalists also strongly criticized the role of women in Egypt, claiming that the limited steps made toward equality with men were contrary to Islam.

As debate became somewhat freer in Egypt in the 1970s, the Aswan High Dam turned out to be a common topic of disagreement. The direct costs of the dam and power station were about $800 million, but far more was ultimately spent on other aspects of the project. There were other problems as well: its electric power generation had fallen short of what had been promised, a number of associated land reclamation projects had failed, each year many tons of rich silt were being blocked from the Nile delta and profitable fishing was being ruined in the Mediterranean, and new currents were causing severe erosion along the coast. Defenders of the dam, however, pointed out that electric power had been quadrupled, flooding had been curtailed, productivity had increased, and the water supply and control system had saved crops in 1972, when water levels in the Nile would have been ruinously low without the dam.

Egypt's economy was affected by war losses. Its need for foreign aid seemed astronomical, although the reopening of the Suez Canal in 1975 did bring in some welcome revenue. The increase in world oil prices resulted in economic growth in addition to that caused by the Aswan Dam. A powerful demand for Egyptian professionals and skilled laborers was created in the oil-producing states of the Middle East.

Foreign pressure for economic liberalization pushed the regime to loosen economic controls. This opening to foreign investment and domestic capitalism was a substantial ideological change from the Arab socialism of the Nasser years. Remittances from Egyptians working abroad, particularly in Libya and Saudi Arabia, increased sharply. Petroleum exports, construction activity along the Suez Canal, aid from the United States, and tourism revenues all helped the economy grow during the 1970s while compensating for the relative stagnation of agricultural revenues. By 1979 oil provided about half of all government revenue.

The government viewed industry as a way to overcome the stagnation of the agriculture sector and provide jobs for the urban masses. Egypt's population dramatically rose, from 33 million in 1970 to 39 million in 1976. Urban areas especially grew. Between 1960 and 1982 the urban population increased from 38 percent to 45 percent of the total.

Government policies after the 1973 war helped especially the small upper class and the expanding middle class, but most Egyptians gained at least some advantages from the changing economy. From 1973 to 1984, Egypt's gross domestic product increased at about 8 percent per year, while real per capita income almost doubled. Life expectancy grew by about 11 years between 1960 and 1982.

Sadat Veers toward the West

In foreign policy, Sadat sought to remove Israel from the Sinai peninsula through new U.S.-brokered step-by-step disengagement agreements. By 1975 Israel had surrendered strategic passes and given up oil fields; in return, Egypt agreed that Israeli nonmilitary cargoes might pass through the Suez Canal. U.N. forces remained between Egyptian and Israeli units. This 1975 agreement infuriated Syria's al-Assad, who feared Israel was now free to attack elsewhere, but Sadat pointed out that Egypt's economy demanded peace.

Relations with the erratic leader of Libya fluctuated, but usually they were not pleasant; Qadhdhafi viewed Sadat as a weak reed. Sudanese ties were much warmer; tentative joint defense plans were drafted, although the idea of any union was shelved.

Sadat turned away from the Soviet Union, seeking aid and diplomatic support chiefly in the west. Part of Egypt's problem was its huge debt to the Soviet Union and other countries. Because of the debt, unfavorable trade balances, and Egypt's burgeoning population, Sadat needed peace, loans, and capital for development. The oil-rich Arab states, western Europe, and the United States were his best hope. In 1977 Sadat postponed all

Soviet debt payments indefinitely. He was convinced that only the United States, not the Soviet Union, could pressure Israel for peace and withdrawal from Egyptian territory.

Even with massive foreign aid, ends still did not meet. Half of the rural population owned no land at all in 1972; their standard of living was deplorable. Sadat tried belt tightening in the cities, but in 1977 when prices were increased on basic commodities, the worst riots since 1952 broke out in Cairo and were quelled only with difficulty. The cries of the people calling, "Nasser, Nasser," must have sent chills through Sadat. Removing the bread subsidy might well bring revolution, since so many poor people depended on cheap bread to live. Although Sadat backed away from changing the bread subsidy, there was no doubt that he had moved away from Nasser's path. The middle classes and the rich were now the beneficiaries of government, at the expense of the workers, peasants, and the poor generally. Sadat favored a more open economy in place of a highly centralized regime; he looked first to Egypt rather than to Pan-Arab nationalism; his policies veered to the right, not to the left; and his ear was attuned to Washington instead of Moscow.

Peace with Israel

Sadat astonished the world by flying to Jerusalem in 1977 and speaking before the Knesset, where he boldly announced that he recognized Israel as a state and was ready to make peace; however, he also stated that Israel must return the Arab lands it had seized in 1967 and recognize the right of self-determination for the Palestinian people. By this audacious trip Sadat demonstrated to the world his sincere desire for peace with Israel. Egypt agreed at Camp David in 1978 and in the 1979 peace treaty to a separate peace with Israel and to arrangements for the Palestinians that were unacceptable to them. Sadat received a number of benefits for his country, including the return of the Sinai Peninsula, increased U.S. aid, and termination of war with Israel.

Israel then embarked on a series of steps, such as the annexations of East Jerusalem and the Golan Heights, that severely tested Egyptian willingness to abide by the 1979 peace treaty; however, it did return the Sinai to Egypt in phases, culminating in April 1982, and Egypt did establish diplomatic relations with Israel. When Israel invaded Lebanon in 1982, Egypt virtually sat back, thereby demonstrating that direct Egyptian-Israeli military confrontations were indeed a thing of the past.

As a multinational force oversaw the Israeli withdrawal from Sinai and the implementation of limited Egyptian control, most of the Arab states vigorously condemned Sadat. The Arab League headquarters was moved from Cairo to Tunis, Egypt's membership in the League was suspended, most Arab governments broke diplomatic relations with Egypt, and the Palestinians referred to Sadat as a traitor to Arab nationalism.

Internal opposition also emerged as many groups viewed both Sadat's foreign and domestic policies as failures. Islamic fundamentalists particularly objected to Sadat's peace with Israel, his corruption, his secularism, and his dependence on the United States. A greater emphasis on the shariah as the source of constitutional legitimacy did not gain the regime support from the fundamentalists. Sadat permitted the Muslim Brotherhood to operate with some freedom, since it did not pose a direct danger to the regime, but other, smaller, and more radical groups engaged in violence and murder. On October 6, 1981, Sadat was assassinated by a small fundamentalist organization.

Sadat had accomplished many of his goals by 1981. The basic continuity of the revolutionary regime was preserved while some of Nasser's policies were changed; the 1973 war led to an opening to the United States, peace with Israel, and the return of the Sinai to Egypt; and some economic progress was made, although daunting problems nevertheless remained. Despite Sadat's accomplishments, the Egyptians did not love him as they had Nasser. Nasser was a heroic figure whose successes and failures were on an epic scale. Sadat was a more limited and less emotionally effective leader, although successful in many ways.

Continuity in the Mubarak Era

Vice President Husni Mubarak (b. 1928), former commander of the air force in the 1973 war, who succeeded Sadat, repressed the Islamic fundamentalists who had assassinated his predecessor. Although Egypt's basic political, foreign policy, and economic policies remained much as they had been under Sadat, there were some alterations, especially the reappearance of competing political parties and a more balanced foreign policy.

Changes after 1981 included the emergence of political parties in the parliamentary elections of 1984. Using a system of proportional representation for every party that gained more than 8 percent of the vote, the government's National Democratic party (N.D.P.) secured over 70 percent of the vote. The N.D.P. had its greatest strength in rural areas and especially from the still-important rural notables. Copts, Christians who were upset over the growth of fundamentalist Islam and numerous attacks upon them by fundamentalists, also tended to vote for the N.D.P. The Wafd (legalized yet again in 1983!), allied with the Muslim Brotherhood, gained 15 percent of the vote, and was the only other party represented in the lower house of parliament. These elections were the most open and freest in many years, although there was a low voter turnout and substantial government manipulation. New elections in 1987 were again fairly open and strongly contested. The National Democrats once more took about 70 percent of the votes, with 17 percent going to a leftist and Muslim Brotherhood coalition and 11 percent to the Wafd.

President Mubarak also clearly controlled the military, which he had purged of possible opponents, and thus he was undeniably in control of the whole state apparatus. Nevertheless, he permitted judges greater independence, and on occasion they ruled against government actions, as when they declared the 1987 elections invalid. The government also was able to punish Muslim fundamentalists who engaged in assassinations and other violence.

Mubarak retained the essentials of Sadat's foreign policy while adding flexibility. Egypt successfully kept friendly relations with Israel and the United States, while at the same time cooperating with other Arab states. The peace with Israel was maintained but not expanded, while the U.S. poured billions of dollars of military and economic assistance into Egypt. The two nations also conducted frequent joint military maneuvers. Mubarak balanced Egypt's relationship with the United States by restoring contacts with the Soviet Union. Egypt aided Iraq in its war with non-Arab Iran, and gradually Arab states reestablished diplomatic relations with Egypt. In 1989, the Arab League readmitted Egypt as a full member. Gulf Arab oil states resumed financial aid to Egypt. Libya's al-Qadhdhafi sought to intervene in the internal affairs of the Sudan and Egypt, both of which cooperated in various measures directed against him. By 1990 Mubarak had retained the foreign policy benefits of the 1979 peace treaty while overcoming most of its drawbacks.

In economic matters, the Mubarak regime was not as successful as in foreign questions. Government deficits ballooned, increased food imports became far more expensive, Egypt's oil exports fell in value, and money coming from the 2 million or so Egyptians who lived abroad, though still substantial, decreased. In 1985 Egypt imported almost $6 billion more than it exported, and its foreign debt by 1991 had increased to about $50 billion. Many countries, including the United States, rescheduled payments on Egypt's debt, but this was contingent on Egypt's enacting economic reforms, such as privatization of government-owned enterprises, cutting subsidies to consumers, reducing inflation, and freeing interest rates.

A substantial sector of the population continued to be extremely poor. The subsidies that kept food prices low helped these people, but the subsidies represented a great expense for the state. The subsidy for bread was more than the annual income from the Suez Canal!

Economic policy was greatly affected by continuing rapid population growth, which took place despite a decline in the fertility rate. Such large numbers of people necessitated ever-growing investments in capital as well as jobs, facilities, and services. The quality of urban life inevitably deteriorated as crowding became ever more intense. Greater Cairo, with as many as 14 million people, was especially affected as people moved there from the countryside. Urban congestion was slightly alleviated when the first subway opened in 1987, but transportation, housing, and enough good jobs remained difficult problems for most Cairenes.

Government development planners, recognizing these difficulties, were more realistic in the mid-1980s than earlier. They sought to encourage agriculture-related industries. New oil and natural gas discoveries were a cause for some optimism amid the general gloom. Government employment and spending rose sharply in the 1980s. In the first part of that decade the gross domestic product continued the sharp growth witnessed in the 1970s, but from 1986 to 1991 it barely kept up with the population increase. The unofficial black market sectors of the economy flourished in the 1980s and 1990s, thus adding to overall consumption.

Egypt after 1990

The remarkable continuity found in Egyptian politics lasted into the 1990s, but Mubarak's rule and the dominance of the military-bureaucratic elite that supported him were challenged by an intensification of Islamic fundamentalist attacks. Despite this challenge, Egypt played a leading role in the 1990–1991 crisis over Kuwait, and it continued to grapple with economic development and cultural issues.

From at least the 1970s onward, Muslims, Christians, and Jews throughout the Middle East (and in other parts of the world as well) experienced a growing involvement in fundamentalist religious movements that sought to expand the role of religion in public life. In Egypt, most Muslims and Coptic Christians who favored fundamentalism expressed their views peacefully. Some expressions of this were a revived interest in scriptural study, a growth in Sufi activities, the appearance of Islamic companies and banks based on profit sharing rather than interest, and the multiplication of private mosques, staffed by popular preachers. Muslim religious figures recorded cassettes, spoke on television, and formed many societies. The expansion in the numbers of non-government organizations (N.G.O.s), especially those of a charitable and religious nature, represented a change in civil society separate from the far-reaching powers of government, and therefore a challenge to it. The government hoped to co-opt relatively moderate Islamic fundamentalists, such as those in the Muslim Brotherhood, while separating them from radicals who engaged in violence. The government permitted the Muslim Brotherhood to operate quietly.

Small splinter groups rejected the Muslim Brotherhood's approach, opting instead for a violent rejection of the government system and calling their opponents renegades from true Islam who merited death. The small groups based their theology and politics largely on the writings of Sayyid Qutb (1906–1966), who had been executed during the Nasser years. According to Qutb, only a fundamental change in society, including the complete restoration of the shariah, could renovate Muslim societies so they could deal with the great power and sinful temptations of the Christian west. Some Egyptians who served in Afghanistan fighting against Communism returned to their homeland full of enthusiasm for waging holy war against secularists. At various times the Egyptian government accused the Islamic Republic of Iran, the Sudanese military, and the Libyans of aiding the violent fundamentalists.

The fundamentalists acted on their beliefs by assassinating the speaker of parliament in 1990 and later attempting to kill Naguib Mahfouz, the Nobel Prize–winning writer. In the 1990s they also engaged in numerous attacks on Egyptian Copts, foreign tourists, government police, and soldiers, and they took part in the 1993 New York City bombing of the World Trade Center. Attacks were most frequent in southern Egypt, where the violent groups had the most support; by 1995 a low-level insurgency was under way in that region.

The radical fundamentalists launched even more attacks in 1996–1997, by which time about 1000 people had been killed. Severe government repression ultimately was successful, and the remnants of the Egyptian fundamentalist leadership fled abroad to Afghanistan and the United States, taking an active role in al-Qaida. The government also regained control over mosques and their imams. However, the Islamization of public life accelerated as moderate Islamists and al-Azhar University's theologians gained public support and penetrated such state institutions as the judiciary, media, and education.

While fighting the radical Islamic fundamentalists, President Mubarak retained his own power as he was periodically re-elected. He also maintained control over the legislature. In the 1990 and 1995 parliamentary elections the government used direct and indirect coercion to guarantee the victory of the National Democratic Party, which won about 70 percent of the seats, with most of the rest going to nominally independent candidates who were actually affiliated with the government. Increased judicial oversight in 2000 allowed a somewhat fairer election and the victory of a few candidates from the Muslim Brotherhood opposition.

Egypt's foreign policy was firmly pro-American in the period after 1990, as seen in the Kuwaiti crisis and war in 1990–1991. Mubarak's quiet diplomacy had led to the reintegration of Egypt into the Arab regional diplomatic system; the headquarters of the Arab League was moved back to Cairo in 1991 after ten years of being located in Tunisia. As Iraq unexpectedly invaded and annexed Kuwait in 1990, Egypt led the Arab opposition, voting in the League for the use of force to compel an Iraqi withdrawal. Acting under the overall leadership of the United States, Egypt sent 38,000 troops to Saudi Arabia, the largest Arab contingent (the Egyptian troops in the war had only a few casualties). Egyptian critics of the government, including Islamic fundamentalists, thought the 1990–1991 policy confirmed the country's role as a puppet of the United States and also pointed to the $52 billion in U.S. aid to Egypt from 1974 to 2000. Backers of Mubarak argued that his course of action was the only possible one given Iraq's intransigence over a peaceful withdrawal from Kuwait.

Egypt suffered economic losses from the 1991 war. In addition to its direct military expenses, the numerous Egyptian workers in Iraq returned home, tourism in Egypt declined sharply, and Suez Canal revenues fell. On the other hand, the United States and other countries reduced Egypt's foreign debt as a reward for Egyptian participation, and the Arab oil countries of the Persian Gulf provided substantial subsidies to Egypt.

The Iraqi government, Arab Palestinians, and many Pan-Arab nationalists had harshly criticized Egypt since the 1979 peace treaty with Israel, but in the 1990s President Mubarak seemed to find vindication for Sadat's actions as various Arab states also moved toward peace. Egypt was influential in the peace process, helping with the crucial Madrid Peace Conference of 1991, the Palestinian-Israeli Accord of 1993, and the Jordan-Israel Peace Treaty of 1994. Despite this trend, Egypt publicly pressured Israel on its possession of nuclear weapons, asking for Israel to renounce them as part of the international nonproliferation agreement in 1995.

President Mubarak tried with little success to mediate between the Palestinians and Israelis in the late 1990s as the peace process collapsed; in 2000–2002 Egyptians often publicly demonstrated in favor of the Palestinian cause. Egypt condemned the September 11, 2001 attacks by Islamic fundamentalists against the United States and cooperated in intelligence matters with America.

An Egyptian Copt, a diplomat and former deputy prime minister, Boutros Boutros-Ghali (b. 1922), grandson of an earlier prime minister of Egypt, became secretary-general of the United Nations in 1992. He was prominent because of his activist leadership and as the first Arab and African to be the leader of the world organization.

Military policy was coordinated with the United States as Egypt secured most of its weapons and military assistance funding from America. Spending on the military in real terms from the 1980s to the 1990s fell by about half, representing roughly 10 percent of total government expenditures. About 420,000 men were still under arms. Nevertheless, Egypt's economy enjoyed something of a peace "bonus" as compared to the massive spending on the armed forces during the height of the Arab-Israeli wars.

Although Egyptian diplomacy, military policy, and suppression of internal fundamentalist opposition were generally successful in the 1990s, economic problems persisted. The most dramatic change was the growing importance of oil, which became a valuable source of revenue for the government. Oil, remittances from workers overseas, tourism, and Suez Canal tolls placed cotton as fifth in value, thereby indicating a healthy diversification. But all of these activities were subject to extreme fluctuations; for instance, tourism fell off during periods of war and internal violence. The government continued reforms demanded by international groups, such as selling state enterprises and reducing the budget deficit, but the bureaucracy of 4 million government employees was not significantly reduced, in large part because of already high unemployment. Foreign aid helped infrastructure investment, particularly in communications, but this did little for most poor Egyptians, who saw a greater inequality in society as the chief consequence of the government's economic policies.

In the late 1990s and early 2000s the economy showed some signs of progress. Per capita income in the 1990s almost doubled. Government deficits and inflation declined, but much of this was the result of lessening subsidies on food. Some more state-owned enterprises were sold, though the pace of privatization was slow. On the other hand, unemployment was growing; much economic activity took place by using informal and unregulated means, often with unfortunate consequences for consumers; the government tended to favor a kind of crony capitalism and local oligopolies; exports did not keep pace with imports; and industry was stagnant as the service sector expanded. The peasants, who still constituted one-half of the population, were negatively affected by the government's decision to phase out rent ceilings on leased land, thereby transferring more power to the owners of land at the expense of their tenants.

The half of Egyptians who were women saw little real change in their status during this time. Representation of women in parliament declined substantially when the quota system ended in 1986. In the parliamentary election of 2000, for instance, only seven women were elected. More boys and girls went to the public schools in the 1990s and about 90 percent of the eligible girls attended the primary grades. Employment for women working outside the home was adversely affected as the government no longer automatically hired all university graduates. More women wore clothing that reflected conservative Muslim ideals. New legislation in 2000 established family courts and enhanced the legal status of women in marriage and divorce cases.

As child mortality rates fell the population grew substantially, though at a slower rate than in earlier times. The population of Egypt, about 50 million in 1988, reached an estimated 65 million in 2001, of which 40 percent was under the age of 15.

Although government funding of cultural activities was cut and conservative Muslims attempted to censor the public expression of secularist values, Egypt maintained its position as the leading Arab producer of books, newspapers, television and radio shows, the studio arts, and popular music. Perhaps because the government spent less money subsidizing films, there was more innovation in the films that were produced. Public libraries were hard hit by budget cuts, but newspaper readership steadily expanded. Television programs, especially comedies and melodramas, were very popular inside Egypt, and they were exported as well. The government allowed eight television channels to exist but real competition came from satellite television broadcasts. In 1998 there were about 12,000 private Internet subscribers and only about 350,000 computers in Egypt, so the electronic revolution had not permeated most sectors of society.

As the government in 2002 celebrated the fiftieth anniversary of the 1952 revolution, Egypt's culture, politics, diplomacy, and economy continued to have a particularly great influence on its southern neighbor, the Sudan.

THE SUDAN

Numairi and Military Rule

On May 25, 1969, about a year before the death of Nasser, Colonel Jaafar Muhammad al-Numairi (b. 1930; also spelled Nimeiri, Numeiri, and Numayri) and other young officers seized the government, overthrew the civilian democratic system, and established the ruling Revolutionary Command Council (R.C.C.) in Sudan. Numairi's cabinet, composed of officers and Nasserite socialists, offered a policy of "freedom and socialism" and pledged to find a solution for integrating the southern Sudan and ending the civil war. Numairi rapidly consolidated power. Civilians were placed in most cabinet posts, and Numairi became both prime minister and head of the R.C.C. All political parties were outlawed. Numairi's actions were clearly modeled on those of Nasser of Egypt, but the Sudan did not join in any meaningful union with its neighbor to the north.

Numairi's chief opponents were the Mahdists and the Communists. In 1970 the Mahdists tried to overthrow Numairi, but the army easily defeated and killed many of them. Then it was the turn of the Communists, who had an active membership estimated at between 5000 and 10,000. In 1971 the leader of the Communist party escaped from jail, and a few days later, his followers captured Numairi. The Sudanese people and the army, however, did not rally to support the Communists; instead the army took control, arrested the instigators of the coup, and reinstalled Numairi. The coup leaders were executed, and leftists within the government and army were dismissed.

Once again in control, Numairi tried a dual policy in the south. He attempted a compromise while also battling the guerrilla forces. The south itself was so divided that Numairi hardly knew who represented the majority. He extended amnesty to rebels, announced that a provisional government for the south would be established, and offered regional autonomy to the three southern provinces, but he could not end the insurgency.

The revolutionary regime of Numairi inherited a formidable set of economic challenges. Sudan's foreign debt was rapidly increasing, reliance on cotton as the only major earner of foreign exchange continued, strikes by trade unions hampered economic growth, and the railways and Gezira cotton area showed increasing inefficiencies. On the other hand, light manufacturing had increased, and agriculture had expanded in terms of both the amount of land cultivated and mechanization.

To deal with these problems, all banks and cotton exporting firms and some foreign companies were nationalized, and newspapers were taken over. Numairi's brand of socialism put an end to large foreign and domestic private companies.

Reconciling the Southern Sudan

Numairi tried to broaden his base of support by pushing through a new constitution for the Democratic Republic of Sudan, having himself formally elected president by the people, and including in the cabinet representatives of a variety of groups and regions. But his most important goal was ending the southern war, which had hampered every action in Khartoum since the early 1960s.

After negotiating with southern leaders, the central government in 1972 signed agreements in Addis Ababa, the capital of Ethiopia, giving local autonomy to the south and amnesty to all; arranging for a cease-fire, the return of refugees, and the assimilation of the guerrillas into the army; and paving the way for political participation by southern leaders. By the end of the year, the three southern provinces had been united into south Sudan, which had an elected assembly, a chief executive answerable to it, and an executive council responsible for all government except defense, currency, and foreign affairs, which remained under the control of Khartoum. Six thousand guerrillas and a similar number of regular soldiers became the southern command under General Joseph Lagu, whose military rank equaled that of Numairi. Abel Alier became president of south Sudan, still holding the rank of vice president for Sudan. One of the greatest problems facing these new leaders was that of resettling more than 400,000 refugees. Autonomy turned out to be real, as English rapidly replaced Arabic in southern government affairs, although Arabic was supposed to be the official language.

At the end of 1973 Numairi opened the first People's Regional Assembly of South Sudan, an act marking autonomy from Khartoum. In the 1978 regional elections, Alier was replaced by Lagu as head of the regional authority. Most observers, remembering earlier bitter feuds and bloodshed, marveled that peace was at hand.

Consolidating Power and Changes in Foreign and Economic Policy

Numairi centralized power ever more surely into his own hands while seeking peaceful foreign relations and substantial economic development. By 1972 he held the offices of president, prime minister, and minister of defense. By 1974 Numairi felt secure enough to release large numbers of political prisoners, including Sadiq al-Mahdi, who in 1976, with Libyan backing, attempted a coup that was soon suppressed. Numairi's susceptibility to this and numerous other attempted coups derived from an inability to institutionalize his support, tolerate dissent, or unite a highly pluralistic body politic.

Numairi's paramount foreign relations concern was peace and cooperation with Egypt and other Arab states, for they exercised the most influence over affairs in the Sudan. Sudanese troops helped Egypt in the Arab-Israeli War of 1973, and Egyptian troops repeatedly backed the regime in Khartoum. The Sudanese Socialist Union, Sudan's sole political party, followed the programs of Egyptian government-sponsored parties.

Hundreds of thousands of Sudanese worked abroad in the oil-rich Arab states of the Persian Gulf. Prospecting for oil in the Sudan itself was widespread, and major discoveries were made in 1979; however, oil operations were interrupted as a result of the renewed southern uprising in 1983. Investments in basic infrastructure became urgent: the railway system was revitalized, and some all-weather roads were built. Education expanded as enrollments doubled to 1.5 million between 1969 and 1982.

Since the end of the nineteenth century, many had seen Sudan's potential as one of the great food producers of the world. In 1904, the British had proposed cutting a channel for the White Nile to bypass the Sudd swamp area, where the Nile floods every August. Such a bypass canal would save some 4 million cubic feet of water. Called the Jonglei Canal, it would be about 224 miles (360 km.) long. In 1975 a French consortium entered into a contract with Egypt and Sudan to build it so as to open a vast area to cultivation. Numairi hoped that such projects, oil money, and western technology would develop the Sudan into a food power.

Social and Cultural Developments

The extraordinary diversity of the people of the Sudan continued with little change throughout the period after independence. The population increased to 18 million by 1976. More than 400 languages and dialects were spoken by more than fifty ethnic or tribal groups, although Arabic has been by far the most widespread language.

Poetry, storytelling, pottery, and music reflected this diversity, although written cultural expressions were mostly in Arabic. About 40 percent of the population considered itself to be Arab in ancestry and language, but a larger proportion spoke the Arabic language. A new generation of Sudanese Arab poets flourished in Egypt after World War II and demonstrated the strength of the Arabic tongue in the Sudan. The post–World War II generations of poets in the Sudan sought to find, define, and express a national identity that would include African as well as Arab elements. In the southern third of the country, English served as a common language to be used for communication by the speakers of the many regional languages. Television broadcasts, which began in 1962, were increased in power so as to reach much of central Sudan by the 1970s.

Religious diversity often coincided with regional and language factors; Muslims were overwhelmingly the majority in the northern two-thirds of the Sudan but a small minority in the south. About 5 percent of the total population was Christian, and 30 percent believed in tribal and animist faiths. The cultural unity of the Sudan was further weakened by the relatively small proportion of the citizenry who lived in urban areas. More than 80 percent of the Sudanese lived in the countryside, where they were widely separated from each other in an enormous nation one-quarter the size of the continental United States. Literacy was low; only about 20 percent of the adults could read and write, thereby limiting the effectiveness of newspapers as a unifying factor. In addition to language, religion, ethnic, and regional differences, there were also remarkable variations in attitude and behavior between the rich and the poor, the educated and the uneducated, and men and women.

The Last Years of Numairi

By 1977 Numairi had stabilized his regime to the extent that he sought to conciliate his opponents. Sadiq al-Mahdi and Hasan Turabi of the Sudanese Muslim Brotherhood returned from exile and accepted the framework of government. Numairi especially appealed to the Brotherhood as his regime adopted an Islamic fundamentalist tone in the 1980s, a step that brought the greater application of Islamic law based on the shariah, even for non-Muslims, in all parts of the country in 1983. Numairi showed his growing egotism by requiring military officers to swear allegiance to him in 1984 as the imam (leader of the Muslim faithful).

In the south, political and tribal infighting among local leaders allowed the central government in Khartoum great leeway. Numairi played the leaders off against each other and then divided the south into three distinct regions with separate governments. This step, plus the Islamic policy and the inefficient dictatorship of Numairi, ultimately united the southerners against the northern-dominated government. The civil war heated up again in 1983. Colonel John Garang led the Sudanese Peoples Liberation Movement in victories over the hapless central government armed forces, and by 1986 he controlled most of the south. The civil war stopped construction on the Jonglei Canal.

Sudan's foreign policy in the last years of Numairi was closely allied with that of Egypt and the United States. Sudan signed a mutual defense pact in 1977 with Egypt, and Numairi supported Sadat's peace initiative with Israel. Because of a perceived threat from Libya, the Sudan and Egypt acted closely together to formulate joint steps against al-Qadhdhafi. Sudan was especially concerned about Libya's ambitions in Chad, so Numairi backed Chadian leaders opposed to those favored by al-Qadhdhafi. As Sudan adopted a more conservative domestic economic policy and an alignment with Egypt and Saudi Arabia, it tended to ally frequently with the United States. In return, the United States provided strong economic and military support to Numairi against both Libya and Communist Ethiopia.

Sudan needed to diversify its agriculture beyond cotton, whose production fell in the 1970s. Imports and government spending led to a foreign debt that grew to more than $9 billion. Other problems included a devaluation of Sudan's currency, an increase in corruption, and an annual inflation rate of around 60 percent. Imports by the early 1980s were three times the value of exports! The already precarious economy was devastated by the famine and drought that hit the Sudan and neighboring Ethiopia in the mid-1980s. The Sudan's own severe problems were made worse by the need to feed hundreds of thousands of starving Ethiopians who fled their country. Perhaps as many as 500,000 Sudanese died as a result of starvation and malnutrition, a disaster that Numairi denied or whose importance he sought to minimize.

Civilian Control Returns

In 1985, General Abd al-Rahman Siwar al-Dhahab, the minister of defense, announced an armed forces coup that ousted Numairi. The causes of the coup included the resumption of the civil war in the south, economic catastrophe, famine, Numairi's growing political isolation as he suppressed even the Muslim Brotherhood, and popular unhappiness with the removal of government food subsidies. Large-scale riots and demonstrations broke out, trade unions and professional associations led the call for the overthrow of Numairi, and the army then joined the civilians at a later stage.

Siwar al-Dhahab dissolved the government party and pledged the military to turn over power to civilian authority. The pattern of events that then ensued, from 1985 to 1989, closely resembled the earlier era of civilian government from 1964 to 1969. Elections to a constituent assembly took place in 1986. Numairi's shariah legislation of 1983 was retained, much to the displeasure of the southerners. The civil war, which persisted, precluded elections in some of the southern districts. The Ummah, though it lacked a majority, was the largest single party and thus formed a coalition with other groups. Sadiq al-Mahdi became prime minister. The Muslim Brotherhood (Islamic Front), popular because of its dynamic leadership and association with the Islamic banks, emerged as the leading element within the opposition. The army actually did turn over effective power to the civilians as the Sudan completed still another cycle in the continuing pattern of alternating military and civilian governments.

The new regime had to deal quickly with the dreadful famine, made worse by locusts and the civil war in the South. Inflation rapidly increased as the weak and unsure government resumed subsidies and resisted austerity measures suggested by the International Monetary Fund, which declared the Sudan to be bankrupt in 1986.

Sadiq al-Mahdi sought friendship particularly with Numairi's enemies, Libya and Ethiopia, which had supported the southern insurgents in the civil war. Libya then dropped this support as its ties with the new government warmed, but Ethiopia and apparently Israel continued to aid the rebels. Assistance to the central government by the United States was endangered by Sudan's increasingly pro-Libyan policy, while ties with Egypt were somewhat strained for the same reason.

There was little agreement among the northerners about what steps to take and how far to go to meet the demands of the south. Over 1 million southerners fled to the outskirts of Khartoum, seeking food and a respite from the fighting as the devastation of the south worsened. Little progress seemed possible in the late 1980s on the key issues of the south, the economy, and the political system as the military, led by General Umar Hasan al-Bashir, once again seized power in 1989.

A Military and Fundamentalist Regime

The new regime was ruled by General Bashir and his colleagues on the R.C.C., but its political base of appeal came from the support of Hasan Turabi's National Islamic Front. Both the military and the fundamentalists wanted to stop the possibility of yet another civilian overturn of a military dictatorship, so they embarked on a systematic and widespread purge of judges, teachers, journalists, civil servants, and politicians. All political parties were outlawed, and a harshly repressive political system was established. In 1993 Bashir assumed the office of president; although he created a cabinet and a parliament, he retained real power in his own hands as he was elected president in 1996 and 2000.

The Sudan central government's foreign and domestic policies reflected its fundamentalist core of support. Sudan received aid from the Islamic Republic of Iran. Many governments, including Egypt, accused the Sudan of supporting violent Islamic fundamentalists in various countries. During the Kuwait crisis in 1990, Sudan abstained in the Arab League vote on the use of force against Iraq, thereby gaining the enmity of the United States and Saudi Arabia. Turabi thoroughly implemented shariah in 1991, including the death sentence for apostasy from Islam. Arabic became the official language of instruction at all levels of education in 1992, and the arts and culture in general were made to conform to Islam as interpreted by the National Islamic Front. These actions ensured the continuation of the civil war in the southern Sudan.

Foreign observers proposed compromise solutions to end the fighting, but reconciliation foundered on the issues of the shariah and power sharing. The northerners who controlled the central government and its army wanted to win the war in the south and west by imposing their own views. A government offensive in 1991–1992 that was successful in taking control of most urban areas owed its effectiveness chiefly to new internal disagreements among the southerners, who split along tribal and ethnic lines and started to fight each other as bitterly as they fought the central authorities.

The central government in Khartoum in the late 1990s attempted to impose its narrow definition of Islam on the entire Sudanese population. Women, Mahdists, Sufis, and non-Muslims were especially affected negatively by the new interpretations of shariah. The civil war in the south was termed a holy war, or jihad.

In 1995 Sudan seemed to back the goup responsible for an assassination attack on Egypt's president Mubarak. The United States, infuriated by Sudan's hosting of Usama bin Ladin, the leader of al-Qaida, the organization responsible for devastating attacks on U.S. embassies in East Africa, bombed an alleged terrorist site near Khartoum in 1998.

Turabi and Bashir worked together to create a new, Islamically oriented constitution in 1998. The government also successfully organized Asian and Canadian oil companies to start the export of oil via a pipeline from the south to the Red Sea in 1999. The regime in 2000 received as much as $1 billion in greatly needed income from this source. However, the economy remained in dire straits, with a continuing emigration of skilled labor, especially to Saudi Arabia, and a renewal of drought in 2001.

A power struggle between the two heads of the government led President Bashir to oust Hasan Turabi from the leadership in 1999. Bashir then attempted to decrease disagreements with the Mahdists and other northern political groups as well as with various foreign countries.

Despite these changes, the civil war continued and even intensified. An appalling situation emerged in the 1990s: the government collapsed in much of the country, and public education, health measures, and economic stability in the south came to an end. Massacres, mass expulsions, summary executions, enslavement, looting, and rapes took place on a wide scale. These events were made worse by repeated famines and droughts, resulting in the movement of more than 3 million refugees to internal and foreign destinations. Although all sides in the civil war took some part in the violence against civilians, the central government bore the chief responsibility, even while it denied the existence of mass starvation and seemed unconcerned about the fate of its own citizens. Perhaps as many as 2 million Sudanese died. International agencies tried to assist the refugees and those starving, but the civil war interfered greatly with their efforts.

Indeed, for the Sudan the whole issue of national identity remained open and unresolved as the twenty-first century began. The appropriate balance among language groups, religions, ethnicities, and regions was unclear and bitterly contested.

LIBYA

Independence, Monarchy, and Oil

In the first half of the twentieth century, Libyans suffered greatly from wars, foreign occupation, brutal exploitation, and poverty. The Italian conquest of Libya and Fascist policies resulted in massive losses, made worse during World War II as Allied forces fought their way from Egypt into coastal Libya. The peace treaty with Italy in 1947 opened the way to a disposition of Libya, and in 1949 the United Nations General Assembly voted to create an independent Libyan state.

A Libyan National Assembly drafted a constitution, selected Tripoli in the west and Benghazi in the east as alternating capitals, and decided on a constitutional monarchy under Idris, head of the Sanusi Sufi order and long-time leader of eastern and parts of southern Libya. Despite the wishes of many western Libyans, a majority of the country's population, the state was to be federal in structure, comprising three provinces: Cyrenaica (coastal eastern Libya), Tripolitania (coastal western Libya), and Fezzan (the lightly populated southern interior). Libya became formally independent on December 24, 1951.

All government actions during the monarchy, from 1951 to 1969, were taken in the context of the regional rivalry between Tripolitania and Cyrenaica; passports were even needed to travel from one to the other! Only the elderly king, the ultimate source of authority in the administration of the state, preserved national unity.

The king and the conservative tribal and merchant notables who backed him gained a large majority in the first parliamentary elections. Such elections involved only a small number of voters, even after women gained the right to vote in 1963. Political parties were banned, apathy was general, and there were few issues that could overcome the provincial distinctions, economic deprivation, and illiteracy of most Libyans.

Libyan foreign policy was caught between the urgent need for western economic aid and the appeal of Egyptian-led, neutralist Pan-Arabism. Usually the king opted for the United States and Britain, which gave Libya money and in return secured for those countries the right to control and use air force bases in Libya as part of their Cold War activities. Egyptian radio, newspapers, and teachers nevertheless permeated Libya. Libya also aided the struggle for independence from France of its neighbors, Tunisia and Algeria, but Libya still needed the money flowing from the foreign bases.

Oil dramatically changed this situation. Exploration by a variety of foreign oil companies started in the 1950s, and production, mostly from Cyrenaica, began in 1959, with the first major export of petroleum beginning in 1961. Government revenues from oil rose rapidly during the 1960s, from just $3 million in 1961 to $1 billion in 1968. By 1965 Libya produced about 10 percent of the world's oil exports; its chief market was western Europe. Instead of being one of the poorer countries in the world, Libya suddenly became rich.

The kingdom's new wealth encouraged, in 1962–1963, the centralization of authority and administration at the expense of the provinces. New wealth also opened the way to increased patronage and corruption.

The majority of the population nevertheless remained poor and resented the obvious wealth of the rich. Social change was rapid, causing many strains on the people and administration, as seen in the increased rate of divorce, although the spread of consumer goods, such as automobiles, was very welcome. Nomadic tribesmen moved to the cities, fleeing droughts in the late 1950s and seeking a share in the new oil wealth of the 1960s. The population of Tripoli doubled to 300,000. Geographic mobility coincided with the appearance of a small number of educated Libyans who formed a middle class, which was often unhappy with the government. During the 1967 Arab-Israeli War, this unhappiness found vent in demonstrations, attacks on Libyan Jews, and an oil embargo. Libya now aided Egypt, with few strings attached to the aid.

Domestically, the government spent the new oil revenues on infrastructure development, agriculture, and social services. Government provided new roads, encouraged irrigation, and imported foreign workers, especially Egyptians, to help in development. Spending on education caused dramatic change; by 1968 most Libyan male children attended free schools with enrollments eleven times larger than in 1950. But the results of these projects were not immediate, and in the short run, Libyans viewed their king as too removed from them to govern effectively. The social, economic, international, and ideological climate of the late 1960s made the regime and its policies seem hopelessly out of date.

The Libyan Revolution and al-Qadhdhafi

On September 1, 1969, a military coup led by Captain Muammar al-Qadhdhafi overthrew King Idris and set up a republican system of government initially similar to Nasser's Egypt or Numairi's Sudan. Idris accepted the coup, settled in Egypt, and died there in 1983. The young Qadhdhafi (b. 1942?) chaired the Revolutionary Command Council, became prime minister, and headed the army. He had no important opposition to his consolidation of power.

Qadhdhafi was born into a poor seminomadic tribe with a record of fighting the Italian occupiers; the tribe was located in an area between the chief population zones and therefore not identified with either Cyrenaica or Tripolitania. He was educated by Egyptian teachers and grew up listening to Egyptian radio. Nasser was his hero. Qadhdhafi graduated from the military academy in 1965 and was the chief figure in planning the 1969 revolution.

Feeling threatened by plots from abroad, Qadhdhafi consolidated his power by purging the police, expanding the size of the army, hiring Egyptian security officials, outlawing political parties, and banning trade unions. The government propagated its views through the media. Influence, appropriations, and prestige moved from Cyrenaica to Tripoli, which became the sole capital of the country.

Qadhdhafi and his associates favored Pan-Arab nationalism, Islamic socialism, and Nasserism while opposing Western imperialism and Zionism. Pan-Arab nationalism, the chief field of action for the new leadership of Libya, was evident in the Revolutionary Command Council's decision, enthusiastically supported by most Libyans, to secure the rapid closing of U.S. and British military bases. Libya then purchased advanced weapons from France and the Soviet Union, even though Qadhdhafi was vehemently anti-Communist. As Italian residents were forced out, they were replaced by Egyptian and other Arab skilled laborers and technicians. An example of Arab cultural nationalism was the new rule that all public signs be written only in Arabic.

After Nasser's death in 1970, Qadhdhafi aspired to become his successor as the leader of Pan-Arabism. Libya proposed to unite with Egypt (now headed by President Sadat) and Sudan, and it aided the Palestinian Arabs and other revolutionary groups. But the rash, impulsive, and sometimes erratic behavior of Qadhdhafi offended many leaders of other countries, including Anwar Sadat, whose policies in regard to Israel and the United States were the opposite of those advocated by the Libyan leader. Libya and Egypt became deeply suspicious of each other as Qadhdhafi was increasingly isolated in the Arab world. Libya intervened in a wide variety of places, using its funds to back revolutionary movements or governments. Such policies upset most foreign states; even revolutionary Algeria, freed from French control in 1962, did not trust Qadhdhafi, whose border dispute with Chad and desire to interfere in that country upset Libya's neighbors as well as France. In 1977 Egypt easily won a short border war with Libya, which subsequently strongly condemned Egypt's 1979 peace accord with Israel. The United States was opposed to nearly all aspects of Libya's foreign activities.

A larger and better-armed military stood behind Libyan foreign policy and also helped guarantee the domestic political structure. In the 1970s the armed forces tripled in size. Conscription was introduced in 1978. Purchases of sophisticated Soviet weapons were supplemented by hiring foreigners to train the Libyan armed forces and even serve in its ranks. Libya bought so many tanks and advanced airplanes that it was not possible for Libyans to maintain or use them all!

The "State of the Masses" and Oil Policy

The Revolutionary Command Council sought a new and radical way to organize Libyan society. Starting in 1973 and based on tribal habits of consensus, popular organizations were set up with the goal of arousing enthusiasm for a new social system. One of the main purposes of the new order was to break down regional and tribal loyalties and bureaucratic structures and to replace them with a sense of participation in, and loyalty to, the nation and Islam. Social justice based on Islam was to replace materialism, capitalism, Communism, and other ideologies in Libya and, ultimately, throughout the rest of the world. In 1977 the country's official name was changed to reflect the current ideology: Libya was now to be called the Socialist People's Libyan Arab Jamahiriyya, with the last term a newly coined word meaning "state of the masses." However, despite the desires of the regime, the "state of the masses" remained limited to Libya. Internally, the country was under the control of Qadhdhafi, the remaining members of the Revolutionary Command Council, and the army, not the popular committees. However, some changes along the lines of the new ideology did take place: shariah was promoted in the courts, usury was forbidden, and the People's Congresses and secretariats replaced other governing institutions. Opposition to the state of the masses was crushed ruthlessly.

Libya could afford to experiment with its new governmental structures because of the enormous revenues flowing to the state from oil production. Libya led the way in putting pressure on foreign-owned oil companies; it secured a higher price for oil in 1970–1971 and nationalized a portion of the companies, opening the way for similar efforts by other governments, with crucial consequences for the world economy. Income from oil, $2.2 billion in 1973, soared to $6 billion in 1974 and then to an amazing $27 billion in 1980. This dollar increase took place even as the number of barrels exported in the 1970s fell. (The world price for oil increased greatly during the 1970s, partly in response to growing demand and partly because of the efforts of O.P.E.C.) Libyan authorities used their increasing wealth to promote social and economic change.

Economic and Social Changes

Starting in the 1970s, Qadhdhafi presided over substantial changes in Libyan society, culture, and economy. The changes included fluctuations in oil revenues, efforts to broaden the non-oil sectors of the economy, new views of the basic nature of Islam, expansion of historical research, and rapid population growth.

Oil prices and revenues were higher in the first half of the 1980s; but beginning in 1982, production dropped and in the mid-1980s, prices dramatically decreased. In 1988 Libya received only $5 billion from oil operations. Government spending had to be cut, and a few steps were taken toward privatization. In the 1990s oil production averaged around 1.4 million barrels per day. While world oil prices were initially quite low, they increased from 1997 onward, resulting in Libyan government income from petroleum rising to $9 billion in 1997 and about $11 billion in 2000. Using this money, grandiose projects continued, the most notable of which was the Great Man-Made River, designed to tap underground water in the Sahara, bring it to population centers, use it for consumption and for agriculture, and ultimately broaden the base of the economy—all at an estimated cost of $25 billion. The first stage opened successfully in 1991, but the plan could not easily overcome the shortage of Libyan laborers and the high cost of foodstuffs grown. By 1994 about 1 million Egyptians were working in Libya, some on the Great Man-Made River project. The second phase of the plan was completed in 1996, but a debate about its viability commenced thereafter, as the price of desalinated water became equal to the cost of water brought by the Great Man-Made River.

Economic development outside the petroleum sector was a top priority of the government, which spent about half of its budget on such purposes in the 1970s. Development, however, was limited by the scarcity of natural resources in Libya. Most of the land was desert; only 1 percent could be farmed. Although the government expended large sums on agricultural development, most of these expensive efforts resulted in depletion of subsurface water and other ecological damage and little economic gain. Industrial growth was also sponsored by the regime, but here again there were shortages of resources, particularly trained laborers. Many well-educated Libyans had left the country and settled elsewhere because they disliked the regime's policies. Qadhdhafi's mandated nationalization of concerns and worker seizure of management functions also tended to reduce commercial and industrial productivity.

Qadhdhafi believed himself to be capable of reinterpreting the bases of Islam. Considering Islam to be the key to social behavior, Qadhdhafi argued that a revitalized Islam was central to social life. He viewed the Quran as the primary source of knowledge and rejected other sources of judgment, such as hadith, scholarly consensus inside the Muslim community, and the elaborate structure of law built over the centuries. One example among his many revisions of the faith was a ruling that the pilgrimage to Mecca was not mandatory. His views on religious matters were taught in the schools, although they were widely opposed by the Libyan ulama, and, indeed, by most Muslims outside Libya.

Libyan history was rewritten so as to glorify nationalism, earlier resistance to the Italians, and the current regime. New historical research institutes expanded studies of the ancient Greek and Roman periods in Libya, and they added a new emphasis on social history and the accumulation of archives and oral history recordings. Scholars especially concentrated on the jihad (holy war) against the Fascist Italians in the 1920s and 1930s. Historians and other scholars and teachers took part in a general expansion of the size of the educational system, but the regime closely monitored academics and severely limited freedom of expression and investigation.

As in most other parts of the Middle East, the number of young people steadily increased. Libya's population swelled rapidly, from about 1 million in 1954 to 3.6 million in 1984, including about 600,000 resident foreign workers. By 2001 the total population stood at 5.4 million. Urbanization also took place at a fast pace; over two-thirds of the population lived in towns and cities by 1990. About half of the population was under the age of 19, so providing education, health care, and other social services to youth was important.

Oil revenues did allow the government to distribute wealth and therefore create a general prosperity. By the late 1970s, free housing, education, medical care, and transport were available; 900,000 students were enrolled in all levels of schooling. By the 1990s 1.5 million students attended educational facilities.

The standard of living of Libyans compared very favorably to that of their neighbors. Average income for a Libyan in 1988 was eight times that of an Egyptian and twelve times that of a Sudanese, and Libyans had the highest average income in all of Africa.

The Isolation of Libya

During the 1980s and 1990s, Libya became increasingly isolated as a result of its extraordinary foreign policies. Its isolation was not total, since Libya had found a few allies, most notably Syria during the 1980–1988 Iran-Iraq War, when both countries favored non-Arab Iran. Nevertheless, most of the rest of the world opposed Qadhdhafi. Diplomatic isolation was particularly dangerous to the Qadhdhafi regime when it involved confrontations with the United States.

Libyan diplomatic isolation was ironic in the light of Qadhdhafi's repeated attempts to merge his country with other states. At various times he proposed the union of Libya with Syria, Chad, Morocco, Algeria, Sudan, Tunisia, and Mauritania. Although agreements were signed, no unions actually took place. Foreign governments were chiefly interested in economic assistance from Libya, allowing their workers to be employed in Libya, and in trying to reduce Libyan interventionism.

Libya sent its troops into Chad on several occasions. The Libyans wanted to retain control of a strip of disputed territory along the Chadian border, and they also wished to establish a government in Chad that would be sympathetic to Libya. France backed the Chadians who opposed Libya's goals. After Libyan armed forces were decisively defeated in 1987, the Libyan government signed a peace agreement in 1989 and withdrew its troops. The International Court of Justice awarded the disputed border zone to Chad in 1994.

The U.S. government accused Libya of sponsoring terrorist attacks directed against American citizens. In addition, the United States vigorously criticized Libya's aid to revolutionary organizations in many parts of the world. Although the Soviet Union and Libya cooperated from time to time in the 1980s, the Soviet Union was not prepared to back Libya in a direct struggle against the United States. A long series of confrontations ensued between the United States and Libya: a 1981 naval crisis; the sending of U.S. aid to Chad, Sudan, and Egypt in 1983; another naval face-off; and, most serious, the 1986 U.S. air attack on Tripoli and Benghazi. Perhaps because of this attack, Libya apparently did reduce its aid to revolutionaries abroad; the number of assassination attempts initiated by Libyan agents decreased in later years. Despite this change, in 1991–1992 the United States, Great Britain, and France charged that Libya had been involved in the sabotage of civilian aircraft and demanded the extradition of Libyan officials they said had been responsible. When Libya refused the extradition requests, the United Nations placed sanctions on air travel and the sales of weapons to Libya. In 1999 Qadhdhafi sent the two men accused of sabotaging the aircraft for a trial conducted by Britain but held in the Netherlands, while the United Nations dropped its sanctions against Libya. One of the two suspects was convicted in 2001, opening the question of the level of complicity of the Libyan government in the aircraft bombings.

The domestic ramifications of Libya's diplomatic isolation were mixed. Some Libyans favored compromise and a more conciliatory foreign policy, but many others rallied to the Qadhdhafi regime, seeing foreign pressure as an affront to the nation. A more serious threat to the government's stability came from relatively low oil revenues and some dissatisfaction inside the armed forces, but no immediate danger appeared likely to overthrow Qadhdhafi as he celebrated the thirtieth anniversary of the revolution. As oil prices rose again in the late 1990s and early 2000s, the regime appeared to become ever more solidly entrenched, despite such developments as the spread of satellite television reception in the 1990s.

The diverse circumstances of Libya, Sudan, and Egypt contributed to numerous differences in their historical evolution after 1969–1970. Libya's wealth in oil, the role of southern Sudan, and Egypt's military power especially contributed to their unique features. In contrast, the three countries also shared many similar experiences in terms of political systems, the importance of the military in society, a growing place for Islam in public life, an interest in Arab cooperation, and a strong desire for economic development and diversification.

REFERENCES

References cited at the end of Chapters 20, 24, 28, 34, and 43 are pertinent to this chapter as well.

Adams, Richard H., Jr.: "Evaluating the Process of Development in Egypt, 1980–97." *International Journal of Middle East Studies* 32 (2000): 255–275. A specialized economic study.

Anderson, Lisa: "Legitimacy, Identity, and the Writing of History in Libya." In Eric Davis and Nicolas Gabrielides, eds., *Statecraft in the Middle East: Oil, Historical Memory, and Popular Culture,* pp. 71–91. Miami: Florida International University Press, 1991. This book also features somewhat similar chapters on the Arab states of the Persian Gulf.

Beattie, Kirk J.: *Egypt during the Sadat Years.* New York: Palgrave, 2000. An excellent detailed political history.

Botman, Selma: *Engendering Citizenship in Egypt.* New York: Columbia University Press, 1999. The author situates the history of women within the general history of modern Egypt.

Burr, J. Millard, and Robert O. Collins: *Africa's Thirty Years War: Libya, Chad, and the Sudan 1963–1993.* Boulder, Colo.: Westview, 1999. An incisive study of the political, geographical, diplomatic, and military factors surrounding the lengthy conflict.

——:*Requiem for the Sudan: War, Drought, and Disaster Relief on the Nile.* Boulder, Colo.: Westview, 1995. An angry discussion of the catastrophe affecting the Sudan and an assigning of responsibility for the terrible situation.

Daly, M. W., and Ahmad AlAwad Sikainga, eds.: *Civil War in the Sudan.* London: British Academic Press, 1993.

El-Ghonemy, M. Riad: "Food Security and Rural Development in North Africa." *Middle Eastern Studies* 29 (1993): 445–466. An analysis of all the countries of North Africa, including Egypt, Sudan, and Libya.

Gurney, Judith: *Libya: The Political Economy of Oil.* Oxford: Oxford University Press, 1996. This work covers all aspects of the oil and gas industry.

Hale, Sondra: *Gender Politics in Sudan: Islamism, Socialism, and the State.* Boulder, Colo.: Westview, 1997. An anthropological study based on interviews with women in the northern Sudan.

Hinnebusch, Raymond A., Jr.: *Egyptian Politics under Sadat: The Post-Populist Development of an Authoritarian-Modernizing State.* New York: Cambridge University Press, 1985.

Ismail, Salwa: "Confronting the Other: Identity, Culture, Politics, and Conservative Islamism in Egypt." *International Journal of Middle East Studies* 30 (1998): 199–225.

El-Kikhia, Mansour O.: *Libya's Qaddafi: The Politics of Contradiction.* Gainesville: University Press of Florida, 1997. A good introduction to the political history of Libya.

Lesch, Ann Mosely: *The Sudan—Contested National Identities.* Bloomington: Indiana University Press, 1998. A balanced exposition of events after 1985 by a leading political scientist.

Lorenz, Joseph P.: *Egypt and the Arabs: Foreign Policy and the Search for National Identity.* Boulder, Colo.: Westview, 1990. A short introduction with an emphasis on the Nasser and Sadat years.

Niblock, Tim: *"Pariah States" and Sanctions in the Middle East: Iraq, Libya, Sudan.* Boulder, Colo.: Lynne Rienner, 2001. The origins and impact of United Nations sanctions on the three countries.

el-Sadat, Anwar: *In Search of Identity: An Autobiography.* New York: Harper & Row, 1977.

el-Shazly, Saad: *The Crossing of the Suez.* San Francisco: American Mideast Research, 1980. An anti-Sadat account of the 1973 war by the chief of staff of the Egyptian army.

Sidahmed, Abdel Salam: *Politics and Islam in Contemporary Sudan.* New York: St. Martin's, 1996. A good introduction to the topic.

Springborg, Robert: *Mubarak's Egypt: Fragmentation of the Political Order.* Boulder, Colo.: Westview, 1989. Particularly useful for its coverage of political economy.

Sullivan, Denis J., and Sana Abed-Kotob: *Islam in Contemporary Egypt: Civil Society vs. the State.* Boulder, Colo.: Lynne Rienner, 1999. A short survey of Islamism, the nature of Islam in Egypt, the Muslim Brotherhood, militant fundamentalism, civil society, and gender issues.

Texas, University of, at Austin, Center for Middle Eastern Studies: Middle East Network Information Center at http://link.lanic.utexas.edu/menic/. This home page has a wide variety of links to many sources dealing with the contemporary Middle East, organized both by country and by topic.

Vandewalle, Dirk: *Libya since Independence: Oil and State-Building.* Ithaca, N.Y.: Cornell University Press, 1998. An excellent review that points out comparisons with other oil-producing states, such as those in the Arabian Peninsula.

Wikan, Unni: *Life among the Poor in Cairo.* Translated by Ann Henning. London: Tavistock, 1980. A gripping account based on in-depth interviews and observations in the early 1970s.

CHAPTER 45

Independent Lebanon and Syria

When Lebanon and Syria were French mandates, their political, economic, and social systems were intertwined; after independence, they often followed quite different historical patterns, diverging according to their varying physical geography and societal groupings. Although Lebanon is smaller than Syria, it has more religious communities, which, along with a service-oriented economy, profoundly influenced its politics, diplomacy, military, and culture.

The United States and the Soviet Union recognized the unconditional independence of Syria and Lebanon in 1944. This meant that France, under the leadership of General Charles de Gaulle, would have to withdraw its troops from its two former mandates of the now-defunct League of Nations, but de Gaulle hoped to retain French influence. Open resistance to the French erupted, and the French shelled Damascus in May 1945. The U.N. Security Council, prodded by the Soviet Union and the United States, recommended that foreign troops leave Syria and Lebanon. French troops finally departed from Lebanon and Syria in 1946. The two countries had achieved independence.

Lebanon prospered mightily for many years after independence, but it then entered into a protracted civil war, with international ramifications, that totally dominated its public life. Syria after independence was initially famous for its political instability, but a Ba'th party dictatorship emerged in the 1960s and provided a long-lasting regime. Syria espoused Pan-Arab nationalism and participated in most Arab-Israeli hostilities; the Syrians played a large part in the Lebanese civil war and eventually secured an important role in that country.

REPUBLIC OF LEBANON

Political power, economic prosperity, foreign policy, and cultural issues in Lebanon were all tied to the religious-communal groups composing the social base of identity in the country. In independent Lebanon, power was based on the confessional system, by which posts in government were allotted according to religious group identity in proportion to the population standing of the group. The presidents would be Maronite Christians, the prime ministers Sunni Muslims, the speakers of parliament Shii Muslims, and the commanders of the military, Maronites. Representation in parliament was also according to religious group category, with the deputies of the several Christian sects having a majority over the various Muslim groups' deputies. Although most law codes applied to all Lebanese regardless of religious community, personal status issues such as marriage and divorce went to separate communal courts. This emphasis on religious identity existed despite the fact that no official state religion was enshrined in the constitution.

The political system was strained by such issues as the problem of Palestine, the economic restructuring resulting from independence, and Cold War crises. Perhaps the small size of the country, the lack of natural resources, and the diversity of religious affiliations bound political leaders together. Among themselves they quarreled over prestige, position, and power, but they usually closed ranks on foreign crises. Cabinets changed frequently, but the leaders shuffled the various ministerial posts among themselves, and policies did not change much. In the three decades following the departure of the French, fifteen different men occupied the position of prime minister, many of them on several different occasions. Even when President Bishara al-Khuri was overthrown in 1952 by a bloodless public strike and he was charged with mismanagement and corruption, few could detect a great alteration in the public life of the country. Camille Shamun (Chamoun; d. 1987) was elected as the new president, and Lebanon continued in its basic business of commerce and providing services, rather than concentrating on ideology or politics.

Fringe parties did not succeed in winning many supporters, but they did pose some challenge to the Lebanese merchant republic as dominated by its commercial upper class. Communists tried to promote class struggle. Some Lebanese wanted a close relationship with France, even at the expense of an Arab identity. Kamal Jumblat, a Druze, pursued a utopian socialist doctrine. Pan-Syrian nationalists strove for the reunion of Lebanon with Syria, especially after the customs union between the two countries was dissolved in 1950.

Lebanon's political system and economy interacted closely, with government playing a small but significant role as the country grew increasingly prosperous. From 1950 to 1974 the economy grew at a rate of about 3 or 4 percent per year, with the service sector expanding as fewer people worked in agriculture. Wealth was extremely skewed, with the top 4 percent of the population gaining about one-third of all personal income, while the bottom 50 percent of the people obtained only about one-fifth of personal income. Beirut led the way to wealth as it became one of the most important Middle Eastern commercial and financial centers. It was a beautiful and cosmopolitan city, filled with excellent restaurants, cinemas, newspapers, publishing houses, and a vast array of consumer goods.

Lebanon did not have any oil of its own, but it nevertheless prospered from the oil wealth of Saudi Arabia and Iraq. Oil pipelines from those countries reached the coast of the Mediterranean in Lebanon. Rents paid by the pipelines, new refineries built in Lebanon, and remittances from Lebanese working in oil-producing countries helped the Lebanese economy.

Every year after World War II, Lebanon had a sizable unfavorable balance of trade, but it was more than redressed by commercial services, tourism, and investments of foreign capital. Since banking was one of the leading businesses in Lebanon and the principal occupation of many political figures, the security and integrity of banking was a prime concern of the government. Because of its openness and unregulated economy, Lebanon became a haven for the rich in other parts of the Middle East who feared their money might be taken by their own governments. One example took place in 1958, just before the formation of the United Arab Republic, when large sums flowed to Beirut from Syria.

Three-fourths of the Lebanese economy stemmed from commerce, and any restraint on the movement of goods was felt immediately. Wealth piled up in the hands of merchants and bankers while poverty was widespread in the cities and villages. Strikes and student demonstrations were manifestations of an escalating revolt against the growing inequities in Lebanese society: the poor countryside versus the wealthy in the city, the poor southern districts versus the north, the poor Palestinian refugees and Shii Lebanese versus the generally richer Maronite Christians.

Rapidly expanding population (about 3 percent a year), a great increase in the urban population at the expense of the countryside, and unemployment offered a severe challenge to the Lebanese political system and economy. Lebanon initiated various projects, the most promising being the Litani River irrigation and hydroelectric power plan, which also met some of the need for economic development in the Shii south.

Lebanon in the main remained a Western-oriented nation, although the Muslim majority emphasized its Arab heritage. The American University of Beirut created much goodwill toward the West, as did the presence in the United States of numerous Lebanese immigrants, most of them Christians.

By far the greatest difficulty for Lebanese foreign policy after 1945 arose from the partition of Palestine and the birth of Israel. In the Arab League and the United Nations, Lebanon argued against the partition of Palestine in 1948, but Lebanon's part in the first Arab-Israeli War, in 1948, was small. The chief immediate consequence of the war was that many Arab refugees from Palestine settled in camps in Lebanon. Most did not become citizens of Lebanon; instead, they hoped to return to their homeland eventually.

Although Lebanon's military prowess was limited, it became famous in the Arab Middle East for its cultural accomplishments. Beirut was a publishing and media hub, producing newspapers, novels, poetry, literary criticism, films, television programs, songs, paintings, and other such items. Radio was a government monopoly, but when television began in 1959, it was in private hands. By 1975 Lebanon had 400,000 television sets. Freedom of thought and expression and an openness to ideas from abroad existed in Lebanon to a greater degree than in most other parts of the Middle East, and this outlook encouraged cultural, artistic, and scientific creativity. Literacy rates were high for both men and women, and most school-age children received at least some formal schooling. In 1972 there were about 660,000 students attending a wide variety of schools, often religiously based, with almost as many female as male pupils. Cultural pluralism found expression in diverse educational arrangements, which reinforced separate identities rather than helping to create a sense of common Lebanese national culture.

Lebanese Politics

Women gained the right to vote in 1953 but the first woman was elected to parliament later, in 1963. No more women would be elected to the national level until 1991.

The relative calm of post–World War II Lebanese political life was shattered by the 1956 Suez crisis. As soon as the 1956 Arab-Israeli War ended, Lebanese leaders engaged in a bitter parliamentary election won by Shamun's backers.

The politicians who found themselves frozen out of office began a battle to regain power and discovered eager allies in Syria and Egypt. When the new United Arab Republic of Syria and Egypt came into existence in 1958, the Maronite leaders announced that Lebanon would not join it. They hoped that the United States would help them block Pan-Arab nationalism and thereby maintain Lebanon's independence.

Political demonstrations and outbreaks of violence erupted and a mild civil war broke out. The opposition, mostly by Muslims, was based in the areas annexed to Mount Lebanon by the French in 1920: parts of Beirut, the Druze central region, most of the south, and Tripoli. The opposition was in favor of union with Syria and Egypt, against a second term for Shamun, and in favor of government measures for the poor. On the other side were Shamun and his supporters, who wanted to amend the constitution so he could have a second term; most of the Christian communities; and those who favored the continued independence of a separate Lebanon under the control of the commercial upper and middle classes. Syria and Egypt helped the rebels, but matters remained stalemated, as General Fuad Shihab refused to commit the army to either political camp.

Shamun called on the United States for urgent support. The landing of American Marines in Beirut heightened the quarrel among local politicians to the level of the Cold War between east and west, because the Americans felt that the Soviets were behind Egypt and Syria. A compromise deal was brokered with American help and pressure. The elements of the compromise were that General Shihab, who was acceptable to both sides in the civil war, was elected president; Lebanon did not join the United Arab Republic; U.S. troops withdrew; and Shihab's foreign and domestic policies aimed at reconciliation with Muslims.

Some of the open wounds of the battles began to heal, and calmer relations with the United Arab Republic alleviated much of the bitterness. Shihab aligned Lebanon with Arab causes. In 1964, a pro-Shihab candidate, Charles Hilu, the minister of education, was elected president. Hilu continued Shihab's policies and managed to preserve Lebanon from the general catastrophe of the 1967 Arab-Israeli War when Egypt, Syria, and Jordan lost territory to Israel. After the fighting was halted, Lebanese politics returned to the usual competition for position, influence, and money.

Throughout the two terms of Presidents Shihab and Hilu from 1958 to 1970, some reforms were undertaken as the state controlled dissent through internal security forces. Social services were extended to the poor, infrastructure development took place, and the presidents managed to offend few people while many Lebanese enjoyed increasing prosperity.

Despite the national reconciliation and reforms, Shihab and Hilu did not change the confessional basis of the state. The number of members in Lebanon's parliament was usually divisible by eleven so that the accepted ratio of six Christians to five Muslims could be easily maintained. No official census was taken after 1932, as the ruling Maronites did not wish to upset this ratio. The membership in 1960, for instance, was ninety-nine deputies: thirty Maronites, twenty Sunnis, nineteen Shiis, eleven Greek Orthodox, six Druzes, six Greek Catholics, four Armenian Orthodox, one Armenian Catholic, one Protestant, and one other Christian. The unwritten national pact—that the president be a Maronite, the prime minister a Sunni, and other officials belong to other religious groups—was reaffirmed by all leaders.

With the election of Sulaiman Franjieh as president in 1970, the compromise and conciliation of the Shihab and Hilu terms came to an end. Franjieh had a more combative personality, and his victory represented a triumph for Shamun and others in the opposition.

The Arab-Israeli Dispute in Lebanon

In the late 1960s and early 1970s, the Palestinian refugee problem became more pressing. The influx of over 100,000 Arab Palestinian refugees in the late 1940s, mostly Sunni Muslims and almost 10 percent of the total population of Lebanon, had injected an explosive factor into that country. They became natural allies of the Lebanese Muslims, the poor, and the Pan-Arab nationalists.

From 1968 on, the Palestinians launched attacks from Lebanon against Israeli territory and Israeli interests abroad, and in return the Israelis attacked the Palestinians and Lebanese. This cycle of violence continued to escalate. The Lebanese armed forces could not defend their country against the Israeli assaults or control the Palestinians within their borders. Some Lebanese demanded measures such as conscription so that Lebanon could fight Israel, while others wanted the Lebanese authorities to crack down on the Palestinian guerrillas. When the Lebanese army moved against the Palestinians, guerrilla forces seized control of most of the refugee camps in the country.

Palestinian guerrilla operations throughout 1970 brought repeated retaliatory raids from Israel. Christian and Shii Muslim leaders demanded that the government act to curtail the Palestinians; Sunni Muslims supporting the Palestinians called on the government to strengthen the army. Armed clashes occurred in Beirut between Palestinians and Pierre Jumayyil's Christian Phalangist private militia. Political violence increased dramatically as even organizations inside the various communal groups vied brutally with each other for power. Signs of incipient civil war were everywhere.

Palestinian forces poured into Lebanon, after their defeat in Jordan in 1970, in such numbers that they seized full control of a 35-kilometer strip along the southern border. Martial law was invoked throughout the country. Palestine Liberation Organization (P.L.O.) leader Yasir (Yasser) Arafat, headquartered in Beirut, agreed in 1972 that the guerrillas would consult with the Lebanese government, which would hold ultimate veto power over any action. Large sections of the Lebanese population, however, subscribed to the Palestinian aims; sympathy strikes were frequent; to many university students, Palestinian activists were neither guerrillas nor terrorists but heroic national freedom fighters.

During the 1973 Arab-Israeli War, Lebanon maintained an official neutrality, to the disgust of most Palestinian groups. Clashes multiplied in 1974, and the Palestinian armed forces grew to 10,000.

Lebanese Civil War

The causes of the civil war lay in part with the personal and group rivalries and antagonisms endemic in Lebanese political, social, economic, and religious life and in part in the inflexibility of Lebanon's political and governmental structures and leaders. The war was made worse by the participation of foreign powers desiring to determine its outcome. Fundamental causes of the civil war in Lebanon were reinforced by the Arab-Israeli dispute, as local political and economic problems were exacerbated by foreign intervention and the issue of the Palestinians.

Most Lebanese supported the aims of the Palestinians and viewed their plight with sympathy, but did not wish to participate in the struggle. Above all, the Lebanese Christians abhorred the idea that the Palestinians might somehow have an overriding voice in Lebanon's political future. Thus, they were greatly distressed as the Palestinians increased their use of Lebanon as a base of operations against Israel, fearing especially that Israel might seize south Lebanon up to the Litani River. Christian conservative militants like Shamun, Jumayyil, and Franjieh, finding their government incapable of controlling the Palestinians, organized to combat them privately.

The Palestinians for their part saw in Lebanon a staging area for incursions into Israel; they used Beirut as a convenient spot for plotting actions against Israel throughout the world. Leftist Muslim groups in Lebanon accepted their Palestinian co-religionists as useful allies in the contest against the well-armed and wealthy Christian rightist minority.

Quite apart from the Palestinians, Lebanon's political structure was askew. No official census had still been taken since 1932. Most knowledgeable observers judged that the ratio of six Christians to five Muslims in parliament and the civil service no longer reflected Lebanon's demography; it might even have changed to a ratio of four Christians to six Muslims. Tampering with the original ratios would alter the power lines within the state, and any suggestion of this infuriated Shamun, Jumayyil, and Franjieh. Furthermore, the Christian rightist minority was considered the party of the wealthy, while the Muslim leftist majority was the party of the poor and underprivileged. Separated by religion, political philosophy, and economics, the two sides seeking power had drifted into civil war.

On April 13, 1975, a busload of Palestinians was massacred by Christian Phalange militia, and widespread violence broke out. The Palestinians joined the leftist parties, largely Muslim in composition, while Shamun's National Liberal party cooperated with Jumayyil's Phalange in supporting President Franjieh, to form a Maronite-dominated coalition of the Christian right. The experienced Sunni politician Rashid Karami tried for compromise, but calls to end the national pact ensured the continuation of the civil war.

Bitter fighting continued through 1975 and most of 1976. The Lebanese army, which for a time had remained aloof, entered the war in September 1975. In Beirut house-to-house fighting devastated sections of the city. It was calculated that \$3.4 billion in damages was incurred in 1975–1976 as homes and businesses were bombed, burned, or looted. By March 1976 between 15 and 20 percent of the heart of Beirut had been destroyed, and at least 10,000 people had died.

Franjieh continued to refuse to step down, and the Lebanese army began to experience massive defections. In the army most of the 18,000 men, including many of the junior officers, were Muslims, while the senior officers were almost all Christians. The army soon split when it was called into the war; most of the Muslims formed the Lebanese Arab Army and united with leftist Muslims and Palestinians, as Christian soldiers joined the rightist militias or stayed in garrisons.

President Franjieh joined with President Hafiz al-Asad of Syria to put together a compromise plan to modify the national pact in various ways, but as the fighting wore on in 1976, it began to look as if victory for the leftist Muslim-Palestinian coalition was close. Then al-Asad cut off all supplies going from Syria to the Palestinians. Perhaps he switched sides because he did not relish the idea of a Palestinian-dominated Lebanon that could involve him in a war with Israel at a time he did not choose. Pan-Arab nationalists in Syria viewed Lebanon as a part of Syria that had been artificially detached by the French, so al-Asad and other Syrian leaders felt that Lebanon should follow Syria's lead on major questions.

The Christian militias and the Syrian army were now aligned against the Palestinians and Muslim Lebanese leftists, and neither side was prepared to compromise. Syrian troops entered Lebanon in 1976 and opposed victory for any Lebanese party.

Syria obtained the necessary votes to elect as president Ilyas Sarkis, who assumed office in September 1976, but the war continued. Israeli naval units were preventing arms shipments from reaching the Muslim leftists and were supplying arms to the Christian militias; ironically, Israel and Syria, deadly enemies, were indirectly allied. By October, more than 20,000 Syrian troops were in Lebanon.

With the internationalizing of the Lebanese civil war, the Arab League called for a joint Arab force to police a cease-fire. Major resistance ended when the Tel al-Zaatar Palestinian refugee camp fell to Syrian and Christian forces. The Syrian troops were warned by Israel not to enter the area south of the Litani River. The war was not over, however, for the shelling, bombing, ambushing, and killing continued, although at a reduced rate.

One casualty of the continuing violence was the assassination of Kamal Jumblat in 1977. The Christian and Muslim militias were larger than ever, and public recruitment had lifted their numbers to 45,000, ten times the size of the Lebanese army. No parliamentary election was held in 1976 or for many years subsequently, and the question of representation, one of the roots of the civil war, was not resolved.

Most of the fighting occurred in the sensitive area south of the Litani River along the Israeli frontier, where Muslim and Maronite villages and enclaves are next to each other in an irregular pattern. In 1978 Israel, acting in retaliation for a Palestinian attack on the Israeli coast, invaded southern Lebanon up to the Litani River. U.N. peacekeeping forces took up positions there, but considerable fighting continued in scattered areas between Israelis and Palestinians and between Lebanese Christian militias and Lebanese Muslim and army groups. World opinion obliged the Israelis to pull back, which they did in stages. Israel turned over a narrow but long strip of Lebanese territory along the Israeli border to Major Saad Haddad and his pro-Israeli Lebanese militia, who held on to this area. Meanwhile, several hundred thousand Lebanese villagers, many of them Shiis, had become refugees.

In the late 1970s, the youthful Bashir Jumayyil, son of the veteran Lebanese politician Pierre Jumayyil, brutally consolidated the rightist militias under the name of the Lebanese Forces. With secret Israeli and American help, he was strong enough to extend his control over the Maronite enclave stretching through east Beirut northward along to the coast, to south of Tripoli, and inland into Mount Lebanon. The leftists, on the other hand, disintegrated; Kamal Jumblat's son Walid proved unable to keep that disparate grouping in west Beirut and the south together. President Sarkis, presiding over what remnants of a government still endured, was ineffectual, in large part because he was perceived as the tool of Syria, which would not, or could not, deliver sufficient force to impose its will on all the Lebanese factions.

Economic and cultural injury was severe: infrastructure and industry were heavily damaged, schools were closed, and patronage of the arts nearly ceased. The service sector was especially hard hit; tourists and businesses feared to operate in Beirut, which ceased to be the international hub of the Middle East. Nevertheless, Lebanon had substantial financial reserves, remittances from overseas increased in the late 1970s, smuggling and illegal drug marketing grew, and foreign governments pumped in large sums to support various factions. The Lebanese currency remained relatively stable in value until 1982.

The Fifth Arab-Israeli War

Israel was under the leadership of Prime Minister Menachem Begin in 1977. Begin concluded a series of arrangements culminating in the peace treaty with Egypt in 1979. In accordance with the exchange of land for peace, Israel returned all of Sinai to Egypt by the spring of 1982; in return, Egypt guaranteed Israel that it would not go to war. Since Israel's southern border was now safer, Begin and Defense Minister Ariel Sharon hoped to destroy the P.L.O. in Lebanon and to impose a peace treaty on Lebanon.

On June 6, 1982, Israel invaded Lebanon with overwhelming force. The stated goal of the Israelis was to clear the P.L.O. guerrillas from a security zone north of Israel. Bypassing U.N. troops, Israel fought P.L.O. forces and pushed rapidly north in a leapfrog pattern toward Beirut. An enormous land and air battle between Syria and Israel for control of Lebanon then ensued. Israel shot down around 100 Syrian airplanes and destroyed Syrian surface-to-air missile batteries while pushing Syrian troops back toward the Beirut-Damascus road.

By June 13 Israel had reached the outskirts of Beirut. There it linked up with Bashir Jumayyil's Lebanese Forces in east Beirut. Egypt and the other Arab states did nothing but protest while Israel cordoned off the P.L.O. and some Syrian and Lebanese forces in west Beirut and bombarded them by land, sea, and air. The 600,000 or so civilians and the thousands of combatants in the Lebanese capital's western half underwent a siege, and television cameras sent around the world extraordinary images of modern warfare devastating an already damaged city.

On August 21 the P.L.O. started to evacuate west Beirut according to conditions agreed on by the United States and other parties. A multinational force of U.S., French, and Italian troops guaranteed security in west Beirut. Bashir Jumayyil was elected president under Israeli supervision; the victory of the rightist and Christian side in the civil war finally seemed to be definitive.

Violence robbed Lebanon of whatever small chance of peace and national reconciliation this situation might have allowed, for Bashir Jumayyil was assassinated. Israel then moved into west Beirut, and the Lebanese Forces killed hundreds of Palestinian civilians. Bashir's older brother, Amin Jumayyil, a more moderate figure, was elected president of Lebanon as the multinational force returned. The Lebanese desperately hoped the carnage might end.

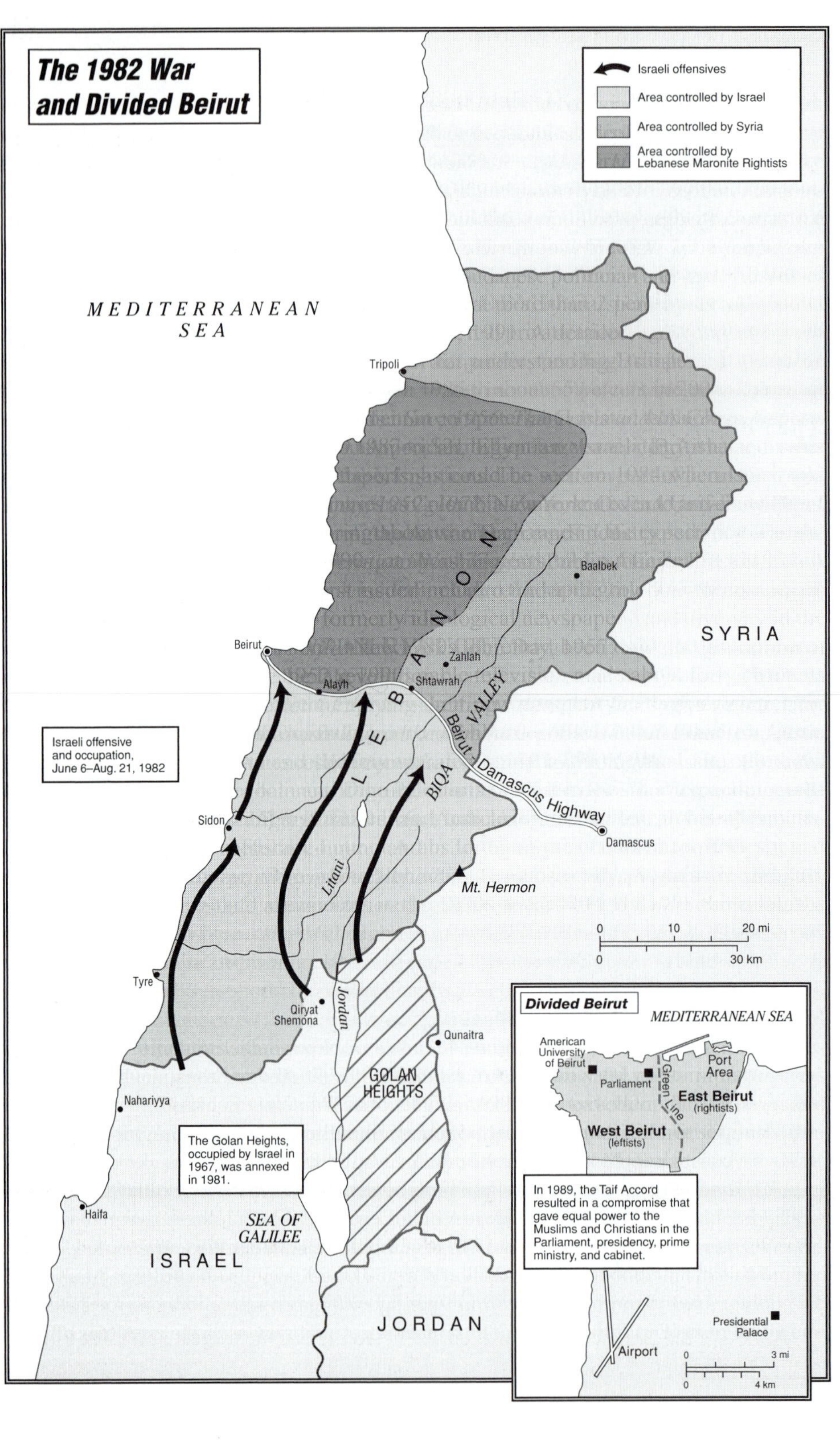
The 1982 War and Divided Beirut
Israeli offensives
Area controlled by Israel
Area controlled by Syria
Area controlled by Lebanese Maronite Rightists
MEDITERRANEAN SEA
Tripoli
Baalbek
SYRIA
LEBANON
Beirut
Zahlah
Alayh
Shtawrah
BIQA VALLEY
Beirut Damascus Highway
Damascus
Israeli offensive and occupation, June 6–Aug. 21, 1982
Sidon
Litani
Mt. Hermon
0 10 20 mi
0 30 km
Tyre
Qiryat Shemona
Jordan
Qunaitra
GOLAN HEIGHTS
Nahariyya
The Golan Heights, occupied by Israel in 1967, was annexed in 1981.
Haifa
SEA OF GALILEE
ISRAEL
JORDAN
Divided Beirut
MEDITERRANEAN SEA
American University of Beirut
Parliament
Port Area
Green Line
East Beirut (rightists)
West Beirut (leftists)
In 1989, the Taif Accord resulted in a compromise that gave equal power to the Muslims and Christians in the Parliament, presidency, prime ministry, and cabinet.
Presidential Palace
Airport
0 3 mi
0 4 km

Syria Regains Limited Preeminence in Lebanon

In late 1982 the United States tried to increase the strength of Lebanon's Israeli-backed central government and its army by sending arms, trainers, and money to help Amin Jumayyil. This seemed a feasible policy since many groups in southern and central Lebanon had initially accepted Israel's invasion, welcoming the Israelis as a better alternative than the P.L.O., whose control had grown increasingly oppressive. However, the actions of the Lebanese Forces soon alienated these groups. The Shiis, backed by Iran, were especially vigorous in launching suicide attacks against Israel and the multinational forces.

Jumayyil signed a quasi–peace treaty in May 1983 with Israel calling for a termination of the state of war, an Israeli withdrawal, and a special security region in southern Lebanon. Syria strongly opposed this agreement, and so did many Lebanese. Syria helped the Shiis and Druzes as they battled the central government army and the U.S. navy for control of west Beirut and central Lebanon. Guerrillas attacked the U.S. barracks in Beirut on October 23 and killed 241 marines. In 1984 President Ronald Reagan ordered the withdrawal of American forces from Lebanon.

Shiis of the Amal ("Hope") organization now controlled much of Lebanon, and President Jumayyil turned to Syria for help, thereby demonstrating his own remarkable flexibility and bringing Lebanon back to the situation that had existed before the 1982 war. The Israeli-Lebanese agreement of 1983 was abrogated by Lebanon. Israel retreated southward, completing its withdrawal from most of Lebanon in June 1985 and leaving the bulk of Lebanon under the control of Syria. It became clear that Palestinian forces supported by Syria were staying in Lebanon.

In the mid- and late 1980s, many groups in Lebanon suffered internal schisms as the state finally collapsed. The Maronite Lebanese Forces rejected President Jumayyil's leadership over whether to accept a large role for Syria. Amal and the Shiis split internally as they battled over Iranian influence, theocracy, hostage taking, and the acceptability of compromise with other Lebanese groups. The leftist Lebanese of various stripes fought the P.L.O., which was also divided against itself.

Under such circumstances Lebanon floundered, the economy disintegrated, each small area stood on its own administratively, and government debt increased dramatically. Emigration abroad grew in the 1980s: from 1975 to 1989 about 1 million Lebanese emigrated, though many ultimately returned to their homeland. In 1987 inflation reached about 500 percent, unemployment rose, and personal income fell by 80 percent from 1982 levels.

Culturally, Lebanon in the 1980s continued to be so diverse as to be without any real national unity. In radio and television broadcasting, newspapers, education, and even language (Arabic versus French as the language of high culture), the various confessional and political groups and factions each had its own choice. The extreme cultural diversity reflected and contributed to a fragmented political order. Female and male writers who broke out of the despair and numbness caused by interminable violence and the chaos of daily life captured many individual aspects of the civil war. Despite the death and destruction caused by the prolonged civil war, Lebanon continued to produce about as many books as Egypt and usually did so in a freer atmosphere with less censorship than in Cairo.

Although the Shiis clearly replaced the Maronites as the largest and most important element in Lebanon's mosaic, they were too divided to provide a generally accepted philosophy that could make a new and united Lebanon work. Instead, kidnappings, especially of foreigners, became frequent, and anonymous car bombings symbolized Lebanon's collapse. About 160,000 people were killed in Lebanon from the beginning of the 1975 civil war to 1990!

The 1987 assassination of Rashid Karami, the able Sunni leader from Tripoli who had so often served as a focus of compromise while prime minister, epitomized the degradation of Lebanese politics and the Lebanese polity. When President Jumayyil's term of office expired in 1988, parliament could not agree on his successor. Instead, the incumbent Sunni prime minister was challenged by Jumayyil's appointment of Maronite general Michel Aoun as head of a caretaker cabinet. Lebanon now had two prime ministers but no president.

The Lebanese army, the Maronite militia, Israel, and Iraq backed General Aoun, but Syria strongly opposed him. Severe fighting in Beirut in 1989 demonstrated that Syria could defeat his forces, and it opened the way to a compromise ending of the civil war.

Lebanon after the Taif Agreement

Syria, Saudi Arabia, the Arab League, and the United States encouraged the surviving members of the Lebanese parliament to endorse a comprehensive agreement to end the civil war in October 1989 in Taif, Saudi Arabia. The Taif Agreement called for the abolition of the confessional system in government administration in the long run. Christian Maronites retained the presidency, although its powers were reduced in favor of a strengthened cabinet, Sunni prime ministry, and Shii speaker of parliament. Representation in parliament was changed so that half of the deputies would be Christians and half Muslims. Among the Muslims, Shiis were now equal in number to the Sunni representatives.

As a beginning for the Taif accords, a president was elected by the old parliament. After the assassination of this newly elected president, Elias Hrawi was elected in 1989 with Syria's blessings. (The Syrians in 1995 persuaded parliament to extend his term to 1998.) President Hrawi now declared the beginning of a Second Republic for Lebanon, but few basic changes in Lebanese politics took place. General Aoun refused to accept the accords, so Syrian troops, taking advantage of the situation created by the Iraqi invasion of Kuwait in 1990, successfully attacked him, and eventually he left the country. Syria and Lebanon signed a treaty in 1991 that made clear Syria's influence over Lebanon.

The Syrian-dominated Hrawi administration now embarked on a reconstruction and reconciliation process designed to overcome the destruction and damage of the 1975–1990 civil war. Beirut was reunited, most militias were disbanded, foreign kidnapping victims were released, a government of national unity was created, physical rebuilding of Beirut began, and the central authorities slowly expanded their sway over most of the nation. This process was limited by Israeli control over parts of southern and eastern Lebanon, battles fought there by Shii Lebanese and Palestinians against the Israelis and their Lebanese allies, and Syrian military occupation of other parts of the country.

Parliamentary elections in 1992, the first in twenty years, resulted in equal numbers of Christian and Muslim delegates, with Maronites still the largest group but with the new prime minister, Sunni billionaire businessman Rafiq Hariri (b. 1944), the leading voice in administration and economic reconstruction. During his long service as prime minister, from October 1992 to December 1998, and then again after October 2000, Hariri followed Syrian wishes on most matters.

In 1992 many Christians who rejected the implications of the Taif accords boycotted the election on the grounds that the continuing Syrian occupation made it impossible to conduct elections fairly. Winners included most of the regional warlords, some Islamic fundamentalists, and many in the old notable families.

Lebanon's foreign policy in the 1990s was largely determined by Syria and by rapid changes in the Arab-Israeli dispute. While Lebanon was represented at the Madrid Conference of 1991 and at subsequent negotiations, it became clear that peace with Israel awaited the conclusion of a Syrian-Israeli agreement on the Golan Heights issue. Syria encouraged groups based in Lebanon to attack Israel and its Lebanese allies so as to apply pressure on Israel for a settlement. In 1993, 1996, and 2000, Israeli attacks against Lebanese infrastructure and Shii guerrillas in southern Lebanon, designed to curb their attacks on northern Israel, led to numerous civilian casualties and forced hundreds of thousands of Lebanese to flee for safety.

Continuing attacks by the Shii fundamentalist Hizb Allah (Hizbullah) group in southern Lebanon helped induce Israeli prime minister Ehud Barak in May 2000 to unilaterally and quickly withdraw Israeli forces from that area. Hizb Allah subsequently dominated the region with the support of Syria. While the United Nations certified a complete Israeli withdrawal, Syria and Hizb Allah picked a quarrel over a small border area so as to justify possible future attacks against northern Israel and to maintain leverage for Syria in bargaining with Israel over the Golan Heights.

The Lebanese economy stagnated after touching bottom in the late 1980s and early 1990s, although there was economic recovery by the mid-1990s. Infrastructure replacement and a construction boom in Beirut fueled the new growth, while education, sports, and cultural life revived enough to remind the rest of the Middle East of the Lebanon that had existed before 1975. The population began to increase again as emigration slowed. However, government deficits, corruption, and uncertainty about the durability of the Taif accords made the steps toward economic expansion tentative. The substantial real growth of the economy in 1993–1997 was followed by slower growth, even though some infrastructure rebuilding now reached completion. Government deficits were covered by borrowing, so that Lebanon became one of the most heavily indebted countries in the world by 2002. Servicing the debt took most of the government's income. On the other hand, in the first decade of peace most Lebanese and the hundreds of thousands of Syrians working in Lebanon were far better off than they had been during the 1975–1990 civil war.

Politics in the late 1990s and early 2000s witnessed increased participation by Christian voters. Parliamentary elections in 1996 and 2000 returned a pro-Hariri majority willing to accept Syrian dominance, while parliament in 1998 elected Emile Lahoud, a reforming Maronite Lebanese general, to replace Hrawi as president. The Lebanese government and Syrian forces in Lebanon periodically took severe steps against the media and others who questioned Syrian control over Lebanon.

Sectarian identity was still strong. Members of religious groups had become more segregated from each other during the civil war and after the Taif accords continued to live separately from each other. In the Christian regions, there were almost no Muslims, and in the Muslim areas a 10 percent Christian minority resided. The compromise ending of the civil war at Taif seemed to be based chiefly on the exhaustion of the contestants rather than on a clear resolution of the problems that had brought it about in 1975. Lebanon after 1990 enjoyed an uncertain and potentially precarious period of peace and recovery from the terrible events of the long civil war.

REPUBLIC OF SYRIA

When World War II ended, the Syrian political leaders who had battled for independence in the mandatory period had the satisfaction of forming the first fully sovereign Syrian republic. The early years of independence were dominated by debates about Pan-Arab nationalism, allocating blame for the loss of the 1948 Arab-Israeli War, and trying to develop a satisfactory political system.

Nationalist feelings in Syria ran higher than in Lebanon since the actions of the French had been more drastic in Damascus than in Beirut. Three times the French had shelled Damascus, the capital of Faisal's short-lived Arab kingdom in 1920. All French schools in Syria were closed in 1945.

Nationalism in Syria was not just anti-imperialist. The goal of a united Pan-Arab state was alive in Syria; indeed, many Syrians regarded it as almost a necessity. Each Arab state separately was weak; together they would have strength. Yet there were many barriers in the way of Fertile Crescent unity, including the separate historic experiences of each country after the area had been divided between England and France in the 1920s. There was also the issue of who would control a united state: Syrians or others.

Syria played an active part in the formation of the Arab League in 1945 and promised to cooperate militarily against the formation of a Zionist state in Palestine. In the first Arab-Israeli War of 1948, Syria took part, but the very small Syrian armed forces did not fight well. There was no great enthusiasm for shedding Syrian blood so that Amir Abd Allah in Transjordan or King Faruq in Egypt might have more influence.

In 1949, Chief of Staff Husni Zaim carried out a bloodless coup d'état. Zaim arrested the president and the leading political figures. The public approved for a number of reasons: the urban Sunni families that controlled politics were not popular, the war in Palestine was a failure, corruption was rampant, and the constitution had been amended to permit the president to succeed himself. Zaim became prime minister, and political parties were outlawed.

Husni Zaim started out strongly, arranging a cease-fire agreement with Israel and proposing unity with Iraq. Fearing Hashimite rule in Syria, Egypt and Saudi Arabia rushed diplomatic and financial support to Zaim, causing him to abandon unionist policies and become president of a new Syrian republic. Worst of all for Arab nationalists, he showed an inclination to restore some aspects of French cultural influence. French, for instance, became an official language, along with Arabic. After about four months in power, Zaim was arrested by General Sami al-Hinnawi, who had him executed. Four months after this event, Colonel Adib Shishakli ousted al-Hinnawi; Syria seemed to be headed toward political chaos with three different political leaders in one year, but Shishakli soon established his dominance.

In 1953 Shishakli became president and prime minister, but his personal dictatorship lacked an institutional base. When the army revolted, he fled. The 1950 constitution was reinstated, and the chamber of deputies was recalled. A wide variety of ideological groups entered the political system. Ex-president Shukri al-Kuwatli was elected president in 1955. A succession of prime ministers battled with the complex problems of Syria, but none found a way toward Pan-Arab union, largely because of the political turmoil created by a rivalry for influence in Syria among Egypt, Saudi Arabia, and Iraq.

Despite the political turmoil, some economic progress took place. Changes affecting agriculture were important since a majority of the population gained its livelihood from farming. The chief area of growth was in the agriculture of the northeastern part of the country. Thanks to increased production there, the wheat grown in Syria in the 1940s had doubled, and in the 1950s it increased by another 50 percent. With the growth of agriculture the Bedouin tribes increasingly became sedentary. Plans for land reform to help the poor and landless peasants were enacted into law but were not implemented to any great extent.

A frenzied political atmosphere developed in Damascus with a series of plots, accusations of treason, scandals, and political witch-hunts. The leftist Syrian politicians used American-backed discussions by Saudi Arabia, Iraq, and Turkey for armed intervention in Syria to whip up enthusiasm and support. The regime needed arms to prevent an internal coup and to strengthen Syria's position against invasion. Following Nasser's example, Syria bought weapons from the Soviet Union and secured Soviet help in forestalling American plans.

Syrian foreign policy was dominated by its antagonism toward Zionism and the new state of Israel. Raids and counterraids occurred frequently on the Syrian-Israeli cease-fire lines. In 1955 Israeli forces mounted a massive attack on Syria. Since the western powers, and particularly the United States, were identified with colonialism and the foundation of the Zionist state, Syrians blamed the west for their defeats and frustration. When the Soviet bloc became anti-Israeli, Syria put into effect the old saying that my enemies' enemies are my friends and allied itself with the Soviet Union.

With the emergence of Nasser as Egypt's leader, many Syrians favored a pro-Egyptian orientation. Young army staff officers were especially ardent supporters of Nasser and his revolution.

Syria Unites with Egypt

In February 1958, the union of Egypt and Syria was officially declared, though the pressure for full union came chiefly from Syria. Nasser became president and al-Kuwatli vice president of the United Arab Republic, which was divided into two regions, Egypt and Syria. All political parties in Syria were dissolved.

Unlike most of the other supposed unions of Arab states, which have existed mostly on paper, Syria and Egypt actually developed a united military and political structure. However, the United Arab Republic faced a geographic problem that could not be easily overcome: Egypt and Syria were separated from each other by nearly 600 miles (950 km.). In addition, Syria and Egypt had quite different economies and social customs. Another difficulty was that Egypt was in control of the new state because of its much larger population and more cohesive leadership, and it imposed Egyptian patterns on Syria. A key example was in the area of land reform, where Egyptian ideas were extended to Syria.

All of this might have been acceptable had there not been severe droughts and crop failures between 1958 and 1960. Export trade with Lebanon, Syria's best customer, was shattered by the difficulties and border closing of 1958, the shift to a Soviet orientation and Egyptian controls, and the scarcity of commodities.

The new social and economic forces at work in Syria freed the imaginations of Syrians who had been suffocated by politics since the end of World War I. However, the better-established elite groups and notable families discovered that the union relegated them to less prominent positions. Land reform sapped their privileges and power; trade quotas, import licenses, and nationalization hampered their business opportunities; and army officers were frustrated by Egyptian domination of the military.

The army, banding together with other dissident groups, staged a successful coup in September 1961. Nasser reluctantly accepted the secession of Syria from the United Arab Republic and Syria emerged again as an independent state.

The Ba'th Takes Power

The new civilian government reversed many measures adopted during the United Arab Republic, but it kept the land reform. Parliamentary elections returned a moderately conservative majority whose programs offended leftist and Pan-Arabist politicians and military officers, many of whom identified themselves with the Ba'th political party.

The Ba'th ("Renaissance"), developed during World War II by Michel Aflaq, a French-educated Christian, and Salah al-Din al-Bitar, a Sunni Muslim, stressed secularist Pan-Arab nationalism, freedom from imperialism, and socialism as the three forces that Arab society should embrace in order to rejuvenate the Arab world and thereby create a renaissance for the Arabs. Most of the Ba'th party members were students, educators, professionals, civil servants, or soldiers. Persons from the provinces and from the Muslim religious minorities were especially numerous; they welcomed the secular ideology of the party. The Ba'th party was relatively well organized, and it profited from its ideological and lower-middle-class appeal. Branches of the party existed in other Arab states, particularly in Iraq, where Ba'thists took power in 1963.

On March 8, 1963, when the Syrian Ba'thists seized power, the party's army officers became the new ruling elite in Syria. Sunni large landowners, urban politicians, and merchants were replaced as the ruling class by the sons of the lower-middle class and the sons of peasants. These army officers were young and locally educated, and most of them were Alawi Shiis. (The Alawis composed about one-tenth of the total population of Syria; many Sunni Muslims considered them not to be Muslims at all.) The Ba'thists instituted a tightly-controlled political system, declaring martial law in 1963—a legal declaration that remained in effect permanently thereafter. Censorship of the media and repression of political opponents were prevalent. During the next seven years, segments of the army and party struggled against each other to gain power.

The new regime planned for a tripartite union with Iraq and Egypt, but because Syria and Iraq insisted on equal votes whereas Nasser demanded that voting should depend on population, the proposed union was never established. However, as long as the Ba'thists dominated the government in Iraq, the two states cooperated in many affairs, and the Pan-Arab executive of the Ba'thist party directed policies. Syria also joined with Lebanon, Jordan, and Egypt in plans for diverting water that would otherwise flow into Israel.

Nationalization, industrialization, and economic development proceeded rapidly. Land reform continued, and by 1972 about 40 percent of the total land under cultivation had been taken from rich landowners. In 1965 the Syrian government nationalized all major manufacturing and processing plants, public utilities, domestic and foreign oil companies, and many export-import firms.

Incidents between Syria and Israel increased in 1966, especially as Israel attacked Syria's water-diversion efforts. Raids against Israel were frequently carried out by members of al-Fatah, a society of Palestinians dedicated to the regaining of their homeland. A crisis flared in May 1967 when Syria claimed that Israel was preparing so massive an attack that even Damascus might fall. Syrian leaders called on Egypt for assistance and protection.

When Israel attacked Egypt on June 5, 1967, Syria chose to come to the aid of Nasser. The main fighting occurred in Sinai, but on the fourth day of the short war, Syria felt the full brunt of the Israeli forces. By the time the cease-fire became effective, Syria had lost to Israel the Golan (Jawlan) Heights above the Sea of Galilee, and tens of thousands of Syrians fled the area and became refugees. To regain the Golan Heights now became Syria's chief foreign policy goal.

Hafiz al-Asad as President

Hafiz al-Asad (b. 1930; also spelled al-Assad), who was minister of defense, moved carefully into a position of dominance in the Ba'th party. He was pragmatic and little concerned with ideology. Al-Asad seized control in a bloodless coup in 1970 and became president in 1971. He was born near Latakia, the son of a peasant. An Alawi Muslim, he had found opportunity for education and advancement only in the military. As a leading officer and minister of defense, he had visited the Soviet Union and much of Europe. To the surprise of most Syrians, he established a personal dictatorship that lasted for decades and thereby ended the political instability for which Syria had become famous.

Al-Asad consolidated power by eliminating his opponents within the Ba'th party and by rewarding his friends and followers. A parliament led by the Ba'th but including some representatives of other groups was appointed. Only the Ba'th party, however, had the right to engage in political activity in the army! Syria under the Ba'th established a security state—a regime that tightly controlled the media, opinion, and institutions, while also gaining support from successful policies.

A new constitution approved in 1973 stated that Syria was democratic and socialist, with sovereignty belonging to the people, and that laws were to be based on the shariah. The Ba'th was declared to be the leading political organization. A personality cult like that of Stalin in the Soviet Union featured propaganda, statues, and mass public gatherings—all designed to give at least the appearance of broad-based support for the regime. The Ba'th party subsequently increased to over 1,000,000 members by the 1990s.

Defeat in war and conflict within the Ba'th did not injure Syrian economic life. Al-Asad benefited from the beginnings of Syrian oil production. In 1968 oil began to flow, and in the 1970s Syria was a net exporter of small amounts of oil, which replaced cotton as the chief source of foreign exchange. Good cotton crops during these years also contributed to economic growth. The government in 1968 had moved the first earth for the Euphrates Dam—one of the largest such projects in the world—which was intended to irrigate lands and to create more electric power. When the dam was completed in 1974, it made available irrigated land that proved expensive to reclaim. Later the Syrian government turned its attention toward more pragmatic and smaller-scale agricultural improvements. Once in use, the dam also brought acute disagreements with Turkey over amounts of water flow. Al-Asad expanded government-backed industry and built roads, railways, and ports.

Syria witnessed major economic growth in the 1970s, with the gross domestic product increasing by almost 10 percent every year. Remittances from Syrians working abroad, foreign aid from Arab governments, and inexpensive weapons from the Soviet Union also helped the national budget and the economy.

Al-Asad's foreign policy was based on friendship with the Soviet Union. The Soviet Union moved its Mediterranean fleet base from Egypt to Syria in 1972 and transferred to Syria massive quantities of arms, including surface-to-air missiles. Ironically, Syria's relations with Iraq became strained after the Iraqi Ba'thists seized power again in 1968, since the new regime in Baghdad became a rival for leadership of the Pan-Arab cause. Iraq gave sanctuary to Syrian Ba'thists out of favor in Damascus. Syria also was on poor terms with King Husain of Jordan after it intervened on behalf of Palestinians who fought against the royal Jordanian army.

The most immediate task facing al-Asad, however, was the struggle against Israel. Syria supported one faction of the Palestinian Arab movement while trying to influence all other such groups so as to channel their activities in ways that would advance Syria's interests. However, nothing al-Asad could do seemed to be able to induce Israel to withdraw from its occupation of the Golan Heights.

The Fourth Arab-Israeli War

In conjunction with Egypt, Syria launched a massive attack on Israel on October 6, 1973. With more than 1000 tanks, the Syrians crossed the cease-fire line and captured much of the Golan Heights. Then Israel counterattacked, bombing key military and economic targets throughout Syria, and by October 10 it had pushed to within 25 miles (40 km.) of Damascus, thereby reaching even farther into Syrian territory than had been the case in the 1967 war. Egypt deserted Syria. Before the war began, its leaders had agreed to act jointly during the fighting, but Egypt's president, Anwar al-Sadat, withdrew from the war first. The cost of war damage to Syria was $2.4 billion, but in this war, unlike those of 1948 and 1967, the Syrian armed forces performed very well, although they were ultimately defeated.

Within weeks after the beginning of the war, immense quantities of arms and munitions were being airlifted to Syria from the Soviet Union. After a trip to Moscow by American Secretary of State Henry Kissinger, the two great powers forced a cease-fire on the three belligerents on October 23, under the auspices of the U.N. Security Council.

In May 1974, Syria and Israel, acting through the United States, agreed to limited disengagement by the establishment of a U.N. neutral zone on the Golan Heights and to a partial Israeli withdrawal. The U.N. force was to remain for six months, when a more permanent settlement was expected, but its mandate was renewed periodically by the United Nations, and it continued on the Golan Heights indefinitely. Al-Asad's stand continued to be that Israel must give up all the lands it had taken in 1967. But Israel extended its law to the Golan Heights of Syria in 1981, in effect annexing the region.

The shifting sands of Arab diplomacy created a constant challenge for al-Asad. He denounced President Sadat after Egypt signed a disengagement pact with Israel in 1975. Although at first he mildly favored Palestinian aspirations in Lebanon, by the spring of 1976 he opposed the victory of any one faction in the Lebanese civil war. Al-Asad sent thousands of troops into Lebanon, and about 20,000 or more remained in that country permanently. Syria expended much of its wealth on subsequent developments in Lebanon. One of al-Asad's continuing concerns was to dominate Lebanon by a policy of divide and rule. Syria, however, took great care to avoid stationing Syrian forces close to the Israeli borders, fearing that their presence in large numbers might invite a full-scale Israeli invasion. Even during the Israeli incursion into south Lebanon in 1978, Syrian units were ordered not to confront the Israelis, though Syria did give aid to Shii Lebanese organizations that fought Israel.

Continuity after 1980

President al-Asad, his family, and the Alawi army officers retained their power, but their popularity apparently diminished in the early 1980s as some of their policies seemed to fail. Pan-Arabism became a fiction. In Syria the Alawi minority control of all power increasingly alienated many in the Sunni Muslim majority, and especially the fundamentalists among them. Many people within Syria accused the regime of corruption, oppression, and torture of prisoners. Assassinations of Alawi officials and military cadets led the government to attack the central Syrian city of Hama in 1982, where a general insurrection by the fundamentalists was crushed as military forces caused thousands of casualties.

Overcoming such opposition, al-Asad provided remarkable stability to Syria. There was, however, no clearly recognized principle of succession, and members of the president's family and entourage intrigued against each other for positions in the military and security forces.

Much of the regime's energies continued to be devoted to foreign policy and military issues, especially Lebanon. The fifth Arab-Israeli War in 1982 in Lebanon saw a marked defeat of the Syrian armed forces as Syria fought the Israelis with only limited help from Lebanese and Palestinian allies. No other Arab country came to the aid of Syria, which was soon outnumbered by Israeli troops and weapons.

The subsequent course of events in Lebanon brought Syria a victory of sorts. Israel and the United States withdrew; President Jumayyil accepted Syrian guidance; Syria occupied much of the country, including west Beirut; Syria's allies overcame their local foes; and the Syrian-backed faction within al-Fatah gained the upper hand in northern Lebanon. Syria was predominant in chaotic Lebanon.

Another bitter rivalry for Syria was with the fellow Ba'thists who ruled Iraq. During the Iran-Iraq War of 1980–1988, Syria backed Iran despite the claims of Arabism, socialism, and secularism that might have inclined it toward Iraq. In return, Iran granted Syria oil—some free and some at special rates. This policy, along with Syria's closeness to Libya's erratic leader, Muammar al-Qadhdhafi, made Syria somewhat of an outcast among the Arab states. Syria was especially cool toward Egypt and Jordan, and al-Asad strongly opposed U.S. and Egyptian attempts to bring Jordan and the mainstream of the P.L.O. into peace talks with Israel.

With the Soviet Union, on the other hand, Syria retained close ties during the 1980s as military purchases increased. When Soviet Communism collapsed in the early 1990s, Asad turned toward the United States through necessity. Although it could purchase weapons from China and North Korea, only the United States had real leverage with Israel in regard to the Golan Heights. Relations with the United States up to this time had usually been tense, in part because of strong differences between the two countries in regard to Israel, the Palestinians, and Lebanon but also because of Syrian involvement in kidnappings, hijackings, and bombings directed against Americans. Now Syria reversed itself and aided the United States in some ways, particularly during the 1990 Kuwait crisis, when it strongly backed Saudi Arabia by sending an armored division. Although Syrian troops provided artillery support for the 1991 war, the chief consequence of Syrian participation was psychological: Ba'thist Syria opposed Ba'thist Iraq and thereby helped legitimize the allied campaign to liberate Kuwait from Iraqi control.

The consequences of the Kuwait crisis for Syria included economic assistance from Saudi Arabia and a more sympathetic attitude in Washington toward Syrian goals in Lebanon. Syria participated in the Madrid peace conference in 1991 while making clear that its view of peace entailed nothing less than the return of the Golan Heights from Israeli occupation. Subsequent negotiations between Israel and Syria held out the prospect of peace between the two bitterly suspicious rivals.

The economic growth of the 1970s changed to stagnation in the 1980s as increasing world prices for cotton did not compensate Syria for the fall in the value of oil, its chief export. Natural gas discoveries provided a new source of income, but the Syrian balance of trade was often negative. Syria's foreign debt, especially to the Soviet Union (perhaps as much as $15 billion), alarmingly increased in the 1980s. A source of help for the Syrian economy was foreign aid from the oil-rich Arab states such as Saudi Arabia or Libya, but this help was conditional on their approval of Syrian foreign policy, and aid fell along with the price of oil in the mid-1980s. The Syrian black market, including large-scale smuggling, continued to flourish into the 1990s, when economic prosperity began to return. Some measures were taken to promote the privatization of government enterprises so as to encourage efficiency. Greater production of oil brought in more revenue for the state, and the number of tourists reached about 1.5 million.

One cause of the economic downturn in the 1980s was the heavy continuing drain on the economy resulting from military expenditures, which took between one-third and one-half of the budget. In the 1980s Syria maintained 500,000 in the armed forces, which were armed with 4400 tanks, 650 combat aircraft, and a chemical warfare capacity. As Syria sought military equality with Israel, the Syrian people paid and paid for it.

Social change during the Ba'thist era was rapid, as was evident in the growth of population and the concentration of persons in the cities. From 1945 to 2002 the population increased from 2.5 million to 17 million as infant mortality fell. More than half the people now lived in cities. Damascus grew from 300,000 in 1945 to 800,000 in 1970 and about 1.5 million in the 1990s. New apartment buildings rose everywhere, and new roads helped bring rural dwellers into the urbanized areas—this despite government efforts to encourage development of the small towns and villages by providing schools, electricity, and health care. Education increased remarkably; in the 1980s there were more than 2 million students at all levels, including those attending the four universities. Almost half of the population was less than 15 years old, and by the 1990s more than half of the adult population was literate.

Female students attended schools in record numbers as the status of women in public life changed rapidly. Women had gained the right to vote as early as 1947, and many became government employees during the Ba'thist era, constituting about one-fourth of such workers by 1975. Women played a notable but not leading role in the party, the parliament, commercial offices, and the professions. Women were especially prominent among writers of short stories.

Starting in the late 1980s the government quietly encouraged family planning. The fertility rate fell in the 1990s, though Syria's rate of population increase still remained among the highest in the world.

Culture in Ba'thist Syria was tightly controlled by the regime through censorship as well as by rewards to those who promoted the aims of the government. Poetry remained a crucial medium of expression, with many poets employing Arab nationalist and pro-Palestinian themes. Social realism flourished in the 1960s among novelists and short story writers, but justice for the poor remained a major topic even in subsequent decades. The Syrian authorities sponsored the theater and films. State-run television, which began in 1960, grew to reach more than one-half million sets by the late 1980s. Ironically, the most famous Syrian cultural figure, Ali Ahmad Said (b. 1930), known as Adunis, lived in exile in Beirut and Paris after 1956. His modernist, symbolist, and surrealist poetry was highly influential in all parts of the Arabic-speaking world. The life of Adunis indicated some of the multiple ways Syria and Lebanon interacted with each other.

Transition to a Dynastic Republic

In the late 1990s and early 2000s Syria manifested remarkable continuity despite the death of Hafiz al-Asad on June 10, 2000. In political, diplomatic, military, economic, and cultural matters the long-awaited transition to new leadership seemed to have only limited consequences.

The worldwide trend toward more democratic regimes had little echo in Syria in the late 1990s as al-Asad groomed his son Bashar to be his successor. The Alawi power brokers in the intelligence services, security guards, and armed forces supported this choice, even though Bashar al-Asad had little experience in politics or administration. Bashar al-Asad was also elected president of Syria with the backing of the Ba'th party, the civil bureaucracy, and all those who had gained from the long rule of his father. A slight relaxation in controls over public discussion of political matters was the only change made in the political environment in the first two years of Bashar al-Asad's presidency.

The foreign policy of Syria continued to be dominated by the long-standing goal of regaining control of all the Golan Heights from Israel. When Turkey and Israel concluded an alliance in 1996, Syria felt under pressure from its two neighbors, a pressure that became clear in 1998 when Turkey used military threats to compel Syria to expel the Kurdish leader Abd Allah Ocalan. Syria suspended peace talks during 1996 to 1999 when the hard-line Likud party controlled the Israeli government, but resumed them when Labor once again came into power. In January 2000, acting under the supervision of the United States, Syria and Israel came close to a settlement but were unable to reach a comprehensive agreement. Later that year, the outbreak of the second Palestinian intifada and the transition to Bashar al-Asad's rule put negotiations with Israel on hold.

The Syrian economy grew substantially in the 1990s. Oil production, agricultural exports, tourism, and investments in the private sector led to an increase of about 7 percent per year in the gross domestic product from 1990 to 1994. From 1995 to 2002 per capita economic growth continued but at a very slow rate due largely to the rapid increase of population. However, the drain on economic resources from spending on the armed forces fell in the 1990s, with military costs from the middle 1980s to the late 1990s sinking by about one-half. Syria abandoned the futile goal of military equality with Israel, opting instead for a strong deterrent force.

Cultural changes in the late 1990s included gradual governmental approval of new communications media. Up to the early 1990s owners of typewriters had to register them with the government. Although many Syrians had satellite television dishes, their possession was legalized only in 2000 by the new president. Even before Bashar al-Asad became president he encouraged access to the Internet, beginning with universities. However, the general public who wished to obtain computer linkages had to operate through Lebanon, where communications were far more open and social and political controls were far more relaxed than in Syria.

Lebanon and Syria differed in multiple ways following the establishment of their independence, but after Syria's intervention in Lebanon's civil war in 1976, the two countries intensified their many cultural, economic, military, and political ties. Despite the opposition to Syrian preponderance strongly felt by most Maronite Lebanese, Syria played a major role in such events as the Arab-Israeli War of 1982 in Lebanon. Nevertheless, the histories of Lebanon and Syria also diverged quite sharply. Their political systems, economies, and cultural orientations remained distinctive. Both Syria and Lebanon endured as separate national units, as they rejected such options as Syria's union with Egypt or the disintegration of Lebanon into smaller political entities.

REFERENCES

References cited at the end of Chapters 35, 37, 41, 42, and 43 are pertinent to this chapter as well.

Abul-Husn, Latif: *The Lebanese Conflict: Looking Inward.* Boulder, Colo.: Lynne Rienner, 1998. In this excellent examination of the Lebanese civil war, the author argues that the chief causes were internal structural failures.

Batatu, Hanna: *Syria's Peasantry, the Descendants of Its Lesser Rural Notables, and Their Politics.* Princeton, N.J.: Princeton University Press, 1999. An extraordinary work of scholarship.

Cobban, Helena: *The Making of Modern Lebanon.* Boulder, Colo.: Westview Press, 1985. An excellent general survey that shows historical continuity underneath the surface pattern of events.

Cooke, Miriam: *War's Other Voices: Women Writers on the Lebanese Civil War.* Cambridge: Cambridge University Press, 1988.

Devlin, John F.: *The Ba'th Party: A History from Its Origins to 1966.* Stanford, Calif.: Hoover Institution, 1976. A detailed account of the origins, doctrine, and political fortunes of the Ba'th.

Gates, Carolyn L.: *The Merchant Republic of Lebanon: Rise of an Open Economy.* London: Centre for Lebanese Studies and Tauris, 1998.

Ghadbian, Najib: "The New Asad: Dynamics of Continuity and Change in Syria." *Middle East Journal* 55 (2001): 624–641. A useful study of the transition to Bashar al-Hafiz and ensuing policies in Syria.

Gordon, David C.: *The Republic of Lebanon: Nation in Jeopardy.* Boulder, Colo.: Westview, 1983. A very good survey of geography, history, and politics.

Hinnebusch, Raymond A.: *Authoritarian Power and State Formation in Ba'thist Syria: Army, Party, and Peasant.* Boulder, Colo.: Westview, 1990. A comprehensive study by a leading authority on modern Syria.

———: "The Political Economy of Economic Liberalization in Syria." *International Journal of Middle East Studies* 27 (1995): 305–320. A useful introduction to the subject.

———: "Pax-Syriana? The Origins, Causes and Consequences of Syria's Role in Lebanon." *Mediterranean Politics* 3 (1998): 137–160. This thorough review untangles a complicated set of events.

———: *Syria: Revolution from Above.* London: Routledge, 2001. A short and incisive work on Syrian politics, economics, foreign policy, and the military, mostly since the 1970s.

Hiro, Dilip: *Lebanon: Fire and Embers—A History of the Lebanese Civil War.* New York: St. Martin's Press, 1993. A detailed recounting of the key events.

Hopwood, Derek: *Syria 1945–1986: Politics and Society.* London: Unwin Hyman, 1988. A clear and concise introduction to political, economic, educational, and cultural matters.

Kerr, Malcolm H.: *The Arab Cold War: Gamal 'Abd al-Nasir and His Rivals, 1958–1970.* 3d ed. London: Oxford University Press, 1971. A subtle and profound analysis of the alliances and enmities of the period by a political scientist who became president of the American University of Beirut before being tragically assassinated there.

Khalaf, Samir: *Civil and Uncivil Violence in Lebanon: A History of the Internationalization of Communal Conflict.* New York: Columbia University Press, 2002. The author, a prominent Lebanese social scientist, places much of the responsibility of the civil war on external causes, as compared to the book by Abul-Husn cited above.

Ludvigsen, Borre: *Al-Mashriq: The Levant—Cultural Riches from the Countries of the Eastern Mediterranean* at http://almashriq.hiof.no. This web site hosted at Ostfold College, Norway, centers on Lebanon and includes historical documents, images, links to other useful sites, many specialized cultural topics, and current events.

Najem, Tom Pierre: *Lebanon's Predicament: The Political Economy of Reconstruction.* Reading, England: Ithaca Press, 2000. Covers the economic reconstruction of Beirut in the 1990s and its links to political processes.

Norton, Augustus Richard: *Amal and the Shi'a: Struggle for the Soul of Lebanon.* Austin: University of Texas Press, 1988. Valuable for southern Lebanon; written by an eyewitness.

Perthes, Volker: *The Political Economy of Syria under Asad.* London: Tauris, 1995. A good description of Syria's statist economy and its impact on various groups.

Picard, Elizabeth: *Lebanon: A Shattered Country, Myths and Realities of the Wars in Lebanon.* Translated by Franklin Philip. New York: Holmes and Meier, 1996. This general history of Lebanese politics concentrates on communal relations.

Roberts, David: *The Ba'th and the Creation of Modern Syria.* New York: St. Martin's Press, 1987.

Rugh, William A.: *The Arab Press: News Media and Political Process in the Arab World.* 2d ed. Syracuse, N.Y.: Syracuse University Press, 1987. An excellent work that covers television and radio, as well as newspapers.

Salibi, Kamal S.: *Crossroads to Civil War: Lebanon, 1958–1976.* Delmar, N.Y.: Caravan Books, 1976. Deals well with complex elements.

Seale, Patrick: *The Struggle for Syria: A Study of Post-War Arab Politics, 1945–1958.* New ed. London: Tauris, 1986. Advances the thesis that dominating the Middle East requires controlling Syria.

———: *Asad of Syria: The Struggle for the Middle East.* Berkeley: University of California Press, 1989. A lengthy and well-researched biography of the Syrian leader.

Shehadeh, Lamia Rustum, ed.: *Women and War in Lebanon.* Gainesville: University Press of Florida, 1999. The chapters in this book discuss the role of women in the civil war and its consequences for them.

Van Dam, Nikolaos: *The Struggle for Power in Syria: Politics and Society under Asad and the Ba'th Party.* 3rd ed. London: Tauris, 1996. An updated version of a classic study of sectarianism and regionalism in Syrian politics.

Wedeen, Lisa: *Ambiguities of Domination: Politics, Rhetoric, and Symbols in Contemporary Syria.* Chicago: University of Chicago Press, 1999. An interesting description of how the government manipulated the public so as to secure compliance with the cult of the leader, Hafiz al-Asad.

CHAPTER 46

Iraq after World War II

Religious and linguistic diversity has strongly influenced the history of Iraq. Most Iraqis belonged to one of three groups: Shii Muslim Arabic speakers, who constituted over one-half of the total population; Sunni Muslim Arabic speakers, who numbered about 25 percent of the people; and Sunni Muslim Kurdish-language speakers, about 20 percent of the total. Despite this diversity, Sunni Arabs have held political power since independence from the Ottomans, including the monarchy, early republic, and Ba'thist eras.

Already nominally independent even before World War II, the Iraqi Hashimite monarchy was closely tied to Great Britain. As oil wealth increased after the republic was created in 1958, Iraq expanded the size and activities of government while adopting a new foreign policy. Once the Ba'th party established its dictatorship, the country set out on foreign adventures, which led to a prolonged war with the Islamic Republic of Iran and a disastrous conflict over the annexation of Kuwait.

KINGDOM OF IRAQ

During the fifteen years from the declaration of war against the Axis in 1943 until the republican revolution of 1958, Iraq underwent twenty-one changes of prime minister, with thirteen different men holding the office. But despite this apparent political instability, on six different occasions Nuri al-Said (1888–1958), a Sunni Arab nationalist and ex-Ottoman officer, was prime minister, and at all times he was the most powerful political leader in Iraq. When he was not prime minister, he still pulled the strings to direct the policies followed by others, even when Shiis held the post of prime minister.

Nuri was appointed to office by the young Hashimite king Faisal II (b. 1935), behind whom stood Abd al-Ilah, regent and crown prince. The regent's influence was felt in all quarters through the difficult years of World War II and the 1948 Arab-Israeli War. In 1953 King Faisal II reached his eighteenth year and nominally assumed full power.

Iraqi politics was strongly influenced by memories of the British invasion of Iraq during World War II, which inflamed Iraqi nationalism. Even the British recognized that their position in Iraq had to change. Iraqi leaders pressed for a new treaty to replace the one of 1930, but the Anglo-Iraqi treaty of 1948, whereby Britain retained the right to send troops in case of war, led to bitter riots and was not ratified.

Foreign policy also became entangled in the Arab Palestinian cause. In 1947 Iraq protested the partition of Palestine and sent about 18,000 soldiers to fight alongside the Arab Legion of Transjordan. The loss of the war led many Iraqis to criticize their government. Although the geographic position of Iraq meant that few Arab refugees from Palestine located there, sympathy for them ran high. Ill feeling against the Jews of Iraq mounted in proportion to the misery of the refugees and the general disillusionment over the war's outcome. In 1950, a law was passed permitting Jews to renounce their Iraqi citizenship and their property, and in the following months thousands left for Israel. Before 1951 was out, almost all of Iraq's Jews had left, creating a gap in the economy soon filled by an emerging Shii middle class.

Frustration and unrest mushroomed in Iraq, especially in Baghdad, whose population was expanding rapidly. In the countryside where the peasants were brutally oppressed and degraded by landlords, there was also widespread unhappiness with the regime. A few families owned most of the land: four-fifths of the population owned no land at all in 1958, and 2500 people held half of all the arable land. Since the landlords were highly influential in parliament, basic land reform was impossible. Other grievances included lack of full independence from Great Britain, the loss of the 1948 war, political corruption, nationalization of oil in Iran and the new fifty-fifty profit-sharing arrangement in Saudi Arabia, the high cost of living, poor harvests, and the disastrous annual flooding of sections of Baghdad.

Liberal democracy seemed a sham to many Iraqis, since elections for the chamber of deputies were usually managed by Nuri al-Said. All political parties were dissolved in 1952 and again in 1954 in an effort to force parties to reapply for licenses, some of which might be denied. The Communist party, which remained underground, found many followers in the educated youth of the lower-middle class in the large cities, in anti-imperialist nationalists, and among Shiis, the religious minorities, intellectuals, and some workers.

Increasing oil revenues helped the political incumbents maintain power. Oil production, because of the nationalization crisis in Iran, had been greatly expanded; more important, the Iraq Petroleum Company agreed in 1952 to a new schedule of royalties, increasing them to 50 percent of the profits before taxes. As world petroleum requirements spurted, royalties mounted, reaching an estimated $250 million in 1955.

After 1950 most oil royalties were devoted to economic development, especially flood control and irrigation projects on the Euphrates and Tigris rivers. By 1956 a barrage prevented serious flooding in Baghdad, and it became possible to reclaim valuable land by irrigation. Other programs cleared vast slum areas in Baghdad and built public housing.

Oil revenues allowed the monarchy to expand education. Schools were extended to push down illiteracy rates, and the University of Baghdad opened in 1957; nevertheless, the peasants in the countryside remained illiterate. While many Shiis went to secular schools and some became integrated into Iraqi society on the national level, most Kurds remained untouched by the changes of the late 1940s and 1950s. In 1951 Iraq adopted a new legal code based on a mixture of Islamic and European concepts, one of the few real reforms of the period. Iraqi short story writers, journalists, painters, and other artists and intellectuals strongly criticized the regime and described the plight of the poor in their works. The influential poet Badr Shakir al-Sayyab espoused nationalism and anti-imperialism. Despite this opposition, many Sunni Iraqi leaders saw in the future a great and prosperous Iraq; others were extremely impatient and believed that the government of Nuri al-Said moved too slowly to achieve a better life for Iraqis.

By the 1950s, Nuri and his advisers were on the U.S. side in the Cold War. In 1955, Iraq signed the so-called Baghdad Pact with Turkey, an arrangement that included military cooperation and coordination. Britain adhered to the pact by signing an important agreement with Iraq. Among other things, this agreement wiped out the treaty of 1930, provided for Britain to evacuate its troops and air force, and gave fuller sovereignty and independence to Iraq. Soon Iran and Pakistan joined the Baghdad Pact, making a chain of allied states separating the Soviet bloc from the rest of the Middle East. The United States did not join the pact but did support it in several ways.

Egypt, which viewed the Baghdad Pact as a threat to its leadership in the Arab world, accused Nuri al-Said of being the tool of Great Britain. Inside Iraq, those who were Arab nationalists or who favored neutrality in the Cold War also strongly opposed the Baghdad Pact. Nuri al-Said was confident that peace and security, as well as economic development, a higher standard of living, and a cultural and social renaissance would create a society in Iraq to parallel the splendor and wealth of Baghdad in the days of the Abbasid caliph Harun al-Rashid (786–809).

When Israel, France, and England invaded Egypt in 1956, Iraq was in an embarrassing position because its pro-western policy seemed to encourage imperialist aggression against Egypt. The Iraqi army entered Jordan, and there was great clamor in Baghdad against Great Britain as Iraqi oil exports through Syria were ended.

When the United Arab Republic began to form, political tension in Baghdad mounted. The possibility of a union between Iraq and Jordan had been discussed for many years, but the union of Syria and Egypt forced the issue. In early 1958 a federation of Iraq and Jordan was proclaimed. King Faisal was recognized as chief of state, with King Husain of Jordan second in leadership. But this attempt to preempt Nasserist Pan-Arab nationalism did not succeed; instead, the Iraqi monarchy was overthrown, and a pro-Nasser republic took its place.

REPUBLIC OF IRAQ

In a swift coup d'état on July 14, 1958, General Abd al-Karim Qasim (1914–1963) overthrew the king and Nuri al-Said, both of whom were massacred in the revolution. Revolutionary mobs in Baghdad became delirious with excitement. Qasim proclaimed the Republic of Iraq and became prime minister of the state. For a short time, oil production and foreign policy continued as before, but when King Husain of Jordan announced he was assuming the position of chief of state of the federation, Qasim renounced the union with Jordan.

The completeness of the revolution and its full acceptance by the general populace throughout the state amazed only those unfamiliar with Iraq's political and social conditions. Nuri al-Said was thoroughly disliked and the crown prince was hated. The same leaders and political system had been in power too long and had failed to satisfy the aspirations of the majority. Many Iraqis sought land reform, measures to alleviate poverty, social advancement for the urban masses, and help for the educated middle class. Most Iraqis also strenuously objected to the government's alliance with Britain and hoped for vigorous action against Israel. In the minds of the people, the old regime had allocated too much of the oil royalties to dams and less useful capital works.

Coming so soon after the birth of the United Arab Republic, General Qasim's revolution raised expectations of an immediate fulfillment of Arab unity by joining Iraq to Egypt and Syria. Colonel Abd al-Salam Muhammad Arif, second in rank among the revolutionaries, led the Nasserite group that favored such a union. Watching the trend in Syria, however, Qasim and other leaders had no desire to be puppets of Cairo. The fundamental Iraqi nationalism of these leaders forced Qasim to dismiss Arif as deputy prime minister.

Until Qasim was overthrown and executed in 1963 in a coup, his primarily Sunni regime was constantly beset by a three-way struggle: Communists and pro-Communists on one side, Nasserite Pan-Arab nationalists on another, and Iraqi Ba'thists on the third. Street fighting erupted in Baghdad at the slightest provocation. In 1959, a revolt broke out in Mosul led by anti-Communist army officers and Pan-Arabists. Blaming the United Arab Republic for plotting it, the army loyal to Qasim crushed the revolt with the aid of Kurdish forces. Qasim increasingly turned to the Communists for support.

In 1961 Qasim laid claim to Kuwait. Because of the return of British forces and the quick adverse reaction by other Arab states, Qasim did not press this claim. Qasim generally remained isolated from other Arab states but became much friendlier with the Soviet Union, Iraq's chief source of weapons.

In domestic policy, Qasim tried to obtain land reform, deal with the increasingly restive Kurds, and overcome his own narrow base of support. The government announced that a new development board would receive 50 percent of the oil royalties and would work to establish Iraq as a welfare state based on practical socialism. Under a new agricultural program, large holdings would be expropriated and distributed to landless peasants. The effect of this program was that much land was confiscated, but uncertainty over distribution meant that relatively few peasants had benefited by 1963. Tribesmen were placed under the same law codes as other Iraqi citizens, women received greater rights, and spending on education doubled.

Iraq had had persistent difficulties with the Kurds in northern Iraq since the end of World War I. The Kurdish tribes wanted independence or at least autonomy in a federalized or decentralized Iraq. Nuri al-Said left the Kurdish problem unsolved. Under the leadership of Mulla Mustafa Barzani (d. 1979), who was from a notable Sufi family, Kurdish resistance increased and then exploded in 1962 into a full-fledged revolt, placing all of rural northeastern Iraq in Kurdish hands. Because the state's major oil resources were in this region, the government was unwilling to tolerate secession or local control. The army had attempted to subdue the Kurdish provinces but had never succeeded. Each time a government in Baghdad hinted at some accommodation with Barzani, the generals showed their disaffection.

Added to the factionalism brought by Nasserism, Communism, and Iraqi nationalism, the Kurdish dilemma set the stage for a successful Ba'th party coup on February 8, 1963. Qasim lacked charisma and had been unable to articulate an appealing ideology.

Iraqi Ba'thists, dominated by the Pan-Arab executive of the Ba'th party, mostly from Damascus, engineered the coup in collaboration with the army; they immediately organized the Revolutionary Command Council and executed Qasim. But the Pan-Arab, secular, socialist, and mostly Sunni Ba'thists had only a small number of members in Iraq and lacked a base of support, so their hold on power was brief.

Colonel Arif was appointed president, and General Ahmad Hasan al-Bakr became prime minister. A roundup of Communists and subsequent murder of hundreds of them indicated the ruthlessness of the Ba'thists. The new regime, pressed by the soldiers, resumed Qasim's campaigns, remaining at odds with the Kurds, the Communists, and Nasser. By autumn Iraqi nationalists in Ba'thist circles resented the domination of the Syrian Ba'thists in every policy dispute, so all non-Iraqis were forced out of positions of influence. President Arif took power into his own hands. From 1963 to 1968, Iraq was under the personal rule of one or another of the Arab Sunni Arif brothers. When Abd al-Salam Muhammad Arif was killed in an accident in 1966, his elder brother, General Abd al-Rahman Arif, was elected president and pursued the same fundamental program and political orientation.

Neither the Arifs nor the first Ba'thist regime could alter Barzani's refusal to bargain for anything short of Kurdish autonomy and a statement in Iraq's constitution that "Iraq is a federative state of Arabs and Kurds." Barzani asserted autonomy for Iraqi Kurdistan and established a parliament. Fighting between the Kurds and the central government's army continued as in the 1966 campaign, when an offensive with 65,000 troops and heavy bombing by the air force failed, and the Kurdish forces (with help from Iran) scored some notable victories. Baghdad then tried compromise, formally accepting Kurdish nationality, language, and tradition. The central authorities said they would recognize Kurdish cultural and political autonomy, institute the decentralization of the government, permit proportionate Kurdish representation in the cabinet and the army command, and appoint Kurdish officials in Kurdish areas. Barzani accepted these proposals, but Pan-Arabs and the army were incensed at the implied surrender of the Kurds.

Inter-Arab relations in the 1960s, particularly those with Cairo, had been difficult for Iraqi leaders, and no thorough or real union with Egypt or Syria took place. At the onset of the 1967 Arab-Israeli crisis, Iraq as a sign of Pan-Arab solidarity sent 30,000 troops to Jordan to reinforce King Husain. As it turned out, Nuri al-Said, Qasim, and the two Arifs all experienced similar problems with Pan-Arabism after World War II. The first ten years of the Iraqi republic were notable for an uncertain political process based on violence, repression, the use of armed force to determine power, and repeated coups and plots. Iraq did not create institutions that could lead to the inclusion of such groups as women, Shiis, Kurds, and the poor in the political process.

BA'THIST RULE IN THE 1970s

On July 17, 1968, Arif was removed by a coup plotted by a small group of young, secularist, Arab nationalist army officers in collaboration with the Ba'th party. They coalesced under a group of leaders called the Revolutionary Command Council (R.C.C.). Controlled by the Ba'th, it named General Ahmad Hasan al-Bakr president, prime minister, and commander in chief of the armed forces.

Political existence was so dangerous for the new rulers that they constantly saw themselves confronted by spies and plotters. In the first eight months of 1969, at least fifty-four people were executed for spying for the United States, Israel, or Iran or for seeking to overturn the administration. Arrayed against the regime were conservative forces on one side and ardent Communists and left-wing Ba'thists supported by Syria on the other. In addition, the Kurds in the north continued to fight for full local autonomy, while Iraqi Shiis in the south sought religious support from the ulama in Iran. Although the Shiis of Iraq were a majority of the population, no Shii served on the R.C.C. from 1968 to 1977, and even after that real power was held by the Sunni Arab Ba'thists.

In the late 1960s a new strongman appeared, Saddam Husain al-Takriti (b. 1937), an Arab Sunni civilian from a poor family, who became assistant secretary-general of the Ba'th party, vice chairman of the R.C.C., and vice president of Iraq. Saddam Husain was gradually gaining more and more control of the government and party as the political clout of the military wing of the Ba'th party ebbed rapidly. For the next several years, there were no major challenges to the Ba'th party's power.

The new regime tended to represent the interests of the rural and small-town lower-middle class. Power was increasingly in the hands of those linked to Saddam Husain personally, whether as recipients of patronage or as relatives, fellow clansmen from the town of Takrit, others from the Sunni Arab northwestern part of the country, and those involved in the violence, murder, and intimidation used against possible opponents.

The Ba'thists now turned their attention to economic issues. In the 1960s the government had nationalized all banks, insurance companies, and some industries, and it had gained control of imports. Iraq acquired state planning and direction of the economy, of which the most important sector was oil.

Under al-Bakr and the restored Ba'thist rule, the importance of oil to the general economy increased in the 1970s. With royalties and taxes raised from 50 to 55 percent, Iraq garnered substantial oil income: about $900 million in 1971. Despite this, Iraq nationalized the Iraq Petroleum Company in 1972 and subsequently the Basrah Petroleum Company. The amount of oil produced and world oil prices continued to mount, bringing in more than $9 billion in 1976. An oil pipeline from the Kirkuk area northward and then across Turkey to the Mediterranean was completed in 1977. With the pipeline to Fao in the south, Iraq had outlets on the Persian Gulf and through Turkey, Syria, and Lebanon, ensuring multiple access to world markets. As oil wealth mounted, inflation increased, and Iraq brought in hundreds of thousands of foreign workers, especially Egyptians. Oil production in 1979 grew to more than 3 million barrels per day, and oil revenues rose to more than $21 billion!

Iraq's other economic concerns were infrastructure development, heavy industry, increased government employment so as to provide services, and agriculture. Of these, spending in agriculture had perhaps the greatest utility. Under Nuri al-Said, great emphasis had been laid on irrigation projects and dams, since a large majority of the population earned its livelihood from the land. Though later regimes were more concerned with finding income for the inhabitants of the teeming slums of Baghdad, economic plans also carried development programs for irrigation, such as the one linking the Tigris River to the Euphrates. With the completion of Syria's Euphrates Dam in 1973, Iraq worried about the possibility of war over the distribution of water, and in

1966 began construction of a large dam on the Euphrates. Salinization annually created new problems as land was lost to farmers; reclaiming land formerly farmed became a major priority of the agricultural sector.

Even though about one-half of the labor force still worked in agriculture, Iraq became a net importer of food in the 1970s. Much land that had been seized by the government was now leased or given to supporters of Saddam Husain. Land reforms by the late 1970s had led to the government's farming one-third of the land. The Ba'th party initially encouraged the formation of collectives along the model of Soviet agriculture and also state cooperatives, with greater peasant rights. In the 1980s, collectives were nearly abolished as inefficient.

Iraq in the 1970s was rich enough to undertake substantial reforms in cultural matters. The regime greatly expanded the educational system as the number of students more than doubled between 1968 and 1983. About one-third of the students were women, and many organizations were established so as to mobilize women behind the Ba'th party. While a larger proportion of Shii children attended the secular government schools than had earlier been the case, educational opportunities in Kurdish areas were still relatively sparse. Ba'thist Iraq especially encouraged scientific and technical education as new universities opened. Television broadcasts, which had begun in 1956, expanded to reach more than 350,000 receivers. About half of television programming consisted of imported shows and about half, locally produced shows. The government sponsored production of documentary films, but most films shown on television were imported.

Urban areas grew rapidly in population as their higher standard of living attracted people from the rural districts. By 1965 a majority of the population lived in cities, and by 1981 more than two-thirds of Iraqis dwelled there. Baghdad's population swelled to more than 4 million, about one-quarter of the country's population.

The Kurds continued to press for autonomy or independence in the 1970s, and Iraq responded by alternatively undertaking military campaigns and compromising with Kurdish demands. Serious fighting broke out again in 1974. The leftist Patriotic Union of Kurdistan party, led by Jalal Talabani, from time to time allied with the Ba'th against Barzani. Barzani's forces maintained a stout resistance, supplied with arms and funds from Iran, Israel, and the United States.

A diplomatic settlement in 1975 between Iran and Iraq spelled disaster for the Kurds. Iran abandoned them, while the Iraqi army mounted an offensive that killed many Kurds and gave Baghdad control of the north. The government uprooted hundreds of thousands of Kurds from their homes and scattered and transplanted them in the south as the Kurdish nationalist movement split into several factions.

Relations with Iran during most of the period after 1968 had been poor. Besides the Kurdish irritant, the two states quarreled over their Shatt al-Arab River border and the Persian or Arabian Gulf. In 1971 diplomatic relations were cut when Iran occupied Abu Musa and the Tunb Islands in the southern Gulf. In 1975 Iran and Saddam Husain struck a deal: Iraq relinquished exclusive control of the Shatt al-Arab, and the shah deserted the Kurds.

The Ba'thist regime acted to improve relations with the Soviet Union, which generally supported Iraqi policies and supplied loans for the Euphrates Dam. A Soviet-Iraqi treaty of friendship in 1972 was based on the trading of Iraqi oil for advanced Soviet weapons.

Iraq took a hard-line position against Israel and any Arab state that might be willing to compromise with it. In the 1973 war, Iraq sent an armored division to help Syria, but the hostility and rivalry between Iraqi Ba'thists and Syrian Ba'thists was so extreme that Iraq quickly withdrew its forces after the end of the fighting. In following years, Iraq gave financial and diplomatic support to the Palestinian cause. Saddam Husain denounced the Egyptian-Israeli Peace Treaty of 1979. In 1981 Israel bombed an Iraqi nuclear facility said to be ready to help produce atomic weapons for Iraq.

SADDAM HUSAIN AND THE WAR WITH IRAN

Iraqi history in the 1980s was completely dominated by the consolidation of power in the hands of Saddam Husain and the Iraqi-Iranian War of 1980–1988. President al-Bakr resigned in 1979 and was immediately succeeded by Saddam Husain, who also became chairman of the Revolutionary Command Council, secretary-general of the Ba'th party regional (Iraq) command, and head of the armed forces. Saddam Husain then conveniently discovered a plot that made it necessary for him to execute his chief rivals and consolidate all power in his own hands. A personality cult centered around Saddam made his image familiar to all Iraqis, while a semblance of democracy was created. After a lapse of twenty-two years, an Iraqi parliament met once again: a national assembly was elected in 1980. It included a substantial Shii as well as female membership but lacked any substantial power and was completely subordinate to Saddam Husain and the Ba'th party. The party grew in the 1980s and was put in charge of all the key positions in trade unions, the schools, and the government. It even had its own militia, a counterbalance to the regular armed forces.

Saddam established a security state, similar to that in Syria and in some other parts of the Middle East. Opponents were ruthlessly persecuted by the internal security forces, who executed a large number of persons in the 1980s. The government secretly killed the Iraqi Shii religious leader and theologian Baqir al-Sadr, and the Ba'th militia destroyed an underground Shii fundamentalist organization. The Sunni ulama were already state employees and the government would later add the Shii ulama as paid employees, while also closely monitoring the content of Friday sermons. Censorship was pervasive, and the media were tightly controlled.

The regime used the carrot as well as the stick. The government built roads and schools, and it refurbished mosques in Shii southern Iraq and in Kurdish northern Iraq. The Ba'th also took into the power elite young Shiis and Kurds who would cooperate with the party. Saddam Husain appointed more Shiis to party and government positions in the mid-1980s, while the Kurdish nationalists became divided after the death of Mustafa Barzani in 1979 as they split along various ideological and leadership lines. Saddam tried to gain popular support by using symbols to evoke the historical legacy of pre-Islamic and early Islamic Iraq, including such projects as the rebuilding of a version of ancient Babylon and promoting the works of the ninth-century writer al-Jahiz. Sculptors, architects, cartoonists, and artists of all kinds were co-opted by the regime to create elaborate propaganda. By 1980 the Iraqi rulers seemed in complete political, economic, and military control of their once-chaotic country, while Iran was undergoing a revolutionary upheaval.

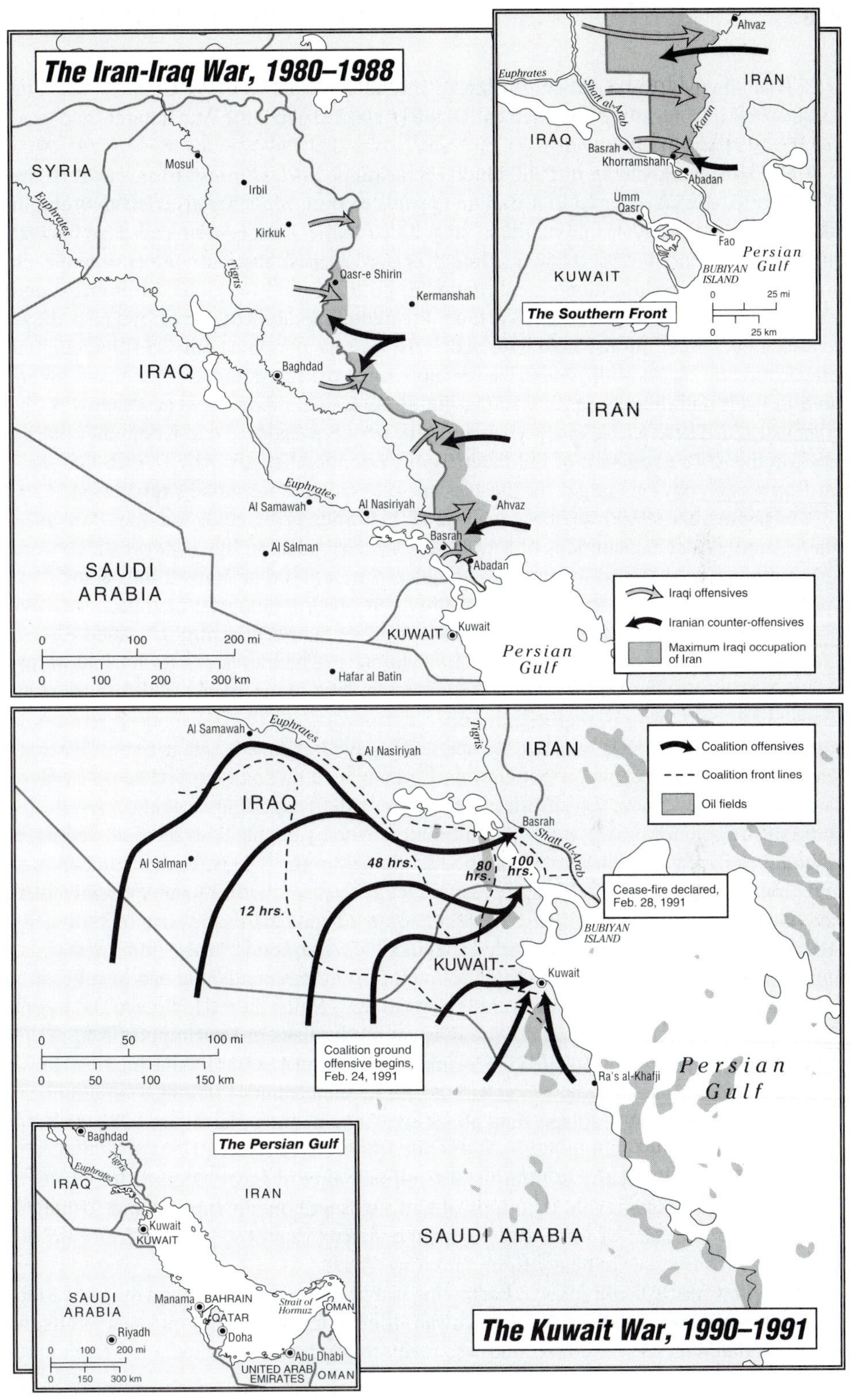

The Iran-Iraq War, 1980–1988
SYRIA
Mosul
Irbil
Kirkuk
Euphrates
Tigris
Qasr-e Shirin
Kermanshah
IRAQ
Baghdad
IRAN
Euphrates
Al Samawah
Al Nasiriyah
Ahvaz
Al Salman
Basrah
Abadan
SAUDI ARABIA
KUWAIT
Kuwait
Hafar al Batin
Persian Gulf
0 100 200 mi
0 100 200 300 km
Iraqi offensives
Iranian counter-offensives
Maximum Iraqi occupation of Iran
The Southern Front
Ahvaz
Euphrates
Shatt al-Arab
IRAN
Karun
IRAQ
Basrah
Khorramshahr
Abadan
Umm Qasr
Fao
Persian Gulf
KUWAIT
BUBIYAN ISLAND
0 25 mi
0 25 km
The Kuwait War, 1990–1991
Al Samawah
Euphrates
Al Nasiriyah
Tigris
IRAN
IRAQ
Basrah
Shatt al-Arab
Al Salman
48 hrs.
80 hrs.
100 hrs.
12 hrs.
Cease-fire declared, Feb. 28, 1991
BUBIYAN ISLAND
KUWAIT
Kuwait
Coalition ground offensive begins, Feb. 24, 1991
Ra's al-Khafji
Persian Gulf
SAUDI ARABIA
0 50 100 mi
0 50 100 150 km
Coalition offensives
Coalition front lines
Oil fields
The Persian Gulf
Baghdad
Tigris
Euphrates
IRAQ
IRAN
Kuwait
KUWAIT
SAUDI ARABIA
Manama
BAHRAIN
QATAR
Doha
Strait of Hormuz
OMAN
Riyadh
Abu Dhabi
UNITED ARAB EMIRATES
OMAN
0 100 200 mi
0 150 300 km

This situation led Saddam Husain to invade Iran in 1980 (see Chapter 40). The 1980–1988 Iraq-Iran War has been called the (first) Persian Gulf War, a name also used for the 1991 war over Kuwait.

Saddam attacked Iran in 1980 chiefly to advance his own prestige as leader of the Arab world. He also feared that Iranian appeals to Iraqi Shiis for his overthrow might lead to serious upheavals that might endanger his regime. Longer-term causes of the war included the rivalry between Iran and Iraq over border questions; the competition of each for regional leadership; ideological, national, political, and religious differences; and mutual interference in each other's affairs. President Saddam Husain of Iraq also chose to attack because of more immediate concerns. He saw an opportunity to fill a regional power vacuum. In addition, Iraq's leadership sought to secure border alignments favorable to itself and thereby to reverse the humiliating deal made between the two countries in 1975. There was also a personal rivalry between Saddam and Khomeini, dating back to the 1978 expulsion of the latter from Iraq. Socialist, secularist, Arab nationalist Iraq was an obvious target for the export of the Islamic Republic's revolution.

In September 1980 Iraq abrogated the 1975 border agreement, and then it invaded Iran. Initially Iraqi expectations of a rapid victory over a demoralized and weak foe were substantiated. Iraq seized much of southwestern Iran and then moved into Kurdistan, while Saddam appealed to memories of the Arab Muslim conquest of Iran in the seventh century. Iran spent months mobilizing, training, and organizing its armed forces, including the Revolutionary Guards. By March 1981, Iraq reached its maximum advance into Iran, but Iran assumed the offensive, first in air attacks and then, despite internal political turmoil, on the ground.

Iraq had many limitations that subsequently gave Iran an advantage in the fighting. These included Iraq's smaller population; limits placed on Iraqi exports of oil by Syrian and Iranian actions; the surprising strength of the Iranian government, despite its internal struggle for power, a struggle ultimately won by people who seemed incapable of compromise; and, most important, the fact that although Iraq was unable to conquer and hold all of Iran, Iran could aspire to conquer at least southern Iraq and possibly even take Baghdad. On the other hand, Iraq had some advantages in the war, including its superior armaments. Once Iran invaded Iraq in 1984, Arab Iraqis, both Sunnis and Shiis, fought with great enthusiasm for their country, putting nationalism ahead of religion.

The Soviet Union was slow to supply arms to Iraq, which turned to France and Egypt for additional sources of weapons. Arabic-speaking Iranians did not support Iraq in the war; instead, they remained loyal to the Islamic Republic, just as Iraqi Shiis remained loyal to Iraq. In general, the Iraqi invasion had the unintended result of uniting many Iranians behind their leaders. Subsequent Iraqi attacks on Iranian cities, starting in 1983, seemed to have the same effect.

Iran had great difficulty in securing new military aircraft and spare parts for its older, U.S.-built planes. As a result, its troops often fought without air support and sustained heavy losses, while the air force was occupied in defensive roles. However, Iran enjoyed some limited successes in heavy fighting during 1982.

Iraq, now nearly bankrupt, was borrowing heavily from the French and the Gulf Arab oil states, especially Saudi Arabia and Kuwait. Iranian revenues from oil sales were sufficient to maintain its war effort. Iraq was ready to accept foreign mediation to end the war, but Iran rejected this possibility. Iran's position was that Iraq had started the war, and its ruling group must pay a heavy price for doing so, including the payment of reparations and the punishment and/or overthrow of Saddam Husain and his regime. The Islamic Republic of Iran hoped to see a government similar to its own created in Baghdad.

In early 1984, Iran launched major attacks on south-central Iraq, expecting to isolate Basrah. Nearly 500,000 soldiers fought each other in difficult terrain, and casualties were heavy, especially for Iran. Iraq's use of poison gas, its aerial superiority, and the relative lack of offensive heavy equipment on the Iranian side led to Iran's greater casualties. But since the Iranian population was about three times larger than that of Iraq and since many of the Iranian fighters believed that death would make them religious martyrs entitled to enter paradise, Iran accepted heavy casualties. Massed human waves of Iranians attacked entrenched Iraqi positions. By early 1984, perhaps 170,000 Iranian combatants had been killed versus 80,000 Iraqis. Many hundreds of thousands on both sides had been wounded, and millions of civilians had become refugees.

Iraq intensified its efforts to stop Iranian exports of oil. Attacks on Iranian oil facilities and tankers increased, but Iranian exports of oil reached about 1.5 to 2 million barrels per day. Iran stopped the export of Iraqi oil through the Persian Gulf, but Iraq did export some petroleum through Turkey. Iraq's economy slowed as it proved impossible to pay for the war and maintain regular civilian expenditures at the same time. From 1981 through 1985, Iraqi oil production averaged slightly more than 1 million barrels per day, and income from oil was about $10 billion per year. In 1983 austerity measures had to be taken.

A shortage of civilian workers led to the employment of women in greater numbers. The government banned contraception and abortion so as to increase the population, thereby replacing Iraqis killed in the war. The status of women did not substantially improve as a result of the war, as could be seen in 1988 when a new law legalized so-called honor killings, in which men killed female relatives who were accused of adultery.

In 1987 the regime reorganized the state-owned sector of the economy and increased the role of private entrepreneurs in industry. Iraq also turned ever more to the Soviet Union for help, buying about half of its weapons from that source at a cost of around $23 billion. Iraq did reestablish full diplomatic relations with the United States in 1984, although the Iran-Contra arrangements disillusioned the Iraqi leadership about the supposed tilt of the United States toward Iraq. Saddam also received substantial assistance from Jordan and Egypt.

In the spring of 1985, Iran began a major offensive across the Shatt al-Arab River, and Iraq responded with the so-called war of the cities. Iraq heavily bombed Tehran, Isfahan, and other cities, while Iran responded with missile attacks against Baghdad. In a surprise attack, Iran took the Iraqi Fao peninsula close to Kuwait in 1986.

From 1980, and particularly between 1985 and 1988, Iraqi Kurdish rebels backed by Iran fought against the Baghdad government with some considerable local success. Iraq ultimately crushed them, in part through the use of poison gas attacks, executions, and massive deportations. Saddam Husain ordered the destruction of about 80 percent of Kurdish villages and the killing of between 150,000 and 200,000 Kurdish civilians in an extraordinary demonstration of brutality aimed at the forcible ending of Kurdish resistance in the northern part of Iraq. International sponsors of Iraq, such as France and the United States, did little to stop these events.

Iran came within 10 kilometers of Basrah as a result of large-scale campaigns in early 1987, but that nearly deserted and heavily damaged city remained in Iraqi hands. Iraq then assumed the offensive and retook the Fao peninsula. Iraq was advancing in most sections of the front lines in 1988 when suddenly the morale of the Iranian armed forces collapsed. On July 18, 1988, Iran accepted a truce with Iraq. A cease-fire soon took effect as United Nations observers were deployed.

Casualties were high: about 300,000 Iranians and 135,000 or more Iraqis killed and about 750,000 on both sides wounded. Economic destruction was enormous. The total direct and indirect cost of the war to Iraq was more than $400 billion, and to Iran more than $600 billion. Iraq's foreign debts also mounted rapidly during the war. Taking into account inflation, Iraq's per capita gross domestic product in 1990 had fallen by more than one-half from the level of 1979. Yet despite these staggering human and economic losses, the war essentially ended as a stalemate with neither side gaining any significant territorial, political, or economic advantage.

THE KUWAIT WAR

Iraq's history in the 1990s was dominated by the events associated with the 1991 war for Kuwait, a conflict also called the Second Persian Gulf War. The causes of Iraq's 1990 invasion of Kuwait, the reaction of the world community, the 1991 combat, the ensuing Shii and Kurdish uprisings, and the resulting weakness of Iraq's central government have all profoundly affected the population of Iraq in recent years.

The 1991 war for Kuwait was triggered by Saddam Husain's invasion of Kuwait on August 2, 1990. Reasons for the decision to invade were diverse, including economic factors, a new international environment, Pan-Arab nationalism, domestic pressures, and personal motives. Iraqis argued that the enormous oil wealth of Kuwait should be spread more evenly and justly among all Arabs, starting with the Iraqis, rather than accruing to the small population of Kuwaitis. World oil prices were said to be low because of overproduction of oil by several countries, including Kuwait, and this meant less money for Iraq. If Iraq and Kuwait united, they would have about 20 percent of the world's oil reserves. Iraq's dire domestic situation also put pressure on Saddam: to restore the damage caused by the Iran-Iraq War of 1980–1988 was extremely costly, yet Iraq was heavily burdened by external debts owed to many countries, including Kuwait. Internationally, the end of the Cold War between the United States and the Soviet Union, and the lessening of Soviet backing for such countries as Iraq, seemed from Iraq's perspective to create in the Middle East a temporary power vacuum, but one that might be filled by the United States in the long run. Iraq was, at least for the moment, the leading military force in the Arab East and in the Persian Gulf region, possessing a large and experienced military, with expensive, secret programs aimed at developing atomic, chemical, and bacteriological weapons. Demobilization of the large Iraqi army seemed politically and economically risky. Pan-Arab nationalists in Iraq argued that Kuwait should not exist as a separate city-state; it was, they claimed, a creation of British imperialism, artificially separated from Ottoman-ruled southern Iraq. Iraq also needed a greater water frontage on the Gulf and disputed the location of its border with Kuwait. The Iraqi regime had emerged from the war with

Iran without any major gains to justify the enormous casualties; a short, decisive campaign against Kuwait could provide Saddam and the Iraqi Ba'th with needed glory, legitimacy, and prestige. Saddam Husain had already displayed his aggressive expansionism, use of violence, impulsive behavior, poor judgment, and ignorance of international diplomacy on earlier occasions, and particularly when he chose to invade Iran in 1980; in 1990 he exhibited the same characteristics and brought further disaster on his country while preserving his own rule.

Kuwaitis systematically rejected the arguments used by Iraq, pointing to the international consensus opposed to the forcible annexation of one country by another. In terms of political legitimacy, Kuwait had existed under its ruling dynasty for considerably longer than had independent Iraq. Kuwait had financially aided Iraq and other Arab states, as well as the Palestinians. Iraq's real economic difficulties, according to Kuwaitis, had arisen from the Iran-Iraq War, not from the international price of oil. Kuwait's neighbors, and particularly Saudi Arabia, were convinced that Saddam Husain was intent ultimately on annexing more than just Kuwait. He aimed to control the entire Arab world.

When Iraq invaded and occupied much smaller Kuwait quickly, Kuwaiti authorities fled to Saudi Arabia, where they established a government in exile. Reaction to Iraq's actions in most parts of the world was negative. Whatever Iraq's grievances were, most governments argued that the Iraqi invasion and annexation of Kuwait were illegal according to both United Nations and Arab League charters.

The United States had earlier adopted a pro-Iraqi position during the Iran-Iraq War and had taken steps over 1988–1990 demonstrating its friendship for Iraq, including diplomatic support, agricultural credits, intelligence information derived from satellites, and some dual-use military equipment. Despite this, Washington was now gravely concerned that if Saddam were successful in Kuwait, he would be able to intimidate and possibly even invade Saudi Arabia, thus adversely affecting the price and availability of oil, as well as upsetting the regional balance of power and opening the way for other countries throughout the world to invade and annex small neighboring states at will. The United Nations, the Soviet Union, a majority of the Arab League countries, Iran, Turkey, Israel, and the European Community nations condemned the invasion and urged Iraq to withdraw from Kuwait. Actions taken by the United Nations Security Council included economic sanctions, a blockade, and eventually an authorization to use "all necessary means" to compel Iraq to retreat.

Limited support for Iraq emerged among Palestinian Arabs, some Pan-Arab nationalists, and a few governments such as Jordan, the Sudan, and Yemen (which had a seat on the U.N. Security Council). These sources opposed the use of force by external powers to compel Iraq's withdrawal, and some among them viewed Saddam as the only person who could unite the Arabs, defy the United States, and forcibly oppose Israel.

The United States gradually sent more than 500,000 troops and many aircraft and warships to eastern Saudi Arabia and the Persian Gulf as the major part of the Desert Shield project to protect Saudi oil fields. Ultimately then president George Bush expanded his goals to include the liberation of Kuwait. Saudi Arabia, the other Gulf Arab states, France, Britain, Egypt, and even Ba'thist Syria contributed large numbers of soldiers, totaling about 200,000, while symbolic units or financial aid came from Germany, Japan, and some other countries. After much negotiating, a dual chain of command was created:

Middle Eastern and other Muslim forces operated under the coordination of Saudi Arabia, and all other forces accepted the leadership of the United States. President Bush and King Fahd of Saudi Arabia jointly decided all key issues after consulting the various allies and the United Nations.

Iraq reacted to the military buildup in Saudi Arabia by seizing foreign hostages, increasing its military mobilization, and harshly administering and looting Kuwait. Saddam and the Iraqi Ba'thists, who had been famous for their secularism, sought to appear more devout, declaring the struggle over Kuwait a jihad. There was also an attempt to link the Kuwaiti issue to the question of an independent Palestinian state, Iraq pointing to the inability of the United Nations to enforce its resolutions pertaining to Israel. Iraq yielded territory to Iran, hoping to reinforce its neutrality. Most important, Saddam refused to accept compromise suggestions presented by mediators, such as the Soviets or King Husain of Jordan, with the key issue being Iraq's guaranteed withdrawal from Kuwait.

The day after the expiration of the United Nations deadline of January 15, 1991, the allied coalition launched a massive air war, Operation Desert Storm, against Iraq and occupied Kuwait. Enormous numbers of bombs were used—more than the total destructive force against Nazi Germany during all of World War II. Damage to Iraqi troops, weapons, infrastructure, and morale was substantial. Iraq had close to 1 million men under arms and more than 5000 tanks, but its armed forces were weakened by political interference and the apparent hopelessness of fighting against so many other countries. Iraq sent much of its air force to Iran, where it was interned. Iran. Jordan, and Turkey remained neutral during the fighting, but Turkey permitted U.S. airplanes to attack Iraq from Turkish bases, while Jordan and its Palestinian Arab citizens were sympathetic to Iraq. At the request of the United States, which feared the Arab states might break away from the coalition, Israel did not join in the fighting even when Iraq launched missiles against it.

The second phase of the war was a ground attack starting on February 24, 1991, and lasting a mere four days. Allied forces directly invaded Kuwait on the eastern part of the front while the crucial strategic thrust was around the Iraqi lines to the west, as American and other forces moved into southern Iraq, nearly surrounding the Iraqis, who hurriedly retreated from Kuwait. Many Iraqi soldiers deserted; others surrendered in large groups to the allies. Iraq had to accept a cease-fire on allied terms.

Iraq suffered many military casualties during the war as compared to a much smaller number of allied losses. But Iraq's travail did not end with the war, since there immediately ensued two separate uprisings against the Ba'thist administration. In southern and central Iraq, Shii Iraqis rebelled, and in northern Iraq Kurds resumed their struggle. Saddam crushed the Shii rebellion with great brutality, and more than 1.5 million Kurds fled to Iran and Turkey as he attacked the north. Eventually Saddam had to yield autonomy to Kurds operating in a small zone in northern Iraq, because the allied forces, chiefly the United States, sent in troops and enforced a no-fly order forbidding Iraqi airplanes to fly over northern (and southern) Iraq.

Other consequences of the war included the restoration of independence for Kuwait and, ironically, the continuation in power of Saddam Husain. Even though Iraq suffered enormous damage and the war was clearly a disastrous defeat, Saddam Husain continued to preside over a devastated and greatly weakened country.

The consequences of the Kuwait War extended beyond Iraq and Kuwait. Hundreds of thousands of refugees fled to other countries during the crisis. The war also opened the way to actions by the United States designed to secure an end to the Arab-Israeli dispute, the first step of which was the peace conference held in 1991 in Madrid. Pan-Arab nationalism was in disarray as a result of the war, which pitted Arab country against Arab country. Although in 1990–1991 the Soviet Union had played a substantial role, its collapse and the ending of Communist rule ended Russian power in the Middle East, at least for a time. Instead, in this first major post–Cold War crisis the United States and a weakened Soviet Union cooperated on most foreign policy issues while strengthening the United Nations. The United States emerged as the dominant external force in the Middle East and, indeed, in the entire world. For the peoples of the Middle East, the Kuwait War marked the most extreme outside intervention in their region of the globe since the two world wars.

IRAQ AFTER THE KUWAIT WAR

Saddam Husain's power was seemingly absolute in most parts of Iraq, but the United Nations, the United States, the Iraqi Kurds, the economic catastrophe caused by the war, and the endemic uncertainty about national unity raised substantial doubts about the longevity of his regime and even the durability of the state.

The United Nations, led by the United States, was determined to set limits on Iraq's military capabilities and alter its international and domestic behavior. A series of U.N. resolutions aimed at disarming Iraq, acquiring full information about its weapons programs, having Iraq pay war reparations, establishing new and clearly demarcated borders for Kuwait, and compelling Iraq to acknowledge Kuwait's sovereignty. Slowly Iraq complied with most of the resolutions, but it attempted to delay their effects or to alter records so as to retain hidden military strength.

Using secret funds kept overseas, Iraq imported food, but the United Nations would allow it to export oil and freely import other items only if Saddam Husain fully accepted all U.N. resolutions. The effect of the U.N. embargo was mixed. Spare parts for military weapons became harder to acquire, the standard of living of most Iraqis fell considerably (even compared to the Iran-Iraq War years), and inflation grew drastically. The Iraqi economy recovered somewhat from the terrible effects of the 1991 bombing: most infrastructure was restored, enough oil was produced for domestic needs and some was smuggled to neighboring states, rationing of essential items was handled well, and crops were planted so that Iraq grew much of its own food. Taking inflation into account, oil revenue in 1994 was about what it had been in 1960, although Iraq's population had tripled in the meantime. In May 1996 Iraq and the United Nations agreed that every three months Iraq could sell $1 billion worth of oil under strict U.N. supervision and required that the proceeds be used for humanitarian supplies and war reparations. While the Ba'th party elite, the security forces, and the military continued to live well, poorer Iraqis, and particularly the very young and the very old, suffered enormously.

Elections in the Kurdish zone of northern Iraq resulted initially in a compromise government in which power was shared between the two chief Kurdish groups—Masud

Barzani's Kurdish Democratic Party and Jalal Talabani's Patriotic Union of Kurdistan. In 1996 and 1997 the two groups fought each other, ending their joint government and establishing two separate regimes. Divided by region, ideology, foreign allegiances, and personal struggles for power, the two groups' mutual enmity severely weakened Kurdish power vis-à-vis Baghdad and diminished the possibility of overthrowing Saddam Husain. Nevertheless, the Iraqi Kurds preserved their autonomy under the umbrella of protection and aid provided by the United States.

The central government in Baghdad started to enjoy greater income as the United Nations Security Council, acting under pressure from Russia, China, and France, authorized Iraq to sell more oil abroad. By October 1999 Iraq could legally export about $8 billion worth of oil every six months, although some of the resulting revenue had to be spent on the Kurdish north and for war reparations. Income from oil was about $4 billion in 1997, but, including illegal exports, it rose to about $20 billion in 2000 as the world price of oil increased. Much of this money was spent on rebuilding the Iraqi military and maintaining the extensive secret police forces.

Economic conditions for most of the population remained grim. About 3 million Iraqis left the country to live abroad. Infant mortality was high, unemployment and crime increased, the quality of education steadily declined, interruptions in the supply of electricity were frequent, and groups suspected of political disloyalty—such as the Shiis—were punished economically. Despite these developments, overall population increased to an estimated 22 million by 1997, as compared to 12 million people in 1977, and the birthrate was among the highest in the world. The central government administered food rationing so as to increase its political control over the people. Bribery and corruption became widespread as the state of the economy destroyed the savings and livelihood of the middle class, while many poorer Iraqis were in truly desperate circumstances.

Continuing disputes between the government of Iraq and the United Nations inspectors searching for prohibited weapons of mass destruction escalated in 1998, eventually leading to the withdrawal of all inspectors and joint American and British air attacks in December on suspected Iraqi storage and production facilities. In subsequent years the two allies attacked Iraqi anti-aircraft facilities on many occasions, while also threatening to overthrow the government of Saddam Husain by supporting political opposition groups, backing coup attempts, and aiding Kurdish resistance in northern Iraq. The reaction by the Ba'th regime was to further crush any potential internal opposition, intensify patronage and rewards for tribes and the elite military units that were wedded to the government, and seek diplomatic support abroad. Using the promise of commerce and military sales, Iraq appealed to European and Arab governments and companies as well as to those who opposed American influence in the Middle East. By 2000–2001 this policy was successful to some degree, as could be seen in the reestablishment of diplomatic ties with Bahrain, Qatar, and the United Arab Emirates and the friendlier economic relationship with Syria. However, the United States seemed implacably opposed to Saddam Husain's regime because of its failure to eliminate weapons of mass destruction and its military adventurism.

U.S. President George W. Bush in 2002 repeatedly condemned Iraq for hiding weapons of mass destruction as he led a military and diplomatic effort to compel Saddam Husain to destroy the weapons or to be overthrown. The United States began to move tens of thousands of its soldiers close to Iraq, while also trying to mobilize an allied coalition. On November 8, 2002, the United Nations Security Council unanimously passed Resolution 1441, which called for the return of U.N. arms inspectors to Iraq and the strict application of new rules designed to discover Iraqi weapons. The U.N. arms inspectors had received only limited cooperation from Iraqi authorities as of late 2002.

Despite Iraq's many problems, the regime resisted all attempts to overthrow it, thereby preserving Sunni Arab rule. The unity of Iraq has been maintained although integrating Shii Arabs and Kurds fully into the political process has not yet been successfully achieved and, in the case of the Kurds, real doubt must exist as to their ultimate allegiance to the concept of Iraq. The reasons for the longevity of the Ba'th and Iraqi centralism included the loyalty of most of the armed forces, resulting in part from favorable treatment by the government, plus repeated purges and executions of all persons who might oppose Saddam. Another factor was fear among Iraqis and foreign governments alike that removing the Ba'th dictatorship would open Iraq to a civil war similar to the 1975–1990 conflict in Lebanon. Many in the Sunni Iraqi minority dreaded a Shii-dominated Iraq or the possible secession of Kurdish northern Iraq and the annexation of parts of Iraq by neighboring states. The most important long-range issues facing Iraq remain those of national integration of ethnic and religious groups in a diverse society.

REFERENCES

References cited at the end of Chapters 32, 35, and 44 are pertinent to this chapter as well.

Alnasrawi, Abbas: *The Economy of Iraq: Oil, Wars, Destruction of Development and Prospects, 1950–2010.* Westport, Conn.: Greenwood Press, 1994. An excellent overview by a leading authority on the subject.

Baram, Amatzia: *Culture, History and Ideology in the Formation of Ba'thist Iraq, 1968–89.* London: Macmillan, 1991. Shows how the regime has used the early history of Iraq to promote its political agenda.

———: "The Effect of Iraqi Sanctions: Statistical Pitfalls and Responsibility." *Middle East Journal* 54 (2000): 194–223. A thorough review of the suffering of Iraqis since 1990.

Bin, Alberto, *et al.,* eds.: *Desert Storm: A Forgotten War.* Westport, Conn.: Praeger, 1998. An excellent military history, including firsthand accounts by American participants.

Birdwood, Lord: *Nuri al-Said: A Study in Arab Leadership.* London: Cassell, 1959. A political biography.

Cordesman, Anthony H.: *Iraq and the War of Sanctions: Conventional Threats and Weapons of Mass Destruction.* Westport, Conn.: Praeger, 1999. A lengthy study of Iraq's military in the 1990s and early 2000s.

DeYoung, Terri: *Placing the Poet: Badr Shakir al-Sayyab and Postcolonial Iraq.* Albany: State University of New York Press, 1998. A complex analysis of the life and works of the Iraqi poet.

Elliott, Matthew: *'Independent Iraq': The Monarchy and British Influence, 1941–58.* London: Tauris, 1996. Political history based chiefly on the British archives.

Farouk-Sluglett, Marion, and Peter Sluglett: *Iraq since 1958: From Revolution to Dictatorship.* 3d ed. London: Tauris, 2001. An excellent general history.

Fernea, Robert A., and Wm. R. Louis, eds.: *The Iraqi Revolution of 1958: The Old Social Classes Revisited.* London: Tauris, 1991. Twelve essays on internal and foreign themes.

Gause, R. Gregory: "Iraq's Decision to Go to War, 1980 and 1990." *Middle East Journal* 56 (2002): 47–70. This prominent analyst of Arab politics argues that the chief cause for Saddam Husain going to war in both 1980 and 1990 was his perception of a threat to his power.

Gunter, Michael M.: *The Kurdish Predicament in Iraq: A Political Analysis.* New York: St. Martin's, 1999. Useful for the 1990s.

Hassanpour, Amir: *Nationalism and Language in Kurdistan, 1918–1985.* San Francisco: Mellen Research University Press, 1992. Concentrates on the Kurdish language.

Helms, Christine Moss: *Iraq: Eastern Flank of the Arab World.* Washington, D.C.: Brookings Institution, 1984. Contains especially useful chapters on the Ba'th party and the war with Iran.

Hiro, Dilip: *The Longest War: The Iran-Iraq Military Conflict.* New York: Routledge, 1991. The best summary of the 1980–1988 Iraq-Iran War.

———: *Desert Shield to Desert Storm: The Second Gulf War.* New York: Routledge, 1992. A lengthy account of all aspects of the 1990–1991 Kuwait crisis and war.

Hopwood, Derek, et al, eds.: *Iraq: Power and Society.* Reading, England: Ithaca, 1993. Essays by British, French, and German scholars on Iraqi politics, economics, and foreign relations.

Karsh, Efraim, and Inari Rautsi: *Saddam Hussein: A Political Biography.* New York: Free Press, 1991. Ascribes Saddam's actions to a search for absolute power and personal glory.

Khadduri, Majid: *Republican Iraq: A Study of Iraqi Politics since the Revolution of 1958.* New York: Oxford University Press, 1969. Detached and objective, with painstaking attention to detail and accuracy.

———: *Socialist Iraq: A Study in Iraqi Politics since 1968.* Washington, D.C.: Middle East Institute, 1978. A continuation of *Republican Iraq* by the same author.

Khadduri, Majid, and Edmund Ghareeb: *War in the Gulf, 1990–91: The Iraq-Kuwait Conflict and Its Implications.* New York: Oxford University Press, 1997. This careful account of the war gives the official Iraqi point of view much weight.

Mahdi, Kamil A.: *State and Agriculture in Iraq: Modern Development, Stagnation and the Impact of Oil.* Reading, England: Ithaca Press, 2000. A survey of the history of Iraqi agriculture from the nineteenth century to the 1970s.

Makiya, Kanan: *Republic of Fear: The Politics of Modern Iraq.* 2d ed. Berkeley: University of California Press, 1998. A highly critical and well-informed discussion of how the Iraqi regime has been able to maintain itself in power.

Musallam, Musallam Ali: *The Iraqi Invasion of Kuwait: Saddam Hussein, His State and International Power Politics.* London: British Academic Press, 1996. A clear account of various explanations for Saddam Husain's 1990 decision to invade Kuwait.

Roy, Delwin A.: "The Educational System of Iraq." *Middle Eastern Studies* 29 (1993): 167–197. Covers the subject up to the 1980s, including the status of women and technological change.

Smolansky, Oles M., and Bettie M. Smolansky: *The USSR and Iraq: The Soviet Quest for Influence.* Durham, N.C.: Duke University Press, 1991. Demonstrates a complicated interaction between the two countries, with Iraq often having acted against Soviet wishes.

CHAPTER 47

Smaller Arabian States

South of Iraq, the Arabian Peninsula is divided among seven Arab states. On the east, along the Persian Gulf, are the small countries of Bahrain, Kuwait, Qatar, and the United Arab Emirates. Oman is on the southeastern and southern shores of the Arabian Peninsula. The great central mass of the peninsula consists of the Kingdom of Saudi Arabia, which also controls the region of al-Hasa facing the Persian Gulf between Kuwait and Qatar, and the eastern shore of the Red Sea from the Gulf of Aqaba southward through Asir. United Yemen occupies the south and southwest of the peninsula. (Yemen will be discussed in Chapter 48; Saudi Arabia and the history of oil in Chapter 49.)

Bahrain, Kuwait, Qatar, the United Arab Emirates, and Oman have shared many similar characteristics. Most of these states have been sparsely inhabited and have only small amounts of arable land. Some areas of Oman form an exception to this rule; there one can find substantial agricultural regions and a denser concentration of people. The peoples of the various states share a similarity in language, religion, and culture. Almost all citizens speak Arabic, although there are substantial dialectical differences. A majority are Sunni Muslims. In Bahrain, however, there is a Shii majority, and a substantial Shii minority resides in other countries as well. Oman has a slight Ibadi (Kharijite) majority. Most of the countries have witnessed only a slow rate of political change, although their economies and societies have seen a great deal of modernization. Ruling families have permeated the institutions of government, thereby helping to ensure, along with considerable wealth derived from oil, the longevity of conservative monarchies in power.

All of the countries were controlled or substantially influenced by Great Britain throughout most of the twentieth century. One example of this far-reaching British influence was the use of the Indian rupee as the currency in the Gulf states, to be supplanted by their own separate national currencies between 1961 and 1970. The United States replaced Britain as the chief military power in the area by the 1980s. All of the states joined the United Nations, the Arab League, and the World Trade Organization. Bahrain, Kuwait, Qatar, the United Arab Emirates, and Oman in 1981 formed the Gulf Cooperation Council, led by Saudi Arabia, so as to coordinate policies in a number of areas. All of the states were substantially affected by the Kuwait War of 1991, with all assisting in the liberation of Kuwait from Iraqi control.

The presence or absence of oil has been the chief variable among the various states. Those with oil are said to have rentier systems of government. In a rentier state, vast oil wealth, gained without much effort, is kept in part by the ruler and his family and partially distributed by the ruler to various elements in society so as to maintain their loyalty. Such distribution of oil wealth by the rulers allowed them to become very powerful. The rentier states established pervasive welfare measures on behalf of all the people. Most rulers kept power in their own hands rather than sharing it, substituting for the slogan of the eighteenth-century American colonists—no taxation without representation—the concept of no taxation *and* no representation.

Those countries possessing quantities of oil undertook massive social and economic change; the most notable example is Kuwait. Those countries with little oil, or which only recently discovered their oil and natural gas, have continued to be relatively poor. Oil had a large impact first on Bahrain and Kuwait, then Qatar, the United Arab Emirates, and Oman.

BAHRAIN

Bahrain is a kingdom composed of several islands totaling about 240 square miles (620 square km.) and standing about 20 miles (30 km.) off the coast of Saudi Arabia and the Qatar peninsula in the Persian Gulf. Its population in 2001 numbered about 640,000.

Inhabited largely by Arabs and ruled by Iran from 1602 to 1782, Bahrain was taken in 1783 by Sunni Arabs led by the Al Khalifah family. It was contested between the Saudis, Iran, and Oman, but it ultimately became a British dependency, with a quasi-protectorate established by agreements made in 1880 and 1892. Local political power was held by the Al Khalifah rulers, who were notable for their longevity: the period from 1869 to 1961 was divided among only three princes. Except for pearl fishing, Bahrain was quite unimportant until the presence of oil was suspected in the 1920s.

Two U.S. companies, Standard Oil of California and the Texas Company, formed the Bahrain Petroleum Company (Bapco) and obtained the concession. Oil in commercial quantities was discovered in 1932, and Bahrain oil entered world markets in 1934. A refinery was constructed to handle Bahrain's output of 30,000 barrels a day and, later, an additional 125,000 barrels coming from Saudi Arabia by an underwater pipeline. In 1952 Bapco entered into an equal profit-sharing agreement with Bahrain's ruler, which gave him about $8 million a year in royalties to add to his $3 million income from taxes. Bapco signed an agreement with the amir in 1974, turning over 100 percent of the company to the government. In 1976, the Bahrain National Oil Company was formed by the government to hold the oil rights; Bapco, however, continued to manage the business. Bahrain's oil reserves were quite limited, but improved production techniques increased output in the 1970s to about 66,000 barrels daily.

Bahrain's financial condition remained stationary until oil prices jumped in 1973 and Bahraini oil revenues topped $100 million a year. The government in the 1970s tried for economic diversification through building a tanker dry dock to service ships, a smelter for aluminum, and a satellite station for communications, as well as continuing the British naval base, which provided income and jobs. As its oil became less abundant in the 1980s,

Bahrain turned to its remaining natural gas and to aid from Saudi Arabia. Bahrain was the first country of the region to enter the post-oil economic era. It has sought to become the banking, communications, and services center of the Gulf Arab states.

Life on the islands has been secure and not too harsh, and the political system has shown a good deal of durability. The appeal of political opponents has usually been temporary. Foreign relations of the state were in British hands, exercised from 1926 to 1956 by Sir Charles Belgrave, the ruler's adviser. The advent of air-conditioning in 1937 meant a notable change for the wealthy who could afford it as an alternative to the sultry heat of the Gulf area.

The period 1953 to 1956 saw sectarian rioting, labor unrest, and a general strike, and Pan-Arab nationalism threatened the ruler's power. Bahrain turned to Saudi Arabia for protection. After the immediate danger passed, the government opened its first radio station in 1955. From time to time the Arab Nationalist Movement instigated strikes; trade unions were banned.

Amir Isa ibn Salman Al Khalifah (b. 1933) succeeded his father in 1961. Great Britain dropped a bombshell by announcing the end of its special treaty position with the states of the area as of 1971. Bahrain, Qatar, and the seven small amirates of the southern Gulf discussed a federation. Encouraged by Saudi Arabia and Kuwait, numerous conferences were held to draw up the structure of such an entity. To the dismay of Arab leaders, however, Iran reasserted its old claim to Bahrain. When a mission from the United Nations in 1970 ascertained that Bahrain desired independence, Iran indicated that Bahraini wishes would be honored. After the proposed federation rejected Bahrain's demand for representation according to population, Amir Isa declared Bahrain an independent and sovereign state on August 14, 1971. When the British left in 1971, the United States assumed responsibility for their base and continued to maintain a military presence there.

In 1972, the amir convened a constituent assembly, half appointed and half elected. A constitution was approved by the amir and by popular referendum. It declared that the amir, not the parliament, appoints the prime minister. When elections for thirty seats in the national assembly were held, with only males voting, political parties were banned, and the government appointed fourteen ministers as members of parliament. Still, eight young leftists were elected, as well as a Shii religious bloc, and a number of notables were defeated. Then, in 1975, the amir dissolved parliament, refused to schedule the election of a new parliament, and transferred its responsibilities to the cabinet, which he expanded. A number of leftists were arrested, and the parliament has not met since then, although an appointive Consultative Council began functioning in 1993.

Many Shiis, a substantial majority of the Bahraini population, resented the Sunni control of the political system, the military, the judiciary, and the economy. Shiis were of mixed ancestry; most were Arabs, while others were from Iran. In 1981, Iran attempted to bring about an Islamic fundamentalist coup, but it was suppressed by the regime.

Bahrain has created a comprehensive social welfare system including free education, medical care, and subsidized housing in newly built towns. Urbanization has been substantial throughout the century, with about an 80 percent rate by the 1970s. Literacy has been widespread, and poetry has flourished. Local television broadcasting began in the mid-1970s. Since foreigners constitute only about one-third of the total population, it has been easier for Bahrain to maintain its cultural integrity than has been the case for some of the other small oil states of the Arabian Peninsula.

The opening of a causeway to Saudi Arabia in 1986, physically linking Bahrain to its much larger, conservative neighbor, plus Saudi financial aid, have helped the Bahrain government meet the needs of its people. Bahrain bought sophisticated military aircraft from the west and expanded its small armed forces, fearing the extension of the Iran-Iraq War. In 1990–1991 U.S. and other allied forces used Bahraini facilities during the Kuwait War. Bahrain's security and prosperity ultimately depend on Saudi Arabia and the United States.

Political and economic unrest beginning in 1994 steadily escalated as thousands of Bahrainis, primarily Shiis but including some Sunnis, demanded a return of parliament and an end to government discrimination and repression. Demonstrations, riots, and petitions for change brought about little or no change until the death of Amir Isa on March 6, 1999 opened the way to new policies. The next ruler, Hamad ibn Isa (b. 1950), rapidly implemented many popular reforms. Male and female Bahrainis voted in municipal elections held on May 9, 2002, and parliamentary elections took place later that year. Amir Hamad changed the status of Bahrain from an amirate to a kingdom that same year, assuming therefore for himself the title of king.

KUWAIT

North of Bahrain on the mainland of Arabia, near the head of the Persian Gulf and bordering Saudi Arabia and Iraq, lies the small principality of Kuwait, with its Sunni majority and Shii minority. The Sunni Al Sabah family has ruled since about 1752, basing its status on support from nomads and merchants. The city-state of Kuwait was long a port, a center for pearling, and the seat of a profitable shipping trade. Kuwait first came to world attention when the British agreed in 1899 to protect it against the imposition of direct Ottoman rule in order to stop the building of the last part of the Berlin-to-Baghdad railroad south to the Gulf. Thereafter Kuwait lapsed into oblivion, except to the British colonial office, until the end of World War I. The Saudis tried to dominate Kuwait during the 1910s and 1920s, but British guns stopped them.

Kuwait and Oil

After oil was struck on Bahrain, world oil companies turned to Kuwait. The Kuwait Oil Company, a corporation owned equally by the British Petroleum Company and the American-owned Gulf Oil Company, received a concession in 1934. Oil was found in 1938, much to the relief of the amir, whose revenue that year was only $40,000. The Burghan field was tapped and has proved to be the largest known pool of oil in the world. Since pearling collapsed in the Gulf about 1930 with the advent of Japanese cultured pearls, oil became the best hope for Kuwait's prosperity. Commercial production, however, was stalled during World War II and did not begin in earnest until 1946. Even then operations went slowly. In 1950, as troubles loomed in Iran, production was increased rapidly.

The original concession provided for a low royalty payment. A new agreement in 1951, following the examples of Saudi Arabia and Venezuela, called for equal sharing of company profits. In 1955 production soared over 1 million barrels a day, and payments to Kuwait's ruler, Amir Abd Allah al-Salim Al Sabah (1950–1965), exceeded $250 million. Oil production passed 2 million barrels per day in 1960, which was about twice as much as Iraqi production. Royalties that year stood at $600 million and petroleum exports at well over $1 billion.

Kuwait could hardly spend all its oil income; nevertheless, in 1968 the amir urged the oil companies to increase production and royalties. In the mid-1970s, concerned about the effects of worldwide runaway inflation and fearing the depleting of proven reserves too rapidly, Kuwait began to limit its oil production. To leave much of the oil safe in the ground rather than bring it to the surface had considerable appeal. Despite this, in 1976 oil revenues were nearly $8 billion. Between 1974 and 1977 the government fully nationalized its oil.

Revenues were so great that the state and wealthy individuals invested large sums abroad. Kuwaiti merchants lost the political influence they had formerly exerted on the ruler, but in return they gained access to great sums of money. Kuwait developed an official stock market and another unofficial, free-wheeling, and extremely risky market for Gulf securities. The crash of the unofficial market in 1982 wiped out $40 billion in real terms. This financial catastrophe plus lower world oil prices and the Iran-Iraq War caused an economic slowdown throughout the 1980s. In 1984, however, new oil reserves were discovered, sharply increasing Kuwait's future ability to pump oil: there were about 200 years of petroleum in reserve at current rates of extraction. In 1987 oil revenues were about $6 billion, and from foreign investments Kuwait gained $4 billion more. Oil production averaged about 1 million barrels per day in the first half of 1990.

In a country with a total population of fewer than 200,000 before 1950 and about 990,000 by 1975, fewer than half of them native born, the wealth pouring in changed the life of the people rapidly. Amir Abd Allah used half his royalties to build schools, roads, hospitals, electrical plants, and the other requirements of a modern community. Television broadcasting began in 1962, and Kuwait University opened in 1966, while newspapers flourished. Because Kuwait's water resources are negligible, large seawater conversion plants were built in the 1950s. Water use in the three decades after 1954 increased by 150 times!

By 1960 Kuwaitis were saying that all needed infrastructure, including oil refineries and modern port terminals, was completed. But when new building slowed down and government land purchases stopped, everyone complained of a recession. Government leaders realized that continued expansion is essential in a rentier-state economy. Despite spending on welfare measures, income in Kuwait remained heavily skewed toward the ruling family and wealthy merchants. The surge in oil income beginning in 1973 increased per capita income dramatically; by 1976 it reached $11,500, the highest in the world.

Increases in oil revenues made possible more government spending to help people and provide for a vast expansion of government employment. In Kuwait, education, aid to artists, medical attention, and hospital care have been available for citizens, who were not required to pay taxes, but noncitizens were less favorably treated. As far back as

1969, foreigners had to be invited in, and the government enacted laws making the obtaining of Kuwaiti citizenship almost impossible. From 1965 on, Kuwaitis were a minority within their own country. Most of the immigrants, who formed the majority, were laborers—chiefly Palestinians, Egyptians, other Arabs, and workers from south and southeast Asia. By 1985 Kuwaitis numbered around 680,000, and there were more than 1 million foreign residents.

The city of al-Kuwait, with the highest per capita income in the world, became a modern town with more automobiles per capita and more air conditioners per habitation than any other city in the world. Its wealth attracted people from many parts of the world.

Kuwaiti Politics

Kuwait was declared free and independent on June 19, 1961, after discussions with Great Britain led to a peaceful termination of the treaty of protection. In less than a week Amir Abd Allah was threatened by Iraq, which sought to annex Kuwait. The amir received forces from Great Britain until troops from Saudi Arabia, Jordan, and the United Arab Republic replaced them.

At Amir Abd Allah's behest, a constituent assembly in 1962 called for a national assembly to be elected by adult males whose ancestry in Kuwait could be established. The new assembly in 1963 repeated some of the experiences of the earlier 1938 legislative council, which had ultimately been abolished. A majority of those elected in the 1960s supported the rule of the Sabah princely family; parliament also included some members of the Arab Nationalist Movement. Many opponents were handsomely rewarded for muffling their criticisms, but few were brought directly into the government. Sabah al-Salim Al Sabah (1965–1977), the amir's brother, was named prime minister and heir to the throne; he became the new ruler when Abd Allah died. The royal family occupied the key cabinet posts. The new amir chose his cousin Jabir al-Ahmad al-Jabir Al Sabah as prime minister and heir to the throne. When Amir Sabah died in 1977, Jabir was recognized immediately as amir of Kuwait.

During the 1960s and 1970s there were three more national assembly elections. Of the members elected in 1975, half had not served before. They were younger, better educated, and less conservative than those they replaced. The new national assembly chose to be active, but the ruling family wished to retain its power, so in 1976 Amir Sabah dissolved parliament and declared he would rule by executive decree.

Kuwait's tremendous wealth and oil resources were constant temptations to aggression. To provide a buffer, Kuwait's rulers initiated a policy of granting and lending significant sums to other Arab states. In 1962, the Kuwait Fund for Arab Economic Development was established. By 1989 Kuwait had given out more than $17 billion to Arab states and groups. But Amir Sabah recognized that a state as small as his could not hope to withstand the armed might of any of the regional powers. His only hope was to conduct a foreign policy that would maintain friendly relations with all, and particularly Iraq, Iran, and Saudi Arabia. Kuwait financially supported the Palestine Liberation Organization and the Arab confrontation states against Israel. Yet Palestinians, as foreigners, were not permitted to settle permanently in Kuwait, and many Arabs living outside the Gulf came to view Kuwait's rulers as corrupt and arrogant. Pan-Arab nationalists argued that Kuwait's enormous wealth should become the joint property of all Arabs.

The Iran-Iraq War of 1980–1988 threatened to involve Kuwait directly. Kuwait was officially neutral, but unofficially it was pro-Iraq, lending Saddam Husain large sums of money. As a result, Iran attacked Kuwaiti oil tankers in 1984. To counterbalance the danger from Iran, Kuwait cooperated closely with Saudi Arabia and the Gulf Cooperation Council in military matters, and bought quantities of weapons from both the United States and the Soviet Union. In 1987 Kuwait registered its oil tankers as American or Soviet, securing U.S. and Russian protection in the Gulf.

In domestic matters, Jabir reinstituted parliament in 1981. In the ensuing elections, Bedouins and Sunnis were heavily represented, while only a few Shiis, Muslim fundamentalists, and Pan-Arab nationalists were elected. Despite lobbying by women's groups, the franchise remained for males only, although the employment of women outside the home increased substantially from the 1960s. Economic difficulties following the crash of the unofficial stock market, the fall of the price of oil, internal corruption, and the question of what to do about the Iran-Iraq War all caused severe disagreements among Kuwaitis. And the parliament, intent on securing a cabinet truly responsible to it, was prepared to express no confidence in some of the princes who held cabinet rank. In 1986, the amir once again dissolved the national assembly.

The War for Kuwait

On August 2, 1990, Iraq invaded Kuwait and then annexed it, thereby setting in motion a chain of events that included international condemnation of Iraq's action, United States and Saudi leadership in forming an international coalition to reverse the invasion, and a United Nations–authorized war in 1991 that expelled Iraq from Kuwait and reestablished it as an independent state. (These matters are more fully discussed in Chapter 46.) The 1991 Kuwait War is sometimes called the Persian Gulf War or the Second Persian Gulf War, with reference to the Iran-Iraq War of 1980–1988 as the first Persian Gulf War.

Iraq invaded Kuwait for a variety of reasons. Some of the long-term causes included Pan-Arab nationalism, a feeling that Kuwait had historically and culturally been linked to Iraq, a desire to harness Kuwait's enormous present and future oil wealth, and the need for a larger territorial access to the waters of the Gulf. There were short-term causes as well, including the charge that Kuwait had produced oil beyond its quota, thereby reducing the international value of Iraqi oil. Iraq also did not wish to repay the money Kuwait had supplied to it during the Iran-Iraq War. Kuwait agreed to compromises on some issues, but it resisted any territorial concession; after the invasion, Kuwaitis appealed to the international community chiefly on the grounds that the annexation at will of small countries by their larger neighbors was a dangerous precedent.

Iraq quickly occupied Kuwait, but Amir Jabir Al Sabah fled to Saudi Arabia, where he headed a government in exile. About 500,000 other Kuwaitis and many resident foreigners also left Kuwait. The brutality of the Iraqi occupation helped to provoke resistance and a sense of national unity. Saudi Arabia and the United States led the international opposition to the annexation of Kuwait, securing widespread support from most Middle Eastern and European governments. The United Nations condemned the invasion and repeatedly undertook actions in 1990 designed to secure an Iraqi withdrawal. With the failure of diplomatic approaches to secure this goal, a coalition with hundreds of thousands of troops fought against Iraq, first in a massive air campaign lasting from January 17, 1991, to late February and then in a short but decisive ground war.

Kuwait after the War

When Iraqi forces left Kuwait, the country was in a shambles. Systematic looting by the Iraqis, damage from the bombing and ground fighting, and the deliberate sabotage of Kuwait's oil wells by the departing Iraqi troops created a terrible situation. Restoring housing, infrastructure, the economy, and the environment began immediately, but full recovery was a long process, hampered by continuing uncertainty as to Iraq's future intentions and Saddam Husain's renewed threats of intervention against Kuwait. The United Nations demarcated new borders with Iraq, created a demilitarized zone there, and staffed it with soldiers. Iraq finally officially acknowledged the independence and territorial integrity of Kuwait in 1994. Kuwait purchased weapons and began to rebuild its small armed forces, but it had to depend ultimately on external countries, and particularly the United States, to save its national existence.

Kuwaitis were bitter toward those who had collaborated with the Iraqi occupiers and the governments that had opposed the use of force to expel Iraq from Kuwait. Under Kuwaiti government pressure, Palestinians living in Kuwait declined from 450,000 to only 50,000, and Kuwait acted diplomatically against Jordan and Yemen. By 1993, although Kuwaitis were still less than half the total population in their own country, the number of resident expatriates was smaller than it had been in 1989.

Recovery from the war was expensive. Kuwait paid the allied countries for part of their expenses, including $13 billion to the United States. Little oil could be produced to generate new revenues until the oil well fires were finally extinguished in late 1991. And by 1993 Kuwait reached its production quota limit of 2 million barrels of oil per day. Rebuilding universities, pipelines, port facilities, and all manner of other projects was so expensive that the country's enormous overseas investments, a reserve against the day the oil ran out, had to be tapped.

Elections to a restored national assembly or parliament in 1992 resulted in a victory for the opposition. Many questions were now raised about members of the royal family and military officers who had been in charge of operations during 1990. New elections in 1996 yielded a parliament with fewer opposition deputies and more who were moderately in favor of the status quo. The July 1999 elections resulted in still another opposition victory, but the opposition was fragmented between Shii and Sunni Islamists and some liberals. While the three parliamentary elections of the 1990s were generally conducted in a democratic manner, most political power continued to reside in the hands of the amir and his family. Many Kuwaitis saw parliament as incompetent or they opposed its decisions, as in its 1999 reversal of the amir's decree granting women the right to vote.

Kuwait's prosperity fluctuated with the price of oil. In the middle 1990s, when prices were low, government income fell, but it then increased substantially in 2000 and afterward as the world paid more for petroleum products. Kuwaitis delighted in the restoration of government-paid benefits such as free education and free health care.

The United States maintained a military presence in the country, thereby securing it from a potential renewed invasion by Iraq. At the Arab summit conference in Beirut in 2002 the government of Iraq once again affirmed its respect for Kuwait's "independence, sovereignty and security"; while welcoming this declaration, Kuwait again called for Iraq to carry out all United Nations resolutions fully rather than selectively. Kuwait's pre-1990 diplomatic, political, and economic situation seemed to be more or less fully restored as of the early 2000s.

QATAR

Qatar was ruled by the Al Khalifah dynasty of Bahrain until the emergence of Muhammad ibn Thani as local leader in 1868. His successor fought off Ottoman expansion and established an alliance with the Saudis, becoming a Wahhabi Muslim in the process. The ruling shaikh in 1916, fearing conquest by the Saudis, concluded a treaty with the British recognizing Britain's control over foreign relations. Occupying a barren peninsula of more than 4000 square miles (11,000 square km.) jutting northward into the Persian Gulf, the amirate had one principal town, Doha, and was ruled absolutely by the Al Thani family.

Qatar entered the oil age when the Qatar Petroleum Company, a subsidiary of the Iraq Petroleum Company, started exploiting a mainland concession in 1949. Offshore rights were held by Shell Qatar, which began producing in 1961 and was reorganized in 1967 to include an Italian company. By 1966 Qatar was receiving over $100 million annually in royalties, and production stood at 276,000 barrels daily. A decade later annual income was over $2 billion, oil production had doubled, and the population had increased tenfold to 220,000, about 80 percent of whom lived in Doha. Most of the population were expatriate non-Qataris.

Qatar was admitted to the Organization of Petroleum Exporting Countries (O.P.E.C.) in 1968. In 1974 the government agreed to buy 60 percent of Qatar Petroleum Company and Shell Qatar. In 1977, Qatar Petroleum Company relinquished all control of its oil operations to the government but continued to provide services, managerial assistance, and trained personnel.

A religious scholar of Arab history and Islamic law, Shaikh Ali ibn Abd Allah Al Thani acceded to rule in 1949. He found the problems of family quarrels, oil development, and riches so vexing that he retired in 1960 to Switzerland, abdicating in favor of his son Shaikh Ahmad, who also preferred Switzerland. Ahmad in the 1960s kept one-fourth of all revenues for himself. His cousin and heir, Shaikh Khalifah ibn Hamad Al Thani, was in charge of governing.

The British departure from the Persian Gulf in 1971 gave birth to a federation of Gulf states, but after due consideration Qatar decided not to join. On April 2, 1970, Amir Ahmad declared he was independent and issued a constitution. Khalifah was named prime minister; nine of the other ministers were from the Thani family as well. In 1971 Amir Ahmad proclaimed Qatar's separation from the British.

Shaikh Khalifah staged a bloodless coup in 1972, replacing Ahmad as ruler. He formed an appointive advisory council to discuss draft legislation and the budget. Amir

Khalifah took an active role in Arab affairs. He made loans or grants to Arab states for military preparedness against Israel and for economic development. In addition, he arranged for an earth satellite communications system centered at Doha to carry telephone, television, and radio transmissions. Oil ensured growing prosperity. In 1975, per capita income in Qatar rose to $8300, behind only Kuwait and the United Arab Emirates.

Since there was only a little agriculture and industry was limited, the economy was dominated by oil, and oil was controlled by the government. Because of the need to diversify the economy, after basic infrastructure was built, the amir turned to industrial development, using natural gas and its by-products. But with the decline in world oil prices, Qatar's income by the mid-1980s fell by half, and government deficits became typical.

Qatar tried to promote a sense of national identity, while values and attitudes changed rapidly, creating strong generational gaps. In 1982 the Arab states of the Gulf created in Qatar a folklore center whose purpose was to promote the common cultural heritage of the region and in particular oral, written, and material data from seafarers and nomads. Poetry often reflected the rapid social changes, resulting in a sense of alienation from the present and nostalgic yearning for the past. The government introduced television broadcasting in 1970; in the 1980s and 1990s videocassette recorders became very popular in Qatar as in other parts of the Gulf. Modern international styles of architecture predominated in Qatar and throughout the rest of the Gulf, but the 1970s and 1980s witnessed a growing interest in earlier designs and renovating existing old buildings. Shariah courts used Hanbali interpretations of holy law for personal and family matters. The government conducted Qatar's first census in 1986.

Like all the other Gulf Arab states, Qatar was closely involved with the Kuwait War of 1991, providing troops who fought as part of the allied armies. Internally, the 1990s were chiefly marked by Crown Prince Hamad's replacement of his father in a bloodless coup in 1995. Hamad, born in 1950, had to deal with oil price fluctuations that lowered Qatari government and personal income in the 1990s. However, Qatar was estimated in 1998 to have the third largest reserves of natural gas in the world, after those in Russia and Iran. To protect this wealth Qatar turned to the United States, welcoming the stationing of American troops there in 2001, and permitting the United States to use Qatari facilities during the war in Afghanistan.

The new amir also encouraged a broadening in communications policy and the political process. In 1996 al-Jazeera (al-Jazira) television, an all-news satellite channel whose broadcasts ultimately reached about 35 million viewers, was established. Since al-Jazeera carried highly controversial programs, Amir Hamad earned the wrath of countries who opposed the station's point of view; the United States, for instance, condemned some of its shows that seemed to be supportive of Usama bin Ladin. A sign of political opening was the March 1999 elections for the Doha Municipal Council. This was the first election ever allowed in Qatar, and a process also notable for the full participation of women as both voters and candidates.

Amir Hamad's political, economic, and diplomatic successes received a wide recognition in 2001 when Qatar was elected for a three-year term to head the Organization of the Islamic Conference, a group of 57 countries.

UNITED ARAB EMIRATES

Seven Arab amirates or shaikhdoms lie along a 510-mile (825 km.) strip of the coastland of Arabia on the Persian Gulf, from the Qatar peninsula to the Strait of Hormuz, and along the Gulf of Oman, to the territory of the sultan of Oman. These seven are Abu Dhabi, Dubai, Sharjah, Ajman, Umm al-Qaiwain, Ras al-Khaimah, and Fujairah. Since only about 5 percent of the land is arable, the inhabitants for centuries earned their livelihood from the sea by pearl diving and commerce.

In 1820 a British naval expedition forced a treaty on each of the seven rulers by which they agreed not to make war on each other, not to raid shipping, not to traffic in slaves, and not to make treaties with other powers. Great Britain in return agreed to protect them from outside aggression. In 1853 a Perpetual Maritime Truce was signed, and by another treaty in 1892 Britain assumed responsibility for foreign relations.

Each of the seven Trucial States was little more than a small coastal town with a desert hinterland, although Abu Dhabi held several of the settlements in the inland Buraimi oases. Multiethnic Dubai was the largest town; Sharjah was the location of the British political resident agent, a small military force, and an airstrip; Abu Dhabi was the largest. Population was quite small: about 180,000 in 1968, 750,000 in 1982, and 2.7 million in 1999, but with noncitizens in the majority. The seven shaikhs met twice a year in a kind of council, but no formal organization or federation developed.

Pearling reached its peak about 1925, at which time the revenue in the pearl trade for all of the Persian Gulf area, including Kuwait and Bahrain, was about $10 million. Less than a tenth of this came to the seven rulers of the Trucial States. The marketing of cultured pearls hurt the trade, and the 1930s depression finished it off. After World War II, as the total value of the pearling industry in the Persian Gulf dropped to $250,000, the towns of the Trucial States were in the doldrums. Abu Dhabi witnessed the first impact of oil, to be followed by Dubai.

Abu Dhabi

Abu Dhabi in 1961 was still insignificant, with a population of about 15,000 and a total revenue of a little under $150,000 for its ruler Shaikh Shakhbut ibn Sultan Al Nahyan, who had acceded to his position in 1928. For more than a decade, the Abu Dhabi Petroleum Company, a subsidiary of Iraq Petroleum Company, held the concessions for the seven shaikhdoms. Offshore concessions were given by Abu Dhabi and Dubai to Abu Dhabi Marine Areas Ltd., owned by British Petroleum Company and a French company. Oil was exported in 1962 in commercial quantities from Abu Dhabi, Shaikh Shakhbut receiving $20 million in royalties. By 1966, royalties had reached $84 million. Production jumped rapidly to reach 367,000 barrels daily, more than in Qatar.

What to do with all this money? Shaikh Shakhbut's wants were simple and inexpensive. His major recreation was hawking. It was only in 1965 that he accepted the fifty-fifty split in profits. Changes were everywhere. He was not convinced all this was for the betterment of his people. Since political and social development was slow, a family council with British blessings sent Shakhbut into exile in 1966, placing his youngest brother, Shaikh Zaid ibn Sultan Al Nahyan in control. Shaikh Zaid, ebullient, lighthearted, and possessing great physical strength, had been raised in the informal nomadic life of the desert.

Zaid initiated plans for a covered market, a seawall, a dual highway from the interior oasis of Buraimi to Abu Dhabi, and water pipelines from Buraimi. His income was initially $170 million. Ten years later, after production had quadrupled and prices had risen, revenues reached nearly $8 billion. Despite increased pumping, oil reserves were expected to last for a century at least at the 1976 rate of production. Zaid settled border disputes with Qatar and with Saudi Arabia, the latter being an especially contentious issue pertaining to the ownership of the Buraimi oases. And Abu Dhabi gradually gained ownership of the oil company. Oil income attracted newcomers as the population jumped to 100,000, only a third of whom had been born in Abu Dhabi.

In 1967 the Abu Dhabi Investment Board was established to invest the growing surplus funds; in 1976 they were estimated at roughly $6 billion. Money was given or loaned to less affluent Arab states, neighboring shaikhs, and Bedouin chiefs. The consumer society that rose up in Abu Dhabi had enormous wealth at its disposal, and it drew artists and writers from Egypt and other parts of the Arab world, thereby becoming famous as the home of the most widely circulated Arabic-language childrens' magazine. Still, what to do with the mounting cash balances created a controversy in governing circles.

With the 1971 British pullout and the apparent failure of a Persian Gulf states federation, Zaid declared Abu Dhabi to be an independent amirate.

Dubai

Northeast of Abu Dhabi along the Persian Gulf coast toward the Strait of Hormuz lies the small amirate of Dubai, the most populous of the seven amirates. Based on an estuary of the Gulf, Dubai had been the main commercial and smuggling center on the coast for more than a century. Its ruler, Amir Rashid ibn Said Al Maktum, who succeeded his father peacefully in 1958, had considerable knowledge of foreign trade and international finance, skills acquired from his mother, who was the real power in Dubai for fifty years.

Oil, discovered in commercial quantities in 1967 by the Dubai Petroleum Company offshore, was first exported in 1969. By 1977 daily exports neared 300,000 barrels, and yearly revenues exceeded $1 billion. Many millions were spent to enlarge the airport to accommodate jumbo jets, build a new air terminal complex, construct the biggest deepwater port in the Persian Gulf, and establish a free port.

Angry at the building of a large dry dock in Bahrain, Dubai in the 1970s built its own. Dubai remained the chief business center for the entire coast, and in the mid-1960s several banks joined the British Bank of the Middle East, long the sole banking house in Dubai and an enterprise that had been highly influential in Kuwait and Oman as well.

Sharjah

The amirate of Sharjah lies next to Dubai on the north and east. Included in its territory is the strategic island of Abu Musa in the Strait of Hormuz, with offshore oil fields. Until

1971 the British located their military and air bases in Sharjah, which was the headquarters of the Trucial Scouts. Sharjah's Amir Saqr ibn Sultan Al Qasimi irritated the British by his pro-Egyptian policies, so London suggested in 1965 that he be replaced. His cousin Khalid ibn Muhammad Al Qasimi, at that moment operating a paint store in Dubai, became amir. As the British were preparing to withdraw their forces from Sharjah, Iran occupied Abu Musa with no interference. An arrangement was made whereby the inhabitants of the island would remain under Sharjah rule, offshore oil revenues would flow to Sharjah, and Iran paid for the military bases. Soon after, former Amir Saqr staged an unsuccessful coup; Amir Khalid was killed, but the rebels were captured by troops of the recently organized United Arab Emirates. Khalid's brother Sultan ibn Muhammad Al Qasimi then became the new Sharjah ruler.

Ras al-Khaimah, Ajman, Umm al-Qaiwain, and Fujairah

These four amirates were poorer than Abu Dhabi and Dubai, the two political units that would dominate the United Arab Emirates. The four small amirates had few resources and only small numbers of people living in them, and their hereditary rulers played a minor role in political affairs as compared to the dynasties governing the larger states.

Forming the United Arab Emirates

All seven of these states realized that with the anticipated end of British protection, they would be too small to maintain their own separate identities. Kuwait and Saudi Arabia encouraged their federation, while Iraq and Iran opposed it. On July 18, 1971, six of the seven formed the United Arab Emirates (U.A.E.) and accepted the provisional constitution. Ras al-Khaimah joined the U.A.E. in 1972.

The federal constitution recognized the continuing independence of each member, each with its own flag and in control of local affairs. It provided for a Supreme Council, consisting of the rulers of the states, each with one vote. Decisions on procedural matters were to be reached by majority vote; substantive issues required a five-vote majority that had to include Abu Dhabi and Dubai. Important matters had to be approved by the Supreme Council.

Amir Zaid of Abu Dhabi was chosen president, and he continued to be reelected to that post. Amir Rashid Al Maktum, the amir of Dubai, eventually became prime minister. (Following his death, his son, Maktum ibn Rashid Al Maktum, became in 1990 both amir of Dubai and prime minister of the United Arab Emirates.) A forty-member council appointed by the rulers consisted of eight members each from Abu Dhabi and Dubai, six each from Sharjah and Ras al-Khaimah, and four from each of the others. The Trucial Scouts were taken over from the British, and the United Arab Emirates became a member of O.P.E.C.

In 1973 most local cabinets were disbanded, and education, public works, industry, agriculture, and justice were added to the responsibilities of the federal cabinet. Except for the ruler of Abu Dhabi, however, the heads of state were reluctant to surrender much of their power. There was an absence of overall planning as the rulers attempted to outdo each other's construction programs.

By the census of 1985, only 20 percent of the residents of the U.A.E. were citizens. The rest were foreign residents—Indians, Pakistanis, Omanis, Iranians, Palestinians, and others. Oil wealth increased urbanization—three cities accounted for 80 percent of the residents—while youths constituted a large proportion of the total population. The National University at al-Ain graduated its first class, including men and women, in 1982. Sports (such as soccer), radio and television, and plays competed among the young for their attention, although poetry still played a large cultural role.

Oil and natural gas revenues, which peaked at $20 billion in 1980, caused rapid social transformation. Per capita income for U.A.E. citizens was close to $100,000. Production in the mid-1980s fell, though, as low as $13 billion in 1982–1983, although reserves were abundant for the foreseeable future. Each member state controlled pricing and oil production policy, but the U.A.E. presented a common front in O.P.E.C.

The great sums of the 1970s and the more modest revenues of the 1980s built roads, airports, seaports, and hotels and provided the foundation for a social welfare system. This prosperity was threatened by the Iran-Iraq War, whose possible extension to the area caused grave concern. The U.A.E. turned mainly to Saudi Arabia for support and to France for weapons. Its own armed forces included many noncitizens and seemed incapable of defending the federation against attack from a major regional power, although emirati troops served in the 1991 Kuwait War.

A financial scandal in 1991 affected Shaikh Zaid of Abu Dhabi, still the president of the U.A.E., when the Bank of Credit and Commerce International was closed after the embezzlement of as much as $12 billion was discovered. The bank was owned by Zaid and his family, who eventually helped creditors in the United States and Britain.

As oil prices moved to higher levels in 2000, the already substantial income of Abu Dhabi rose dramatically. In addition, the U.A.E. had the fourth largest reserves of natural gas in the world, promising even more prosperity in the future for the minority of its population who were citizens and the large majority who were resident aliens. An extensive physical infrastructure, including numerous seaports and air facilities, combined with new colleges and an emphasis on the most technologically advanced communications systems to provide a notable advance in the standard of living. However, the seven member states of the U.A.E. still retained a somewhat separate organization and identity, even while their rulers' subjects increasingly interacted with each other inside the common framework provided by the U.A.E.

OMAN

The Sultanate of Oman, situated at the southeastern corner of Arabia, is larger than all the other states of the peninsula except for Saudi Arabia and Yemen. Members of the Al Bu Said dynasty were Ibadi Muslims who ruled in Oman starting in about 1749. They expelled Iranian forces and expanded their sway to include areas in the Gulf, Dhufar province to the south, and the rich area of Zanzibar off the shore of east Africa. Zanzibar was lost after 1856, and the interior of Oman came under the control of rivals. European steamships also curtailed the importance of Omani shipping.

By the Treaty of Sib of 1920, Sultan Taimur (1913–1932) acknowledged the division of the country between his own dynasty and the tribes of the interior, which were to be governed by an elected Ibadi imam with political and religious authority over them. No great difficulties arose with the imam, who served from 1920 until 1954, but the selection of a new imam was against the strong wishes of Sultan Said ibn Taimur (1932–1970). War broke out between the two in 1955, with Sultan Said aided by British soldiers. The sultan was highly dependent on Great Britain, which for many years had managed his foreign relations. By 1959 the imam and his followers had been routed from their mountain strongholds and fled into neighboring Saudi Arabia. In the meantime, in 1955, the sultan had visited the interior where the imam had held sway, the first such trip by any sultan of the coast since 1886.

Sultan Said defeated the imam, but Said's reign was affected by his autocratic character and slowness to modernize. He feared accumulating a foreign debt and preserved his rule by dividing the tribes and isolating Oman from most contact with the outside world. Said himself stayed in Dhufar and never went to the capital city of Muscat after 1958.

In 1970 Sultan Said was overthrown and exiled by his English-educated son Qabus (b. 1940). Sultan Qabus ended Oman's isolation but preserved power in his own hands. Hampered by the massive expenses incurred in fighting the rebellion in Dhufar, Qabus declared that Oman was not yet prepared for responsible ministerial government.

In 1963, oil in commercial quantities was discovered by Petroleum Development (Oman) Ltd. In 1967 a new agreement was reached with Sultan Said, giving him a percentage of the royalties and splitting the profits on the usual fifty-fifty basis. Oil production averaged 300,000 barrels through the 1970s. Although not a member of O.P.E.C., Qabus followed it carefully, and government revenues soared from about $6 million in 1966 to $1.4 billion in 1976. In 1974 Oman acquired 60 percent of the oil company, which it retained in subsequent reorganizations.

The greatest problem facing Sultans Said and Qabus over the years was the guerrilla warfare and open rebellion in Dhufar province in the southwest. The struggle began to go the sultan's way in 1972, when most of the tribesmen and nationalists gave their allegiance to Qabus. He married King Husain's daughter in Amman and arranged for a Jordanian military mission. Oman received substantial aid from Britain, Saudi Arabia, and Iran, including Iranian troops. Qabus also obtained the backing of the United States, which later acquired the right to use prepositioned military supplies under certain conditions.

Convinced that the rebellion in Dhufar had been crushed, Qabus in 1976 began to devote more than half of his budget to development. A five-year plan called for expending $8 billion for education, harbors, roads, and electrification. Qabus built radio and television stations, and the first newspapers appeared. A desalinization plant opened, and education rapidly expanded. In 1970 there were only about 900 students in secular government schools; in 1985 there were 200,000 in 560 schools, mostly staffed with foreign teachers. Qabus University, which used English as the language of instruction for most classes, opened in 1986. This development of infrastructure began to affect the lives of most, although some tribes remained beyond the reach of government. Peasants tilled the 1 percent of the land that was arable to raise dates and other crops, generally using traditional irrigation methods.

Justice was still based on the shariah. Although there was no constitution or parliament, Qabus named an appointed State Consultative Council in 1981 to offer advice periodically on economic, social, and legal matters. In 1991 the Council became partially elective. The small army became less dependent on foreigners, except in the area of armaments, most of which were purchased from Britain.

Oman helped form the Gulf Cooperation Council in 1981. The Omanis, Yemenis, Emiratis, and Saudis also cooperated in delimiting their mutual borders in the 1990s. Another aspect of the sultan's security policy has been a close friendship with the United States and Great Britain. Sultan Qabus assisted the Arab-Israeli peace process in the 1990s and allowed the United States to use Omani facilities during the 2001 war in Afghanistan.

Oman in the 1990s and early 2000s made progress in reaching many of the domestic goals set by Sultan Qabus. Gross domestic product growth in the 1990s was about 5 percent per year. Oil production averaged close to 900,000 barrels per day, with estimated reserves that could last for about 15 years. The government took measures to develop natural gas production, increase tourism, and improve the ports. Political changes included a Basic Law, a sort of proto-constitution, issued by the sultan in 1996. The Consultative Council remained a partially elected and partially appointed body, with elections held in 1997 and 2000. Women first became members of the Council in 1994. Social developments included increases in those receiving an education—enrollment in the schools by 2001 was about 540,000, one-half of whom were female. The first-ever national census in 1993 showed the population to consist of about 1.5 million Omanis and about 500,000 foreign residents.

Problems faced by Oman included excessive reliance on foreigners, rapid population increase, governmental corruption, the continuing strength of tribalism, and the lack of a clear successor to Sultan Qabus. On the other hand, unlike some of the Arabian Peninsula countries, Oman had a long history with a well-established national identity.

Oman, Bahrain, Kuwait, Qatar, the United Arab Emirates, and Saudi Arabia found in the Gulf Cooperation Council (G.C.C.) a means for securing mutually beneficial cooperation without losing their separate national identities. While military and diplomatic coordination was only partially successful, the G.C.C. countries took serious steps toward establishing a common market and customs union. One example of this was that it became possible for a citizen of any one of the countries to work in any of the others without obtaining a work permit. The G.C.C. states also enacted similar regulations in regard to commerce, culture, the professions, and social issues, thereby reinforcing a sense of common interests.

The five small members of the Gulf Cooperation Council have, since the discovery of oil, all witnessed extraordinary changes in their economies, urbanization, degree of independence, foreign policies, the numbers of expatriate residents, and strategic situations. They also have demonstrated a surprising degree of continuity in such basic matters as political systems, language, religion, and popular culture. Yemen, another country in the Arabian Peninsula discussed in Chapter 48, experienced upheavals in its political system and in the nature of its national cohesion not present in the experience of the states discussed here.

REFERENCES

References cited at the end of Chapters 40 and 46 are pertinent to this chapter as well.

Allen, Calvin H., and W. Lynn Rigsbee: *Oman under Qaboos: From Coup to Constitution, 1970–96.* London: Frank Cass, 1999. In this general survey the authors discuss the rentier state approach, continuity with earlier times, and economic diversification beyond oil.

Anscombe, Frederick F.: *The Ottoman Gulf: The Creation of Kuwait, Saudi Arabia, and Qatar.* New York: Columbia University Press, 1997. An excellent study of eastern Arabia in the late nineteenth century, based on the Ottoman archives.

Clarke, Angela: *Bahrain: Oil and Development.* London: Immel, 1990. The story of Bapco and its impact on Bahrain.

Cottrell, Alvin J., ed.: *The Persian Gulf States: A General Survey.* Baltimore, Md.: Johns Hopkins University Press, 1980. A massive and important study with chapters on early as well as recent times; includes Saudi Arabia, Iran, and Iraq as well as the smaller states of the Gulf.

Crystal, Jill: *Oil and Politics in the Gulf: Rulers and Merchants in Kuwait and Qatar.* Cambridge: Cambridge University Press, 1990. An excellent study of the influence of oil revenues on domestic politics that thoughtfully illustrates the rentier state concept.

———: *Kuwait: The Transformation of an Oil State.* Boulder, Colo.: Westview, 1992. A short but remarkably valuable study.

Fuller, Graham E., and Rend Rahim Francke: *The Arab Shi'a: The Forgotten Muslims.* Basingstoke, England: Macmillan, 1999. Based on numerous interviews, this book concentrates on Bahrain, Kuwait, Iraq, Saudi Arabia, and Lebanon.

Gause, F. Gregory, III: *Oil Monarchies: Domestic and Security Challenges in the Arab Gulf States.* New York: Council on Foreign Relations, 1994. An outstanding short work on recent developments, including discussion of politics, economics, religion, and social change.

Graham, Helga: *Arabian Time Machine: Self-Portrait of an Oil State.* London: Heinemann, 1978. Extensive interviews vividly showing the transformations in people, as well as the general society of Qatar.

Heard-Bey, Frauke: *From Trucial States to United Arab Emirates: A Society in Transition.* New ed. London: Longman, 1996. An indispensable guide to the history of the United Arab Emirates and its constituent elements.

Herb, Michael: *All in the Family: Absolutism, Revolution, and Democracy in the Middle Eastern Monarchies.* Albany: State University of New York Press, 1999. In this fascinating study, a political scientist seeks to explain the unexpected survival of monarchies in some Middle Eastern countries, including those of the Persian Gulf.

Ismael, Jacqueline S.: *Kuwait: Dependency and Class in a Rentier State.* Gainesville: University Press of Florida, 1993. Treats Kuwait before and after oil, with an emphasis on economic factors.

Lawson, Fred H.: *Bahrain: The Modernization of Autocracy.* Boulder, Colo.: Westview, 1989. A good introduction to all aspects of Bahrain's history, politics, and economics.

al-Naqeeb, Khaldoun Hasan: *Society and State in the Gulf and Arab Peninsula: A Different Perspective.* Translated by L. M. Kenny. London: Centre for Arab Unity Studies, 1990. A complex, thoughtful, and highly critical interpretation of the history of Arabia since the sixteenth century.

Peck, Malcolm C.: *The United Arab Emirates: A Venture in Unity.* Boulder, Colo.: Westview Press, 1986. An informative general survey.

Peterson, J. E.: *Oman in the Twentieth Century: Political Foundations of an Emerging State.* London: Croom Helm, 1978.

———: "The Arabian Peninsula in Modern Times: A Historiographical Survey." *American Historical Review* 96 (1991): 1435–1449. The best bibliographical beginning point for researchers on the subject.

———: "The Political Status of Women in the Arab Gulf States." *Middle East Journal* 43 (1989): 34–50. Also covers education, employment, and women's organizations.

Riphenburg, Carol: *Oman: Political Development in a Changing World.* Westport, Conn.: Praeger, 1998. A useful survey that includes politics, the economy, the status of women, and foreign policy.

Rivlin, Paul: *Economic Policy and Performance in the Arab World.* Boulder, Colo.: Lynne Rienner, 2001. Important for the 1990s, especially for the role of oil.

Rumaihi, Muhammad: *Beyond Oil: Unity and Development in the Gulf.* Translated by James Dickins. London: Saqi Books, 1986. A broad and pessimistic overview of the smaller Arab states of the Gulf.

Schofield, Richard: *Kuwait and Iraq: Historical Claims and Territorial Disputes.* 2d ed. London: Royal Institute of International Affairs, 1993.

Soffan, Linda Usra: *The Women of the United Arab Emirates.* London: Croom Helm, 1980.

Tétreault, Mary Ann: *Stories of Democracy: Politics and Society in Contemporary Kuwait.* New York: Columbia University Press, 2000. An expert on Kuwait analyzes the chief themes of modern Kuwaiti history and the events of the 1990s.

Wilkinson, John C.: *Arabia's Frontiers: The Story of Britain's Boundary Drawing in the Desert.* New York: St. Martin's Press, 1991.

Winckler, Onn: "The Immigration Policy of the Gulf Cooperation Council (GCC) States." *Middle Eastern Studies* 33 (1997): 480–493. Valuable for information on the ratio of citizens to foreign residents at various periods.

Zahlan, Rosemarie Said: *The Making of the Modern Gulf States: Kuwait, Bahrain, Qatar, the United Arab Emirates and Oman.* 2d ed. Reading, England: Ithaca Press, 1998. This outstanding survey should be the beginning point for the reader seeking information on these five countries.

CHAPTER 48

Yemen

Yemen in the twentieth century was divided into two parts—south and north—although in earlier times the country was often unified. This division, along with the late discovery of oil, profoundly affected the history of Yemen and served to differentiate it from other parts of the Arabian Peninsula. Unlike the countries discussed in Chapter 47, many parts of Yemen are suitable for agriculture, and most Yemenis have earned their livelihood from farming. Among the countries of the Arabian Peninsula Yemen has a large population, almost entirely Muslim in religion and Arabic-speaking in language. Political and economic ties between Yemen and Saudi Arabia have been influential for both countries, while many Yemenis have resented what they considered to be Saudi interference in their internal affairs and many Saudis have feared the possible emergence of a revolutionary or democratic Yemen as a threat to their interests. The processes of political centralization, economic development, fostering of nationalism, and cultural opening to the world that shaped most Middle Eastern societies earlier in the twentieth century reached Yemen at a later stage.

In South Yemen, Britain ruled the port of Aden as a colony starting in 1839. After World War I the British gradually extended control over parts of South Yemen's interior, although they never completely integrated the area into their empire. South Yemen became independent in 1967, only to embark on the construction of a radical Marxist government unlike all those in the rest of the Middle East outside Soviet central Asia.

North Yemen emerged from Ottoman control as an independent state, but one that was poor and isolated from the rest of the Middle East. The Zaidi Shii imamate loosely dominated the country until a republican revolution broke out in 1962. Throughout subsequent events, popular sentiment in the North as well as the South favored the union of the two Yemens, despite their substantial and increasing differences.

SOUTH YEMEN AND THE BRITISH

The Arabian Peninsula port of Aden is located 700 miles (1100 km.) west of the Dhufar border of Oman. Aden juts out from the south coast of Arabia into the Indian Ocean about 100 miles (160 km.) east of Bab al-Mandeb, the narrow strait controlling the southern entrance to the Red Sea. Aden has been important for trade between east and west, including Africa, since antiquity. Local shaikhs seized Aden in 1735 and occupied it until the British annexed it as a colony in 1839.

After the opening of the Suez Canal connecting the Red Sea and the Mediterranean in 1869, Aden grew rapidly into one of the great British coaling stations, a submarine cable center, and, as a free port, a trading center. From the Crown Colony of Aden, the British spread their influence along the entire southern Arabian coast, and by treaties with local rulers they established what came to be known as the Eastern Aden and the Western Aden protectorates. The Eastern Aden protectorates were five independent sultanates and two shaikhdoms; the two largest sultanates together were usually called the Hadhramaut, from which originated many of the prosperous Arab merchants of Indonesia and India. In the Western Aden protectorates, which surrounded the city of Aden, there were seven sultanates, six shaikhdoms, two amirates, and one confederation of tribes. By World War I the total population in all of South Yemen was about 500,000.

During the 1930s Britain slowly and gradually extended its influence into the interior of the protectorates. After World War II social and political attitudes in Aden and the protectorates changed markedly. During the war, the mountains of supplies on their way to Middle East theaters of war raised Aden to the third-ranking port in the British Empire, after London and Liverpool. In 1954 the Anglo-Iranian Oil Company erected a $150 million refinery there and almost overnight created a new city, Little Aden, to support it. In the protectorates a new generation of rulers wanted more independence. Aden governors were dependent directly on London, and the individual princes longed for home rule.

Talks in London led to the creation in 1959 of a small federation of six of the states of the Western Aden protectorates. Later, others joined, to make a total of seventeen. The name was changed in 1962 to the Federation of South Arabia.

North Yemen refused to recognize the federation because it had claimed the territory as part of a united Yemen for centuries. In Aden many North Yemeni workers and refugees mounted a Free Yemeni Movement. As long as Imam Ahmad ruled in Sana in North Yemen, they did not want a union, but the revolution of 1962 and the birth of a republic in North Yemen (now called the Yemen Arab Republic) altered conditions. President al-Sallal of North Yemen urged Aden and the Federation of South Arabia to join with his country, and he was strongly supported in this demand by President Nasser of Egypt. Pro-independence guerrillas in 1963 launched a small civil war. To the surprise of many, in 1964 Great Britain unexpectedly promised independence for 1968 and announced later that its troops would be withdrawn from Aden.

Agitation grew as competition developed in Aden and the federation states among Arab nationalists for the role of the successor to the British. One important group was the Front for the Liberation of Occupied South Yemen (F.L.O.S.Y.), sponsored by Egypt. Among the others, only the radical National Liberation Front (N.L.F.) survived. Through coups, the N.L.F. gained control of all the states of the federation, whose officials declared the conservative union to be at an end. As the position of the British grew untenable, the date of withdrawal was moved up to November 1967. Qahtan al-Shabi, the N.L.F.'s leader, formed a group that assumed office as the British left, and South Yemen became an independent state with its capital at Aden.

INDEPENDENT SOUTH YEMEN

Extreme radicals were able to take power in South Yemen because of the great chasms in its society: Aden versus the hinterland, class-conscious Adeni workers versus "feudalistic" tribal autocrats, a national structure versus petty principalities. The indigenous middle class was small and politically inexperienced, while those who wanted rapid change, complete independence from Britain, and national unity believed that they needed a totalitarian state to achieve those goals and also to preserve themselves in power against their numerous opponents.

The N.L.F. controlled all the states, but only a small minority of politically minded individuals felt any national sentiment for South Yemen or any devotion to a socialist society. Popular opinion was more devoted to family, region, tribe, Islam, and a vague concept of a united south and north Yemen than to Marxist state socialism. Rebellions against the N.L.F. and its edicts broke out in every part of the state. Within the N.L.F., there was constant bickering and rivalry over programs and positions. Saudi Arabia refused to recognize the new regime and gave asylum to former rulers of the federation. F.L.O.S.Y. exiles continued to operate in North Yemen, serving as a magnet for malcontents. Despite these problems, South Yemen (now officially the People's Republic of South Yemen) repulsed attacks originating in Saudi Arabia and the Yemen Arab Republic.

Qahtan al-Shabi, the N.L.F. leader, became the president, prime minister, and commander in chief of the armed forces in South Yemen. All those in government were inexperienced in administrative matters. Before the end of 1967, South Yemen had been admitted to the Arab League and the United Nations. The new defense minister hastened to Moscow for aid and arms at the same time as al-Shabi was proposing complete harmony with the Yemen Arab Republic.

In modern times the chief reason for the development of Aden, and the main source of its income, was the servicing and repairing of ships in connection with the Suez Canal. When the Suez Canal was blocked to international commerce, especially oil tankers, during the third Arab-Israeli War of 1967 (just before the republic was formed) and was not reopened until 1975, the cessation of traffic produced economic disaster. In response, the new regime adopted austerity measures, which aroused considerable discontent among the populace. In 1969 young leftists removed al-Shabi, accusing him of dictatorial rule. A five-man presidential council under the chairmanship of Salim Rubay Ali took power.

The new administration, however, could not alter the nation's basic difficulty: the collapse of trade and the resulting massive unemployment. It adopted stringent economic measures, including the raising of tariffs to 300 percent to inhibit imports. The new leaders sought funds from the Communist countries, particularly the Soviet Union.

The presidential council purged the government and army of nearly all their officials. Foreign concerns were nationalized, religious foundations (waqfs) were taken over by the government, peasants and workers seized control of property, and a complete revolution of society was attempted. About one-fourth of the population fled abroad as the secret police crushed internal opposition. Nearly half of the land was redistributed to 26,000 families by government decree, and most of the farmland was organized into agricultural cooperatives. Late in 1970, after the publication of the draft of the new constitution, the name of the People's Republic of South Yemen was officially changed to the People's Democratic Republic of Yemen.

Conditions still did not improve. Before the Suez stoppage, at least 500 ships a year dropped anchor in Aden harbor; there were fewer than fifty in 1972. Higher taxes imposed on foods brought insurrection in many rural areas. With N.L.F. extremism and ineptitude aggravating the economic difficulties and inciting more rebellions, other Arab countries began to question South Yemen's policies and leadership. The government generated considerable domestic and international criticism when it celebrated Lenin's birthday for a week, while not acknowledging the prophet Muhammad's birthday.

Poverty nevertheless did not halt military and ideological ambitions. China set up a military mission in Aden alongside Moscow's, which was arming the southern forces. The arms often went to the insurrectionists engaged in a guerrilla war in Dhufar against Oman. The radical regime in South Yemen lost nearly all its friends except China, the Soviet Union, and Iraq.

This international hostility toward South Yemen coincided with a continuing popular desire for union among many of the people in both Yemens. After secret meetings, the prime ministers of both Yemens signed a document pledging to halt acts of hostility, such as the short war of 1972. Subsequent negotiations on unity revealed, however, that each side was ready to absorb the other but not to cooperate with each other in peaceful ways.

During the fourth Arab-Israeli War in 1973, South Yemen declared the Strait of Bab al-Mandeb a war zone and consented to the stationing of other Arab troops there. South Yemen leased Perim, an island in the strait, to Saudi Arabia for ninety-nine years for $150 million. Relations slowly improved with Egypt and Saudi Arabia; the Dhufar conflict with Oman that had begun in 1965 ended in 1975. Salim Rubay Ali then pronounced a policy of coexistence with all Arab states.

The Suez Canal reopened for traffic in 1975, and life began to stir in Aden, but shipping patterns had changed, and fewer of the new oil supertankers now called at Aden. Plans were made to recondition harbor facilities. British Petroleum in 1977 transferred title to its large refinery in Aden to the government, but in subsequent years, the refinery often operated at a loss.

Internal disputes repeatedly tore apart the ruling Marxist-Leninist party. In 1978 Salim Rubay Ali and several hundred others were killed during severe fighting, and in 1980 his successor as chief of state and head of the party was deposed. The prime minister, Ali Nasser Muhammad, added the post of secretary-general of the Yemeni Socialist party to his duties and became the chief political figure from 1980 until the bloody fighting of 1986, when he was replaced as leader by Haidar Abu Bakr al-Attas, the prime minister. Al-Attas was chosen president and was then elected in 1986, following new elections to parliament. In the 1986 fighting, more than four thousand people had been killed and a small-scale civil war broke out in Aden. The party leaders in such crises differed about ideology, tribalism, relations with conservative regimes, and personal rivalries for power.

The constitution proclaimed Islam the state religion (South Yemeni emulation of the Soviet Union did not extend as far as atheism, but only to a cautious secularism). New legal codes were gradually adopted, but Islamic and tribal law remained widely used. Personal status law declared women and men equal in family relations, and women served in the parliament and as judges. In the first elections for parliament in 1978, non-party independents held many seats, but power was in the hands of the party apparatus. The party used education to encourage Marxist values, expanded the number of students greatly, sent thousands of youths to the Soviet Union for training, and opened the University of Aden in 1975. The government strongly encouraged female education.

In the economic sphere, the regime achieved some limited success for its 2 million people. Agricultural goods had to be sold to the state at prices fixed by it. Production fell following independence, although the standard of living of many of the peasants may have improved. Yemenis living abroad sent remittances back home; this was the country's largest source of foreign exchange, helping to provide foreign exchange to pay for imports. In the early 1980s imports were worth more than twenty times the value of exports. Contact with the richer societies elsewhere in the peninsula stimulated comparisons with the poverty back home; expectations for consumer durables, especially, were stimulated but not fulfilled. Redistribution of wealth and particularly the extension of services to the countryside, formerly available only in Aden, were undertaken by the government. The basic poverty of the country, however, remained unchanged, and South Yemen accumulated a large external debt. South Yemen discovered oil and natural gas fields long after they had been found elsewhere in the Arabian Peninsula. Oil exports starting in 1987 promised better times for the economy.

In its foreign policy, the regime provided access to military facilities and allied itself very closely with the Soviet Union, which provided armaments, training, financial aid, and a treaty of friendship signed in 1979. The Rubay Ali government may have had a hand in the assassination of North Yemen's leader in 1978, which alienated many nearby states. This situation led to a second border war between the two Yemens in 1979. However, a more pragmatic foreign policy emerged in the 1980s, with friendly ties to Saudi Arabia, Oman, and North Yemen. Despite periodic meetings and discussions, little real progress toward uniting the very different political and economic systems of the two Yemens was made in the 1980s; such a union seemed less possible than ever as the two societies increasingly diverged.

THE IMAMATE IN NORTH YEMEN

The Zaidi Shii imamate in mountainous independent North Yemen controlled one of the most remote and isolated spots in the world. At various times the Ottoman Empire ruled coastal Yemen, and occasionally parts of the interior as well. Zaidi tribes in the steep mountains and interior plateaus were able to resist Ottoman expansion, while the Sunni tribes living on the coastal plain had to acknowledge the supremacy of the sultans. As a result of World War I, Imam Yahya of the Hamid al-Din dynasty gained independence for the North, whose population then was around 3 to 4 million. The imam was not able to create some of the most important benchmarks of a nation-state: a unified national market, a common currency, or a standing army. Nevertheless, Yahya argued that all of Yemen, including Aden and the southern regions dominated by the British, should be part of one united state.

In 1934 King Abd al-Aziz of Saudi Arabia defeated the armies of the imam and annexed the province of Asir, but did not push on to destroy Yemen's independence. The British in Aden had a running quarrel with Imam Yahya over the frontier of South Yemen, somewhat abated by the British-Yemeni Treaty of 1934. To counterbalance the Saudis and the British in the period between the two world wars, the imam turned to Italy for support. A treaty was signed, and a Yemeni mission visited Italy to obtain arms and munitions. Yemeni students were also sent to Iraq and Egypt for military training, but the imam's army consisted mostly of tribal contingents. During World War II, North Yemen remained neutral but ousted Germans and Italians from its territory. North Yemen was admitted to the Arab League in 1945 and to the United Nations in 1947.

Society changed slowly in Yemen. Imam Yahya remained a rather old-fashioned despot, and Zaidi Shiis dominated the government, much to the displeasure of Shafii Sunnis who lived in the coastal and southern parts of Yemen. Many of the younger generation wanting more rapid modernization plotted to remove the imam. In 1948, Imam Yahya was assassinated, and a member of a notable family became imam in his place. However, Yahya's eldest son, Ahmad Hamid al-Din, overthrew the insurgents, and many rebels were beheaded as he became imam in turn.

Yemen's political development proceeded at a snail's pace, and the forces for change attempted a coup against Imam Ahmad in 1955. The revolt was led by his brother Prince Abd Allah, who had represented Yemen at the United Nations. It was crushed by the imam's eldest son, Prince Muhammad al-Badr, who freed his father and executed Prince Abd Allah.

The attempted coup, however, stirred up action in Yemen. Imam Ahmad appointed al-Badr deputy prime minister, foreign minister, and minister of defense. A trade mission from the Soviet bloc arrived in Taizz, the imam's favorite residence and thus the capital, and negotiated trade agreements for the Soviet Union, and China signed a five-year trade agreement and provided credits for economic development.

After the formation of the United Arab Republic of Egypt and Syria, Crown Prince al-Badr visited Cairo, where he signed a pact in 1958 creating the United Arab States, a vague federation of Yemen and the United Arab Republic.

Yemen remained politically frozen until Imam Ahmad's death in 1962, whereupon his son became Imam Muhammad al-Badr. The new ruler appointed his friend, Soviet-trained Colonel Abd Allah al-Sallal, army chief of staff and promised that Yemen would begin to modernize. A week later, on September 26, a military junta bombarded the royal palace at Sana, declared that Imam al-Badr had been killed, and formed a republic with al-Sallal as leader. However, al-Badr was not dead, as he demonstrated by holding a news conference in the mountains of northern Yemen.

CIVIL WAR IN NORTHERN YEMEN: ROYALIST VERSUS REPUBLICAN

At the outset, al-Sallal arranged a military defense pact with Cairo. Initially 20,000, ultimately as many as 60,000 Egyptian troops were sent to Yemen to ensure al-Sallal's position and to solidify control by Nasser over republican Yemen. The modernized Egyptian army, finding it difficult to fight in the mountain areas, restricted its activities to the plains and larger towns. The royalists were supplied with arms and ammunition by Saudi Arabia; their fighting forces were almost entirely made up of Zaidi mountain tribesmen who fought willingly against the Egyptian foreigners. Furthermore, they were eager to capture weapons and stores of ammunition. No one doubted that they could conquer the plains within hours if the Egyptian troops departed. As the war dragged on, Nasser became bogged down in Yemen, as the French had in Algeria. At the same time, support for the republic slowly grew in the cities of northern Yemen and among the Sunni and even some of the Zaidi population.

Toward the end of 1962, after the Yemen Arab Republic had been recognized by the Soviet Union and the United Arab Republic, the United States proposed the withdrawal of all foreign troops from Yemen. On this basis the United States recognized the republican regime, which was admitted to the United Nations. Not until Egypt's setbacks in the 1967 war with Israel, however, did Nasser give his word to King Faisal of Saudi Arabia that Egyptian troops would depart from Yemen and that support for al-Sallal would be terminated.

Republican Yemen had great difficulty in forming a stable government that could gain the support of the people. As well as being a hard man to please, al-Sallal was in poor health, and he was forced to remain in Cairo for medical treatments for protracted periods. Amid jealousy and distrust, one prime minister after another would be turned out to escape to Cairo with his life, often to return when his replacement fled. After an attempted coup, al-Sallal reassumed the post of prime minister and reestablished his absolute authority. Nasser hoped al-Sallal would hold Yemen until the British departed from Aden, but Nasser had to abandon him. In 1967, on his way to Moscow, al-Sallal was overthrown in a bloodless army coup. The civil war finally ended in a compromise: the creation of a tribally dominated conservative republic in 1970.

YEMEN ARAB REPUBLIC

With al-Sallal gone, the last Egyptian troops departing, and King Faisal demanding compromise, the civil war lost its drive. The army turned over the government to a group of civilian "Third Force" anti-Egyptian moderate Zaidi republicans under Qadi Abd al-Rahman al-Iryani and a presidential council. When Saudi Arabia halted the flow of arms and money, al-Badr gave up the struggle and left.

The new national assembly reelected al-Iryani president at its first meeting. Twelve of the seats in the assembly remained empty, reserved for members from South Yemen, a gesture on the part of the Yemen Arab Republic or North Yemen toward union of the two Yemens.

Society was in chaos, and the economy was in a shambles: famine stalked a land devastated by a drought as well as a lengthy civil war. The moderately socialist government was staffed by able and earnest people, but they could do little to overcome these problems. Governments were only temporary, and no faction could establish general legitimacy. Early in 1970, negotiations with wealthy and conservative Saudi Arabia, the key to peace and economic progress for Yemen, led to an agreement to end friction along the frontier, to promote reconciliation among all the factions within northern Yemen, and to take back all exiles except al-Badr. After royalist leaders returned to Sana, regained their property, and had one of their number elected to the presidential council, Saudi Arabia recognized the republic.

A border war with South Yemen superseded all else in 1972. The prime ministers of the two Yemens next approved detailed agreements to unify. Yet little was done to obtain the popular but elusive goal of unity because the two countries differed sharply in political system, economic situation, and foreign orientation. In 1973, though the talks with South Yemen continued, so did border raids and assassinations.

One prime minister followed another until 1974, when the Zaidi-controlled army staged a bloodless coup, suspended the constitution, dissolved the assembly, and removed the prime minister and cabinet. Leading the coup was the Ruling Command Council under Colonel Ibrahim al-Hamdi, who became chairman and head of state. Yemen developed closer ties with Saudi Arabia, which provided aid. Saudi financing helped Yemen buy weapons from the Soviet Union and the United States. The military sought to advance their own interests through cooperating with the newly installed technocrats in expanding the size of government. A sign of growing central government power was the first census, completed in 1975. The new military rulers sought gradually to expand the authority of the central government at the expense of the tribes. At the same time, though, governmental weakness opened the way for private initiative. Using remittances from abroad that came into Yemen through informal money changers, local cooperative societies built roads, opened schools, and provided other public services.

Al-Hamdi was assassinated in 1977, and his successor was killed by a bomb in 1978. The constituent assembly then elected Colonel Ali Abd Allah Salih as president in 1978. Salih conciliated all factions and foreign states, and he managed to establish a more permanent regime as he brought his family and a wide array of groups into governing circles. He introduced conscription for the army in 1979. Elections in 1988 for a consultative council also resulted in the renewal of Salih's tenure. However, the military remained the only institution that could hold the country together. Foreign policy during the Salih years was designed to secure the approval of both the United States and the Soviet Union.

Border fighting with South Yemen intensified into full-scale war in 1979, although a cease-fire was concluded with the withdrawal of troops from the border areas of both Yemens and a reopening of unification talks. Unity continued to be the stated goal of both Yemens, but no real change took place in the relations between the two countries.

North Yemen concluded economic development and trade agreements with the European Economic Community and the Soviet Union in 1984 and continued to rely on international assistance to relieve its persistent budget deficits. Yemeni prosperity and economic growth depended on the employment situation in Saudi Arabia, where hundreds of thousands of North Yemenis (out of the total North Yemeni population of more than 9 million) resided and worked. Remittances from Saudi Arabia and workers' returning to live in North Yemen began to change the Yemeni countryside in terms of both new capital available for a higher standard of living and a decreasing pool of agricultural labor available for the terraced farming of the hillsides. Other changes resulted from the discovery and exploitation of oil in North Yemen itself; exports commenced in 1987.

Education expanded dramatically in the 1970s and 1980s, as seen in the opening of the University of Sana in 1971. Illiteracy, however, remained widespread. Television broadcasting began in 1975, and it has affected the lives of North Yemenis, especially women, by showing alternatives to strict gender segregation practices. While most Yemeni poets have not experimented as radically in form as elsewhere in the Arab world, they have been deeply committed to reforms and the process of change. The development of painting and sculpture started in the 1980s, with the first piece of modern public sculpture commissioned for the new Sana airport late in the decade. Folk art continued to an extent, as in working in glass and with the making of daggers, while the preservation of old sectors of Sana drew the attention of Yemenis and the United Nations.

Rapid increases in population and movement to the cities, especially Sana, influenced all aspects of culture. The capital grew from a small town of about 35,000 in 1962 to over 200,000 twenty years later. By 1993 the population of Sana was estimated at as many as 1 million people.

Cultural, social, and economic transformations took place inside the political tranquility provided by the relatively stable regime of Ali Abd Allah Salih. The military solidly supported him, but the integration of Sunnis into the Zaidi-dominated northern government took place only to a limited degree. And the government remained smaller and weaker than in most other parts of the Middle East.

THE UNION OF NORTH AND SOUTH YEMEN

North Yemen and South Yemen fully united on May 22, 1990, with Sana as the capital. This surprising event had many causes, the most important of which was the general desire among most Yemenis for a union. In the short run, the democratic reforms in the Soviet Union during the late 1980s helped induce a collapse of faith in scientific socialism in South Yemen, while the Soviets sharply reduced their financial aid to it, thereby ruining its economic prospects.

Since the leaders of the North and South agreed to share power jointly, the existing cabinets and parliaments united. President Salih of the North stayed in that post for united Yemen; the head of the southern-based Yemen Socialist party became vice president, and the prime ministry went to another southerner. Military units were exchanged as well, but they continued to be chiefly northern or southern in composition. A plebiscite in 1991 approved the new constitution. The Communist-style rule in the South and the dictatorship in the North were both relaxed. Despite all these measures, it was clear that most internal policies would follow northern patterns, for instance, in the presidential decree of 1992 on personal status law for women, which abolished most of the changes in southern legal codes pertaining to marriage in favor of a more conservative approach to such issues.

The newly united Yemen had to face an external diplomatic issue almost immediately following its creation, when Iraq invaded and annexed Kuwait in 1990. Yemen opposed the use of force to compel the withdrawal of Iraq from annexed Kuwait, a position that was particularly important because of Yemen's presence on the United Nations Security Council. Saudi Arabia and the other Gulf Arab states were furious at Yemen's actions. As a result 800,000 Yemeni expatriate workers were expelled, and unemployment rates in Yemen increased to about 40 percent. The Yemeni economy suffered severely in the 1990s, although oil production increased to about 200,000 barrels per day.

Since the North had more than four times the population of the South and Salih was popular there, it was to be expected that his political supporters would win the 1993 election. President Salih's General People's Conference did better than the Yemen Socialist party, while a third group, the Islah party, represented the views of Islamists and moderate tribal conservatives in both the North and South. The ex-Marxist Yemen Socialist party was deeply upset by the results of the election as well as assassinations of some of their leaders. However, the chief problem facing both northerners and southerners was the integration of two very different political systems at a time of great economic difficulty.

Full-scale civil war broke out among military units in 1994, with southerners attempting to break away from northern control. Northern units launched tank, artillery, rocket, and bomber attacks on southern targets as leaders in the South proclaimed their renewed independence. In a little over two months, the North defeated the South amid heavy and brutal fighting, taking Aden and inflicting much damage on civilians.

While Yemen remained united, the victory was based on the supremacy of the North and its leaders, army, customs, and institutions. Even though President Salih allowed the reappearance of the Yemen Socialist party, he cracked down on political opposition, newspapers, and freedom of expression in the middle 1990s. In the parliamentary elections of 1997 the General People's Conference won a clear majority of the votes, with the Islamists coming in second, and the Yemen Socialist party boycotting the election. In 2001 the president appointed a new upper house of parliament, thereby further strengthening his power.

Yemen's leaders were, however, faced with extraordinary economic difficulties. Saudi Arabia and the other Gulf Arab states in 1990 had suspended economic assistance as well as deporting Yemeni workers. (Saudi Arabia even went so far as to support the southern secessionists in 1994.) Yemen curbed government spending and subsidies to the poor, as unemployment, rapid population growth, and inflation remained major problems. Some economic progress became apparent by the late 1990s as oil prices became higher and Yemeni production increased, more Yemeni workers returned to Saudi Arabia and other oil-producing states, and Yemen became friendlier with the United States.

Yemen emerged from its international isolation slowly—an example was the resumption of foreign relations with Kuwait in 1999. Military cooperation with the United States was disrupted when Islamic fundamentalists linked to Usama bin Ladin's al-Qaida organization attacked the USS Cole in Aden harbor in October 2000. Yemen worked with the United States in attempting to locate those responsible for the attack and also in tracking down adherents of al-Qaida following the September 11, 2001, terrorist attacks in the United States. (This cooperation was difficult because the Yemenis who had fought with the Taliban in Afghanistan, and other so-called Arab Afghans, were often sheltered in tribally controlled rural areas of Yemen outside the direct control of the central government.) Yemen also concluded, in 2000, an agreement with Saudi Arabia about its long and vaguely defined border, thereby promising to end one of the irritants that had often poisoned relations between the two neighbors. For Yemen, ties to Saudi Arabia, the wealthiest and most influential of the countries in the Arabian Peninsula, and a leader in oil policy issues and Islamic matters worldwide, were of paramount importance.

REFERENCES

References cited at the end of Chapter 47 are pertinent to this chapter as well.

Bidwell, Robin: *The Two Yemens.* Boulder, Colo.: Westview Press, 1983. A comprehensive history of both the North and South by an outstanding scholar.

Boxberger, Linda: *On the Edge of Empire: Hadhramawt, Emigration, and the Indian Ocean, 1880s–1930s.* Albany: State University of New York Press, 2002. A fine account of identity, emigration, politics, and social structures.

Burrowes, Robert D.: *The Yemen Arab Republic: The Politics of Development, 1962–1986.* Boulder, Colo.: Westview Press, 1987. Especially valuable for the Salih years.

Carapico, Sheila: *Civil Society in Yemen: The Political Economy of Activism in Modern Arabia.* New York: Cambridge University Press, 1998. Discusses non-governmental civil society in the 1950s, the 1970s, and the early 1990s in both parts of Yemen.

Chaudhry, Kiren Aziz: *The Price of Wealth: Economies and Institutions in the Middle East.* Ithaca, N.Y.: Cornell University Press, 1997. This careful comparative study of Yemen and Saudi Arabia from the 1920s to the 1980s tests some aspects of the rentier theory about merchants and government bureacracies.

Cigar, Norman: "Islam and the State in South Yemen: The Uneasy Coexistence." *Middle Eastern Studies* 26 (1990): 185–203.

Halliday, Fred: *Revolution and Foreign Policy: The Case of South Yemen, 1967–1987.* Cambridge: Cambridge University Press, 1989.

Ismael, Tareq Y., and Jacqueline S. Ismael: *The People's Democratic Republic of Yemen: Politics, Economics and Society.* Boulder, Colo.: Lynne Rienner, 1986. A thorough and somewhat favorable view of South Yemen; very useful for the detailed history of internal political struggles.

Kostiner, Joseph: *Yemen: The Tortuous Quest for Unity, 1990–94.* London: Royal Institute of International Affairs, 1996.

Makhlouf, Carla: *Changing Veils: Women and Modernisation in North Yemen.* Austin: University of Texas Press, 1979. Discusses upper-class women in Sana, the capital.

Molyneux, Maxine: "Women's Rights and Political Contingency: The Case of Yemen, 1990–1994." *Middle East Journal* 49 (1995): 418–431.

Peterson, J. E.: *Yemen: The Search for a Modern State.* Baltimore, Md.: Johns Hopkins University Press, 1982. Political history and development with a concentration on institutions.

Serjeant, R. B., and Ronald Lewcock, eds.: *San'a': An Arabian Islamic City.* London: World of Islam Festival, 1983. Excellent scholarly essays on all aspects of Sana, contemporary and historical.

Stookey, Robert W.: *South Yemen: A Marxist Republic in Arabia.* Boulder, Colo.: Westview Press, 1982. An outstanding general survey.

al-Suwaidi, Jamal S., ed.: *The Yemeni War of 1994: Causes and Consequences.* London: Saqi, 1995. Essays on the causes of the civil war and the role of tribes, internal politics, and external powers in it.

Wenner, Manfred: *The Yemen Arab Republic: Development and Change in an Ancient Land.* Boulder, Colo.: Westview, 1991. A useful concise history of northern Yemen.

CHAPTER 49

Saudi Arabia and Oil

The collapse of the Ottoman Empire in 1918 opened the way to the expansion of two dynasties: the Saudis in eastern Arabia and the Hashimites in western Arabia. Both were founded on claims to religious legitimacy predating World War I, both had an insecure economic resource base, and both sought alliance with Great Britain. The Saudi royal house ultimately defeated the Hashimites and established the Kingdom of Saudi Arabia. After the end of World War II, oil provided enormous wealth to the Saudi state, enabling it to transform an economy that had been notable for its poverty. Saudi Arabia became one of the most significant of Middle Eastern countries and the most influential country in the Arabian Peninsula.

BRITAIN AND SHARIF HUSAIN OF MECCA

World War I created in the Arabian Peninsula a partial political and power vacuum, although Britain assumed that Arabia was to be a British sphere of influence. In the nineteenth century, the Persian Gulf had come under the control of England; official British residents and agents controlled the foreign affairs and advised the rulers of the small states on the eastern coast of the Arabian peninsula from Kuwait to Oman. On the southern shore of Arabia, Britain held its colony of Aden and protected or had treaty rights with nearby sultans, imams, and amirs. But along the western coast of Arabia, the Ottoman Empire predominated. Communications from Istanbul by sea via Suez, land routes from Damascus, and the Hijaz Railway enabled the Ottoman Empire to maintain substantial power. From this coast and from Ottoman Syria and Iraq, the empire found it possible to keep a hand on the precarious balance among the Arab tribes of the interior deserts and to sway decisions favorable to the Ottomans.

In essence, the British inherited the Ottoman role in 1916, when they subsidized the Hashimite Sharif Husain of the Hijaz on the western coast and recognized and subsidized the Saudi ruler Abd al-Aziz in central and eastern Arabia. They gave Sharif Husain nearly $1 million in gold each month and supplied him with arms to captain the

Arab rebellion against the Ottomans. Husain proclaimed himself king of the Arabs and was promised a united Arab state at the end of the war. When the mandate system was established and Syria, Palestine, and Iraq were taken by France and England, he was disillusioned and provoked. In 1921 the British proposed a treaty that recognized Husain as the sovereign of the Hijaz and continued his subsidy indefinitely. Yet his pride would not permit him to accept the clauses that mentioned Britain's "special position" in Palestine. British payments of gold suddenly ceased, and Husain was on his own.

Without British protection and assistance, Husain of Mecca, although he styled himself king of the Arabs, reverted to being only an independent Arab ruler, and by no means the strongest. He had taken the lead in the discussions with the British regarding Syria and Iraq; now the burden of failure was his, although he always acted as if his sons Abd Allah and Faisal in Transjordan and Iraq were only his viceroys. Unfortunately for his son Ali, heir in the Hijaz, his viceroys had taken with them most of the army built up during the Arab Revolt in World War I. Husain's prestige came from his descent from the prophet Muhammad, but this honor did not necessarily make him popular with many of the nomadic tribes in the Hijaz. He looked down on such individuals as Abd al-Aziz, the Saudi-Wahhabi leader, as uneducated Bedouins. For their part, they considered him to be a protégé of the British. In addition, Husain was a poor administrator. Almost the sole income of the Hijaz was derived from the annual pilgrimage to Mecca. Husain mismanaged it, and he permitted pilgrims to be fleeced by the merchants until it became a scandal throughout the Muslim world. His final mistake was assuming the title of caliph in 1924 after the Turkish Republic abolished the Ottoman caliphate.

Abd al-Aziz boiled in rage that that "sinful man" should so desecrate the position held by the caliphs Abu Bakr and Umar. Moreover, Abd al-Aziz had several old scores to settle with Husain, and he wanted the income from the pilgrimage. Most important was Abd al-Aziz's inclination to unite the Arabian Peninsula under his own rule.

ABD AL-AZIZ

Abd al-Aziz ibn Abd al-Rahman Al Saud, known in the West as Ibn Saud, was born about 1880 to the Saud family of Riyadh in the Najd. Since the middle of the eighteenth century, his princely family had been the political mainstay of the puritanical sect of Islam originated by Muhammad ibn Abd al-Wahhab, and the Saudis aided in the propagation of Wahhabism throughout Arabia. The first Saudi kingdom was ended by Mehmet Ali of Egypt, who invaded Arabia on behalf of the Ottoman Empire. In the late nineteenth century, the most serious rivals and enemies of the Saudis were the Rashidi family of the Shammar tribe to the north, centered on the town of Hail. Abd al-Aziz's father and uncles lost out to the Rashidis in various battles in large part because of an internal struggle for power, thereby ending the second Saudi state. At an early age Abd al-Aziz had to go into exile in Kuwait. In 1902, against seemingly impossible odds, Abd al-Aziz, in a stroke of derringdo, led forty young men up tilted palm trunks over the walls and rooftops of Riyadh to recapture the city from the Rashidis for himself and his family, thereby establishing the third Saudi kingdom.

In the years that followed, Abd al-Aziz was able to ward off the declining Rashidis. Using an appeal to Wahhabi religious solidarity and dynastic loyalty, Abd al-Aziz was able to construct an alliance of townspeople, settled tribesmen, and nomadic tribes to begin building state authority. In 1913, he captured from the Ottomans the province of al-Hasa on the Persian Gulf, not knowing that the province was practically floating on oil. When World War I reached the Middle East, Abd al-Aziz was visited by British officers and agreed to accept a subsidy not to join the Ottomans. Upon the defeat of the Ottoman Empire in Arabia, the entire peninsula seemed open to another wave of Saudi-Wahhabi expansion, but Abd al-Aziz soon encountered strong opposition from the Hashimites of Mecca, who were also intent on expanding their rule.

In 1919, Abd Allah, Husain's second son, led a column of armed men to seize a disputed oasis. The Saudis annihilated his army, Abd Allah barely escaping with his life, and the British informed Abd al-Aziz that he could keep his conquests but must not invade the Hijaz.

When Britain installed Husain's sons Abd Allah in Transjordan and Faisal as king of Iraq in 1920 and 1921, Abd al-Aziz felt surrounded by Husain and the Hashimite clan. The apparent encirclement spurred the Saudis to move outward. Abd al-Aziz sent his son Faisal in 1920 across difficult trails to acquire the highlands of Asir and the realm of the Idrisi family south of the Hijaz.

Forging a strong bond of friendship with the Idrisis and obtaining their allegiance, Abd al-Aziz next turned to settling his family feud with the Rashidis. In a series of swift and daring expeditions, the Saudis captured Hail in the autumn of 1921. A number of the Rashidis were then forced to reside as his "guests" at Riyadh, and Abd al-Aziz became the sole power in the interior expanses of Arabia. A provisional settlement was made with the British with regard to their protected areas; the 1922 protocol of Ukair loosely defined Saudi versus British areas and districts. Two neutral zones were set up on the boundaries of the Saudi domain: one faced Iraq, and the other was next to Kuwait. These neutral zones served as buffer regions, so that wandering tribes would not create incidents.

The extension of the Saudi realm led to serious economic problems. At that time the annual income of the kingdom, treated as the king's own personal income, was about $750,000, to which was added a subsidy from the British. For a state that had just doubled its responsibilities, however, this was insufficient, and to augment it in Arabia seemed exceedingly difficult. In the winter of 1923, a foreign syndicate was granted an oil concession for a rental of $10,000 a year. Ironically, only two years' rental was paid; then, upon the advice of geologists, the concession was abandoned.

KING OF SAUDI ARABIA

In 1923 Great Britain held a conference of Arab leaders who were receiving subsidies and told them that payments would stop in 1924; a lump sum payment was handed them forthwith. Abd al-Aziz had hardly reached Riyadh after leaving the conference when Husain arranged to be proclaimed caliph. The announcement shocked the Saudis, who felt that the holy places of Islam were being ruled by a presumptuous person. In September, the Saudis attacked the Hashimites at Taif, and in October they occupied Mecca. Husain fled to Jidda and abdicated in favor of his eldest son, Ali. (He then took up residence with his son Abd Allah, until the British conveyed him to Cyprus. He died in 1930 in Amman.) Abd al-Aziz could have pressed on easily and defeated Ali at Jidda, but he realized that this might involve the European powers. Obtaining no aid from Great Britain, Ali surrendered Jidda to the Saudis in 1925 and went to Baghdad to live at his brother Faisal's court.

Abd al-Aziz of the House of Saud was now master of most of Arabia, including the Hijaz. He added the title of king of the Hijaz to that of sultan of Najd. In taking Mecca, the Wahhabis destroyed a number of the shrines that they considered the works of the devil and then Abd al-Aziz refurbished the holy places. In 1926 he held an Islamic congress in the Hijaz that brought Islamic leaders to see him and the administration he was inaugurating. In effect, it legitimized his rule and indicated that the pilgrimage, now the Saudis' greatest source of income, was again safe.

Abd al-Aziz was a born leader. He inspired confidence, was just and honorable in his administration, and made decisions and took actions promptly. He observed the Wahhabi code yet carefully appraised and judged social innovations. The introduction of the telephone and the radio into Arabia, for instance, was bitterly opposed by the archconservatives among his ulama, who argued that these instruments must be agents of the devil since they could carry the voice so far. Abd al-Aziz neatly disputed that contention by pointing out that these instruments would bring the word of God and that the faithful would be able to hear the Quran read by worthy ulama. The telephone and the radio thus came to Saudi Arabia, in the process helping to centralize and stabilize the power of the state over all its far-flung territories.

Life around Abd al-Aziz, whether he was at the capital of Riyadh or staying in the provinces, was simple and direct. The business of the government was dispatched with efficiency in a patriarchal atmosphere. Abd Allah Sulaiman, the treasurer, on most occasions kept the state's money in his bedroom at the palace in Riyadh. At one time he commented on his anxiety over the risk when the balance rose to $50,000 in cash. Other advisers, besides members of the royal family, included Arab political refugees, ulama, merchants, and the British convert to Islam H. St. John Philby.

Military power in the third Saudi state rested on a combination of groups, including the town militias, tribal units, and the Ikhwan (Brotherhood). The founding of Ikhwan communities starting in 1908 or 1912 proved significant in the Saudi rise to power. The first brotherhood was established around desert wells, where the fighting Bedouins were settled. Its motive was partly economic. The state provided funds for a mosque, religious schools for reading and writing, wells, agricultural irrigation, arms, and ammunition. This settlement, a religio-socio-military camp, became the prototype of many such towns. From the brotherhoods Abd al-Aziz received his most devoted soldiers and the necessary stiffening for the regular levies that made his army so feared.

Abd al-Aziz's power was extended over the nomadic tribes. Traditionally independent, they rebelled against Saudi justice, military control, peace, and taxation. When the Ikhwan joined the tribes, claiming Abd al-Aziz was too sympathetic to the British and that he had compromised the Wahhabi cause by settling for peace with Iraq and Transjordan rather than further expansion, a small-scale civil war broke out. This struggle of 1928–1930 ultimately was won by Abd al-Aziz, who received the backing of the ulama and most of the settled population.

Abd al-Aziz tied the tribes to his rule by holding suitable hostages at his court, by cash grants, and, if necessary, by armed subjugation. In 1932, the official name of the state was changed from the Kingdom of the Hijaz and of the Najd and Its Dependencies to the Kingdom of Saudi Arabia, a name that reflected the centrality of the dynasty to the identity of the state.

After the occupation of Jidda, Abd al-Aziz in 1925 arranged treaties with Britain that defined the frontiers with Iraq and Transjordan. However, no mention was made of the districts of Maan and Aqaba, which the Saudis claimed but which were joined to Transjordan. Two years later, in the Treaty of Jidda, Great Britain recognized Abd al-Aziz as a sovereign and independent ruler. He pledged to "maintain friendly and peaceful relations" with Kuwait, Bahrain, Qatar, and the Oman Coast, all of which were under the protection of Great Britain.

The problem of Asir, south of the Hijaz, troubled Abd al-Aziz for many years. After the death of Muhammad Idrisi in 1923, his heirs mismanaged affairs and quarreled continually. When Imam Yahya of Yemen supported the Idrisis, hostilities broke out in 1934, with the Saudis fighting the Yemenis. Abd al-Aziz's armies won a quick and crushing victory, yet in the Treaty of Taif, peace was established on the basis proposed before the Saudis attacked, since there was a suspicion that Italy might intervene if too harsh a peace was imposed on Yemen.

DISCOVERY OF OIL

The worldwide depression of the early 1930s upset the Saudi economy. The government had depended on the pilgrimage traffic, which in the late 1920s had amounted to over 100,000 visitors each year. In 1931, however, the traffic dropped to 80,000; in 1932, to 40,000. The total income of the government was only about $2 million. Abd al-Aziz granted a concession to the Standard Oil Company of California.

Standard Oil of California and the Texas Company formed the California Arabian Standard Oil Company to undertake mapping, geologic surveying, and drilling in al-Hasa province. Engineers came across to the Saudi mainland from nearby Bahrain, where oil had been found in 1932. With the deepening of well 7 at Dhahran in 1938, oil was found in quantity and shipped to Bahrain. Piers were quickly constructed, and the first tanker was filled in May 1939, Abd al-Aziz turning the first valve. Exploration spread, and other producing wells were located, but when World War II broke out, Saudi Arabia was not yet a substantial producer of oil. Lack of personnel and equipment kept Saudi production down during the war.

Although Saudi Arabia was neutral during most of World War II, the decline of the pilgrimage to Mecca reduced the country to desperate financial straits. The oil company advanced some money, but more was needed, and Britain began to advance sizable sums to Saudi Arabia in 1941. American lend-lease was later made available. Saudi Arabia had not joined the League of Nations, but in 1945 the kingdom declared war on Germany so as to become a member of the new United Nations.

A refinery was built at the request of the American army. The oil company, now called the Arabian American Oil Company (Aramco), in 1945 built an underwater pipeline to Bahrain, enabling the flow of oil to be increased. The total income of the Saudi government jumped from about $7 million in 1939 to over $200 million by 1953 because of oil revenues. As a result of inadequate banking facilities, much of the cash journeyed to Cairo, where it was turned into luxury articles of small bulk that could be easily shipped to the Arabian coast. Lavish living and enormous incomes for the royal family and their friends became the custom, and a great part of the income of the state was squandered. In the postwar era, Saudi Arabia became entirely dependent on oil royalties.

EXPANSION OF OIL PRODUCTION

Toward the end of World War II, the demand for petroleum products became staggering, and the need for a pipeline prompted Aramco to seek additional capital for construction. In 1946 arrangements were made for Standard Oil of New Jersey and Socony-Vacuum to acquire 30 and 10 percent, respectively, of Aramco stock. Work on the pipeline was soon started, although all work on the line ceased during the 1948 Arab-Israeli War. Syria, Lebanon, and Jordan declared that the line would not be permitted as long as the United States supported the creation of Israel. King Abd al-Aziz, however, announced that he would not revoke the American oil concessions. The oil companies thereupon organized the Trans-Arabian Pipe Line Company. Over half a billion dollars was expended between 1948 and 1953 in constructing the line and developing new fields and facilities for Aramco. In 1950 the 1068-mile (1719 km.) pipeline was completed, and 300,000 to 500,000 barrels a day began to flow from Dhahran to Lebanon. New production was brought in every year, and by 1956 oil was being produced at a rate exceeding 1 million barrels a day.

As production increased and Aramco profits began to swell, Abd al-Aziz pressed for greater returns. At the end of 1950 a new concession gave Saudi Arabia considerably more money, including a guaranteed 50 percent of Aramco profits. The announcement of these terms led to the breakdown of oil discussions in Iran and a change in the rates in Iraq. In fact, the Aramco–Saudi Arabia concession terms in 1950 established a new general pattern of royalties throughout the Middle East. Saudi Arabia increased production during the controversy over Iranian oil nationalization.

Such high levels of income posed many new problems to government leaders. The first budget, of $55 million, was drawn up for fiscal year 1948, but no budget was published again until 1952. Moreover, budgets were not necessarily followed, especially since a distinction between the public treasury and the private purse of the king and the royal family had not yet been drawn.

KING SAUD AND KING FAISAL

King Abd al-Aziz, who died in 1953 after a fifty-year reign, was succeeded by the eldest of his thirty-five living sons, Saud ibn Abd al-Aziz. (Subsequently, other sons of Abd al-Aziz succeeded to the throne, with each one reaching power according to a consensus based on the general principle of the ablest among the elder sons receiving the endorsement of senior princes inside the very large royal family.) In the king's last years, Prince Saud had been declared heir apparent and begun to participate in governmental

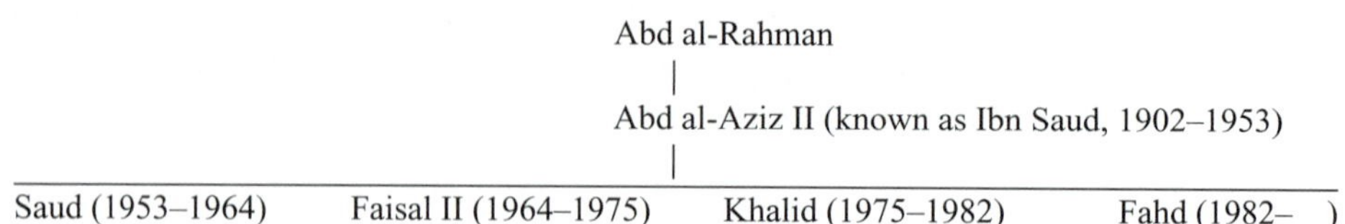

The Later Saudi Rulers

activities. Other sons shared duties of administration; the most prominent of these was Prince Faisal. Definite ministries of government were established, and a formal cabinet was organized. The new King Saud served as his own prime minister, while Faisal was declared heir to the throne and continued his work in foreign affairs.

Extravagant spending led to government deficits and even foreign borrowing. Corruption spread rapidly, especially in the awarding of contracts. Many Saudi officials were able to buy estates in Egypt or apartment houses in Beirut, and the construction of new palaces proceeded rapidly. Problems of finance, bitter rivalry with the leaders of other Arab states, internal social upheaval, the Cold War, the issue of Palestine, traditional nepotism, and the impact of modern living produced such strong conflicts as to demonstrate that King Saud was unequal to the task of governing. Suddenly, in 1958, after a royal family conference, King Saud agreed to transfer authority over the government to Prince Faisal, who was generally acknowledged as a more talented administrator than his brother.

Faisal ibn Abd al-Aziz was born in Riyadh in 1904 and grew up in the household of his maternal grandfather, where he was toughened in the ways of desert warriors. As early as 1919 he undertook various missions for his father, becoming viceroy of the Hijaz and foreign minister in 1926. Although Faisal had traveled widely, he remained austere and simple in his personal tastes and was known for his fairness and integrity.

The question of highest priority for Faisal was how to cope with the ineptness of King Saud in a society in which the king's wish could not be publicly challenged. Faisal had promised Abd al-Aziz many years before that he would never raise a hand against his older brother. When King Saud reasserted his authority in 1960, Faisal dutifully stepped aside. The drastic measures Faisal had adopted to end corruption and waste, institute efficiency and tighten authority, and modernize the state and society had irritated many influential figures. In the struggle against Saud, Faisal was supported by the National Guard, many of the royal princes, the ulama, and those who favored change and reform.

King Saud's return did not improve the situation. The army revolt in Yemen opened the eyes of even the most conservative elements as to what could happen at home, and they called for Faisal to run the government. Refusing to be king, he again took over as prime minister, forming a new cabinet and removing from office all of King Saud's sons. Faisal outlined a new program calling for the organization of a consultative council, the establishment of a ministry of justice, the abolition of slavery (which took place in 1963), and rapid economic and social development. King Saud failed miserably in a second bid to regain his powers. In 1964 he renounced his right to rule and left Saudi Arabia. Faisal was recognized as king, and the popular Prince Khalid, another son of Abd al-Aziz, was named deputy prime minister, crown prince, and heir to the throne.

For a decade King Faisal managed the affairs of Saudi Arabia astutely. In spite of the billions that began to pour into the treasury in the 1970s, King Faisal stood fast in the conservative management of affairs. Faisal drew heavily on family talents. In 1967, Minister of the Interior Prince Fahd was named second deputy prime minister and second in line to succeed to the throne.

Following the death of Egypt's president Nasser in 1970, King Faisal became the dominant figure among the Arabs, as well as the leader of Islamic society. An avowed enemy of communism and Zionism, he used his influence, power, and resources against both. He was assassinated on March 25, 1975, at the hands of a disgruntled nephew, who three months later was beheaded publicly, as tradition demanded.

KING KHALID AND KING FAHD

Following the assassination of Faisal, power continued in the hands of the extremely numerous royal family. The hundreds of royal princes in effect delegated their potential authority to a dozen or so senior princes, and especially to the surviving sons of Abd al-Aziz. Politics in Saudi Arabia was the struggle for influence and position among this small group. Saudi Arabia had no constitution or parliament for many years, and there were also no political parties, while the press and other media were indirectly controlled by the monarchy. The kings appointed some technocrats to the cabinet, but the key posts were reserved for royal princes. Descendants of Muhammad ibn Abd al-Wahhab, the eighteenth-century religious reformer, also occupied prominent places in government. In general, the royal family relied on the ulama for legitimacy and in return supported the ulama and their ideas on social and legal policy. The basis of the state was dynasty and religion, not nationalism.

Since the government controlled enormous oil riches, it was able to accommodate most forms of dissent. Rapid economic development, large-scale weapons purchases, personal advancement and high salaries to deserving commoners, economic subsidies to tribes and peasants, and commercial prosperity enhanced the monarchy's popularity with various sectors of society. The kings opted for rapid economic change, but without corresponding political change; this choice excluded most groups from a role in political decision making. A prudent foreign policy also was a hallmark of Saudi Arabia, which managed to avoid direct warfare, and the destruction and chaos that often ensued, until the Kuwait crisis of 1990.

Within hours of Faisal's murder, the council of royal princes installed Prince Khalid ibn Abd al-Aziz (b. 1912) as king and prime minister. Prince Fahd became crown prince, first deputy prime minister, and minister of the interior; Prince Abd Allah was named second deputy prime minister and commander of the National Guard. Shunning public life as much as possible and loving the desert, many assumed that Khalid would be overshadowed by his aggressive brother, Prince Fahd, but Khalid, extremely popular with the tribes, rapidly learned to wield his power in a quiet but forceful way. However, his poor health made him delegate more and more power to Fahd.

A severe and unexpected threat to the royal rule took place on November 20, 1979, the first day of the Muslim lunar year 1400, when some hundreds of armed men seized the central Muslim shrine, the Kaba, and the enormous mosque built around it in Mecca. The rebels, most of them tribal Saudis, declared that one of them was the expected Mahdi, or divinely guided messiah, and that they were now entitled to rule the state. They denounced corruption and demanded a moral cleansing of the country. Saudi forces carefully took the mosque in bitter fighting, and more than sixty of the rebels were subsequently executed. Surprisingly, this event caused very few repercussions. There were minor and unrelated Shii uprisings in eastern Arabia, where that sect was locally numerous and had been repressed, but the main effect was to decrease the already small chances of official secularization. Fahd peacefully became king after King Khalid's death in 1982, naming his brother Abd Allah as crown prince.

One of the most notable events of the 1980s involving the Saudi royal family took place well above the kingdom, and even the world, as Prince Sultan bin Salman, a nephew of the king, flew aboard the U.S. space shuttle *Discovery* in 1985. He thus became the first Saudi, the first Arab, and the first Muslim in space. The ulama dealt with the thorny issue of which direction to face—normally toward the Kaba in Mecca—for a person praying in space by declaring that one could pray while facing in any direction at all.

Royal prestige was convincingly demonstrated in 1986 when King Fahd dismissed long-time oil minister Ahmad Zaki Yamani from that position. Although Yamani had served for twenty-four years and he had been the most important figure in the Organization of Petroleum Exporting Countries (O.P.E.C.) for nearly as long, he had no political base of support when the king named a replacement and opted for a new oil strategy.

THE OIL BOOM AND O.P.E.C.

Each year Saudi oil production increased beyond all predictions. In 1966 it topped 2.5 million barrels a day, making Saudi Arabia the fourth largest world producer, after the United States, the Soviet Union, and Venezuela. Offshore discoveries, added to new finds, more than maintained the quantities of proven oil reserves, which were 50 billion barrels in 1960, 81 billion by 1967, and 175 billion ten years later. Into the 1980s and 1990s new reserves continued to be discovered. Saudi Arabia had about one-quarter of the world's oil!

One of the difficult problems for Saudi Arabia, as well as for the oil companies, was the vagaries of supply and demand. These were made more complex by discoveries of oil in many new regions. Although increases in world oil consumption did not always keep pace with production, any reduction in exports hurt Saudi Arabia's budget, since it was tied to oil exports. Moreover, larger exports from one country too frequently meant that the international oil companies would curtail production in another country. The oil-producing countries wished to gain control over their own natural resources and thereby reduce the influence of foreigners on their economies.

To meet these goals, Abd Allah al-Tariki, Saudi director of petroleum affairs, initiated in 1960 at Baghdad the Organization of Petroleum Exporting Countries, comprising Iran, Iraq, Kuwait, Saudi Arabia, and Venezuela. O.P.E.C. sought to gain information and influence gradually in oil matters. After its formation, Libya, Algeria, Indonesia, Qatar, Nigeria, the United Arab Emirates, Gabon, and Ecuador also joined, making it by

1973 a powerful force in the world. (Ecuador and Gabon subsequently left O.P.E.C. in 1992 and 1996.)

Initially O.P.E.C. attempted to protect its members, each one a weak developing nation, against the informal cartel of the international oil companies, sometimes referred to as the "seven sisters." In the mid-1970s, however, the tables were turned. The oil companies, through the nationalization or purchase of oil-producing resources by the host country, had become subservient to the O.P.E.C. members, while the petroleum-importing states were reeling from O.P.E.C. price fixings and increases that were moving billions of dollars out of their economies and into the treasuries of the oil producers.

In 1968 Kuwait, Libya, and Saudi Arabia also joined together in the Organization of Arab Petroleum Exporting Countries (O.A.P.E.C.), with the stipulation that membership was reserved to Arab states whose oil production constituted a major part of the nation's economy. Because of their almost total dependence on their petroleum resources, the Arab oil-producing countries determined a need to enter the oil business on their own. Some countries, such as Iraq, simply nationalized the foreign companies, but Saudi Arabia gradually bought Aramco, completing the process in 1980. The settlement allowed the former owners of Aramco to market 80 percent of Saudi oil production, receiving a fee per barrel for their services. Furthermore, they would be paid to explore, expand facilities for refining, and ship petroleum. The oil-producing countries of the Middle East finally had control of their chief natural resource.

Except for 1967, when oil revenues faltered because of the third Arab-Israeli War, the closing of the Suez Canal, and a temporary freezing of shipments to Great Britain and the United States, Saudi oil production broke one record after another. World economies were prospering, and their petroleum requirements mounted. By the end of 1971, output was over 5 million barrels per day, and the government budget reached $2.4 billion. However, Saudi Arabia cut production somewhat during the oil embargo directed by the Arab states against America for its support of Israel in connection with the 1973 Arab-Israeli War. In 1974, Saudi Arabia averaged 8 million barrels a day.

The world consumed more than five times as much oil in 1972 as in 1948, and demand was outrunning supply. With no end of the seller's market in sight, O.P.E.C. raised prices several times in 1973 and 1974, and by the end of 1974, the price of Saudi Arabian crude oil stood between $11 and $12 a barrel. This quadrupling of price disturbed world economic and financial relationships, spurring a worldwide recession. With inflated prices, Saudi Arabian budgets escalated, jumping to $32 billion in 1976–1977. Foreign reserves invested abroad by Saudi Arabia rose $12 billion or more each year.

In the mid- and late 1970s, Saudi oil production increased, and so did Saudi revenues from it, despite worldwide inflation that decreased the value of payments. Following the Iranian revolution of 1979 and the outbreak of the Iran-Iraq War in 1980, oil production was increased to over 9 million barrels per day, and Saudi Arabia became the second largest producer of oil in the world, exceeded only by the Soviet Union. Output reached almost 10 million barrels per day in 1981 as the price of oil rose to $34 a barrel, while Saudi revenues were more than $110 billion!

O.P.E.C. oil prices doubled in 1980–1981. As world demand for oil began to decline in the face of such high prices, and as production by non-O.P.E.C. countries increased, prices started to fall. O.P.E.C. exports declined from 31 million barrels per day in 1979 to only 17 million per day in 1983. By 1982 the Saudis cut their output to 6 million barrels per day. Oil minister Yamani tried to persuade other O.P.E.C. countries to reduce production and lower prices, but the market operated more quickly than Saudi diplomacy. By early 1983, Saudi Arabia produced only 3.6 million barrels per day, and in the same year O.P.E.C. cut its official prices, assigned production quotas, and gave the Saudis the swing role in production. Since the population of the kingdom was so small and its oil reserves were so great, the Saudis agreed to vary their production as world demand varied so as to help prop up the price of oil.

While the government budget fell into deficit, Saudi foreign reserves were tapped to provide cash. Yet Saudi Arabia at this time made some progress in reaching at least one of its goals: a Saudi for the first time became president of Aramco (later called Saudi Aramco) in 1984.

Oil production in Saudi Arabia reached a twenty-year low in mid-1985 at 2.2 million barrels per day, and the Saudis unilaterally cut their oil prices. Then, tired of the cheating of some O.P.E.C. members who produced more than their quotas while leaving the Saudis holding the bag, they began to increase output. The Saudi goal was to pressure the rest of O.P.E.C. into more equitably applied restrictions on output and pricing. Yamani sharply increased pumping to 7 million barrels per day in mid-1986. World oil prices fell sharply to a six-year low, and O.P.E.C. agreed to try the Saudi strategy. All O.P.E.C. countries agreed on a quota system for limiting their total production to 18.5 million barrels of oil per day, including limits of about 2.6 million barrels each for Iraq and Iran, who were fighting each other. But although this strategy ultimately was adopted, Saudi revenues were falling; they had been $43 billion in 1984 but were only $22 billion in 1987. Uncertainty within Saudi Arabia was so great that the government never issued an official budget for 1986–1987.

Saudi Arabia had a preeminent role in O.P.E.C. because it sold a large share of O.P.E.C. production, but it has not had complete control, and O.P.E.C. itself has not totally dominated the world oil market. In the 1980s only about one-third of world oil came from the O.P.E.C. countries. Each member of O.P.E.C. has had its own interests, and internal disagreements have been deep and varied. Algeria, Libya, Iraq, and Iran often pushed for higher prices than Saudi Arabia wished. The Saudi position was based on its enormous reserves, a relatively small population, and its pro-American policies, which resulted in a long-range view of oil issues favorable to international stability. The enormous riches of Saudi Arabia gave it a margin enabling variation in pricing policies, while at the same time Saudi wealth posed an alluring opportunity for poorer and ambitious neighbors.

MILITARY FORCES

For all of Abd al-Aziz's character and personality, he never forgot that his position rested on military power. Saudi Arabia did not fight in any major wars after 1934 in a substantial way up until the 1990s; Kings Saud, Faisal, Khalid, and Fahd also preserved the peace. In fact, the chief purpose of the military and National Guard was to secure domestic order and preserve the regime. Two parallel organizations existed: the regular armed forces and their rivals, the tribally based National Guard. Despite some occasional plots aimed at military coups, the two institutions remained loyal to the government and the monarchy.

In 1951 Saudi Arabia signed a mutual defense assistance agreement with the United States. The most powerful military base in that part of the Middle East was located at Dhahran. Here, toward the close of World War II, the United States constructed a mighty airfield and installations from which planes could control much of the Middle East and bomb strategic spots in the Soviet Union. The United States promised to train a small Saudi navy, organize and instruct a Saudi air force at Dhahran, and expand the army school. However, the lease for the base was not renewed, and in 1962 it was relinquished to Saudi Arabia.

The outbreak of civil war in Yemen in the autumn of 1962 reemphasized the military aspects of life in Saudi Arabia, as President Nasser of Egypt supported the Yemeni republican forces while the royalists sought protection from Saudi Arabia. Egypt bombed Saudi border towns. In the northeast, Kuwait looked to Saudi Arabia to help ward off the danger of invasion from Iraq. Jet fighters were quietly invited back from the United States in 1963, American paratroopers participated in training the Saudi Paratrooper Corps, and a British military mission arrived to advise the Saudi army.

Saudi Arabia felt weak and vulnerable, since its population was small compared to those of Iran, Iraq, and Egypt. This feeling was reinforced with the British withdrawal from the Persian Gulf in 1971. King Faisal aided Oman's monarchy against leftist guerrillas. As Iran, Israel, and other possible enemies acquired vast supplies of weapons, an arms race in the region began. In 1973 Saudi military purchases topped $1 billion.

In 1975–1976 Saudi Arabia spent $4 billion in the United States for military goods and $4 billion more the next year. It seemed that the military could escalate its requirements to almost any height. About one-quarter to one-third of the national budget went in various ways for military expenditures.

By 1979 more than half of all U.S. foreign military sales went to the Saudis. In the 1980s there were several instances, however, when Saudi Arabia wished to buy weapons systems but pro-Israelis in the U.S. Congress objected, fearing such arms would be used against Israel. Saudi Arabia therefore sought to diversify. There ensued a $4 billion purchase of weapons from France in 1984 and sales in 1985 and 1988 by Great Britain that totaled considerably more than $14 billion. Saudi Arabia secretly bought Chinese surface-to-surface missiles that were capable of hitting any targets in the Middle East, and they were installed in 1987–1988.

Pakistan sent an armored brigade of about 10,000 troops to Saudi Arabia in the early 1980s in return for money and new schools. The troops were later withdrawn because Pakistan, although willing to have them used against Israel, was not agreeable to their employment against Iran, should a war take place.

Saudi Arabia spent enormous sums on its military, including especially infrastructure, technical training, and arms acquisitions and maintenance, but this money did not buy security from attack. Instead, the Saudi government depended on its foreign policy to gain allies and deter enemies.

SAUDI FOREIGN RELATIONS

Saudi Arabia's foreign interests have been based on preserving the regime and maintaining the status quo in the region through an unofficial alliance with the United States.

Saudi kings saw Soviet Communism, Israeli Zionism, and Pan-Arab nationalism and socialism as their chief enemies. This view implied a basic contradiction in Saudi policy, however, for although a close reliance on American power for opposing the Soviet Union was desirable, the United States was also the major backer of Zionist Israel. Another basic aspect of Saudi policy pertained to the pilgrimage to Mecca: the Saudis were the protectors of the holy places and came to play a major role among the Muslim countries of the world as a result of this and their wealth. (The pilgrimage season was highly significant for the government, much of which moved to Mecca every year at that time.)

Saudi Arabia participated in the deliberations of the Arab League starting in 1945, but it was not one of the leading countries in that group until much later. In 1948, for instance, the Saudis sent only a nominal force to fight Israel.

In 1953 a serious dispute arose with Great Britain over the possession of the Buraimi oases, which Abu Dhabi also claimed. The question remained unsettled until 1974, when Saudi Arabia and Abu Dhabi divided the area. Saudi borders to the south and east were still largely undemarcated, which led to this sort of problem.

Saudi Arabia during the 1956 Arab-Israeli War supported Egypt. Throughout the union of Egypt and Syria between 1958 and 1961 and the vagaries of Nasserism, King Saud tended to support Egypt, while King Faisal strongly opposed Nasser. Conservative, monarchical, fundamentalist, rich, and pro-American, Saudi Arabia naturally clashed with revolutionary, republican, secularist, poor, and pro-Soviet Egypt. Pan-Arab nationalism was a threat to the Saudi royal family's power and wealth and to the identity of the country.

In 1962 Saud and Faisal condemned Egypt's intervention in northern Yemen on the side of the republican regime. Faisal believed that the republican regime in Yemen would collapse if Egyptian forces were withdrawn. Only in the aftermath of the 1967 Arab-Israeli War did Nasser withdraw his forces and permit a compromise, and Saudi Arabia ultimately recognized both the relatively conservative government of the (northern) Yemen Arab Republic as well as the leftist People's Republic of South Yemen.

In 1968, when Great Britain announced its intention to give up special privileges in the Persian Gulf, Saudi Arabia began to exert its influence in the Gulf. The Saudis denied Iran's claim to Bahrain, but King Faisal did agree to divide the continental shelf in the Gulf with Iran. The seven shaikhdoms of the Trucial Coast began to discuss forming the United Arab Emirates, and King Faisal unsuccessfully urged Qatar and Bahrain to join. Other disputes were settled by agreements with Kuwait and Iraq that divided the former neutral zones equitably.

Saudi Arabia began to take an active role in Arab-Israeli affairs after the 1967 war. King Faisal, who was personally very devout, expressed sorrow at the annexation of the Muslim parts of Jerusalem by Israel in 1967; he repeatedly stated his desire to pray at the holy places there. The Saudis came to subsidize Egypt, Jordan, Syria, and the Palestine Liberation Organization in their confrontation with Israel. Faisal declared publicly in 1971 that there could be no peace in the Middle East without Israeli evacuation of Muslim holy places in Jerusalem, withdrawal from 1967 conquests, and recognition of Palestinian rights. In 1973 Faisal was one of the leaders of the oil embargo against the United States, reducing Saudi Arabia's production levels and signaling his solidarity with the Arab cause against Israel. Saudi Arabia broke diplomatic relations with Egypt in 1979 following Egypt's peace treaty with Israel. The Saudis also stopped paying Egypt a subsidy of nearly $1 billion per year. By 1982, however, the Saudi king came to accept Egypt again as a partner in discussions and resumed formal relations in 1987.

Even more pressing than the Arab-Israeli question, from the Saudi viewpoint, was the 1980–1988 Iran-Iraq War, in which Saudi Arabia backed Iraq financially and diplomatically. Khomeini of Iran attacked the Saudi royal family as despots and criticized their claims to Islamic legitimacy. The Saudis feared the possible expansion of the war into Kuwait and Saudi Arabia and repeatedly encouraged a cease-fire and peace.

Kings Khalid and Fahd often sought to bring about compromise solutions to Middle Eastern problems as part of the general Saudi practice of reinforcing the status quo. Outside the Middle East, Saudi Arabia played a prominent role in the affairs of the world's Muslim community, sponsoring the Organization of the Islamic Conference (founded 1969), a summit of all Muslim nations and peoples, and the World Muslim League, established in 1962 with its headquarters in Mecca.

One way to increase Saudi security was through regional hegemony, and the kingdom in 1981 joined with Bahrain, Kuwait, Oman, Qatar, and the United Arab Emirates to create the Gulf Cooperation Council for coordinating military, diplomatic, and other matters. Another device was the increased purchase of arms, particularly from the United States. President Ronald Reagan repeated the pledges of earlier presidents in assuring the Saudis of U.S. military intervention if the royal government was under direct attack, from within or without. King Fahd secretly gave millions of dollars to the Nicaraguan Contras and other groups at the request of the U.S. government, and Saudi Arabia thus became involved in the Iran-Contra affair in the United States.

Saudi Arabia has granted large amounts of its oil wealth to various Muslim countries and groups abroad, and it has built mosques, trained preachers, and printed Qurans to help spread Islam in such places as central Asia. The kingdom helped fund the Palestine Liberation Organization, the Eritrean rebels in Ethiopia, and the anti-Communist Afghan guerrillas.

DEVELOPMENT IN SAUDI ARABIA

The considerable influx of money following World War II generated many plans for the improvement of Saudi Arabia, which lacked almost every prerequisite of a modern society, particularly infrastructure. Attention was first turned to massive construction projects: highways, ports, airfields, schools, hospitals, electric power plants, irrigation systems, and means of supplying water to Jidda, Mecca, and Riyadh. Aramco proved an interested ally in these programs and located able engineers for many of the projects. The railway between Dammam and Riyadh was completed, the port of Dammam was reconstructed, and, to serve as a gateway to Medina, the port of Yanbu was developed on the Red Sea.

The Saudi authorities spent large sums of money developing all aspects of education. Students numbered only 33,000 in 1953; by 1970, this number grew to 550,000, and by 1990 to 3.1 million. Elementary schools appeared in all parts of the kingdom in great numbers; in 1963 alone there were one hundred new schools for boys and sixty-two for girls. About half as many girls attended schools as boys, and they were taught separately. By the 1980s, however, nearly as many girls attended school as boys, although their career opportunities were quite restricted. While in the 1960s most teachers were Arabs from outside Saudi Arabia, this began to change as thousands of Saudis educated abroad returned and Saudi universities also produced many graduates. Careers in teaching, government, and business opened up to them. The first secular university was opened in Riyadh in 1957, while the Islamic Shariah College of Mecca had been created in 1949. What is now the King Fahd University of Petroleum and Mining at Dhahran graduated its first class in 1972. Several other universities, institutes, and educational centers were built.

Construction radically transformed the appearance of Riyadh and the other large cities; most of the older buildings were torn down as new buildings rose up everywhere. Many government offices were moved to Riyadh from Jidda. Hospitals were built not only in the capital but throughout the country. Each year transportation and communications were vastly improved, financed by ever larger budget appropriations, thereby extending the power of the central government over all areas.

Under Faisal, economic development had the highest priority, receiving 40 percent of the budget. Surveys revealed sizable deposits of iron, copper, and silver, and the amounts of sulfur obtained from oil were vast. Some industries developed, but most of the non-oil economic activities involved construction, services, commerce, and the expansion of government. In 1975, a second five-year development plan was announced, at a cost of $150 billion. Allocations were still chiefly for infrastructure and social development—roads, housing, harbors, and irrigation—but one-sixth of the plan's cost was to go to industrial development.

As infrastructure projects were completed in the late 1970s, the Saudis turned to the long-range issue of future sources of income other than exporting oil. Natural gas utilization and petrochemicals were obvious choices. A new pipeline linking the Persian Gulf and the Red Sea opened in 1981, and a $12 billion natural gas system was completed later. The new industrial cities of Jubail and Yanbu were opened in the late 1980s. Jubail on the Gulf, which cost more than $45 billion to complete, soon began to export chemicals based on petroleum.

The government also sponsored agriculture. Since only about 2 percent of the country's land was arable, the rest being desert or mountainous, farming prospects were limited. Nevertheless, wells were cleaned, pumps were installed, and desalinization projects built. Intensive hydrological surveys were carried out in several areas as the supply of water became critical in Riyadh. Dams and desalination plants were built, with the hope that Saudi Arabia could gain some independence from the need to import nearly all its food.

In 1970, agriculture was responsible for 70 percent of employment, but by 1980 this fell to only 25 percent as a majority of the population became urban. Peasants and nomads moved to the cities, although governments paid much higher than world prices for their products. Poultry and dairy farming flourished, and heavily subsidized farmers in the 1980s produced enough grain to feed the kingdom on their own and even to export wheat. The Saudi government also helped agriculture by bringing electricity to 2000 villages in the 1970s.

Agriculture produced only a small part of the Saudi gross national product. Even after oil revenues sharply declined in the mid-1980s, oil was by far the most important aspect of the Saudi economy. Private companies, especially those engaged in construction, suffered losses, but major projects were completed, while the government became as interested in the full and efficient use of existing facilities as in the building of new enterprises.

The sums spent on development were allotted to contractors, many of whom were foreigners and who needed to hire foreign laborers, who totaled perhaps 3 million by the early 1980s. Hundreds of thousands of North Yemenis, Palestinians, Egyptians, Pakistanis, Koreans, and others were brought into the kingdom. They often lived apart from the Saudis, but there was inevitably some interaction and diffusion of new ideas, values, and patterns of living. Saudi tourists who traveled abroad also encountered different lifestyles than those they were accustomed to at home.

SOCIAL AND CULTURAL CHANGES

A large gap between high urban and low rural income led many peasants and tribesmen to move to the bigger cities. This urban settlement by nomads was encouraged in part by a government land policy that fostered private property at the expense of tribal jurisdiction. By 1981, two-thirds of the Saudis lived in cities, one-quarter were villagers, and only about one-tenth percent were nomads or seminomads. The townspeople had greater access to educational facilities and other government services than the rural population. Population growth rates were high, and in the 1970s school enrollments almost doubled while university students' numbers increased four times. By 1992 about half of the population was under the age of fifteen, creating enormous demands for services from the state.

Although wealth was concentrated in the hands of the royal family, many others also became wealthy, and a great deal of money trickled down even to the poor. Social services improved greatly in quality and availability. Radios, television sets, automobiles, and other consumer goods of all sorts were widely available.

The new media gave even the rural population access to information. National radio broadcasts began in 1949, and television service commenced in 1965. Religious programming occupied a substantial proportion of broadcast time, as did entertainment from other Arab countries and abroad. Since public cinemas were not permitted, private rentals of movies and, more recently, videocassettes have been the means of dissemination of films. The Saudi government in the 1970s sharply increased the number of public libraries to about forty, while the new Department of Antiquities surveyed archaeological sites, opened museums, and encouraged historical research. Youth groups sponsored poetry recitals, musical performances, and literary clubs. An annual national heritage and culture festival near Riyadh starting in 1985 featured poetry, artisans, and racing events. Jidda became famous for its public sculptures, found amid traffic circles and along the Red Sea. The modern international style of architecture became the basis of design for the many new buildings dotting the city centers throughout the country. Probably soccer was the most popular form of entertainment, with enormous enthusiasm among the male population for the various teams. Saudi Arabia participated in a wide variety of cultural events by hosting many Arab, Muslim, and other international conferences and congresses. In all cultural fields, however, the ulama played a leading role in shaping discourse so as to preserve the religious and social heritage of the past.

In literature Saudi Arabia followed the same trends as in many other Arab countries. Saudi poets exhibited the modernist versus classical or romantic split in poetry, as well as popular local folk poetry. New forms included the use of free verse, and there has been some following of European examples as well as a good deal of originality. Short stories and novels frequently stressed change and separation, themes widespread in Saudi social life, as well as depictions of local and regional life.

In all of these activities, women have had either no part or a very limited role. Despite increasing literacy, Saudi women were denied active participation in public or political life; males ran the government, the religious system, courts, and most economic institutions. Gender segregation in public places was strictly enforced. Women were not allowed to drive automobiles and were sharply restricted as to places where they could work outside the home. The legal system has changed in some ways, particularly in regard to commercial and administrative law, but personal matters have been adjudicated on the Wahhabi interpretation of the Quran and the hadiths (sayings) of the Prophet. Therefore, the legal status of women and their dependence on men have continued as before, even as many more women have graduated from the schools and universities and have moved into such professions as writing and teaching.

THE KUWAIT WAR

The Iraqi invasion and annexation of Kuwait, the resulting international crisis, and the Kuwait War of 1991 dramatically affected Saudi Arabia in the 1990s. (These events are more fully discussed in Chapter 46). After King Fahd's attempted mediation of the differences between Iraq and Kuwait failed, Saddam Husain's armed forces seized Kuwait on August 1, 1990, although the Kuwaiti royal family and tens of thousands of Kuwaitis escaped to Saudi Arabia, where a government in exile was established. The United States convinced Saudi Arabia that Iraq would not be content with Kuwait; Saddam might well invade the Saudi kingdom or would desire to dominate it through intimidation.

Since the Saudi armed forces, though well equipped with sophisticated weapons, numbered only about 70,000 men, Fahd invited American troops to defend Saudi Arabia's eastern oil fields. Saudi Arabia mobilized its own forces and also provided assistance to the hundreds of thousands of troops who arrived in the next few months from the United States and to the soldiers also arriving from Egypt, the Arab states of the Persian Gulf, Britain, France, Syria, and several other countries. Saudi general Prince Khalid ibn Sultan coordinated the actions of about 200,000 non-western troops, and the United States supervised the arrangements for the other 600,000. King Fahd and then president George Bush of the United States jointly determined grand strategy after consulting the leaders of the chief allied nations.

Diplomats from the kingdom helped coordinate the successful international effort to condemn Iraq's actions at the United Nations and the Arab League. Saudi diplomacy was assisted by financial aid freely extended to a number of countries and by the opening of diplomatic relations with China and the Soviet Union. Saudi finances were strained by the cost of the war preparations, but they benefited from increased production and the higher price for oil brought about by the crisis.

The Iraqi response to all these Saudi actions was to accuse King Fahd of being a puppet of the United States and to condemn the presence of so many non-Muslim soldiers on the territory of a state home to the holy cities of Mecca and Medina. Saddam claimed to be willing to work toward a peaceful compromise resolution of the Kuwait crisis, but repeated efforts in this direction by Soviet, Jordanian, and other leaders failed. When Yemen, Jordan, and the Palestinians seemed to support Iraq against Saudi Arabia, the Saudi government retaliated by compelling hundreds of thousands of Yemeni workers to leave, ending economic aid to Jordan, and cutting off support of the Palestine Liberation Organization.

The United Nations Security Council authorized the use of all necessary force to compel Iraq to withdraw from Kuwait, if it had not already done so on its own, no later than January 15, 1991. Just after the expiration of this deadline the allied countries launched a massive air war from Saudi Arabia, the Gulf, and Turkey against Iraqi targets. The Saudi air force fought efficiently, though most action was undertaken by U.S. airplanes. Iraq fired missiles at Saudi cities but caused only slight damage. Saudi ground forces took an active part in the ground war of February 24–28, which crushed the Iraqi army and brought about the liberation of Kuwait.

The allied victory was not total. Saddam Husain remained in power in Baghdad after suppressing two insurrections. Although most foreign troops left Saudi Arabia, some stayed behind as part of an operation using bases there and in Turkey to enforce no-fly zones in northern and southern Iraq. Bomb attacks killed U.S. troops stationed in Saudi Arabia in 1995 and 1996.

The war cost Saudi Arabia about $55 billion. Part of this money came from current income, but the rest had to be drawn from overseas investments and borrowing. Despite this, the royal family felt it necessary to spend large sums on weapons purchases, mostly from the United States.

Saudi oil production remained constant at about 8 million barrels per day in the 1990s, with world demand slowly increasing, while prices and O.P.E.C.'s share of total supply remained roughly as before the Kuwait War. By 1992 Saudi Arabia was the world's largest producer of oil, with vast underground proven reserves yet to be tapped. To protect this wealth, the Saudis sought peace abroad; they opened ties to the Islamic Republic of Iran, demarcated the border with Oman and Yemen, and participated in the Arab-Israeli peace process, but maintained an avowed and deep hostility to the regime of Saddam Husain in Iraq.

SAUDI ARABIA IN THE 1990s AND 2000s

Political power after the Kuwait War continued to reside in the hands of the king and royal family, although as the health of King Fahd deteriorated, Crown Prince Abd Allah gained most of the responsibility for day-to-day affairs. In 1992–1993 King Fahd authorized a substantial political reform as an appointed consultative council (majlis al-shura) finally came into existence. The council could consider only matters assigned it by the king, but its members, many of whom were highly educated, came to play a role in the formation of policy. Basic laws issued by Fahd also opened the way for a new generation of the royal family to be considered for succession to the throne. As Saudi Arabia faced a plethora of political, economic, military, and diplomatic issues in the 1990s, two very different internal groupings favored changes in government policies: Islamic fundamentalists, who criticized the regime for its alleged laxity, pro-Western leanings, and liberalism, and Western-style liberals, who criticized the authorities for their alleged severity, cultural dogmatism, suppression of women, and conservatism.

The most famous Saudi Islamic fundamentalist was the radical Usama bin Ladin. Even though he was stripped of his Saudi citizenship in 1994, Usama bin Ladin still managed to attract some Saudis to his al-Qaida organization, employing his great personal wealth and the religious and cultural antagonism felt by a minority of Saudis toward the United States. Fifteen of the nineteen persons directly involved in the September 11, 2001, attacks on America were Saudis. Usama bin Ladin also strongly condemned the Saudi government for its dependence on the United States.

Saudi Arabia had been one of the few countries in the world to recognize the Taliban government of Afghanistan, but the kingdom suspended diplomatic relations in 1998 because of terrorist attacks launched by bin Ladin's followers in East Africa. The Saudi authorities criticized the 2001 terrorist attacks and joined the United States in seeking to curb financial support for al-Qaida in 2002. Diplomatic relations with the United States nevertheless remained strained, in part because of feelings among some American leaders that Saudi Arabia had not done enough to curb extremist Wahhabis and also because of the general feeling among Saudis that unquestioning American support of Israel during the second intifada was wrong. At an Arab summit conference in March 2002, Saudi Arabia launched a proposal for ending the Arab-Israeli dispute on the basis of a compromise.

In the ten years after the Kuwait War, the Saudi economy fluctuated in response to dramatic variations in world oil prices, which in turn responded to supply and demand factors. By 1996 Saudi Arabia had become the world's largest exporter of oil, producing about one-third of O.P.E.C.'s sales and about 12 percent of all the world's oil. Because of increased efficiency, the development of alternative sources, and occasional economic slowdowns, the price of oil fell substantially in the middle and late 1990s, reaching a low point of $10 per barrel in late 1998. With a rapid yearly increase in the Saudi population, real per capita income was far less than it had been earlier, falling by three-fourths between the early 1980s and 2001. However, careful management of production quotas by O.P.E.C. began to change this situation, with the price of oil steadily rising starting in 1999. By October 2000 the world price of a barrel of oil had reached $37 and Saudi income from oil was about $60 billion. Saudi Arabia increased oil production, partially in response to American requests, achieving a more stable price range by 2002.

Increased oil revenues permitted the Saudi government to end the long-established practice of running budget deficits and borrowing money to pay for them. While government subsidies had been cut in the middle 1990s, especially to agriculture, in the early 2000s more money was available, in particular for educating the almost 5 million students in Saudi schools and universities. The government sought to train Saudi workers to replace the quarter of the population who were foreign residents and who filled most private-sector jobs. Such training involved computers, whose use became much more widespread in 1999 when direct dialing to the Internet became available for the first time, even while Saudi censors employed filters to limit access to some sites, whose content was deemed to be morally offensive or politically suspect.

Criticisms from within and abroad did not change the basic outlines of Saudi government and society, in which the importance of oil prosperity and religious legitimacy remained dominant. While Saudi Arabia sought entrance to the World Trade Organization, the Saudis also continued to manage the pilgrimage to Mecca, which now attracted 2 million or more pilgrims every year. Saudi Arabia thus remained the leading Islamic country in the world, and the country's wealth, even though less than formerly, gave it a considerable degree of domestic prosperity and international influence. The state—that is, the king and royal family—kept economic and political power within the hands of the ruling elite.

Compared to such Middle Eastern countries as Iraq, Syria, Egypt, and Turkey, Saudi Arabia was distinctly different in that its political system and public life were based on royal rule, conservative religious values, and a large role for the ulama in cultural matters. The Saudi dynasty had acted since World War II on the belief that rapid economic growth, extraordinary social alterations, and Saudi dependence on external military guarantees for security need not entail changes in basic political and religious patterns.

REFERENCES

References cited at the end of Chapters 27, 46, 47, and 48 are pertinent to this chapter as well.

Abdalla, Abdelgadir Mahmoud, et al., eds.: *Sources for the History of Arabia.* Riyadh: Riyadh University Press, 1979. 2 vols. The best beginning place for historiographical studies; a mine of information about events and sources.

Abir, Mordechai: *Saudi Arabia: Society, Government and the Gulf Crisis.* London: Routledge, 1993. Concentrates on the period since the death of King Abd al-Aziz.

Almana, Mohammed: *Arabia Unified: A Portrait of Ibn Saud.* Rev. ed. London: Hutchinson Benham, 1982. A colorful and personal account of administration in the days before oil.

Alnasrawi, Abbas: *Arab Nationalism, Oil, and the Political Economy of Dependency.* New York: Greenwood Press, 1991.

Altorki, Soraya: *Women in Saudi Arabia: Ideology and Behavior among the Elite.* New York: Columbia University Press, 1986. Shows the changes in the patterns of living for urban elite women.

Altorki, Soraya, and Donald P. Cole: *Arabian Oasis Town: The Transformation of 'Unayzah.* Austin: University of Texas Press, 1989. How economic and social change has affected one town in central Arabia.

Amuzegar, Jahangir: *Managing the Oil Wealth: OPEC's Windfalls and Pitfalls.* London: Tauris, 2001. The author discusses each OPEC country's economic history, chiefly for the period 1974 to 1994, and then compares them, with a supplement bringing his analysis up to 2000.

Arebi, Saddeka: *Women and Words in Saudi Arabia: The Politics of Literary Discourse.* New York: Columbia University Press, 1994. Examines Saudi women writers of the 1980s.

Bogary, Hamza: *The Sheltered Quarter: A Tale of a Boyhood in Mecca.* Translated by Olive Kenny and Jeremy Reed. Austin: University of Texas, 1991. A charming account of life in pre-oil days, with information on social history, religion, education, and gender relations.

Cordesman, Anthony H.: *Saudi Arabia: Guarding the Desert Kingdom.* Boulder, Colo.: Westview, 1997. A complete look at all aspects of the subject.

De Gaury, Gerald: *Faisal, King of Saudi Arabia.* New York: Praeger, 1967. A perceptive study of a complex ruler.

Fandy, Mamoun: *Saudi Arabia and the Politics of Dissent.* New York: St. Martin's Press, 1999. Examines the fragmented political and religious opposition to the ruling dynasty, especially in the 1990s.

Gause, F. Gregory, III: *Saudi-Yemeni Relations: Domestic Structures and Foreign Influence.* New York: Columbia University Press, 1990. How domestic factors influenced foreign policy from 1962 to 1986.

Habib, John S.: *Ibn Sa'ud's Warriors of Islam.* Leiden: Brill, 1978. An examination of the Ikhwan.

Helms, Christine Moss: *The Cohesion of Saudi Arabia: Evolution of Political Identity.* Baltimore, Md.: Johns Hopkins University Press, 1981. An analytical work emphasizing geography and its effects, as well as history and diplomacy for the early twentieth century.

Jayyusi, Salma Khadra, ed.: *The Literature of Modern Arabia: An Anthology.* London: Kegan Paul, 1988. This massive anthology of poetry and short stories includes Saudi Arabia and the other countries of the Arabian Peninsula; a valuable introduction provides an overview of recent literature.

Katakura, Motoko: *Bedouin Village: A Study of a Saudi Arabian People in Transition.* Tokyo: University of Tokyo Press, 1977. Shows the impact of change and the resilience of tradition among tribal villagers near Mecca. Most useful.

Kostiner, Joseph: *The Making of Saudi Arabia 1916–1936: From Chieftaincy to Monarchical State.* New York: Oxford University Press, 1993. Argues that tribal considerations were major factors in determining Abd al-Aziz's policies.

Kramer, Martin: *Islam Assembled: The Advent of the Muslim Congresses.* New York: Columbia University Press, 1986. Deals with the Hijazi congress and other such gatherings in the 1920s and 1930s. Well researched and well written.

Long, David E.: *The Kingdom of Saudi Arabia.* Gainesville: University Press of Florida, 1997. An excellent short survey.

McLoughlin, Leslie: *Ibn Saud: Founder of a Kingdom.* New York: St. Martin's Press, 1993. A concise biography of King Abd al-Aziz, emphasizing his personal life and accomplishments.

al-Mani, Muhammad Abdullah, and Abd ur-Rahman Sbit as-Sbit: *Cultural Policy in the Kingdom of Saudi Arabia.* Paris: UNESCO Press, 1981.

Monroe, Elizabeth: *Philby of Arabia.* London: Faber & Faber, 1973. A vivid picture of the man, the times in which he lived, and the journeys by which he most deserves to be remembered.

Munif, Abdelrahman: *Cities of Salt: A Novel.* New York: Random House, 1987. In this first volume of a trilogy, the author examines the negative impact of oil development on tribal society.

Niblock, Tim, ed.: *State, Society and Economy in Saudi Arabia.* London: Croom Helm, 1982. A fine collection of essays on various topics; especially valuable for diplomatic and economic matters.

Ochsenwald, William: "Saudi Arabia." In *The Politics of Islamic Revivalism: Diversity and Unity.* Edited by Shireen T. Hunter. Bloomington: Indiana University Press, 1988.

Philby, H. St. John B.: *Arabia.* New York: Scribners, 1930. Philby was a British convert to Islam who served as adviser to Abd al-Aziz and was one of the outstanding explorers of Arabia; his many books are excellent sources of information on Saudi Arabia.

———: *Saudi Arabia.* London: Benn, 1955. A history of that state.

Rasheed, Madawi Al: *Politics in an Arabian Oasis: The Rashidi Tribal Dynasty.* London: Tauris, 1991. An anthropological-historical discussion told from the point of view of the Rashidis.

Salibi, Kamal: *A History of Arabia.* Delmar, N.Y.: Caravan Books, 1980. A fine general survey of the whole peninsula's history, including early as well as recent times.

Teitelbaum, Joshua: *The Rise and Fall of the Hashimite Kingdom of Arabia.* New York: New York University Press, 2001. A fine account of the rule of Sharif Husain of Mecca in western Arabia.

Troeller, Gary: *The Birth of Saudi Arabia: Britain and the Rise of the House of Sa'ud.* London: Frank Cass, 1976. Of particular value for the period from 1910 to 1926.

Twitchell, Karl: *Saudi Arabia.* Princeton, N.J.: Princeton University Press, 1953. A fundamental work by a mining and hydraulic engineer who did much of the original work in exploring Arabia.

Vassiliev, Alexei: *The History of Saudi Arabia (1745–1994).* London: Saqi Books, 1998. A Russian author provides a detailed and sometimes critical political history.

Vogel, Frank E.: *Islamic Law and Legal System: Studies of Saudi Arabia.* Leiden: Brill, 2000. Based on firsthand study of Saudi courts, this scholarly analysis concentrates on the ulama, the rulers, and the day-to-day practice of law.

Winder, R. Bayly: *Saudi Arabia in the Nineteenth Century.* New York: St. Martin's Press, 1965. A valuable and comprehensive political history. Indispensable.

al-Yassini, Ayman: *Religion and State in the Kingdom of Saudi Arabia.* Boulder, Colo.: Westview Press, 1985. An excellent survey of the subject.

Yergin, Daniel: *The Prize: The Epic Quest for Oil, Money, and Power.* New York: Simon & Schuster, 1991. A lengthy and well-written history of oil in all parts of the world.

CHAPTER 50

Trends after 1945

Following World War II, nationalism became the chief force in the Middle East as nationalists won victories over Britain and France, the retreating imperial powers. The independent nation-state was the victor in the historical process. Most of the history of the period since 1945 has therefore been told in regard to each country. Some broad trends, already seen in those earlier chapters in regard to various countries, are rapid population growth, urbanization, changes in gender relations, mass involvement in politics, expansion of the size of governments, and the growing impact of oil revenues. Other trends and themes that affected the whole region broadly and generally can best be seen in a separate discussion. These trends include, among others that could be cited, the decline of the former Great Powers, the increasing importance of the new superpowers, the widening gap in scientific and technological fields between the Middle East and the west, the working out of the implications of Pan-Arab nationalism, the rise of religious fundamentalism, and growing militarization and terrorism.

THE DECLINE OF THE OLD POWERS

After World War II, the world at large became greatly concerned with the affairs of the Middle East. The advent of the state of Israel and the enormous flow of oil focused attention on the area and emphasized its importance in matters of politics, transportation, communications, religion, culture, markets, military strategy, imperialism, and nationalism.

Until 1956 the British enjoyed the dominant role in the Middle East. Although its involvements in this part of the world were various and comprehensive, Britain was chiefly interested in the fact that the Middle East lay astride the route to India, the jewel in the crown of the British Empire.

The British used many devices to maintain their imperial position in the Middle East. Britain often wished to rule indirectly through indigenous elites and princes, as in the Gulf Arab states. Elsewhere, as in Iraq, the British sought to create a government similar to their own, expecting that it would act in a friendly and peaceful manner within the British family of nations.

In any case, the British by economic, financial, military, and ideological means fully intended to retain their dominant position in the Middle East. However, weakened at home by losses in World War II, Great Britain found the retention of India and the Middle East beyond its means. Rising nationalism and growing economic strength and determination among Turks, Arabs, Israelis, and Iranians spelled the end of British dominance. Withdrawal of the British, partial though it was in the 1940s and 1950s, led to a realignment of the power and position of foreign states and internal factions. Readjustment of these forces gave rise to uncertainty, evidences of which were particularly noticeable in such issues as oil in Iran, the status of Cyprus, control of the Suez Canal, the 1958 revolution in Iraq, Kuwait's and South Yemen's independence, and the Arab-Israeli dispute in Palestine.

The second Arab-Israeli War in 1956 marked the real end of major unilateral British military excursions in the Middle East. Britain intervened in Jordan in 1958 and in Kuwait in 1961 to protect those allied regimes, but these interventions were the last direct attempts to show military strength. The eclipse of British power in the Middle East became nearly complete in the 1960s, when the British pulled out of the Gulf and southern Arabia.

Never able to match the power of England and plagued by miserable governments in Paris, French empire builders, except for their success in North Africa, Syria, and Lebanon between World Wars I and II, devoted their energies to spreading and establishing French culture among the elite of the local peoples. However, the utter defeat of France in World War II and the subsequent weakness of its economy dispelled most of the prestige held by France in the Middle East. Admiration for French manufactures and French ways largely vanished in the postwar period, although the French language remained popular as a means of communication in cultured circles.

In 1956, France, along with Great Britain and Israel, attacked Egypt. In subsequent years France supported Israel in various ways, but in the 1967 crisis the French maintained a neutrality, which to the Arabs appeared to be a sympathetic position, in sharp contrast to British and American attitudes.

In the 1970s, 1980s, and 1990s Great Britain and France still played a role in the Middle East, although it was less prominent than formerly. They sold weapons on a large scale to such countries as Saudi Arabia, Oman, Iraq, and Jordan. Both countries were members of the European Economic Community (E.E.C.; later, the European Union), which undertook a multitude of diplomatic and economic actions that affected the Middle East. Trade with the area increased as a result of one set of agreements made in the late 1970s and then a second round of negotiations in the late 1980s. In addition, a great deal of oil revenue was invested by Middle Eastern governments in European banks and industries. Hundreds of thousands of Middle Easterners worked and resided in Europe. Greek membership in the E.E.C. as of 1981 and the tangled and troubled relationship between Greece and Turkey were of major concern to those Turks who saw the future of their country lying in Europe. An E.E.C. declaration in 1980 supported "the legitimate rights of the Palestinian people" as well as of Israel. In the 1980s Britain and France increasingly turned their attention to the Gulf Cooperation Council countries and the Iran-Iraq War.

Britain and France participated in the multinational force in Beirut following the 1982 Israeli invasion and also, although with more success, in the Sinai observer force after 1979, and in the fleets that stood outside the Persian Gulf in the 1980s ready to intervene to protect shipping. France vigorously and directly backed those forces in Chad opposed to Libya's al-Qadhdhafi; both France and Britain cooperated with the United States in bringing about U.N. sanctions against Libya. Britain closely coordinated its policies with those of the United States in the Middle East. Britain, France, Germany, and several other European countries sent troops or financial assistance to help oust Iraq from its occupation of Kuwait in 1990–1991.

In the 1990s and early 2000s the European Union (E.U.) countries were preoccupied by the process of moving closer to a full merger of their economies, while also bringing eastern Europe and the Balkans into their system. Nevertheless, the E.U. maintained an interest in the Middle East and North Africa, particularly in regard to increasing commerce, keeping access to energy, and supporting political stability, the latter being important as a means of restraining the flow of immigrants into Europe. The European-Mediterranean Economic Area agreement of 1995 linked almost all the countries of the southern and eastern Mediterranean basin to the European Union in a pledge to move toward freer trade, while the E.U. promised economic assistance. In addition, a number of countries signed individual agreements on trade and aid with the E.U., as in the case of Jordan in 1997.

In military matters the E.U. tended to support the United States, as in the 2001 American campaign against the Taliban and al-Qaida in Afghanistan. Individual E.U. countries subsequently sent troops as part of the international peacekeeping force in Kabul. However, most of the European Union countries tended to question some aspects of U.S. policy in the Middle East. The European states were generally more sympathetic to the Palestinians and more critical of Israel than was the United States, and many Europeans decried what they viewed as American unilateralism in regard to Iraq.

THE NEW SUPERPOWERS

After the 1956 second Arab-Israeli War, the most important powers for the Middle Eastern countries were clearly the United States and the Soviet Union. These two countries each had enormous armed forces, large nuclear weapons stockpiles, and considerable economic and technological strengths. They also were the leaders of worldwide ideologies and alliance systems. Operating from positions of strength, they were often able to reach their goals in the Middle East, but their mutual competition hindered their effectiveness, and some states in the area were able to resist their influence or were capable of shaping relationships with the superpowers on their own terms.

U.S. goals in the Middle East were chiefly strategic, aimed at containing and curbing the power and expansion of the Soviet Union. Just after the end of World War II, the United States supported pro-western regimes in Turkey, Iran, Greece, and other countries against Soviet pressures. However, the welfare and security of Israel evoked greater popular concern in the United States than any other Middle Eastern issue. Although American devotion to Israel fluctuated somewhat, there was little domestic support for aid to the Arab states, even those allied with the United States against Communism.

When the United States strongly supported Israel, as in the 1967 third Arab-Israeli War, American prestige suffered among the Arabs. Such moves had a tendency to polarize the Arab states and people into those who maintained a pro-U.S. foreign policy and those who sought an alliance with the Soviet Union. American oil investments in the area were extensive, but they were purchased by the oil-producing countries in the 1970s. Still, the United States remained gravely concerned about the availability and price of oil coming from the Middle East.

The Soviet Union's chief aims in its Middle Eastern policies were also strategic rather than ideological: to break through the pro-American alliances, secure the friendship of Middle Eastern peoples, and win the diplomatic cooperation of their governments. Attainment of these objectives was sought by a mixture of pressure and inducement on nationalist and anti-imperialist political figures to pursue pro-Soviet policies and to oppose the United States and its allies. Beginning in 1955, Soviet arms were supplied in ever-increasing quantities to Middle Eastern Arab states as a further move to draw them closer to the Soviet orbit. Complementing these arms were general diplomatic support and sizable developmental grants and loans given to select countries for such important and visible items as the Aswan High Dam in Egypt. The third and fourth Arab-Israeli Wars demonstrated Soviet commitment to their allies, but at great risk that international combat would break out. Still, the initial results brought them favor among many Arabs.

The two superpowers dramatically increased their involvement in the Middle East after 1967. The United States continued to maintain its military commitment to the defense of Turkey, despite conflicting views over the actions of Turkey in Cyprus. President Richard Nixon assigned to the shah of Iran a role as policeman of the Persian Gulf, as a sort of surrogate for direct U.S. involvement. Iran was able to purchase enormous quantities of sophisticated weapons from the United States. U.S. foreign policy in regard to both Turkey and Iran was predicated on the desire to contain the Soviet Union while avoiding situations that might lead to nuclear war.

Another basic ingredient in U.S. foreign policy was support of Israel. In 1971 aid to Israel was increased fivefold. During the 1973 Arab-Israeli War, the United States went to the brink of nuclear conflict with the Soviet Union, causing a shock that impelled Secretary of State Henry Kissinger to throw himself into the search for peace in the region. Throughout the following dramatic developments—disengagement, step-by-step withdrawals, the 1978 Camp David Accords, and the peace treaty of Washington in 1979—it was the United States that provided the diplomatic energy, pressure, and financial and other guarantees that permitted Egypt and Israel to bring about a mutual peace.

U.S. commitment to Israel became even stronger in the 1980s. The Reagan administration tacitly approved Israel's invasion of Lebanon in 1982 and its subsequent support of a pro-Israeli Lebanese government. The United States directly aided the new Lebanese administration and then underwent the humiliation of being forced out of Lebanon. America accepted numerous actions by Israel that were generally opposed by nearly all the countries of the world. U.S. financial, military, and diplomatic aid to Israel and then Egypt continued at high levels in the 1980s, 1990s, and 2000s.

In other parts of the region, the United States faced grave threats to its predominant role. Two of the chief purposes of U.S. diplomacy were to maintain access for itself and its allies to Middle Eastern resources, especially oil, and to secure a general stability in that part of the world. Both purposes seemed threatened by the Islamic fundamentalist revolution in Iran and the ensuing Iran-Iraq War, which began in 1980. Presidents Carter and Reagan became closely involved with Iran, and they were substantially hurt by their failures to effect changes in Iranian foreign policy. On the other hand, the United States and other countries were successful in keeping open the sea lanes for the shipment of oil. The United States was publicly committed to the defense of Saudi Arabia in particular and to the freedom of navigation for neutral shipping in the Gulf in general. At the same time, the United States sought to curb Soviet domination in Afghanistan following Soviet invasion of that country in 1979.

Soviet policy in the Middle East in the 1970s was oriented primarily toward the extension of Soviet influence through alliances and cooperation with friendly, non-Communist regimes. Replacement from the Soviet bloc of the weapons expended in the disastrous 1967 war gave courage to the Arab military. The Soviet Union aided Egypt and Syria in their 1973 war with Israel and provided arms to Iraq during the 1980–1988 war with Iran. Between 1967 and 1973 the Soviet Union supplied $3 billion in arms to the Middle East, including almost $2 billion to Egypt. Soviet influence in Egypt was then lost as President Sadat turned to the United States. As the conservative monarchies in the Gulf region gained wealth, they tried to diminish the appeal of Soviet aid by providing an alternative source of assistance. Saudi Arabia criticized the officially atheistic Soviet Union while helping Egypt, Syria, Jordan, Lebanon, Iraq, the Palestinians, North Yemen, and others. In some cases these countries and groups also continued to accept Soviet aid, but in other instances they left their prior relationships with the Soviets.

The only Communist government in the Middle East outside Soviet central Asia, the Caucasus, and Afghanistan was that of South Yemen, which was closely dependent on the Soviet bloc. Internal government structures were modeled on the Soviet system, but South Yemen was not a total satellite.

Soviet influence in the Middle East diminished in the 1980s, and the appeal of Marxism-Leninism steadily declined. The Soviet Union vacillated over what course of action to take in the 1980–1988 Iran-Iraq War, but it usually sided with Iraq. The Soviets also had close ties with Syria and the Arafat-led majority of the Palestine Liberation Organization (P.L.O.). The Soviet Union was consistent in opposing the United States's step-by-step peace process. After 1985 the new Soviet leader, Mikhail Gorbachev, redefined foreign policy goals and the means of achieving them. The Soviet withdrawal from Afghanistan in 1988 was an acknowledgment of the failure of Communism in the face of a nationalist and Islamic resistance aided by many foreign countries.

The losses in Afghanistan were one of the many factors that helped cause the collapse of Communism in the Soviet Union and, in December 1991, the dissolution of that country into fifteen sovereign states. As independent republics emerged in central Asia and the Caucasus, their foreign policies and domestic political, religious, and cultural structures became independent from the Russian Republic.

Because of military, political, and economic transformations, Russia under the leadership of President Boris Yeltsin was less able to influence the central parts of the Middle East. Foreign aid was sharply reduced or eliminated, with drastic consequences, especially for South Yemen.

Russia also cooperated with the United States, most notably during the diplomatic crisis over the Iraqi occupation of Kuwait in 1990. Although the Soviet Union did not directly fight Iraq, it did vote in the U.N. Security Council to authorize the use of force to compel Iraq to withdraw. Russia was nominally co-chair with the United States of the Arab-Israeli peace talks, but its fading power meant that the United States would be the chief party. Hundreds of thousands of Jews who had lived in the former Soviet Union immigrated to Israel.

Earlier American diplomatic losses, such as the 1982–1983 Lebanese intervention, were forgotten now. It was mostly the United States that gained as the Soviet Union lost its post-1956 role in the Middle East. Increased arms sales by China, a greater economic role for Japan, a resurgence of interest in the European Union: all of these matters did not detract from the emergence of the United States as the greatest power in the world during the 1990s. The United States led the coalition of countries that defeated Iraq in 1991, and U.S. prepositioned military equipment and guarantees became the chief safeguard of the independence of the Arab states of the Persian Gulf. Armament sales by the Americans increased dramatically amid signs that U.S. culture was becoming even more popular with Middle Eastern elites. U.S. influence now extended even into the former Soviet areas of the Caucasus and central Asia. The United States helped secure Israel's arrangements with the Palestinians, and it brokered the Jordanian-Israeli peace treaty of 1994, while striving to bring about a Syrian-Israeli peace.

The growth of American power and influence throughout most parts of the Middle East was welcomed in some quarters but opposed in others. Iran, Iraq, Sudan, and Libya, and most Islamic fundamentalists resisted what they regarded as the forcible imposition of American policies, values, interests, and attitudes upon the peoples of the region.

Russia in the late 1990s and early 2000s attained more internal political and economic stability, thereby permitting it to adopt a more forcible, but still modest, role in the Middle East. Pursuing its own national interests in the Caucasus and Central Asia, Russia no longer based its policies on ideology or rivalry for power with the United States. As the Russian state sought to suppress renewed Chechen separatism within its borders, foreign policy was largely oriented toward economic factors. Russian exports of oil became more valuable in the late 1990s, trade with Turkey and Iran increased, arms sales in the Middle East earned substantial sums, and Russia played a part in the economic development of oil pipelines in central Asia. Russian policy sometimes differed from that of the United States, especially in regard to Iraq and Iran. However, Boris Yeltsin's successor as president in 2000, Vladimir Putin, continued his predecessor's basic alignment on crucial issues with Washington. Putin assisted the United States in Afghanistan by not raising objections to a substantial American military presence in central Asia, which acted in support of the Northern Alliance and Americans fighting against the Taliban.

In the late 1990s and early 2000s the United States continued its prior policies in the Middle East including "dual containment" of both Iraq and Iran, large-scale arms sales to allies, support of friendly regimes including many dictatorships, and pressure for the faltering Palestinian-Israeli peace process. The failure of President Bill Clinton to secure agreement between Israel and the Palestinian Authority in 2000 and the extraordinary degree of support for Israeli prime minister Ariel Sharon expressed by Clinton's successor, President George W. Bush, showed the limits of American abilities as a peacemaker. Widespread unhappiness in the Middle East with the course of the Arab-Israeli dispute threatened many American policies and interests in the region, including the campaign against terrorists launched after the attacks of September 11, 2001, on the United States. Most Middle Eastern governments initially supported the American-led war against the

Taliban and al-Qaida in Afghanistan, but the same governments seemed dubious about United States policy in Iraq, which sought to stop the proliferation of weapons of mass destruction by the overthrow of the Saddam Husain government.

THE WIDENING SCIENTIFIC AND TECHNOLOGICAL GAP

The influence of the Soviet Union and the United States in the Middle East after 1945 was based in large part on their accomplishments in science and technology and the inability of most countries in the Middle East to compete with the superpowers in these fields. This inability was linked to a number of social and economic trends in the Middle East. Population, particularly in the cities, grew at such a rapid pace as to make necessary the creation of millions of new jobs. Demand for water also grew very rapidly. At the same time, the highly unequal concentration of wealth in the hands of small urban elites and the control of resources by governments often worked against the interests of the poor and the rural population. There was a clear and pressing need for balanced economic growth in industry, agriculture, and services. Scientific and technological advancement seemed to be one of the main keys to obtaining such development. Governments usually concentrated on the so-called hard sciences and technology, feeling that investment in fields such as chemistry and engineering would be more immediately rewarding than concentrating resources in the social sciences, such as sociology or psychology.

Middle Easterners had come to understand after World War II that there was a decided gap between scientific and technological knowledge, education, and application in the western and Communist blocs on the one hand and the Middle East on the other. This gap was most clearly shown in military technology. It also appeared in the ceaseless stream of new discoveries and inventions that enabled the more developed societies to boost their standards of living. In order to obtain an improved position in science and technology, most countries in the Middle East increased the size and sophistication of their educational institutions and sought to replace foreign scholars with their own citizens. Policies encouraged students to study abroad, especially for advanced degrees, and sought to allocate resources for local research and development projects. Foreign aid also helped to develop science and technology. These measures resulted in great progress in some cases, but the even more rapid rate of advances in the developed world was such that the scientific and technological gap grew, except perhaps in the case of Israel.

Technology and science flourished in Israel, originating at the Haifa Technion and the Weizmann Institute of Science, which conducted research in the natural sciences. Teachers in such fields as aeronautical engineering, nuclear physics, medical technology, space sciences, and computer research trained scientists and engineers, who directly helped Israel's military efforts. Many scientists sought advanced degrees abroad; 15 percent of Israel's workforce held academic credentials by the mid-1970s. The need for scientists and technologists increased in the late 1970s and 1980s because of Israel's economic difficulties. Jewish immigrants from the former Soviet Union provided many new skills in the 1990s. Persons who specialized in dry farming techniques, solar energy, medical imaging devices, electronic software, and especially armaments research and development helped the Israeli economy through increasing exports. By 2000, Israel had more scientists per capita than any other country in the world. Over one-half of Israelis had computers and about 700,000 Israelis subscribed to Internet connections. Israel produced computer equipment and software in such fields as data compression, encryption, and anti-virus programs. Government, science, and industry cooperated closely as high technology seemed the best hope for Israeli economic development as well as a key ingredient in Israeli military superiority over its Arab enemies.

Iran and Turkey followed basically similar policies until the Iranian Islamic Revolution of 1979. Under Muhammad Reza Shah, Iran undertook an ambitious expansion of universities and scientific institutes, including an atomic energy program. The transfer of technology from foreign firms, particularly U.S. companies, ran into a number of problems, including the sometimes inappropriate technology being transferred as well as a shortage of trained Iranian technicians. Vocational education in Iran was often poor in quality and inadequate in comparison to demand. The Islamic Republic of Iran reorganized the educational system and commissioned the writing of new textbooks after 1979. Science policy has been aimed at rural development and indigenous industrial research, while involving the development of a more religious approach to science and technology. After a slow beginning, Iran has recently seen a burgeoning in the use of new computer and communications technology. Videocassette recorders (VCRs) became legal in 1993. The two Internet cafes in Tehran in 2000 had mushroomed to about 1500 by June 2001. Satellite television dishes were technically illegal in the 1990s but were nevertheless widely used, with an estimated 500,000 such dishes in Tehran in 1995.

Turkish scientific growth has been directed by the Science Policy Unit of the Scientific and Technical Research Council, created in 1963. The Science Policy Unit has emphasized technology transfer from the west and has spent research funds on such fields as local geology, ecology, agronomy, vocational schools, and medical and engineering studies. Particular attention was devoted in Turkey to documentation services so that Turkish scientists could stay up to date with scientific research done elsewhere using languages other than Turkish. Turkish scientists in 1980 published around 250 scholarly articles, which represented about one-half of one percent of all such articles in the world. By 2001, Turks wrote almost 6,400 scientific studies, or about 5 percent of the world's scientific articles. In the area of new computer technology, Turkey gained access to the Internet in 1993, and Turks by 2002 were major users of mobile telephones, computers, and advanced information technology. Turkish advances in science and technology resulted in part from a considerable expansion in the number of and enrollment at universities, both public and private, including a program of sending young scholars abroad for training.

In the Arab world, higher education expanded dramatically after 1945. By the early 1980s there were over fifty universities, with an enrollment of about 1 million students. The universities were generally teaching institutions; their research budgets were very low. Scientific periodicals showed growth in numbers. However, the gap between Israeli and Arab research, as measured by various quantitative factors, persisted and remained roughly constant. In the 1950s Egypt dominated scientific publishing among Arab countries. There and elsewhere in the Arab world, most scientific research centered initially around medicine. By the mid-1970s medicine and agriculture were the two primary topics, and most published research dealt with local applications and field research. Egypt,

Lebanon, Sudan, Iraq, and Saudi Arabia led in research, but political and military developments in Iraq and Lebanon later decreased the opportunities for research. Since Egypt produced so many graduates, particularly in engineering, that it could not provide jobs for them all, many educated Egyptians worked abroad, especially in the Persian Gulf region and Libya.

In the 1990s the Arab states witnessed some changes in science and technology, including a dramatic increase in the number of educational institutions. By 1995 there were about 175 universities and over 300 colleges and technical schools in the Arab countries. Arab scholars published about 7,100 scientific articles in 1995, with Egypt, Saudi Arabia, Morocco, and Kuwait producing the most. However, with a population somewhat smaller than that of Egypt, France had nearly 20 times as many scientific papers issued that year. Most of the Arab countries were relatively slow to adopt new computer and communications infrastructure and technology. By 1999 there were only about 300,000 subscribers to the Internet, a number that rapidly increased, rising to about 550,000 in 2000. Only about 1 percent of the World Wide Web pages appeared in Arabic. The wealthier oil-producing Arab states—the United Arab Emirates, Qatar, Bahrain, and Kuwait—led the way in the new technology, with Lebanon and Jordan also participating substantially. Most countries tried to stop access to web sites deemed offensive for sexual, religious, and political reasons. Despite these attempts, political opponents often used the Internet to send their messages. Cellular phones became widespread, with an estimated 2.5 million in use in Saudi Arabia alone by 2002. Women in particular profited from using the new technology, since it obviated to some degree the problems of gender separation in the workplace and seclusion in the home that were prevalent in the more conservative Arab countries.

Arab governments developed institutes, councils, and committees to promote science and technology. Most were national in scope, but some included cooperation with the United Nations or involved persons from several countries in the region. The Kuwait Institute for Scientific Research, one example of a national coordinating institution, was founded in 1967. By the mid-1970s it had thirty-five researchers, several with specializations in solar energy. The Institute's operations were suspended during the Iraqi occupation of Kuwait, but it resumed research in fields such as water availability by 1994. Another example of a research institute was the International Centre for Agricultural Research in the Dry Areas, established in 1977 in Aleppo, Syria. The Centre has studied planting seasons, herbicides, planting patterns, and disease-resistant plant varieties. In the 1990s two of the most prominent research centers were the Emirates Center for Strategic Studies and Research in the United Arab Emirates and the King Abd al-Aziz City for Science and Technology in Saudi Arabia. The chief difficulties such institutes faced were in maintaining high standards and in linkages with government and business so that discoveries could be practically applied.

There was little original research conducted in most parts of the Middle East (or in other less developed regions), and the quality of applied technology also remained fairly low. Reasons included the poverty of many countries; the dependence on foreigners for large projects; a tendency to buy from abroad "turn-key" factories, which came complete, thereby giving little scope for local initiatives; the underdevelopment of local high-technology industries; the newness of scientific and technological programs in some of the wealthier states; the inadequacy of many libraries and laboratories; heavy demands placed on university scholars faced with enormous classes to teach; and the intolerance of higher authorities toward criticism and dissent among scholars. Thousands of scientists and engineers moved to western countries and to the oil-rich countries of the Middle East, thereby creating a brain drain that stifled creativity in the poorer nations. In the 1980s and 1990s developments such as growth in education and literacy rates, more government investment in research and development, and larger numbers of published scientific articles suggested that some improvement in research productivity was underway. On the other hand, in the late 1990s and early 2000s the development and use of science and technology depended increasingly on factors largely absent from most of the Middle East: freedom in the exchange of information, transparency of economic operations, rewards for flexibility and innovation, employment of women and their promotion to positions of responsibility, and acceptance of international competition. Population was rapidly growing throughout the region and economic progress per capita was very slow. Most governments still did not invest sufficiently in science and technology; Arab nations, for instance, spent only about a percent of gross national product on research and development, well below the world average.

Continuing problems were the issues of which language to use in science education and the proper role of religion. Arab nationalists pushed for the use of Arabic in the classroom and the coinage of Arabic words for scientific concepts, although English was the language most often used in the international scientific exchange of information. Some Muslim scientists, especially those in the social sciences, argued that the quest for value-free, objective science was inherently unattainable and could lead to an immoral use of new knowledge. They urged a reconstruction of the understanding of science so as to place it within a religiously supportive societal framework. Islamic fundamentalism gained a considerable following among scientists in the 1980s and 1990s. Fundamentalist engineers in the 1980s acquired prominent roles in Egyptian and Turkish professonal organizations.

Despite these and other disputes and difficulties, some major research and engineering projects aimed at economic development or military security were underway in the Middle East during the 1980s and 1990s. Turkey, Libya, and several other countries dramatically increased investments in water management. Saudi Arabia built two new industrial cities that became closely involved in the manufacture of petroleum by-products. Iran, Israel, and other countries developed plans for atomic energy plants to reduce the need for oil or coal. Israel, which had developed the ability to produce atomic weapons in the late 1960s, now launched its own space satellites.

Changes in communications technology became particularly important in the late twentieth century. The Arab Satellite Communications Organization's permanent communications satellites were launched by the United States and France starting in 1985. In the 1990s most Arab governments obtained their own satellite television broadcasting facilities, while private companies based in Europe that could evade governmental censorship proved quite popular. A Turkish telecommunications satellite went into space in 1994. New telephone lines were added in many countries; the number of telephones in Iran increased from 800,000 in 1978 to about 4 million in 1994. Computer use also grew rapidly in many countries. The expense of computer equipment and the costs of using lines to gain access to the worldwide Internet meant that at first primarily universities, research facilities, and the wealthiest segments of society had access to the new technology. An Iranian firm in the 1980s tried to make its own minicomputer operating system, but competition from abroad resulted in Iranian companies' assembling imported components or buying new or used foreign-made computers. Middle Eastern computer users faced the difficulty that software was usually in English; adaptations for Middle Eastern alphabets and languages required additional work. A Windows 2000 operating system platform in Arabic met some of this need. Nevertheless, dependence on Western science and technology remained considerable in order to achieve most of these undertakings.

PAN-ARAB NATIONALISM AND THE ARAB LEAGUE

From 1945 to the late 1960s, many Arab states sought to gain or expand their independence from Great Britain and France. In addition to international recognition of sovereignty, this struggle included several other goals: expelling foreign troops, nationalizing major enterprises owned by foreigners, selecting political systems attuned to the perceived needs of the nation, and advancing local culture while lessening cultural borrowing from abroad. Arab nationalists also sought to spread the basic concepts of nationalism to groups whose political values were not yet nationalistic: the masses of society and especially the rural and urban poor, as well as some ethnic, linguistic, and religious minorities. Most Arab nationalists also favored the goal of Arab unity. They argued that the Arabs constituted one ethnic unit and that separate political categories such as Jordanians, Iraqis, Saudis, and Egyptians were artificial and should give way to one large, powerful, and united people living in one state. Such a political entity would have the ability and wealth to accomplish many things that each separate government could not hope to do. Since actual historical experience was such that most Arabs lived in individual nation-states rather than in one united Arab country, Pan-Arab nationalists had to struggle against pragmatists who identified more with existing governments.

An alternative to Pan-Arab unity was the League of Arab States (also called the Arab League), based on the idea of cooperation among existing states. During World War II, Great Britain and Iraq supported the creation of such an organization. Representatives of Iraq, Syria, Lebanon, Transjordan, Saudi Arabia, and Egypt signed the Arab League pact at Cairo in 1945. Other members joined later: North Yemen, 1945; Libya, 1953; Sudan, 1956; Morocco, 1958; Tunisia, 1958; Kuwait, 1961; Algeria, 1962; South Yemen, 1967; Bahrain, 1971; Qatar, 1971; Oman, 1971; United Arab Emirates, 1971; Mauritania, 1973; Somalia, 1974; Palestine Liberation Organization, 1976; Jibuti, 1977; and the Comoros Islands, 1993. (The Arab League did not include non-Arab Middle Eastern countries such as Iran, Turkey, and Israel.) The pact provided for a council, composed of a representative of each member state, and a secretary-general, whose permanent seat was to be in Cairo. From the League's inception, Egypt was the most important member. The League's second and longtime secretary-general was Abd al-Khaliq Hassunah, former Egyptian foreign minister. In 1960 the United Nations officially accepted the Arab League as a regional organization, which facilitated agreements between the League and such U.N. bodies as the World Health Organization.

The purpose of the League was to seek cooperation of member states in health, economic, cultural, and social affairs, in communications, and in matters affecting nationality. It embodied a guarantee of the sovereignty of each member and a promise to respect the systems of government established in other member states and to abstain from any interference in internal affairs of other member states.

The Arab states found in the League a promise of unity against the partition of Palestine and the Zionist state of Israel. In practice, however, the League was often divided internally on which steps to take against Israel. As defeat was experienced during the first Arab-Israeli War in Palestine in 1948, the Arab League declared that any member that made peace with Israel would be expelled. It also voted to oust Jordan, which annexed most of the remaining Arab portions of Palestine, although Jordan successfully defied this decision and was readmitted. The Arab boycott of Israel was organized by the League.

An Economic Council of the League was created to coordinate and unify economic policies, commerce, trade, and financial developments. However, Arab countries traded for the most part with nations outside the Middle East rather than with each other, except for the movement of workers to the oil-producing states. The League also helped to establish a number of joint ventures in such fields as cement manufacturing, pharmaceuticals, and leather industries, but political differences precluded full economic integration. Arab councils and federations for education, science, communications, public relations, labor, the practice of law, and aviation were formed. Conferences and congresses were sponsored on a wide variety of subjects: medicine, Islam, Arab history, banking, chemistry, tourism, and engineering. Government officials met with their counterparts from other Arab League countries to correlate policies and to formulate plans for joint ventures. These undramatic meetings were steps in the direction of real cooperation. Yet mutual distrust, the gap between the rich oil states and the poorer non-oil states, and ideological rivalry meant that the Arab countries found it difficult to surrender their own national interests.

International diplomacy and politics were the Arab League's underpinnings. The League declared its sympathy for Arab independence struggles in Morocco and Algeria, supplied funds to nationalists there, granted asylum to the leaders, and urged that economic measures be taken against France. Egypt was supported in its struggle with Britain over Suez Canal bases; North Yemen and Saudi Arabia were aided in their disputes with Britain. However, divisions between revolutionary, pro-Soviet Arab states versus conservative, pro-United States governments led to frequent confrontations inside the League in the 1950s, 1960s, and 1970s.

The Arab League also became weaker as Pan-Arabism seemed likely to unite the Arabs through other means than the cooperation of independent states. However, when the United Arab Republic of Egypt and Syria split up in 1961, and, still later, when the failure of Ba'thism and Nasserism to bring about real unity became apparent, the League seemed one of the few avenues for fruitful cooperation. In the 1970s and 1980s, with the resurgence of Islamic fundamentalism and the rise of Arab oil wealth, both secular Pan-Arabism and cooperation through the League generally faded. An additional reason was the ineffectiveness of the League in intra-Arab disputes. The League tried to use its good offices to keep peace but usually was not very effective, as in the quarrels between Oman and South Yemen and the dispute over the water of the Euphrates River between Iraq,

Syria, and non-Arab Turkey. The Arab League played only a limited role in Lebanon's civil war, providing additional troops to help Syria in the late 1970s.

Two other channels for Arab cooperation outside the League were the Arab heads of state who made mutual commitments in summit conferences, and Arab cooperation in oil matters. The first summit conference was held in 1964. Another Arab summit meeting was held in Khartoum in the summer of 1967 to assess the disastrous third Arab-Israeli War. The conferees pledged to ensure the withdrawal of Israeli forces from occupied Arab territory, but they did not achieve much. Another summit, held in Rabat in 1974, reached the important decision to make the P.L.O. the sole legitimate representative of the Palestinian Arabs. Periodic conferences thereafter included in 1990 such bitterly divisive matters as the decision on the use of force against Iraq to compel it to withdraw from Kuwait. Arab oil-producing countries mostly belonged to the Organization of Petroleum Exporting Countries (O.P.E.C.). In addition, they had their own separate organization, founded in 1968, that sponsored conferences on such subjects as mineral resources, new techniques in petroleum production, and the petrochemical industry.

Pan-Arabism and the League were severely strained by the 1979 peace treaty between Egypt and Israel. Most Arab governments opposed the terms of the treaty. They suspended Egypt's membership in the Arab League, moved its headquarters from Cairo to Tunis, and broke diplomatic relations with Egypt. These actions were reversed in 1989 when Egypt was readmitted to the Arab League. Another source of strain took place when Syria and Libya supported non-Arab Iran in its 1980–1988 war against Arab Iraq, while Egypt, Jordan, Saudi Arabia, Kuwait, and other Arab states backed Iraq. Only with the cease-fire in 1988 did this diplomatic dispute end.

Despite numerous disagreements, many Arab goals, hopes, and dreams were nevertheless accomplished. By the end of the 1980s, nearly all the Arab states except Palestine were clearly independent, sovereign, free of unwanted foreign troops, in control of their own natural resources, and energetically spreading nationalist values through education. Existing political systems claimed to be legitimate and in tune with the desires of the people (despite the prevalence of many unpopular dictatorships and one-party regimes). Cultural borrowing was still widespread, but governments could freely alter the pace and direction of such borrowing, and the Arabic language was predominant.

One remaining threat to Arab unity of feeling and cooperation by 1990 came from some members of minority groups, such as the Kurds in Iraq, Lebanese Maronites, and southern Sudanese. Where minority religion, language, and ethnicity overlapped in one geographic region, such opposition to centralizing nationalist governments was especially strong.

Ironically enough, the primary problem for Arab state nationalism was that of Pan-Arab unity—a result of the very successes of the nationalists, for as each country gained independence, its leaders and many of its people savored the benefits of a separate existence while coming to fear and distrust union with another Arab country. The failure of the Egyptian-Syrian union of 1958–1961 showed this trend. Repeatedly, various Arab governments announced their intention to unite, but these unions were only on paper. In fact, the pressure for union became a cause for disunity, since the various leaders and parties sharply disagreed with each other over methods of achieving union and who should control a united state once established.

Arab politics evolved then on a country-by-country basis. Even when regimes were supposedly committed to unity, they often actually opposed each other, as in the case of Ba'thist Syria versus Ba'thist Iraq. Egypt under Sadat put its own national interests first while making peace with Israel. The Palestinians wanted to have their own country rather than be part of a greater Pan-Arab nation. Rich oil states, such as Saudi Arabia and Kuwait, helped their fellow Arabs financially in a number of ways but with no lessening of their separate sovereignties. Technocrats in the oil states were bored with nationalism and turned to economic development as a panacea for questions about identity.

As the decades passed, national borders that had been created by the European powers and that had been regarded by the Pan-Arab nationalists as unreal took on an air of permanency. It was often difficult for the citizens of one Arab country to visit, telephone, work in, or trade with neighboring Arab states. Despite these factors, the desire for Arab cooperation and for the close coordination of military and foreign policy still ran deep among the Arabs of the Middle East. The issue was how to obtain such cooperation among sovereign states that were very different. When Iraq invaded and annexed Kuwait in 1990, Arab nationalists were deeply divided in their views. On the one hand, many regarded Kuwait as an artificial state and the annexation to Iraq as a highly desirable first step toward a larger union. On the other, some opposed this action on the grounds that the violent overthrow of one Arab state by another would open the Arab Middle East to constant war, that it was contrary to the concept of voluntary Pan-Arabism, and that Saddam Husain should not become the chief leader of the Arabs. Several Arab armies participated in the 1991 Kuwait War, thereby increasing the sharp differences among the Arab political leadership.

Many Arabs in the 1980s and 1990s turned away from grandiose and unrealistic pronouncements about Pan-Arab unity and looked to local regional cooperation, taking as models the United Arab Emirates, the Gulf Cooperation Council, the merger of the two Yemens, the occasional cooperation of Sudan and Egypt, and the 1989 Arab Maghrib Union in North Africa. Such local measures did not provide much help for the Palestinians, who sought a nation-state of their own, so they sought compromise with Israel, leading in the 1990s to mutual recognition and some degree of autonomy.

The apparent collapse of the Palestinian-Israeli peace process and especially the outbreak of the second intifada in 2000 resulted in widespread sympathy for the Palestinian cause and the reinvigoration of Arab common identity. The 1996 Arab summit conference, the first since 1990, was held in response to a deterioration in the relations between Palestinians and Israelis, and subsequent conferences in 2000 and 2001 condemned Israel and supported the Palestinian Authority. A new generation of pragmatic Arab leaders seemed willing to accept the goal of cooperation among the Arab states rather than union, even though the constitutions of many countries still enshrined the principle of full political integration. The impulse for Arab integration remained strong among the general population, based on cultural, religious, and historical commonalities. However, in the late 1990s and early 2000s few substantive measures were taken in the direction of Arab unity, and many Arabs assumed Pan-Arabism was dead. Sharp differences separated the Arab leaders, including such issues as whether to ally with the United States, how or whether to reintegrate Iraq into the Arab system, and the role of Islam in public life.

THE FUNDAMENTALIST CHALLENGE

In the 1980s and 1990s many Muslim and non-Muslim scholars opposed the widespread use in the west of the term *Islamic fundamentalism.* Instead, they want to describe this phenomenon by such words as *Islamism* or *Islamic resurgence, militancy, activism, renewal,* and *revival,* because Muslims have been "fundamentalists" throughout their history, with a continuing strong emphasis on the Quran and the earliest period of Islamic experience in the seventh century. Despite this legitimate argument, no more satisfactory term has yet been sufficiently accepted in the Middle East or the west to replace *fundamentalism.*

The causes of the rise of fundamentalism go back to the period after 1945, when, from the perspective of many Muslims, Jews, and Christians in the Middle East, both secular nationalism and Marxism were seen as failures. The leaders of the secular nation-states seemed to want to modernize and transform their societies into copies of the United States or the Soviet Union. Usually they were unable to do so. A bitter underground opposition to Communism was particularly widespread in Soviet central Asia and the Caucasus.

The small oil-rich states were successful to a degree, but they were only beginning the process of transformation. Larger and relatively poorer countries such as Turkey and Egypt had considerable experience in westernization, modernization, and incorporation into the world economy, but with questionable results. The nationalists promised far more than they were able to deliver, so that rising expectations were disappointed, thereby creating a potentially revolutionary situation. Many people living in the Middle East felt a sense of powerlessness and alienation from the ruling elites. In those societies where the desire to imitate other countries was at least partially realized, many of the lower classes were either unaffected or alienated by the transformation.

Many intellectuals wondered if either the west or the Soviets were really worth imitating. Instead of such mimicking, they said, it was time for one of those periodic waves of reform and renewal that had so often revived religious communities in the past. Many Muslims argued that revitalization of Islam would address the severe stress and dissatisfaction with prevailing norms that permeated most developing and peripheral Third World societies. Extremely rapid changes led many intellectuals to seek an ideal Islamic society, while the growing social base of educated people brought into the public arena masses committed to Islamic values, dubious about nationalist secularism, and opposed to American-led globalization. Political opposition groups facing heavy-handed dictatorial rule supported by elaborate security agencies tended to turn to Islam as the only viable means of securing change.

Economic development in the Middle East had often led to an abandonment of the national past and to the loss of newly gained independence to imperialism and then neoimperialism. Most important, westernizers abandoned their own culture, religious systems, and values in favor of secular law, individualism, materialism, and the creation of security-oriented states. The rich in such societies got much richer, while the poor were given platitudes about social justice, land reform, and national glory. Even the most modern and autocratic secular rulers were unable to secure many of the basic goals and needs of the population, examples being the failure of Nasser's Egypt in wars against Israel and the uninvolvement of Iran's villagers in oil prosperity. Islam seemed the only channel by which radical changes could be made and the evils of westernism overthrown.

As a result of all these factors, a reemphasis on religious values in public life grew in appeal by building on the model established by the Muslim Brotherhood in Egypt even before World War II. The Brotherhood and similar groups spread throughout many Muslim countries in the 1950s and 1960s, but they became particularly important in the 1970s and 1980s. The most spectacular case showing this trend was the Islamic Republic of Iran, where the ulama who had led the mass struggle against the shah in 1978 gained power and created a theocratic state. But in many other countries, fundamentalism or communal religious parties, movements, and ideas increased their followings. Both Christians and Muslims in Egypt became more conscious of their separate communal existence. In the 1980s and 1990s Egyptian Islamic fundamentalists attacked persons they viewed as secularists, such as the famous novelist Najib Mahfuz (Naguib Mahfouz). The governments of Libya and the Sudan propagated fundamentalist ideas. Lebanese Maronites led one side in the civil war that devastated their country between 1975 and 1990. In Israel, fundamentalist Orthodox Jews helped gain power for the Likud bloc, and they strongly influenced policy on domestic matters as well as on the question of retaining the occupied territories.

In some places the fundamentalists seemed to have only a small following. Saudi radical fundamentalists seized the Kaba in Mecca in 1979, but they were soon repressed in Saudi Arabia. In Turkey, Syria, Iraq, Jordan, the Persian Gulf Arab states, and united Yemen, fundamentalist movements emerged, often as the only viable political opposition, but were either suppressed or assimilated into the existing system of governance. Iraqi Shii fundamentalists were isolated, executed, or co-opted. In this and other cases, however, many of the national governments found it desirable to adopt symbolic gestures showing a greater commitment to Islam, thereby defusing the appeal of the fundamentalists. In addition, nonpolitical expressions of Islamic concern grew stronger throughout the Middle East, including banks that did not pay interest, conservative clothing for women, and more media attention to religion.

The controversy created by the fundamentalists over Salman Rushdie's 1988 novel, *The Satanic Verses,* illustrated the symbolic side of their movement. Rushdie (b. 1947) was an Indian Muslim writer who had become a British citizen. His novel contained passages concerning the prophet Muhammad that many Muslims found deeply offensive, and a number of countries, including Egypt, banned the book. Iran went beyond this, as the Ayatollah Khomeini called for Rushdie's assassination as punishment for blasphemy, apostasy from Islam, and slander against Muhammad. Despite Rushdie's apology, Iran subsequently broke diplomatic ties with Britain since the British government refused to ban sales of the novel.

The fundamentalists wanted far more than symbols. Their goals included the establishment of an Islamic moral order; the banning of sinful behavior; social and legal justice for all, irrespective of wealth; the greater application of religious precepts to all areas of life; struggle to remove Western imperialism, both direct and indirect; and the search for Pan-Islamic unity. The fundamentalists tended to reject such traditional Islamic institutions as the Sufi orders.

Most fundamentalists favored gradual reform and the reinvigoration of Islam's role in public life, while not necessarily wanting the immediate establishment of a new system of government. On the other hand, some radicals adopted a strident revolutionary tone, severely criticized the ulama, and advocated violence, attitudes deeply offensive to many other Muslims. Quranic literalism, impractical utopianism, and political demagoguery also limited the appeal of many of their leaders. Despite this, fundamentalism seemed to present an opportunity to overcome the deep schisms between elites and masses in culture, values, and identity.

The fundamentalists came to power through the Islamic revolution in Iran, the Turabi-military regime in the Sudan, and the Taliban movement in Afghanistan. Even in those countries not ruled by fundamentalists, religious fundamentalism became an important element in the ongoing debate about political legitimacy, democracy, identity, and the ultimate meaning of life for individuals and for groups. One reason for the relatively slow spread of fundamentalism in the 1980s was that the Shii Iranian experience had shown several problems that resulted from the actual implementation of fundamentalist ideals. The sovereignty of God, as interpreted by the ulama, conflicted with popular sovereignty, which was the theoretical basis on which most nation-states were founded. Harsh internal actions, repression of domestic opposition, and an unwillingness until 1988 to compromise with Iraq so as to bring about peace discredited Iran's regime in the eyes of many Muslims. The Iranian and other fundamentalists were also unclear about a number of economic issues. Land reform, banking, the role of women in society, education, technology and science, and the adaptation of certain aspects of shariah to new circumstances were only a few of the matters still being debated among fundamentalists.

The Soviet Union and the United States opposed the spread of fundamentalism and the Iranian revolution to other countries. It also became clear to the kings, generals, and politicians who controlled politics in the Middle East that the victory of fundamentalism could come about only following their own ouster.

Radical fundamentalist rule in the Sudan and in Afghanistan prompted doubts about the ability of Islamic idealists and violent revolutionaries to achieve goals worthy of imitation elsewhere. In the Sudan between 1989 and 1999 the fundamentalist Hasan Turabi put into effect many of his key concepts before being ousted from influence by the military. The harsh regime was unable to end the civil war that devastated the country and impoverished its people. While the fundamentalist Taliban movement brought peace to most of Afghanistan after 1996, its repressive policies, intolerance of opposition, and failure to promote effective economic recovery caused many Muslims in the Middle East to view it with disdain.

More moderate Islamic fundamentalists increasingly came into prominent positions in the 1990s. The collapse of atheistic Communism in the Soviet Union opened the path to a revival of Islam in central Asia and the Caucasus. In Jordan and Turkey the Islamic opposition parties played a considerable role in politics. The status of women, gender issues, and the question of veiling were widely debated. Even though a large majority of fundamentalists were moderates who deplored the use of violence in most cases, it was the increasing role of violence, whether through the militarization of society or the outbreak of radical terrorist attacks, that dominated public attention in the 1990s and early 2000s.

MILITARIZATION AND TERRORISM

The many nationalist, political, economic, religious, and other conflicts in the Middle East since World War II led to a steady growth in the importance of the military in the governments of most of the countries involved. These countries experienced a dramatic increase in the amounts spent on armaments, more reliance on foreign sources of weapons and military assistance, and an exaltation of military values at the expense of civilian goals.

Most countries in the Middle East saw the military seize power for varying periods of time, as in Egypt, Syria, Iraq, Sudan, Libya, North Yemen, and Turkey. The Pahlavi dynasty in Iran had come to power in a similar fashion in the 1920s. While civilians retained power in Israel, the military played a large role in society and consumed a significant part of national resources. In other cases the armies tried to seize power but were defeated. The reasons for their actions depended in part on specific conditions in each country, but they also resulted from such general factors as their monopoly of legitimate power, the desire to win wars and the feeling that military governments might prosecute wars more efficiently, the tendency for the military to be the most efficient and modernized sector of society, and the incompetence and corruption of many civilian governments.

The pattern of events following the military seizures of power varied sharply. In some cases the military returned rule to civilians after a relatively short period of time, as in Turkey. Alternatively, in Egypt after 1952 and Syria after 1970, the military or leading personalities within it retained power indefinitely. The actual accomplishments of each military regime also varied quite substantially. Occasionally the military would fall from power through sheer ineptitude, as in the Sudan. Competition between military and guerrilla groups fueled civil wars in Lebanon and Afghanistan.

While the evaluation of military rule was the subject of much debate, it was clear that far more was being spent on weapons in the 1980s and the 1990s than in the 1950s. The size of most armed forces grew greatly; one example was Egypt's army, which went from 60,000 to about 450,000 by 1989. From 1967 to 1991 the Iranian, Israeli, Saudi, and Sudanese armed forces roughly doubled in size, while the increases in Iraqi, Libyan, Syrian, and Yemeni forces were even greater. Israel's military continued to involve a very high proportion of the total population even as Israel added to its nuclear weapons stockpile. Iraq in the 1980s spent enormous sums on a program to manufacture its own nuclear weapons, but as a result of the 1991 defeat, it had to destroy its nuclear capability under United Nations supervision. In constant 1982 dollars, annual military expenditures in the Middle East increased from $24 billion in 1973 to $61 billion in 1983, for a total of $542 billion in ten years. Military spending took about one-quarter of government expenditures in the 1980s and early 1990s. The need to buy ever more complex and expensive weapons in the 1990s led to constant military reorganizations and retraining programs.

The Middle East bought more than one-third of total world weapons imports. Major purchasers of weapons in the 1980s were Iraq, Saudi Arabia, Iran, Egypt, Libya, Syria, and Israel. The two major suppliers of weapons to the Middle East were the Soviet Union and the United States, but Britain, France, Germany, China, and other countries also exported armaments to the Middle East.

Toward the end of the 1980s, as the Iran-Iraq War ended, the Arab-Israeli dispute started to decline in intensity, the price of oil declined, and the Soviet Union and the United States resolved aspects of the Cold War, spending on the arms race in the Middle East fell. However, in the 1990s, the opposite situation evolved, with the Kuwait War and its consequences spurring on the countries of the Persian Gulf region to even greater spending on the military. The proliferation of ballistic missiles and weapons of mass destruction and the collapse of the Soviet Union also contributed to a strategic uncertainty, and the level of mutual hostility among many countries remained high. In 1997 the core

Middle Eastern countries spent about $57 billion on defense, not including payments on debts related to past wars or pensions to former soldiers. The highest amounts were spent by Saudi Arabia, Israel, Turkey, and Iran. As a proportion of total government spending, military expenditures were particularly high in Afghanistan, Sudan, and the United Arab Emirates. The Middle East continued to be the chief market for the world's international armaments sales. Extraordinary amounts were spent by societies that ranged from a few extremely wealthy countries that could perhaps afford such expenses to some of the poorer nations on the planet, where the diversion of large sums meant real deprivation for already desperately poor people and severe damage to prospects of future economic improvement.

The militarization of society contributed indirectly to the growth of terrorism in the Middle East. Definitions of terrorism have varied sharply, but the core concept has included the use of violence directed against noncombatant civilians by unofficial covert organizations for political purposes. Thus, terrorism differs from guerrilla warfare. Persons engaging in terrorist acts view themselves as victims of injustice and use the label "terrorist" for their enemies, not for themselves. They see their own causes as absolutely moral and good and their enemies as absolutely immoral and evil; any kind of action can be moral under such circumstances. Often the terrorists have been psychologically and physically brutalized as children; most identify with groups of people deprived of their basic identity and human and political rights. The terrorist groups justify their actions by pointing to their goals, citing their frustration arising from the seeming impossibility of securing those goals by peaceful means, and seeking to create feelings of terror among populations, who will then pressure their governments into political concessions. Any harm the terrorists might inflict on their victims is said to be justifiable so as to create publicity for their causes.

While similar in some ways to terrorism conducted by small groups, state terrorism is usually more organized, systematic, and directly linked to specific goals. Some states in the Middle East directly or indirectly supported small-group terrorists by means of financial or military aid. Of the seven governments the United States listed in the 1990s and 2000s as sponsors of international terrorism, five were in the Middle East: Iran, Iraq, Libya, Sudan, and Syria. In return, the leaders of those countries on occasion accused the United States of indirect sponsorship of terrorism through its support of Israel, whose attacks on Palestinians were viewed as examples of state terrorism.

Frequent targets of terrorism in the Middle East included Palestinians, Israelis, Turks, Lebanese, and non–Middle Easterners residing in Lebanon. The chaotic situation of Lebanon following the 1975 civil war allowed terrorist groups to operate in relative safety; often these bands became simple bandit gangs seeking cash and masquerading behind ideological, nationalist, and religious rhetoric. As order was restored in Lebanon in the early 1990s, hostages were gradually released.

A small number of Muslims, including the Shii leaders of revolutionary Iran, argued that struggle against the enemies of Islam through the use of terrorism was justifiable. Some Israelis and Armenians said that reprisals against perpetrators of violence were justified because of past injustices against their communities. They also wished to achieve future expansion, more security, or statehood. Palestinians who attacked Israeli civilians used nationalistic and/or religious arguments. In most cases, however, a majority inside each of the highly diverse groups and countries in the Middle East opposed terrorism, including random violence, individual assassinations, collective punishments, bombings of civilian settlements, kidnappings, and similar events.

In 1998–2000 the number of terrorist attacks launched by Middle Eastern groups or states declined substantially as Libya, Iran, Syria, and Sudan moderated their policies, while the Palestinian-Israeli dispute seemed to once again be more open to a peaceful settlement. The collapse of the peace process in late 2000 led to a resumption of violent attacks by both secular-nationalist and religiously based Palestinian groups on Israelis and extremely repressive Israeli actions, including the near destruction of the Palestinian Authority in the occupied territories. This situation inflamed public opinion throughout the Middle East against Israel and its chief international supporter, the United States. Many Arabs and Muslims in the Middle East experienced a deep sense of anger, despair, and helplessness—feelings that provided increased opportunities for radical Islamic fundamentalists based in Afghanistan to attract people who would be willing to launch attacks against the United States.

As discussed in Chapter 40, the radical Islamic fundamentalist Taliban movement came to power in Afghanistan by 1996. The Afghan Taliban government hosted Usama bin Ladin and his al-Qaida organization, a loosely structured but highly trained and well-financed group of radical fundamentalists who drew their followers from Saudi Arabia, Yemen, Egypt, and, in fact, the world. Using sophisticated technology, bin Ladin declared a holy war or jihad against the United States, citing its military presence in the holy land of Islam in Saudi Arabia, its backing of anti-fundamentalist dictatorial regimes throughout the Middle East, its support for Israel, and its alleged responsibility for Iraqi suffering after the 1991 Kuwait War. Along the lines of other radical fundamentalists, bin Ladin claimed to be re-creating the circumstances of the early Muslim community while rejecting medieval and modern developments that he said had corrupted Islam. Like the Qarmatians and Assassins of earlier days, bin Ladin felt that most Muslims were not "real" Muslims because they did not believe in the narrow definition of the faith and the terrorist use of violence against civilians that he espoused. After struggling in Afghanistan against the Soviet Union and then attempting to establish a headquarters in Sudan, bin Ladin returned in 1996 to Afghanistan, where he planned numerous terrorist attacks.

The success of Egyptian efforts to suppress radical fundamentalism in the 1990s resulted in the fleeing abroad of the remnants of the terrorist organizations. Many radical fundamentalist young men from Egypt, Pakistan, Algeria, Central Asia, western Europe, the United States, and southeast Asia trained in al-Qaida camps in Afghanistan and subsequently became members of terrorist cells under the direction of Usama bin Ladin.

Terrorism became a deep concern for the United States in the 1970s and afterward, because many terrorist acts were undertaken against Americans living abroad. Terrorism from the Middle East reached the United States directly in the first attempt to destroy the World Trade Center buildings in New York City on February 26, 1993. Al-Qaida carried out attacks on United States embassies in Africa in 1998 and on a United States naval vessel, the U.S.S. *Cole,* in the Aden, Yemen, harbor on October 12, 2000. The most devastating suicide attacks took place on September 11, 2001, when members of al-Qaida hijacked American civilian aircraft. One airplane flew into the Pentagon just outside Washington, D.C., one crashed in Pennsylvania, and two others crashed into the World Trade Center twin towers, thereby killing thousands of innocent civilians.

Governments in the Middle East and Muslim religious officials condemned these attacks and cooperated with the United States in its efforts to punish the violent fundamentalists responsible for them. Throughout the Middle East and in other parts of the world, countries curbed local groups linked to al-Qaida. Saudi Arabia and Yemen especially cracked down on radical fundamentalists within their borders and gave tacit backing to the United States war in Afghanistan against the Taliban and al-Qaida that started in October 2000. While the United States and its Afghan and other allies were successful in defeating the Taliban by December, the disappearance of Usama bin Ladin and the dispersal of much of al-Qaida into Pakistan indicated that the terrorist threat from this organization might well continue in the future. Addressing the underlying causes of radical Islamic fundamentalism was likely to remain an even more important task for the world community of nations than the immediate necessity of eliminating the capacity to perform more attacks such as those of September 11, 2001.

The peoples of the Middle East sought to maintain their religious beliefs while dealing with increased pressures for secularization, globalization, and rapid social change. Most Muslims in the Middle East rejected radical Islamic fundamentalism and the use of terrorism even though societies moved closer to having a larger role in public life for religion. Middle Eastern countries sought success in scientific and technological development as in the quests for complete national independence, resistance to foreign domination, and military strength. A desire to continue earlier basic patterns in social values and everyday life met with conflicting pressures associated with widespread technological and cultural changes. It was frustrations in these areas that increasingly impelled scientists and others toward their own cultural roots, particularly toward fundamentalist religious values, structures, and institutions.

Dependence on other societies and states was a grave threat to both fundamentalism and nationalism. The search for religious, ideological, and military independence and separateness conformed to the long historic identity of the Middle East. It remains to be seen how growing world interdependence will influence the various national and religious loyalties of the Middle East and the peoples who so strongly believe in them.

REFERENCES

Many works cited earlier pertain to this chapter, especially references found at the end of Chapters 37 through 49.

Ajami, Fouad: *The Arab Predicament: Arab Political Thought and Practice since 1967.* Updated ed. Cambridge: Cambridge University Press, 1992. A pessimistic analysis of Arab society and the decline of Pan-Arabism.

Barnett, Michael N.: *Dialogues in Arab Politics: Negotiations in Regional Order.* New York: Columbia University Press, 1998. Deals with Arab nationalism and unity from the 1920s onward.

Bergen, Peter L.: *Holy War, Inc.: Inside the Secret World of Osama bin Laden.* New York: Free Press, 2001. This is a fine account by a leading television reporter.

Bowen, Donna Lee, and Evelyn A. Early, eds.: *Everyday Life in the Muslim Middle East.* Bloomington: Indiana University Press, 1993. These readings about families, gender relations, work, religion, and entertainment present a lively, sympathetic, and informative picture of continuity and change in the contemporary Middle East.

Brown, L. Carl: "The Middle East: Patterns of Change 1947–1987." *Middle East Journal* 41 (1987): 26–39. A superb overview of general trends.

———: *Religion and State: The Muslim Approach to Politics.* New York: Columbia University Press, 2000. A good general introduction to the history and present-day aspects of this matter.

Choueri, Youssef: *Arab Nationalism: A History—Nation and State in the Arab World.* Malden, Mass.: Blackwell, 2000. Emphasizes the ideology of Arab nationalism.

Cordesman, Anthony H.: *After the Storm: The Changing Military Balance in the Middle East.* Boulder, Colo.: Westview, 1993. A perceptive, lengthy work filled with illuminating detail by an outstanding authority on the subject.

Dekmejian, R. Hrair: *Islam in Revolution: Fundamentalism in the Arab World.* 2d ed. Syracuse, N.Y.: Syracuse University Press, 1995.

Enayat, Hamid: *Modern Islamic Political Thought.* Austin: University of Texas Press, 1982. Discusses the connections between nationalism, democracy, socialism, and religion; particularly valuable for a discussion of Sunni and Shii points of view.

Esposito, John L.: *Unholy War: Terror in the Name of Islam.* Oxford: Oxford University Press, 2002. Discusses jihad, radical Islamic fundamentalists, Usama bin Ladin, and policy options.

Findley, Carter Vaughn, and John Rothney: *Twentieth-Century World.* 5th ed. Boston: Houghton Mifflin, 2002. An outstanding world history with particularly good treatment of the Middle East.

Franda, Marcus: *Launching into Cyberspace: Internet Development and Politics in Five World Regions.* Boulder, Colo.: Lynne Rienner, 2002. This excellent study compares electronic communications in several regions, including the Middle East.

Freedman, Robert O.: "Russian Policy toward the Middle East: The Yeltsin Legacy and the Putin Challenge." *Middle East Journal* 55 (2001): 58–90.

Hinnebusch, Raymond, and Anoushiravan Ehteshami, eds.: *The Foreign Policies of Middle Eastern States.* Boulder, Colo.: Lynne Rienner, 2002. An overview and country-by-country survey.

Hudson, Michael G., ed.: *Middle East Dilemma: The Politics and Economics of Arab Integration.* New York: Columbia University Press, 1999. Includes a particularly useful chapter on science and technology in the Arab countries by A. B. Zahlan.

Humphreys, R. Stephen: *Between Memory and Desire: The Middle East in a Troubled Age.* Berkeley: University of California Press, 1999. Thoughtful essays on contemporary issues and their historical origins.

Hunter, Shireen T.: *The Future of Islam and the West: Clash of Civilizations or Peaceful Coexistence?* Westport, Conn.: Praeger, 1998. A lucid consideration of relations between the Islamic world and the west, with an emphasis on foreign policy.

Jawad, Haifaa A.: *Euro-Arab Relations: A Study in Collective Diplomacy.* Reading, England: Ithaca, 1992. This detailed book examines political, economic, and military matters.

Juergensmeyer, Mark: *Terror in the Mind of God: The Global Rise of Religious Violence.* Updated ed. Berkeley: University of California Press, 2002. Analysis of religious terrorism among Christians, Jews, Muslims, Sikhs, and Buddhists, based in part on interviews.

Kaufman, Burton I.: *The Arab Middle East and the United States: Inter-Arab Rivalry and Superpower Diplomacy.* New York: Twayne, 1996. An excellent book on U.S.-Arab relations since 1945.

Kavanaugh, Andrea L.: *The Social Control of Technology in North Africa: Information in the Global Economy.* Westport, Conn.: Praeger, 1998. A fine study that demonstrates the abilities of some governments to control new media.

Long, David E., and Bernard Reich, eds.: *The Government and Politics of the Middle East and North Africa.* 4th ed. Boulder, Colo.: Westview, 2002. Perceptive studies of each country in the region by authorities in the field.

Moore, Clement Henry: *Images of Development: Egyptian Engineers in Search of Identity.* 2d ed. Cairo: American University in Cairo Press, 1994. An outstanding study.

Moussalli, Ahmad S.: *Moderate and Radical Islamic Fundamentalism: The Quest for Modernity, Legitimacy, and the Islamic State.* Gainesville: University Press of Florida, 1999. A complex and sophisticated analysis of doctrine and theory.

Murden, Simon W.: *Islam, the Middle East, and the New Global Hegemony.* Boulder, Colo.: Lynne Rienner, 2002. A useful review of recent developments.

Nizameddin, Talal: *Russia and the Middle East: Towards a New Foreign Policy.* New York: St. Martin's, 1999. Concentrates on the 1990s.

Owen, Roger: *State, Power and Politics in the Making of the Modern Middle East.* 2d ed. London: Routledge, 2000. A general treatment of the twentieth-century Middle East with insights on religion, the military, the economy, and politics.

Rugh, William A.: "Arab Education: Tradition, Growth and Reform." *Middle East Journal* 56 (2002): 396–414. The author concludes that as the quantity of students has greatly expanded, there has been a loss of quality in Arab educational systems.

Sakr, Naomi: *Satellite Realms: Transnational Television, Globalization and the Middle East.* London: Tauris, 2001.

Salem, Paul: *Bitter Legacy: Ideology and Politics in the Arab World.* Syracuse, N.Y.: Syracuse University Press, 1994. Treats Pan-Arab and regionalist nationalism, Islamic fundamentalism, and Marxism, chiefly in Egypt, Lebanon, Syria, and Iraq.

Voll, John Obert: *Islam: Continuity and Change in the Modern World.* 2d ed. Syracuse, N.Y.: Syracuse University Press, 1994. An outstanding book that deals with the whole Muslim world; the discussion of the relationship between fundamentalism and earlier periods is exceptional.

Zahlan, A. B.: *Science and Science Policy in the Arab World.* London: Croom Helm, 1980. A full account of the subject by the leading authority.

Zebiri, Kate: *Mahmud Shaltut and Islamic Modernism.* Oxford: Clarendon Press, 1993. This discussion of the life and thought of the theologian Shaltut (1893–1963), the head of al-Azhar University in Cairo, can serve as a useful alternative to discussions of modern Islam that overly emphasize fundamentalism.

Glossary

Some concepts, terms, and abbreviations are briefly defined here; for place names and persons, see the Index.

abu (äb'o͞o) father of

adet (ād't) customary law and taxes, as opposed to shariah

aga, agha, aqa (ãg'ə) generally a high-ranking officer; title of respect

Alids (älĭds) descendants of Ali, the cousin of the prophet Muhammad, and their backers

alim (plural, ulama) (ãlĕm) a religious scholar, official, theologian

Allah (äl'ə) God

amir (ā-mîr') prince, military commander, governor

amir al-umara (ā-mîr' äl-ômärä) commander of commanders, supreme commander

anjuman (ä'njô-mãn) a society of Muslims, especially used in Iran

Aramco the Arabian American Oil Company, in Saudi Arabia

ayatollah (ī'yə-tō'lə) a high-ranking Twelver Shii religious scholar

b. born; in the middle of a name this means son of, as in Ahmad b. Mustafa, or Ahmad the son of Mustafa

B.C.E. Before the Common Era; equal to the chronological designation B.C.

Bedouin (bēd'wĭn) a pastoral nomad

bey (bā) army officer, ruler, official; a title of respect

beylerbey (bā'lər-bā) a high-ranking Ottoman soldier or governor

ca. circa, about

caliph (kə-lĭf) a successor of Muhammad, the messenger of God, as leader of the Muslim community

capitulations treaties granting legal and tax privileges to foreigners

C.E. Common Era; equal to the chronological designation A.D.

chador (chä-dôr') a woman's robe or dress, covering most parts of the body

d. died

derebey (dîr-bā') a valley lord, an Ottoman local leader

devshirmeh (dĕv-shĭrmāh) an Ottoman conscription system for Christian youths

dhimmi (thĭm'-ē) a protected non-Muslim

diwan (divan) (dĭwän') a poetry collection; register for tax purposes; council

E.E.C. European Economic Community

E.U. European Union

fatwa (făt'wä) a religious opinion issued by a mufti

futuwwa (fo͞oto͞owə) associations of youths and the ideals associated with them

ghazi (gä'zē) a raider, a warrior for the faith of Islam

ghulam (ghô-Läm') a male slave soldier and administrator, especially in Safavid Iran

hadith (hə-dēth') an account of a saying or action of the prophet Muhammad

hajj (hāj) pilgrimage to Mecca

Hamas an abbreviation for the Palestinian group, the Islamic Resistance Movement

hijrah (hĭj-rə) the movement of Muslims and especially the prophet Muhammad from Mecca to Medina in the year 622

ijma (ĭj'mə) consensus of the Muslim scholars

ijtihad (ĭj-tî-häd') individual examination of the basic elements of the Muslim faith, especially in law

ikhwan (ĭkh-wän) a brotherhood, an organization of fellow believers, especially in Saudi Arabia and Egypt

imam (ĭ-mäm') leader in prayer; leader of the Muslims, especially used by Shiis

intifada (ĭn'tə-fä'də) shaking off, an Arab insurrection in Palestine

iqta (ĭk'tə) a ruler's grant of the right to collect government revenues from land in return for services by a subject

janissary (jăn'ĭ-sĕr'ē) an Ottoman infantry soldier

jihad (jĭ-häd) inner struggle for religious improvement; holy war

jizyah (jĭz-yə) a poll tax on non-Muslims

kanun (qanun) (kä'no͞on) a law or regulation issued by a government and based on the opinion of a ruler

khan (kän) Turkish or Mongol chieftain, prince, ruler

khedive (kə-dēv') prince, especially used in nineteenth-century Egypt

khutbah (khŭt-bə) sermon

kibbutz (plural, kibbutzim) (kĭ-bo͞ots') a Jewish collective settlement, village

madrasah (mäd-rä-sə') an upper-level Muslim school specializing in religion and law

Mahdi (mä'dē) the rightly guided one, the Messiah

majlis (məj'lēs) political assembly, parliament, council

majlis al-shura (məj'lēs äsh-o͞o-rä) consultative council

mamlachtiut the concept of state power in Israel, involving government control over all institutions, secular civil law, and consensus

Mamluk (mam'lo͞ok) a military slave soldier; a ruling system based on freed military slaves, especially in Egypt

mawla (plural, mawali) (mäw'lă) a client; a person brought into a tribe or group

mihrab (mî'rəb) niche indicating direction for prayer in a mosque

millet (mĭl'ĭt) semiautonomous religious community in the Ottoman Empire

minbar (mĭn'bər) a pulpit in a mosque

mufti (mŭf'tē) a Muslim legal consultant who issues fatwas

mujtahid (môj'ta'hēd) an interpreter of Islamic law

mullah (molla) (mŭl'ə) religious teacher and leader; alim

N.A.T.O. the North Atlantic Treaty Organization

O.P.E.C. the Organization of Petroleum Exporting Countries

Orientalists western scholars of Islam and the Middle East

Pan-Arabism an approach to Arab nationalism that argues for a large, inclusive Arab state to include all Arabs

Pan-Turkism an approach to Turkish and Turkic nationalism that argues for a large, inclusive Turkish state to include all Turks

pasha (pä'shə) an Ottoman title, originally military

Phanariot (fănar-yôt) a Greek Ottoman official

P.L.O. the Palestine Liberation Organization

qadi (kă'dē) judge

qizilbash (kēzèl'bōsh) pro-Safavid tribal and Sufi groups

r. reigned

ray (rī) personal opinion in Islamic law

reaya (rēə'îə) taxpaying subjects of the Ottoman Empire

rentier state a government that controls and distributes large sums of money derived from the foreign sale of oil

riddah (rĭd'dah) apostasy or breaking away from Islam

sabra (sä'bra) a native-born Israeli Jew

sadr (sädĕr') a Safavid religious official

sayyid (sä'yĭd) a descendant of Husain, the son of Ali and grandson of the prophet Muhammad; also a title of respect

shah (shä) king, emperor

shaikh (shāk) a chief; a Sufi leader; an elder; also a title of respect

shaikh al-Islam (shāk äl-Ĭsläm) the leading Muslim religious official; the chief Ottoman mufti

shariah (shä-rē'ä) the holy law of Islam; also the right path

sharif (shə-rēf') a descendant of Hasan, son of Ali and grandson of the prophet Muhammad

Shii (shē'ē) a Muslim who believes Ali and his descendants to be the rightful leaders of the Islamic community

sipahi (sî-pä-hē) an Ottoman cavalryman

Sufi (so͞o'fē) a Muslim mystic; a mystical approach to religion

sultan (sŭl'tən) the holder of power

Sunni (so͞on'ē) a follower of the sunnah—the custom, usual procedure, and behavior of the prophet Muhammad and his companions

surah (so͞or'ə) a chapter of the Quran

tanzimat (tän-zē'māt) reforms, in particular those in the Ottoman Empire during the nineteenth century

themes (thēm's) Byzantine military districts

ulama (o͞o'lə-mä) plural of alim

ummah (ôm'ä) the community of Muslim believers

valide sultan (väl'ē-dĕ sŭl'tən) mother of the sultan

vilayet (vĕl'äyət) an Ottoman province

vizir (wazir, vezir, vizier) (vä-zēr') a high-ranking deputy to the ruler

wafd (wäfd') a delegation; especially refers to an Egyptian political movement in the twentieth century

waqf (wäkf') an endowed charitable or religious trust

zakat (zä-kät') a tax imposed upon Muslims for charity

Zionism (Zī'ŏn-ĭsm) Jewish nationalism

Chronology

570	Birth of Muhammad, the Prophet
610	Revelations to Muhammad begin about this time
622	Migration of Muslims to Medina, year 1 of Islamic hijri lunar calendar
632	Death of Muhammad
632–634	Reign of caliph Abu Bakr
634–644	Reign of caliph Umar
636–637	Battles of Yarmuk and Qadisiyyah, Muslim victories over Byzantines and Sasanians
644–656	Reign of caliph Uthman
656–661	Reign of caliph Ali; first civil war
661–680	Reign of caliph Muawiyah I of the Umayyad dynasty
661–750	Umayyad dynasty of caliphs
680	Death of Husain, son of Ali, at hands of Umayyads
ca. 685	Construction starts on Dome of the Rock in Jerusalem
685–705	Reign of caliph Abd al-Malik, re-establishes Umayyads
705–712	Muslim conquest of Central Asia and India begins
711	Muslim conquest of Spain begins
750–1258	Abbasid dynasty of caliphs
762	Founding of city of Baghdad
767	Abu Hanifah, theologian, dies
786–809	Reign of Abbasid caliph Harun al-Rashid
820	Al-Shafii, theologian, dies
869–883	Rebellion of the Zanj
874	Disappearance of the twelfth imam of the Shiis
874–999	Samanid dynasty in Iran and central Asia
909–1171	Fatimid dynasty in North Africa and Egypt
923	Al-Tabari, historian, dies

935	Al-Ashari, theologian, dies
945	Buyid Shiis take Baghdad, control Abbasid caliphate
969	Founding of city of Cairo by Fatimids
973	Founding of Al-Azhar University in Cairo
1020	Firdawsi, Persian-language poet, dies
1030	Mahmud of Ghaznah, conqueror of northern India, dies
1037	Philosopher, physician, scientist Ibn Sina (Avicenna) dies
1054	Great schism between Catholic Church of the West and Orthodox Church of the East
1055	Sunni Seljuk dynasty begins rule of Baghdad and the East
1071	Battle of Manzikert, victory of Seljuk ruler Alparslan over the Byzantines
1092	Death of the Seljuk vizir Nizam al-Mulk, founder of the Nizamiyah school in Baghdad
1097–1291	Christian Crusades in eastern Mediterranean
1111	Theologian and Sufi al-Ghazali dies
1171–1250	Ayyubid dynasty, founded in Egypt by Salah al-Din (Saladin)
1204–1261	Western Catholics rule Constantinople
1219–1335	Mongols raid, conquer, and then rule in Middle East as I-Khans
1227	Genghiz Khan, Mongol ruler, dies
1250–1517	Mamluks rule in Egypt, Syria, and other lands
1258	Baghdad falls to Mongols who kill the Abbasid caliph
ca. 1299	Ottoman principality begins expansion
1326	Bursa becomes first urban capital for Ottomans
1347–1350	Black Death in Middle East
1360–1389	Reign of Murad I, Ottoman sultan
1380–1405	Conquests in Middle East and India by Timur Leng (Tamerlane)
1389	Battle of Kosovo, Ottoman victory over Serbia
1402	Battle of Ankara, Timur Leng captures Bayezid I, Ottoman sultan
1405–1506	Timurid dynasty in eastern Iran and Afghanistan
1406	Ibn Khaldun, historian, dies
1413	Mehmed I reunites Ottoman state
1453	Mehmed II, Ottoman sultan, captures Constantinople (Istanbul)
ca. 1465	Construction completed of Ottoman royal palace of Topkapi Saray in Istanbul
1500–1617	Ottomans build imperial mosques in Istanbul
1501–1722	Shii Safavid dynasty rules Iran
1514	Ottoman sultan Selim I defeats Safavid shah Ismail I
1517	Selim I conquers Egypt
1520–1566	Reign of Suleiman I, Ottoman sultan
1529	First Ottoman siege of Vienna
1588–1629	Reign of Abbas I, Safavid shah

1656–1702	Köprülü family members serve much of this time as Ottoman vizirs
1669	Ottoman capture of Candia in Crete
1683	Second Ottoman siege of Vienna
1699	Treaty of Karlowitz marks Ottoman defeat
1736–1747	Nadir Khan rules as shah in Iran
1745–1818	First Saudi state in central Arabia
1774	Treaty of Kuchuk Kainarji between Ottomans and Russians
1783	Russian annexation of Crimea
1789–1807	Reign of Selim III, Ottoman sultan and reformer
1794–1925	Qajar dynasty rules in Iran
1798	Napoleon Bonaparte conquers Egypt
1804	Serbia rebels against Ottoman rule
1805–1848	Mehmet Ali (Muhammad Ali) controls Egypt
1808–1839	Reign of Mahmud II, Ottoman sultan and reformer
1811	Mehmet Ali destroys Mamluks in Cairo
1813	Iran cedes much of the Caucasus to Russia by the Treaty of Gulistan
1821–1829	Greek revolt against Ottoman rule
1826	Mahmud II destroys the Janissaries
1829	Ottoman-Russian Treaty of Adrianople (Edirne)
1839	Ottoman reform decree, Hatt-i Sharif
1839–1876	Era of reforms (Tanzimat) in the Ottoman Empire
1840	Treaty of London limits Mehmet Ali
1844	Beginnings of Babi-Baha'i faith
1848–1896	Reign of Nasir al-Din, Qajar shah of Iran
1853–1856	Crimean War
1856	Ottoman reform decree, Hatt-i Humayun
1858	Ottoman Land Law
1863–1879	Reign of Ismail, viceroy and khedive of Egypt
1866	Ismail begins Assembly of Delegates
1869	Opening of the Suez Canal
1871–1897	Career of Jamal al-Din al-Afghani, Islamic opponent of imperialism
1875	Ottoman government becomes bankrupt
1876	Egyptian government becomes bankrupt
1876	Ottoman constitution
1876–1909	Reign of Abdulhamid II, Ottoman sultan
1878	Congress of Berlin
1879	Cossack Brigade is organized in Iran
1881	Ottoman Public Debt Administration begins

1881	Muhammad Ahmad in the Sudan says he is the Mahdi
1882	Britain occupies Egypt
1883–1907	Lord Cromer controls Egypt
1890–1892	Tobacco concession crisis in Iran
1892–1914	Reign of Abbas Hilmi II, khedive of Egypt
1894–1897	Massacres of Armenians in Anatolia
1897	Theodor Herzl founds the World Zionist Organization
1898	British-Egyptian forces conquer Sudan
1899	Publication of Qasim Amin's book favoring improvement in the status of women
1899–1905	Muhammad Abduh, Islamic reformer, is grand mufti of Egypt
1900–1908	Construction of the Hijaz Railroad
1902	Abd al-Aziz begins third Saudi state
1905–1906	Iranian Constitutional Revolution begins; Muzaffar al-Din, shah of Iran, convenes a parliament, issues a constitution
1906	Dinshaway affair in Egypt
1908	Major oil production in Iran begins
1908–1909	Committee of Union and Progress wrests power from Ottoman sultan
1911–1912	Italian-Ottoman War
1912–1914	Ottomans lose almost all of their Balkan territories
1914	Britain declares a protectorate over Egypt
1914–1918	World War I
1914	Iran declares neutrality in the War
1914–1918	Ottomans are allies of Germany and Austria-Hungary in World War I
1915	Husain-McMahon correspondence begins
1915–1916	Battles at Gallipoli; Entente forces withdraw
1915–1916	Ottomans commit large-scale massacres of Armenians in Anatolia
1916	Sykes-Picot Agreement
1916	Sharif Husain of Mecca begins Arab Revolt against Ottomans
1917	Balfour Declaration
1917	Communists seize power in Russia
1917–1936	Reign of Ahmad Fuad, king of Egypt
1919	Egyptian national uprising against British control
1919	Mustafa Kemal (Atatürk) begins resistance to Entente forces in Anatolia
1919–1929	Reign of Aman Allah (Amanullah) in Afghanistan
1920	San Remo agreement on division of Ottoman lands, oil, and the Mandates
1920	French occupy Damascus
1920	National uprising against British in Iraq
1920	Treaty of Sèvres devastates Ottoman Empire
1921	Reza Khan gains control of Iran

1921	Abd Allah, Hashimite prince of Transjordan, begins rule
1921–1933	Reign of Faisal I, Hashimite king of Iraq
1922	Britain unilaterally declares Egypt independent
1922	Turkey defeats Greece
1922	Turkish nationalists end the Ottoman sultanate
1923	Treaty of Lausanne recognizes Turkish independence
1923	Establishment of the Turkish Republic
1923–1938	Mustafa Kemal Atatürk is president of Turkey
1925	Reza Khan becomes shah of Iran, founds Pahlavi dynasty
1925	Gezira cotton development begins in Sudan
1925	Kurdish rebellion in Turkey
1926	Lebanese Republic is proclaimed
1927	Death of Saad Zaghlul, Wafdist leader of Egypt
1929	Western Wall incident and riots in Palestine
1932	Independence of Iraq
1936	Anglo-Egyptian Treaty
1936	Abortive French treaties with Syria and Lebanon
1936–1938	Palestinian Arabs undertake a national uprising; Peel Report
1936–1952	Reign of Faruq, king of Egypt
1938	Completion of Trans-Iranian Railroad
1938	Discovery of oil in Saudi Arabia
1938–1950	Ismet Inönü is president of Turkey
1939–1945	World War II
1941	British and Free French invasions of Syria, Lebanon, and Iraq
1941	British and Soviet invasion of Iran; reign of Muhammad Reza Shah begins
1942	Battle of al-Alamain in Egypt
1945	Creation of the League of Arab States (the Arab League)
1947	United Nations calls for partition of the Palestine Mandate
1948	David Ben-Gurion declares the independence of the State of Israel, becomes first prime minister
1948	First Arab-Israeli War
1950	Turkey conducts first national democratic elections
1951	Libya becomes independent
1951–1953	Crisis over Iranian oil nationalization ends with ouster of Prime Minister Mosaddeq
1952	Military leads a revolution in Egypt, declares the Republic in 1953
1952–1999	Reign of Husain, Hashimite king of Jordan
1953	Death of King Abd al-Aziz of Saudi Arabia
1954–1970	Gamal Abd al-Nasser (Jamal Abd al-Nasir) is leader of Egypt
1956	Independence of the Sudan

1956	Second Arab-Israeli War, includes Britain and France
1958	Lebanese civil war
1958	Military leads a revolution in Iraq, ends the Hashimite monarchy
1958–1961	United Arab Republic, Egypt and Syria
1960	Military seizure of power in Turkey
1960	Formation of the Organization of Petroleum Exporting Countries (O.P.E.C.)
1961	Britain ends protectorate over Kuwait
1962–1970	Civil war in North Yemen
1963	Ba'th Party begins rule in Syria
1964	Creation of the Palestine Liberation Organization (P.L.O.)
1964–1975	Reign of King Faisal of Saudi Arabia
1967	Third Arab-Israeli War
1967	Independence of South Yemen from Britian
1968	Ba'th Party rules in Iraq
1969	Libyan revolution, Muammar al-Qadhdhafi becomes leader
1969–1985	Jaafar al-Numairi is leader of Sudan
1970	Aswan High Dam is completed in Egypt
1970	Qabus becomes sultan of Oman
1970–1981	Anwar al-Sadat is president of Egypt
1970–2000	Hafiz al-Asad is leader of Syria
1971	Creation of the United Arab Emirates (U.A.E.)
1973	Fourth Arab-Israeli War
1973–1974	Notable increases in the price of oil
1974	Coup in Cyprus is followed by Turkish invasion
1974–1975	Step-by-step disengagements between Israel and Egypt, Syria
1975–1990	Lebanese civil war
1977	Menachem Begin, leader of Likud, becomes the first non-Labor prime minister of Israel
1978	Ali Abd Allah Salih becomes president of North Yemen
1978–1979	Revolution in Iran leads to ouster of Muhammad Reza Shah and creation of the Islamic Republic
1978–1979	Camp David agreements, Egyptian-Israeli peace treaty
1979	Saddam Husain becomes president of Iraq
1979–1989	Soviet occupation of Afghanistan
1980	Military seizure of power in Turkey
1980–1988	Iran-Iraq War (also known as the Persian Gulf War)
1981	Creation of the Gulf Cooperation Council
1981	Husni Mubarak becomes president of Egypt
1982	Fifth Arab-Israeli War
1983	Civil War in Sudan resumes

1984–2000	Kurdish insurrection in Turkey
1985	Notable decline in the price of oil
1985–1991	Reforms in the Soviet Union result in the Caucasus and central Asian states becoming independent
1987	First Palestinian intifada against Israel begins
1988	Najib Mahfuz (Naguib Mahfouz), Egyptian novelist, wins Nobel Prize for literature
1989	General Umar Hasan al-Bashir gains power in Sudan
1989	Death of Ruh Allah Khomeini in Iran
1990	Union of North and South Yemen
1990–1991	Iraq invades and annexes Kuwait; an international war in January–February 1991 results in Iraq being expelled from Kuwait and United Nations limitations placed on Iraq and its military
1993–1997	The Oslo agreements and other measures taken by Israel and Palestinians lead to the creation of a Palestinian Authority and the extension of its administration to most of the West Bank and Gaza Strip
1994	Peace treaty between Israel and Jordan
1994	Civil war in Yemen, ends with victory of the North over the South
1996	The Taliban establish their rule over most of Afghanistan
1997	Election of the reformer Muhammad Khatami as president of the Islamic Republic of Iran
1999	Abd Allah II, Hashimite King of Jordan, begins reign
1999	Turkey becomes a candidate for full membership in the European Union
2000	Israeli Prime Minister Ehud Barak ends the occupation of southern Lebanon in May but he and Yasir Arafat fail to conclude an agreement at Camp David, Maryland, in July
2000	Bashar al-Asad becomes president of Syria
2000	The second intifada of the Palestinian Arabs against Israel breaks out in September
2001	On September 11 al-Qaida terrorists attack targets in the United States, resulting in an invasion of Afghanistan by the United States and its allies, the fall of Qandahar in December, and the collapse of Taliban rule
2002	On June 14 a national council selects Hamid Karzai to be leader of Afghanistan

List of Websites

Ahlul Bayt Digital Islamic Library Project: www.al-islam.org/organizations/dilp, for many Shii works, guides, and references.

Bilkent University (Ankara, Turkey), Department of History: "The Topkapi Palace Museum." www.ee.bilkent.edu.tr/~history. Omer Nezih Gerek, Russel Johnson, and Mehmet Kalpakli have compiled an attractive site for the Ottoman imperial center, featuring historical background, a virtual tour, discussion of the collections, and bibliography.

Blake, Corinne: "Teaching Islamic Civilization with Information Technology." *Journal for MultiMedia History* 1 (1998) at www.albany.edu/jmmh/vol1no1/teach-islamic. Direct links to, and critical discussion of, on-line sites for the Quran, hadith, Shiism, Sufism, Islamic literature, and art.

Chicago, University of, Joseph Regenstein Library: www.lib.uchicago.edu/e/su/mideast/Photo Archive.html. Photo Archive. Early photographs, especially of Cairo, Jerusalem, Damascus, and Istanbul.

Halsall, Paul: *Internet Islamic History Sourcebook—Islamic History Section of Internet Medieval Sourcebook* at www.fordham.edu/halsall/islam/islamsbook.html. A very useful web site that includes maps, primary sources, and secondary articles on Islamic history.

Halsall, Paul: *Internet Medieval Sourcebook* at www.forham.edu/halsall/sbook.html. Contains many documents, particularly relating to religious issues, as well as links to other sites.

Islamic Arts and Architecture Organization: www.islamicart.com. This site features discussions of Islamic coins, rugs, wood and metal objects, and the decorative arts.

Ludvigsen, Borre: Al-Mashriq: The Levant—Cultural Riches from the Countries of the Eastern Mediterranean at http://almashriq.hiof.no. This web site hosted at Ostfold College, Norway, centers on Lebanon and includes historical documents, images, links to other useful sites, many specialized cultural topics, and current events.

Middle East Institute, Washington, D.C.: www.mideasti.org. A site with many links to other resources, compiled by the publishers of the *Middle East Journal*. Especially useful for foreign policy and current affairs.

Middle East Studies Association of North America: www.mesa.arizona.edu. This home page of a major academic association for the study of the Middle East has many useful links to a variety of other sources.

Muslim Students Association of the University of Southern California: www.usc.edu/dept/MSA/fundamentals, for hadiths and sunnah.

Norton, Claire, and Marios Hadjianastasis: www.ottoman-links.co.uk. The Ottoman Studies Resource Index. Contains many useful links to sites for a wide variety of subjects including Ottoman chronology, flags, literature, and the study of the Middle East.

Olnon, Merlijn: *Memalik-i Mahruse—The Ottomanist's Domain:* http://members.lycos.nl/molnon. Based at Leiden University, this site includes recent book and article citations, sections on transliteration and paleography, and information on Ottoman court music.

Qadiri-Rifai Tariqa: www.qadiri-rifai.org, for the history, leaders, and beliefs of a Sufi brotherhood.

Rochefort, Thomas C.: http://isfahan.anglia.ac.uk/. Isfahan Web Server. Photos and descriptions of buildings in Isfahan are artfully combined with historical descriptions, links to other sites, and a bibliography.

Texas, University of, at Austin, Center for Middle Eastern Studies: Middle East Network Information Center: http://link.lanic.utexas.edu/menic/. This home page has a wide variety of links to many sources dealing with the contemporary Middle East, organized both by country and by topic.

Index